AVIATION HISTORY

by Anne Millbrooke

ISBN-13: 978-0-88487-433-1
ISBN-10: 0-88487-433-8

Cover: NASA photograph of the Space Shuttle Atlantis on the STS-84 mission. Airline Transport Pilot Eric R. Baldwin stands in front of Carl M. William's 1929 A2 Alexander Eaglerock at Centennial Airport, Denver, Colorado.

Library of Congress Cataloging-in-Publication Data

Millbrooke, Anne Marie.
    Aviation history / by Anne Millbrooke.
        p.   cm.
    Includes bibliographical references and index.
    ISBN 0-88487-433-8
    1. Aeronautics--History.   I. Title.
TL515.M443   1999
629.13' 09--dc21   99-16561
                                                        CIP

Jeppesen
55 Inverness Drive East
Englewood, CO 80112-5498
Web Site: www.jeppesen.com
Email: Captain@jeppesen.com
Copyright © Jeppesen
Published 1999, 2000, 2006

10001810-002

Acknowledgements

Writing a textbook makes an author depend upon many colleagues, including those who share their research in person or via publications, those who refer the author to appropriate primary and secondary literature, those who facilitate access to sources, and those who discuss the subject of the book or the process of writing a book. In preparing a new edition, the author's debt extends again to these professional colleagues and also to the kind readers of the first edition who forwarded comments, corrections, and questions to the publisher or author.

I have attempted to acknowledge published authors in the source notes within the information boxes throughout the text as well as in the brief bibliographies that conclude each chapter. Photographs and illustrations were obtained from many sources, and these are acknowledged in Appendix D.

I sincerely thank the Jeppesen team and my editor, Richard Snyder, for helping me produce the award-winning first edition of Aviation History, and now — under the lead of editor Chuck Stout — for helping produce this second edition of Aviation History. Dick Snyder gave accurate, consistent, and valuable input, as well as encouragement and gentle though effective reminders about deadlines. Chuck Stout followed his example. The publication teams turned out this fine publication. Special thanks to Matt Ruwe and Chuck Stout, who used my sketchy outlines to draft chapters 9 and 10 respectively for the first edition. I have rewritten those chapters for this new, updated edition, yet their influence lingers.

Among the team members deserving special thanks are Richard Hahn, Jeppesen Media Productions Manager; Patrick Brogan and Paul Gallaway, artists extraordinaire; Grace Cooke and Darrel Schultz, eagle-eyed copy editors; and Alan Lathan of Jeppesen's Frankfurt office. I'd also like to thank Gary Kennedy and Dave Chance for all their work obtaining permission to use photos in this book. A number of people were involved in both editions, including Liz Bartlett, Susan Beale, Marsha Beardsley, LeAnna Diercks, Jug Eastman, Michelle Gable, Judi Glenn, Dave Goehler, Mike Lawrence, Dan Marin, Lawrence Montano, Rick Patterson, Dan Reece, Scott Saunders, Nancy Silverthorne, Sandy Stedman, Andrea Stevens, Dawn Stevens, and Jay Weets.

Libraries are important resources to any historian, and I especially thank librarians Kay Hansen at Northwest Campus in Nome, Alaska; Bonnie Williamson at the Havre-Hill County Public Library in Havre, Montana; Valerie Cole, Montana State University — Northern in Havre; and the entire inter-library loan and circulation departments in the library at Montana State University in Bozeman, Montana. These professional librarians facilitated access to printed sources.

Some colleagues provided encouragement, sympathy, stimulating discussion, and source material during my work on this book, some on the first edition, some on this new edition, and many on both. Peter J. Capelotti and Pierre Lissaragues read chapters of the original manuscript and provided comments, corrections, and sources useful in revising the text of the first edition. Tom Crouch and Dominick A. Pisano at the National Air and Space Museum, Smithsonian Institution, also provided timely and helpful assistance, and Tom provided key insights for improving the coverage of the Wright Brothers. Martin Reuss and Martin K. Gordon, Office of History, U.S. Army Corps of Engineers; J.D. Hunley, History Office, Dryden Flight Research Center, National Aeronautics and Space Administration; and Hervé Brun, Armée de l'Air, provided valuable assistance at different stages of my work. Herman Van Dyk generously provided his drawings of airships. Paul Lagasse, Jay P. Spenser, and Charles Steffens encouraged me and provided helpful comments as well as information. Robert N. Harvey, Liv and Bryan Morgan, and Steven J. Pilling forwarded me useful material. I extend special thanks to my friends John C. Greene, Valerie Hemingway, Pascal J. Imperato, Michael Sokal, and Frances & Bryan Sterling, who have encouraged me directly and by example.

After the first edition appeared, two NASA-ASEE fellowships at the NASA Langley Research Center in Virginia enriched my understanding of aeronautical and space topics. Thank you to NASA and ASEE for support, and to Samuel E. Massenberg, Director of the Office of Education at Langley, to Debbie Murray, administrator for the ASEE program, Larry E. Tise, office mate one summer, and NASA scientists, engineers, librarians, and information officers who enabled me to have two delightful, informative, and productive summers at Langley.

To these folks I name and to the many others who helped me, thank you. Given the widespread, in-depth, and high-quality support that I received, I accept full blame for any errors remaining.

Anne Millbrooke

AVIATION HISTORY

Table of Contents

AVIATION HISTORY

Using the Book

Aviation History is structured to give you a well-rounded review of the significant events, people, places, and technologies in aviation throughout history. To get the most out of this book, you may want to review the major design elements that are presented on the next few pages.

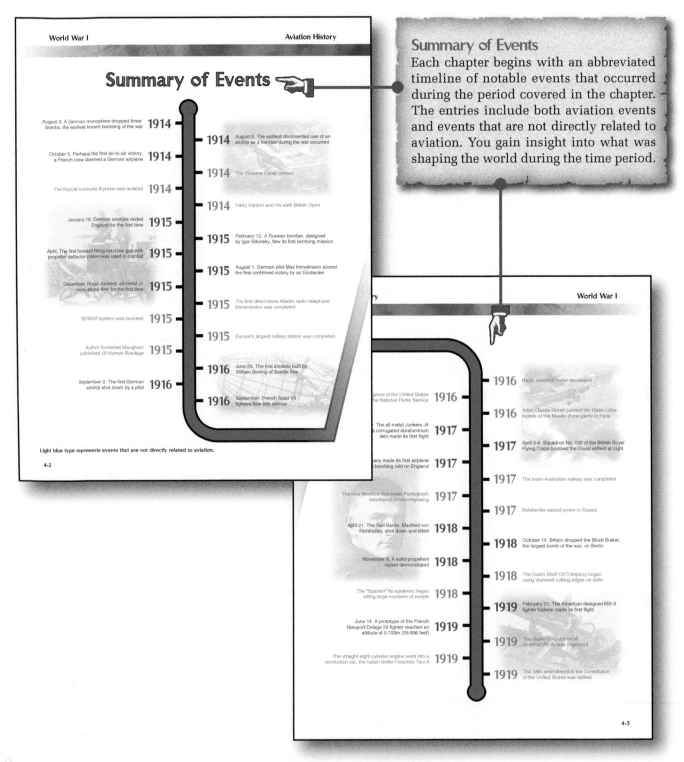

Summary of Events
Each chapter begins with an abbreviated timeline of notable events that occurred during the period covered in the chapter. The entries include both aviation events and events that are not directly related to aviation. You gain insight into what was shaping the world during the time period.

Key Terms

Red type identifies a key term that is used and defined for the first time in the book.

Historic Note

This type of box includes supplemental information about the topic being covered and helps you gain additional insight into the subject.

SECTION C

DIRIGIBLES

In the 19th century, aviation became more than hot air and hydrogen balloons. The technology evolved to include dirigible balloons — that is, directable, steerable balloons, and from there to airships with semi-rigid or rigid frames. Navigation of dirigibles and airships also evolved from ballooning.

A dirigible is an aircraft that can be directed or steered. The origin of the word is French: *diriger* — to direct, to aim, to guide. In aviation the French word "dirigible" began as an adjective for the dirigible balloon, a balloon with sufficient power to overcome the resistance of air and thereby to be directionally controlled in flight rather than simply floating with the fluid air. To be dirigible, a balloon thus required power as well as directional control. In the early contemporary literature, a dirigible might be called a flying ship, aerial steamer, steam balloon, flying machine, or airship. Only gradually did the noun dirigible come to mean non-rigid dirigible balloons, and the term airship become associated with the dirigible balloons that have semi-rigid or rigid internal framework. Rigidity refers to the **form**. The form of a non-rigid dirigible is maintained by the internal pressure of the gas in the balloon envelope. A semi-rigid form is acquired by using the internal pressure in the gas container *and* a keel structure. The rigid form is supported by a rigid structure or framework within the envelope. This text will distinguish between non-rigid dirigible and more rigid airship, though even today the word dirigible is sometimes used to include semi-rigid and rigid airships as well as non-rigid dirigible balloons. This section will discuss non-rigid dirigibles and a few contemporary semi-rigid airships, and the next section will cover the semi-rigid and rigid airships of the late 19th century and early 20th century. (Figure 1-17)

Directional Control

Almost as soon as the Montgolfier brothers had demonstrated the flight of free balloons, and manned flight, the question of directional control attracted attention. John Jeffries and Jean Pierre Blanchard made one of the early attempts to steer a balloon on

Balloon

Non-rigid

Semi-rigid

Rigid

Figure 1-17. These drawings illustrate the difference between balloons, non-rigid and semi-rigid dirigibles, and rigid airships.

1-25

Historical Note

Anthony Fokker defined the problem and solution of forward firing:

"The technical problem was to shoot between the propeller blades, which passed a given point 2,400 times a minute, because the two-bladed propeller revolved 1,200 times a minute. This meant that the pilot must not pull the trigger or shoot the gun as long as one of the blades was directly in front of the muzzle. Once the problem was stated, its solution came to me in a flash.

"The obvious thing to do was to make the propeller shoot the gun, instead of trying to shoot the bullets through the propeller. Inasmuch as the machine gun would shoot only about 600 times a minute this required some practical working out, but the principle had been found, which was the important thing.

"For a temporary device, I attached a small knob to the propeller which struck a cam as it revolved. This cam was hooked up with the hammer of the machine gun, which automatically loaded itself, of course. Thus as I slowly revolved the propeller, I found that the machine gun shot between the blades."

Fokker in his book *Flying Dutchman, the Life of Anthony Fokker*, by Fokker and Bruce Gould (1931; New York: Arno Press, 1972).

Gentleman's Warfare

Pilots were officers. They had name, rank, and privilege, unlike the anonymous mass of conscripts and enlisted men dying in the trenches. The airmen flew, observed, and reported. According to a German pilot, "Yes, our profession is wonderful. I fly once every three days." Echoed an American pilot, "We have absolutely no duties but flying, and no discipline except to be here when we are wanted to fly." "The early war pilot went into battle armed more as a sportsman than a soldier," according to a British officer. Even the vocabulary of the early military pilots was sporting, like ace meaning top sportsman and a mission being called hunting.

Forward firing led to the classic dog fights, the dueling pilots, the gentlemen in one-on-one sporting combat.

Flight Lines

"After we flew around and about each other nine or ten times, unable to get each other in our sights, I saw my opponent more closely. He wore a scarf flying in the wind and black headcovering . . . . He looked at me for a long time, then raised his right hand and began to wave. I don't know why, but all at once I felt very sympathetic to the man in the Spad. Without a thought, I waved back. This went on for five or six curves. Suddenly I had the strange feeling that I wasn't confronting an opponent but practicing turns with a comrade."

German pilot Ernst Udet describing an aerial duel, as translated and quoted in Peter Fritzsche, *A Nation of Fliers*.

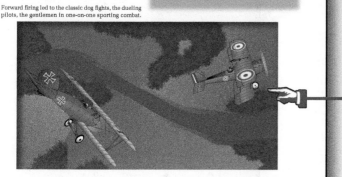

4-28

Flight Lines

Firsthand accounts of what happened in aviation give you an up close and personal view of the events in aviation history. These boxes provide that valuable information and insight.

Graphics

Full color graphics are used throughout the book to enhance the historic content. These elements appear with the boxed information, in figures, and as stand-alone illustrations.

Historic Event

A single, significant event in aviation history is contained within this box. The event typically was a defining moment in aviation. A review of these elements will give you an overview of aviation's significant achievements.

Historical Evidence

A discussion of the evidence of what happened in history is included here. This is a unique look at the artifacts and records of aviation from a historian's point of view. You'll experience how historians use a variety of information to glean important clues about events in aviation history.

Historic Event

On 23 February 1909 Canadian pilot J.A.D. McCurdy flew the Aerial Experiment Association's Aerodrome No. 4, *Silver Dart*, for the first airplane flight in Canada. The location was Baddeck, Nova Scotia, summer home of Alexander Graham Bell who had organized the Aerial Experiment Association for the purpose of building a practical airplane.

Historical Evidence

The Alexander Graham Bell Museum at Baddeck, Nova Scotia, displays artifacts and documents of the experiments and researches of Bell, including his aviation endeavors with the Aerial Experiment Association. Those artifacts and documents are primary sources, contemporary evidence of what happened. The museum labels are secondary sources, as they present information interpreted by curators who decide what is important to tell museum visitors about Bell.

Augustus Herring, who was a shady individual, Curtiss organized several companies of his own: the Curtiss Aeroplane Company and the Curtiss Exhibition Company in 1910 and the Curtiss Motor Company in 1911.

...irplanes

...as manufacturing motorcycles and ...rs in Hammondsport when dirigible ...s Baldwin first approached him.

Baldwin wanted light-weight and powerful motors for his dirigibles. Curtiss provided the motors, and he rode in Baldwin dirigibles. He then joined the Aerial Experiment Association, which gave him solid scientific knowledge of heavier-than-air craft as well as practical experience with airplanes. He thereafter flew and designed airplanes.

Personal Profile

Glenn Hammond Curtiss (1878-1930) was second only to the Wright brothers in influence on the early development of American aviation. Interested in mechanical matters, he became a bicycle racer and then a bicycle manufacturer. He added motorcycle racing and motorcycle production to his activities. He participated in Alexander Graham Bell's Aerial Experiment Association that produced the successful *June Bug* and *Silver Dart* airplanes. In 1909 he founded the first aircraft manufacturing company in the United States; this was more than a year before the Wright brothers organized the Wright Company. His company and the successor Curtiss Aeroplane Company made pusher biplanes that incorporated ailerons. Curtiss became embroiled in patent litigation with the Wright brothers. He died in 1930, but his name continued in the aviation industry until the 1947 sale of the Aeroplane Division of Curtiss-Wright to North American, and the concurrent demise of Curtiss-Wright.

Glenn Hammond Curtiss

SECTION A

AIRSHIPS, DIRIGIBLES, AND BALLOONS

Q & A

What? The development of aircraft as weapons and the evolution of aerial warfare

When? 1914-1918 — During World War I

Where? Europe

Who? Combatant nations, both the Allies and the Central Powers

Why? To promote national interests and to defend national interests

RETOURNEMENT
(Side View)

Control in Center, Right Foot Well Forward

Feet Straight – Control Center; Slightly Forward

Mounting Steeply, Control Well Back

Feet Straight Slightly Forward Sharply to Right

Control Back to Center, Still Slightly Forward– Feet Straight

Normal Flight

Mounting

Normal Flight

World War I opened in 1914 with mobility as German troops stormed through Belgium and into France. The troops moved by train, truck, car, horse, and on foot. Aircraft observed the situation. Airplanes, balloons, dirigibles, and airships flew reconnaissance missions; the crews looked at the enemy, recorded their position, and reported. On occasion an airman dropped a little bomb, with little effect on the war below. Within months the movement stopped as troops on both sides dug into trenches. The war reached a stalemate. As one British pilot said, "flying was a soft job compared to what the infantry had to go through in the trenches." Indeed, the war was mostly down in the trenches where dirt could shelter a soldier from a bullet, and where long lines of opposing trenches faced each other and any head popping above a trench might become a target. The air provided a dramatic alternative to the positional war of attrition on the ground. Germany, France, Great Britain, and other nations had lighter-than-air crafts and crews in their air forces.

German Airships

When war broke out in Europe, the German Army had six operating airships, and the German Navy had two. At the time Germany had little strategy for using these rigid-frame airships, but the zeppelins were the pride of Germany's air-minded public which demanded they be used. Zeppelins, regardless of make, were *wunderwaffen* — wonder weapons. Thus, when the war began, the German Army flew airships on reconnaissance flights to observe the enemy, and occasionally an airship crew would drop a bomb or two. Soon Germany developed the airship as a bomber, though these aircraft proved most effective throughout the war as reconnaissance vehicles. The

---

Personal Profile

These boxes contain biographical information about important individuals who were instrumental in making aviation history. You will learn what made them noteworthy and how they achieved their success.

Question and Answer Boxes

Section A of each chapter begins with a Q&A box that answers the questions: What? When? Where? Who? and Why? This element helps to define the topic of the chapter.

Historical Evidence

Post-war disillusionment with World War I was expressed in novels and films.

Paramount released the motion picture *Wings* in 1927. *Wings* is a silent film about air warfare and the devastation of war. The film contains lots of footage of air battles. Richard Arlen and Buddy Rogers starred as two young men who joined the United States Air Service; Clara Bow played their romantic interest. The film won the first Academy Award for Best Picture. John Monk Saunders wrote the novel *Wings* in 1927 based on the movie.

The German novel *All Quiet on the Western Front* (1928), by Erich Maria Remarque, became a best-selling book not only in Germany but also through translations in other countries. It is about the war in the trenches, the war experienced by many more soldiers than the comparatively few airmen who participated in the air war. The Universal film version of *All Quiet on the Western Front*, starring Lew Ayres as German soldier Paul Baumer, won the Academy Award for Best Picture of 1930.

fighters, bombers, and scout craft. The end of the war struck the aircraft industry with cancellations of government contract, liquidations of contractual assets, contracts adjustments, and war surplus equipment — all of which curtailed the industry in the immediate post-war years. Finally, the Treaty of Versailles and its harsh treatment of Germany influenced international aviation developments.

Study Questions

1. Regarding airships during World War I, who made airship raids against whom — and why?

2. How effective was the airship as a bomber?

3. What wartime technological developments contributed to the fighter as a military type of airplane?

4. By the end of the war, what airplanes demonstrated the bomber as a mature-for-the-time technology?

5. Which source listed in the bibliography would you use to determine if a specific person served in an air arm of the United States during World War I?

6. What were the major steps or processes in the production of aircraft during World War I?

7. During the war, why did the United States fail to produce significant numbers of aircraft for use in Europe?

8. What affect did the Armistice and the various peace treaties have on aircraft production and military aviation?

4-48

Photographs

Both color and black and white photographs from a variety of sources are included to enhance the historic content. These elements can appear with the boxed information, in figures, and as stand-alone illustrations

Questions

Questions at the end of each chapter help you evaluate your understanding of the material. They cover not only events in aviation history, but also the relationship of events, people, and technology.

...tions did the Treaty of Versailles place on German aviation?

...ce or sources listed in the bibliography would you read for a first-hand or eye-witness account of wartime aviation?

Bibliography

Aviation Issue. *National Geographic Magazine*, 33/1 (January 1918): Major Joseph Tulasne, "America's Part in the Allies' Mastery of the Air"; Captain Jacques De Sieyes, "Aces of the Air"; Captain Andrè de Berroeta, "Flying in France"; Major William A. Bishop, "Tales of the British Air Service"; General P. Tozzi, "Italy's Eagles of Combat and Defense"; Lieutenant Colonel Hiram Bingham, "Building America's Air Army"; Stuart Walcott, "The Life Story of an American Airman in France"; Rear Admiral Robert E. Peary, "The Future of the Airplane"; and "Germany's Air Program."

Christienne, Charles and Pierre Lissarague. *A History of French Military Aviation*. Translated by Francis Klanka. French edition, 1980; Washington: Smithsonian Institution Press, 1986.

Finne, K.N. *Igor Sikorsky, the Russian Years*. Edited by Carl J. Bobrow and Von Hardesty. Translated by Von Hardsety. Russian edition, 1930; Washington: Smithsonian Institution Press, 1987.

Fritzsche, Peter. *A Nation of Fliers, German Aviation and the Popular Imagination*. Cambridge, MA: Harvard University Press, 1992.

Hallion, Richard P. *Rise of the Fighter Aircraft, 1914-1918*. Baltimore: Nautical & Aviation Publishing, 1984.

Jane's Fighting Aircraft of World War I. 1919; revised edition, London: Studio Editions, 1990.

Kennett, Lee. *The First Air War, 1914-1918*. New York: Free Press, 1991.

Richthofen, Manfred von. *The Red Baron*. Translated by Peter Kilduff. Edited by Stanley M. Ulanoff. 1969; New York: Barnes & Noble, 1969.

Robinson, Douglas. *The Zeppelin in Combat, a History of the German Naval Airship Division, 1912-1918*. 1962; Atglen, PA: Schiffer Publishing, 1994.

Sloan, James J. *Wings of Honor: American Airmen in World War I, a Compilation of All United States Pilots, Observers, Gunners and Mechanics Who Flew against the Enemy in the War of 1914-1918*. Atglen, PA: Schiffer Military/Aviation History, 1994.

Timeline

Light blue type indicates an event not directly related to aviation

1914	August 3. A German Taube monoplane dropped three bombs on Lunéville, France, in the earliest known bombing of the war.
1914	August 6. The German airship Z 6 bombed Liège, Belgium. This is the earliest documented use of an airship as a bomber during the war.
1914	August 26. An unarmed Morane Type Monoplane flown by P.N. Nesterov of Imperial Russian Army rammed an Austrian plane midair, because the Austrian plane was attacking the Sholkiv airfield where Nesterov was based; both pilots died.
1914	October 5. The crew of a French two-seat Voisin shot down a German two-seat Aviatik in air-to-air combat, perhaps the first successful victory of one airplane over another in battle.

4-49

Bibliography

Each chapter contains a bibliography of the books and other references used by the author in the preparation of the chapter. This list helps you locate additional information on the topics presented in the chapter.

Timeline

An expanded timeline is included at the end of each chapter. As with the overview at the beginning of the chapter, it covers both aviation events and those that are not directly related to aviation. Valuable insight can be gained by reviewing what was happening in the world during the time period covered in the chapter.

CHAPTER 1

EARLY AVIATION (1783-1914)

AVIATION HISTORY

Summary of Events

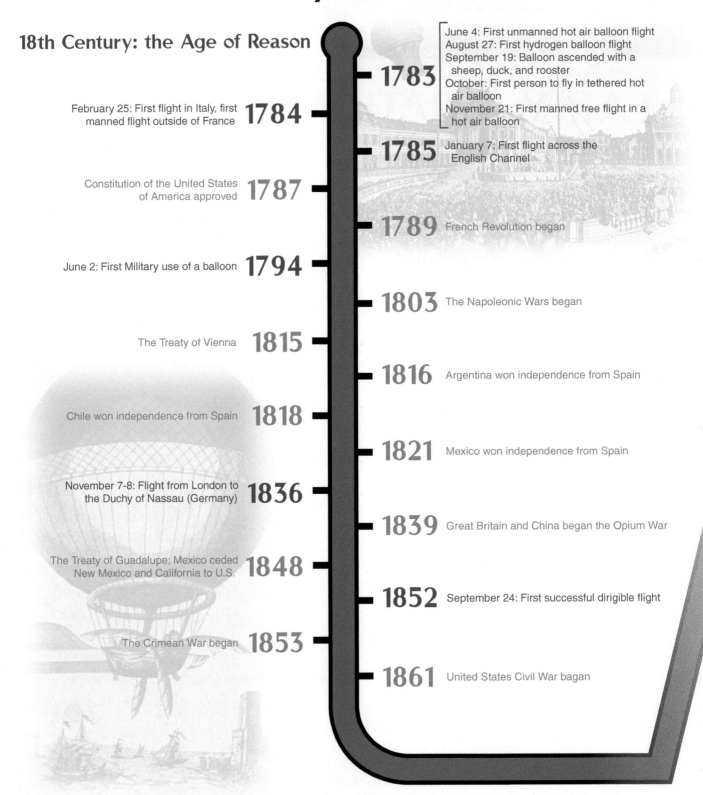

18th Century: the Age of Reason

February 25: First flight in Italy, first manned flight outside of France **1784**

Constitution of the United States of America approved **1787**

June 2: First Military use of a balloon **1794**

The Treaty of Vienna **1815**

Chile won independence from Spain **1818**

November 7-8: Flight from London to the Duchy of Nassau (Germany) **1836**

The Treaty of Guadalupe; Mexico ceded New Mexico and California to U.S. **1848**

The Crimean War began **1853**

1783 June 4: First unmanned hot air balloon flight
August 27: First hydrogen balloon flight
September 19: Balloon ascended with a sheep, duck, and rooster
October: First person to fly in tethered hot air balloon
November 21: First manned free flight in a hot air balloon

1785 January 7: First flight across the English Channel

1789 French Revolution began

1803 The Napoleonic Wars began

1816 Argentina won independence from Spain

1821 Mexico won independence from Spain

1839 Great Britain and China began the Opium War

1852 September 24: First successful dirigible flight

1861 United States Civil War bagan

Light blue type represents events that are not directly related to aviation.

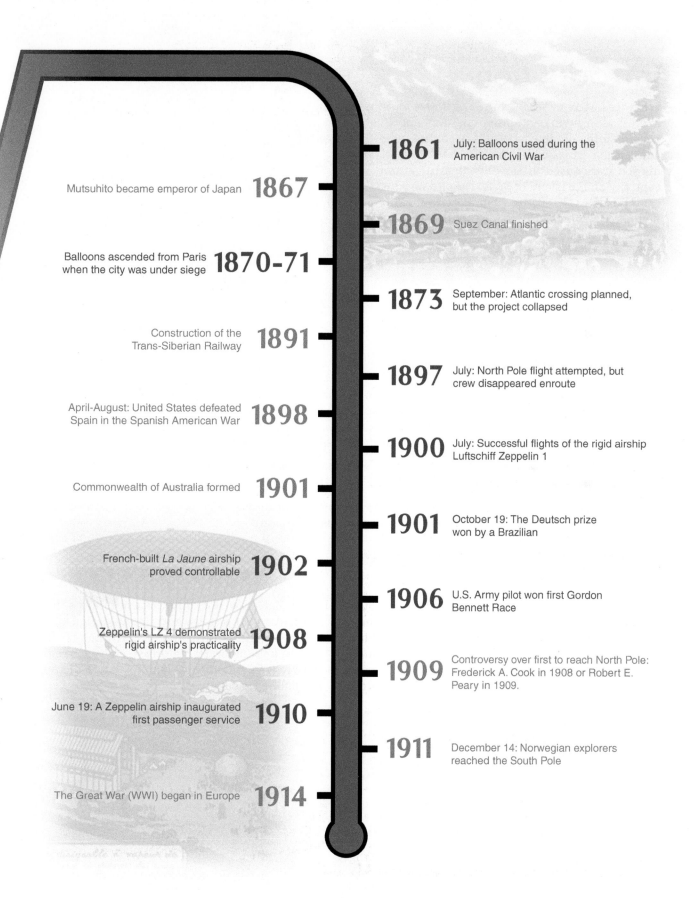

1861   July: Balloons used during the American Civil War

Mutsuhito became emperor of Japan   **1867**

1869   Suez Canal finished

Balloons ascended from Paris when the city was under siege   **1870-71**

1873   September: Atlantic crossing planned, but the project collapsed

Construction of the Trans-Siberian Railway   **1891**

1897   July: North Pole flight attempted, but crew disappeared enroute

April-August: United States defeated Spain in the Spanish American War   **1898**

1900   July: Successful flights of the rigid airship Luftschiff Zeppelin 1

Commonwealth of Australia formed   **1901**

1901   October 19: The Deutsch prize won by a Brazilian

French-built *La Jaune* airship proved controllable   **1902**

1906   U.S. Army pilot won first Gordon Bennett Race

Zeppelin's LZ 4 demonstrated rigid airship's practicality   **1908**

1909   Controversy over first to reach North Pole: Frederick A. Cook in 1908 or Robert E. Peary in 1909.

June 19: A Zeppelin airship inaugurated first passenger service   **1910**

1911   December 14: Norwegian explorers reached the South Pole

The Great War (WWI) began in Europe   **1914**

Introduction

What was early aviation? Initially, it was an idea expressed in myths and proposals. Ancient Greek legend told of the skillful Daedalus who constructed wings of wax and feathers. He and his son Icarus used these wings to escape from captivity on the island of Crete. Despite warnings from Daedalus, Icarus flew too close to the Sun and melted his wings. From the mythological Icarus comes the modern adjective icarian, meaning someone with high-flying or bold ambition.

Icarus and Daedalus

Historical Evidence

The story of Daedalus and Icarus comes from the oral tradition of ancient Greece. In the 8th century B.C. the Greek poet Homer composed epic poetry about Greece's past. Homer's *Illiad* is the story of the Greek military expedition against the Trojans of Troy. In the poem, Homer mentioned the skill of Daedalus and the Icarian Sea where Icarus fell. Homer recited his poems in order to entertain and inform his audiences. He was a superb storyteller in the oral tradition of his day.

Later Greeks wrote the Homeric epics on papyri, writing material made from reeds of the papyrus plant. The English word "paper" is derived from the Greek word for "papyrus."

Homer's *Iliad* remains a classic of literature, translated from the ancient Greek into many modern languages. From such writings that survived through time, scholars learned the story of Daedalus and Icarus. The Latin poet Ovid (43 B.C.–18 A.D.) told the whole story in book eight of his *Metamorphosis*. A popular English-language version of the story is in Thomas Bulfinch's *The Age of Fable*, originally published in 1855 and often reprinted as *Bulfinch's Mythology*.

During the Italian Renaissance, about the year 1500, Leonardo da Vinci designed several flying machines. Like the mythological Daedalus, he based his flapping-wing aircraft on the flight of birds. Such wing-flapping aircraft got the name ornithopter from the Greek words for bird and wing. Leonardo's drawings show not only the use of arms, but also the movement of legs, and in one design the head, to power and control the aircraft. Leonardo even drew a helicopter. His impressive designs remained drawings in manuscripts and notebooks unknown to the public for centuries.

Flying Machines of Leonardo da Vinci

In the seventeenth and eighteenth centuries there were various proposals for flying "ships"; for example, Father Francesco de Lana in 1670 proposed a ship carried into the air by four copper vacuum spheres.

When manned flight became a reality, aviation was called aerostation, levitation, or ballooning. It began in France in 1783 when Joseph and Étienne Montgolfier invented the hot air balloon. The Montgolfiers not only invented the balloon and ballooning, but also created the new field of aviation. They moved flight beyond mythology and speculation to practice. They invented, constructed, demonstrated, and improved the balloon as an aircraft. Others quickly joined the Montgolfiers in ballooning and further improved the design, construction, and operation of balloons.

Francesco de Lana's
Copper-Sphere Aerial Ship.

The Montgolfier brothers are the focus of Section A of this chapter. Their successors in ballooning are featured in Section B. Nineteenth-century advances in technology produced the dirigible balloon, which was directable or steerable due to the addition of power and control mechanisms. Dirigibles, such as those created by Brazilian aviation pioneer Alberto Santos-Dumont, are the subject of Section C. Section D covers semi-rigid and rigid airships; that is, dirigible balloons with supporting framework within the balloon envelope, like the famous German airships of Count Ferdinand von Zeppelin. In other words, this chapter covers the history of lighter-than-air craft, including free balloons (balloons that float freely without any means of controlling horizontal direction), nonrigid dirigible balloons (balloons with power and directional control), and semi-rigid and rigid airships (dirigible balloons with internal framework).

By studying this chapter, you should become familiar with what happened in lighter-than-air aviation and when it happened during the period from the invention of aviation in 1783 until the start of World War I in 1914. What happened — the main events — includes the people associated with aviation. It also includes the technologies of the time. Specifically, after studying this chapter, you will be able to identify the Montgolfier brothers and discuss their invention of the hot air balloon. You should also be able to identify the Montgolfiers' main competitor, J.A.C. Charles, and discuss the competing technology of the hydrogen balloon. You will be able to cite several examples of aviators and balloon flights from the late 18th century into the early 20th century. You should understand the development of dirigibles and airships, the relationship of these developments to basic balloon technology, and the contributions of aviation pioneers like Santos-Dumont and von Zeppelin to these newer technologies. For all these early lighter-than-air technologies, you should be able to discuss the motives behind the development and use of the aircraft, including research, transportation, military, sport, and exploration.

SECTION A

THE INVENTION OF AVIATION

Q & A

What? The invention of the hot air balloon and thereby the invention of aviation

When? 1783 amid the Enlightenment enthusiasm for science and technology

Where? Annonay, France

Who? Joseph and Étienne Montgolfier

Why? To experiment with converting heat into mechanical energy and to fly

Aviation began in the provincial French town of Annonay, where the brothers Joseph and Étienne Montgolfier lived. The year was 1783.

The Montgolfier Brothers

Joseph and Étienne Montgolfier were two of sixteen children in the wealthy bourgeois family of Montgolfier, papermakers. The family owned and operated two papermills on the Deûme River upstream from Annonay; the steep flow of the river provided the waterpower to turn the wheels of their mills. In 1783 there were four papermills on the Deûme, two operated by the Catholic Montgolfiers and two competing mills owned by the Protestant Johannot family. Joseph was the 12th child in the

Montgolfier family and Étienne the 15th. Joseph was 43 years old, and while he was absent-minded and a careless dresser, he was the creative and enthusiastic partner in the balloon project. Practical Étienne, 38 and a neat dresser, managed the family's papermills and brought business and organizational skills to the balloon project.

Although mechanics and science interested both brothers, it was Joseph who conceived the idea of aviation. He had read Joseph Priestly's 1774 scientific treatise on oxygen and had heard of Henry Cavendish's 1766 discovery of hydrogen. Joseph was experimenting with heat and mechanical work in the form of steam engines and heat pumps when he turned his attention to aviation. He defined the problem in aviation as one of heat applied to air, a problem of chemistry in the language of that day. He

Historical Note

Joseph Montgolfier performed experiments relating to flight in order to understand the mechanical nature of heat, a technical problem. He may have defined flight also as a military problem. At the time, as thirteen American colonies fought for independence from Great Britain, Spain besieged the British territory of Gibraltar. This Great Siege lasted from 1779 into 1783. Contemporary evidence suggests that Joseph Montgolfier realized that the long siege of Gibraltar might be broken from the air.

observed clouds in suspension in the air and explored the analogy of enclosing a cloud in a bag. He saw smoke rise from a fire and experimented with a paper bag over a fire. The warmed air lifted the bag. He then constructed a model of taffeta on a thin wood form, lit a fire, and watched the model rise to the ceiling.

Joseph informed Étienne of the experiment with the taffeta model, and the two brothers began to build larger models with wood forms and to conduct more experiments. This was a rational approach, an Enlightenment approach, familiar to Joseph in his scientific and mechanical investigations and similar to that used by Étienne in improving and rationalizing the manufacture of paper in the family's mills. In order to protect their priority, their claim of developing the first ascending machine, Étienne Montgolfier in December 1782 reported on the experiments in progress to Nicolas Desmarest, an official of the national Bureau of Commerce and a member of the Academy of Science. Joseph and Étienne thought of their invention as a machine, a scientific and mechanical device, as revealed in their initial use of the term *machine diöstatique* (static air machine). Étienne suggested this new machine might be used to transmit communications, to conduct scientific experiments, to carry people, drop bombs, or transport goods.

The two brothers, with the help and support of the family, proceeded to construct a full-size machine. Only the brothers' elderly father thought the project a folly. While the family constructed the full-size balloon for unmanned flight, he forbade Joseph and Étienne from flying — just in case they had any such

ideas, which they did. Still, they promised him they would not fly. For the full-scale balloon, Joseph and Étienne eliminated the wood form that had shaped their models. Instead of this rigid form, the brothers adopted a flexible bag or envelope, reinforced with rope. They considered using "inflammable air," as hydrogen was then called, due to its lightness and to its relative permanence compared with hot air (which would cool), but the cost of obtaining hydrogen prompted them to continue using hot air. Étienne performed mathematical analyses to determine dimensions, weight, volume, lifting force, rate of ascent, fuel consumption, and cost. Unlike the models, this full-scale balloon was lined with paper, which was in plentiful supply at the Montgolfier mills and which insulated the fabric to hold hot air. Joseph and Étienne performed a series of tethered tests, which permitted them to refine their techniques for filling and releasing the balloon.

The First Balloon Ascension

The brothers scheduled the first public ascension of the balloon for 4 June 1783 to coincide with a meeting of the *Etats particuliers de Vivarais* (the assembly of the district of Vivarais). This legislative assembly represented the nobility (the second estate) and the commons (the third estate) of the Vivarais district; the clergy (the first estate) were not represented in the assembly. Annonay was a market and industrial town in the northern end of Vivarais, near the Rhône River, south of Lyons. In 1783 Annonay was the site of the annual meeting of the *Etats particuliers*, which met in

Historical Note

The paper used in the Montgolfiers' balloons was different and stronger than the wood-pulp paper in routine use today. Then, paper was made of cotton and linen fibers, often made literally of rags. It was called rag paper.

various towns in the district. The brothers invited the officials to view the ascension and to document the event.

Before the launch, a crowd of invited officials and curious people had gathered in the rain to watch four workmen inflate the balloon. Joseph and Étienne supervised the workers, who first constructed a wooden frame and then hung the balloon over the frame. This balloon consisted of linen sackcloth lined with rag paper. The four fabric panels of the balloon — one for the dome and three for the sides — were held together by sewn seams and approximately 1,800 buttons. The workers placed a brazier or tray holding a fire under the mouth of the balloon; wool and straw were the fuels. This fire gradually heated the air that rose and filled the balloon. When filled, the balloon displaced nearly 28,000 cubic feet of air and weighed approximately 500 pounds. The diameter was about 35 feet and the circumference about 110 feet. Ropes covered and thereby reinforced the balloon. (Figure 1-1)

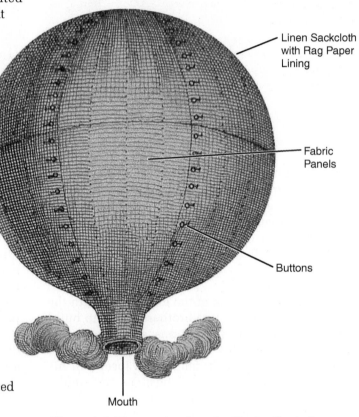

Linen Sackcloth with Rag Paper Lining

Fabric Panels

Buttons

Mouth

Figure 1-1. The construction of a Montgolfier balloon.

As the balloon tugged at its tether lines, the brothers instructed the workers to attach the brazier below it. This was an improvised effort to counter the cooling effects of the day's rain. Since the official observers from the *Etats particuliers* were present, the brothers refused to postpone the flight. Once released, the balloon rose to almost 3,000 feet (500 *toises* in the French measurement of the day). Air currents carried the balloon about a mile and a half. Warm air leaking out the numerous button holes limited the duration of the flight. As the balloon landed, the brazier spilled embers onto the fabric and started a fire that consumed the balloon. Startled peasants near the landing spot watched the strange thing burn. Despite the destruction of the balloon, the Montgolfiers' experiment had been a success. The brothers had demonstrated their invention: the hot air balloon, a flight vehicle lifted and held aloft by heated air. The hot air balloon was soon called a *montgolfière* after its inventors.

Given the successful demonstration in Annonay, and the fire that destroyed that balloon upon landing, the brothers immediately began to make another balloon. They planned a demonstration of their invention in Paris. The Academy of Science appointed a committee to consider this new subject of aviation. Among the members were Desmarest, a geologist; the marquis de Condorcet, a mathematician; and Antoine Lavoisier, a famous chemist. In Paris the Montgolfier brothers sought government funds to reimburse their ballooning expenses to date and to finance further development of aviation; they also sought publicity for their balloon and orders for their papermaking business. In time they partly achieved all these objectives.

Historic Event

On 4 June 1783 a balloon ascended from a town square beside the Deûme River in the French town of Annonay. It traveled a distance of about one and a half miles and remained in the air about ten minutes. The event is now history: the first public ascension of a balloon and the beginning of aviation. The hot air balloon became known as a *montgolfière* after the Montgolfier brothers who invented and launched this first balloon.

the hydrogen in the envelope. Instrument makers A.J. and M.N. Robert, brothers, had discovered how to dissolve rubber in turpentine, and this allowed them to rubberize the silk taffeta fabric used in construction of the envelope. The envelope thus consisted of taffeta and india rubber, and the exterior was decorated with red and blue stripes. Given the lightness of hydrogen, the balloon's diameter was only twelve feet, yet that required 900 cubic feet of a gas previously produced in only small, experimental quantities. The Robert brothers solved this problem too. After considering various means of obtaining large quantities of hydrogen, they decided to use an oak barrel filled with iron filings. They poured vitriolic (sulfuric) acid over the filings in the barrel, and a copper tube carried the hydrogen from the barrel to the valve opening on the balloon. When the tethered balloon was partly filled, it rose about 100 feet above Paris and attracted an unanticipated crowd. This prompted Charles to move the partly inflated balloon at night through the streets of Paris to the Champ de Mars, the site scheduled for a public ascension the next day.

On the 27th of August 1783, Charles and his crew produced the additional hydrogen necessary to finish filling the envelope of the balloon, while troops kept the park clear of people. Ticket holders gained admission to the park at 3 p.m. Beyond the park, people crowded roof tops and Paris streets. Charles released the balloon at 5 p.m. The balloon rose quickly, about 1,500 feet in two minutes, and disappeared in clouds. These clouds both rushed the

Competition

Étienne Montgolfier represented the brothers in Paris. When he arrived, the city already knew of the balloon ascension in Annonay. The French Academy of Sciences had already awarded a grant for the development of another balloon, and ticket sales were underway to underwrite experiments of a competitor! Each ticket holder would be admitted to view a balloon ascension yet to be scheduled. The grant and ticket sales both supported the work of J.A.C. Charles, a physicist. Charles decided to use hydrogen as the lifting agent, so his design was called a hydrogen balloon. Unlike Annonay, Paris had both the financial and chemical resources necessary for him to develop the hydrogen balloon.

Aided by Parisian artisans, Charles constructed a hydrogen balloon. He needed a tight sealant to hold

Personal Profile

Jacques Alexander César Charles (1746-1823), a physicist and popular lecturer, had extracted hydrogen from acids in reaction with metals. For visual effect, he had even soaped the opening of the experimental container in order to create hydrogen soap bubbles. This experience he applied to ballooning when he learned of the *montgolfière* demonstration at Annonay. Charles employed hydrogen as the lifting agent in his balloons, but that agent presented the challenge of finding an air-tight fabric for the balloon envelope. Rubberized silk proved to be the answer.

Jacques Alexander
César Charles

its steady pressure while rising through thinning atmosphere. Like the first *montgolfière*, this first *charlière* or hydrogen balloon proved successful despite being totally destroyed.

Historic Event

The French physicist J.A.C. Charles launched a hydrogen balloon on 27 August 1783. This was the second public ascension of a balloon and the first launch of a hydrogen balloon. Like the first *montgolfière*, this first *charlière* was an unmanned experimental aircraft.

First *Charlière* balloon ascent

Hot Air Development

The Montgolfier brothers, their priority well recognized, continued work on their balloon. In Paris, Étienne arranged for the Academy of Science to temporarily finance the balloon under assembly at the Réveillon wallpaper factory, and he eventually convinced the government Ministry of Finance to assume this financial responsibility. The second *montgolfière* was similar to the first, yet improved. At forty feet, its diameter was a little bigger. When inflated, it weighed 2,500 pounds and displaced 4,500 pounds of atmosphere. Paper lined the interior and exterior of taffeta cloth; the Montgolfiers still considered paper adequate reinforcement for a hot air balloon. Étienne designed the balloon in three sections: a center panel, a top cap, and a base cone. Étienne's friend J.B. Réveillon decorated this balloon elegantly in wallpaper style with decorations of gold on a background of azure.

Held captive by ropes and men, the second *montgolfière* passed a test flight. The next day, 12 September 1783, the balloon was ready for demonstration to the Academy of Science. It rained that day, but a crowd gathered, so Étienne continued preparations despite the weather. Briquettes of straw and shreds of wool fueled the fire below the envelope. As the filled balloon pulled at its tether lines, the rain increased. The rain gradually washed off the paper covering the cloth envelope, and this forced Étienne to cancel the ascension. The lesson of the failed experiment, he wrote Joseph, was to build a machine not vulnerable to fire, wind, or water. The Montgolfier brothers and their associates rushed to build a new balloon for their next launch, which was scheduled to carry animals aloft in a demonstration before King Louis XVI and Marie Antoinette at Versailles.

launching of the balloon and obscured most of its flight from view. Less than an hour later the balloon burst and fell to the ground north of Paris, near Ecouen. Frightened peasants attacked the wreck with pitchforks. (Figure 1-2) Charles determined that the balloon burst due to

Figure 1-2. When the first *charlière* landed, the locals attacked it and beat it to death.

Completed within a week, the new *montgolfière* consisted of brightly colored, varnish-coated taffeta. The balloon had a diameter of 41 feet, a displacement of 3,192 pounds of air, and a cage for a sheep, a duck, and a rooster. On 19 September at Versailles the balloon rose about

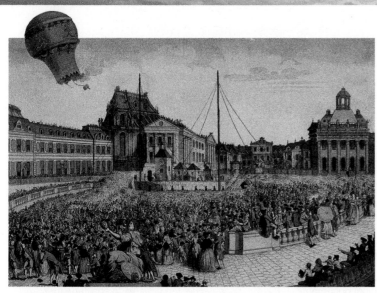

Figure 1-3. The cage below the Montgolfier balloon carried the first passengers aloft: a sheep, duck, and rooster.

1,500 feet. Gusty winds tilted the balloon, which allowed hot air to escape and limited the duration of the flight; nonetheless, the balloon traveled a little more than two miles (1,800 fathoms). The king watched the eight-minute flight with field glasses. Both the balloon and the animals landed safely. The experiment was a great success. (Figure 1-3)

Manned Flight

Manned flight also began in 1783. In October, Étienne Montgolfier tested a new balloon built for carrying people. This balloon had a diameter of forty-six feet. Still financed by the French government, the Montgolfiers again employed Réveillon to decorate the envelope. Below the envelope hung a burner and below that a wicker gallery. Fire aboard a manned balloon would allow the aerialist to control altitude; for that reason, the hot air or *montgolfière* balloon also became known as the fire balloon. As the balloon neared completion, Étienne rode in the gallery in tethered flight. This test was the first manned flight in the history of aviation! In a letter from Annonay, Étienne's wife congratulated him for embarking successfully and especially for returning safely. Due to the Montgolfier brothers' promise to their father not to fly, Étienne did not publicize this experimental flight made in the privacy of the Réveillon courtyard.

Later that month Jean-François Pilâtre de Rozier made solo, tethered flights in the same balloon used by Étienne. Passengers accompanied him on two test flights. Pilâtre de Rozier promoted aviation, and he generated publicity for his test flights. He and the marquis d'Arlandes, François Laurent, made the first

public manned flight in a free (untethered) balloon on 21 November 1783. The event had been postponed twice, for rain the previous day and for wind earlier on the 21st. The well-publicized free flight of a manned *montgolfière* lasted 25 minutes, passed over Paris, and covered five miles. (Figure 1-4) The American diplomat Benjamin Franklin, then assigned to Paris, was among the official observers who signed a *procès-verbal* documenting the flight; *procès-verbal* is French for a written report of proceedings.

Figure 1-4. The first public ascent of an untethered balloon with human passengers on 21 November 1783.

 ## Historic Event

In October 1783 Étienne Montgolfier became the first person to fly — the first airman. He went aloft in a hot air balloon. He tested the balloon in tethered flight in the privacy of the Réveillon courtyard in Paris. This was in the routine course of his developing balloon technology.

 ## Historic Event

The first public manned flight and the first manned flight in a free balloon occurred on 21 November 1783, in Paris, France. Jean-François Pilâtre de Rozier and François Laurent, the marquis d'Arlandes, went aloft in a *montgolfière* hot air balloon.

Historical Evidence

For years history books named Jean-François Pilâtre de Rozier as the first person to fly. This "fact" was based on the tethered solo flights by Pilâtre de Rozier in October of 1783. That is because Pilâtre de Rozier spoke publicly of his flights, and written reports of his flights survive, and because Étienne Montgolfier did not mention flying earlier except in private communications, which remained private for two hundred years.

In the 1980s a historian named Charles Coulston Gillispie conducted research using the Montgolfier family papers. He found correspondence about Étienne and Joseph promising their father not to fly, as well as about Étienne's flying. In one surviving letter, Étienne's wife Adélaïde wrote, "I have just received your letter, my dear, where you tell us about your embarking. Although it did not give me much pleasure, I congratulate you on your success and specially on your safe return. I don't much like these aerial voyages." The family tried to keep Étienne's flying secret from his father, but failed. The father again demanded that his children not fly, but Joseph later went aloft.

The Montgolfiers' letters of 1783 are primary sources of historical information. Gillispie's book *The Montgolfier Brothers and the Invention of Aviation* is a secondary source, as the 20th-century historian had no first-hand or primary knowledge of 18th-century events. In the book are English translations of parts of the original documents — the evidence — that led Gillispie to conclude that Étienne Montgolfier was the first person to fly.

Hydrogen Balloon Development

Meanwhile the instrument makers A.J. and M.N. Robert also developed a manned balloon. They improved the hydrogen design of Charles, whom they had assisted earlier in the year. In particular, the Robert brothers improved the method of generating large quantities of hydrogen by arranging barrels in a ring, each barrel containing metal scraps and each connected to a central tube. They recharged the barrels in sequence, and used a less concentrated form of sulfuric acid than they had used to fill Charles' balloon. (Figure 1-5) The Roberts' envelope was 26 feet in diameter and reinforced with netting. A new feature was altitude control: a valve and a secondary opening through which the pilot could release pressure. Like the earlier ascension of a *charlière*, this new hydrogen balloon was financed through the advance sale of tickets to the launching. On 1 December 1783 M.N. Robert and J.A.C. Charles flew the balloon from Paris to Nesle, a distance of about 17 miles (43 kilometers). (Figure 1-6) After the pair landed, Charles ascended solo to a height of 9,000 feet (2,743 meters) and recorded scientific observations. The rapid ascent to such a high altitude, however, frightened him, and he never again flew.

Aviation thus began in 1783. That year Joseph and Étienne Montgolfier and J.A.C. Charles designed and launched two types of balloon: the hot air and the hydrogen. Both types became known by the names of their respective designers, establishing a practice still in use today. Though certainly recognizing the value of public recognition, the Montgolfier brothers and Charles referred to their early launches as experiments, since they applied the scientific method as then understood. Their first experiments were unmanned tests of machinery and

Figure 1-5. To inflate the hydrogen balloon, the Robert brothers use a central tube connected to a ring of barrels filled with metal scraps. The barrels were recharged in sequence by adding sulfuric acid to each barrel in turn. The acid's action on the metal generated hydrogen.

Flight Lines

"I stood up in the middle of the gondola, and lost myself in the spectacle offered by the immensity of the horizon. When I took off from the fields, the sun had set for the inhabitants of the valleys. Soon it rose for me alone, and again appeared to gild the balloon and gondola with its rays. I was the only illuminated body within the whole horizon, and I saw all the rest of nature plunged in shadow."

J.A.C. Charles, 1 December 1783, as translated and quoted in Charles Coulston Gillispie, *The Montgolfier Brothers and the Invention of Aviation.*

theories of flight. Less than six months after the first public ascension of a *montgolfière*, aviation evolved to manned flight. In a very short time, aviation moved from fancy to fact. The fact included the technology of aircraft, the airmanship of new aerial pilots, the infrastructure — designers, constructors, suppliers, financiers — on the ground, as well as popular and press interest in aviation.

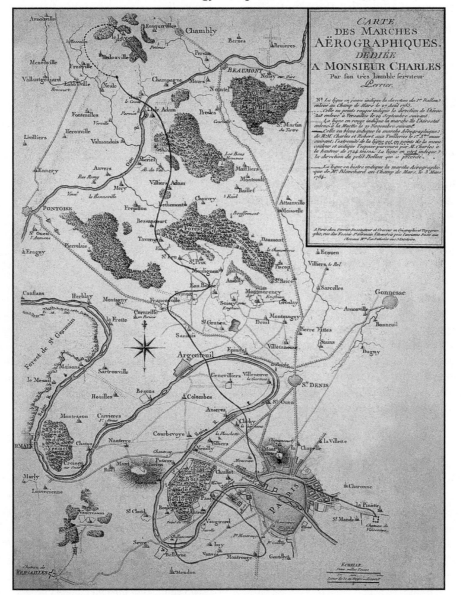

Figure 1-6. Flight of M.N. Robert and J.A.C. Charles from Paris to Nesle on 1 December 1783.

SECTION B

BALLOONS

What the Montgolfier brothers had begun in Annonay in 1783 quickly spread. Ballooning became immediately popular throughout Europe and soon spread across the Atlantic Ocean. As new names entered aviation, some of the pioneers left. The marquis d'Arlandes stopped flying after his one flight in November 1783. Preferring scientific work to fast ascent, J.A.C. Charles quit flying after his two flights on the first of December 1783. But the Montgolfier brothers were not through yet.

The Montgolfiers Continue

At the end of 1783, Joseph Montgolfier was constructing a large 100-foot diameter balloon in Lyons. The heat source for it was a wood burner, more powerful than straw- and wool-burning braziers and, therefore, capable of generating more lift. This fifth *montgolfière* built for public display was called the *Flesselles*, after a local government official and supporter, though this project was financed through the advance sale of tickets. Joseph supervised the final assembly and when he attempted to inflate the balloon, repairs had to be made. After the repairs, he completed a tethered test flight with six passengers aboard in January 1784. In the twenty-four hours before a planned free flight with six passengers, rain and sleet damaged the aircraft. Then a fire burned the cap and necessitated substantial repairs. Snow fell, and the fabric froze stiff. Workers thawed and reinflated the balloon, which now had holes in its weakened fabric.

Contrary to safety considerations and reasonable advice, four noblemen insisted upon ascending in the damaged craft — insisted with guns! Jean-François Pilâtre de Rozier decided to board too. So then did Joseph Montgolfier and a fifth nobleman. That made seven passengers in the balloon. The crowd in attendance pressed for a show. The balloon was released. Initially, it dragged, but gradually the *Flesselles* rose to a height of approximately 2,500 feet. Fabric tore, and the balloon descended rapidly. It landed hard, yet the event was another successful demonstration of flight, and as such was duly celebrated by the crowd and town. (Figure 1-7)

Figure 1-7. Heavily laden with seven passengers, the *Flesseles* rose above the town of Lyons, France.

Historic Event

On 4 June 1784 Madame Thible became the first female aboard a balloon in free flight. At least four French women preceded her aloft in tethered flight. With a male pilot, Madame Thible flew in a *montgolfière* named *Le Gustav* after the king of Sweden, who was among the spectators watching that flight.

Historic Event

Jean-François Pilâtre de Rozier and Pierre Romain became the first aerial fatalities. Under a grant from the French government, and in a balloon that mixed hot air and hydrogen, they attempted to cross the English Channel from east to west; that is, from France to England. Their balloon caught fire, and they crashed near Boulogne, not far from the launch site. The date was 15 June 1785, less than two years after the first manned flights.

Historical Note

Balloonists introduced the sport and the safety of parachutes to aviation. The French balloonist André Jacques Garnerin was an aerial showman. In Paris on 22 October 1797, he made a successful parachute jump from a balloon about 3,000 feet in the air; this is the earliest known drop from substantial altitude. Garnerin died in a parachute descent 21 September 1802. In September 1815 Garnerin's niece, Eliza Garnerin, became the first woman to drop by parachute from a balloon. Her ascent by balloon and descent by chute were over Paris. The earliest known case of a pilot parachuting to safety happened on 24 July 1808: R. Jordarki Kuparanto abandoned his burning hot air balloon over Warsaw.

Joseph and Étienne Montgolfier collaborated on ballooning into the summer of 1784, when Étienne left Paris and returned to full-time management of the family papermills. Joseph helped develop a parachute in 1784, but soon turned his inventive attention away from aviation.

Military Aviation

France led the world in aviation, including military aviation. In fact, military aviation began in France. In 1793 Napoleon's revolutionary government assigned a confiscated balloon to the Republican army. With this balloon, the army started its air arm. In 1794 the French army formally organized the *Compagnie d'Aerostiers* (company of balloonists). Aerostat was a balloon, aerostier a balloonist, and aerostation ballooning. The military *compagnie* consisted of balloonists trained to work in pairs as observers of enemy troop positions and movements, as well as command and support personnel. That June, in the hydrogen balloon *Entreprenant* (*Enterprise*), these military aeronauts went into action against the Austrian army. They launched from the French base at Maubeuge, and they observed Austrian maneuvers at Charleroi. When the Austrians saw the balloon, they realized their positions were known to the French, and surrendered. Military aeronauts also participated in the battle of Fleurus a month later, and during the siege of Mainz the following year. (Figure 1-8) Unable to retreat quickly enough, however, the balloon corps was captured by Austrians at Würzburg in September 1796. The Austrians imprisoned the men and preserved the balloon (which is still in the military museum in Vienna). Napoleon Bonaparte also used a second balloon company against the Italians at the siege of Mantua in 1796.

Although Napoleon's two balloon companies provided valuable information during several campaigns, in

Figure 1-8. The use of balloons during the battle of Fleurus.

1799 the army disbanded both companies and the training school for military balloonists at Meudon. For the most part, warfare diverted French interest and resources away from flying — despite the temporary military use of balloons. The French Revolution had plunged France into war in 1789, and conflict continued through the Napoleonic Wars, which concluded with the Treaty of Vienna in 1815. All that time aviation activities increased in other countries.

International Aviation

The achievements of Joseph and Étienne Montgolfier had attracted immediate and international interest to aviation. On 25 February 1784 Paolo Andreani, Charles Gerli, and Augustin Gerli made the first balloon ascension in Italy. This was the first manned flight outside of France. In 1784 manned flight was also achieved in Ireland, Scotland, England,

Historical Note

On 3 December 1804 piloted and pilotless balloons filled the air above Paris in celebration of Pope Pius VII crowning Napoleon Bonaparte emperor of France. In 1799, a few years after the French Revolution, Napoleon had seized power in France. He refused to recognize the Pope's authority, but he appreciated the public relations value of the Pope officiating at his coronation. Military aviation had begun in France during the revolutionary period, but the Napoleonic Wars of the early 19th century diverted French resources and attention away from aviation.

Figure 1-9. As ballooning spread outside France, it quickly became a favorite pastime, as seen in this countryside painting.

and the United States. Clearly, the technology and techniques of ballooning quickly became international. (Figure 1-9)

Jean-Pierre Blanchard was a French balloonist who helped spread aviation to other countries. Blanchard had experimented with flapping-wings prior to the Montgolfiers' demonstration of the hot air balloon. Upon news of the Montgolfiers' achievement, he became a balloonist and showman. He demonstrated his aerostatic skills and his aerostat — a hydrogen balloon — in England in 1784. While in London, he met an American expatriate named John Jeffries. A native of Massachusetts, Jeffries had graduated from Harvard College and had studied medicine in England and Scotland. A loyalist during the American Revolution, he moved to Canada and then to London. While in London, he became interested in levitation, as ballooning was sometimes called, and in the possibilities of studying the atmosphere aloft. In order to make scientific observations, Jeffries employed Blanchard.

Blanchard and Jeffries made two "aerial voyages" together, the first from London to Kent on 30 November 1784, and the second from England to France on 7 January 1785. On the first voyage, while floating over London, Jeffries wrote four cards, addressed them to friends, and dropped them out of

the car — an event sometimes cited as the first airmail, informal though it was. By wearing hidden weights, Blanchard had tried to trick Jeffries out of accompanying him on the second voyage, but Jeffries prevailed. That voyage crossed the English Channel and made both men famous, as it was the first flight of a balloon over a major body of water. To reward the Frenchman, Louis XVI granted Blanchard a pension. During both voyages Jeffries observed meteorological and aeronautical phenomena. More specifically, he studied the power of ascending and descending and the effect of oars or wings — attached to what Jeffries called the aerial car — for the purpose of steering the balloon. He also studied air currents, temperature, barometric pressure, and hydrometric and electrometric readings of the atmosphere at different altitudes. After the flights Jeffries published *A Narrative of the Two Aerial Voyages*, a volume described as the first book on aviation written by an American, albeit an American expatriate living in England. Jeffries later moved back to the United States and practiced medicine in Boston. (Figure 1-10)

Figure 1-10. Jean-Pierre Blanchard and John Jeffries became the first people to cross the English Channel by balloon on 7 January 1785.

Historic Event

On 7 January 1785 the French balloonist Jean-Pierre Blanchard and the American doctor John Jeffries crossed the English Channel in a hydrogen balloon. This was the first flight of a balloon over a major body of water. The balloon's car is preserved at the Calais Museum in Calais, France, near where the pair landed.

Flight Lines

"At half past one o'clock, the Balloon seemed to be distended to its utmost extent, and thereby (as in our former experiment) drew up the Car close to it; on which occasion, recollecting the importance of a sufficiency of inflammable air, to the completion of our Voyage, and that it was not possible to determine exactly, how much of it might escape if we opened the valve, we *only untwisted the two tubes at the bottom of the Balloon*, by which it had been filled with the gaz, and cast them over the sides of the Car; and in a minute or two we had the pleasure to see them become distended through their whole length, beginning at the ends attached to the Balloon. We also had the farther satisfaction to observe, that by this method, no more of the gaz or inflammable air would escape, than was absolutely necessary to relieve the Balloon, and to prevent it from bursting."

John Jeffries, 7 January 1785, on a flight across the English Channel; in Jeffries, *A Narrative of the Two Aerial Voyages*.

Ballooning in the United States

Blanchard soon left revolutionary France and traveled to the United States. He made a tour of the States where ballooning was already popular. Doctor John Foulke of Philadelphia had studied aerostation (ballooning) in France in 1783. Back in the States the next year Foulke lectured about ballooning and released a six-foot diameter hot air balloon made of paper. This was possibly the first unmanned balloon released in the States. Launching small paper balloons quickly became popular sport. In 1784 the College of William and Mary in Virginia established a Balloon Club, which within a couple of years succeeded in making both hot air and hydrogen balloons. Also in 1784, a tavern owner and lawyer, Peter Carnes of Maryland, used silk to make a 35-foot

Historical Note

Water challenged balloonists, as water provided no landing ground. In 1785 Richard Crosbie made three unsuccessful attempts to fly across the Irish Sea. On the third attempt he descended into the sea, from which a barge rescued him. Also in 1785, Richard McGwire attempted the crossing. He came down about ten miles off the Irish shore from which he had departed. Finally in 1817, Windham Sadler achieved the first aerial crossing of the Irish Sea. (His father James Sadler had become a balloonist in 1784).

diameter hot air balloon. He exhibited this "American Aerostatic Balloon" in Baltimore in June. He sold tickets to the public for watching flights on the 19th and the 24th. Carnes had planned and advertised that he would ride in the balloon on those days, but damage to the balloon during transportation prevented any attempt on the 19th and his large size — he was a big man — grounded him on the 24th. That day a youth of thirteen years, Edward Warren, volunteered to ride in the balloon. Carnes consented, and Warren — in tethered flight — achieved the first manned ascent in the United States. Thereafter other manned, tethered flights occurred in the country.

Historic Event

French balloonist Jean-Pierre Blanchard made the first free flight of a manned balloon in all of the Americas. He ascended from Philadelphia, Pennsylvania, and descended in rural New Jersey. The date was 9 January 1793.

What Blanchard accomplished on 9 January 1793 was the first manned free flight of a balloon in all the Americas. This was the 45th ascension in the aeronaut's career. As a gesture of goodwill, President George Washington presented Blanchard a written passport for safe conduct wherever he might land. Washington joined the crowd who watched the ascension from the Walnut Street Prison in Philadelphia; the prison yard was large enough to hold the more than four thousand ticket holders. Blanchard traveled with the wind and landed in Gloucester County, New Jersey, about 15 miles from his launch site. With only broken English at his command, he used the passport given him by Washington to befriend local residents who came to the landing site. He financed this event and his American tour through the sale of tickets and of his

Personal Profile

Jean-Pierre Blanchard (1753-1809) began his aviation career by experimenting with flapping-wing or ornithopter designs. He tested parachutes by dropping sheep off roofs. Upon learning of the Montgolfiers' invention, he immediately turned to ballooning. He continued experimenting with mechanical devices. On 16 October 1784 he attempted to propel a balloon by hand-turning a propeller that he had attached to the basket. On 7 January 1785 he and John Jeffries made the first aerial crossing of the English Channel. His rewards were fame and a French pension. On 9 January 1793 he made the first manned free flight of a balloon in the Americas. He was an accomplished aviator who suffered a heart attack while in flight in 1808 and who died on 7 March 1809.

Jean-Pierre Blanchard

Historic Event

Madeleine-Sophie Blanchard, widow of Jean-Pierre Blanchard, was the first woman to die in a flying accident. An aerial performer, she specialized in night flights lit by fireworks. She died when fireworks ignited her balloon, and she and the balloon fell onto a Paris roof, on 7 July 1819.

own publications about ballooning. Blanchard continued flying into 1808, when he suffered a heart attack while aloft and fell about 50 feet. He died the next year.

Exhibition Flying

By the early 19th century, the basic equipment for ballooning was well developed. The spectacle of flight, not the technology, held the attention of both balloonists (increasingly

called aeronauts) and the public. Aeronauts rather than designers dominated ballooning. The professional aeronauts flew for exhibition and distance. Since flight was dominant, 19th-century development focused on improving performance and lowering costs, and balloonists did the development work.

The English balloonist Charles Green achieved success in exhibitions and development. In the early 1820s Green tried using coal gas instead of hydrogen. He obtained the coal gas from the Westminster and London Gas Light and Coke Company. Though heavier than hydrogen, this gas was readily available, took less time to inflate the balloon, and proved less acidic and therefore less harmful than privately generated hydrogen. In the 1830s Green invented the **dragline**, a rope attached to the balloon basket and used when the balloon was near the ground to slow the speed of descent or ascent. On descent, dropping the line on the ground reduced the weight supported by the balloon and thereby slowed the descent. On ascent, carrying the dragline in the basket increased the weight to be lifted aloft and thereby slowed the ascent. (Figure 1-11)

Figure 1-11. In addition to slowing the ascent and descent of the balloon, the dragline created by Charles Green also was used in conjunction with a moveable sail to help steer the balloon.

Personal Profile

Charles Green (1785-1870) was an English balloonist known for performing stunts and for advancing the science and technology of flight. Among his stunts was riding a pony into the basket of a balloon and into flight. He discovered that gas from the municipal gas lines could be used in balloons at less cost than hydrogen. He invented the dragline and developed its applications. He set a balloon distance record of 480 miles (772km) with his 1836 flight from England to Germany. Green was also a frequent flyer: He made over 500 ascents!

Charles Green

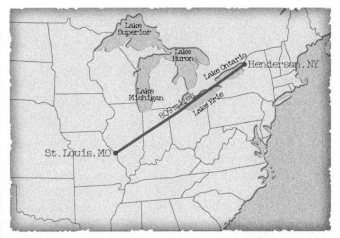

Figure 1-12. Long distance flight of Wise, Gager, and La Mountain from St. Louis to Henderson N.Y.

Green ascended for the hundredth time in 1832; he was possibly the first person to have made that many flights. A few years later, in 1836, he set a world distance record of 480 miles (772 kilometers) by flying from England to Germany, from London to the Duchy of Nassau. He carried two passengers on the 18-hour flight. Before the flight he called his balloon *Royal Vauxhall Balloon*; after the flight, *Great Balloon of Nassau*. On this flight he demonstrated the applications of the dragline and the feasibility of night flights.

In the United States, ballooning entered a golden age in the 1830s. Charles Ferson Durant, for example, studied ballooning in France and made one ascension there. He returned to the United States and on 9 September 1830 made his American flying debut as "The American Aeronaut" in a hydrogen balloon. An English immigrant, Richard Clayton, set a world distance record for free balloons when he flew the *Star of the West* from Cincinnati, Ohio, to Monroe County, Virginia, 350 miles, in 1835. In an effort to carry mail east later that year, Clayton crashed the heavy and slowly rising balloon into a building. He later experimented with using city-illuminating gas to lift the balloon that replaced the *Star of the West*. Once a spectator's cigar lit gas escaping from Clayton's balloon, destroying his balloon and injuring five people. Another world distance record was set by Americans in 1859 when aeronauts John Wise, O. Gager, and John La Mountain flew from St. Louis, Missouri, to Henderson, New York, 809 miles. (This

distance record held for more than sixty years, until 1900 when Count Henry de La Vaulx flew 1,195 miles from Paris to Korostichev, Russia.) (Figure 1-12)

Crossing the Atlantic Ocean became a popular challenge during the mid 1800s. In 1844 the *New York Sun* reported that a manned balloon had crossed the Atlantic Ocean, but this flight was merely a journalist trick played on the newspaper and its readers by author Edgar Allan Poe. Wise, Gager, and La Mountain were on their way to attempt a transatlantic crossing in 1859 when the storm forced them down in Henderson, New York. John Wise was one of the leading balloonists in the United States. Wholly dependent upon ballooning for his living, John Wise barnstormed, made balloons, sold balloons, and taught male and female would-be aeronauts. Sponsored by the *New York Daily Graphic*, he planned a transatlantic balloon flight for 1873. That attempt ended on the ground, before launch, when the hydrogen balloon called *Daily Graphic* collapsed while being inflated. These examples merely highlight some of the newsworthy flights in a period when balloonists were barnstorming the country. During the same period, balloonists like Eugène Godard and his siblings were barnstorming across Europe.

Historic Event

On 7 November 1836 Charles Green and two passengers — Robert Holland and Monck Mason — ascended from Vauxhall Gardens in London. The next day they descended near Weilberg in the German Duchy of Nassau. That flight covered 480 miles (772 km). It demonstrated the utility of the dragline and the feasibility of night flights.

Historical Note

The Atlantic Ocean challenged aeronauts of the 19th century. Several had already announced plans to fly across the ocean when Edgar Allan Poe's spoof appeared in the *New York Sun* in 1844. Poe reported that a manned balloon had crossed the Atlantic Ocean, but he was joking. The aeronauts were not. English balloonist Charles Green published his plan for an aerial voyage across the ocean, but he never made the flight.

The American balloonist John Wise (1808-1879) pursued the dream of crossing the Atlantic for decades. From the early 1840s, his plan was to travel with the west-to-east air currents. Raising the necessary funds delayed his first attempt that was originally scheduled for 1843. Finally in 1859 he and colleagues in the Trans-Atlantic Balloon Corporation ascended from St. Louis in their balloon *Atlantic*. They were bound for the east coast and the crossing when a storm damaged the balloon and forced a landing in Henderson, New York. They had traveled 809 miles, including across Lake Erie, and they set a world distant record, but their venture was over. Wise spent years raising funds to attempt another transatlantic crossing. In the 1870s, with a young partner named Washington Donaldson, Wise again prepared to cross the ocean. This time poor construction of the balloon led him to withdraw from the venture in 1873.

On 10 August 1978 Ben L. Abruzzo, Maxie L. Anderson, and Larry M. Newman began a five-day flight across the Atlantic in the gas balloon *Double Eagle II*. For balloons, this was the first successful transatlantic crossing.

John Wise

Military Aviation Developments

Aviation earned only a small role in the military during the age of ballooning. Napoleon used balloons for reconnaissance in the 1790s. The Austrian military launched unmanned balloons — each carrying a bomb — against Venice in 1849; and balloons carried passengers, mail, and propaganda from Paris while that city was under siege in 1870-71. The United States Army made limited but regular use of balloons during the Civil War that began in 1860. Early in the war, the Union Army of the northern states organized a Balloon Corps. Thaddeus Lowe designed balloon equipment, including the balloon *Eagle*, and developed aerial reconnaissance techniques for the Union Army during the war. In July 1861 a Union officer aloft in a balloon directed artillery fire during the siege of Washington. That same year the Union soldiers converted the coal barge *G.W. Parke Custis* into a balloon carrier (an operational aircraft carrier); thereafter, the Union

Personal Profile

A leading name in 19th-century aviation was Eugène Godard (1847-18–). He was the head of a French family of balloonists who performed in Europe, Asia, Africa, and North America. In Paris the family operated a large manufacturing shop to produce balloons for Godard. Godard made his first balloon ascension in 1847 in a hot air paper balloon. Thereafter, in balloons, he crossed the Alps, the Carpathian Mountains, and the English Channel. He carried passengers with him, suspended gymnasts beneath his car, and parachuted from balloons. He promoted his ascensions as "either scientific or eccentric," and he received a silver medal for "improvements in aerial ascension" at the New York World's Fair of 1853. He contributed to French military aviation by participating in France's military campaign against Italy in 1859 and in the defense of Paris during the siege of 1870-71. Godard was a professional aviator and a professional showman.

Eugène Godard

Historical Note

During the Franco-Prussian War, the Prussian army besieged Paris and bombarded the city with its new steel cannons. The city's residents sent mail out via the *Balloon Post*. Hot air balloons carried over two-million letters out of the city, and also carried crates of carrier pigeons. *Pigeon Post*, using the Paris-supplied birds, transported mail into the besieged city. After four months, the siege ended when France surrendered.

launched a balloon from its deck for reconnaissance missions. (Figure 1-13) The Union disbanded the Balloon Corps in 1863; the war continued into 1865. Despite the proven effectiveness of balloons in reconnaissance, the balloonists had never meshed into the organizational structure of the Army.

Figure 1-13. A reconnaissance balloon attached to a barge was able to view troop movements and direct artillery fire while keeping out of the reach of enemy fire.

Exploration

While barnstorming and exhibition flying continued, exploration by air became big news in the late 19th century. One of the biggest stories featured the Swedish aeronaut S.A. Andrée who attempted to fly across the North Pole. Andrée had excelled in his studies and graduated from the Royal Institute of Technology in Stockholm. Visiting the Centennial Exposition in the United States in 1876, he met the prominent aeronaut John Wise. Andrée received his introductory education in aviation from Wise. Back in Sweden, Andrée developed what he called a distaste for business. In 1882-83 he participated in the International Polar Year by recording aero-electrical observations at the Swedish base on Spitsbergen. He later became an engineer and manager with the government patent office. In 1893 the Lars Hierta Foundation gave him a grant with which he purchased a balloon. Andrée named this French-made balloon *Svea* (*Sweden*). He made various ascents and documented each one. He approached aeronautics as scientific work, not sport or adventure, even before deciding in 1894 to fly over the North Pole.

Andrée announced his planned polar expedition at a meeting of the Swedish Academy of Sciences in February 1895. He explained that "the expedition must not be equipped in such a way as to deprive it of its character of a *balloon expedition*, for the journey is to be carried out by *balloon*, and the travelers are to rely on the balloon." He turned to the public in order to collect funds for the expedition. On special order, Henri Lachambre of Paris made the expedition balloon *Örnen (Eagle).* (Figure 1-14) As Andrée had specified, it was made of Chinese silk, seams sewn with silk too. Varnish covered the inside and outside. Andrée ordered a special hydrogen gas generator from Ernst Eck. He recruited a small crew: Dr. Nils Ekholm of the Meteorological Institute of Stockholm

Figure 1-14. Illustration of the *Eagle* that was used by Andrée in his attempt to reach the North Pole in 1896.

and physics professor Nils Strindberg. Strindberg traveled to Paris to study ballooning and make ascensions. In 1896 the crew and balloon boarded the ship *Virgo* for transport to Spitsbergen. The ice pack around the island delayed their arrival at Dane Island. Unfavorable winds on the island delayed their launching the balloon, and gas leaked out of the silk cloth of the inflated balloon. With insurance

Personal Profile

Considered Sweden's first aeronaut, Salmon Auguste Andrée (1854-1897) worked in the Patent Office. He acquired an interest in aviation while visiting the United States. In Sweden, he applied that interest to exploration. He wanted to fly across the North Pole. Weather delayed his flight from 1896 to 1897. Once aloft, he and his two colleagues disappeared. Thirty-three years later, in 1930, a Norwegian scientific expedition discovered their bodies, diaries, and undeveloped film.

Salmon Auguste Andrée

about to expire on the *Virgo*, they abandoned their attempt and returned to the ship and to Sweden.

Determined to reach the pole by air, Andrée quickly raised money to cover expenses of a second attempt. Alfred Nobel, Axel Burman, and Baron Dickson were among the supporters to contribute again. Andrée sent the balloon to Paris to be enlarged about 10,000 cubic feet, to 170,000 cubic feet, to better lift the weight of the fabric used in its construction. Dr. Ekholm left the crew, in a large part due to his concern over the amount of gas that had escaped the balloon in 1896 and the amount that would probably escape the balloon when inflated for another attempt. Civil engineer Knut Fraenkel replaced him and, in the spring of 1897, Fraenkel traveled to Paris to study ballooning. That summer Andrée tried again. On 11 July 1897 he, Strindberg, and Fraenkel ascended in the *Eagle* from a base on Spitsbergen. They disappeared. (Figure 1-15)

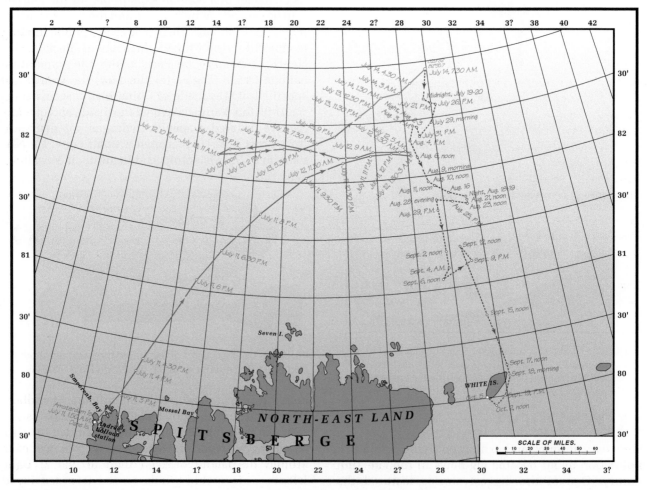

Figure 1-15. Map of Andrée's arctic flight path. The solid line represents the flight path of Andrée's balloon between July 11 and 14. The dashed line shows Andrées march and drift over the ice from July 14 to October 5, 1897.

Flight Lines

"Our journey has so far gone well. We are still moving on at a height of 800 feet in a direction which at first was N. 10° E. declination but later N. 45° E. declination. Four carrier-pigeons were sent off at 5.40 p.m. Greenwich time. They flew westerly. We are now in over the ice which is much broken up in all directions. Weather magnificent. In best of humours."

S.A. Andrée, Nils Strindberg, and Knut Fraenkel on 11 July 1897, at about 6 p.m., in a dispatch thrown overboard in a mail-buoy that was found in 1900; quoted in *Andrée's Story, the Complete Record of His Polar Flight, 1897.*

Flight Lines

"It is not a little strange to be floating here above the Polar Sea. To be the first that have floated here in a balloon. How soon, I wonder, shall we have successors? Shall we be thought mad or will our example be followed. I cannot deny that all three of us are dominated by a feeling of pride. We think we can well face death, having done what we have done. Isn't it all, perhaps the expression of an extremely strong sense of individuality which cannot bear the thought of living and dying like a man in the ranks, forgotten by coming generations? Is this ambition?"

S.A. Andrée, on 12 July 1897, at about 11 p.m., in his diary; quoted in *Andrée's Story, the Complete Record of His Polar Flight, 1897.*

Historical Evidence

In 1897 Swedish aviator S.A. Andrée and two colleagues disappeared while attempting to fly a balloon over the North Pole. In 1930 a Norwegian scientific expedition discovered their frozen bodies about 500 miles from the Pole. Also found were the men's diaries and undeveloped film. A month and a half after being forced down on ice, Andrée had written, "No one has lost courage; with such comrades one should be able to manage under, I may say, any circumstances."

Using the diaries and film found with the bodies, experts determined what had happened. The Eagle had remained airborne for 65 hours, then the weight of fog on the balloon and the loss of guide ropes forced it to land on ice. The flight thus ended on the morning of 14 July. It had reached 82° 56' North latitude and 29° 52' East longitude. Then the three men walked across ice until early October, when they camped on White Island (Kvitøya). There they died.

Turn of the Century

Andrée's disappearance was news, big news, international news. Newspaper publishers recognized that, and in the early 20th century newspapers sponsored "newsworthy" expeditions for the publicity and for exclusive rights to an expedition's story. W.D. Boyce, publisher of the *Chicago Blade* and the *Chicago Ledger*, led the African Balloonograph Expedition to British East Africa and the Kijabe. There he invited Mickie Akeley for a ride. She was the wife of Carl Akeley, wildlife collector, photographer, and taxidermist for the American Museum of Natural History in New York. She accepted, and she became a Chicago news story: the first woman to ascend over British East Africa. That 1909 Balloonograph Expedition competed with news in the rival Chicago *Record-Herald* about Walter Wellman's expedition to fly over the North Pole in the airship *America*. Wellman had attempted an unsuccessful polar flight in 1907 and this 1909 expedition failed to reach the Pole as well.

From scientific and mechanical experimentation in the 18th century, through showmanship, military applications, scientific research, and exploration, ballooning had become mostly sport for wealthy people by the early 20th century. These wealthy balloonists started aero clubs in France (1898), Great Britain (1901), and the United States (1905), and they organized the Fédération Aéronautique Internationale (1905). Wealthy sportsmen also acted individually to promote ballooning. New York *Herald* publisher and yachtsman Gordon Bennett sponsored the first of his annual balloon races in 1906. Contestants raced for distance. Lieutenant Frank P. Lahm of the United States Army in the balloon *United States* won by floating from the starting point in Paris, France, to Yorkshire, England, a distance of 402 miles (647 km); governments could compete with wealthy sportsmen. (Wilbur Wright later taught Lahm how to fly airplanes.) (Figure 1-16)

Figure 1-16. The first Gordon Bennett balloon race was held in Paris, France in 1906. It was won by American Lieutenant Frank Lahm (left). This photograph shows Lahm and his companion, Major Henry B. Hersey, ready for ascent on 30 September 1906.

Among "The Perils and Pleasures of Ballooning" listed in a 1906 article of that title were the perils: a mistake on the ground in assessing the condition of the balloon could cause catastrophe in the air, flying into cold air currents or clouds can cause the gas to contract and the balloon to descend rapidly, one could get lost in the fog or caught in a storm, lightning might strike the balloon, or the balloon might drift over the sea or other large body of water. The main peril, of course, was death. Among the pleasures were: "neither fear [of falling] nor the wish to jump," "all is quiet and calm," "a sense of tranquillity," "a sense of lightness and freedom," "wonderful sensations," including "the element of excitement," yet safe enough to take the wife and children along for a ride. "The real pleasure of a balloon trip," the author concluded, is "the sailing over the earth where the city and the country can be seen as a bird sees them."

SECTION C

DIRIGIBLES

In the 19th century, aviation became more than hot air and hydrogen balloons. The technology evolved to include dirigible balloons — that is, directable, steerable balloons, and from there to airships with semi-rigid or rigid frames. Navigation of dirigibles and airships also evolved from ballooning.

A **dirigible** is an aircraft that can be directed or steered. The origin of the word is French: *diriger* — to direct, to aim, to guide. In aviation the French word "dirigible" began as an adjective for the dirigible balloon, a balloon with sufficient power to overcome the resistance of air and thereby to be directionally controlled in flight rather than simply floating with the fluid air. To be dirigible, a balloon thus required power as well as directional control. In the early contemporary literature, a dirigible might be called a flying ship, aerial steamer, steam balloon, flying machine, or airship. Only gradually did the noun dirigible come to mean non-rigid dirigible balloons, and the term **airship** become associated with the dirigible balloons that have semi-rigid or rigid internal framework. Rigidity refers to the **form**. The form of a non-rigid dirigible is maintained by the internal pressure of the gas in the balloon envelope. A semi-rigid form is acquired by using the internal pressure in the gas container *and* a keel structure. The rigid form is supported by a rigid structure or framework within the envelope. This text will distinguish between non-rigid dirigible and more rigid airship, though even today the word dirigible is sometimes used to include semi-rigid and rigid airships as well as non-rigid dirigible balloons. This section will discuss non-rigid dirigibles and a few early semi-rigid airships, and the next section will cover the semi-rigid and rigid airships of the late 19th century and early 20th century. (Figure 1-17)

Directional Control

Almost as soon as the Montgolfier brothers had demonstrated the flight of free balloons and manned flight, the question of directional control attracted attention. John Jeffries and Jean Pierre Blanchard made one of the early attempts to steer a balloon on

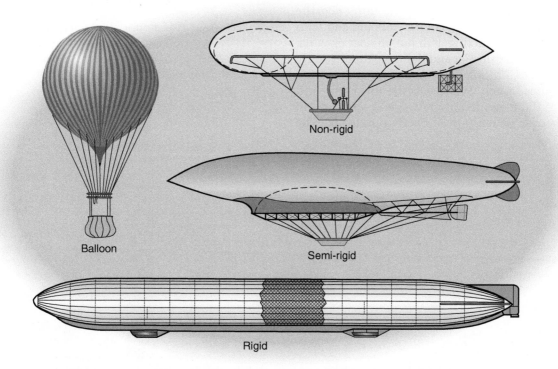

Balloon

Non-rigid

Semi-rigid

Rigid

Figure 1-17. These drawings illustrate the difference between balloons, non-rigid and semi-rigid dirigibles, and rigid airships.

30 November 1784. That day they ascended and traveled with the air from London to Kent. Blanchard, the French balloonist, attended "to the state and management of his Aerial Car and Balloon," in accordance with his employment agreement with Jeffries. Jeffries, the American expatriate and physician, made scientific observations during the flight. One of his research points was "the effect which oars, or wings, might be made to produce toward this purpose [power], and in directing the course of the Balloon." Thus for the flight, Blanchard's hydrogen balloon had "wings or oars" attached to car. (Figure 1-18)

Figure 1-18. One of the earliest experiments with dirigible flight was John Jeffries attempts to control a hydrogen balloon with wings or oars.

During the flight, Jeffries wrote, "Blanchard applied himself to his oars, which he had made some experiment of on our first ascent, and which (though inadequate to the *government* of the Balloon) appeared to me very materially to *influence* the course, ascent, and progress of the Balloon; and with which we could, by acting with but one oar or wing, always turn round the Car and Balloon, either wholly or in part, *ad libitum* [at one's pleasure]; which circumstance much increased the pleasure and variety of the magnificent view under and around us." This observation proved overly optimistic. The wings or oars could neither govern nor steer the balloon, and their value as a power source was limited indeed. The attachments could merely spin the aircraft in the air. In fact, Jeffries spent most of the flight recording data on the atmosphere, winds, and temperature. Regarding the wings or oars, he concluded "that with some future improvements . . . they may be of material service . . . especially whenever the wind is not strong."

Less than two months later Jeffries and Blanchard again attached the wings or oars to the car of Blanchard's hydrogen balloon, this time for their historic flight across the English Channel. In Jeffries' account of this flight and in the diary he kept during the flight, there is no mention of any experiments with the wings or oars. Over the channel, the balloon repeatedly descended. Each time Jeffries and Blanchard cast out items of weight — sacks of ballast till all the ballast was gone, then parcels of pamphlets, food, and then one wing, and then the other wing, followed by the lining and ornaments cut away from the car, by the anchors and cords, and even some of their clothing. Discarding weight helped keep them out of the water, and falling barometric pressure and coastal winds finally lifted the balloon to the coast of France. Neither aviator used the wings on this voyage. Blanchard later tried a rotating fan to power a balloon,

Historical Note

In 1941 the Institute of Aeronautical Sciences and the Works Projects Administration reprinted John Jeffries' 1786 *Narrative of the Two Aerial Voyages.* The reprint identifies the original publication as "the first book written by an American on aeronautics."

Flight Lines

"Upon examining the Compass, to try to find our course, I was surprized to find the needle changing, and appear to be running all around the card, almost continually. The earth now appeared to be exactly like a beautiful coloured map or carpet, not having the least appearance of hill, elevation of buildings, or inequality of surface whatever; but almost continually changing its position, as to the prospect before me, owing, I apprehend, to the almost incessant *rotary* and *semicircular* motion of the Balloon around its own axis."

John Jeffries, 30 November 1784, while making scientific observations from a balloon equipped with "wings or oars," in Jeffries, *A Narrative of the Two Aerial Voyages.*

John Jeffries

but that too proved ineffective, as did ideas explored by others in the late 18th and early 19th centuries.

Dirigible Flight

In 1852, on 24 September, a Frenchman named Henri Giffard succeeded in making the first dirigible flight. He used a three-horsepower steam engine to power an elongated hydrogen balloon. The powerplant and operator's car were suspended forty feet below the gasbag. Giffard's powerplant weighed 350 pounds, which was lightweight for a steam engine of that era. His 88,000 cubic foot balloon measured 144 feet long and 40 feet in diameter. He departed from the Paris Hippodrome, flew 17 miles, and in the process demonstrated directional, horizontal control of his aircraft. His speed was six miles per hour, too slow to fly into a wind. As an inventor, Giffard had to adapt

the steam engine to his aeronautical application, to produce an entire engine in a lightweight version for flight. Steam was the industrial power of the 19th century; the alternatives were waterpower, animal power, or hand power. Steam was used to power ships and trains, mills and factories, water pumps, and mine drains. Giffard's choice of steam power was logical — and it was an indirect extension of work pursued by Joseph Montgolfier, who had experimented with steam power before and after developing the hot air balloon. Giffard made additional flights in the same aircraft, but firing a steam engine aboard a highly flammable hydrogen airship had obvious dangers. Instead of seeking a more powerful and still lightweight engine, Giffard turned his efforts to making large balloons. At the Paris World's Fair of 1878, one of his captive balloons lifted 52 passengers aloft at one time.

Dirigible Development

After dirigible flight was demonstrated, innovators built their own designs, including early semi-rigid airship designs. The focus remained on dirigible flight, on controlling the flight path of an aircraft.

Paul Haenlein, a German engineer, used the newly invented internal combustion engine to power his dirigible in 1872. The 3.6-horsepower internal combustion engine drew coal gas from the aircraft's envelope for fuel. Haenlein flew the ship in tethered flight at Brunn in the Austro-Hungarian Empire (later Brno, Czechoslovakia).

French balloonists and brothers, Albert and Gaston Tissandier, built experimental models and, in 1883, a full-size electrically powered airship. The craft carried both a battery and a Siemens 1.5 horsepower electrical motor. The Tissandiers' airship reached only three miles per hour in speed and thus proved very difficult to steer.

Historic Event

The first flight of a dirigible, that is, the first powered flight of a balloon, occurred on 24 September 1852. Henri Giffard piloted the steam-powered aircraft. The three-horsepower (2.24 kW) engine drove a propeller. The engine produced sufficient power for Giffard to fly six miles per hour, but insufficient power for him to fly into even a light wind, so he steered the aircraft in circles.

Le dirigeable à vapeur de Giffard au dessus du parc de Châlais-Meudon (1852)

Henri Giffard's Steam-powered Dirigible

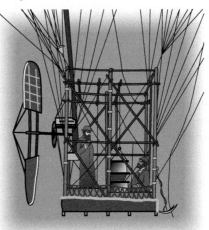

Albert and Gaston Tissandier's Electric-powered Dirigible

Personal Profile

Alberto Santos-Dumont (1873-1932) was the son of a Brazilian coffee planter. Santos-Dumont learned mechanics working on the railway system of his father's large plantation. He read Jules Verne and on holiday in Paris in 1891 he saw balloons in flight. He moved to Paris in 1898. Best known for his dirigible designs and flights, he flew in an airplane of his own design in 1906. For two years Europeans honored him as the first person to fly an airplane, a heavier-than-air flying machine, because they did not believe that the Wright brothers had flown in the United States. Wilbur Wright's 1908 visit to France, and flights there, corrected the credit for first airplane flight. A couple years later multiple sclerosis ended Santos-Dumont's flying career. He returned to Brazil. The development of military aviation in general and the use of airplanes to drop bombs in particular distressed him in his later years.

Alberto Santos-Dumont

Flight Lines

"I had navigated the air. . . . I had mounted without sacrificing ballast. I had descended without sacrificing gas. My shifting weights had proved successful; and it would have been impossible not to recognize the capital triumph of these oblique flights through the air. No one had ever made them before."

Alberto Santos-Dumont referring to his first cruises in dirigible balloons in 1898; in Santos-Dumont, *My Air-ships*.

The French government awarded a grant to Charles Renard and A.C. Krebs, both captains in the French Engineering Corps, to build an electrically powered dirigible. This aircraft, called *La France*, used a 211-pound, eight-horsepower motor that was then considered both light and reliable. The two captains made the first flight in the dirigible on 9 August 1884. They flew a round trip from Chalais-Meudon to Villacoublay and back, a total distance of five miles. *La France* flew at least five more times, but twice heavy wind prevented it from flying back to its base. These 19th-century developments proved that dirigible navigation, and yes airship navigation, was practical; thereafter, sport and exhibition flyers often built their own, sometimes primitive, dirigibles.

Alberto Santos-Dumont, son of a Brazilian planter, became a French hero for designing, building, and flying dirigibles in France around the turn of the century. His first flight was in a balloon in 1897. That same year, he designed a small, one-person hydrogen balloon, called the *Brazil*. At five feet and 110 pounds, Santos-Dumont did not need a large balloon. He used *Brazil* as a training balloon. By the end of the year he had already made 25 ascensions. In 1898 he began designing dirigibles, which he called airships in what was common usage at that time. French

engineer Albert de Dion designed the 3.5-horsepower, air-cooled, gasoline engine used in Santos-Dumont's first dirigible; the engine weighed only 66 pounds. Santos-Dumont learned to fly the dirigible at a slight nose up angle, much like an airfoil, to add to the lift provided by the buoyancy of the gas enclosed in the elongated envelope. He also would drop the nose down to reduce lift without releasing gas. In 1899 he built two small dirigibles, which he flew over Paris.

To promote aviation, Henry Deutsch de la Meurthe offered a prize of 100,000 francs to the first person to fly from the Aero Club of France headquarters at St. Cloud to the Eiffel Tower in Paris, and back, a seven-mile route, in less than a half hour. That meant the winner would have to fly at a ground speed of at least 14 miles per hour. Santos-Dumont selected that prize as his goal. He built his airship No. 5 for the competition. This airship had a pinewood keel, joints of aluminum, and wire instead of rope for reinforcement and suspension. These features cut weight and air resistance. The four-cylinder engine produced 12 horsepower. Cool air and high winds greeted him on the morning of his scheduled competition flight in July 1901. He flew the route and finished eleven minutes too late. Before he could land, the motor failed. The wind carried the balloon, and he crashed into a chestnut tree. In the repaired airship, he tried again in August. Equipment problems and wind resulted again in his crashing. He built a new airship, No. 6. In October he flew that airship in the Deutsch competition. A change in rules meant that he now needed to launch and land within the 30 minute limit. He exceeded the limit by half a minute, but in response to popular sentiment, he received the prize. Brazil awarded him an additional 125,000 francs. (Figure 1-19)

Santos-Dumont built several more airships. His No. 7 had 60 horsepower. He called No. 9 his "little runabout...the smallest of possible dirigibles, yet very practical indeed." It was powered by a 26.5-pound, three-horsepower Clément motor; note that the first successful dirigible flight had used a 350-pound engine for the same horsepower. Santos-Dumont then shifted his attention to airplanes. Other aviation-minded individuals were exploring the possibilities of semi-rigid and rigid envelopes in the late 19th century.

Figure 1-19. Dumont and his Dirigible No. 6 winning the Deutsch competition in August 1901.

AIRSHIPS

Count Ferdinand von Zeppelin, a retired German Army officer, developed the large rigid airship with multiple gas compartments — a type of airship that immediately became known as Zeppelin. He dominated airship development from the construction of his first Zeppelin in 1900 until his death in 1917. There are, however, other names and other designs of significance in the history of airships.

Airship Development

David Schwartz of the Austro-Hungarian empire designed two all-metal airships. The first proved structurally unsound. He made the second of aluminum sheet and powered it with a twelve horsepower Daimler gas engine connected to three propellers. Schwartz died in 1897, shortly before the airship was completed. In November of that year, a volunteer flew it at Templehof near Berlin. He launched the airship, moved it through the air, lost control and crashed, but survived. Von Zeppelin was among the spectators of this rigid airship's debut and demise.

Airship development, like aviation in general, was an international activity. In 1897 Major August von Parseval of the Germany army invented the Drachenballoon, or kite balloon, which was a tethered or captive balloon with an elongated bag to give it more stability in wind than the standard spherical balloon. The military forces of several European nations used Parseval's design for observation and reconnaissance, including in the Balkans and in Africa. Almost a decade later Parseval made his first semi-rigid, flexible airship. He built five *Parsevals* between 1906 and 1911. Others were constructed during World War I, which was called the Great War until the second World War. (Figure 1-20)

The British government built five small airships in 1907. In France the brothers Paul and Pierre Lebaudy, owners of a sugar refinery, commissioned the design and construction of the semi-rigid *Jaune* in 1902. The French company Societe-Zodiac built an airship *pour le sport* (for sport), but airships did not become popular sport aircraft. Umberto Nobile led the Italian government's *Stablimento di Construzioni Aeronautiche* (Establishment for Aeronautical Construction) which produced P-type (173,000 cubic feet) and M-type (441,000 cubic feet) airships before the Great War; both types used external keels. In the United States, balloonist Thomas S. Baldwin — who had built an unsuccessful pedal-powered dirigible balloon in 1892 — built the *California Arrow* in 1904. This simple dirigible used a ten-horsepower Curtiss motorcycle engine, a gasoline engine. That was the only airship to achieve flight at the 1904 World's Fair in St. Louis. (Figure 1-21) Baldwin made more airships, mostly for exhibition ascents. In 1908 he sold the U.S. Army Signal Corps an improved Baldwin dirigible, powered by a twenty-horsepower Curtiss engine; this machine was the Army's first powered aircraft.

Figure 1-20. Major August von Parseval built several airships that were a semi-rigid, flexible design.

Figure 1-21. The Thomas Baldwin-designed *California Arrow* in flight during the 1904 St. Louis World's Fair.

Personal Profile

Walter Wellman (1858-1934) was a Chicago journalist who wrote for several newspapers. In 1894 he unsuccessfully attempted to reach the North Pole by ship and sled. He planned to fly a Paris-made airship over the North Pole in 1906. Engine problems on the *America* prompted him to cancel the flight. He attempted to fly over the North Pole in 1907 and 1909. Both attempts failed to reach the pole. Wellman made the news again in 1910 when he attempted to fly the same airship across the Atlantic Ocean. The airship departed Atlantic City on 15 October. Engine failure over the ocean forced Wellman to make a radio distress call. A steamship in the area happened to see the craft and rescued the crew on 17 October.

Walter Wellman

Exploration

Walter Wellman's polar airship expeditions of 1906, 1907, and 1909 were the first aerial attempts to reach the North Pole after the disappearance of S.A. Andrée in 1897. A Chicago journalist, Wellman had already led two land-based expeditions in search of the geographic North Pole. For his flight over the pole, he ordered a semi-rigid airship from Paris and christened it *America*.

In 1906 Wellman built a base camp, complete with airship hangar, for his aerial expedition to the Pole.

Historic Event

On 2 September 1907 Walter Wellman, Melvin Vaniman, and Felix Reisenberg boarded the airship *America* for a flight to the North Pole. A storm enroute changed their plans. Although they did not reach the North Pole, these men in the *America* made the first motorized flight in the Arctic.

Flight Lines

"The engine was started, and the *America* leaped forward. With a thrill of joy we of the crew felt her moving through the air. Looking down from our lofty perch, we could see the equilibrator [dragline] swimming along in the water, its head in the air, much like a great sea-serpent.... Soon the wind freshened from the northwest, accompanied by snow. We were in danger of being driven upon the mountainous coast...."

"Everything depended upon the engine. Vaniman kept it running, and increased its effective output as the danger of shipwreck became most pressing. Inch by inch we fought our way past the mountains, one after another, clearing the last by only a few rods. The open Arctic Ocean was before us; and well satisfied with the working of engine and ship up to this time, it was with great satisfaction I gave the order to Riesenberg at the wheel to 'head her north!'"

Walter Wellman describing his polar flight of 1907; in Wellman, *The Aerial Age.*

Flight Lines

"Remembering the compass derangement of 1907, I climbed to the upper deck, hung there suspended between the heavens and the earth, and noted with content that the reserve or standard compass was steady and true, though the steering compass below was a little erratic, due to the vibration of the ship. Then I returned to the work of writing up the log and preparing the data for the navigation of the ship.

"In a pause I looked over the side at the waters far below, now flecked with small fields of floating ice, the main pack being but a few miles farther north. At that instant I saw something drop from the ship into the sea. Could one believe his eyes? Yes — it was the equilibrator [dragline].

"The leather serpent, so thoroughly tested two years before, had played us false ....

"Instantly we all knew the voyage was at an end, that without the equilibrator the ship would soon become unmanageable."

Walter Wellman describing his polar flight of 1909; in Wellman, *The Aerial Age.*

Historical Evidence

Historians use multiple sources to find the best evidence of what happened in the past. Many of these sources are written documents, like Walter Wellman's autobiography (*The Aerial Age*), Wellman's letters, drawings, photographs of his airship, and newspaper articles about his aerial expeditions. While historians also glean information from historical sites and historical artifacts, archeologists specialize in artifacts and the sites where artifacts are found. Archeologists also use documentary sources, but their emphasis is on artifacts. Using related but distinct methodologies, historians and archeologists can conduct research on the same topic and share their results with each other.

Historical archeologist P.J. Capelotti surveyed Wellman's polar base camp in 1993. He concluded that "Wellman had constructed a spectacular infastructure little more than 700 miles from the North Pole" and that "the consistent Wellman failures cannot be traced to his technology." Wellman lacked the skill, the nerve, and the faith to complete his mission. According to Capelotti, Wellman's failure to reach the North Pole was also a failure "to inaugurate a radically new method of scientific and geographic exploration" — the aerial method. These conclusions and the supporting evidence are in Capelotti's report on *The Wellman Polar Airship Expeditions at Virgohamna, Danskøya, Svalbard.*

The camp was at Virgo Harbor on Danes Island, Spitsbergen. Wellman used it for three years. The first year, 1906, he never launched his airship because of problems with the engines. The next year, in *America*, he made the first motorized flight in the Arctic, but failed to reach the Pole.

Again in 1909, he flew but not to the Pole. Early in this flight Wellman later recalled, "At the rate we were going we could reach the Pole in less than thirty hours!" As the flight progressed, the dragline disengaged, and a Norwegian survey vessel towed the airship — in the air — to base. With explorers Robert Peary and Frederick Cook both claiming to have reached the Pole, Wellman abandoned his effort. In 1910 he attempted to cross the Atlantic Ocean in his airship. The

America lost one engine only eighty miles out from Atlantic City, the departure point, yet Wellman persisted. He eventually sent a radio distress signal, and on the third day of the flight and about a thousand miles from shore, he was rescued by a steamer. (Figure 1-22)

Figure 1-22.
Wellman's rescue.

Historic Event

Walter Wellman claimed that he and his crew aboard the airship *America* were "the first to send wireless messages from airship to shore." The day was Saturday 15 October 1910. The occasion was their attempt at transatlantic flight. As the airship drifted farther from shore, distance between stations disrupted service. On Tuesday the 18th the crew used the wireless to communicate with a ship at sea. The message from the *America* was that it needed emergency help, which the sea-going ship provided. Aviators in the United States and France had experimented with wireless communication earlier that year, but those experiments involved airplanes, not airships, so Wellman possibly did sent the first airship-to-shore message as well as the first aerial radio distress message. At the time the radio was new in aviation.

Personal Profile

Count Ferdinand Adolf August Heinrich von Zeppelin (1838-1917) was a career
Army man. He was also a wealthy aristocrat. During the American Civil War he
traveled to the United States and inspected the Union Balloon Corps. He became directly
involved in aviation after retiring from the cavalry. He designed his first airship in the early
1890s. In 1898 he organized a joint stock company *Luftschiffbau Zeppelin* GmbH. He
established a small factory in Manzell and built a construction hangar on pontoons on Lake
Constance. Zeppelin's first aircraft was the *Luftschiff-Zeppelin 1*, or *LZ 1*, which first flew on 2
July 1900. His primary interest was military aviation, but he introduced passenger service and
thereby started commercial aviation in 1910. He refined the Zeppelin design until a dispute with
the German Naval Office in 1915. Von Zeppelin died two years later.

Count Ferdinand von Zeppelin

Zeppelins

The premier airships were those identified by the
name of Count Ferdinand von Zeppelin of Germany.
Zeppelin was a retired cavalry officer with a continuing
interest in military matters, particularly military
aviation. He watched the progress of aviation in
France and believed that French aviation threatened
the security of Germany. He recognized a military
need for aircraft that were capable of long-range
flight, could fly in bad weather, and carry bombs,
arms, and crew. Based on these military requirements,
he developed large rigid airships with aluminum
frames and numerous compartments for the hydrogen
gas. (Figure 1-23)

Historic Event

Starting 19 June 1910, Zeppelin airships went
into service with the new *Deutsche Luftschiffahrts
A.G. (DELAG)* company, a commercial airline without scheduled
service or fixed routes. In the few years before the start of
World War I, this company transported 34,000 people, mostly
on sightseeing trips between German cities. Germany's express
trains traveled faster than the 40 miles per hour averaged by
the airships. During the years 1910-1914, DELAG flew seven
different Zeppelin airships.

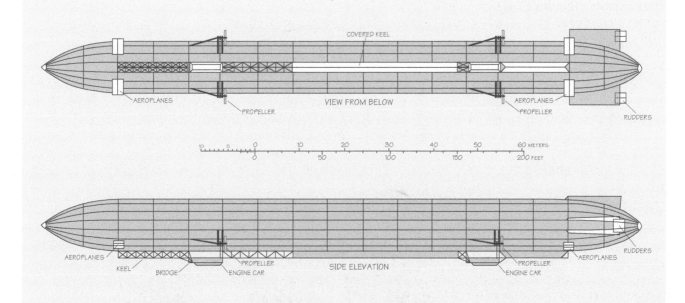

Figure 1-23. Schematic of a Zeppelin airship.

Figure 1-24. The airship *Schwaben* was typical of the designs used by DELAG to transport people.

Zeppelin's first airship was the *Luftschiff-Zeppelin 1*, or LZ 1, which first flew on 2 July 1900. This aircraft had a 420-foot long envelope with a capacity of 400,000 cubic feet. Hydrogen gas provided the lift and the power was supplied by two 14-horsepower engines, but its speed was less than 20 miles per hour. The second Zeppelin was completed in 1905, the third in 1906, the fourth in 1908, and more after that. Each Zeppelin represented an improvement over its predecessors. The LZ 7 *Deutschland* inaugurated passenger service with the commercial *Deutsche Luftschiffahrts A.G. (DELAG)* company in 1910, and Zeppelin supplied that airline with seven airships by the start of World War I, but Count von Zeppelin's primary interest remained military aviation. (Figure 1-24)

Conclusion

Lighter-than-air technology evolved from balloons to dirigible balloons to dirigible balloons with semi-rigid or rigid forms; that is, from balloons to dirigibles to airships. The appearance of a more advanced form of technology added to the number of technologies in aviation; the new did not close or replace the old. In fact, ballooning — the oldest aviation technology — experienced a major revival in the 1960s and 1970s.

Study Questions

1. What was aviation as invented by Joseph and Étienne Montgolfier in 1783?

2. In what ways did the Montgolfier brothers and J.A.C. Charles finance their balloon experiments?

3. What were the military applications or uses of balloons?

4. Why did balloonists ascend during the 19th century?

5. How are balloons, dirigibles, and airships similar? and how different?

6. What makes a balloon dirigible?

7. Who was the Brazilian aviation pioneer who built and flew dirigibles and an airplane?

8. Why were lighter-than-air craft used in the Arctic?

9. Of the two sources pertaining to Walter Wellman that are listed in the bibliography, which one is a primary source and which one is a secondary source?

10. What was a Zeppelin?

Bibliography

Andrée, S.A. and others. *Andrée's Story, the Complete Record of His Polar Flight, 1897, from the Diaries and Journals of S.A. Andrée, Nils Strindberg, and K. Fraenkel, Found on White Island in the Summer of 1930.* Edited by the Swedish Society for Anthropology and Geography. Translated by Edward Adams-Ray. New York: Viking Press, 1930.

Capelotti, P.J. *The Wellman Polar Airship Expeditions at Virgohamna, Danskøya, Svalbard — a Study in Aerospace Archaeology.* Meddeleser No. 145. Oslo: Norsk Polarinstitutt, 1997.

Crouch, Tom D. *The Eagle Aloft, Two Centuries of the Balloon in America.* Washington: Smithsonian Institution Press, 1983.

Eckener, Hugo. *Count Zeppelin, the Man and His Work.* Translated by Leigh Farnell. London: Massie Publishing Company, 1938.

Gillispie, Charles Coulston. *The Montgolfier Brothers and the Invention of Aviation, 1783-1784.* Princeton: Princeton University Press, 1983.

Jeffries, John. *A Narrative of the Two Aerial Voyages of Doctor Jeffries with Mons. Blanchard; with Meteorological Observations and Remarks.* London, 1786. Reprinted as Two *Aerial Voyages of Dr. Jeffries with Mons. Blanchard*, by the Institute of the Aeronautical Sciences and Works Projects Administration [New York, 1941] and by Arno Press (New York, 1971).

Payne, Lee. *Lighter Than Air, an Illustrated History of the Airship.* 1977; New York: Orion Books, 1991.

Porter, Rufus. *A Yankee Inventor's Flying Ship, Two Pamphlets by Rufus Porter.* Edited by Rhoda R. Gilman. St. Paul: Minnesota Historical Society, 1969. (Reprint of Porter's *Aerial Navigation*, 1849, and *An Aerial Steamer*, 1850)

Santos-Dumont, A. *My Air-ships.* New York: Century Company, 1904.

Wellman, Walter. *The Aerial Age, a Thousand Miles by Airship over the Atlantic Ocean, Airship Voyages over the Polar Sea, the Past, the Present and the Future of Aerial Navigation.* New York: A.R. Keller & Company, 1911.

Timeline

Light blue type indicates an event not directly related to aviation

18th Century: Étienne and Joseph Montgolfier invented the hot air balloon during the 18th-century Enlightenment, the Age of Reason. Traits of this period include a belief in human progress and in the capacity of people to reason, also an enthusiasm for scientific and intellectual pursuits. The Industrial Revolution had begun to centralize production in factories increasingly equipped with manufacturing machinery.

Year	Event
1783	June 4: At Annonay, France, Joseph and Étienne Montgolfier launched an unmanned hot air balloon of their invention into the air. This was the first public ascension of a balloon.
	August 27. Jacques Alexandre César Charles sent the first hydrogen balloon, which he invented, aloft unmanned from Paris. It landed about fifteen miles away.
	September 19. At Versailles, Étienne Montgolfier sent aloft a hot air balloon with a sheep, duck, and rooster in the basket. King Louis XVI, Marie Antoinette, and the royal court watched the launch.
	October. Étienne Montgolfier became the first person to fly when he made private and tethered experiments in which he ascended in a *montgolfiére* balloon; and later in the month J.F. Pilâtre de Rozier completed captive flight tests in the same balloon.
	November 21. J.F. Pilâtre de Rozier and François Laurent, marquis d'Arlandes, flew a montgolfiére in public demonstration of manned, free flight — the first manned free flight on record.
1784	February 25. Paolo Andreani completed a balloon flight in Italy, the first in that country and the first manned flight outside of France.
1785	January 7. Frenchman Jean Pierre Blanchard and American John Jeffries make the first flight across the English Channel in a hydrogen balloon; this was the first balloon crossing of a major body of water.
1787	The Philadelphia Convention of 1787 wrote and approved the Constitution of the United States of America. The next year this Constitution superseded the Articles of Confederation under which the young country had been governed since 1781. In 1791 ratification of the Bill of Rights added the first ten amendments to that Constitution.
1789	The social and political upheaval of the French Revolution began when a Paris mob stormed the fortified prison of Bastille in July. The French Revolution continued until Napoleon (Napoleon Bonaparte, 1769-1821) became consul, or ruler, of France in 1799.
1794	June 2. Napoleon's army organized, trained, and on this date sent into action a Compagnie d'Aerostiers.
1803	The Napoleonic Wars began. Napoleon tried to conquer much of Europe. The wars ended more than a decade later after Napoleon's disastrous invasion of Russia and after an alliance of Prussia, Britain, Sweden, and Austria invaded France.
1815	The Treaty of Vienna contained terms for the territorial balance of power in Europe following the Napoleonic Wars. Among the results were the partition of the Italian states among various

powers, the creation of the Confederation of the Rhine, the unification of the Netherlands, the extension of Russian control over Finland and into Poland, and the expansion of Prussia.

1816   Argentina won independence from Spain. Two years later, after years of insurrection, Chile also won independence from Spain. In 1821 Mexico became independent. After leading successful revolutions against Spanish rule, Simón Bolívar (1783-1830) organized governments in Colombia (1824), Peru (1824), and Bolivia (1825). The Spanish empire declined as these American colonies achieved independence.

1836   November 7-8. English aerial pilot Charles Green and two passengers flew from London to the Duchy of Nassau (Germany); they demonstrated the feasibility of long-distance and night flying.

1848   The Treaty of Guadalupe Hidalgo ended the Mexican War begun two years before. Mexico ceded New Mexico and California to the victorious United States.

1839   Great Britain and China began fighting the Opium War. The war was a British attempt to open trade with China, including opium trade. When the war ended in 1842, the Ch'ing dynasty ruling China ceded Hong Kong to Britain and granted several countries concessions of "extraterritoriality."

1852   September 24. Henri Giffard of France made the first successful dirigible flight.

1853   The Crimean War began. Russia fought an alliance of Turkey, England, France, and Sardinia, over the "Eastern Question" of European control of territory in the declining Ottoman Empire. During this war the English nurse Florence Nightingale (1820-1910) introduced reforms to the care of wounded and sick soldiers. The war ended in 1856 with Russian expansion blocked.

1861   In the United States, Southern states ceded and joined the Confederacy. This began the Civil War between the Confederacy and the Northern states remaining in the Union. The Union prevailed in 1865.

1861   July. During the American Civil War, a Union officer aloft in a balloon directed artillery fire during the siege of Washington.

1867   Displacing the military rule of the Tokugawa shogunate, Mutsuhito (1852-1912) became emperor of Japan. During his reign, from 1867 to 1912, he was known by the name Meiji. The Meiji Restoration (also called Meiji Reform) began in 1868. The reforms ended feudalism, centralized government administration, and generally westernized and industrialized Japan.

1869   French engineer Ferdinand de Lesseps (1805-1894) finished building the Suez Canal between the Mediterranean Sea and the Gulf of Suez. Great Britain acquired the canal in 1875.

1870-1871 Sixty-four balloons ascended from Paris when the city was under siege; fifty-nine landed in friendly territory.

1873   September. John Wise planned to cross the Atlantic Ocean by balloon, but the project collapsed.

1891   Tsar Nicholas I (1796-1855) initiated construction of the Trans-Siberian Railway. Construction continued for more than a decade and opened Siberia for settlement and development, as well as for geopolitical objectives in the Pacific region.

1897   July 11. Swedish aeronaut S.A. Andrée and his crew of two ascended with the intent of flying across the North Pole, but they disappeared.

1898   In the Spanish-American War the United States supported the independence of Cuba and defeated the Spanish in Manila harbor in the Philippines. Through the Treaty of Paris, Spain freed Cuba, ceded Puerto Rico and Guam to the United States, and sold the Philippines to the United States. The United States thereby became an imperial power.

1900   July. In Germany, Count von Zeppelin's rigid airship the *Luftschiff Zeppelin 1, or LZ-1,* made three test flights during which the craft proved to have too little power and control, but to be otherwise sound.

1901   British colonies on the continent of Australia became federated states in the new Commonwealth of Australia. Britain was fighting the South African or Boer War, which began in 1899 when the Dutch in the Boer states of Transvaal and Orange resisted British settlement in those territories. With the Treaty of Vereeniging in 1902, the Boers agreed to British rule.

1901   October 19. In France, Alberto Santos-Dumont of Brazil won the Deutsch prize for flying his airship No. 6, a dirigible balloon, over a course around the Eiffel Tower in record time.

1902   The French-built *La Jaune* airship proved controllable due to adequate power.

1906   F.P. Lahm of the U.S. Army won the first Gordon Bennett Race, a balloon race founded by James Gordon Bennett. The race was for distance — the farthest distance from the starting point. That first race began in France and ended in England.

1908   Zeppelin's LZ 4 flew down the Rhine River in demonstration of the rigid airship's practicality, a demonstration staged for the German army.

1909   Controversy arose over whether Frederick A. Cook (1865-1940) successfully led an expedition to the North Pole in 1908, or whether the first to the Pole was Robert E. Peary (1856-1920) in 1909, or if either had reached the Pole.

1910   June 19. A Zeppelin airship inaugurated passenger service with the new Deutsche Luftschiffahrts A.G. (DELAG) company, a commercial airline without scheduled service.

1911   December 14. Norwegian explorer Roald Amundsen (1872-1928) reached the South Pole. A month later British explorer Robert F. Scott (1868-1912) also reached the South Pole, but he died on the trek homeward.

1914   The Great War began in Europe; it later became known as World War I.

CHAPTER 2

WRIGHT BROTHERS (1896-1914)

AVIATION HISTORY

Summary of Events

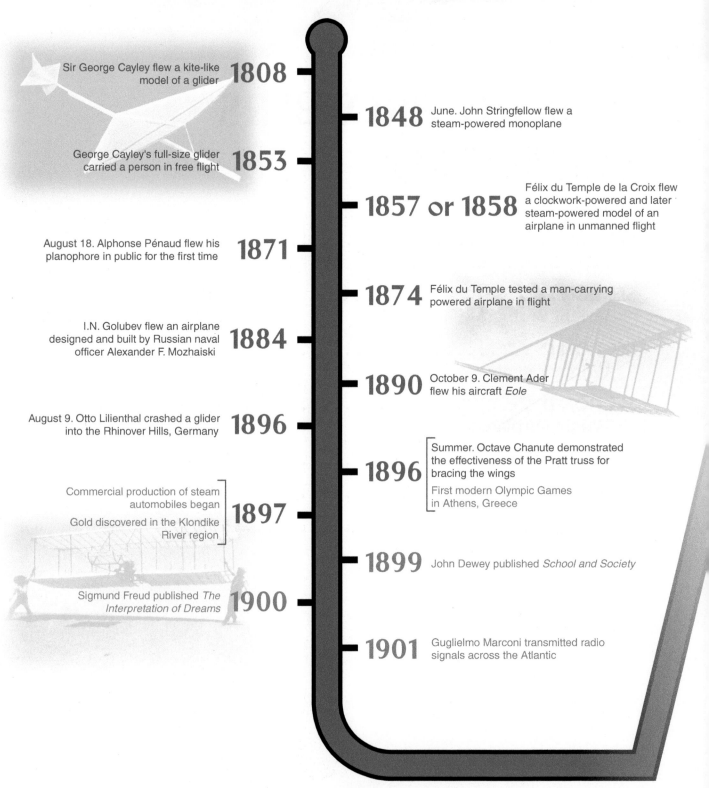

Sir George Cayley flew a kite-like model of a glider
1808

1848 June. John Stringfellow flew a steam-powered monoplane

George Cayley's full-size glider carried a person in free flight
1853

1857 or 1858 Félix du Temple de la Croix flew a clockwork-powered and later steam-powered model of an airplane in unmanned flight

August 18. Alphonse Pénaud flew his planophore in public for the first time
1871

1874 Félix du Temple tested a man-carrying powered airplane in flight

I.N. Golubev flew an airplane designed and built by Russian naval officer Alexander F. Mozhaiski
1884

1890 October 9. Clement Ader flew his aircraft *Eole*

August 9. Otto Lilienthal crashed a glider into the Rhinover Hills, Germany
1896

1896 Summer. Octave Chanute demonstrated the effectiveness of the Pratt truss for bracing the wings

First modern Olympic Games in Athens, Greece

Commercial production of steam automobiles began

Gold discovered in the Klondike River region
1897

1899 John Dewey published *School and Society*

Sigmund Freud published *The Interpretation of Dreams*
1900

1901 Guglielmo Marconi transmitted radio signals across the Atlantic

Light blue type represents events that are not directly related to aviation.

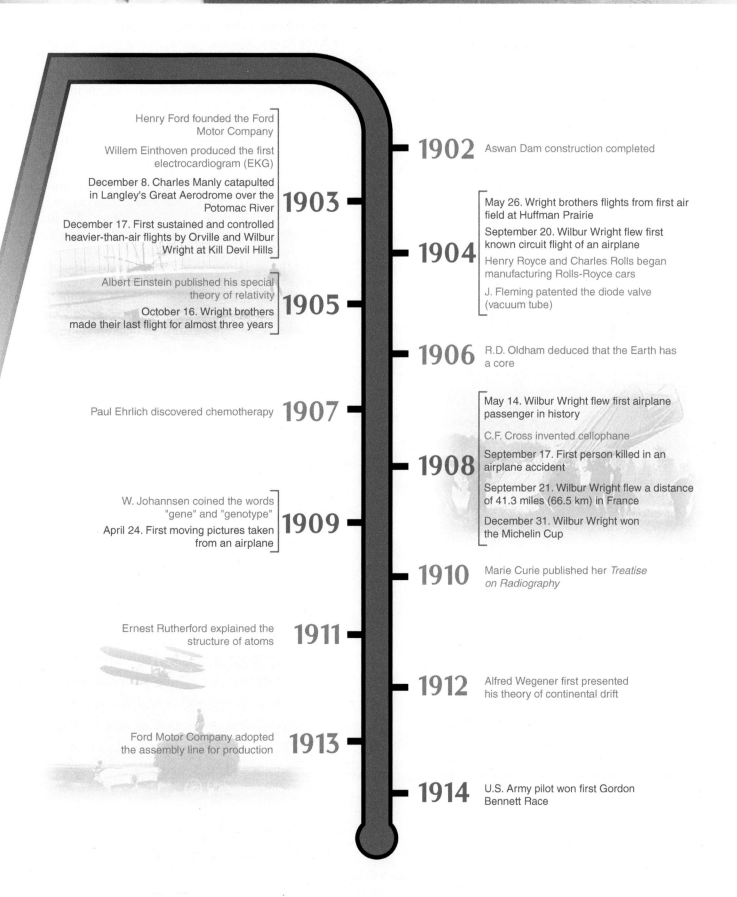

Henry Ford founded the Ford Motor Company

Willem Einthoven produced the first electrocardiogram (EKG)

December 8. Charles Manly catapulted in Langley's Great Aerodrome over the Potomac River

1903

December 17. First sustained and controlled heavier-than-air flights by Orville and Wilbur Wright at Kill Devil Hills

Albert Einstein published his special theory of relativity

1905

October 16. Wright brothers made their last flight for almost three years

Paul Ehrlich discovered chemotherapy **1907**

W. Johannsen coined the words "gene" and "genotype"

1909

April 24. First moving pictures taken from an airplane

Ernest Rutherford explained the structure of atoms **1911**

Ford Motor Company adopted the assembly line for production **1913**

1902 Aswan Dam construction completed

May 26. Wright brothers flights from first air field at Huffman Prairie

September 20. Wilbur Wright flew first known circuit flight of an airplane

1904

Henry Royce and Charles Rolls began manufacturing Rolls-Royce cars

J. Fleming patented the diode valve (vacuum tube)

1906 R.D. Oldham deduced that the Earth has a core

May 14. Wilbur Wright flew first airplane passenger in history

C.F. Cross invented cellophane

September 17. First person killed in an airplane accident

1908

September 21. Wilbur Wright flew a distance of 41.3 miles (66.5 km) in France

December 31. Wilbur Wright won the Michelin Cup

1910 Marie Curie published her *Treatise on Radiography*

1912 Alfred Wegener first presented his theory of continental drift

1914 U.S. Army pilot won first Gordon Bennett Race

Introduction

What was aviation during the development of heavier-than-air flight? For more than a century, aviation was lighter-than-air aircraft: balloons, dirigibles, and airships. These developments produced a heritage of flight and experienced pilots, yet the enthusiasm for ballooning, and later dirigibles and airships, diverted resources from the mechanical and aeronautical development of airplanes; that is, heavier-than-air craft.

Birds embodied the dream of flight, and early designers tried to imitate bird flight. Leonardo da Vinci's amazing flapping-wing ornithopters were theoretical attempts to define heavier-than-air flight. The designs could not have flown. The movement of the wings and the reliance upon human muscle for power could not have propelled the aircraft through the air. Leonardo was one of many who explored the analogy of man in flight and birds in flight. Unlike other ornithopter designers of the 16th, 17th, and 18th centuries, however, Leonardo studied the problem of flight. In 1505 he investigated the flight of birds and recorded his observations and theories in a notebook. Though he never solved the problem, later in life he drew some fixed-wing gliders in what was a more practical approach to flight than his ornithopters. All his designs remained relatively unknown till publication in the late 19th century and, therefore, did not influence the early development of heavier-than-air aviation, so the focus remained on birds. This was particularly the case of "tower jumpers," would-be flyers who in their home-built wings jumped from high buildings, an often deadly endeavor, from the 12th century to the 20th century. Even early fixed-wing designs relied upon the shape of birds. That was the case of the glider model *Passarola* or *Great Bird* launched in Lisbon in the early 18th century. Mechanical designs just before the Montgolfiers invented ballooning include A.J.P. Paucton's

Leonardo da Vinci drawings of an ornithopter.

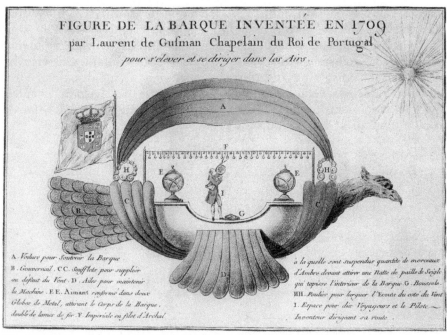

The Passarola or Great Bird designed by Father Laurençe de Gusmão.

man-powered aircraft that had one rotor for vertical lift and another for horizontal propulsion, Canon Desforges' flying carriage with flapping wings and a safety parasol, and Jean-Pierre Blanchard's ornithopter, which he built but could not get off the ground.

This chapter discusses the origins of heavier-than-air flight, including concepts, models, experiments, and eventually the successful flights of Wilbur and Orville Wright. Section A covers the heavier-than-air developments prior to the Wright brothers, including 19th-century designs and models of heavier-than-air craft, scientific and engineering studies and experiments, gliders, and the people promoting heavier-than-air flight.

Section B discusses the research, development, and flights of Wilbur and Orville Wright from 1896 until they achieved manned, controllable, sustained, powered flight in late 1903. At that time, and aside from lighter-than-air flights, the two brothers and their Wright Flyer represented the state of the art in aviation. In 1903 the Wrights applied for a patent for their "flying machine." This patent was awarded in 1906. Section C discusses the definition of an airplane contained in the patent and the importance of patents in the development of aviation. Section D continues the story of the Wright brothers developing and demonstrating the airplane.

Historical Evidence

In 1505 Leonardo da Vinci made a scientific study of how birds fly. He recorded his work in a notebook entitled *Sul Volo degli Uccelli (On the Flight of Birds)*. That notebook was finally published in 1892. Leonardo described his idea about imitating birds:

"A bird is an instrument working according to mathematical law, an instrument which it is within the capacity of man to reproduce with all its movements, though not with a corresponding degree of strength, for it is deficient in the power of maintaining equilibrium. We may therefore say that such an instrument constructed by man is lacking in nothing except the life of the bird, and this life must needs be supplied from that of man."

Historical Evidence

Historians use many souces of information. One is fiction. Fictional stories reveal contemporary ideas about topics like flying. Among the early aviation-related literature is the 1759 novel *Rasselas*, written by the famous Samuel Johnson. It is the story of Rasselas, Prince of Abyssina, traveling to Egypt. The book contains "A Dissertation on the Art of Flying" and this explanation of flight:

"So fishes have the water, in which yet beasts can swim by nature, and men by art. He that can swim needs not despair to fly: to swim is to fly in a grosser fluid, and to fly is to swim in a subtler."

Like Leonardo da Vinci, a fictional character, *Rasselas,* believes manmade wings would enable man to fly. The wings are made, but they fail the one and only flight test.

By studying this chapter, you will develop an understanding of what happened during the development of heavier-than-air aviation from the endeavors of the 19th century through the Wright brothers' contributions during the 1896-1914 period. After studying this chapter, you should be able to cite several examples of 19th-century people who contributed to the development of heavier-than-air aviation. You will be able to identify Orville Wright, Wilbur Wright, and the Wright Flyer. You should have a basic understanding of what a patent is and be able to discuss the content and significance of Wrights' patent of a "flying machine." Finally, you should be able discuss the development and marketing of Wright airplanes during the years before World War I.

Historical Note

The early literature of flight includes both fact and fiction, like these examples:

1627   Friedrich Hermann Flayder, *De arte volandi (The Art of Flying)* — proposal for a flapping-wing ornithopter

1638   Francis Godwin, *The Man in the Moone: or a Discourse of a Voyage Thither* (written under the pseudonym Domingo Gonsales, the Speedy Messenger) — a fictional story about flying a kite-like craft pulled by birds

1648   John Wilkins, *Mathematical Magic* — a book that examines several possible methods of flight, including the "probable" method of a flying chariot

1670   Father Francesco Lana de Terzi, *Prodromo dell' Arte Maestra (Introduction to the Master Art)* — an article about proposed aerial ships and the prospect of aerial warfare

1680   Giovanni Alfonzo Borelli, *De Motu Animalium (On the Movement of Living Things)* — an argument that human muscles are insufficient to propel an aircraft the way wings enable a bird to fly

1726   Jonathan Swift, *Travels into Several Remote Nations of the World* (written under the pseudonym Lemuel Gulliver and more commonly known as *Gulliver's Travels*) — a satire that includes a flying island powered by a big magnet

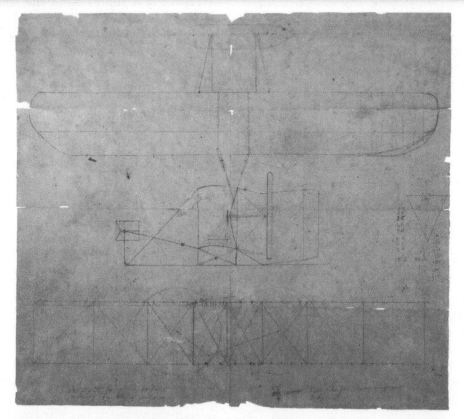

Preliminary three-view sketch of the 1903 Flyer, drawn in pencil on brown wrapping paper. The notations are in Wilbur Wright's handwriting.

HEAVIER THAN AIR

Q & A

What? The invention of the airplane and the inauguration of heavier-than-air flight

When? Flights of 17 December 1903 demonstrated and confirmed the invention

Where? Kitty Hawk, North Carolina

Who? Orville and Wilbur Wright

Why? To fly

Two technologies that influenced aviation were much older than their aeronautical applications. One was the kite, a Chinese invention. It is in essence a flying wing that dates from the 1st century or earlier. The other is the windmill, which originated in ancient Rome, but the form that influenced aviation appeared in 12th-century Europe. According to British historian Charles Gibbs-Smith, "the kite is in reality a primitive aeroplane — a craft supported in the air by the action of wind upon an inclined surface — and the windmill is a propeller." The aeronautical significance of the windmill as a propeller was recognized in 1784. That year two Frenchmen, Professors Launoy and Bienenu, devised a simple helicopter with rotors on both ends of a pole. Also that year, Monsieur Vallet

Historical Note

Chinese aviation began with the kite in the first century or earlier. Like western aviation, the eastern version has a history filled with legends, proposals, reports of military intelligence gathering, and fanciful attempts to fly like a bird or in aerial carriages. But it was in the West that the kite, and the later Chinese inventions of gunpowder and rockets, were applied to practical aviation.

developed a propeller that he tested on a river boat and later, in 1785, on balloons. With only muscle to power the propeller, it proved ineffective, but the idea remained popular in attempts to propel balloons. The **propeller** was called an airscrew in British usage and a *moulinet* (revolving fan) in French usage. The word propeller comes from the Latin *propellere* meaning to drive forward. The aeronautical significance of the kite as a wing was recognized in 1804 by the Englishman who first conceived of the modern airplane: George Cayley.

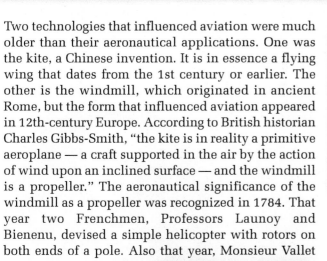

Sir George Cayley

The modern airplane originated with Sir George Cayley who conceived the idea. Inspired as a youth by the invention of the balloon, he pursued a scholarly

Historical Evidence

The Science Museum in London preserves a silver disc on which George Cayley engraved a diagram of the forces of lift, drag, and thrust. The disc is dated 1799. On the reverse side is a sketch of a fixed-wing glider, with a seat for the pilot and with manually operated "assisters" instead of a propeller. In accompanying documentation, Cayley addressed the issue of weight by applying the weight of the craft and his own weight. These artifacts are evidence (1) that Cayley identified the four forces acting on an object in flight: lift, weight, drag, and thrust; and (2) that he applied this information to powered and manned flight of a heavier-than-air craft.

Other evidence of Cayley's accomplishments appear in the series of articles on aerial navigation that he published in *Nicholson's Journal of Philosophy* in 1809 and 1810 and a later article on that topic in *Mechanics Magazine* in 1843. Also, Cayley's *Aeronautical and Miscellaneous Notebook* was published in 1933.

Personal Profile

Sir George Cayley (1773-1857) was a wealthy land owner in Yorkshire, England. He established the scientific principles for heavier-than-air flight and used glider models for research. He built and flew man-carrying gliders. He suggested using multiple wings — biplanes or triplanes — to achieve maximum lift with minimum structural weight, and he recognized that curved surfaces provide greater lift than flat surfaces. He suggested that an internal combustion engine be used to power an airplane, and suggested jet propulsion. In addition to aviation designs and devices, Cayley invented railroad and agricultural equipment, including the Caterpillar tractor that he patented under the name "universal railway" in 1825.

Sir George Cayley

interest in aviation throughout his life. Late in the 18th century he defined the problem of mechanical flight (distinct from the chemical flight of balloons): "to make a surface support a given weight by the application of power to the resistance of the air." He also drew a diagram of the forces of lift, drag, and thrust; and he sketched a fixed-wing glider complete with vertical and horizontal control surfaces on the tail, a fuselage seat for the pilot, and manually operated "assisters" to propel the craft. He clearly distinguished between the mechanism for lift — the wing — and the mechanism for thrust — the assisters. By the turn of the century, Cayley had thus identified the problem of flight, and he identified the basic elements of the solution, which was the airplane.

Cayley read studies of air resistance in regard to ballistics and windmills. He applied that knowledge to experiments with a whirling arm device in order to understand air resistance in relation to aircraft. That was in 1804, the year he recognized the aeronautical significance of the kite. He proceeded to make a model glider. This model used a common paper kite as the wing; the wing is the airfoil that creates a pressure differential in the air and thereby produces lift. The kite sat on a pole that served as the aircraft's body or fuselage. The word fuselage comes from a French word meaning spindle-shaped, and Cayley wrote of an aeronautical experiment that showed "that the shape of the hinder part of the spindle is of as much importance as that of the front in diminishing resistance." The five-foot model had an empennage, or tail assembly, that combined a rudder and elevator; that is, a tail rudder or fin controlled the rotation about the vertical or yaw axis and the tail elevator or stabilizing surface controlled movement about the lateral or pitch axis. The word empennage comes from the French term to feather, as to add a feather to an arrow or in Cayley's case to a glider. The 1804 model even had a movable weight whereby Cayley could shift the center of gravity; the center of gravity, or CG, refers to the center of the aircraft's total weight, the point about which the aircraft can be balanced and the point around which all movements of the aircraft rotate. He flew the unmanned model. At times, he had a man run with the model, and that man would be lifted into the air for several yards at a time. The experiments were successful, and this simple experimental aircraft became the model for the modern airplane. (Figure 2-1)

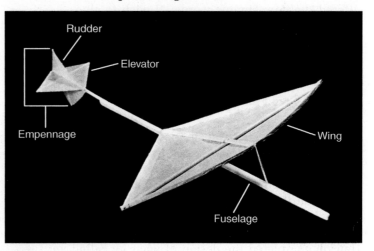

Figure 2-1. 1804 Cayley glider. It included a wing, fuselage, empennage, rudder, and elevator.

In 1809 Cayley built a full-size glider with a wing area of 200 square feet. This glider flew unmanned and successfully. Cayley recognized the need for power if an aircraft were to transport people and freight, so he turned his attention to the problem of power. For years he investigated motorized flight by focusing on flapper power, both ornithopter flapping and flapping propulsion on fixed-wing machines, but he failed to develop a successful motor. He even designed a convertiplane for vertical liftoff and horizontal flight. Late in life he built and flew gliders again. One small glider towed by a rope carried a ten-year-old boy aloft. In 1853 a larger glider carried a man in free flight. This man was Cayley's coachman and a reluctant flier. The coachman glided across the valley near Cayley's home. On the far side of the valley he crashed a bit hard on the tricycle undercarriage. He then uttered the now famous words: "I wish to give notice, I was hired to drive and not to fly."

Henson and Stringfellow

Inspired by Cayley's substantial contributions to aeronautics, two Englishmen continued development of heavier-than-air aircraft. William Samuel Henson and John Stringfellow collaborated on several aviation projects during the period from 1835 to 1847. Henson had already experimented with gliders, and Stringfellow had launched a couple balloons. In 1842 Henson completed the design of what he called an aerial steam carriage. It was a steam-powered airplane design that benefited from Cayley's work. Henson and Stringfellow enlisted attorney D.E. Colombine and newspaperman Frederick Marriott to join them in organizing the Aerial Transit Company in 1842-43. This company tried to raise funds to construct and fly the steam carriage. The full-size airplane was never built, but Henson and Stringfellow built and tested a twenty-foot model of the monoplane. A monoplane has one (mono) lifting plane or surface, that is, one wing (a biplane has two, a triplane, three). The wing was a unique feature of Henson's design. It was cambered (curved), braced with king posts, and constructed with supporting spars and connecting ribs. Henson's design also included a vertical rudder. The steam engine turned two six-bladed pusher propellers. In a flight test at Chard in 1847, the model achieved only a descending powered glide. It failed to fly. Henson abandoned the project and left England, but his design had demonstrated the *possibility* of powered heavier-

than-air flight. Stringfellow, on the other hand, persisted. In 1848 he built a ten-foot model of a monoplane, an improved version of Henson's design. This was a "launch by wire" aircraft. It hung suspended from an inclined wire, and as the engine literally built up steam, the craft would move down the wire. At a certain point, it detached itself from the

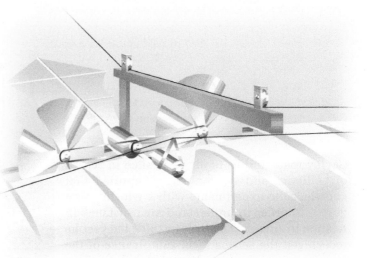

Stringfellow's launch by wire monoplane

Personal Profile

John Stringfellow (1799-1883) was a specialist in lace-making machinery. He collaborated on aircraft design and construction with W.S. Henson from 1835 into 1847 on several aviation projects. His particular contribution was designing light- weight steam engines. Their final project together was building a 20-foot model of Henson's steam-powered monoplane. After Henson emigrated from England to the United States, Stringfellow made a ten-foot model of a monoplane. With this steam-powered model of a monoplane, according to his biographer, Stringfellow established the world's first unmanned, powered, winged flight — a claim sometimes disputed, because the model was launched by wire and stayed in flight too short a time to prove *sustained* powered free flight. Stringfellow later exhibited a triplane and a steam engine at Britain's first aviation exhibition, held at Lydenham, London, in 1868.

John Stringfellow

Personal Profile

Frederick Marriott (1805-1884) was an English newspaperman who joined the venture to build W.S. Henson's aerial steam carriage for the Aerial Transit Company. Marriott promoted the venture and placed prints of the steam carriage in the press. He is credited with coining the word aeroplane, which became the British term for airplane. He soon left the partnership and immigrated to the United States. Settled in San Francisco where he founded the *San Francisco Newsletter*, Marriott organized the California Aerial Steam Navigation Company in the 1860s. This company built the *Avitor*, a winged, steam-powered dirigible, called an aerial steam car. It first flew on 2 July 1869 at the San Jose racetrack. That was a tethered flight. Later flights were also tethered or indoors. Promotion of the *Avitor* included a poetry contest won by Bret Harte with a poem of the same name. Fire destroyed the *Avitor*, and Marriott's last venture in aviation was designing a heavier-than-air "aeroplane steam carriage," a further development of the steam-powered airplane concept and a design not complete at the time of his death.

wire and flew. The craft was launched at Chard and at Cremorne Gardens in London. The publicity, started by Marriott, for Henson's steam carriage and the work of Henson and Stringfellow revived popular interest in aviation and inspired later aeronautical efforts.

Félix du Temple, a French naval officer, also made an early heavier-than-air craft in the nineteenth century. He flew a steam-powered model in 1857. He developed his ideas and eventually built a full-size airplane. The powerplant consisted of a steam engine and a **tractor propeller**; that is, a propeller located on the front of the aircraft. The aircraft had a tail feature and plenty of wingspan for lift. In 1874 this aircraft rolled down an inclined ramp on its wheeled undercarriage and under its own power. It hopped into the air and landed. Some proponents claim this 1874 event as the first powered flight of a heavier-than-air craft, others argue that it was simply the first powered takeoff, and still others note that du Temple's early and somewhat practical design almost flew.

Historical Note

"First" is a loaded term for historians who want to know how the word is qualified. Historians, for example, disagree on who achieved the first powered flight of an airplane. The honor is sometimes given to John Stringfellow of England for his 1848 flights of a steam-powered model airplane, and sometimes to Félix du Temple of France for his 1857 flights of a steam-powered airplane model. Du Temple's supporters argue that Stringfellow's flight did not demonstrate *sustained* flight, while du Temple's did. Advocates of Stringfellow's claim simply argue powered free flight of an airplane, without reference to sustained flight. The flights differed significantly in takeoff: Stringfellow's model was launched by wire, du Temple's took off under its own power. Did the wire launch of Stringfellow's model propel its short flight, or did the aircraft fly on its own? The limited evidence allows historians to differ in their conclusions.

Historians are not interested in the first time something happened for the sake of firstness. What interests historians is the first *known* event that *influenced* other events, or the *historically significant* event regardless of its number in any sequence of events.

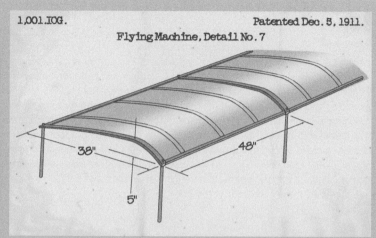

1,001,IOG.   Patented Dec. 5, 1911.

Flying Machine, Detail No. 7

38"   48"

5"

The first major society devoted to flying was the *Société Aérostatique et Météorologique de France* (Aerostatic and Meteorological Society of France), founded in 1852. It became the *Société Française d'Aviation Aérienne* (French Society for Aerial Aviation) in 1873. More influential was the Aeronautical Society of Great Britain, founded in 1866 and renamed the Royal Aeronautical Society in 1918. The British society attracted scientifically trained men who addressed the problem of mechanical flight. It was at the first meeting of that society that F.H. Wenham (1824-1908) presented the results of his years of study and experimentation with wing design: a cambered or curved wing set at an angle to the wind obtains most of its lift nearing the front part of the wing and thus a long wing (with high aspect ratio) generates the most lift. In 1871 Wenham and John Browning built the earliest known wind tunnel for aeronautical research, and in it Wenham continued investigating the properties of airfoils. The Aeronautical Society provided meetings to discuss ideas, technical journals in which to publish works, and information disseminated by other members and from outside sources.

Otto Lilienthal

In 1889 a German engineer named Otto Lilienthal published an important book on bird flight as the basis of aviation. Although he believed that the powered airplane would be an ornithopter and, in fact, experimented with ornithopters as a youth, he accomplished his most productive and influential work with fixed-wing gliders. Starting in 1891, Lilienthal constructed and flew gliders. He made five types of monoplane gliders and two biplane gliders, all fixed-wing aircraft, but the wings were shaped like bat wings. His favorite form of takeoff was a hill launch with the pilot running forward. In Grosskreuz he actually built a conical hill on which to conduct his experiments. The gliders allowed the pilot's hips and legs to hang free for use during takeoff and for flight control. Control was achieved by the pilot swinging his body and thereby changing the center of gravity. Flight was an athletic activity for Lilienthal, who was in his 40's when he conducted the gliding experiments. He logged nearly 2,000 flights in glides that covered distances of 300 to 750 feet. He made cambered wings that were foldable for transport of the gliders. In addition, he experimented with the tailplane, a leading-edge flap device, rear elevator, and ornithopter wingtips. Lilienthal demonstrated that man could fly heavier-than-air craft without an engine and thereby gain the flight experience he believed necessary for the design and control of a powered airplane.

Personal Profile

Otto Lilienthal (1848-1896) was a German engineer who balanced theory and practice when he turned his attention to aviation. He wanted to fly and directed his experiments toward that goal. He studied bird flight, particularly the type, structure, area, and lift of the wings of different birds. He experimented with fixed-wing gliders, published his technical notes, and allowed photographs of his glides. Lilienthal logged almost 2,000 flights. He convinced many people that powered flight was possible through the dissemination of information about his gliding.

Otto Lilienthal

Lilienthal's interest in ornithopters represented his ties to the past, and his gliders placed him at the state of the art in aviation. He crashed a glider into the Rhinower Hills on 9 August 1896, and died the next day. On his death bed he uttered his last words: "Sacrifices must be made."

Flight Lines

"Once, on a soaring flight which started from a greater height, my body and outstretched arms fell into a position in which the centre of gravity was shifted too far back, and I was so exhausted that it was impossible for me to bring my arms forward again. As I sailed along at a height of sixty feet and a speed of about fifty kilometres per hour, the apparatus, which was heavily weighted behind, tipped up more and more, and at last, owing to its motive power, shot up vertically into the air. Desperately I held fast, seeing only the blue sky flecked with white clouds, and expecting from moment to moment that the machine would turn over backwards and end my soaring experiments, perhaps for ever. Suddenly, however, it ceased climbing and began to drop backwards; it was steered into short circling curves by the horizontal tail which was now slanted upwards, until it turned over so far that it stood on its head and plunged down with me perpendicularly earthwards."

Otto Lilienthal on a crash that he survived with a cut head and sprained wrist, as quoted by Ann & Lorne Welch in *The Story of Gliding* (London: John Murray, 1965).

Personal Profile

As a child, Octave Chanute (1832-1910) immigrated with his family to the United States from France. He became a civil engineer known for designing railway bridges. Chanute built a variety of gliders and became a trusted colleague of the Wright brothers. In 1903 Chanute informed the French Aero Club in Paris of the Wrights' glider flights, and he wrote articles on American aviation for French journals. It was he who informed Europe of the Wrights' powered flights.

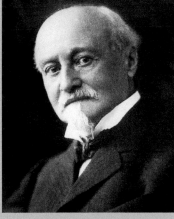

Octave Chanute

Octave Chanute

Civil engineer Octave Chanute was in his 60's when he shifted his pursuits from railway bridges to aviation. He had for years collected information about flight, and his first endeavor was writing a history of *Progress in Flying Machines*, published in 1894. Following Lilienthal's example, Chanute began building man-carrying gliders in 1896. He improved the Lilienthal design by abandoning the bat-wing shape, and using a Cayley-type tail unit. His goal was

inherent stability. He made three basic types of gliders. One was a multiple-wing glider with movable wings, another a triplane glider, and the third a biplane glider. He tried various modifications of his machines. An innovation he introduced with the biplane glider was the Pratt truss to brace the wings; he adapted the truss from bridge technology. Chanute used Lilienthal's swinging-body control system. Given his age, he hired a young man with an established interest in aviation, Augustus Herring, as test pilot. In Chanute's gliders, Herring flew over the Indiana Dunes on the shore of Lake Michigan, east of Chicago. The Wright brothers read Chanute's book and contacted him; thereafter, Chanute and Herring visited the Wright brothers' camp at Kill Devil Hill, North Carolina. Chanute disseminated information about flying through his book and other communications, and he encouraged the Wrights on their quest for powered flight.

Nineteenth-Century Aeronautics

Cayley, Henson, Stringfellow, Lilienthal, and Chanute were influential in the development of heavier-than-air aviation, but they were not alone. Throughout the 19th century many individuals experimented with flight. Often they attempted flight in aircraft that were more curiosities than flying machines, like the ornithopters of Clement Ader in France, Jacob Degen in Switzerland, and W.J. Lewis in the United States; or the kite-drawn carriage of George Pocock in England, or the steam-powered test rig of Hiram S. Maxim in England. Ader, by the way, named a couple of his aircraft *Avion* which became the French word for airplane. Some 19th-century efforts were more practical, like the steam-powered helicopter of Enrico

Forlanini in Italy, the glider experiments of Jean-Marie Le Bris in France, and the model airplanes and box kites of Lawrence Hargrave in Australia. In 1871 Alphonse Pénaud of France built and flew an innovative and influential planophore. This planophore was a monoplane driven by twisted rubber (like the child's toy that followed Pénaud's innovation). *Plano* comes from a Greek term meaning capable of movement, and *phore* from the Greek meaning bearer, as in bearing a pilot on board. Pénaud achieved lateral stability by means of dihedral or the upward angling of the wing and longitudinal stability by the position and angle of the fixed tailplane. Pénaud later designed and patented, but did not build, an amphibious tractor monoplane. By the close of the 19th century, heavier-than-air machines were under development in Australia, Britain (both England and Scotland), France, Germany, Italy, Poland, Russia, the United States, and other countries, though airships, dirigibles, and balloons still dominated flight.

WRIGHT BROTHERS

Personal Profile

Wilbur Wright (1867-1912) was 5'9 1/2", 140 pounds with a dark complexion. He was a few years older and a bit thinner than his brother, Orville. He was neat and his manner was controlled, cool, even aloof, yet outgoing and thoughtful. He was the public speaker of the pair. The airplane was his idea.

Wilbur Wright

Personal Profile

Orville Wright (1871-1948) was 5'8", 140 pounds, with a pale complexion, dark hair, and a reddish mustache. He was particular in dress, though impulsive and enthusiastic in general. Although timid in public, he was quick thinking and optimistic. He was the more mechanical of the brothers.

Orville Wright

Personal Profile

The brothers Wilbur and Orville Wright achieved the first significant flights of an airplane: they flew sustained flights of a powered airplane under the control of the airborne pilot. Later they developed a practical airplane, and they built a passenger-carrying airplane. Among the honors they earned were the 1908 Gold Medal of the Aero Club of France, the 1909 Gold Medal of the Royal Aeronautical Society, and the 1909 Langley Medal of the Smithsonian Institution.

Wilbur and Orville Wright were the first two individuals inducted into the Aviation Hall of Fame (posthumously); the year was 1962. They entered the International Aerospace Hall of Fame with its first group of honorees in 1965.

Wilbur and Orville Wright

Wilbur and Orville Wright lived in Dayton, Ohio, and were the sons of a bishop in the United Brethren Church. As youths, they showed an interest in aviation, but pursued more immediate and practical endeavors. They tried working in a print shop, but disliked the business. Each bought a bicycle in 1892, rode together, and soon joined the bicycle craze sweeping the country. Wilbur rode the back roads, and Orville raced around tracks. They became known as bicycle mechanics prior to opening their bicycle sales and repairs shop. The next step was to make their own cycles. The Wrights' bicycles were handcrafted originals made in their shop, while other cycle makers at the time were mass-producing bikes in factories.

The Wrights did buy some stock components, such as seats, tires, and handlebars. They were skilled craftsmen — ingenious mechanics.

News of Lilienthal's death in 1896 kindled Wilbur Wright's interest in aviation. He studied bird flight, read Étienne-Jules Marey's book on *The Animal Machine*, and decided to enter aviation. He wrote the Smithsonian Institution in Washington for information about aviation. The Smithsonian responded with a reading list that included Chanute's *Progress in Flying*. Wilbur's enthusiasm for aviation spread to Orville. Lilienthal was a favorite subject of both Wrights. Through reading, discussing, corresponding, and experimenting, the brothers learned to be engineers and inventors in the field of aeronautics.

Personal Profile

Étienne-Jules Marey (1830-1904) was a French physician whose photography informed and influenced the Wright brothers. When their interest turned toward aviation, the brothers repeatedly read *The Animal Machine (Le Machine Animale)*, written by Marey in 1873 and translated into English in 1874. In the book Marey tried to explain animal locomotion, particularly how a bird's wings flap, and he printed a rapid sequence of photographs of flying birds. He later photographed the flow of smoky or steamy air over objects of different shapes in a wind tunnel. Marey introduced these photographic techniques to aeronautical research.

Étienne-Jules Marey

The Wright brothers started modestly by constructing a **biplane kite** in August 1899. The kite had aeronautical controls.

1. There was a fixed horizontal rear stabilizer.

2. The wings could be moved forward or backward to adjust the center of gravity.

3. Cords allowed the wings to be warped for lateral stability.

Wilbur got the idea of wing warping from watching buzzards in flight and noticing the twisting of their wingtips as they recovered balance. The brothers tested the craft like a kite with control strings to the operator on the ground. The sophistication of the Wrights' first, simple aircraft indicated the depth of what they had learned as well as their originality. (Figure 2-2)

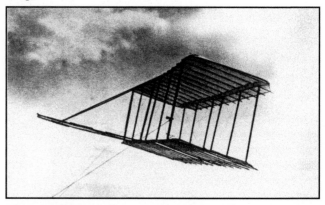

Figure 2-2. The Wright's biplane kite during tethered tests in August 1900.

Famous Flights

The first week of August 1899 Wilbur Wright flew the brothers' first aircraft, a kite. He was able to control it during climbs, dives, rolls left, and rolls right. The control system consisted of four lines from the kite, two from the upper wing surface and two from the lower. The strings attached to the ends of two sticks held by the operator on the ground. One string from each wing surface went to an end of a stick, so that each stick had a string from each wing surface. Each stick was attached to the aerodynamic surfaces on one side of the kite, one end of the stick to the upper wing and the other end to the lower wing. Adjusting the sticks would thereby adjust the wings on both sides of the kite. These kite flights of 1899 proved the correctness of the Wright brothers' initial concepts of control.

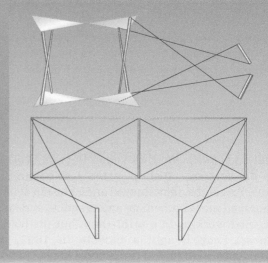

Flight Lines

"Well, after erecting a derrick from which to swing our rope with which we fly the machine, we sent it up about 20 feet, at which height we attempt to keep it by the manipulation of the strings to the rudder [elevator]. The greatest difficulty is in keeping it down. It naturally wants to go higher & higher. When it begins to get too high we give it a pretty strong pull on the ducking string, to which it responds by making a terrific dart for the ground. If nothing is broken we start it up again. This is all practice in the control of the machine."

Orville Wright referring to the biplane kite, in a letter to his sister Katharine Wright, 14 October 1900, as quoted in Tom D. Crouch, *The Bishop's Boys, a Life of Wilbur and Orville Wright.*

Historical Note

Bicycle technology influenced the Wright brothers. The cycle business supplied them:

- funds that covered the expenses of developing a flying machine.

- wood-working and metal-working tools and skills that they used in constructing gliders and the airplane.

- cycle technology, like the chain-drive transmission system, that they adapted to their aviation work.

- knowledge of and experience with balance and control. Both the cycle and the plane require controlling motion around the roll and yaw axes, and the operator is part of the balance and control system of both the cycle and plane.

- the awareness that a pilot must learn to fly as a cyclist learns to ride a bike — by practice.

- a consciousness of weight, for both cycles and planes are designed to be light and swift.

The genius of the Wright brothers went beyond their bicycle experience, but their genius recognized and applied lessons from cycling to flying.

The Problem of Mechanical Flight

At this early stage the Wrights recognized the whole problem of mechanical flight: plane *and* pilot, stability *and* maneuverability. They identified the pilot as part of the machinery and experience of flight. They did not isolate aspects of flight; for example, they did not separate the stability of the aircraft from the maneuverability achieved by pilot control. Stability is the tendency of the airplane to return to equilibrium once it is disturbed; an inherently stable plane, once disturbed, would return to its original attitude. Maneuverability is the ability to turn, climb, descend, roll, and yaw. A plane which is too stable would be hard to maneuver, as it would tend to return to its original attitude despite actions of the pilot to disturb that attitude for the purpose of maneuvering. Early unmanned gliders needed to be stable, but that stability was often designed into the early manned gliders as well. That is why most early glider pilots

needed to be athletically fit, like Lilienthal swinging his body with sufficient force to overcome the stability inherent in the glider. As a result of their insight into the whole problem of flight, the Wrights intended to design a relatively unstable airplane so that a pilot could control and maneuver the aircraft. But first, there was a lot of work to be done developing lift, power, and control, as well as gaining experience through glider flights.

Gliders

The Wright brothers finished building their first full-size glider in 1900. By design, this glider was unstable and required pilot skill to fly. It had wing warping for lateral stability that was controlled by the pilot. The warping would increase the curvature or twist at one end of the wing and decrease it at the other end. This action would bank the glider or return it to a horizontal attitude. Since the glider was a biplane, the control warped both wings. Other features were a movable forward elevator and a prone position for the pilot. Since the winds around Dayton were

Historical Evidence

Place is a type of evidence for a historian. By understanding place, the historian can better understand what happened there. Kitty Hawk is an excellent example. Why did the Wright brothers of Dayton, Ohio, travel to Kitty Hawk, North Carolina, in 1900, and again in 1901, 1902, and 1903, to conduct their flight experiments? The answer is simple: wind. According to the United States Weather Bureau then (and now), the Kill Devil sand dunes on the coast of North Carolina, near Kitty Hawk, experience strong and steady winds. Wind power keeps a kite in the air. In 1900 Wilbur and Orville Wright were flight testing a kite. In 1901 and 1902 the brothers flight tested biplane gliders. Among other things, the

movement of the air over a glider, particularly the wings, is necessary to create lift. Their 1903 airplane also utilized two airfoils and the winds of Kitty Hawk to achieve flight. The higher the winds, the less power was needed from the airplane motor, and the Wrights had developed only a low-power engine in order to minimize the weight that the engine would add to the airplane. Kitty Hawk provided the best place to conduct tests of their machines. The Wright Brothers National Memorial at Kill Devil Hills is listed on the National Register of Historic Places.

THRUST — LIFT — DRAG — WEIGHT

generally mild, too mild for the flight tests, the brothers traveled to Kitty Hawk, North Carolina, a place known for steady strong winds. They established camp on the Kill Devil Hills sand dunes outside of town. There they tested the kite glider and a manned glider with Wilbur as the test pilot. (Figure 2-3)

Each subsequent glider incorporated lessons learned from earlier models or versions. The 1901 model, for example, was larger than the 1900 glider, wingspan of 22 feet versus 17 feet and wing area of 290 square feet versus 165. It was larger to provide more lift, deemed necessary by the 1901 focus on manned glider tests. To launch the glider, Orville held one wingtip and a local Kitty Hawk resident held the other wingtip. The

Figure 2-3. Wilbur Wright during a glider flight in October 1902.

Historical Note

The Wright brothers used formulas they found in the publications of Lilienthal and Chanute to predict the performance of a wing.

One lift equation was:

$$L = k \times S \times V^2 \times C_L$$

with L being lift in pounds, k: coefficient of air pressure, S: total area of the lifting surface, V^2: velocity squared (velocity being airspeed), and C_L: coefficient of lift.

This formula required the researchers to know the particular wing to be tested and the conditions under which it would be tested. Each angle of attack represented a new test condition and required computation, so each wing would undergo a series of tests. The result of a single test was an experimentally determined number for the lift of the wing at the set angle of attack.

The Wrights used a similar formula to compute the *predicted* amount of drag of the wing under the conditions of the test.

Historical Note

In 1901 the Wrights constructed a wind tunnel in order to predict more precisely wing performance. Wind tunnel data influenced the Wrights' 1902 glider and subsequent designs.

Flight Lines

"Day before yesterday we had a wind of 16 meters per second or about 30 miles per hour, and glided in it without any trouble. That was the highest wind a gliding machine was ever in, so that we now hold all the records! The largest machine that we handled in any kind [of weather], made the longest distance glide (American), the longest time in the air, the smallest angle of descent, and the highest wind!!!"

Orville Wright referring to the 1902 glider, in a letter to his sister Katharine Wright, 23 October 1902, as quoted in Tom D. Crouch, *The Bishop's Boys, a Life of Wilbur and Orville Wright.*

two men ran with the glider until it became airborne with Wilbur prone in the pilot's place. During one of the early test flights, the glider became uncontrollable in pitch (nose up-down) and crashed. The brothers investigated and determined that the ribs in the wings flexed. Their solution was to add middle spars and brace the wings. That was done on version two. In a subsequent flight test, version two went into a stall-spin (commonly called well-digging). The problem was identified as adverse yaw while wing warping, though at the time the brothers were not familiar with the term adverse yaw, which means the aircraft yaws in the direction opposite to the turn being performed. The solution showed up on the next version: a double vertical surface fixed as a tail. On the 1902 glider, that double vertical surface was identified as the cause of slipping while wing warping, so the Wrights adopted a single vertical surface that was movable and connected to the wing warping system (that is, a rudder). The rudder appeared on the next configuration tested that year at Kitty Hawk.

Control

In 1902 the Wright brothers made almost a thousand glides at Kitty Hawk, and they solved the problem of control. The final version of that year's glider demonstrated systems that successfully controlled the three axes of the airplane. If the pilot moved the elevator control bar backward or forward, the elevator in the front of the airplane moved and the nose would pitch up or down respectively. The forward elevator thus provided control around the lateral or pitch axis. The French called the forward elevator a *canard*, or duck, due to its resemblance to the head at the end of the long neck of a duck in flight. If the pilot moved the hip cradle, the wing warping control cables moved and the wings warped. Wing warping controlled movement around the longitudinal or roll axis. The

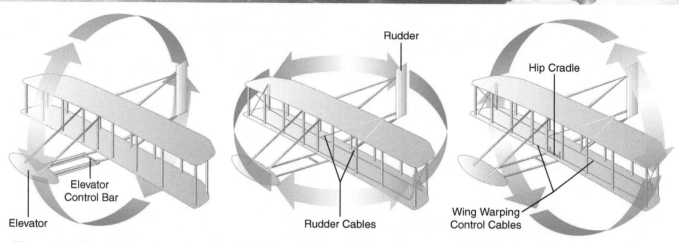

Figure 2-4. This diagram shows how the 1902 Wright glider controlled pitch (left), yaw (middle), and roll (right).

rudder was connected to the wing warping system to offset the increased drag known as adverse yaw; therefore, rudder movement provided control around the vertical or yaw axis. Pilot skill gave stability and control to the unstable glider. (Figure 2-4)

Engine

Control was the Wrights primary concern from the beginning. Wilbur explained: "When once a machine is under proper control under all conditions, the motor problem will be quickly solved." The engine problem was secondary to control, but with the control problem solved in late 1902, the Wrights needed an engine to power their next aircraft. They looked at automobile engines, but found none light enough. Their solution was a specially designed engine derived from the four-stroke gasoline engine invented by N.A. Otto in 1876. The brothers and machinist Charles Taylor designed and built the 200-pound, 4-cylinder, 12-horsepower engine for the 1903 Flyer. It was water cooled, a heavier alternative than air cooled, but more reliable than air cooled; for manned flight, the brothers chose reliability over lightness. (Figure 2-5)

Historical Note

Throughout the 19th century, the problem of an aviation engine had proved unsolvable. Human muscle was inadequate, as the many ornithopter designers repeatedly proved. The industrial power of the century came from water or steam. Watermills were obviously impracticable aboard a flying machine, and even light-weight steam engines proved too heavy for full-size airplanes. Indicative of the many efforts to solve the problem, fifteen different engines were exhibited at the British Aeronautical Society's aviation exhibition in 1868. Steam, guncotton, gas, and oil drove the various engines. The power to weight ratio was key. Early engines simply weighed too much for the power produced; there was insufficient power to carry the weight of engine and aircraft. The Wright brothers used a simple four-cycle engine; whereas, Samuel Pierpont Langley used Charles M. Manly's more complicated engine on his *Great Aerodrome*. At that time the four strokes of an engine were described as suck, squish, pop, and ptui.

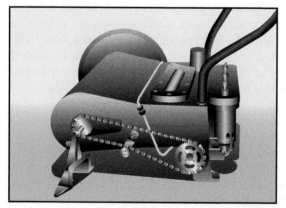

Figure 2-5. This is a close up of the water-cooled engine that powered the 1903 Wright *Flyer*.

Airplane engines drive propellers, so the Wrights applied their engineering skills to solve the propeller problem. Soon they discovered that a propeller was an airfoil that rotated. It generated thrust in the same way the wing created lift. They applied the formulas used to study wings to their investigation of propellers. They wanted to understand propellers theoretically, but the problem was complex. Orville explained, "With the machine moving forward, the air flying backward, the propellers turning sidewise, and nothing standing still, it seemed impossible to find a starting point from which to trace the various simultaneous reactions." Yet they did. They decided upon two pusher propellers with counter-rotating blades. **Counter-rotation** meant the blades would turn in opposite directions and would counter the torque of each other. The propellers had a diameter of 8.5 feet. The Wrights adapted the chain transmission system of the bicycle to link the propellers to the engine.

Airplane Flight

In 1903 the Wrights built their first powered aircraft which they called the *Flyer*. They took the machine to Kitty Hawk for testing. Their careful preparations included gliding flights in the 1902 glider. In appearance, the old glider and the new airplane looked similar, though the Flyer had an engine, propellers, a double rear rudder, and a double front elevator. The Wrights laid rail downhill and into the wind for launching the Flyer, which had no wheels. The landing gear consisted of skids. These skids rested on a cart-like structure which rode the rail on bicycle hubs. A wire held the Flyer while its engine gained power. When the wire was released, the airplane on the launch cart rolled along the rails until the airplane took off. All power came from the airplane's engine. After various delays, the first flight was scheduled for 14 December. Wilbur won the coin toss and the privilege of piloting the first flight. Invited witnesses were present. The Flyer rolled along and took off. It climbed steeply, stalled, and crashed with minor damage. Wilbur admitted the cause was pilot error: he brought the nose up too high.

Three days later the Wright brothers were ready to try again. The airplane had been repaired, and the rails had been moved to level ground, so this takeoff would not be assisted by gravity. Five witnesses and a camera were present to verify the event. Orville got in the plane, as now it was his turn to try. He flew for 12 seconds and attributed the shortness of the flight to his inexperience. Wilbur then made a flight of about 11 seconds. Orville went next and remained in flight 15 seconds. The final flight that morning, with Wilbur flying, lasted 59 seconds! They had taken off from a level surface under the power of the plane, with no assistance. They had controlled the airplane in flight, and they had landed on skids on the ground at least as high as the starting point. They had achieved the first, manned, powered, controlled, and sustained flights of an airplane!

Flight Lines

"Success four flights Thursday morning all against twenty one mile wind started from level with engine power alone average speed through air thirty one miles longest 57 seconds"

In fact, the longest of the four flights lasted 59 seconds. Orville Wright in a telegram to his father Bishop Milton Wright, 17 December 1903, as quoted in *The Papers of Wilbur and Orville Wright, Volume One: 1899-1905.*

Historic Event

On 17 December 1903 Wilbur and Orville Wright flew an airplane in manned, powered, controlled, and sustained flights of a heavier-than-air aircraft. The flights were well documented and verified at the time. Orville made the first flight and thus was the first airplane pilot. Wilbur followed within the hour. Each made a second flight that morning.

Flight	Pilot	Distance	Duration
First	Orville Wright	120 feet	12 seconds
Second	Wilbur Wright	175 feet	11 seconds
Third	Orville Wright	200 feet	15 seconds
Fourth	Wilbur Wright	852 feet	59 seconds

Historical Evidence

The Wright brothers kept diaries and recorded their work in progress in notebooks, and they corresponded with family and colleagues. They arranged to have photographers document the progress of their work. These diaries, notebooks, letters, and photographs provide primary evidence of what the brothers did and thought. Scholars studying these and other documents have produced secondary literature about the Wrights, like Tom Crouch's biography of *The Bishop's Boys, a Life of Wilbur and Orville Wright*. After extensive research, Crouch concluded, "They were acute observers, who moved beyond surface appearances to achieve an understanding of fundamental principles. Both of them understood the world in terms of graphic and concrete images; more important, they could apply these observations of physical and mechanical reality to new situations. It was the very core of their shared genius."

Historic Event

The hundredth anniversary of the Wrights' first airplane flights of 17 December 1903 gave cause for celebration across the United States, in the United Kingdom, in China, and elsewhere around the world. Air shows, glider competitions, kite festivals, parade floats, lectures, exhibits, conferences, web sites, books, aviation film festivals and documentary films were among the celebrations taking place in 2003. Kitty Hawk, North Carolina, and Dayton, Ohio, celebrated their ties with the Wright brothers by hosting series of celebrations culminating on 17 December 2003.

Honoring the Wright brothers and rediscovering the challenges of flight were behind numerous reproductions of the Wright Flyer. The Wright Experience group in Virginia built Wright kites, gliders, and airplanes, including an exact replica Wright Flyer for the Wright Brothers National Memorial at Kitty Hawk. Students at Utah State University made a modified Flyer out of modern composite materials. Taking a scientific approach to understanding the Wright Flyer, the Los Angeles Section of the American Institute of Aeronautics and Astronautics undertook a 20-year project culminating in 2003 with a replica of the Wright Flyer on national tour. The Los Angeles team built and tested a 1/8th scale radio-control model. They built two sub-scale wind tunnel models for testing. They also built a full-scale replica and reinforced it for wind tunnel tests at the Ames Research Center of the National Aeronautics and Space Administration. They concluded that "the aircraft was very unstable and almost impossible to fly."

In a foreign tribute to the Wright brothers, the Aero Club of South Africa sponsored the Flying Lion project. The club encouraged pilots to take stuffed-toy lions, dressed as pilots, on flying adventures. The rules required recording each adventure in a logbook, taking photographs on each leg of the adventure, and staying in one place no longer than three days at time. The Flying Lion adventure ended appropriately on 17 December 2003.

SECTION C

WRIGHT PATENT

On the 23rd of March 1903, Orville and Wilbur Wright applied for a patent for a "flying-machine." Why did they apply for a patent? A **patent** is a

Historical Note

According to the Constitution of the United States, Congress has the power "to promote the progress of science and the useful arts by securing for limited times to authors and inventors the exclusive rights to their respective writings and discoveries." The first act of Congress under the Constitution gave the Secretary of State, the Secretary of War, and the Attorney General the responsibility of granting patents. In 1836 Congress created the Patent Office to administer the program. A patent is a contract between the inventor and the government, wherein the government represents the public. It contains information about the invention. The public obtains free use of information about the invention once the patent expires.

government document granting certain rights to an inventor, usually the exclusive right to manufacture and sell the invention for a specific period of time. The Wrights applied specifically for a **letters patent**, which is an open letter; that is, a document open for public inspection. Through the dissemination of information about inventions contained in patents, governments encourage innovation and invention. By obtaining a patent, the inventor obtains exclusive rights to the invention for a certain number of years. The Wrights sought exclusive right to make, use, and sell their invention for 17 years, the term specified by law in the United States at that time. They had a product to sell, and that is why they wanted a patent.

The Patent Office summarily dismissed the Wrights' application as a nuisance. Over the years the government had received many applications pertaining to flying machines that could not fly. The Wrights sent additional information, and the application was dismissed again. That meant no legal protection for

Historic Event

Orville and Wilbur Wright submitted their first application for a patent on 23 March 1903, nine months before they achieved powered flight. They sought protection for their ideas, notably what worked with their 1902 glider. The United States issued the patent three years later. The patent was for a broadly defined "flying machine."

UNITED STATES PATENT OFFICE.

ORVILLE WRIGHT AND WILBUR WRIGHT. OF DAYTON, OHIO.

FLYING-MACHINE.

Patented May 22, 1906.

Specification of Letters Patent.

Application filed March 23, 1903 Serial No. 149,220

No. 821,393.

To all whom it may concern:
Be it known that we, ORVILLE WRIGHT and WILBUR WRIGHT, citizens of the United States, residing in the city of Dayton, county of Montgomery, and State of Ohio, have invented certain new and useful Improvements in Flying-Machines, of which the following is

that class of fly...sustained...

ous disturbing forces which tend to shift the machine from the position which it should occupy to obtain the desired results. It is the chief object of our invention to provide means for remedying this difficulty, and we will now proceed to describe the construction by means of which these results are accomplished.

In the accompanying drawings we have shown an apparatus embodying our invention in one form. In this illustrative embodiment the machine is shown as comprising superposed aeroplanes 1 and 2, ...prefer, although our ...structure...

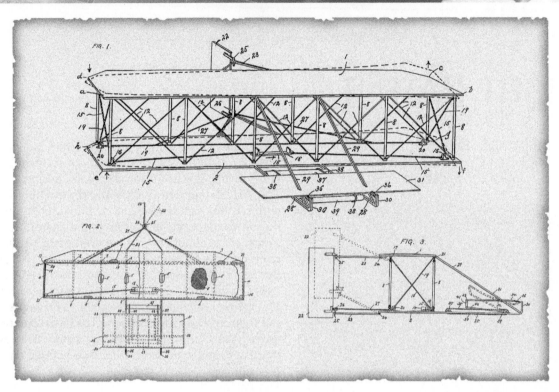

Figure 2-6. These are the first three figures from the Wright flying machine patent of 22 May 1906.

their ideas, which through Chanute were becoming known in Europe, so they hired a patent attorney. He drafted a broad claim intended to make any flying machine by someone else an infringement. Belgium, France, and Great Britain awarded the Wrights patent rights in 1904, and finally the United States granted their patent in 1906. That same year Austria, Germany, and Italy also granted patent rights. In the United States, the patent was assigned the number 821,393. The various patents gave the Wrights legal protection in the world's major aviation centers.

Wright Flying Machine

What was the invention patented by the Wrights? The term flying machine is vague, and it refers to the class of invention. That class, as explained in the patent, relates to those machines "in which the weight is sustained by the reactions resulting when one or more aeroplanes are moved through the air edgewise at a small angle of incidence, either by the application of mechanical power or by the utilization of the force of gravity"; that is, a heavier-than-air, aerodynamic flying machine, either glider or airplane. The Wrights specified either monoplane or biplane in the text. They patented their general principles, very broadly:

"The objects of our invention are to provide means for maintaining or restoring the equilibrium or lateral balance of the apparatus, to provide means for guiding the machine both vertically and horizontally, and to provide a structure combining lightness, strength, convenience of construction, and certain other advantages . . . ."

They patented their ideas of control and construction. They wanted a broad patent and they got it, yet the emphasis of the patent, like the focus of their development work, was control. The engine was not included in the patent even though it was essential for powering an airplane through the air. Control was the important issue in the Wrights' scheme. (Figure 2-6)

Historical Evidence

Patent No. 821,393 is a primary source. The patent is included in Appendix B of this text. It is a historical document that contains evidence of what the Wright brothers claimed as their invention. Close or analytical reading of the document can uncover evidence from the obvious like vocabulary to the obscure like pulley-rope connections between operator and control surfaces. When reading the patent, for the sake of clarity, it is important to note the Wrights' odd use of the word aeroplane for wing and airfoil in general. Their definition of aeroplane as an airfoil appears on page 5 of the patent.

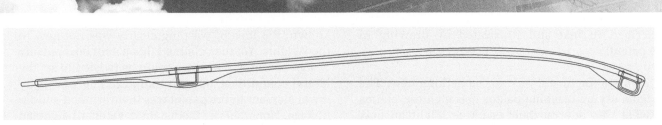

Figure 2-7. This is a cross-section of the Wright Flyer's wing showing the spars (one front and one rear) that ran lengthwise along the wing. Ribs and rib-like bows connected the spars.

Wings

The flying machine described in this patent had many features. The main lifting surface was the wing or wings in the case of a biplane. The wings were airfoils, what the Wrights called "aeroplane" in the patent. The wing frame was made of spars, bows, and ribs covered with fabric. The two transverse spars extended from wingtip to wingtip, one near the front of the wing and the other near the rear. The ends of the parallel spars were connected by rib-like bows at the wingtips. Ribs connected the front spar and the rear spar. The threads in the cloth cover were arranged to provide support like a truss. Control wires connected to the wingtip ends of the rear spar; the pilot used these wires to warp the wing for banking and turning. If the aircraft was a biplane, straight rigid standards and diagonal wire stays connected the two wings, and truss struts and truss skids braced the wings. The Wrights had learned the truss system from Chanute. (Figure 2-7)

Control

The pilot, called an "operator" in the patent, was essential to the control system. This operator lay prone, face down, on the lower wing (or only wing of a monoplane). By laterally moving the hip cradle, the operator would warp the wing because there was a guide-pulley-and-rope link between the operator's hip cradle and the wing's outer corners. In the patent, the Wrights defined wing warping as "any construction whereby the angular relations of the lateral margins of the aeroplanes [wings] may be varied in opposite directions with respect to the normal planes." (Figure 2-8)

Other features of the airplane described in the patent include a vertical rudder or tail that can turn around a vertical axis; a pulley-rope connection between the cradle and rudder, and a connection between the rudder and the lateral margins of the wings; a front horizontal "rudder" (elevator). Each feature is

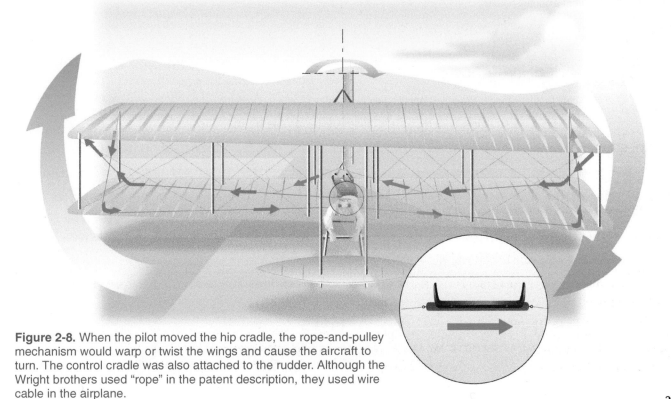

Figure 2-8. When the pilot moved the hip cradle, the rope-and-pulley mechanism would warp or twist the wings and cause the aircraft to turn. The control cradle was also attached to the rudder. Although the Wright brothers used "rope" in the patent description, they used wire cable in the airplane.

described in text and illustrated by drawing in the patent.

Patents are for inventions, for something new. The Wrights' flying machine patent lists eighteen claims of what was new in their machine. Eighteen new elements is an exaggeration of reality. Many of the claims related to wing warping; but, unknown to the Wrights, that concept had been patented before. Clement Ader in France had patented a form of warping in 1890, and Friedrich Robitzch in Germany had obtained a 1902 patent for altering surfaces for the purposes of stability and control. Though little known, the idea of warping clearly was not new to the Wrights. Yet they claimed this patent covered any design in which the wings could be twisted to set the lateral margins at opposite angles. The one truly novel element in the patent was the warp-and-rudder linkage. Nonetheless, the patent covered all eighteen claims and reflects the brothers' ability to conceive of the airplane as a whole solution to the problem of flight. The Wrights sought and obtained more than one patent during their career, but this first patent — No. 821,393 — best describes their invention, which was basically the Wright biplane glider of late 1902.

Historical Evidence

Orville and Wilbur Wright obtained several patents from the United States government. They applied for the basic airplane patent in 1903 and received that patent in 1906. In 1908 they applied for four patents later granted.

No. 821,393 for Flying-Machine, patented 22 May 1906 (the basic Wright patent based on the 1902 glider, with wing warping and rudder linkage).

No. 908,929 for Mechanism for Flexing the Rudder of a Flying Machine or the Like, patented 5 January 1908 (horizontal "rudders" or elevators as well as vertical rudders)

No. 987,662 for Flying-Machine, patented 21 March 1911 (lateral stability achieved by use of horizontal surfaces adjustable to different angles of incidence on the right and left sides: wing warping, without reference to rudder)

No. 1,075,533 for Flying-Machine patented 14 October 1913 (automatic stability about longitudinal, lateral, and vertical axes, by use of pendulum and vane to detect changes in attitude)

No. 1,122,348 for Flying-Machine, patented 29 December 1914 (lateral balance regulated with wing warping and vertical rear rudder as well as vertical front-mounted rudder)

Historical Evidence

The Wright brothers sought exclusive rights to their technology in other countries by obtaining foreign patents.

Austria: Österreichische Patentschrift No. 23,174 (1906) and No. 36,566 (1909)

Belgium: Brevet d'invention No. 176,292 (1904), No. 211,970 (1908), No. 211,971 (1908), No. 213,823 (1909), and No. 217,586 (1909)

France: Brevet d'invention No. 342,188 (1904) and No. 384,124 (1908), No. 384,125 (1908), No. 401,905 (1909), No. 404,866 (1909)

Germany: Patentschrift No. 173,378 (1906), No. 240,181 (1911), No. 240,702 (1911), No. 259,339 (1913), No. 258,732 (1913), No. 259,811 (1913), No. 260,050 (1913)

Great Britain: Patent Specification No. 6,732 (1904), No. 24,076 (1909), No. 24,077 (1909), No. 2,913 (1909), No. 16,068 (1909)

Hungary: Szabadalmi leírás No. 44,407 (1909), No. 44,408 (1909), and 47,943 (1910)

Italy: Registro generale No. 227/184.81601 (1906), No. 99,047 (1908), No. 99,048 (1908), No. 100,791 (1909), 103,685 (1909), No. 124,336 (1912)

Russia: Gruppa V No. 15,010 (1909)

Spain: Patente de invención No. 44,332 (1908), No. 44,333 (1908), No. 44,860 (1909), and No. 45,940 (1909)

SECTION D

WRIGHT AIRPLANES

Historic Event

On 26 May 1904 the first flights of the Wright Flyer No. 2 took place at the newly established airfield called Huffman Prairie, near Dayton, Ohio. Torrence Huffman lent the 90-acres of pasture land to the Wright brothers for their aeronautical use. This was the first airfield for airplanes, and the Flyer No. 2 was the first plane to use the field. During 1904 the Wright brothers made a total of 105 takeoffs from that field. Huffman Prairie is now a National Historic Landmark in recognition of its role in the Wrights' development of the airplane there.

The delay in winning government approval of their patent kept the Wrights from exhibiting their airplane and releasing detailed information about the operation of the aircraft. Their reticence affected the initial dissemination of information about their 1903 accomplishments, but they never stopped development of the airplane. They knew the 1903 Flyer was not a practical machine, and that 59 seconds was not a practical flight time. In 1904 they built a new airplane called Flyer No. 2, and a new airplane motor.

They also developed an airport, or aerodrome in British usage. The developments included removal of barbwire fences, construction of a hangar, and installation of launching rails. This field was at Huffman Prairie, a pasture, eight miles east of Dayton, literally across the fence from the end of the Dayton trolley line. The brothers agreed to herd any horses or cows from the pasture before flying on any given day.

Flyer No. 2

Flyer No. 2 had less camber and more horsepower than No. 1, and the propeller gearing was new. Each of the brothers made numerous short flights in No. 2 as they familiarized themselves with airplane controls and maintenance. In September they adopted an assisted takeoff device. A rope routed over a pulley was connected on one end to a weight and the other end to the cart, or truck, that was attached to the launch rail. As before, the Flyer would rest on the truck. When the weight was released, the truck would speed along the launch rail, and the plane would take off. The flights were experiments, test flights, and training flights. Having invented the airplane, they were teaching themselves to fly and trying to determine how to make the craft more practical. They kept the plane low to the ground so that they might survive a crash. No. 2 developed a problem during right turns in which the wing failed to warp adequately enough to avoid a stall. They finally solved this problem in their next airplane the following year.

Flight Lines

"We have found great difficulty in getting sufficient initial velocity to get real starts. While the new machine lifts at a speed of about 23 miles, it is only after the speed reaches 27 or 28 miles that the resistance falls below the thrust. We have found it practically impossible to reach a higher speed than about 24 miles on a track of available length, and as the winds are mostly very light, and full of lulls in which the speed falls to almost nothing, we often find the relative velocity below the limit and are unable to proceed."

Wilbur Wright in a letter to Octave Chanute, 8 August 1904, as quoted in Tom D. Crouch, *The Bishop's Boys, a Life of Wilbur and Orville Wright.*

Flight Lines

"When it turned that circle, and came near the starting-point, I was right in front of it; . . . it was . . . the grandest sight of my life. Imagine a locomotive that has left its track, and is climbing up in the air right in front of you — a locomotive without any wheels. . . . Well now, imagine that locomotive with wings that spread 20 feet each way, coming right toward you with the tremendous flap of its propellers, and you have something like what I saw."

Businessman Amos Root on witnessing the 20 September 1904 "first circular flight of an airplane in the history of the world," as quoted in Tom D. Crouch, *The Bishop's Boys, a Life of Wilbur and Orville Wright*.

Flyer No. 3

Wilbur and Orville Wright completed Flyer No. 3 in 1905. It was a new machine, except for the 1904 engine. There were numerous improvements, adjustments, and refinements over earlier models. No. 3 met the criteria of a practical airplane. In it the Wrights learned to avoid the right-turn stall by technique: put the nose down and increase speed. They made 49 flights in No. 3 that year. Many of the flights were long, several so long — 18 to 38 minutes in duration and 12 to 24 miles in distance — that they ended when the fuel ran out. For later flights that season, the brothers separated the controls of the wing warping and tail rudder and thereby gained control and coordination. With these developments, the Wrights believed "the age of the flying machine had come at last."

Marketing Attempts

Fearful of commercial or military spies trying to steal the technology, the Wright brothers grounded themselves in October 1905. They were still without patent protection in the United States and therefore reluctant to reveal too much technical information. They now had a practical airplane, so they began to market it. They approached the United States government to no avail for several years. They offered their product to the British government, which declined the offer. They approached governments because they foresaw military use of airplanes and recognized government funding as sufficient to pay for their development work as well as products.

The Wrights were known among the European aviation circles through Chanute's 1903 visit to Europe and through correspondence of the Wrights and Chanute

with members of the Aeronautical Society of Great Britain. The British War Department even sent emissaries to the United States to learn more about what the Wrights were doing aeronautically. The superintendent of the British Government Balloon Factory, Colonel J.E. Capper, met the Wrights and affirmed that they had indeed accomplished what they said. C.S. Rolls of the Rolls-Royce car company met the Wright brothers in New York City in 1906. He later bought a Wright airplane, and shared information about the Wrights' airplanes with the British government. But the British government did not buy Wright airplanes.

In December 1907 the United States Army Signal Corps invited proposals for a heavier-than-air flying machine. The government received forty-one bids, but only three met the specifications. The Wrights received the government contract for one airplane in February 1908. This government contract and hopes of selling airplanes in Europe prompted the brothers to resume flying in May 1908.

Refurbished Flyer No. 3

When the brothers took to the air that May, it was in a refurbished Flyer No. 3. New features included seats for the pilot and one passenger on the leading edge of the wing. Hand levers replaced the hip cradle. The brothers refreshed their piloting skills at Kitty Hawk, away from the centers of publicity, as they still wanted to protect their technology from public disclosure. There they carried the first airplane passenger in history: Wilbur Wright took mechanic Charlie Furnas for a ride in the refurbished Flyer No. 3, the first passenger plane in history. There too at Kitty Hawk, Orville crashed and wrecked the plane. He explained that he had grasped the wrong control lever of the newly installed steering system, which had one lever to guide the plane downward and a separate lever to direct the plane upward.

The Wright brothers built a flyer for the Army, designated by the Army as Model A. It was the Army's first airplane. Based on the modified Flyer No. 3, this two-seat biplane had a gross weight of 1360 pounds, a wingspan of 36′ 5″, and a length of 32′ 8″. The engine was a Wright model 4, that delivered 25 horsepower and a top speed of 40 miles per hour. This twin-propeller pusher crashed on 17 September 1908, at Fort Myer, Virginia. Pilot Orville Wright sustained serious injuries. His passenger, Lieutenant

Historic Event

On 14 May 1908 two people flew together in an airplane. That was a first-in-the-world event. Wilbur took mechanic Charlie Furnas up for over four minutes. Orville then tried to take Charlie up but had three false starts instead. The refurbished Wright Flyer No. 3 in 1908 became the first passenger plane in history.

Thomas Etholen Selfridge, became the first airplane fatality. The accident marred an otherwise successful demonstration of the military capabilities of aviation, and the Army continued its relationship with the Wrights. The brothers delivered to the Army a rebuilt Model A, designated by the Army as Model B, in June 1909.

Historic Event

On 17 September 1908, at Fort Myer, Virginia, Lieutenant T.E. Selfridge became the first fatality of an airplane accident. He was a passenger on a demonstration flight being given by Orville Wright, who was seriously injured in the crash.

European Tour

Concurrent with Orville Wright representing the brothers with the United States Army in 1908-09, Wilbur Wright toured Europe to demonstrate the Wright airplane there. He flew the Hunaudières Race and at Camp d'Auvourst Course in Le Mans, France. In December he won the Michelin Cup for the longest flight over a closed circuit: two hours, 18 minutes and 33 seconds. He demonstrated the Wright airplane and took passengers aloft one at a time. Wilbur flew and gave rides at Pont-Long, Pau, France; Centocelle Field, Rome, Italy; Tempelhof Field, Berlin, and Bornstedy Field, Potsdam, Germany.

Historical Note

On 16 September 1908 Wilbur Wright in a two-seat Flyer in France carried his first European airplane passenger: Ernest Zens. On 7 October he carried his first female passenger: Mrs. Hart O. Berg, whose skirt was tied down to avoid flight hazard and personal embarrassment. Orville took up the first cinematographer in April 1909, in Italy. He took up the first royalty in October of that year: Crown Prince Frederick William of Prussia.

Flight Lines

"Having clambered in among various rods and wires one struggles into the little seat arranged on the front edge of the lower plane, and places one's feet on a small bar in front. . . . Then the driver bends down and releases the catch which holds the anchoring wire. The machine is off! It bounds forward and travels rapidly along the rail. The foreplanes are meanwhile pressed down to prevent the machine lifting prematurely, but when about half the length of the rail has been traversed, the lever is pulled back, the planes come into operation, and the whole machine rises almost imperceptibly off the track. The ascent must be very gradual. . . . So steady and regular is the motion that it appears exactly as if it were progressing along an invisible elevated track. Only just now and again, as a swirl of wind catches it, does it make a slight undulation like a boat rising to a big wave. Mr. Wright, with both hands grasping the levers, watches every move, but his movements are so slight as to be almost imperceptible. . . . All the time the engine is buzzing so loudly and the propellers humming so that after a trip one is almost deaf."

Passenger Baden Fletcher Smyth Baden-Powell (founder of the Boy Scouts) on a flight with Wilbur Wright, at Le Mans, France, 1908, as quoted in Tom D. Crouch, *The Bishop's Boys, a Life of Wilbur and Orville Wright.*

In 1909 both brothers carried passengers, civil and military, male and female, European and American, on both sides of the Atlantic Ocean. In addition to the United States Army, the brothers sold planes to a French syndicate and to English customers. They also trained pilots, civil and military, mostly customers who had purchased their airplanes. The Wrights and their planes were suddenly popular, famous, and honored, but the brothers longed to return to research and development.

More Military Sales

In 1910 the Wrights began using wheels on their aircraft, on the Model B and subsequent models. That year the Wrights made two revised Model B airplanes for the Army, which used them at the Army field in College Park, Maryland, in 1911 and seven Triad Scout planes, Army Model C, in 1912. For these two seaters, the brothers moved the elevator to the rear of the plane. The Model B's engine generated 30 horsepower and a top speed of 42 miles per hour, and the C's 50 horsepower and 48 miles per hour. In 1913 the brothers delivered two one-place pushers to the Army, which the Army designated Model D Scouts. Its 50-horsepower Wright engine could reach a top speed of 67 miles per hour.

Wright Company

Late in 1909 the Wright brothers incorporated the Wright Company. The company acquired the Wright patents, and patent infringement cases, and the brothers received cash and shares. Wilbur became company president, Orville vice president. Neither was interested in running the company, but they did supervise the production side — from the construction of a factory in Dayton in 1910 to the fabrication of two prototypes of a new design. The new models were the two-seat Model B and the one-seat racing Model R, both with a new four-cylinder engine sufficiently powerful — 40 horsepower — for the aircraft to takeoff on wheels rather than be launched from rails. That first year their Dayton factory reached the production level of two airplanes per month.

Historical Note

The Wright Company provided flight training to civil and military customers. One of the military students at Huffman Prairie in 1911 was Lieutenant Henry H. "Hap" Arnold of the U.S. Army. Arnold described his experience at the Wright flying school.

The training actually began at the Wright factory in Dayton, "for in addition to learning to fly we found we would have to master the construction and maintenance features of the Wright machine."

Flight training began with an old airplane mounted on a sawhorse:

"The lateral controls were connected with small clutches at the wing tips, and grabbed a moving belt running over a pulley. A forward motion, and the clutch would snatch the belt, and down would go the left wing. A backward pull, and the reverse would happen. The jolts and teetering were so violent that the student was kept busy just moving the lever back and forth to keep on an even keel. That was primary training."

From the simulator in the factory, the student moved to Huffman Prairie. An average flying student, Arnold completed his flight training in ten days. During those ten days he logged 28 training flights for a total of three hours and 48 minutes of dual time. The last three flights he "landed without assistance."

H.H. Arnold in his autobiography *Global Mission* (New York: Harper & Brothers, 1949).

Despite their hopes, however, the brothers became absorbed in defending their priority and patents in the courts. Employees designed and built Wright airplanes; in 1913-14, for example, engineer Grover

Loening designed the first Wright flying boat, called the Model G. Like the Model G, the Wright Company failed to keep up with the competition during the years immediately preceding World War I. That competition is the subject of the next chapter.

Historical Note

Wilbur Wright (1867-1912) became ill in 1912. The initial diagnosis was malarial fever but the doctors changed the diagnosis to typhoid. On 30 May 1912 Wilbur Wright died. He was 45 years old.

Wilbur Wright

Historical Note

Orville Wright (1871-1948) sold his manufacturing and patent rights a few years after Wilbur's death in 1915. Throughout his long life he accepted awards for their shared accomplishments, starting with the Collier Trophy in 1913. That award recognized their development of the automatic stabilizer, described in Letters Patent No. 1,075,533.

Orville Wright

Conclusion

Wilbur and Orville Wright earned the distinction of being the first men to fly an airplane in *manned, powered, controlled, and sustained flight*. They were not the first people to be lifted by an aircraft, not even the first by a heavier-than-air craft, and they and their contemporaries knew it. Their achievement was greater than simply getting up into the air and back onto the ground. Through their three gliders (1900, 1901, and 1902) and three Flyers (1903, 1904, and 1905), they developed the technology and principles of heavier-than-air flight into a practical airplane. This fact is often lost on the many claimants who vie for the honor of first flight. Clement Ader in France laid claim to the honor, not for his 1890 flight inches above the ground in his steam-powered *Eole,* but for a short flight in the multi-engine, steam-powered *Avion III* in October 1897. The military witnesses at Ader's demonstration could not verify the craft flew! One of the more interesting examples is Samuel Pierpont Langley of the United States. Langley died in 1906, a few years later it was argued that his gasoline-powered and catapult-launched *Aerodrome* of 1903, despite two plunges into the Potomac River, was *capable* of manned flight. Like the Wrights' contemporaries, historians honor the brothers because they were the first to fly an airplane that influenced the concept as well as the practice of aviation. They added to the 1903 accomplishment by

Historical Note

One of many current claims that someone other than the Wrights achieved the first powered flight comes from Bridgeport, Connecticut. A contingent there argues for recognition of Gustave Whitehead *and* for the development of a tourist industry based on Whitehead. Born Gustav Weisskopf in Bavaria in 1874, Whitehead immigrated to Brazil and later, in 1895, to the United States. He moved to Bridgeport in 1900. There he built gliders, monoplanes, biplanes, triplanes, and a helicopter, as well as aviation motors. He flew on 14 August 1901 according to reports in the *Bridgeport Herald*, *New York Herald*, and *Boston Transcript*, though there is no evidence that a reporter witnessed any flight or interviewed any witness. Whitehead flew again on 17 January 1902, according to reports. Again, reliable evidence is elusive. Stanley Beach, son of the editor of *Scientific American* and himself the aviation editor of that magazine, financed Whitehead for a while in 1902-03, but this relationship did not result in the magazine crediting Whitehead with the first flight. Whitehead and Beach applied for a patent for a glider; the application was dated December 1905. Lee S. Burridge of the Aero Club of America funded Whitehead's helicopter work for a while in about 1911. Eventually Burridge sued Whitehead and acquired his shop; that apparently ended Whitehead's endeavors in aviation. Whitehead died in 1927 at the age of 53.

developing a practical airplane that could be maneuvered with relative ease and by making a passenger-carrying airplane. These significant accomplishments were carefully documented and established at the time, and they contributed to the advance of aviation.

Study Questions

1. Who was the first to aeronautically identify the basic form and elements of a modern airplane?

2. What glider experiments influenced the design of the airplane?

3. How did the Wrights' bicycle business help their aviation ventures?

4. What did the Wright brothers accomplish in 1903?

5. What distinguishes the Wrights' flights of 17 December 1903 from earlier heavier-than-air flights?

6. Why did the Wright brothers apply for patents?

7. What was an airplane as defined by the Wright patent of 1906?

8. When did the passenger plane become a reality?

9. Orville Wright won the 1913 Collier Trophy for what achievement in aeronautics?

10. Why did the Wright brothers leave the Wright Company, Wilbur in 1912 and Orville in 1915?

Bibliography

Crouch, Tom D. *The Bishop's Boys, a Life of Wilbur and Orville Wright*. New York: W.W. Norton and Company, 1989.

Crouch, Tom D. *A Dream of Wings, Americans and the Airplane, 1875-1905*. New York: W.W. Norton and Company, 1981. Reprinted, Washington: Smithsonian Institution Press, 1989.

Gibbs-Smith, Charles H. *The Aeroplane, an Historical Survey of Its Origins and Development*. London: Her Majesty's Stationery Office, 1960.

Gibbs-Smith, Charles H. *Sir George Cayley's Aeronautics, 1796-1855*. London: Her Majesty's Stationery Office, 1962.

Gollin, Alfred. *No Longer an Island, Britain and the Wright Brothers, 1902-1909*. Stanford, CA: Stanford University Press, 1984.

Jakab, Peter L. *Visions of a Flying Machine, the Wright Brothers and the Process of Invention*. Washington: Smithsonian Institution Press, 1990.

Lilienthal, Otto. *Birdflight as the Basis of Aviation, a Contribution towards a System of Aviation*. Translated from the second German edition entitled *Der Vogelflug als Grundlage der Fliegekunst* by Adolf William Isenthal. London: Longmans, 1911.

McFarland, Marvin W., editor. *The Papers of Wilbur and Orville Wright, including the Chanute-Wright Letters and Other Papers of Octave Chanute, Volume One: 1899-1905* and *Volume Two: 1906-1948*. New York: McGraw-Hill Book Company, 1953. Reprinted, New York: Arno Press, 1972.

Penrose, Harald. *An Ancient Air, a Biography of John Stringfellow of Chard, the Victorian Aeronautical Pioneer*. Washington: Smithsonian Institution Press, 1989.

Renstrom, Arthur G. *Wilbur & Orville Wright, a Chronology Commemorating the Hundredth Anniversary of the Birth of Orville Wright, August 19, 1871*. Washington: Library of Congress, 1975.

Timeline

Light blue type indicates an event not directly related to aviation.

Year	Event
1808	Sir George Cayley flew a kite-like model of a glider as part of his investigations of the center of gravity; obviously, he used a scientific approach to the problems of flight.
1848	June. John Stringfellow of England flew a steam-powered, ten-foot model of a monoplane at Chard, and in August the model also flew at Cremorne Gardens in London. No one was aboard the aircraft during the flights. According to Stringfellow's biographer, the June flight was "the first power-driven self-supported flight in world history."
1853	Summer. George Cayley's full-size glider carried a reluctant coachman in free flight from Brompton Hall, near Scarborough, England. This flight is the earliest-known successful manned heavier-than-air free flight.
1857	French seaman Félix du Temple de la Croix flew a clockwork-powered and later steam-powered model of an airplane in unmanned flight; this event rivals the Stringfellow claim of first powered heavier-than-air flight.
1871	August 18. Alphonse Pénaud flew his planophore in public for the first time. This rubber-driven monoplane had dihedral in the main wing, a tailplane, a vertical rudder, and pusher propeller.
1874	Félix du Temple tested a man-carrying powered airplane in flight with a young sailor as pilot at Brest, France; the power came from either a hot-air engine or a very light steam boiler. The flight was probably more of a hop off the inclined takeoff ramp. Some claim this flight as the first full-size, powered, manned airplane to leave the ground.
1884	Near St. Petersburg, Russia, I.N. Golubev as pilot flew an airplane designed and built by Russian naval officer Alexander F. Mozhaiski. He "flew" in the sense that the plane apparently left the ground briefly after rolling down the inclined ski-jump-like ramp. This "flight" rivals the 1874 flight of Félix Du Temple.
1890	October 9. Clement Ader became airborne at Armainvilliers, France, in his aircraft *Eole*. This flight prompted later claims of "first airplane," but like other 19th-century heavier-than-air flying machines, the *Eole* failed to achieve sustained flight. Ader's attempts to fly his *Avion III* on 12 and 14 October 1897 would again result in claims of "first flight."
1896	August 9. Otto Lilienthal crashed a glider into the Rhinover Hills, Germany. His death the next day from injuries sustained in the crash became an international news story and thereby spread information about his glider experiments.

1896   Summer. Octave Chanute flew gliders, piloted by A.M. Herring, on the windy shore of Lake Michigan near Chicago. His experiments demonstrated the effectiveness of the Pratt truss for bracing the wings of biplanes and other multi-wing aircraft.

1896   In April, Athens, Greece, hosted the first modern Olympic Games.

1897   In Massachusetts, the brothers Francis E. and Freelan O. Stanley began producing steam automobiles commercially.

1898   Miners continued to rush to the Klondike River region of the Territory of Canada, in response to the 1897 news that gold had been discovered there.

1899   American philosopher and educator John Dewey (1859-1952) published his book *School and Society*, in which he advocated progressive education.

1900   Austrian psychiatrist Sigmund Freud (1856-1939) published *The Interpretation of Dreams* about his investigations of unconscious mental processes; this was an influential publication during the early years of psychoanalysis.

1901   Italian inventor Guglielmo Marconi (1874-1937) transmitted radio signals across the Atlantic Ocean, from Poldhu, Cornwall, England, to St. John's, Newfoundland. Marconi and the German physicist Karl Braun (1850-1918) shared the 1909 Nobel Prize in physics for their work on wireless telegraphy (radio).

1902   For irrigation and the economic development in Egypt, Great Britain completed construction of the Aswan Dam on the upper Nile River, near the town of Aswan. Originally, the dam measured 6,400 feet (1,950 meters) in length and 65.5 feet (20 meters) in height. It was raised to 88.5 feet (27 meters) in 1912 and to 118 feet (36 meters) in 1933.

1903   In the United States, Henry Ford founded the Ford Motor Company; and the next year in Britain Henry Royce and Charles Rolls began manufacturing and selling Rolls-Royce cars.

1903   Dutch physiologist Willem Einthoven (1860-1927) developed a means to record on a graph the electrical activity of the heart; that is, he invented the string galvanometer to produce electro-cardiograms (EKGs). He won the 1924 Nobel Prize in physiology or medicine.

1903   December 8. Samuel Piermont Langley catapulted his *Great Aerodrome* over the Potomac River beside the capital city of Washington. This full-scale, man-carrying, gasoline-powered aircraft — piloted by Charles Matthews Manly — failed the flight test. It broke apart and fell into the river, but it led to claims that the *Aerodrome* was the first airplane capable of flight.

1903   December 17. Orville and Wilbur Wright made four flights over the North Carolina sand dunes called Kill Devil Hills, near the town of Kitty Hawk. Their Flyer left the ground under its own power, moved forward far enough to demonstrate the aircraft could sustain flight, landed safely on land at least as high in elevation as their takeoff point, and did so under the control of the pilot. Wilbur made the first flight and thus became the first pilot of an airplane, as defined by the *Wright Flyer*.

1904   In Great Britain, J. Fleming patented the diode valve (vacuum tube).

1904   May 26. The Wright brothers made the first flights of their new Flyer No. 2 from Huffman Prairie, near Dayton, Ohio, and in so doing they inaugurated flights at the first air field specially designed for airplane use.

1904   September 20. Wilbur Wright flew an airplane in a circle; this was the first known circuit flight of an airplane, and it demonstrated the extent of control the pilot had over the Wright Flyer No. 2.

1905   German physicist Albert Einstein (1879-1955) published his special theory of relativity regarding uniform motion, and he proposed light quanta or photons in an explanation of photoelectric effect.

1905   October 16. Having demonstrated that Flyer No. 3 was fully controllable during the summer and fall season, the Wright brothers made their last flight for almost three years. They stopped flying on this date in order to protect the intellectual property of their airplane, which was not yet protected by a United States patent. By the time they resumed flying on 6 May 1908, they had lost much of their technical lead in aviation.

1906   Based on his seismological studies, British geologist R.D. Oldham deduced that the Earth has a core.

1907   German bacteriologist Paul Ehrlich (1854-1915) discovered chemotherapy, the injection of chemicals as a treatment for diseases. In 1908 he and Russian biologist Ilya Metchnikov (1845-1916) won the Nobel Prize in medicine for their research on the immune system. A few years later, in 1910, Ehrlich discovered a cure for syphilis — an arsenic compound he called 606 because it was the 606th compound he tested for that purpose.

1908   C.F. Cross invented cellophane.

1908   May 14. Wilbur Wright took mechanic Charlie Furnas for a ride in the refurbished Flyer No. 3; refurbishment included the addition of two seats, one for the pilot and one for a passenger. That made Furnas the first airplane passenger in history and the modified Flyer No. 3 the first passenger airplane in history.

1908   September 17. Lieutenant Thomas Etholen Selfridge, of the United States Army Signal Corps, died in the crash of a Wright biplane at Fort Myer, Virginia, and thereby became the first person killed in an airplane accident. Pilot Orville Wright was injured.

1908   September 21. Wilbur Wright demonstrated the endurance of his Wright airplane by flying a distance of 41.3 miles (66.5 km) in France.

1908   December 31. Wilbur Wright won the Michelin Cup by flying 77 miles (124 km) at Camp d'Auvourst, France. This newsworthy flight lasted two hours, eighteen minutes, and thirty-three seconds.

1909   Danish scientist W. Johannsen coined the words "gene" and "genotype."

1909   April 24. Wilbur Wright flew a Wright biplane over Centocelle, Italy, while a photographer shot the first aerial motion-picture film from an airplane.

1910   French physicist Marie Curie published her *Treatise on Radiography*. She had won the 1903 Nobel Prize in Physics for her work on radioactivity. She won the 1911 Nobel Prize in Chemistry for the discovery of radium and polonium.

1911   British physicist Ernest Rutherford explained his theory of the structure of atoms, that the atom was not an indivisible unit, but a structure with a nucleus surrounded by protons and electrons.

1912   German astronomer, meteorologist, and polar explorer Alfred Wegener (1880-1930) presented a talk on "The Geophysical Basis of the Evolution of the Large-scale Features of the Earth's Crust (Continents and Oceans)" at the Geological Association in Frankfurt am Main. He further developed his theory of continental drift in articles, in his 1915 book *The Origin of Continents and Oceans,* and five subsequent editions of that book.

1913   Henry Ford (1863-1947), who had founded the Ford Motor Company in 1903, adopted the assembly line for production of the Model T car. The assembly line concept used machine-made interchangeable parts in continuous movement on a line (or conveyor). The assembly line was an innovation in mechanization and industrial organization.

1914   E. Kleinschmidt invented the teletypewriter.

CHAPTER 3

EARLY FLIGHT (1904-1914)

AVIATION HISTORY

Summary of Events

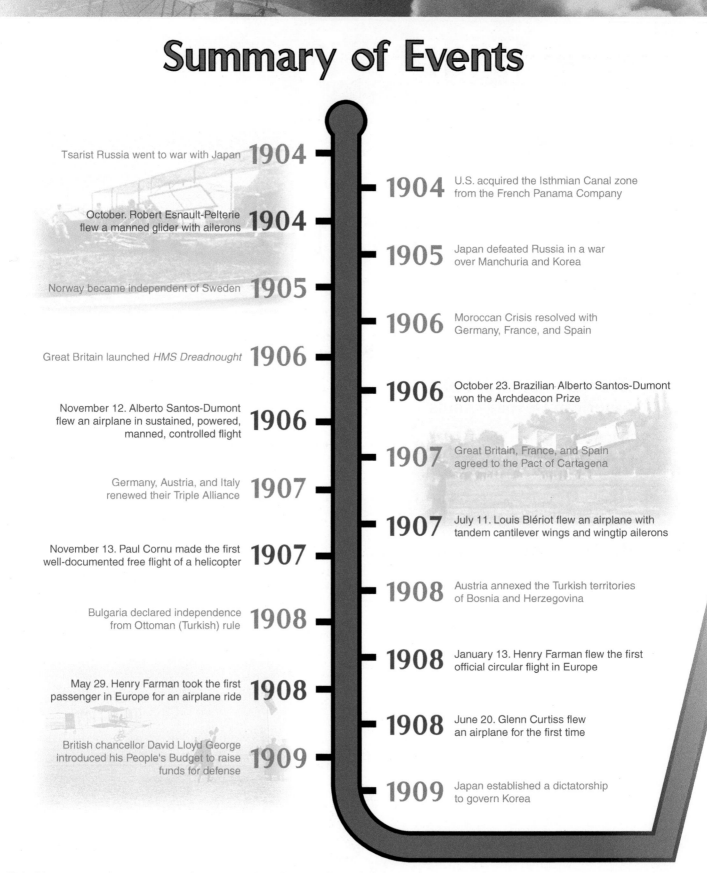

Tsarist Russia went to war with Japan **1904**

1904 U.S. acquired the Isthmian Canal zone from the French Panama Company

October. Robert Esnault-Pelterie flew a manned glider with ailerons **1904**

1905 Japan defeated Russia in a war over Manchuria and Korea

Norway became independent of Sweden **1905**

1906 Moroccan Crisis resolved with Germany, France, and Spain

Great Britain launched *HMS Dreadnought* **1906**

1906 October 23. Brazilian Alberto Santos-Dumont won the Archdeacon Prize

November 12. Alberto Santos-Dumont flew an airplane in sustained, powered, manned, controlled flight **1906**

1907 Great Britain, France, and Spain agreed to the Pact of Cartagena

Germany, Austria, and Italy renewed their Triple Alliance **1907**

1907 July 11. Louis Blériot flew an airplane with tandem cantilever wings and wingtip ailerons

November 13. Paul Cornu made the first well-documented free flight of a helicopter **1907**

1908 Austria annexed the Turkish territories of Bosnia and Herzegovina

Bulgaria declared independence from Ottoman (Turkish) rule **1908**

1908 January 13. Henry Farman flew the first official circular flight in Europe

May 29. Henry Farman took the first passenger in Europe for an airplane ride **1908**

1908 June 20. Glenn Curtiss flew an airplane for the first time

British chancellor David Lloyd George introduced his People's Budget to raise funds for defense **1909**

1909 Japan established a dictatorship to govern Korea

Light blue type represents events that are not directly related to aviation.

1909 July 25. Louis Blériot made the first airplane flight across the English Channel

1909 August 29. Glenn Curtiss won the first Gordon Bennett speed race

1910 King Edward VII died; George V became king of the United Kingdom

1910 King Manuel II fled Portugal

1910 March 28. French pilot Henry Fabre made the first known takeoff and landing on water

1910 November 14. Eugene Ely made the first takeoff from a platform on the deck of a ship

1911 Porfirio Díaz's presidency of Mexico ended

1911 Tibet became an autonomous region under British control

1911 January. Glenn Curtiss made the first water takeoff and water landing in America

1911 January 18. Eugene Ely made the first landing of an airplane on the deck of a ship

1912 The Manchu dynasty formally abdicated, and a republic replaced the Chinese or Ch'ing empire

1912 May 2. C.R. Samson made the first British flight from a ship under way

1913 Greece obtained Crete and many Aegean islands from Turkey

1913 The Triple Alliance — Germany, Austria-Hungary, and Italy — held a naval convention

1913 April 16. Maurice Prévost won the first Schneider Trophy race

1913 September 21. Adolphe Pégoud flew the first sustained inverted flight under the control of the pilot

1913 September 13. French pilots M. Seguin and Henry Farman set a world distance record in an airplane (634 miles)

1913 November. Two airplanes engage in aerial combat for the first time

1914 January 1. Pilot Anthony Jannus flew the first scheduled airline flight in an airplane

1914 July. German pilot H. Oelerich set a new international altitude record in an airplane (26,700 feet)

1914 World War I began as a Balkan War that escalated into a Great War in Europe and finally into a World War

Introduction

What was aviation during the decade before World War I? It was biplanes and experimental aircraft, as well as balloons, dirigibles, and airships. It was first flights and record flights. It was individuals building and flying their own aircraft. It was an industry being created by adventurous and practical airmen, as well as by engineers and businessmen. It was business with financiers, lawyers, publicists, and customers. It was test pilots, military aviators, and sport flyers. It was exhibition flying. It was activity, sometimes private, often public, at local, national, and international levels. It was the development of technology and infrastructure. It was, in the words of historian Robert Wohl, "a passion for wings." The early 20th century was the beginning of a long romance with aviation.

With the Flyer in December 1903 and again with Flyer No. 3 in 1905, Wilbur and Orville Wright clearly represented the state of the art in airplane design and operation. They retired from flying for almost three years to improve their invention. When they resumed flying in 1908, they found a highly competitive field. Aviation-minded Europeans were fueled by nationalistic pride, by the increasing threat of war, by government procurement policies designed to encourage aviation development, and by frequent air shows, speed races, and distance competitions. France led the world in aviation by 1910,

Igor Sikorsky

Cromwell Dixon

1911 Chicago International Meet

Katherine Stinson

but even Britain, Germany, Russia, and Italy were soon ahead of the United States in terms of research and development and government support. While Europeans were developing the technology and infrastructure of an aviation industry, the Wright brothers turned their attention to defending their invention through patent litigation. Even in the United States, the competition—the one competitor, Glenn Curtiss — left them behind.

Section A of this chapter discusses the early airplanes and airmen *in Europe* during the decade after the historic flights of 1903. Section B describes developments *in the United States* during that period. Section C covers early flying competitions and the role of competitions in early aviation. Section D examines the small aviation industry that emerged in the decade before World War I.

By studying this chapter you will become familiar with the major events, people, and planes associated with the early development of airplanes. Specifically, you should be able to discuss the first airplane flight in Europe. You should be able to identify Henry Farman, the Short brothers, Louis Blériot, and Igor Sikorsky, the pioneers of aviation in Europe. You should also be able to discuss the Aerial Experiment Association and Glenn Curtiss. You should be able to explain importance of flying competitions. And you should be able to list multiple reasons that European nations surged ahead of the United States in aviation.

AIRPLANES AND AIRMEN IN EUROPE

Q & A

What? The birth of an aviation industry

When? Approximately 1904-1914

Where? United States and Europe

Who? Orville and Wilbur Wright, Glenn Curtiss, Henry Farman, and many others

Why? Challenge of research and development, adventure and romance, business opportunities and employment

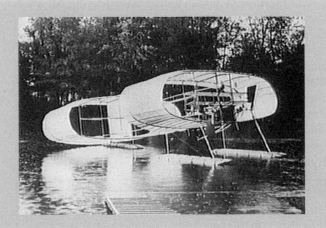

The Wrights defined the airplane in 1903 and refined the definition in 1905, but they sheltered their technology, and others pursued the problems of flight independently. The independent and simultaneous development of heavier-than-air craft continued after the Wrights' achieved powered flight in 1903 and even after they demonstrated a practical, fully controllable airplane in 1905. For several years much of the development work in aviation was done without knowledge of the Wrights' technology, at least without detailed knowledge of the technology. The work was experimental, even the flights were experimental. Octave Chanute inspired some of the European efforts.

European Developments

Chanute lectured in Paris in 1903 on his own gliders and on the Wrights' gliders, including wing warping in simultaneous operation with a rear rudder. He provided information for his French audience, and he spurred their pride. Aviation, thanks to the Montgolfier brothers, was a French invention, and so too should be the airplane. Inspired by Chanute's lecture, Robert Esnault-Pelterie tried to reproduce the 1902 Wright glider, including wing warping. Without the specifications for the Wrights' machine, without the experience of hundreds of gliding flights, and

without the Wrights' theoretical understanding of flight, he failed. Such failures made Europeans skeptical of aviation news received from the United States. Esnault-Pelterie devised his own glider, used ailerons instead of wing warping, and flew it in October 1904. Esnault-Pelterie is but one example of French interest in aviation. (Figure 3-1)

In 1905 aviation enthusiast Gabriel Voisin and attorney Ernest Archdeacon organized the Syndicat d'Aviation to build aircraft; this was one of the first companies organized to make heavier-than-air craft. The company produced two gliders, one for Archdeacon and one for engineer Louis Blériot. Mounted on floats, both of these boxkite-like biplane

Figure 3-1. Esnault-Pelterie tested a modified Wright-type glider which incorporated ailerons in front of the wings rather than wing warping.

gliders took off from the Seine River towed by a motorboat. Pleased with his glider, Blériot joined Voisin in organizing the Blériot-Voisin Company. This company made a glider and a powered airplane, neither of which was successful. On the side, Voisin constructed the 14-*bis* airplane for Brazilian dirigible pioneer Alberto Santos-Dumont. The Blériot-Voisin partnership broke up in 1906, partly because of Voisin's independent actions. That same year Voisin established a factory at Billancourt to make gliders and airplanes. He gradually developed an airplane controlled by neither wing warping nor ailerons, but by boxkite- like features. In 1906 Voisin and Blériot developed a biplane powered by a remarkable little *Antoinette* motor, designed by Léon Levavasseur for motorboats and named after the daughter of his financial backer. For a few years thereafter this was the most popular airplane motor in Europe. (Figure 3-2)

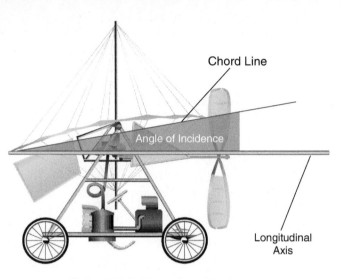

Trajan Vuia's Monoplane No. 1

Figure 3-2. Boxkite airplane designed by Voisin at an airshow in Breacia, Italy.

France had talented and enthusiastic aviators and wealthy patrons of aviation, but airplane development was underway in other countries too. In 1906 Romanian aviator Trajan Vuia flew his monoplane No. 1, or at least the plane hopped briefly into the air. Among the aircraft's features was the variable incidence of the wing; incidence is the angle between the airplane's longitudinal axis and the wing's chord line, that imaginary line from the leading edge of the airfoil to the trailing edge. Vuia's plane also had pneumatic tires. Also in 1906, the Danish pilot Jacob C.H. Ellehammer began making powered hops in a plane of his own design. Such experimental flights contributed to understanding various aspects of the problem of flight. Of course, not all would-be aviators were practical. Horatio Phillips in England, for example, built and flew a powered *Multiplane* that had 160 narrow-chord wings.

First Airplane Flight in Europe

Alberto Santos-Dumont, the Brazilian aviation pioneer living in Paris, turned his attention from dirigibles to airplanes, from lighter-than-air to heavier-than-air, upon hearing Octave Chanute's reports of what the Wright brothers were doing in the United States. In 1906 Santos-Dumont designed a biplane he called 14-*bis*. He hired Gabriel Voisin to build the plane, and he began flight testing in September. The 14-*bis* was a biplane with boxkite-like wings and with a boxkite unit in front; the front unit served as both elevator and rudder. The first tests were conducted with the airplane hanging

 Historic Event

Alberto Santos-Dumont made the first officially recognized airplane flight in Europe on 12 November 1906.

under Santos-Dumont's dirigible No. 14. The French word *bis* means twice or again, and dirigible No. 14 was twice an aircraft with the airplane hanging below it. The aircraft took to the air with a 50-horsepower Antoinette motor. In October 1906 Santos-Dumont won the Archdeacon Prize, offered by French attorney and aviation enthusiast Ernest Archdeacon, for the first flight of at least 25 meters (82 feet).

Historical Note

The airplane was an international technology, despite national patents and the loyalties of aviators. Shown are some generally recognized first flights by country.

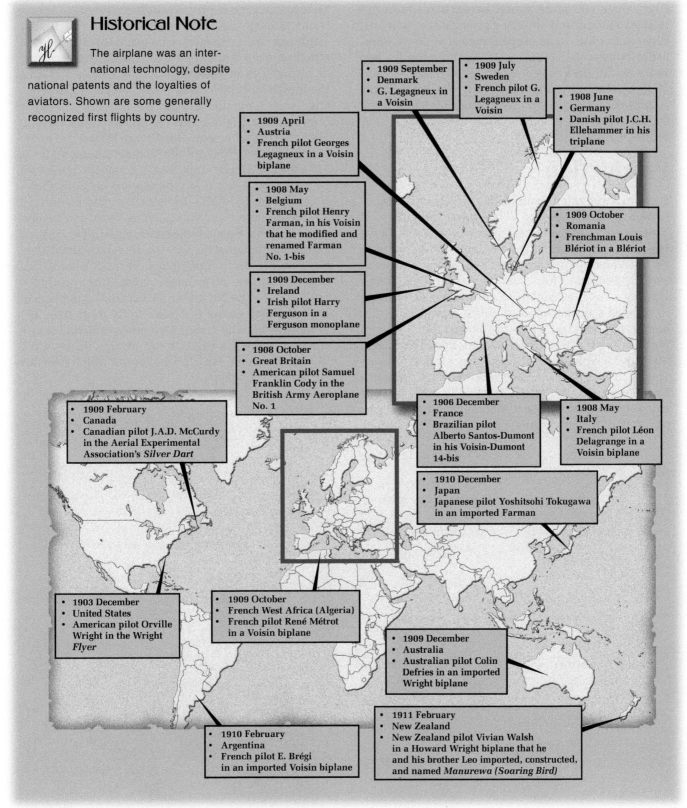

- 1909 September
- Denmark
- G. Legagneux in a Voisin

- 1909 July
- Sweden
- French pilot G. Legagneux in a Voisin

- 1908 June
- Germany
- Danish pilot J.C.H. Ellehammer in his triplane

- 1909 April
- Austria
- French pilot Georges Legagneux in a Voisin biplane

- 1908 May
- Belgium
- French pilot Henry Farman, in his Voisin that he modified and renamed Farman No. 1-bis

- 1909 October
- Romania
- Frenchman Louis Blériot in a Blériot

- 1909 December
- Ireland
- Irish pilot Harry Ferguson in a Ferguson monoplane

- 1908 October
- Great Britain
- American pilot Samuel Franklin Cody in the British Army Aeroplane No. 1

- 1906 December
- France
- Brazilian pilot Alberto Santos-Dumont in his Voisin-Dumont 14-bis

- 1908 May
- Italy
- French pilot Léon Delagrange in a Voisin biplane

- 1909 February
- Canada
- Canadian pilot J.A.D. McCurdy in the Aerial Experimental Association's *Silver Dart*

- 1910 December
- Japan
- Japanese pilot Yoshitsohi Tokugawa in an imported Farman

- 1903 December
- United States
- American pilot Orville Wright in the Wright *Flyer*

- 1909 October
- French West Africa (Algeria)
- French pilot René Métrot in a Voisin biplane

- 1909 December
- Australia
- Australian pilot Colin Defries in an imported Wright biplane

- 1910 February
- Argentina
- French pilot E. Brégi in an imported Voisin biplane

- 1911 February
- New Zealand
- New Zealand pilot Vivian Walsh in a Howard Wright biplane that he and his brother Leo imported, constructed, and named *Manurewa (Soaring Bird)*

Flying the 14-*bis* on 12 November 1906, Santos-Dumont made the first officially recognized airplane flight in Europe. He made several flights that day, one lasting 21 seconds and covering 722 feet (220 meters). He won the French Aero Club's prize offered for the first flight over 100 meters, and he earned the club's official recognition for the first manned powered flight in Europe. To a Europe skeptical of the Wrights' achievements, Santos-Dumont was honored for two years as the first person to fly an airplane — until Wilbur Wright's 1908 European tour proved the American claims. A few years later Santos-Dumont tested small tractor monoplanes called *Demoiselle (Young Lady)*.

Production

Early aviators often made their own aircraft. France turned production into a business, and the first Frenchman to make aircraft production his business was Gabriel Voisin. After building Santos-Dumont's 14-*bis*, Voisin joined his brother Charles in forming Voisin Frères. This company built airplanes. Influenced by the Wright airplane, the Voisin brothers developed a pusher biplane with a forward elevator and a tail rudder. They produced about twenty airplanes by the time World War I started in Europe in 1914. Like Voisin, most European aircraft makers were strongly influenced by Wilbur Wright's European tour of 1908. The Wright airplane was evidence of what had been accomplished, and it was a stimulant to achieve more.

Henry Farman

Henry Farman was an Englishman, born and raised in France, who became France's leading aviator and eventually a French citizen. He and his brother Maurice had raced bicycles in their twenties. Henry raced motorcycles, then automobiles, and finally airplanes. A near-fatal car accident turned his attention from automobiles, and in 1907 he ordered an airplane from Voisin. He improved this airplane, the fourth built by Voisin Frères, by adding ailerons and modifying the tail. In the airplane he made Europe's first flight around a circular route early in 1908; for this he won the Grand Prix d'Aviation, 50,000 francs donated by Henry Deutsch de la Meurthe and Ernest Archdeacon. Later the same year he made a sixteen-mile (26km) cross-country flight, from Châlons to Rheims (now Reims), and he ordered a second plane from Voisin. Voisin sold the second plane built for Farman to someone else. That angered Farman enough that he, Farman, promptly established his own production company. Farman established his factory at Billancourt where he produced biplanes. At the Rheims International Air Meet in 1909, he became the first pilot to fly more than 100 miles. He actually flew 111.8 miles (180km) over a closed circuit. He was the top prize winner at the Rheims air meet, which was good publicity for his production company.

Historic Event

On 13 January 1908 Henry Farman flew a Voisin airplane around a circular route at Issy, France, in the first circular flight in Europe. Flying in a circle proved pilot control of an airplane to a greater degree than linear flight.

Personal Profile

Henry Farman (1874-1958), shown on the left, was born to English parents living in France. He lived his entire life in France and became a naturalized French citizen. He was a superb pilot, one of the best in Europe in 1908-1909. He became an aircraft manufacturer. On the right is Gabriel Voisin, who built Farman s first airplane.

Henry Farman and Gabriel Voisin

Historical Note

Dates suggest the concurrent development of the passenger plane in the United States and France:

14 May 1908 — Wilbur Wright in the United States carried the very first airplane passenger, Charles W. Furnas.

29 May 1908 — Henry Farman took the first passenger aloft in Europe; the passenger was Ernest Archdeacon, a French lawyer and promoter of aviation.

8 July 1908 — Lèon Delagrange took a female passenger named Thérèse Peltier for a ride in a Voisin biplane; Peltier later became the first woman to solo in an airplane.

7 October 1908 — Wilbur Wright in France took a woman, Mrs. Hart Berg, along as the first female passenger *on a Wright airplane*

Personal Profile

The brothers Horace Leonard Short (1872-1917), Albert Eustace Short (1875-1932), and Hugh Oswald Short (1883-1969) established the first British company to manufacture airplanes. They learned airplane design by making six Wright airplanes under license. In 1913 they designed and produced a seaplane, the first in a long line of successful seaplanes.

Hugh Oswald Short

Horace Leonard Short

Albert Eustace Short

Historical Note

Henry Farman's brother Maurice established an airplane manufacturing company in competition with his brother. That company introduced the *M.F. Longhorn* training plane in 1912. During the war Maurice and Henry merged their companies to produce military planes.

Short Brothers

Horace, Albert, and Hugh Short organized a company to build airplanes in 1908, the first airplane manufacturing company in Britain. Horace and Albert were experienced balloon makers who had constructed balloons for the British Army, for C.R. Rolls of the Rolls-Royce car company, and for other private customers. The Short company built two airplanes, one for Rolls and the other for Frank McClean, but neither plane was a success. In February 1909 Albert Short obtained a license from Wilbur Wright to manufacture six Wright airplanes in Britain. This

volume order made the Short company the first in the world to produce airplanes in a series. In order to make the planes, Horace traveled to France and prepared drawings of the Wright plane that Wilbur was demonstrating there. The Short company produced the six Wright airplanes and, in the process, learned enough to thereafter design their own aircraft. Horace designed the Short biplane No. 2, the first successful Short airplane. In 1913 the brothers produced a seaplane with folding wings for parking on ships.

Louis Blériot

In 1909 Blériot produced his first successful aircraft: the Blériot XI, a monoplane. The designer was Raymond Saulnier, one of the engineers in his employment, yet the design incorporated features from earlier Blériot aircraft. Some of these features were a three-wheel undercarriage, pylons supporting the wings, rectangular fuselage, small rudder, and rear elevator. The Blériot XI used wing warping for

Personal Profile

Louis Charles-Joseph Blériot (1872-1936) was a wealthy French engineer experienced in automobile headlamps. He gradually entered aviation, first trying a flapping-wing device, then a brief cooperation with Voisin. He hired his own staff and developed aircraft, personally test flew each one, and crashed often. Seeing Wilbur Wright demonstrate the Wright airplane in 1908 gave him a better understanding of flight. He had spent most of his wealth by this time on failed aircraft.

Louis Charles-Joseph Blériot

lateral control, something Blériot learned from Wilbur Wright the previous year. The first flight was a hop of 200 meters on 23 January 1909. Blériot increased the wing area from twelve square meters to fourteen before the next flight, which was in February. That time the plane flew 700 meters. Blériot continued flight testing and modifying the XI even after his larger model XII entered flight testing. The engine was of particular concern. Blériot replaced the original seven-cylinder REP (Robert Esnault-Pelterie) engine with a three-cylinder, 25-horsepower Anzani, designed by the Italian bicycle racer Alessandro Anzani.

Historic Event

In 1909 Louis Blériot and Gabriel Voisin won the Osiris Prize awarded by the Institut de France for "the most important discovery or work in the department of Science, Literature, and Art, or in anything that may be of conspicuous public interest." Was aviation "science, literature, and art," *or* a thing of "conspicuous public interest"?

To demonstrate his new airplane and to attract customers, Blériot selected a challenging flight. He chose to fly for the prize offered by the London *Daily Mail* to the first pilot to fly an airplane across the English Channel. English pilot Hubert Latham made an attempt, but ditched due to engine problems.

Latham's attempt was significant because the preparations included receiving weather information transmitted via wireless telegraphy. Flying the new Blériot XI monoplane, Louis Blériot won the prize. The flight served as an advertisement for Blériot's new plane. Wilbur Wright had considered competing, but decided the channel represented too much risk for the only Wright airplane in Europe, a plane he needed for his marketing efforts.

Historic Event

On 25 July 1909 Louis Blériot flew the Blériot XI from Calais, France, to Dover, England. He was the first person to fly an airplane across the English Channel.

After crossing the English Channel, Blériot flew numerous demonstration flights of the model XI; in Vienna he attracted a crowd of 300,000 spectators! He crashed in Romania in December 1909; this was his 32nd crash. Seriously injured, he restricted his flying for a few years then stopped altogether. He had a business to run and orders to fill.

Flight Lines

"Below me is the sea, the surface disturbed by the wind, which is now freshening. The motion of the waves beneath me is not pleasant. I drive on. . . . For ten minutes I am lost. It is a strange position to be alone, unguided, without compass, in the air over the middle of the Channel. I touch nothing. My hands and feet rest lightly on the levers. I let the aeroplane take its own course. . . . I steered toward the white cliffs. But the wind and fog caught me. I fought with my hands, with my eyes. I kept steering toward the cliffs, but I couldn't see Dover. Where the devil was I?"

Louis Blériot recalling his historic flight across the English Channel, as quoted in Tom D. Crouch's *Blériot XI*.

Historical Note

The British B.E.2 attained the all-round inherent stability sought for decades by airplane designers. The B.E.2 represented compromises from the unmanned model goal of full inherent stability to the Wright brothers' intentional instability to facilitate pilot control of an aircraft. The B.E. stood for Blériot Experimental, a two-seat reconnaissance airplane designed by Geoffrey de Havilland after the example of Blériot's biplanes in France. The Royal Aircraft Factory made the airplane and assigned the designation. Introduced in 1912, the B.E.2 went into production for the war.

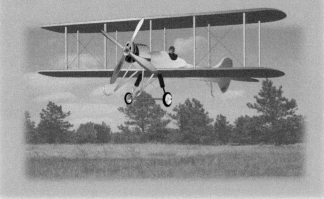

Historical Note

The Wright brothers were bicycle makers before they became aviation pioneers. Many leading bicyclists in the United States and in Europe became prominent aviators, including Glenn Curtiss in the United States, Henry Farman in France, August Euler in Germany, Alessandro Anzani in Italy, and Helene Dutrieu in Belgium.

Igor I. Sikorsky

While many aviation pioneers had experience in lighter-than-air craft or with racing bicycles, some did not. One of these was the Russian Igor I. Sikorsky. The young Sikorsky studied at the Russian Naval Academy in Petrograd and the Polytechnic Institute of Kiev. Traveling in Germany in 1908, Sikorsky read of flights by the German Count von Zeppelin and the American Wright brothers. He toyed with the idea of a flying machine lifted by the propeller, not by wings. In Paris, the center of European aviation, he visited various flying fields, saw flying machines, purchased a motor, and bought parts of the machine he planned to build. Back in Russia, he built a helicopter. It was "a failure to the extent that it could not fly," he concluded, but he gained experience and acquired

engineering information. He built a second helicopter in 1910. It too could not fly. He turned his full attention to airplanes. (Figure 3-3)

Figure 3-3. Igor Sikorsky beside 1910 helicopter design.

Like the Wright brothers in the United States, but without their glider experience, Sikorsky had to teach himself to fly. He did this in an airplane of his own design. The S-1 lacked the power necessary for flight, so he installed an Italian 25-horsepower Anzani engine — taken from his first helicopter — in the second plane. That S-2 flew, and in the process Sikorsky began to teach himself to fly. He quickly built improved airplanes. In 1911 he produced the successful model S-5, powered by a 50 horsepower Argus engine and controlled by pedals for the rudder and by a single wheel instead of two sticks for the ailerons and elevator. In that plane in 1911 he qualified for a pilot's license, *Fédération Aéronauticque Internationale* license number 64 issued by the Imperial Aero Club of Russia. (Figure 3-4)

Figure 3-4. Igor Sikorsky's pilot license number 64 with photo of Igor in an S-5.

Historical Note

Regarding his first helicopter of 1909, Igor Sikorsky recalled:

"The tests and experimental work, however, proved to be very interesting and instructive. I learned much by working from early morning until late in the night and by gradually eliminating the few major, and multitude of minor, troubles. This was all excellent training. By fixing the troubles, reinforcing the parts which would not stand up, adjusting the various mechanisms which would permit the whole machine to run for several minutes at a time at full power, I could learn what could not be obtained from books. The practical experience gained was very valuable, but with knowledge came the realization that the first helicopter would never get me in the air."

Igor I. Sikorsky in *The Story of the Winged-S, an Autobiography* (New York: Dodd, Mead & Company, 1958)

Flight Lines

"In the morning of the next day, June 3, 1910, on the way to the field, we made plans for the first test of the *S-2*. The cloudiness and very light wind appeared favorable. The *S-2* was wheeled out of the hangar, I checked the controls, climbed into the seat behind the motor, and shouted,

'Contact.'

"The engine was quickly started. While three men held the plane, I gradually opened the throttle, and a few moments later the good sound of the motors, the propeller blast, and the smell of burned castor oil told me that it was time to try.

"I gave the signal, and the plane was released. The *S-2* had a much better acceleration. From the very first moment I could feel that the stronger propeller blast made the control more effective and the tail went up at once. I had no tachometer, not a single instrument, in the *S-2*. A few seconds later, feeling that the speed was already well in excess of what the previous plane could ever do, I gradually started to move the stick back. A moment later, I was in the air. All my attention was concentrated on the controls. Having never before been in the air, even as a passenger, I had to learn quickly the necessary movements which were familiar in imagination but not yet in reality. By delicately pushing or pulling the stick I could hold the plane at two to four feet of altitude for a time, which appeared quite long to me, as well as to the witnesses of this first flight.

"Finally, the plane, for some reason, settled down. Feeling that the wheels were again on firm ground, I cut the ignition."

Igor I. Sikorsky in *The Story of the Winged-S, an Autobiography* (New York: Dodd, Mead & Company, 1958)

Sikorsky continued to design improved and larger airplanes. In 1912 he won a military flying competition with the *S-6* and took a job designing airplanes for the Baltic Railroad Car Company. The next year he introduced his four-engine *Grand* with an enclosed cabin and an observation platform. The size and sophistication of this aircraft stunned the aviation world. (Figure 3-5)

Figure 3-5. Igor Sikorsky seated in the cabin of the S-21 *Grand* in 1913.

Flight Lines

"Having reached some four hundred feet, I started to turn to the left. The plane performed nicely. A little later, a second turn at some 600 feet altitude was made, this time passing over the hangars and the point of departure. The mechanic on the front bridge was happily waving his hand to the huge crowd below, the co-pilot behind in the large cabin was looking down through the window. For a short moment a happy realization that this was the long desired achievement flashed through my mind. The next instant, however, I was again busy with the routine test flight. . . . Finally, it was possible to make what appeared the most important item of the test, namely, the 'landings.' While still some seven or eight hundred feet high, I tried twice to put the plane in a gliding position, and then by pulling the wheel reproduced a maneuver of normal landing. The plane obeyed so satisfactorily that, contrary to the original program, I decided to make an ordinary landing and not a power stall. About one mile from the field, I turned around and started to come down gradually, aiming at the beginning of the runway. The plane was well under control and having reached the field at an altitude of some fifty feet, I could increase the power slightly and continue to fly over the runway toward the hangars. Having reached the middle of the runway, I cut the engines and easily made an ordinary, reasonably smooth landing."

Igor Sikorsky describing the first flight of the *Grand*, 13 May 1913, in his book *The Story of the Winged-S, an Autobiography* (New York: Dodd, Mead & Company, 1958)

German Airplanes

Germany initially lagged behind the United States and the rest of Europe in the development of airplanes and the airplane production industry. To catch up, German companies obtained licenses to produce foreign designs. The first German airplane works was

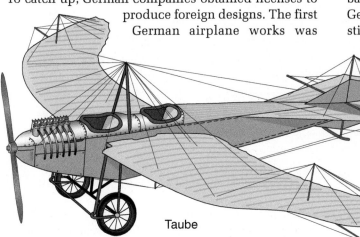
Taube

Rumpler, founded by E. Rumpler. It started production with an Etrich license for the Taube. The Austrian designer Igo Etrich had designed a bird-like monoplane that he called the *Taube (Dove)* in 1910, and introduced a two-seat version in 1912. Etrich sold a Taube license to Rumpler who put the aircraft into German production. Etrich soon waived German patent and license rights, and this made the basic Taube design available to any German manufacturer who wanted to copy or modify the design. Thereafter, Taube-type aircraft were produced by many German companies, including the pre-war companies Albatros, Aviatik, A.E.G. (Allgemeine Elektrizitäts Gessellschaft), D.F.W. (Deutsche Flugzeug Werke), Euler, Gotha, and Otto, as well as companies established during World War I.

In all, Germany had about twenty-five aircraft production companies before the war. Most started like Rumpler with an existing design of another maker, often a French design. Albatros, for example, began in Berlin in 1910 under heavy French influence. Its first products were Farman boxkite type airplanes and Antoinette monoplanes. Albatros added the Austrian Taube-type monoplane to its line, and one of its Taubes won the 1913 Italian seaplane circuit; that particular airplane was equipped with both wheels and floats. Aviatik, founded in 1910, entered production with licenses for two French aircraft — the Farman boxkite type plane and for the Hanriot monoplane. Emil Jeannin left Aviatik to form his own Jeannin company that made racing monoplanes designed after the French Nieuport example. As the name suggests, the Deutsche Bristol Werke

began operations under the influence of the British Bristol company.

Deutsche Flugzeug Werke (D.F.W.) was one of several aircraft companies established with government backing, as the German government strove to advance German airplane development and production, but still under foreign design influence. Founded in 1910 as the Mars Company, D.F.W. entered production with the Maurice Farman biplane. D.F.W. later designed a monoplane that won the 1913 Prince Henry trophy, and it produced the Mars biplanes used in the Balkan conflicts. D.F.W. gradually developed its own aircraft. Its two-seat B.I tractor biplane came standard with a 100-horsepower Mercédés engine; Benz, Mercédés, and Rapp also made 150-horsepower engines for the aircraft. H. Oelerich set a new world's record for altitude in a standard D.F.W. B.I, which he flew to 8,150 meters (26,740 feet) in July 1914.

Historical Evidence

German pilot H. Oelerich set a new world's record for altitude in July 1914. He flew a standard D.F.W. B.I, powered by a 100-horsepower Mercédés engine, to an altitude of 8,150m (26,740 feet)!

The first aviator to obtain a German pilot's license was August Euler, founder of the Euler works in Frankfurt. He began production by making Voisin biplanes under license. German pilot Gustav Otto began manufacturing aircraft under license with Henry Farman and then developed his own Otto tractor biplane. Ago was a spin-off of Otto; it initially

Historical Note

A Dutchman founded one of the more successful early German companies. Anthony Fokker (1890-1939) founded the Fokker company in 1911. His first airplane was the *Spin* monoplane. He built and sold several airplanes before World War I. He remained in Germany and greatly expanded production during the war. Fokker moved his company to the Netherlands after the war in order to avoid the restrictions that the victorious nations imposed on the defeated.

Anthony Fokker

specialized in pusher planes. Schwade started by making Henry Farman biplanes. When the Zeppelin airship company established a seaplane division at Friedrichshafen in 1912, that division began production under heavy Curtiss influence, as seaplanes were the one area in which the United States remained highly competitive with European makers.

AMERICAN DEVELOPMENTS

The Wright brothers were number one in American aviation, but they were not alone. They led American aviation through 1908 and even 1909, but they increasingly faced competition. Competitors challenged the Wrights in technological matters, commercial sales, and popular opinion.

Aerial Experiment Association

In the autumn of 1907 inventor Alexander Graham Bell, best known for inventing the telephone, organized an Aerial Experiment Association (AEA) for the purpose of building a practical airplane. Members included J.A.D. McCurdy of Canada, Lieutenant Thomas Selfridge of the United States Army, balloonist and dirigible pioneer Thomas Baldwin, and bicycle and motorcycle maker Glenn Curtiss. Like Samuel Pierpont Langley, they called an airplane an "aerodrome," which is the British term for airfield. Bell had been experimenting with tetrahedral kites, and he continued those experiments with the AEA. The members studied the problems of flight and they built kites and gliders and even powered a kite. Curtiss' motorcycle company, the Curtiss Manufacturing Company, developed engines for some of the AEA's experiments.

The AEA as a team built four airplanes in 1908. No. 1, *Red Wing*, was a biplane with a forward elevator and fixed rear stabilizer and a movable rear rudder, but with no system to control lateral stability; that is, no wing warping or ailerons. Its undercarriage consisted of ice skids, for takeoff and landing on a frozen lake. Baldwin made the first two flights in March 1908, and crash landed both times. Airplane No. 2, *White Wing*, was also a biplane, but with tricycle landing wheels. This plane had movable control surfaces on its four wingtips; these surfaces later were called ailerons. Baldwin, Curtiss, and McCurdy made successful flights in *White Wing*; however, McCurdy also crashed it. With No. 3, *June Bug*, they improved upon Nos. 1 and 2. *June Bug* flew numerous flights. In June, Curtiss flew it to win the *Scientific American* Trophy, awarded by the Aero Club of America and offered at that time to a pilot who would fly one kilometer (3,280 feet) or more in a straight line. When equipped with pontoons, No. 3 was called *Loon*. No. 4, *Silver Dart*, first flew at Hammondsport, New York, home of the Curtiss company that supplied the 50-horsepower, water-cooled, V-8 engine. The AEA then moved the plane to Baddeck, Nova Scotia, where Bell lived during the summers. There the *Silver Dart* made the first airplane flight in Canada on 23 February 1909; appropriately, the Canadian McCurdy was the pilot.

Flight Lines

For what turned out to be the last trial of Aerodrome No. 3, the aircraft was equipped with pontoons and renamed *Loon*. As pilot J.A.D. McCurdy taxied the *Loon*, a pontoon caught on the dock and the aircraft sank. Glenn Curtiss and McCurdy described the events in a message to Alexander Graham Bell:

"GAVE VAUDEVILLE PERFORMANCE TONIGHT BY MOONLIGHT WITH LOON FIRST HYDRO TEST SUCCESSFUL, SECOND AERODROME TEST FAIRLY SUCCESSFUL, THIRD SUBMARINE TEST MOST SUCCESSFUL OF ALL. EXPERIMENTS ENDED."

Curtiss and McCurdy, January 1909, as quoted in Robert Scharff and Walter S. Taylor's *Over Land and Sea*.

The Aerial Experiment Association disbanded on schedule at the end of March 1909. It had completed its experimental agenda and applied for several patents, including a patent for the wingtip aileron system. Its immediate and lasting legacy was the aircraft manufacturing company established by Glenn Curtiss at Hammondsport. From 1909 to 1911 the company name was Herring-Curtiss, but Curtiss provided the expertise, the financing, the management, and the substance. Having difficulty with his partner

Historic Event

On 23 February 1909 Canadian pilot J.A.D. McCurdy flew the Aerial Experiment Association's Aerodrome No. 4, *Silver Dart*, for the first airplane flight in Canada. The location was Baddeck, Nova Scotia, summer home of Alexander Graham Bell who had organized the Aerial Experiment Association for the purpose of building a practical airplane.

Historical Evidence

The Alexander Graham Bell Museum at Baddeck, Nova Scotia, displays artifacts and documents of the experiments and researches of Bell, including his aviation endeavors with the Aerial Experiment Association. Those artifacts and documents are primary sources, contemporary evidence of what happened. The museum labels are secondary sources, as they present information interpreted by curators who decide what is important to tell museum visitors about Bell.

Augustus Herring, who was a shady individual, Curtiss organized several companies of his own: the Curtiss Aeroplane Company and the Curtiss Exhibition Company in 1910 and the Curtiss Motor Company in 1911.

Curtiss Airplanes

Glenn Curtiss was manufacturing motorcycles and motorcycle motors in Hammondsport when dirigible designer Thomas Baldwin first approached him.

Baldwin wanted light-weight and powerful motors for his dirigibles. Curtiss provided the motors, and he rode in Baldwin dirigibles. He then joined the Aerial Experiment Association, which gave him solid scientific knowledge of heavier-than-air craft as well as practical experience with airplanes. He thereafter flew and designed airplanes.

Personal Profile

Glenn Hammond Curtiss (1878-1930) was second only to the Wright brothers in influence on the early development of American aviation. Interested in mechanical matters, he became a bicycle racer and then a bicycle manufacturer. He added motorcycle racing and motorcycle production to his activities. He participated in Alexander Graham Bell's Aerial Experiment Association that produced the successful *June Bug* and *Silver Dart* airplanes. In 1909 he founded the first aircraft manufacturing company in the United States; this was more than a year before the Wright brothers

Glenn Hammond Curtiss

organized the Wright Company. His company and the successor Curtiss Aeroplane Company made pusher biplanes that incorporated ailerons. Curtiss became embroiled in patent litigation with the Wright brothers. He died in 1930, but his name continued in the aviation industry until the 1947 sale of the Aeroplane Division of Curtiss-Wright to North American, and the concurrent demise of Curtiss-Wright.

Figure 3-6. On the left is a Curtiss Model D Pusher. Female pilot Julia Clark is behind the wheel. On the right is a drawing of a Curtiss tractor.

Curtiss designed mostly pusher airplanes and only a few tractor models before the war. A **pusher** airplane has the propeller behind the engine and usually behind the trailing edge of the wing; the generated thrust pushes the airplane. In contrast, a **tractor** airplane has the **powerplant** — the engine and propeller — in the front where the thrust draws or pulls the airplane; the term comes from the Latin *tractus*, to draw. Curtiss placed ailerons midway between the wings of his pusher biplanes. His use of ailerons, not the placement thereof, brought him into a lengthy legal dispute with the Wrights. (Figure 3-6)

Seeking orders from the United States Navy, Curtiss designed and demonstrated airplanes that could take off from and land on ships, and he designed hydroplanes and flying boats. His **hydroplanes** or

"hydro-aeroplanes" were simply landplanes with floats in place of wheels, initially one float per plane. The use of pontoons or floats for landing gear meant the aircraft were **seaplanes**. The first Curtiss **flying boat** underwent tests at the naval facility at San Diego, California, in January 1912. As the name implies, this type of aircraft has a boat-like hull which settles on the water rather than a float or pontoon that holds the aircraft above water. The hull is the bottom of the fuselage, and it serves as the undercarriage of the flying boat. The Navy purchased fourteen pusher seaplanes from Curtiss during the years 1911-1914. The Navy also purchased Curtiss flying boats and Curtiss airplanes equipped with wheels during this period, and the Army bought Curtiss landplanes. (Figure 3-7)

Figure 3-7. View of an early Curtiss seaplane. Note the single pontoon for the landing gear.

Historic Event

On 10 November 1910 pilot Eugene Ely flew a Curtiss biplane off the USS *Birmingham*, a Navy cruiser. The plane was a pusher powered by a 50 horsepower engine. The wheeled undercarriage rolled down a wooden takeoff platform built on deck. Ely flew the plane from the ship to Hampton Roads, Virginia.

Historic Event

On 18 January 1911 Eugene Ely flew a Curtiss pusher biplane from shore to the USS *Pennsylvania* in San Diego Bay, California. He landed on a platform on the deck of the ship. A hook on the airplane caught an arrester that shortened the landing roll. He then took off from that same platform. He and the Curtiss airplane thus proved the practicality of using ship-based aircraft.

Exhibition and Stunt Flying

Beyond aviators, few people had ever seen an airplane. That fact drew crowds to advertised airplane flights. At first, people simply came to see an airplane fly. They kept coming to watch speed races, to witness exhibition and stunt flying, and to see crashes. The first exhibition flyers were the men who designed, built, and flew the first airplanes — men like Wilbur and Orville Wright and Glenn Curtiss; their European counterparts were Alberto Santos-Dumont, Louis Blériot, and Henry Farman.

Both Wilbur Wright and Glenn Curtiss scheduled exhibition flights for the Hudson-Fulton Tercentenary Celebration in New York in 1909. For several days, wind grounded both pilots, except for short flights. Without flying a major exhibition, Curtiss finally left for an engagement in St. Louis. Two days later the winds quieted and Wright flew up the Hudson River, around Grant's Tomb, and back. About a million people saw some part of this flight, which proved a publicity bonanza for the Wrights and a publicity disaster for Curtiss.

Curtiss made successful exhibition flights in St. Louis and then Chicago. Based on his success, and the greater success of Orville Wright, Curtiss decided to form an exhibition team of two pilots and two planes. He soon had several teams touring the country. The pilots, in addition to him, were Charles Willard, Jack McCurdy, J.C. (Bud) Mars, Charles Hamilton, and Eugene Ely. Others joined later. Curtiss personally taught many to fly; lessons came with the purchase of a Curtiss plane. Though Curtiss sometimes performed stunts in the air, his exhibition flyers did not. Their job was to exhibit the airplane and to promote aviation, not to scare people with needless crashes. Yet their income was 50% of the take, and this incentive sometimes overshadowed safety considerations as the pilots performed for audiences and competed for prizes. (Figure 3-8)

Figure 3-8. Charles Hamilton flying a Curtiss Rheims Racer at an airshow at Meadows Race Track in Seattle, Washington, on 11 March 1910. The next day he crashed the aircraft.

Recognizing Glenn Curtiss as competition, the Wright brothers organized an exhibition team of their own in the summer of 1910. They recruited pilots Roy Knabenshue and Tom Baldwin to fly Wright machines at fairs, air meets, and other public events. Soon the Wrights recruited more team members, who received their pilot training from Orville at Huffman Prairie. The Wright Fliers, as members of the exhibition teams were called, earned salaries, not percentage of revenues, and thus were modestly paid compared to the Curtiss pilots and independent showmen. Still accidents happened. Ralph Johnstone died in a crash in Denver in November, and Arch Hoxsey died in a Los Angeles crash in December. Four more Wright Fliers died in accidents before the brothers disbanded their exhibition team in late 1911.

Among the Curtiss exhibition flyers was Cromwell Dixon of Columbus, Ohio. Dixon once billed himself as "the youngest aeronaut in the world," a title he was outgrowing. In 1911 he brought his Curtiss pusher to Montana. The biplane had a Curtiss water-cooled engine and the characteristic aileron between the wings. On 30 September, nineteen-year old Dixon flew from Helena to Blossberg, Montana, a distance of

Historic Event

On 21 June 1913 Georgia Broadwick parachuted from an airplane over Los Angeles. This is the earliest known parachute jump from an airplane by a female.

loop. Curtiss had taught Beachey exhibition flying, but Beachey preferred stunt flying. He flew a Curtiss pusher, then a Curtiss tractor, then a Warren Eaton pusher, then a Glenn L. Martin tractor monoplane. He raced his airplane against cars and flew in the mist of Niagara Falls. He performed at fairs, air meets, and air races. As he advertised, "BEACHEY FLIES 3 P.M. RAIN, SHINE OR CYCLONE." He even talked aviation on the vaudeville circuit. He died in 1915 when the wings broke off his Martin *Little Looper* in a dive at the Panama-Pacific International Exposition in San Francisco. Of course, not all exhibition flyers and not all stunt pilots were American, but Americans pursued exhibition and stunt flying more enthusiastically and extensively than European pilots.

Figure 3-9. In 1911 exhibition flyer Cromwell Dixon flew this Curtiss pusher across the Continental Divide. This was the first flight over the Divide.

17 miles. He navigated by smoke from a fire lit in Blossberg for that purpose. This flight made him the first person to fly across the Continental Divide, and this feat earned him the $10,000 prize offered by a railroad executive, land developers, and the Montana State Fair organization. Dixon performed daily at the Montana State Fair that year and made his historic flight as part of the fair's program. (Figure 3-9) Only days later, while performing at the Interstate Fair in Spokane, Washington, Dixon crashed and died.

Lincoln Beachey was one of the most famous daredevils in the United States, known almost as much for his crashes as his flights. His trademark stunt was the

Historical Note

Exhibition flying and stunt flying differed. Cortlandt Bishop, President of the Aero Club of America, promoted exhibition flying and discouraged what he called aerial showmen. As he explained, "But, we, the leaders of the aero-age must make every effort to combat the ruthless destruction of a great enterprise and a delightful sport through an excess of promotional vigor."

Bishop as quoted in Robert Scharff and Walter S. Taylor's *Over Land and Sea* (New York: David McKay Company,

Historical Note

"O fatal art!"

— Ovid referring to flight

Aviators died. That was a common fact during the early years of aviation, though the lowness and slowness of flights often saved pilots. The first airplane fatality was Lieutenant Thomas Etholen Selfridge, a passenger killed in a crash of a Wright airplane at Fort Myer, Virginia, on 17 September 1908. Pilot Orville Wright survived that crash. Among the early airplane fatalities were:

- Eugène Lefèbvre who crashed a Wright Model A at Port Aviation Juvisy, France, 7 September 1909. Lefèbvre was the first pilot killed in an airplane accident.

Selfridge Crash

Charles Rolls Crash

- Ferdinand Ferber who crashed on takeoff at Boulogne, France, 22 September 1909.

- Charles R. Rolls who crashed his Wright biplane during the Bournemouth Aviation Week, England, 12 July 1910.

- Georges Chavez of Peru who flew from Switzerland over the Alps and crashed in Italy, 23 September 1910.

- Cal Rodgers who crashed the Wright-built *Vin Fiz* on the beach at Long Beach, California, 3 April 1911.

Cal Rodgers Crash

- Edouard Nieuport who crashed while demonstrating a plane to the military, France, 15 September 1911.

- Samuel F. Cody whose plane broke apart in flight near Farnborough, England, 7 August 1913. He had designed and built the airplane.

- Gustav Hamel who crashed after takeoff from Calais, France, 23 May 1913.

Historical Note

A 1911 report listed the four leading causes of airplane accidents:

1. faults of construction,

2. mistakes of the pilot,

3. state of the weather, and

4. fault of the public, or special or unknown factors.

The report covered 47 accidents and three fatalities in 1909, and 101 accidents and 28 fatalities in 1910. Almost half of the accidents and more than half of the deaths were due to construction problems. Faulty turns were the leading pilot errors. The public cause of accidents involved the "imprudences of spectators," according to the *Scientific American* summary of the French-prepared report.

Historical Note

Regarding the safety of aviation, British pilot Claude Grahame-White in 1912 wrote:

". . . The ordinary man regards the pilot of an aeroplane as an individual who runs a dreadful risk every time he makes an ascent. He is fostered in this belief by the great amount of space which has been devoted in popular journals to aerial catastrophes. It has become the habit to open a newspaper and exclaim, 'Ah! Another airman killed!' Thus, the casual reader comes to form an opinion that the ranks of airmen are being so steadily depleted that there will soon be very few left.

"As a matter of fact, quite the reverse is the case. The army of pilots is growing so rapidly that, even at the end of last flying season, there were estimated to be 6,000 men in the world capable of handling an aeroplane; nowadays the lists of men who have secured their pilot's certificates are augmented from week to week so rapidly that it is impossible to keep count of all the newcomers to the pastime. And the important point to be made in this connection is: all this flying is being accomplished with diminishing risk to the pilots taking part in it."

Among the recent safety improvements were duplicate control wires, improvements in design, more powerful engines, more efficient propellers, and use of metal in construction of the framework.

Claude Grahame-White, "The Safety of Flying," *Outing Magazine*, 1912, as reprinted in *Early Flight from Balloons to Biplanes*, edited by Frank Oppel (Secaucus, NJ: Castle, 1987).

FLYING COMPETITIONS

Reflecting the popularity of aviation around the turn of the century, flying clubs were organized in France, Italy, the United Kingdom, and elsewhere. The main purpose of these aero clubs was to promote aviation. They were initially formed for the sport of ballooning, enjoyed by many of the wealthy founders, but soon they supported airplane flight as well. In their respective countries, these national clubs sanctioned aviation competitions, certified flight records, presented awards, lobbied on behalf of aviation, and issued pilot licenses.

Aero Clubs

Eight national aero clubs — representing Belgium, France, Germany, Italy, Spain, Switzerland, the United Kingdom, and the United States — organized the Fédération Aéronautique Internationale (FAI or International Aeronautical Federation) in Paris in October 1905. At the time, the membership of the national clubs consisted mostly of wealthy balloonists who flew for sport, but the emphasis soon shifted to airplanes. Founded in 1905, the Aero Club of America was the first organization to provide "official" support of the Wright brothers' claims and, in the club's words, "their great achievement in devising, constructing,

and operating a successful man-carrying dynamic flying machine." That was a key activity of the aero clubs — to provide "official" recognition of aviation events and achievements. Within the respective nations, the national clubs provided witnesses, documentation, and verification of official flying records.

Through participation in the international body, national clubs recognized international licensing standards. The Fédération Aéronautique Internationale issued international pilot licenses based on the participating clubs meeting the international standards on the national level. The various clubs issued pilot licenses to promote safety. They encouraged participation in their licensing programs by excluding unlicensed pilots from club-sanctioned competitions and from attempts to establish official records. The pilot license had no sanction of law until governments began requiring and issuing them in the 1920s, yet insurance companies often required early aviators to obtain the license in order to qualify for insurance. The clubs began granting airplane pilot licenses in 1910; this expanded existing programs to license balloon and dirigible operators. The Royal Aero Club of Great Britain, for example, issued its first Aviator Certificate to J.T.C. Moore-Brabazon on 8 May 1910.

 ## Historical Note

In 1910 the Royal Aero Club of Great Britain began awarding pilot licenses to airplane pilots. The first ten licenses went to:

1. J.T.C. Moore-Brabazon
2. C.S. Rolls
3. A. Rawlinson
4. Cecil S. Grace
5. G. B. Cockburn
6. Claude Grahame-White
7. Alex Ogilvie
8. A. Mortimer-Singer
9. S. F. Cody
10. Lieutenant L.D.L. Gibbs

The Royal Aero Club awarded 863 pilot licenses by 4 August 1914.

Some British subjects obtained licenses in France and the United States, sometimes in addition to a British license, and sometimes instead of one.

These and many more names of British aviation pioneers appear in *History of British Aviation, 1908-1914*, by R. Dallas Brett (1933; Surrey, England: Air Research Publications, 1988).

Historical Note

The first ten airplane pilot licenses issued by the Aero Club of America, all in 1910, went to:

1. Glenn H. Curtiss
2. Lieutenant Frank P. Lahm
3. Louis Paulhan
4. Orville Wright
5. Wilbur Wright
6. Clifford B. Harmon
7. Captain Thomas S. Baldwin
8. J. Armstrong Drexel
9. Todd Schriver
10. Charles F. Willard

The American Aero Club issued licenses for spherical balloon, dirigible balloon, aeroplane, hydroaeroplane, and expert aviator. It issued over 3,500 airplane pilot licenses by 1919.

Various lists of early American aviators appear in *For the Greatest Achievement, a History of the Aero Club of America and the National Aeronautic Association*, by Bill Robie (Washington: Smithsonian Institution Press, 1993).

The first five airplane licenses issued in the United States went in alphabetical order to pilots well known in aviation circles: License No. 1 to Glenn H. Curtiss, No. 2 to Frank P. Lahm, No. 3 to Louis Paulhan, No. 4 to Orville Wright, and No. 5 to Wilbur Wright. License No. 6 went to Clifford B. Harmon who had to pass a flight test before club representatives. At that time, the Aero Club of America required an applicant to be 21 years old, to make three solo flights under the supervision of the club, and demonstrate safe flight skills. Traditionally, the club's agents stayed on the ground and watched an applicant take the flight test. The Aero Club of America (and its successor, the National Aeronautic Association) licensed airplane pilots from 1910 into 1927, when the Federal Government began to license pilots.

A few women were among the early pilots who earned licenses. The Baroness Raymonde de la Roche became the first female pilot or aviatrix to obtain a pilot license. The Aéro Club de France issued her the certificate in 1910. Harriet Quimby became the first American woman to earn a pilot license; that was license No. 37, issued in 1911.

Air Shows

The first international air show was at Rheims, France, in August 1909. Twenty-three aircraft entered this *La Grande Semaine d'Aviaton* (grand air meet) to compete in speed, distance, and duration races. Records were set and reset. On the 23rd of the month

Historic Event

On 2 August 1911 Harriet Quimby became the first American woman to earn a pilot license. The Aero Club of America awarded her license number 37. She had learned to fly at the Garden City, Long Island, flying school of Alfred Moisant, an exhibition flyer. She toured with the Moisant International Aviators, though she was an aviatrix (female aviator). She was the first female pilot to fly an airplane across the English Channel. On a flight over Boston Harbor, the rudder and warping lines of her Blériot tangled. She crashed and died on 1 July 1912.

Glenn Curtiss flew the *Golden Flyer* at the record speed of 43.385 miles per hour (69.821km/h). The next day Louis Blériot flew his Blériot XI at a speed just over 46 miles per hour (74 km/h). A few days later Curtiss won the speed prize with a speed of 47 mph (75.7 km/h). Similarly, British pilot Hubert Latham flew a closed circuit in an Antoinette IV for a total distance of 96 miles (154.6km), only to be bettered another day by Henry Farman, who flew a closed circuit for more than 111.8 miles (180km).

Figure 3-10. A Curtiss pusher prepares to compete in the International Aviation Meet in Chicago in August 1911.

In January 1910 the Aero Club of California, an affiliate of the Aero Club of America, hosted an international air show at Dominguez Field near Los Angeles. Louis Paulhan of France was the top winner among aviators attending that meet. American air meets were held in Boston, Baltimore, and Asbury Park, New Jersey, during the year. In August 1911 Chicago hosted the second international air show in the United States. Flyers competed in several categories — endurance (time in the air), altitude, passenger-carrying, and speed, monoplane or biplane. Scottish pilot James Martin in a Grahame-White machine won the alighting (spot landing) contest, and British aviator Thomas Sopwith in a Blériot won the monoplane passenger-carrying event; he carried one passenger for six laps at speeds up to sixty miles per hour. Canadian pilot J.A.D. McCurdy flew his plane into electrical wires, but walked away uninjured. William Badger died from crash injuries after the wings of his Baldwin biplane ripped apart in the air, and St. Croix Johnstone died when his Moisant monoplane crashed into Lake Michigan. The show went on. (Figure 3-10)

Newspaper Competitions

Newspapers had sponsored balloon and dirigible flights in the nineteenth century, and newspapers sponsored airplane competitions in the early twentieth century. The *Daily Mail* of London expressed particular interest in aviation as news. In 1906 it assigned Harry Harper full time to the aviation beat; he was apparently the first full-time aviation reporter. The next year the newspaper sponsored its first competition, which was a "fly off" for model aircraft. The winner, Alliott Verdon Roe, used the prize money to build a full-size airplane. In 1909 the newspaper awarded British pilot J.T.C. Moore-Brabazon a prize of a thousand pounds for being the first Briton to fly for one continuous mile in a British-made airplane. Moore-Brabazon used the Short No. 2 biplane in the competition. Another

Historical Note

Flying competitions effectively promoted aviation. The Rheims Meet in 1909, for example, drew Claude Grahame-White to aviation. After the meet, Grahame-White purchased a Blériot airplane and taught himself to fly. He earned British certificate No. 6. Having crashed several times while teaching himself to fly, Grahame-White opened several flying schools in 1910 — at Pau, Brooklands, and Hendon. He developed Hendon as a place for exhibition flying. To increase public awareness of the importance of aviation, in 1912 he flew across England in an airplane labeled "Wake up England." When the war began, he enlisted in the Royal Naval Air Service and became a bomber pilot.

Claude Grahame-White

Figure 3-11. Louis Paulhan flies his boxkite-type biplane. He won the Daily Mail Prize in 1910 for his London-to-Manchester flight.

Daily Mail competition was the English Channel crossing, won by Blériot in 1909. (Figure 3-11)

The next year the *Daily Mail* sponsored a prize worth ten-thousand pounds for a London-to-Manchester race. French pilot Louis Paulhan won the race. During that race British aviator Claude Grahame-White earned the distinction of making the first night flight of an airplane in Britain. The 1911 *Daily Mail* competition was a five-day "Round Britain" air race won by a French naval pilot in a French-made airplane, the Blériot XI. The *Daily Mail* called its 1913 race around the United Kingdom the Hydro-Aeroplane Trial; it was a seaplane race that no pilot or plane finished. The Great War in Europe started in 1914 and interrupted the newspaper's sponsorship of aviation events, but after the war the *Daily Mail* resumed awarding prizes to pilots competing to achieve newsworthy goals in aviation.

Other newspapers followed the *Daily Mail's* example and created aviation news by sponsoring competitions. In the United States, the *New York World* sponsored a prize for the first flight between New York and Albany. Glenn Curtiss won the prize with his round trip flight of May 1910, and he stopped only twice for fuel. The flight took 2 hours and 51 minutes. The *New York Times* and *Philadelphia Public Ledger* offered $10,000 for a round trip between New York and Philadelphia. Charles Hamilton won the prize in the summer of 1910. With each long-distance flight, the

distance increased. The *New York Times* offered a prize for the first flight from New York City to Chicago. Publisher William Randolph Hearst offered a $50,000 prize for the first transcontinental flight across the United States, the entire distance to be flown within thirty days and the offer to expire in one year. (Figure 3-12)

Figure 3-12. Cal Rodgers following historic flight from New York to Pasadena, California in 1911.

Competing for the Hearst Prize in 1911, Cal Rodgers took 49 days to fly from Sheepshead Bay, New York, to Pasadena, California. Crashes, repairs, and convalescence interrupted the trip, but he made the flight. It took him 19 days too many for the Hearst Prize, but this newsworthy flight was the first transcontinental.

Rodgers flew a Wright Model B biplane named *Vin Fiz* after the grape drink company that was sponsoring the trip. He flew without paying the Wrights royalties, but when he reached the West Coast, the Wrights gave him the royalties as a reward and thanks for putting their airplane in the news for so long. Five months later Rodgers died in an airplane accident.

Gordon Bennett Races

Gordon Bennett, publisher of the *New York Herald*, established prizes to encourage aviation and to generate news for his paper. The first Gordon Bennett International Cup balloon race was held in 1906. That competition was held in France, where Bennett lived. Sixteen contestants entered the long-distance race, which Frank P. Lahm of the United States won. The

Bennett cup went to the aero club that sponsored the winning pilot, and that club would host the next competition, so the Aero Club of America sponsored the second Gordon Bennett balloon race in 1907. American, British, French, and German balloonists competed; Oscar Ebersloh of Germany won with a flight of over 872 miles. The cup and the race moved to Germany.

But in 1908 the airplane was the big news. Practical machines were being flown on both sides of the Atlantic. Bennett's response to the new technology was to establish an annual airplane race to promote the airplane and generate airplane news. The first Gordon Bennett or Blue Ribbon race was held at Rheims in 1909, at the international air show. Bennett's *Herald* called the race a "fight for supremacy of the air." Each contestant flew two rounds, the winner had the lowest total time. The winner was Glenn Curtiss of the United States, who flew a Curtiss biplane. French pilots Louis Blériot, Hubert Latham, and Eugène Lefèbvre placed 2nd, 3rd, and 4th respectively. Blériot flew a Blériot monoplane, Latham an Antoinette monoplane, and Lefèbvre a Wright biplane. (Figure 3-13)

Figure 3-13. Glenn Curtiss flew a biplane similar to the one shown here when he won the first Gordon Bennett airplane race at Rheims in 1909. The photograph shown here was taken during a Curtiss exhibition at Atlantic City, New Jersey, in 1911.

The cup and the race moved to the United States for 1910. The race was held at Belmont Park. British pilot Grahame-White won in a Blériot monoplane. John B. Moisant of the United States finished second. He too flew a Blériot monoplane. At Eastchurch, England, in 1911, Charles T. Weymann of the United

Personal Profile

James Gordon Bennett, Jr. (1841-1918), succeeded his father as publisher of the *New York Herald*. Bennett not only printed news, he made news. He sent reporter Henry Stanley to Africa to find the medical missionary David Livingstone. As a yachtsman who lived in Paris, Bennett began European editions of the *Herald*. He sponsored boating, automobile, and air races. In 1906 he founded the annual Gordon Bennett International Cup balloon race, and in 1909, he started the Gordon Bennett Cup airplane race, also known as the *Coupe Internationale d'Aviation*. He was a patron, promoter, and publicist of aviation.

James Gordon Bennett, Jr.

States flew a Nieuport monoplane to victory. French pilots in French-made planes, one a Blériot and the other a Nieuport, finished second and third. French pilots — Jules Védrines, Marcel Prévost, and André Frey — and French planes — two Deperdussin monoplanes and a Hanriot monoplane — swept the competition at Chicago in 1912. Overwhelmed by the French performances in Chicago, the American pilots did not even fly. At Rheims in 1913, Prévost in a Deperdussin set a speed record of 126.67 miles per hour. The French swept the competition again. They placed first, second, and third.

The Atlantic Crossing

Competitive attention was already on crossing the Atlantic Ocean before the *Daily Mail* provided monetary incentive. The early attention was lighter-than-air: Walter Wellman failed to cross in his semi-rigid airship *America* in 1910. Joseph Brucker of Austria planned to cross in a dirigible named *Suchard* in 1911, but canceled the plans. Melvin Vanniman died in his attempt in 1912, when his semi-rigid airship *Akron* exploded. In 1913 the *Daily Mail* offered its generous prize of ten thousand pounds for the first transatlantic flight of an airplane. One detractor of the *Daily Mail* called the offer "an inducement to suicide." Contenders announced themselves in Belgium, France, Germany, Great Britain, Italy, and the United States. Planes were readied: MacKay Edgar's Martinsyde monoplane, Rodman Wanamaker's Curtiss flying-boat *America*, Princess Anne Löwenstein-Wertheim's Handley Page biplane. The race to cross the Atlantic was interrupted by world events before any planes took off. The approaching war overshadowed this and other competitions, as designers, manufacturers, and flyers directed their efforts toward preparedness and then toward the military emergency.

 ## Historical Evidence

Aviation novels for boys became popular in the United States starting in 1909. Inspired by the Wright brothers, exhibition fliers, air races, and by aviation news in general, these novels stressed the adventure of flying over technical accuracy. Among the series that appeared in 1909-1910 were *The Boy Aviators* by Captain Wilbur Lawton, *The Airship Boys* by H.L. Sayler, *The Aeroplane Boys* by Ashton Lamar, and *The Bird Boys* by John Luther Langworthy. The Boy Aviators located Toltec treasure in Nicaragua, worked for the Secret Service in Florida, hunted ivory in Africa, and raced to the South Pole. In each book the boys flew their homebuilt airplane to fame and fortune. The Airship Boys flew balloons, dirigibles, and airplanes on aerial adventures from Mexico to the North Pole. The Flying Machine Boys and Rover Boys soon joined the boy adventurers in the air. Even The Motor Boys took flight in several novels. In a series of books published in 1913, young Dave Dashaway flew a hydroplane on the Great Lakes, an airship across the Atlantic, and an airplane around the world. Tom Swift too began flying — a glider, airship, and airplane. The Great Marvel Series flew boys to the North Pole, the Moon, and Mars. After the Great War began in 1914, the Boy Allies and Air Service Boys flew and fought for freedom. After the war Andy Lane, Ted Scott, and Don Sturdy found adventure in the increasingly crowded skies. Advertised as "modern" stories, these books reflect both the popularity and the popular perceptions of aviation.

AVIATION INDUSTRY

In the decade after the Wright brothers' 1903 flights, a small, diverse, lively aviation industry gradually emerged. The industry was larger, more diverse, and livelier in Europe than in the United States. By 1910, Europe clearly led the world in aviation. The European surge to world leadership has often been explained as a result of the patent wars that the Wright brothers initiated in the United States in 1909 and spread to Europe in 1910. The brothers sought injunctions against airplane makers, airplane pilots, and the sponsors of various air races, air meets, and air shows. They did not want to stop the use of airplanes. They wanted to sell licenses and to receive revenue for all the flying machines that infringed on their patent rights. The litigation continued for years. The patent cases diverted Orville and Wilbur Wright from the technical development of airplanes, their area of expertise and greatest contribution. While other factors explain the differential development rates of the aviation industry in the United States and Europe, the patent wars explain the decline of the Wrights' role in aviation. Since the legal cases were also tried in the court of public opinion, the patent wars also affected the reputation and legacy of the Wrights, even raised questions about their priority and achievements.

Patent Wars Begin

In August 1909 the Wright brothers obtained a court order restraining the Aeronautical Society of New York and its Aeronautical Exhibition Company from exhibiting the group's one and only airplane, the brand new Curtiss *Gold Bug*. This airplane, also called Curtiss No. 1, was a single-seat pusher. Curtiss did not place the ailerons on the wingtips as the Aerial Experiment Association had done on its planes, rather, he attached the ailerons as supplementary surfaces midway between the biplane's wings. The ailerons, regardless of placement, in combination with a tail rudder were what prompted the Wrights to claim patent infringement and to obtain the court order forbidding exhibition of Curtiss-designed and Curtiss-made

aircraft. The court order also required paying the Wright brothers for any exhibition of the airplane prior to the court order. Later that month the maker of the Curtiss *Gold Bug* — the Herring-Curtiss Company — received a similar court order. This injunction prohibited Herring-Curtiss from manufacturing, selling, or exhibiting airplanes, in essence, from doing business. The charge behind the court orders was infringement of the Wrights' 1906 patent. (Figure 3-14)

The Wright Company versus The Herring-Curtiss Company and Glenn H. Curtiss and the sequel case of The Wright Company versus The Curtiss Aeroplane Company are representative of the many lawsuits, counter suits, and appeals that resulted from the Wrights' efforts to bar others from using what they considered their technology. The Wright brothers argued that the 1906 patent granted them exclusive rights to the principle underlying the wing-warping control system; therefore, anyone making, selling, or exhibiting an airplane based on that principle was infringing upon their rights. A patent confers exclusive rights to an inventor.

Enforcement of patent rights is a national matter, so in the United States the federal courts and in Europe national courts heard the cases. There are several possible remedies if a court determines that infringement has occurred. The infringing party may be ordered to stop the infringing behavior. The patent holder may recover damages suffered as a result of the infringement, or receive any profits the infringer may have earned as a result of infringing. Orville and Wilbur Wright wanted to receive license fees from anyone using their technology.

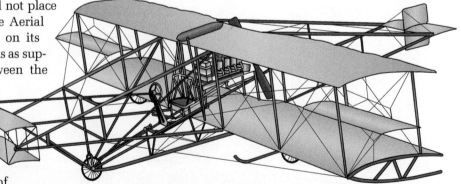

Figure 3-14. The Curtiss *Gold Bug* was the center of a patent fight between the Wrights and the Herring-Curtiss Company.

Curtiss Defense

Curtiss's first defense was to deny infringement. He argued that the supposed infringements were covered by Herring's patents that preceded the Wrights' patent. Herring, formerly Chanute's glider pilot, complicated the case. He and Curtiss were quarreling over proceeds from sales, exhibitions, and prizes. Herring owned controlling interest in the Herring-Curtiss Company, which he had received as payment for his aviation patents; however, he had never given the patents to the company. Faced with the Wrights' suit, Curtiss sued his controlling partner, Herring, for the patents. Herring fled, but a court ruling finally forced him to turn over his patents. This revealed his scam, because he had no patents, only old applications that had never received government approval. He had parlayed his former relationship with Chanute, and his having met the Wrights and seen their work in progress, into controlling interest of the company. With the litigation and resulting poor press, as well as the injunction against making and selling airplanes, Herring-Curtiss soon filed for bankruptcy. Herring was out of the company. He sued Curtiss in a case that dragged on for years before one court finally awarded him damages; he died before collecting.

Meanwhile the Wright brothers formed the Wright Company in 1909, which placed a financially powerful company rather than two inventors against Curtiss and other alleged infringers. Basically, the Wrights claimed that the use of ailerons in conjunction with a rudder infringed upon their control of lateral stability by linking wing warping and the rudder. The linkage was crucial to the case. In January 1910 a judge, who had never seen an airplane, ruled that a broad claim like the Wrights when liberally interpreted established infringement. The court's liberal interpretation was that at some point in flight Curtiss used the rudder in synchrony with the ailerons to restore lost balance. The legal issue was not one of copying, but one of exclusive rights. There had been no copying, as the ailerons were installed and demonstrated on the Curtiss airplane before the Wrights demonstrated their machine in public in 1908. Under the injunction, Curtiss posted bonds in order to remain in business while fighting the Wrights' claim. That was the flying business, as the injunction effectively halted production and sale of airplanes. On appeal, the injunction was lifted, but the legal wrangling continued.

With the injunction lifted, Curtiss could again manufacture and sell airplanes. He organized the Curtiss Aeroplane Company, resumed business, and continued to fight the Wrights' patent. He argued that the aileron system differed in a major way from the control system in the Wrights' patent. He explained that the Wright pilot controlled wing warping and rudder simultaneously, whereas ailerons operated independently of rudder. He also claimed that ailerons provide structural strength that wing warping does not allow. Curtiss argued that ailerons were supplementary surfaces, whether trailing edge or wingtip devices, and that they did not require the wing to flex and thus they added strength to the wing. (Figure 3-15)

Another approach used by Curtiss, and other possible infringers, was to direct effort toward discovering an

Historical Note

In 1868 M.P.W. Boulton of England patented a control system for lateral stability. It was the aileron system, but the invention became lost for nearly a hundred years because it was in Boulton's patent for an ornithopter. The aileron was later developed again, and independently from the Wright brothers' wing-warping.

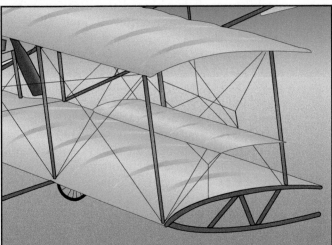

Figure 3-15. The position of the ailerons on the Curtiss *Gold Bug* and the fact that the rudder operated independently of the ailerons were the basic elements of the Curtiss defense against the Wright patent infringement lawsuit.

alternative to ailerons other than wing warping, and many experiments were conducted. He also tried using only one aileron at a time in order to remove any analogy with wing warping. Curtiss even rebuilt Langley's *Aerodrome* in an attempt to prove that the aircraft was "capable" of flight, in an effort to invalidate the Wrights' patent. Nonetheless, the patent controversy dragged into the war years.

Other Patent Battles

The Wright Company sued the International Aviation Meet Association while the 1911 Chicago air show was in progress, and the threat of legal action threatened the Bennett Race. In the United States, the Wright brothers also brought legal action against French aviator Louis Paulhan and British pilot Claude Grahame-White, who visited the country to exhibit their aircraft and to compete for monetary prizes. Finally, the Aero Club of America mediated the Wright patent dispute as it related to club sanctioned events in the United States, notably flying competitions and attempts to set flying records. The Aero Club and the Wright Company signed a contract under which the club sanctioned only those events approved by the Wrights, and the Wrights licensed club-approved promoters and allowed competitive aircraft to participate.

Historical Note

The Voisin biplane, with a pusher powerplant behind the pilot, achieved lateral stability through the suspension of fins or curtains from the upper surfaces of the wing and the tail. This gave the aircraft the appearance of being a boxkite. Voisin made 75 biplanes based on the successful 1907 design. In 1908 Henry Farman used one of the planes to win the 50,000-franc prize for first European flight over a one-kilometer circuit. Farman used the rudder alone to make the required turn. Voisin's system was an exception in that the Wright brothers did not claim any infringement of their patent.

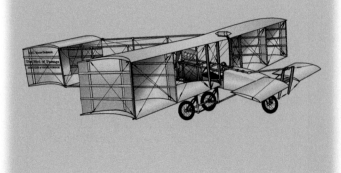

In Germany a German Wright Company represented the American Wright Company and built Wright airplanes. In 1913 a German court invalidated the Wright brothers' German patent. The court determined that Octave Chanute had described wing warping in a lecture at Berlin University before the Wrights had applied for the patent. Since public disclosure of the invention preceded the application, according to German law, the patent was void. The Curtiss aileron patent suffered a similar French fate, based on French airplanes having used ailerons prior to 1908—for example, on Robert Esnault-Pelterie's 1904 glider.

In France the Compagnie Générale de Navigation Aérienne (General Company for Aerial Navigation) represented the Wright brothers and Wright Company in legal actions against six aircraft makers: Antoinette, Blériot, Clément-Bayard, Esnault-Pelterie, Farman, and Santos-Dumont. A French tribunal initially ruled in the Wrights' behalf in five of the six cases. As an individual without a commercial company, Santos-Dumont was cleared of the infringement charge. The remaining five alleged infringers defended their interests in French courts until the Wrights' French patent expired in 1917.

Due to distance and different laws, the Wright brothers enforced their patent rights less effectively in Europe than in the United States. Only Great Britain paid. Organized in 1913, the British Wright Company made few planes but pursued the patent claim and eventually received a settlement from the British government for the unauthorized use of the Wright patent.

Automatic Stability

Patent litigation diverted Orville and Wilbur Wright from developing airplane technology, though they repeatedly tried to return to technical work. The brothers found some time to develop automatic stability, their last shared technical contribution to aviation. The innovation refined their balance between stability and control. Orville Wright tested the automatic stability system on glider flights at Kitty Hawk in 1911. They received Letters Patent No. 1,075,533 in 1913 for this new system. A pendulum detected changes in attitude around the yaw and roll axes, and a vane detected changes in pitch. Feedback mechanisms automatically activated wing-warping and elevator controls to restore equilibrium. This system has been called an automatic pilot for straight-and-level flight, but it was soon overshadowed by a competitor's technology, in this case by the gyroscopic stabilizer demonstrated by Lawrence Sperry in 1914. (Figure 3-16)

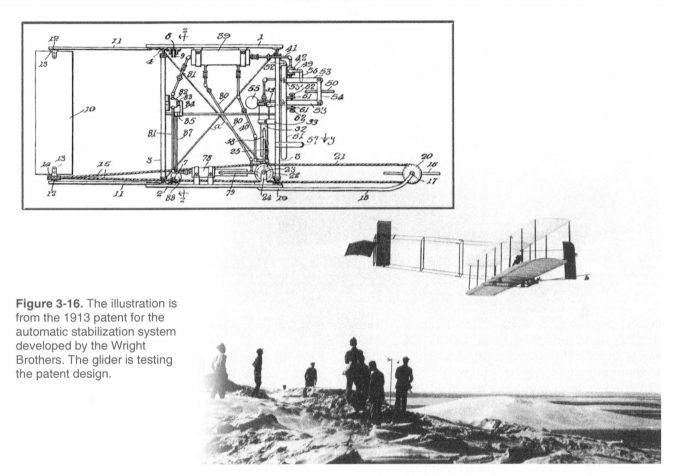

Figure 3-16. The illustration is from the 1913 patent for the automatic stabilization system developed by the Wright Brothers. The glider is testing the patent design.

The Wrights' automatic stability system is one example of how their technology failed to keep pace with the rapid developments of their competitors. Ailerons versus wing warping is another; ailerons were more effective. The Wrights adopted wheels for the undercarriage relatively late, in 1910. At that time a Wright pilot used one hand lever to warp wings, another lever to set the rudder, and a third lever to adjust the elevator. In contrast, Curtiss aircraft were equipped with a control wheel that the pilot pulled or pushed to control the elevator and turned to set the rudder, also a shoulder yoke to adjust the ailerons.

Engine Production

Airplane engines went into production. One of the first was made by relatives of the Montgolfier brothers, Laurent and Louis Séguin. The Séguins made automobile engines through their French company Société des Moteurs Gnôme. In 1907 they began producing airplane engines, seven-cylinder rotary engines that weighed only 165 pounds (75kg) and generated 50 horsepower (37kw). This one Gnôme engine started a family of engines. Léon Levavasseur's Antoinette, Robert Esnault-

Historical Note

Engineer Elmer Sperry (1860-1930) worked for the United States Navy on developing marine gyroscopes, like the gyro compass. His son Lawrence Sperry (1892-1923) took lessons at the Curtiss flying school in Hammondsport, New York. The father and son then collaborated with Glenn Curtiss in the development of an automatic stabilizer for aircraft. This stabilizer used two gyroscopes, one for yaw (rudder control), and the other for the roll and pitch (aileron and elevator controls).

ENV V-type Engine

Langley Radial Engine

Anzani "Fan" Type Engine

Pelterie's REP, and Alessandro Anzani's Anzani engines went into production too. In the United States, at least thirty-four manufacturers produced aeronautical motors before the war. These motors had from 2 to 16 cylinders arranged in vertical, horizontal, radial, V, opposed, or tangent format. They weighed from 90 to 325 pounds, and they produced from 25 to 200 horsepower. In contrast, by 1914, the French military standardized its equipment sufficiently to use only three types of airplane engines, all with horsepower in the 70 to 85 range: the Gnôme rotary, the Renault, and the Canton-Unné. Germany had less than ten engine makers, including Argus, Benz, Daimler, Mercédés, and Rapp.

Flight Lines

"The grease-covered mechanics wheeled out one of the patched-up machines kept especially for 'taxi-drivers' like myself, and I clambered into the cockpit. . . . I had been told to steer for a pylon at the other end of the field, and as my little monoplane bumped unevenly over the ground, I must have concentrated too much on the pylon and not enough on what I was doing. I pressed my feet so heavily on the rudder cross bar that the back of the seat gave way, and I slipped over onto the bottom of the fuselage, pulling the elevator control to me as I went. Not realizing in the least what had happened, I scrambled back into position as quickly as I could. Instead of being on the ground as I supposed, I was three hundred feet in the air and still rising."

Student Earle Ovington on his first solo flight at the Blériot school near Pau, as quoted in Tom D. Crouch's *Blériot XI.*

Flight Schools

After his successful year of 1909, winning the Osiris Prize, crossing the English Channel, and demonstrating the Blériot XI, Louis Blériot had orders to fill and a factory to expand. In 1911 the 500th Blériot airplane rolled out of the factory. All those airplanes needed pilots, and Blériot opened flying schools at Etampes outside of Paris, at Canbois near Pau in southern France, and at Hendon near London. Lessons were free to buyers of Blériot airplanes. Other students paid a fee plus the cost of any damage to aircraft. One student at Pau observed that "learning aviation lacks poetry": there were dirt, replacement parts, and the smell of oil.

Manufacturers typically taught their customers how to fly. In Britain alone, between 1910 and the start of the war in 1914, British civilian flying schools trained 664 pilots. Bristol taught almost half of these, at the Brooklands and Salisbury Plain aerodromes. Vickers and Grahame-White each trained more than seventy pilots at Brooklands. The other aircraft makers taught fewer pilots, which reflected their lower production levels. Avro, Hewlett and Blondeau, Sopwith, Hanriot, and Ducrocq also trained pilots at Brooklands. Ewen, Blériot, Deperdussin, Aeronautical Syndicat, Temple, Beattie, British Caudron, and Hall used Hendon for their training field. The seaplane maker Lakes used Windermere, Melly used Freshfield, and McArdle and Drexel used Beaulieu aerodrome. In 1914 there were thirteen civilian flying schools in Britain, down from seventeen the year before. Brooklands was the busiest training field, followed by Hendon, and then by Salisbury Plain. Also, the Royal Flying Corps trained military pilots at Upavon and Hendon fields. The number of student pilots, the number of manufacturers providing pilot training, and the number of airfields where training occurred reflected the diverse aviation industry in Britain.

Airports

Early airfields were just that — fields. The Wright brothers used pasture land known as Huffman Prairie in Ohio. Fort Myer, Virginia, used its parade ground for the 1909 trials of the first airplane the United States Army purchased from the Wrights. The Army leased a field at College Park, Maryland, in 1909. This field was developed by clearing the land, adding acreage, constructing four wooden hangars and one barracks, digging a well, and installing telephones. Selection criteria for that and other early airfields included size of open space, access to the public, weather conditions, hangars for sheltering aircraft and maintenance equipment, like mowers and scrapers, and facilities for student pilots. Lights at the field were appropriate for the occasional night flight. The military used fields mostly for training and maneuvers, and manufacturers used air fields for test flights and demonstration flights. One pre-war criteria favored

Wright Flyer at Ft. Myer, Virginia

Wright Flyer at Ft. Myer, Virginia

for civil and military fields was proximity to both land and water for either wheel or float takeoffs and landings.

Everywhere there were airplanes, there were airfields. The French established one of the more exotic pre-war airports at Biskra, Algeria. The military aviation unit assigned to French West Africa used this field for its Farman airplanes. Municipal governments and aero clubs around France maintained fields for airplanes. Aero clubs in other countries also encouraged and maintained fields.

French aero clubs urged the construction of "aerial roads" to guide pilots between air fields, as did other clubs in others countries. An aerial road was a line of visual aids set to guide pilots visually along a route. It was an airway marked on the ground, on ground-based structures or by captive balloons. Rooftop paintings of letters, numbers, and arrows were popular in many locations. Tall markers constructed specially

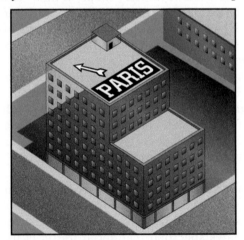

for pilots were tried. For a while Germany used translucent red balloons, each containing an electric light, to guide night flights, mostly airship flights. Belgium used the white cross symbol, made of stone or wood on the ground; the pointed top of the cross pointed north. France experimented with silvered glass balls on the ground. Developing a system of symbols involved local, national, and international efforts.

Publications

Publishers recognized a growing market for aviation literature. Some was serious aeronautical material, like F.W. Lanchester's 1907 *Aerodynamics* and his 1908 *Aerodonetics*. Other publications were more popular, like *Jane's All the World's Aircraft*, the first edition edited and published by Fred T. Jane in 1909.

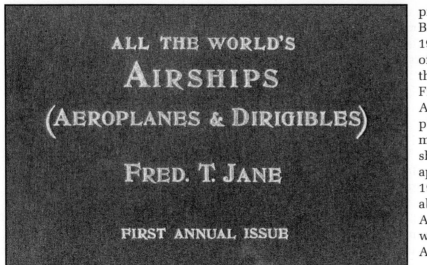

Jane's 1909 Cover

Since pilots navigated mostly by visual contact with the ground, aided by the compass, they used road maps and general military maps, if maps at all. In 1911, however, the armies of France and Germany prepared and published aeronautical maps of their respective countries. The British Ordnance Survey produced maps (and still does today).The Royal Prussian Land Survey also printed aeronautical maps of parts of Germany. These Prussian maps used the scale of 1 to 300,000 and used colors to indicate elevations. The Royal Prussian Aeronautical Observatory at Lindenberg, by the way, organized an aeronautical weather service in 1911.

International aerial laws first appeared in print in 1911. These were the product of the First International Congress of Aerial Law that met in Paris that summer. These laws specified that aerial traffic is free, yet subject to regulations by whatever nation is under the airspace in question; also that each aircraft be registered with only one country and that country be determined by the residency of the owner of the craft; that each aircraft display a mark of nationality. International law permitted landing in open fields, but not within cities or military fortifications, and forbade the "jettison" or dropping of objects that might hurt people or property. Wrecked or abandoned aircraft could be claimed by the owner within one year of discovery of the aircraft and upon payment of finder, salvage, and preservation costs.

Airmail

Airmail before World War I consisted of numerous single-flight and short-lived services. German pilot and airplane designer Hans Grade operated a privately run airmail service between Borck and Brück, Germany, starting in 1909. C.S. Rolls made a one-time delivery of one letter on his round trip flight over the English Channel in 1910. While over France, he dropped this letter for the Aéro Club de France. Another British pilot, Claude Grahame-White, carried mail on a flight in 1910, but he landed short of his destination. Official airmail apparently began in India on 18 February 1911, when Henri Pequet flew airmail aboard his Humber biplane from Allahabad to Naini Junction. The occasion was a Universal Postal Exhibition at Allahabad. Pequet and W.G. Windham continued to fly mail between those towns for a while thereafter. The correspondence was placed in special envelopes labeled "First Aerial Post." Back in Great Britain, the Blériot and Grahame-White flying schools carried official airmail between Hendon and Windsor for two weeks in September 1911. That same month airmail service began in Italy, between the cities of Bologna, Venice, and Rimini. Also in September 1911, the United States Postmaster-General named Earle L. Ovington Air Mail Pilot No. 1. Ovington flew mail in a Queen monoplane, which was like a Blériot. Exhibition flyer Katherine Stinson became the first American female to fly official airmail. She did that as a government-approved stunt at the Montana State Fair in Helena in 1913. She flew the mail from the fairgrounds to downtown. (Figure 3-17)

Figure 3-17. Katherine Stinson flew airmail in this Wright Model B biplane at the Montana State Fair in 1913.

Historical Note

The Stinsons were a flying family. Two Stinson sisters and a brother became pilots, and together they opened the Stinson School of Flying in San Antonio, Texas. Katherine Stinson (1891-1977) was the first to learn to fly. She was the fourth woman in the United States to earn a pilot's license. A founder of the flying school, she did not teach. She raised capital by stunt flying. As part of the Montana State Fair in 1913, she became the first female pilot to carry U.S. mail, which she flew from the fairgrounds outside Helena into the city. Her plane was a Wright Model B biplane. A few years after performing in Montana, Katherine Stinson went on an exhibition tour of China and Japan. In Tokyo 25,000 people attended one of her acrobatic shows. Marjorie Clair Stinson (1896-1975) taught Canadian military pilots to fly and worked as an aeronautical draftsman for the U.S. Navy during World War I. Eddie Stinson (1893-1932) was the last of the three to become a pilot. He worked as a mechanic and taught at the family's flying school, and he flew exhibition flights. After World War I he barnstormed, worked as a test pilot, flew air taxi, and set several endurance records. In 1925 he established the Stinson Company that manufactured commercial airplanes and general aviation aircraft. He died in an airplane crash. The Stinson siblings were part Cherokee, as one grandparent was a Cherokee Indian.

Commercial Aviation

As mentioned in chapter one, Ferdinand Graf von Zeppelin organized DELAG (Die Deutsche Luftschiffahrt Aktiengesellschaft) as a commercial airline in 1909. That airline used airships for charter and tour service. Commercial airplane operations began on a very limited basis before World War I. There is the case of Philip O. Palmalee flying freight in a Wright Model B biplane in 1910; he transported 542 yards of silk between a Dayton, Ohio, factory and a Columbus, Ohio, store. Pilots flew short-term jobs in several countries, but not often or regularly. In 1913 Thomas Benoist, aircraft manufacturer, and Paul E. Fansler, electrical engineer, organized the St. Petersburg-Tampa Airboat Line. This airline provided regularly scheduled service between St. Petersburg and Tampa from December into April 1914. The city of St. Petersburg subsidized the service. These commercial ventures never rivaled exhibition and prize income during the pre-war period.

Military Air Forces

During the decade 1904-1914 many nations added small, low-budget aviation units to their military forces. In 1907 the United States Army established an Aeronautical Division within the Signal Corps. Brazil organized a balloon corps in 1908 and, in 1909, Austria formed a military air unit. Also in 1909, Japan established a Provisional Committee for Military Balloon Research. In 1910 France, Romania, and Russia created military air units; in 1911, Belgium; and in 1912 Argentina, Australia, Bulgaria, Greece, Japan, Portugal, and Turkey. Aviation gradually earned military respect as reflected in organizational changes, like Britain's formally establishing the Royal Flying Corps, Germany creating its Military Aviation Service, and Italy the Italian Air Service — all in 1912.

The military encouraged aviation by participating in development not only of aircraft, but also of accessories like radios. In 1909 the U.S. Army Signal Corps experimented with wireless communication using a Baldwin-type dirigible that received signals broadcast from two ground stations; the "aerial wireless set" weighed approximately 70 pounds. The next year French military personnel experimented with wireless apparatus for dirigible balloons. The apparatus weighed from 225 to 900 pounds, depending upon its power. Airships obviously could carry more weight and more crew than the airplanes of the time. In 1910 James McCurdy communicated by wireless from an airplane to a temporary land station at the Sheepshead Bay race track. According to *Scientific American* magazine, the transmitter was "an ingenious sending apparatus, which was affixed to the steering wheel of an aeroplane. The energy was derived from a vest-pocket battery. The aerial was fifty feet of wire . . . trailing after the machine." McCurdy and his ground station operator, H.M. Horton, continued their experiments at Hammondsport, New York, headquarters of the Curtiss Aeroplane Company, under the watchful eye of a Signal Corps lieutenant assigned to observe the experiments. The British Navy, for a final example, used two Short seaplanes in communication experiments in 1913. The planes were equipped with French-made, lightweight, wireless-telegraphy transmitters. The range of these radios was 20 miles. One sent a message to King George V aboard the royal yacht *Victoria*. Yet, until World War I, the radio in aviation remained experimental.

Many air forces bought airplanes. Some bought balloons, dirigibles, or airships. Most operated flying schools for military aviators. The military forces proved significant customers of the fledging aviation manufacturers, but not as significant as the

Historical Note

The one aspect of aviation that frightened many Europeans — British, Russian, and French — was the success of Count von Zeppelin's airships. British statesman David Lloyd George described the unease he felt in 1910: "Whether the peril would come from the air or from under the waters, I knew not . . . There were ominous clouds gathering over the Continent of Europe and perceptibly thickening and darkening. The submarine and the Zeppelin indicated a possible challenge to the invincibility of our defence."

Lloyd George in his *War Memoirs*, as quoted in Alfred Gollin's *No Longer an Island, Britain and the Wright Brothers,* The1909, 1911, and 1912 editions, Stanford, CA: Stanford University Press, 1984.

David Lloyd George

"One cannot doubt that flying, to judge from the position which it has reached even today, must in the future exercise a potent influence, not only upon the habits of men, but upon the military destinies of states," said Winston Churchill in early 1914 (as published in various collections of his speeches). At the time Churchill was First Lord of the Admiralty. After World War I, while Secretary of State for War, Churchill became an airplane pilot.

manufacturers wanted. Both manufacturers and military forces demonstrated military applications of aviation. In at least two conflicts, airplanes flew missions. An Italian Air Flotilla dropped grenades from French-made Blériot airplanes onto Turkish ground forces in northern Africa as part of the Italo-Turkish War in 1911. In 1913 combatants dropped bombs from airplanes and engaged in air-to-air combat in the Mexican revolution. The aerial combat involved handguns fired by pilots of two airplanes: Dean Ivan Lamb flying for one side and Phillip Rader flying for the other.

The many Balkan crises, the Moroccan crisis, and German and Italian imperialism highlighted growing tensions among nations and fueled preparations for possible war. Aviation was an important, though minor aspect of the preparations. Germany with its Zeppelins and France with its airplanes led the military development of aviation. The French military, for example, sponsored competitions among manufacturers to encourage the design of military airplanes. The 1911 competition was held at Montcornet, near Rheims, in October and November. The military issued specifications for aircraft: three seats (one for pilot, one for observer, and one for co-pilot), capable of flying the distance of 300 kilometers, and landing on short air fields, including agricultural fields. Nine planes qualified. To be ranked, they competed in speed races. The French military placed an order for ten airplanes of the winning model: a Nieuport powered by the Gnôme engine;

ordered six of the second-place finisher, a Gnôme-powered Breguet; and ordered four of the third-place aircraft, a Gnôme-powered Deperdussin. The top five airplanes were powered by the Gnôme engine, which was determined by this competition to be the best available. France continued to develop its military aviation and, in the first half of 1913, ordered 400 new airplanes.

Historical Note

In 1914 France led the world in military aviation. This was in part a result of the Franco-Prussian War of 1870-1871. In that war, France had lost Alsace, Lorraine, and Sarre, and with these provinces coal, iron, and heavy industry. France shared its wide northern border with Germany, and France felt vulnerable. Germany had population and other resources that France lacked. French aviation pioneer Clement Ader thought the airplane could compensate for the imbalance. He published the important book *L'aviation militaire* in 1909 and expanded it twice in 1911. Other editions appeared in 1912 and 1916. The 1909, 1911, and 1912 editions influenced the prewar mobilization of air resources in France.

Conclusion

Courtesy of Orville and Wilbur Wright, the United States led the world in heavier-than-air aviation in 1903, in 1905, even in 1908. Competition among

European nations, among equipment makers of different nations, among pilots seeking to win races and capture prizes for the glory for their respective nations, and among militaries seeking air strength in the event war happens, helped Europe take the lead in aviation from the United States. Both national pride and the threat of war fueled activity on the continent and in Great Britain. European governments purchased aircraft partly to stimulate technological development and partly to build national capacity to fight if need be. Aviation sales and therefore production in Europe far exceeded the activity level in the United States. France placed large military orders for aircraft. Great Britain operated the Royal Aircraft Factory at Farnborough as well as purchased aircraft from private industry. Czar Nicholas II supported the research, development, and production of Sikorsky aircraft, including the large multi-engine planes capable of carrying bombs.

The lack of government funds and the lack of nationalistic competition with neighboring states, more than the disrupting effect of the Wrights' patent wars, hampered aviation in the United States. As the United States entered the World War in 1917, the War Department identified only six American aircraft companies that had made more than ten airplanes. In contrast, in 1911 alone, French companies had produced 1,350 airplanes, 1,400 airplane engines, and 8,000 propellers — many of these products for export. The United States lagged behind Europe, and France led European aviation into the war.

Study Questions

1.　What was the first airplane flight in Europe, and why does that flight receive the credit?

2.　Who were Henry Farman, the Short brothers, Louis Blériot, and Igor Sikorsky?

3.　What was the Aerial Experiment Association?

4.　What kinds of airplanes did Glenn Curtiss build?

5.　How did exhibition flying and stunt flying differ?

6.　When did the Fédération Aéronautique Internationale form and why?

7.　Why did newspapers sponsor flying competitions, and why did aviators compete?

8.　What was Glenn Curtiss's position regarding the Wrights' patent for a flying machine?

9.　How did France become the leading aviation country in the world before the war?

10.　Which sources listed in the bibliography are biographies?

Bibliography

Barnes, C.H. *Shorts Aircraft since 1900.* 1967; revised, Annapolis, Maryland: Naval Institute Press, 1989.

Bowers, Peter M. *Curtiss Aircraft, 1907-1947.* 1979; reprinted, London: Putnam, 1987.

Brett, R. Dallas. *History of British Aviation, 1908-1914.* 1933; reprinted, Surbiton, Surrey, England: Air Research/Kristall Productions, 1988.

Crouch, Tom D. *Blériot XI, the Story of a Classic Aircraft.* Washington: Smithsonian Institution Press, 1982.

Harper, E.H. and Allan Ferguson. *Aerial Locomotion.* Cambridge Manuals of Science and Literature. Cambridge, England: Cambridge University Press, 1911.

Lebow, Eileen F. *Cal Rodgers and the Vin Fiz, the First Transcontinental Flight*. Washington: Smithsonian Institution Press, 1989.

Oppel, Frank, editor. *Early Flight from Balloons to Biplanes*. Secaucus, New Jersey: Castle, 1987.

Scharff, Robert and Walter S. Taylor. *Over Land and Sea, the Dramatic Story of the Great Aviation Pioneer Glenn H. Curtiss*. New York: David McKay Company, 1968.

Villard, Henry Serrano. *Blue Ribbon of the Air, the Gordon Bennett Races*. Washington: Smithsonian Institution Press, 1987.

Wohl, Robert. *A Passion for Wings, Aviation and the Western Imagination, 1908-1918*. New Haven, Connecticut: Yale University Press, 1994.

Timeline

Light blue type indicates an event not directly related to aviation.

1904	October. Robert Esnault-Pelterie flew a manned glider with ailerons for control of lateral stability. This is the first full-scale aircraft known to have ailerons installed on the wings.
1904	Tsarist Russia went to war with Japan. Domestically, the Russian Social Democratic Workers' Party promoted socialism. That party had two factions, the "majority" or "Bolshevik" faction led by V.I. Lenin (1870-1924) and the "minority" or "Menshevik" faction led by G.V. Plekhanov (1857-1918).
1904	The United States acquired control of the Isthmian Canal zone from the French Panama Company. The United States then built a canal across the isthmus, a job completed in 1914.
1905	Japan defeated Russia in a war over their conflicting interests in Manchuria and Korea, a war begun in 1904. The Russian construction of the Trans-Siberian Railway, completed in 1905, was a factor in the war. This Russo-Japanese War marked Japan's emergence as a world power.
1905	Norway became independent of Sweden.
1906	October 23. Brazilian Alberto Santos-Dumont flew his *14-bis* biplane almost 197 feet (60m) and won the Archdeacon Prize for accomplishing an airplane flight of more than 82 feet (25m).
1906	November 12. Alberto Santos-Dumont flew his biplane *14-bis* in sustained, powered, manned, and controlled flight over a distance of 722 feet (220m) in 21 seconds. At the time and for two years, Europeans questioned news of the Wright brothers' flights in the United States and credited this Santos-Dumont flight as the first airplane flight. It was the first flight to gain international recognition as a world distance record; that recognition was granted by the *Fédération Aéronautique Internationale*.
1906	The Moroccan Crisis was resolved when Germany dropped its demands and when France and Spain divided control of Morocco.
1906	Great Britain launched HMS *Dreadnought*, which at the time was more heavily armed and faster than any existing battleship. This was part of the naval arms race that preceded World War I.
1907	July 11. Louis Blériot flight tested the Type VI *Libellule*, which had cantilever wings in tandem and wingtip-type ailerons. He flew about 80 feet (25m).

1907	November 13. French bicycle maker Paul Cornu flew a helicopter with paddle-shaped blades to a height of about one foot (30cm) above ground for about 20 seconds. This is the first well-documented free flight of a helicopter. Later that day he lifted his brother as a passenger to a height of about five feet (1.5m). He was one of several aviators experimenting with vertical lift at the time.
1907	Great Britain, France, and Spain agreed to the Pact of Cartagena regarding the Balearic Islands in the Mediterranean Sea and the Canary Islands in the Atlantic Ocean, and Britain and Russia signed a convention on Persia, Afghanistan, and Tibet. Both treaties were to block German expansion.
1907	Germany, Austria, and Italy renewed their Triple Alliance, originally formed in 1882. The Triple Alliance balanced the power of the Triple Entente of Russia, France, and Britain in international affairs. The main areas of disagreement in the early twentieth century were Morocco and the Balkans.
1908	January 13. Henry Farman won the Grand Prix d'Aviation, sometimes called the Deutsch-Archdeacon Prize after its sponsors, for flying the first official circular flight in Europe; Wilbur Wright in Ohio in the Flyer No. 2 had flown the first known circular flight on 20 September 1904.
1908	May 29. Only two weeks after Wilbur Wright had carried the first airplane passenger aloft, pilot Henry Farman took the first passenger in **Europe** for an airplane ride. The passenger was Ernest Archdeacon, a French lawyer and promoter of aviation.
1908	June 20. Glenn Curtiss flew an airplane for the first time. It was the *June Bug* that he designed for the Aerial Experiment Association. Less than a month later, on 4 July, Curtiss won the *Scientific American* Trophy for flying nearly a mile (1.6km) in *June Bug*.
1908	Austria annexed the Turkish territories of Bosnia and Herzegovina on the Balkan Peninsula, and the major powers failed to reach an agreement at the London naval conference which ended without regulations regarding warfare.
1908	The Balkan state of Bulgaria declared its independence from Ottoman (Turkish) rule and crowned a German prince King Ferdinand (1861-1948).
1909	July 25. Louis Blériot won the *Daily Mail* prize by flying an airplane across the English Channel in the first airplane crossing of that body of water. He flew at altitudes between 150 and 300 feet (45 and 90m) above water. He made the 24 mile (36.5km) flight in 37 minutes.
1909	August 29. Glenn Curtiss flew his *Rheims Racer*, powered by a Curtiss V-8 engine, to victory in the first Gordon Bennett speed race. He achieved an average speed of 47 miles per hour (75.7km/h). French pilots — Louis Blériot, Hubert Latham, and Eugene Lefèbvre — placed second, third, and fourth in the race. George Cockburn of Great Britain finished fifth.
1909	British chancellor David Lloyd George (1863-1945) introduced his People's Budget to raise funds for defense.
1909	After the murder of a Japanese official in the Japanese protectorate of Korea, Japan established a dictatorship to govern Korea; Japan formally annexed Korea the next year.
1910	March 28. French pilot Henry Fabre flew his *Hydroavion* floatplane off water and landed on water in the first known flight to take off from and land on water. Nearly a year later, in January 1911, American aviator Glenn Curtiss accomplished his first water takeoff and water landing at the San Diego Harbor.

1910	November 14. Exhibition pilot Eugene Ely flew a Curtiss airplane called the *Hudson Flier* off the USS *Birmingham*. The Navy had constructed a takeoff platform over the ship's bow for this experiment.
1910	King Edward VII (1841-1910), successor of Queen Victoria (1819-1901), died. George V (1865-1936) became king of the United Kingdom and emperor of India.
1910	A revolution forced King Manuel II (1889-1932) to flee Portugal, which then became a republic.
1911	January 18. Eugene Ely landed a Curtiss pusher biplane on the deck of the USS *Pennsylvania*, which was anchored in San Francisco Bay. This was the first time an airplane landed on the deck of a ship, and it demonstrated the naval potential of airplanes. He took off from the deck of the ship later that day to return to Selfridge Field in California.
1911	The 35-year dictatorship-like presidency of Porfirio Díaz (1830-1915) ended with his resignation during this opening year of what turned out to be a prolonged revolution in Mexico.
1911	With the collapse of the Chinese empire in 1911, Tibet became an autonomous region under British control, and remained so until the Chinese invasion of 1950.
1912	May 2. C.R. Samson took off from HMS *Hibernia* in a Short S.27 biplane. This was the first British flight from a ship under way. Once an aviation feat had been accomplished, like Eugene Ely's successful takeoff from a ship, the feat was likely to be repeated by others.
1912	The Manchu dynasty formally abdicated, and a republic replaced the Chinese or Ch'ing empire.
1913	April 16. Maurice Prévost flew a Deperdussin to victory in the first Schneider Trophy race. He averaged 45.75 miles per hour (73.63km/h).
1913	September 13. French pilots M. Seguin and Henry Farman set a world distance record by flying an airplane 634 miles (1,021km).
1913	September 21. Adolphe Pégoud flew his Blériot monoplane in sustained inverted flight, the first such upsidedown flying under the control of the pilot.
1913	November. Two airplanes engage in combat for the first time. The scene was the Mexican revolution. The weapons were handguns fired by the pilots of two airplanes: Dean Ivan Lamb flying for one side and Phillip Rader flying for the other. Bombs had been dropped from an airplane during the Mexican conflict earlier, in May.
1913	By the Treaty of London, Greece obtained Crete and many Aegean islands from Turkey.
1913	The Triple Alliance — Germany, Austria-Hungary, and Italy — held a naval convention.
1914	January 1. Pilot Anthony Jannus of the Benoist Company flew one passenger from St. Petersburg, Florida, to Tampa, Florida. This was the first scheduled flight of an airline using an airplane in regularly scheduled service (as opposed to charter service or airship travel).
1914	July. German pilot H. Oelerich flew a DFW B.I. to an altitude of 26,700 feet (8,150m) and thereby set a new international altitude record.
1914	In June a Bosnian Serb assassinated Archduke Franz Ferdinand of Austria-Hungary, and in July Austria-Hungary declared war on Serbia. This started the third Balkan War of the young century. In August, Germany declared war on Russia and France, and Britain declared war on Austria-Hungary. By the end of the year, Japan, Belgium, East Prussia, Montenegro, Canada, Australia, and Turkey had joined the conflict. World War I thus began as a Balkan War that escalated into a Great War in Europe and finally into a World War.

CHAPTER 4

WORLD WAR I (1914-1919)

AVIATION HISTORY

Summary of Events

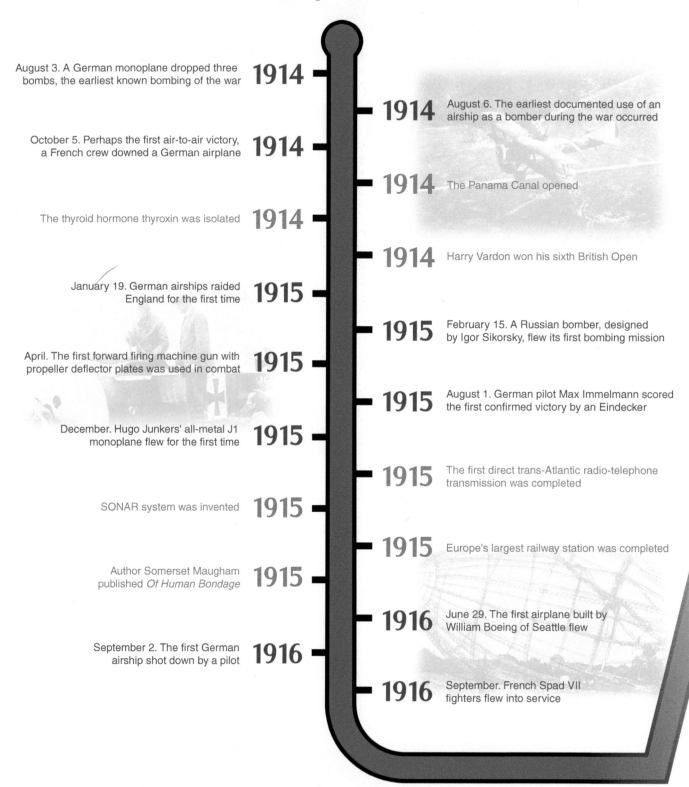

August 3. A German monoplane dropped three bombs, the earliest known bombing of the war

1914

1914 August 6. The earliest documented use of an airship as a bomber during the war occurred

October 5. Perhaps the first air-to-air victory, a French crew downed a German airplane

1914

1914 The Panama Canal opened

The thyroid hormone thyroxin was isolated

1914

1914 Harry Vardon won his sixth British Open

January 19. German airships raided England for the first time

1915

1915 February 15. A Russian bomber, designed by Igor Sikorsky, flew its first bombing mission

April. The first forward firing machine gun with propeller deflector plates was used in combat

1915

1915 August 1. German pilot Max Immelmann scored the first confirmed victory by an Eindecker

December. Hugo Junkers' all-metal J1 monoplane flew for the first time

1915

1915 The first direct trans-Atlantic radio-telephone transmission was completed

SONAR system was invented

1915

1915 Europe's largest railway station was completed

Author Somerset Maugham published *Of Human Bondage*

1915

1916 June 29. The first airplane built by William Boeing of Seattle flew

September 2. The first German airship shot down by a pilot

1916

1916 September. French Spad VII fighters flew into service

Light blue type represents events that are not directly related to aviation.

1916 Radio direction finder developed

1916 The Congress of the United States established the National Parks Service

1916 Artist Claude Monet painted his *Water Lilies* murals at the Musée d'orangierie in Paris

1917 February. The all-metal Junkers J4 airplane with a corrugated duraluminum skin made its first flight

1917 April 5-6. Squadron No. 100 of the British Royal Flying Corps bombed the Douai airfield at night

1917 May 25. Germany made its first airplane mass bombing raid on England

1917 The trans-Australian railway was completed

1917 The new Bowtree Automatic Pantograph introduced photocomposing

1917 Bolsheviks seized power in Russia

1918 April 21. The Red Baron, Manfred von Richthofen, shot down and killed

1918 October 14. Britain dropped the Block Buster, the largest bomb of the war, on Berlin

1918 November 6. A solid-propellant rocket demonstrated

1918 November 11. Germany agreed to an armistice and thereby ended the Great War.

1918 The "Spanish" flu epidemic began killing large numbers of people

1919 February 21. The American designed MB-3 fighter biplane made its first flight

1919 June 14. A prototype of the French Nieuport-Delage 29 fighter reached an altitude of 9,100m (29,856 feet)

1919 The Radio Corporation of America (RCA) was organized

1919 The straight-eight-cylinder engine went into a production car, the Italian Isotta-Fraschini Tipo 8

1919 The 18th amendment to the Constitution of the United States was ratified

Introduction

During World War I aviation was lighter than air and heavier than air. The technology and missions of airships and airplanes developed in both unique and complementary ways — military ways. Aviation was largely a European activity, supported by production and training on other continents. Production of large quantities of aircraft and engines became a wartime imperative and transformed a young industry consisting of many small airplane and engine makers into large-scale production previously unknown in the industry. Aviation was new, progressive, and technological. It was modernism in flight. It was movement and liberation from earthly bonds. It was patriotic and nationalistic — particularly during World War I.

The war began locally as one more of the many Balkan crises. The assassination of the heir to the Austro-Hungarian throne in late June 1914 sparked the Balkan conflict, because Austria-Hungary blamed Serbia for the assassination. Due to a well established "alliance system," as well as to nationalistic and imperialistic objectives, the dispute quickly expanded across Europe into a Great War. The many nations of Europe belonged to different alliances and by agreement went to the aid of their alliance partners. As an ally of Austria-Hungary, Germany declared war on Russia, which was an ally of Serbia.

Historical Note

The Alliance System basically divided Europe into two hostile camps by 1914. Some of the alliances were:

Austrian-German Alliance, 1879-1918

Triple Alliance, 1882-1915 (Austria, Germany, and Italy)

Russian-French Alliance, 1891-1917

Anglo-Japanese Alliance, 1902-1915

Anglo-French Entente, 1904

Anglo-Russian Agreement, 1907

Germany-Turkey Treaty, 1914

Triple Entente, 1914-1918 (Russia, France, and England)

That was the first of August. Germany declared war on France, an ally to Russia, on the fourth of August. That same day Germany invaded Belgium, which was in its path to France. Also that day, Britain declared war on Germany. Europe thus divided into two armed camps: the Allies, also known as the Entente Powers, on one side versus the Central Powers, also known as the Central Empires, on the other side.

The Allies and Central Powers "raced" to the sea in September and October 1914. This race established the Western Front as a line from the North Sea through Belgium and France to Switzerland. That is where the British, French, and German air forces concentrated for the next four years. The Eastern Front brought German and Russian air forces into conflict. What Europeans called the Great War became the First World War. Its battlegrounds involved the territories of Britain, Germany, Japan, and eventually China as well as European colonies in Africa, factions in the Middle East, and parties on the Balkan Peninsula, including the Austrian Front. In February 1917 Germany formally declared its policy of unrestricted submarine warfare, and implementation of that policy finally brought the United States into the war on the side of the Allies.

Nationalism is devotion to one's nation and a desire to secure one's national interests over the interests of other nations. It is the aspiration to advance one's nation. Nationalism was a cause of the war; that is, different nations each with their own national agendas competed economically, diplomatically, and finally militarily. Nationalism also found expression in aviation.

Aviators, and the public in their respective nations, took national pride in capturing the Bennett Cups or other honors in prewar flying competitions. During the war, the combatant nations used aircraft as nationalistic symbols. Nationalistic pride in aviation went beyond the romance and fads of aviation, to national identity and claims of distinctiveness and superiority. This was true of the German Zeppelin perhaps more than any other aircraft, but airplanes too kindled pride. Legends grew around the British S.E. (scout experimental, made by the Royal Aircraft Factory), the French Spad, and the German Fokker. These were the new fighter planes, envisioned before the war and produced and proven during the war. Bombers too gave a visual representation of nationalism, again led by the zeppelins, but also including airplanes like the Russian Il'ya Mourometz and the German Gothas. In the United States, far from

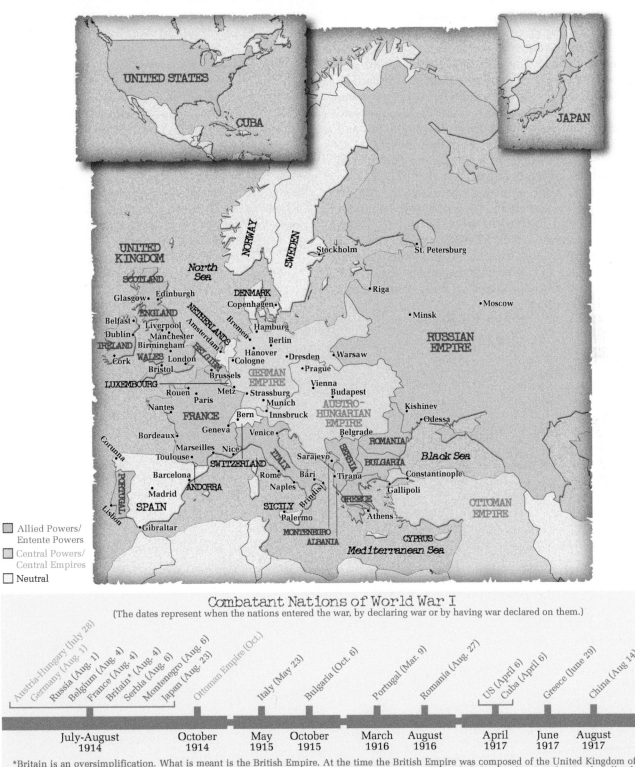

Allied Powers/
Entente Powers
Central Powers/
Central Empires
Neutral

Combatant Nations of World War I
(The dates represent when the nations entered the war, by declaring war or by having war declared on them.)

Austria-Hungary (July 28)
Germany (Aug. 1)
Russia (Aug. 1)
Belgium (Aug. 4)
France (Aug. 4)
Britain * (Aug. 4)
Serbia (Aug. 6)
Montenegro (Aug. 6)
Japan (Aug. 23)
Ottoman Empire (Oct.)
Italy (May 23)
Bulgaria (Oct. 6)
Portugal (Mar. 9)
Romania (Aug. 27)
US (April 6)
Cuba (April 6)
Greece (June 29)
China (Aug 14)

| July-August 1914 | October 1914 | May 1915 | October 1915 | March 1916 | August 1916 | April 1917 | June 1917 | August 1917 |

*Britain is an oversimplification. What is meant is the British Empire. At the time the British Empire was composed of the United Kingdom of Great Britain and Ireland which included England, Scotland, Wales, and Ireland. The Empire also included Australia, Canada, Newfoundland, New Zealand, and South Africa. All these peoples were "British" in the imperial sense of the word.

the combat overseas, it was a trainer — the Curtiss JN Jenny. Aircraft were of course more than symbols, and wartime aviation represented great advances in the technical and industrial aspects of aviation as well as in the tactical use of aircraft.

Airships, dirigibles, and balloons are the subject of Section A of this chapter, and airplanes the focus of Section B. Aviation production is discussed in Section C. The armistice and transition to peace as related to aviation are the subject of Section D.

By studying this chapter, you should be able to provide information about airship raids: Who raided whom? Why? What routes did airships fly? What damage was done? How effective was the airship as a bomber? As a reconnaissance aircraft? You should be able to discuss the development of military airplanes for reconnaissance, artillery spotting, fighting, and bombing, and to name specific developments and aircraft of the war period. You should be able to define the term ace and to name specific examples of aces of different nationalities. You should be able to outline the major steps or processes in aircraft production at that time, to name several major producers, and to explain why the United States failed to produce aircraft in significant numbers or quality to meet the wartime needs. Finally, you should be able to cite specific examples of how the terms of peace influenced and even regulated aspects of post-war aviation.

Historical Evidence

Popular perceptions of World War I were shaped in part by what people read, including novels. That was true even before the war started. In 1908 English writer H.G. Wells wrote *War in the Air,* and in 1909 German author Rudolf Martin wrote *World War in the Air.* Wells described an air war involving German, American, and Asiatic airships. Wells' world war destroyed civilization. One character asks, "But why did they start the War?" The answer: "They couldn't stop theirselves. 'Aving them airships made 'em." In Martin's novel, German airships win an empire in Europe for Germany.

AIRSHIPS, DIRIGIBLES, AND BALLOONS

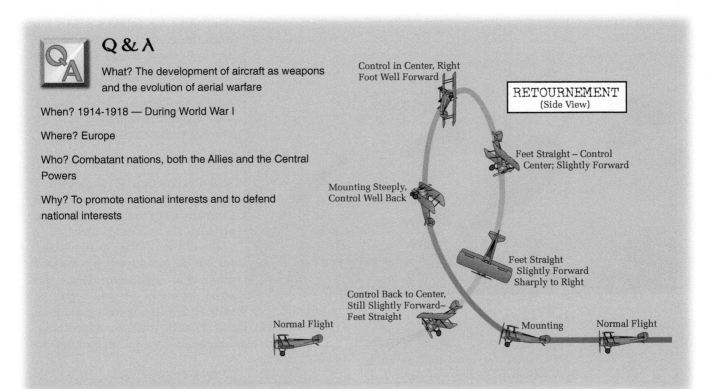

Q & A

What? The development of aircraft as weapons and the evolution of aerial warfare

When? 1914-1918 — During World War I

Where? Europe

Who? Combatant nations, both the Allies and the Central Powers

Why? To promote national interests and to defend national interests

RETOURNEMENT (Side View)

Control in Center, Right Foot Well Forward

Feet Straight – Control Center; Slightly Forward

Mounting Steeply, Control Well Back

Feet Straight Slightly Forward Sharply to Right

Control Back to Center, Still Slightly Forward– Feet Straight

Normal Flight

Mounting

Normal Flight

World War I opened in 1914 with mobility as German troops stormed through Belgium and into France. The troops moved by train, truck, car, horse, and on foot. Aircraft observed the situation. Airplanes, balloons, dirigibles, and airships flew reconnaissance missions; the crews looked at the enemy, recorded their position, and reported. On occasion an airman dropped a little bomb, with little effect on the war below. Within months the movement stopped as troops on both sides dug into trenches. The war reached a stalemate. As one British pilot said, "flying was a soft job compared to what the infantry had to go through in the trenches." Indeed, the war was mostly down in the trenches where dirt could shelter a soldier from a bullet, and where long lines of opposing trenches faced each other and any head popping above a trench might become a target. The air provided a dramatic alternative to the positional war of attrition on the ground. Germany, France, Great Britain, and other nations had lighter-than-air craft and crews in their air forces.

German Airships

When war broke out in Europe, the German Army had six operating airships, and the German Navy had two. At the time Germany had little strategy for using these rigid-frame airships, but the zeppelins were the pride of Germany's air-minded public who demanded they be used. Zeppelins, regardless of make, were *wunderwaffen* — wonder weapons. Thus, when the war began, the German Army flew airships on reconnaissance flights to observe the enemy, and occasionally an airship crew would drop a bomb or two. Soon Germany developed the airship as a bomber, though these aircraft proved most effective throughout the war as reconnaissance vehicles. The Navy soon took the

Historic Event

On 6 August 1914 the German airship Z 6 bombed Liège, Belgium. Fire from a Belgian gun on the ground hit the airship and damaged it, but Z 6 returned to base. This is the earliest documented use of an airship as a bomber during the war.

lead, buying more airships, flying more raids, and using airships till the end of the war. On the other hand, the Army dismantled its airship program in 1916. A certain competitive friction existed between army and naval branches of aviation not only in the German airship program, but also throughout military aviation in Germany *and* in the other combatant nations. (Figure 4-1)

The Germans used airships during their advance into Belgium and France at the beginning of the war. The Zeppelin Z 6 was hit by enemy fire from the ground, so too were Z 7 and Z 8; the Z 8 was shot down.

Figure 4-1. German airships, like the Z 6 shown here, were used initially for reconnaissance missions.

The designation Z indicated a Zeppelin made before the war. Germany designated wartime army airships LZ and naval airships L, and used still other designations for ships produced by makers other than Zeppelin. What the army learned in the opening months of war was that airships were vulnerable. They offered large, highly visible, low-flying, and slow-moving targets for guns on the ground, so

Historical Note

The influence of Ferdinand *Graf* or Count von Zeppelin was so great that German airships, regardless of designer and maker, were called zeppelins. In this textbook, airships built at the Zeppelin factory are identified by capitalizing the word Zeppelin. A lower case zeppelin identifies airships without reference to the manufacturer.

Flight Lines

"Dinner was ready in a large tent, and we had scarcely sat down when a Zeppelin was reported on the horizon. [Charles] Longcroft jumped into a scout, flung a handful of bombs into it, and in a moment was soaring into the sunset. We walked up on to the hill, and we could see the Zeppelin a thin, black mark on the low horizon. Longcroft was not away long, because directly he got up into the air he said it was impossible to see anything for the mist. In the meantime the sun had thoroughly set, and it grew dark. Flares were lit on the Aerodrome, and soon we heard Longcroft's machine buzzing in the air. He flew in through two trees, and made a perfect landing in the dark."

British officer Maurice Baring describing a Zeppelin incident at Baillel, France, on 31 May 1915, in *Flying Corps Headquarters, 1914-1918*, by Maurice Baring (1920; Edinburgh: William Blackwood & Sons, 1968).

Figure 4-2. The downing of this zeppelin demonstrated the vulnerability of airships. French soldiers surround the airship to keep spectators at a distance.

the German Army reduced its use of airships over the land and during the day on the Western Front. (Figure 4-2)

While the army was already curtailing — but still continuing — its use of airships, Peter Strasser, as head of the naval airship division, argued for increased use of airships, particularly for raids against England. Although England lacked air defenses at the beginning of the war, Germany launched no coordinated series of attacks in 1914 or 1915. In fact, Germany did not launch its first raid against England until January 1915. An airship raid was a bombing mission. On the first raid German airships bombed Yarmouth. That and subsequent early raids on England targeted docks, coastal military facilities, and war production plants; later raids included civilian targets. Since battleships could cause much more damage than the comparatively small load of bombs that an airship could carry, the

Historic Event

On 19 January 1915 Germany made the first zeppelin raid on England. The German naval airship division launched three airships. L 3 and L 4 reached the Norwich region of England. Each dropped fifteen bombs on Yarmouth. Twelve were 110-pound bombs, and eighteen were incendiary bombs. This raid damaged a town square, destroyed several small buildings, killed four people, and injured sixteen.

Compare that first airship raid with Germany's first airplane mass bombing of England on 25 May 1917, when 21 Gotha bombers killed 95 people and injured 260. The Gotha was named after one of its builders. It was a twin-engine G-plane or *Grossflugzeug* (large plane).

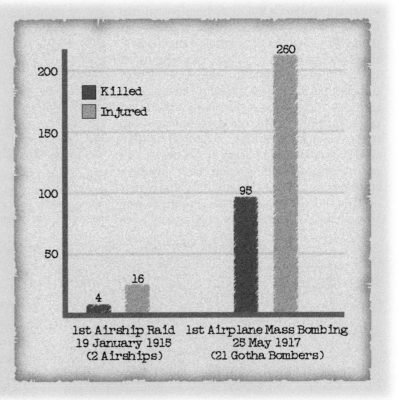

German airships targeted British morale as well as British property. This was terror bombing, designed to lure Britain into a separate peace. Yet the raids apparently raised German morale more than lowered English morale. As one German newspaper raved after the Yarmouth raid, "The most modern air weapon, a triumph of German inventiveness and the sole possession of the German military, has shown itself capable of crossing the sea and carrying the war right to the sod of old England!" German airships continued raiding England into 1918.

The early raids startled and shocked the English, but soon the attacks rallied the English in support of their country's war effort. The British even responded with humor; for example, the War Office called a loft atop its building the Zeppelin Terrace. The British also developed their home defense system. They established observation patrols to watch for incoming aircraft, and installed searchlights that nightly lit up the sky. They erected wires to entangle airships; tethered balloons held the wire webs in suspension in the air. Also, they designed and produced more powerful fighter planes capable of flying at the increasingly higher altitudes flown by airships.

The German Navy launched a total of 53 airship missions against England. A single mission involved a 20- to 24-hour round-trip flight across the North Sea. Each mission was dangerous due to the weather over the sea, the observation balloons, wire nets suspended in the air, searchlights, anti-aircraft guns, and planes that defended England. As England improved its defenses, Germany scheduled raids at night during the dark phase of the moon. Navigation at night improved in 1916 when Germany began using newly developed radio direction-finding equipment. Britain's response was to develop night fighter planes and tactics. To counter the zeppelins, the British Navy adopted twin-engine seaplanes

and used pursuit planes that took off from pontoon platforms at sea.

Cold temperatures were a problem whether due to altitude or weather. Cold thickened an airship's oil and sometimes froze its coolant. Ice on the hull added dangerous weight to a ship and could interfere with rudder movement, while ice thrown from propellers could puncture gas cells. To limit the weight of an airship, and thereby increase the load of bombs carried, fuel was carefully allotted, no more than necessary for the planned flight plus a small reserve, which meant a problem for the crew if the wind or a navigation error took the ship off course. (Figure 4-3) Weather and mechanical problems actually downed more German airships destined for England than did British anti-aircraft fire, airplanes, and bombs combined. Survival required luck and

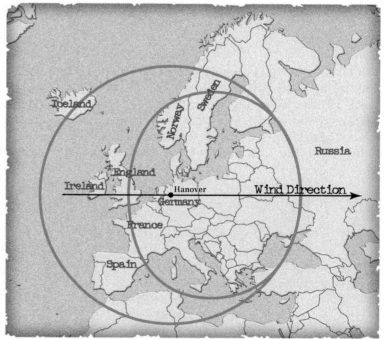

Figure 4-3. The range of airships defined a wide radius of action where Germany might achieve *raumbeherrschung* — dominion over space. The outer circle is the no wind radius and the inner ellipse is the radius with a west wind.

Flight Lines

"The only certain thing about airship travel is uncertainty."

German Captain Martin Dietrich about wandering somewhere unknown over England on a raid in September 1916, as translated and quoted in Peter Fritzsche, *A Nation of Fliers* (Cambridge, MA: Harvard University Press, 1992).

Historic Event

On 2 September 1916 Lieutenant William Leefe Robinson of the Royal Flying Corps shot down the zeppelin SL 11, or Schütte-Lanz 11, the first airship to be shot down during World War I. Robinson was flying a B.E.2 mission to intercept airships approaching London. He received the Victoria Cross for this deed.

Historic Event

On 8 September 1915 Heinrich Mathy led a German airship raid against England and caused considerable damage, especially to the warehouse district of London. There were 109 casualties. This turned out to be the most destructive airship raid of the entire war. Mathy's L13 and three other naval zeppelins participated in the raid.

Compare that damaging airship raid with Germany's Gotha bomber raid on London 13 June 1917, when 162 people were killed and 432 injured. Twenty planes participated in the raid.

On 1 October 1916 Germany launched 10 naval airships against England. Mathy commanded the L31. The Germans flew into a storm. The failure to forecast this and other storms demonstrated weaknesses in the meteorological support for weather-sensitive airships. Nine ships diverted to industrial targets in the Midlands. Mathy continued to London, where he was shot down.

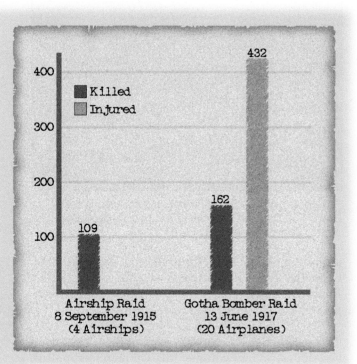

Flight Lines

"It is only a question of time before we join the rest. Everyone admits that they feel it. Our nerves are ruined by mistreatment. If anyone should say that he was not haunted by visions of burning airships, then he would be a braggart," wrote German airship commander Heinrich Mathy. When in the fall of 1916 a British pilot fired and ignited Mathy's L31 airship, Mathy had a choice — to burn or to jump. Either way, the result would be death. He jumped.

Historic Event

On 21 March 1915 German airships attacked Paris for the first time. A British officer in Paris at the time said the raid was "not of any importance," and that there was a "zeppelin alarm" the next night. During the alarm the city turned out its lights in a defensive effort to darken, or blackout, the city from view. The blackout was a new defense, an innovative response to raids earlier in the war. German airships raided Paris for the last time on 29 January 1916. A German Taube airplane had made the first aerial attack on Paris on 30 August 1914.

skill, for the technology was not enough to protect the crews or the airships.

German airships also raided France, Belgium, the Eastern Front, and the Balkan Peninsula, as well as attacked battleships and submarines at sea. Given the Allied shortage of anti-aircraft guns on the Eastern Front, the German Army continued to make daytime airship raids there into 1916. Using bases in Lithuania, Poland, Hungary, and Bulgaria, German zeppelins bombed a variety of eastern targets, including Warsaw, Sebastopol, Odessa, and Bucharest. After Italy joined the war on the side of the Allies, German airships targeted Italian ports on the Adriatic Sea. In 1917 the German Army replaced the airship as a land bomber with the new airplane bombers, though the Navy continued to use airships effectively along the coasts. It is estimated that German airships flew about 250 army missions during the war, a couple hundred naval bombing missions, and well over a thousand naval reconnaissance flights.

German Technology

Throughout the war, Germany continued to produce airships. They built airships that were bigger, more powerful, and flew higher than earlier models. Having built twenty airships before the war, Count von Zeppelin had the most experience and the greatest expertise in building airships. There were other

Figure 4-4. Many Zeppelins were constructed in the Zeppelin factory in Friedrichshafen. This aerial photograph of the factory was taken in 1918.

airship makers, like Schütte-Lanz, Parseval, and Gross-Bassenach. The process as well as the product improved, and in 1917 the Zeppelin factory took only six weeks to build an airship. (Figure 4-4.)

To fly higher required more gas and therefore larger envelopes. The volume of German zeppelins increased in steps during the war — from 22,000 cubic meters in 1914, to 32,000 in 1915, to 55,000 in 1916, to 68,000 in 1918. Power and speed also increased, the former from 600 horsepower when the war began to 1,600 horsepower late in the war, and the latter from 75 to 120 kilometers per hour. Load capacity increased as well and reached approximately four tons of bombs by the end of the war. Bodies of the airship became more streamlined. (Figure 4-5)

Figure 4-5. This 1916 Zeppelin L 30 was one of the first of the new streamlined airships.

A German government official estimated that 80 airships could be built at the cost of a single battleship, but airships proved no bargain. They were expensive to maintain and operate in terms of both money and manpower; for example, they required large ground crews and large facilities. During the war Germany

Historical Note

The Daimler L motor, shown here, was the engine used in the first Zeppelin that flew on 2 July 1900. Thereafter Maybach engines powered most of Germany's zeppelins. The CX model in particular was a reliable engine. Designed by Wilhelm Maybach (1846-1929), this engine used low-octane gasoline as fuel, and it was powerful enough to turn large propellers. Electrical components, like spark plugs, were shielded to keep sparks away from the hydrogen compartments. Maybach made a practical carburetor. His Zeppelin subsidiary made engines for the zeppelins, and his company later produced automobiles.

constructed airship hangars at Frankfurt, Düsseldorf, Leipzig, Potsdam, and Hamburg; some hangars revolved in order to reduce the wind damage while pulling out or pushing in an airship.

How did German airships fare in warfare? Not well. The German Navy lost 53 of its 73 airships, and lost 389 men with those ships. The German Army lost 26 of 52 airships and 52 men during the war. Germany thus lost 441 aircrew men, but England suffered only 556 casualties from the German airship raids. The death rate of airship crews exceeded that of airplane crews and that of submarine service. The Germans tended to mistake lucky hits for precision bombing, and the crews often overstated the damage in reports to military authorities. The raids failed to demoralize the civilian population, which was one of the German goals; nonetheless, the raids did reveal civilian vulnerability during an air war. The airship proved effective flying reconnaissance over water, away from anti-aircraft guns, and out of range of fighter planes. There was no instance of airship fighting airship during the war. The overall war experience

Flight Lines

"The airplane appears to slither over the zeppelin. It is as certain of its task as a spider waiting in ambush. Then we hear what sounds like the long rat-a-tat-tat of the machine gun. . . . The airship suddenly begins to glow bright yellow-red. A darting flame shoots out of the hull. Then a fine smoke creeps over the ship, the stern drops, and the ship plunges down into the depths. It is a column of fire, like a meteor hissing out of the heavens. They are finished over there."

Crew member on the German Zeppelin L 42 giving eye-witness account of the destruction of the airship L 48 over Suffolk, England, 17 June 1917, as translated and quoted in Peter Fritzsche, *A Nation of Fliers* (Cambridge, MA: Harvard University Press, 1992).

demonstrated the failure of the airship as a land bomber and its effectiveness for naval reconnaissance.

French Dirigibles and Airships

French dirigibles and airships, like the German airships, were used initially for reconnaissance and artillery ranging, but also were vulnerable during daylight and over land. Thus France used its lighter-than-air craft mostly at night over land and increasingly for naval rather than army missions. After mobilization, France's aerostation section consisted of four stationary companies based at Toul, Epinal, Belfort, and Verdun; eight port companies at Toul, Epinal, Belfort, Verdun, Maubeuge, Langres, and Versailles (two companies). The section had approximately 4,000 men, including 70 commissioned officers. It had six ships, three Clément-Bayards, one Astra, one Zodiac, and one Chalais-Meudon — all assigned to the army, none to the navy. The section added several Zodiac and Astra-Torrès machines in 1915. (Figure 4-6)

Figure 4-6. Among the airships of the French aerostation section at the start of World War I were those similar to this Clément-Bayard design.

Historic Event

On 19 August 1914 the French dirigible *Fleurus*, a Chalais-Meudon product, made the first wartime Allied lighter-than-air military flight over Germany. This night reconnaissance flight passed over the Saar region and penetrated Germany as far as Treves.

The army suspended use of dirigibles and airships for awhile due to several instances of the aircraft being damaged by friendly fire, by French forces who did not recognize the nationality of the aircraft; Germany painted the Iron Cross insignia on its aircraft for recognition purposes. From April to September 1915 the army launched numerous bombing missions against enemy railroads and troops. The French Army stopped using dirigibles and airships altogether during the war — after flying 63 missions over land. In 1917 it transferred its remaining three serviceable aircraft to the navy.

The French Navy created a dirigible division during the war. It acquired numerous machines, some from Britain, and demonstrated the effectiveness of the dirigibles and airships at sea. Also, the Navy developed the streamlined CM-T especially for naval missions. The airship had a longer range of action

Historical Note

The French dirigible *Adjudant Vincenot* was a
9,000-cubic meter Clément-Bayard produced in
1911. It was a frequent flier. During one six-month period in 1915,
it flew 31 military missions. During the same period the dirigible
was struck by over a hundred bullets. Its Captain Joux requested
that newer machines be equipped with anti-aircraft machine
guns. The French complied and introduced anti-aircraft-armed
craft in late 1915. The Germans followed the French example by
arming their airships. The *Adjudant Vincenot* was destroyed at
the Battle of Verdun in June 1916, but the crew survived.

and higher bomb-carrying capacity than airplanes. At
sea neither anti-aircraft artillery nor fighter planes
threatened the airships and dirigibles. Like Germany,
France used naval aircraft for both bombing
and reconnaissance. The reconnaissance missions
provided protection for naval vessels, including
coastal minesweepers. The dirigibles and airships
protected ship convoys by scouting for enemy
submarines and mines. Lighter-than-air craft
routinely provided surveillance along the country's
coastlines. When the war ended, the French Navy
had 37 dirigibles and airships.

British Dirigibles and Airships

Great Britain started the war with four lighter-than-air
craft: a French-made Astra-Torrès dirigible, a German-
made Parseval, and two English-made balloons. As
an island nation, Britain naturally used aircraft as
naval weapons. The dirigible proved highly
effective for reconnaissance and surveillance
of sea coasts. Among the British innovations of
the war was the Sea Scout (SS) blimp, a small
(2,000 to 3,000 cubic meters) dirigible. Sea Scouts
were designed and constructed for patrolling
coasts and spotting floating mines, submarines,
and other enemy vessels. (Figure 4-7)

England also developed the larger C type
Coastal Patroller and even larger NS or North
Sea dirigibles. During the war Britain produced
over 200 dirigibles and provided some to
France and other Allied nations. British
airmen in dirigibles logged over 300 hours in
flight in 1915, 7,000 hours in 1916, 22,000
hours in 1917, and 53,000 hours in 1918. The

British used downed German zeppelins as models for
the design and construction of several rigid airships:
R.23, R.24, R.25, and R.26. None matched the quality
of the German-made zeppelins. At the end of the war,
Britain had the largest fleet of lighter-than-air craft,
103 craft.

Italy constructed and used semi-rigid Forlanini-type
airships during the war. These airships flew bombing
and reconnaissance missions over land and sea.

Drachen and Free Balloons

Both the Allies and the Central Powers used tethered
and free balloons during the war. The Drachen,
Drachenballoon or kite balloon, was a balloon tethered
to the ground or to a naval vessel on water. These
elongated and stable balloons had an advantage over
airships and airplanes in their direct connection by
telephone line with forces on the ground. This
allowed better direction of artillery fire. Later
balloons had radio transmitters in case the telephone
lines broke, and some had receivers so the balloonists
could listen to airplane transmissions. The kite balloon
was used for observation, sector reconnaissance,
artillery spotting, battery ranging, and verification
of demolition. It proved so effective that it was
used throughout the war by the various combatant
nations. (Figure 4-8)

France had no captive observation balloons when the
war started, but following Germany's successful
example, France acquired and used both kite balloons
and spherical balloons. A French officer described

Figure 4-7. The British Sea Scout served a valuable role as a coast
patroller and spotting blimp.

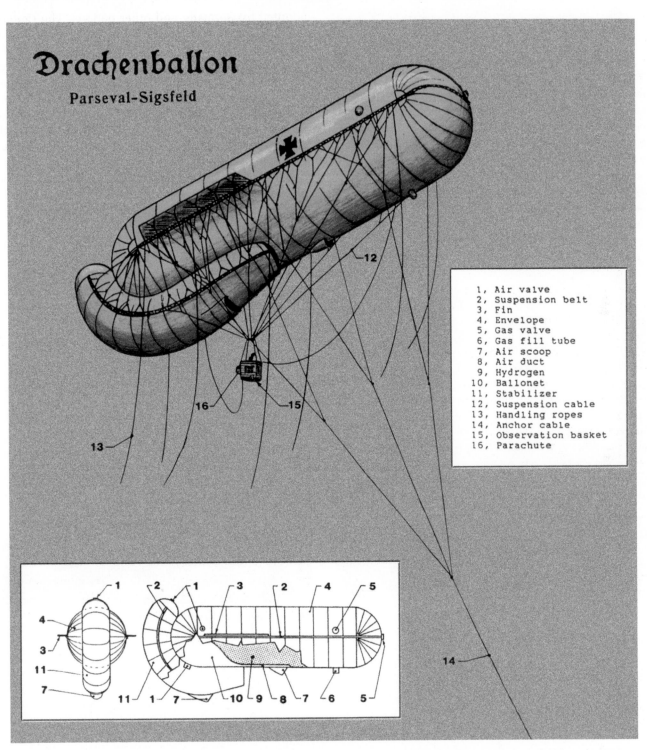

Drachenballon
Parseval-Sigsfeld

1, Air valve
2, Suspension belt
3, Fin
4, Envelope
5, Gas valve
6, Gas fill tube
7, Air scoop
8, Air duct
9, Hydrogen
10, Ballonet
11, Stabilizer
12, Suspension cable
13, Handling ropes
14, Anchor cable
15, Observation basket
16, Parachute

Figure 4-8. This German Drachenballoon was designed by Parseval and Sigsfeld. It was tethered either to the ground or a vessel and allowed the observer in the basket to report on enemy movements or to direct artillery fire.

one battlefield situation, "That day the situation before Verdun was grave, and the precariousness of our communications was such that only the balloon could report the facts." A balloonist could report enemy positions and direct fire accordingly. When the balloon came under fire, the balloonist could see the shot, count the seconds, and telephone for the winch to rapidly raise or lower the balloon out of the way.

In 1916 British Captain Albert Caquot devised an improved version of the German Drachen that was

Historical Note

Belgian ace Willy Coppens gained added fame as a balloon killer, a dangerous occupation given that observation balloons were often protected by a ring of anti-aircraft batteries. Like other Belgian pilots, Coppens flew old airplanes discarded by the British or French. He flew low enough and close enough to ignite balloon bags with incendiary bullets that he got from the French. Germans added little balloons on cables around an observation balloon in order to entangle any airplane and thereby protect the observation balloon. Coppens learned to avoid the defensive cables by diving onto the large observation balloon. His flying career ended in 1918 when a bullet tore apart one of his legs while he was attacking a cluster of balloons.

Flight Lines

"I swung around to the south, and suddenly saw a strange object, apparently bearing down upon me at high speed, which I almost immediately recognized as a kite covered in white silk. It was, of course, stationary, supported by the wind, and its apparent forward movement was due to the fact that I was approaching it at a speed of over 120 mph. I immediately pulled my nose around and up, and began a spiral climb to avoid the apron of steel cables that I guessed must be stretched between the kites surrounding the balloon I had just sent down in flames."

Willy Coppens describing a narrow escape while balloon hunting for the Belgian Air Force, as translated and quoted in Stephen Longstreet, *The Canvas Falcons, the Men and Planes of World War I* (1970; New York: Barnes & Noble Books, 1995).

adopted by Germany and other nations. The *Caquot* dangled light cables down in order to entangle enemy airplanes. The British deployed the *Caquot* in defensive barrages, one barrage was 50-miles long. The unmanned balloons were linked by horizontal cables from which additional cables dangled. Other nations copied this British technique. France was the first nation to equip its military balloonists with parachutes. Parachutes were used when a balloon was damaged by fire or aircraft strike, or when the balloon drifted away from its tether. During the final Allied offensive of 1918, when the war became highly mobile, the captive balloons went with the troops.

Free balloons were also used during the war. Among the ballooning innovations of the war were the development of drift indicators, recognition signal projectors, and bombs and bombsights. But it was the kite balloon that proved effective for military applications during World War I.

Defensive line of *Caquot* balloons

MILITARY AIRPLANES

Most air forces entered World War I with aircraft and crews suitable for only reconnaissance, observation, and scouting missions. The airplanes were mostly two-seat and relatively low-powered biplanes with limited maneuverability and limited load-carrying capacity. That was consistent with prewar planning, as this 1910 American statement about airplanes illustrates:

"From a military standpoint, the first and probably greatest use will be found in reconnaissance. A flyer carrying two men can rise in the air out of range of the enemy, and passing over his head out of effective range, can make a complete reconnaissance and return, bringing more valuable information than could possibly be secured by a [ground] reconnaissance in force."

That indeed is how the various air forces operated as they entered the conflict, but the military utilization of aircraft expanded to other missions and the development of aircraft for the new military applications transformed military aviation into a specialized and diversified field during the course of the First World War.

Combatant Air Forces

When the war started, the German Army had the largest air force: over 230 airplanes. Russia had approximately 190 airplanes, France had 160 airplanes, Austria-Hungary about 110, and Great Britain about 80. The United States had only 15 airplanes in military service in 1914 and still had no combat-ready planes in 1917 when the country finally entered the war. (Figure 4-9)

Other lands that joined the conflict also had military aviation in 1914, but these were minor aspects of their military programs. The Japanese Army and Navy, for example, had a total of 28 airplanes in 1914; during the war Japanese forces flew a total of 135 sorties against German positions in the Orient. Australia, Canada, New Zealand, and South Africa, even Ireland, contributed to the air might of the British Empire; and one Indian pilot in the Royal Air Force became an ace. The contributions and the sacrifices of these lands were valuable, despite the relatively small size and numbers involved.

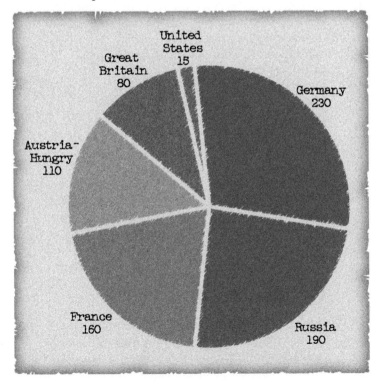

Figure 4-9. This chart represents the approximate number of airplanes each nation had at the start of World War I. The exact number of aircraft in any one nation's service varied according to whether the sum was based on orders, deliveries, combat readiness status, army or naval aircraft, military reports, or contemporary estimates.

Germany

When Germany declared war against Russia and France and invaded Belgium in early August 1914, German aviation included two aeronautical societies, the Imperial Aero Club and the Automobil-und Flugtechnische-Gesellschaft, and two military air forces, the large army air force, and a small naval air section. The German Army had four battalions and more than 15 army flying schools. Germany's 230 military airplanes were far short of the military goal of a thousand planes. The aircraft were of two basic types: the Taube or monoplane type and the Arrow or biplane type. There were more biplanes than monoplanes and more two-seaters than single-seaters; the extra wing and extra seat facilitated carrying both pilot and observer aloft.

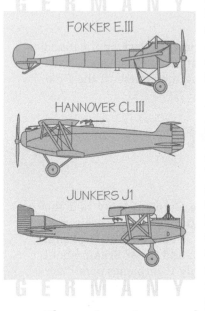

FOKKER E.III

HANNOVER CL.III

JUNKERS J1

The equipment was made by a variety of German companies, including Albatros, Aviatik, Euler, Fokker, Gotha, Jeannin, and Rumpler. The German Navy had 36 biplanes, again mostly German makes and mostly biplanes. Like the landplanes, seaplanes entered wartime service in patrol and reconnaissance duty. Also like the landplanes, the seaplanes were soon drawn into combat roles.

Historical Note

Igo Etrich (1879-1967) of Austria designed the Taube (Dove) monoplane in 1909. The design grew out of his observations of a leaf floating to the earth and his ideas about building an all-wing aircraft. His tailless design lacked stability, so he added the empennage. This redesigned Taube became a classic aircraft. Etrich released the patent for German use, and German companies made Taube-type airplanes.

Austria-Hungary

The Austro-Hungarian air force consisted of an Army section with 110 airplanes of mostly German and some Austrian makes: 60 monoplanes made by Albatros, Lohner-Daimler, and Etrich-Taube, and 50 Albatros and Lohner-Daimler biplanes. They also had a Navy section but the number of seaplanes was unknown. The notable domestic maker of army aircraft was the Lohner Aircraft Works of Vienna; however, the country also relied upon German-made aircraft and German models built in Austria-Hungary under license. This reliance upon German support in aircraft production remained the case throughout the war, though domestic factories produced adequate supplies of Hiero and Austro-Daimler aircraft engines.

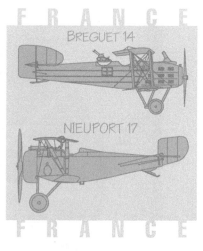

ALBATROS D III

PHÖNIX D.1 SCOUT

France

France had the leading air force among the Allies. In 1914 the French organized its air force into 21 flights of six airplanes and about 50 men each, plus 2 Blériot cavalry flights of four airplanes each. It also had nearly 300 airplanes on order when the fighting started. France had 3,500 military aviation personnel, including 240 commissioned officers and 240 non-commissioned officers. It had four military airports: Rheims, Belfort, Verdun, and Camp Châlons. France also had a Central Establishment for Aerostation Matériel for ballooning and Le Service des Fabrications de l'Aviation (Service for Aircraft Production) that controlled production in the factories of various airplane makers and that centralized the purchase of military airplanes. They also had two laboratories: an aeronautical laboratory in Chalais-Meudon and an aviation laboratory in Vincennes. The young French naval air service had the St. Raphael technical center at Fréjus that included about 10 planes and 200 men when the war began.

BREGUET 14

NIEUPORT 17

Great Britain

Established in 1912, the British Royal Flying Corps represented the state — **not** the state of the art — of military aviation at the start of the war. Officers of the Royal Flying Corps arrived by boat in France on 11

August 1914, only one week after Britain entered the war. This advance team prepared for the arrival of the British flight squadrons by obtaining water carts, pegs for airplanes, oil, and other supplies. The Royal Flying Corps lost its first two airmen before they left England when their Blériot monoplane crashed enroute to Dover for the departure to France. On 13 August all four squadrons — Nos. 2, 3, 4, and 5 — of the Royal Flying Corps flew from England to Amiens airfield in France. The first plane to arrive was the new model B.E.2a which, like most of the other planes, was a two-seat biplane scout. Within days the British airmen — pilots, observers, and mechanics — moved to Maubeuge airfield. Their temporary headquarters was in a tin shed next to a French airship hangar that housed two airships. In total, this British Expeditionary Force of the Royal Flying Corps consisted of 105 officers, 755 men, and 63 airplanes. The aircraft were B.E.2, 2a, and 2b reconnaissance planes, as well as Avro, Bristol, and Sopwith scouts. French-made Farman biplanes and Blériot monoplanes were used as trainers in France. Within two weeks the Royal Naval Air Service started arriving in France with landplanes, seaplanes, and lighter-than-air aircraft.

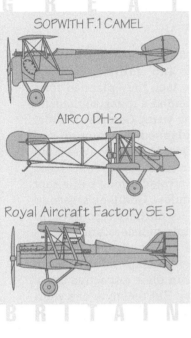

SOPWITH F.1 CAMEL

AIRCO DH-2

Royal Aircraft Factory SE 5

Russia

Russia's relatively large air force consisted of Russian-made aircraft, most notably Sikorsky machines, as well as foreign models like the French Deperdussin, Farman, and Nieuport; the German Albatros, Aviatik, and Rumpler; and the British Bristol. Many of the foreign makes were built under license in Russia. Despite the large number of aircraft, Russia had maybe fifty airplanes that were

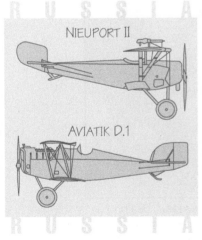

NIEUPORT II

AVIATIK D.1

combat ready and fewer than a hundred military pilots when the war came. Russian naval air resources consisted of about fifty seaplanes, mostly Curtiss aircraft, but also a few Astra, Bréguet, Donnet-Levêque, Farman, Nieuport, and Sikorsky craft.

Italy

The Italian Aeronautical Corps actually had prewar combat experience, albeit limited, in the Tripoli campaign during the Italo-Turkish War. The effectiveness of a few planes against tribesmen on the ground placed aviation firmly, if not largely, in the domain of the Italian Army. Italy's inland waterways and vast coast supported naval aviation. In addition to a large airship division, the Navy had flying boats and seaplanes made domestically by Lohner, Macchi, and others, as well as imported Curtiss planes. But the Italian military and naval air sections remained small until the First World War started elsewhere in Europe. The war spurred domestic production and military acquisition of aircraft. The Italian military studied the use of aircraft in the war before Italy finally joined the conflict in May 1915.

ANSALDO SVA5

CAPRONI CA 3

United States

Safely removed from the European War by geography, the United States did not formally enter the war until April 1917. The Army and Navy air services recruited, trained, and transported airmen to Europe, but other Americans were already engaged in the air war. Some had gone to Canada or Britain to enlist, often under assumed names to avoid losing their citizenship. Some served in the Canadian Royal Flying Corps, others in the British Royal Flying Corps. Still others enlisted in the French Foreign Legion — the *Légion Étrangére* — that allowed them to retain their United States citizenship. The Legion

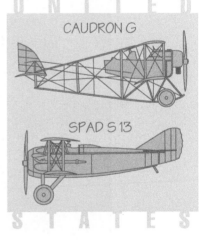

CAUDRON G

SPAD S 13

did not require men to swear allegiance to France. The Americans who joined the Foreign Legion's Flying Corps trained at French military flight schools at Avord, Pau, Le Plessis-Belleville, or elsewhere. They flew French airplanes, including Blériots, Nieuports, and Spads. They served with a variety of French squadrons.

LaFayette Escadrille

The LaFayette Escadrille was originally called Escadrille Americaine and flew at the front for a short period under this name. Germany quickly protested this designation, since the United States was supposedly a neutral country. The Escadrille was forced to change its name to LaFayette Escadrille. The men trained and served as an American unit within the French Foreign Legion. They tallied 39 confirmed victories while with the N.124, which was the numerical designation of the LaFayette Escadrille. (Figure 4-10)

When the United States entered the war in 1917, most of the Americans in the LaFayette and other French *escadrilles* (squadrons) transferred to the U.S. Army's Air Service or the U.S. Naval Air Service. One pilot who did not transfer was the first black American military aviator, Eugene Bullard. He stayed in the French service, but ended the war as he began it, as an infantryman in the trenches. Since the United States had little equipment in Europe, the Americans transferring from the various French squadrons were often assigned to fly with French, British, or Italian units.

Slowly Expanding Air Forces

When the local Balkan crisis exploded into a World War in 1914, political and military leaders anticipated a short war; in fact, they planned for a short war. But events prevented a quick settlement, and the war lasted four long years. Germany's initial push was not as hard as planned, Belgium offered unanticipated local resistance, and Germany ravaged Belgium in retaliation for its resistance. The Allies raced Germany to the coast and created a long battlefront between the opposing armies. Germany's second front with Russia diluted its military resources. In protective trenches, conscripts, enlistees, and officers dug into a stalemate and a war of attrition. Duty — personal duty to one's nation — kept soldiers at the fronts. Both sides believed in their respective cause and in their ultimate victory. But the myth of a short war slowed the initial expansion and development of military programs, including aviation.

Figure 4-10. The LaFayette Escadrille at Chaudun. Front row, left to right: Didier Masson, J. Ralph Doolittle, Chouteau Johnson, William Thaw, Georges Thenault, Edwin Parsons, Thomas Hewitt Jr., Harold Willis, unknown. Second row, left to right: Ray Bridgman, Robert Rockwell, Dudley Hill, David Peterson, William Dugan, Douglas MacMonagle, Walter Lovell, and Arnoux de Maison-Rouge. Several other pilots not shown in this photograph were assigned to the squadron at the time.

Race to the Channel

The air war began early with Germany's invasion of Belgium and the subsequent race to the English Channel. The Central Powers, led by Germany, and the Allied forces of France and Britain raced their forces toward the strategic ports on that waterway. At the beginning of the war, German aircraft dominated the skies, though the early missions were mostly reconnaissance in nature. The German troops were advancing, and the air forces moved with their respective armies. German planes flew from protected positions behind German lines, while French and British planes retreated with the Allied troops. In 1914 German Navy pilots fought Allied aircraft over the coast of Flanders, raided military installations on the coast of Kent, and participated in naval actions in the North and Baltic seas.

The British Royal Flying Corps arrived in France during the Allied retreat from Mons, a Belgian town just north of France. This retreat was also a race to the Channel ports, which were strategic military sites. Immediately British pilots, observers, and planes joined their French colleagues in flying reconnaissance. After each mission the pilots or observers turned in their road maps, marked with new positions of the advancing enemy. On 22 August a British pilot was wounded by ground fire; he was apparently the first British air casualty of the war. Guns at the front could be heard at Maubeuge the next day. On the 24th the British and French retreated from Maubeuge.

Airfields

The French and British — and other air forces engaged in the war — created airfields (aerodromes in British usage) as they moved. During the retreat from Mons and the race toward the English Channel, this required what the Flying Corps called "one night stands." Pilots took off from one field in the morning and landed on a newly prepared field later in the day. The day the British left Maubeuge, they established a field at Le Cateau. The next day British pilots exchanged shots in the air with German airmen. A German plane flew over the newly established airfield. Soldiers fired at it, but they missed. After one night at St. Quentin, the British retreated toward LaFère, then to Compiègne. During the retreat planes flew reconnaissance, landed on hastily prepared fields as well as existing airfields, and

operated in the rain. Moving the Flying Corps also required trucks (lorries) to carry gasoline (petrol), oil, and other supplies, including typewriters and stationery for headquarters clerks, and light tenders and automobiles to transport ground personnel. Beyond Compiègne the British cleared corn from a field that became their latest airfield. The ideal field was wide, smooth, grass. (Figure 4-11)

Figure 4-11. This French training airfield was typical of the airfields used early in the war. In the background is the "start house" which was used mainly for instructional purposes. The aircraft on the left is a Caudron G.III and on the right is a Maurice Farman M.F.11.

Historical Evidence

A British officer in France reported that "the Germans dropped the first bomb of the war on our Aerodrome" at Compiègne on 29 August 1914. This was obviously the first bomb to come to that officer's attention and probably the first at that airfield. It was not the first of the war. From other contemporary sources, historians know that a German Taube monoplane bombed Lunéville, France, on 3 August 1914; and the German Zeppelin Z 6 bombed Liége, Belgium, on 6 August. Often, "first" means only the earliest known to the speaker or writer.

At Juilly the Germans nearly caught the Flying Corps because the airplanes could not be flown at night. A North Irish Horse troop and some French Territorials guarded the airfield and planes that night, and all departed safely in the morning. That afternoon the British spotted a German observation airship and chased it, but did not catch it. Outside of the village of Touquin the British used a flower garden as their airfield. The next night they parked at Melun. Finally, on the 6th of September, the battle of Marne began and the Allied retreat ended. The British Flying Corps awarded medals to pilots and mechanics. A day later they returned to Touquin, which the Germans had only briefly occupied. The Allied

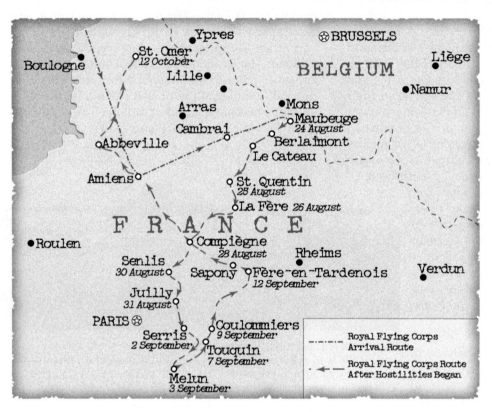

Figure 4-12. The Royal Flying Corps arrived at Maubeuge, France on 24 August 1914. The next day began an almost two week retreat from the advancing German Army. The retreat ended near the town of Melun during the battle of Marne. In early September the Allies advanced.

advance was on. Gradually through the fall, the front line stabilized as the Allies and Central Powers reached a stalemate. (Figure 4-12)

Expansion

In the fall of 1914, after the war started, Britain began expanding the Royal Flying Corps. The recruiting, training, and organizing of new squadrons took place in England. Replacements and additional units joined the expeditionary forces in France. With the new men came wireless officers (radio operators), and a few observers got cameras and began taking reconnaissance photographs from the air. The air force was expanding its capabilities as well as its numbers. It was February 1915 before the Corps received the first of its ordered Voisin machines. The

Corps had wings, squadrons, depots, and aircraft parks (major supply depots) established in France, and the Corps obtained supplies from French aviation manufacturers.

The German aircraft industry's ability to replace aircraft and to produce new types of aircraft, and the military's ability to train pilots, observers, and ground crews, helped Germany's army air force maintain the dominant aerial position through 1915 and into 1916. In general, the tactical application of German aircraft to the war effort paralleled Allied developments. Sometimes the Central Powers led the way and, at other times, the Allies introduced the newest technology or technique, but successful practices of any combatant were quickly adopted by other nations in the conflict.

Historical Note

France's initial response to the German invasion of 1914 nearly crippled its aviation industry. Anticipating a short war and relying upon newly developed heavy artillery, one army general canceled airplane orders and required aviation factory workers to join the ground fighting. Since Great Britain and Russia bought most of their airplanes from France, this disrupted Allied aviation in general, albeit temporarily. When French observation planes provided crucial intelligence about German troop movements at the Marne and allowed the Allies to stop the German advance on Paris, France reorganized and strengthened its military aviation. General August Edouard Hirschauer became director of the aircraft industry at the rear and Commandant, later General, Joseph Barès became director of aeronautics at the front.

Historical Note

During World War I the camera became a weapon used in general reconnaissance and in making military maps. An aerial photography mission usually used a two-seat plane. The pilot maneuvered the plane into position and held it level and stable while the observer snapped the pictures. Both pilot and observer had machine guns to defend themselves from aerial attack, but there was no defense other than altitude from anti-aircraft artillery.

"As the airmen have become the eyes of the land forces, so the camera has become the eyes of the airmen," reported the *Scientific American* magazine.

Early cameras used glass plate negatives. The observer loaded a negative plate, pushed the lever to expose the negative, removed the exposed plate, and started over in a timed sequence.

One wartime development was the automatic plate loading apparatus that could handle up to 200 plates. This apparatus loaded an unexposed plate, released the shutter, and removed the exposed plate, in timed sequence.

Another innovation was the chronophotographic apparatus that used roll film. The operation of this camera used an electric or clockwork mechanism. Three magazines of film used on a single mission would provide a thousand pictures.

The development of a long-focus apparatus allowed negative plates to be exposed at focal lengths of 0.25, 0.50, or 1.2 meters.

Headquarters

Airfield of von Richthofen's Jaqdegeschwader Nr. I

Some later cameras came with electric heating devices in order to avoid condensation, and some came with yellow screens to improve contrast when photographing detail in shades of green.

The various combatants developed defenses against enemy cameras such as,

- camouflaging trenches, roads, buildings, and aircraft with terrain colors or with shades of green
- hiding camps and supplies in greenery as shades of green blurred details on pictures
- moving troops, equipment, and supplies at night
- performing night maneuvers
- building falseworks to deceive the enemy, like false batteries and false camps
- increasing the range of anti-aircraft fire so as to keep photographic planes at a greater distance than the effective range of cameras

Military Aviation Developments

The military development of aviation — the technology, techniques, and tactics — occurred while the combatant nations fought. Through 1914 and into 1915, reconnaissance was the aviation mission. Observing more than fighting, aircraft had little impact on the overall course of the war, and the number of aircraft on the side of the Allies or on the side of the Central Powers made very little difference. Observation was the mission in late August and early September 1914 when French pilots detected and confirmed a change of direction for part of the advancing German army, which was moving around rather than toward Paris. With the help of this information, the Allies won the battle on the Marne River.

Aerial Combat

The role of the pilot gradually changed over the course of the war. Early on, pilots learned to carry pistols for defensive reasons. On the Eastern Front an unlucky, unarmed, but brave Russian pilot rammed his airplane into an attacking Austrian plane in order to defend the airfield under attack; both pilots died. Occasionally opposing pilots shot at each other, usually from too great a distance to do any harm. In October 1914 the two-man crew of a French Voisin biplane shot down a two-man German Aviatik biplane. They used a pivoting machine gun mounted on their airplane. The pilot, Sergeant Joseph Frantz, maneuvered the airplane and the observer, Corporal Louis Quénault, fired the Hotchkiss machine gun. This was the beginning of air-to-air combat. (Figure 4-13)

Figure 4-13. The front-mounted, pivoting machine gun made this aircraft a deadly combatant. The aircraft shown here is a Voisin type 3, #V.1346, with a Fiat machine gun. This particular Voisin was in the Italian service.

Historic Event

On 5 October 1914 French pilot Joseph Frantz and observer Louis Quénault shot down an enemy airplane. They were flying in a French Voisin biplane equipped with a pivoting Hotchkiss machine gun. They shot down a German Aviatik biplane that was on a reconnaissance flight over Rheims (now Reims). This was the first French air-to-air combat victory of the war, and perhaps the first aerial victory of the war, not counting the ground-to-air fire that had downed airplanes, like a British Avro 504 over Belgium on 22 August or the two German airships shot down the next day, also over Belgium.

Bombing

In 1914 the various air forces became interested in bombing. This was a practical field of interest unlike prewar bombing experiments that yielded no operational results. The British Royal Flying Corps was an example. According to a staff officer in France, "On September 18th the first experiments with dropping bombs from the air were made by Major Musgrave. One bomb was dropped, and it exploded, but not exactly where nor how it was expected to explode." In February 1915: "On the 10th we had experiments in bomb-dropping on the Aerodrome. [Charles] Longcroft went up and dropped a bomb; it fell in a slightly unexpected place, and went off as it was supposed to do with a bang." At the time the word bomber still referred to a soldier who tossed small pocket bombs at the enemy, and the term bombardment referred to artillery shells. Still aircraft began going on bombing missions, and pilots tossed small pocket bombs from their airplanes. On 14 March 1915 a British pilot named Barton went on a night bombing mission, flew into a tree, and survived. His bombs did not explode — thus illustrating the danger of night flying, the relatively safe slowness of flight, and the relative harmlessness of aerial bombs during this early stage of the war. A favorite target for 1915 bombers of all nations was an enemy train, since trains carried supplies for fighting troops and fuel for aircraft. That fall the Royal Flying Corps, the German Air Service, and the French military all issued directions that bombs were to be carried on reconnaissance flights. (Figure 4-14)

Artillery

At the start of the Neuve Chapelle push in March 1915, the British Flying Corps adopted the new practice of artillery spotting in which aircraft and artillery cooperated during a battle. Pilots or their radio operators/observers sent wireless messages to ground personnel to guide the artillery gunners toward enemy targets. The initial resistance to the

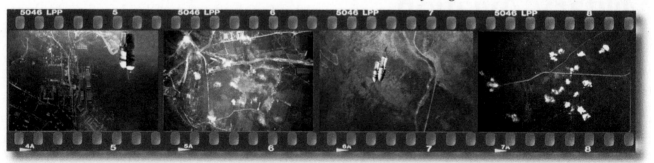

Figure 4-14. Early in World War I, the bombs dropped from aircraft were small and inflicted very little damage. Later in the war, bombing became much more sophisticated.

Figure 4-15. In the fall of 1914 some British fliers at the Western Front called the one anti-aircraft gun that bothered them an Archibald after the song "Archibald, certainly not." Soon *archie* became the British term for anti-aircraft guns. This particular unit is an Austro-Hungarian "flak" unit.

Historic Event

March 10, 1915, "was the first time during the war that aircraft co-operated with artillery in battle. Some of the pilots were up nearly all day sending wireless messages." This was a British first. Although the author did not record when other air forces began artillery spotting, such new military practices tended to spread quickly — even to the enemy. The source of the quotation is Maurice Baring, *Flying Corps Headquarters, 1914-1918* (1920; Edinburgh: William Blackwood & Sons, 1968).

new technique came from the gunners, not the aircrews. The various combatant nations used airplanes, airships, dirigibles, and balloons for artillery spotting. (Figure 4-15)

Communications

Early in the war, military forces tried various methods for air-to-ground communications. One of the simpler methods was dropping message bags connected to long streamers. At the time, radio was a complicated way to communicate. One-way, air-to-ground wireless radios could send information in code, but three problems limited the use of these radios. One was the weight of wireless equipment in the light aircraft of the day. Another was the danger of a fire being started by sparks from the radio equipment, a serious threat to aircraft constructed of wood and cloth. And, finally, an airborne radio required a radio operator skilled in Morse code, which added the weight of the operator to the load.

Signaling by lamps similarly required a second person in the aircraft, whereas signaling by the Grubb reflector — reflecting a beam projected up from the ground — did not require a second person. A simple sound signal could be given by interrupting the aircraft engine in a coded sequence, but the sound had limited range and was subject to the interference of combat noise. Flying a prearranged maneuver, such as dipping, circling, or banking, proved

Historical Evidence

Development of military aviation occurred in the field as well as in the laboratories and factories and at the flying fields behind the lines. Eyewitnesses recorded these often ad hoc developments in diaries and memoirs. In 1915, for example, a staff officer with the Royal Flying Corps in France reported on a competition within the Corps:

"On the 9th of October, in the afternoon, we had a glorious exhibition of machines. Each squadron sent a machine fitted up with its pet gun — mountings, and gadgets — and one got the prize. The following questions were dealt with: —

Bomb sights.	Wireless accumulators.
Camera.	Wireless instruments.
Incendiary bomb-tubes.	Signalling keys (they must be inside)
Wireless reel.	Heating the carburettor [sic].
Bomb-carrier fittings (standard position close to fuselage).	Holes in planes.
	Colour of cowl.
Release gear (cam gear for releasing bombs).	And, if *extra tanks are carried*, petrol, oil, pump, instruments, control pillar.
Gun mountings.	
Ammunition.	Map case."

This particular reporter did not list the winner; from Maurice Baring, *Flying Corps Headquarters, 1914-1918* (1920; Edinburgh: William Blackwood & Sons, 1968).

effective except when attacking enemy aircraft disrupted the maneuver. A properly equipped aircraft, when the weather was just right, could communicate effectively with smoke signals. Or a pilot could shoot signal guns that projected colored flares.

Personnel on the ground could communicate with aircraft by placing white canvas on a landing strip, by flashing colored lights in code, by artillery fire (mainly used to get the attention of the flight crew), or by sending wireless messages to aircraft equipped with a receiver. One method of communicating, well known in naval circles, was the semaphore alphabet. This system sent information based upon the positions and movements of two flags. The system signaled letters of the alphabet that spelled out words. A military standard was to send or receive eight words per minute, a word defined as any five letters. This was one-way communication from the signal officer on the ground or carrier ship to the pilot in the plane. Signal squares and other shaped flags were also displayed or hoisted on halyards to communicate with aircraft.

Despite the early limitations, radios had obvious advantages over all the other methods of communication in aviation. This was especially true as airplanes became faster, flew higher and farther, and operated at night. During and after World War I, aviation radios were under development. The early wartime low-powered radios, with long trailing antennas, were used mostly along the front in reconnaissance and artillery-spotting aircraft.

When Germany began nighttime airship raids against Britain in early 1915, the flight crews were guided by the lights of cities and towns. The British monitored the wireless telegraphy transmissions between the enemy airships to get an early warning of airships enroute. Radio interception also allowed the British to obtain direction-finding positions of the conspicuous and cumbersome intruders. The Germans responded by raiding Britain with bombers as well as airships.

Forward Firing

Military airplanes of World War I were mostly tractor machines, not the traditional Wright and Curtiss pushers that had dominated American aviation in the prewar years. The early airplanes were mostly two-seat observation planes with the firepower coming from the installation of a machine gun or two. Pusher planes, like the Vickers Gun Bus and various Farman planes, allowed machine guns to be mounted in front of the propellers and, therefore, were capable of shooting forward without damaging the airplane. Tractor machines used side or ring mounted guns, which required careful maneuvering by the pilot in order to give the observer/gunner a clear view of and a clear shot at enemy aircraft.

In March 1915 a French pilot serving with the French Flying Corps, Escadrille M.S. 23, had his airplane modified. Escadrilles were designated by the type of aircraft that a unit flew. M.S. was a Morane-Saulnier unit, and this pilot — Roland Garros — flew a Morane Type L monoplane. Raymond Saulnier added metal deflector plates to Garros' propeller blades and mounted a machine gun to the top of the fuselage of his one-seat tractor machine. This enabled him to fire forward without damaging his propeller because the bullets that did not go between the blades would ricochet off the deflector plates. (Figure 4-16)

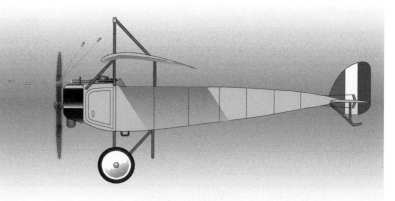

Figure 4-16. Raymond Saulnier added steel wedges to the propeller blades directly in front of the gun barrel. When Roland Garros fired through the propeller arc, most of the bullets missed the spinning blades. Those that hit the blades ricocheted off the deflector plates.

Garros flew his modified Morane against the enemy. In April he downed five German airplanes and became the first ace of the war. An **ace** is defined as a pilot with five or more victories over enemy aircraft. A few days after his last kill, enemy fire severed the fuel line on Garros' airplane, and he crashed into German territory. He tried but failed to burn the Morane before the Germans captured him.

The Germans turned Garros' innovations over to Dutch engineer Anthony Fokker, who devised improved versions for German use. Fokker developed and produced a machine gun that was synchronized with the propeller by an interrupter gear. The idea of synchronization had been explored by several people in different nations before the war, but Fokker devised the new technology and his innovation

Historic Event

In April 1915 a French pilot named Roland Garros scored victories against five German planes. He downed the first with machine-gun fire on the first of the month. He shot down four more planes in the next sixteen days. The French public and press called him an *as* or **ace**, literally meaning top card (like ace of diamonds) but figuratively meaning top sportsman. That impromptu accolade led to the term ace defining a pilot with five or more victories over enemy aircraft.

Morane Type N

revolutionized aerial warfare. The synchronized machine gun installed on a single-seat Fokker Eindecker E.1 airplane initiated the "Fokker scourge." This aircraft proved so effective that Allies began calling their own airplanes "Fokker fodder." For a while Germany dominated the sky. That was the situation in late 1915 and early 1916, until the Allies produced their own forward-firing technology, fittingly adapted from a captured German machine. Soon both sides were using synchronized machine guns, and that made the aircraft even more deadly than the simple fighter/reconnaissance planes of earlier days. (Figure 4-17)

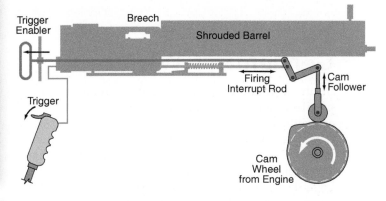

Figure 4-17. The cam mechanism developed by Anthony Fokker allowed a forward-firing machine gun to fire the gun between the propeller blades. All the pilot needed to do was pull the trigger and the mechanism did the rest.

Personal Profile

Roland Garros (1888-1918) was a music student who operated an automobile repair shop until the Rheims air meet of 1909 lured him into aviation. He purchased a Clément-Bayard Demoiselle and took flying lessons at Issy. He became an exhibition pilot, flying for a while with the Moisant International Aviators. In 1913 he flew across the Mediterranean Sea, from France to Tunisia, a distance of 453 miles (729 km). When the war started, he joined the French air force as a scout pilot. In March 1915 Raymond Saulnier modified Garros' Morane Type L airplane by adding propeller deflector shields and a machine gun. In April Garros downed five German airplanes and became the first ace of the war. A couple of days later enemy fire caused him to crash and he was captured by the Germans. Garros remained a prisoner of war into 1918, when he escaped. He trained again as a combat pilot and returned to action. He was flying a Spad when he was shot down and killed that summer.

Roland Garros

Personal Profile

Anthony Herman Gerard Fokker (1890-1939) was born in Java where his Dutch father owned a plantation. Educated in Holland, Fokker moved to Germany to study airplane mechanics. He founded an aircraft manufacturing company in Germany, but sold few airplanes until he received wartime military orders. He made monoplanes, biplanes, and triplanes. It was the synchronized machine gun more than the aeronautics of his designs that made his fighters deadly effective. After the war he moved his factory to Holland, which had remained neutral throughout the war. He later established a short-lived subsidiary in the United States.

Anthony Herman Gerard Fokker

Historical Note

Anthony Fokker defined the problem and solution of forward firing:

"The technical problem was to shoot between the propeller blades, which passed a given point 2,400 times a minute, because the two-bladed propeller revolved 1,200 times a minute. This meant that the pilot must not pull the trigger or shoot the gun as long as one of the blades was directly in front of the muzzle. Once the problem was stated, its solution came to me in a flash.

"The obvious thing to do was to make the propeller shoot the gun, instead of trying to shoot the bullets through the propeller. Inasmuch as the machine gun would shoot only about 600 times a minute this required some practical working out, but the principle had been found, which was the important thing.

"For a temporary device, I attached a small knob to the propeller which struck a cam as it revolved. This cam was hooked up with the hammer of the machine gun, which automatically loaded itself, of course. Thus as I slowly revolved the propeller, I found that the machine gun shot between the blades."

Fokker in his book *Flying Dutchman, the Life of Anthony Fokker*, by Fokker and Bruce Gould (1931; New York: Arno Press, 1972).

Gentleman's Warfare

Pilots were officers. They had name, rank, and privilege, unlike the anonymous mass of conscripts and enlisted men dying in the trenches. The airmen flew, observed, and reported. According to a German pilot, "Yes, our profession is wonderful. I fly once every three days." Echoed an American pilot, "We have absolutely no duties but flying, and no discipline except to be here when we are wanted to fly." "The early war pilot went into battle armed more as a sportsman than a soldier," according to a British officer. Even the vocabulary of the early military pilots was sporting, like ace meaning top sportsman and a mission being called hunting.

Forward firing led to the classic dog fights, the dueling pilots, the gentlemen in one-on-one sporting combat.

Flight Lines

"After we flew around and about each other nine or ten times, unable to get each other in our sights, I saw my opponent more closely. He wore a scarf flying in the wind and black headcovering . . . . He looked at me for a long time, then raised his right hand and began to wave. I don't know why, but all at once I felt very sympathetic to the man in the Spad. Without a thought, I waved back. This went on for five or six curves. Suddenly I had the strange feeling that I wasn't confronting an opponent but practicing turns with a comrade."

German pilot Ernst Udet describing an aerial duel, as translated and quoted in Peter Fritzsche, *A Nation of Fliers* (Cambridge, MA: Harvard University Press, 1992).

The publicly popular, even romantic, image of the airman became the lone pilot, the aerial knight, the ace, the sportsman. Up until the Fokker scourge, the Allies had suffered few air casualties. That changed in late 1915 when the names Immelmann and Boelcke became internationally known. Max Immelmann and Oswald Boelcke served in the German Imperial Air Service. They received two of the first Fokker airplanes equipped with forward-firing machine guns; Immelmann scored the first confirmed victory in an Eindecker on the first of August 1915. With forward-firing guns, an airman above and behind his enemy had a deadly advantage, so pilots learned to loop and climb and circle to get into the desired relative position. Immelmann and Boelcke quickly became aces by downing more than five enemy aircraft, and they continued to shoot down Allied airplanes. Immelmann scored 16 victories before his death in 1916, and Boelcke scored 40 victories before his death that same year. Immelmann died in combat, and Boelcke died when a student's plane struck his in midair.

One of Boelcke's students was Manfred von Richthofen, an experienced bomber pilot learning advanced fighter techniques. Richthofen became known as the Red Baron. He specialized in attacking slower, two-seat reconnaissance planes that could not maneuver as well as his single-seat fighter. He downed 80 Allied aircraft before being shot down himself in 1918. The Red Baron is an example of the mythical and knightly gentlemen, an ace among pilots, doing honorable battle one-on-one in the skies. The reality is he aimed for enemy fuel tanks which gave victims the choice of burning or jumping to their deaths; 54 of his victories were "burns."

Historic Event

On 9 May 1918 French pilot René Fonck flying a Spad fighter downed three German airplanes and on another flight later in the day downed three more German planes. Fonck (1894-1953) thus became one of only a few pilots to score six verified victories in one day. Within months Fonck became the only World War I pilot to score six victories in a day *twice!* When the war ended, Fonck claimed over a hundred victories, 75 of which were confirmed.

Personal Profile

Max Franz Immelmann (1890-1916) served in the German Air Force during World War I. He received one of the first Fokker airplanes equipped with a forward-firing machine gun. With that airplane in 1915, he shot down a French bomber. This was the first confirmed German scout victory over enemy aircraft. He introduced what became known as the Immelmann turn.

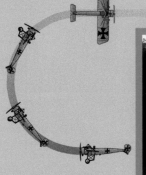

Max Franz Immelmann

His effectiveness on the Western Front earned him the nickname "Eagle of Lille." He won the German Blue Max award. He downed sixteen enemy aircraft before being killed in aerial combat on 18 June 1916.

Flight Lines

"I was on patrol that day and observed three Englishmen who had nothing else in mind than to hunt. I noticed how they ogled me, and since I felt ready for battle, I let them come. I was lower than the Englishmen; consequently, I had to wait until they came down to me. It did not take long before one dove for me, trying to catch me from behind. After a burst of five shots the sly fellow had to stop, for I was already in a sharp left curve. The Englishman attempted to get behind me while I attempted to get behind him. So it went, both of us flying like madmen in a circle, with engines running full out at three-thousand-meter altitude. First left, then right, each intent on getting above and behind the other. I was soon acutely aware that I was not dealing with a beginner, for he did not dream of breaking off the fight. He had a very maneuverable crate, but mine climbed better, and I finally succeeded in coming in above and behind him."

"Red Baron" Manfred von Richthofen describing his victory over British ace Lanoe Hawker on 23 November 1916, in Richthofen's *The Red Baron* (Garden City, NY: Doubleday, 1996).

Historic Event

On 21 April 1918 Canadian pilot Roy Brown in a Sopwith Camel and Australian ground fire brought down the Red Baron, Manfred von Richthofen, who died of a bullet wound following the crash of his Fokker Dr I triplane. The Allies gave Richthofen a formal burial with military honors.

Brown had learned to fly at Huffman Prairie, Ohio, in a Wright airplane. He was flying fighter cover for Australian camera planes at the time of the encounter with Richthofen. Australian Lewis field machine guns and artillery also fired at the Red Baron's plane. Brown never claimed that he shot down the Baron, only that he shot at a red triplane. Witnesses never agreed upon who shot the Baron down, though the Royal Air Force generally credited Brown. Taken ill days after the encounter, Brown was sent to England for medical treatment, and he never flew combat again.

Flight Lines

"Fighting in the air is not a sport. It is scientific murder."

American ace Eddie Rickenbacker, as quoted in Peter Fritzsche, *A Nation of Fliers* (Cambridge, MA: Harvard University Press, 1992).

As gentlemen, pilots dropped messages — news of captured or killed, questions regarding their own missing in action — as well as funeral wreaths and bombs. On 28 July 1915, for example, German pilots dropped three bombs and a message on the town of St. Omer, France. The message was a warning that they would be bombing the town daily throughout the next week, which they did, though the small bombs caused little damage. Despite favorable press for friendly exchanges and gallant behavior, the purpose of destroying one's enemy remained the reality of war.

Historical Note

Different nations used different methods to verify air victories; for example, some required one witness, others two, in addition to the pilot making the claim. Lists of aces, pilots who downed at least five enemy aircraft, differ in the number of victories confirmed for each pilot. The lists have been modified with post-war confirmations, clarifications, and compilations. Among the top aces of several combatant countries are the following:

Ernst Udet

Manfred von Richthofen

Frank Luke, Jr.

- Australia
  Robert A. Little with 47 victories
  Roderic S. Dallas with 32 victories

- Austria-Hungary
  Godwin Brumowski with 35 victories
  Julius Arigi with 32 victories

- Belgium
  Willy Coppens with 37 victories
  Andre de Meulemeester with 11 victories

- Canada
  William A. Bishop with 72 victories
  Raymond Collishaw with 61 victories

- France
  René Fonck with 75 victories
  Georges M.L.J. Guynemer with 53 victories

- Germany
  Manfred von Richthofen with 80 victories
  Ernst Udet with 62 victories

- Great Britain
  Edward Mannock with 61 victories
  James T.B. McCudden with 57 victories

- Italy
  Francesco Baracca with 34 victories
  Silvio Scaroni with 26 victories

- New Zealand
  Keith L. Caldwell with 25 victories
  Keith R. Park with 20 victories

- Russia
  Alexander A. Kozakov with 20 victories
  Vasili Yanchenko with 16 victories

- United States
  Edward V. Rickenbacker with 26 victories
  Frank Luke, Jr. with 18 victories

Fighter Planes

With improvements in anti-aircraft guns and with the synchronized machine gun, pilots wanted to fly higher, climb quicker, turn sharper, loop, circle, and dive; to shoot, strafe, and bomb — to maneuver, to survive, to kill. Designers responded with the general-purpose fighter. Many airplanes in the category had the synchronized machine gun, usually a Vickers gun on British and French aircraft. Britain installed synchronized machine guns on its new designs, like the Sopwith 1 1/2 Strutter and Bristol Scout C. The French also installed synchronized guns on new models, like the Nieuport Type 23 biplane and Morane Parasol monoplane. The Germans armed the Halberstadt D II and Albatros Dr I fighters and other planes. The new planes allowed pilots, actually required pilots, to develop and learn new flying skills. (Figure 4-18)

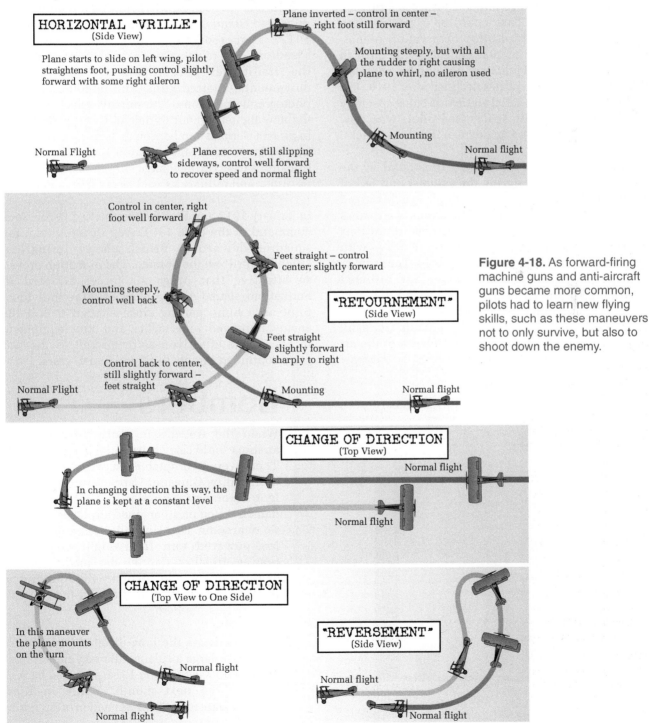

Figure 4-18. As forward-firing machine guns and anti-aircraft guns became more common, pilots had to learn new flying skills, such as these maneuvers not to only survive, but also to shoot down the enemy.

In addition to new technology, the fighter brought new tactics and techniques to military aviation. The fighter helped merge pilot and plane into the war machine. In 1916 German Lieutenant General Ernst von Hoeppner of the Imperial Air Service approved formation flying then being developed by Hauptmann Boelcke and other German pilots. Instead of single planes going on missions, squadrons of up to 10 planes went out together. Squadrons were called *Jagdstaffeln* or *Jastas*. A wing, or *geschwader*, might have as many as 50 planes flying a mission. Planes in formation made mass attacks. They could be aggressive and offensive. They could destroy observation planes, bombers, and escort scouts. Reflecting the shift in strategy and tactic to formations, the number of classic duels between two airplanes declined after 1916. The *Jastas* defined classic aerial warfare as being specially equipped planes, with specialized pilots who flew specific missions. These "gentlemen" hunted in packs!

Changes in aerial warfare were illustrated at the Battle of the Somme during the summer and fall of 1916. With their newly acquired synchronized machine gun, the Allies massed hundreds of airplanes that strafed trenches as well as bombed munitions depots, and transportation and supply routes — with demoralizing effect on the German troops. The number of aircraft as well as the damage they inflicted contributed to the effect. The Allies ended the reign of the Fokker scourge, which encompassed the more common Aviatik as well as Fokker aircraft. Germany responded with the *Jasta*, and the balance of the air war shifted back to Germany's favor. As shown in the bar chart below, Britain and France lost a total of 123 aircraft in September compared to Germany's loss of only 27. October too was bad for the Allies at the Somme: 88 planes lost to Germany's 12.

British and French air forces effectively challenged the German Air Force in 1916 at the Battle of the Somme. The German Army elevated its air force to the status of a separate army corps that year, but continued British and French developments prompted Germany to reorganize its Flying Corps in 1917. That reorganization created Army air squadrons. The reconnaissance squadrons performed the traditional observation of enemy troop movements, spotted guns, and conducted aerial photography missions. The pursuit squadrons used the new fighter aircraft to defend German positions, to protect German bombers on missions, and to attack kite balloons and transportation lines. The bomber squadrons used the new large aircraft to bomb enemy positions and military as well as civilian targets.

In January 1917 von Richthofen, the Red Baron, took command of the Jasta 11. Flying in formation, the squadron downed 83 British planes during that "Bloody April" on the Somme. The formation proved so effective that other air forces adopted it. Formations shared one problem with the individual pilot on a hunt: getting close enough to kill the enemy. Improved guns, sights, and other equipment increased the effectiveness of aircraft as the war continued into its third and fourth years.

Bombers

When the war began, only dirigibles and airships could carry substantial loads of bombs. There were two notable exceptions: airplanes designed by Giovanni Caproni in Italy and by Igor Sikorsky in Russia. In 1914 these men demonstrated multi-engined airplanes designed to overcome the limited lifting power of low-powered and lightweight engines of prewar airplanes. Caproni designed the three-engine biplane and Sikorsky the four-engine Il'ya Mourometz, named after a legendary tenth century Russian hero.

To demonstrate the long-distance capabilities of his new large airplane, Sikorsky flew it from Moscow to Kiev in June 1914, and then back to Moscow the next month. While in Kiev, Sikorsky learned of the assassination of Archduke

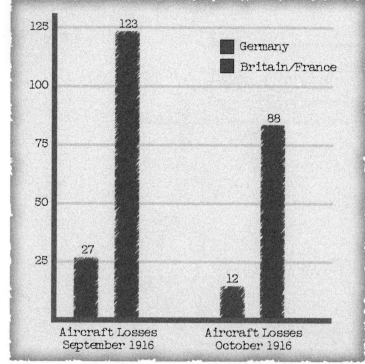

Franz Ferdinand, the heir to the Austro-Hungary throne. The Baltic Railroad Car Company, Sikorsky's employer, placed the Il'ya Mourometz into production and the airplane flew into action on the Eastern Front. There, as part of a squadron of "flying ships" (airplanes), the Il'ya Mourometz flew reconnaissance and bombing missions. Caproni's bomber also went into almost immediate service with the Italian Air Service, but Italy remained neutral in the World War into the spring of 1915. (Figure 4-19)

Figure 4-19. An Italian Caproni Ca3 bomber. This particular aircraft is parked at a training station in New York (1918-1920), but it still has the Italian marking with the inscription "Mayflower Maid N.Y." below the cockpit.

Historic Event

On 15 February 1915 a Russian-designed and Russian-built Il'ya Mourometz flew the first bombing mission for that model of airplane. It was a large airplane with an enclosed cabin and separate compartments for the pilot and passengers. The plane also had an outdoor observation deck. The Il'ya Mourometz could carry 1,500 pounds (680kg) of bombs and a crew of up to sixteen men. During World War I, 42 Il'ya Mourometz airplanes were built. These airplanes flew more than 400 wartime missions over Germany and Lithuania. In 1915 the Il'ya Mourometz was state of the art. When the war ended in 1918, it was obsolete.

Historical Note

The Russian Il'ya Mourometz demonstrated its effectiveness on the Eastern Front. Russian pilot Alexey Ponkratieff won the Order of St. George medal for flights he made in the Il'ya Mourometz II during May 1916. The official report of this award cites:

"While performing reconnaissance flights in the region between Yazlovetz and Bugatch, he personally piloted the ship and, facing danger to his life from incessant enemy battery fire, obtained accurate information about the strength and location of the enemy gun batteries and the bridges spanning the Strypa River. During the battle of May 26, 1916, in the sector Yazlovetz-Lussiloff, he discovered the absence of enemy reserves, a fact which was utilized by our forces during further development of military operations.

"He inflicted heavy losses to the enemy troops and transports by bombs, arrows and machine gun fire; by direct hits at Yazlovetz which caused several fires and aided our troops in capturing the town. He later destroyed the railroad track west of Bugatch railway station, making evacuation by the enemy forces more difficult. By accurate machine-gun fire he silenced the enemy's anti-aircraft battery which was firing at the ship, and brought down an enemy plane which tried to prevent its operation. By accurate marksmanship he silenced an enemy anti-aircraft battery near Bugatch railway station. During the reconnaissance flights he photographed the enemy positions; the photographs being used by our troops during the battle of Yazlovetz."

Russian Seventh Army Report, 6 October 1916, as translated and quoted in Igor I. Sikorsky, *The Story of the Winged-S, an Autobiography* (1938; New York: Dodd, Mead & Company, 1958).

While dirigibles and airships initially dominated bombing on the Western Front, several combatant nations developed airplanes as bombers in order to have aircraft that were less vulnerable to defensive fire and weather. Germany recognized the limitations of its airship and developed airplane bombers during the war. It produced multi-engine G and R planes. The G plane or *Grosßflugzeug* (large plane) was a twin-engine bomber, often called the Gotha after one of the German companies that built this type of plane. It was used mainly on the Western Front, and the multi-engine R plane or *Reiesenflugzeug* (giant plane) was used mostly on the Eastern Front. The electrical company A.E.G. (Allgemeine Elekrizitäts Gessellschaft) established an aviation subsidiary in 1913 that specialized in military airplanes. During the war it produced the G.I and G.IV twin-engine biplane bombers and one R-type four-engine plane. These bombers were unique at the time for the amount of steel used in their construction — in the fuselage, nacelle, landing gear, and even the wings. Standard armament on the G.IV consisted of two machine guns. Each engine was a 260-horsepower Mercédès. The Aviatik company produced the G.III Großflugzeug as a medium bomber. The aviation department of Gathaer Waggonfabrik made the twin-engine, three-seat biplane — the Gotha bomber. The Gotha began as a pusher landplane, but later tractor and seaplane versions also were produced. The airship maker Zeppelin produced a four-engine biplane bomber, the Zeppelin-Staaken R.VI, called the "Gigant" which is German for Giant. There also was a five-engine version. Like Zeppelin airships, these planes used Maybach engines, 260-horsepower engines in this case. (Figure 4-20)

Figure 4-20. Two German bombers. The rear view is a captured Friedrichshafen G.IIIa, 1056/17, that has the French cocarde superimposed over the Balkan Kreuz. The front view is a Gotha G.V, 904/16, assigned to the Kagohl (Bombing Group) 3.

Having learned from German airship raids, Britain added bombers to its air force and used the bombers to take the war into Germany. British bombing missions targeted German industrial centers and sources of war supplies, including the Zeppelin factory at Friedrichshafen. This was strategic bombing — a German innovation turned on Germany.

Historic Event

On 1 April 1918 Great Britain established the first independent air force, the first military air arm independent of both army and navy. Britain merged its Royal Flying Corps and Royal Naval Air Service into the new Royal Air Force, called the Independent Air Force during a transitional period.

On 14 October 1918 the British Independent Air Force flew a Handley Page bomber over Germany and dropped the largest bomb of the war — the Block Buster, which weighed 1,650 pounds (747kg) — on Berlin. This was the British reprisal to Germany's Gotha raids on London.

Both sides in the war had difficulty locating and stopping enemy bombers at night. Both used anti-aircraft guns and searchlights. One British defense was tracking enemy aircraft and reporting their position by radio; the British called the radio-equipped planes used for this purpose tracker aircraft. A plane on patrol would spot the invaders, track them, broadcast the fact, and permit fighter planes to home to the area. During the war the Germans developed propeller-driven generators to power aircraft radio equipment, and the British devised a three-beacon radio position system to aid navigation. By the end of the war, radios had become cockpit equipment in some fighters and bombers. Yet rapid disarmament after the war obscured some of the wartime advances.

Bombing dominated French aviation during the war. Of all the combatant nations, France dropped more bombs during the war. French bombers flew *en masse*, in V formations of 3 to 5 planes, but on missions involving up to hundreds of planes. The French developed the fast and powerful Breguet XIV bomber and the Caudron R XI fighter to provide close cover, and these aircraft enabled France to bomb in the daytime at a time when most bombing raids occurred under the cover of night. In 1918 the French organized the First Air Division (*Première division aérienne*) for large offensives, like that September's Saint Mihiel offensive. About 900 French planes, 400

American planes, and 160 British planes supported the drive led by General John Pershing. Pilots from the United States flew mostly fighters. In 1918 four American bomber squadrons organized. The pilots received bomber training in France. They flew mostly the French-made Breguet XIV on daytime missions, as the United States delivered no American-made heavy bombers to the war. Despite the French training and French equipment, American bombers suffered heavy losses due to the inexperience of young pilots in what was by then an old European war.

Flying Boats

Flying boats (with hulls) and seaplanes (with floats) patrolled and protected coasts, ports, and convoys at sea. They scouted for submarines and sometimes attacked and destroyed them. They dropped bombs and torpedoes, and they detected floating mines.

Several nations contributed to the wartime development of flying boat and seaplane technology. France, in particular, developed the Maritime Aeronautical Service. This naval force expanded its flying boat and seaplane fleet from 8 planes at the start of the war in 1914 to over 1,200 at the time of the Armistice in 1918. French flying boats and seaplanes were assigned to duty along France's Atlantic and Mediterranean coasts as well as along French Africa shores. The French flying boats — F.B.A. (Franco-British Aviation), Donnet, Lévy-Besson, Coutant, and Tellier types — were biplanes used mostly for bombing. The floatplanes were used for pursuit. France also deployed an aircraft carrier — the *Caminas*. Planes landed on water, cranes lifted the planes onto the deck, and the planes catapulted off the carrier. The French Navy operated three flight training schools during the war — Berre, Hourtin, and Saint Raphaël — as well as schools for ground personnel. (Figure 4-21)

Figure 4-21. Britain and Germany also produced both seaplanes and flying boats. For example, the Short 184 seaplane (upper left) was a prototype seaplane being tested by the British before it was put into service. Approximately 900 were produced with 300 still in service at the end of the war. The Felixtowe F.5 flying boat (lower left) was a British antisubmarine patrol bomber. The Zeppelin-Staaken Type L (upper right) was a German naval version of the Fliegertruppen (German Air Service) land based bomber, the R.VI. The seaplane version had 2 large pontoon floats that replaced the 16 wheels. The Hansa-Brandenburg W.33 (W represents *Wasser* or Water), in the lower right, was a monoplane version of the H.B. W.19 biplane.

Radio usage increased in naval aviation during World War I. In one successful combat action, a seaplane on patrol flew over a submerged German submarine. The aviation officer spotted the submarine. He sent a radio message to a nearby destroyer and fleet of trawlers. The seaplane then circled above the submarine until the destroyer and trawlers arrived and destroyed the submarine. (Figure 4-22)

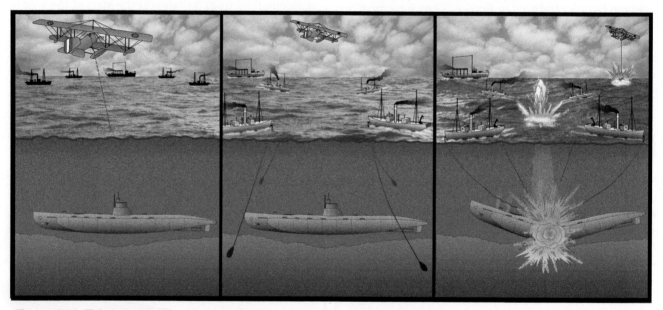

Figure 4-22. This recreation from a 1918 *Electrical Experimenter* article describes the almost uncanny, hawk-like qualities of the modern radio-equipped seaplane. An Allied seaplane spotted a German submarine (U-boot or Unterseeboot) lying on the ocean bed. The pilot radioed a fleet of trawlers to converge on its position. Under direction of the seaplane, the trawlers got out their sweeps and steamed toward each other. With the cable holding the submarine, the seaplane gave the command and the TNT was discharged, destroying the submarine. The seaplane then sped off to destroy a floating mine.

AIRCRAFT PRODUCTION

World War I was a grand stimulant to the aviation industry. It created a demand for aircraft that far exceeded the prewar capacity of the industry, and also exceeded the industry's wartime production. Government contracts subsidized the expansion of the industry. An order for airplanes, for example, might include funds to build a new wing on a factory so that a company could produce the necessary planes. Some governments assumed direct management of aircraft production to one degree or another, others coordinated, often with the threat of taking control if cooperation was inadequate.

The war experience with aircraft production varied among the combatant nations. France was the leading producer of aircraft before and during World War I; though in 1917-1918, British production began to rival the French, partly because the war, at least the Western Front, was being fought in France. The French government produced aviation equipment, including dirigibles and captive balloons, at its aviation center in Chalais-Meudon, and purchased equipment from domestic and foreign companies. Both France and Britain were known for multiple manufacturers, multiple designs, and a general lack of standardization early in the war. That last feature — lack of standardization — posed training, parts, and maintenance challenges.

Standardization developed as the war was fought and as the combatants selected what designs would be appropriate to their respective and changing needs. Germany investigated over 600 different models and placed 72 into production, whereas Britain tested over 300 prototypes and produced 73 models. In contrast, the French tested fewer than 300 prototypes and selected only 38 for large-volume production. When the United States belatedly entered the war, it followed the French example of standardization; standardization was already a well-established feature of the American system of manufacturing sewing machines, bicycles, and other products.

Assembly of wing structures at the Albatros factory in Germany

Fabric covering applied to Albatros wings

Females worked in the Albatros works and other wartime factories in Germany and in other nations

Installation of engines at the Albatros factory

Final assembly of Albatros military planes

Albatros biplanes assembled and ready for delivery

Historic Event

In October 1917 the German company Junkers formed as a cooperative venture with airplane maker Fokker. At the time Junkers made diesel engines and designed airplanes. The formal name of the new company was Junkers-Fokker Werke, *werke* meaning works or factory. Junkers-Fokker advertised "metal aeroplane building." The metal was duraluminum — a strong, hard, lightweight, workable alloy of aluminum. Earlier that year Junkers produced an all-metal, low-cost reconnaissance biplane and an experimental monoplane, low-wing fighter, also all metal. Still earlier, in 1910, Hugo Junkers (1859-1935) had patented the thick-section cantilever wing.

The final production figures reveal the results. France produced 51,700 airplanes and 92,386 airplane engines during the 1914–1918 period. In comparison, Great Britain produced 55,092 airplanes and 41,034 airplane engines during the same period. The United States produced fewer than 20,000 airplanes — and delivered fewer than 2,000 — during the war. It managed to produce nearly 30,000 airplane engines, but too late in the war.

Germany was a large producer of aircraft but, as the war continued year after year, production lagged. By 1916 shortages of coal, skilled workers, and supplies hampered production; the war of course limited Germany's access to imported goods from the Allied nations. Nonetheless, the German aircraft industry employed approximately 35,000 people late in the war.

The war disrupted production as well as stimulated production through large military orders; for example, until the war broke out, Britain purchased all its aircraft magnetos from Germany, and Germany imported many raw materials from countries it would fight in the war. Moreover, the initial presumptions that the war would be short, maybe six to eight weeks in duration, delayed decisions necessary for a long-term build-up of the military air forces and the industrial bases that supplied such forces.

British Production

The United Kingdom produced over 55,000 aircraft during World War I and developed a vast industry of aircraft, engine, armament, and instrument makers. The British government's Royal Aircraft Factory, formerly the Royal Balloon Factory, in Farnborough, manufactured equipment. The military branches purchased equipment from companies too. The aviation industry was a competitive system when the war began, but as the war created demand far beyond existing production capabilities, the competitive system broke down. Government interference increased, to protect the government and public from profiteering, but also to ensure adequate production for the wartime emergency. Government interference took several forms: rationing to get raw supplies to manufacturers, price fixing, control of distribution — notably of steel, and control of the labor pool to get skilled workers where the skills were needed most and to prevent labor slowdowns or stoppages. The British government was slow to enact some of these measures; for example, it waited until 1917 to create an Air Board for coordinating aircraft supplies.

An amazing feature of British aircraft production was the number and variety of producers from the government's own shop in Farnborough to the many manufacturing firms. The Aircraft Manufacturing Company (later called Airco), a maker of Henry and Maurice Farman types before the war, produced de Havilland biplanes throughout the war, including the famous D.H.4 adopted as a model for United States production. (Figure 4-23) Builders such as Armstrong-Whitworth, Austin Motors, Avro, B.A.T. (British Aerial Transport), Beardmore, Blackburn, Blériot & Spad Aircraft Company, Boulton & Paul, Bristol, British Caudron, and others made airplanes of all sorts of designs, sizes, and specifications.

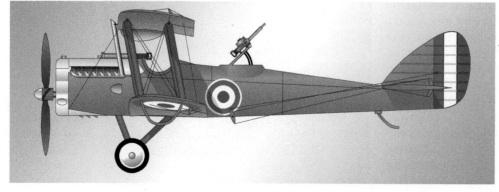

Figure 4-23. One of the most famous British World War I designs was the de Havilland D.H.4, which was later adopted by the United States.

Personal Profile

Geoffrey de Havilland (1882-1965) graduated from the Crystal Palace Engineering School in England. He worked briefly in the automobile industry. In 1908 and 1909 he built both a biplane and a motor for the aircraft. A few hops and a crash later, de Havilland began construction of his second airplane. This aircraft proved flyable. The government Balloon Factory in Farnborough gave him a job as an airplane designer and test pilot; the factory had expanded its production beyond balloons. He designed a variety of airplanes for Airco starting in 1914, including the famous D.H.4 that came out during the war. He founded his own company after the war in 1920, and that de Havilland company merged into the Hawker Siddeley Group in 1966.

Geoffrey de Havilland

Sopwith is an example of one British manufacturer. When the war began, Sopwith was the foremost airplane manufacturer in Great Britain. Thomas Octave Murdock Sopwith founded the company in 1911. He held British Aviator's Certificate No. 31, and he won the 1914 Schneider Cup race in a Gnôme-powered Tabloid airplane on two pontoons. The wartime focus of the company was production. It designed and manufactured fighter planes heavily used by the British Royal Flying Corps. The Type 9700 or 1 1/2 Strutter got its name from the W-shaped struts that connected the wings of this biplane. Sopwith also produced the lightweight Pup, known for its high altitude flying and ability to attack enemy aircraft from above. (Figure 4-24)

The company built almost 150 Triplanes, called Tripe or Tripehound, that were used by Canadian military pilots as well as British and French pilots. The three staggered wings provided exceptional maneuverability, and Germany copied the feature into the Fokker triplane. Sopwith's last wartime product was the best: the Camel. This single-seat biplane had a rotary engine and 2 machine guns under the cowling which gave the cowling a Camel's hump. It was an agile fighter developed for high performance and maneuverability. It required skilled pilots; many military Camels went down because pilots lacked the necessary skill to control the plane. Sopwith built 5,000 Camels.

Regarding Fokker airplanes dominating the skies in late 1915, a British officer explained that the problem was production:

"... in aviation during the war everything was a compromise between progress and supply. As it took more than nine months for anything new in the shape of a machine or an engine to be available in any quantity, it generally happened that by the time a machine or an engine or the spare parts of both were available in sufficient quantities, the engine or machine or spare parts in question by that time were out of date."

Both Britain and the United States vastly expanded their manufacturing efforts in 1917. The British expansion was to meet Allied needs, which were compounded by French retreats on the front that affected French production capabilities. The United States expanded because it had finally joined the Allies in war against the Central Powers.

Figure 4-24. The Sopwith "1 1/2 Strutter" (left) was named for the extended fuselage-to-wing strut arrangement that forms a "W." The Sopwith 9901 "Pup" (right) got its name from the similarities it bore with the larger 1 1/2 Strutter.

United States Production

The United States waited until it joined the war in 1917 before developing production capabilities, though individual companies had won large European orders and expanded their operations independent of the government. Those contracts actually blocked the companies from accepting some orders from their own government. American companies supplied more than aircraft; for example, France and Britain used American machinery and agricultural equipment to make airfields.

The country's belated entry to the war prompted the government to forge cooperation among companies that had been engaged in patent litigation and competition for almost a decade. The result was the formation of the Manufacturers Aircraft Association, a patent pool wherein companies cross-licensed their inventions for a fee; the greater the number or the more important the invention, the larger the fee. The largest fees were two million dollars that went to the Wright and Curtiss companies. World War I thus effectively ended the patent wars. Both the British and American governments bought manufacturing rights from Wright *and* Curtiss in order to facilitate war production.

Airplanes Made in the USA

When the United States entered World War I, the Navy established a Naval Aircraft Factory at the Philadelphia Naval Yard for both the development and production of naval aircraft. The first airplane the Navy designed and built was the N-1 Davis Gun Carrier in 1918. During World War I the Naval Aircraft Factory built four Davis Gun Carriers. The Navy produced mostly Curtiss Flying Boats: 137 H-16s, plus 17 sets of H-16 spare parts. Also, the Navy built 31 F-5-L flying boats, plus 8 sets of F-5-L spares. The F-5-L was a derivative of the H-16; the F referred to the British naval air station at Felixstowe. It was a new and improved flying boat. (Figure 4-25)

The production of naval aircraft at the Naval Aircraft Factory and by the Curtiss Aeroplane Company remained separate from the larger production program for military landplanes and free of the scandal that engulfed that aircraft production program.

When the United States entered the war, the government made the decision to concentrate production on one airplane for the Army — the most efficient foreign plane then in service. The War Department sent the Bolling Commission, headed by Raynal C. Bolling of United States Steel, to Europe to inspect equipment in use in the war. The industrialists on the Bolling Commission failed to realize the strengths and weaknesses of various European designs examined. They selected the de Havilland 4, a British plane, as the model to be produced in the States. The commission selected the D.H. 4 in part because the British granted free use of its license whereas the French required royalties for any French license. By focusing on one plane, the U.S. hoped to avoid the confusion faced by the British and French, both of whom, in the opinion of the United States, were producing too many different types of planes for efficient, large-scale production. (Figure 4-26)

The aviation industry employed more than 200,000 people during peak production late in 1918. There was an east coast center and a midwest center. Most of the airplanes came out of the factories of Dayton Wright in Dayton, Ohio, Curtiss in Buffalo, New York, Fisher Body in Detroit, Michigan, and Standard Aero in New York. There were problems, beginning with delays in getting the designs, drawings, and machine

Figure 4-25. The basis for the Navy F-5-L flying boat was the Curtiss H-16 and the Felixstowe F-5, the latter a British design, and both the H-16 and F-5 were derived from earlier Curtiss and Felixstowe flying boats.

Figure 4-26. The British de Havilland D.H.4 was the model selected for United States production. The airplane in this photograph is an American D.H.4 with a Liberty engine.

Historical Note

Historical Note

The wartime Dayton-Wright Airplane Company was independent of the Wright Company and its successor Wright-Martin. Founded in 1916 by automotive engineer Charles F. Kettering, Dayton-Wright employed Orville Wright as a consulting engineer and used his name. Its purpose was to make military airplanes under government contract. During the war, Dayton-Wright produced about 3,000 de Havilland D.H.4 biplanes. The size of its government orders, given the company's total lack of experience, contributed to charges of misconduct in the wartime production program. Dayton-Wright also built about 400 standard J.1 trainers.

After the war, General Motors bought the company. In 1923 General Motors decided to leave the aviation field and dissolved Dayton-Wright. It sold its trainer designs to Ruben Fleet of the newly incorporated Consolidated Aircraft Corporation. The lineage, but not the Wright name, continued. In 1941 Consolidated merged with Vultee to form Consolidated Vultee Aircraft, better known as Convair. General Dynamics acquired Convair in 1953.

tools needed for production. One criticism was that the program was run by people without expertise or knowledge about aircraft. This was certainly the case early in the war, though a couple of reorganizations lessened the problem. The government awarded contracts to companies without experience in the aircraft industry, and the government failed to place orders with some established aviation firms. Another allegation was that the manufacturers given contracts lacked the information needed to estimate the cost of production, a part of the cost-plus-fee contracting system in use; less polite critics simply said the manufacturers inflated costs to inflate profits. Even the government's aircraft production board eventually admitted the narrow plan to adapt one European airplane to all the American requirements was folly, and ultimately abandoned the program. By then it was too late for the change in policy to impact the war.

Despite the United States wartime effort, it was French arms manufacturers who supplied not only the French armies, but also the American Expeditionary Force in Europe. Most of the artillery pieces and tanks used by the Americans were made in France. Of the 43 American squadrons in France on Armistice Day, only 10 used American-made planes. American pilots were still assigned to French and Italian units and they flew the equipment of those units. France, in fact, supplied the United States with over 2,500 airplanes, while the United States shipped less than 1,400 airplanes to Europe.

The highlight of the American production program was Curtiss. This New York company produced seaplanes for the Allies and for the United States Navy, seaplanes that saw action in Europe from 1914 onward. Curtiss also manufactured the JN-4 Jenny, a trainer widely used in the United States. Under United States government contracts, Curtiss produced 5,221 airplanes, about a third of all airplanes delivered to the government during the war. Curtiss also made about 5,000 airplane motors.

Historical Note

One criticism of the wartime airplane production of the D.H.4 is that the selected airplane later earned the nickname Flaming Coffin. Burning planes were not new to the war. Two monoplanes, for example, caught fire and fell during the 1911 race from Paris to London. Sticks, cloth, and glue burned easily, and gasoline motors ignited fires, which usually started in the carburetor. Fires prompted efforts to move the gasoline tank behind the pilot and away from the tractor engine, and to use metals in the construction of airplanes.

Historical Note

The Curtiss JN-4 trainer was a tractor airplane. The engine was up front, from where it could not fall on the student pilot in the event of a crash since planes tended to crash nose first. Crashes were a normal part of pilot training at that time.

Spruce Production

The aircraft production program needed spruce for propellers and much more. Spruce was valued for its lightness and its strength. It was essential for the construction of the framework of the planes. A single D.H.4, for example, required 1,600 feet of rough lumber for 400 feet of finished spruce (351 actual board feet). Similarly, a JN 4D required 1,200 feet of rough lumber and 262 feet of actual footage, and the Bristol USB-1 (planned American version of the F.2 fighter) required 1,500 feet rough lumber and 330 feet actual footage.

Figure 4-27. Spruce was a key product in the development and production of airplanes during World War I. The "Spruce Squadron" were soldiers, loggers, and lumbermen in the American Northwest who kept the Allied forces supplied with airplane lumber.

The Pacific Northwest was the principal source of spruce, but the mills in the Northwest were not equipped to cut the straight-grain timber required for aircraft production. Also, the main spruce area was in Clark County, Washington, and it was almost inaccessible. Furthermore, a strike involving the Industrial Workers of the World union — the Wobblies — almost halted production. Despite experiments with plywood and alloys, the Allied governments relied heavily upon spruce throughout the war.

Allied buyers (United States, United Kingdom, France, and Italy). The result was a supply of spruce adequate to meet domestic wartime needs and to ship 120 million board feet to our Allies. (Figure 4-27)

Liberty Engine

For World War I the United States initially wanted one engine, like one plane. The government looked into selecting a foreign engine, but the foreign engines were basically handmade and therefore not adaptable to American machine tool production. The United States decided to produce an all-American engine that would lend itself to quantity production and that would have higher horsepower than other engines; this despite the fact numerous aircraft motor companies had experience making motors under contract and sometimes under license for the Allies. The Wright-Martin Company, for example, built the Hispano-Suiza engine for the French government. While the United States was designing its Liberty engine in May 1917, England was manufacturing or experimenting with 37 different kinds of airplane engines; France with 46; and Germany was producing five different engines. The United States had access to British and French designs and performance figures in hand, and information on captured German engines, while designing the "all-American engine."

Once the design was completed, the Liberty engine was submitted to American aircraft engine makers to check the design, and to machine tool makers who would produce the nearly 3,000 machine tools

Historical Note

While the use of metals in airplane construction increased during World War I, many airplanes used extensive amounts of spruce. Some of the spruce parts were:

- fuselage — struts, blocks, tail skids, posts, shafts, sticks, braces, plugs, pilot's seat

- wings and wing post — spars, beams, ribs, supports, aileron, posts, block reinforcements, braces, cap strips, bracing, stiffener, struts

- engine section panels — stringer, spar, rib, strip, trailing

- horizontal stabilizer, vertical stabilizer, and elevators

In response to the wartime emergency, the U.S. Army established the Spruce Production Division of the Signal Corps and imposed a military-style order on the program. Headquartered in Portland, Oregon, the Spruce Production Division mobilized 25,000 soldiers and sent them to the Northwest forests and mills. It recruited 75,000 men for the Loyal Legion of Loggers and Lumbermen, whose slogan was "No strikes, fair wages, meet the country's needs in spruce at any cost." It standardized specifications of the four needed to build the engine. The design was also submitted to automobile manufacturers because the engine "must be a producer's engine" and the American auto companies were the world's leading producers. Left out were the thirty or so aircraft motor makers in the country.

The first trial Liberty engine was completed by July 4th, 1917, and that date was heralded as the day American aviation became free of the dependence upon foreign engines — Liberty Day and thus the name Liberty engine.

Automobile companies — Ford, Packard, Pierce Arrow, Duesenberg, and others — had made auto engines before the war and during the war joined in aircraft engine production (as auto companies would again do during World War II). By Armistice Day, the United States had produced 24,478 Liberty engines in 23 engine plants. Six thousand Liberty engines had gone to the American Expeditionary Force in France, others to the U.S. Navy, to the Allies, and for use on training planes. The Liberty engine did not "win" the war. It arrived too late to play a significant role in the war.

ARMISTICE AND PEACE

Armistice Day — Paris 1918.

An **armistice** is an agreement to stop fighting. The First World War fighting ended with a series of these agreements. The first concerned Germany's Eastern Front with Russia, where Germany and Russia on 8 November 1917 agreed to stop fighting. The subsequent Treaty of Brest-Litovsk of March 1918 listed the terms of peace. Another armistice quieted the Bulgarian/Macedonian line on 29 September 1918. An Ottoman armistice was agreed to at Mudras, on the island of Lemnos, on 30 October 1918. Austria-Hungary ceased fighting on 3 November 1918, and the last of the Central Powers still in the conflict — Germany — agreed to an armistice on 11 November 1918. Thus the war as an armed conflict ended 11 November 1918. Since an armistice is preliminary to peace, more negotiations were to follow, these were peace negotiations.

As soon as the fighting ceased and armistice agreements promised no more fighting, the need for war supplies of all types disappeared. The various governments canceled existing and pending orders because they did not want to pay for the undelivered portions of the contracts, particularly not at the high prices wartime shortages support. Companies and governments negotiated settlements of these unfinished contracts. Workers were laid off, factories closed, and some companies went out of business. Some reorganized; for example, wartime airplane manufacturer Wright-Martin reorganized into post-war airplane engine producer Wright Aeronautical. Companies and governments began the process of liquidating unneeded assets, everything from excessive production capacity (excessive for peacetime needs) to war surplus equipment. In most countries, the end of the war also brought government and public investigations of military procurement in general, and in the United States aviation procurement in particular.

Treaty of Versailles

Just as there were several armistice agreements to end fighting, there were multiple treaties ending the war. These treaties emerged from peace conferences and defined the terms of peace. The major conference was the Paris Peace Conference at Versailles in 1919-1920. There the nations negotiated peace treaties. The Big Four nations, which had done most of the Allied fighting, sent their representatives: France — Georges Clemenceau, United States — Woodrow Wilson, Italy — Vittorio Orlando, and Britain — David Lloyd George; Russia did not attend since it had turned from World War to revolution and civil war at home. (Figure 4-28)

Figure 4-28. Vittorio Orlando, Lloyd George, Georges Clemenceau and President Woodrow Wilson at the Paris Peace Conference in 1919.

Historical Note

The Wright patents finally proved useful to American aviation in 1919, when the American aviation industry used the patents to stop the importation of surplus British military aircraft. The United States had sufficient American-made war-surplus equipment to stifle its industry for years.

Historical Note

The Treaty of Versailles contained a controversial "war-guilt" clause, actually it was an article — Article 231 — which stated:

"The Allied and Associated Governments affirm and Germany accepts the responsibility of Germany and her Allies for causing all the loss and damage to which the Allied and Associated Governments and their nationals have been subjected as a consequence of the war imposed upon them by the aggression of Germany and her allies."

Germans called this the *Schuldartikel* (article on guilt) or *Schuldspruch* (guilt sentence). It became a point of honor for Germans who denied sole responsibility for causing the war. This provision also became part of the peace treaties with Austria and Hungary. It provided the justification for the defeated nations to pay reparations. German Chancellor and Führer Adolph Hitler repudiated Article 231 in 1937.

The Paris Peace Conference established a League of Nations, forerunner of the United Nations. The participating nations agreed to the mandate form of international trusteeship to administer former German colonies and Ottoman provinces. The conference also negotiated specific peace treaties and recognized treaties already negotiated: Treaty of Versailles with Germany, June 1919; Treaty of St-Germain with Austria, September 1919; Treaty of Neuilly with Bulgaria in November 1919; Treaty of Trianon with Hungary, June 1920; and the Treaties of Sèvres and Lausanne with the Ottoman Empire, 1920 and 1923. The Treaty of Versailles was the first of these to be signed, the first to come into force, and the first in importance.

Formally known as the Treaty of Peace between the Allied and Associated Powers and Germany, the Treaty of Versailles contained fifteen parts defining the terms of peace. Imposed upon Germany by the victors, it required that Germany accept responsibility for provoking the war. This war guilt clause was a source of public humiliation for Germans, and many German people did not believe that Germany was guilty of anything more than protecting its national interests against nations which would infringe upon those interests.

Through various parts of the treaty, Germany lost land, colonies, money, rights, and freedoms. For example, it *gave* — as in returned — Alsace and Lorraine to France, which had bore the brunt of the war for four long years. In all, Germany lost about 25,000 square miles in total area plus all its colonies in Africa and in the Pacific. In Part V, the treaty addressed military, naval, and air matters. These clauses required reductions of men, supplies, ships, and aircraft, and set maximum size restrictions on Germany's post-war military forces and equipment. The treaty also prohibited conscription and specified all-volunteer forces. Through the treaty, the victorious nations tried to remove Germany's capability of making war and to prevent a post-war arms race.

The Treaty of Versailles required Germany to pay reparations, the exact amount to be determined later by a Reparations Commission. Reparations are compensation of damage done in the war — that is, restitution — paid by the defeated. After World War I the international Reparations Commission decided that Germany owed 132,000 marks as its share of the war costs. The reparations that went to the victors were based upon wartime losses. France received half the sums collected from Germany. Reparations also went to Great Britain, Italy, and Belgium, and small percentages to British Commonwealth countries, Japan, Portugal, and Balkan states. Reparations contributed to the economic depression that hit Germany after the war and thereby restricted the government's ability to participate in civil and commercial aviation, but the Treaty of Versailles more directly restricted post-war German aviation.

The Air Clauses

The air clauses were among the harshest terms of the treaty. Germany was prohibited from having any naval or military air force of any kind. The air clauses were explicit and restrictive.

Under these terms, Germany turned over to the Inter-Allied Commissions of Control over 15,000 pursuit and bombing planes and over 2,500 airplane motors. Most of the materiel covered in Article 202 went to the victors — approximately 30% to France, 30% to

Great Britain, 15% to the United States, 15% to Italy, 5% to Belgium, and 5% to Japan. German aeronautical materiel sold by the Allied and Associated Powers was not credited to Germany's reparation account, though that was standard practice for non-aeronautical material.

PART V. SECTION III.—AIR CLAUSES

ARTICLE 198.

The armed forces of Germany must not include any military or naval air forces.

Germany may, during a period not extending beyond October 1, 1919, maintain a maximum number of one hundred seaplanes or flying boats, which shall be exclusively employed in searching for submarine mines, shall be furnished with the necessary equipment for this purpose, and shall in no case carry arms, munitions or bombs of any nature whatever.

In addition to the engines installed in the seaplanes or flying boats above mentioned, one spare engine may be provided for each engine of each of these craft.

No dirigible shall be kept.

ARTICLE 199.

Within two months from the coming into force of the present Treaty the personnel of air forces on the rolls of the German land and sea forces shall be demobilised. Up to October 1, 1919, however, Germany may keep and maintain a total number of one thousand men, including officers, for the whole of the cadres and personnel, flying and non-flying, of all formations and establishments.

ARTICLE 200.

Until the complete evacuation of German territory by the Allied and Associated troops, the aircraft of the Allied and Associated Powers shall enjoy in Germany freedom of passage through the air, freedom of transit and of landing.

ARTICLE 201.

During the six months following the coming into force of the present Treaty, the manufacture and importation of aircraft, parts of aircraft, engines for aircraft, and parts of engines for aircraft, shall be forbidden in all German territory.

ARTICLE 202.

On the coming into force of the present Treaty, all military and naval aeronautical material, except the machines mentioned in the second and third paragraphs of Article 198, must be delivered to the Governments of the Principal Allied and Associated Powers.

Delivery must be effected at such places as the said Governments may select, and must be completed within three months.

In particular, this material will include all items under the following heads which are or have been in use or were designed for warlike purposes:

Complete aeroplanes and seaplanes, as well as those being manufactured, repaired or assembled.

Dirigibles able to take the air, being manufactured, repaired or assembled.

Plant for the manufacture of hydrogen.

Dirigible sheds and shelters of every kind for aircraft.

Pending their delivery, dirigibles will, at the expense of Germany, be maintained inflated with hydrogen; the plant for the manufacture of hydrogen, as well as the sheds for dirigibles, may, at the discretion of the said Powers, be left to Germany until the time when the dirigibles are handed over.

Engines for aircraft.

Nacelles and fuselages.

Armament (guns, machine guns, light machine guns, bomb-dropping apparatus, torpedo-dropping apparatus, synchronization apparatus, aiming apparatus).

Munitions (cartridges, shells, bombs loaded or unloaded, stocks of explosives or of material for their manufacture).

Instruments for use on aircraft.

Wireless apparatus and photographic or cinematograph apparatus for use on aircraft.

Component parts of any of the items under the preceding heads.

The material referred to above shall not be removed without special permission from the said

9. What restrictions did the Treaty of Versailles place on German aviation?

10. Which source or sources listed in the bibliography would you read for a first-hand or eye-witness account of wartime aviation?

Bibliography

Aviation Issue. *National Geographic Magazine*, 33/1 (January 1918): Major Joseph Tulasne, "America's Part in the Allies' Mastery of the Air"; Captain Jacques De Sieyes, "Aces of the Air"; Captain Andrè de Berroeta, "Flying in France"; Major William A. Bishop, "Tales of the British Air Service"; General P. Tozzi, "Italy's Eagles of Combat and Defense"; Lieutenant Colonel Hiram Bingham, "Building America's Air Army"; Stuart Walcott, "The Life Story of an American Airman in France"; Rear Admiral Robert E. Peary, "The Future of the Airplane"; and "Germany's Air Program."

Christienne, Charles and Pierre Lissarague. *A History of French Military Aviation*. Translated by Francis Klanka. French edition, 1980; Washington: Smithsonian Institution Press, 1986.

Finne, K.N. *Igor Sikorsky, the Russian Years*. Edited by Carl J. Bobrow and Von Hardesty. Translated by Von Hardsety. Russian edition, 1930; Washington: Smithsonian Institution Press, 1987.

Fritzsche, Peter. *A Nation of Fliers, German Aviation and the Popular Imagination*. Cambridge, MA: Harvard University Press, 1992.

Hallion, Richard P. *Rise of the Fighter Aircraft, 1914-1918*. Baltimore: Nautical & Aviation Publishing, 1984.

Jane's Fighting Aircraft of World War I. 1919; revised edition, London: Studio Editions, 1990.

Kennett, Lee. *The First Air War, 1914-1918*. New York: Free Press, 1991.

Richthofen, Manfred von. *The Red Baron*. Translated by Peter Kilduff. Edited by Stanley M. Ulanoff. Garden City, NY: Doubleday, 1969.

Robinson, Douglas. *The Zeppelin in Combat, a History of the German Naval Airship Division, 1912-1918*. 1962; Atglen, PA: Schiffer Publishing, 1994.

Sloan, James J. *Wings of Honor: American Airmen in World War I, a Compilation of All United States Pilots, Observers, Gunners and Mechanics Who Flew against the Enemy in the War of 1914-1918*. Atglen, PA: Schiffer Military/Aviation History, 1994.

Timeline

Light blue type indicates an event not directly related to aviation

1914	August 3. A German Taube monoplane dropped three bombs on Lunéville, France, in the earliest known bombing of the war.
1914	August 6. The German airship Z 6 bombed Liège, Belgium. This is the earliest documented use of an airship as a bomber during the war.
1914	August 26. An unarmed Morane Type Monoplane flown by P.N. Nesterov of Imperial Russian Army rammed an Austrian plane midair, because the Austrian plane was attacking the Sholkiv airfield where Nesterov was based; both pilots died.
1914	October 5. The crew of a French two-seat Voisin shot down a German two-seat Aviatik in air-to-air combat, perhaps the first successful victory of one airplane over another in battle.

1914	The Panama Canal opened providing a sea route through the Isthmus of Panama and linking the Atlantic and Pacific oceans.
1914	Biochemist Edward Kendall of the Mayo Clinic in Minneapolis isolated the thyroid hormone thyroxin.
1914	At Prestwick, Harry Vardon won his sixth British Open Golf tournament.
1915	January 19. German airships raided England for the first time. The naval airships L 3 and L 4 dropped bombs on Yarmouth.
1915	February 15. The Russian bomber Il'ya Mourometz, designed by Igor Sikorsky, flew its first bombing mission.
1915	April. French pilot Roland Garros in a Morane Type L airplane equipped with a machine gun and deflector plates on the propeller blades shot down five German airplanes and thereby became the first ace of the war.
1915	August 1. German pilot Max Immelmann flying a Fokker E.1 Eindecker monoplane with a synchronized, forward-firing machine gun scored the first confirmed victory by an Eindecker, soon to be known as the Fokker Scourge; he shot down a British B.E.2 that was over Germany on a bombing raid.
1915	December. Hugo Junkers' all-metal J1 monoplane flew for the first time; it had the thick-section cantilever wing that Junkers had patented in 1910.
1915	The first direct transatlantic radio-telephone transmission relayed speech from Canada to Paris.
1915	P. Langevin of France invented the <u>so</u>und <u>n</u>avigation <u>a</u>nd <u>r</u>anging (SONAR) system, to enable ships to detect icebergs and submarines.
1915	Construction of Europe's largest railway station is completed at Leipzig.
1915	Author Somerset Maugham published his novel *Of Human Bondage*.
1916	June 29. The first airplane built by William Boeing of Seattle, partner in the firm B & W, flew powered by a Hall-Scott engine.
1916	September 2. A British Royal Flying Corps pilot named William Leefe Robinson shot down a German Schütte-Lanz airship, the first airship shot down during the war.
1916	September. The French single-seat Spad VII fighter planes flew into service with Allied air forces.
1916	Frederick A. Kolster developed a radio direction finder for marine navigation; thereafter, ships could take bearings off radio beacons installed along coastlines.
1916	Canadian Peter Nissen invented the bow-shaped Nissen hut, used by the Allies as temporary shelter for troops.
1916	The Congress of the United States established the National Parks Service.
1916	Artist Claude Monet painted his *Water Lilies* murals at the Musée d'orangierie in Paris.
1917	February. The Junkers J4 made its first flight. This all-metal airplane had corrugated duraluminum skin. That summer it went into production as the JI, and 227 were built.

1917   April 5-6. Squadron No. 100 of the British Royal Flying Corps made its first raid; it bombed the Douai airfield at night. This squadron was formed specifically for night bombing, and it used F.E.1b and B.E.2e biplanes for that purpose.

1917   May 25. Germany made its first airplane mass bombing raid on England. Twenty-one Gotha bombers killed 95 people and injured 260.

1917   The trans-Australian railway was completed providing an east-west link in that country.

1917   The new Bowtree Automatic Pantograph introduced photocomposing, printing by photography.

1917   Bolsheviks seized power in Russia and confiscated property of the wealthy, of the royal family, and of the church.

1918   April 21. Canadian pilot Roy Brown in a Sopwith Camel and Australian anti-aircraft fire brought down the famous German ace, the Red Baron, Manfred von Richthofen, who died.

1918   October 14. A large Handley Page bomber flown by the British Independent Air Force dropped the largest bomb of the war — the Block Buster — on Berlin; the bomb weighed 1,650 pounds (747kg).

1918   November 6. At the Aberdeen, Maryland, army proving ground, Robert H. Goddard demonstrated rockets by launching a solid-propellant rocket that he designed as an artillery weapon.

1918   German scientist W. Schottke identified the cause of interference on a line as random fluctuations in the power of the electrical current.

1918   The Dutch Shell Oil Company began using diamond cutting edges on drills.

1918   The "Spanish" flu epidemic began killing large numbers of people, especially in Europe, the United States, and India.

1919   February 21. The Thomas Morse MB-3 biplane made its first flight; this became the first American-designed fighter to enter large-scale production.

1919   June 14. A prototype Nieuport-Delage 29 fighter reached an altitude of 9,100m (29,856 feet); the French biplane then went into production.

1919   The Radio Corporation of America was organized.

1919   The straight-eight-cylinder engine went into a production car, the Italian Isotta-Fraschini Tipo 8.

1919   The United States adopted prohibition of alcoholic beverages by ratifying the 18th amendment to the Constitution of the United States — effective in January 1920.

CHAPTER 5

PEACETIME AVIATION (1919-1927)

AVIATION HISTORY

Summary of Events

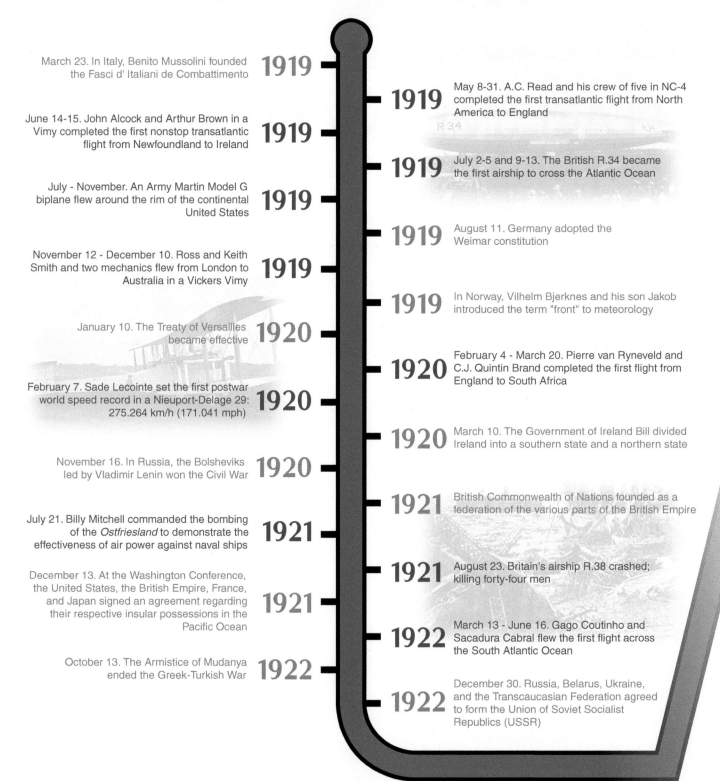

March 23. In Italy, Benito Mussolini founded the Fasci d' Italiani de Combattimento

1919

1919 May 8-31. A.C. Read and his crew of five in NC-4 completed the first transatlantic flight from North America to England

June 14-15. John Alcock and Arthur Brown in a Vimy completed the first nonstop transatlantic flight from Newfoundland to Ireland

1919

1919 July 2-5 and 9-13. The British R.34 became the first airship to cross the Atlantic Ocean

July - November. An Army Martin Model G biplane flew around the rim of the continental United States

1919

1919 August 11. Germany adopted the Weimar constitution

November 12 - December 10. Ross and Keith Smith and two mechanics flew from London to Australia in a Vickers Vimy

1919

1919 In Norway, Vilhelm Bjerknes and his son Jakob introduced the term "front" to meteorology

January 10. The Treaty of Versailles became effective

1920

1920 February 4 - March 20. Pierre van Ryneveld and C.J. Quintin Brand completed the first flight from England to South Africa

February 7. Sade Lecointe set the first postwar world speed record in a Nieuport-Delage 29: 275.264 km/h (171.041 mph)

1920

1920 March 10. The Government of Ireland Bill divided Ireland into a southern state and a northern state

November 16. In Russia, the Bolsheviks led by Vladimir Lenin won the Civil War

1920

1921 British Commonwealth of Nations founded as a federation of the various parts of the British Empire

July 21. Billy Mitchell commanded the bombing of the *Ostfriesland* to demonstrate the effectiveness of air power against naval ships

1921

1921 August 23. Britain's airship R.38 crashed; killing forty-four men

December 13. At the Washington Conference, the United States, the British Empire, France, and Japan signed an agreement regarding their respective insular possessions in the Pacific Ocean

1921

1922 March 13 - June 16. Gago Coutinho and Sacadura Cabral flew the first flight across the South Atlantic Ocean

October 13. The Armistice of Mudanya ended the Greek-Turkish War

1922

1922 December 30. Russia, Belarus, Ukraine, and the Transcaucasian Federation agreed to form the Union of Soviet Socialist Republics (USSR)

Light blue type represents events that are not directly related to aviation.

1923 January. French and Belgian forces occupied the Ruhr region because Germany failed to make reparation payments

1923 January 9. Juan de la Cierva made the first official flight of his first successful autogyro, the C.4

1923 May 2-3. Oakley G. Kelly and John A. Macready made the first nonstop transcontinental flight in the United States

1923 June 17. The United States Army refueled a de Havilland DH-4B light bomber in flight

1923 September 1. An earthquake destroyed Yokohama and most of Tokyo, Japan

1924 January 21. Soviet Leader Vladimir Ilich Lenin died, and Josef Stalin succeeded him as chairman of the Politburo

1924 Summer. At the eighth Olympic Games, held in Paris, Finnish runner Paavo Nurmi won a record five gold medals

1924 September 28. The first round-the-world flight in history was completed

1924 October 13-15. The Zeppelin *LZ 126* flew from Friedrichshafen, Germay to Lakehurst, New Jersey, where it was turned over to the United States Navy and christened the *Los Angeles (ZR-3)*

1925 January 3. Benito Mussolini became the dictator of Italy

1925 In Paris, France, the Exposition Internationale des Arts Décoratifs et Industriels Modernes introduced the world to the Art Deco design

1925 November 16 - 1926 March 13. Alan Cobham, A. Elliott, and B. Emmott flew a de Havilland DH 50 to make the first round-trip between Croydon, England, and Cape Town, South Africa

1926 May 9. Naval Lieutenant Commander Richard E. Byrd and army pilot Floyd Bennett made the first airplane flight over the North Pole

1926 May 11-14. Roald Amundsen, Lincoln Ellsworth, and Umberto Nobile made the first airship flight over the Pole

1926 September 5. Ford Motor Company introduced the eight-hour work day and the five-day work week

1926 September 8. The League of Nations admitted Germany to membership

1926 September 14. The Russian Dobrolet airline provided the first service to Kabul

1927 Helen Wills of the United States won her first ladies-singles title at Wimbledon

1927 January 7. British Imperial Airways opened its airline route to Basra, Iraq, and Cairo, Egypt

Introduction

World War I ended with the armistices of 1918 and the treaties that followed. The postwar period opened with surplus airmen and aircraft no longer needed by the air forces of the former combatants, and surplus production capacity no longer needed to supply war materiel. The airmen and equipment makers with war experience dominated postwar aviation.

Immediately after the war, military and civil aviators turned their efforts toward long-distance flight. That is the subject of Section A of this chapter, which discusses peacetime application of capabilities developed during the war. Section B covers airships, the commercial hopes for lighter-than-air airliners for long-distance routes. Section C describes barnstorming and competing in the postwar environment, including a variety of record-setting flights made using military and military surplus equipment as well as postwar products designed for the new civil market. Section D describes the emergence of commercial aviation, such as airlines and airmail services.

After studying this chapter, you will be able to identify several transatlantic fliers of 1919 and the aircraft used to cross the Atlantic Ocean. You will be able to compare airship development in Britain, France, Italy, the United States, and Germany. You will be able to explain the relationship of the airship *Shenandoah* to the court martial of Billy Mitchell. You will be able to explain the importance of gliding to German aviation in the 1920s and to discuss the relationship between military surplus equipment and barnstorming. Finally, you will be able to explain why and how airmail service began in several countries and to name major airlines and airliners of the 1920s.

Vickers Vimy

Army World Flight Crew

Shenandoah

Boeing 40A Mailplane

PEACETIME DISTANCE FLYING

Q & A

What? The transition of aviation from wartime to peacetime activities

When? 1919-1927

Where? Worldwide

Who? Airmen with wartime military experience and often with war surplus aircraft and engines

Why? To fly, to race, to develop commercial aviation, to maintain a strong defense

Three historic flights across the Atlantic Ocean in 1919 demonstrated the shift in aviation from wartime to peacetime pursuits. Those and other long-distance flights further demonstrated the capabilities of aircraft developed during the war as well as the skill and experience of pilots, navigators, and mechanics. Compared to prewar equipment, military aircraft at the end of the war were larger and stronger, engines more powerful and reliable, and instruments and radios more developed and more frequently installed in aircraft. Military aviation influenced the immediate postwar activities in civil as well as military aviation.

Navy Flight Across the Atlantic

Late in World War I, after the United States joined the Allied side in 1917, the Navy and the Curtiss Aeroplane Company designed a new military flying boat to bring the war to German submarines at sea. These were NC flying boats. The NC stood for Navy/Curtiss; the usual pronunciation was simply "Nancy." The NCs were designed to fly across the Atlantic Ocean because wartime shipping space was in short supply and the need for patrol aircraft was pressing. The aircraft were to patrol wherever submarines might be, which was another reason for long-range capability. This long-distance requirement meant a large aircraft with multiple engines and

with structural strength enough to land on rough seas. The Navy provided its new hull design, and the Curtiss Aeroplane Company drafted plans for the biplane. Like traditional Curtiss flying boats, the NC had a hull made of laminated wood veneer, but the new Navy version was shorter and came with a superstructure or boom of spruce that supported the tail surfaces. The supported tail enabled rear machine gunners to shoot straight back. The design called for a big flying boat, with the upper wing spanning 126 feet, the lower wing 96 feet, and the length measuring 68 feet. The fully loaded weight was 28,000 pounds. (Figure 5-1)

Figure 5-1. Tom Hamilton in the foreground with NC-4 on a dock near a hangar.

Curtiss built four NCs at its Garden City, Long Island, New York, plant. The Navy assembled these four at the nearby Rockaway Naval Air Station. The first one made its maiden flight in October 1918 — too late to participate in the war that ended a month later. The Navy gave the four experimental aircraft distinct designations rather than the single model designation normally used for production aircraft. NC-1 had three Liberty engines installed in the tractor mode. After the armistice, this airplane set a world's record for highest number of passengers carried; 51 people were on board a 25 November 1918 flight. Nonetheless, tests of the NC-1 showed that it was underpowered for transatlantic flight. The Navy, therefore, installed four engines on NC-2, NC-3, and NC-4, and added a fourth engine, a pusher, to the NC-1. NC-2, completed in early 1919, had its engines in two tandem pairs, one pair on each side of the fuselage; the pilot sat in a nacelle between the two engine pairs. The Navy finished assembling NC-3 in April and NC-4 on the first of May. Both NC-3 and NC-4 had three tractor engines plus one pusher engine; the pilot sat in the hull ahead of the lower wing. All the engines were Liberty 12s; that is, twelve-cylinder, 400-horsepower Liberty engines. (Figure 5-2)

Flight Lines

"I was privileged to be an observing passenger aboard the NC-1 on an eight hour non-stop proving flight. I thought it would never end. Its cruising speed was slow, 80-85 mph, and there was no shelter for a 'super cargo' like me, and it was cold and windy almost beyond endurance for so long a time. No lunch either."

Grover Loening in *Take Off into Greatness*, as quoted by Peter Allen in *The 91 before Lindbergh.*

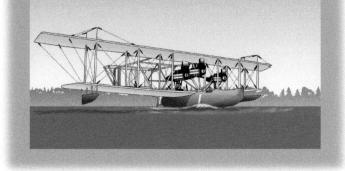

Portugal, and Great Britain for landing and passage of the aircraft. Prior to the attempted crossing, the NC-2 failed to meet the Navy's expectations because of its engine arrangement, and the NC-1 was damaged in a storm. The Navy removed the wings from NC-2 and installed them on NC-1. A fire in the hangar damaged the tail of NC-4 and a wing of NC-1. Both were repaired.

Historic Event

Between 8 May and 31 May 1919, A.C. Read and his naval crew flew the Navy-Curtiss flying boat NC-4 across the Atlantic Ocean and thereby completed the first transatlantic flight. He made the flight by hopping from stop to stop and by following a line of naval ships across the ocean.

Figure 5-2. The NC-4 flying boat during preflight check by a small crew in 1919.

With the war over, the Navy decided to fly the NCs across the Atlantic Ocean anyway, to demonstrate their capabilities and for the United States to win the honor of being the first to fly across the "pond." The Navy redesignated the four aircraft NC-TAs for Navy/Curtiss-Transatlantic, and made arrangements with the governments of Canada, Newfoundland,

The crossing consisted of stages, first to Nova Scotia, then to Newfoundland, the Azores, Portugal, and Britain. The Navy marked the route with over sixty naval ships stationed at intervals to guide the flying boats and monitor their progress. On 8 May three planes — NC-1, -3, and -4 — left Rockaway, Long Island, for the transatlantic flight. Commander John H. Towers, who held Naval Aviator Certificate No. 3, was in the flagship NC-3. He was in charge of this small NC Seaplane Division One. During the flight to Halifax, Nova Scotia, NC-4 developed engine trouble and stopped in Massachusetts for a replacement

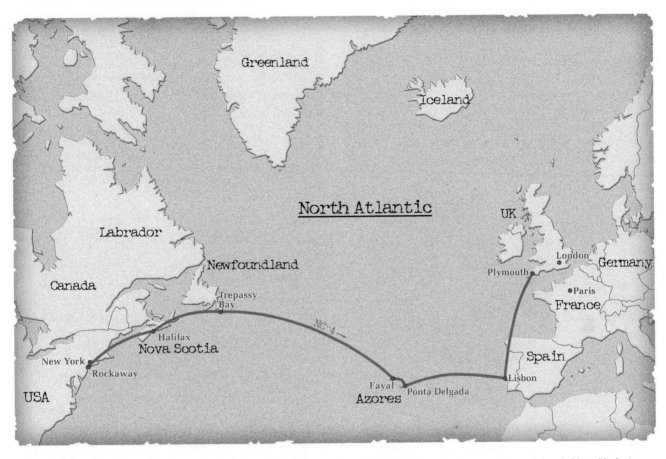

Figure 5-3. This map shows the route flown by Commander Read in NC-4 from Rockaway, Long Island, New York, to Plymouth, England.

engine. NC-1 and NC-3 continued to Trepassy Bay, Newfoundland, where NC-4 caught up to them. (Figure 5-3)

Meanwhile, the Navy launched a non-rigid dirigible from Rockaway for a transatlantic crossing just days after the three NC flying boats departed from the same air station. The dirigible, C-5, was a coastal patrol aircraft no longer needed to patrol the coasts. It was 192 feet long, held 182,000 cubic feet of gas, and it had two Union 120-horsepower engines. C-5 flew over a thousand nautical miles and reached Newfoundland ahead of NC-4. Winds there blew the dirigible from its outdoor mooring and out to sea. C-5 was lost, but its crew of six was safe in Newfoundland.

At Trepassy Bay, NC-4 got another replacement engine. On the next stage of the transatlantic flight, radio communications failed on two planes, but worked for the NC-4; this proved decisive when the planes encountered bad weather. Both NC-1 and NC-3 ditched at sea. A naval ship rescued the crew of the NC-1, which sank, and NC-3 taxied 200 miles to the Azores. NC-4 completed the flight to the Azores

and landed at the shore of Horta on the island of Fayal. NC-4 continued to Ponta Delgada in the Azores, to Lisbon, Portugal, and to Plymouth, England. (Figure 5-4)

Figure 5-4. NC-4 taxis into Lisbon harbor, 27 May 1919, following the transatlantic flight from Rockaway, Long Island.

A.C. Read was commander and navigator of NC-4. His crew consisted of two pilots, W. Hinton and E.F. Stone, the latter a Coast Guard officer. The crew also included two engineers, J.S. Breese and E.S. Rhoads,

Personal Profile

Albert Cushing Read (1887-1967) attended the Naval Academy at Annapolis, Maryland. He began his naval career with assignments on ships. In 1916 he learned to fly at the naval flight school in Pensacola, Florida. The next year he commanded a naval air station and flew anti-submarine patrols along the East Coast of the United States. He commanded the NC-4 on the historic transatlantic flight of 1919. Read rose through the naval ranks with assignments that included commanding aircraft carriers, teaching at the Naval War College, and serving in the naval Bureau of Aeronautics. He retired at the rank of an admiral.

Albert Cushing Read

Flight Lines

"As in everything else, there is no royal road to long-distance flying. Physical fitness and technical knowledge are essential, for the strain is certainly heavy both on man and machine."

Sir John Alcock writing about his 1919 flight across the Atlantic Ocean, in John Alcock and Arthur Whitten Brown, *Our Transatlantic Flight*.

Historical Note

Between 14 June and 15 June 1919 two British airmen named John Alcock, pilot, and Arthur Whitten Brown, navigator, flew a modified Vickers Vimy biplane across the Atlantic Ocean, from Newfoundland to Ireland. In so doing, they made the first nonstop transatlantic flight.

and a radio operator, H.C. Rodd. In May 1919 these six men completed the first transatlantic flight in NC-4. At the time, other airmen — mostly British and American — were preparing to fly across the Atlantic. In fact, two British attempts failed while the American fliers were enroute. The British magazine *Flight* noted at the time that the NC-4's flight was "a triumph of organisation." The British *Aeroplane* praised the American crew, the American flying boat, and American engines, and added, "But above all it was a triumph of organisation." The Navy organized and flew across the Atlantic in a professional, carefully planned, and safe manner.

Alcock-Brown Crossing

World War I had interrupted the *Daily Mail* prize competition for the first transatlantic flight. The competition resumed in 1919. Still sensitive about the war, Alfred, Lord Northcliffe, publisher of the *Daily Mail*, excluded from the competition airplanes and pilots from the countries that had fought against Britain and the Allies during the war. The prize was "to be awarded to the aviator who shall first cross the Atlantic in an aeroplane in flight from any point in the United States, Canada, or Newfoundland to any

point in Great Britain or Ireland, in 72 consecutive hours. (The flight may be made either way across the Atlantic.)"

The *Daily Mail* competition attracted eleven entries. As a government agency, the United States Navy chose not to compete for the prize. Three teams gathered at St. John's, Newfoundland, in May 1919. They had chosen St. John's as the departure point in order to take advantage of the prevailing wind. Another team never made it to Newfoundland, for they crashed their four-engine Handley Page V1500 biplane before leaving Europe. The Handley Page was a bomber, a product of the war, designed and produced for military use. The Navy's three NC flying boats were en route when the British team of H.G. Hawker and H. Mackenzie-Grieve took off in their Sopwith *Atlantic* on 18 May. The biplane was derived from the Sopwith B1 bomber, which in turn was based on the Cuckoo torpedo bomber. Hawker and

Figure 5-5. This photograph is John Alcock and Arthur Brown's Vickers Vimy prior to their transatlantic crossing on June 14 and 15, 1919.

of John Alcock and Arthur Whitten Brown flew a modified Vimy called the *Atlantic*. This Vimy was smaller than the flying boats used by the United States Navy. Its wingspan was 68 feet (versus 126 for the NCs). It had two Rolls Royce Eagle engines (instead of the NC's four). Its fully loaded capacity was 13,500 pounds (compared to 28,000). Its crew was two (rather than six). Built at the Brooklands Aerodrome, the *Atlantic* made only one test flight prior to being disassembled, crated, and shipped to Newfoundland. (Figure 5-6)

Mackenzie-Grieve made it two-thirds of the way to England before the *Atlantic* experienced radiator failure, and they ditched beside a Danish steamer. Also on 18 May, F.P. Raynham and C.W.F. Morgan tried to take off in the Martinsyde *Raymor*, but crashed during the attempt. Their small biplane was named after themselves — Raynham and Morgan. The third team's airplane had arrived in 13 crates, and mechanics spent two weeks assembling and preparing the airplane. It was a Vickers Vimy, a Vickers FB27 heavy bomber. (Figure 5-5)

The Vimy was a state-of-the-art bomber when the war ended and cut short its production run. Late in the war the British needed long-range bombers that could deliver heavy loads to Germany. That was the criteria for the Vimy design, but the aircraft appeared too late for active duty during the war. The transatlantic team

The Alcock-Brown team left Newfoundland on 14 June. Loaded with over a thousand gallons of fuel (860 imperial gallons of petrol, in British usage), the *Atlantic* barely made it off the ground. British war hero John Alcock was the pilot, and British veteran Arthur Whitten Brown was the navigator. Brown used celestial navigation; that is, he "shot" the sun or stars, depending upon time of day, with a sextant. Brown also took drift sightings to determine course variations. That meant the Vimy had to ascend above the clouds for position readings and descend below the clouds for course information repeatedly throughout the long flight. Given the heavy clouds, Alcock and Brown flew at altitudes of 100 to 11,000 feet.

They experienced mechanical problems: a broken exhaust pipe, an inoperative intercom, radio failure, one misfiring engine, iced fuel overflow gauge, and a frozen airspeed indicator. Caught in a cloud bank and unaware of the airspeed, as the "meter" was stuck at

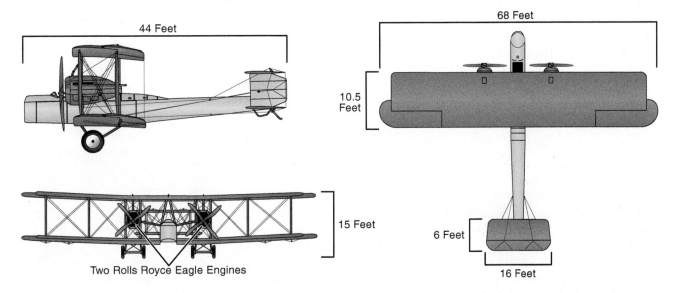

Figure 5-6. The Vimy was designed as a heavy bomber. It could carry up to four people and cruise at about 80 knots.

Flight Lines

"And then we 'stalled'. The Vickers-Vimy hung motionless for a second, while our speed dropped below the minimum necessary for heavier-than-air flight; after which it heeled over and fell into what was either a spinning nose-dive or a very deep spiral.

"The compass needle continued to revolve rapidly, showing that the machine was swinging as it dropped; but, still, hemmed in as we were by the thick vapour, we could not tell how or in which direction we were spinning. Before Alcock could reduce the throttle, the roar of the engines had almost doubled in volume, and instead of the usual 1,650 to 1,700 revolutions, they were running at about 2,200 per minute. The pilot throttled down, and the vibration ceased.

"Apart from the changing levels marked by the aneroid, only the fact that our bodies were pressed tightly against the seats indicated that we were falling. How and at what angle we were falling, we knew not. Alcock tried to centralise the controls, but failed because we had lost all sense of what was central. I searched in every direction for an external sign, and saw nothing but opaque nebulousness."

Sir Arthur Whitten Brown describing the stall and spin over the Atlantic Ocean, in John Alcock and Arthur Whitten Brown, *Our Transatlantic Flight*.

ninety knots, Alcock once stalled the plane, but he recovered from the resulting spin.

Alcock and Brown landed in the Galway region of Ireland, 16 hours 27 minutes and 1,980 miles (3,186km) from their starting point. They thus completed the first nonstop transatlantic flight, and they won the *Daily Mail* prize; King George V knighted both of them. *Flight* magazine commended the "British aviators, flying a British machine which is British in design and construction down to the last detail — not forgetting the engine." Aviation remained a nationalistic symbol, and the *Atlantic* went to the London Science Museum for preservation. (Figure 5-7)

In competing for a prize that had been suspended during the war, Alcock and Brown demonstrated the return to peacetime pursuits in aviation. Their military

Figure 5-7. The Alcock and Brown memorial commemorates the first non-stop transatlantic west-east flight by John Alcock and Arthur Whitten-Brown. They crash landed in Derrygimlagh Bog below the memorial on June 15th 1919 after a flight of 16 hours and 27 minutes from Newfoundland.

Flight Lines

"We have had a terrible journey.

"The wonder is we are here at all. We scarcely saw the sun or the moon or the stars. For hours we saw none of them. The fog was very dense, and at times we had to descend to within 300 feet of the sea.

"For four hours the machine was covered in a sheet of ice caused by frozen sleet; at another time the sleet was so dense that my speed indicator did not work, and for a few seconds it was very alarming.

"We looped the loop, I do believe, and did a very steep spiral. We did some very comic 'stunts,' for I had no sense of horizon.

"The winds were favourable all the way . . ."

John Alcock, "The Pilot's Story," June 1919, as photo-reproduced in Peter Allen, *The 91 before Lindbergh*.

service during the war, in which one learned to fly and the other to navigate, and their use of an airplane designed for the military illustrated the wartime contributions of training, experience, and equipment to postwar aviation.

Personal Profile

John Alcock (1892-1919) became an airplane mechanic and then a pilot. During World War I he served in the Royal Naval Air Service first as a flight instructor at the naval school at Eastchurch and later as a combat pilot in the Aegean Sea. He once single-handedly attacked three enemy planes, a deed for which he won the Distinguished Service Cross. Turkish anti-aircraft fire shot him down in September 1917. He spent the remainder of the war as a prisoner. Alcock and Arthur Whitten Brown flew nonstop across the Atlantic Ocean in 1919, a deed for which both were knighted. Later in 1919 Alcock died while attempting to land an airplane in fog in France.

John Alcock

Airship Roundtrip

Soon after the armistice with Germany in 1918, the British Admiralty offered to loan now-unneeded

Historic Event

From 2 July to 13 July 1919 the British-made rigid airship R.34 became the first lighter-than-air aircraft to cross the Atlantic Ocean, the first aircraft to cross the Atlantic east to west, the first aircraft to make a round-trip flight over the Atlantic, and the first airship to attempt to use a direction-finding radio on a transoceanic flight.

naval airships to the British Air Ministry for the newly formed Air Force. The idea was to explore the commercial potential of airships. The newest airship included in the offer was still in the construction hangar. It was the R.34, a British copy of the German naval airship L 33 that was captured in England in September 1916. The German crew of the L 33 had set the grounded airship on fire, but the fire consumed only the gasbags and outer fabric. The structure remained intact. This L 33 proved to the British military that their designs were far behind German airship technology, so Britain decided to base future airships on the German technology. The first product of this decision was the R.33, built by the Armstrong-Whitworth firm at Barlow. The second was the R.34.

The R.34 was assembled at the William Beardmore & Company's factory at Inchinnan, near Glasgow, Scotland. It was completed in December 1918, but bad weather kept it in the hangar until March. Compared to the German L 33, the British R.34 was a little longer (643 feet versus 600 feet). It held a little less hydrogen (less than two million cubic feet compared to two million), and it had one less engine (five instead of six). The R.34's engines were an English make; they were 250-horsepower, V12,

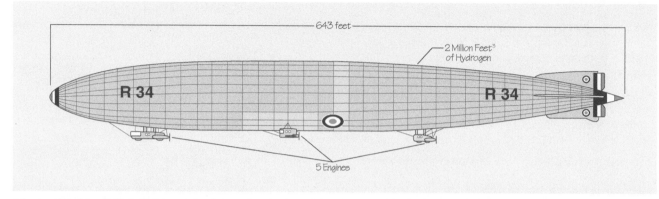

643 feet

R 34

2 Million Feet³ of Hydrogen

R 34

5 Engines

Figure 5-8. The British R.34 was based on the design of the German Naval airship L 33.

water-cooled Sunbeam-Coatalen Maori engines. The frame was duraluminum. The varnished and rubberized cotton fabric of the gasbags was lined with gold-beater's skin; that is, the outer layer of the guts of 600,000 oxen lined the gasbags as a seal to hold the hydrogen inside. The fuel tanks could hold 6,000 British gallons (21 tons) of gasoline. (Figure 5-8)

The R.34 rolled out on 14 March 1919 and made a five-hour maiden voyage. The Aero Club of America, the Aerial League, and the Pan American Aeronautical Federation invited Britain to send an airship to an aeronautical meeting and show in Atlantic City, New Jersey, in May, but arranging for such a trip took time. The airship was damaged on its second trial flight in April, but its third trial flight in May included its delivery to the East Fortune base in East Lothian, near Edinburgh. The United States had no large airships, no rigid airships, and no large hangars in which to house a ship. Landing the R.34 there would require a level field about two square

miles in size and free of obstructions. A landing crew of at least 300 men would be needed; the British used more than 500 on the ground at East Fortune. Supplies would be needed for the return trip. These requirements exceeded the capabilities of the flying clubs so the United States Navy agreed to provide mooring and supplies. The British sent an advance party and spare parts to the United States; the advance party was to organize and train the ground crew. As preparations for a transatlantic flight were underway, the air show in Atlantic City took place without any airships. The British Secretary of State for Air, Winston Churchill, urged, "We ought to go through with this. Unlike aeroplane attempts, it is a practical proposition which has been approached in a businesslike way with adequate preliminary tests." Later tests included a proving flight over the North Sea and Baltic Sea in June.

For the transatlantic crossing, the R.34 lifted off from East Fortune on 2 July 1919. Brigadier General

Flight Lines

"The speed of the crossing was not too impressive, but the landing was. As the ship floated stationary over the field at an altitude of 1000 feet, a sudden burst of white fell from its control cabin. In a moment the object opened into a parachute and with a sangfroid and a chic that only the English can put over, the executive officer of the R.34, Squadron Leader Pritchard, landed lightly and unconcerned in full beribboned uniform, carrying a swagger stick! Efficiently he commanded the landing operations."

Grover Loening referring to 6 July 1919 arrival of the R.34 in New York, as quoted in Peter Allen, *The 91 before Lindbergh*.

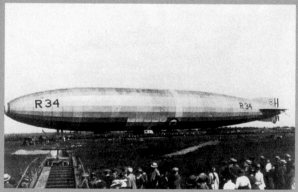

Historical Note

An early stowaway on an aircraft was William Ballantyne on the R.34 airship in July 1919. He worked on the airship prior to the transatlantic flight. He hid on board until the airship was too far from port to return. Once discovered, he assumed his usual duties. He rode to the United States, where he became a media favorite. Grounded — but not court martialed — by British authorities, he returned to Britain by surface ship.

Some writers report that a stowaway was among the 51 people on board the prototype of the NC flying boat when it set a number-of-passengers-carried record on 25 November 1918.

Who was the first aerial stowaway? It may have been the NC flying boat passenger number 51, or William Ballantyne on the rigid airship, or someone on a less newsworthy flight and, therefore, lost to posterity.

Edward M. Maitland was the senior officer on board. Major George Scott was the captain. The crew consisted of eight officers and 22 men. An American naval officer rode as an observer. There were two stowaways on board — an aircraft man named William Ballantyne and a tabby cat named Wopsie. The crew nicknamed R.34 "Tiny." The airship carried mail and film of the Peace Conference then in progress in Paris. It also carried chewing gum as a substitute for smoking because of the flammability of hydrogen gas. The wireless direction-finding equipment did not work well enough to be helpful. The airship flew through Atlantic storms and

landed on Long Island 108 hours after departure from Britain.

After a few days in New York, R.34 returned to Britain. It left the United States with mail, film of its arrival, and a United States Army observer instead of the naval officer. The R.34 landed in Pulham on 13 July, 75 hours after leaving New York. The airship was successful but already obsolete, as the British were then constructing airships based on German technology obtained at the end of the war.

Australian Flight

In addition to the flights across the Atlantic Ocean in 1919, Lieutenant Ross Smith, his brother Lieutenant Keith Smith, and two mechanics — Sergeants James M. Bennett and W.H. "Wally" Shiers — flew from England to Australia. Ross Smith was in command. He was an experienced pilot, an ace, and a war hero. The plane was a Vickers Vimy; G-EAOU was the registration designation. Two Rolls Royce Eagle VIII engines, 360-horsepower units, powered the new bomber, fresh from the factory and only lightly modified for the long-distance flight. Instead of military equipment, the plane was stocked with tropical stores and rigged with extra fuel tanks. The incentive for this flight came from the Australian Prime Minister William Hughes, who was in Paris for the Peace Conference. He announced that the Australian government was offering a prize of 10,000 pounds to the first Australian to fly from Britain to Australia, to do so in 1919, and to complete the entire flight within 30 days.

Historic Event

Over the twenty-eight day period from 12 November to 10 December 1919, Ross Smith, Keith Smith, J.M. Bennett, and W.H. Shiers flew from England to Australia. Their 28-day flight covered 11,294 miles (18,172 km) and won a prize offered by the Australian government for such a flight. More importantly, the flight symbolically linked the ends of the British Empire and illustrated the possibilities of an imperial air route.

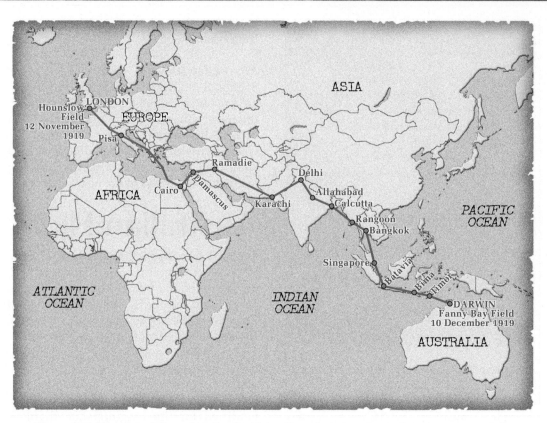

Figure 5-9. The route followed by the Smith brothers from London to Darwin was carefully planned to take advantage of supplies along the way.

Personal Profile

Ross MacPherson Smith (1892-1922) joined the Australian cavalry when World War I started and served in Gallipoli. In 1916 he transferred to the Australian Flying Corps, which taught him to fly. He flew combat missions against German and Turkish aircraft and downed nine. As the pilot, he flew Lawrence of Arabia on secret missions in the Middle East. He and three others completed the first flight from England to Australia. Smith and his crew won an Australian prize, and Ross and his brother Keith won knighthood, for completing the flight. Smith died on 13 April 1922 when the Vickers Viking he was testing crashed.

Ross MacPherson Smith

Ross Smith and his crew departed Hounslow Field, London, on 12 November. They flew a carefully planned route that had been specially supplied to support the flight. En route they logged 235 hours and 55 minutes of flight time. They landed at Darwin on the afternoon of 10 December. The landing marked the formal opening of Darwin's new Fanny Bay Field, a strip of hard, gravelly land which had been cleared of 700 yards of wire fencing, two banyan trees, two earth mounds, and several small trees. Hudson Fysh of the Defense Department was on hand to present the fliers the ten-thousand-pound prize for completing the flight. His words revealed Australia's pride and interest in the flight, "one of the greatest flights, if not the greatest, in the history of aviation, and a great initial fillip [stimulus] for civil aviation in Australia, for no one had ever flown across the world before." (Figure 5-9)

Other Long-Distance Flights

While the Smiths were en route to Darwin, Australia, so too were H.N. Wrigley and A.W. Murphy. Wrigley and Murphy departed Point Cook, Victoria, near

Figure 5-10. The Vickers Vimy proved to be an excellent choice for post-war distance flying. The Vimy pictured here is a replica, flown by Lang Kidby and Peter McMillan in 1994, that successfully retraced the Smith brothers' flight.

Melbourne on the southern coast of Australia, on 16 November. They flew a military B.E.2.E. biplane over 2,500 miles north by west to Darwin. They logged 46 hours in the air by the time they landed at Darwin on the northern coast on 12 December; two days after the Smiths arrived from England. Flying for the Australian Defense Department, they were surveying an air route between Melbourne and Darwin. In so doing, they completed the first transcontinental flight across Australia.

Long-distance flying began in 1919, and the quest for distance remained thereafter an aviation pursuit. Like Alcock and Brown and the Smith brothers, other distance fliers used the Vimy. A Commercial Vimy attempted a flight from England to South Africa. It departed England in January 1920 and prematurely stopped in Tanganyika a month later. The flight ended there due to radiator problems. The next month another Vimy, a military model, left England for South Africa. This time Lieutenant Colonel Pierre Van Ryneveld and Major C.J. Quintin Brand of the South African Air Force flew the Vimy. They departed Brooklands Field on 4 February 1920 and headed southeast. They crossed Europe, stopped in Cairo, and headed south again. When a radiator began to leak, the Egyptian Air Force came to their aid with another Vimy. In this loaned aircraft, Van Ryneveld and Brand continued southward. At Bulawayo, Southern Rhodesia, they damaged the plane while attempting takeoff. The persistent fliers borrowed a de Havilland DH 9 and flew to Cape Town. They

landed at the Wynberg Aerodrome on 20 March and collected the prize offered by the South African government. Like the Smith brothers, Van Ryneveld and Brand were knighted for helping to tie the British Empire closer together.

Vickers delivered 99 Vimys to the Royal Air Force for postwar duty, including the Vimys flown by the newly established air forces of Egypt and South Africa. The Vimy demonstrated the transition of an airplane from wartime to peacetime use. In fact, the Vimy proved so successful after World War I that some people accused Vickers of using wartime resources to develop a commercial plane for the eventual postwar market. Profiteering was the charge but, in this case, it did not stick. Vickers built only a few Commercial Vimys. (Figure 5-10)

Research and Development

The immediate postwar achievements in distance flying utilized the military developments of wartime aviation, but the experience of war included research and development. Steady technical progress followed the end of the war. In the United States, for example, a lone scientist pursued an aeronautical adventure of a different sort with the 1919 publication of his book *A Method of Reaching Extreme Altitudes*. The scientist was Robert H. Goddard and his method was the liquid-fueled rocket. In 1919 the method was an exploration on paper, but that effort took flight in 1926 when Goddard successfully launched a rocket. (Figure 5-11) Goddard's German counterpart was Hermann Oberth, who presented the idea of escape velocity in *The Rocket into Interplanetary Space (Die Rakete zu den Planetenräumen*, 1924).

Historical Evidence

The space-oriented work of American Robert H. Goddard (1882-1945), German Hermann J. Oberth (1894-1989), and Frenchman Robert Esnault-Pelterie (1881-1957), inspired science fiction writers. The popularity of science fiction about space, indicated by sales, is evidence of public interest in space travel. The first major science fiction magazine *Amazing Stories* was an immediate popular and financial success. In the 1920s several space adventure books appeared in print; for example:

Edgar Rice Burroughs, *The Chessmen of Mars*, 1922: about space travel

Otto Willi Gail, *Der Stein vom Mond (The Stone from the Moon)*, 1926: about a space station and a three-stage rocket with wings

Miral-Viger, *L'Anneau de Feu (Ring of Fire)*, 1922 — about an atomic-powered spaceship

Figure 5-11. Dr. Robert Goddard with his first successful liquid fueled rocket ready for launch.

AIRSHIPS

Postwar aviation included an enthusiasm for airships and activities such as "prospecting" or surveying air routes for possible airship lines. The airship proved itself during the war as a naval coastal patrol ship and in 1919 as a long-distance aircraft. The Treaty of Versailles prohibited Germany from having any military air force and, under the terms of the treaty, Germany delivered all its aircraft and airplane engines to the Allied and Associated Powers. The Allied restrictions also required the dispersal of German military airships among the Allies and limited German production and operation of airships. Despite the Allied terms, German crews destroyed some airships, and the Allies imposed restitution payments for the losses. Prohibited from military aviation, Germany turned its postwar interest to commercial air travel by airship. Outside of Germany, the airship remained mostly a military aircraft — yet one heavily influenced by German airship technology and with commercial potential. German airships remained the standard reference by which all airships were judged.

Zeppelins

As soon as the war ended, the Zeppelin company built LZ 120, *Bodensee (Lake Constance)*, and LZ 121, *Nordstern (North Star)* for passenger service. *Bodensee* made more than a hundred flights between Friedrichshafen and Berlin in late 1919, but the

Allies then confiscated both the *Bodensee* and *Nordstern* as restitution for German equipment destroyed after the war. Italy received the rigid airship *Bodensee* and renamed it *Esperia*, but the Italians in general pursued the development of semi-rigid airships. *Nordstern* and the naval L 72 went to France, which renamed the *Nordstern* the *Mediterranee* and the L 72 the *Dixmude*. France studied the German airships for a couple of years before flying them.

Flight Lines

"The Dixmude, once more under control, is obedient to those who sail her. The [rigid] dirigible rises, dips its prow, turns upward again, maneuvers to the right, and performs evolutions to the left. The Algerians look up at us, entranced. The citizens have climbed upon their terraces, have filled the squares, and are spread out over all the roads. The tramways are blocked, and no vehicles can move anywhere in the city. Thousands of admiring looks, and some possibly a little anxious, are fixt upon the Dixmude."

Passenger Maxine Baze describing an airship flight over North Africa in 1923, published in *The Literary Digest* (12 January 1924), and quoted in Lee Payne, *Lighter Than Air, an Illustrated History of the Airship*.

In 1923 France launched both *Mediterranee* and *Dixmude* for flights between France and its African colonies. These were "prospecting" flights to survey possible routes for commercial airline development. As such, they were relatively low-altitude flights, low relative to the high altitudes for which the Germans had designed the rigid Zeppelin. Low altitude placed an airship in the turbulence of weather below the calm higher altitudes, and high-altitude designs featured light frames for the calm flight environment. The *Mediterranee* made several trips, then France dismantled the aircraft. In September the *Dixmude* flew from Toulon, France, across the Mediterranean Sea to Oran, Bizerte,

LZ 120 *Bodensee*

and Sardinia; and then back across the Mediterranean, over Nice and Paris, to Toulon: 4,500 miles. On another trip to North Africa in December, the *Dixmude* disappeared into the Mediterranean Sea — downed by lightning or turbulence from a storm encountered en route. Thereafter, the French enthusiasm for lighter-than-air aircraft waned, though the Zodiac Company built a few small non-rigid dirigibles and small semi-rigid airships.

Belgium, Great Britain, and Japan also received German military zeppelins as restitution of war losses. The airships were dismantled for shipment, and Belgium and Japan apparently never reassembled their respective ships. Britain had already benefited from captured German airship technology, as illustrated by the R.34. Late in the war, Britain captured more modern German airships on which it based its later rigid designs, like the R.38.

R.38

The R.38 was under construction at the Short Brothers' plant at Cardington in 1919. Britain, continuing its wartime practice of nationalizing parts of its aviation industry, turned that plant into the Royal Airship Works. The government finished building the large R.38 airship, which held more than two and a half million cubic feet of hydrogen gas. The United States planned to buy this rigid ship, to accept delivery in Britain, and to fly it across the Atlantic Ocean. Test flights preceded the delivery of the airship, which the United States designated ZR-2; the naval ZR-1 was under construction in the United States. On one high-speed test flight of the R.38, the crew made a sharp turn. This maneuver was prohibited in Germany due to the light frame design for rigid airships. The frame snapped, gas burned, and the

R.38 fell into the Humber River. Forty-four airmen died, including the core of the British airship program and sixteen observers and trainees from the United States. Five men survived, one American and four Englishmen. (Figure 5-12)

Historic Event

On 24 August 1921 the British airship R.38 crashed. During a flight test, the crew made a high-speed turn. The resulting stress snapped the light frame, and the hydrogen gas ignited. Forty-four men died, and only five survived. This incident was the worst aerial disaster to date.

Flight Lines

"I had just reached the cockpit when with a tremendous crash, the girders amidship broke, and the ship split in halves and started to descend towards the river. I cannot describe my sensations but I certainly thought my end had come. I made a rush for the tail to get a parachute, but found two of my enlisted comrades, Harry Bateman and Walter Potter, already there. I know there was only one chute there for the three of us. Bateman had the chute and jumped, but the chute fowled, and he hung to the tail. Both Potter and I started to run forward for other chutes but just as I got in the keel either the petrol tanks or the hydrogen exploded.

"Flames immediately began to sweep the forward part of our half of the ship. . . .

"We could not use the parachute as we were too low, being only a few hundred feet up. I saw we were going to land in the water, and so climbed up on the fabric forward of the tail cup. When I thought we were going to strike, I jumped."

Bateman and Potter survived.

United States Navy rigger Norman Walker describing his surviving the crash of R.38 on 24 August 1921, quoted in Lee Payne, *Lighter Than Air, an Illustrated History of the Airship.*

Figure 5-12. The British Short Brothers designed the R.38, the Royal Airship Works at Cardington constructed the ship, and 44 airmen died when the airship crashed on its final test flight.

Roma

In addition to R.38, the United States explored a variety of airship designs. The Navy bought the Italian-made semi-rigid *Roma*, which was war surplus equipment as soon as it was completed in 1920. Italy sold it to a businessman who planned an airship airline but he, instead, sold it to the United States. It held over a million cubic feet of hydrogen. The Navy disliked the flight characteristics exhibited by the *Roma* during flight tests in early 1922, so the Navy modified the aircraft. On 21 February 1922 that modified aircraft crashed and burned. Thirty-four airmen died and only eleven survived. This accident followed closely the British R.38 disaster. The American response was to abandon flammable hydrogen for the safer, but more expensive, helium. While hydrogen could be produced anywhere, helium was extracted from natural gas by freezing the natural gas to hundreds of degrees below zero. That process made it expensive. (Figure 5-13)

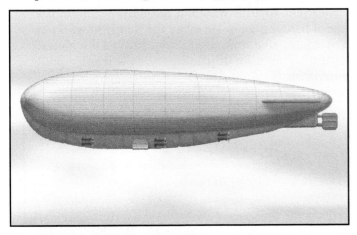

Figure 5-13. The semi-rigid airship *Roma* was an Italian-made aircraft purchased by the United States Navy. This was one of the last American airships to use hydrogen.

Shenandoah

The first helium airship was also the first rigid airship made in the United States. It was the ZR-1, better known as the *Shenandoah*. The design was based on captured German technology, specifically the L 49 Zeppelin that the French downed in 1918. The French copied the German design and provided the plans to the United States. The Navy built this airship at the Naval Aircraft Factory at the Philadelphia Navy Yard, strengthened the framework over the German design, and assembled it at the Lakehurst Naval Air Station. The ZR-1 used over two million cubic feet of gas. Since the construction of the airship was finished after the R.38 and *Roma* crashes, helium was

Figure 5-14. The ZR-1, *Shenandoah* is moored on the mast of a Navy ship, the *USS Patoka* in July 1925.

used. The airship weighed 40 tons and could lift 62 tons. Six 300-horsepower Packard engines provided the power. The maiden flight was 4 September 1923. (Figure 5-14)

The *Shenandoah* had a colorful and short life. The Navy planned to send it to the North Pole, which no aircraft had yet reached. The Navy constructed mooring masts along the planned route as flight tests were conducted. One test was to determine if the airship could ride out a storm while moored to high mast. During the test the ZR-1 was damaged. It tore loose from its mooring and drifted off. It eventually returned safely due to the efforts of the partial crew

 ## Historic Event

On 4 September 1923 the United States airship ZR-1, better known as the *Shenandoah*, made the first flight of a helium airship. Fires that burned the R.38 in Britain and the *Roma* in the States, killing many airmen, prompted the change from flammable hydrogen to safer helium.

Figure 5-15. The airship *Shenandoah* at the St. Louis air race in 1924.

on board, but it failed the test. The Navy canceled the polar flight and planned instead a transcontinental flight. With Rear Admiral William Moffett on board, the airship left Lakehurst on 7 October 1924. It flew west, crossed the Rockies near Denver, went to San Diego, California, and up the coast to Fort Lewis, Washington. It returned to Lakehurst over the reverse route. *Shenandoah* flew more than nine thousand miles in 19 days. (Figure 5-15) On a naval publicity tour of the Midwest in September 1925, the *Shenandoah* was caught in a violent storm, a squall line, and crashed. Although it did not burn like hydrogen airships did, it was destroyed and fourteen naval airshipmen died, including the commanding officer, Zachary Lansdowne.

Los Angeles

Although the Allies prohibited German production of military aircraft, and even scheduled the destruction of the Zeppelin works in Friedrichshafen, the United States in 1922 requested an exception. The United States asked that one airship be built at the Zeppelin works before the planned destruction of the factory. The airship, the United States argued, would be compensation for a war claim. The Allies approved the request, and the LZ 126 was built as a civil airship. This allowed the Zeppelin plant to stay in the airship business but out of military aviation.

Count Zeppelin's former assistant, and now successor, Hugo Eckener personally delivered the airship to the United States Navy. That required a flight across the Atlantic Ocean, made in October 1924. LZ 126 was the second airship to make a transatlantic crossing, after the R.34. The United States

Navy designated LZ 126 the ZR-3, christened it the *Los Angeles*, and used it as a training ship. Though the LZ 126 went to the Navy and, therefore, became a military airship, Eckener eventually convinced the Allies that airships were not militarily viable in the age of fighter planes. He saved the Zeppelin works at Friedrichshafen from destruction and led the revival of the German airship industry as a wholly civil enterprise. (Figure 5-16)

Figure 5-16. The ZR-3, *Los Angeles*, was built by the Zeppelin works in Germany and delivered to the United States Navy following a transatlantic crossing in October 1924.

The LZ 126 (ZR-3) arrived after the American decision to switch to helium gas. The Navy only had enough helium for one large airship, so either the *Shenandoah* or the *Los Angeles* could be flight ready (inflated) at any one time. The *Los Angeles* was the shorter of the two, by 22 feet, but the wider, by 12 feet; therefore, it could hold half a million more cubic feet of gas. It was suspended in the hangar when the *Shenandoah*, with its smaller requirement for gas, went on the publicity tour in 1925.

Personal Profile

Hugo Eckener (1868-1954) was a news reporter when he watched Ferdinand Zeppelin's first airship take flight in 1900. At that time he thought the airship was a folly. Six years later he went to work for Zeppelin. He piloted zeppelins, taught zeppelin pilots, devised improvements in zeppelin technology, and publicized the company. He also organized the airship airline DELAG. During World War I, he managed Zeppelin's military programs. After Count Zeppelin died in 1917, Eckener led the company into commercial airship development. The Nazi party acquired control of the Zeppelin company. Eckener opposed the Nazis. He disagreed with Goering about the display of the Nazi swastika on the *Graf Zeppelin* at the Chicago World's Fair of 1933-34, and other propaganda uses of Zeppelins, and he lost his job. By then, he had made over 2,000 airship flights!

Hugo Eckener

Germany

As the various Allied restrictions on German aviation were lifted, the Zeppelin company began making the LZ 127, better known as the *Graf Zeppelin*.

Construction began in late 1926. The LZ 127 was a commercial airliner specially designed for regular transatlantic service and, therefore, larger than LZ 126. Public contributions helped finance the construction, as Germans still had pride in zeppelins, a pride renewed by the historic transatlantic crossing of the LZ 126 in 1923. The *Graf Zeppelin* was under construction when Lindbergh crossed the Atlantic Ocean in 1927. (Figure 5-17)

The development of airship technology included setbacks as well as progress, setbacks like the 1921 British R.38 disaster, the 1923 French *Dixmude* disappearance, and the 1925 American *Shenandoah* crash. In fact, Britain, France, and the United States lost over 150 airmen to airship accidents during the postwar years. This loss of life and lack of expertise hindered the airship programs in those nations. Germany retained the leadership in airship technology.

Figure 5-17. The LZ 127, *Graf Zeppelin*, arriving in the United States (left) and moored in Los Angeles (right).

Barnstorming and Competing

Early Barnstormers

During the postwar period pilots — many with military flight experience — became popular with public audiences by displaying aircraft and flying abilities through barnstorming and competitions. The pilots chased speed in races, reached for altitude records, and attempted long-distance flights. This was an international phenomenon. Military surplus equipment helped make this possible, affordable, but economic recovery after the cancellation of war contracts required new production and new designs too. Nationalists of various nations competed to be the first to fly around the world, the first to North Pole, South Pole, or other geographical goal. The military services allowed their pilots to participate in attention-grabbing flights — to demonstrate military equipment and skills, and to attract public funding for military aviation. Gliding too became popular, especially in Germany under the postwar restriction that the Allies had imposed upon civil and military aviation.

Gliding

After World War I, Germany revived gliding as a major aeronautical activity. Civil engineer Oskar Ursinus edited the popular *Flugsport* magazine in which he promoted gliding for science and sport. The science was a return to prewar research on the aeronautics of light aircraft. Ursinus organized Germany's first gliding rally in 1920. Held at the Wasserkuppe peak in the mountainous Rhön region,

this rally began modestly. Eleven gliders registered for that first rally. Four were determined to be fit for flight, and three actually flew. The late arrival of an academic flying group from the German town of Aachen, near the Belgian border, saved the show. Former Austrian air force pilot Wolfgang Klemperer skillfully flew the group's *Black Devil* monoplane glider. Over twenty gliders registered for the second Wasserkuppe rally in 1921. There Arthur Martens established a new world record for distance at 8.9 kilometers; he flew the Hanover academic flying group's *Vampyr*, a high-wing monoplane glider (now in the collections of the Deutsches Museum in Munich). Friedrich Harth set an endurance record of 21 minutes.

The sport of gliding quickly became nationalistic as well as popular. A common German response to the Allied restrictions on aviation was: "If we can't fly with motors, we'll fly without them." Fifty-three aircraft registered for the third annual Wasserkuppe rally in 1922. New records were set, like an endurance record of more than three hours! The rally attracted international attention, as Germans declared gliding a German national sport. Veteran pilots came to Wasserkuppe to learn to glide. A memorial to Germany's fallen airmen — the Ring of German Fliers — was erected on the slopes of Wasserkuppe in 1923. Gliding became so popular that a hotel, theater, post office, restaurants, and other facilities were constructed at the rally site. A second gliding camp opened at Rossitten in East Prussia, beside the Baltic Sea, and a third at Grunau in Silesia. The German government encouraged gliding and sponsored the founding of the Rhön-Rossitten Society to organize competitions and scientific research. In 1926 the Allies prevented the German government from financing sport groups as a condition of the Allies removing postwar restrictions on German civil aviation. The Allies feared that sport groups like gliding clubs might be paramilitary units.

The German glider pilots learned to ride for hours in the warm air rising along the slopes. They observed topography favorable to updrafts and the horizontal winds in valleys, and they mapped the "air roads" as determined by ground features. With this information, Johannes "Bübi" Nehring accomplished a round-trip glider flight in 1926. A thunderstorm in August of that year caught pilot Max Kegel in a thermal updraft. He landed more than 55 kilometers from Wasserkuppe and thereby doubled the distance record for gliders. Kegel did not recognize the significance of the thermals that he had discovered, and, for a couple years, he and other glider pilots continued to fly with reference to terrain rather than clouds.

Though Germany adopted gliding as a national sport, there were gliders and glider pilots in other countries too, but never on a scale to rival German gliding.

Flight Lines

"It's raining — it's hailing! Already the ground below has disappeared from view . . . my wingtips are no longer visible. [Suddenly I rise] like a piece of paper that is pulled up a chimney."

Max Kegel on getting caught in a thunderstorm updraft in 1926, as translated and quoted in Peter Fritzsche, *A Nation of Fliers, German Aviation and the Popular Imagination* (Cambridge: Harvard University Press, 1992).

Barnstorming

Barnstorming became an American passion in much the same way that gliding became a German passion. As war surplus equipment became available and affordable after the war, former military pilots and civilians who wanted to fly became enthusiastic fliers. Top pilots flew great distances for prize money, honor, and adventure; but everyday pilots could fly from town to town, performing stunts, playing the fairs, and selling rides to earn a living. Still, in the early 1920s, most of the barnstorming pilots were former military aviators out of a job, but trained and experienced in flying. Barnstorming became popular in many countries, but it became a passion in the United States. The United States had developed its aviation production capabilities effectively but too late for most of the products to be shipped to the war. Similarly it had trained thousands of pilots, most of whom never went into battle. Furthermore, the United States homeland was undamaged by the combat and bombardment that scarred postwar Europe, and it was free of the need to recover from wartime damage. In addition, American audiences had no experience with the horrors of the air war fought beyond the ocean.

The Curtiss Jenny was the barnstormer's airplane of choice. It was actually the JN-4 through JN-4D series of trainers produced during World War I, including the Jennies made in Canada, which were called Canucks. The JN aircraft merged features of the Curtiss J and the N models. Curtiss alone produced almost five thousand Jennies during the war. Six other firms also had war contracts to build the aircraft. Approximately 95% of the pilots who trained in the United States or Canada during the war flew the Jenny as part of their training. They knew the plane and liked its characteristics. (Figure 5-18)

Figure 5-18. Many of the pilots trained during the war flew the Curtiss JN-4, like the ones shown above. Following the war, the Jenny was the airplane of choice for the barnstormers and flying clubs. The one shown in the lower photograph was from the Carrollton Aero Club in Texas.

The Curtiss OX-5 engine that powered the Jenny during and after the war was a water-cooled, V-engine that produced 90-horsepower at 1,400 rpm. This was not a combat engine; it weighed about 400 pounds with water, oil, and radiator. During the war, it was troubled by bad magnetos because of the severed supply of German magnetos to engine makers in the United States. The OX-5 realized improved reliability in the postwar years with the substitution of Bosch or Splitdorf magnetos. The valve mechanism and leaking coolant system remained problems, but the engine was readily available, relatively cheap and, therefore, met the criteria of barnstormers. How cheap? In 1919 Curtiss sold a new OX-5 for a thousand dollars. By the time Lindbergh flew the Atlantic in 1927, the price was around $250 to $300. (Figure 5-19)

Figure 5-19. The Curtiss OX-5 engine.

The United States Army listed 3,285 Jennies in its inventory of equipment in 1919 and only 37 in 1927, which was the year the Army withdrew the last ones from service. Curtiss bought more than twenty million dollars worth of surplus Jennies and engines. It reconditioned these in Curtiss factories and sold them for public use. During the war, a Jenny with engine and instruments sold for about $8,000; the airframe alone cost between $3,500 and $4,800 depending upon the maker and when it was produced. After the war, the price of a Jenny varied widely. A reconditioned Canuck could be purchased for $2,600 to $3,000 in 1919. In the 1920s, the price for a reconditioned Canuck was as little as $1,500. The price for an unused Jenny was $3,250, and $2,000 or more for a rebuilt Jenny. Used aircraft, of course, cost less than new or surplus equipment. After changing owners several times, a Jenny might sell for $250–$500. These were cheap prices compared to postwar production models like the Curtiss Oriole at $8,000 or the Laird Swallow at $6,500.

The Jenny had a short but colorful civil career as the most common **barnstorming** airplane. The word barnstorming accurately described the association of airmen flying from farmer's field to farmer's field, like theatrical performers who played in barns as they traveled about the country. To the audience, barnstorming was entertainment. To the fliers, it was their livelihood. They worked alone, formed teams, and joined flying circuses. They played small towns and large cities. Barnstormers walked on wings, often aided by the struts and wires used in the construction of biplanes. Ormer Locklear was a famous wing-walker; his partner Milton Elliott flew the plane. Locklear starred in an early aviation movie, the 1920 silent film "The Great Air Robbery." Some transferred from a moving automobile to a flying Jenny, or from a Jenny in flight to another Jenny in flight. Clyde Pangborn popularized the car-to-plane stunt, and Gladys Ingle became known for transferring between planes in flight. Jack Shack was among the stuntmen who performed trapeze acts below planes in flight. The Dance of Death required two biplanes which flew with their wingtips overlapping. (Figure 5-20)

Aided by the lack of formal registration and airworthiness guidelines in United States (unlike in Europe where regulation came with peace), airmen modified their planes and held them together with whatever wire or glue they had. In fact, when the United States adopted airworthiness requirements in 1927, it grounded many Jenny pilots; others continued to fly outside the regulations.

Europe had barnstormers too. Britain's Percival Phillips, for example, went from the Royal Flying Corps to his own Cornwall Aviation Company that toured resorts and pastures where he performed in an Avro biplane. As soon as the Allies lifted restrictions on German civil aviation, air shows became popular throughout Germany. They attracted large crowds in the cities and played small towns as well. Ace Ernst Udet performed acrobatics. One of his popular stunts was using a wingtip to pick up a handkerchief from the ground. Other pilots raced their planes and some sold rides. Air shows demonstrated a revival not only

Figure 5-20. Stuntman Ormer Locklear, the first of the wing-walking barnstormers, does a handstand on the wing of a Curtiss Jenny JN-4D biplane in 1920.

of German aviation, but also of Germany in general, to the crowds who came to see Germans literally rise above the postwar landscape. German pilots competed in international as well as domestic competitions flying in new airplanes built by German manufacturers like Junkers and Heinkel.

Army World Flight

The United States Army's Air Service actively pursued altitude records, speed records, endurance records, technological advances, and publicity for its aeronautical accomplishments. From a wartime high of nearly nine thousand pilots, the Air Service shrank to about one thousand in the early 1920s. The Air Service considered itself a neglected arm of the military. To improve its plight, the Army Air Service promoted aviation and lobbied for more support for military aviation. Newsworthy flights were part of the campaign for popular, political, and military support. The Army sponsored the first flight around the rim or border of the United States (1919), completed a round-trip between the continental United States and territorial Alaska (1920), sank a captured battleship with bombs dropped from airplanes (1921), achieved the first nonstop transcontinental flight across the United States (1923), and conducted the first aerial refueling using a plane modified into the first aerial tanker (1923). What was next? (Figure 5-21)

Major General Mason Patrick, head of the Air Service, devised "The Plan" for a round-the-world flight. This was to be the Army's equivalent of the Navy's 1919 transatlantic crossing. The Army ordered four aircraft for the flight around the world — a flight to be accomplished through careful planning, generous provisioning, a large support infrastructure, international

Figure 5-21. The sinking of the giant battleship *Ostfriesland* in 1921 left no doubt that air power would play a dominant part in future warfare at sea.

cooperation, and war-derived equipment. According to an Army announcement, the purposes of the proposed circumnavigation of the globe were to "point the way for all nations to develop aviation commercially and to secure for our country the honor of being the first to [circle] the globe entirely by air." (Figure 5-22)

Figure 5-22. Major General Mason Patrick (center) was the mastermind behind the U.S. Army World Flight. The Plan called for four specially built Douglas World Cruisers to fly around the globe. On the left is Lester Maitland and on the right is Albert Hegenberger.

The Air Service brought the Navy, Coast Guard, and Bureau of Fisheries into The Plan in order to provide naval support for the Army fliers who were to cross two oceans on their way around the world. This was an unusual case of interservice cooperation in a time better known for interservice rivalry. After international negotiations involving the U.S. State Department and more than twenty countries, the Army sent personnel and supplies to the more than fifty locations around the globe. The Army divided the global route into six support districts. Radio equipment was carefully prepared at every planned stop and on naval support vessels at sea.

The Army used a competitive process to select the four pilots: Major Frederick L. Martin, flight leader, and Lieutenants Erik Nelson, Lowell H. Smith, and Leigh Wade. Martin had served as a supply officer in France during the war. He was a career officer who learned to fly in his late thirties. Nelson, a Swedish immigrant, was an engineering officer and helped select and customize the aircraft for the world flight. Nelson also had previously circled the globe under sail. Smith won several prizes in the Trans-Continental Speed, Reliability, and Endurance Contest from San Francisco to New York City and return; he was the first to return to San Francisco. Wade was a test pilot at McCook Field, Dayton, Ohio.

Figure 5-23. The Army World Flight crew: (left to right) Maj. Fredrick Martin, Lt. Leslie Arnold, Lt. Lowell Smith, Sgt. Alva Harvey, Lt. Leigh Wade, Sgt. Henry Ogden, Lt. Erik Nelson, Lt. John Harding.

He set a multi-engine altitude record of 27,120 feet. (Figure 5-23)

The pilots selected their respective mechanics: Martin — Sergeant Alva L. Harvey, Nelson — Lieutenant John Harding, Smith — Lieutenant Leslie P. Arnold, and Wade — Sergeant Henry H. Ogden. The mechanics were experienced airmen too. Harding had been the flying mechanic for the Army's 1919 flight around the rim of the United States. Arnold, home from occupation duty in postwar Europe, had flown stunts at county fairs to promote his military unit. Ogden began the flight as a sergeant and received a promotion to lieutenant during a stop in Japan. Arnold, Nelson, and Wade were among the aviators who bombed the captured German battleship *Ostfriesland* in the 1921 demonstration of Army airpower.

The eight men went to Langley Field, Virginia, for special training in aerial navigation, meteorology, and first aid. The pilots also learned to take off and land seaplanes, as they would be flying both land and seaplanes on the global route. At Langley they also got to fly the prototype of the aircraft selected for the trip: the Douglas World Cruiser. (Figure 5-24)

The prototype of the Douglas World Cruiser was a converted Navy torpedo bomber. Douglas built the four at its Santa Monica, California, factory. The four

teams chose to name their aircraft after American cities representing the cardinal points of the compass: *Boston*, *Chicago*, *New Orleans*, and *Seattle*. The World Cruisers were two-seat, open-cockpit biplanes with wings of wooden construction and

Figure 5-24. The Douglas World Cruisers were designed with a landing gear that could be switched from wheels to floats to allow both land and sea operations.

Historical Note

In 1924 the United States was one of six countries with teams striving to be the first to fly around the world. The other countries were Argentina, France, Great Britain, Italy, and Portugal. Five teams were private ventures. In only one case did a national government provide full logistical support to its team. That was the United States, and that made the difference.

A pilot with military experience, A. Stuart MacLaren led the British World Flight eastward from England. He was one of the two men who had made the first flight from England to Egypt in 1918. On his world flight attempt in 1924, MacLaren ditched his Vickers flying boat off the coast of Akyab, Burma (Myanmar), in late May. The American World Flight airmen were in Tokyo when they heard the news. They arranged for United States naval ships to transport a spare Vickers amphibian that was among the British team's provisions stored in Tokyo. At Akyab, the British airmen assembled the plane and departed to continue their flight. The British and American teams passed each other in Burma, but neither saw the other due to heavy rain. MacLaren ditched the second plane in the sea beyond the Japanese Kuril Islands and near the Soviet Komandorski Islands. That ended the British World Flight.

Italian ace Antonio Locatelli commanded a team of four airmen on Italy's World Flight. The team had one airplane, a German-designed, but Italian-made twin-engine Dornier Wal monoplane with a metal hull. The Italian team met the remaining two American teams in Iceland, and they departed together for Greenland as a flight of three planes. Caught in thick fog, Locatelli landed in order to avoid crashing into an iceberg. The landing damaged the aircraft's engine mounts, and rough seas damaged the ailerons, stabilizer, and elevators. That was on 21 August. Three days later, the American navy cruiser *Richmond* rescued the four Italian airmen, but not their plane.

These private ventures lacked the logistics adequate for the round-the-world flight. Much has been written about the successful U.S. Army flight around the world. The teams that achieved less than round-the-world flight are mostly forgotten, but they too contributed to the development of aviation by exploring routes and testing equipment, and by exposing the limitations of airplanes and infrastructure.

Seattle (foreground) and Boston in Santa Monica, CA, 17 March 1924.

fuselages of tubular steel. The wingspan was 50 feet, and the fuel capacity was 450 gallons (2,700 pounds). Empty weight when equipped with wheels was 4,300 pounds, with pontoons 5,500 pounds. The Army pulled 35 Liberty engines from its inventory of war surplus engines; that inventory once included about twelve thousand engines. Four engines were immedi-

ately installed — one on each plane. The others were distributed along the planned route (a total of seventeen engines were replaced during the World Flight). The instruments on board were a compass, airspeed indicator, altimeter, turn and bank indicator, tachometer, and gauges for water temperature, oil temperature, and oil pressure. To save weight, no radios were installed or carried on the aircraft. The airmen would use hand signals to communicate with each other and with personnel aboard ships or on the ground.

Weather was a determining factor for the schedule and direction of the planned route. May was the month of least fog in the Aleutians and Kurils of the northern Pacific, and August had the best flying weather in the northern Atlantic around Iceland and Greenland. The flight would proceed westward from the West Coast, against the prevailing winds, to enable the airmen to cross the two oceans at the most favorable times in terms of weather.

On 6 April 1924 the airmen and airplanes took off from Lake Washington beside the Sand Point airfield

Historical Note

The Army started the round-the-world flight with four planes.

Major Frederick L. Martin, flight leader, and Sergeant Alva L. Harvey, mechanic, crashed the *Seattle* (DWC 1) into an Alaskan mountain less than a month after starting the long-distance flight. They survived, but did not continue.

Lieutenant Lowell Smith, pilot and the flight leader after Martin's crash, and Lieutenant Leslie Arnold, mechanic, in the *Chicago* (DWC 2) completed the world flight from Seattle to Seattle.

Lieutenant Leigh Wade, pilot, and Sergeant Henry H. Ogden, mechanic, ditched at sea near the Faroe Islands between Great Britain and Iceland. The flagship USS *Richmond* rescued the crew, but the *Boston* (DWC 3) sank.

Lieutenants Erik Nelson, pilot, and John Harding, mechanic, in the *New Orleans* (DWC 4) completed the flight.

The *Chicago* and *New Orleans* landed at Sand Point side by side, simultaneously. Both were the first to finish a round-the-world flight.

near Seattle. They flew north to Prince Rupert, British Columbia, to Sitka and then Seward, Alaska, and southwest along the Alaska Peninsula. After leaving Chignik in bad weather, Martin crashed the *Seattle* into a mountain on that peninsula. The three remaining planes flew on along the Aleutian islands chain and across the North Pacific; however, bad weather sent them to the Soviet Komandorski Islands. Lack of diplomatic relations between the United States and the young Soviet Union prevented the American airmen from going ashore. On shore was the village of Nikolski, Bering Island, where wireless towers were

Flight Lines

"At 11.35 on the morning of May 15th, we set forth [from Attu] across the Pacific, and at five minutes past midday we passed over the last bit of American soil that we were to see for a long time. At 12.20 we passed the [Coast Guard cutter] *Haida*, and circled low to wave to our Coast Guard friends who had worked so enthusiastically for us. Bering Sea is one of the roughest bodies of water in the world, as we had long since discovered, and right here where it joins the North Pacific is the roughest part. So the *Haida* was rolling and tossing about like a cork, yet every man on board was hanging on with one hand and waving good-bye to us with the other.

"By now the sky in the southwest in the direction of Paramushiro had suddenly turned black, while due west it was still clear. So we headed toward the Komandorskis, deciding to take our chances with the Bolsheviks rather than face the wrath of the storm. For three hours we flew out of sight of land, wondering all the time what the Russians would think when they saw three giant planes swoop down out of the sky in this remote region where even ships only come about once a year.

"After we changed our course to avoid the storm and headed for the Komandorskis, our nearest land was Copper Island, two hundred and seventy miles away. This island is nine miles long and one mile wide — not a very large object, and one that could be easily missed in an ocean had our navigation been at fault. This was our first long water flight and consequently our first real test, so that, after straining our eyes for hours in an effort to sight Copper Island, it was rather a triumph to see it eventually 'dead ahead,' over our radiator caps."

Lowell Smith describing the first flight from an American continent across the Pacific Ocean to Asia, part of the Army World Flight of 1924, in Lowell Thomas, *The First World Flight*.

Historic Event

In 1924 United States Army airmen attempted to complete the first round-the-world flight. Eight airmen in four Douglas World Cruisers departed westward from Sand Point, Seattle, Washington, on 6 April. Five months later, on 28 September, four airmen and two airplanes completed the flight.

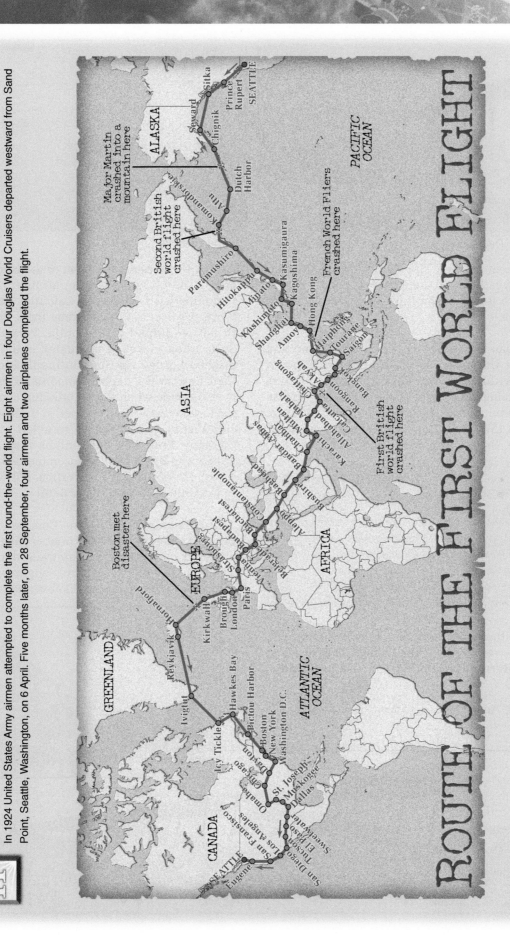

ROUTE OF THE FIRST WORLD FLIGHT

Figure 5-25. Douglas World Cruiser in Shanghai (left) and flying over Calcutta (right).

the prominent feature. The next morning brought improved weather, and the American airmen flew to Paramushiro Island in the Kurils, which was then a part of Japan.

Despite Japan expanding in the Pacific Ocean and despite the United States restricting the rights of Japanese within the United States and limiting Japanese immigration to the States, the Army airmen received warm receptions at their six stops in Japan. From Japan, the airmen flew to Shanghai, Hong Kong, and Saigon. Saigon in French Indochina (Vietnam)

Historical Note

Some famous stowaways were not stowaways at all. The Associated Press reporter Linton Wells hitched a ride — with permission of the flight crew — on a Douglas World Cruiser flying over India in 1924, but other journalists reported Wells was a stowaway.

was the southernmost latitude reached on the flight. They flew west to Bangkok, Siam (Thailand), to Rangoon, Burma (Myanmar), and Calcutta, India. (Figure 5-25)

Figure 5-26. Army World Flight during their stopover in Baghdad, Iraq.

Having flown around the rim of the North American and Asia continents, the airmen replaced the pontoons with wheels at Calcutta. They flew the World Cruisers as landplanes from there to Great Britain — inland across India, Persia (Iran), Iraq, Syria (then a French mandate), and Turkey. They reached Europe via Constantinople (now Istanbul), then flew to Bucharest, Romania. They flew right over Belgrade when a good tailwind convinced them not to stop there. They stopped at Budapest, Hungary, and Vienna, Austria, and refueled at Strasbourg, Germany. From Paris to London, they navigated by following a British airliner! Commercial airlines then served the major cities of Europe, but were still rare in the United States. (Figure 5-26)

At the Blackburn Aeroplane Company's airfield in Brough, a field beside the Humber River, the airmen prepared their planes for the transatlantic crossing. They replaced the Liberty engines, performed extensive maintenance, and substituted pontoons for

Flight Lines

"On this flight across the North Arabian desert to Aleppo, we saw scores of 'sand devils' whirling about the desert. They seemed to travel at great speed and reminded us somewhat of the pictures of waterspouts that we used to see in our school geographies. They made the air extremely 'bumpy,' but the stimulus of the desert air at five thousand feet, the great panorama of desert that spread out before us on every side, and above all the fact that we were well on our way now to the accomplishment of our task, contributed to render that day's flight particularly enjoyable."

Erik Nelson describing an over-land part of the 1924 flight, as quoted in Lowell Thomas, *The First World Flight*.

Flight Lines

"For another hour we dodge icebergs and shadows that fairly seemed to leap at us out of the fog. . . . First, we would dodge a white shadow, and then a black one would suddenly loom up on the opposite side. Once in a while, when concentrating all our attention on a particularly ominous-looking patch of cliff to our right, we would instinctively feel something sliding by the wing on our left. Turning quickly we would be just in time to see a ghostlike berg that we had missed by only ten feet or so, melting into the gloom. Perhaps it was a sudden icy draft from the berg, like the cold hand of death, that would cause us to turn our heads."

Lowell Smith's description of flying low en route to Greenland, as quoted in Lowell Thomas, *The First World Flight*.

wheels. They flew the Douglas World Cruisers as seaplanes from Great Britain, but loss of oil pressure caused Wade and Ogden in the *Boston* to ditch between the Orkneys and the Faroe Islands. The naval flagship USS *Richmond* rescued the men, but the *Boston* sank. The *Chicago* and *New Orleans* flew on to Iceland, Greenland, Labrador, Nova Scotia, and then across the United States to Seattle. (Figure 5-27)

Lowell Smith and Leslie Arnold in the *Chicago* and Erik Nelson and John Harding in the *New Orleans* landed at the Sand Point airfield on 28 September — after logging 363 hours and 7 minutes of flight time in

their single-engine, open-cockpit biplanes. They had flown 26,345 miles in six months, and they were the first to fly around the world.

The Army's success demonstrated the vast resources necessary at that time to support the airplanes of the period, particularly in contrast to the failure of competing attempts by Argentinean, British, French, Italian, and Portuguese airmen. The Army had replaced 17 engines, lost two airplanes, made five forced landings, and created an international line of support to achieve the first World Flight. Flying around the world was impressive and daring, but it was not sufficient to garner political support for military aviation. The hopping from stop to stop, the

Figure 5-27. The *Boston* ran into trouble after leaving Great Britain and sank between the Orkneys and Faroe Islands. The *Chicago* and *New Orleans* completed the World Flight by returning to Sand Point Airfield on 28 September 1924.

repairs, the weather delays, the loss of two airplanes, and the expensive support network strung along the route actually suggested that the airplane might not be the future of long-distance travel and that, instead, airships might be the future of long-distance and transoceanic flying. That the LZ 126 crossed the Atlantic Ocean in only a few days time in October 1924 only reinforced the view, particularly in regard to aircraft large enough to carry passengers and freight commercially.

Billy Mitchell

The Army completed the World Flight of 1924 without any fatalities, but that in no way meant that military aviation in the United States was state of the art. The Army sponsored the flight to garner support, and a vast Army-arranged infrastructure supported the flight. One of the most vocal proponents and clearest critics of military aviation in the postwar period was Brigadier General William Mitchell. He supported all aviation. In 1920 he organized the Army's aerial mapping expedition to Alaska and, in 1921, he advocated airship development. Regarding airships, he argued, "For commercial purposes the airship offers very interesting possibilities. There is no dust or smoke or unpleasant experience travelling by them. The degree of safety, with the proper ground organization of airship stations, is very good." He was certain that military aviation was essential to national security, and he said so to anyone who would listen.

He routinely criticized the military for failing to develop aviation to his standards, and he argued for a strong and independent air force. His public agitation got him demoted to colonel and assigned to an out-of-public-view base in Texas.

The loss of the *Shenandoah* and 14 airmen on 3 September 1925, the day after the disappearance of two Navy airplanes attempting to fly from California to Hawaii, inspired him to speak again, or rather to write. Mitchell issued a 17-page statement to the press that blamed military aviation in general: "These accidents are the direct result of the incompetency, criminal negligence and almost treasonable administration of the national defense by the Navy and War departments." He accused the Army and Navy of allowing aviation decisions to be made by officers with no knowledge of aviation. He claimed they made bad decisions, like sending the *Shenandoah* on a publicity tour of the Midwest against the advice of the airship's commanding officer who warned of violent summer storms like the squall line that brought the *Shenandoah* down.

The Army held a general court martial that found Mitchell guilty of insubordination. Suspended for five years, Mitchell resigned. He lost his rank, his job, and his military career for promoting military aviation too much, but he focused public attention on the problem. As the *New York Evening Post* reported, "Getting rid of Col. Mitchell will not, however, get rid

Personal Profile

William "Billy" Mitchell (1879-1936) attended college in Washington, DC. He sat in the gallery of the United States Senate when that assembly passed a declaration of war against Spain in 1898. He promptly enlisted as a private in the Army. He wanted to go to war, but his influential father, United States Senator John Mitchell of Wisconsin, intervened. Young Mitchell was soon an officer in the Signal Corps, then being organized by polar explorer Adolphus W. Greely. Lieutenant Mitchell strung telegraph wire in Cuba, the Philippines, and Alaska. In 1903, in recognition for his work in Alaska, Mitchell received a promotion to the rank of captain, which made him the youngest captain in the Army. He learned to fly in 1916 — on his own time and at his own expense since he was too old, 36, to qualify for military flight school. As a licensed pilot, he was able to join the Aviation Section of the Signal Corps, soon to be the Air Service. He went to France with the American Expeditionary Force. He served as Chief of the Air Service for the First Army and later as an Air Service Commander, and he received two Distinguished Service Cross medals. After the war he promoted a strong and independent air force. In 1925 an Army general court martial found him guilty of insubordination for criticizing the War Department for failing to develop military aviation, specifically for blaming the War Department for the crash of the airship *Shenandoah*. That court suspended him from service, and he resigned.

William "Billy" Mitchell

Historical Evidence

Army officer Billy Mitchell was an author too. He published six books, one on field signal communication, one a biography of General A.W. Greely, and four on aviation. He also wrote more than a hundred articles. Regarding his opinions, see some of his 1925 articles:

"Every Nation Is Developing Aviation — We Are Slipping Backward," *New York Sunday American*, 1 February 1925.

"How Should We Organize Our National Air Power?" *Saturday Evening Post*, 14 March 1925.

"Neither Armies nor Navies Can Exist Unless the Air Is Controlled over Them," *U.S. Air Service*, May 1925.

"Full Texts of Statements Leading to Court-Martial," *Aviation*, 14 September 1925

"Our American Air Agitation," *The Aeroplane*, 7 October 1925

"Col. Mitchell Explains His Plan," *Liberty*, 21 November 1925

"Our Problem of National Defense," *Liberty*, 5 December 1925

"Our Military Organizations Obsolete," *Liberty*, 19 December 1925

of the issues he has raised nor will it greatly better the conditions in American aviation."

Speed

During World War I the fastest airplanes exceeded the speed of the fastest automobiles for the first time, but the Féderation Aéronautique Internationale suspended recognition of records for the duration of the fighting. At the end of the war, the prewar records stood. The absolute world air speed record is an example. As an absolute, this record defined the fastest airplane of any type at a given time. The record in 1919 was the 1913 record of 126.667 mph (203.850 km/h) set by Marcel Prevost in a Deperdussin at Reims. That record fell in February 1920 when Joseph Sadi-Lecointe achieved the speed of 171.041 mph (275.264 km/h) in a Nieuport-Delage 29V. The record changed seven times in 1920! Sadi-Lecointe regained it at the end of the year with a speed of 194.516 mph (313.043 km/h). Sadi-Lecointe moved the record beyond 200 mph in 1921. American military pilot Billy Mitchell captured the

record in 1922 when he flew a Curtiss R-6 222.970 mph (358.836 km/h) at Selfridge Field, Michigan. French military pilot Florentin Bonnet in a Bernard V.2 set a record of 278.481 mph (448.171 km/h) in December 1924. This record held for almost three years, until November 1927, when an Italian military pilot named Mario de Bernardi reached 297.817 mph (479.290 km/h) in a Macchi M.52R. (Figure 5-28)

In addition to absolute speed, there were records by type and size of aircraft as well as races over specified courses. The first postwar and final Gordon Bennett

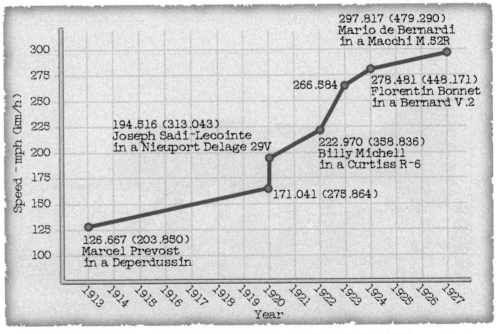

Figure 5-28. This chart shows steady increase in speed from 1913 to 1927.

race was held in France in 1920. One pilot and one plane came from Great Britain — F.P. Raynham and his Nieuport Martinsyde biplane. From the United States came two competitors, R.W. Schroeder with a Verville Scout biplane and Howard Rinehart with the new Dayton-Wright monoplane; a third American air racer, Roland Rohlf, crashed his Curtiss biplane upon arrival at the Étampes airfield. France fielded three entrants: Georges Kirsch in a Nieuport biplane, Bernard de Romanet in a SPAD-Herbemont S.20 biplane, and Sadi-Lecointe in a Nieuport biplane 29V. The Dayton-Wright RB racer was considered a top contender with its Hall-Scott motor, retractable wheels, and cantilever and variable camber wings, but a broken rudder cable prematurely ended its flight. Sadi-Lecointe won the race, and Romanet placed second.

Among the international races were the Deutsch de la Meurth that attracted few competitors for its two races, the first in 1920 and the last in 1921, and both won by Nieuport-Delage airplanes. Similarly, the two Coupe Commodore Louis D. Beaumont races in 1924 and 1925 were won by Nieuport-Delage airplanes, both times the model 42. Schneider Trophy races resumed in 1920 and became very popular. Britain, Italy, and the United States won the Schneider seaplane titles during the postwar years. The winning aircraft were a Savoia S.12 (pilot L. Bologna) in 1920, a Macchi M.7 (pilot G. de Briganti) in 1921, a Supermarine Sea Lion II (H. Baird) in 1922, a Curtiss CR-3 (D. Rittenhouse) in 1923, a Curtiss R3C-2 (Jimmy Doolittle) in 1925, a Macchi M.39 (Mario de Bernardi) in 1926, and a Supermarine S.5 (S. Webster) in 1927. No plane, pilot, or nation dominated the event. (Figure 5-29)

Some races were national in character, like the British Aerial Derbies and King's Cup races that attracted sportsmen and amateur fliers as well as professional pilots. In the United States the six Pulitzer Trophy races, 1920-1925, awarded prestige as well as prizes. Four of the six winning airplanes were Curtiss racers; the 1920 winner was a Verville VCP-R and the 1923 a Verville-Sperry R-3. These were the aircraft of professional pilots. The last Pulitzer race was won by a Curtiss R3C racer just one month after that new aircraft's maiden flight. An offshoot of the Pulitzer races, the National Air Races began in 1926. The first was held in Philadelphia. George Cuddihy won with a closed-course speed of 180 mph. He flew a naval Boeing FB-3 biplane fighter. The National Air Races in 1927 were in Spokane, Washington. Lieutenant E.C. Batten in a Curtiss Hawk XP-6A, an Army "service test" biplane, won with a speed of 201 mph.

There were still races at state and county fairs in the United States, and local aviation days and city festivals throughout Europe, but those were more entertainment and demonstration. Speed had become a professional pursuit. Even barnstorming pilots raced, but air races were dominated by professional pilots. These professionals were often manufacturer's test pilots, and often military aviators, or at least full-time pilots with corporate sponsors. Their support organizations provided financial and technical assistance. Racing had practical value to the sponsors, including publicity and the development of speedy features wanted by many customers. Racing was sport, but it was also business — the business of developing and marketing efficient aircraft, and speed was a major criteria of efficiency.

Figure 5-29. A Macchi M.39, piloted by Mario de Bernardi won the 1926 Schneider Cup on 13 November 1926.

Polar Flights

Three teams raced toward the North Pole in 1926: George Wilkins of Australia led one team, Richard Byrd of the United States led an expedition, and Roald Amundsen of Norway and Lincoln Ellsworth of the United States led an expedition. Their motivations were personal, technological, and scientific, including the personal and nationalistic desire to be first to the pole and the urge to explore. It was a test of man and machine against arctic conditions. Of the three teams,

two succeeded. One in an airplane and one in an airship flew over the North Pole. Wilkins did not make it to the North Pole in 1926. He and his pilot Carl Eielson failed in their attempt in 1926, and again in 1927. They finally reached the pole by air in 1928. All three times Wilkins started at Point Barrow, Alaska.

The two successful teams started from Spitzbergen, Norway. Amundsen and Ellsworth on one team and naval Lieutenant Commander Byrd and army pilot Floyd Bennett on the other were at Spitzbergen, at Kings Bay specifically, at the same time. On 9 May 1926 Byrd and Bennett reached the North Pole in the Fokker Trimotor *Josephine Ford*, which had been built in Fokker's postwar factory in Holland. They flew back to Spitzbergen where Amundsen and Ellsworth warmly congratulated them.

Norwegian explorer Roald Amundsen had tried to reach the pole by airplane in 1925, but engine trouble in one of two Dornier-Wal seaplanes stopped the

Historical Evidence

The North Pole's aerial explorers wrote autobiographical accounts of their adventures:

Roald Amundsen and Lincoln Ellsworth, *First Crossing of the Polar Sea* (New York: George H. Doran, 1927). This book contains chapters by other members of the expedition too.

Richard Evelyn Byrd, *Skyward* (New York: G.P. Putnam's Sons, 1928).

Umberto Nobile, *My Polar Flights*, translated by Frances Fleetwood (New York: G.P. Putnam's Sons, 1961).

George H. Wilkins, *Flying the Arctic* (New York: G.P. Putnam's Sons, 1928).

Personal Profile

Richard Evelyn Byrd (1888-1957) traveled around the world at the age of twelve. He later graduated from the Naval Academy, but a football injury kept him in administrative jobs for a while. During World War I he completed the naval pilot training program. In 1919 he helped plan the transatlantic crossing of the NC flying boats. He and Floyd Bennett flew over the North Pole in 1926. The next year Byrd competed for the Orteig Prize, but Charles Lindbergh beat him across the Atlantic Ocean. Byrd flew over the South Pole in 1929. He holds the distinction of being the first man to fly over the North Pole, the first over the South Pole, and the first over both poles. He participated in the aerial exploration of Antarctica through the International Geophysical Year of 1957-58.

Richard Evelyn Byrd

Historic Event

On 9 May 1926 naval Lieutenant Commander Richard E. Byrd and army pilot Floyd Bennett made the first airplane flight over the North Pole. They flew the Fokker Trimotor *Josephine Ford*.

A few days later on 12 May 1926 the airship *Norge (Norway)* definitely passed over the North Pole. The Norwegian explorer Roald Amundsen and American adventurer Lincoln Ellsworth led the expedition from Spitzbergen on the 11th, over the North Pole on the 12th, and to Teller, Alaska, on the 14th.

Flight Lines

"The first stage of our navigation was the simple one of dead reckoning, or following the well-known landmarks in the vicinity of Kings Bay, which we had just left. . . .

. . .

As there are no landmarks on the ice, Polar Sea navigation by aircraft is similar to that on the ocean, where there is nothing but sun and stars and moon from which to determine one's position. The altitude above the sea horizon of one of these celestial bodies is taken with the sextant. Then, by mathematical calculations, requiring an hour or so to work out, the ship is located somewhere upon an imaginary line. The Polar Sea horizon, however, cannot always be depended upon, due to roughness of the ice. Therefore, we had a specially designed instrument that would enable us to take the altitude without the horizon . . .

. . .

"Bennett and I took turns piloting. . . . Once every three minutes while I was navigating I checked the wind drift and ground speed, so that in case of a change in wind I could detect it immediately and allow for it.

. . .

"We were aiming for Grey Point, Spitzbergen, and finally when we saw it dead ahead, we knew that we had been able to keep on our course! That we were exactly where we had thought we were!

. . .

"It was a wonderful relief not to have to navigate any more."

Richard Byrd describing the aerial navigation of his polar flight of 9 May 1926, in Byrd's *Skyward* (New York: G.P. Putnam's Sons, 1928).

Historical Evidence

Proponents of Italian aviation and of Norwegian aviation seeking first-flight honors for their respective nations, and opponents of Richard Byrd, have questioned whether Byrd indeed flew over the North Pole. The main objection is that his Fokker trimotor was not fast enough to make the distance in the time and weather of 9 May 1926, but his actual flight time was only minutes short of the minimum estimated time for the flight. There is evidence to suggest that Byrd did fly over the Pole as accurately as instruments and techniques of that time allowed.

Richard Byrd's polar diary was published in 1998 in a volume that also reprinted Byrd's navigational instructions to his pilot Floyd Bennett and Byrd's navigation report on the polar flight. The book also contains the report of the special committee of the National Geographic Society that verified Byrd's claim to have flown over the North Pole. The National Geographic Society studied Byrd's documentation and concluded,

"The feat of flying a plane 600 miles from land and returning directly to the point aimed for is a remarkable exhibition of skillful navigation and shows beyond a reasonable doubt that he knew where he was at all times during the flight."

See *To the Pole, the Diary and Notebook of Richard E. Byrd, 1925-1927,* edited by Raimund E. Goerler (Columbus: Ohio State University Press, 1998).

attempt. Those German-designed Dornier-Wals, by the way, were constructed in Italy to bypass Allied restrictions on German aircraft production. That 1925 failure led Amundsen to select the airship for his 1926 attempt. The airship attempt was financed by American adventurer Lincoln Ellsworth and supported by the Aero Club of Norway. They purchased a semi-rigid Italian airship made at the Italian government aircraft factory. This N-1 had a metal hull 348 feet long and 62 feet in diameter. It held 645,000 cubic feet of hydrogen in ten gas compartments. (Figure 5-30)

Figure 5-30. The Dornier-Wal seaplane used by Roald Amundsen in his attempt to reach the North Pole. Although he failed in the seaplane, he succeeded in an airship.

Amundsen and Ellsworth hired the director of the Italian government aircraft factory to be the pilot. This colorful and soon controversial man was Umberto Nobile. He later claimed nearly full credit for the 1926 flight and, in 1928, he crashed the airship *Italia* in the Arctic. Amundsen disappeared looking for survivors of the *Italia*. Nobile had helped to design and construct the N-1 and now supervised modifications for the new owners, who called the airship *Norge (Norway)*. The polar flight crew consisted of eight Norwegians, six Italians, one American, and one Swede; there was also ground support. (Figure 5-31)

Under the Norwegian flag, the Amundsen-Ellsworth expedition departed Spitzbergen on 11 May. They flew across the North Pole on 12 May, and used a sun compass to navigate toward Point Barrow, Alaska. En route the explorer Amundsen looked for undiscovered land, a northern continent or islands, but saw only ice on the Polar Sea. On 14 May the expedition landed at Teller, Alaska, about 60 miles north of Nome, after flying about 4,500 miles over the Arctic. They accomplished the first airship crossing of the North Pole only days after the first airplane reached that geographically remote spot.

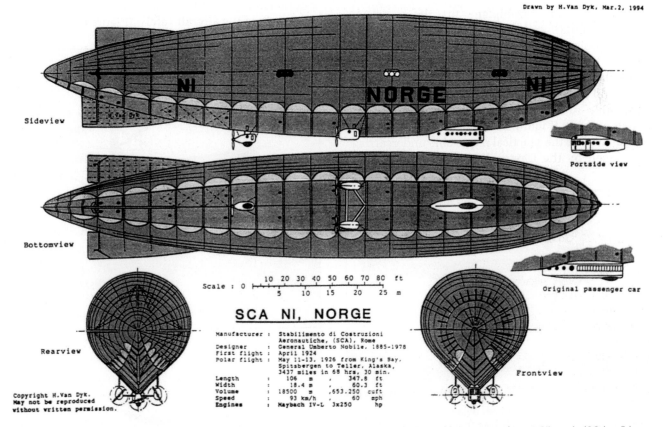

Drawn by H.Van Dyk, Mar.2, 1994

Sideview

Portside view

Bottomview

Original passenger car

Scale : 0 ⊢⊣⊢⊣ 10 20 30 40 50 60 70 80 ft
        5   10   15   20   25 m

Rearview

Frontview

Copyright H.Van Dyk.
May not be reproduced
without written permission.

SCA NI, NORGE

Manufacturer :	Stabilimento di Costruzioni Aeronautiche, (SCA), Rome	
Designer :	General Umberto Nobile, 1885-1978	
First flight :	April 1924	
Polar flight :	May 11-13, 1926 from King's Bay, Spitsbergen to Teller, Alaska, 3437 miles in 68 hrs, 30 min.	
Length :	106 m ,	347.8 ft
Width :	18.4 m ,	60.3 ft
Volume :	18500 m ,	,653.250 cu.ft
Speed :	93 km/h ,	60 mph
Engines :	Maybach IV-L 3x250 hp	

Figure 5-31. The *Norge* first flew in April 1924. Its Maybach engines enabled the *Norge* to cruise at 60 mph (93 km/h). This is the airship used by explorers Amundsen and Ellsworth to reach the North Pole in May 1926.

Flight Lines

"After our departure we first kept in communication with the small private wireless station at King's Bay, and afterward with the large, coastal station at Green Harbour.

"In order to accurately keep on the meridian of King's Bay up to the Pole, the course was constantly corrected with radio-bearings, taken to King's Bay and later to Svalbard wireless station, and we also took, when opportunity offered, long-distance bearings to Stavanger wireless station [the large Norwegian Trans-Atlantic Station, call sign LCM], Nauen, and the large American stations in the vicinity of New York."

Captain Birger Gottwaldt describing the radio navigation of the *Norge* from the 11th to the 14th of May 1926, in Roald Amundsen and Lincoln Ellsworth, *First Crossing of the Polar Sea* (New York: George H. Doran, 1927).

Research and Development

The postwar period was a time of change from war to war surplus to postwar products — military and civil. Research and development influenced the changes. Several navies, for example, converted war surplus ships into aircraft carriers. Britain's HMS *Hermes*, completed in 1923, was the first carrier designed as a carrier.

The de Havilland *Moth* biplane, first flown in 1925, became popular with European flying clubs and flight schools because it was cheap and lightweight, yet reliable, with a simple four-cylinder *Cirrus* engine. This light airplane was an important draw for private pilots, and it prompted de Havilland to open overseas companies to meet the demand throughout the British Empire. (Figure 5-32) Products were further developed, like the practical retractable undercarriage introduced by the Dayton-Wright company on its RB Racer.

Figure 5-32. According to British aviation historian Gibbs-Smith, the de Havilland Moth was "the most successful light aeroplane in history."

In addition to final products, there was experimentation. In Spain, Juan de la Cierva developed the autogiro and the principle of autorotation in which the engine set the rotor in motion but, once airborne, the motion continued via the slipstream acting upon the blades.

The challenge of vertical flight attracted international interest. In the United States alone Émile Berliner, George de Bothezat, M.B. Bleeker, and the Curtiss Aircraft company experimented with helicopters in the 1920s. A.G. von Baumhauer in the Netherlands and Étienne Oehmichen in France built experimental helicopters too. One of the most fruitful research efforts was that of Marquis Raul Pateras de Pescara,

an Argentine engineer working in France and Spain. Pateras de Pescara experimented with counter rotating biplane rotors. He invented the cyclic control, a mechanism to change the pitch of individual blades during rotation and thereby to vary the thrust as needed to tilt the plane of the rotor. Tilting was a change of attitude that allowed the craft to fly forward, backward, or sideways. Pateras de Pescara also applied the concept of autorotation to the helicopter. He demonstrated that if an engine stopped, the upward rush of air against the descending machine would automatically rotate a free rotor. The free rotor's energy could be stored until needed by the pilot to land the aircraft safely. (Figure 5-33)

Figure 5-33. The 1920s saw more research and development in rotorcraft. This produced such aircraft as the Pescara Helicopter No. 3 (top), and the Berliner helicopter (bottom).

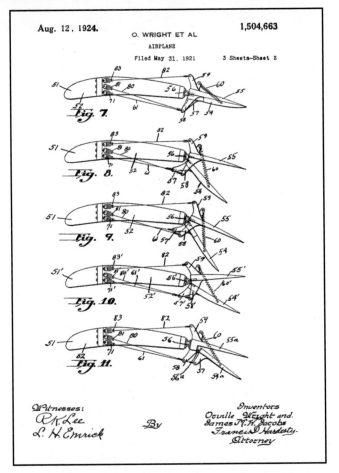

Aug. 12, 1924.

O. WRIGHT ET AL

AIRPLANE

Filed May 31, 1921   3 Sheets-Sheet 2

1,504,663

Witnesses:
R. K. Lee
L. H. Emrick

By

Inventors
Orville Wright and.
James N. H. Jacobs
Francis Hardesty.
Attorney

Figure 5-34. Orville Wright applied for a patent on 31 May 1921 that can best be described as the split flap. Among other things, the invention increased the lift of the airfoil thereby permitting considerably lower flying speeds than previously possible.

In the United States Orville Wright patented the split flap to increase the lift of an airfoil and thereby permit flying at lower speeds. (Figure 5-34) In Britain, A.A. Griffith envisioned turbine-driven propellers for aircraft (turbo-prop powerplants). He described the axial flow turbojet in his 1926 paper on *An Aerodynamic Theory of Turbine Design.*

The postwar period was obviously a time of activity and change. Airship development, barnstorming, and competitions of the postwar period continued into the Golden Age of Aviation, the late 1920s and 1930s, but that later period also included commercial airlines and airmail service, the foundations of which were laid in the postwar period.

Airlines and Airmail

After World War I, airmail and airlines usually developed together, but not always. Several airmail services actually began during the war. The Italian military air force, for example, began carrying airmail between Turin and Rome in May 1917. The next month the commercial Società Industrie Meridionali began transporting airmail between Naples and Palermo. That August airmail service opened between the French cities of Paris, Le Mans, and St. Nazaire. Scheduled international airmail service began in March 1918 with German Hansa-Brandenburg C.I biplanes flying between Kiev and Vienna; this was after Germany and Russia achieved their armistice.

Using Curtiss JN4 and Standard JNS biplanes, the United States Army established an airmail service between New York City and Washington in May 1918. The Canadian Royal Air Force started an airmail service in Canada the next month. Despite military participation and leadership in early airmail ventures, airmail quickly became a civil aviation activity and mostly a commercial activity.

France was the leading aviation country before the war. When the war ended, France had about 12,000 pilots and almost as many aircraft in the military, as well as a well-developed aviation production industry. With these resources and with government support, France reestablished its leadership in aviation after the war. The French government encouraged aviation through its National Weather Bureau and its Comité Francais de Propagande Aéronautique (French Committee to Promote Aeronautics), and by subsidizing the training of pilots, the development and sale of aircraft, and by providing subsidies to private individuals buying airplanes for personal use. This was while other governments reduced support for aviation in the absence of any wartime emergency.

Latécoère

French industrialist Pierre-Georges Latécoère began planning a commercial airmail venture even before the armistice. He wanted a postwar aviation venture that would not compete with existing railroads nor subject passengers to the discomforts of open-cockpit flights. His plan was to establish an airmail airline to link France with French territories on other continents. Africa was his first priority. He employed the Italian military pilot Beppo de Massimi to help plan and operate the airmail service. He named the company Lignes Aériennes Latécoère (Latécoère Air Lines). He obtained French government approval and Spanish government authorization to overfly Spain and Spanish territories in Africa, and to construct and operate the necessary airfields within Spanish borders. He hired pilots, built airfields, and initiated airmail service.

Personal Profile

Pierre-Georges Latécoère (1883-1943) was a French industrialist, wealthy from railroad and munitions contracts. He entered aviation during World War I. In October 1917 he obtained a government contract to manufacture a thousand Salmson reconnaissance planes within a year, and he filled the contract. As soon as the Armistice ended fighting in 1918, he established the Lignes Aériennes Latécoère (Latécoère Air Lines), sometimes called Compagnie Latécoère (Latécoère Company). His company flew airmail and later designed and produced airplanes specifically for airmail service. He sold the airmail company in 1927, and the new owner renamed it Aéropostale. Latécoère continued to make airplanes until his death during World War II.

Pierre-Georges Latécoère

Flight Lines

"When the night is very fine and you are at the stick of your ship, you half forget yourself and bit by bit the plane begins to tilt on the left. Pretty soon, while you still imagine yourself in plumb, you see the lights of a village under your right wing. There are no villages in the desert. A fishing-fleet in mid-ocean, then? There are no fishing-fleets in mid-Sahara. What —? Of course! You smile at the way your mind has wandered and you bring the ship back to plumb again. The village slips into place. You have hooked that particular constellation back in the panoply out of which it had fallen. Village? Yes, village of stars."

Antoine de Saint-Exupéry describing night flying over Africa in 1927-28, in Saint-Exupéry's *Wind, Sand and Stars* (1939), reprinted in his *Airman's Odyssey* (New York: Reynal & Hitchcock, 1943).

The first airmail flights covered the 200 miles between Toulouse, France, and Barcelona, Spain, in December 1918. Within months *la Ligne* (the Line) extended another 250 miles to Alicante in southern Spain. The condition of the new Latécoère airfield there contributed to the crash landings of the first two flights to arrive from France. In March 1919 Latécoère began to explore a route south to Dakar, the administrative capital of French West Africa. It was September before regularly scheduled airmail service reached Casablanca and 1925 before the airmail service finally reached Dakar.

The Toulouse-Dakar route covered over sixteen hundred miles. The first aircraft used to carry mail over *la Ligne* were the Latécoère-built Salmson biplanes. In the twenties Latécoère used mostly war-surplus Breguet 14 biplanes; more than five thousand had been produced during the war. The Breguets were open cockpit biplanes with wooden propellers, a 300-horsepower engine, and a range of about 400 miles. The range of the aircraft determined where the company-established airfields were located to refuel, maintain, and rescue aircraft en route. The Breguets required frequent maintenance, but the machines were simple enough to be easily repaired.

Flight Lines

"The trip went well, aside from a breakdown and the plane crashing into the desert."

Antoine de Saint-Exupéry describing a February 1927 flight on which he was a passenger and the pilot was his friend Henri Guillaumet, in a letter from Africa to his mother, quoted in Stacy Schiff's *Saint-Exupéry, a Biography*.

Adventurous pilots like Henri Guillaumet, Jean Mermoz, and Antoine de Saint-Exupéry flew the "southern mail" over France and Spain and sometimes over hostile territory. Moors routinely shot at the mailplanes, which low-powered engines and desert-high temperatures sometimes combined to keep the altitudes below a thousand feet. The Moors occasionally killed, sometimes wounded, and regularly captured French pilots who made unscheduled landings in the desert. Their objective was to rob the mail of cash and to ransom the crew. Latécoère thus flew planes in pairs, one to carry the airmail and the other to fly escort in case the mailplane went down and required aid. The company even hired native interpreters to ride the mailplanes in order to negotiate ransom should the French crew be captured. Planes also went down because the Breguets were old in

Historical Evidence

French author Antoine de Saint-Exupéry wrote a children's tale about *The Little Prince* (*Le petit prince*, 1943) from Asteroid B612 who visited Earth. Saint-Exupéry was an aviator who wrote about aviation too. His first books were novels, fictional stories that he made up based upon his own experiences in aviation: *Southern Mail* (*Courrier sud,* 1929) was about flying airmail in Africa, and *Night Flight* (*Vol de nuit,* 1931) about flying the mail in South America. Saint-Exupéry also wrote autobiographies, factual accounts of his life, like *Wind, Sand and Stars* (*Terre des hommes,* 1939) about his flying the mail in Africa and South America, or his later *Flight to Arras* (*Pilote de guerre,* 1942) about flying reconnaissance during World War II. Autobiographies and even autobiographical novels provide primary evidence of what happened.

Another type of evidence is the biography, an account of someone's life written by someone else. A biography is a secondary source. An example is Stacy Schiff's *Saint-Exupéry, a Biography.*

Saint-Exupéry wrote in his native French. Lewis Galantiére and Stuart Gilbert translated his books into English.

design as well as age. Sand fouled carburetors and fuel. Coastal humidity soaked the cloth fabric covering the wings and separated the fabric from the structure, and the dampness also corroded metal parts. Of the 126 pilots recruited by Latécoère between 1923 and 1926, seven died from work-related injuries and another 55 left the company.

Latécoère built a prototype mailplane — the Latécoère or simply Laté 17 — in 1924. It had room for passengers as well as mail; after all, if a plane were flying between two points, why not transport whatever load — mail or passengers— would pay. In 1927 a Frenchman living in Brazil bought the Latécoère airline, changed the name to Compagnie Générale Aéropostale or simply Aéropostale, and began the expansion across the South Atlantic Ocean and throughout South America. The Laté 25 and Laté 26 mailplanes with space for passengers went into service after the airline was sold and renamed. Latécoère was not the only French airmail line during the postwar period, but it was the largest and most ambitious.

Aerial Diplomacy

The Paris Peace Conference of 1919 provided the opportunity for the Allied and Associated Powers to adopt an international convention regarding aerial navigation. These nations shared the wartime experience of cooperating in the air. The 1919 international convention drafted a multilateral system for managing airspace over the various participating nations. This facilitated the development of airlines throughout Europe during the postwar period. Allied reparations and restrictions imposed on Germany prompted Germany to choose a different diplomatic route to managing its own airways and to establishing international airways.

The Treaty of Versailles had prohibited only German *military* aviation, but the subsequent London Ultimatum of May 1921 forbade German production of *all* aircraft for the rest of that year, and the Allies later extended that prohibition into mid-1922. In 1922 the annual international Conference of Ambassadors acknowledged that Germany had delivered "all military and naval aeronautical material" required by Article 202 of the Treaty of Versailles; therefore, Germany was allowed to resume manufacturing, exporting, and importing *civil* aviation equipment, **but** with new restrictions. These restrictions specified airplane engines of no more than 60 horsepower, airplane speeds not to exceed 170 kilometers per hour (about 106 mph), airplanes not to fly higher than 4,000 meters (around 13,000 feet), and cargo limited to less than 600 kilograms (a little over 1,300 pounds). On 1 January 1923, the civil aviation restrictions of the Treaty of Versailles expired, but the 1922 restrictions remained.

Paris Peace Conference, 1919. Left to right, Lloyd George, Vittorio Orlando, Georges Clemenceau and President Woodrow Wilson

When the Treaty of Versailles clauses expired, the Allies invited Germany to accept the international convention for air navigation. Germany chose to remain outside the multilateral system. Germany instead reached a series of bilateral agreements to establish commercial air routes for German airlines. It required all commercial airlines flying over Germany to obtain special authorization, with the exception of airlines of nations with which Germany had bilateral agreements (initially Switzerland, Denmark, Netherlands, and the Free City of Danzig). In other words, Germany restricted its airspace. Under this decree, Germany confiscated fourteen French aircraft! In 1926 Germany and France reached an agreement regarding air navigation and the confiscation ceased. That May the German airline Luft Hansa and the French airline Farman began flying between Berlin and Paris. Also in 1926 the last of the restrictions imposed upon German civil aviation were lifted. Soon Germany signed air treaties with Belgium, Czechoslovakia, Great Britain, Italy, and Spain. These bilateral agreements and the end of restrictions opened the air for German commercial aviation, which literally took off.

Germany

Despite being hamstrung during the postwar period, Germany produced many airlines. More than 50 German companies applied for airline licenses in 1920 alone! Deutsche Luftschiffahrts A.G. (DELAG), the German airship airline organized in 1909) resumed service in 1919. For several months it provided scheduled airship service by flying the Zeppelin LZ 120 *Bodensee*. DELAG carried more than two thousand passengers before the Allies requisitioned the airship as a war reparation. (Figure 5-35)

The airline Deutsche Luft-Reederei (D.L.R.) registered in 1918 in anticipation of the postwar resumption of civil aviation and, in February 1919, D.L.R. started service between the former capital of Berlin and the new government seat of Weimar. The first flight carried newspapers, the second carried mail, and within a week D.L.R. transported passengers between the cities. In its first six months of operations, D.L.R. expanded its routes within Germany and carried 1574 passengers. At the time it used war-surplus bombers, the four-engine Staaken R XIVs, but Allied restrictions soon forced it to use smaller airplanes, like the A.E.G. J II produced by Allgemeine Elektrizitäts-Gesellschaft (A.E.G.) and converted from the wartime J II biplane; conversion included adding a roof over the open cockpit.

D.L.R. was a founding member of the International Air Traffic Association organized during the summer of 1919. In 1920, it formed an airline service pool with the Royal Dutch Airline K.L.M. (Koninklijke Luchtvaart Maatschappij voor Nederland an Kolonien) and the Danish company D.D.L. (Det Danske Luftfartselskab); a pool is an association of competitors who agree to cooperate for mutual benefit. The airline continued operations despite temporary fuel shortages, Allied occupation of the Ruhr and Rhineland districts (which meant no flying there), and internal reorganizations. The holding company Aero-Union acquired D.L.R. in 1921; that linked the airline with the Luftschiffbau Zeppelin, Hamburg-Amerikanische Paketfahrt, and the joint German-Russian airline Deutsch-Russische Luftverkehrsgesellschaft (Deruluft) for about a year. In 1922 D.L.R. became part of the Deutsche Aero Lloyd corporation. The scene continually shifted until January 1926 when Deutsche Aero Lloyd group and Junkers Luftverkehr group merged into Deutsche Luft Hansa (D.L.H.).

Figure 5-35. The airship *Bodensee* (LZ 120) was used by DELAG to resume passenger service in Germany following the war.

Figure 5-36. Luft Hansa acquired and flew a variety of aircraft in the 1920s, such as this Dornier Komet III.

Luft Hansa acquired the many airlines associated with Lloyd and Junkers groups, including Junkers aerial services in South America. One of Luft Hansa's first initiatives was sponsoring a 1926 prospecting flight to Peking, China.

Luft Hansa also acquired the aircraft of the many airlines: Dornier Komet IIs and IIIs, Fokker-Grulich FIIs and FIIIs, Junkers F-13s, G-24s, A-20s, and a variety of other aircraft. The most popular airliner was the F-13, and Luft Hansa acquired a total of 55 F-13s. The F-13 was a postwar design, an airline design. It was a metal monoplane with a low cantilever wing. The enclosed cabin could carry four passengers in addition to crew members. Junkers produced 322 F-13s from 1919 into the early 1930s; Junkers designated the plane J13 during development. It exported the aircraft to North and South America as well as to European countries. (Figure 5-36)

During the early 1920s when the Allies restricted German civil aircraft production, the F-13 and other German designs, including Dornier and Rohrbach, were made under license or in German-run factories in other countries, such as Italy, the Soviet Union, Sweden, and Switzerland. The Dornier Komet III was another postwar German design for a metal airliner, this one a high-wing monoplane with enclosed cabin and seating for six. The Japanese Kawasaki company bought a license and began producing the Komet III in Japan in 1926.

Imperial Airways

In contrast to the French and German competitive efforts in commercial aviation, the United Kingdom used a conservative approach. Several airlines began

operation in the postwar kingdom. Encouraged by the British government, several of these — British Marine Air Navigation, Daimler Airways, Handley Page Transport, and Instone Airline — merged in 1924 to form a national airline called Imperial Airways. The merged fleet consisted of old airplanes: seven de Havilland D.H. 34s, three Handley Page W.8b's, two Sea Eagles, and one Vimy Commercial. The new airline developed routes to India and Africa, but largely ignored domestic and European routes, with the exception of a few major European cities like Paris and Zurich. For the popular Paris-London run, Imperial acquired new three-engine Armstrong Whitworth A.W. Argosy biplanes in 1926. These were luxury planes for the luxury-class passengers Imperial targeted.

Africa, Asia, South America, and South Pacific

During the postwar period American, British, French, Dutch, German, and Russian companies explored the globe in search of air routes because airlines provided comunication with colonies. The process was gradual. During the 1920s, for example, British Imperial Airways developed airline service along routes of British colonial ports: Croydon/London to Gibraltar to Malta to Baghdad to Aden to Karachi to India, between Cairo and Basra, and into British Africa. Such air routes conferred commercial and political advantage. Great Britain sought an air route to India and to independent China; the Netherlands sought a route to resource-rich Netherlands East Indies (Indonesia); France to French Indochina (Vietnam,

Figure 5-37. The Singapore I was based on this prototype N-C Cromarty flying boat of 1921. It was flown by Sir Alan Cobham in a survey flight around Africa in 1928.

Cambodia, and Laos); the United States to the Philippines; and the Soviet Union to northern Asia and Afghanistan. (Figure 5-37)

Some efforts were small and local. A couple of former American military pilots established the Philippine Airway Service between the cities of Cebu and Iloilo on neighboring islands, and a Filipino established a charter service between sugar-rich Iloilo and the nearby island of Negros. Mining airlines in South America, that flew supplies to interior mines, are another example. Mexico's Compañia Mexicana de Transportación, founded in 1921, specialized in serving oilfields while it tried to develop intercity routes.

United States

After the military proved the route and the concept, the United States Post Office assumed responsibility for airmail service. The first route, in August 1918, was between New York and Washington, the same route on which the Army had made the maiden airmail flights in May. During 1918 over seven hundred airmail flights were made covering a total distance of over 80,000 miles, and airmail pilots made 46 forced landings. In 1919 the figures leaped to over 1,600 airmail flights, nearly 400,000 miles flown, and over 160 forced landings.

In 1919 the Post Office Department's Air Mail Service began development of a transcontinental airmail service. It opened the first segment between New York and Cleveland with a stop at Bellefonte, Pennsylvania, and a second segment between Cleveland and Chicago with a stop at Bryan, Ohio. At the time pilots normally flew mail during the day and transferred the mail to trains for night transportation.

Historic Event

On 15 May 1918 the United States Army began airmail service by flying mail over the New York – Washington route with a stop in Philadelphia. The maiden service required four Curtiss JN-4H airplanes and four pilots, all Army lieutenants. The plan was for southbound mail to leave New York on one plane, change planes in Philadelphia, and continue on to Washington, and for the northbound mail to do the reverse. Torrey H. Webb flew the southbound mail from New York to Philadelphia, and James C. Edgerton carried it from there to Washington. The northbound pilot leaving Washington became disoriented, flew south, decided to land for directions, and flipped the plane. Without the Washington mail, H. Paul Culver flew from Philadelphia to New York. Thus the Army provided the first successful airmail service and logged the first mailplane accident on the same day.

The third and fourth segments opened in 1920. The western segments covered the route between Chicago and Omaha via Iowa City and the longer Omaha/San Francisco route with stops at North Platte, Nebraska; Cheyenne, Rawlins, and Rock Springs, Wyoming; Salt Lake City, Utah; and Elko and Reno, Nevada. The first transcontinental all-airmail trip took place that September and required nearly 83 hours to complete.

Historic Event

On 8 September to 11 September 1920 the U.S. Air Mail Service completed the first transcontinental airmail service. This experimental delivery involved numerous planes and pilots flying in relay between New York and San Francisco. Randolph Page, James P. Murray, and Edison E. Mouton were pilots on different stages. The trip was a series of daytime flights that took nearly 83 hours.

An experimental coast-to-coast flight of the mail happened in February 1921. Jack Knight and two other pilots, flying day and night in relay fashion, crossed the United States to demonstrate the feasibility of transcontinental airmail. In the process, they set the west-to-east transcontinental flying record of 33 hours and 20 minutes. To achieve this feat, the Air Mail Service started two planes westbound from New York and two planes eastbound from San Francisco. Icing forced one westbound plane down in Pennsylvania, and weather — snow, rain, and fog — grounded the other westbound effort in Chicago. One eastbound flight crashed when the pilot stalled the plane on takeoff from Elko, Nevada. The pilot was

Historic Event

Between 22 February and 23 February 1921, airmail pilots flying in relay and flying day and night carried mail from San Francisco to New York in a total elapsed time of 33 hours and 20 minutes, a record time. Their planes were Liberty engine-powered de Havillands.

killed, but a reserve plane picked up his mail and flew eastward. Only one pilot braved the weather between Omaha and Chicago — James H. Knight. In one plane the mail continued east, via relay, and reached New York City. Months later the Air Mail Service began regularly scheduled night flying. (Figure 5-38)

The Air Mail Service experimented with fire protection, ignition systems, flight instruments, radio navigation aids, light beacons, and night flying. Night flying, for example, remained experimental through 1923. The Air Mail Service used a variety of airplanes, though for three years the wartime de Havilland D.H. 4 was standard. The Service won two Collier trophies: the 1922 trophy "for a year's operation without a single fatal accident" and the 1923 trophy "for night flying in commercial transportation." Its transcontinental airmail route became the main airway across the country. But the number of forced landings went up as the number of miles flown climbed: over 800

Figure 5-38. James H. Knight was one of three pilots who took part in the record breaking transcontinental airmail flight in February 1921.

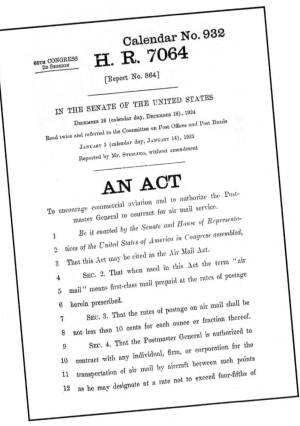

Figure 5-39. The Air Mail Service involved many different people and modes of transportation.

forced landings in 1920 and over 1,400 in 1921. Reorganized, the Air Mail Service flew fewer miles in 1922 and 1923 and greatly reduced the number of forced landings, only about 550 in 1922 and about 500 in 1923. Airmail was becoming a safer industry, though a government industry still. In the Air Mail Service in 1925, the Post Office Department employed 745 people. Of that number, 699 or 94% were ground personnel, including 353 mechanics and mechanic's helpers who maintained the postal fleet of 96 aircraft. (Figure 5-39)

Flight Lines

Airmail pilot Dean Smith wrote of "the pleasure and excitement of those first hesitant probes across the dark plains. We were like children venturing from home, each time daring a bit farther, then running back filled with awe at what we had done. It felt empty and lonesome out there, even with the beacons flashing, four or five visible ahead; we felt the fear of the unknown, the excitement of pioneering, and the satisfaction of accomplishment."

Quoted in William M. Leary, *Aerial Pioneers, the U.S. Air Mail Service, 1918-1927*.

Two acts of Congress would gradually transform aviation into a regulated and subsidized industry. One was the Air Mail Act of 1925, also known as the Kelly Act after its sponsor, Congressman Clyde Kelly of Pennsylvania. The second was the Air Commerce Act of 1926, sometimes called the Bingham Bill, after Senator Hiram Bingham of Connecticut. The Air Mail Act of 1925 led to the contracting of airmail service to commercial airlines, and many airlines organized in anticipation of the act and in response to the act. The act phased the Post Office out of transporting airmail and subsidized airlines that won airmail contracts. With the passage of the Air Commerce Act in 1926,

the Department of Commerce assumed aviation tasks that had been performed by the Post Office Department, notably the maintenance and operation of airways. This Air Commerce Act also provided for the licensing of pilots, airworthiness regulations, and other federal activities in civil aviation.

Calendar No. 932

68TH CONGRESS
2D SESSION

H. R. 7064

[Report No. 864]

IN THE SENATE OF THE UNITED STATES

DECEMBER 16 (calendar day, DECEMBER 18), 1924
Read twice and referred to the Committee on Post Offices and Post Roads

JANUARY 5 (calendar day, JANUARY 14), 1925
Reported by Mr. STERLING, without amendment

AN ACT

To encourage commercial aviation and to authorize the Postmaster General to contract for air mail service.

1   *Be it enacted by the Senate and House of Representa-*
2 *tives of the United States of America in Congress assembled,*
3   That this Act may be cited as the Air Mail Act.
4   SEC. 2. That when used in this Act the term "air
5 mail" means first-class mail prepaid at the rates of postage
6 herein prescribed.
7   SEC. 3. That the rates of postage on air mail shall be
8 not less than 10 cents for each ounce or fraction thereof.
9   SEC. 4. That the Postmaster General is authorized to
10 contract with any individual, firm, or corporation for the
11 transportation of air mail by aircraft between such points
12 as he may designate at a rate not to exceed four-fifths of

The most immediate results of the Air Mail Act and the Air Commerce Act were a sudden growth of airlines in the United States that had lagged far behind Europe and the development of mailplanes and airliners in a country that had thus far neglected commercial designs. T. Claude Ryan in California incorporated his Ryan Airlines to provide service

Figure 5-40. Many different aircraft were used to carry airmail in the mid-1920s.

between Los Angeles and San Diego in 1925. He started operations with modified Curtiss Standard biplanes powered by the new 150-horsepower Hispano Suiza engine. Henry Ford backed aircraft designer William B. Stout, and together they produced the Stout metal airplane and opened airline service between Chicago, Detroit, and Cleveland in 1925. These and other companies vied for the new federal airmail contracts. Some companies, like Ryan, failed to obtain mail contracts and went out of business; for example, Ryan carried over 5,500 passengers in 1926, but ceased operation in 1927. A few commercial ventures survived without airmail contracts. These were air taxi, air charter, or air show companies, many of which also provided lessons to would-be fliers.

Eleven companies became airmail carriers in 1926: Colonial Air Transport, Colorado Airways, Florida Airways, Ford Motor Company, National Air Transport, Northwest Airways, Pacific Air Transport, Robertson Aircraft, Stout Air Services, Varney Air Lines, and Western Air Express. These were all new companies established in the mid-twenties to take advantage of the business opportunity presented by privatization of airmail. They provided feeder service to the main transcontinental line still operated by the Post Office during the transition from government to commercial aircraft. Some of the new mail carriers transported only mail, like Varney which flew Swallow biplanes over the Pasco-Boise-Elko route, but most also carried passengers, and some even carried express cargo. (Figure 5-40)

Conclusion

The postwar years were a transitional period: from war to peace, from war surplus to new products, and from government and military aviation to private and commercial aviation. It was a time to set aside the past and to prepare for the future.

Study Questions

1. What types of aircraft flew across the Atlantic Ocean in 1919?

2. What enabled aircraft to fly long distances in 1919?

3. Given the Allied restrictions upon German aviation during the postwar period, how did Germany maintain its lead in airship technology?

4. Why did the United States switch from hydrogen to helium gas in military airships?

5. Who was the first to fly around the world, when, and why?

6. How might an autobiographical account of an event differ from a journalistic account of the same event? Hint: Compare the writings of Alcock and Brown with the book by Lowell Thomas listed in the bibliography section of this chapter.

7. A general court martial found Billy Mitchell guilty of what?

8. Who was Pierre-Georges Latécoère?

9. Why did imperial powers prospect, survey, and establish long-distance air routes?

10. Why did airmail service and commercial passenger service often develop together?

Bibliography

Alcock, John and Arthur Whitten Brown. 1919-1920 magazine articles; reprinted as *Our Transatlantic Flight*. London: William Kimber, 1969.

Allen, Peter. *The 91 before Lindbergh*. Shrewsbury, England: Airlife Publishing, 1984.

Arnold, Henry H. *Airmen and Aircraft, an Introduction to Aeronautics*. New York: Ronald Press Company, 1926.

Davies, R.E.G. *A History of the World's Airlines*. London: Oxford University Press, 1964.

Davies, R.E.G. *Lufthansa, an Airline and Its Aircraft*. Rockville, MD: Paladwr Press, 1991.

Gunn, John. *The Defeat of Distance, Qantas, 1919-1939*. 1985; St. Lucia: University of Queensland Press, 1988.

Leary, William M. *Aerial Pioneers, the U.S. Air Mail Service, 1918-1927*. Washington: Smithsonian Institution Press, 1985.

Payne, Lee. *Lighter Than Air, an Illustrated History of the Airship*. 1977; New York: Orion Books, 1991.

Schiff, Stacy. *Saint-Exupéry, a Biography*. New York: Alfred A. Knopf, 1994.

Thomas, Lowell. *The First World Flight*. Boston: Houghton Mifflin, 1925.

Timeline

Light blue type indicates an event not directly related to aviation.

1919	March 23. In Italy, Benito Mussolini (1883-1945) founded the Italian fascist movement in the form of the Fasci d'Italiani de Combattimento.
1919	May 8-31. A.C. Read was commander of the crew of five and Navy-Curtiss flying boat designated NC-4 ("Nancy"-4) that completed the first transatlantic flight, from North America to England. He made the flight by hopping from stop to stop and by following a line of naval ships drawn across the ocean.
1919	June 14-15. Demonstrating a return to peacetime aviation, British airmen John Alcock and Arthur Brown flew a Vimy biplane powered by two Rolls Royce Eagle engines across the Atlantic Ocean from Newfoundland to Ireland, and thereby completed the first nonstop transatlantic flight.
1919	July 2-5 and 9-13. The British R.34 became the first airship to cross the Atlantic Ocean, the first aircraft to cross the Atlantic east to west, the first aircraft to make a round-trip flight over the Atlantic, and the first to attempt to use a direction-finding radio on a transoceanic flight.
1919	July - November. An Army Martin Model G biplane, designed as a Glenn Martin bomber (GMB) for use in World War I, but configured as an observation plane, flew around the rim of the continental United States.
1919	August 11. In Germany the national assembly of the newly formed republic adopted the Weimar constitution, which was named after the town of Weimar.
1919	November 12 — December 10. The brothers Ross and Keith Smith and two mechanics flew from London to Australia in a Vickers Vimy. They flew the 11,294 miles (18,172 km) in less than a month and won a prize offered by the Australians for such a flight.
1919	In Norway, Vilhelm Bjerknes (1862-1951) and his son Jakob Bjerknes (1897-1975) introduced the term "front" to meteorology.
1920	January 10. The Treaty of Versailles became effective after ratification by 29 countries; among the Allies, the United States, China, Ecuador, and Nicaragua failed to ratify it.
1920	February 4 - March 20. Pierre van Ryneveld and C.J. Quintin Brand completed the first flight from England to South Africa, via the outposts, like Cairo, in the British Empire.
1920	February 7. At Villacoublay, France, Joseph Sadi-Lecointe flew a Nieuport-Delage 29 to set the first postwar world speed record: 275.264 km/h (171.041 mph). At the time, for speed records, the Fédération Aéronautique Internationale required four runs over a one kilometer course, including runs in both directions to cancel the effect of wind.
1920	March 10. In the United Kingdom the Government of Ireland Bill divided Ireland into a southern state and a northern state; the act became effective in April 1921, and Michael Collins became the first prime minister of the southern Irish Free State in January 1922.
1920	November 16. In Russia the Bolsheviks led by Vladimir Ilyich Lenin (1870-1924) won the Civil War.
1921	The British Commonwealth of Nations was founded as a federation of the various parts of the British Empire.

1921   July 21. Billy Mitchell of the Army Air Service commanded the bombing of the captured German battleship *Ostfriesland* by Army Martin MB-2 biplane bombers; he thereby demonstrated air power's effectiveness against naval ships.

1921   August 23. Britain's airship R.38 on a test flight made a high-speed turn and snapped its light frame. The airship crashed, killing forty-four men, including the core of the British airship program and sixteen observers or trainees from the United States Navy.

1921   December 13. At the Washington Conference, the United States, the British Empire, France, and Japan signed an agreement regarding their respective insular possessions in the Pacific Ocean; this Washington Conference of 1921-1922 produced seven treaties, including the February 1922 Washington Treaty limiting naval armaments signed by Italy in addition to the four powers involved in the insular-possessions treaty.

1922   March 30 — June 17. Two Portuguese pilots, Gago Coutinho and Artur Sacadura Cabral, flew the first flight across the South Atlantic Ocean; they flew from Lisbon, Portugal, to Rio de Janiero, Brazil, and wrecked two planes enroute.

1922   October 13. The Armistice of Mudanya ended the Greek-Turkish War.

1922   December 30. Russia, Belarus, Ukraine, and the Transcaucasian Federation agreed to form the Union of Soviet Socialist Republics (USSR); this new confederation and its constitution became effective the next year.

1923   January. French and Belgian forces occupied the Ruhr region because Germany failed to make reparation payments.

1923   January 9. Spanish designer Juan de la Cierva made the first official flight of his first successful autogiro, the C.4.

1923   May 2-3. Military pilots Oakley G. Kelly and John A. Macready of the Army Air Service made the first nonstop transcontinental flight in the United States; they logged 26 hours and 50 minutes in the air in a Fokker T-2 between the departure from Roosevelt Field, Long Island, New York, and the landing at Rockwell Field, California.

1923   June 17. Using a de Havilland D.H. 4B light bomber modified into a tanker, the United States Army refueled a de Havilland D.H. 4B light bomber in flight.

1923   September 1. An earthquake destroyed Yokohama and most of Tokyo, Japan.

1924   January 21. Soviet Leader Vladimir Ilyich Lenin (1870-1924) died, and Josef Stalin (1879-1953) succeeded him as chairman of the Politburo or central committee of the Communist Party.

1924   April 6 — September 28. Four Douglas World Cruisers attempted to fly around the world, from Seattle to Seattle. Two completed the flight — the first round-the-world flight in history. Army airmen Lowell Smith and Leslie Arnold in the *Chicago* and Erik Nelson and John Harding in the *New Orleans* completed the flight.

1924   Summer. At the eighth Olympic Games, held in Paris, Finnish runner Paavo Nurmi won a record five gold medals.

1924   October 13-15. The Zeppelin *LZ 126* made a transatlantic crossing by flying from the factory in Friedrichshafen to Lakehurst, New Jersey, where Germany turned the airship over to the United States Navy; the Navy christened this ship the *Los Angeles (ZR-3)*.

1925   January 3. Benito Mussolini (1883-1945) became the dictator of Italy.

1925	In Paris, France, the Exposition Internationale des Arts Décoratifs et Industriels Modernes introduced the world to the Art Deco design style that featured slender forms, straight lines, and sleek appearance.
1925	November 16 - 1926 March 13. Alan Cobham, A. Elliott, and B. Emmott flew a de Havilland DH 50 round-trip between Croydon, England, and Cape Town, South Africa; they reached Cape Town on 17 February and began the return trip. This was the first round trip between the two points. Later in 1926 Cobham made the first round-trip flight between England and Australia (June 30 to October 1) and lost his engineer to a Bedouin bullet fired from the desert below the plane.
1926	May 9. Naval Lieutenant Commander Richard E. Byrd and army pilot Floyd Bennett made the first airplane flight over the North Pole; they flew the Fokker Trimotor *Josephine Ford*.
1926	May 11-14. Roald Amundsen led the expedition of the airship *Norge* from Spitzbergen on the 11th, over the North Pole — the first airship flight over the Pole — on the 12th, and to Teller, Alaska, on the 14th; with Amundsen of Norway were Lincoln Ellsworth of the United States, Umberto Nobile of Italy and others.
1926	September 5. In the United States the Ford Motor Company introduced the eight-hour work day and the five-day work week.
1926	September 8. The League of Nations admitted Germany to membership.
1926	September 14. An airplane of the Russian Dobrolet airline arrived in Kabul, Afghanistan. It was a Junkers F-13 probably built at the Fili factory in Moscow, which made Junkers aircraft under license; Dobrolet provided service to Kabul thereafter.
1927	Helen Wills (1906-) of the United States won her first ladies-singles title at Wimbledon; she won a record eight Wimbledon titles during her tennis career.
1927	January 7. British Imperial Airways opened its airline route linking the colonial cities of Basra, Iraq, and Cairo, Egypt.

CHAPTER 6

GOLDEN AGE (1927-1939)

AVIATION HISTORY

Summary of Events

May 20-21. Charles Lindbergh flew nonstop and solo from New York to Paris. **1927**

1927 September 16. German President Paul Hindenburg refused to accept the war guilt clause of the Treaty of Versailles.

October 14-15. The first nonstop airplane flight across the South Atlantic Ocean. **1927**

1927 Chinese civil wars began.

April 12-13. The first nonstop, east-to-west flight across the Atlantic Ocean. **1928**

1928 October 1. The Soviet Union began its first Five-Year Plan.

August 8-29. The *Graf Zeppelin* flew around the world. **1929**

1929 October 24-29. The U.S. stock market crashed.

November 28-29. The Byrd Antarctic Expedition flew over the South Pole. **1929**

1930 March 12. Mahatma Gandhi led the "salt march."

October 5. The British airship R.101 crashed. **1930**

1930 Construction continued on the Maginot Line of defense between France and Germany.

February 2. The Geneva Disarmament Conference opened. **1931**

1931 June 23-July 1. Wiley Post and Harold Gatty flew around the world in 8 days, 15 hours, 51 minutes.

September 18. Japan began its siege of Mukden (now Shenyang), Manchuria. **1931**

1931 October 3-5. Clyde Pangborn and Hugh Herndon, Jr. flew from Japan to Wenatchee, Washington.

May 20-21. Amelia Earhart became the first woman to fly across the Atlantic Ocean nonstop and solo. **1932**

1932 June 15. The Chaco War started.

March 4. Franklin Delano Roosevelt became the 32nd president of the United States. **1933**

1933 April 3. Lord Clydesdale and Stewart Blacker, and David McIntyre and Sidney Bonnet flew over Mount Everest.

Light blue type represents events that are not directly related to aviation.

1933 October 14. Adolf Hitler withdrew Germany from the Geneva Disarmament Conference and from the League of Nations.

1934 October 21 - 1935 October 20. Mao Tse-tung led the Chinese Communist on the "Long March" from southern China to northern China.

1935 May 28. The first flight of the Messerschmitt Bf 109 was made.

1935 October 2. Italy invaded Ethiopia; later in the month, the League of Nations denounced action and imposed sanctions on Italy.

1936 January 20. King George V of the United Kingdom died, and his oldest son became King Edward VIII. Edward abdicated in December, and his brother George VI became king.

1936 July 17. Generals Francisco Franco and José Sanjurjo led an uprising in Spanish Morocco that began the Spanish Civil War.

1937 May 6. The *Hindenburg* caught fire and crashed at Lakehurst, New Jersey.

1937 November 6. Italy joined the Anti-Comintern Pact.

1938 March 13. Germany annexed Austria.

1939 August 27. The Heinkel HE 178 jet-powered airplane made its maiden flight.

1933 July 15-22 Wiley Post flew solo around the world in 7 days, 18 hours, and 49 minutes.

1934 October 20 - November 4. C.W.A. Scott and T. Campbell Black won the MacRobertson air race from England to Australia.

1935 March 16. Germany renounced the Treaty of Versailles and began full rearmament.

1935 July 28. The first flight of the Boeing Model 299, later known as the B-17 Flying Fortress, was made.

1935 November 22. Pan American started transpacific airmail service with a flight from San Francisco via Honolulu, Wake, and Guam, to Manila in the Philippines.

1936 June 26. The Focke-Achgelis Fa 61 dual-rotor helicopter made its maiden flight.

1936 September 29. F.R.D. Swain flew a Bristol Type 138 wooden monoplane to a world altitude record of 49,967 feet (15,223 meters).

1937 June 20. A Russian ANT-25 flew the first nonstop, great-circle flight from the Soviet Union to the United States.

1937 December 13. Japan captured Nanjing, China, and began the Nanjing Massacre.

1938 July 10-14. Pilot Howard Hughes and his crew of four flew around the world in a Lockheed 14 in a record setting elapsed time of 3 days, 19 hours, and 17 minutes.

1939 September 1. Germany invaded Poland and, thereby, began the combat of World War II.

Introduction

In 1927 the young American pilot Charles Lindbergh flew alone across the Atlantic Ocean to France and fame. More than ninety people had flown across the Atlantic Ocean before Lindbergh's historic flight, so his flight both closed the postwar period of long-distance flying and opened the Golden Age of Aviation in which new aircraft and new aviators met new aeronautical challenges. Lindbergh and his flight became symbols of what was good in society, of man and machine in harmony, of individual success in a modern technological and mobile world. He was the Golden Boy of the Golden Age — the new Icarus, a man raised rather than felled by manufactured wings.

The Golden Age of Aviation featured flying for adventure, exploration, and sport and, also, the flying boats, airships, mailplanes, and airliners that flew with increasing safety, reliability, and frequency over the expanding air routes of commercial airlines. The operation of the new aircraft involved communication and navigation radios, new and improved flight instruments, and the developing procedures for instrument flying. The period was peaceful, though only relatively speaking, as aircraft went into combat in small wars on several continents and as growing international tensions prompted nations to prepare for war.

Lindbergh's historic transatlantic flight is the subject of Section A of this chapter. Flying adventures like Lindbergh's flight, aerial surveys and expeditions, and sport flying made private flying popular, and new aircraft made private flying more accessible to more people. That is the subject of Section B. Section C discusses the growth of commercial aviation around the world, including the declining French influence, the strong German network, the conservative British approach, and the ascending American industry. Section D covers the development of radio communication and navigation during the Golden Age of Aviation, and the development of military aviation during the interlude between world wars.

After studying this chapter, you will be able to identify Charles Lindbergh and to discuss the significance of his 1927 flight. You will recognize the aviators and aircraft involved in the major aviation events that provided the news media with stories of flying farther, faster, and higher. You will be able to cite examples of people and planes influential in the development of private flying. You will be able to explain the role of airmail in the development of commercial aviation in general and, specifically, in the French and American aviation scandals of the early thirties. You will be able to identify the modern airliners introduced in the thirties and name the features that made them modern. You will be able to list the major components of the four-course radio navigation system and to explain how the system operated. You will be able to name the military conflicts in which aircraft were used during the late twenties and the thirties, and you will be able to discuss the peacetime development of military aircraft.

Charles A. Lindbergh

CHARLES LINDBERGH

Q & A

What? Nonstop and solo flight across the Atlantic Ocean and the start of the Golden Age of Aviation

When? 1927 May 20-21

Where? The flight was from New York to Paris, and the celebration and impact of the event extended worldwide

Who? Charles Lindbergh who, through this flight, came to represent aviation in general

Why? To compete, to win, to fly

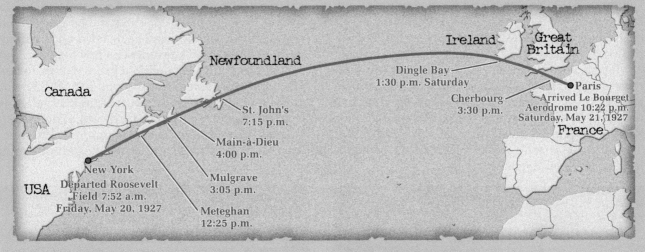

Lindbergh's Solo Atlantic Crossing

Charles Lindbergh was a youth in rural Minnesota during World War I. He worked on a farm in lieu of attending high school as part of an educational program supporting the war effort, and he earned his high school diploma by examination. Later he dropped out of the University of Wisconsin for lack of interest in his engineering studies. He learned to fly in a Lincoln Standard biplane, powered by a 150-horsepower Hispano-Suiza engine. The Nebraska Aircraft Company in Lincoln was refurbishing the war-surplus aircraft and selling them as "turnabouts," and that is where Lindbergh took his first flying lessons in 1922. He received eight hours of dual instruction and then joined friends barnstorming. They flew, he wingwalked and parachuted. He bought his own airplane in 1923: a war-surplus Curtiss JN-4D Jenny. In it he finally soloed for the first time. As a pilot, he continued to barnstorm.

His serious education in aviation began in 1924 at Brooks Field, Army Air Service, San Antonio, Texas. He was an aviation cadet, one of 104 cadets beginning flight training that April. They flew in the morning, attended ground school in the afternoon, and studied at night. Six months later Lindbergh was one of only 32 cadets continuing to the second six-month phase of the training program. He learned to fly in formation, and he practiced bombing and strafing. In March 1925 he graduated first in a class of 18 remaining cadets, and he received his commission as a Second Lieutenant in the Army Air Service Reserve. The military had a surplus of pilots left over from war, so Lieutenant Lindbergh was released from active duty.

Lindbergh joined the Robertson Aircraft Corporation of St. Louis as an airmail pilot. Established by war veteran William B. Robertson in 1921, this company bought

Personal Profile

Charles A. Lindbergh (1902-1974) was an aviator. His early career included stints as a flying circus performer, a military aviation cadet, an airmail pilot, and a long-distance flier. He made a historic transatlantic crossing in May 1927. After that his public image reached extremes. In 1927 he was acclaimed the "new Christ" risen from the ruins of a world crucified by World War I. In 1941 he was reviled as the Anti-Christ sympathetic to Adolf Hitler's National Socialism and opposed to the United States participating in any European war. After World War II he was dismissed as an environmental nut. The reality was less extreme and more complex. Lindbergh was a pilot: he won the Orteig Prize, he toured the United States and Latin America promoting aviation, he surveyed routes for airlines, he advised aircraft makers and, as a civilian, he flew World War II combat missions in the Pacific theater. He was a caring husband to a loving wife. He was a father who lost one child in a highly publicized kidnapping. He became a graceful writer whose 1953 book *The Spirit of St. Louis* won a Pulitzer Prize. He also became a conservationist. He was a quiet man with a very public life.

Charles A. Lindbergh

war-surplus airplane parts and engines, assembled them into airplanes, and sold the products. When the United States replaced the Post Office Department's Air Mail Service with contract airmail, Robertson won a contract to carry mail over Commercial Airmail Route 2 (CAM 2), which connected St. Louis and Chicago. Lindbergh tested airplanes and organized the mail route. He hired pilots, employed people along the route to operate signal lights, and arranged for trucks to deliver fuel to the various fields. Lindbergh flew Robertson's first airmail run on 15 April 1925. Thereafter, Robertson's airmail planes made five round-trip flights a week. (Figure 6-1)

Lindbergh prepared to compete. He raised financial support among the St. Louis business community. He ordered a plane to be made to his specifications. He selected a monoplane for the reduced drag of one wing compared to two, and he decided upon a single engine, for it would consume less fuel than multiple engines. He ordered a modified Ryan M-1 mail plane and one 223-horsepower Wright J-5C Whirlwind radial engine. An additional fuel tank installed in front of the cockpit blocked forward vision, so he added a periscope to his cabin equipment. He named the plane *Spirit of St. Louis* in recognition of the source of his funding. (Figure 6-2)

Figure 6-1. Charles Lindbergh flew airmail for the Robertson Aircraft Corporation, which had won Commercial Airmail Route 2 (CAM 2).

Orteig Prize

The Orteig Prize lured Lindbergh from flying the mail to planning a long-distance flight. French-born, New York City businessman Raymond Orteig offered a $25,000 prize for the first nonstop airplane flight between New York and Paris in either direction.

Figure 6-2. The financing for the Lindbergh transatlantic attempt came from a group of St. Louis businessmen. The aircraft, a Ryan M-1, was built by Ryan Aircraft in San Diego, California.

Lindbergh's proving flight took the aircraft from the Ryan factory in San Diego, via St. Louis, to Long Island, New York, in 21 hours and 20 minutes; this set a new coast-to-coast speed record. In New York, Lindbergh plotted his course, the shortest or great-circle route between New York and Paris. He studied the weather over the Atlantic. Finally he packed refreshments for the trip: four sandwiches, two canteens of water, and army rations.

More than ninety people had already crossed the Atlantic Ocean by air. Some flew in airplanes, namely the Navy's NC-4, Alcock and Brown's Vimy, and the Army's Douglas World Cruisers. Others flew nonstop in airships, either the R.34 or the LZ 126. The crew of the R.34 even crossed the Atlantic in both directions. But no one had made a nonstop airplane crossing from New York to Paris. People tried. Competing for the Orteig Prize, on 21 September 1926, French ace René Fonck and his crew crashed their fuel-heavy, three-engine Sikorsky S-35 on takeoff. Pilot Fonck and navigator Lawrence W. Curtin jumped out of the aircraft. Radio operator Charles Clavier and mechanic Jacob Islamov were trapped in the burning wreck. They died. But the Orteig Prize attracted many aviators to the challenge. In 1927 there were more than twenty transatlantic attempts. Only three planes made it across the Atlantic, and only the first won the Orteig Prize. (Figure 6-3)

Figure 6-3. Igor Sikorsky (left) and René Fonck (right) waving from cockpit of the S-35 in 1926, before Fonck's ill-fated attempt at the Orteig Prize.

Historical Note

The competition for the Orteig Prize was deadly, as these several examples illustrate:

21 September 1926 — During takeoff French ace René Fonck and his crew crashed their fuel-heavy Sikorsky S-35; radio operator Charles Clavier and mechanic Jacob Islamov died in the burning wreck.

26 April 1927 — Noel Davis and Stanton Wooster crashed their fuel-heavy Keystone Pathfinder trimotor *American Legion* on takeoff; both died.

8 May 1927 — French airmen Charles Nungesser and Francois Coli left France in the single-engine Levasseur PL.8 *l'Oiseau Blanc (White Bird);* they were never seen again.

Lindbergh's successful flight proved that the Atlantic could be flown solo, so some of the teams he beat for the Orteig Prize continued their efforts to fly across the Atlantic Ocean. The results were sometimes fatal:

31 August 1927 — Three pilots — Princess Anne Löwenstein-Wertheim, Leslie Hamilton, and Fred Minchin — flew the single-engine Fokker *St. Raphael* west from England; they disappeared.

Historic Event

Between 20 and 21 May 1927 Charles Lindbergh flew the Ryan monoplane *Spirit of St. Louis* nonstop from New York to Paris. He departed a few minutes before eight in the morning. He landed 3,600 miles away and 33 hours and 29 minutes later. He won the $25,000 prize offered by Raymond Orteig for the first nonstop flight between New York and Paris.

American Legion

Nonstop Transatlantic Flight

On the drizzling morning of 20 May the highly trained, experienced, and well-prepared Lindbergh took off from Roosevelt Field. His heavily loaded plane barely cleared the tractor, gully, and telephone wires at the end of the field. He flew northeast on the great-circle route. He passed St. John's, Newfoundland. He flew over the ocean and flew day and flew night. When he saw fishing boats, he knew he was approaching land. Then he saw the coastline. He flew over Ireland and England and the English Channel. From the French coast he followed the light beacons that lit the Paris-London airway. He reached Paris after ten in the evening on the 21st, and after 33 hours and 29 minutes in the air. We made it, he wrote: *"We"* referred to man and machine and became the title of his 1927 book about the transatlantic flight. His 1953 book, *The Spirit of St. Louis*, won a Pulitzer Prize.

Lindbergh won the Orteig Prize — and much more. French President Gaston Doumergue awarded Lindbergh

Flight Lines

"As the fog cleared I dropped down closer to the water, sometimes flying within ten feet of the waves and seldom higher than two hundred.

"There is a cushion of air close to ground or water through which a plane flies with less effort than when at a higher altitude, and for hours at a time I took advantage of this factor.

"Also, it was less difficult to determine the wind drift near the water. During the entire flight the wind was strong enough to produce white caps on the waves. When one of these formed, the foam would be blown off, showing the wind's direction and approximate velocity. This foam remained on the water long enough for me to obtain a general idea of my drift."

Charles A. Lindbergh describing his transatlantic flight of 20-21 May 1927, in Lindbergh's book *"We"* (New York: G.P. Putnam's Sons, 1927).

Flight Lines

"During long ages between dawn and sunrise, I'm thankful we didn't make the *Spirit of St. Louis* a stable plane. The very instability which makes it difficult to fly blind or hold an accurate course at night now guards me against excessive errors. It's again a case of the plane and me compensating for each other. When I was fresh and it was overloaded, my quickness of reaction held its nose from veering off. Now that I'm dreaming and ridden by sleep, its veering prods my lagging senses. The slightest relaxation of pressure on either stick or rudder starts a climbing or a diving turn, hauling me back from the borderland of sleep. Then, I fix my eyes on the compass and determine again to hold it where it belongs. . . . I react from my stupor, level out, kick the rudder back onto the compass heading, shake myself to half awakeness — and let the needle creep again. I'm asleep and awake at the same moment, living through a reality that is a dream."

Charles A. Lindbergh, *The Spirit of St. Louis* (New York: Charles Scribner's Sons, 1953).

the Legion of Honor. Belgian King Albert decorated him with the Chevalier of the Royal Order of Leopold. Back in the United States, President Calvin Coolidge pinned the Distinguished Flying Cross on Lindbergh's lapel. The flight also won the reserve officer promotion to colonel and, after Lindbergh visited Congress, the Congressional Medal of Honor. Lindbergh became a popular hero. He represented youth and newness and modernism. He was not a war veteran associated with the past. He was a peacetime pilot with the romantic experience of flying the mail. He was young with the freedom not only of youth but of mobility. He escaped daily life via the modern machine — the airplane. Daringly, bravely, heroically, he crossed the Atlantic Ocean nonstop *and* solo. (Figure 6-4)

Figure 6-4. A photomontage depicts the Spirit of ST. Louis, flown by Charles Lindbergh across the Atlantic on May 20-21, 1927, in the air above Paris, France.

Historical Note

A single Wright Whirlwind engine powered Charles Lindbergh's Ryan on the historic transatlantic flight of May 1927. The engine was a product of the Wright Aeronautical Corporation.

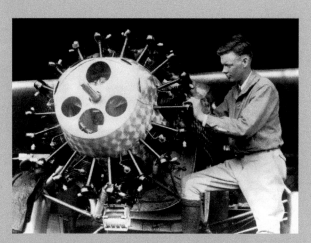

Former automotive engineer Charles L. Lawrance designed the Whirlwind, which reached the market in 1923. It had proven its reliability by the time of the 1927 flight, and its air-cooling was considerably lighter in weight and simpler in construction than water-cooled alternatives. Lawrance won the 1927 Collier Trophy "for development of radial air-cooled aircraft engines."

The Wright Whirlwind also powered the two other airplanes that flew nonstop across the Atlantic Ocean in 1927. In early June, Clarence Chamberlin and Charles Levine flew the Wright-Bellanca W.B.2 *Columbia* across the ocean. With no reason to fly to Paris, as Lindbergh had already won that prize, they flew the "first" nonstop flight from New York to Berlin and set a distance record in the process since Berlin was almost 300 miles farther than Paris. In late June the explorer Richard Byrd, his pilot Bert Acosta, copilot Bernt Balchen, and wireless operator George O. Noville flew the Fokker trimotor *America* to the coast of France. With clouds obstructing their view and fuel running low, they ditched. All survived. Chamberlin and Levine's *Columbia* had one Wright Whirlwind engine. Byrd's *America* had three.

Aircraft engine makers followed the Wright Whirlwind example. Bristol made the Jupiter, Continental developed the A-70, Fiat the A, Kinner the K-5, and Pratt & Whitney the Wasp — all air-cooled, radial engines, some large, some small. In contrast, de Havilland produced the inline, air-cooled Gipsy; Rolls Royce the inline, liquid-cooled Kestrel; and Napier the W-type, liquid-cooled Lion.

Historical Note

The Wright engine got its name from Wilbur and Orville Wright. The brothers had founded their Wright Company in 1910. That company in 1916 merged with Glenn L. Martin into the Wright-Martin Aircraft Corporation. The end of World War I left military customers and equipment makers with surplus equipment. The cancellation of war contracts and the shortage of new orders hurt companies. In response, Wright-Martin reorganized into the Wright Aeronautical Corporation in 1919. Wright Aeronautical merged with the Curtiss companies in 1929. The result was Curtiss-Wright, an aviation equipment maker. Curtiss-Wright remained in operation through World War II. The contract cancellations at the end of that war hit the company hard. Curtiss-Wright closed factories and, in 1946, sold its assets to North American, which did not use either the Curtiss or Wright name.

Goodwill Tours

Lindbergh's flight proved the reliability of aircraft and aircraft engines designed and built after the war. The flight demonstrated the safety of civil aircraft and of aviation in general. Now Lindbergh wanted to sell aviation and to promote commercial aviation in particular. He did this through goodwill tours. With the support of the newly formed Daniel Guggenheim Fund for the Promotion of Aeronautics and the United States Department of Commerce, Lindbergh flew the *Spirit of St. Louis* on a tour of the United States. Between 20 July and 23 October 1927, he visited all 48 states. He covered 22,000 miles, and he logged 260 hours and 45 minutes in the air. (Figure 6-5)

That December he made his second goodwill trip. This was a nonstop flight between the capital cities of Washington and Mexico City. On the cloudy morning of 13 December 1927 he left Washington. He flew both day and night, through clouds and, over Mexico the next morning, through fog. The flight lasted 27

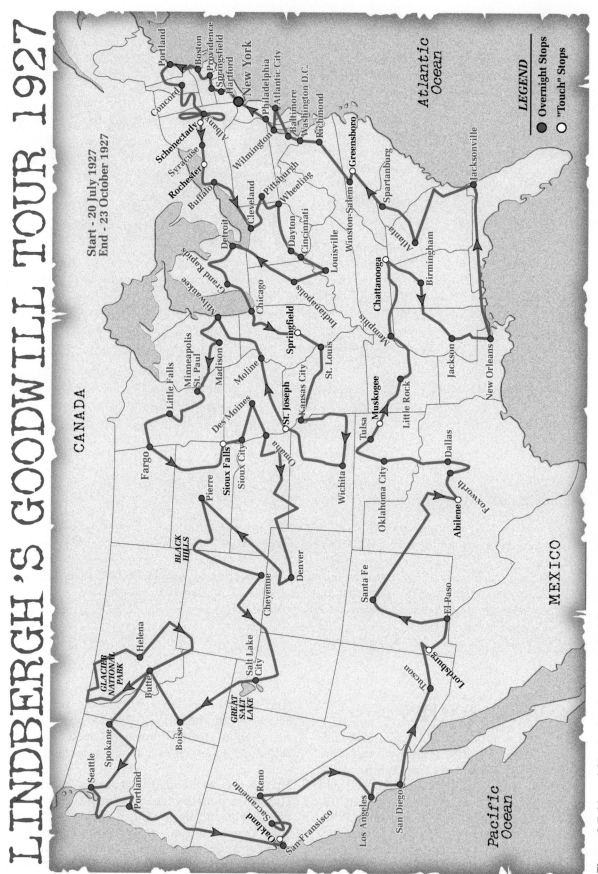

LINDBERGH'S GOODWILL TOUR 1927

Start - 20 July 1927
End - 23 October 1927

LEGEND
● Overnight Stops
○ "Touch" Stops

Figure 6-5. Map of Charles Lindbergh's United States goodwill tour in 1927.

Flight Lines

"This has been in some ways the most interesting flight I have ever made. I managed to get completely lost in the fog over Mexico. Something went wrong. I guess it was me. I am sorry that those waiting for me had such a long time under the hot sun, but I was just as anxious to come down as they were to have me. It was far from pleasant flying. Unable to get beneath the fog, I went up again and set a compass course for Mexico City. I got completely lost. I knew I was in a bad country to play around in. I tried to puzzle it out by the watersheds, but it was not until I saw a sign of the Hotel Toluca that I really managed to get located and then set my course again for Mexico City."

Charles Lindbergh describing a goodwill flight to Mexico City, 14 December 1927, in a telegram quoted in *Time Capsule/1927, a History of the Year Condensed from the Pages of Time* (New York: Time-Life Books, 1968); the text of the actual telegram was in all capital letters and without punctuation marks.

hours and 15 minutes, a couple of hours longer than planned because he had gotten lost in the fog. His next tour started from Mexico City. He flew the *Spirit of St. Louis* to 17 Latin America countries and covered 9,000 miles.

The New York-to-Paris flight and the goodwill tours demonstrated the reliability of aircraft and the safety of flying. They also raised public interest in aviation. The future of aviation, according to Lindbergh, lay in commercial flying, and to that he turned his attention and efforts. He got jobs with two airlines: Pan American Airways, the American pioneer in international airline service, and Transcontinental Air Transport (TAT) , a domestic carrier known for years as "The Lindbergh Line."

Historical Evidence

In 1928 the *Spirit of St. Louis* went to the Smithsonian Institution, the national museum in Washington, D.C. It is an artifact of a remarkable flight and evidence of the technology that made the flight possible. Lindbergh's flight log recorded 174 flights in the plane and revealed the plane's total flying time of 489 hours and 25 minutes.

ADVENTURE, EXPLORATION, AND SPORT

Aviation was sport and spectacle. It was an adventure in the exploration of the planet, the plane, and the pilot. Charles Lindbergh and his transatlantic crossing combined these elements. Pilots promoted themselves, their aircraft, and their flights; this is how many supported their flying. Some publishers, like George Putnam in New York, specialized in aviation adventures. Geographical and scientific expeditions used airplanes not only as service vehicles, but also for recording the spectacular and newsworthy elements that attracted supporters. Filmmakers used airplanes both for aerial photography and for subject matter; for example, Martin and Osa Johnson used airplanes to get to remote regions of Africa and Borneo and to enhance their nature films for techno-logically savvy audiences. Newsworthy flights and their news coverage helped make aviators the heroes of the day and inspired private individuals to fly. Light airplanes enabled the private pilot to develop as a class of fliers distinct from the transport pilots and other commercial aviators. Homebuilt aircraft opened aviation to ordinary people, and gliders pro-vided sport, instruction, and entertainment. All these were part of the Golden Age of Aviation.

Dole's Pacific Air Race

While Lindbergh was conquering the Atlantic and winning the Orteig Prize, James D. Dole organized a Pacific Air Race with a $35,000 prize. The rules were simple: fly nonstop from Oakland, California, to Honolulu, Hawaii. Three planes crashed and three people died just trying to get to Oakland for the start of the race. Fifteen pilots drew for takeoff position, but on Tuesday 16 August 1927 only nine planes were ready. Beginning just before noon, the planes took off one by one. One did not leave the ground. Two fuel-heavy aircraft crashed on takeoff. Six flew west. One turned back, another made an emergency landing, and two disappeared with the loss of seven lives. One of these was the *Golden Eagle*, the first Lockheed Vega ever built. A search plane was lost too, adding two more fatalities to the race's toll. Two planes completed the race; Wright J-5 engines powered both of the planes. Art Goebel and navigator William V. Davis flew the winning airplane, the *Woolaroc*, which was a modified Travel Air 500 high-wing monoplane. A modified Breese high-wing monoplane named *Aloha* finished second. The race proved transpacific air travel possible but expensive in terms of aircraft and life. (Figure 6-6)

Figure 6-6. Art Goebel and William V. Davis in a modified Travel Air 500 won the Dole Pacific Air Race from Oakland, California, to Honolulu, Hawaii. Of the 15 aircraft entered in the race, only two finished.

Flight Lines

"The rainstorms surged in round us again. We were 600 feet up, and as we had been flying for only six and a half hours, our petrol load was still tremendous. To fly low in such atrocious conditions, heavily overloaded, was an experience that did not at all add any to the peace of mind.

"To dodge around the fringes of the storm and to climb through the murk were the kind of maneuvers that were going to mop up our gasoline at a disconcerting rate. To fly low overloaded in the face of the savage chopping gusts with visibility shrinking to a few hundred feet was to flirt a little too dangerously with risk. We were indeed on the horns of a dilemma. We were forced to decide on a policy, as we had not the faintest idea how long this battering by the storms might continue. That policy was to climb, to risk a heavier petrol consumption, and hope for the best. So we opened up the motors to 1,775 revolutions, and plowed up through rain and storm and a jolting nasty wind which blew in sudden gusts."

C.E. Kingsford-Smith and C.T.P. Ulm, "The Flight of the *Southern Cross*" — about their transpacific flight of 1928, reprinted in *Men in the Air, the Best Flight Stories of All Time from Greek Mythology to the Space Age*, edited by Brandt Aymar (New York: Crown Publishers, Wings Books, 1990).

Other airmen attempted transpacific flights. The Australians Sir Charles Kingsford-Smith and Charles T.P. Ulm, with the American crew of Harry Lyons as navigator and James Warner as radio operator, made a flight in the Fokker *Southern Cross* from Oakland to Honolulu to Suva, Fiji, to Sidney, Australia, in 1928. They started 31 May, finished 9 June, and logged 83 hours and 38 minutes in flight. In October 1931 Clyde Pangborn and Hugh Herndon, Jr. , flew a Bellanca from Japan across the Pacific to Wenatchee, Washington.

Atlantic Crossing

Still others retained interest in the Atlantic Ocean. The Italian pilot Francesco de Pinedo crossed the South Atlantic Ocean in stages in 1927. He flew a Savoia-Marchetti flying boat to South America then north to Mexico and the United States. Amelia Earhart — the Lady Lindy — in 1932 became the first female pilot to make a solo, nonstop transatlantic flight. She flew a Wright-powered Lockheed Vega 5B that had been modified from a Vega 1. That fall James Allan Mollison, a commercial transport pilot and former military pilot, made the first east-to-west solo crossing, although he was not the first to make the crossing in this direction. He flew a light airplane, the de Havilland D.H. 80A Puss Moth, *Heart's Content*, which he had previously flown from England to Cape Town. In 1932 a total of five planes carried twenty-two people across the Atlantic, while the airship *Graf Zeppelin* made 18 crossings of the South Atlantic.

In 1936 Beryl Markham became the second person and the first female to fly the North Atlantic solo east

Personal Profile

James Allan Mollison (1905-1959) was born in Scotland. He served in the Royal Air Force in the early twenties and flew airmail for the Australian National Airways. He became a competitive pilot. He set records for long-distance flights, including Australia to England, London to Cape Town, England to South America, London to New York, and New York to London. During World War II he served as a ferry pilot. His wife Amy Johnson (1903-1941) learned flying through the London Aeroplane Club. She completed an England-to-Australia flight, the first by a female pilot. The couple once crashed a plane arguing whom would fly and apparently neither did the flying during the argument. After they divorced, she served as a pilot in Britain's wartime Air Transport Auxiliary Service. Tangled in a parachute, she drowned in the Thames after bailing out of an airplane.

Amy Johnson and James Allan Mollison

to west and nonstop, and the first woman to complete an east-to-west airplane flight. Her autobiography *West with the Night* (1942) describes the flight. Also in 1936, Mollison made his third transatlantic flight, this one being the first nonstop solo flight from North America to London; he flew from Harbor Grace, Newfoundland, to London in a Bellanca monoplane powered by a 700-horsepower Pratt & Whitney Twin Wasp Junior radial engine. Douglas Corrigan, whose nickname was Wrong-Way Corrigan, flew across the Atlantic in 1938.

Personal Profile

Douglas Corrigan (1907-1996) was a native of Texas. He learned to fly, and he went to work at the Ryan flying school in San Diego. He worked on the construction of Charles Lindbergh's *Spirit of St. Louis.* He later became a barnstormer. A fan of Lindbergh, he decided to fly across the Atlantic Ocean. He failed to obtain the necessary authorizations because his old plane, powered by a 175-horsepower Wright Whirlwind engine, did not meet transoceanic standards. He made the flight anyway. On 17-18 July 1938 Corrigan flew a Curtiss Robin from Floyd Bennett Field, New York, to Dublin, Ireland. Due to lack of authorizations, he claimed that he intended to fly to California and simply, and

Douglas Corrigan

mistakenly, flew the wrong way. That prompted the nickname Wrong-Way Corrigan. As a civilian pilot during World War II, he ferried aircraft for the military. After the war he became an airplane salesman.

Flight Lines

"We fly, but we have not 'conquered' the air."

Beryl Markham writing about her 1936 transatlantic flight that ended with a crash landing in Nova Scotia, in Markham's *West with the Night* (Boston: Houghton Mifflin, 1942).

German Flights

Germans repeatedly flew the North Atlantic Ocean. In April 1928 the Junkers W 33 *Bremen* became famous as the first plane to fly across the Atlantic Ocean nonstop from east to west. Hermann Köhl and Baron von Hünefeld of Germany and James Fitzmaurice of Ireland were the airmen who made the flight. They carried no radio, and en route not a single ship spotted the plane. They did not land in New York City as planned, but crashed on Greenly Island, Newfoundland, but they had indeed crossed the ocean. Germany celebrated this flight and the German fliers in a manner similar to the United States honoring Lindbergh. (Figure 6-7)

Figure 6-7. Herman Köhl, Baron von Hünefeld, and James Fitzmaurice became famous when they flew a Junkers W 33, called the *Bremen,* across the Atlantic from east to west. Their flight ended on Greenly Island, Newfoundland, where they crashed.

Reflecting the increasingly popular view that seaplanes were more appropriate than landplanes for transoceanic flights, a German pilot sought a practical, rather than record-setting, route across the North Atlantic. Wolfgang von Gronau was director of the Deutsche Verkehrsfieger-Schule seaplane flying school on the island of Sylt, in the North Sea near the Danish border. In 1930 von Gronau and crew flew the Dornier 15 Wal flying boat from Sylt to New York by numerous stages along the perimeter of the North Atlantic. *Wal* is the German word for whale, an apt descripton of this large seaplane. Its successor was the Dornier 18. The 1930 flight took nine days. The next year the Dornier Do X Teutonic flying boat made the flight from Germany to New York via the South Atlantic Ocean. This trip took ten months. Also in 1931, von Gronau flew a Wal from Sylt, over the Greenland icecap, to Chicago.

Figure 6-8. Dornier aircraft made a number of long-distance flights, such as the Dornier Wal that flew along the perimeter of the North Atlantic and the Dornier Do X that flew around the world.

In 1932 German crews in the Do X made a round trip Germany-New York-Germany flight and then flew around the world, from Sylt to Montreal, across Canada, through Alaska, along the coast of Asia, and back to Germany. The round-the-world flight began 22 July and ended 111 days later back in Germany on 23 November. (Figure 6-8)

Round the World

Von Gronau's round-the-world flight was one of several during the Golden Age of Aviation. The airship *Graf Zeppelin* made a circumnavigation in 1929. Pilot Wiley Post and navigator Harold Gatty flew around the world in 1931. Von Gronau's flying-boat trip was in 1932. Post again circled the world in 1933, this time solo. Post flew his Lockheed Vega monoplane *Winnie Mae* on both his trips. In the summer of 1931 he completed the loop in eight days, 15 hours, 51 minutes, and two summers later in a new record time of seven days, 18 hours, and 49 minutes. (Figure 6-9)

Personal Profile

Claudius "Claude" Dornier (1884-1969) was a Bavarian who studied engineering in Munich. As a Luftschiffbau Zeppelin employee, he calculated airship stresses before the Great War and designed floatplanes during the war. After the war he established his own Dornier company, but located the manufacturing facilities in Switzerland and Italy in order to avoid Allied restrictions on German production. He produced a line of all-metal flying boats, including the large twin-engine Wal (Whale) and the huge twelve-engine Do X. The Do X engines were American-made Curtiss Conqueror engines that provided a combined 7,800 horsepower. The X or experimental Dornier boat was the largest airplane in the world when it was launched in 1929. That year the Do X became the first airplane to fly with 100 people on board, and that same year it carried 169 on one flight. In 1932 the Do X flew around the world. Dornier led his company into military production during World War II and back into civil aviation after the war.

Claude Dornier

Figure 6-9. Wiley Post sitting on his Lockheed Vega, *Winnie Mae*, at Floyd Bennett Field following his solo around the world flight in July 1933. Post flew the *Winnie Mae* around the world twice: once with navigator Harold Gatty in 1931 and again solo in 1933.

Howard Hughes made the trip around the world in 1938. He, his flight engineer Eddie Lund, radio engineer

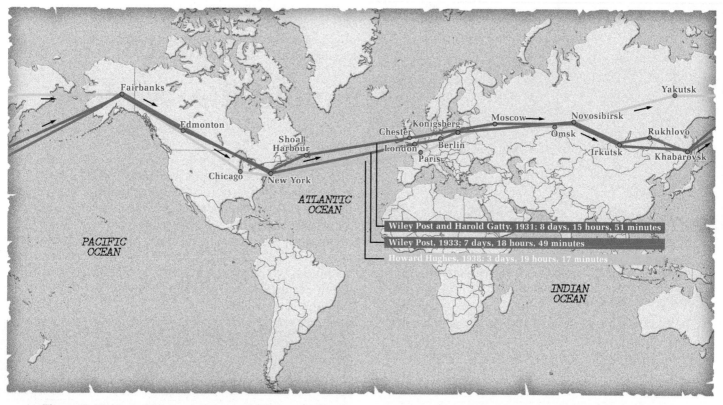

Figure 6-10. Map of the around the world flights of Wiley Post in 1931 and 1933, and the flight of Howard Hughes in 1938. Over the course of seven years, nearly five days were trimmed from the around the world flight time.

 ## Flight Lines

"Many years of research have produced tables which give the exact locations of stars, sun, and moon at every minute of every 24 hours in each of the 365 days of the year. They all pass through regular cycles of time and space, and by the use of a standard time their position-charting may be reversed, so that taking the positions charted for them as fact, we may locate our own exact position on the earth.

"Of course, I had all the changes in course figured out before I started on the trip. But with no knowledge of what winds would prevail, or at what altitude we were going to fly, and with no advance check on our ground speed, I had to make observations every half hour on that flight through the night. For these I used three instruments: a sextant, a drift indicator, and a ground speed indicator. The sextant is an instrument for measuring the vertical arc between the horizon and a star, or other celestial body. To make sure of the time, I carried three chronometers, because a minute of error in time meant a 15-mile error on the equator in the final calculation of position.

"I also used a special series of star curves of progression compiled some time earlier by Commander P.V.H. Weems and myself. By using the chart I eliminated the necessity for long mathematical computations which would have told me, on completion, only the position I had been in before I started the plotting.

"This fixing of position was a serious business with me and kept me busy during most of the flight. When sights were not available, I had to keep rapid check on the course Wiley took and to instruct him from a graph made up from dead reckoning, on which the course was figured according to the last known limits of error and the known amounts of variation over the course to be followed."

Harold Gatty describing his work as navigator on a transatlantic night flight in 1931, in Wiley Post and Harold Gatty, *Around the World in Eight Days, the Flight of the Winnie Mae* (Garden City, NY: Garden City Publishing Company, 1931).

Richard Stoddart, and navigators Thomas Thurlow and Harry P.M. Conner flew a twin-engine, Wright Cyclone-powered Lockheed 14 that averaged 206 miles per hour during the 91 hours of flight. Their total elapsed time was three days, 19 hours, and 17 minutes. Such long-distance flights demonstrated the capabilities of the aircraft; proved the routes could be flown; tested engines and instruments in flight; established speed, endurance, and distance records; and garnered honor to the airmen, sponsors, and nations involved. (Figure 6-10)

Polar Flights

After Richard Byrd and Floyd Bennett reached the North Pole in 1926, polar exploration routinely employed aircraft. The Byrd Antarctic Expedition flew to the South Pole in November 1929. Byrd, Bernt Balchen, Harold June, and Ashley McKinley flew over the pole in a Ford trimotor called *Floyd Bennett*, named after the pilot who had died the previous year. In 1928 the Australian explorer Hubert Wilkins and his American pilot Ben Eielson flew from Barrow, Alaska, to Spitzbergen in 20 hours, 30 minutes. They flew the high latitudes of the north. In one international example of 1937, a Russian Tupolev ANT-25 flew from Moscow over the North Pole to Vancouver, Washington. The three-man crew — pilot Valeri Chkalov, co-pilot Georgi Baidukov, and navigator Alexander Beliakov — completed this first nonstop, great-circle flight from the Soviet Union to the United States in 63 hours

Historic Event

On 28-29 November 1929 Richard Byrd and colleagues in a Ford trimotor made the first flight over the South Pole.

Flight Lines

"Aboard airplane *Floyd Bennett* in flight 1.55 Greenwich Mean Time Friday Nov. 29. My calculations indicate that we have reached the vicinity of the South Pole. Flying high for a survey. Airplane in good shape, crew all well. Will soon turn North. We can see an almost limitless polar plateau."

Richard Byrd in a message radioed by Harold June, 1929, as quoted in C.B. Allen and Lauren D. Lyman, *The Wonder Book of the Air* (1936; Chicago: John C. Winston Company, 1941).

Flight Lines

"The Stinson machines were warmed up and an hour later Pilot [Alger] Graham in No. 2 machine, with [wireless operator] Howard Mason as passenger, tried to get off. The temperature had warmed towards the middle of the day and the sharp tail-skid cut deeply into the snow. Several attempts to get off failed and we had to delay long enough to install the wide-set wooden tail-skids prepared for such an emergency. These tail-skids, while assuring a quicker take-off, were likely to interfere slightly with the performance of the machine in the air. With the tail-skids attached Graham got off without further trouble. Eielson and I followed immediately in the *Detroit News No. 1* and set our course for Wiseman."

George H. Wilkins describing a departure from Fairbanks, Alaska, in 1927, in Wilkins' *Flying the Arctic* (New York: G.P. Putnam's Sons, 1928).

ANT-25

Personal Profile

Andrei Nikolayevich Tupolev (1888-1972) studied engineering at a technical school in Moscow. With his professor N. Y. Zhukovskii, he founded the Central Aerodynamics and Hydrodynamics Institute. He supervised airplane design and construction. He was a member of the Soviet committee that, in response to Junkers aircraft, investigated metal airplane construction. He became the Soviet in charge of heavy aviation, and he became the leading Soviet airplane designer. He designed numerous airplane models, each designated ANT after his initials. For a while, the twelve-engine ANT-26 was the largest plane in the world. Early in World War II, while imprisoned in Joseph Stalin's gulag or network of labor camps, Tupolev designed a strategic bomber and a twin-engine bomber. Stalin gave him a pardon and awarded him the Stalin Prize. Tupolev continued to design large airplanes.

Andrei Nikolayevich Tupolev

and 17 minutes. The distance flown was 5,288 miles. These are just a few examples of the many Arctic flights made during the Golden Age of Aviation.

Italian Distance Flight

National pride was often at stake. Fascist leader Benito Mussolini, for example, sent his Minister of Air Italo Balbo to the Chicago World's Fair in 1933. Balbo led a squadron of Italian airplanes to Chicago. The planes were Savoia-Marchetti SM.55X flying boats, each powered by two 750-horsepower Isotta-Fraschini Asso engines. Twenty-five planes left the Orbettol seaplane base north of Rome on the first of July. One plane and one airman were lost in Amsterdam on the way to America. Twenty-four planes flew in formation over the Chicago World's Fair. Another plane and another airman were lost in Lisbon on the return flight. Of the hundred airmen on the flight, there were only two casualties.

Figure 6-11. Italo Balbo, the Italian Minister of Air, led a squadron of 25 Savoia-Marchetti SM.55X flying boats to the 1933 Chicago World's Fair.

The long distance, the transatlantic crossings, the remarkable safety record, and the spectacle of the formation flying made fascism look good, though only briefly. (Figure 6-11)

MacRobertson Air Race

National pride showed in international competitions too. One of the most influential competitions of the thirties was the 1934 MacRobertson Air Race, named after Australian philanthropist Sir MacPherson Robertson who put up the prize money. Contestants were to race the 12,300 miles from England to Australia. Twenty contestants took off on 20 October, and ten completed the distance to Australia. C.W.A. Scott and T. Campbell Black of Great Britain won the race. A former Qantas Airline employee, Scott had already set records for England-to-Australia and Australia-to-England. Black had opened an airline in British East Africa (now Kenya). The two flew in a special de Havilland 88 Comet. (Figure 6-12)

K.D. Parmentier and J.J. Moll of KLM (Koninklijke Luchtvaart Maatschappij, the Royal Dutch Airlines) placed second in a regular Douglas airliner, and Clyde Pangborn and Roscoe Turner of the United States placed third in a Boeing 247D. The Comet was one of three racers that were specially made for the race and sold to the race teams at only a nominal cost in exchange for publicity. Powered by two de Havilland Gipsy engines, it was a low-wing monoplane with a manually retractable undercarriage, variable pitch propellers, and split trailing edge flaps. The second and

Figure 6-12. The 1934 MacRobertson Air Race was won by C.W.A. Scott and T. Campbell Black flying a de Havilland 88 Comet like this replica.

third place finishers were airliners designed and produced in the United States, a reflection of the growing importance of the American aviation industry.

Altitude Flights

Among the many flights for distance and adventure were some noteworthy for altitude too. In April 1933 Lord Clydesdale and Stewart Blacker in a Westland PV.3 torpedo bomber and David McIntyre and cameraman Sidney Bonnet in a Westland Wallace military plane flew over Mount Everest (29,030 feet, 8,848 meters). (Figure 6-13)

Balloonists also competed for altitude records. The manned balloons *Explorer I* and *Explorer II* were launched from a "strato-bowl," a deep canyon in the Black Hills of South Dakota. Army balloonist Major William Kepner was the pilot in charge, and Captain Orvil A. Anderson was the associate pilot. In the *Explorer I* in 1934, with observer Captain A.W.

Figure 6-13. Flying over Mount Everest was a challenge in 1933.

Stevens, they rose to more than eleven miles above the earth. The next year Kepner and Anderson in the *Explorer II* reached 72,395 feet or 13.7 miles — a world absolute altitude record.

The world-flier Wiley Post developed a pressure suit for use in stratospheric flights because his plane did not have a pressurized cabin. The development was cut short when Post and humorist Will Rogers died in an airplane crash in northern Alaska in 1935. Setting altitude records was the sole goal of some flights. In 1936, for example, F.R.D. Swain of Britain's Royal Air Force flew a Bristol Type 138 wooden monoplane powered by a special Pegasus engine to a world altitude record of 49,967 feet (15,223 meters). He wore an air-tight suit and obtained oxygen from a tube to his helmet.

Speed Flights

Speed meant beating another pilot's time, getting somewhere ahead of others, flying faster than other aircraft in the type or category, and setting absolute speed records. When Lindbergh crossed the Atlantic in 1927, the world absolute speed record was held by a French pilot at 278.481 mph (448.171 km/h). The record was broken by an Italian pilot who, flying Macchi planes, set it at 297.817 mph (479.290 km/h) in November 1927 and at 318.624 mph (512.776 km/h) in March 1928. A British pilot in a Supermarine established the record in 1931 of 407.001 mph (655 km/h). Competitive race times were usually considerably slower than the absolute record; for example, the Gee-Bee 7-11 *Super Sportster* won the 1932 Thompson Trophy with a speed of only 294.4 mph. An Italian pilot in a Macchi-Castoldi set a new absolute record in 1933 and again in 1934. The record remained at 440.678 mph (709.202 km/h) until new German military planes appeared in 1939: the Heinkel He-100V-8 set the record in March at 463.921 mph (746.604 km/h) and the Messerschmitt Me-209V-1 set it at 469.224 mph (755.138 km/h) in April. (Figure 6-14)

French Raids

The type of French flight known as a **raid** began as exploratory flight, but during the 1930s it became classed as sport *(l'aviation sportive)*. At that time, it lost the practical association with surveying commercial

Figure 6-14. Jimmy Doolittle flew the Gee Bee Super Sportster R-1 to victory in the 1932 Thompson Trophy race. He flew 252.686 miles per hour (406.286 km/h) in that race. Also in 1932, he flew the R-1 to a new speed record of 296.287 mph (476.828 km/h).

Figure 6-15. Antoine de Saint-Exupéry was a famous French flyer and former airmail pilot who flew exploratory flights and competed for distance and speed records.

routes. The government's air ministry offered prizes for first flights to far destinations. As most destinations were reached, it offered additional prizes for the fastest flights. In 1935, for example, it offered two prizes, one for the fastest flight from Paris to Tananarive (now Madagascar). The other prize was for the fastest flight from Paris to Saigon — won by André Japy with a time of 98 hours and 52 minutes. The former airmail pilot Saint-Exupéry competed for the Paris-to-Saigon prize, but he only got as far as the Egyptian desert. Flying blind and without a radio, he was unable to ascertain the barometric pressure which was necessary to set the altimeter. He flew his Simoun into the sand! He and his mechanic wandered on foot for days. Their crash was bad for aviation, even by the standards then, but their heroic survival made good press. Saint-Exupéry's final raid was an attempt to fly the length of both American continents. His airplane was a light Caudron Simoun made by Renault. On the flight, Saint-Exupéry admired the radio navigation system installed in the United States, and he followed the Latin American airway established by Pan American. He considered both the radio navigation system and the international airway to be superior to counterparts in French aviation of that period. He flew 3,400 miles — less than half the planned distance — and crashed at Guatemala City's La Aurora field. (Figure 6-15)

Light Airplanes

The famous transatlantic flight of Lindbergh and his monoplane popularized both the man and the machine. The airplane, in Lindbergh's case, was small and lightweight. Manufacturers responded to the popularity of aviation by producing light airplanes for ordinary fliers: for the Saturday Lindberghs and Lady Lindy's, for ranchers and farmers, and businessmen and school teachers. Some light airplanes were high-performance, like Saint-Exupéry's Simoun. Others were built for the competitive aviator. Most were for private pilots, an emerging class of pilots distinguished by their license, their aircraft, and their non-commercial flying.

The de Havilland D.H. 60 Moth biplane became so popular by the late twenties that the word *Moth* came to denote every small airplane, similar to the earlier word *Zeppelin* referring to all rigid airships regardless of make. The construction was simple, as the fuselage was basically a wooden box of plywood covering four spruce framing members running fore and aft, which were called longerons; screws, not glue or dope, attached the plywood. De Havilland delivered the first Moth in 1925 and the first seaplane version in 1926, and it produced over four hundred of the aircraft by the end of 1928. De Havilland granted licenses for Moth production to companies in Australia and Finland. This two-seat biplane was usually powered by a single Cirrus engine, 60- to 105-horsepower. New and improved versions appeared, including the D.H. 60G Gipsy Moth, D.H. 60GIII Moth Major, D.H. 60M Moth, D.H. 60T Moth Trainer; 100- to 133-horsepower de Havilland Gipsy engines usually powered these airplanes. De Havilland produced 595 of the wooden Gipsy Moths from 1928 into 1934. Introduced in 1928, the 60M Moth had a welded steel tube fuselage. It was produced in Australia and Norway as well as Britain. Moths flew long distances, raced fast, entered the fleets of flying clubs around the world, joined military air forces, carried mail and supplies in the back country, and served private pilots. (Figure 6-16)

In the United States numerous companies produced light airplanes for private pilots, the technological leader being the Taylor Aircraft Company which built the Model A Cub. C.G. Taylor and William T. Piper founded this company and placed the Cub into production in 1930. the Model A was powered by a little 37-horsepower engine. It began a line of Cubs. From 1931 to 1936 the company built about 350

Figure 6-16. Geoffrey de Havilland produced many variations of the Moth. Shown here is a replica of the Tiger Moth.

of the popular E-2 Cub, powered by either a 37- or 40-horsepower Lycoming A-40 engine. Taylor produced Cub models through the J-2. A fire at the factory in Bradford, Pennsylvania, the opening of a new factory at nearby Lock Haven, a dispute between the partners, and a reorganization transformed the Taylor company into the Piper Aircraft Corporation in 1937. The first Piper Cub was the J-3.

The Stinson Reliant, Model SR, introduced in 1933 was another technological leader. It combined features of the Stinson S and R models, used a new 215-horsepower Lycoming engine, came equipped with more flight instruments, and had seats for four. This high-wing monoplane was an immediate sales success. Stinson made hundreds of civil model Reliants during the 1930s, and hundreds of military Reliants, trainers, and utility planes during World War II. Aeronca, Beech, Bellanca, Cessna, Fairchild, Porterfield, Rearwin, Taylorcraft, and Waco were among the other lightplane makers during the Golden Age of Aviation. (Figue 6-17)

Autogiros

Among the light aircraft of the period were autogiros, sometimes spelled autogyros and sometimes called windmill planes. Many of these were small enough to fit into an automobile garage. An **autogiro** has both a rotor and propeller. The rotor blades are airfoils, like the wings of an airplane or the blades of a propeller. When the blades turn around through the air, the rotor generates lift. The autogiro's propeller draws the aircraft forward. That forward motion and not the motor turns the rotor blades, which thus are freely

Figure 6-17. The Golden Age of Aviation produced several well known light airplanes such as (clockwise from upper left) the Taylor E-2 Cub, Piper J-3 Cub, Stinson Junior, and Waco straight wing.

and material for the Blériot XI, Santos Dumont Demoiselle, Farman biplane, and Curtiss biplane; the company also made "expanding pitch" propellers of Oregon spruce and Honduras mahogany. For the customer with a small budget, the Hull Monoplane Company of Marshalltown, Iowa, sold blueprints and instructions for making an airplane from a bicycle! Homebuilt aircraft became a standard feature of aviation, particularly in the United States.

Early American homebuilts were sometimes the maker's personal designs of a single aircraft. Often, however, the homebuilt was based on the design of a factory-made airplane that could be built at home. The Heath Parasol was one of the first aircraft to be marketed explicitly as a homebuilt. Ed Heath of Chicago, assisted by Clare Linsted, built the prototype Heath Parasol in 1926. Heath published the plans for the Parasol in *Popular Mechanics*, and he made a few factory-built Parasols. More importantly, he focused his business on selling kits to home-builders. In 1930 he introduced the Super Parasol kit. His factory-made kits could be assembled at home and would qualify for a government license if the various government inspections were passed. The Heath company continued selling kits after Heath died. (Figure 6-18)

Bernie Pietenpol's Air Camper, which first flew in 1928, became one of the more popular American

rotating. Juan de La Cierva of Spain dominated autogiro development.

Companies in several countries built autogiros, the majority under Cierva license, but there were other proprietary designs too. The United States and the United Kingdom became involved with autogiros in a bigger way than other countries. The Autogyro Company of Philadelphia, Buhl Aircraft Company of Marysville, Michigan — maker of the first pusher autogiro, Kellet Aircraft Corporation of Philadelphia and, particularly, the Pitcairn Autogiro Company of Pennsylvania entered the autogiro business. Avro was the largest British producer, but the Hafner, Kay, and Weir companies entered the business in small ways. In France Cierva-Lepére, Lioré-et-Oliver, and Wymann built the machines. Focke-Wulf was the chief maker of German autogiros, and Shiro Kayabawas the Japanese autogiro maker. The Soviet Central Aerodynamics and Hydrodynamics Institute also produced autogiros; it started with a Cierva design but quickly moved to Soviet designs. Sales figures remained more modest than the press coverage of these little aircraft. Included in that press coverage was Amelia Earhart who in 1931 flew a Pitcairn autogiro to an unofficial altitude record of 18,451 feet and a different Pitcairn on a promotional tour for Beech Nut.

Homebuilt Aircraft

Starting with the Montgolfier brothers' balloon of 1783, aircraft have been built at home. Early balloons, dirigibles, and airplanes were often designed at home too. Given the enthusiasm for aviation generated by the Wright brothers' demonstration flights of 1908-1909, companies began selling airplane plans to would-be homebuilders. Some even sold complete bills of material with blueprints for the desired type of airplane. In 1911, for example, R.O. Rubel, Jr., & Company of Louisville, Kentucky, offered plans

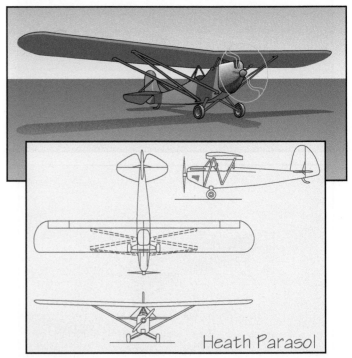

Figure 6-18. Ed Heath was instrumental in developing the homebuilt aircraft in the United States. Shown here is the Heath Parasol (top) and the 3-view plans (bottom).

Personal Profile

As a youth, Bernard H. "Bernie" Pietenpol (1901-1984) of Cherry Grove, Minnesota, worked on tractors and motorcycles. He learned to fly in a war-surplus Curtiss Jenny. He built an airplane powered by a Ford automobile engine, readily available since he repaired and sold cars for a living at the time. *Modern Mechanix* magazine published the plans for his two-seat Air Camper in 1932 and for his single-seat Sky Scout in 1933; both sets of plans specified automobile engines, the Ford Model A engine for the Air Camper and the Model T engine for the Sky Scout.

The Air Camper became a popular homebuilt, built from the published plans. Pietenpol remained in the car business until World War II, when he became a flight instructor. After the war he went into the television repair business.

Bernard H. Pietenpol

Air Camper

homebuilts and one made from the published plans alone. The Crawford Motor and Airplane Manufactory at Long Beach, California, sold plans, instructions, and materials for a "wonderful two-place, companion-type, small, high-lift wing monoplane." The Guardian Aircraft Company of St. Louis sold plans and materials for a low-wing, open-cockpit, two-seat light airplane. There were other companies who sold homebuilt plans and materials too. The situation in Europe was different.

Flying Fleas

In Europe building airplanes had become an establishment activity; that is, the activity of established companies and government factories. Henri Mignet changed that. He built his own planes and inspired a homebuilding movement. Mignet built his eighth aircraft in 1927. This HM.8 was a modest machine by any standards. It was small and light weight and powered by the ten-horsepower Anzani engine. Its

Personal Profile

Henri Mignet (1893-1965) grew up in western France. At age 18 he began corresponding with the German glider pioneer Gustav Lilienthal, and in 1912 Mignet built a glider. He attended the technical *École Philomatique* (School of Electro-Physics) in Bordeaux. He worked in a factory until World War I. During the war, he served as a radio-telephonist in an artillery unit. After the war he built the HM.2 monoplane, which had features adapted from Louis Blériot and Willi Messerschmitt designs. He

made both airplanes and gliders. HM.7 was a helicopter powered by a ten-horsepower Anzani motorcycle engine; though man and machine were lifted into the air, HM.7 crashed. Mignet worked for the Philips radio company while continuing experiments in aviation. The 1927 HM.8 was his most successful aircraft to date. It was a little light airplane with parasol wings and a ten-horsepower engine. It sparked a homebuilding movement in France, and its successor the HM.14 made the movement international.

Henri Mignet in Flying Flea

parasol wing was foldable and pivoting — folding to facilitate transporting the aircraft on the ground and pivoting to change the angle of attack during flight. Mignet published an article in *Les Ailes (Wings,* March 1928) about this successful venture into *l'aviation de l'amateur* (amateur aviation). The magazine then printed letters from admirers and critics who debated the viability of homebuilt aircraft, as well as additional articles by Mignet. In the magazine and his book *Le Sport de l'Air (Air Sport,* 1931), Mignet gave instructions and plans for homebuilders. Mignet knew of the amateurs in Germany's glider movement, and he was aware of companies in the United States providing products to amateur aviators. He argued for amateur builders everywhere. Over a few years time and mostly in France, but sometimes elsewhere, about 200 amateurs built HM.8s.

Mignet continued to experiment with aircraft design and even built his own wind tunnel to help develop a better and safer amateur airplane. He searched for natural controls that would make a plane incapable of stalling or spinning. The press gave a design in progress the nickname *Le Pou du Ciel* — The Flea of the Sky or simply Flying Flea. The name stuck to the HM.14, the prototype of which Mignet built in 1933. The HM.14 solved the problem of stalling by using two wings that were almost tandem and almost stagger. The lower wing was positioned close enough to the trailing edge of the upper wing to create a venturi between the wings and thereby delay the upper wing from stalling. Mignet described the Flea as "a kite with an auxiliary engine"; it was an ultralight made of wood, fabric, dope, nuts, and bolts. It became known partly for what it did not have. It did not have ailerons, slots, elevators, or cowling. (Figure 6-19)

Homebuilt Movement

Mignet wrote a book about the HM.14 entitled *Le Sport de l'Air (Air Sport,* 1934). That year he exhibited his Flea at the Paris Air Show and demonstrated it at the Orly grass field near Paris. The response was tremendous. *Les Ailes* and *The Aeroplane* ran feature stories; hundreds of amateurs built the aircraft. The *Réseau des Amateurs de l'Air* (network or organization of air amateurs, RAA) formed in France, and in Britain the Air League took up the cause of amateur builders. The Air League published a translation of Mignet's 1934 book under the title *The Flying Flea* (1935) and organized a Pou Club (*pou* the French for flea) to assist amateur airplane makers. Mignet earned income from publication royalties, not from selling

Figure 6-19. Henri Mignet designed the homebuilt aircraft called the HM.14, *Flying Flea*, in 1933. The staggered wing design made it stall resistant. The design is still being built today.

plans or materials. Nine Fleas and their builders and about 15,000 spectators attended a Flea rally at Orly in 1935. In August that year, Mignet flew his Flea, powered by a 17-horsepower Aubier et Dunne engine, across the English Channel to Britain, where his presence further inspired the new homebuilt movement there.

An immediate problem for Flea builders was the fact that neither pilot nor plane could be licensed under French or British aviation regulations of the time. The fatal crash of a Flea in the French colony of Algeria prompted the local government there to ban the aircraft type, and the popularity of the machine attracted the attention of government regulators elsewhere. The French Air Ministry soon banned unlicensed aircraft from using licensed flying fields; fortunately, Mignet's designs did not require an airfield, since it was able to take off and land in less than a hundred feet. The British Air Ministry issued special permits for homebuilts between July 1935

 Historic Event

In 1935 French amateur builders of the Mignet HM.14 Flea organized the *Réseau des Amateurs de l'Air* (RAA), *réseau* being a network or organization and this one being for homebuilders. Henri Mignet called airplane homebuilders *amateurs de l'air* or air amateurs. His term for homebuilding was *autre aviation* — alternative aviation.

Current homebuilder associations include the French *Réseau du Sport de l'Air*, the British Popular Flying Association, and the American Experimental Aircraft Association (founded in 1953).

Historical Evidence

Government documents are sources of historical information. In the case of a government permit, the document enables the recipient to do something. The British Air Ministry began to issue special permits to fly homebuilt aircraft in 1935. These permits enabled a homebuilt industry to develop and grow.

A permit allowed the specified aircraft "to be flown without having been certified as airworthy . . . and without carrying a certificate of airworthiness." The authorization was subject to conditions and limitations:

1. The permit was valid only in Great Britain and Northern Ireland.

2. The aircraft could not fly over populated areas or groups of people.

3. The aircraft could not carry passengers, goods, or mail for hire.

4. The aircraft was not allowed to fly acrobatic maneuvers.

5. The aircraft could be flown only when in good repair and working order.

6. The aircraft could be flown only when covered by insurance for any third party damage to persons or property on the ground.

7. The aircraft could not be flown in any manner that would invalidate its insurance policy.

8. The permission could be withdrawn at any time, and if not withdrawn or renewed it would expire on the specified date.

This is according to Authorisation No. 21, dated 24 December 1935, as photo-reproduced in Ken Ellis and Geoff Jones. *Henri Mignet and His Flying Fleas* (Somerset, England: Haynes Publishing Group, 1990).

and May 1939, during which time 76 Fleas received authorization. As the number of Fleas increased so did the number of fatal accidents, which led both France and Britain to impose bans in 1939. The war then interrupted homebuilding activity in Europe.

Gliding

Light airplanes and homebuilts often involved the individual flier, but gliders attracted teams. This was the case internationally. In Germany, where gliding was already a popular national sport, gliding became a craze. Gliding camps and schools opened around the country, and enrollments in the schools increased year after year. Academic flying groups and Young Flier Groups proliferated. "Young fliers" were age eighteen to twenty-six years, and the Young Flier Groups alone enrolled nearly ten thousand members in the early 1930s. Local *Sturmvogel* or Storm Bird groups also organized. The allure of gliding included going to camp for weeks at a time in the summer, participating in the sport, and singing patriotic songs around the campfire. The various gliding groups usually made their own aircraft: the academic flying groups built aircraft from their own designs and other flying clubs built them from purchased blueprints and plans. The "group" was also important when it came time to fly. Six to ten people would pull a rope and thereby pull the glider into the air for takeoff and

the group would transport the glider back up the hill after a flight. (Figure 6-20)

Figure 6-20. During the early 1930s, gliding was a popular team activity in Germany.

Flight Lines

"I want to climb higher, ever higher, until I reach the stars and can look back at the planet and its rivers, mountains, and oceans through the dark light of the universe."

German glider pilot Robert Kronfeld, as translated and quoted in Peter Fritzsche, *A Nation of Fliers, German Aviation and the Popular Imagination* (Cambridge: Harvard University Press, 1992).

German glider pilots began investigating thermals in the late 1920s. Robert Kronfeld deliberately flew into a storm on 20 July 1929. The thermals carried him up to 3,000 meters, and he glided to a landing spot 143 kilometers from his departure point at the Wasserkuppe. He proved that thermals could be used to aid flight, and that gliders could fly away from the updrafts of sloping terrain. Pilots began to fly in front of storms and to catch the thermal updrafts in order to gain altitude. From altitude, they glided long distances. They began using clouds as indicators of thermal activity. The German pilots learned to ride the fair-weather thermals of forming cumulus clouds. As pilots had once glided from slope to slope to catch updrafts, they now glided from cloud to cloud to ride thermals. They also learned to ride thermals produced by dry, sun-warmed ground and by cities and industrial sites. Wolf Hirth demonstrated city thermals in flights over Berlin and New York City. He and other expert gliding pilots held a "C" license, whereas the majority of German glider pilots earned only the "A" rating, which meant that they could glide for about a minute and that they could land safely. The National Socialist Party militarized the gliding clubs in Germany, but government-subsidized

Flight Lines

"In a long glide, my Sperber carried me to Cologne, and I soon fell to 1,300 ft. In wide circles, I searched for the aerodrome, but could not find it anywhere. The situation was becoming critical and I was only 700 ft above the rooftops, when literally at the last moment a power-plane came to my rescue. As it was climbing towards me still at a very low altitude, it could not have taken off so very long ago. So, pushing the stick forward, I flew rapidly in the direction from which it had come. At last the aerodrome appeared in sight, and clearing the last obstacles with 6 ft to spare I landed right in front of the hangars at 1735 hrs completely exhausted after a 6-hr flight. I was almost too tired to climb out of the cockpit; but I was in high spirits, for I had flown 206 miles: the longest goal-flight ever made in a glider."

Erwin Kraft describing the end of his glide on 21 August 1935, as quoted in translation in Ann and Lorne Welch, *The Story of Gliding* (London: John Murray, 1965).

Soviet gliders outdistanced German pilots by the late 1930s. (Figure 6-21)

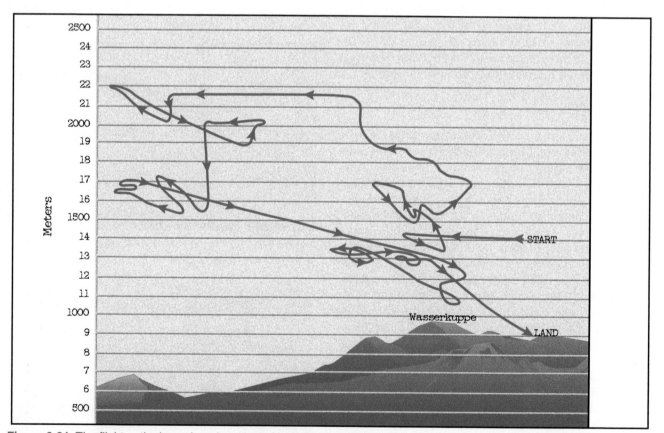

Figure 6-21. The flight path shown here is typical of how German glider pilots used the thermals over Wasserkuppe. Pilots such as Wolf Hirth learned to ride the thermals of cumulus clouds as well as those produced by warm ground and city thermals.

SECTION C

COMMERCIAL AIRLINES AND AIRLINERS

Commercial aviation established regularly scheduled domestic and international routes during the Golden Age of Aviation. There was variety, also competition and growth. There were mergers, acquisitions, and reorganizations, even scandals and failures. Airlines ranged from the mundane to the grand. On the mundane side were three specially modified Junkers G 31s transporting men and freight to gold fields in the mountains of New Guinea. These operations remained relatively unchanged throughout the decade as the mining companies continued operation and as the land lacked the cities and population that supported airline development elsewhere. A grand airline of this period was TACA, the Transportes Aéreos Centro-Americanos, established by New Zealand-born Lowell Yerex in 1931. At the time Yerex had one airplane, a Stinson, in Mexico. His

company expanded from Mexico to Panama and beyond into an international network from Miami to Rio de Janeiro. TACA specialized in carrying freight.

Politics and diplomacy also influenced airline development. The Australian Queensland and Northern Territory Aerial Services (Qantas) relied upon government airmail contracts and cooperation with Britain's Imperial Airways. It faced domestic competition and developed its own international routes. The airline changed its name to Qantas Empire Airways (QEA) in 1934. A Curtiss mechanic, pilot, and representative to Peru, founded a Peruvian airline in 1928. His name was Elmer J. "Slim" Faucett, and the company was Compañía de Aviatión Faucett. Faucett managed to see his company expand and survive despite Peru's terrain, the formation of a

government airline, and politics. Revolutions and civil wars, and changing fortunes of French, German, and American airlines affected the development of commercial service in South America as well as colonial Africa. For example, Imperial Airways operated airmail service between London and Cape Town and that prompted the private Union Airways to organize in 1929 to carry airmail between South African cities, and that domestic airline expanded to passenger service in the thirties.

Aéropostale

One of the most influential airlines on three continents in the late twenties was Compagnie Générale Aéropostale, owned by the Brazil resident Marcel Bouilloux-Lafont. In 1928 Aéropostale started airmail service between France and South America via the African route established by *la Ligne* of Latécoère, and in 1929 Aéropostale began regular night flights along the African route and on South American routes. New planes made these services possible. The Latécoère 25 appeared in 1928, followed by the Laté 26 and then the closed-cabin Laté 28. (Figure 6-22)

Figure 6-22. Aéropostale flew regular scheduled airmail flights in the late 1920s and early 1930s in aircraft such as this Latécoère 28.

Jean Mermoz and two crewmen flew a Laté 28 floatplane from St. Louis, Senegal, to Natal, Brazil, in less than twenty-two hours in 1930. This experimental flight demonstrated the aerial possibilities of service across the South Atlantic, and proved the reliable power and long range of the Laté mailplane. The Latés had space for passengers as well as mail and also had radios for night flying. A private company, Aéropostale had strong government support in the

form of subsidies as well as contracts. This allowed Aéropostale to link the vast French empire together and compete with the German Luft Hansa line. The French-German competition extended beyond Europe to South America, where Aéropostale operated the long coastal Patagonia line in Argentina, as well as routes in Bolivia, Brazil, Chile, Paraguay, Peru, Uruguay, and Venezuela. Deutsche Luft Hansa, the German Condor Syndikat, and associated German-sponsored companies operated in Brazil and on the west coast. In 1930 Aéropostale carried 32 million letters on three continents. The airline had the longest line of routes in the world.

The economic and territorial grandeur of Aéropostale disappeared amid scandal in the early 1930s. The jealousy and resulting politics of France's four other airmail lines were contributing factors. The 1929 stock market crash in the United States and the ensuing depression of the world's economy, the 1930 revolt in the Republic of Brazil and the resulting dictatorship of Getúlio Vargas, and the failure of three banks owned by Aéropostale's owner Bouilloux-Lafont brought public attention and financial investigation to the large and successful airline. The press reported all charges, substantiated or not. Company executives were attacked for alleged mismanagement and financial improprieties. In March 1931 the French Chamber of Deputies refused to grant Aéropostale its annual government subsidy, a subsidy routinely awarded in order to promote French trade with other continents. The immediate financial emergency caused by the loss of the subsidy forced the company into liquidation and bankruptcy.

A government-appointed board of directors assumed management of the airline. Routes were closed, services in various regions suspended, personnel laid off, and development of the new long-distance Laté 38 stopped. The *Journal de l'aviation Française* blamed "banking rivalries, envious foreigners, jealous Frenchmen, and socialist intrigues."

Early French postal airplane

Aéropostale failed in 1931 due to its earlier success, according to several contemporary and historical sources. The new management tried to save the airline. In 1932, for example, it issued a 25-page brochure entitled *Le Vérité sur [The Truth about] l'Aéropostale*. New charges emerged. One was that the operations manager tampered with mail and another that Bouilloux-Lafont's son André had documents falsified. The operations manager lost his job, and André Bouilloux-Lafont went to prison for several months. Government officials were accused of collusion with company executives in a supposed effort to obtain control of the airline. International conspiracy charges arose when the press reported that French and German officials had discussed

possibly merging South American operations. The French press and public debated capitalism versus nationalization. In the end, nationalization won.

On 30 August 1933 France merged its five airlines into one. The government initially owned one-fourth of the new national airline, which soon became known as Air France. This French government, by the way, changed several times just during the Aéropostale scandal; in fact, France had 43 different governments from 1919 to 1939! The air minister changed frequently too, almost annually. This instability certainly contributed to the decline of Aéropostale, once the pride of France.

French Aviation

In 1934 Air France joined the same international airline pool as Deutsche Luft Hansa, so its chief competition was now a collaborator. Latécoère, by the way, continued as an airplane maker in Toulouse, independent of Aéropostale in the end and of Air France in the beginning. From inception, Air France was a national airline, but France permitted other airlines. In 1935 Didier Daurat, formerly of Aéropostale and its predecessor Latécoère, established an airmail line called Air Bleu. It began operations with the Caudron-Simoun 180-horsepower airplane, the first French airplane equipped with the variable-pitch propeller. It was also equipped for instrument flying.

By the mid-1930s the French were tired of the airmail scandal and apparently of aviation in general. The poor domestic economy, the 1934 Paris riots, government corruption, Italy's 1935 invasion of Ethiopia, the 1936 outbreak of civil war in Spain, the spread

Historic Event

On 30 August 1933 France merged its five airlines into one that soon became known as Air France.

The five airlines were Air Orient, Air Union, CIDNA (Compagnie Internationale de Navigation Aérienne), S.G.T.A. (Société Générale de Transport Aérien, also known as Farman), and Compagnie Générale Aéropostale (formerly Latécoère). Earlier that year four of the airlines, all except Aéropostale, had formed SCELA (Société Centrale pour l'Exploitation de Lignes Aériennes) in order to promote a national airline system. The French government owned 25 percent of the new airline, and the four SCELA companies owned varying shares too. Aéropostale, being bankrupt, did not purchase any share of Air France.

Once merged, Air France had a fleet of 259 aircraft. These included 25 different types. Of the 259, over half — 172 — were single-engine airplanes; that is, they were obsolete in a commercial-transport era of tri-motors and multi-engine flying boats.

Historical Note

Variable pitch, controllable pitch, and constant speed all refer to a propeller that allows a pilot to adjust the angle of the propeller blades in flight (like a driver shifting the gears of a car). A low or fine pitch is for takeoff and climb, and a high or coarse pitch for cruise. The purpose is to convert as much engine power to thrust as possible over a range of engine speed and airspeed combinations.

A variety of engineers experimented with controlling the pitch of propeller blades before, during, and after the First World War.

H.S. Hele-Shaw and T.E. Beacham in England developed and patented a hydromechanically activated variable-pitch airscrew in 1924. Development continued and, in 1937, Rotol Airscrews Limited organized in England to produce propellers based on the Hele-Shaw design.

In Germany, Junkers experimented with an electrically activated controllable propeller, and Ratier in France produced a pneumatically actuated propeller.

In the United States, the Hamilton Standard Propeller Company and its chief engineer Frank Caldwell won the 1933 Collier Trophy for developing a practical controllable pitch propeller. Patented after the Hele-Shaw version, the Hamilton Standard hydromechanically activated propeller went into production more quickly. It went into service on the new modern airliners of the 1930s — the Douglas DC-2, the Boeing 247D, and the Lockheed Electra. In the 1930s Hamilton Standard licensed production of its controllable propeller to Hispano-Suiza in France, Junkers in Germany, Fiat in Italy, and Sumitomo in Japan.

1933 Collier Trophy winners, Hamilton Standard and Chief Engineer Frank Caldwell (second from left).

The development work of the 1920s and early 1930s led to the widespread use of controllable-pitch propellers in the 1930s and thereafter.

Personal Profile

Frederick B. Rentschler (1887-1956) founded Pratt & Whitney Aircraft. As a young Army officer during World War I, he had inspected aircraft engine production at Wright-Martin plants. From 1919 to 1924 he served as the president of the Wright Aeronautical Corporation. In 1925 he founded Pratt & Whitney Aircraft as a division of the Pratt & Whitney tool company in Hartford, Connecticut. A few years later, in December 1928, Rentschler and his Pratt & Whitney company merged with William E. Boeing and his Boeing Airplane & Transport Corporation. In 1929 Boeing Airplane & Transport changed its name to United Aircraft & Transport Corporation. As a result of the airmail scandal of 1934, United Aircraft & Transport dissolved. Rentschler took its Pratt & Whitney division and other manufacturing operations east of the Mississippi River and placed them in a new United Aircraft Corporation. Years later Time magazine recognized Rentschler's emphasis on aircraft engines and impact on the industry with a cover story about "Mr. Horsepower."

United Aircraft changed its name in 1975 to United Technologies.

Frederick B. Rentschler

of fascism on the continent, and fear of Germany's growing economic and military strength seemed more important. Nationalization of the aviation industry and labor strikes also hurt French aviation. By 1937 French airplane makers were producing only 37 planes a month; this in the country that had led wartime and postwar production. French customers began ordering airplanes from manufacturers in the United States, where mass production techniques developed in the American automobile industry influenced production of aeronautical products. French industry in general still relied upon custom craft techniques in both its automotive and aeronautical industries. The beneficiaries of France's decline in aviation were Germany, Great Britain, and the United States.

Deutsche Luft Hansa

The German national airline of the late 1920s and the 1930s was Deutsche Luft Hansa. This line made use of the increasing number and reliability of instruments, newly improved aircraft radios, and multi-engine airplanes that improved the safety of air transport. After consolidating the resources obtained when the company formed, the young Deutsche Luft Hansa introduced new equipment and procedures. It began installing radios on large transport planes in 1926, and it made the instrument rating compulsory for transport pilots in 1929. (Figure 6-23)

Luft Hansa acquired some multi-engine aircraft, like the Junkers G 24 previously used by the Junkers lines.

Figure 6-23. During the late 1920s and early 1930s, Deutsche Luft Hansa introduced new aircraft, such as this Junkers G24, and procedures which improved airline safety.

Historical Note

The pride of French aviation in the mid-thirties was the prototype Latécoère 521, called *Lieutenant de Vaisseau Paris.* Built in 1933-1935, the 521 was the world's largest flying boat. The plane had two decks and numerous passenger cabins, some with beds and baths. The six 800-860 horsepower Hispano-Suiza engines turned three-bladed Ratier controllable-pitch propellers. A hurricane sank the *Lieutenant* at Pensacola, Florida, in 1936. Air France's Henry Guillaumet flew the rebuilt *Lieutenant* to five world records in 1937, including the seaplane distance record (3,586 miles nonstop from Morocco to Brazil). With new 920-horsepower Hispano-Suiza engines, the plane made three round-trips between France and the United States. A sister ship, the Laté 522, was completed in 1939, but the war interrupted the development of these large French flying boats, and turned the 521 and 522 into naval patrol ships. The development of the practical transport Laté 631 was delayed by the war, and its production postponed until after the war.

Henry Guillaumet

Historical Note

In Germany, instrument flying evolved in steps similar to those taken in other countries:

- daytime flying in visual contact with the ground

- visual night flying, as done by the German lines of Aero Lloyd and Junkers Luftverkehr in 1924

- following lighted airways at night, modeled after the United States Post Office Department's airmail routes

- installing radios in larger transports, which Deutsche Luft Hansa began doing in 1926. The weight of a radio and the need for a radio operator initially limited radios to larger aircraft.

- voluntary instrument flying, introduced in Germany by Luft Hansa's Willi Polte flying a Junkers G-24 in 1927

- requiring an instrument rating for airline pilots, which Luft Hansa began doing in 1929 (four years before the United States required air transport pilots to obtain the instrument rating)

The predecessor, Aero Lloyd, had ordered Rohrbach Roland monoplanes, and Luft Hansa accepted delivery of the prototype in 1926. Designed by Adolph Rohrbach and produced at his firm's factory in Copenhagen, the Roland had three 320-horsepower BMW Va engines. It seated ten. With this aircraft Luft Hansa made a trial flight over the Alps in 1927. The airline began regular service carrying mail and freight over the mountains to Italy in 1928. That same year the airline experimented with a steward serving refreshments during passenger flights. Given the safety record compiled by multi-engine transports, Luft Hansa started passenger service from Munich, over the Alps, to Milan in 1931. By then, Luft Hansa's multi-engine fleet included Junkers G 24s and G 31s, as well as Albatross L 73s. (Figure 6-24)

Figure 6-24. Luft Hansa used this Rohrback Roland II during trial flights over the Alps in 1927.

With increased safety and greater range of aircraft, Luft Hansa expanded its operations and created a large European network. While Aéropostale had the longest line of routes, Luft Hansa flew more miles due to the numerous routes throughout Europe. The North Atlantic Ocean challenged Luft Hansa. In order to get bases along the route, Luft Hansa leased equipment and wrote off losses to support Flugfélag Island, an Icelandic airline formed in 1928. Flugfélag Island used Junkers F 13 floatplanes in its four years of seasonal operation. The airline ultimately failed, but it developed a floatplane base at Reykjavik that remained, and Deutsche Luft Hansa established a favorable reputation in the country.

Transoceanic

Luft Hansa initiated an experimental ship-to-land airmail service in the North Atlantic in 1929. It flew a Heinkel He 12 floatplane off the passenger ship *Bremen* and carried airmail to New York. A catapult assisted the takeoff from the *Bremen*. From 1929 through 1935 German planes were catapulted off ocean liners a total of 198 times. Three types of planes were used, the Heinkel He 12 and He 58 and the Junkers Ju 46. Two ocean liners were used as launch sites, the *Bremen* and the *Europa*. The catapult launch reduced the amount of fuel needed for takeoff and increased the load size at takeoff, so a catapulted plane could carry more mail or fuel than one taking off from water, or it could achieve greater range with the same takeoff load. The oceanic flights generated publicity and support for German aviation but provided scant savings of time as the planes usually departed the ocean liners only 300 miles from their final destination. (Figure 6-25)

Figure 6-25. A Heinkel low-wing seaplane being catapulted from the *Bremen* in 1929. Luft Hansa used this innovative method of delivering the mail from ships to land bases.

In 1933 Deutsche Luft Hansa improved the experimental airmail system by posting a depot ship at the end of each flight and occasionally en route. That June the Dornier Wal *Monsun* made a catapult-assisted takeoff and crossed the South Atlantic Ocean, from Bathurst, West Africa, to Natal, Brazil. In 1934 Luft Hansa began scheduled airmail service across the South Atlantic, Berlin to Rio in four days. Planes landed and deployed a drag sail. A crane hoisted the aircraft onto the deck, where crews refueled and serviced them. From a sled on a rail, aircraft were launched by hydraulic catapult. The depot ships also were deployed in the South Atlantic. Germany converted the *Westfalen* to a depot ship, a merchant ship 410 feet long. The *Schwabenland*, *Ostmark*, and *Friesenland* also entered depot service during

Figure 6-26. Officer on a depot ship *Schwabenland* prepares to launch a Luft Hansa Dornier Wal (left). On the right, the Wal is shown shortly after launch.

the thirties. These depot ships were substitutes for territory that Germany did not have, and they were mobile. (Figure 6-26)

Cooperation

Luft Hansa entered into a partnership with a Spanish consortium to establish the Sociedad Iberica de Aviación (Iberia) in order to link the two countries by air. The Spanish venture provided stops between Germany and Latin America where Luft Hansa cooperated with existing companies with German ties. The companies included Sociedad Colombo-Alemana de Transportes Aéreos (SCADTA) in Colombia, Lloyd Aéreo Boliviano (L.A.B.) in Bolivia, and airlines supplied by the new Condor Syndikat, like the Syndicato Condor Limiteda established in Brazil in late 1927. The German airline also cooperated with French airlines to reduce competition along international routes. The Aéropostale scandal opened South Atlantic opportunities to Luft Hansa, which for three years carried mail between Europe and the Canary Islands. An ocean liner carried the mail toward South America and, as it neared that continent, Syndicato Condor would catapult a Dornier Wal into flight to finish the crossing. On

the return trip, Luft Hansa used the catapult-launch technique to hurry mail to Europe. In the South Atlantic, like the North Atlantic, Luft Hansa converted to using depot ships. With depot ship support, Luft Hansa flew mail over the entire transoceanic route.

Having lost its colonies at the end of World War I, Germany nonetheless tried to expand its commercial influence. In 1930 Luft Hansa reached an agreement with the Kuomintang government of China to form a joint company. This Eurasia Aviation Corporation, one-third German and two-thirds Chinese, began scheduled airmail service in 1931. During the thirties the Eurasia airline used Junkers airplanes: two single-engine F 13s and twenty-two multi-engine planes — W 33s, W 34s, and Ju 52/3m's, and one Ju 160. Luft Hansa made several efforts for Eurasia to link with the Soviet Dobrolot line, but these efforts failed — once when a plane was shot down over Mongolia, and another time when worsening of Sino-Soviet relations grounded aircraft. Eurasia Aviation developed and operated a domestic Chinese network of routes, but the Chinese civil war and the Japanese invasion of China hindered the further development of Chinese aviation.

British Airlines

Continuing its conservative approach, Imperial Airways carried up-scale passengers in luxury planes between distinguished points. It was the sole national airline serving the British empire, but it carried far fewer customers than airlines serving Germany, France, and Italy. Its neglect of domestic routes led several private companies to establish supplemental service within the United Kingdom. Among the domestic carriers of the 1930s were Hillman, British Airways, and the Scottish Motor Traction Company. Imperial's fleet, like its marketing approach, was conservative too; it included none of the modern airliners produced in Germany and the United States. Imperial also did not aggressively improve its colonial routes. In 1931 Imperial had only 22 airplanes, all British makes, in comparison to Aéropostale's 172 French-made planes and Deutsche Luft Hansa's 145 airplanes of German and Dutch make. Nonetheless, Imperial provided comfortable service to distant points in the British empire. Its 1932 African service, for example, involved 33 stages and six changes of vehicles. Passengers traveled in a Handley Page H.P. 42 from London to Paris; a train from Paris to Brindisi, Italy; a Short Scipio from there to Alexandria, Egpyt; an Armstrong Whitworth Argosy south to Khartoum in the Anglo-Egyptian Sudan; a Short Calcutta to Kisumu, Kenya; and, finally, another H.P. 42 to Cape Town.

During the 1930s Imperial upgraded its fleet, but not to international standards. In 1931, for example, it placed into service the safe and comfortable 40-seat Handley Page Type 42, but Imperial kept the aircraft in service long after faster foreign-made airliners were introduced. The pride of the Imperial fleet were its Empire Flying Boats, four-engine Short aircraft popularly known as Empire Boats. The first few were launched in the summer of 1936. (Figure 6-27)

Britain continued to develop conservative four-engine landplanes too. At the end of the decade, Imperial, for example, acquired the large 40-seat Armstrong Whitworth A.W. 27 Ensign and the impressive 20-30 seat de Havilland Type 91 Albatros. Both were monoplanes. The Ensign was an underpowered, high-wing all-metal model, and the Albatros was a low-wing aircraft with good aerodynamic performance but obsolete wooden construction.

A British government commission in 1938 recommended improving airline service by dividing international routes between two companies. Under the proposal, Imperial would operate long Empire routes and British Airways would operate shorter European routes. Imperial was still a very conservative line with only 71 British-made airplanes, whereas smaller British Airways was more aggressive. It operated 13 Lockheed and three Junkers airliners. In comparison, Deutsche Luft Hansa had a fleet of 230 aircraft, mostly Junkers; and Air France operated 104 planes, mostly French makes but also several Fokkers. Commercial aviation in Britain simply was not keeping pace, much less catching up, with foreign competition. Parliament tried to solve the problems. In 1939 it passed an act to create the British Overseas Airways Corporation, which in 1940 acquired the assets of both Imperial and British Airways. Numerous small companies still provided domestic service within the United Kingdom.

United States

The Air Mail Act of 1925 stimulated the formation of airlines in the United States; airlines organized to carry airmail under government contract. The Air Mail Act of 1930, called the Watres Act or McNary-Watres Bill after Congressman Laurence Hawley Watres of Pennsylvania and Senator Charles D. McNary of Oregon, amended the act of 1925. The 1930 law provided a premium to airlines that carried passengers in addition to airmail. In this way, the federal government explicitly subsidized the transportation of passengers as well as the transportation of mail. The federal incentive prompted airlines to order new and larger planes, and manufacturers responded in 1933-1934 with the Boeing 247, the Douglas DC-2, and the Lockheed 10 Electra. These were the first of the "modern" airliners, two-engine,

Figure 6-27. Nacelles built into the leading edge of the Empire Flying Boat acted as shock-absorbing spring mechanisms between the floats and wing.

Historic Event

On 8 February 1933 at Boeing Field, Seattle, test pilot Les Tower took the Model 247 on its first flight. Boeing based the 247 on the Boeing YB-9 bomber. At the end of March, Boeing delivered the first aircraft to an airline, Boeing Air Transport.

The 247 airliner was an all-metal, monocoque, low-wing, twin-engine monoplane with stressed skin, controllable-pitch propellers, retractable undercarriage, and Pratt & Whitney Wasp radial engines that were in nacelles and cowled to enhance cooling and reduce drag. Another innovation was the use of trim tabs on all control surfaces to allow pilots to make minor adjustments to the airplane's attitude.

The 247 was also the first air transport with wing and tail deicing. The flight instruments — artificial horizon, directional gyro, vertical speed indicator, sensitive altimeter (sensitive to the setting of the barometric scale), and navigational radios — were also modern. Pilots flew by instruments before the 247, but the 247 came equipped with instruments that allowed the pilot to navigate by the federal airway system. It was one of the first aircraft used in instrument flight as currently defined.

Boeing had competitors, as Douglas first flew its DC-1 in July 1933, DC-2 in May 1934, and DC-3 in December 1935. Lockheed first flew its Electra 10 in February 1934. The Douglas DC-1 and Lockheed Electra also had flaps, another feature that came to be recognized as modern. Being first gave Boeing's 247 a successful initial year of production and sales.

The Boeing 247 influenced foreign aircraft design, as evidenced in the Bristol 142, Junkers Ju 86, and Heinkel He 111, all of 1935.

Historical Note

Football coach Knute Rockne died in an airline crash near Bazaar, Kansas, on 31 March 1931. He was a passenger on board a Transcontinental Air Transport (TAT) flight. The aircraft was a Fokker F-10A trimotor. The sporting fame of the Notre Dame University coach made the crash front-page news.

The Fokker trimotor had a good safety record and a good corporate reputation. General Motors then owned the American Fokker company that made the F-10A. The aircraft was a high-wing trimotor monoplane. Its composite construction included a fuselage of welded steel tubes covered with fabric. The cantilever wing was made of wood covered with plywood skin.

What caused the accident? The Aeronautics Branch of the United States Department of Commerce looked at pilot error, a broken propeller, and weather as causes for the accident. It finally determined that the wood-and-glue construction of the wing was the fault. Federal inspectors removed the plywood skin of the wing and found moisture, deteriorated glue, and a weakened structure. The spruce and birch spars were literally coming unglued.

What was the result? The Aeronautics Branch grounded the Fokker aircraft from carrying passengers, which affected 35 planes: 15 at American Airways, 10 at Pan American, 7 at TAT, and 3 at United. After passing inspection, an airplane could return to service subject to periodic inspection. The inspection was expensive because it required removal of the skin. Some Fokkers returned to passenger service briefly, but the public and the airlines had lost confidence. The publicity was so bad that General Motors renamed its Fokker division the General Aviation Manufacturing Corporation and phased out production of Fokker designs. The American Fokker company, which had ignored the international trend toward metal aircraft construction, was out of business.

Coach Knute Rockne

all-metal transports with seating for passengers. As these new airliners became available, the Department of Commerce banned single-engine aircraft in scheduled service from carrying passengers at night or over terrain like the mountainous west without suitable emergency landing sites.

The many airlines organized in the mid-twenties to carry airmail began merging and consolidating in the late twenties. Further reorganization and consolidation of the emerging airline industry came in response to the Air Mail Act of 1930. The Big Four conglomerates formed. One was William Boeing's United Aircraft & Transport Corporation (UAT or UATC) that acquired Boeing's production and operating divisions; that is, divisions that made aircraft equipment and divisions that operated the equipment in service: Boeing Airplane Company, Boeing Air Transport, Pacific Air Transport. It also acquired the Pratt & Whitney aircraft engine maker, the Hamilton and Standard propeller companies which it merged into Hamilton Standard, the Chance Vought supplier of naval aircraft, Stearman Aircraft Company, Sikorsky Aviation, National Air Transport, and Varney Airlines. United Airlines became a separate company in 1934.

The Big Four also included North American Aviation, led by C.M. Keys and best known for its Eastern Air Lines Division (later Eastern Air Lines). North American also acquired the General Aviation manufacturing divisions of General Motors. The so-called Western group of aviation equipment makers and airlines included Western Air Express (WAE), Transcontinental Air Transport (TAT), Pacific Marine, and other operating airlines that merged into Transcontinental and Western Air (TWA). The Aviation Corporation (AVCO) consolidated Colonial, Embry-Riddle, Southern, Universal, and other airlines into American Air Lines. Many investments crossed lines as companies were bought and sold. Equipment maker Curtiss Aeroplane & Motor Company, for example, had ties with National of the United group, Pitcairn of the North American group, and Transcontinental Air Transport of the Western or TWA group, as well as with the Wright Aeronautical Corporation that made aircraft engines. Relatively few aviation companies, whether equipment makers or operating airlines, remained independent during the early 1930s. Some, like Braniff, briefly joined a hold-

ing company but later became independent again. Many changed names several times during this period, like Western Air which became General Airlines and then Western Air Express again.

Air Commerce Act

The federal government became increasingly involved in aviation from 1926 to 1934, when the Department of Commerce implemented the Air Commerce Act through several bureaus. Three existing bureaus within the Commerce Department initially assumed new aviation duties. The Bureau of Lighthouses acquired responsibility for airway development and maintenance. It thus undertook the construction of light beacons and other navigational aids, similar to its long-standing duties associated with building lighthouses and other equipment for water navigation. The Bureau of Standards, a government laboratory, undertook aeronautical research; and the Coast and Geodetic Survey began mapping airways. The Commerce Department established several new divisions for air regulations, information, and administration of the Aeronautics Branch established under the Air Commerce Act. Furthermore, Congress directed the Weather Bureau, then part of the Department of Agriculture, to collect weather data, to investigate weather phenomena, and to provide weather reports and forecasts in support of aviation activities.

In 1934 the Department of Commerce consolidated its aviation activities in the Bureau of Air Commerce. The Weather Service and Coast and Geodetic Survey

Historic Event

Through the air Commerce Act of 1926, the United States government established its first civil aviation office: the Aeronautics Branch of the Department of Commerce.

In 1934 the Aeronautics Branch became the Bureau of Air Commerce. That Bureau became an independent agency, the Civil Aeronautics Authority, in 1938. Two years later (in 1940) the office moved back into the Department of Commerce where it had the new title Civil Aeronautics Administration. Civil aviation again acquired independent status in 1958 with the establishment of the Federal Aviation Agency, successor of the Civil Aeronautics Administration. That organization changed its name to Federal Aviation Administration when it moved into the Department of Transportation in 1967. Today the United States still administers civil aviation through the Federal Aviation Administration within the Department of Transportation.

remained outside the Bureau of Air Commerce, yet active in aviation. Local, state, and federal governments cooperated in the construction and expansion of airports and air fields. President Franklin D. Roosevelt's New Deal programs provided construction jobs at the airports, as well as on the airways, to relieve the unemployment of the Great Depression. The federal government subsidized and regulated aviation. Also, the state aeronautics agencies provided regulation, encouragement, and coordination of aviation activities within each state. The development of federally equipped and federally regulated airways helped all of aviation in general, not just the commercial airlines the airways were constructed to serve.

Jeppesen

While commercial aviation grew, pilots needed detailed information about the routes over which they flew. Even on the national airway system and with documentation provided by the government, pilots wanted more information for their own safety. An airmail pilot named Elrey B. Jeppesen began recording in a notebook detailed notes about the routes over which he flew. He charted "letdown" procedures for emergency fields along the routes, procedures defined in part by the four-course radio ranges along government airways. At the request of other pilots, Jeppesen in 1934 began publishing the airway information he compiled. (Figure 6-28)

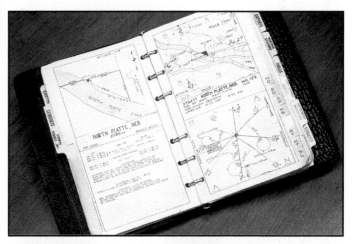

Figure 6-28. E. B. Jeppesen was the first person to produce detailed letdown procedures to help airmail pilots operate in all types of weather conditions.

Personal Profile

Elrey B. Jeppesen (1907-1996) went for his first airplane ride in a war-surplus Curtiss Jenny. He learned to fly while a teenager. Instead of a high school diploma, he earned a pilot's license. It was signed by Orville Wright and issued by the National Aeronautic Association (successor to the Aero Club of America). He bought a Jenny, then an Eaglerock. He barnstormed, flew with Tex Rankin's Flying Circus, and for Fairchild Aerial Surveys.

Jeppesen became an airmail pilot and flew for Varney, Boeing Air Transport, and later United Air Lines. During these airmail runs he began collecting information about routes. He started a publishing business to make the information available to other pilots. The first Jeppesen Airway Manual appeared in 1934. He married a stewardess, kept flying airliners, and developed his publishing business.

In 1965 the National Business Aircraft Association presented Jeppesen its Meritorious Service Award for aiding business aviation and, in 1983, the National Aeronautic Association named him an Elder Statesman of Aviation for making a significant contribution to aviation over the years. Jeppesen was inducted into the National Aviation Hall of Fame, and he received the Distinguished Service Award from the Federal Aviation Administration. The terminal at Denver International Airport, which opened in 1993, is named after Jeppesen.

Elrey B. Jeppesen

Historic Event

Ellen Church, a registered nurse, became the first stewardess on an American airline. On 15 May 1930 she made her first flight as a stewardess in a Boeing Model 80 flown by Boeing Air Transport between San Francisco, California, and Cheyenne, Wyoming. European airlines already used stewards.

Ellen Church

Airmail Scandal

On 9 February 1934 Postmaster General James A. Farley canceled all airmail contracts covering routes within the United States, effective nine days later. He charged collusion between the previous Postmaster General and the airmail contractors, and he objected to the rates paid to the contractors. Partisan politicians and the press debated the scandal, and Congress investigated the airmail contracts. The focus of the scandal was on meetings that occurred in 1930 between the then Postmaster General

Only two cents of every dollar spent by the United States Post Office Department in fiscal year 1934 went to airmail, but that sum represented an important subsidy to the air transport industry and became the subject of public scandal, congressional investigations, and new legislation.

Walter F. Brown and the airmail contractors. Together they redrew the map of airmail routes, included themselves, and left out any new or future companies that might want to enter the lucrative airmail business. The purpose of the government policy behind these meetings was to support fewer and, therefore, stronger air carriers. The results were economical and practical, but the meetings became known as "spoils conferences."

President Franklin D. Roosevelt issued an executive order directing the Army Air Corps to fly mail until the Post Office Department resolved the issue. That expanded the airmail scandal beyond commercial aviation to military aviation. For over three months, from 19 February to 1 June, the Army flew the mail. Pilots crashed and died. Ten days was not enough time to prepare military pilots and planes for the airmail assignment, not even to become familiar with the airmail routes. The fighter planes and trainers were inappropriate for the airmail task. There was not enough space for the mail bags, and the planes were inadequately equipped for instrument flight. The military pilots were poorly trained for scheduled day and night operations over unfamiliar terrain regardless of weather and for cross-country flying in general. Many were Reserve officers with little experience in terms of flight time. The winter weather was severe. Beacons en route were not state of the art, and inaccuracy was common. The

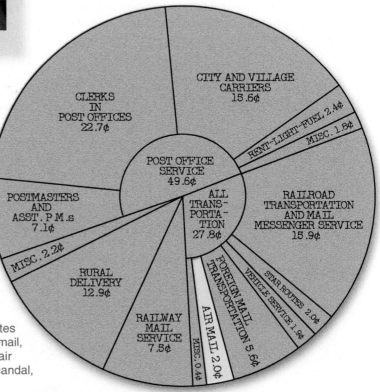

Army suspended flights briefly, from 10 to 19 March, in order to reorganize its efforts toward safer operations.

The Army logged 14,745 hours transporting mail and flew 1,707,559 miles. There were 66 accidents, and twelve men died. The total cost of the military effort was over 3.76 million dollars. The per-mile cost of $2.21 was considerably higher than the per-mile cost of 54 cents previously charged by the contractors. Major General Benjamin B. Foulois, chief of the Air Corps, received criticism for having accepted the assignment given the condition of Army aviation at that the time. In general, the Army failed the test of readiness, but passed the tests of willingness and courage. The Army concluded the airmail assignment with new evidence to support its requests for planes, personnel, and training. Hap Arnold, who had been in charge of the western district of the Army's airmail system, looked on the bright side: "It gave us wonderful experience for combat flying, bad weather flying, night flying; but best of all, it made it possible for us to get the latest navigational and night-flying instruments in our planes."

The airmail scandal, despite the military endeavor, was a civil matter. Postmaster General James A. Farley reorganized and extended the airmail system, and Congress forced the separation of airlines flying mail from companies that produced aviation equipment used in the flying of mail. The rationale was that the government subsidized airmail. If the airmail carrier bought its equipment from other divisions of the same parent corporation, that government airmail subsidy would extend to those manufacturing divisions. Forcing airmail carriers to purchase equipment competitively would, theoretically, bring their costs down. At least that was the idea, and to a limited extent, it worked. Separating companies that made airmail equipment from companies that flew airmail effectively split all aircraft equipment makers from aircraft equipment operators.

One result of the airmail scandal was the DC-3, an aircraft that emerged from the requirement that airlines carry passengers without major federal subsidy. First test flown as the Douglas Sleeper Transport (DST) on 17 December 1935, the DC-3 became the transport that carried many of the airlines successfully through the end of the decade. The DST entered service with American Airlines in 1936. The sleeper had sleeping berths. Douglas removed the berths and designated the aircraft the DC-3. The aircraft proved safe and reliable and immediately became popular with passengers as well as airlines in the United States and abroad. Douglas produced five versions of the DST/DC-3 before the war, when the aircraft became a military transport. Douglas built over ten thousand DC-3s and its derivatives in the 1930s and 40s. (Figure 6-29)

Figure 6-29. Soon after entering service in 1936, the Douglas DC-3 became a mainstay of the airlines.

Pan American

Pan American Airways incorporated and began scheduled service in 1927. As the name implied, this airline intended to provide international service on the American continents. It entered business with an airmail contract to fly the route between Key West, Florida, and Havana, Cuba. Cy Caldwell flew the first airmail flight under the contract in October 1927, on

Historic Event

On 28 October 1927 pilot Hugh Wells in a Fokker F-VII made the inaugural flight of regularly scheduled service by Pan American Airways.

the last possible day to begin the service under the terms of the contract. He flew a borrowed Fairchild FC-2 called *La Niña*. Regularly scheduled service began nine days later when the Fokker F-VII *General Machado* flew from Meacham Field, Key West, to Havana. Hugh Wells was the pilot and Ed Musick was the navigator. (Figure 6-30)

Figure 6-30. Pan American Airways began scheduled service to Havana, Cuba, in October 1927.

President Calvin Coolidge encouraged American airmail service to South America, in part to stem the rapidly developing French and German networks there. The Foreign Air Mail Act of 1928 made the routes competitive. Juan Trippe of Pan American secured a monopoly on landing rights in Cuba and that gave his venture an advantage. Trippe was a Yale graduate with financial backing from New York businessmen. Several companies vied for Latin American business, but Trippe's Cuban tactic advanced his influence and remained an effective approach as he expanded Pan American's routes. Charles Lindbergh served as a technical advisor on Caribbean, Latin American, and later on North Atlantic, South Atlantic, and Pacific Ocean routes. Pan American opened its own ocean-flying laboratory in Miami to support the development of transoceanic routes.

As the Pan American routes expanded, Trippe acquired airlines in Latin America and China and melded them into the Pan American giant. Pan American opened regularly scheduled passenger

service across the Pacific Ocean in October 1936, and airmail service started in November, but only after thoroughly surveying and preparing the route. Preparations included 51 flights between San Francisco and Honolulu and 23 round-trip flights between California and the Philippines. It involved constructing bases at Midway Island, Wake Island, and Guam — the steps between Hawaii and the Philippines. Pan American initiated service across the North Atlantic in 1939. Charles Lindbergh and his navigator-wife Anne Morrow Lindbergh had surveyed routes across both oceans for the company.

Historical Note

Flying long distances often meant crossing oceans and seas. The airlines competing on overseas routes placed flying boats into passenger and airmail service. The French Latécoère, British Short, German Dornier, and Italian Savoia-Marchetti flying boats competed with Boeing, Martin, and Sikorsky craft built in the United States. Several manufacturers produced four-engine flying boats: the Martin Model 130 and Sikorsky S-42 appeared in 1934, the Short Empire in 1936, and the Boeing 314 in 1938. Pan American used Sikorsky and Martin boats on transocean routes.

Dornier Do X

Historical Note

For landplanes, Pan American favored the Fairchild FC-2, Ford Trimotor, and Fokker F-10A trimotors until it upgraded to the new modern airliners, the Lockheed L-10 Electra, Douglas DC-2, and DC-3 twin-engine monoplanes.

Ford Trimotor

Historical Note

Did Pan American have competition on the transpacific routes? Hypothetically, yes. An airship proponent argued the economic advantage of using airships rather than airplanes. He considered specifically the San Francisco — Canton route:

"The present Clippers require more than six days to make this voyage, over a route 8,770 statute miles in length, and with overnight stops at five places, including Wake and Midway islands, which are of no interest, commercially or otherwise. The great circle route between the same terminal points is but 6,891 miles long. A modern airship could traverse this in about four days without a stop, carrying a payload of over 20 tons, equal to the capacity of a fleet of fifteen Clippers. Instead of the inconvenience of occupying cramped quarters by day, and transferring to hotels at night, the airship passengers could sleep in their own comfortable cabins, and enjoy various diversions without annoyance from vibration or noise. They are served with hot, well-cooked meals, instead of lunches. Airsickness is unknown aboard an airship, and this is an important consideration with many travelers. With all of these advantages, the cost of the single airship would be only one-third the cost of the fifteen Clippers. And the expense of maintaining the given intermediate landing points is an additional charge against the Clipper that does not apply to the airship."

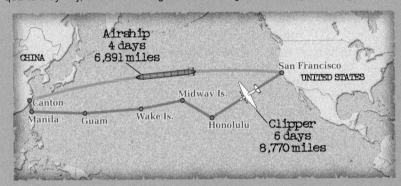

The chief problem with this proposal, its author noted, was that the United States had produced no commercial airships. He based his argument on Germany's commercial airship experience. See his argument in his article: Francis H. Knauff, "The Future of the American Airship," *Military Engineer* (July-August 1938).

Airships

The United States did not have a commercial airship program, but the United Kingdom had a short-lived program that literally crashed. Lord Thomson, Secretary of State for Air, foresaw airship transports linking the British Empire. Britain built two rigid ships modeled after German Zeppelins: the R.100 and R.101. Both held 5 million cubic feet of hydrogen. Both were designed to carry up to a hundred passengers plus 8 tons of mail and cargo. Private industry built the R.100 and the Royal Airship Works at Cardington built the R.101. The 101 was finished first. At 732 feet in length by 140 feet in width, and with the 5 million cubic feet volume, it was the largest aircraft in the world when completed in June 1929. The R.100 was completed soon thereafter. The relatively heavy weight of the airships meant that the payload of these ships was less than half the projected amount; for example, the R.101 weighed 113 tons instead of the planned 90 tons. (Figure 6-31)

In 1930 the R.100 made a round-trip flight to Canada and encountered dangerous weather conditions en route. The R.101 was to prove itself on a flight to India. Lord Thomson boarded this flight to realize his dream of imperial airship transportation. Other

Figure 6-31. The British hoped that the R. 100 and R. 101 airships would usher in a new era of long-distance air transportation.

airship leaders, like the director of airship development at Cardington, R.B.B. Colmore, joined him. The flight had one scheduled stop at Ismailia, Egypt, 2,235 nautical miles from Cardington, and the final destination was another 2,135 nautical miles away in Karachi, where an airship shed (hangar) had been built. On 4 October 1930 the R.101 with 54 people on board took off in bad weather. The total load was 160 tons, the greatest lifted to that date by any aircraft. The airship flew south by east over London and across the English Channel, while rain gradually added about five tons to its weight. Still in bad weather, the airship crashed near Allone, France, and quickly burned. Forty-eight people died, including Britain's airship leadership. Also dead was the British airship program. The R.100 never flew again, and the R.102 and R.103 plans were abandoned.

German Airships

In September 1928 the first postwar civil airship made in Germany, the LZ 127, rolled out of the construction hangar at Friedrichshafen. The American publisher William Randolph Hearst contributed significant funds for the completion of the airship in exchange for rights to the story of a planned transatlantic crossing. Named after Count Zeppelin, this *Graf Zeppelin* made several trial flights in Germany. In October it made the flight from Friedrichshafen, Germany, to Lakehurst, New Jersey. The flight took three days. Later that month the *Graf Zeppelin* flew back to Germany. The press monitored the round-trip flight via radio transmissions from the airship.

Yet *Graf Zeppelin* is most remembered for a historic flight around the world in August 1929. Hearst also financed this flight in return for non-European rights to the story, so the flight began and ended in the United States. European rights went to the Ullstein Press in Berlin and the *Frankfurter Zeitung*. During the trip around the world, the *Graf Zeppelin* logged 7 days and 11 minutes in the air. Flying around the

world generated publicity and proved the long-distance capability of the airship, but *Graf Zeppelin* was built for transport service and to that duty it was now assigned. (Figure 6-32)

The *Graf Zeppelin* carried a crew of forty, twenty passengers, and up to 26,000 pounds of mail and cargo. In 1930 it flew from Germany to Brazil on an experimental flight, and in 1931 the airship made three round-trip proving flights carrying mail between Brazil and Germany. Lufstchiffbau Zeppelin began scheduled passenger service across the South Atlantic in 1932. That year the *Graf Zeppelin* completed nine round trips. Some flights were nonstop between Friedrichshafen, Germany, and Pernambuco (Recife), Brazil. Other flights made a stop en route at Seville, Spain. The service was seasonal, summer only. Between 1931 and 1937, *Graf Zeppelin* completed a total of 124 transatlantic flights across the South Atlantic, and the Brazilian government constructed an airship terminal at Santa Cruz, near Rio de Janeiro, to support the future of the airship service.

In 1935 the Nazi government merged airship and airplane lines in Germany. The Reichsluftfahrt-minisisterium (R.L.M. or Imperial Air Ministry)

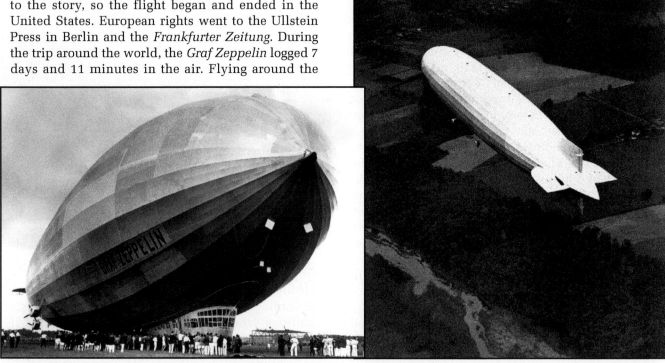

Figure 6-32. The photograph on the left shows the relative size of the *Graf Zeppelin*. On the right, the *Graf Zeppelin* glides over the New Jersey countryside.

Figure 6-33. The *Hindenburg* (left) and *Graf Zeppelin* (right) in formation over Germany.

combined Luftschiffbau Zeppelin and Deutsche Luft Hansa into Deutsche Zeppelin-Reederei, transport company. Luft Hansa still operated the airplane lines, but it now provided the financing needed for the construction of a new airship — LZ 129, the *Hindenburg*. As Germany had the only prominent and commercial airship program, the public began to associate airships with the Nazis. Hugo Eckener, still head of the Zeppelin company, disliked Nazi politics and Nazi use of airships for propaganda. The German government and the airship company received bomb threats, which were dismissed as crank nuisances. The company did, however, implement security measures to screen passengers and baggage in order to protect airships from sabotage. (Figure 6-33)

In 1936 the *Hindenburg* joined the *Graf Zeppelin* in commercial airline service. The *Hindenburg* was the world's largest airship. It crossed the South Atlantic 12 times (six round trips) and the North Atlantic 32 times in 1936. The 1937 season began with the *Hindenburg* making a round-trip flight to South America. Its next scheduled trip was across the North Atlantic. It left Germany the evening of 3 May. Max Pruss commanded the aircraft. Three days later it arrived at Lakehurst, New Jersey. Windy weather delayed the landing. Once the weather front had moved through the area, the airship came in, descended, and maneuvered for landing. In the process, the airship caught fire and crashed. The hydrogen-fed fire burned the airship quickly, but diesel fuel for the engines kept the wreck smoldering for several hours. Thirty-five people died, many others suffered injuries, yet 62 of the passengers and crew survived. The crash, aided by the press

coverage of it, taught the Germans what the Americans had learned with the *Roma*: hydrogen gas was too expensive in terms of safety and the public perception of safety. But the public generally did not distinguish between types of airships. The safety of all airships became suspect. The *Hindenburg* crash proved to the public and, more specifically to travelers, that the airship was not viable as a commercial transport.

 Flight Lines

"It is burning, bursting into flames and is falling on the mooring mast and all the folks . . . this is one of the worst catastrophes in the world! . . . Oh, it's four or five hundred feet into the sky, it's a terrific crash, ladies and gentlemen. . . . Oh, the humanity and all the passengers!"

News reporter Herbert Morrison describing the crash of the Hindenburg on 6 May 1937, as quoted in Rick Archbold, *Hindenburg, an Illustrated History* (Toronto: Warner/Madison Press Book, 1994).

Historic Event

The German airship *Hindenburg* crashed on 6 May 1937. Hydrogen gas fed a fire that started as the ship was landing at the Lakehurst Naval Air Station. The fire quickly engulfed the entire ship. People jumped and fell to their deaths. Others were burned horribly. "Oh, the humanity," cried one eye-witness. Yet only 36 people died — 22 crew members, 13 passengers, and one member of the ground crew. Of the 97 people on board the *Hindenburg*, 62 survived.

It was not the death toll that made this catastrophe so grand a news story. It was the press coverage. Reporters, photographers, and newsreel cameramen were there. They captured the event in pictures, in sound, and in print. This on-site coverage of a disaster was new to journalism. Newsreels showed the disaster in movie theaters. Radios repeatedly broadcast the recorded on-the-spot description of the event as it happened. Newspapers printed pictures and news stories. Survivors told their stories.

Why did the *Hindenburg* crash? Sabotage was immediately suspected. Perhaps the Communists blew up the ship, or Nazi sympathizers, or anti-Nazi partisans. The flash of a camera bulb might have ignited the fire. Maybe a mooring line dropped to the ground transferred static electricity, or the airship brushing the clouds caused a type of discharge known as St. Elmo's fire, or lightning may have hit the airship. Less reasonable theories blamed a ray gun, incendiary bullets, rare bacteria that ignite hydrogen, and a rocket shot off from the Berkshire Hills of Massachusetts. The United States Department of Commerce conducted an inquiry. The Federal Bureau of Investigation (FBI) investigated. Cooperating with the Americans, Eckener testified that landing ropes brushing the ground *could have* transferred static electricity and ignited some hydrogen that escaped from a stern gas bag torn by a bracing wire. In the end, the American investigating commission agreed that was the "most probable" cause. A German investigation reached a similar conclusion.

The reason why the *Hindenburg* crashed became irrelevant to the popular perception that airships were unsafe. The German airship program gradually wound down. The hydrogen *Graf Zeppelin* was immediately pulled from service and never returned.

The *Graf Zeppelin II* (LZ 130) , under construction at the time of the *Hindenburg* crash, was completed, filled with hydrogen, and placed into service. It was treated with graphite to eliminate sparking between the covering fabric and the supporting girders. In addition, a new landing procedure required careful monitoring of the electrical gradient between airship and ground. This German airship flew mainly over Germany, though it was also used for electronic espionage beyond Germany's borders. Nonetheless, the public romance with airships was gone.

Commercial Aviation

Airlines that carried mail, passengers, or freight dominated commercial aviation, but the airplanes were increasingly used for other commercial purposes during the Golden Age of Aviation: aerial mapping, aerial photography, aerial tourism, air ambulance, bush flying, charter, crop dusting, flying physicians, forestry — especially fire spotting and fighting, even experimental smokejumping at the end of the thirties, and taxi service. Many of these operators used small, light airplanes.

SECTION D

AVIATION RADIO AND MILITARY AVIATION

In a 1923 radio broadcast General Billy Mitchell announced that the "American aviation radio is rotten." Despite some development work by the Post Office Department and the military services, the radio remained an experimental device into the late 1920s as far as American aviation was concerned. The two flights to the North Pole in May 1926 demonstrated the nation's lag behind its European counterparts, for the Norwegian airship expedition relied upon radio navigation through its voyage and communicated by radio, while the American airplane pilots navigated by celestial means and used their radio for occasional communications. The situation changed under the Department of Commerce's aeronautical program. From the late twenties through the thirties, the Department developed, installed, operated, and upgraded radio navigation aids on the nation's ground-based airway system.

Under the Air Commerce Act of 1926, the Department of Commerce built the Federal Airways System by constructing and operating aids to air navigation. The Federal Airways System began small in 1927 with the transcontinental airway acquired from the Post Office Department. The total mileage was only 4,121 miles. The system added mileage yearly and reached a total of 13,459 miles in 1930, including feeder lines. The system grew to 19,339 miles in 1932 and peaked at 23,110 miles of airways in 1936. When the decade of the 1930s opened, expenditures went mostly for airway lighting and intermediate (emergency) air fields. By the end of the decade, radio and communication programs dominated the Department's aviation activities and expenditures. (Figure 6-34)

The military also participated in radio communications and radio navigation development during this period. In 1929 Lieutenant Jimmy Doolittle used a direction finder radio beacon on his historic "instrument" flight. Flying a Consolidated NY-2, in a hood-covered cockpit, he took off, flew a circuit, and landed — all without being able to see either the horizon or the

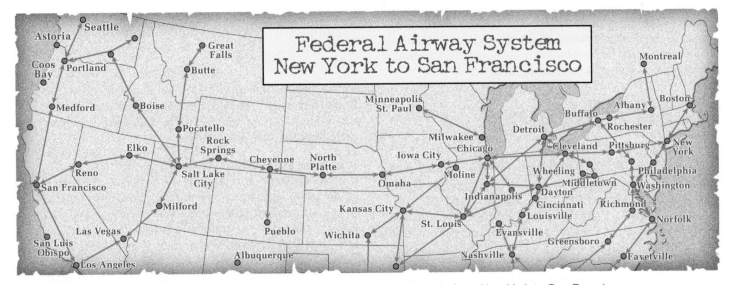

Figure 6-34. This map shows the Federal Airway System on the main route from New York to San Francisco.

Figure 6-35. Jimmy Doolittle, in his Consolidated NY-2, flew the first true "instrument flight" in September 1929.

ground. Yet as late as 1929, the four-volume *Text Book on Aviation* did not even cover radios in its course to prepare pilots for commercial careers. (Figure 6-35)

The first radio-equipped control tower was not built until 1930 (at Cleveland's municipal airport), and the federal Bureau of Air Commerce did not establish an instrument rating for pilots until 1933. Army Captain Albert F. Hegenberger won the Distinguished Flying Cross Oak Leaf Cluster and the Collier Trophy in 1934 for developing the Army's blind landing system, an instrument landing system that the Bureau of Air Commerce adopted for civil use. In contrast, the German airline Deutsche Luft Hansa began installing radios in its larger planes in 1926 and began requiring pilots to be instrument rated in 1929.

Early Radios

Harold Gatty served as navigator aboard Wiley Post's historic round-the-world flight of 1931, He had studied navigation under Lieutenant Commander Philip Weems, a pioneer in aero-navigation, notably celestial navigation. After racing around the world with Post aboard the Lockheed plane known as the *Winnie Mae*, Gatty wrote,

"The time may come when navigators may not depend so much on celestial observations and use the radio instead, as is done to a greater extent now than formerly by navigators on ships.

"Our radio, however, proved to be very nearly just so much dead weight. We regarded the transmitter as more important than the receiver because of its usefulness in an emergency. We signaled on it considerably as we were nearing Ireland, then again on the way to Nome, but as far as I know, nobody heard us.

"As far as radio weather reports were concerned, we didn't get any. . . . The weather reports are usually sent out on long waves, and long-wave equipment weighs too much at present to be desirable on an airplane that is making a long-distance flight."

Gatty concluded that "airplane radios must be improved a lot." That described the state of the art in aviation radios in 1931, but that state changed considerably during the 1930s.

Airplanes were increasingly equipped with radios — mostly military and airline planes, but gradually some commercial and private airplanes too. Of the over 8,000 civil aircraft — transport, commercial, and private planes — operating in the United States in late 1934, 775 had radios aboard, and less than half of these radios — only 326 — had two-way capability. Many military aircraft of the time were still without radios too. Obviously, there was a gulf between the

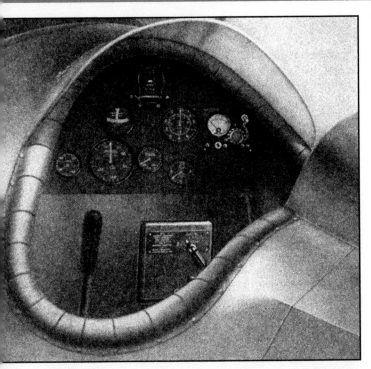

Figure 6-36. This is the view of a typical airmail airplane radio installation. The navigation indicator is in the upper center, the receiver control panel is on the right, and the receiver is in the lower portion of the instrument panel.

state of the art and the state of common practice regarding aviation radios. The weight, cost, reliability, and usability of the radios of the time contributed to the gulf. Radios, for example, had to be shielded from the ignition system to prevent ignition interference; shielding added weight. By the late 1930s Western Electric was marketing compact radio receivers for private pilots flying small airplanes that weighed only 11 to 16 pounds depending upon the model and its features. A transmitter, however, was a separate device and an additional 25 pounds. (Figure 6-36)

The early aircraft radios could receive information, and the two-way radios could also send information, in voice or code form. Ground stations often transmitted in voice and, thereby, communicated weather or other information valuable to a pilot; but, distance, static, and noise could interfere with voice communications. The code transmitter-receiver was called variously code set, telegraph radio, and wireless telegraph. A code receiver, in contrast to a code set, could only receive. The code set was a simple and sturdy device with greater range than the two-way radio telephone system then available for voice communications. A range receiver was the instrument needed for radio navigation — for receiving navigation information. With a range receiver, a pilot could navigate by reference to the radio signals transmitted from the ground stations known as radio ranges. These low and

medium frequency facilities marked four courses to and from stations constructed along Federal Airways in the late twenties and throughout the 1950s. Marker beacons were low-power radio markers located en route between directional beacons. They were used to indicate a location along the route and, therefore, measure distance. Both radio ranges and marker beacons became visual landmarks with the construction of flashing beacon lights at the respective locations. Radio ranges remained in operation for decades. The last four-course range in the United States was not decommissioned until 1974; other countries continued to use radio ranges after that.

Four-Course Radios

A four-course beacon broadcast two directional signals — the letter N (dash dot in Morse code) and the letter A (dot dash) — each of which radiated out in a figure eight pattern. When off course, the pilot would receive either an N or an A. Where the two signals overlapped with equal intensity, the signals merged into a steady dash — that was the on-course signal. A pilot would align the flight path of the plane with an on-course signal heard in a headset or visually displayed on an indicator in the airplane. In other words, the pilot flew a course by following a radio signal. The radio range beacon's course signal was customarily interrupted at intervals of about 12 seconds for the transmission of the code for the identification letter of that beacon, and it was regularly interrupted for broadcast of weather information. A modernization of the Federal Airways System, between 1937 and 1939 upgraded or replaced radio ranges so the stations could simultaneously transmit course and voice on the same frequency, actually one kilocycle apart. Only then could a pilot receive both broadcasts simultaneously. (Figure 6-37)

Figure 6-37. This diagram illustrates the sectors or quadrants of a four-course radio range. The aircraft position is determined by the relative strength of the A or N signals. Where the signals overlap with equal strength, a steady dash, or monotone hum, will be heard. This is the "on-course" signal.

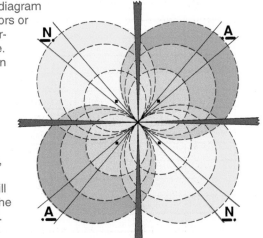

The most common code in aviation (both then and now) was the Morse Code. This telegraphic code of dots, dashes, and spaces had been devised by the nineteenth-century inventor Samuel F.B. Morse and standardized as the International Morse Code. A specific combination of short and long sounds represents each letter of the alphabet and each number. These dots (dits) and dashes (dahs) were taught via the phonic method that required students to learn to recognize each letter from its sound. *Di-dah*, for example, means A, whereas *dah-dit* means N. The *dah* is three times as long as the *di* (or *dit* if it comes at the end of a letter). In Morse Code words are spelled out letter by letter. For the sake of brevity, operators often use abbreviations and cipher groups; that is, coded messages. To obtain a military pilot's rating in the early 1940s a person had to demonstrate the ability to send and receive at least 20 words per minute; a word is defined as five letters. (Blinker lights also relied upon the Morse Code. Long and short flashes of light replaced the long or short sounds of the radio signal. Memorization of the visual code was recommended *only after* the code had been learned by sound.)

	Current International Phonetic Alphabet	1942 U. S. Phonetic Alphabet	Morse Code
A	Alpha	Able	• —
B	Bravo	Baker	— • • •
C	Charlie	Charlie	— • — •
D	Delta	Dog	— • •
E	Echo	Easy	•
F	Foxtrot	Fox	• • — •
G	Golf	George	— — •
H	Hotel	How	• • • •
I	India	Item	• •
J	Juliett	Jig	• — — —
K	Kilo	King	— • —
L	Lima	Love	• — • •
M	Mike	Mike	— —
N	November	Nan	— •
O	Oscar	Oboe	— — —
P	Papa	Peter	• — — •
Q	Quebec	Queen	— — • —
R	Romeo	Roger	• — •
S	Sierra	Sugar	• • •
T	Tango	Tare	—
U	Uniform	Uncle	• • —
V	Victor	Victor	• • • —
W	Whiskey	William	• — —
X	X-ray	X-ray	— • • —
Y	Yankee	Yoke	— • — —
Z	Zulu	Zebra	— — • •

Accidents

Accidents illustrate how systems work and fail to work, including the radio navigation system. A big problem for pilots in the thirties was a lack of familiarity with radio navigation. Faulty reception of radio signals was also a common problem. In the period of one month, beginning December 1936 and ending in January 1937, five airliners crashed in the United States. Two approaching Los Angeles hit the mountains near Burbank's Union Terminal. One of those accidents killed filmmaker Martin Johnson and injured his wife Osa. (Figure 6-38)

Figure 6-38. Martin and Osa Johnson were nature cinematographers who flew extensively in Africa and Borneo. Most of their flying was "contact" or visual flying with little or no use of radio navigation.

On a lecture tour, Martin and Osa Johnson were en route from Salt Lake City to Los Angeles on 12 January 1937. Salt Lake had clear weather. California did not, but California had state-of-the-art airports and airways equipped with radio ranges so the airlines could fly by radio beam when weather obscured visibility. In Salt Lake the Johnsons boarded a Boeing 247D airliner owned and operated by Western Air Express. Headquartered in Burbank, Western Air used Burbank's Union Air Terminal for its Los Angeles stop. The airline was a pioneer in both the "new meteorology" of airmass analysis and radio communication, including radio direction finding. The airliner was the two-engine, all-metal, stressed-skin Boeing 247 introduced in 1933. Powered by Pratt & Whitney Wasp engines, it was a low-wing monoplane with an insulated and heated cabin with seating for ten passengers. Among the plane's equipment were three radio receivers, a radio transmitter, a carburetor de-icer, and propeller de-icers.

Personal Profile

Martin Johnson (1884-1937) and his wife Osa (1894-1953) were from Kansas. They filmed nature in exotic locations. They produced movies like *Simba* (1928) and *Wonders of the Congo* (1931), and they wrote books about their travels like his *Camera Trails in Africa* (1924) and her *Jungle Babies* (1930). To attract and hold public interest in their films, and to facilitate travel, they added aircraft to their expeditions. Each earned a pilot's license, but they hired professional pilots to fly their Sikorsky amphibians on expeditions to Africa and Borneo. Both their single-engine S-39CS scouting plane and their twin-engine S-38 explorer's yacht appear in their films *Wings over Africa* (1934) and *Baboona* (1935) and in his book *Over African Jungles* (1935). They took only the S-39 to Borneo. It appears in the film *Borneo* (1937) and in her book *Last Adventure* (1966).

When the Johnsons boarded the craft, William W. Lewis was the pilot and Clifford P. Owens the copilot. Both held valid transport pilot licenses, with instrument ratings, and both had passed their recent federally required medical examinations. This was their first flight together. The third member of the crew was Esther Jo Conner, a stewardess. From Salt Lake City to Las Vegas, the flight was uneventful. It made a scheduled stop in Vegas. Beyond there, the weather was bad enough that the departure was delayed more than twenty minutes for detailed analysis of the weather conditions. The crew studied weather reports for four locations along the airway — Daggett, Palmdale, Saugus, and Burbank. At 9:00 a.m. the plane was cleared from Las Vegas to Daggett; clearance into Burbank was pending continued favorable weather there.

The plane, when nearing Daggett, received the clearance into Burbank. Long Beach and Palmdale were given as alternate destinations. Authorization for instrument flying accompanied the clearance into Burbank, as the weather en route was changing conditions of clouds, rain, and temperature. When the flight reached Palmdale, pilot Lewis reported being at 7,000 feet and over broken clouds, but also under broken clouds. Southwest of Palmdale, near Acton, the flight crew lost visual contact with the ground as the plane flew into a solid overcast. From there, the radio transmission from the Saugus range guided the plane along its course. The flight followed the Saugus leg aligned with magnetic course 221° and passed over the Saugus cone of silence at 10:50 a.m. Following instrument flight procedure for Saugus,

Lewis turned the plane to the right onto the Bakersfield leg, magnetic course 316°, and followed that northwest leg of the radio range for three minutes. He descended to approximately 5,500 feet, lowered the landing gear, and slowed the airspeed to 120 miles per hour — all in preparation for landing at Burbank and all in accordance with procedures established by Western Air Express and approved by the national Department of Commerce.

He then turned the plane 180° back toward Saugus and Burbank. Flying through turbulence at the lower altitude, the pilot approached Saugus again and radioed that ice was accumulating on the plane. He crossed the Saugus cone of silence this time at 5,200 feet and continued south toward Burbank. But turbulence increasingly buffeted the plane and distracted the pilot as he passed Saugus the second time and at a lower altitude and lower airspeed than before. Lewis switched the radio from the Saugus frequency to that of Burbank, but he did not immediately receive Burbank's directional signal. Burbank had temporarily suspended broadcast of its range signal in order to use its frequency for voice communication with planes in the area. Burbank was operating normally, as it could not transmit voice and range signals at the same time.

To pilot Lewis, the voice transmission meant that he was flying blind with no radio signal to guide him. From Saugus to Burbank was approximately 17 miles, and the instrument course passed through Newhall Pass. Lewis flew by averaging readings from a magnetic compass made unstable by turbulence. He was trying to hold the compass course of 125° into Burbank. That was a form of instrument flying known as dead reckoning. Unlike radio navigation, dead reckoning was not approved by either the airline or the Bureau of Air Commerce for an instrument approach to Burbank.

After a few minutes Lewis requested that Burbank turn on its range signal, and the station promptly complied. Over his earphones, Lewis detected a Morse code N. Since he was approaching from the north, he knew that not only was he off course, but also east of course. East of course meant mountains. Lewis immediately started to turn in order to get over lower terrain again. The plane crashed at 3,550 feet elevation on the side of Los Pinetos in the San Gabriel Mountains, near the town of Newhall. Everyone aboard was injured or killed. Martin Johnson died the next day. The copilot Owens and three others also died. Osa Johnson and pilot Lewis were among the injured who survived.

Figure 6-39. In November 1935, a Pan American crew flew from Alameda, California, to the Philippines. Captain Ed Musick, navigator Fred Noonan, and radio operator Wilson Jarboe relied upon radio navigation during this transoceanic flight.

The government accident report pointed to significant errors made by Lewis. At Saugus he had switched to the Burbank frequency although company rules prescribed that pilots on instrument approaches follow the Saugus south leg for two minutes before switching to Burbank. When he switched to Burbank and heard voice transmission, he could have switched back to the Saugus frequency and flown guided by its signal. He did not. A pilot was responsible for requesting continuous operation of a radio range when needed, and Lewis had delayed his request to Burbank. In turbulent conditions known to interfere with a compass, he had flown by average compass readings for several minutes. Also, he had lowered his altitude during that time. The pilot had descended "to a dangerously low altitude without positive knowledge of his position." The probable cause of the accident, the report concluded, was pilot error.

Pacific Radios

The four-course radios relied upon the Adcock antenna fixed to four poles, a low-frequency and short-range system. Hugo Leuteritz of Pan American experimented with the Adcock system in attempts to develop a long-range radio navigation aid. He achieved

long range, with short wave and high frequency, by adding a dipole to each antenna. Juan Trippe, founder and head of Pan American, had this long-range direction-finding equipment installed on Pacific islands in preparation for opening transpacific air service. These radio facilities helped guide the *China Clipper*, a Martin M-130 flying boat, on its historic November 1935 airmail flight from the Alameda, California, seaplane base via Honolulu, Midway, Wake, and Guam, to the Philippines. Under the command of Captain Ed Musick, navigator Fred Noonan plotted the radio direction-finder bearings and celestial fixes necessary to locate the islands in the vast ocean. Wilson Jarboe operated the radio. On the way to Wake, Noonan used the "aim off" technique, aiming off to one side of Wake Island and then flying a sun line to the destination; he did not rely solely upon the new radio equipment. (Figure 6-39)

For Amelia Earhart's planned flight around the world in 1937, radios were installed in her new Lockheed Electra: Western Electric radio equipment that could send and receive both voice and code across all wave bands, and also a Bendix radio direction finder (or radio compass, also called homing compass). Coast Guard radiomen were unfamiliar with the Bendix homing device, so the emergency band of five hundred kilocycles would be used as a backup. To improve the range of the radio, Western Electric recommended a 250-foot trailing aerial. It would have to be reeled out in flight and reeled in before

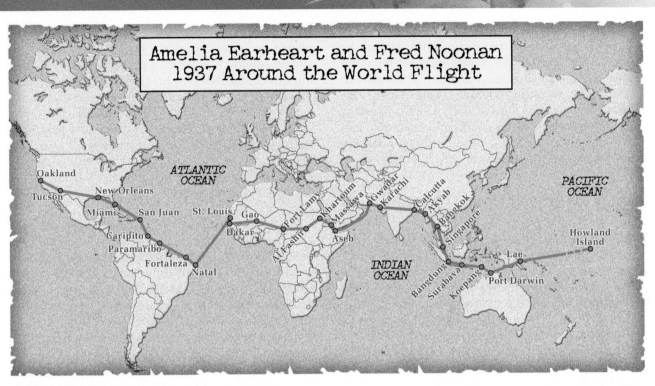

Figure 6-40. This map shows the planned route of Amelia Earhart's 1937 around the world flight. The use of radio navigation was to be an integral part of the flight. The flight ended near Howland Island when Earhart and navigator Fred Noonan disappeared.

landing. Earhart knew how to use the radio equipment. In March of 1937 she passed a radio test required by the federal Bureau of Air Commerce, but her radio proficiency was not up to the standards some considered appropriate for the transpacific flight, particularly the 2,500-mile segment over water from New Guinea to little Howland Island. (Figure 6-40)

Before Earhart departed from the United States, both the trailing aerial and the code wireless set were removed from the Electra. The removal of this equipment reduced the pilot's workload and the weight of the aircraft and, eventually, contributed to Earhart's failure to locate Howland Island in the Pacific Ocean. A code set was known to be more dependable than voice transmitting and receiving equipment and, at the time, code sets were more common on aircraft than voice communications. But code sets were heavy and required skill to send and receive code, and Earhart and her navigator, Fred Noonan, lacked the speed of code operation that they thought was necessary to justify carrying the weight. Earhart decided to broadcast only by voice — on frequency 6210 kilocycles during the day and on 3205 at night. (Figure 6-41)

Confusion over broadcast frequencies and radio procedures between the flight crew and the Coast Guard support personnel in ships and on Howland Island — that is, lack of preflight preparation and coordination — contributed to Earhart's disappearance. Without effective communications between aircraft and support personnel, the support personnel were unable to render the necessary navigational assistance at the crucial time and place. Earhart and Noonan disappeared en route to Howland Island.

Radios became standard equipment in airliners in the 1930s and contributed to the regularity of service; that is, to maintaining schedules of operation regardless

Figure 6-41. Amelia Earhart and Fred Noonan in Los Angeles as they complete preparations for their ill-fated flight.

of weather. These commercial aircraft often carried two or three radios: two-way radio telephone for voice communication, a receiving set for radio navigation, and an emergency receiver. These aircraft also carried a radio operator. Pan American's transoceanic aircraft carried both a radio operator and a navigator and both a communication radio and a navigation radio. Less state-of-the-art airliners carried at least a code receiver, usually a code set.

Military Aviation

The Golden Age of Aviation was a period of peace in comparison to the preceding and following world wars. World leaders tried to hold together a fragile peace defined by the multiple treaties consummated at the end of World War I, but those very treaties, notably the harsh Treaty of Versailles, threatened the peace by limiting the options for economic and political expansion of various nations. Despite the relative peace, aircraft went into battle on several continents.

Chaco War

Tension along the border between Bolivia and Paraguay threatened peace in the late twenties and early thirties. On 15 June 1932 a border dispute started the Chaco War, named after the disputed Chaco Boreal territory. The combatants in this small South American war used reconnaissance, bomber, fighter, fighter-bomber, transport, ambulance, trainer, and general purpose aircraft. During the course of the war Bolivia operated approximately 60 combat

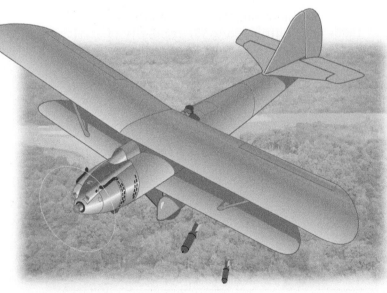

Figure 6-42. The Breguet 19 illustrated here was used during the Chaco War in 1932.

aircraft and approximately 20 support and training planes. Paraguay used fewer aircraft, about 30 combat and 30 support and training planes. The planes were imported: Curtiss-Wright Osprey, Potez 25 A-2, Vickers Type 149, Junkers K 43b, Breguet 19, Curtiss Falcon, Macchi M.18.R., de Havilland D.H.9, and many other models. There was no standardization of equipment. The Chaco War continued till June 1935 when Paraguay won most of the territory — per an armistice agreement. A peace treaty was not signed until 1939. (Figure 6-42)

Aerial warfare was relatively undeveloped in South America until this conflict, which was won on the ground, but it prompted the improvement of the air forces of various South American nations. After the armistice, for example, Bolivia ordered modern aircraft from Germany and the United States, including three Klemm Kl 25 trainers, two Junkers Ju 86 bomber-transport planes, and ten Curtiss-Wright 19R fighters. Paraguay had won the war, but not the aerial competition of the war. After the war, Paraguay purchased aircraft from Italy, including a Breda Ba 25 float trainer for its Navy, three Ba 25 landplanes for its Army, three Caproni Ca 309 Ghibli bomber-transport planes, and five Fiat CR.32 fighters. Lack of funds, international opposition to arming belligerent nations, and unstable governments limited the numbers and types of aircraft purchased by Bolivia and Paraguay.

Fascism

More threatening to the fragile world peace were the rise of fascist leaders in Europe and the expansionist program of imperial Japan. Benito Mussolini's Fascist dictatorship in Italy, Francisco Franco's Falange movement and rebellion in Spain, and particularly Adolf Hitler's National Socialist or Nazi Party in Germany were the most powerful and, therefore, the most threatening forms of fascism in the world. The word fascism came from the Italian word *fascio* for bundle or political group. It referred to a movement or governmental system led by a dictator and characterized by extreme nationalism, imperialism, militarism, violence, nonrationalism (rejection of reason as authority or source of knowledge), anti-communism, anti-liberalism, and anti-conservatism. Fascism promoted common good over individual will, one-party dictatorship, and the cult of the leader. Mussolini was *il Duce* (the leader), Franco *el Caudillo* (the leader), and Hitler *der Führer* (the leader). Fascism was authoritarian in that individual political freedom was subordinate to the authority or power of the state.

Abyssinia

Benito Mussolini rose to power in Italy in 1921 on the fascist ideal of building a new Roman Empire. First he developed a dictatorship at home, and then he ventured militarily into Africa in an effort to create the new Italian empire. Unified only in the 1870s, Italy was a relatively young nation without the foreign possessions of older empires like Britain and France. Mussolini wanted to conquer Abyssinia, also called Ethiopia, and combine it with Italian Eritrea and Italian Somaliland into Italian East Africa. War broke out in 1935 when Italian troops invaded Abyssinia. The Italian forces fought with airplanes, tanks, machine guns, and poison gas. Italian bombers dropped bombs and mustard gas; a single Savoia S-81 could carry and drop two tons of bombs. The Ethiopians used spears and obsolete rifles.

Benito Mussolini (1883–1945)

Italy was the fourth largest air power in the world at the time; fourth behind France, Russia, and Britain. The Italian Air Force had 2,000 pilots, 20,000 other personnel, and 2,300 combat aircraft at the beginning of 1935, and it increased its manpower and combat airplane strength during the war in eastern Africa. It also increased the range and speed of its aircraft. All fifteen airplane factories in Italy engaged in war production. Savoia and Caproni produced long-range bombers, and Savoia also built flying boats for coastal air stations. Fiat built fighter planes, Romeo made pursuit and observation planes, and Piaggio made seaplanes. The war lasted a year. Italy ended the war with victory and with improved airplane production and new aircraft. Before, during, and after the invasion of Abyssinia, the League of Nations condemned the Italian aggression and such international action

threatened to expand the conflict in East Africa into a wider war. Guerrilla fighting continued for years (until an Allied campaign of World War II forced Italy out of Eritrea, Somaliland, and Ethiopia).

Spanish Civil War

Francisco Franco was one of two Spanish generals who led revolts against the leftist republican government in Spain in 1936. A civil war followed the initial revolts, and Franco emerged as the leader of the fascist Falange party, the military, and Church groups who favored more authoritarian government. They became known as Nationalists as opposed to the Republican or Loyalist forces loyal to the elected government. Italy and Germany sent aircraft and personnel to support Franco. Initially, aircraft were operated during an airlift of Nationalist rebels from blockaded Morocco to Seville. Later combat planes targeted military and civilian targets. Many nations, like the Soviet Union, sided with the legitimate government, or at least preferred the Republican concept of government over fascist dictatorship. The Soviet Union sent men and machines, including airplanes, to support the leftist cause. In addition to the Soviet support, British, French, American, and other foreign volunteers joined international brigades to fight Franco's forces. Fascist Germany and Italy sent approximately 60,000 men to support the Nationalists, while the international brigades provided about 20,000 men to the Loyalist cause.

Francisco Franco (1892–1975)

Both sides in the conflict used aircraft. A total of about 15,000 people — civilians as well as combatants — were killed in air raids. The most famous use of airplanes during the Spanish Civil War was the bombing of the Basque town of Guernica. On 27 April 1937 Germany's Condor Legion, fighting for Franco, destroyed Guernica with bombs. Spain was a proving ground for German and Italian military aircraft, and airplanes provided Franco's forces with a significant advantage that contributed to victory and the establishment of Franco's right-wing dictatorship in 1939.

Nazi Germany

Adolf Hitler led the Nazis to power in 1933. He established the Third Reich, the third German empire. The first was the Holy Roman Empire that began with the coronation of Otto I as emperor in 962 and ended when Francis II renounced the title emperor in 1806, and the second empire lasted from the 1872 unification of Germany by Otto von Bismarck to the 1918 abdication of Kaiser Wilhem, *kaiser* being the German word for emperor. The Nazi version of fascism was unique with its extremely racial definition of the "new man" — an Aryan superman — to evolve from the new order. Either a racially pure Germany would beat its racially impure and inferior enemies or Germany would perish, Hitler claimed. This idea extended to world power or extinction. Nazi doctrine advocated racially oriented violence, particularly anti-Semitic violence. It also rejected Western culture epitomized by Germany's historical enemies: France and Britain. In addition to being authoritarian, German fascism was totalitarian in that the ruler or regime held absolute and centralized control over not only the political, but also the economic, social, educational, and cultural aspects of life in the country.

Adolf Hitler (1889–1945)

Hitler withdrew Germany from the Geneva Disarmament Conference, renounced the Treaty of Versailles, and rearmed Germany, including the air force. He supported gliding schools, flight instruction, and the National Socialist Flying Corps, and he excluded Jews from all air sports. He created an Air Defense League for civil defense. He sent German military forces into the Rhineland bordering France and, thereby, confirmed that neither France nor Britain wanted to go to war. He negotiated the Munich Agreement over the future of Czechoslovakia and sent German troops into that disintegrating country. He annexed Austria; this *anschluss* or union was prohibited by the 1919 treaties of Versailles and St. Germain. Without actually going to war, Hitler scared the world into believing a war was coming, that only a war would stop German aggression.

Sino-Japanese Conflict

The Japanese imperial government of the 1930s was considered authoritarian, totalitarian, aggressive, even racist, but not fascist in the European sense (and fascism was a European movement). The Showa emperor, constitutionalism (rule by constitution), and traditionalism dominated the leadership, but political pluralism as illustrated by multiple political parties remained a factor of Japanese politics into the late 1930s. Yet Japan shared some traits with the fascist regimes of Europe: racism, nationalism, imperialism, and militarism. Japan embarked on what became its Fifteen Year War in 1931 by invading the Asian mainland. Japan used seaplane bombers during the initial assaults on Manchuria, which was quickly captured and renamed Manchukuo. Guerrilla opposition kept the occupying forces on alert.

Japan was in the process of industrializing, and its big three aircraft makers — Kawasaki, Mitsubishi, and Nakajima — in the 1930s finally began producing Japanese designs rather than relying upon foreign airplanes, technology, and designs. Some of these airplanes were ready in 1937 when Japan entered a full-scale war with China. The Mitsubishi twin-engine Ki-21 and G3M1 dropped bombs on China, and the Mitsubishi Ki-15 flew reconnaissance missions. The Japanese Navy used carrier-based aircraft against the Chinese, including the Nakajima B5N1 bomber and the Mitsubishi A5M1 fighter. In 1938 Japan further encouraged its aircraft industry by exempting it from taxes and duties. Aircraft were needed not only for the China campaign, but also for home defense and defense of Japan's far-flung empire in the Pacific. Still, bombing proved decisive and devasting during the China campaign. (Figure 6-43)

Figure 6-43. Mitsubishi produced this Ki-15-I Karigane that was used as a civil transport.

After years of civil war, China had acquired aircraft, but too few and too old to match the Japanese air attacks. General Chiang Kai-Shek personally used the DC-2 *Flying Palace* for his travels. Chinese military aircraft attacked and bombed Japanese positions, like the flag ship *Idzuma* in the occupied section of Shanghai in 1937. The Japanese responded by bombing and strafing Shanghai. The fighting disrupted commercial air travel. The British Crown Colony of Hong Kong became a refuge for aircraft and people fleeing China, but Japanese forces bombed nearby Sham Chun (Shenzhen) and almost circled the colony by the end of 1937. Air France, Pan American, and other airlines experienced declining numbers of passengers on their Asian flights as well as a significant decline of airmail to a war-torn China. Imperial Airways painted large Union Jacks on the wings and sides of its DH.86 transports to avoid being shot down

mistakenly by Japanese forces along China's southern coast. Japanese fire damaged some commercial aircraft in flight, like Imperial's *Dorado* and a Eurasia Junkers Ju 52, and downed others, like the China National Aviation Corporation's DC-2 called *City of Kweilin*. In the *Kweilin's* case, Japanese fighters strafed the downed aircraft and killed 14 passengers. Some airlines ceased operation, while others repeatedly suspended operations. Hong Kong Air Services turned to night flights and preferably cloudy nights for service between the colony and unoccupied cities in China. Meanwhile, in 1939, the German airline Deutsche Luft Hansa opened service between Berlin and Tokyo, via British Hong Kong.

Military Expansion

The world tensions justified research and development of military aviation technology. In 1935, for two significant examples, Germany's Hans-Dietrich Knoetzsch first flew the prototype of the state-of-the-art German fighter Messerschmitt Bf 109 and Leslie Tower of the United States first flew the Boeing Model 299, later known as the B-17 Flying Fortress strategic bomber. These military aircraft were based on the technologies developed for and used in the modern airliners of the day. Some lines of development wound down, like the United States Navy's rigid airship program. The Navy awarded contracts for two large airships in 1928. It received the USS *Akron* (ZR-4) in 1931 and the USS *Macon* (ZR-5) in 1932. The Navy lost the *Akron* in a storm in 1933 (72 men lost) and the *Macon* was lost at sea in 1934 (two men died).

Some development work pointed toward new technologies of flight, like Ewald Rohlfs' 1936 maiden flight of the Focke-Achgelis Fa 61 dual-rotor helicopter (this flight lasted 28 seconds) and Erich Warsitz's 1939 maiden flight of the Heinkel He 178 jet-powered airplane (this flight lasted 15 minutes). In France, military aviation mirrored the instability in civil aviation. The country's air force, for example, had eight different chiefs of staff in eight years; though France did send 576 military planes into the air to celebrate Bastille Day 1935.

By 1937 the major powers were expanding their air forces in preparation for war. The United States considered itself first in the world in terms of air transport and private flying, which it was, but it was only sixth in terms of combat aircraft. Russia's goal was 10,000 airplanes by 1939, and it was producing

MILITARY PLANES BY NATION				
The Seven Air Powers	January 1932	January 1935	January 1936	January 1937
France	4,000	3,600	3,400	4,000
British Empire	2,000	2,800	3,600	4,000
Italy	1,800	2,300	2,800	3,200
United States	1,800	2,060	1,900	2,200
Russia	1,500	3,000	3,300	3,400
Japan	1,300	1.850	1.800	2,000
Germany	------	600	1,600	3,000

Estimated combat airplane strength of the seven powers, from The Aircraft Yearbook for 1935 and The AircraftYear Book for 1937 (New York: Aeronautical Chamber of Commerce, 1935 and 1937 respectively).

Figure 6-44. The late 1930s was a time of gradual military aviation buildup as countries prepared for war.

military aircraft in eleven factories. Germany in full mobilization produced 800 to 1,000 airplanes a month in 1937. (Figure 6-44)

In Germany in March 1939 the French pilot and author Saint-Exupéry observed the large number of airplanes in excess of hangar space. To him, this foreshadowed war. After German troops went into Czechoslovakia in March 1939, in violation of the Munich Agreement, France mobilized its military.

Conclusion

The fatalities in sport and commercial flying, the decline of Aéropostale, the airmail scandals in France and the United States, and airship accidents demonstrated that not everything was golden during the Golden Age of Aviation. Yet much was golden. The late twenties and the thirties were golden to the new class of private pilots, the homebuilders, the lightplane manufacturers, the designers of modern airlines, the commercial pilots surveying and serving transport routes, the regulatory agencies developing civil aviation policy, and the infrastructure behind the radio navigation system. The growing military air forces in the mid to late thirties also cast a shadow over the goldenness of the age, but the developments transformed several air forces from small biplane fleets into modern fighting units. Lindbergh visited Germany in 1936, 1937, and 1938. He toured the aircraft factories, watched demonstration flights, and talked with aircraft designers and military leaders. He concluded that Germany "cannot be kept down except by war, and another European war would be disastrous for everyone."

Study Questions

1. What distinguished Charles Lindbergh's transatlantic flight of 1927 from earlier and later transatlantic flights?

2. Who flew around the world and why did they do it?

3. What aircraft contributed to the growth of private flying during the Golden Age of Aviation?

4. What airlines competed for international routes during the late twenties and the thirties?

5. What features defined the modern airliners of the thirties, and what airliners met the definition?

6. What was a four-course radio?

7. How did the advent of instrument flying change the nature of aircraft operation?

8. What kind of aircraft were the *Graf Zeppelin* and *Hindenburg*?

9. Where were airplanes used in military conflicts during the period between the world wars?

10. Which publications listed in the bibliography are secondary sources of historical information?

Golden

Bibliography

Davies, R.E.G. *Charles Lindbergh, an Airman, His Aircraft, and His Great Flights.* McLean, VA: Pa

Davies, R.E.G. *Airlines of Latin America since 1919.* 1983; Washington: Smithsonian Institution Press, 1984.

Dick, Harold G. with Douglas H. Robinson. *Graf Zeppelin & Hindenburg, the Golden Age of the Passenger Airships.* Washington: Smithsonian Institution Press, 1985.

Gandt, Robert L. *China Clipper, the Age of the Great Flying Boats.* Annapolis, MD: Naval Institute Press, 1991.

Gwynn-Jones, Terry. *Farther and Faster, Aviation's Adventuring Years, 1909-1939.* Washington: Smithsonian Institution Press, 1991.

Komons, Nick A. *Bonfires to Beacons, Federal Civil Aviation Policy under the Air Commerce Act, 1926-1938.* 1977; Washington: Smithsonian Institution Press, 1989.

Lindbergh, Charles. *The Spirit of St. Louis.* New York: Charles Scribner's Sons, 1953.

Lindbergh, Charles A. *"We".* New York: Grosset & Dunlap, 1927.

Montague, Richard. *Oceans, Poles, and Airmen, the First Flights over Wide Waters and Desolate Ice.* New York: Random House, 1971.

Rae, John B. *Climb to Greatness, the American Aircraft Industry, 1920-1960.* Cambridge, MA: MIT Press, 1968.

Wright, Monte Duane. *Most Probable Position, a History of Aerial Navigation to 1941.* Lawrence: University Press of Kansas, 1972.

Timeline

Light blue type represents events that are not directly related to aviation

1927	May 20-21. Charles Lindbergh flew the Ryan monoplane *Spirit of St. Louis* nonstop and solo from New York to Paris.
1927	September 16. German President Paul Hindenburg (1847-1934) refused to accept the war guilt clause (article 231) of the Treaty of Versailles.
1927	October 14-15. Dieudonné Costes and Joseph le Brix completed the first nonstop airplane flight across the South Atlantic Ocean; they flew a Breguet 19 from Saint-Louis, Senegal, to Port Natal, Brazil.
1927	Chinese civil wars began with purges to remove Communists from the ruling Guomindang or National People's Party that had overthrown the Qing dynasty in 1912; the wars also began with Communist uprisings that year and with the government's ongoing Northern Expedition to pacify northern China. The civil wars continued until the Communist victory in 1949.
1928	April 12-13. The Junkers W 33 monoplane *Bremen* made the first nonstop flight east-to-west, against the prevailing winds, across the Atlantic Ocean; the airmen on the flight were Hermann Köhl and Baron von Hünefeld of Germany and James Fitzmaurice of Ireland.

1928   October 1. The Soviet Union began its first Five-Year Plan for a state-directed economy and for agricultural collectivism.

1929   August 8-29. The German airship *Graf Zeppelin* flew around the world; financed in large part by American publisher William Randolph Hearst and, therefore, beginning and ending the flight in the United States. The round-the-world flight logged seven days 11 minutes in the air.

1929   October 24-29. From Black Thursday through Black Tuesday, the American stock market crashed; this led to a worldwide economic collapse and the subsequent Great Depression.

1929   November 28-29. Norwegian pilot Bernt Balchen flew American adventurer Richard Byrd and others in the Byrd Antarctic Expedition over the South Pole.

1930   March 12. In India, Mahatma Gandhi (1869-1948) led the "salt march" from Ahmedabad to the coast where he seized salt to protest the British-imposed salt tax; this opened Gandhi's civil disobedience movement in colonial India.

1930   October 5. The British airship R.101 crashed in France; 48 men died.

1930   France continued construction, begun the previous year, of the Maginot Line of defensive fortifications along the border between France and Germany; named after Minister of War André Maginot (1877-1932), the line remained under construction until completion in 1940.

1931   February 2. Sixty countries participated in the Geneva Disarmament Conference that opened this day; it was a diplomatic attempt to reach an international agreement of disarmament, but the conference ended in June 1934 without an agreement.

1931   June 23-July 1. Pilot Wiley Post and navigator Harold Gatty flew the Lockheed Vega monoplane *Winnie Mae* around the world in eight days, 15 hours, 51 minutes; and 15-22 July 1933 Post flew the *Winnie Mae* solo around the world in the record time of seven days, 18 hours, and 49 minutes.

1931   September 18. Japan began its siege of Mukden (now Shenyang), Manchuria, and extended its power to all Manchuria the next year; Japan occupied Manchuria, called Manchukuo during the occupation, until expelled by the Soviets in 1945.

1931   October 3-5. Clyde Pangborn and Hugh Herndon, Jr., in a Bellanca completed a transpacific flight by flying from Japan to Wenatchee, Washington.

1932   May 20-21. Amelia Earhart became the first woman to fly across the Atlantic Ocean nonstop and solo; she flew a Lockheed Vega from Newfoundland to Ireland and beat the record time set by Alcock and Brown in 1919.

1932   June 15. A border dispute started the Chaco War, named after the disputed Chaco Boreal territory, between Bolivia and Paraguay; the war continued till June 1935 when Paraguay won most of the territory.

1933   March 4. Franklin Delano Roosevelt (1882-1945) was inaugurated as the 32nd president of the United States, and he immediately began his New Deal program for domestic economic relief from the Great Depression.

1933   April 3. Lord Clydesdale and Stewart Blacker in a Westland PV.3 torpedo bomber and David McIntyre and cameraman Sidney Bonnet in a Westland Wallace flew over Mount Everest (29,030 feet; 8,848 meters).

1933   October 14. In office since January, the new chancellor of Germany Adolf Hitler (1889-1945) withdrew Germany from the Geneva Disarmament Conference and from the League of Nations and, thereby, from international scrutiny of German armament; he had already introduced laws excluding Jews from government jobs, boycotting of Jewish businesses, and denying police protection for Jews and their property.

1934   October 20 - November 4. Twenty contestants began and ten completed the MacRobertson air race from England to Australia, one of the last great long-distance air races; C.W.A. Scott and T. Campbell Black of Great Britain in a special de Havilland 88 Comet won the race, and K.D. Parmentier and J.J. Moll of the Royal Dutch Airlines in a regular Douglas DC-2 airliner placed second, and Clyde Pangborn and Roscoe Turner of the United States in a Boeing 247-D placed third.

1934   October 21 - 1935 October 20. Pursued by government troops of Chiang Kai-shek (1887-1975), Mao Tse-tung (1893-1976) led the Chinese Communists on the "Long March" of about 6,000 miles (9,600km) from southern China to northern China.

1935   March 16. Germany renounced the Treaty of Versailles and began full rearmament; later in the year Germany passed the Reich Citizenship Law that defined German citizenship by a Nazi-defined racial purity and that made Jews subjects rather than citizens of Germany.

1935   May 28. The first flight of the prototype of the state-of-the-art German Messerschmitt Bf 109 fighter was made; Hans-Dietrich Knoetzsch was the pilot.

1935   July 28. The Boeing Model 299, later known as the B-17 Flying Fortress strategic bomber, completed its first flight; Leslie Tower was the pilot.

1935   October 2. Italy invaded Ethiopia; later in the month, the League of Nations denounced the Italian action and imposed sanctions on Italy.

1935   November 22. Pan American started transpacific airmail service with a flight from San Francisco via Honolulu, Wake, and Guam, to Manila in the Philippines. Edwin C. Musick was the captain of the Martin M.130 flying boat named *China Clipper* that made the flight.

1936   January 20. King George V (1865-1936) of the United Kingdom died, and his oldest son became King Edward VIII (1894-1972). Edward abdicated in December to marry a divorcee, so Edward's brother George VI (1894-1952) became king.

1936   June 26. Ewald Rohlfs flew the Focke-Achgelis Fa 61 dual-rotor helicopter on its maiden flight, which lasted 28 seconds.

1936   July 17. Generals Francisco Franco (1892-1975) and José Sanjurjo (1872-1926) led an uprising in Spanish Morocco against Spain's Republican government and, thereby, began the Spanish Civil War; in 1939, Franco's forces won the war and Franco became the *caudillo* (leader) and dictator of the country.

1936   September 29. F.R.D. Swain of the Royal Air Force flew a Bristol Type 138 wooden monoplane powered by a special Pegasus engine to a world altitude record of 49,967 feet (15,223 meters); he wore an air-tight suit and obtained oxygen from a tube to his helmet.

1937   May 6. The *Hindenburg*, the world's largest airship, arrived on schedule at Lakehurst, New Jersey, caught fire and crashed.

1937   June 20. A Russian Tupolev ANT-25 completed its flight from Moscow over the North Pole to Vancouver, Washington; pilot Valeri Chkalov, co-pilot Georgi Baidukov, and navigator Alexander Beliakov flew this first nonstop, great-circle flight from the Soviet Union to the United States: 5,288 miles in 63 hours and 17 minutes.

1937   November 6. Italy joined the Anti-Comintern Pact formed by Germany and Japan the year before, and Hungary and Spain joined the Pact in 1939. Pact members opposed international communism represented by the Comintern (Communist International organization based in the Soviet Union, founded in 1919 and disbanded in 1943).

1937   December 13. After a week of battle, Japan captured Nanjing, China, and began the "rape of Nanjing," also known as the Nanjing Massacre, that claimed over two hundred thousand victims.

1938   March 13. Germany annexed Austria; this union or *anschluss* (connection) was prohibited by the 1919 treaties of Versailles with Germany and of St-Germain with Austria.

1938   July 10-14. Pilot Howard Hughes, flight engineer Eddie Lund, radio engineer Richard Stoddart, and navigators Thomas Thurlow and Harry P.M. Conner flew around the world in a twin-engine, Wright Cyclone-powered Lockheed 14 that averaged 206 miles per hour during the 91 hours of flight time, total elapsed time three days, 19 hours, and 17 minutes.

1939   August 27. Erich Warsitz flew the Heinkel He 178 jet-powered airplane on its maiden flight, which lasted 15 minutes.

1939   September 1. Germany invaded Poland and, thereby, began the combat of World War II.

CHAPTER 7

WORLD WAR II (1939-1945)

AVIATION HISTORY

Summary of Events

September 1. Germany invaded Poland — **1939**

1939 — September 1. German fighters and dive bombers used in *blitzkrieg* invasion of Poland

September 14. Igor I. First flight of Sikorsky VS-300 helicopter — **1939**

1940 — January 6. Finnish Air Force Lt. Jorma Sarvanto shot down six Soviet bombers during the Winter War

May 26 - June 4. British Spitfires successfully defended troops being evacuated from Dunkirk — **1940**

1941 — April 8. P.E.G. Sayer of Great Britain flew the Gloster-Whittle jet-powered plane.

March. The United States Congress passed the Lend-Lease Act — **1941**

1941 — May 20. The German *Luftwaffe* landed over 22,000 men on the Island of Crete

June 22. German aircraft attacked the Soviet Union in Operation Barbarossa — **1941**

1941 — August 14. Winston Churchill and Franklin D. Roosevelt agreed to the Atlantic Charter

December 7. Japanese naval aircraft attacked Pearl Harbor, Hawaii — **1941**

1941 — In China the Viet Minh league for the independence of Vietnam formed

The Alaska Highway was constructed — **1942**

1942 — April 18. American B-25 bombers raided Tokyo

May 4-8. The Battle of the Coral Sea fought with aircraft — **1942**

1942 — July 18. German pilot Fritz Wendel flew the first jet-powered Messerschmitt Me 262

October 1. United States pilot Robert Stanley flew the jet-powered XP-59A Airacomet — **1942**

1943 — January 14-24. Winston Churchill and Franklin Roosevelt convened the Casablanca Conference

April 18. American pilots shot down Admiral Isoroku Yamamoto's Mitsubishi G4M1 Betty bomber — **1943**

1943 — May 31. Tuskegee airmen flew their first combat mission

July 10. The Allied invasion of Nazi-controlled Europe began with Operation Husky — **1943**

1943 — November 6-22. Winston Churchill, Franklin Roosevelt, and Chiang Kai-shek attended the Cairo Conference

Light blue type represents events that are not directly related to aviation.

June 6. Allied pilots supported the D-Day landings at Normandy **1944**

1944 June 13. The first jet-powered V-1 flying bombs struck London

June 15. United States B-29 Superfortress bombers attacked Japan for the first time **1944**

1944 July. Forty-four nations participated in the Bretton Woods Conference

July 20. Plot to assassinate Adolph Hitler failed **1944**

1944 August-October. Poles in Warsaw forced to surrender after the Warsaw Rising

August-October. China, Great Britain, the Soviet Union, and the United States drafted a charter for United Nations **1944**

1944 September. Egypt, Iraq, Lebanon, Saudi Arabia, Transjordan, Yemen, and Palestinian Arabs organized the Arab League

September 8. The V-2 ballistic rocket launched against Paris and London **1944**

1944 Iceland became an independent republic

February 13. Allied bombers dropped firebombs on the German City of Dresden **1945**

1945 March. Finland declared war against Germany

May. Palestine partitioned into Jewish and Arab sectors and Israel became a nation on 14 May **1945**

1945 May 7. Germany surrendered

May 10. The United States Army Air Forces tested strategic nighttime firebombing by raiding Tokyo **1945**

1945 June 26. Fifty nations signed the United Nations Charter

July 17 - August 2. Winston Churchill, Joseph Stalin, and Harry Truman attended the Potsdam Conference **1945**

1945 August 6. Atomic bomb dropped on Hiroshima, Japan; and on August 9th another atomic bomb dropped on Nagasaki

Soviet Union declared war on Japan **1945**

1945 August 14. Japan surrendered

August 17. Indonesia declared independence from the Netherlands and gained it four years later **1945**

1945 August 20. Emperor Bao Dai of Vietnam abdicated, and within two weeks the Democratic Republic of Vietnam was proclaimed

September 2. Japan formalized its surrender **1945**

Introduction

Unlike World War I, World War II involved a multitude of aircraft from the start, as well as new classifications of aircraft and new aviation technologies that rose during the war. There were bombers — light, medium, and heavy. There were fighters — day fighters, night fighters, fighter bombers, even ground-attack fighters. There were trainers — primary, basic, and advanced. There were gliders, helicopters, jet planes, and rockets, though reciprocating-engine airplanes dominated the aerial combat at all fronts. There were transports, observation aircraft, seaplanes, and photo-reconnaissance aircraft. There were wood-and-glue models as well as all-metal aircraft. There were lots of aircraft!

One estimate is that Great Britain and the United States together produced over 380,000 aircraft during the war years.

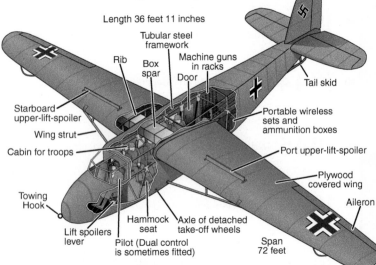

Length 36 feet 11 inches
Tubular steel framework
Rib
Box spar
Machine guns in racks
Door
Tail skid
Starboard upper-lift-spoiler
Wing strut
Cabin for troops
Portable wireless sets and ammunition boxes
Port upper-lift-spoiler
Plywood covered wing
Aileron
Towing Hook
Hammock seat
Axle of detached take-off wheels
Lift spoilers lever
Pilot (Dual control is sometimes fitted)
Span 72 feet

German Light Assault Glider

Many names in aviation during the war were familiar: Boeing, Curtiss, Douglas, Grumman, Lockheed, Martin, and Northrop in the United States; Bristol, de Havilland, Fairey, Handley Page, Hawker, Short, and Supermarine in Great Britain; Dornier, Focke-Wulf, Heinkel, Junkers, and Messerschmitt in Germany; Caproni, Fiat, Macchi, and Savoia-Marchetti in Italy; and Kawasaki, Mitsubishi, and Nakajima in Japan. Some names were new, or at least new outside their respective home countries, like Commonwealth in Australia, Federal in Canada, Aichi and Yokosuka in Japan, and Lavochkin and Yakovlev in the Soviet Union. Some of the pilots also had familiar names, like Charles Lindbergh who as a civilian flew 50 combat missions in the Pacific, Antoine de Saint Exupry who disappeared on a flight over the Mediterranean Sea in 1944, and Adolf Galland who had flown with

Germany's Condor Legion during the Spanish Civil War before becoming a World War II ace and Germany's youngest general. Well-known female pilots also contributed to the war efforts, like Soviet pilot Marina Roskova who organized women's air regiments for the Red Air Force and her American counterpart, Jacqueline Cochran, who organized the United States Army's Women's Airforce Service Pilots (WASPs).

North American P-51 Mustang

The most famous of the new names were the pilots who flew wartime missions, including the top aces of various countries like Clive Robertson Caldwell of Australia, Pierre H. Clostermann of France, Erich Hartmann of Germany, Saburo Sakai of Japan, and Richard Ira Bong of the United States. Women also became involved in military aviation like Hanna Reitsch, the German test pilot, and Lilya Litvak, the Soviet's top female ace. There were also famous groups like the Tuskegee Airmen who under the command of Benjamin O. Davis proved black airmen were effective in combat; Jimmy Doolittle's Raiders who made the first attack on Tokyo; and Claire Lee Chennault's Flying Tigers who flew for China against Japanese forces during the war. Britain's Dambusters, a special

Flying Tigers P-40s

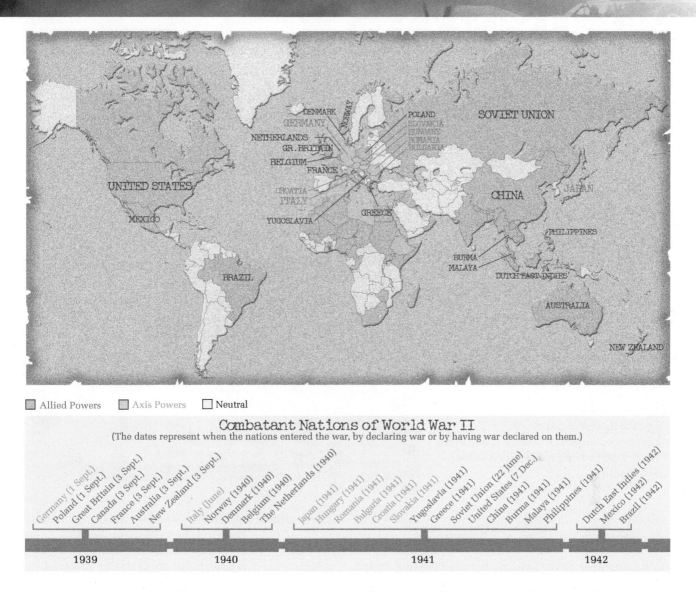

■ Allied Powers   ■ Axis Powers   □ Neutral

Combatant Nations of World War II
(The dates represent when the nations entered the war, by declaring war or by having war declared on them.)

Germany (1 Sept.)
Poland (1 Sept.)
Great Britain (3 Sept.)
Canada (3 Sept.)
France (3 Sept.)
Australia (3 Sept.)
New Zealand (3 Sept.)
Italy (June)
Norway (1940)
Denmark (1940)
Belgium (1940)
The Netherlands (1940)
Japan (1941)
Hungary (1941)
Romania (1941)
Bulgaria (1941)
Croatia (1941)
Slovakia (1941)
Yugoslavia (1941)
Greece (1941)
Soviet Union (22 June)
United States (7 Dec.)
China (1941)
Burma (1941)
Malaya (1941)
Philippines (1941)
Dutch East Indies (1942)
Mexico (1942)
Brazil (1942)

| 1939 | 1940 | 1941 | 1942 |

unit organized by Guy Penrose Gibson, bombed German dams.

The fame came from war, from a war many had tried to avoid through participation in the League of Nations, through attendance at disarmament conferences, through overlooking Japan's 1937 invasion of China, through appeasement of Adolf Hitler as he moved German troops into Austria in 1938 and Czechoslovakia in 1939, through inaction regarding Italy's invasion of Albania in 1939, through international alliances like the Soviet-German non-aggression pact of 1939, and through neutrality acts. But the imperialist, nationalist, and militarist goals of a few countries pulled others into a new world conflict: World War II.

Section A of this chapter discusses the war emergency that arose in 1939. In this section the student will learn how the war began, the early progress of the war, and the training of personnel for this growing conflict. Section B covers military research and development and military production. After reading this section the student will be able to answer questions about helicopter development, gas turbine research, and rocketry. The western air war in the North Atlantic, Europe, North Africa, and the Middle East is the subject of Section C, and the Pacific air war in Asia and in the Pacific Ocean is covered in Section D. The student will learn about the air battles, air equipment, and airmen in various theaters of operations.

SECTION A

WAR EMERGENCY AND RESPONSE

Q & A

What: World War II

When? 1939 - 1945

Where? Worldwide, with concentrations of fighting in Europe and in the Pacific

Who? The Axis Powers of Germany, Italy, Japan, and other nations versus the Allied Powers of Britain, France, Soviet Union, United States, and other countries

Why? Imperialism, nationalism, and militarism, as well as defense of homelands and of political values like democracy (in the case of the United States) and communism (in the case of the Soviet Union)

On 1 September 1939 Germany invaded Poland. That day the Polish Supreme Command Staff announced:

> "In the early hours of this morning the Germans invaded our country in a surprise attack by their air force and ground troops, without a declaration of war. The German Luftwaffe carried out a number of attacks on individual targets throughout the territory of Poland."

Germany wanted the Free City of Danzig and the Polish Corridor that linked Poland and the Baltic Sea, both granted to Poland by international agreement at the end of World War I. On the first evening of this new war the German Wehrmacht (Armed Forces) High Command announced:

> "Today, in a series of vigorous operations, the German Luftwaffe attacked and destroyed the military installations on numerous Polish airfields including Rumia, Puck, Grudziadz, Poznan, Plock, Lodz, Tomaszow, Radom, Ruda,

Katowice, Krakow, Lvov, Brest, [and] Terespol. In addition, several air combat wings are effectively supporting the advance of the army."

Thus began the German blitzkrieg campaign against Poland. *Blitzkrieg* is German for lightning war and described fast-moving assaults using motorized infantry and tanks supported by aircraft, particularly fighters and dive bombers. Attacks on enemy aircraft, airfields, and aircraft-making capabilities were strategic missions, whereas supporting the land troops were tactical missions. On the initial raids against Poland, the German Luftwaffe (air force) used Messerschmitt

Historic Event

Germany's invasion of Poland on 1 September 1939 began the conflict soon known as World War II. Germany used aircraft both strategically and tactically during this offensive.

Flight Lines

"The target sheets show us everything clearly: the hangars — the depots — the repair hangar — the radio-telegraph installations. Focus of the attack: recognized enemy aircraft on the field. . . .

. . .

"Another squadron is flying to our left: we see that it is being fired on. Then a cloud of black smoke on the horizon shows us our target. We are alongside, we see fire, smoke, more fire and explosion after explosion. We nose our aircraft to 150 feet so that the bombs will bite on impact. Then a short distance ahead at the edge of the airfield, we see a neatly arranged string of Polish fighter planes. The bomb trail is launched. The bombs batter our enemy to pieces. Red explosions are bursting all over the ground, the threads of enemy anti-aircraft shells pull around us. Our machine-gun barrels are hot; probably the turrets have never been rotated so fast. Then, pressed close to the ground, we race off on the course for home."

German pilot of a Dornier Do 17 describing the 1 September 1939 raid on Krakow, Poland, as translated by Han van Heurck and quoted in Janusz Piekaltiewicz, *The Air War, 1939-1945*.

Bf 109 single-engine and Bf 110 twin-engine fighters, Junkers Ju 87 *Stuka* dive bombers, Heinkel He 111 and Dornier Do 17 bombers, and other aircraft.

Poland Falls

On 2 September Germany continued its invasion of Poland, and Poland used PZL (Panstwowe Zaklady Lotnicze) P.11a and 11c fighters and P-23 Karas light bombers to raid Germany. Britain and France aligned with Poland in the conflict and issued Germany ultimatums. When Germany failed to respond, Great Britain and France declared war on Germany. That was on the 3rd, when Australia and New Zealand joined Britain's side. On the 4th Britain's Royal Air Force raided German naval units at Wilhelmshaven and Cuxhaven, but met strong resistance and lost several aircraft. Strong resistance also met the British fighters that attacked Wilhelmshaven and Cuxhaven the next day. With the Polish Air Force heavily damaged, though not destroyed, and greatly out-numbered and out-classed by the German Luftwaffe, German aircraft attacked railroads, roads, bridges, and troop columns to disrupt any Polish retreat. Within a week of the start of the war, French and German fighters met in the air over both French and German territory. (Figure 7-1)

As Germany crushed Poland from the west, the Soviet Union invaded Poland from the east. On the

first day of the Soviet invasion — the 17th of September 1939 — the Red Air Force reported downing seven Polish fighters and three Polish bombers. Germany used artillery and aircraft against a heavily defended Warsaw and systematically destroyed the city, including civilian targets selected to lower Polish morale. The city's defenders managed to shoot down more than a hundred German aircraft in the futile effort to stop the invaders. British and French aircraft pulled German aircraft to a western campaign, but Germany with approximately 1,500 fighter planes, in addition to other types of aircraft, had sufficient air power to cover both the Polish campaign and the western action. German air forces,

Figure 7-1. A PZL P.11c Polska flown by the 121st Fighter Squadron of the 2nd Air Regiment, Polish Air Force.

for example, attacked British naval vessels in the North Sea; Germany reported destroying one aircraft carrier, but Britain reported no losses of ships nor men. French and British planes met German aircraft in various skirmishes, but these failed to save a heavily bombed Poland. The nation surrendered on 5 October 1939, and Germany and the Soviet Union quickly partitioned the land. Poland as a nation vanished, but Britain welcomed Polish airmen to organize Polish wings to fly with the Royal Air Force. With Germany's initial objective achieved, there was a lull in the war.

The Phony War

From October 1939 the war entered what became know as the "Phony War" or in German the *Sitzkrieg* phase. During this time there was fighting in Europe, but the winter weather restricted aerial operations. Germany began air raids against England in October, and German radio followed its daily news report with the song "We Ride against England." The Royal Air Force, in turn, continued to attack Wilhelmshaven and other German targets, most well defended with air raid warning service, fighters, and destroyer aircraft. The British used Vickers Wellington bombers flying in formation to attack German positions. The French Air Force — *l'Armee de l'Air* — engaged in skirmishes along its border with Germany. Its main fighters were the French-made Morane Saulnier MS.406 and the American-made Curtiss Hawk 75, both single-seat planes. The former had a water-cooled Hispano-Suiza engine and the latter an air-cooled Pratt & Whitney radial engine. (Figure 7-2)

A Luftwaffe Front-Line Bulletin in December 1939 commented that the "coloring of the [British] aircraft differed considerably from the German. Their dominant feature was their camouflage paint of wavy brown, green and yellow lines. For the first time we observed clearly visible national markings, printed on both sides of the fuselage." The same bulletin reported that the Messerschmitt Bf 110 fighter easily caught the Vickers Wellingtons. In combat the British planes closed ranks. Already at this early date, according to the German bulletin, "the English aircraft flew their course smartly and could not be diverted: the formations could be broken up only after hard attack." The Germans recognized a major weakness in these early British bombers: they caught fire easily — the engine, the fuel tanks, and the fabric.

Winter War

The Soviets invaded Finland late in November and thereby began a short Winter War. During this northern conflict the Soviets used Tupolev SB-2 bombers previously used in the Spanish Civil War, as well as other aircraft. The Red Air Force dropped incendiary bombs and high-explosive bombs on the Finnish capital of Helsinki. The Red planes were based in nearby Soviet-occupied Estonia. The Finnish pilots flew Fokker D-XXI and other aircraft. In one of Finland's finest aerial moments, on 6 January 1940 Air Force Lieutenant Jorma Sarvanto shot down six Soviet Ilyushin DB-3 bombers.

The Soviets soon sent more aircraft to attack Finland. Britain, France, Italy, Sweden, the Union of South Africa, and the United States sent airplanes to supply the Finnish Air Force. The Finnish pilots thus flew a

Figure 7-2. A British Vickers Wellington IV bomber with a Spitfire escort during World War II

Figure 7-3. Finland flew aircraft such as this U.S.-built Brewster during the Continuation War of 1941 — 1944. The blue swastika in a white circle was the symbol of the Finnish Air Force from 1918 through World War II.

wide variety of aircraft including British Gladiators, Hurricanes, Lysanders, and Blenheims; French Morane-Saulniers and Koolhovens; Italian Fiats; Swedish-made Gladiators; South African Gladiators; and American Brewsters. (Figure 7-3)

Finland lost 67 aircraft in this Winter War. The Soviets lost 684, but the Soviets won the war against their small neighboring country. The Soviet-Finnish Peace Treaty of Moscow ended the heroic resistance by the Finns in March 1940, and gave some strategic territory to the Soviet Union. Despite losing the war, Finland found itself in the awkward position of having fought an Allied Power once the Soviet Union joined France and Britain in war against Germany.

The Russian-Finnish war was a local conflict involving two countries not yet involved in the main war in Europe, where the Phony War continued through April 1940. That May, Germany began its next major campaign which was a blitzkrieg through the Low Countries and into France. This war was real!

The Battle for France

Germany began its battle for France by invading Belgium and Holland (the Netherlands) in May 1940. It selected this route to France because the fortified Maginot Line protected the French border with Germany, but not the border between France and Belgium. Germany simply went around the north-western end of the line. It began by sending the

Luftwaffe against the Belgian and Dutch air forces, which were caught on the ground and mostly destroyed. To limit French interference with the German invasion of Belgium and Holland, the Luftwaffe also bombed French airfields, including those at Dijon, Lyons, Metz, Nancy, and Romilly. The German fighters and bombers outnumbered French aircraft and the supporting British planes. The Royal Air Force flew Hawker Hurricane fighter-bombers, powered by Rolls Royce Merlin engines, in defense of France and the Low Countries.

Some of the German pilots, like Adolf Galland, had experience in the Spanish Civil War. Galland in a Bf 109E shot down three Hurricanes over Belgium in one day — the first three of the 104 victories that he scored during World War II. At the age of 29, he became Germany's youngest general. He favored using fighter planes for air superiority rather than ground attack, but German policy continued to assign

Photo of Maginot Line Fortification

German route around Maginot Line

Figure 7-4. The primary fighter-bomber for the RAF was the Hawker Hurricane powered by a Rolls Royce Merlin engine.

ground, but Germany pushed through toward the French ports on the English Channel. French and other Allied forces retreated, abandoned airfields, and moved equipment to emergency landing fields.

Dunkirk

In late May and early June 1940 the British Expeditionary Force and part of France's Northern Army evacuated across the English Channel to Britain. Hundreds of naval ships, merchant vessels, and private boats transported men from France to Britain. During the evacuation Allied aircraft heavily defended Dunkirk, the departure site. There, the new British Spitfires encountered German fighters for the first time. To the German's surprise, this British plane was more maneuverable than the Messerschmitt Bf

fighters to ground attack missions that proved so effective in the early blitzkrieg campaigns against Poland, the Low Countries, and France. (Figure 7-4)

As France fought for its survival, Britain brought Gloster Gladiator biplanes into the fight. Germany rounded the end of the Maginot Line at Sedan in May, and Belgium surrendered on the 28th of that month. Fighting was fierce in the air and on the

Flight Lines

"The enemy was attacked from a position of advantage above and astern. The first burst with machine guns and cannon hit the enemy aircraft. When I broke away Lieutenant Rödel fired and scored hits. The enemy machine spiraled down and I followed, firing from a distance of

between 50 and 70m. Parts of the aircraft were observed to break off and it spun down into the clouds. Ammunition used: 90 cannon shells; about 150 machine gun bullets. The Hurricanes appeared poorly trained and failed to support each other."

German pilot Adolf Galland describing an encounter between Messerschmitt Bf

Adolf Galland

109Es and Hawker Hurricanes near Liege, 12 May 1940, as translated and quoted in Mike Spick, *Luftwaffe Fighter Aces*.

Flight Lines

". . . over Dunkirk, about three miles away, a gaggle of swift-growing dots. He knew what they were instantly. The 110's wheeled inland without dropping their bombs, but the sky was empty of cloud and the Spitfires leapt after them, blaring on full throttle. No time for thinking, but as he turned his reflector sight on and the gun button to 'fire,' he knew he was going to shoot. A glance back through the perspex; the straining Spitfires were stringing out in a ragged line and up to the left four grey shapes were diving at them — Messerschmitt 109's, the first he had seen. From the beam they flicked across in front like darting sharks, winking orange flashes in the noses as they fired."

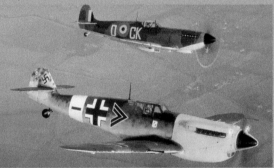

British pilot Douglas Bader describing his Dunkirk sortie, as retold by Paul Brickhill in *Reach for the Sky, the Story of Douglas Bader, Legless Ace of the Battle of Britain* (New York: W.W. Norton & Company, 1954). Bader had lost both legs in a 1931 airplane crash. He "killed" a Messerschmitt 110 on the mission described above.

109E. British fighters were attacking German bombers, and German fighters protecting those bombers were attacking British fighters.

Germany won the air battle over Dunkirk in terms of fighter statistics. German fighters flew 2,000 sorties and lost 37 aircraft, whereas British fighters flew 1,764 sorties and lost 106 aircraft. By a different measure, the British won: British fighters succeeded in protecting the evacuation of 330,000 men! A sortie is one mission by a single military plane.

Flight Lines

"We circled over the city for a while, throttled the engines, let them run again full blast, then repeated the process. We wanted to create the impression that a whole formation was over Berlin. Then we turned off toward a northern suburb and dropped our payload there on one of the numerous factories. The attack certainly did not cause any great destruction, but after all we were more concerned with the psychological effect."

A French officer describing the first air raid of the war on Berlin, 7 June 1940, as translated and quoted in Janusz Piekaltiewicz, *The Air War, 1939-1945*.

Flight Lines

"There it lay before us, clearly visible through the drifting cloud cover: Paris. Never will we forget the moment when the bombs left our bays and whistled down onto the square. Then we heard a crashing sound down below, where the flights that came after us had hit their targets. Impact after impact, flash after flash, one explosive cone after another over the whole expanse of the [Le Bourget] air base — an overpowering picture of the fearful effects of mass bombing."

German Heinkels over Paris

German pilot describing June 1940 raid on Paris, as translated from a German newspaper and quoted in Janusz Piekalkiewicz, *The Air War, 1939-1945*.

After the evacuation of Dunkirk, Germany turned toward the rest of France and pressed toward Paris. The French Havas News Agency gave a brief summary: "The German Luftwaffe has bombed French airfields and connections leading to Paris." In a desperate attempt to stop the German advance, the French Navy sent one plane to bomb Berlin. This was the Farman 223.4 long-range bomber *Jules Verne*, commanded by Captain de Corvette Daillire and navigator Paul Comet. That sortie reached Berlin, dropped bombs, and caused minimal damage. Soon the Germans reached Paris.

Mediterranean Region

While Germany advanced toward Paris in 1940, it also sent troops to the Mediterranean Sea. In May 1941 it launched a major airborne paratroop attack against Crete, at the time defended by British and Greek forces. In addition to transporting paratroopers to the island, German planes supported the invasion by bombing, fighting, and dive bombing defensive positions on the island and at sea. The large number of German troops that landed on Crete and the bloody fighting that followed caused Britain to withdraw with heavy losses after 12 days; the British withdrew to Egypt.

Italy, which had sold airplanes to France early in the war, declared war on France and Great Britain in June 1940. Italy's entrance to the war also expanded the Mediterranean conflict, as the Italians bombed British territories in Malta and North Africa — in the Sudan, Kenya, Egypt, and Tunisia. (Figure 7-5)

Figure 7-5. German paratroopers leave a transport plane in an attack similar to that used against Crete.

France collapsed that month. The French armistice with Germany came on 22 June 1940. General Charles de Gaulle explained, "It is quite true that we were, and still are, overwhelmed by enemy mechanized forces, both on the ground and in the air. It was the tanks, the planes, and the tactics of the Germans, far more than the fact that we were outnumbered, that forced our armies to retreat. It was the German tanks, planes, and tactics that provided the element of surprise which brought our leaders to their present plight."

French Governments

With the fall of France in June 1940, Germany occupied Paris and northern France. Germany ruled this occupied French territory, simply called occupied France. By terms of the armistice, France canceled its military orders for aircraft, stored its military aircraft, and disabled its war-production factories, including the six state-owned *sociétés nationales* (nationalized companies) that manufactured airplanes.

In the town of Vichy, Marshal Henri-Philippe Petain organized a Vichy authoritarian government for the unoccupied two-fifths of the country; he became a puppet of Nazi Germany. His government ruled Vichy France and collaborated with the Germans ruling occupied France. In 1941, for example, the Vichy Government agreed that French aircraft production facilities in the occupied territory could produce aircraft of German designs for Germany.

In London, General Charles de Gaulle organized the Free French and included French territories in North Africa in this new organization. A French resistance movement also formed.

Battle of Britain

Having won the Battle of France, Germany began the Battle of Britain. This was an air war intended to precede an invasion of the British Isles, a plan given the German code name Sea Lion. The German Navy

Aircraft spotter on a London roof during the Battle of Britain. St. Paul's Cathedral is in the background.

and Luftwaffe initially targeted British shipping, its supply lines. Then, starting in August 1940, Germany attacked southern England and bombed airfields and factories. Adolf Hitler directed the strategy; in his words: "The German Air Force will use all available means to destroy the British Air Force as soon as possible. Attacks will be directed primarily against the flying units, ground organization, and supply installations of the Royal Air Force and, further, against the air armaments industry, including factories producing anti-aircraft equipment." This German assault failed to destroy the Royal Air Force on the ground or in the air, so the Luftwaffe began what the British called the *Blitz*, an air attack against London and other British cities that began in September.

St. Paul's Cathedral amid the rubble

Throughout the Battle of Britain, British Air Chief Marshal Hugh Dowding led the defensive effort that utilized about 700 Hurricane and Spitfire fighter planes against the numerically superior German Luftwaffe force of nearly a thousand fighters, over 800 long-range bombers, and over 300 dive bombers. Germany targeted British cities in addition to London. German day bombing missions caused heavy damage to the British cities and heavy losses to the German air forces; for example, on 14 September 1940, British forces downed 56 German bombers. The high losses prompted Germany to switch to night bombing in October. Again, Germany suffered the loss of many bombers. Britain's use of the newly invented radar system contributed to the effective defense of its homeland. The ability to track incoming aircraft allowed Dowding to keep his fighters on the ground until the enemy was in range. The Hurricanes and Spitfires had ample fuel to attack incoming German bombers.

Flight Lines

"I trimmed up and the controls seemed quite all right. The windscreen was black with oil. Temperatures were up round the clocks and pressures had dropped to practically zero. But she kept on flying after a fashion. . . . I decided I'd have to bail out into the Channel. It wasn't a very pleasant prospect. . . . But the only alternative was to try to ditch her, and a Spit was notoriously allergic to landing on water . . . The cockpit was full of glycol fumes and the stink of burning rubber and white-hot metal . . ."

British Spitfire pilot Robert Stanford Tuck describing limping across the English Channel and parachuting onto English soil after an encounter with a German Junkers Ju 88 during the 1940 Battle of Britain, as quoted by Larry Forrester in "Spitfire Tales," in *War in the Air, True Accounts of the 20th Century's Most Dramatic Air Battles — by the Men Who Fought Them,* edited by Stephen Coonts (New York: Pocket Books, 1996).

Historical Note

During the 1930s researchers in Germany, Great Britain, and the United States explored the electronics necessary for a radar system. The word radar began as an acronym for radio detection and ranging. Under threat of war, Britain accelerated its research program and put bulky ground radar units to use in the defense of Britain during 1940. These units detected German aircraft before the enemy reached the British Isles. Britain developed a lighter unit for airborne use. Radar was particularly effective in bombers and night fighters. The equipment improved navigation as well as targeting techniques. In 1940 Germany, too, installed defensive radar. Soon most countries used both ground and airborne radar, which was continually being improved under the pressure of war.

Historical Note

During the Battle of Britain, British Prime Minister Winston Churchill gave credit to the Royal Air Force:

"The gratitude of every home in our Island, in our Empire, and indeed throughout the world, except in the abodes of the guilty, goes out to the British airmen who, undaunted by odds, unwearied in their constant challenge and mortal danger, are turning the tide of the world war by their prowess and by their devotion. Never in the field of human conflict was so much owed by so many to so few. All hearts go out to the fighter pilots, whose brilliant actions we see with our own eyes day after day; but we must never forget that all the time, night after night, month after month, our bomber squadrons travel far into Germany, find their targets in the darkness by the highest navigational skill, aim their attacks, often under the heaviest fire, often with serious loss, with deliberate and careful discrimination, and inflict shattering blows upon the whole of the technical and war-making structure of the Nazi power. On no part of the Royal Air Force does the weight of the war fall more heavily than on the daylight bombers who will play an invaluable part in the case of invasion and whose unflinching zeal it has been necessary in the meanwhile on numerous occasions to restrain."

Winston S. Churchill, 20 August 1940, in *Parliamentary Debates*, 5th series, volume 364 (1940), as quoted in *Aspects of Western Civilization, Problems and Sources in History*, edited by Perry M. Rogers (1988; 3rd edition, Saddle River, NJ: Prentice Hall, 1997).

Winston S. Churchill (left)

Germany realized that its Luftwaffe alone could not destroy the Royal Air Force and, with that Air Force defending Britain, no safe invasion could be achieved. So in October 1940 Germany decided to postpone the invasion of Great Britain, but Germany continued air raids on British cities into 1941. Britain thus won this battle, but the losses were high on both sides. Britain lost about 900 airplanes and over 400 airmen, and Germany lost 1,700 planes. During this phase of the war, Britain fought alone, for Poland, Belgium, France, Norway, and other countries had fallen, and the United States remained officially neutral though sympathetic to the Allied cause.

Battle of the Atlantic

The maritime battle of the Atlantic began when the war started in 1939. That September, German submarines sank the British passenger liner *Athenia,* the British aircraft carrier *Courageous,* and 41 merchant ships. In October a single submarine, the U-47, snuck into Scapa Flow basin in the Orkney Islands and sank the British battleship *Royal Oak.* The U designating U-boats was for *unterseeboot,* undersea-boat or submarine. Germans called their submarines sea wolves, and they often traveled in packs. The submarines fought an unrestricted war; that is, they targeted all enemy vessels, not simply warships. The Battle of the Atlantic was over supply routes in the Atlantic Ocean and adjoining Caribbean Sea and northern European waters. The Germans used mines, airplanes, and warships, as well as submarines, to interfere with the shipping that supplied Britain's economy and military. The British responded with warships, aircraft patrols, and torpedo bombers.

The British had few submarines when the war began because the Admiralty had placed reliance upon asdic which was a device developed by the Allied Submarine Detection Investigation Committee late in World War I. The United States called their device sonar. Asdic still had technical difficulties early in World War II. To escape asdic or sonar detection, submarines operated mostly at the surface after dark; danger of visual detection existed during daylight. The German submarines wreaked havoc on Allied shipping between 1939 and 1941. Developing anti-submarine aircraft became an Allied priority.

Germany's most powerful battleship was the new *Bismarck,* launched in 1939. A British reconnaissance plane, a Spitfire, photographed the *Bismarck* in the Norwegian fjord of Grimstad in May 1941. On the 24th of that month the famous old British warship the *Hood* engaged the *Bismarck.* The *Hood* lost. Only three of its crew survived; 1,416 men died. The next day British Swordfish torpedo bombers flew off the carrier *Victorious* against the *Bismarck.* These fabric-covered biplanes flew more than a hundred miles to the target. *Bismarck's* anti-aircraft guns repelled the assault, but all the planes returned to the *Victorious.* On the 26th a British Catalina spotted the German battleship. Swordfish bombers from the *Ark Royal* attacked the *Bismarck* with torpedoes. Anti-aircraft shells tore the fabric planes, but the aircraft remained intact. Swordfish were not invincible, and all the torpedo bombers that attacked two German battleships on 12 February 1942 were shot down. On the 26th of May 1941, however, the Swordfish launched two torpedoes that struck the *Bismarck.* One hit the steering engine room and jammed the rudders. Unable to maneuver, the *Bismarck* was incapacitated while British battleships and cruisers closed in for the kill. The *Bismarck* sank on the 27th; 110 of the more than 2,000 crew members survived. (Figure 7-6)

Figure 7-6. A broadside view of the 35,000-ton German battleship *Bismarck.* Air power helped sink her on 27 May 1941.

Aircraft thus participated in a significant manner in the major surface conflict of the Battle of the Atlantic. After that, submarines dominated German strategy in the Atlantic, and Germany used over 1,000 submarines during the war.

U.S. Neutrality

The United States was not initially a combatant in World War II, as there were many isolationists in the country opposed to any entanglement in Europe. The isolationists argued that World War I would have been merely a European war if other nations had stayed out of European affairs. President Franklin D.

Roosevelt and others in the country wanted to oppose the aggression of Germany in Europe, Italy in Africa, and Japan in the Pacific; they wanted to intervene without going to war. Congress passed neutrality acts to keep the United States out of combat. This was the popular position of the day. Nonetheless, the United States started preparing for war and increasing production of military goods, especially to fill orders from France and Britain. The United States also created a Civilian Pilot Training Program, planned to defend the hemisphere, raised the number of recruits in the armed forces, and even initiated a peacetime draft. (Figure 7-7)

Figure 7-7. Republic P-47s in assembly for the war in Europe.

The neutrality was partial. The objective was to aid Allies fighting the Axis Powers, particularly Nazi Germany, without being drawn into the war. Initially, the United States sold war materials to France and Britain on a cash-and-carry basis. At the same time the United States built up its military preparedness. Italy joined the war on the side of Germany in June 1940, and France fell that month. As the war continued through 1940, Britain began to run short of cash needed to buy American-made airplanes, airplane engines, munitions, and other supplies. The United States adopted a policy of "all aid short of war." That included the Destroyers-Bases Agreement of September 1940 whereby the United States traded destroyers to Britain in exchange for 99-year leases on bases in the Caribbean and Newfoundland.

Britain requested more equipment on a credit basis. In a fireside-chat radio broadcast to the American people and later in a message to Congress, President Roosevelt proposed that the neutral United States become an "arsenal of democracy" by lending and leasing supplies to Great Britain. This proposal quickly became the Lend-Lease Act of 1941. This

act represented a shift of American public opinion from the isolationism of 1939 to an undeclared war in 1941.

Lend-Lease Act

The Lend-Lease Act of 1941 permitted the United States to lend or lease supplies to allies fighting aggression. Passed in March, the act intended weapons and supplies to go particularly to Great Britain but allowed shipments to any country whose defense was "vital" to the interests of the United States. Under the Lend-Lease Act, payment could be in kind, in property, or in any benefit accepted by the United States, and payment could be deferred to a later date. In secrecy, the United States had already

Historic Event

On 11 March 1941 the United States Congress passed the Lend-Lease Act in order to assist the Allies in fighting fascist regimes in Europe. This act authorized the country to provide supplies to any foreign country deemed "vital to the defense of the United States."

begun to construct bases for Britain in Scotland. United States supplies were to help Britain fight the Battle of Britain; that is, to prevent Germany from capturing Britain. Supplies went to Great Britain by convoy and by ferrying. Developed by the British as a strategic means of air transport, ferrying entailed delivering aircraft under the aircraft's own power.

The United States provided over 46 billion dollars in Lend-Lease aid to the Allies during the war. Great Britain received the most: 69% of the total. The Soviet Union received 15% — billions of dollars in aid. Thirty-one other nations received lesser amounts of aid.

National Defense

National defense measures affected all aviation in the United States. New Deal programs of the 1930s, like the Civil Works Administration, the Public Works Administration, and the Works Progress Administration, had provided funds for the construction of airports, emergency landing fields, radio ranges, course lights, and rotating light beacons that served the nation through the war. Before the United States joined the conflict in Europe, the Civil Aeronautics Authority (later Administration), the Works Projects Administration, and other agencies sponsored further development of these aviation resources in the name of national defense. This aviation infrastructure supported transport and training during the war. (Figure 7-8)

Figure 7-8. The United States preparation for war included building the aviation infrastructure through construction of airports and navigation aids.

In 1940 Congress approved the massive Development of Landing Areas for National Defense that provided construction funds for 535 airports nationwide. In conjunction with this program, the Civil Aeronautics Administration changed the system for numbering runways. Before the change, runways had been numbered consecutively from the number one, starting at the northerly most runway and proceeding counterclockwise. Introduced in the summer of 1941, the new numbering system indicated the magnetic heading (with the last zero omitted) of takeoffs and landings on a particular runway.

For defense purposes, the Civil Aeronautics Administration assumed operation of airport traffic control in 1941 and extended air traffic control to all airways in 1942. With the extension of en route air traffic control to all airways, the agency expanded its flight advisory service beyond airlines to all pilots flying the airways. These defense measures — airport construction, airport traffic control, airway traffic control, and flight advisory service — became permanent operations of the federal civil agency.

Spreading War

Hitler formulated war strategy as he went along. The invasion of Poland in 1939 was a rousing success. There followed a lull as he decided on the next move. The fall of France in 1940 was another success, followed by another lull before the Battle of Britain. The British, aided by supplies from the United States, fought back. At times the Luftwaffe was not only matched in the skies, but also sometimes beaten. Even Germany's ally, Italy suffered defeats in Africa. Hitler's solution was to turn east.

Hitler thought that invading and defeating the Soviet Union would so strengthen Japan, the Soviets' competitor in Asia, that the United States would be unable to join the war in Europe. That would leave Great Britain alone in the fight against Germany and, therefore, Germany would be able to defeat Britain. He timed the invasion for the spring of 1941 so that the war could be fought during favorable weather. He simply ignored his August 1939 non-aggression pact with Joseph Stalin and the Soviet government.

Operation Barbarossa

On Sunday 22 June 1941 Radio Moscow announced,

> "At four o'clock this morning, without declaration of war and without any claims being made on the Soviet Union, German troops attacked our frontier in many places and bombed from the air Zhitomir, Kiev, Sebastopol, and Kaunus. This unheard of attack on our country is an unparalleled act of perfidy in the history of civilized nations."

Germany had in fact attacked the Soviet Union all along the line from the Baltic Sea in the north to the Black Sea in the south. This was Germany's Operation Barbarossa. Germany planned to overrun the Soviet Union in a *blitzkrieg* ten-week summer campaign. Up until the attack, the Soviets were shipping grain, petroleum, and ores to Germany.

Historic Event

On 22 June 1941 Germany attacked the Soviet Union. This was Operation Barbarossa, an invasion opened by German air and ground troops. Germany had a non-aggression pact with the Soviet Union that this invasion violated. The attack brought the Red Air Force into combat with the Luftwaffe on Germany's Eastern Front.

The surprise attacks on Soviet airfields destroyed many Soviet planes on the ground and achieved immediate air superiority. The Soviet fighter planes were concentrated at a few airfields as the Soviet Union was in the process of building new fields with longer runways for its newest planes. The Soviet pilots who made it into the air were no match for the Germans. They did, however, slow down the

Figure 7-9. The Soviet Air Force flew aircraft such as this I-16 fighter plane. During the first days of Operation Barbarossa, they lost many of these aircraft.

Germans, which gave the Soviets time to dismantle and move aircraft factories away from the advancing Germans. (Figure 7-9)

The Soviets had counted over 500 German flights into Soviet territory prior to the invasion, flights later known to have been reconnaissance for the invasion. Not wanting to offend Adolf Hitler, the Soviet Union had not responded to the reconnaissance flights. Even to the invasion, the Soviets initially responded politically rather than militarily in hopes Germany might withdraw. For two months German forces pushed the Eastern Front eastward.

The initial invasion was a disaster for the Soviet Union, which lost 2,000 aircraft in two days! The losses mounted. The commander of a bomber unit that lost over 500 planes committed suicide, and an air general in the northwest was convicted of treason for having been defeated by German forces. By November, however, the German's lack of a clear objective within the Soviet Union hampered

German soldiers in Russia

operations. The northern arm of the German forces had surrounded Leningrad and stalled there. A central drive had reached within twenty-five miles of Moscow and stalled. The southern assault captured the Crimea.

Like Napoleon's troops in an earlier century, the Germans froze with the Russian winter of 1941. The Germans had entered the Soviet Union blitzkrieg-style, but the forces lacked clear objectives and were disoriented by the Soviet's lack of a coordinated defense. By the time the Germans gained focus, so had the Soviets.

Most of the Red Air Force had been destroyed during the early months of fighting, but the bombers at bases away from the frontier survived. The Soviets acquired airplanes and other supplies from Allies who adamantly wanted the Soviets to keep fighting on Germany's second front, and the Soviets rushed men and, starting in late 1941, women through aviation training and to the front.

Ferry Routes

With Germany as the common enemy, the Soviet Union and the United States became "cautious allies" in an alliance held together by Lend-Lease. Lend-Lease deliveries to this new ally became a high priority. In March 1942, for example, President Roosevelt had requested that all Lend-Lease material for the Soviet Union "be released for shipment at the earliest possible date regardless of the effect of these shipments on any part of our war program." The Soviet fighting presence prevented Germany from transferring troops from the Eastern Front to assault England or to enter the Pacific conflict. Until the invasion of Normandy in June 1944, the war in Europe was fought by the Soviets on Germany's Eastern Front and by strategic bombing groups flying from England against German targets. Under Lend-Lease, the United States supplied the Soviet forces as well as the British.

The United States used several routes to transport Lend-Lease goods to the Soviet Union. North Atlantic convoys carried equipment for complete rolling mills, tire plants, and petroleum refineries, as well as railroad locomotives, trucks, cars, airplanes, munitions, and other supplies to the northern Soviet ports of Murmansk, Archangel, and Molotovsk. The losses were high. Over twenty percent of the cargo shipped over the North Atlantic route was lost to German aerial and surface attacks, submarines, or weather. The busiest shipping route, in terms of tonnage, was the North Pacific shipping route to Vladivostok on the Sea of Japan, but no armaments could go through Japanese waters per a Soviet neutrality agreement with Japan. (Figure 7-10)

Figure 7-10. An East Coast naval convoy comprising 24 merchants, mostly colliers, steaming in the North Sea.

Lend-Lease goods also traveled to the Soviet Union via the Persian Gulf and overland through Iran. To reach the Persian Gulf, goods went by ship around the southern tip of Africa; or by ship to the Gold Coast of Africa and then by air across that continent and on to the Gulf. After the Allies secured the Mediterranean Sea, material was shipped through the Mediterranean and the Suez Canal. When opening this Persian route, the United States initially used British facilities in Basra, Iraq. Later in 1942 the United States opened and operated an aircraft assembly plant in Abadan, Iran. This Abadan facility closed in 1944 when the United States decided to transfer all Lend-Lease aircraft bound for the Soviet Union via Alaska. Most Lend-Lease supplies and equipment went to the Soviet Union by sea, but the urgent materiels went by air — mostly from the Great Falls Army Air Base across Canada and into Alaska (the Northwest Staging Route) and from Fairbanks, Alaska, across Siberia (the Alaska-Siberia Route, ALSIB).

Great Falls personnel ferried airplanes, materiel, and other goods — free from the threat of German attack, but subject to Japanese threat and northern weather. The United States delivered 14,000 Lend-Lease aircraft to the Soviet Union, more than half via the Alaska-Siberia air route with its staging base in Great Falls, Montana.

A Pacific War

After years of fighting the Chinese in a campaign to conquer that land, Japan attacked United States and British territories in the Pacific region. One target was the United States naval fleet at Pearl Harbor, Hawaii. The Japanese sent a task force of 31 vessels, including six aircraft carriers, toward Pearl Harbor. The 432 Japanese planes on board the carriers included fighters, dive-bombers, level-bombers, and torpedo planes. On the morning of the attack a mobile radar unit in Hawaii detected the incoming aircraft, but the newness of radar technology and the possibility that the aircraft were American prompted the watch officer to ignore the warning. The Japanese thus struck without warning. (Figure 7-11)

Figure 7-11. Japanese photograph taken during the 7 December 1941 attack on Pearl Harbor. In the distance, the smoke rises from Hickam Field.

President Franklin D. Roosevelt responded with his famous war message:

> "Yesterday, December 7, 1941 — a date which will live in infamy — the United States of America was suddenly and deliberately attacked by naval and air forces of the Empire of Japan.
>
> . . .
>
> "The attack yesterday on the Hawaiian Islands has caused severe damage to American naval and military forces. Very many American lives have been lost. . . .
>
> "Yesterday the Japanese Government also launched an attack against Malaya.
>
> "Last night Japanese forces attacked Hong Kong.

"Last night Japanese forces attacked Guam.

"Last night Japanese forces attacked the Philippine Islands.

"Last night the Japanese attacked Wake Island.

"This morning the Japanese attacked Midway Island.

"Japan has, therefore, undertaken a surprise offensive extending throughout the Pacific area.

. . .

"Hostilities exist. . . .

. . .

"I ask that the Congress declare that since the unprovoked and dastardly attack by Japan on Sunday, December seventh, a state of war has existed between the United States and the Japanese Empire."

USS *Shaw* exploding at Pearl Harbor 7 December 1941.

Historical Note

Japan's multiple attacks happened on December 7 and 8, yet almost concurrently, because the International Dateline divides the places attacked in that massive offensive around the Pacific and in Asia.

Congress complied. The United States was at war with Japan. Japan had two European allies, Germany and Italy; the three had signed a military alliance pact in Berlin in September 1940. Several days after Japan attacked Pearl Harbor, its allies declared war on the United States, so the United States was suddenly at war in Europe as well as in the Pacific — as was Great Britain and the British Empire. The world was at war — again.

Training

Training began as war preparedness programs, but as more and more nations joined the conflicts around the world, the training became specific to the military needs on various fronts. Military forces expanded existing training programs. The United States Army, for example, built over fifty air bases to train airmen and aircrews in the Rocky Mountain region. This region had available land and open spaces, people, and politicians eager for defense investments, generally good flying weather, aerial crossroads suitable for the wartime emergency, inland location (assumed safe from air raids and invasion), and dispersal (protection against a single attack destroying too much air power). The Civilian Pilot Training Program (CPT) was one training program that shed its civil disguise and became explicitly military under the new name War Training Service.

Civilian Pilot Training

In anticipation of war, Congress had passed the Civilian Pilot Training Act of 1939, and President Roosevelt created the Civil Air Patrol in late 1941. Through these programs civilians received flight instruction and opportunities to fly despite wartime restrictions on private flying. The Civilian Pilot Training Program and its successor the War Training Service contracted with many colleges and universities to train civilian pilots. These schools provided classroom instruction while local flying schools provided the flight instruction. At the same time, many of these schools were training students in an Army Air Force Training Command program, in Army Specialized Training Units, the Navy's V-12 officer training program, and other military programs. (Figure 7-12)

Figure 7-12. A Craig Field Cadet in the Advanced Flying School climbing into the cockpit of his training ship, Selma, Alabama.

The Civil Aeronautics Administration also offered a non-college component to the Civilian Pilot Training Program/War Training Service. In communities with neither a college or university, the local flight school sometimes provided both ground and flight instruction. In some communities, the local high schools obtained contracts to provide the classroom instruction for civilian student pilots and adult students. The high schools then hired local pilots to give the flight instruction. The Civilian Pilot/War Training programs were separate from the high schools' normal programs, though there was one experimental program whereby 21 high schools enrolled their own students in Civilian Pilot Training, but this experiment was never repeated. As was expected during the war, the new pilots enlisted after completing civilian flight training. The Army Air Forces provided additional training in aerobatics and simulated instrument training, as well as flight training in the respective military aircraft the pilots would be assigned to fly.

As part of the Civilian Pilot Training Program, psychologists participated in a Standard Testing Program conducted in association with the National Research Council's Committee on Selection and Training of Aircraft Pilots. The committee experimented with a variety of tests used for pilot selection, developed "patter" or talk for the flight instructor to use in flight with a student pilot, and evaluated pilot performance. In general, the committee encouraged, organized, and coordinated research in aviation psychology.

From its establishment in 1939 through the end of the war, the Civilian Pilot Training Program and War Training Service trained over 375,000 people. It was a financial boon to campuses and fixed-base operators across the country. The civilian training relieved the Army Air Corps and later the Army Air Forces from conducting basic ground and flight training. The War Training Service also trained Army and Navy reservists during the war. Some civilian graduates joined the Army and others the Navy, but some remained civilian pilots.

Commonwealth Air Training

The British also started a training program as the war began. Called the British Commonwealth Air Training Plan, this program established 107 training centers in Canada. The first opened in the summer of 1940. Located from Vancouver in the west to Charlottetown in the east, these centers trained aircrews of recruits from Australia, Great Britain, and New Zealand, as well as Canada. More than 130,000 students graduated from this Commonwealth program;

another 5,000 British airmen received their training in Canadian Royal Air Force schools. Of the 49,808 pilots who graduated from the Commonwealth Air Training program, over 25,000 flew for the Royal Canadian Air Force, over 17,000 for the British Royal Air Force and Fleet Air Arm, over 4,000 with the Royal Australian Air Force, and over 2,000 with the Royal New Zealand Air Force. The other graduates were navigators, bombers, wireless operators, gunners, and flight engineers.

Tuskegee Airmen

As the United States mobilized and prepared for war, on 19 July 1941 twelve African-American aviation cadets and one African-American officer reported to the Tuskegee Army Air Field, Alabama, for flight training. These men received ground instruction at the nearby Tuskegee Institute. Primary flight instruction utilized PT-17 primary trainers at the new Moton Field at Tuskegee. Basic training used BT-13 basic trainers at the Tuskegee Army Air Field. Maxwell Field and Gunter Field were used for night flights. Advanced flight training employed AT-6 advanced trainers at the Tuskegee Army field as well as at Dale Mabry Field in Tallahassee, Florida. The first class of African-American airmen — minus eight "washouts" — graduated from Tuskegee and received wings on 7 March 1942. Lemuel Custis, Benjamin O. Davis, Charles DeBow, George Roberts, and Mac Ross thereby became the first African-American pilots in the United States Army Air Forces. (Figure 7-13)

Figure 7-13. Lt. Col. Benjamin Davis, on wing, giving pointers to Lt. Charles W. Dryden.

Historic Event

The first class of African-American airmen graduated from Tuskegee and received wings on 7 March 1942. These five men were the first African-American pilots in the United States Army Air Forces: The photograph shows (left to right) Roberts, Davis, DeBow, Lieutenant R.M. Long (advanced flight instructor), Ross, and Curtis.

• Lemuel Custis

• Benjamin O. Davis

• Charles DeBow

• George Roberts

• Mac Ross

The Tuskegee-trained African-American aviators, air crew, and ground support personnel became known as the Tuskegee Airmen. Their training and wartime service took place under the Army's "separate but equal" policy that kept black aviators segregated from white fliers and black units in conditions unequal to those of white units. This policy led to the Tuskegee Airmen's nickname "Lonely Eagles."

During the war the Army opened another training center for black airmen at Walterboro Air Base in South Carolina. Replacements in the all-black combat units came from Walterboro or Tuskegee. African-American airmen also served in the 477th Bombardment Group, but that group had not reached combat readiness by the end of the war and thus did not go overseas. An all-black paratroop unit formed and trained during the war. Known as the Triple

Historical Note

The Tuskegee Airmen trained and served under the Army's "separate but equal" policy that kept black aviators segregated from white fliers and black units in conditions unequal to those of white units.

After the war, on 26 July 1948, President Harry S. Truman signed an executive order that desegregated and integrated the American military forces, including the new independent Air Force.

Nickles or simply the Nickles, this 555th Battalion of the 82nd Airborne was sent to jump fires out West rather than to fight enemy forces overseas.

Soviet Women Pilots

As Operation Barbarossa continued, the Soviets realized their need for pilots and ground crews exceeded the available number of men. Marina Raskova organized female flying regiments to supplement the male forces and to fight alongside them in the air war against the German invaders. She was a Hero of the Soviet Union, a distinction earned for a long-distance flight by an all-female crew. She recruited female pilots for combat duty as pilots and navigators as well as female crews for ground duties. Many of the recruits had learned to fly in local flying clubs, and some had given flight instruction at those clubs. To be accepted for military pilot training, a woman needed to have already logged at least 500 hours in flight.

Military flight training for the women began at Engels, beside the Volga River, hundreds of miles north of Stalingrad. A thousand women were in the first training group under the command of Major Raskova and her assistant Major Yevdokia Bershanskaya, a former civilian airline pilot. The pilots-in-training took ground instruction and flying lessons up to 14 hours a day. Like the male programs, the female training program was compressed into six months in order to get crews to the front quickly. Women destined for ground crews also spent long days learning their assignments. Most of the instructors

Figure 7-14. Female bomber pilots of the Soviet Union standing in front of a PO-2 trainer.

were male for the first class of female students; some of the instructors had acquired combat experience in the Spanish Civil War or the Winter War against Finland.

The primary trainers were the U-2 trainers, better known by the later designation PO-2. This biplane, designed by Nikolai Polikarpov and his design team, remained in production from 1930 until 1945 (and remained in service until 1962). Many Soviet flying clubs had used the PO-2 before the war. In these planes the students practiced flying, navigating, and bombing. They were training to join all-female fighter and bomber regiments.

Would-be fighter pilots flew the Yak-1 in advanced training; Alexander Yakovlev and his staff designed this single-seat, low-wing fighter; thus the Yak designation. The powerplant included a 1,100-horsepower, 12-cylinder, liquid-cooled V-type engine and a three-bladed, constant-speed, metal propeller.

Flight Lines

"To fly a combat mission is not a trip under the moon. Every attack, every bombing is a dance with death."

Soviet bomber pilot Serafima Amsova-Tararenko as translated and quoted in Anne Noggle, *A Dance with Death, Soviet Airwomen in World War II* (College Station: Texas A&M University Press, 1994). Amsova-Tararenko served in the all-female 588th Night Bomber Regiment.

The women selected for bomber duty trained in old PO-2s converted to night bombers or in newer Pe-2s, which were low-wing dive bombers. The Pe-2 was designed by V.M. Petlyakov and powered by two 1,100-horsepower, liquid-cooled V-type engines. Soviet factories produced over 11,000 Pe-2s for use mainly as tactical bombers during the war.

These three planes — Yak-1, PO-2, and PE-2 — were the aircraft the women's regiments flew into combat after they finished training in May 1942.

The women joined three all-female regiments: the 586th Fighter Regiment equipped with Yak-1s, the 587th Bomber Regiment equipped with PE-2s, and the 588th Night Bomber Regiment (later the 46th Guards Regiment) equipped with PO-2s. These regiments remained intact and in combat throughout the war in Europe. After training the initial recruits, Colonel Yevdokia Bershanskaya took command of the night bombers. Marina Raskova, the woman who organized the program, died in a crash while leading the 587th Dive Bomber Regiment on a mission in 1943. Fighter pilot Lilya Litvak became known as the Rose of Stalingrad, where she flew sorties. She shot down 12 German planes and became the Soviet's top female ace of the war. She died in the air battle over Orel in 1943. Navigator Galina Markova was one of many female fliers who won the Hero of the Soviet Union Award; she was in the day bomber regiment. (Figure 7-15)

Figure 7-15. The Soviet women flew PE-2s into combat after finishing training.

The three female regiments flew more than 30,000 combat sorties during the war. In addition, some Soviet women served in regular Red Air Force male units. Senior Lieutenant Anna Timofeyeva-Yegorova, for example, became a Hero of the Soviet Union while serving as pilot with the 805th Ground Attack Regiment; she flew Ilyushin Sturmovik Il-2 aircraft. Soviet women were the only women who were assigned to regular combat duties during World War II.

WASPs, WAVEs, etc.

Women in the United States also wanted to serve their country during time of war. Some served in the Air WAACs, that is, the Women's Army Auxiliary Corps air arm, as instructors, mechanics, and radio operators. Some women also served in the Aircraft Warning Service. In 1943 the auxiliary Air WAAC became the military Air WACs, Women's Army Corps air arm. The naval WAVES — Women Appointed (later Accepted) for Volunteer Emergency Service — trained women in many aviation billets; a billet is a naval term for job. WAVES thus served as tower operators, aviation ordnance personnel, aerological engineers, gunnery instructors, aviation machinist's mates, parachute riggers, and radio operators. They did not fly aircraft.

Women wanting to be service pilots joined the Women's Flying Training Detachment (nicknamed "woofteds" after the abbreviation WFTD), the Women's Auxiliary Ferry Squadron (WAFS) , and their successor organization the Women Airforce Service Pilots (WASPs). During the war the female pilots ferried aircraft from factories to military bases, flew transport flights, towed aerial targets for practice exercises, tested aircraft in flight, and provided flight instruction to student pilots, male and female. Organized by veteran flier Jacqueline Cochran, the WASP pilots flew every type of airplane in service during the war. (Figure 7-16)

Of the 1,074 women who graduated from the WASP training program, 38 died due to accidents; their accident and fatality rates were comparable to male pilots in similar assignments. They served in support, not combat, roles. They relieved men for assignment to combat zones. In her autobiography, Cochran voiced a common but not universal sentiment of women who served: "My inability to so fight in the last war was my greatest disappointment."

Figure 7-16.
Jacqueline Cochran organized the Women Airforce Service Pilots (WASPs) during WWII.

MILITARY R&D AND PRODUCTION

World War II ended the flying boat era by stimulating development of transport landplanes and by encouraging the construction of landplane fields. The United States Navy used blimps as coastal reconnaissance aircraft during the war. It had the only lighter-than-air fleet of World War II, because firepower made the craft obsolete in combat. The war also ended the autogiro era by supporting the development of helicopters. Helicopters, jets, and rockets were new aircraft employed during the war, but they remained under development throughout the war and had little impact on the outcome of the war.

Helicopters

The helicopter was a European invention of the 1930s. There was no one single inventor as various individuals and groups simultaneously developed the technology. Various European prototypes flew in the 1930s, notably the Breguet Gyroplane that stayed in the air for more than one hour in 1936 and the Focke-Achgelis Fa 61 dual-rotor helicopter that first flew in 1936 — for 28 seconds! The Nazi Party in Germany touted the Fa 61 as evidence of Germany's technological superiority, but German technological resources were diverted from helicopter development during the war. The Focke-Achgelis Fa 223, first flown in 1940, was the world's first production helicopter, but it was not produced in large quantities. Germany even experimented with a rotor-kite autogiro for observation of submarines. Anton Flettner in Germany developed canted intermeshing rotors. (Figure 7-17)

Despite its European origin, the helicopter was made practical and was produced in quantity in the United States in the 1940s. Its development and production was accelerated by the wartime emergency. Several designers in the United States developed helicopters of their own designs that incorporated scientific and technical advances from the international development of the technology. Igor Sikorsky not only developed helicopters, but also placed helicopters into volume production during the war. Sikorsky utilized a single main rotor over the fuselage and a small anti-torque rotor attached to the tail. Germany and most of Europe were literally in the midst of the war when the United States, not yet a combatant nation, assumed the lead in helicopter technology.

Federal Aid

The promise of federal funds encouraged helicopter design in the United States. The initial promise came in the 1938 Dorsey Bill (House of Representatives 8143, Public Law 787, but commonly referred to by the name of the congressman who introduced the legislation, J.G. Dorsey). The Dorsey Bill intended to support the development of autogiros, but military and civil customers wanted an aircraft with more capabilities and the money went to helicopter research and development. In response to the Dorsey Bill, in early 1940 the United States Army issued helicopter specifications drafted by an autogiro pilot, Captain H. Franklin Gregory, even though the country had no helicopters or helicopter pilots. The prospect of government contracts, particularly military production contracts, also inspired private and corporate investment in helicopter research and development. Based on the autogiro's limited success, there was speculation about personal helicopters too.

Figure 7-17. German helicopter designed by Heinrich Focke.

Historical Note

In the 1930s autogiro makers in the United States built about 300 autogiros. An autogiro uses the vertical rotor for lift and an airplane powerplant for thrust. In contrast, the helicopter uses the vertical rotor or rotors for both lift and thrust.

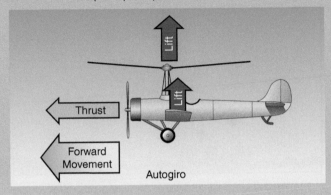

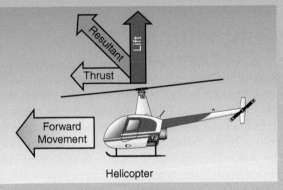

Sikorsky Helicopter

Russian émigré Igor I. Sikorsky built two helicopters in Russia before that nation's revolution prompted him to leave — neither helicopter flew. In France briefly and in the United States thereafter, Sikorsky designed fixed-wing aircraft in the teens, twenties, and thirties. In the 1930s he turned his efforts again toward rotorcraft.

Sikorsky's experimental helicopter was the VS-300, VS for Vought-Sikorsky. Due to the declining market for Sikorsky amphibians and flying boats, the parent United Aircraft Corporation had merged its Sikorsky division with its Vought fighter division. Igor Sikorsky made his first "hop" in the VS-300 on 14 September 1939. The aircraft was tethered during early test flights to limit its height. Initially, the unstable craft had four landing wheels — two main-gear wheels under the body, one under the nose, and another under

Figure 7-18. Igor Sikorsky during test flight of his VS-300 helicopter.

the tail. The powerplant consisted of a 75-horsepower Lycoming air-cooled airplane engine and a three-bladed rotor. (Figure 7-18)

It flew without tether lines in May 1940, the same month Igor Sikorsky received the first helicopter pilot

Personal Profile

As a youth, Igor Ivanovich Sikorsky (1889-1972) read Jules Verne's *Clipper of the Clouds* and studied reproductions of Leonardo da Vinci's drawings of flying machines. Sikorsky received a technical education and began a prominent career in aviation in imperial Russia. That is where he became a pioneer in multi-engine aircraft — his first was the Grand in 1913. Later, in the United States, he became an industry leader in amphibious aircraft — most notably the S-38 used by airlines and explorers in the 1930s, also the larger S-42 and S-43 flying boats. He did not invent the helicopter, though he designed his own line of helicopters. On 14 September 1939 he made what he called his "first hop" in a helicopter, his prototype VS-300A. The VS was for Vought-Sikorsky, 300 for the design number, and A for the first version. Sikorsky became the "father of the helicopter" because he was the first to place helicopters into volume production, which he did during World War II.

Igor Ivanovich Sikorsky

license issued in the United States. In testing his design, he had taught himself to fly a helicopter — much as he had taught himself decades earlier to fly an airplane of his own design. In July the VS-300 remained aloft for 15 minutes, a new record for this experimental machine.

Competition

Sikorsky lost the competition for the first Army development contract under the Dorsey Bill. In 1940 the Army chose a design with twin-lateral rotors; that is, side-by-side rotors like those used on the German Fa 61 helicopter. Laurence LePage and Haviland Platt, the designers, called the design the Platt-LePage PL-3. The Army designated it XR-1, experimental rotary-wing number one. A 450-horsepower Pratt & Whitney radial engine powered the two rotors. Platt-LePage built and tested the aircraft, crashed it in July 1943, and rebuilt it as the XR-1A. The Army abandoned that program in April 1945 because by then other designs had proved more promising.

Autogiro makers Kellett and Pitcairn developed helicopter concepts during the war. Engineer Frank N. Piasecki successfully brought autogiro experience to the design of helicopters. He foresaw a market for personal helicopters and released a newsreel touting an *Air Flivver in Every Garage* (1943); the "flivver" being a reference to the once popular and affordable Ford Model T automobile. During the war Piasecki developed a large tandem-rotor helicopter intended for use by the Coast Guard in rescuing people from ships torpedoed by enemy submarines.

Inventor Arthur M. Young experimented with helicopter concepts, particularly those concerning stability. Young acquired the backing of Bell Aircraft, which built P-39 and P-63 fighters and B-29 bombers during the war and which was looking for a postwar civil product. A privately owned aircraft analogous to cars appealed to Lawrence D. Bell, founder and head of the company. The Bell Model 30 prototype first flew in 1943, but went into production after the war. (Figure 7-19)

Similarly, Hiller's XH-44 flew in 1944 and entered production later. It was the first helicopter with all-metal rotors. It had a coaxial configuration, like those designed by Louis Breguet in France. Entrepreneur Stanley Hiller, Jr. , focused on the business aspects of marketing personal and commercial helicopters after the war.

Sikorsky Development

The experimental VS-300 was continually being modified and improved: rotors of different sizes,

Figure 7-19. The Bell Model 30 was a one-seat, open-cockpit aircraft that could reach airspeeds of 100 mph.

different engines, changes in landing gear, temporary tail booms, and various trial mechanisms for controlling flight. In addition to the Army, the United States Coast Guard and the British Purchasing Commission for the Royal Air Force discussed their needs with Sikorsky engineers. These engineers discovered that a cyclic control problem was caused by gyroscopic precession that caused pilot commands to be 90° off; they corrected the problem by adding a tail rotor. Sikorsky retired the VS-300 in October 1943, after the aircraft had logged 102.5 hours in flight. By then the company had a new helicopter in development, one incorporating what was learned from the VS-300. This new aircraft was the Sikorsky VS-316, better known as the Army XR-4.

The XR-4 built in 1941 was a prototype of a planned production helicopter. It was a practical two-seat machine powered by a 165-horsepower Warner radial engine. In May 1942 a Sikorsky pilot flew the XR-4 from the plant in Connecticut to Wright Field in Ohio,

Flight Lines

"We had drifted across the street in the meantime and now the rear rotor was getting the additional lift from the west wind while the front rotor was shielded by some more trees, causing the nose to point downward. It felt like we were almost perpendicular to the ground but actually it was quite a bit less."

Frank Piasecki describing a demonstration flight of the XHRP-1 Dogship prototype before Navy officers in the spring of 1945, as quoted in Jay P. Spenser, *Whirlybirds, a History of the U.S. Helicopter Pioneers.*

Flight Lines

"The helicopter, in its present stage of development, has many of the advantages of the blimp and few of its disadvantages. It hovers and maneuvers with more facility in rough air than the blimp. It can land and take off in less space. It does not require a large ground handling crew. It does not need a large hangar. There is sufficient range (about two hours) in this particular model to make its use entirely practical for harbor patrol and other Coast Guard duties."

Commander W.A. Burton of the United States Coast Guard describing a demonstration of the XR-4, April 1942, as quoted in Jay P. Spenser, *Whirlybirds, a History of the U.S. Helicopter Pioneers.*

a distance of over 750 miles. Sikorsky engineers still struggled with vibration problems, but the wartime emergency and military funding accelerated development. Dynamically balancing the wooden rotor blades; that is, distributing the internal weight chordwise as well as root to tip, increased stability. This innovation came from competitor Frank Piasecki. Dynamic balancing gave each of the blades of a rotor the same weight, the same center of gravity, and the same center of lift. In 1943 the Sikorsky company built three YR-4As for evaluation by the Army, and Sikorsky began delivering 27 YR-4Bs for service testing. Even before the R-4B went into production, Sikorsky was developing its successor, the R-6, and a larger helicopter, the R-5. The XR-5 first flew in August 1943, and the XR-6 in October of that year.

Sikorsky Production

With production orders for the new product line in hand, Sikorsky separated from Vought and became again an independent division of United Aircraft. Sikorsky built the R-4s and R-5s in its Bridgeport, Connecticut, factory. Due to limited space in the Bridgeport factory, Sikorsky licensed R-6 production to Nash-Kelvinator in Detroit. Nash-Kelvinator built machines on a moving assembly line. Wartime production totaled over a hundred R-4s, 65 R-5s, and some R-6s. (Figure 7-20)

Most of the helicopters went to the United States Army. They used R-4Bs in the Aleutian Islands of the Alaska territory and R-6s in the China-Burma-India Theater of operations. Army helicopters flew rescue

missions, carried supplies from ships to islands, and completed radar calibration missions. Less interested in rotary-wing aircraft, the United States Navy acquired helicopters from the Army, including YR-4Bs (given naval designation HNS-1) and R-4Bs (RHS in naval terminology). The Navy used helicopters for rescue missions and coastal patrol. Some of the naval helicopters went to the Coast Guard, which was under the Navy during the war. The military services also used helicopters as training aircraft.

About 50 R-4Bs went to Great Britain. German "wolf packs" of U-boats (submarines) were attacking Lend-Lease supply routes across the Atlantic Ocean, and sinking supplies vital to Britain's interests. The British wanted to use helicopters to drop depth charges in anti-submarine warfare, but the light R-4Bs had difficulty operating from the pitching decks of ships at sea.

The first successful production of helicopters in volume earned Sikorsky the honorary title "father of the helicopter." That was a wartime achievement, and he was the only one who produced helicopters in quantity during World War II. That wartime production was military production. Sikorsky's wartime production exceeded in numbers the dozens of helicopters of several makes built in Germany during the war, like the Focke-Achgelis Fa 223. Similarly, Austrian wartime designs, like Baron Friedrich von Doblhoff's No. 1 jet-propelled and the piston-powered WN 342, were not produced in quantity.

Figure 7-20. Igor Sikorsky (left) and Orville Wright (right) in front of the Sikorsky R-4.

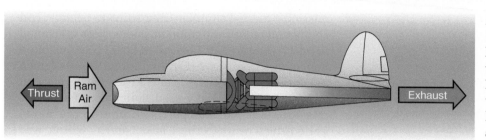

Figure 7-21. Ram air entering the gas turbine engine is compressed, then combined with fuel, and ignited. The exiting exhaust gases produce an opposite force called thrust.

Jets

Two men invented the jet engine — one in Germany and one in Britain. Each had his respective invention in hand prior to the war, and both spent the war developing the technology. Both were trained in science rather than experienced with the existing piston-engine technology. The aerodynamic thrust of a jet engine is an example of Newton's third law of motion: for every action there is an equal and opposite reaction. Rapidly expanding gases in the jet engine are directed rearward which, in turn, produces the forward thrust. The technological precursors of the jet engine were water turbines and steam turbines rather than aircraft piston engines. The jet aircraft engine was a new technology based on science. The science existed when the war started. The war spurred development of service engines. (Figure 7-21)

Frank Whittle

Frank Whittle joined Britain's Royal Air Force in 1923. He attended the Royal Air Force's academy at Cranwell where he wrote a thesis on *The Future*

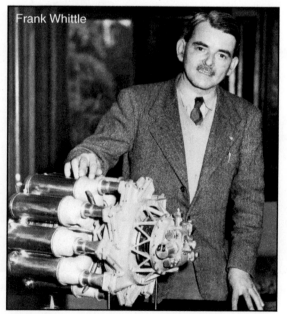

Frank Whittle

Developments in Aircraft Design (1928). That thesis contained his early thoughts on how a gas turbine engine might be built. His post-graduation assignment was as a test pilot, so he had little time to work on a research and development agenda, though he did patent one idea in 1930. He obtained private support and took a leave of absence from the military in order to work on the idea. He built a test model in 1937 and operated a jet engine in 1939. His design first powered an aircraft on 15 May 1941. This Whittle jet engine powered a Gloster E28/39. Whittle developed the technology through a company called PowerJets until the British Government nationalized the company in 1944. That year the Royal Air Force placed jet airplanes into service. (Figure 7-22)

Figure 7-22. Sir Frank Whittle (left), inventor of the first British jet engine with W. G. Carter (right), inventor of the first British jet plane next to the Gloster E28/39 which housed Whittle's engine.

Whittle's contemporary Alan Griffith at the Royal Aircraft Factory developed jet technology in the late 1920s too. He defined axial-flow technology. In 1939

BRITISH JET AIRCRAFT OF WORLD WAR II

Aircraft	Engine(s)	Date of First Jet Flight	Status 1945
Gloster F.9/40 Meteor	Halford H1	March 1943	Prototypes
Meteor I	Rolls Royce Welland I	January 1944	Operational
Meteor III	Derwent I	December 1944	Operational
de Havilland E.6/41	D. H. Goblin	September 1943	In
D. H. 100 Vampire			production

he joined Rolls-Royce and began actual development of gas turbine engines. The development was still in progress when the war ended. During the war the Royal Aircraft Factory built an experimental F.2 turbojet engine. The de Havilland company developed the Goblin which went into production but not squadron service before the war ended. At the time, Britain had the operational Gloster F.9/40 Meteor that had entered service in 1944. Rolls-Royce Welland I engines based on the Whittle design powered the Meteor. Britain also had the prototype de Havilland E.6/41 fighter, better known as the D.H. 100 Vampire with the prototype Goblin engine.

Hans von Ohain

Hans von Ohain in Germany came up with the idea for a continuous-cycle combustion engine in 1933 while a graduate student at Göttingen University. He won the backing of airplane-maker Ernst Heinkel, who wanted high-performance aircraft. Von Ohain built an experimental centrifugal compressor fueled by hydrogen. He then built a flight worthy engine that flew on 27 August 1939, just days before World War II started. Pilot Erich Warsitz flew the Heinkel HE 178 jet-powered airplane on its maiden flight, which lasted 15 minutes. Von Ohain continued to develop the jet engine, including the axial flow compressor, during the war. Herbert Wagner of the Junkers Aircraft Company and Helmut Schelp of the Deutsche Versuchsanstalt für Luftfahrtforschung (DVL, the German aerodynamic institute) also developed gas turbine technology within wartime Germany. Nazi politics interfered with this and other German research and development programs, yet Germany pushed jets into production.

During World War II Germany produced the most jet aircraft and put the most types of jet aircraft into service, and it did so while the war severed trade for strategic materials. The production includes twenty some Ohain HeS-8 and HeS-8A (designated the 001 by the German Air Ministry). In 1942 von Ohain directed development of the 011 engine. Junkers placed the Jumo 004 into mass production; this was the only German mass-produced jet engine of the war and the German engine that used the least strategic materials. Bavarian Motor Works (BMW) built some 003 engines that went into service aircraft, and Diamler-Benz initiated a jet-engine development program.

The German jet engines powered the Messerschmitt Me 262 fighter that first flew in 1942. The aircraft was a low-wing and all-metal plane capable of over 500 miles per hour. Two Junkers Jumo 004B engines powered the production version. Although Messerschmitt built about 1,400 Me 262s, only a couple hundred reached service. They flew fighter, bomber interception, and reconnaissance missions. The Arado Ar 234 bomber-reconnaissance plane was powered by either the Jumo 004 or the BMW 003 engines, one located in a pod below each wing. The plane went into production in 1944. Production of the Heinkel He 162 Volksjager (People's Fighter), powered by the BMW 003 engine, reached a total of only 116 aircraft during the war. Jet engines also powered prototype aircraft, including the Horten-Gotha Go 229 all-wing and no-tail fighter,

GERMAN JET AIRCRAFT OF WORLD WAR II

Aircraft	Engine(s)	Date of First Jet Flight	Status 1945
Messerschmitt Me 262	Junkers Jumo 004 & 004B	18 July 1942	Operational
Arado Ar 234	Jumo 004 & B.M.W. 003	mid 1943	Operational
Heinkel He 162 Volksjager	B.M.W. 003	6 December 1944	Operational
Horten-Gotha Go 220	Jumo 004C	—	Prototype
Junkers Ju 287	Jumo 004 & B.M.W. 003	1945	Prototype
Henschel Hs 132	B.M.W. 003	—	Prototype

Flight Lines

"A runway is never long enough! I was doing 80 m.p.h. when at last the tail rose, I could see, and the feeling of running your head against a wall in the dark was over. Now, with reduced air resistance, the speed increased quickly, soon passing the 120 m.p.h. mark and long before the end of the runway the plane rose gently off the ground.

"For the first time I was flying by jet propulsion! No engine vibration, no torque, and no lashing noise from the air-screw. Accompanied by a whistling sound, my jet shot through the air."

German officer Adolf Galland describing his first test flight of a tail-dragging experimental Messerschmitt Me 262 in May 1943, as translated and quoted in *The War, 1939-1945, a Documentary History*, edited by Desmond Flower and James Reeves (1960; New York: Da Capo Press, 1997).

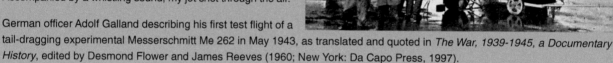

the Junkers Ju 287 heavy bomber, and Henschel Hs 132 dive bomber.

Technology Transfer

While von Ohain and Whittle pursued parallel paths without knowledge of each other, Britain transferred jet technology to its ally the United States. Whittle visited the United States and helped General Electric, a company with experience in steam turbines and not aircraft engines, become a jet-engine maker. General Electric began by copying the Whittle engine. The company also conducted internal studies of jet technology. The General Electric-made jet engine first flew on the Bell XP-59 in 1942, and the following year General Electric had jet engines in production. These were the I-14 and I-16 versions of the Whittle engine. General Electric also developed its own engine designs, the I-40 and TG-180. General Electric received Army contracts for its jet-engine program, whereas the Navy supported Westinghouse's development of a jet engine. (Figure 7-23)

The United States decided to withhold jet technology from aircraft-engine makers like Pratt & Whitney in order not to divert effort from wartime production of piston engines. In secret and at the company's own expense, Pratt & Whitney conducted gas turbine research during the war in order to protect its postwar interests, to have a jet product ready for the postwar market.

During the war the United States produced three reliable (for the time) jet airplanes, the first was the Bell P-59A Airacomet and the others were the Lockheed XP-80 and the McDonnell FD-1 Phantom. The Airacomet had first flown with General Electric engines in 1942; the XP-80 with a de Havilland Goblin engine in early 1944, and the XP-80A with a General Electric I-40 engine later that year, and the Phantom with two Westinghouse 19B engines in 1945. None of these jet aircraft had reached operational status when the war ended.

Figure 7-23. The first jet fighter used by the U. S. military, a Bell P-59A (front) flies alongside a P-63A prop fighter.

UNITED STATES JET AIRCRAFT OF WORLD WAR II			
Aircraft	Engine(s)	Date of First Jet Flight	Status 1945
Bell P-59A Airacomet	G.E. prototypes G.E. I-16	1 October 1942	Training
Lockheed XP-80 XP-80A	D.H. Goblin G.E. I-40(J-33)	9 January 1944	Developmental Developmental
McDonnel FD-1 Phantom	Westinghouse 19B	January 1945	Developmental

The French Société Rateau and Société Turbomeca initiated jet programs early in the war, but the fall of France halted French engine development until the Liberation. Similarly, jet engine development in other countries had neither achieved flight nor reached production by the end of the war.

Rockets

The leading developer of rockets during World War II was Wernher von Braun of Germany, who had been active in the Verein für Raumschiffahrt (VfR, the German Rocket Society) before the war. In 1937, in fact, von Braun and his colleagues had flown a Heinkel He 112 on rocket power alone. Helmuth Walter designed rocket engines for assisting takeoff during the early 1930s, and his engines powered the experimental rocket-powered Messerschmitt Me 163 Komet that achieved a speed of 623 miles per hour in October 1941. The Me 163 entered service in the summer of 1944 as an interceptor. The duration of its powered flight — 8 minutes — was too short for it to prove effective in combat. It was von Braun's work on the V-2 project at Peenemünde that made war news.

Peenemünde

Peenemünde was the German rocket research station near the Baltic Sea in northern Germany. Established in 1937, it was a rare example of effective coordination among military, industrial, and academic scientists in Nazi Germany; though it was reorganized several times during the war. When the German invasion of Russia stalled in late 1941, and when the United States joined the war in late 1941, Adolf Hitler faced the Soviet Union, the United States and Britain — three enemies instead of one. At this time Adolf Hitler committed more resources to Peenemünde, which at its peak employed 2,200 scientists and technicians.

Vengeance Weapons

During the war the Germans developed the revolutionary V-1 flying bomb, or cruise missile, and the long-range ballistic V-2 rocket, or guided missile. The V is for Vengeance weapon. The V-1 was a pilotless jet plane with a high-explosive warhead. It had a range of 150 miles. The V-1 first struck London in June 1944. There it became known as the buzz bomb or doodlebug. The air force's V-1 jet program competed

Personal Profile

Hanna Reitsch (1912-1979) was one of Germany's top pilots. She began flying gliders in the late 1920s and competed in glider contests in the 1930s. She became a test pilot at the German Institute for Glider Research. She test flew the huge Me-321 Gigant glider. She flew the Fa-61 helicopter inside a large auditorium in Berlin in 1938. She also flew airplanes and worked as Adolf Hitler's pilot for a while. During the war she flew acceptance trials of the Messerschmitt Me-163 Komet, a rocket-powered, short-range, single-seat intercept fighter. Reitsch also test flew a piloted version of the V-1 jet-powered plane. As a pilotless craft loaded with a warhead, the V-1 became known as a buzz bomb or doodlebug. She chronicled her career in aviation in her autobiography, published in English originally in 1955 as *The Sky My Kingdom* (reprinted, London: Greenhill Books, 1997).

Hanna Reitsch

Figure 7-24. The German V-1 flying bomb was a pilotless jet plane with an explosive warhead. Its most famous missions were attacks on London where it earned the name "buzz bomb."

for resources with the army's V-2 rocket project headed by von Braun. (Figure 7-24)

Historical Evidence

Military projects competed for resources during the war. In Germany in 1943, one V-2 rocket proponent argued:

"It is urgently necessary that A-4 [V-2] be given a higher priority than the radar program through an order of the Führer. This can be justified with the argument that the A-4 [V-2] has the character of an offensive weapon while radar is a part of the defense."

This writer knew that Adolf Hitler preferred offensive action over defensive.

The competition of the V-2 with the radar as well as with the V-1 jet project is discussed in Michael J. Neufeld, *The Rocket and the Reich, Peenemünde and the Coming of the Ballistic Missile Era* (New York: Free Press, 1995). Neufeld's book is a secondary source that uses and cites primary sources of information, like the above statement.

V-2

The V-2 was a rocket-propelled guided missile. It carried about 1650 pounds of explosives and had a range of approxiately 200 miles. The V-2 first struck London in September 1944, three months after the first V-1. Both "vengeance weapons" were too late to change the outcome of the war, but they produced great panic in Britain. (Figure 7-25)

Figure 7-25. The German V-2 rocket was a long-range ballistic missile. It also was used to attack London.

Radar

Radar was a weapon. It was a defensive weapon that evolved from an idea expressed by Robert Watson Watt in 1934 and from an echo displayed by Arnold Wilkins on a cathode ray tube in 1935. The idea was that radio waves could be used to detect airplanes in flight. The echo was the reflection of a radio signal off a Heyford bomber eight miles away from the British Broadcasting Company's transmitter at Daventry. This demonstrated that reflected radio waves could be used to detect and to determine the position of an object even in flight.

The British initially referred to this technology as reflected direction finding (RDF). The word radar came later; it was an American acronym for RAdio Direction And Ranging. But radar was largely a British invention. It was developed by British scientists like Watt and Wilkins, though personnel from Australia, Canada, New Zealand, and the United States participated in the development of the technology, and the Germans responded by developing radar too.

Great Britain developed radar in the 1930s and 1940s and placed it into operation in 1939. The experimental

Figure 7-26. British Navy radar station in the 1940s.

Chain, Home (CH) system and then more developed Home Chain equipment, including installations that could detect low and extra-low flying aircraft. Even the early experimental version of radar proved effective in the defense of the "homeland." It detected the *Graf Zeppelin II* LZ 130 on a spying mission over Britain in 1939, and it gave warning of German planes approaching Britain in 1940. (Figure 7-26)

Initially, radar was a ground-based system for detecting in-coming aircraft. Soon, however, Great Britain developed an airborne radar that helped nightfighter pilots detect aircraft in the darkness and helped bomber crews locate nighttime targets. Britain's Coastal Command also used radar to detect submarines.

The development of the two-way radiotelephone, that is the very high frequency (VHF) communications radio, enabled radar to be employed in **ground-controlled interception (GCI)**. Long-range radar equipment on the ground would first detect approaching aircraft and ground crew would plot the course. The failure of the aircraft to respond to a radio "identification, friend or foe" message would confirm the hostile identification. The radar station would relay the information to a ground-controlled interception station (which had shorter range capabilities, often 50 miles). This GCI station would accept tracking responsibility and would authorize nightfighters equipped with compact radar equipment to take flight. The GCI station would then track friend and foe and direct the friendly aircraft into position

close enough (within a few miles) for the airborne radar to home in on the enemy.

Development Projects

Research and development also increased the capabilities of aircraft during the war. Speed is an example. The fastest propeller-driven fighters of 1939 were in the 350 miles-per-hour class, like the Supermarine Spitfire MkI and the Messerschmitt Bf 109E-1. In 1945 the fastest propeller driven aircraft were in the 450 miles-per-hour class, like the improved Spitfire MkXIV and Bf 109K-4. Autopilot is another example. During the war, automatic flight control systems were installed in bombers, like the Consolidated B-24 Liberator, to lighten the pilot's workload while flying in tight formation. The pilot worked a "formation stick" rather than manipulating multiple controls.

The United States sponsored many research and development programs during the war. A National Inventor's Council processed suggestions from inventors throughout the country. The National Advisory Committee for Aeronautics employed scientists and technicians in laboratories and conducted wind tunnel experiments to improve the internal combustion engine for aircraft. The Naval Research Laboratory improved radar. The National Bureau of Standards worked on the proximity fuse. The Army Ordnance Corps developed rocket technology, and the Army

Corps of Engineers managed the Manhattan project that developed the atomic bomb.

Deicing

Deicing is an example of an existing technology improved to meet wartime needs. In aviation, icing conditions normally grounded aircraft, but wartime emergencies required flight into icing conditions. Before the war, icing conditions were usually managed by altering routes, canceling, or delaying flights. Wartime military pilots often had to fly regardless of conditions. Two major problem areas for the United States were Aleutian Islands and the Himalayan Mountains. Defending the United States territory of Alaska from attack by nearby Japan, Navy patrol boats in the Aleutian Islands were prone to icing. The United States ferried supplies from India over the Himalayan Hump to China. On that route, ice claimed up to nine aircraft in a single day. These specific problems, as well as the general problem that icing posed to aviation spurred research and development of deicing technology. (Figure 7-27)

Figure 7-27. PBY-5A Catalina on patrol for enemy activity in the Aleutian Islands, March 1943.

The National Advisory Committee for Aeronautics led the wartime research program in the United States. Engineer Lewis A. Rodert was head of the icing research program. The researchers explored pneumatic de-icing rubber boots that worked in limited conditions, but were not aerodynamically clean. B.F. Goodrich cooperated in an effort to improve pneumatic

de-icers, and the Army Air Force retrofitted B-24 bombers with pneumatic de-icers. Rodert's team also experimented with chemical de-icers, both alcohol-based fluids that lowered freezing temperatures and oil-based fluids that prevented ice from adhering to a surface. The British Royal Air Force preferred chemical solutions for raiding Germany via the ice-prone North Atlantic route. (Figure 7-28)

Figure 7-28. A B-24 Liberator with retrofitted pneumatic deicing boots along the leading edge of the wing and tail.

Rodert developed thermal de-icing, the application of heat to melt ice at the time of formation. The idea was not new, as the Germans had installed thermal de-icers on the Junkers Ju 88 and Dornier 217E in the late 1930s. During the war, Junkers used a series of heat exchangers on its military planes to melt ice. A captured German exchanger showed the use of exhaust gas, but Rodert chose heated air versus exhaust gas. His team developed the technology to a higher operational level for Allied use.

LORAN

The United States rushed LORAN (long range aid to navigation) systems into operation for both maritime and aviation use. This low-frequency radio aid to navigation was going through tests at the Massachusetts Institute of Technology in December 1941. The Japanese attack on Pearl Harbor caused the rush from laboratory to military use. The wartime airborne equipment weighed from 35 to 55 pounds, depending upon the model, acceptable weight in military planes. The receiver in an aircraft measured the time difference between the arrival of two radio signals, one signal from a master station and the other signal from a slave or secondary station. Each signal created a line of position from the respective ground station, and the

PRODUCTION OF MILITARY AIRCRAFT					
	1941	1942	1943	1944	Total
Japan	5,088	8,861	16,693	28,180	58,822
Germany	11,766	15,556	25,527	39,807	92,656
Soviet Union	15,735	25,430	34,900	40,300	116,365
United States	19,433	49,445	92,196	100,752	261,826

two lines crossed at the receiver's location. The U.S. Army operated the ten LORAN stations in the China Theater to guide pilots flying the Hump, and a few stations in western Australia. The British Royal Air Force operated ten stations that provided coverage for the northeast Atlantic Ocean, parts of Europe, and the Bay of Bengal. The Royal Canadian Navy operated stations covering the northwest Atlantic, including Nova Scotia and the Grand Banks. The U.S. Coast Guard operated more stations than any other organization. There were 47 pairs of LORAN stations in operation at the end of the war.

Production

World War II was a big war, and it took a big production effort to equip the combat and support personnel. Increasing the size of factories or the number of machines and workers was not enough. How things were made needed to be changed to meet the new demands. With the United States supplying Allies through cash-and-carry and Lend-Lease even before the United States became a combatant, the country became — in President Franklin D. Roosevelt's words — an arsenal of democracy. It became a production center. Aviation companies converted from peacetime job shop methods to wartime line production. The magnitude — not the nature — of demand changed, but both the magnitude and nature of production changed.

Job Shop

In 1940 most manufacturers of aviation equipment still used the job shop or "European" method of production. This method of small-scale production, even intermittent production, met low peacetime demands. Skilled workers and skilled operators achieved generally high standards of quality and precision. They used general-purpose machinery and flexible (multiple-use) tools. Some parts were even handmade or hand-finished; the parts were not designed for line production. Parts were produced in lots or batches, and often workers had to finish parts before they could assemble them into a product; the

general jigs and fixtures lacked the precision necessary for parts to be fully interchangeable. Products were built in place on the assembly floor.

Line Production

Line production was the mass production technique pioneered by Henry Ford and the automobile industry, but prewar aviation lacked the volume of production to justify adopting the method. That changed during the war. The aviation manufacturers did not simply copy automotive practice. They modified the production and management methods of the automotive industry. (Figure 7-29)

Figure 7-29. Woman riveter at the Lockheed Aircraft plant in Burbank, California.

Manufacturers arranged equipment in progressive sequence and adopted special-purpose and multi-station machines, with specialized jigs and fixtures. They used the assembly line for large-volume production. The production line was a moving line where the flow of the product through the plant was controlled, both in the timing and sequence of production tasks. Scheduling was paramount. It balanced the operations of each line, feeder, and final assembly. At the same time, manufacturers introduced flexibility into the production line for changes in design and schedule, as the technology was being developed and improved while in production. They increased the division of labor and decreased the skill in assembly.

Manufacturers also simplified designs for line production; for example, by using interchangeability of parts. They considered ease of production as a factor in design. Components were broken into subassemblies. Engineering and manufacturing divisions worked cooperatively. Production activities, like tool engineering and production control, were centralized. Procedures were developed for handling manufacturing information, drawings, templates, and parts specifications.

This new line method of production used existing resources — skilled workers, foremen, executives — and added personnel from other industries, especially automotive and metalworking. The aviation manufacturers sometimes used outside companies and thereby outside management and workers, such as when Sikorsky Aircraft contracted with Nash-Kelvinator to produce helicopters. Licensing, subcontracting, and purchasing parts and components were ways that they utilized outside expertise, equipment, and methods.

The aviation manufacturers included airplane makers, engine makers, and propeller makers. They opened branch, satellite, and shadow plants. A shadow plant was a shadow or copy of the floor plan of another plant; this allowed personnel and equipment to be moved and utilized efficiently. The manufacturers also used Government Furnished Equipment (GFE) and billed customers for factory additions, like the "French wing" and "British wing" of some plants; these methods allowed a company to expand beyond its prewar and postwar needs without investing in the expansion.

Female Workers

Companies recruited women to increase the workforce and to staff the new and expanded factories. These women came to work with some previous preparation. Many had some previous work experience, usually in inspection, assembly, and light-machine work. New England, for example, had a long tradition of women working in textile factories. Some of the women had World War I production experience. The initial interview and placement proved increasingly important to effective management. Placement sometimes included pre-shop initiation on different machines and mechanical aptitude testing. Schools, companies, and the government also trained women. Unlike prewar trade schools that taught men trades, the wartime courses taught women one operation or skill. On-the-job training was common. (Figure 7-30)

In the aviation industry during the war, women worked in inspection, welding, drafting, toolmaking, bench work, and assembly. They worked as machine operators, stock chasers, laboratory technicians, draftsmen, engineers, and clerks. Women held similar jobs in the nations on both sides of the conflict.

Figure 7-30. Women were an integral part of the war effort. In this photograph they are working on the transparent noses of the A-20 attack bombers.

THE WESTERN AIR WAR

The Western or European Theater of World War II had three main fronts: a Western Front between Germany and Western Europe, including the Atlantic supply routes; an Eastern Front between Germany and the Soviet Union; and a Southern Front between the Axis Powers and Allied forces in the Mediterranean region of North Africa and southern Europe. The Western Front dominated the war in 1939 and 1940. The Southern Front opened when Italy joined the Axis side of the war in 1940, and Germany opened the Eastern Front by invading the Soviet Union in 1941. As the Allies gathered men and materiel for an invasion of Western Europe, and as Germany stalled in the Soviet Union, the Southern Front became the primary place of action in 1942 and 1943. Yet the increasing range of aircraft during the war upset the prewar definition of a war front, as planes could fly over ground troops and strike targets far from any ground fighting.

Southern Front

The Southern Front began as an extension of Italy's prewar imperialistic expansion in Africa. As Hitler's forces swept continental Europe in 1940, Benito Mussolini's Italian armed forces struck British and French positions in Africa, including British Somaliland and Egypt in the east and French Dakar on the west. After the fall of France, the French possessions of Tunisia, Algeria, and French Morocco became independent, but British-held Egypt continued

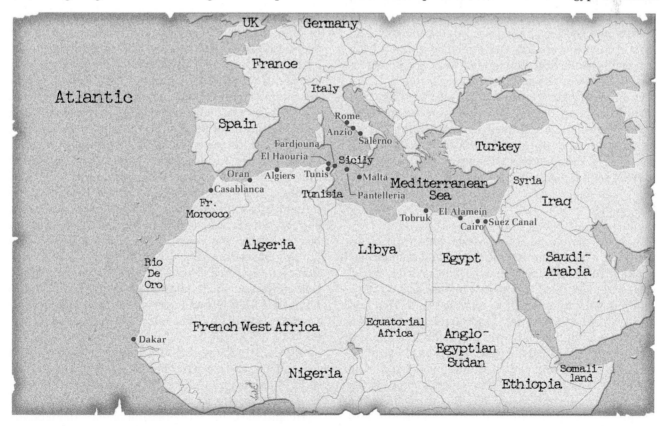

to fight the Italian army. In 1940 ground forces dominated the warfare in Africa. That remained the case when the British began a counterattack in January 1941, and when Germany sent troops to reinforce the Italians in North Africa in February. Ground forces were dominant in April when Ethiopia and Italian East Africa surrendered, and they were dominant thereafter.

Battle of North Africa

The German expeditionary forces in North Africa became known as the Afrika Korps, which incorporated Italian forces under the German command. The British desert forces became the Eighth Army and included troops from throughout the British Empire. Both sides utilized motorized infantry units and armored ground units. Defending the Suez Canal shipping lane and the Middle Eastern oil fields were primary Allied objectives, yet the strategic importance of air fields in North Africa made the ground war of vital importance to future control of the airspace over the Mediterranean region.

Air forces participated in the North African conflict, as permitted by sandstorms, wartime priorities, and availability of aircraft and airmen. Axis air attacks, for example, forced the Royal Air Force to withdraw from besieged Tobruk in 1941, and German dive bombers thereafter raided the garrison defending Tobruk and the naval forces supplying the garrison. Britain lost 34 warships and merchant ships during that eight-month siege. But ground warfare dominated. General Erwin Rommel of the German Army commanded the Afrika Korps, and the German 88-millimeter artillery piece, a dual-purpose anti-tank and anti-aircraft gun, proved effective in the region. Rommel's forces captured Tobruk in June 1942. For over a year Rommel gained fame as the Desert Fox playing with the Allied "Desert Rats."

Malta

The small British island of Malta, south of Sicily, provided a base from which planes and submarines could attack Axis supply lines to North Africa. In the spring of 1942, the Luftwaffe launched an air attack on the island in an effort to remove the British and Allies from the central Mediterranean. German bombers and fighters attacked the island in April and May. The aircraft carrier USS *Wasp* twice slipped into the Axis-dominated Mediterranean Sea during the battle. The Royal Air Force flew Spitfires off the *Wasp* to help defend Malta. The British retained the island, but Malta's infrastructure of airfields and

docks was sufficiently damaged so that it no longer hindered Axis shipping. The problem for Axis forces in North Africa was that too few supplies were shipped in comparison with the resupply of Allied forces. (Figure 7-31)

Figure 7-31. B-25 and P-51 similar to the ones used in Egypt.

El Alamein

Rommel led the German and Italian forces into Egypt in June 1942. This time his ground forces extended beyond Axis fighter coverage and he suffered losses by attacks from the Desert Air Force. According to German General von Mellenthin, "from the moment we entered Egypt the writing was on the wall as far as air support was concerned. Rommel never again enjoyed the advantage of air superiority, and the enemy's air forces grew with terrifying strength." Many of those Allied aircraft came from the United States, like the North American B-25 Mitchell bombers. Also, Britain's Special Air Service units helped upset the balance of supplies by attacking supply depots and airfields behind Axis lines in North Africa; the Special Air Service units were ground forces. At Minqa Qaim, the Allies tried to stop Rommel's advance. The Allies failed there in a battle that ended in such confusion that Allied planes bombed Allied troops and German units fired upon German units. The Allies retreated to El Alamein.

At El Alamein the Axis and Allies faced each other in late October and early November 1942. The geography of El Alamein prohibited the usual maneuverability of desert warfare as the Mediterranean Sea on the north and the Qattara Depression of marshland on the south blocked two flanks. El Alamein was a battle of infantry, tanks, and artillery more than planes. Still the British constructed wooden mock-ups of artillery stations to mislead Axis reconnaissance planes. The Germans in turn planted 250-pound aircraft bombs in the sand as land mines. The Desert Air Force of British and American planes outnumbered Luftwaffe aircraft, dominated the air, and hindered German supply and combat operations. After suffering heavy losses, the Axis forces began to retreat on 4 November. The tide of war in North Africa thus turned largely on the basis of supplies and air power.

Historical Evidence

Field Marshal Erwin Rommel described the enemy's use of aircraft at El Alamein:

"Following on their non-stop night attacks, the R.A.F. sent over formations of eighteen to twenty bombers at hourly intervals throughout the day, which not only caused considerable casualties, but also began to produce serious signs of fatigue and a sense of inferiority among our troops."

This is an eyewitness account of the battle by a participant in the battle. It is a primary source of information. Rommel's statement is translated and quoted in *The War, 1939-1945, a Documentary History*, edited by Desmond Flower and James Reeves (1960; New York: Da Capo Press, 1997).

Field Marshal Erwin Rommel (left)

Operation Torch

Within a grand strategy of wearing Germany and Italy down by attacking the periphery of their frontiers, Great Britain and the United States devised a strategy for the Mediterranean region that required control of all of North Africa. The American assignment became Operation Torch, an invasion of French North Africa. Morocco and Algeria had been neutral since the fall of France and had not been occupied by German forces. Securing this territory would prevent the Axis

from using it, would squeeze the Axis forces now retreating westward from Egypt, and would open Mediterranean shipping lanes to the Allies. It would also secure North African airfields for Allied use to launch air attacks on Axis positions in southern Europe.

Americans landed at Oran, Algiers, and Casablanca on 8 November 1942. This was an amphibious operation employing 650 ships, many British, and including aircraft carriers to provide air cover if needed. Marshal Pétain of the Vichy Government ordered French forces to resist the invasion. Fighter planes from the USS *Ranger* strafed French naval ships resisting the landing at Casablanca, and fighters destroyed French aircraft on the ground at airfields in French North Africa in order to prevent any air resistance and to secure the airfields for Allied use. Several hundred French and American personnel died in brief fighting at Oran and Casablanca.

Allied airmen quickly flew to the French airfields in American Curtiss P-40 Warhawk fighters, Boeing B-17 Flying Fortress bombers, and North American B-25 Mitchell bombers as well as British Spitfires and Hurricanes. The German Luftwaffe responded to the Allied presence with air raids. German bombers, for example, repeatedly struck Algiers. Nonetheless, French North Africa reached an armistice with the Allies and joined the Allied war against the Axis powers. Germany retaliated by occupying Vichy France, which had proven powerless to prevent the Allied actions. (Figure 7-32)

Figure 7-32. A U.S. Army Air Corps P-40 pursuit plane taking off from the USS *Chenango* in the Mediterranean in 1942.

In North Africa the largely American group of Allies in the east pushed west into Tunisia in an effort to sever the Axis sea and air supply lines that ran between Sicily and Tunis. Also, the mostly British Empire group of Allies pushed west after the retreating Axis forces. Sicily still provided supplies and air support to the Axis forces. In fact, Junkers transport planes carried German troops to Tunisian airfields in response to the American landings in North Africa. Luftwaffe planes, including the Messerschmitt Bf 109 fighters, attacked the Allied forces on both sides of the Axis forces. Partly due to rain that mired the tanks and armored vehicles in mud, the Allies and the Axis faced each other in combat and in stalemate in Tunisia during 1942-1943. At this time Allied planes dominated the African skies. On 10 April 1943, for example, Allied B-25 bombers downed 25 Junkers transport planes carrying supplies to Axis forces in Tunisia. A month later the Battle of North Africa was over, and the Allies controlled the entire north shore of the continent.

Operation Sicily

With Allied troops securely in North Africa, and with Allied landing craft in the Mediterranean (left over from Operation Torch), the Allies decided to use the troops in southern Europe — to attack Sicily and go up to Italy. In preparation for the invasion, Allied planes from North Africa bombed Axis airfields and fought Axis planes in the Mediterranean region. The plan was to achieve air supremacy prior to the invasion.

The Allies attacked Sicily from the air and sea on 10 July 1943; this was Operation Husky. Six Italian divisions and two German divisions were known to be defending Sicily's five-hundred miles of coastline. Another four Italian divisions were inland on the island. There were 32 airfields on the island, 8 of which were out of operation due to Allied air raids preceding the invasion. The preliminary attacks on Axis air forces proved effective during the invasion when the Luftwaffe and Italian Air Force failed to launch a major air attack against the landing ships and troops. Axis aircraft sank only 12 of the 1,400 vessels participating in the invasion. Rather than attack in mass, the Axis removed airplanes from Sicilian airports to rearward fields on the Italian Peninsula.

Generals Omar Bradley and George S. Patton of the United States and Bernard Montgomery of the United Kingdom led the invasion of Sicily, which was supported by naval and air forces. General Carl A. Spaatz commanded the American Northwest African Air Force during the invasion. The 99th Fighter Squadron of Tuskegee Airmen escorted bombers to Sicily, and they flew over 175 bombing and strafing missions there. Bombing and strafing delayed German reserves from reaching the beachhead until so many Allied troops had landed that the invading troops could resist counterattacks by the defenders. Troop carrier wings delivered airborne troops and towed troop-carrying Waco CG-4A gliders; combat-inexperienced flight crews during this operation revealed the need for more training of transport crews before sending

---

Historical Note

Among the American airmen who served in North Africa and Sicily during the war were the Tuskegee Airmen, the black airmen in a segregated Army. The first Tuskegee Airmen — the 99th Fighter Squadron — arrived at Fardjouna (Cape Bon), Tunisia, on 31 May 1943 and flew their first mission against the Italian island of Pantelleria a few days later. In late June they transferred to El Haouria on the eastern end of the Gulf of Tunis. They supported the invasion of Sicily, and in July they transferred to Licata, Sicily. They later participated in air raids on Nazi Germany.

During the war Tuskegee Airmen in the 99th Fighter Squadron and 332nd Fighter Group flew over 1,500 missions. They downed more than 250 enemy aircraft and sank one destroyer. While escorting Allied bombing missions in North Africa and Europe, the African-American fighter units lost no bombers. Tuskegee Airmen won a total of 95 Distinguished Flying Crosses during the war, as well as numerous Legions of Merit, Silver Stars, Purple Hearts, and also foreign medals, like the French Croix de Guerre and the Yugoslavian Red Star.

Whereas white airmen rotated home after 50 combat mission, the black airmen flew until black replacements were available, sometimes as many as 70 missions.

them into battle. Weather affected air operations: the weather was so good that there was little down time for maintenance of aircraft, and the high rate of flying meant crew fatigue was a problem. As the Southern campaign continued, many experienced flyers — after completing 50 missions — rotated home. This depleted crews and left inexperienced replacements to continue the battle.

Personal Profile

Benjamin O. Davis, Jr. (1912-2002), was the son of Benjamin O. Davis, Sr., a career military man who rose from private to general in the segregated United States Army. The younger Davis entered the Military Academy at West Point, New York, in 1932. As an African-American, he received the silent treatment from the other military cadets for four years, yet he graduated 35th in a class of 276 students. He requested assignment to the Army Air Corps, but the Air Corps was then all-white by Army policy, so he began his

military career in the infantry. When President Franklin D. Roosevelt directed the War Department to create a black flying unit as part of the nation's mobilization for a war already raging in Europe, Davis became a Tuskegee airman. He organized and led the all-black 99th Pursuit Squadron and the all-black 332nd Fighter Group. He flew combat over North Africa and Europe and won the Distinguished Flying Cross as well as other medals. After President Harry S. Truman desegregated the military in 1948, Davis led white as well as

Benjamin O. Davis, Jr.

During the Sicilian campaign, on 14 July 1943, President Franklin D. Roosevelt of the United States warned Italians, "The skies over Italy are dominated by the vast air armadas of the United States and Great Britain. Italy's sea-coasts are threatened by the greatest accumulation of British and Allied sea power ever concentrated in the Mediterranean. . . . The sole hope for Italy's survival lies in honorable capitulation to the overwhelming power of the military forces of the United Nations." During the war the Allied Powers called themselves the United Nations (not to be confused with the postwar United Nations). Italy responded with a *coup d'tat* that overthrew the fascist *duce* (leader) Benito Mussolini. That was in July 1943. The war continued with Italian General Pietro Badoglio leading the government.

Italy

From Sicily, the Allies launched an attack against the Italian mainland. Over 3,000 Allied aircraft supported this invasion. That was more than twice as many aircraft as the Axis had there for defense. British troops landed in Calabria on 3 September 1943 and met little Italian resistance. Italy surrendered and declared an armistice on the 8th. The Southern Front became a battle of the Allies versus the Germans in Italy, and the Germans now fought the Italians. The Italian government, including the king, queen, and General Badoglio, fled Rome to avoid capture by the Germans. They maintained a wartime government in Allied-occupied southern Italy. Germany occupied northern Italy.

When American troops landed at Salerno on 9 September, the sole enemy was Germany. Luftwaffe reconnaissance flights had discovered the forthcoming invasion of the Italian mainland, but lacked the aircraft to repel the landings. When Allied ground forces got into a difficult situation at Salerno, the Allies dropped airborne troops at night and provided air support and naval bombardment. While the Luftwaffe launched about 450 sorties during a critical two-day period in September, the Allies launched over 2,000 sorties a day. During the invasion, Allied air forces also provided close ground support on beachheads, tactical airlift of supplies and men, and interdiction of enemy lines of communication.

Through the Sicilian and Italian campaigns, Allied air forces acquired airfields in southern Italy. The Allies used these airfields for strategic bombers, as the Italian fields were much closer to European targets than the bases in North Africa. These airfields could provide bombers for missions against Germany when weather grounded bombers in the United Kingdom; thus, weather would no longer give Germany a break from air raids. The Allies also used the fields for missions to the Eastern Front.

Flight Lines

"Our third P-47 mission was penetration escort for B-17s and B-24s to the heavily defended Munich area. As the formation leader I was responsible for the takeoff from Ramitelli [Italy] and joining up in a way that would enable us to rendezvous with the bombers. We had to position ourselves carefully so that we could react to the radio calls announcing the presence and location of enemy fighters. We also had to accommodate the bombers: sometimes they were early, sometimes late; sometimes they changed direction and altitude because of cloud cover. The B-17s usually flew higher than the B-24s, but we had to maintain an altitude that would enable us to take care of the entire force. Bombers dropping to the rear of the formation because of battle damage were also our responsibility. Our pilots had to stay in a position to attack enemy fighters as they made their passes at the friendly formations, and they had to protect our own formation at the same time, so our eyes had to be everywhere. As we approached Munich, I dispatched Capt. Red Jackson's 302d Squadron to meet a threat developing at the high right rear side. Simultaneously, two Me-109s flew through the squadron I was leading. We took our best possible defensive maneuver, turning into them. In the turn, I fired a wide deflection shot at the closest enemy fighter without visible results. Captain Jackson gave this report in his debriefing: 'An Me-109 came in on my tail . . . a dogfight ensued until I shot the Me-109 down . . .' Including Captain Jackson's kill, we destroyed a total of five enemy fighters. Over the Udine area enemy fighters attacked the B-24s, and we were able to damage one Me-109. . . ."

Benjamin O. Davis, Jr., describing an escort mission in June 1944, in *Benjamin O. Davis, Jr., an Autobiography* (Washington: Smithsonian Institution Press, 1991).

The battle for Italy continued into 1945. It was a long Allied drive up the peninsula, hindered by Germany defenses, mountainous terrain, and two winters. Planes and paratroopers participated. French and Polish troops reinforced the British and American units. But it was a slow war of attrition. An attempt to break the impasse by landing at Anzio in early 1944 reached a new stalemate. An Allied officer observed, "Life at Anzio was never dull, easy or quiet. German artillery and aircraft continued to strike almost daily. While mass raids of fifty or more aircraft practically ceased during April, hit and run raids by one or more planes persisted." The war in Italy was bloody but, in 1944 the focus of the European war turned to the Western Front.

Western Front

The Western Front itself contained several distinct but inter-related operations, including naval forces fighting in the Atlantic Ocean, Allied bombing of German cities, vengeance weapons attacking England, and the Allied invasion of German-occupied territories on the continent.

Battle of the Atlantic

German U-boats dominated the Battle of the Atlantic into 1942. By then the Allies returned to the convoy system that had proven effective during World War I. In addition, the Allies built escort vessels to protect the

The Western Front

ENGLAND
London
BELGIUM
FRANCE
Paris
HOLLAND
Berlin
GERMANY
SWITZERLAND
DENMARK
SWEDEN
LITHUANIA
EAST PRUSSIA
Warsaw
POLAND
CZECHOSLOVAKIA
SLOVAKIA
Steyr
AUSTRIA
Budapest
HUNGARY
CROATIA
ROMANIA
Belgrade
Bucharest
ITALY
YUGOSLAVIA
BULGARIA
CORSICA
Rome
SARDINIA
GREECE
SICILY
Madrid
SPAIN
PORTUGAL

Allied Powers
Axis Powers
Neutral

convoys. Still, German submarines attacked Allied ships across the Atlantic Ocean, from the approaches to Britain, along the North Atlantic shipping lane south of Greenland, to the shores of the eastern United States, off the coast of Africa, and in the Caribbean Sea. One U-boat commander sank 44 ships. At least ten commanders scored more than 20 kills. Supplies needed to fight the war went down with the ships; for example, a shipment of crated North American P-51 Mustangs sank en route to Britain.

Convoys became safer as more escort vessels became available, as escort crews received more thorough training, as British asdic and American sonar systems became more effective, and as the Allies applied radar to antisubmarine warfare. Whereas asdic/sonar detected underwater vessels, radar could detect submarines on the surface even at night. The British also developed an electronic submarine finder called HFDF, or Huff-Duff, which was a ship-based high-frequency (H and F in huff) direction finder (D and F in duff) that could tune in on high-frequency radio communication signals from submarines. Ships in a convoy maintained total radio silence; they received radio communications, but sent none; very-high-frequency radio telephones provided ship-to-ship and ship-to-air communications.

Aircraft participated in the maritime Battle of the Atlantic. Escort vessels towed barrage balloons as defense against German aircraft, which would be disabled if flown into the steel cables lifted into the air by the balloons. Patrol planes, flown from atop or aside surface vessels, and coastal patrol planes flew anti-submarine missions. Fighter aircraft based on land protected departing and arriving ships. British Sunderland flying boats carried both bombs and depth charges for use against submarines. Britain's Swordfish biplanes attacked submarines with torpedoes, and laid mines. (Figure 7-33)

Merchant ships equipped with catapult launchers sent Hurricane fighters to strafe German vessels and to fight German aircraft, but the Hurricanes could not return to the ship to land. The United States built air bases in Iceland, Greenland, and Newfoundland for aircraft to support the transatlantic shipping and for use by aircraft being ferried (flown) from the United States to the war in Europe. The Curtiss P-40 Warhawk fighters, the Martin PBM Mariner flying boats, the Consolidated PBY Catalina amphibians, and other aircraft performed air escort as well as patrol duties in the North Atlantic. (Figure 7-34)

Figure 7-33. A Consolidated PBY-5 Catalina taking off on a coastal patrol mission.

Bombing Germany

Britain's Royal Air Force and Germany's Luftwaffe bombed each other routinely. Both struck civil as well as military targets, mostly cities. The Blitz brought German bombers to British cities. The Royal Air Force responded by bombing Germany but with

Figure 7-34. A PBY amphibious airplane is lashed to the deck of the USS *Albemarle* in the midst of a vicious storm off the coast of Iceland.

little effect during 1940 and 1941. When the British began using newly developed radar position-finding devices in 1942, the accuracy of air raids increased, even at night. The early raids targeted the industrial Ruhr valley, then extended to Hamburg, Berlin, and other German cities. The British used the method of dropping bundles of tinfoil strips as a reflective bank that would overwhelm German defensive radar.

Flight Lines

"Our night fighters tried to adjust to the new British methods, and profited by them to a certain extent because the British markers not only showed the way to their bombers but also to our pursuing night fighters. In a certain way the disadvantages of the radio and radar interference were annulled by the effect of the markers. Another means of finding the bomber stream was the burning enemy bombers which had been hit and which could be seen from a great distance. As a result of this, our night fighters found the whereabouts, course and altitude of the bombers, visible in the glow of the fires that attracted our fighters from a distance of sixty miles as a candle attracts a moth. The British bombers were pursued until they were over the target and also on their return journey. The solid system of the limited defense areas was out of date. Now the fighters 'traveled'."

Luftwaffe officer Adolf Galland describing German fighter tactics in defending against Allied bombers, as translated and quoted in *The War, 1939-1945, a Documentary History*, edited by Desmond Flower and James Reeves (1960; New York: Da Capo Press, 1997).

Historical Note

World War I was the war of aces, of gentlemen fighting sportingly in the air. That was the belief during World War II when formation flying and rotation from combat duty limited the role of the individual pilot. Not until after World War II did Allied nations learn the extent to which German fighter pilots outscored their enemies.

The *Jagdflieger* or German fighter pilot of World War II scored victories in numbers that far exceeded pilots of other nations. One hundred and six German pilots scored one hundred or more air victories during the war. Germany's top ace on the Western Front was Hans-Joachim Marseille, who scored 158 victories before being killed in battle in 1942. In comparison, Richard Ira Bong, the top American ace of the entire war scored only 40 victories.

After the United States entered the war, the Army Air Forces sent planes and personnel to bases throughout Britain to join the British air assault against Germany. British pilots flew night raids. Some flew specialty missions; for example, Guy Penrose Gibson organized a "Dambusters" squadron that bombed dams in Germany. The Royal Air Force included Free French pilots like Pierre H. Clostermann, who scored 33 victories against German aircraft, and Czech pilots like Josef Frantisek, who scored 28 kills during the war. The American presence in Britain reached a large scale in 1943. At the time there were so many airfields and airplanes in Britain, the island was referred to as an aircraft carrier. Initially, the United States began flying daylight raids although its bombers lacked long-range fighter escorts. The day bombers suffered high losses, but the precision of the daytime raids caused damage. An early target was the ball-bearing industry in Schweinfurt and the armament industry in general in various German cities. The Allies suffered significant losses on the raids, as German fighter pilots, like Hans-Joachim

Marseille, valiantly defended their homeland. (Figure 7-35)

Often it was the weight of the bombs rather than accuracy that destroyed targets — or the firestorm ignited by the bombs. The Allies dropped high-explosive (H.E.) bombs, incendiary bombs, and phosphorus canisters. One series of raids in late July and early August 1943 destroyed half of Hamburg and killed 40,000 people. The massive formations of bombers, the frequency of bombing, and the resulting damage made the air war a form of psychological warfare delivering terror into the heart of Germany — attacking the working population as well as the public's willingness to continue the war.

The increasing range and number of American fighter planes boosted the Allies air strength and expanded

Figure 7-35. Photograph made from B-17 Flying Fortress of the 8th AAF Bomber Command during an attack on the CAM ball-bearing plant and the nearby Hispano Suiza aircraft engine repair depot.

the effectiveness of air raids on Germany. In 1944 the Allies were able to raid Germany around the clock with bombers escorted by long-range fighters, like the North American P-51 Mustang, powered by the British Merlin engine, and the Republic P-47 Thunderbolt, powered by an American Pratt & Whitney engine. The attacking bombers flying out of Britain or Italy could fly high above bad weather, while defending fighters were forced to take off into bad weather. (Figure 7-36)

Figure 7-36. North American Aviation designed the P-51 Mustang long-range escort to British requirements in 1940 and placed the aircraft into production the next year. The British had more than 200 Mustangs in service by the end of 1942, and received hundreds more the next year.

The Allied bombing reduced Germany's war production. The Luftwaffe, according to Colonel Adolf Galland, placed its hopes in the Messerschmitt Me 262 jet fighter, but it was Germany's vengeance weapons — the V-1 pilotless jet and the V-2 rocket — that brought the psychological war back to Britain in 1944. (Figure 7-37)

Figure 7-37. The Republic P-47 Thunderbolt was the largest single-seat combat airplane of World War II. Its large droppable fuel tanks extended its range for escorting bombers. The painted bands on this Thunderbolt identify it as an Allied aircraft participating in D-Day.

Vengeance

During the summer of 1944, Germany sent about 8,000 V-1 pilotless jet planes carrying high-explosive warheads from German-occupied shores of western Europe across the English Channel against London. Over 2,000 of these buzz bombs penetrated Britain's defense. They caused over 10,000 casualties (wounded and killed). That autumn Germany launched about 1,000 V-2 rockets carrying explosives toward London. About half of these reached the English city and caused an additional 10,000 casualties. Britain sent Spitfires to bomb the launch sites. The United States also sent bombers against the sites. (Figure 7-38)

Figure 7-38. An unexploded German V-1 missile fired at Britain following D-Day.

Flight Lines

"In the distance hummed faintly the engine of a flying bomb.

. . .

"The dull burr became a roar, through which our voices could now only faintly be heard.

. . .

"The roar stopped abruptly as the engine cut out . . .

. . .

"Then there was a noise so loud it was as if all the waters and the winds in the world had come together in mighty conflict. . . ."

Elisabeth Sheppard-Jones describing a V-1 attack on London, 18 June 1944, as quoted in *The War, 1939-1945, a Documentary History*, edited by Desmond Flower and James Reeves (1960; New York: Da Capo Press, 1997).

While the vengeance weapons terrorized Britain, Germany strengthened its military production. In September 1944 German factories delivered more single-seat fighter planes than any previous month of the year. Slave labor and domestic sacrifice overcame shortages of materials and labor. Despite the production, the air force was hampered by the fuel shortage and by ground crews being transferred to combat units. Fog and thunderstorms over Germany in the autumn of 1944 shielded Germany's oil refineries from air raids and allowed the battered nation to replenish that dwindling supply so necessary for its own air force.

D-Day

Germany and the Allies prepared for the invasion of Europe, the opening of a second front on the ground. Germany built defensive fortifications along the occupied French coast. Britain and the United States massed trained personnel and equipment in the British Isles. Knowing that German forces were strongest near Calais, where the English Channel is narrowest, the Allies selected Normandy for the invasion site. The amphibious assault occurred on 6 June 1944. Allied air forces provided cover for the landing troops, dropped paratroopers, and struck railroads, bridges, and other transportation targets to interfere with the movement of German forces. The Allies employed almost 100,000 men, more than 4,000 ships, over 2,000 fighters, and about 1,000 bombers in this Operation Overlord. (Figure 7-39)

Allied air superiority limited German mobility, but the Allied troops could not break into open country.

Figure 7-39. General Dwight D. Eisenhower gave the Order of the Day. "Full Victory — nothing else" to paratroopers in England, just before they boarded their airplanes for the D-Day assault.

Historic Event

On 6 June 1944 the Allies landed at Normandy in a campaign to retake the continent from German forces which had forced the Allies to evacuate Dunkirk four years earlier.

Concentrated bombing of the Germans on 25 July opened the way for Allied troops to sweep through France. United States army forces liberated Paris in August; British forces pushed into Belgium. In December, Hitler ordered German troops transferred from the Eastern Front to this Western Front. He directed one last German offensive, the Battle of the Bulge.

Eastern Front

Germany had a plan when it started the war: to make Europe German by isolating and capturing nations one by one. It had done that with Austria and Czechoslovakia before the war. It then applied the approach to Poland. By signing the nonaggression pact with Joseph Stalin in 1939, Adolf Hitler had hoped to keep Britain and France out of the war and thereby isolate and take Poland. Great Britain and France came to Poland's defense so Germany isolated and took France. Unable to isolate Britain from its chief supplier, the United States, Germany turned to the Soviet Union.

By size and power, by competing revolutionary ideology, and by occupying territory that Hitler wanted for *lebensraum* (living space), the Soviet Union was an obvious enemy. The invasion was consistent with

Personal Profile

As a youth, Oleg K. Antonov (1906-1984) made model airplanes. He completed his studies at the Leningrad Polytechnic Institute in 1930, whereupon he went to work in a glider factory near Moscow. He rose to be chief engineer then chief designer before the war. During World War II, he designed the A-7 cargo gilder used to transport personnel and provisions. After the war, he directed his own airplane design bureau. His An-2 utility biplane won him the Stalin Prize in 1952. He designed a successful line of postwar transports that included the An-8, An-10, An-12, An-22, An-24, and An-26 transport planes. He designed the large four-engine An-124 and the larger six-engine An-225. When the An-22, An-124, and An-225 were first introduced, each one was recognized as the world's largest aircraft.

Oleg K. Antonov

Hitler's isolate and capture approach to the war. Weakening Russia in the Far East would strengthen Japan in the Pacific and thereby preoccupy the United States far from the war in Europe. This would isolate Britain, which Germany could then take. But Hitler's forces stalled in Russia.

On 2 February 1943 the Germans, and some Romanians, attempting to take Stalingrad (now Volgograd) surrendered to the Soviets after five months of battle. The Soviet resistance stopped Germany's advance. Germany lost about 300,000 men at Stalingrad. Its conquest of Europe reached its limits. Italian and Hungarian forces in the southern Soviet Union also withdrew. Germany and the Axis Powers lost men, materiel, and territory on the Eastern Front. In contrast, that year Lend-Lease supplies reached the Soviet Union in volume. Whereas some Allied-supplied materiels were inferior to Russian-made counterparts, North American Mustang fighters, Mitchell medium bombers, and Douglas Dakota transports were better than Russian-made equipment; Soviet transport gliders tended to be well made. All Soviet air crews trained in a hurry and dashed into combat.

Battle of Kursk

After the victory at Stalingrad, the Red Army liberated Kursk. In July, Germany launched a counter-offensive against Kursk using over 2,500 tanks and about 1,000 aircraft. The Soviets then had more aircraft, men, and equipment. This was basically a tank battle. Aircraft attacked armor, notably German *stuka* or dive bombers fired cannon guns against Soviet tanks. Pilot Hans Rudel destroyed 12 tanks in one day. Germany lost 75,000 men. The Soviets suffered more losses, but won the battle. German General von Mellenthin explained, "It is true that Russian losses were much heavier than German; indeed, tactically the fighting

had been indecisive. . . . but our Panzer divisions — in such splendid shape at the beginning of the battle — had been bled white, and with Anglo-American assistance the Russians could afford losses on this colossal scale." Germany's *Panzer* (armored wagon or tank) divisions moved quickly and effectively in previous assaults. From here on, the Germans retreated. So did Italian and Hungarian troops along the southern boundary of the Soviet Union.

The disorderly withdrawal of the Germans from the Soviet Union was reminiscent of the uncoordinated Russian response to the invasion of 1941. At the Orels airfield in 1943 the Russians captured 150 serviceable aircraft, including 119 four-engine Focke-Wulf Fw 200 Condors — planes that normally would have been flown behind the lines or destroyed than allowed to be captured by the enemy. The Soviets pushed to Kharkov, the Dnieper, and Kiev. As the Germans retreated, they scorched the earth of the western Soviet Union. The scorched-earth tactics made it difficult for the Soviets to launch a major assault.

Combat continued along the Eastern Front, including bombing raids and fighter encounters. The inexperience of Soviet crews and their obsolete aircraft that had made them targets of the experienced Luftwaffe pilots early in the war, gave way to experience, but replacements arrived without experience and Soviet pilots in general were not familiar with foreign-made aircraft that they received through Lend-Lease. Germany's highest scoring aces, like Erich Hartmann, served on the Eastern Front.

Hitler favored offensive tactics and provided little support for his retreating troops that in 1944 were driven into Poland in the north and into Romania in the south. When Germans in the far north retreated into Finland, the Finns — already defeated by the

Personal Profile

During World War II, Erich Hartmann (1922-1993) became the highest-scoring fighter pilot of all time.

Hartmann was, in the German term, an *experte,* what the Allies called an ace. His mother had been a glider pilot, and she interested him in gliding when he was 14 years old.

During the war he served with the *Jagdgeschwader* or JG 52 formation at the Eastern Front. His wartime nickname was Bubi, Boy. He flew single-seat Messerschmitt Bf 109G fighters on more than 1,400 sorties. Avoiding dogfights, he preferred the surprise attack. He downed 352 enemy aircraft! These were mostly Russian planes, but the number includes seven American P-51s, North American Mustangs, that he shot down over Romania.

After the war Hartmann served ten years in a Soviet prison. International pressure led to his release in 1955. He promptly joined the air force of West Germany.

Erich Hartmann

Flight Lines

"Finding [the enemy] depended purely on being where the action was concentrated on the ground and on visual look-out. Ground stations called us by radio the position of the enemy after a coordinate system on our maps. So we could search in the right direction and choose our best attack altitude. If I covered the sky, I preferred a full-power, sun attack from below, because you could spot the enemy very far away against a white cloudy sky. The pilot who sees the other pilot first already has half the victory."

German ace Erich Hartmann describing his combat experience, as quoted in Mike Spick, *Luftwaffe Fighter Aces.*

Soviets in the Winter War of 1939-1940 — again fought Soviet invaders, this time the Finns fought along side the Germans. Stalin and Hitler were competitors, two dictators who used similar methods to maintain authoritarian power over the people of their respective nations. Both wanted eastern Europe. Finland wanted neither within its borders.

Closing the Ring

Wartime Germany had no balance of power between its civil administration and military authorities. Hitler was Führer (Leader) and the leader of the Reich (Empire), the military, and the people. Hitler developed and directed military strategy and tactics. Below Hitler there was competition among the Nazi Party, the Army, the Luftwaffe (Air Force), and the police forces (the SS [Schütz Staffeln], Home Guard, and Police). There was also competition within these various groups. Due to the internal disputes and mistrust of his aides, Hitler lacked the good counsel of experts. This lack of strong advice

affected the conduct of the war in 1942 and thereafter. In North Africa, he relied on Axis ground forces without supplying them the necessary war materiel to do the job. Hitler's separateness from good counsel became more evident as the Allies tightened the ring around Nazi Germany.

In January 1945 Soviet forces entered Germany from the east. Allied bombers raided Germany from the west (Britain) and from the south (Italy). In March, Allied forces crossed the Rhine River. As Allied forces advanced on the Western Front, Hitler ordered *all* fighter planes to that front. The Minister for Armaments Albert Speer and Luftwaffe Colonel Adolf Galland visited Hitler to argue against the order and for the use of aircraft to defend the Reich. Hitler threw them out. In February, Allied bombers destroyed Dresden, and on 12 March 1945 the Allies dropped nearly 5,000 tons of bombs on Dortmund alone. That month Britain's Royal Air Force dropped over 65,000 tons total. (Figure 7-40)

Figure 7-40. The 8th Air Force raid on a Focke Wulf plant at Marienburg.

Forces from throughout Europe converged on Germany in 1945. Formed to defend the Soviet homeland from invasion, the all-female air regiments of the Red Air Force advanced on Berlin in 1945. The 588th Night Bomber Regiment helped take Berlin in the spring of 1945 — still flying the old PO-2s which were now heavily patched. The 587th bombers and the 586th fighters, the other all-female air regiments, were in Germany too when the European war ended. The Tuskegee Airmen based in Italy also participated in the approach to Berlin — by escorting bombers to German targets.

In April the United States transferred the 8th Army Air Force to the Pacific, as there were no more targets to bomb in Germany. On 2 May 1945 the remaining German forces in northern Italy surrendered. The Luftwaffe fought to the end — putting Messerschmitt Me 262s into combat in late April and early May. On 8 May 1945 Germany surrendered. The war in Europe was over.

Historic Event

On 13 February 1945 Allied bombers came to Dresden. Firestorms consumed the town, which burned for five days. At least 250,000 people died — refugees as well as residents.

Flight Lines

"The complete superiority of the Messerschmitt 262 was well demonstrated to us one evening when we carried out a dusk patrol over Grave. . . . Suddenly, without warning, an enemy jet appeared about one hundred yards ahead of our Spitfires. The pilot must have seen our formation, since he shot up from below and climbed away at a high speed. Already he was out of cannon range, and the few rounds I sent after him were more an angry gesture at our impotence than anything else."

Johnny Johnson describing an encounter with a Messerschmitt 262 in the spring of 1945, as quoted in *The War, 1939-1945, a Documentary History*, edited by Desmond Flower and James Reeves (1960; New York: Da Capo Press, 1997).

Me 262

THE PACIFIC AIR WAR

In December 1941 Japan attacked Pearl Harbor, the Philippines, and Malaya. By these surprise attacks, Japan intended to destroy the striking power of the United States and United Kingdom in the Pacific. Japan's plan was to capture resource-rich areas for its Greater East Asia Co-Prosperity Sphere, especially the oil-producing Dutch East Indies (today's Indonesia, but then a colony of the Netherlands). Japan also targeted the mineral- and forestry-rich British colonies in southeast Asia. French Indo-China and the United States territory of the Philippines were between Japan and its southern objectives. As the Western powers fought the European war, their Asian-Pacific lands became prey. The Japanese plan was to take these lands and to establish a defensive perimeter far from the Japanese homeland. That perimeter, according to the plan, could be defended against any limited offensives that the Allies might launch. Just as Germany and Italy wanted to establish a "New Order" in Europe, Japan sought to create a "New Order" in Asia.

Surprise Attack

Given Japan's occupation of Manchuria and invasion of China in the 1930s, and given the war waging in Europe, the Allies tried to contain Japan's expansion. The Allies, especially the United States, opposed Japan's expansion into China. While negotiating with

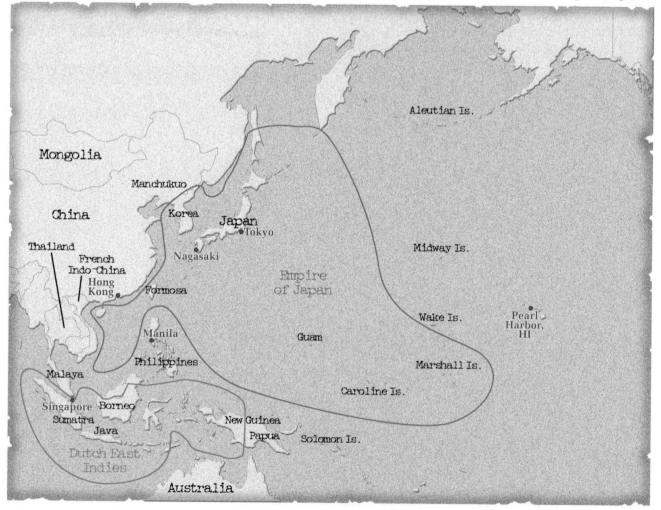

Japan, the United States also traded with Japan. As late as 1940, the United States supplied half of Japan's iron, steel, and oil. On 27 September 1940 Japan joined Italy and Germany in a new Triple Alliance, an Axis defensive pact. The United States responded with an embargo on aviation gas, scrap metal, steel, and iron. The situation remained until the summer of 1941 when Japan pressured Vichy France to allow Japan to have bases in French Indo-China. Indo-China was both a stepping stone on the way to the Dutch oil fields as well as a step between the Chinese enemy of Japan and the Allied forces in the Pacific. Japanese forces moved into northern Indo-China (now Vietnam) on 25 July 1941. The United States recognized Indo-China as a stepping stone for other Japanese objectives — in President Roosevelt's words, "for the purposes of further offense." The day after Japan crossed the border into Indo-China, the United States froze Japanese assets in the United States and closed the Panama Canal to Japan.

Allied with Germany and Italy, Japan intentionally threatened the United States with a war on two fronts should the American country join the war against the Axis in Europe. The United States, Britain, and the Netherlands imposed economic sanctions on Japan, including an embargo on oil, to discourage its expansion. These sanctions pressed Japan to find a solution and to expand before it exhausted its oil reserves. During the tense summer of 1941 the United States Ambassador to Japan, Joseph G. Grew, said that Japan and the United States came "within eight yards of war." The eight yards were between the gunboat USS *Tutuila* on the Yangtze River at Chungking, China, and a bomb dropped by a Japanese Navy aviator. The bomb missed the target, and negotiations postponed the war. The relationship between the Pacific powers grew more strained that fall when pro-war General Hideki Tojo became the premier of Japan.

As the powers continued negotiations, Japan massed troops along the Malayan border. The United States and the United Kingdom expected war. They expected Japan to attack Malaya. The surprise was a three-prong attack on Pearl Harbor and the Philippines as well as Malaya.

Pearl Harbor

The United States had received reports of Japanese plans to attack Pearl Harbor as early as January 1941 but, at the time, the plans seemed fantastic to American officials. Japan recognized Pearl Harbor as a large advance base that threatened its plans for expansion and therefore planned accordingly. In late November

Historic Event

On 7 December 1941 Japanese naval aviators attacked Pearl Harbor in the United States territory of Hawaii. The surprise attack destroyed aircraft and battleships and killed many soldiers and sailors. The attack also brought the United States into World War II.

USS *Arizona*

Japan sent a Pearl Harbor Task Force of ships eastward toward Hawaii. Admiral Isoroku Yamamoto commanded the Japanese Combined Fleet that included the Pearl Harbor Task Force; Vice Admiral Chuichi Nagumo commanded the task force. Yamamoto received his orders on 1 December: "direct an attack on the enemy fleet in the Hawaiian area and reduce it to impotency, using the 1st Air Fleet as the nucleus of the attack force." The next day he received word that the "hostile action . . . shall be commenced on 8 December." Yamamoto sent a radio message to the Pearl Harbor Task Force at sea: "Execute attack. 8 December designated as X day." Japan was on the other side of the International Dateline from the United States, so 8 December in Japan was 7 December in Hawaii and the rest of the United States.

That Sunday morning two U.S. Army privates operated a mobile radar set at Opana Station on the Hawaiian island of Oahu. They detected a big blip 137 miles away, possibly a lot of aircraft, possibly Navy aircraft engaged in an exercise with the Army that Sunday morning. They telephoned a report of their radar readings, but the lieutenant receiving the report dismissed it. It could be U.S. Navy planes flying off a carrier or B-17s arriving from the mainland. The two privates dutifully recorded the path of the incoming blip until their relief arrived. The first Japanese planes struck minutes before 8:00 a.m., and before the privates completed the drive back to their base to submit their report in person. Despite the successful

Figure 7-41. Naval Air Station at Pearl Harbor, Hawaii, 7 December 1941.

those carriers. They arrived in two waves: a first wave of 189 aircraft and a second wave of 171 aircraft. The aircraft included Aichi E13A seaplanes that flew reconnaissance flights for the operation, also Aichi D3A dive bombers, Nakajima B5N2 torpedo bombers, and Mitsubishi A6M2 Reisen (Zero) fighters. The first wave began the attack by dive bombing Army aircraft on the ground at Wheeler Field and Hickam Field, Navy aircraft on Ford Island and at Kaneohe, and Marine aircraft at Ewa. Then torpedo bombers attacked the battleships in Pearl Harbor. Bombers dropped their loads next, and then fighters strafed. Then, a little after 10:00 in the morning, the second wave of Japanese aircraft arrived. A soldier on the ground later wrote home, "All I can say is that my baptism under fire sure was hell on earth and I saw my Maker on Sunday, December 7, 1941."

invention, development, and use of radar in Great Britain, the technology was still new to the United States military. (Figure 7-41)

Japan's Pearl Harbor Task Force consisted of 31 ships, including six aircraft carriers. The attackers flew off

By attacking aircraft first, the Japanese disabled the aerial defense capabilities in Hawaii. They damaged and destroyed the Army's fighters and bombers (B-17s and B-18s), the Navy's patrol planes (over 60 PBYs), and the Marine's aircraft of various types. The main target, of course, was the Pacific Fleet of the

Historical Note

The most heavily produced Japanese aircraft of the war was the Mitsubishi A6M Reisen, also known as Navy Type 0 Carrier Fighter, and better known simply as the Zero.

Engineer Jiro Horikoshi led the Mitsubishi design team that produced the all-metal, low-wing monoplane. The Zero had several engine designs. A 780-horsepower Mitsubishi Zuisei 13 engine powered the 1939 prototype. The Nakajima 940-horsepower Sakae 12, the 1,130-horsepower Sakae 21 and Sakae 31, and the Mitsubishi 1,560-horsepower Kinsei 61 powered the production models. These 14-cylinder radial engines were air-cooled.

Captured Japanese Zero

The Navy fighter flew into action at Pearl Harbor and most other battles of the war in the Pacific. Japan assigned the Zero to all of its wartime aircraft carriers. The fighter had both maneuverability and range. It scored victories against land-based and carrier-based aircraft. The lack of armor and of protection for the fuel tank made the aircraft inappropriate for the defensive nature of its missions in the last couple of years of the war. Since Japan produced no wartime successor to the Zero, the fighter remained in production and in operation until the end of the war.

Both Mitsubishi and Nakajima manufactured the Zero, over 11,000 in all, including more than 300 of the A6M2-N floatplane version.

A Japanese carrier in the Pearl Harbor Task Force, 7 December 1941.

United States Navy. The attackers sank three battle-ships (*Arizona, California,* and *West Virginia*), damaged several battleships (*Maryland, Nevada, Oklahoma, Pennsylvania,* and *Tennessee*), and hit some cruisers. They killed over 2,000 people and wounded over a thousand more. Japan lost only 30 planes in the attack, five midget submarines, and one regular-size submarine. The attack was a surprise for the United States territory — and the nation. It was a Japanese victory! Yet, the U.S. Navy's aircraft carriers *Enterprise* and *Lexington* were at sea during the attack and escaped damage. Also, the Japanese failed to hit the oil storage facilities in Hawaii so the United States still had fuel for Hawaiian-based operations. The Pacific Fleet was damaged, but not destroyed, and the United States rallied to the war against Japan.

Historical Evidence

The United States Congress established a Joint Committee on the Investigation of the Pearl Harbor Attack. After the war the government published 39 volumes resulting from the hearings of this committee: *Hearings before the Joint Committee on the Investigation of the Pearl Harbor Attack* (1946). The volumes contain documents and testimony. They provided the basic information used in many post-war books on Pearl Harbor, like Walter Millis' book *This Is Pearl* (1947). Years later secret government documents in the United States and Japan were declassified, and the declassified information prompted revisions of the story of what happened at Pearl Harbor. See, for example, Akira Iriye's *Pearl Harbor and the Coming of the Pacific War: A Brief History with Documents and Essays* (1999).

Philippines

Months before Pearl Harbor, the United States began reinforcing the Philippines to block the Japanese from the oil-rich Dutch East Indies. The United States also recalled General Douglas MacArthur to active duty — to command all U.S. forces in the Far East. The United States based submarines and aircraft in the Philippines, but the pace of activities on the Philippines remained slow. As of November 1941, the Commander in Chief of the Far Eastern Air Forces (Lewis Brereton) noted a delay in funding that was needed to implement the construction of airports. That same month the Chief of Naval Operations (Harold R. Stark) warned Admiral Hart in Manila of a possible Japanese attack on the Philippines. Furthermore, on 27 November, the United States Department of State warned General MacArthur that "hostile action [was] possible at any moment."

On the morning of 8 December, MacArthur received information about the attack on Pearl Harbor. He did not act. About noon Japanese air forces arrived over Manila and struck Clark and Nichols Fields. The Japanese forces caught and destroyed U.S. aircraft on the ground in the Philippines. In ruins were the modern B-17 bombers in the Philippines, which had been the largest concentration of American aircraft outside the United States. Unlike Pearl Harbor where a naval fleet was the target of a one-day attack, the Philippines themselves were a Japanese objective and, therefore, the attack of 8 December opened a Japanese invasion. By the end of December 1941, the Japanese had two armies on Luzon, the principal island, and the two armies were converging on Manila. General MacArthur declared Manila an open city as the American High Commissioner and the Commonwealth Government of the Philippines withdrew to the fortified island of Corregidor. Most of the military forces left the city for the Bataan Peninsula. Manila fell on 2 January 1942. (Figure 7-42)

Figure 7-42. B-17 damaged during the Japanese attack in the Philippines.

Corregidor, 26 miles west of Manila, is near the mouth of Manila Harbor, south of the Bataan Peninsula. When the Philippines were under Spanish rule, the island was a signal station to alert Manila of incoming ships. After the United States acquired the Philippines in 1898, a pro-independence guerrilla uprising prompted the United States to fortify the island as part of harbor defenses. The island is about four miles long by one-half mile wide at the widest point, and it is only 628 feet high at Topside, the highest point; the total area is about two square miles. General MacArthur and Filipino President Manuel Quezon established offices and quarters in the Malinta Tunnel. Constructed between 1922-1932, the 835-foot long

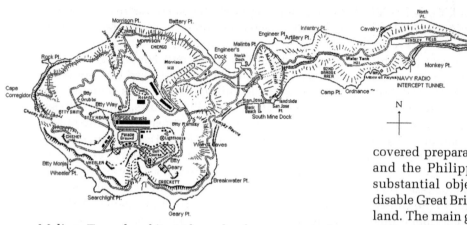

Figure 7-43.
Corregidor is about four miles long and one-half mile wide. This map shows the installations during World War II.

Malinta Tunnel and its 24 branches became central to the island's defense. It was built in the base of the limestone formation that gave the island its nickname — the Rock. Originally built as an arsenal and underground hospital, the tunnel became the bombproof headquarters for the Americans and Filipinos (and later the Japanese) on Corregidor.

The Malinta Tunnel was one of very few installations protected against air attack. The Japanese bombarded Corregidor for five months; for example, on 25 March the Japanese raided Corregidor with 54 bombers. Meanwhile on Luzon, despite odds of 5-1, American and Filipino forces defended the Bataan Peninsula for three months. On 7 April Bataan fell and 76,000 Allied troops surrendered. American and Filipino forces continued to fight and delay the Japanese at Corregidor. This battle of the Philippines was an Allied effort to slow the Japanese drive until troops and materiel could be shipped to the new Pacific war zone. Finally, President Roosevelt ordered MacArthur to Australia. MacArthur left Corregidor on 11 March. The troops on the island held out for almost two more months. On 6 May Corregidor fell. General Jonathan Wainwright surrendered the remaining 10,000 Allied troops in the Philippines. (Figure 7-43)

Malaya

The Japanese attacks of 8 December 1941 included Malaya, Thailand, and Hong Kong as targets. The Thai resistance ceased after the first day, and the Japanese passed through that land unhindered. Hong Kong fell after 17 days of fighting. It took the Japanese only 70 days to capture Malaya though the Allies had expected that invasion. Japan had openly massed troops near Malaya in the fall of 1941. The openness was deceptive as it covered Japanese operations elsewhere. Japan broadcast phony radio messages to mislead the Allies regarding the location and number of ships and squadrons. Japan's Malaya campaign

covered preparations for the attacks on Pearl Harbor and the Philippines, but the campaign had other substantial objectives too. The Japanese sought to disable Great Britain's Pacific Fleet as well as to capture land. The main goal was Singapore at the southern tip of the Malay Peninsula. Singapore was headquarters for the British fleet, which was there to protect British interests, including trade and communication routes, in Asia and the Pacific. Singapore was British territory. It had an established port with commercial dockyards and a new naval base; the Five Power Naval Limitation Treaty of 1922 had not prohibited naval development at Singapore.

The British strategy for Singapore had a flaw, identified if not fully recognized by the Chiefs of Staff at a 1937 Imperial Conference: "The strengths of the fleet that could be sent to the Far East must be governed by consideration of our home requirements." The German threat in Europe meant no fleet in Singapore in the late 1930s and early 1940s. Only two British battleships and a few planes were at Singapore when Japan invaded Malaya. The defensive plans assumed a naval threat, but the Japanese came overland through Malaya. The march through Malaya was jungle warfare, though the Japanese utilized reconnaissance flights and bombed British airfields like Alor Star and Kota Bahru. Britain's Royal Air Force flew Brewster

Flight Lines

"Now great wedges of silver bombers droned across the sky and one after another the cities of Burma spurted with flame and vanished in roaring holocausts. Prome, Meiktila, Mandalay, Thazi, Pyinmana, Maymyo, Lashio, Taung-gyi, largely wooden towns, all of them crumbled and burned. The Japanese used pattern bombing, coming over in faultless formation, giving themselves a leisurely dummy run or two, and then letting all their bombs go in one shattering crump. They were very accurate."

General William Slim describing Japanese bombing techniques used in Burma, spring 1942, as quoted in *The War, 1939-1945, a Documentary History*, edited by Desmond Flower and James Reeves (1960; New York: Da Capo Press, 1997).

Figure 7-44. This captured Japanese aerial photograph showed the British ships *Prince of Wales* and *Repulse* under attack by Japanese bombers.

Buffalo fighters which were too few in number and too limited in capability to halt the invaders who used fighters and bombers, like the twin-engine Mitsubishi 96. High-level bombers and torpedo-bombers sank both the HMS *Prince of Wales* and HMS *Repulse*. The Japanese also bombed Penang, Kuala Lumpur and, finally, Singapore. The defenders could not hold their position until reinforcements arrived. Singapore fell on 15 February 1942, and the Japanese renamed it Shonan. (Figure 7-44)

During the initial drive from December 1941 through spring of 1942, the Japanese captured their objectives, including the Netherlands East Indies and Burma. Japan had relied, like its German model, on surprise attacks, air superiority — bombing and strafing in advance of land troops — and sheer numbers to move quickly in capturing lands. Japan established its defensive perimeter far from the homeland, and even made offensive raids beyond the defense line. Japan now had free movement, food, oil, and raw materials within a large segment of the Asian-Pacific region.

Changing Tide

The surprise attacks on Pearl Harbor, the Philippines, and Malaya destroyed many Allied aircraft, most of which were caught on the ground. These attacks and the subsequent campaigns demonstrated the importance of air power in Japanese military strategy. Japan scored early victories, but not as destructive to the Allies' ability to wage war as planned. While Allied troops fought for time in the Philippines, Malaya, and the East Indies, the Allies began gathering forces and materiel in Australia for a counter-assault. The Allies needed time because military air transport routes had to be established before equipment, supplies, and

reinforcements could be delivered to the Pacific Theater. Commercial airlines based in the United States provided transport support to the military in the South Pacific as well as in places as dispersed as Alaska, India, and Newfoundland. Japan expected limited conflicts after the initial victories, but the Allies did not limit combat in the Pacific. While giving priority to the war in Europe, the Allies still launched a massive offensive led by the United States Navy. This was total war for survival in the Pacific and for geopolitical objectives. In the Pacific war, the Allies had two main objectives: one was to push Japanese forces out of Pacific waters and off Pacific islands and the second was to attack Japan.

Doolittle's Raid

Even as the Japanese continued to advance in Burma and the Philippines, the United States sent a military response to the Japanese homeland. General James H. "Jimmy" Doolittle led a squadron of 16 B-25 bombers on a raid against Tokyo. North America made these modern Mitchell bombers, which had gull wings, and two Wright R-2600 radial engines — each rated at 1,700 horsepower, and a normal bomb load of 2,000 pounds (910 kg). This secret mission took off from the USS *Hornet*. The planes flew undetected into Japanese territory. The pilots ignored the aircraft carrier in Tokyo Bay and headed toward their targets. They avoided barrage balloons defending one side of the city. They dropped their 500-pound bombs from 1,500 feet. The bombs did some damage to the targets, but the effectiveness of the raid was the assault on

 Historic Event

On 18 April 1942 General James H. "Jimmy" Doolittle led an air raid against Japan's capital city of Tokyo.

Flight Lines

"I was almost on the first of our objectives before I saw it. I gave the engines full throttle as Davenport adjusted the prop pitch to get a better grip on the air. We climbed as quickly as possible to fifteen hundred feet, in the manner which we had practised [sic] for a month and had discussed for three additional weeks.

"There was just time to get there, level off, attend to the routine of opening the bomb bay, make a short run and let fly with the first bomb. The red light blinked on my instrument board, and I knew the first 500-pounder had gone."

Captain Ted W. Lawson describing his participation in the Doolittle Raid of 18 April 1942, as quoted in *The War, 1939-1945, a Documentary History*, edited by Desmond Flower and James Reeves (1960; New York: Da Capo Press, 1997).

Historical Evidence

The United States ambassador and embassy staff, who had been confined within the embassy grounds in Tokyo since 8 December 1941 witnessed the Doolittle Raid. Ambassador Joseph G. Grew recorded the event. His account is a primary document. It is eyewitness evidence of what happened. Grew wrote:

". . . before lunch we heard a lot of planes overhead and saw five or six large fires in different directions with great volumes of smoke. At first we thought that it was only maneuvers but soon became aware that it was the first big raid on Japan by American bombers . . . We saw one of them apparently losing altitude and flying very low, just over the tops of the buildings to the west, and at first we feared that it had crashed but then realized that it was intentionally following these tactics in order to avoid the dives of pursuit planes and the anti-aircraft fire."

Grew noted, "We were all very happy and proud in the Embassy."

In June of that year the Japanese transported American diplomats, as well as American missionaries, teachers, newspaper correspondents, and businessman, by ship from Yokohama. That ship sailed to the French territory of Mozambique where an exchange of foreign nationals took place. The ambassador thus was not in Japan to report on subsequent air raids.

This inside account of Japan during the early months of the war appears in Joseph G. Grew, *Ten Years in Japan, a Contemporary Record Drawn from the Diaries and Private and Official Papers of Joseph G. Grew, United States Ambassador to Japan, 1932-1942* (New York: Simon and Schuster, 1944).

Japanese morale. The Japanese homeland could be hit by the war! The daring raid also raised morale in the United States.

One of the B-25s finished the raid low on fuel and landed north of Vladivostok. The Soviet Union interned the crew of five due to a neutrality agreement between the Soviet Union and Japan. The Soviets did not want to risk a war on a second front. The Soviets, allied with the United States during this war, transferred the airmen to Tashkent in south central Asia and later facilitated their "escape" to Allied Iran.

Japan implemented air raid measures and increased air defense operations. It transferred some air squadrons from the front line back to protect the homeland. The raid also prompted Japan to initiate a balloon-development and fabrication program

for a future attack against the United States. Though Japan was still winning the war when Doolittle's Raid struck, that soon changed at the battles in the Coral Sea and near Midway Island.

Coral Sea

As Japan prepared to attack Australia from New Guinea, the United States Navy moved two aircraft carriers, seven cruisers, and naval support vessels into the Coral Sea. The Japanese had three carriers and six cruisers in the Coral Sea. The two sides fought there from the 4th to the 8th of May 1942. Aircraft fought the battle. The opposing fleets never saw each other and never came within firing range of each other. Japan lost three aircraft carriers, one of which — the *Shoho* — sank. The United States lost one carrier, the *Lexington*. Japan lost four cruisers and

Figure 7-45. TBF torpedo planes drop their torpedoes (left). Torpedo explosions consume the burning Japanese aircraft carrier *Shoho* on 7 May 1942, during the Battle of the Coral Sea.

two destroyers, the United States one destroyer. This battle stopped Japan's southward drive. (Figure 7-45)

Midway

The Japanese planned to capture Midway Island, where the United States had a small base that protected Hawaii and that might serve as a forward base of operation against Japanese forces. In June of 1942, as a diversion for the Midway operation, Japanese forces attacked the United States naval base at Dutch Harbor (on the island of Unalaska) in Alaska and captured three islands near the western end of the Aleutian chain. The Japanese held and fortified these islands for a year. Due to intelligence reports, the United States naval forces in the North Pacific intercepted the main Japanese fleet heading toward Midway on 4 June. About 250 miles apart, the carrier ships of the two combatants fought the battle in the air. Aircraft from Midway joined the battle. Japanese and United States pilots flew torpedo bombers, dive bombers, and fighters. Japanese Mitsubishi A6M2 Zero fighters, Nakajima B5N2 Kate torpedo bombers, and Aichi D3A1 Val dive bombers, and American Consolidated

PBY patrol boats, Grumman Avenger torpedo bombers, Grumman Wildcat fighters, Douglas Dauntless dive bombers, Boeing B-17 Flying Fortress bombers, and other aircraft saw combat that day. The United States sank four Japanese carriers (*Akagi, Hiryu, Kaga,* and *Soryu*) and three transports; at least 7,500 Japanese died in the battle. The United States lost one carrier (the *Yorktown*). (Figure 7-46)

Figure 7-46. Navy SBD Dauntless dive bombers flying over burning Japanese ship at Midway, 6 June 1942.

"Midway was a crucial battle which reversed the whole position in the Pacific War," according to Mochitsura Hashimoto of the Japanese Navy. Coral Sea and Midway cost Japan dearly in terms of men

Historic Event

Between 4 and 8 May 1942 opposing navies fought a battle entirely in the air over the Coral Sea. The importance of aircraft in naval combat was reinforced the next month at the Battle of Midway, where again fleets within striking range of aircraft fought using aircraft against their respective opponents. In both cases, the United States Navy defeated the Japanese Navy.

Historical Note

The territory of Alaska figured in the war plans of the United States. It was a corner in the "strategic triangle" for Pacific defense in war plans Orange (1938) and Rainbow (1939). In 1939 the country began improving the defenses of Alaska and Hawaii and Panama, the defense triangle. The United States embarked on programs to construct a road and an airway — inland supply routes by surface and by air — to its distant northern territory. The road was the Alaska Highway (also known as the Alaska-Canada or ALCAN Highway), and the airway was the Northwest Staging Route that connected to the Alaska-Siberia Air Route (ALSIB). Both were important in the defense of that vast and sparsely settled territory, especially after the Japanese attack on the Aleutian Islands in June 1942 and during the campaign to recapture the Aleutian Islands of Attu, Agattu, and Kiska from the Japanese a year later.

and equipment as well as morale. The Allies were overtaking Japan in terms of aircraft development, production, maintenance, and training. Midway also prompted Japan to adopt a defensive position that gave the Allies a reprieve from the previously sustained Japanese offensive operations.

Allied Offensive

The Allies initiated a limited offensive operation at Guadalcanal, one of the Solomon Islands in the southwestern Pacific Ocean. The Japanese were constructing a bomber base there. Allied aircraft could reach Guadalcanal from the base at Port Moresby in southern New Guinea. Japanese aircraft based at Rabaul on New Britain Island were also within range of Guadalcanal. The amphibious invasion involved more than 80 ships, including the transports for the American Marines and fire-support ships. Marines landed at Guadalcanal and neighboring Tulagi island on 7 August 1942. The next day marines captured the airfield under construction which, under Allied control, became Henderson Field. When Allied carriers withdrew, the invading forces lost most of their air protection, and that enabled the Japanese to inflict heavy damages against forces much larger in number. Some of the Japanese pilots, like naval pilot Saburo Sakai, flew as much as 600 miles from base to the battle at Guadalcanal. Logistical problems regarding supplies and reinforcements plagued both sides. Both sides reinforced and attacked from time to time, while aircraft carriers provided support. The outcome on the island depended on the on-going naval contest to control the surrounding sea, which the Allies

tended to control by virtue of aircraft flying from Henderson Field during the day, but which the Japanese dominated at night. Finally in February 1943 the Allies secured the island when the Japanese evacuated. (Figure 7-47)

Figure 7-47. Dauntless dive bomber off Guadalcanal, Japanese transports burning in the background, 16 November 1942.

Personal Profile

Saburo Sakai (1916-2000) dropped out of high school and enlisted in the Japanese Imperial Navy in the early 1930s. He became a Navy pilot in 1937. In August 1942 he flew a long-range Zero over 600 miles from his base to reach Guadalcanal. In battle there he received severe injuries, including the loss of one eye, yet he returned to base! He continued flying. During World War II he flew over 200 combat missions and scored 67 kills. He ended the war as Japan's highest scoring ace. After the war he opened a print shop in Tokyo. He died 22 September 2000 at the age of 84.

Saburo Sakai

Guadalcanal helped the Allies define their Pacific strategy. By the summer of 1942, the plan was for the United States to lead the drive from the South and Southwest to the Philippines, and to drive across the central Pacific Ocean to the Philippines. The strategy called for island hopping, not island by island, but by leaps and bounds that might bypass strongholds and that might catch the Japanese by surprise, but always within range of supporting Allied bombers. The bomber

Figure 7-48. The Chance Vought F4U Corsair fighter-bomber became operational in the Pacific theater of operations in 1943. The Japanese called it Whistling Death for the high-pitched noise that came from the 1,800-horsepower engine as the aircraft dove.

crews appreciated the protective cover of fighter escorts, whether from island or carrier base. Pilots flying the Corsair fighter, for example, downed over 2,000 enemy aircraft and lost less than 200 of their own Corsairs; the Corsair was used heavily in the Pacific. The P-38, a long-range fighter when equipped with drop fuel tanks, also proved effective in the Pacific — offensively as well as defensively. (Figure 7-48)

In April 1943 Army Air Force pilots based at Guadalcanal and flying Lockheed P-38 Lightning fighters shot down the Mitsubishi G4M1 Betty bomber carrying the commander-in-chief of the Japanese Combined Fleet, Admiral Isoroku Yamamoto. That was over the island of Bougainville. Over the Solomon Sea, they also shot down an accompanying bomber carrying the admiral's staff. This seriously weakened the senior military leadership of Japan.

The battle for Rabaul in the summer and fall of 1943 opened the Allied southern drive in the Pacific, and the battle at Tarawa that November was part of the American drive across the central Pacific. This two-paths-across-the-ocean strategy took American forces to the Caroline Islands in the spring of 1944, the Philippine Sea in that summer, and the Palau Islands that fall. By the time Allied forces invaded the Philippines in October 1944, the United States was already sending long-range bombers from newly acquired bases in the Marianas against Japan itself. But Tokyo was beyond the range of U.S. fighters in the Marianas, so the bombers had no fighter cover. Bombers from the Marianas, therefore, flew high-altitude raids. Capturing the little (eight square mile) island of Iwo Jima (literally "sulfur island") in early 1945 gave the United States a fighter base that could provide fighter cover all the way to Tokyo.

The Allied advance was neither neat nor clean as there were counter-offensives and stalemates as well as bloody landings and jungle fighting from the South Pacific northward. Allied carriers remained busy moving into locations for air raids on Japanese positions and Japanese shipping; and Japanese carriers provided defensive support for the retreating forces.

Flight Lines

"The Zero pilots were notified to guard and protect Admiral Yamamoto's Betty . . . The weather at that time, the visibility, was good; the altitude of the two Bettys was 2,500 meters, and the six Zeros flew right behind the rear of the two bombers at 3,000 meters. They were only about ten minutes from the Buin Airfield when they encountered the P-38s. They never suspected the P-38s would approach from a lower altitude, and they were scanning the horizon and above because they had fairly high mountains on their left-hand side. They were surprised to be attacked unexpectedly from the rear and from a lower altitude. . .

"The immediate thought that went through his mind was to not to try and shoot the P-38s, but rather to repel them from the attack mode. So all of the six Zeros made a straight dive from their higher altitude to intercept in between the bomber and the oncoming P-38s. They kept firing, rather than at the P-38s, they kept shooting in front of the path of the P-38s trying to repel the P-38s coming toward the Betty. Of course, after the initial

Admiral Isoroku Yamamoto

attack by the first wave of P-38s they [the Zeros] were all busy trying to recover their altitude and get ready for the second wave of P-38s. By the time he [Zero pilot Kenji Yanagiya] recovered his position, he saw smoke coming out of Admiral Yamamoto's Betty . . ."

Translator Makoto Shinagawa relaying the story told by Zero pilot Kenji Yanagiya, who had been flying cover for Admiral Yamamoto on 18 April 1943; as printed in *Lightning over Bougainville, the Yamamoto Mission Reconsidered*, edited by R. Cargill Hall (Washington: Smithsonian Institution Press, 1991).

Personal Profile

Richard Ira Bong (1920-1945) scored forty confirmed victories in the air during World War II. That made him the leading ace of the United States for both world wars.

A native of Wisconsin, Bong learned to fly in the Army Air Corps. He served briefly as an Army flight instructor. He spent most of the war in the Pacific with the 5th Air Force. Bong flew a Lockheed P-38 Lightning in combat over New Guinea and the Philippines. The large twin-engine P-38 was sometimes called the fork-tailed devil because of the vertical fins on twin booms. It was used for ground-attack and bomber-escort missions. Bong used the plane to dive on enemy aircraft, shoot from close range, and pull up. He had scored his "kills" before later models of the P-38 were equipped with dive brakes that enabled other pilots to dive steeply and recover; dive brakes were flaps attached to the wings near the engine nacelles. General Douglas MacArthur presented Bong the Congressional Medal of Honor in 1944. General George C. Kenney called Bong "Ace of American Aces."

Richard Ira Bong

After completing two tours of combat duty in the Pacific, Major Bong became a test pilot. On 6 August 1945 he was making an acceptance flight of a jet-powered Lockheed P-80A Shooting Star at Burbank, California. The engine flamed out after the plane lifted off the runway. The plane stalled and crashed. Bong died at the age of 24.

Historical Note

The early P-80 jet aircraft experienced a number of crashes. Ace Richard I. Bong was the sixth death in a crash of the P-80, and the Army grounded the planes while investigating his crash. That investigation revealed that

some crashes were due to pilot error, some to structural failure, and some, like Bong's, to the failure of the Allison jet engine. The death of the war ace, the end of the war, and the cancellation of war contracts threatened the P-80, but the nation's first combat jet also served as a trainer for jet pilots going to Korea several years later.

Historical Note

Australian, British, and New Zealand pilots also downed enemy aircraft in the Pacific. Australia's top ace of the war, Clive Robertson Caldwell, scored 28.5 victories — mostly while based in Palestine early in the war, but also eight Japanese planes in the Pacific war.

While the United States pushed Japan from two fronts, the United Kingdom and China were to come overland through Burma and China, and the United Kingdom was to push up from India into the South China Sea. China was key to the United States because Allies in that position could support the Pacific campaigns, so the United States sent forces to the China, Burma, and India (CBI) Theater. Chiang Kai-shek led the Nationalist Chinese forces and commanded the Allied forces within China. Since the fall of Burma in 1942, supporting the Chinese fight against Japanese invaders meant flying men and materiel over "the Hump," the Himalaya Mountains, between British India and Chinese positions in China. The United States accepted responsibility for operating this air route, which was usually short of transport aircraft and trained personnel. In China, the American retired Army officer Claire L. Chennault led a small volunteer air force — the Flying Tigers, which began the war with 100 P-40Bs in summer

Figure 7-49. A bomber takes off above a row of Flying Tiger Curtiss P-40s at a U.S. base in China.

Figure 7-50. A Kamikaze plane moments before impact with a U.S. ship in the South Pacific.

1941. Chennault and the Flying Tigers became part of the regular United States Army Air Forces in July 1942, but the Allied air forces in China often remained short of equipment and personnel. Nonetheless, the combined Allied effort to retake Burma and push Japanese forces from China succeeded to the point that Allied bombers based in China started to raid Japan in June 1944. (Figure 7-49)

The North Pacific Ocean was not a line of advance but, after recapturing Attu and Kiska in the summer of 1943, the United States used the Aleutian Islands to stage bombing raids on Japan, not to invade, but to annoy and to keep Japanese forces defending the homeland.

Divine Wind

Military reverses eroded and nearly eliminated Japan's conventional air power. Production of aircraft and training of replacement airmen failed to keep pace with losses. Japan's declining air power further increased the capabilities of the Allied air forces in the Pacific. In the fall of 1944 Japan converted some air forces to kamikaze missions. *Kamikaze* is the Japanese word for *divine wind*. Kamikaze missions were a last resort that sent pilots in aircraft heavily loaded with explosives on suicide missions against Allied targets. Though state of the art at the start of the war, the Zero fighter was obsolete by this time, and the Navy sent many Zero fighters on kamikaze attacks. From October 1944 to the end of Okinawa in the spring of 1945, Japanese pilots flew 2,550 kamikaze missions, including over 300 during Japan's desperate but unsuccessful battle to hold Okinawa. Kamikaze pilots scored 475 hits or damaging near misses against aircraft carriers, battleships, and

escort carriers; they sank 45 ships. The attacks were damaging, but Japan could not sustain the offensive. It was too costly. (Figure 7-50)

The Japanese also launched its long-planned balloon attack on the United States. From November 1944 through April 1945, Japan launched more than nine

Flight Lines

"I believe in the victory of Greater Asia.

. . .

"I leave for the attack with a smile on my face. The moon will be full tonight. As I fly over the open sea off Okinawa I will choose the enemy ship that is to be my target.

"I will show you that I know how to die bravely."

Kamikaze pilot Akio Otsuka, 1944, as translated and quoted in *The War, 1939-1945, a Documentary History*, edited by Desmond Flower and James Reeves (1960; New York: Da Capo Press, 1997).

thousand bombing balloons. These were paper balloons armed with incendiary and anti-personnel bombs; the balloons measured 32 feet in diameter when inflated with hydrogen. Carried from Japan by the wind, several hundred balloons reached North America; during the war they were found from Alaska to Mexico and inland as far as Michigan. The balloons caused a total of six fatalities, all in one incident when someone on a church outing in Oregon picked up a bomb that then exploded. The incendiary possibilities, particularly during the dry months, seemed the most dangerous aspect of the balloons, so the Air Force stationed troops and paratroopers in western locations for fire-fighting missions. Fighter planes tried to intercept balloons in flight, though planes shot down only two balloons over the United States proper, one over California and the other over Nevada, and several balloons over the territory of Alaska.

Strategic Bombing

According to the United States Strategic Bombing Survey, "The air attack on Japan was directed against the nation as a whole, not only against specific military targets, because of the contributions in numerous ways of the civilian population to the fighting strength of the enemy, and to speed the securing of unconditional surrender." Japan was a single "total target." The United States used B-24s and B-25s from the Army's Eleventh Air Force based in the Aleutian Islands and PV-1s and PV-2s of the Navy Fleet Air Wing Four also based in the Aleutians as well as other carriers at sea. It used B-29s from the Army's Twentieth Bomber Command based in China and on islands in the Pacific. During the war the United States bombed 500 separate targets in Japan including, lastly, Hiroshima and Nagasaki. (Figure 7-51)

Historical Note

Airmen attacking Japan sometimes landed or crashed in Siberia. Of the 291 American airmen interned in the Soviet Union during the war, five were Doolittle raiders — the crew of a B-25 that landed at Vladivostok 16 April 1942. Another 242 had taken off from bases in the Aleutian Islands. These 32 flight crews flew in Army B-24s and B-25s or Navy PV-1s and PV-2s that reached Siberia between August 1943 and July 1945. The other 44 men — four crews — had flown from B-29s bases in China during the July-November 1944 period. The Soviets transferred the airmen via various routes to Tashkent in south central Asia, and on to Ashkhabad or Kizil Arvat or Baku near the Iranian border. The Soviets then facilitated the airmen's "escape" to Allied Iran. Secrecy kept the airmen's adventures in the Soviet Union from the public — and more importantly from the Japanese — until after the war. Their story is told in Otis Hays, Jr., *Home from Siberia, the Secret Odysseys of Interned American Airmen in World War II* (College Station: Texas A&M University Press, 1990).

B-29 Bomber

The B-29 Superfortress was designed for high-altitude missions. It was Boeing's successor to the B-17 Flying Fortress that also was a four-engine bomber. The B-29 was a pressurized, high-speed, long-range, heavy bomber. The power consisted of four supercharged, 2,200-horsepower Wright engines (R-3350 twin-row radials). The first prototype flew in September 1942. The B-29 was built during the war by Boeing in Renton, Washington, and Wichita, Kansas; Bell in Marietta, Georgia; and Martin in Omaha, Nebraska. A large sub-contracting program acquired equipment and subassemblies from throughout the country.

Figure 7-51. On the left, pilots from a U.S. Navy aircraft carrier receive last minute instructions before their attack on Tokyo. On the right, TBMs and SB2Cs from the carrier USS *Essex* drop bombs on Hokadate, Japan.

Figure 7-52. B-29 Superfortresses taxiing on the ramp.

With the capture of the Marianas Islands in the Western Pacific, the United States had accelerated its offensive against Japan. From Saipan in November 1944 the U.S. conducted a raid against Tokyo, 1,500 miles distant. The B-29s on this and later raids used their high-altitude capabilities to stay above anti-aircraft fire and above the effective range of fighter planes. The capture of Iwo Jima in February 1945 facilitated low flight, and from April to the end of the war. Iwo Jima provided fighter escort for the bombers. The bombing was highly effective and losses were only moderate.

Historic Event

On 10 March 1945 the United States tested strategic night-time firebombing. It raided Tokyo. This one raid destroyed one-fourth of the city and killed over 100,000 people.

Production started before all the equipment and installations were ready, so early production aircraft went immediately to modification centers for updating. "The battle of Kansas" describes the six-week period in March and April 1944 when the first B-29s for overseas service were modified. (Figure 7-52)

The first overseas delivery was via the Atlantic Ocean and North Africa to India and China. The first B-29 combat mission was a raid from India on Bangkok in June 1944. The first B-29 raid against Japan was made from four Chinese bases later in June 1944. The B-29 had remote-control power turrets, operated by gunners in sighting stations within the pressurized crew area of the aircraft, and the gunnery was computerized. According to Major General Curtis E. LeMay, "poor gunnery in the Orient was never the dreadful bugaboo which had confronted every commander in the European war, especially in the early days." LeMay transferred from Europe to the Pacific when the new, state-of-the-art B-29s entered service — prior to that Pacific bombers shared the problems of European bombers.

Firebombing

LeMay transferred to the Pacific in the summer of 1944. He observed, "Our big foe in the Pacific war, besides the Japanese, was just the Globe itself: the distances, the water, the weather, the mountains, the ever-acute logistic menace." LeMay directed the bombing of Japan. He developed the strategy of attacking Japan with low-flying B-29s at night. The year was 1945. His strategy was to fly B-29s low — at 5,000 to 9,000 feet — below anti-aircraft fire, and at night, since Japan had few night fighter planes.

LeMay tested his strategy on the night of 10 March 1945 when 325 B-29s, each loaded with ten thousand pounds of firebombs, raided Tokyo. One-fourth of the city, 16.7 square miles burned. A hundred thousand people died. (Figure 7-53)

Figure 7-53. B-29 Superfortress dropping a load of bombs.

LeMay applied this strategy of night fire raids until the end of the war. More than sixty cities were burned. Hundreds of thousands of civilians died. The narrator of the wartime propaganda and documentary film *To the Shores of Iwo Jima* referred to "blasting the enemy into ashes" on that small island — that was literally the case in firebombing Japan. LeMay later explained:

> "Killing Japanese didn't bother me very much at that time. It was getting the war over that bothered me. So I wasn't worried particularly about how many people we killed in getting the job done. I suppose if I had lost the war, I would have been tried as a war criminal. Fortunately, we were on the winning side."

Japan had little defense. Its only operational night fighter equipped with airborne radar was the Navy's Nakajima J1N1-S Gekko; Japan had other night fighters, but they were not radar equipped.

Assessment

The strategic bombing of Japan caused physical destruction as well as social and psychological disruption. Japanese morale was negatively affected by military reverses (especially from the loss of Saipan onward) and by war weariness, social unrest, and consumer shortages. Holding up Japan's declining morale were fear of defeat and its consequences, spiritual faith in the nation, obedience to the Emperor, and the news blackout that prevented them from knowing what was happening. Nonetheless, from mid-1944 onward Japanese morale declined. Aircraft production declined too. Japan had dispersed its aircraft industry in response to bombing, but could not maintain the quantity of production because of lack of supplies, damaging air attacks, and domestic problems.

Air raids destroyed large portions of Japan's 66 largest cities. The raids caused the evacuation of 8.5 million people from Japan's cities, and they brought the war to more than a third of the civilian population. The air raids injured 1.3 million people and killed 900,000. In contrast, LeMay lost a total of about 485 B-29s and about 3,000 men. After the war the Japanese cited air attacks as "the most important single factor" in causing them to doubt victory, in giving them a sense of forthcoming defeat, in making them unwilling to continue the war, and in causing them personal wartime worry.

Atomic Bomb

President Roosevelt died on 12 April 1945. Vice President Harry S. Truman became president. Truman entered office knowing nothing of the secret atomic weapon developed under Roosevelt's administration, but Truman made the decision to use the atomic bombs.

He followed the advice of his advisers: use the bomb against a target that would demonstrate its strengths; that is, against targets not already scarred by war. In fact, the United States had spared Japanese cities from incendiary attacks in order to better assess the effects of the atomic bomb. Kyoto was eliminated from consideration because it was a religious and cultural center. Targets of more military importance were Hiroshima, Kokura, Niigata, and Nagasaki. Weather conditions and operational factors at the time of the mission determined the final selection.

Historic Event

On 6 August 1945 the United States dropped an atomic bomb on the Japanese city of Hiroshima. Three days later, on the 9th, the United States dropped another atomic bomb, this one on the city of Nagasaki.

Nagasaki, Japan

The Commanding General of the Army Strategic Air Forces, Carl Spaatz, issued the order to deliver the "first special bomb as soon as weather will permit visual bombing after about 3 August 1945 on one of the targets." The 509th Composite Group, a special B-29 unit, carried the bombs. They encountered no fighter opposition or flak on two raids. On 6 August 1945 they dropped an atomic bomb on Hiroshima, and on 9 August, an atomic bomb on Nagasaki. Each bomb destroyed about a six-square-mile area. The bombs burned people, collapsed buildings, and started fires; atomic radiation injured and killed too.

In Hiroshima, approximately 60,000 to 70,000 people died and, in Nagasaki, approximately 40,000. Japan surrendered a few days later.

Debating the Bomb

Did the United States need to drop atomic bombs? The answer has been the subject of an on-going debate since August 1945. As early as 1946, the U.S. Strategic Bombing Survey concluded:

"Even without the atomic bombing attacks, air supremacy over Japan could have exerted sufficient pressure to bring about unconditional surrender and obviate the need for invasion, . . . [C]ertainly prior to 31 December 1945, and in all probability prior to 1 November 1945, Japan would have surrendered even if the atomic bombs had not been dropped, even if Russia had not entered the war [in the Pacific, which it did after the first atomic bomb had been dropped], and even if no invasion had been planned or contemplated."

Truman remained convinced "that the bomb did not win the war, but it certainly shortened the war. We know that it saved lives of untold thousands of American and Allied soldiers who would otherwise have been killed in battle."

General LeMay did not understand the point of the debate:

"Incidentally, everybody bemoans the fact that we dropped the atomic bomb and killed a lot of people at Hiroshima and Nagasaki. That I guess is immoral; but nobody says anything about the incendiary attacks on every industrial city in Japan, and the first attack on Tokyo killed more people than the atomic bomb did. Apparently, that was all right."

Or maybe he did understand — from a military perspective: "But all war is immoral, and if you let that bother you, you're not a good soldier."

Historical Note

General Curtis E. LeMay became the model for Stanley Kubrick's character Buck Turgidson, a nuclear-crazed general, in the 1964 movie *Dr. Strangelove*. For LeMay's account of events, see his autobiography : *Mission with LeMay, My Story*, by LeMay with MacKinlay Kantor (Garden City, NY: Doubleday & Company, 1965).

Peace

Germany had surrendered unconditionally on 7 May 1945. Japan surrendered unconditionally on 14 August 1945. The Allied strategy — to weaken the enemy from the perimeter — defeated both Germany and Japan. On VJ Day, 2 September 1945, MacArthur accepted the formal surrender of Japan aboard the USS *Missouri*. The war was over. Peace treaties needed negotiating, but the fighting was over. The troops could go home. (Figure 7-54)

Figure 7-54. General Douglas MacArthur as the Supreme Allied Commander signs the formal surrender document onboard the USS *Missouri* in Tokyo Bay. A formation of Vought F4U Corsairs and Grumman F6F Hellcats flew over as part of the surrender ceremony.

Conclusion

Some European history books call the period encompassing both the First and Second World Wars as the European Civil War and, thereby, stress the European nature of the conflicts on that continent. Similarly, some Japanese history books label the period 1931-1945 the Fifteen Year War and, thereby, emphasize Japan's continuing effort to expand in Asia and the Pacific during that period. For the British and the United States, which fought in both the Eastern and Western Hemispheres. World War II was truly a global war fought against different, albeit allied, enemies. This was a war against the aggressive imperialism, extreme militarism, and ultra nationalism of three authoritarian regimes. As such, the war was won by the Allies. The war overthrew the ruling regimes in Germany, Italy, and Japan, and ended the German, Italian, and Japanese empires. But issues were left unresolved, and these soon became the focus of a Cold War.

Study Questions

1. How did Germany use aircraft during the *blitzkrieg* invasions of Poland, Belgium, and France?

2. What defenses proved effective for Great Britain during the aerial Battle of Britain?

3. In what ways were helicopters and jet airplanes similar and dissimilar during World War II?

4. How did the aviation industry adopt line production during World War II?

5. What distinguished the Tuskegee Airmen and the Soviet airwomen of World War II?

6. How did aircraft support combat in African deserts, on Mediterranean shores, and on Germany's Eastern Front?

7. What were the vengeance weapons and how effective were they?

8. How did naval aircraft fight the war in the Pacific?

9. What aircraft attacked Japan, and what effect did these raids have on the war in the Pacific?

10. Which sources listed in the bibliography would you use to compare and contrast the techniques of different air forces of different countries during the war?

Bibliography

Arnold, H. H. *Global Mission.* New York: Harper & Brothers, 1949.

Bowman, Martin W. *USAAF Handbook*, 1939-1945. Mechanicsburgh, PA: Stackpole Books, 1973.

Constant, Edward W., II. *The Origins of the Turbojet Revolution.* Baltimore: Johns Hopkins University Press, 1980.

Dunmore, Spencer. *Wings for Victory: the Remarkable Story of the British Commonwealth Air Training Program in Canada.* London: McClelland & Steward, 1996.

Francillon, René J. *Japanese Aircraft of the Pacific War.* 1970; Annapolis, MD: Naval Institute Press, 1995.

Janes's Fighting *Aircraft of World War II*. Reprint of Jane's All the World's Aircraft, 1940-1946 editions; New York: Crescent Books, 1989.

Kelsey, Benjamin S. *The Dragon's Teeth? The Creation of United States Air Power for World War II*. Washington: Smithsonian Institution Press, 1982.

Latham, Colin and Anne Stobbs, *Radar, a Wartime Miracle*. Stroud, Gloucestershire, UK: Sutton Publishing Limited, 1996.

Noggle, Anne. *A Dance with Death, Soviet Airwomen in World War II*. College Station: Texas A&M University Press, 1994.

Spick, Mike. *Luftwaffe Fighter Aces, the Jagdflieger and Their Combat Tactics and Techniques*. London: Greenhill Books, and Mechanicsburg, PA: Stackpole Books, 1996.

Timeline

Light blue type represents events that are not directly related to aviation.

1939	September 1. Germany utilized fighters and dive bombers in its blitzkrieg invasion of Poland, an invasion that opened World War II.
1939	September 14. Igor I. Sikorsky made his first flight in a helicopter, the Sikorsky prototype designated VS-300; this VS-300 evolved into the first helicopter placed into production.
1940	January 6. Finnish Air Force Captain Jorma Sarvanto shot down six Soviet Ilyushin DB-3 bombers that invaded Finland during the Winter War of 1939-1940, a war in which losing Finland lost 67 aircraft and winning Soviet Union lost 684.
1940	May 26 - June 4. Fighter planes from Great Britain, notably the new Supermarine Spitfires, successfully defended British and French troops being evacuated by ship from Dunkirk on the coast of France.
1940	September. Great Britain and the United States reached the Destroyer Transfer Agreement whereby the neutral United States would transfer 50 destroyers to Britain in exchange for leases of bases in the British West Indies, Newfoundland, and British Guiana.
1941	March 11. The United States Congress passed the Lend-Lease Act which authorized the United States to lend or lease supplies and equipment to countries deemed vital to the security of the United States. About sixty percent of the aid went to Britain and its territories, about 20 percent to the Soviet Union, and lesser amounts to other countries — 38 countries in all received Lend-Lease assistance by the time the war ended.
1941	May 20. In the largest airborne invasion of World War II, the German Luftwaffe landed over 22,000 men on the Island of Crete; paratroop losses were high.
1941	June 22. German aircraft attacked the Soviet Union in the opening day of Operation Barbarossa and damaged many front-line Soviet aircraft on the ground at various airfields; German pilots destroyed well over 1,000 Soviet aircraft in the one day.
1941	August 14. Winston Churchill (1874-1965) of Great Britain and Franklin D. Roosevelt (1882-1945) of the United States met on board a ship off Newfoundland and agreed to what became known as the Atlantic Charter, by which they agreed to advocate freely chosen governments, free trade, freedom of the seas, and the participation of local populations in territorial changes.

1941   December 7. Japanese naval aircraft flying off carriers at sea attacked Pearl Harbor, Hawaii, and destroyed aircraft and battleships.

1941   In China, the Viet Minh league for the independence of Vietnam formed, and throughout World War II the Viet Minh opposed the Japanese and assisted the Allies.

1942   The 1,500-mile Alaska Highway was constructed to facilitate the defense of the United States territory of Alaska and to use Alaska as a military base of operation in the Pacific Ocean. At the same time the United States constructed the Northwest Staging Route airway along the path of the highway.

1942   April 18. General James H. "Jimmy" Doolittle led an air raid of American B-25 bombers against Japan's capital city of Tokyo.

1942   May 4-8. The navies of Japan and the United States fought the Battle of the Coral Sea when the fleets were within aircraft range, but not artillery range, of each other.

1942   July 18. German pilot Fritz Wendel flew the first jet-powered flight of the Messerschmitt Me 262 fighter; the engines were two Junkers turbojets; a couple hundred Me 262s enter service late in the war.

1942   October 1. Bell test pilot Robert Stanley flew the jet-powered XP-59A Airacomet for the prototype's first flight; the General Electric jet engines were based on British technology developed by Frank Whittle but given to the United States as part of the Allied war effort.

1943   January 14-24. Winston Churchill and Franklin Roosevelt convened the Casablanca Conference to plan war strategy. They agreed to increase bombing of Germany by the United States, to proceed with the invasion of Sicily as planned, and to transfer British forces to the Far East after the fall of Germany.

1943   April 18. American pilots flying Lockheed P-38 Lightning fighters shot down the Mitsubishi G4M1 Betty bomber carrying the commander-in-chief of the Japanese Combined Fleet, Admiral Isoroku Yamamoto.

1943   May 31. Tuskegee Airmen flew their first combat mission; based in North Africa, the black pilots flew fighter cover for a bombing raid against the Italian island of Pantelleria.

1943   July 10. The Allied invasion of Nazi-controlled Europe began with the invasion of Sicily from the air and the sea; the Allies called this Operation Husky.

1943   November 6-22. Winston Churchill, Franklin Roosevelt, and Chiang Kai-shek (1887-1975) of China attended the Cairo Conference to discuss Far East policy and agreed upon the unconditional surrender of Japan and the postwar disposition of various Japanese-occupied or Japanese-administered territories.

1944   June 6. Allied pilots flew almost 5,000 sorties in support of the D-Day landings on the Normandy coast.

1944   June 13. The first jet-powered V-1 flying bomb struck London, where they became known as the buzz bombs or doodlebugs.

1944   June 15. The United States Army Air Forces used the new B-29 Superfortress bomber for the first time to attack Japan; the aircraft were based in Chengtu, China.

1944   June 17. Iceland, long a Danish territory, became an independent republic.

1944   July. Forty-four nations participated in the Bretton Woods Conference, a financial meeting held
            in Bretton Woods, New Hampshire. The conference participants proposed an international
            bank and an international monetary fund to help stabilize the world's economy after the war.

1944   July 20. The July Plot to assassinate German Führer (leader) Adolf Hitler (1889-1945) failed.
            More than 200 plotters were arrested, and many were executed.

1944   August-October. The underground Polish Home Guard staged the Warsaw Uprising, but
            Germany suppressed the uprising with air raids and ground attacks; severed supply lines and,
            thereby, forced the Poles in Warsaw to surrender.

1944   August-October. At the international Dumbarton Oaks Conference in Washington City, China,
            Great Britain, the Soviet Union, and the United States drafted a charter for the proposed United
            Nations.

1944   September. Egypt, Iraq, Lebanon, Saudi Arabia, Transjordan, and Yemen, and Palestinian Arabs
            met in Alexandria to organize the Arab League.

1944   September 8. Germany introduced its new secret weapon, the V-2 ballistic rocket, by launching
            it against Paris and London.

1945   February 13. Allied bombers dropped firebombs on the German city of Dresden; these bombs
            ignited firestorms that consumed the town and killed at least 250,000 people.

1945   March. Having been invaded successfully by Russia in November 1939-March 1940 Winter War
            and having participated in the unsuccessful German invasion of Russia in 1941, Finland
            declared war against Germany. Finland thus fought both the Allied and the Axis Powers.

1945   March 10. The United States Army Air Forces tested strategic night-time firebombing by raid-
            ing Tokyo; this single raid killed over 100,000 people and destroyed a quarter of the city.

1945   May 7. Germany surrendered as Allied forces moved from the West as well as the East; this was
            V-E or Victory-in-Europe Day.

1945   May 14. Palestine was partitioned into Jewish and Arab sectors with the Jewish sector becoming
            the nation of Israel on this date, and with the Arab parts going to Transjordan.

1945   June 26. In San Francisco fifty nations signed the United Nations Charter, which was ratified at
            the first meeting of the General Assembly in October in London.

1945   July 17 - August 2. Winston Churchill, Joseph Stalin (1879-1953), and Harry Truman (1884-1972)
            attended the Potsdam Conference near Berlin to discuss the postwar situation and, in so doing,
            recognized the Soviet Union's influence in Eastern Europe.

1945   August 6. A B-29 of the 509th Composite Group, United States Army Air Forces, dropped an
            atomic bomb on Hiroshima, Japan; and on August 9th the United States dropped an atomic
            bomb on Nagasaki.

1945   August 9. After maintaining neutrality in the Pacific for years, the Soviet Union entered the war
            against Japan.

1945   August 14. Japan surrendered.

1945   August 17. The Parti Nasionalis Indonesia, led by Achmad Sukarno (1901-1970), declared independence from the Netherlands and began a four-year revolution that ended with independence in late 1949.

1945   August 20. Under pressure from the Viet Minh, Emperor Bao Dai (1913-1997) of Vietnam abdicated and within two weeks the Viet Minh proclaimed the Democratic Republic of Vietnam.

1945   September 2. Japan formalized its surrender.

CHAPTER 8

COLD WAR (1945-1958)

AVIATION HISTORY

Summary of Events

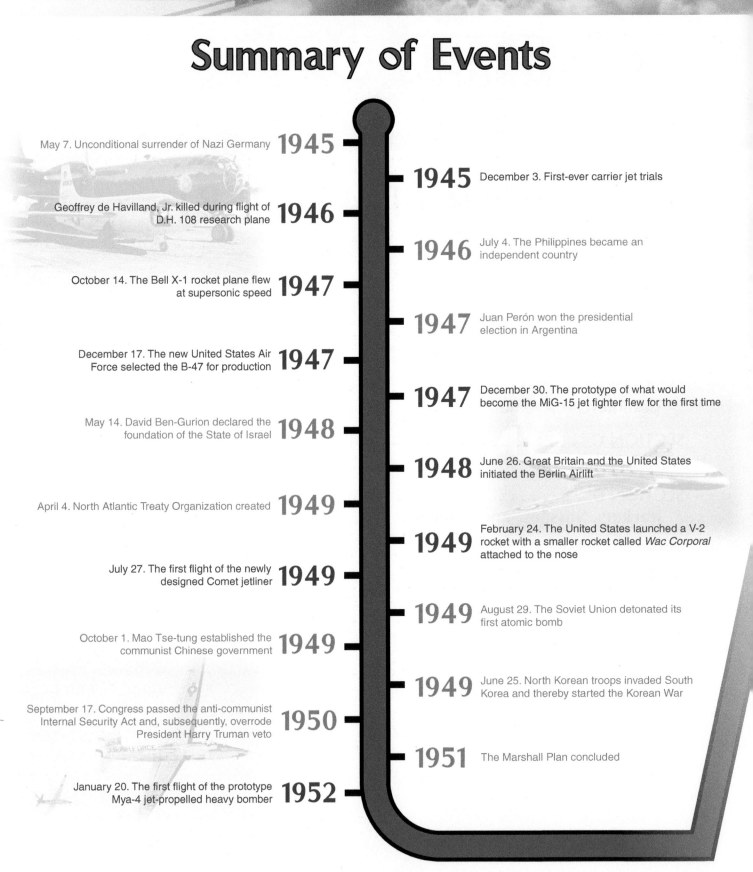

May 7. Unconditional surrender of Nazi Germany **1945**

1945 December 3. First-ever carrier jet trials

Geoffrey de Havilland, Jr. killed during flight of D.H. 108 research plane **1946**

1946 July 4. The Philippines became an independent country

October 14. The Bell X-1 rocket plane flew at supersonic speed **1947**

1947 Juan Perón won the presidential election in Argentina

December 17. The new United States Air Force selected the B-47 for production **1947**

1947 December 30. The prototype of what would become the MiG-15 jet fighter flew for the first time

May 14. David Ben-Gurion declared the foundation of the State of Israel **1948**

1948 June 26. Great Britain and the United States initiated the Berlin Airlift

April 4. North Atlantic Treaty Organization created **1949**

1949 February 24. The United States launched a V-2 rocket with a smaller rocket called *Wac Corporal* attached to the nose

July 27. The first flight of the newly designed Comet jetliner **1949**

1949 August 29. The Soviet Union detonated its first atomic bomb

October 1. Mao Tse-tung established the communist Chinese government **1949**

1949 June 25. North Korean troops invaded South Korea and thereby started the Korean War

September 17. Congress passed the anti-communist Internal Security Act and, subsequently, overrode President Harry Truman veto **1950**

1951 The Marshall Plan concluded

January 20. The first flight of the prototype Mya-4 jet-propelled heavy bomber **1952**

Light blue type represents events that are not directly related to aviation.

May 2. The Comet 1 entered commercial service as the first regular passenger jet service

1952

1952 July 23. The organization called Free Officers overthrew King Farouk of Egypt

November 12. The first flight of the large turboprop Tu-95 bomber

1952

1954 May 1. May Day celebration in Moscow displayed the new Mya-4 Bison heavy turbojet bomber. The TU-95 Bear bomber was demonstrated at the next May Day celebration

September 8. The Southeast Asia Treaty Organization (SEATO) was signed

1954

1954 July. The French withdrew from Vietnam, the United States rejected the Geneva Accords and moved into Vietnam

April 5. The Central or Middle East Treaty Organization was signed

1955

1955 May 14. The Warsaw Treaty of Friendship, Cooperation and Mutual Assistance was formed, commonly known as the Warsaw Pact

July. The United States was fooled into thinking there was a "bomber gap" with the Soviet Union

1955

1955 August 4. The first flight of the U-2 prototype

June 28. Polish workers led an uprising in Poznan, which became known as the Poznan Crisis

1956

1956 July 26. Gamal Abdel Nasser nationalized the Anglo-French Suez Canal Company

September 15. The Tupolev Tu-104 entered airline service

1956

1956 November 5. British and French paratroopers dropped into the Suez Canal zone

July 1. The 18-month International Geophysical Year began

1957

1957 October 5. The Soviet Union launched the satellite *Sputnik* into orbit, *Sputnik II* a month later, on 3 November, with the dog Laika on board, and *Sputnik III* on 15 May 1958

December 6. The first U.S. attempt to launch the Vanguard satellite ended when the rocket burned on the launch pad

1957

1958 January 31. The United States finally achieved its first successful launch of a satellite, *Explorer I*

October 1. The National Aeronautics and Space Administration began operations

1958

1958 October 26. Pan American placed the Boeing 707-120 into commercial service

Introduction

The Cold War began with the division of Europe into two armed camps in 1945 as the Western allies entered Germany from the west and the Soviet Union entered from the east. During World War II the Soviet Union joined a military alliance and received wartime aid, but it did not obtain any postwar commitments from the Western allies. The Soviets lost 25 million people during the war, mostly along the front with Germany. After the war the Soviets wanted a protective barrier of Eastern European nations within its sphere of influence in order to prevent any future attack from the West, like the German invasions of World War I and World War II and the French invasion by Napoleon Bonaparte more than a century earlier. The Western Allies in turn wanted to contain the spread of communism, for Soviet dictator Joseph Stalin had spoken of communist world domination. The failure of the World War II allies to agree on a postwar political structure for Germany divided Germany, Austria, postwar Europe in general, and soon the world. As British statesman Winston Churchill explained, "From Stettin in the Baltic to Trieste in the Adriatic an iron curtain has descended across the continent of Europe."

The Cold War was a rivalry of two superpowers — the United States and the Union of Soviet Socialist Republics (USSR). The Soviet Union adjusted to peace in Europe and strengthened its presence in central Europe while the United States continued fighting in the Pacific. Dropping atomic bombs on Japan was in part a demonstration of the new weapon and in part a warning to Stalin. War-weakened Europe yielded international prestige to the two superpowers, one of which dropped the super weapon — the atomic bomb — in 1945 and the other of which began exploding nuclear weapons in 1949. The Soviet Union and United States engaged in an international power struggle that was an arms race, a scientific and technological race, and a space race, as well as an ideological competition between democratic and communist ideals.

A cold war by definition is conflict short of combat, but the Cold War had its battles, as when the United States and Great Britain countered the Soviet blockade of Berlin with an airlift, or when the left nationalists and right nationalists of Korea waged war for the unification of that divided land and drew support from "cold warriors" in both camps, or when Vietnamese and Algerians waged local wars against foreign imperialist rule while the international community's attention focused on the global Cold War. The Cold War encompassed the two worlds of the superpowers and their respective allies. It also engulfed the Third World of countries outside the spheres of influence of the two superpowers, but within the imperialist objectives of both sides since both the United States and the Soviet Union sought to spread their respective ideologies. The chief weapons were words compiled as propaganda.

In addition to the Cold War, the end of World War II brought a resumption of civil aviation. That is the subject of Section A of this chapter. Section B covers the postwar airlines and commercial aviation in general around the globe. Hot spots are discussed in Section C, and rockets, missiles, and satellites in Section D.

After studying this chapter, you will be able to discuss the international organizations of civil aviation that emerged after World War II. You should also be able to describe the wartime technologies that became the postwar infrastructure of civil aviation. You will be able to draw the lines of the Cold War on a map of Europe and to identify the hot spots where representatives of the first (democratic) and second (communist) worlds and peoples of the Third World met in conflict involving the use of aircraft. You will also be able to discuss the development of rockets, missiles, and satellites during the early years of the Cold War.

SECTION A

RESUMPTION OF CIVIL AVIATION

Q & A

What? Cold War between democracy and communism as political systems and between capitalism and socialism as economic systems; a war of propaganda and ideology; an arms race, including nuclear arms, and a space race; tensions short of combat with a few geographically confined exceptions

When?   1945-1991

Where?   Worldwide

Who?   Two superpowers — the United States and the Union of Soviet Socialist Republics, and the nations aligned with the United States in the Western alliance or those aligned with the Soviet Union in the Eastern Bloc, also the unaligned nations of the Third World

Tupolev Tu-95 Bear

Why?   Failure of World War II allies to agree upon the postwar fate of Germany as well as competition and mistrust between democratic nations and communist countries

Surplus aircraft flooded the market worldwide at the end of World War II. Military transports became available from the various combatant nations as soon as the war ended, because the many nations demobilized — with the notable exception of the Soviet Union. Airlines in government service during the war, either through nationalization or contractual arrangements, returned to commercial ventures, often with war-surplus transports converted to civil use. Customers worldwide bought the war-surplus equipment, while others bought the old equipment being replaced by military and commercial operators. As expected, civil aviation boomed.

International Aviation

Planning for conversion from wartime to peacetime began during the war. Companies made plans, and governments decided national policy. Internationally, companies and governments discussed a wide range of options for postwar civil aviation. There were proposals for the internationalizing of civil aviation; a wartime British report had concluded that "the choice is between Americanization and internationalization." Imperial powers explored imperial plans too. There were bilateral discussions, like the Anglo-Soviet talks on landing rights. There were also many questions. Should there be competition, national monopolies, or international cartels? Should civil aviation be regulated by individual governments or controlled by an international body? Should any international body be controlling or advisory? Should there be regional arrangements or should agreements be global? Should there be bilateral international agreements or multilateral agreements? Should airspace be free and open, or should nations hold sovereignty to the airspace over them? Does national security require national sovereignty over airspace? Should defeated Germany and Japan be banned from having postwar aviation industries? Should an international organization operate airports? Should a country grant reciprocal rights or maintain an exclusionist or a protectionist policy? The planning was political and diplomatic as well as industrial and technical. It covered private flying, general aviation, and commercial transportation, and sometimes military aviation.

Chicago Conference

In November-December 1944 the United States hosted the International Conference on Civil Aviation in Chicago. At issue were the rights of transit and landing, the allocation of commercial air routes, the frequencies of flights over international routes, safety issues, technical matters, and navigation topics. Fifty-two allied, associated, or neutral countries participated in the conference; the Soviet Union chose not to attend. The participants reached agreement on technical matters, like accepting the United States standards for air rules, traffic control procedures, communication practices, and meteorological services.

They readily agreed on the first two "freedoms" of the air. These were the rights of transit and of "technical stop." The right of transit allowed a plane to fly across the territory of a foreign country. Technical stop referred to the right to land for technical, non-traffic, non-commercial reasons, such as refueling or repairs.

These rights applied to private flying as well as commercial aviation. The agreement on these rights of transit and landing might have opened the North Atlantic via British-controlled Newfoundland, but Britain excluded Newfoundland from the agreement because of its strategic position.

Great Britain and the United States disagreed over the commercial privileges, the final three "freedoms" of the air: the right to load passengers, mail, and cargo in the airline's country of origin and transport the same to a foreign country; the right to load a plane in a foreign country and fly to the airline's country of origin; and the right to transport passengers, mail, or cargo from one foreign country to another foreign country beyond the carrier's country. The United States and Britain represented two distinct positions at the conference, and Canada tried to mediate with an intermediary proposal. The United States wanted all Five Freedoms adopted multilaterally. Britain resisted. The British feared the large number of American planes and American pilots could dominate international routes, including those between Britain and Europe and between Britain and its empire; they also disliked the United States tying additional Lend-Lease aid to British concession on the commercial freedoms. Canada negotiated a middle ground on freedoms three and four. This involved an "escalator" clause that would limit the frequency of an airline's international flights depending upon the percentage of capacity filled on a particular route on a regular basis. The fifth freedom, even with an escalator clause, would not adequately

Historical Event

From 1 November through 7 December 1944 the United States hosted the International Conference on Civil Aviation, popularly called the Chicago Conference. The main topics of discussion were the Five Freedoms of the Air. These freedoms were rights or privileges:

1. The freedom to fly over foreign territory without landing.

2. The freedom to land for technical, non-traffic, non-commercial reasons.

3. The freedom to load passengers, mail, and cargo in the airline's country of origin and disembark them in a foreign country.

4. The freedom to take on board passengers, mail, and cargo in a foreign country and to transport them to the airline's country of origin.

5. The freedom to transport passengers, mail, or cargo from one foreign country to another foreign country beyond the airline's country.

Figure 8-1. Pan American Airways represented a threat to British civil aviation after the war. The concern was the U.S. domination of international routes.

limit the number of planes flown over a route, in the British opinion. The matter remained unresolved in Chicago. (Figure 8-1)

Each nation bargained from positions determined in large part by the war still being waged in Europe and the Pacific. The United States had plenty of state-of-the-art transport aircraft, and wartime production capacity that could be converted to civil transports, but the country lacked an international network of air bases. Britain had bases throughout the British Commonwealth, that is, around the world, but the war had made Britain dependent upon the United States for supplies and had opened airspace throughout the British empire to planes from the United States. During the war Britain had agreed to produce fighter planes and night-bombers, while the United States agreed to produce transport and other aircraft, so the U.S. was in a better position to produce civil transports. The war damaged Britain's economy and fueled an economic boom in the United States. During the war airlines based in the United States maintained their independent status while growing with government contracts. In Britain, the British Overseas Airways Corporation became a transport division of the military Air Ministry. In contrast, in the United States, Pan American retained its "favored instrument" status and monopoly of international routes. Moreover, Pan American expanded into British Overseas routes on a wartime basis. Britain had shared Frank Whittle's jet engine technology with the United States as partial payment of the growing Lend-Lease bill, but the United States did not share transport designs. Britain and the United States were wartime allies looking out for their respective national interests in the postwar future.

The Chicago Conference failed to reach multilateral agreements on all Five Freedoms. Freedoms one and two were adopted multilaterally in Chicago and later bilaterally by additional countries. Freedoms three, four, and five of the Air Transport Agreement were formalized through bilateral agreements, if at all. Countries not agreeing to the commercial clauses often cited as the reason fear of American — or sometimes British — domination of commercial aviation. By 1953 only 12 countries had agreed to the Five Freedoms, yet 41 accepted the two freedoms of transit and technical stop.

Within countries there was disagreement too. In the United States, for example, Juan Trippe of Pan American argued for a nationalist "chosen instrument" to be an all-American flag line owned jointly by the domestic airlines. This all-American airline would monopolize international routes. Trippe saw the Freedoms of the Air as an international challenge to the air supremacy of the United States. His proposal did nothing to ease foreign fears of the United States dominating postwar civil aviation. William A. Patterson of United Airlines and Henry Luce of *Time, Life,* and *Fortune* supported Trippe's all-American proposal. (Figure 8-2)

Figure 8-2. Juan Trippe of Pan American Airways pushed for an American flag airline.

In contrast, President Franklin D. Roosevelt favored more competition and more government regulation. Roosevelt wanted governments, rather than airlines, to negotiate foreign civil aviation rights, and that is what happened at the Chicago Conference. One of the achievements of the conference was governments and international bodies replacing airlines in civil aviation negotiations. This was formal and international acknowledgment that civil aviation had become defense, commerce, and foreign policy.

The Chicago Conference reached an Interim Agreement on International Civil Aviation. This created an international advisory body. While the Chicago Convention went to the participating nations for ratification, a Provisional International Civil Aviation Organization (PICAO) organized in 1945. It administered the 96 articles of the convention until the required 26 nations ratified the Chicago Convention. One basic principle was that each nation has exclusive sovereignty over its airspace. A significant action was the PICAO's 1946 adoption of the United States radio and navigation aid system as the world standard; this impacted the electronics industry in the United States and disappointed Great Britain, which had proposed its system for international use. In 1947 the permanent international advisory body replaced the provisional organization.

ICAO

The International Civil Aviation Organization (ICAO), headquartered in Montreal, began with 50 contracting or member nations. Its structure was similar to the new United Nations. It had an Assembly of all members which initially met annually, and a governing Council of leading members which met regularly during the year. In the early years the governing Council was composed of representatives from 21 contracting countries. The purposes of ICAO were (and are) to ensure safety, encourage civil aircraft design, encourage the development of airways, airports, and air navigation facilities, and to promote fair, safe, efficient, and economical operation of international airlines. The organization recognized the need for international standardization to achieve these objectives. The ICAO also entered into an agreement with the United Nations in 1947; by this agreement, the two organizations could participate in the work of the other in order to fulfill the requirements of their respective charges.

The ICAO quickly and efficiently organized and executed its assignments. In 1948 and 1949 the ICAO arranged joint financing for telecommunications services located in Iceland and Greenland. These facilities served many flights across the North Atlantic Ocean, though few flights of Iceland or Denmark (government of Greenland). The agreements covered telecommunications, weather stations, and air traffic control. The agreements were revised at Geneva in 1956. The ICAO's Geneva Convention of 1948 provided protection for the property rights of aircraft owners. The Rome Convention of 1952 defined the absolute liability of an aircraft operator for any damage caused to third parties on the ground. A Hague protocol of 1955 limited the liability of an air carrier to passengers. The ICAO continued to perform its functions routinely year after year.

IATA

Months after the Chicago Conference, in April 1945, representatives of 44 airlines based in 25 countries met in Havana and revived the International Air Traffic Association under the new name International Air Transport Association (IATA). This group focused on air traffic operations and established traffic conferences to set international fares pending the approval of the respective governments involved in a particular case. Soon bilateral agreements referred to fares as set by IATA.

Bermuda Agreement

At Hamilton, Bermuda, in February 1946 Great Britain and the United States resolved the stalemate reached at the Chicago Conference. By this time, Harry S. Truman was president of the United States, and Labour's Clement Attlee was prime minister of Britain; such changes in government brought shifts in the policies of the respective governments. The war was over and the postwar countries were eager to activate international routes. Also, Britain needed modern transport planes which the United States could provide until the British aviation industry developed and produced successful designs. The two countries reached a compromise agreement.

This bilateral agreement on commercial aviation included the three commercial Freedoms of the Air, in addition to the first two freedoms already accepted at Chicago. Britain yielded on the frequency of service United States airlines could offer, and the United States yielded on price by recognizing the IATA as the mechanism for joint rate-setting, subject to the two governments' approval. One United States critic of this feature argued, "Competition by consent is not competition." Britain also extended the freedoms of transit and technical stop to Newfoundland. Britain conceded more than the United States because Britain needed a loan that was before the U.S. Congress for approval, because Britain needed planes, and because Britain recognized the importance of good relations with the United States.

Although the United States had previously entered several bilateral air agreements with Eire (Ireland),

Iceland, Holland, and Sweden, the Bermuda Agreement became the model for postwar commercial aviation. The United States used the one-on-one bilateral approach with other nations thereafter. The Bermuda Agreement was reciprocal and was inclusive of all Five Freedoms, but adherence proved difficult at times for both Britain and the United States. Problems periodically arose over the negotiation of routes and fares. Both countries nonetheless reiterated their support for the bilateral agreement and the principles upon which it was based. The Bermuda Agreement remained in effect for thirty years (until the Bermuda 2 Agreement of 1977). Other nations tended to enter more restrictive bilateral agreements, along the lines of what Britain had proposed at the Chicago Conference.

Bilateral air agreements became a tool of Cold War warriors in the U.S. State Department. They traded air rights for the allegiance and support of foreign governments. In 1947 Britain and the United States held secret talks about coordinating their aviation policies pertaining to the Soviet Union. The two countries, bound by the Bermuda Agreement, thus were prepared to respond together when the communists blockaded Berlin the next year.

Infrastructure

During World War II, national defense and emergency measures justified the wartime trend for governments to intervene in civil affairs. This applied to aviation too and affected the postwar resumption of civil aviation. In the United States, the Civil Aeronautics Administration (CAA) began its first airport construction program in 1940, took over airport traffic control in 1941, and expanded air traffic control to airways in 1942. The Development of Landing Areas for National Defense program built 535 airports designated for civil control once the war ended. The CAA had begun a certification program for municipal airport traffic controllers just before the war. During the war, the CAA staffed over 100 airport control towers and over 20 airway traffic control centers. The federal personnel and the resulting federally imposed standardization of air traffic control procedures remained after the war. Flight advisory service, also begun by the CAA during the war, continued into the postwar period. Wartime and early postwar communication with aircraft was "preventive control" in that the controllers spoke with airline dispatchers or interstate airway communication stations which relayed messages to and from pilots. The expanded wartime infrastructure in the United States — unharmed by the battles that

devastated European and Asian infrastructures — set the standards adopted at the Chicago Conference. The infrastructure also supported a postwar boom in commercial air transportation in the United States.

Civil Aeronautics Administration

Aviation was the number one industry in the United States during World War II. It dropped to 12th place in 1948, mainly due to the loss of military contracts. The industry clearly needed government support despite a congressional tendency to limit funding to government agencies. To do more without more, the Civil Aeronautics Administration (CAA) decentralized. Aeronautical engineer Theodore P. "Ted" Wright led the agency's reorganization. Wright kept policy making at the headquarters in Washington, and he assigned the administration of the policies to the regions; that is, pilots, mechanics, and manufacturers would deal directly with CAA personnel in their respective regions. Under the designee program, the agency designated factory employees, aircraft inspectors, and flight instructors. This relieved the CAA from inspecting parts, planes, and pilots. The agency recognized about 8,000 designees during the first year of this program (1946-1947). It introduced the technical standard order (TSO) that allowed parts manufacturers to certify that their parts met the published performance requirements contained in the orders. Overall, the agency's decentralization made it possible to regulate safety despite being poorly funded during the postwar period. Other nations faced even bigger challenges with infrastructures and economies destroyed by World War II.

Phonetic Alphabet

Internationally, the postwar infrastructure included wartime improvements in voice-communication radios and the wartime Allied "combined" phonetic alphabet, which soon evolved into the international phonetic alphabet. A phonetic alphabet is one in which a spoken word stands for each letter in an effort to avoid confusing similarly sounding or indistinctly spoken letters. In 1942 the Allied forces adapted the spoken equivalent of the semaphore alphabet of flag signals into the combined phonetic alphabet used during World War II. After the war, the International Civil Aviation Organization employed linguists to *scientifically* devise a new international alphabet. That new "Alfa-Bravo-Coca" alphabet replaced the older, military "Able-Baker-Charlie" in 1952. The United States agreed to the changes in exchange for

Historical Note

Languages change. So do alphabets, even phonetic alphabets. Today's phonetic alphabet has a long and colorful past. This table shows the changes from the semaphore alphabet to phonetic alphabet used in modern aviation.

Recognizing obsolete terms in the phonetic alphabet may enable one to date a historical document and may make one a better critic of flying films, but staying current regarding usage facilitates clear communication in the flight environment and thereby promotes safety.

Phonetic Alphabet										
A	Alfa	Adam	Able	Alfa	Alpha	N	Negat	Nan	Nectar	November
B	Baker	Bravo				O	Option	Oboe	Oscar	
C	Cast	Charlie	Coca	Charlie		P	Prep	Peter	Papa	
D	Dog	Delta				Q	Queen	Quebec		
E	Easy	Echo				R	Roger	Romeo		
F	Fox	Foxtrot				S	Sail	Sugar	Sierra	
G	George	Golf				T	Tare	Tango		
H	Hypo	How	Hotel			U	Uncle	Unit	Union	Uniform
I	Item	India	Interrogatory			V	Victor			
J	Jig	Juliett				W	William	Whiskey		
K	King	Kilo				X	X-ray	Extra	X-ray	
L	Love	Lima				Y	Yoke	Yankee		
M	Mike	Metro	Mike			Z	Zed	Zebra	Zulu	

the ICAO designating English the international language of aviation. The ICAO adopted several changes in the international phonetic alphabet after 1952 that yielded the current "Alpha-Bravo-Charlie" alphabet.

Landing Systems

World War II yielded two main landing systems for poor visibility conditions: the military ground controlled approach (GCA) and the civil instrument landing system (ILS) system. The prewar low-frequency four-course radio navigation systems were old and not adequate to meet postwar needs. Both the GCA and ILS systems sent signals from the ground. The GCA required the signals to be highly directional radar beams; in fact, the only equipment needed was ground-based radar and communications radio. Ground equipment would send two radar beams toward an incoming aircraft. One beam pinpointed the aircraft in relation to the lateral approach path (left, right, or on course). The other beam established the aircraft in relation to the vertical glide path (high, low, or on course). The military GCA controller radioed instructions to the pilot and thereby controlled the approach. (Figure 8-3)

In the civil ILS system the pilot "read" the beams on cockpit instruments and adjusted the flight in order to center the beams on the correct glide path. The ILS used a localizer, glide path, and marker beacons, all of which were radio broadcast units and each of which

required a separate receiver in the cockpit of the plane. The third system then in use was the SCS-51, or Signal Corps System 51. It was simply an Army version of the ILS system. The GCA required less equipment and less training of pilots, while the ILS required no ground controller and thus no training of the controller. (Figure 8-4)

The Provisional International Civil Aviation Organization tested European systems, as well as GCA and ILS, in order to determine the preferred system. PICAO selected the ILS, which had the potential of linking with an automatic pilot system. The GCA was notably more precise during this early period, but the ILS was cheaper to install and operate. Commercial pilots argued successfully for the ILS system to be installed at civilian airports. Commercial pilots thus determined what system general aviation pilots would use, though most small planes lacked the instruments necessary to use ILS. The 1945 Collier Trophy for greatest achievement in aviation went to Luis Alvarez, developer of the GCA, rather than to the CAA, developer of the ILS. The CAA finally adopted GCA as a supplement to ILS at busy airports. Airport traffic controllers liked separating traffic by the airport surveillance radar (ASR) used in GCA, rather than by time as previously done. Pilots appreciated the precision of GCA and ILS. Some airports used both systems. By the early 1950s, use of ILS and GCA lowered weather minimums necessary for safe landing and reduced the number of flights canceled due to weather.

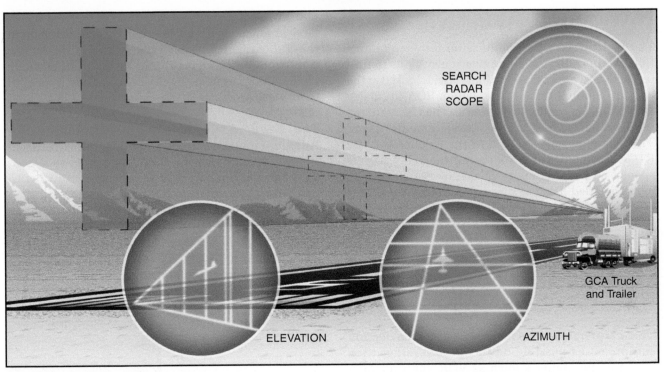

Figure 8-3. The main components of the Ground Controlled Approach system are a ground-based radar site, a surveillance radar unit, and a communication radio for the controller. The controller on the ground monitors the approaching aircraft on the radar screens and radios altitude and heading corrections to the pilot.

Localizer Transmitter

Figure 8-4. The main components of the Instrument Landing System (ILS) are the localizer transmitter, glide slope transmitter, and two marker beacons located along the approach path. A receiver and ILS indicator are located in the aircraft to guide the pilot along the approach path. The basic system adopted after the war is very similar to the one used today.

Glide Slope
Transmitter

Middle Marker

Outer Compass
Locator

Navigation Aids

The Radio Technical Commission for Aeronautics (RTCA) investigated air navigation systems to find one standard for civil and military use. It looked at the omnidirectional radio range, which RCA (formerly the Radio Corporation of America) had announced in 1941, before the United States entered the war. The war sped development of the technology. The RTCA recommended the omnidirectional range in its special committee report, SC-31, of 1948, and also recommended distance measuring equipment (DME) and precision approach radar (PAR). The commission

Historical Note

In 1949 *Aviation Week* coined the term "avionics" to describe aviation electronic devices.

stated a preference for placing as much navigation equipment as possible on the ground rather than in the plane. Better known as VOR, the <u>v</u>ery high frequency <u>o</u>mnidirectional <u>r</u>ange system became operational on VOR or Victor (V) airways beginning in 1952. These airways were highways in the sky. Within two years the United States maintained over 45,000 miles of Victor airways. The technology continued in development — to eliminate FM (frequency modulation) radio interference, to increase the precision of omnirange signals, and to fix other problems. (Figure 8-5)

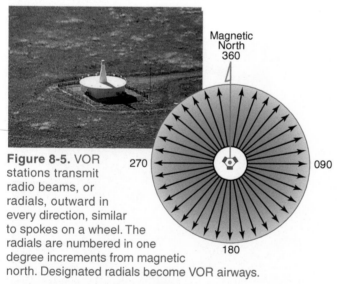

Magnetic North 360

270

090

180

Figure 8-5. VOR stations transmit radio beams, or radials, outward in every direction, similar to spokes on a wheel. The radials are numbered in one degree increments from magnetic north. Designated radials become VOR airways.

The Aircraft Owners and Pilots Association (AOPA) objected to deactivating four-course radio ranges, whose low/medium-frequency signals provided weather information beyond the range of very high frequency signals. Meanwhile, the CAA distance

measuring equipment system competed with the Navy's tactical air navigation (TACAN) system throughout the 1950s. The Korean War, in the early 1950s, interrupted development and installation of many civil avionics systems by diverting money from civil to military programs.

The Navy, Air Force, and Civil Aeronautics Administration established a Landing Aids Experiment Station in foggy Arcata, California, in 1946. Neon-light bars, high-intensity incandescent Bartow lights, colored lights, one-side lighting, two-side lighting, centerline lighting, slopeline lights, European lighting systems, and even fog dispersal were tested before the facility closed in 1950. In the mid 1950s a consensus finally emerged in favor of centerline lighting on 24 T-bars lined up from the runway threshold and extending 3,000 feet along the approach path. This was the British system favored by most international aviation organizations of the time. (Figure 8-6)

Landing Threshold

Figure 8-6. After years of research, a consensus was finally reached on a standard approach lighting configuration consisting of 24 T-bar lights extending out from the centerline of the runway.

World War II also internationalized LORAN (long range aid to navigation) technology, developed in the United States, but operated by British and Canadian military personnel as well as the U.S. Coast Guard during the war. At the end of the war there were 47 pairs of LORAN stations in operation, though the technology mostly supported maritime navigation rather than air navigation during the postwar period.

General Aviation

The United States led the world in military aviation, commercial aviation, and general aviation during the postwar years. The United States sold nearly 8,600

Figure 8-7. The Beechcraft V-tail Bonanza was a popular general aviation airplane built after the war.

trainers before the war ended in the Pacific. Private pilots, flight schools, and fixed-base operators bought the training aircraft, which had to be refurbished and recertified for civil use. New aircraft were also built, such as the Beechcraft Bonanza, North American Navion, Piper PA-11 and PA-12 versions of its earlier Cub J-3 and J-5 aircraft, Republic Seabee amphibian, Stinson Voyager, and the Bell 47 helicopter. The United States had suspended civil aircraft production during the war. Manufacturers resumed production in 1945 and made 2,047 civil aircraft that year. Production quickly rose to 35,001 civil aircraft in 1946. Of that total, 34,568 were personal or general aviation planes and 433 were commercial, transport aircraft. Aeronca alone built 7,555 airplanes that year, mostly the two-seat Model 7AC Champion. Nearly 80,000 aircraft were registered to private owners, fixed-base operators, charter services, and flight schools. (Figure 8-7)

Military pilots returning to civilian life and veterans with educational benefits financing flight lessons increased the number of private pilots. Women too resumed private flying as lessons and aircraft again became available. In 1945 alone the United States awarded pilot certificates to over 20,000 private pilots. By the end of 1946, nearly 190,000 private pilots held certificates. To accommodate the large number of private pilots, the Civil Aeronautics Administration dropped the requirements to learn navigation and meteorology as prerequisites for a certificate; the CAA abandoned this experiment after a few years. The simplification of private flying regulations lasted longer.

The Federal Airport Act of 1946 remained in effect for over 20 years. When Congress considered the act, AOPA objected to the allocation of airport funds at a ratio of 29 fields for small planes to each field for airliners. The pilots' organization argued

unsuccessfully that the ratio of airfields should correspond to the given ratio of 100 small planes for each airliner in the country. Unlike the national highway program, the airport program failed to win adequate appropriations, much less increased appropriations. Cold War sentiments pushed the available funds toward a common system of airports and navigation facilities for defense and commercial aviation; this meant less for general aviation needs and gave a defense appearance to the civil airport program. The total number of federally recognized airports in the United States rose from 4,025 in 1945 to 6,839 in 1955.

The postwar sale of personal aircraft boomed, but only briefly. The pent-up wartime demand lasted into 1947, but then sales began dropping. Production also dropped — to 15,617 civil aircraft in 1947, to 7,302 in 1948, 3,545 in 1949, 3,520 in 1950, and to a low of 2,477 in 1951. According to government figures, the annual cost of operating a small plane in 1947 was approximately half the initial sale price. At the time the Aircraft Owners and Pilots Association objected to costly new electronic navigation aids, like the very high frequency omnidirectional ranges (VORs), that would drive up the cost of flying even higher. The CAA argued that improved air traffic control required that more sophisticated equipment be installed in small planes.

New aircraft continued to become available. Mooney entered production with Al Mooney's single-seat M-18 Mite in 1948. Beechcraft first flew its six-place D-50 Twin-Bonanza in 1949, and Aero rolled out its five- to seven-place Commander executive plane in 1951. Taylorcraft fitted fiberglass molding to the tubular frame of its four-seat Model 20 Ranchwagon introduced in 1955, and Cessna introduced the four-place Model 182 with "Land-O-Matic" tricycle gear in 1956. Despite the development of new general aviation planes,

Mooney M-18 Mite

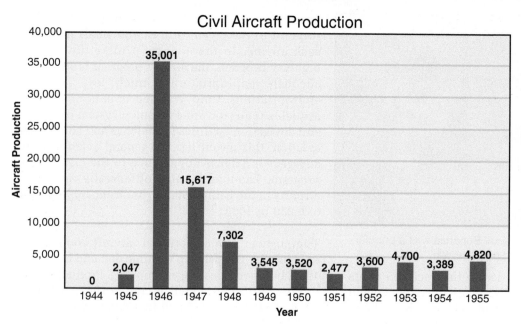

Civil Aircraft Production

Aircraft Production

Year	Production
1944	0
1945	2,047
1946	35,001
1947	15,617
1948	7,302
1949	3,545
1950	3,520
1951	2,477
1952	3,600
1953	4,700
1954	3,389
1955	4,820

Figure 8-8. Civil aircraft production in the United States, 1944 - 1955. Data from the Aircraft Industries Association of America, *The Aircraft Year Book 1956* (Washington: Lincoln Press, 1957).

production figures never again reached the highs of 1946. (Figure 8-8)

Homebuilders

After World War II, homebuilders in several countries organized to protect and promote their interests. In the United Kingdom, they founded the Ultralight Aircraft Association, which later merged into the Popular Flying Association. In France the Réseau du Sport de l'Air took the place of Henri Mignet's prewar Réseau des Amateurs de l'Air. In the United States, in 1953, homebuilders organized the Experimental Aircraft Association.

Agriculture

The postwar boom in aviation affected agriculture in several ways. The Flying Farmers and Ranchers organized as but one of several organizations that encouraged the use of aircraft in agriculture. Spraying and dusting became businesses. The federal government sponsored control programs for grasshoppers, spruce budworms, Mediterranean fruit flies, and gypsy moths. Mosquitoes and other pests, including pesty plants like the western sagebrush, were also sprayed. Coyotes and other animals that preyed on livestock were hunted from planes. Fertilizer and seed were dusted on fields. The airplane replaced the packline to deliver supplies for shepherds and other workers in remote locations. Also, the increased number of people and increased volume of cargo flown across borders introduced foreign diseases,

plants, insects, and animals, and, therefore, increased the need for agricultural inspections at airports of entry. Airplanes were also used by wildlife, forestry, and fisheries personnel in natural resource management.

Historical Evidence

Advertisements are historical documents that contain evidence of how marketers presented products to customers. In 1946 Taylorcraft advertised a plane "for every farmer":

"No more [do] bad roads keep you marooned in winter. Riding fence, checking stock, inspecting crops, trips for implement parts and attendance at stock sales and farm meetings are matters of pleasant minutes with your 'Ace.' Farm wives, too, enjoy the 'Ace,' with its friendly comfortable side-by-side seating."

This was the "modern way of farming," according to the Taylorcraft advertisement, which appeared in the *Montana Farmer* (1 October 1946).

COMMERCIAL AVIATION

Airlines had proved their worth during the war. Some nations nationalized their airlines for the duration of the war. Others, like the United States, contracted with the airlines for services needed in support of the war effort. Airlines of the victorious Allied nations tended to benefit from the war, whereas airlines of the defeated Axis countries suffered in ways that many did not survive. The war left newly constructed airfields and provided newly developed technologies to commercial aviation. The postwar remains reflected the dominance of reciprocating engine-powered aircraft during the war, but the wartime jet technologies became available for commercial development.

After World War II, commercial aviation worldwide experienced a substantial and sustained boom. Some historians call the increase in passengers and in miles flown a transportation revolution. During the postwar period the United States emerged as the clear leader of international aviation. British aviation rose to a prominent position in Europe. Airlines based in Latin American countries formed, struggled, and sometimes succeeded locally, regionally, and even internationally. Africa remained largely in colonial status and that extended to its airways. Asia, like Europe, was rebuilding from the devastation of the war, and it was troubled by the Cold War-era conflicts in Korea and Vietnam. The Cold War affected airline operations near hot spots, diverted production and capital from commercial programs, promoted military development of aviation over commercial, and encouraged standardization of military and civil infrastructures.

United States Airlines

During World War II, the "big five" airlines — American, Eastern, Pan Am, TWA, and United — as well as the smaller airlines like Continental, Delta, Pennsylvania Central, and Northeast transported cargo and troops, spies and diplomats, medical supplies and medical evacuees across continents and oceans, arctic regions and tropical jungles, even deserts. Coordinated by Edgar Stanley Gorrell, president of the Air Transport Association since its founding in 1936, the airlines proved the effectiveness and safety of air transportation. The Army's Air Transport Command and the Naval Air Transport Service

Historical Note

Flying boats as airliners became obsolete during the immediate postwar period. Compared to the postwar landplanes, flying boats were expensive to operate and maintain. They were aeronautically inefficient, and they were unable to serve inland destinations. The wartime development of a global network of land bases eased the airline industry's transition to landplanes.

Most flying boats in postwar service were older prewar or wartime machines, like British Sunderlands converted to Hythe-class airliners, or the Sikorsky S-43 amphibians used in Brazil, or the Boeing 314 clipper ships used across Atlantic and Pacific waters. Developed before the war but constructed after the war, the French flying boat Latécoère 631 flew the Air France route from Biscarosse, France, to Port-Etienne, French West Africa, to Fort-de-France in Martinique. The large Latécoère 631 could carry 46 passengers in luxury and could cruise at 185 mph. The range was nearly 4,000 miles, but the aircraft was not competitive as an airliner. It was soon withdrawn from service.

Landplanes were more efficient than flying boats. Pan American replaced the Boeing 314s in Pacific service with Douglas DC-4s, four-engine planes with a range of 2,500 miles. Pan American stopped using flying boats in 1946, and even the island nation of Great Britain closed the last of its commercial flying boat operations in 1958.

Short Sunderland V

1946		1950		1955	
1	Beechcraft	5	Boeing SA-307B	10	Boeing 377
1	Boeing 247-D	10	Boeing 377	93	Convair 240
5	Boeing SA-307B	103	Convair 240	122	Convair 340
427	Douglas DC-3	388	Douglas DC-3	302	Douglas DC-3
86	Douglas DC-4	150	Douglas DC-4	89	Douglas DC-4
3	Lockheed Electra	111	Douglas DC-6	173	Douglas DC-6
17	Lockheed Lodestar	11	Lockheed Lodestar	63	Douglas DC-7
7	Lockheed Constellation	83	Lockheed Constellation	10	Lockheed Lodestar
1	Sikorsky S-38	33	Martin 202	133	Lockheed Constellation
11	Stinson			18	Martin 202
				100	Martin 404
				5	Vickers Viscount

Figure 8-9. Number of planes and type used by domestic airlines. Data from the Aircraft Industries Association of America, *The Aircraft Year Book 1956* (Washington: Lincoln Press, 1957).

provided the majority of wartime transport service, flying more miles than the civilian airlines, but the civil assistance proved crucial to the global air transport network supporting the Allies. These wartime experiences provided thousands of experienced pilots and ground crews for the postwar airlines.

Grandfather rights eased the transition to peacetime for the major airlines, which emerged from the war with rights to their routes as of 1938. American Airlines returned to the Southern Transcontinental route between Washington and Los Angeles, through Philadelphia, Nashville, Dallas, and El Paso. United Air Lines operated the main Transcontinental route between New York City and San Francisco. Transcontinental & Western Air (TWA) returned to its major "Lindbergh line," which had stops in Pittsburgh, Columbus, St. Louis, Kansas City, and Albuquerque. Northwest Airlines resumed operation of the Northern route between Chicago and Seattle, and extended that route to New York.

Before World War II, airlines based in the United States had used twin-engine Douglas DC-3s and other two-engine, all-metal transports. TWA had just introduced into service the four-engine pressurized Boeing 307 Stratoliner when the war started. After the war, the airlines used much of the same equipment, added war-surplus equipment like the Lockheed Lodestar, and ordered new equipment with features developed during the war. The old DC-3 remained ubiquitous. TWA introduced the Lockheed Constellation to service, and United the Douglas DC-4 (civilian version of the Skymaster). Eastern and TWA purchased the Martin 404 for trunk service. The shifting composition of the fleets was reflected in the increasing speed of the airliners. The average speed of domestic scheduled air carriers in 1946 was 160 miles per hour. In 1950 the average was 182 miles per hour; in 1955, it was 209 miles per hour. (Figure 8-9)

Competition

The airlines competed on speed and service. Accidents and groundings of aircraft temporarily hurt the affected airlines. A fire aboard a TWA Constellation, for example, killed five people in July 1946. The government grounded the 43 Constellations then in service. In October 1947 a fire caused a DC-6 to crash: 52 people died. Another fire, though not fatal, the next month prompted the three airlines operating the DC-6 to ground the aircraft. In both cases, the problem was traced to design features in the fuel system. Modifications were made, the aircraft re-entered service, and both models established good safety records.

Douglas DC-6B

Historical Note

A 12-horsepower engine powered the Wright brothers' flights of 1903. Charles Lindbergh used a 223-horsepower engine to fly nonstop across the Atlantic Ocean in 1927. Four 2,200-horsepower engines provided a total 8,800 horsepower to the Lockheed Constellation airliner introduced to service in 1947.

What is horsepower, and what is the difference between 12 and 8,800 horsepower?

Horsepower is a rate of work: so much force moves so much weight so far in so much time. In an old tradition one horsepower is the equivalent of the output or work of one carthorse. According to the dictionary, horsepower is a foot-pound-second unit of power. One horsepower is 550 foot-pounds, which means one horsepower can move or lift 550 pounds one foot in one second. At the per-minute rate, one horsepower can move 33,000 pounds one foot in one minute.

A piston engine converts the chemical energy in fuel into usable energy by heating a fluid called air. That working fluid turns a shaft that propels the airplane. That is usable or brake horsepower.

Aviation horsepower defines how much weight can be lifted or thrust so far in so much time. Nine horsepower can lift 297,000 pounds one foot in one minute, whereas 8,800 horsepower can lift over 290 *million* pounds one foot in one minute.

Historic Event

On 25 August 1945 Lockheed first flew the commercial Model 049 Constellation, a modified basic model of the four-engine Constellation. In 1939 Lockheed had begun to develop this aircraft for airlines. TWA and Pan American placed orders in 1940. Those orders were under construction when the United States entered the war, and the U.S. Army Air Forces assumed the orders. The Army Air Forces ordered more aircraft to be built to military standards during the war. When the war ended, Lockheed had military versions in production. Lockheed completed the aircraft as commercial airliners. These aircraft went to TWA, Pan American, American Overseas Airlines, British Overseas Airways Corporation, Air France, KLM, and Linea Aeropostal Venezolana. The aircraft combined high speed, reliable performance, long range, and large size. It became available as a civil airliner just as the postwar commercial aviation boom began. Its main competitor in the immediate postwar market was the Douglas DC-4.

Pilots with wartime experience and operators with war surplus aircraft established new nonscheduled airlines, known as nonskeds. These included charter services and freight airlines, also briefly some local-service airlines. In the United States, over 2,500 nonsked operators flew over 5,000 aircraft by the summer of 1946. Many of these small operations failed as businesses. Others became supplemental carriers that conducted regular operations and, in the process, they obtained the necessary government certificate of convenience and necessity that permitted scheduled service. The postwar freight lines used war surplus aircraft. Slick Airways used C-46s. The Flying Tiger Line flew C-54s (refurbished as DC-4s), as did California Eastern Airlines, Pacific Overseas Airlines, and Seaboard & Western Airlines.

Local service airlines fed passengers into large cities served by major airlines and, thus, became known as feeder airlines. They emerged during the immediate postwar period. Among these were Bonanza in the Southwest; Southwest on the West Coast; Empire and West Coast in the Northwest; Monarch in the Mountain West; Wisconsin Central (North Central after 1952), Ozark, and Trans-Texas in the Central part of the country; and Southern, Piedmont, All-American (Allegheny after 1951), and Robinson (Mohawk after 1952) in the East. Bonanza, Southwest, West Coast,

Monarch, Wisconsin Central, Ozark, Trans-Texas, Southern, Piedmont, All-American, and Robinson all began service with Douglas DC-3s; Empire started with Boeing 247Ds. (Figure 8-10)

Figure 8-10. The postwar era saw a growth in regional airlines, such as Pacific Northern Airlines.

For the Chicago Conference, President Roosevelt had suggested "area competition" for international routes. This emerged in 1945. That June the Civil Aeronautics Board awarded TWA and American Export Lines foreign routes across the Atlantic Ocean. American Export, renamed American Overseas Airways later that year, received routes to northern Europe. TWA got the southern Europe routes. This ended Pan American's peacetime monopoly on foreign routes, and left Pan American the routes to central Europe. While domestic carriers expanded into Pan American's foreign routes, the government refused to grant Pan Am any domestic routes for a few years. Pan Am tried to eliminate the domestic competition from foreign routes by fare-cutting, but that undermined the new IATA fare-setting and soon failed.

Airways Crisis

The heavy use of airways by commercial, private, and military planes during the 1950s created an airways crisis. The facilities and equipment along the

federally maintained airways were not adequate for the volume and type of traffic. Inadequate funding had slowed the installation of very high frequency omnidirectional ranges and of distance measuring equipment. By the start of 1955, the country had 383 installed VORs, only 167 operating DMEs, few airport surveillance radar (ASR) systems, and no enroute long-range radar yet. Air traffic controllers still relied upon the scribbled notes and vertical boards of the manual posting system of the 1930s. Pilots and controllers relayed voice messages through ground personnel, and they crowded radio frequencies with location fixes and other information.

To promote safety and to compensate for weaknesses in the traffic control system, controllers spaced aircraft ten minutes apart. Bad weather requiring instrument flight prompted greater separation. Under visual flight rules (VFR) or in mixed visual-instrument conditions, the see-and-be-seen principle provided little protection given the speeds of some aircraft, including the military jets that shared airspace with commercial transports and personal planes. Higher closure speeds meant an increased chance of a mid-air collision. Cancellations, delays, and near-misses were the symptoms of the congested and antiquated airway system.

The airways crisis was brought into sharp focus in 1955. In January a TWA transport and a private DC-3 transport collided midair near Cincinnati. Fifteen

Historic Event

In the New York City area 15 September 1954 became known as Black Wednesday. On that day the air traffic overwhelmed the air traffic control system. Over 40,000 passengers were delayed for hours as the system nearly collapsed.

Flight Lines

"When you come into the area of one of the big terminals like New York or Washington, it's like trying to talk over an old-fashioned party-line telephone, with everyone on the line at once hollering 'Fire.'"

Pilot commenting on airport traffic control, 1950s, as quoted in Stuart I. Rochester, *Takeoff at Mid-Century.*

Historical Note

In the period 1950-1954, the United States recorded 65 midair collisions of civil aircraft. All the fatalities were in light aircraft rather than commercial transports.

People died in various types of civil transport accidents: 96 in 1950, 142 in 1951, 46 in 1952, 86 in 1953, and 16 in 1954.

people died. The British turboprop Vickers Viscount entered service in the United States that summer. Boeing was accepting orders for its new civil jetliner, the 707, and setting speed records by flight testing the Pratt & Whitney-powered prototype in transcontinental flights of about five hours. Douglas announced plans to build the DC-8 jetliner. As planes reached jet speeds, the margin of safety dropped. Although the British-developed de Havilland Comet jet had entered scheduled service elsewhere in 1952, the United States did not get regularly scheduled jetliner service until 1958. Nonetheless, the forthcoming speeds were recognized as a pressing problem in 1955, because military jets and the British Viscount turboprop were flying the country's airways.

Crisis Resolution

The aviation community agreed that it needed a new and modern air navigation and traffic control system. Beyond that, there was less agreement. The airlines and military forces in particular wanted state-of-the-art technology, but identified different technologies for the job. Private pilots consistently argued against any system that would exert positive control over their flights, require expensive instruments in their planes, or necessitate additional training to maintain flight-ready status. Nonskeds and small operators tended to fall somewhere between the high-technology business and the unrestricted private flying.

Air traffic controllers wanted an electronic data storage and retrieval system with visual and graphic displays. Safety experts called for more radar, better radar, long-range radar, and radar beacon systems with airborne transponders and ground interrogators. The Civil Aeronautics Administration was developing a horizontal radarscope to be used in conjunction with markers representing planes ("shrimp boats") on a map. The missile and rocket industries of that time were developing the electronic and computing

Historical Note

The world witnessed the introduction of jetliners in the 1950s, though reciprocating engines powered most of the airliners of that decade. In the United States, for example, reciprocating engines powered all the civil transport airplanes produced through the mid-decade.

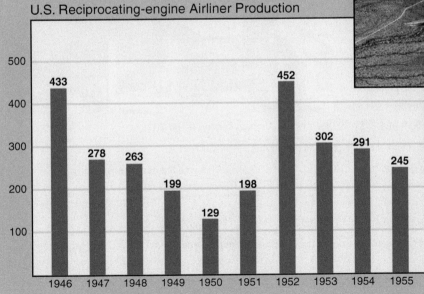

U.S. Reciprocating-engine Airliner Production

Year	Production
1946	433
1947	278
1948	263
1949	199
1950	129
1951	198
1952	452
1953	302
1954	291
1955	245

The data in the chart came from the Aircraft Industries Association of America, *The Aircraft Year Book 1950* (Washington: Lincoln Press, 1951), and *The Aircraft Year Book 1956* (Washington: Lincoln Press, 1957).

capabilities that could solve many of the air navigation and control problems. The Massachusetts Institute of Technology was constructing the Semiautomatic Ground Environment (SAGE) air defense system for the Air Force that used digital computers and networked radar installations. Could it be adapted for civil aviation use? The electronics and avionics revolution presented an array of possibilities, but no products on the shelf.

The airways were underfunded in the postwar period partly due to congressional preference for user-charge funding. There was no consensus regarding a common civil-military system, and there was much technology in development. In 1955 the airways thus lacked an immediate solution to the crisis. The answer came piecemeal over time. United Airlines became the first carrier to install airborne radar equipment in its fleet. The government build a long-range radar facility to serve aircraft approaching Idelewild (later Kennedy), La Guardia, and Newark fields in the New York City area. In the meantime, crashes happened. In June 1956 two airliners over the Grand Canyon collided midair: 128 died. Near misses were more common than crashes. Technologies continued in development. In 1957 the air traffic control radar beacon system (ATCRBS) entered service for operational tests. Though the air navigation and air traffic control systems, and even the nation's runways, were not yet ready for the new jet age, the commercial Boeing 707 with Pratt & Whitney JT3 jet engines and the de Havilland D.H. 106 Comet with Rolls Royce Avon jet engines began operating in the United States in 1958.

Historic Event

On 30 June 1956 a TWA Super Constellation bound from Los Angeles to Kansas City and a United DC-7 en route from Los Angeles to Chicago crashed in midair over the Grand Canyon. The failure of either pilot to report at the Tuba City, Arizona, checkpoint alerted officials to the disaster. Two planes crashing in clear weather, with both pilots flying under air traffic control, publicized the airways crisis, though the Constellation had climbed above its assigned altitude at the time of the crash. The Civil Aeronautics Board clearly stated in its accident report the probable cause of the accident: "the pilots did not see each other in time."

Historic Event

The design, development, and production of the Boeing 707 jetliner was a historic accomplishment.

Mamie Eisenhower christening Pan American 707

On 20 May 1952 the Boeing company initiated a program to develop, build, and demonstrate a prototype designated Model 367-80.

On 15 July 1954 Boeing's prototype Model 367-80 — or simply the Dash 80 — completed its first flight. It combined features from Boeing's experience with both civil and military aircraft.

On 13 October 1955 Pan American World Airways placed the first order for Boeing's Model 707 derivative of the Model 367-80.

On 20 December 1957 Boeing made the first flight of a 707-100, the initial production version of the 707.

On 18 September 1958 the Boeing 707-100 received aircraft type certification number ATC 4A-21.

On 26 October 1958 Pan American placed the Boeing 707-120 into commercial service. This was the aircraft's first commercial flight and the beginning of commercial jet service using aircraft made in the United States. (Boeing publicity referred to this as the -120 though it is the same version referred to in government records as the -100.)

From August 1958 to April 1982, Boeing delivered 916 civil 707 jet airliners.

Also derived from Boeing's Model 367-80 prototype were the commercial Boeing 720 airliner and the military KC-135 tanker, as well as military variants and conversions of the 707.

The history of this and other Boeing aircraft is given in Peter M. Bowers, *Boeing Aircraft since 1916* (1966; 2nd edition, London: Putnam, 1989).

Personal Profile

Leonard S. "Luke" Hobbs (1896-1977) studied engineering at Texas A&M and earned his degree in 1916. He served in an Army engineering division during World War I. He then earned a master's degree at Kansas State College. He went to work as an aeronautical test engineer at the Army's McCook Field in Dayton, Ohio. He later contributed to the design of aircraft engine carburetors while employed at the Stromberg Motor Devices Corporation. He joined Pratt & Whitney Aircraft in 1927, just two years after the company was founded. There he worked on air-cooled radial engines.

During World War II, Hobbs experimented with a free-piston turbine engine despite the government's efforts to keep piston-engine makers solely occupied with wartime production. The government did not share with Pratt & Whitney the wartime jet technology obtained from the British, although Pratt & Whitney did manufacture Rolls Royce jet engines under license after the war.

In 1944 Hobbs became corporate vice president of engineering for Pratt & Whitney's parent corporation, United Aircraft. From that position he oversaw Pratt & Whitney's transition to jet engines. He made the decision to "leap-frog" the competition. He led the design, development, and production of the JT3 jet engine.

Leonard S. "Luke" Hobbs

Given the military designation J57, this engine entered service on the Boeing B-52 bomber in 1952. It powered the new North American F-100 fighter starting in 1953. The JT3 entered commercial service on Boeing's first jet transport, the Boeing 707, in 1958. It also powered Douglas's first jetliner, the DC-8, that entered service in 1959.

Hobbs won the 1952 Collier Trophy for the J57 military version of the engine and the 1972 Elmer A. Sperry Award for the JT3 civil version.

Federal Aviation Agency (FAA)

Amid the airways crisis and efforts to prepare for jet aircraft, there emerged proposals for an independent federal agency for civil aviation. The existing Civil Aeronautics Administration was part of the Department of Commerce. In the summer of 1958, Congress passed the legislation and President Dwight D. Eisenhower signed the Federal Aviation Act into law. This act created the Federal Aviation Agency (FAA) as an independent department within the Executive Branch of the government. The transition from Civil Aeronautics Administration to Federal Aviation Agency occurred that fall. The new agency became fully operational on 1 January 1959.

European Airlines

When European airlines resumed operations after the war, they turned to United States manufacturers for equipment. In war-torn lands and with war-damaged economies, Europeans bought American equipment because it was available, because it was state of the art, because the Marshall Plan (formally the European Recovery Program) provided U.S. aid for purchasing equipment, and because western allies were needed in the fight against communism. Europe returned to the flag airline system of prewar days, with independent companies and secondary lines in many countries.

British Airlines

Despite a good wartime record of producing military planes, Great Britain had not produced transport planes during the war, so it lagged behind the United States in production of aircraft for the postwar transport market. Early in 1946 Britain bought five Lockheed Constellations from the United States. After reaching the Bermuda Agreement on civil aviation, Britain bought more American aircraft — six Boeing Stratocruisers. Its own Tudor long-range aircraft encountered problems, including a crash in 1948. Icing problems grounded its Vickers shorter-range Viking aircraft, and low power hampered its sales of the Bristol Wayfarer. The Brabazon 1 failed without ever reaching commercial flight. The Princess Flying Boat failed too.

Without suitable aircraft, British airlines could not compete economically on international routes. The British were as dependent upon the United States as a supplier of airplanes as the United States was dependent upon the British as a supplier of jet engine technology. Until the aircraft engine industry in the United States developed jet engines, the U.S. companies made British jet engines under license, including the 1947 licenses for the Rolls Royce Nene and Derwent engines. As a temporary measure, the British bought transports made in the United States, including some used Constellations purchased from Eire (Ireland). British airlines used equipment made in the United States until British products became available.

Comet

Great Britain hoped its development of jet-engine airliners would wean British airlines from products made in the United States. In response to British government specifications, the de Havilland company began exploring design possibilities in 1944. The company's chief designer Ronald Bishop directed the secret project. De Havilland revived the Comet name that previously identified five D.H. 88 racers built by the company in 1934-1935. On 27 July 1949 pilot John Cunningham and a crew of three took the prototype designated G-5-1/G-ALVG on the first flight of the newly designed Comet jetliner. At a time when jet aircraft meant military aircraft, this commercial program placed Britain far ahead of other nations in developing civil jet-powered aircraft.

Historic Event

On 27 July 1949 the de Havilland Comet jetliner flew for the first time. Pilot John Cunningham and a crew of three flew the prototype designated G-5-1/G-ALVG.

Cunningham took the prototype through numerous flight tests that year, and he demonstrated the aircraft at the Farnborough Air Show. De Havilland received orders from around the world. A second prototype, designated G-5-2/G-ALZK, was completed in 1950; de Havilland delivered it to the Comet Unit of the national British Overseas Airways Corporation for

proving tests and training crews. Meanwhile, the first production Comet — Comet 1 — began undergoing flight tests in January 1951. Whereas the first prototype and early production Comets had de Havilland Ghost jet engines, the second prototype Comet and later Comets used the Rolls Royce Avon.

Historic Event

On 2 May 1952 the de Havilland Comet 1, powered by de Havilland Ghost engines, entered commercial service. Designated G-ALYP, the jetliner flew from London to Johannesburg with scheduled stops in Rome, Beirut, Khartoum, Entebbe, and Livingstone. This was the world's first regular passenger jet service.

The Comet inaugurated the world's first regular passenger jet service on 2 May 1952. A British Overseas Airways Corporation Comet 1, powered by de Havilland Ghost engines, departed from London bound for Johannesburg with scheduled stops in Rome, Beirut, Khartoum, Entebbe, and Livingstone. This was the world's first regular passenger jet service. The Comet operated successfully for months.

Comet Crashes

In October 1952 a BOAC Comet crashed taking off from Rome's Ciampino airport. No one was killed, but the aircraft was destroyed. Six Comets crashed in 1953-1954. In January 1953 a Comet had an accident while landing and killed one ground worker at the Entebbe airport. In March one crashed on takeoff at Karachi. In May there was an accident amid a violent storm near Calcutta, India, and in June an accident at Dakar in French West Africa. In January 1954 a Comet crashed near Elba, and in April one broke apart in the air near Stromboli; both islands are off Italy's west

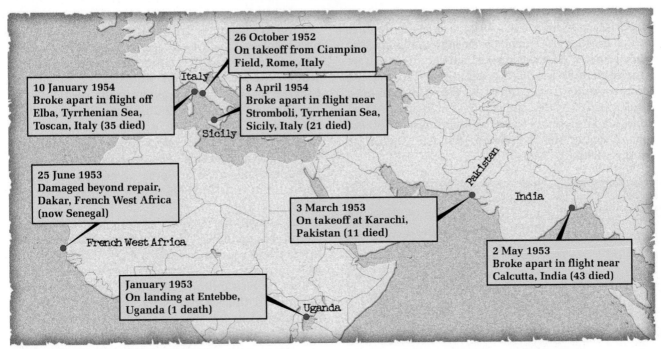

Figure 8-11. Accidents plagued the world's first jetliner.

coast. De Havilland grounded the Comet 1 after the January 1954 crash and again after the April accident. The death toll had reached 111, and the Comet 1 had earned the worst safety record of any airliner then in service. The Ministry of Transport and Civil Aviation withdrew the Comet's certificate of airworthiness. (Figure 8-11)

What had gone wrong? The inexperience and errors of the new jet pilots may explain some of accidents, but the Comet 1 itself apparently contributed to the accidents. The hydraulic flight controls gave the pilot no feedback, no sense of aerodynamic forces, no "Q" feel in the language of the day. Metal fatigue weakened the fuselage and proved to be a problem, but the problem was not detectable using the static strain tests that de Havilland had used. Fatigue was proved in two cases after extensive scientific studies of salvaged parts, conducted at the Royal Aircraft Establishment in Farnborough. Later Comets — the Comet 4 — came with "feel" units. These Comets also featured a modification to the leading edges of the wing to reduce the tendency to stall. The Comet 4s were built structurally stronger, and fatigue inspections became routine. The machines proved safe and reliable! De Havilland built 67 Comet 4s, and 113 Comets in all, before ending production in 1962.

British Leadership

With the Comet, Britain became a leader in commercial jets as well as in air accident investigations. The British Overseas Airways Corporation also provided world leadership in establishing jet service, in developing long-haul routes, and in maintaining a worldwide network of routes. The company also managed to buy U.S.-made aircraft to supplement the miscellaneous British equipment in its fleet and to replace obsolete flying boats with used Douglas DC-4s. The company stopped using flying boats in 1950. British European Airways, founded in 1946, started large and grew larger. Based in London, Europe's largest city, British European started with the European routes of British Overseas and acquired ten domestic airlines in the United Kingdom, like Scottish Airways and Channel Island Airways, in 1947. A few private little airlines remained independent. The main weakness in British aviation remained problems of designing and producing new commercial designs.

French Airlines

French civil air service resumed operation in October 1945. Air France, as a name and a company, reappeared in 1946. Air France established service across Europe and across the Atlantic Ocean. It soon served the French imperial posts in Africa and Asia. It used DC-3s, the Sud-Est SE-1616 four-engine Languedoc (Languedoc is a province in southeast France), and soon DC-4s and Constellations. Air France reorganized and centralized air service in 1948, under the new name Compagnie Nationale Air France. The French government owned 70% of the company. Air France updated its fleet in 1953 when it obtained Super

Constellations from the United States, one Comet jet plus Viscounts from Great Britain, and the double-decker Breguet 763 Provence. Despite the grounding of its Comet 1, Air France remained confident that jet aircraft were its future. It ordered the French-made SE-210 Caravelle jetliners, which it placed into service in 1959. Two independent airlines survived the postwar scramble to establish airlines; the others ceased operations or merged into Air Algérie or another airline. (Figure 8-12)

Figure 8-12. Air France used the Vickers Viscount similar to the one shown here.

Soviet Airlines

After the British Comet, a Soviet Tupolev became the next jetliner to go into commercial service. The Tu-104

Historic Event

On 15 September 1956 the Tupolev Tu-104, powered by Mikulin AM-3M jet engines, entered airline service in the Soviet Union. Aeroflot used the jetliner initially on the Moscow-Omsk-Irkutsk route.

was a derivative of a Cold War bomber. Designed by Andrei N. Tupolev, the Tu-104 first flew in 1955, and it entered airline service with Aeroflot in 1956. This medium-range jetliner soon served points from Petropavlovsk and Khabarovsk in eastern Siberia; to Tiflis and Tashkent in the south; also to the foreign ports of Delhi and Cairo; and to Copenhagen, Amsterdam, and Paris in the west. In the late 1950s the Soviet Union had an extensive network of jet service. The Ilyushin Il-18 Moskva turboprop, designed by Sergei Ilyushin, was undergoing flight tests in 1958.

In the communist Soviet Union the national airline Aeroflot operated as an economic tool of the state. It maintained regularly schedule service, but it also flew military transport flights, government charter flights, and agricultural flights. A Soviet-made DC-3 designated the Lisunov Li-2 was a workhorse of the fleet. During the war the Russian engineer Boris Pavlovich Lisunov had supervised the license agreement with Douglas Aircraft and approved the more than 1,000 engineering changes from the Douglas-provided drawings. Russia produced 4,863 Li-2s between 1940 and 1945, first at a factory in Khimki (that was evacuated in the fall of 1941), then at a factory in Tashkent. Also popular with Aeroflot were the Ilyushin Il-12 and Il-14 twin-engine transports similar to the DC-3. Less successful were the four-engine, piston-powered Il-18s (not the later turboprop planes with the same designation) that did not go into production.

German Airlines

The prewar German airline Deutsche Luft Hansa continued operations till 21 April 1945, when Nazi Germany fell. Defeat left Germany in ruins — disarmed, impoverished, and partitioned. German pilots with wartime experience, mostly with the Luftwaffe, lacked the continuity of flying that pilots of the victorious Allied nations enjoyed after the war; many of the German pilots did not fly for more than five years after the war ended. Germans became familiar with American and British transports and crews from the Berlin Airlift.

In 1953 West German business interests began to organize an airline company called Luftag. The next year they changed the name to Deustche Lufthansa, popularly called simply Lufthansa. British European Airways and TWA assisted Lufthansa in preparing to re-enter service. Lufthansa ordered Convair 340 aircraft for the domestic routes and Lockheed L-1049 Super Constellations for international routes. British

Figure 8-13. The German airline Lufthansa used the Super Constellation to fly international routes.

European helped train Lufthansa personnel, including Convair pilots. Lufthansa contracted with TWA for training the Constellation crews, and TWA sent instructors to West Germany to conduct the training. Lufthansa began service on 1 April 1955 with the Convairs on domestic routes. Two weeks later the Super Constellations began flying the international routes. The TWA instructors flew as pilots and their German students as crews on some of Lufthansa's early transatlantic flights. British and American personnel continued to fly and train Lufthansa crews for a year. Lufthansa crews began to fly alone, without foreign assistance, in March 1956. The company soon provided its own training. (Figure 8-13)

About the same time East Germany decided to establish an airline. It too selected the historic name Deutsche Lufthansa! Established in 1954, this airline began providing transport service on 4 February 1956. This was an international service within the communist bloc of central and eastern Europe. The first flight of the new airline used the new 18-seat Soviet twin-engine Ilyushin Il-14. More than a year later, on 16 June 1957, the East German Lufthansa initiated domestic air service with a flight from Berlin to the Baltic Sea coast resort of Barth, via stops in Leipzig, Dresden, and Erfurt. The Iron Curtain separated the route systems of the two Lufthansa airlines.

European Lines

Numerous airlines reestablished or started service in postwar Europe. The basic pattern was to create a strong national airline, with or without independent airlines in the country. Albania was the one country that did not establish a national airline. In a unique way, Danish, Norwegian, and Swedish airlines formed a consortium after World War II. Founded in 1946, the Scandinavian Airline System (SAS) became a successful example of international airline cooperation. SAS used the DC-6 for long routes and the Convair and various Douglas airliners in Europe. KLM, a big airline in the little country of the Netherlands, resumed operations in 1945 and soon operated around the globe — with some regional disruption as Indonesia struggled toward independence. Achmad Sukarno led the Partai Nasionalis Indonesia that fought the four-year war for independence for Indonesia in the late 1940s. The Belgian national airline SABENA became an international helicopter operator and flew airliners within Belgium and between Belgium and the Belgian Congo. The Spanish national line Iberia flew within Spain and established postwar service between Spain and Spanish-speaking Latin America. The Finnish airline Aero O/Y became Finnair in 1951. Although Italy entered World War II as an Axis power, its status as a non-belligerent in 1945 allowed it to reestablish civil aviation much quicker than the defeated Germany and Austria. Funding came from Britain and the United States. British European Airways invested in Aerolinee Italiane Internazionali (Alitalia), organized in 1946. The two Italian lines merged into Linee Aeree Italiane, a flag line also called Alitalia, in 1957.

Latin American Airlines

The war effort by Allied airlines influenced the fate of Axis-controlled airlines in other countries. Latin America is an example. The war in Europe had little initial impact on commercial aviation in Latin

America. Airlines of the Axis countries had operated there for a decade or more. These airlines provided a much needed public utility service and employed many local nationals. In many locations the Axis-controlled companies provided most if not all of the necessary air transportation. As late as 1941, German-owned airlines operated in Bolivia, Brazil, Chile, Ecuador, and Peru, and an Italian-owned airline operated in Brazil. These airlines provided service to other countries, and other Latin American airlines operated under the influence of German or Italian companies. (Figure 8-14)

Figure 8-14. Prior to World War II, German and Italian airlines controlled the majority of the air service in Latin America. In the postwar era, this influence was dramatically reduced.

Axis Influence

In 1941 the United States established an American Republics Aviation Division within the Defense Supplies Corporation. This Aviation Division provided airplanes, technicians and other personnel, and financing to Latin American and United States companies to replace the Axis influence in Latin

American aviation. The Latin American countries in turn nationalized or requisitioned several Axis-influenced companies under the pretext of the airlines having violated some regulation; for example, Bolivia nationalized German-influenced LAB (Lloyd Aéreo Boliviano) for its poor safety record and because of public dissatisfaction with the airline. Some nations withdrew operating permits from Axis-influenced companies. For example, Peru withdrew Lufthansa Peru's permit because it flew through restricted airspace. Existing airlines of Allied countries duplicated Axis-influenced routes; for example, Pan American-Grace duplicated the service provided by German-controlled SEDTA (Sociedad Ecuatoriana de Transportes Aéreos) in Ecuador and thereby made the routes financially disastrous to SEDTA.

Other Axis-influenced companies were forced out of Latin America less directly. British and American companies provided the aviation fuel throughout Latin America, aviation fuel was legally a "munition of war," and the Allies coordinated control of the fuel to choke some Axis-influenced companies out of business. The Allies similarly controlled spare parts, an essential feature of airline operations. These actions closed both German-owned Condor and Italian-owned LATI (Linee Aeree Transcontinentali Italiane) airlines.

Removal of the Axis influence in Latin America, and from nearly 20,000 miles of air routes, contributed to the development of Latin American-owned airlines. Pan American initially provided much of the replacement service — either directly or through wholly or partly owned subsidiaries. In general, however, ownership of Latin American airlines converted from foreign to domestic.

The war brought an improvement of ground facilities that supported postwar commercial aviation. The United States constructed airports and seaplane bases in Caribbean territories of Great Britain; these supported the wartime ferrying of aircraft and transporting of supplies across the South Atlantic Ocean. Other facilities were constructed to ease the transport of raw materials, like rubber, needed for defense purposes. The defense demand for raw materials also fueled wartime and postwar economic development in Latin America, and economic development in turn increased the loads, destinations, and distances flown by airlines in the region.

Four nations — Argentina, Colombia, Brazil, and Mexico — led Latin American aviation during the postwar period. A single airline emerged as the main operator in Argentina and Colombia, while the larger

Brazil and Mexico developed multiple airlines. In each case, the influence of Pan American continued to decline as domestic-based airlines developed in these countries. Throughout Latin America, new and small postwar airlines emerged — particularly to transport freight. Most used war-surplus aircraft produced in the United States and older aircraft that major airlines had replaced with newer models. The variety of aircraft within fleets contributed to the demise of most of these short-lived companies. Foreign capital helped some companies to survive a bit longer.

Argentine Airlines

During World War II the Argentine Army organized the commercial LASO (Línea Aérea Suroeste) and the Argentine Air Force established the commercial LANE (Línea Aérea Nor-Este). These two airlines merged into LADE (Líneas Aéreas del Estado) in 1945. LADE operated a network of commercial routes into 1947, when newly formed joint-stock companies began operation; thereafter, the military continued to operate LADE as a subsidized service to locations that could not support commercial service. The Argentine government sought Argentine companies to assume cabotage rights then enjoyed by American and European companies; cabotage is commerce between two destinations within a country, a right often reserved for domestic carriers. Postwar Argentine law required that Argentine-owned companies take over cabotage routes then served by foreign companies like Panagra which was a partnership of two companies based in the United States — Pan American Airways and the W.R. Grace shipping line.

Three Argentine companies assumed the cabotage rights in 1947. One was a reorganized Aeroposta Argentina, still influenced by partial ownership by French interests. The other two were the newly organized ALFA (Aviación del Litoral Fluvial Argentino) and ZONDA (Zonas Oeste y Norte de Aerolíneas Argentinas). The government assigned each of the three to different service areas and allowed each to serve neighboring countries. In addition to these domestic carriers, Argentina established a national airline called FAMA (Flota Aérea Mercante Argentina). FAMA began operations with aircraft converted from wartime purposes or civilian versions of military aircraft, like the Avro Lancastrian airliners converted from British bombers and the Douglas DC-4 version of the C-54 military transport made in the United States. A new government-owned airline — Aerolíneas Argentinas — acquired FAMA and the three domestic carriers in 1949.

Aerolíneas Argentinas was a state corporation, a branch of the Ministry of Transport, with both domestic and international routes. When it began in 1949, Aerolíneas Argentinas operated the consolidated fleet of the four predecessor companies. This fleet included Douglas DC-3, DC-4, and DC-6 landplanes. It used Short Sandringham flying boats (converted from wartime Sunderlands) between towns along the Río de la Plata. Aerolíneas Argentinas operated as a monopoly until 1956, when Argentina's new government permitted other airlines to form. Those airlines — Transcontinental, Aerolíneas Ini, Transatlántica, Austral, and Aerotransportes Litoral Argentino — reflected a lessening of government control, but the independents struggled to survive in competition with the experienced, technologically sophisticated, and commercially savvy national airline.

Aerolíneas Argentinas obtained its first jetliners in 1959: the Comet 4. This jet proved itself on trunk or main routes as well as on international routes. With Comets, Aerolíneas Argentina started the first jet service in South America, the first jet service between South America and North America, and the first jet service across the South Atlantic Ocean — all in 1959. In August of that year, the airline crashed a Comet near Asunción; this was a public relations embarrassment as the airline had been promoting the modern jets to improve the company's image after several piston planes crashed in previous years.

Colombian Airlines

By the end of the war, the Colombian airline AVIANCA (Aerovias Nacionales de Colombia) had totally shed its German heritage, even its German-influenced name SCADTA (Sociedad Colombo-Alemana de Transporte Aéreo). The airline, however, remained under the heavy influence of Pan American, which owned more than 50% of the stock. Pan American controlled the route system, including the allocation of aircraft. Older Ford Tri-motors and Junkers W-34 floatplanes flew local routes, Boeing 247s covered the main routes. New Douglas DC-3s were added to the inter-city routes. DC-3s soon replaced all the Boeing 247s, and Sikorsky S-38 amphibians replaced the W-34s. AVIANCA expanded to international service immediately after the war. In 1946 it added service to Ecuador; in 1947 to the Panama Canal Zone and to the United States; and in 1950 to Portugal, Italy, and France, as well as Jamaica. New equipment, particularly the Lockheed Constellation, and Pan American promotion helped these and later expansions of international service. AVIANCA also expanded its domestic service.

Despite the failure of many little postwar airlines in Colombia, a few secondary airlines formed and operated: Taxi Aéreo de Santander (Taxander) in 1947, Lloyd Aéreo Colombiano in 1954, and Aerovías Condor de Colombia in 1955. Lloyd and Condor started with Curtiss C-46s equipped with jet-assisted-take-off (JATO) power. Such airlines provided supplemental service to the AVIANCA operations during the 1950s. Also, the Dutch airline KLM formed ties with the new AVIANCA in order to obtain the right to load and unload passengers and freight in Colombia.

Brazilian Airlines

When World War II began, Brazilian investors owned two Brazilian airlines — VASP (Viação Aérea São Paulo) and VARIG (Viação Aérea Rio-Grandense), which amounted to about a third of the commercial industry in Brazil. German interests owned another third, represented by the Condor airline, and parties in the United States owned the final third in the form of Panair do Brasil. During the war German investment left Brazil, Condor became Serviços Aéreos Cruzeiro do Sul, and Pan American's ownership of Panair do Brasil dropped from 100% to 58%. At the end of the war, Brazilian interests owned about 80% of the airline industry, including VASP, VARIG, Cruzeiro do Sul, NAB (Navegacão Aérea Brasileira), nearly half of Panair do Brasil, and nearly half of Aerovias Brasil. Parties in the United States held about 20% in the form of investments in Panair do Brasil and Aerovias Brasil.

By the end of the war, Lockheed and Douglas aircraft entered Brazilian fleets. These included the Lockheed 10 Electra, 12 Electra Junior, 14 Super Electra, and 18 Lodestar models, and the Douglas DC-3. As the departure point for Allied flights across

the South Atlantic Ocean, Natal became the busiest airport in Latin America. Some of the transport planes, like Curtiss C-46s and Douglas C-47s (military versions of DC-3s), became surplus and available in Brazil at the end of the war. Brazilians also purchased British war-surplus equipment, like Avro Ansons, Percival Princes, and de Havilland Dragon Rapides.

Cruzeiro do Sul and Panair do Brasil maintained national networks. Other airlines served regions within Brazil. Many of these were new. More than 20 new Brazilian airlines formed in the mid to late 1940s. Most of these failed within a few years, though a few struggled along until they were acquired by larger entities. VASD (Viação Aérea Santos Dumont), for example, operated one Budd Conestoga landplane, two Consolidated PBY-5 Catalina flying boats, and three Douglas DC-3s between 1945 and 1952; Nacional acquired VASD in 1952. Transportes Aéreos Nacional, in turn, was purchased by REAL (Redes Estaduais Aéreas Limiteda) in 1956, and VARIG acquired REAL in 1961. Little Sadia adopted the motto: *Pelo Ar Para Seu Lar* (By Air to Your Home). Airlines merged, acquired smaller companies, and associated with partners throughout the 1950s.

To obtain international routes, Brazil followed the postwar example of Great Britain and the United States, specifically the model of the Bermuda Agreement; that is, it used the bilateral agreement. Such postwar agreements were to protect the aviation industries of each nation from domination by the other. Brazil's 1946 agreement with the United States recognized the Five Freedoms. The agreement complied with the fare structures established by the International Air Transport Association. The agreement also limited capacity and protected cabotage rights of both nations. In addition to international agreements, companies needed to qualify under the laws of their respective nations. Panair do Brasil, for example, required proof of Brazilian control in order to qualify under Brazilian law to become an international carrier, so Pan American again reduced its ownership share, this time from 58% to 48%.

Mexican Airlines

Pan American's domination of Mexico's airways, partly through its international routes and partly through financial control of CMA (Compania Mexicana de Aviación), continued into the postwar years. Pan Am provided state-of-the-art equipment to its subsidiaries, like the four-engine DC-4s operated by CMA beginning in 1946, the pressurized DC-6 airliners in 1950, and DC-6Bs in 1953. Mexico's President Miguel Alemán organized a challenge to Pan American's dominance in Mexico. In 1952 Aeronaves de México, then a second-level domestic operator, acquired LAMSA (Líneas Aéreas Mexicanas, S.A., formerly Líneas Aéreas Mineras, S.A.). The next year Aeronave de México bought Aerovías Reforma. This consolidated airline — Aeronaves de México — operated Douglas DC-3s and later Convair CV-340s. During this same time period a road-building program provided motorized land transportation to many isolated communities for the first time, and also contributed to the decline of the small airlines that had served such "bush" communities.

Mexicana, as CMA was called, and Aeronaves began to compete for domestic and international routes. Equipment was a competitive feature. In 1957 both began acquiring long-range airliners. Mexicana got the new Douglas DC-7Cs, and Aeronaves leased Lockheed 049 Constellations. That same year Aeronaves ordered its first turbine-powered planes, the turboprop Bristol Britannia 302 airliners, each with four Proteus engines. Soon Mexicana leased a Britannia from Aeronaves. An international treaty in 1957 divided destinations in the United States between the two Mexican airlines. Mexicana kept the route to Los Angeles and added routes to Chicago and San Antonio. Aeronaves won the New York route, with rights also to Washington, DC. Mexicana ordered de Havilland Comet 4C jet airliners for its routes in 1959. The competition to expand included acquisitions, like Aeronaves' purchase of the border airline Aerolineas Mexicanas and Mexicana buying another border airline, Líneas Transcontinentales de Aero-Transportes. Strikes hit both of Mexico's major airlines in 1959, and the Mexican government temporarily controlled both companies. Throughout these various developments, Pan American's financial investment in Mexican companies declined substantially.

African and Asian Airlines

As of 1952, four airlines served the six continents: Pan American, British Overseas, Air France, and KLM. Some airlines in Africa and Asia were regional or imperial. Like Latin America, Africa and Asia shed the imperial influence and the airlines of Axis Germany and Italy during World War II. The remaining European imperial countries — the United Kingdom, France, and Belgium — returned to their colonies after the war; Italy and Germany had lost their overseas territories in war. The nationalist independence movements and the decolonization trend — what British Prime Minister Harold MacMillan called the "wind of change" — could disrupt service to or through any specific location for a while.

Almost everywhere there were efforts to establish airlines during the postwar years; pilots and planes were readily available. The postwar competition in India was sufficient to fuel government action. The Air Corporations Act of 1953 nationalized Air-India International and allowed a new domestic airline, the Indian Airlines Corporation, to absorb the eight competing companies. Indian Airlines formed an integrated network of routes in India and connected with neighboring states. In the early 1950s, QANTAS in Australia and South African Airways provided a joint service across the Indian Ocean. In another example, Philippine Air Lines (PAL) quickly regrouped after the war, although it had been founded just months before the Japanese invasion of 1941 and it had remained inactive throughout Japan's long occupation of the country. PAL opened service as a scheduled operator in 1946. With independence, the

Philippines decided upon one flag, so PAL bought its nonscheduled competitor. It made use of airports that the Japanese had developed, like Nielson and Nichols fields. It established routes to Europe and North America. It used DC-6s for long hauls and DC-3s for short hauls and brought the Vickers Viscount turboprop into service in 1957.

Japanese Airlines

During World War II, both the Navy and Army of Japan operated scheduled air service through the Asian-Pacific empire. Those networks were destroyed by the Allied forces advancing on the Pacific Island nation. General Douglas MacArthur as Supreme Commander for the Allied Powers (SCAP) issued an instruction (IN) called SCAPIN 301 in November 1945. This banned all civil aviation in Japan for a period of five years. Airlines and flying clubs closed. Even teaching aviation was forbidden. Foreign (non-Japanese) airlines established a Japan Domestic Air Corporation to provide service during the five years. Pan American, Northwest, Canadian Pacific, Philippine Air Lines, and the Taiwanese Civil Air Transport cooperated in this venture.

Five years later SCAPIN 2106 permitted Japan to create a domestic airline. An amendment in 1951 allowed Japan to establish a Japanese airline. Japanese Air Lines (JAL) organized that year. Initially, it leased equipment from the Japan Domestic Air Corporation. Japanese Air Lines hired pilots from Northwest Orient Airlines, as Japanese pilots were forbidden to fly and it contracted with a non-scheduled operation called Transocean Airlines for maintenance. A 1953 law made it the only international Japanese airline. It acquired DC-4s and -6s and ordered jet powered DC-8s.

HOT SPOTS

Joseph Stalin and Harry S. Truman led the Soviet Union and United States respectively into the Cold War. Stalin sought to consolidate the territorial gains won at the end of the war and to destroy Germany as an economic, political, and military threat. He also sought to spread communism throughout the world. He saw Greece and Turkey as potential extensions of the protective shield he was constructing around the Soviet Union. In 1947 Stalin organized the COMINFORM, the Communist Information Bureau, to encourage communism in other parts of the world. He also accelerated the development of nuclear weapons in order to counter the strength of the United States. Stalin's Soviet Union had numerous intelligence operations that gathered information about foreign countries, foreign nationals, Soviet citizens, and even Communist party officials; in 1954, the year after Stalin's death, these operations reorganized into the Komitet Gosudarstvennoy Bezopasnosti (Committee for State Security), better known as the KGB.

Joseph Stalin

Harry Truman

Truman defined the position of the United States in terms of containment and deterrence. In 1947 he established what became known as the Truman Doctrine: "It must be the policy of the United States to support free peoples who are resisting attempted subjugation by armed minorities or by outside pressures." The idea of containment was to contain communism within the Soviet-occupied territories; that is, to stop the spread of communism — initially in Greece and Turkey. The containment policy soon justified actions against communism around the world — and at times the action consisted of threatening to use nuclear weapons. The United States also established the Central Intelligence Agency (CIA) in 1947 to handle foreign intelligence during the Cold War.

Also that year Truman charged an Air Policy Commission with studying the current and future needs of aviation in the United States. The resulting report entitled *Surviving in the Air Age* stated that the long range of aircraft and the destructiveness of atomic weapons meant no one, no industry, no nation, could be secure in a war. This report recommended establishing a strong military force to deter potential aggressors. The deterrence would be the threat of devastating retaliation. Truman and the United States adopted the policy of deterrence. Truman assigned the responsibility for deterrence to the newly independent Air Force, established by the National Security Act of 1947.

Nuclear Weapons

Truman believed that nuclear weapons and strategic bombing were "cheap alternatives" to fighting costly ground wars. The Soviets attempted to neutralize the American nuclear advantage by developing their own nuclear weapons. The United States remained the sole nuclear power through 1948 and well into 1949. The Soviet Union became a nuclear power in 1949 and the United Kingdom in 1952. From 1945 through 1952 these three nations announced a total of 38 nuclear explosions: 34 by the United States, 3 by the Soviet Union, and 1 by the United Kingdom.

Historic Event

Early in the Cold War each detonation of a nuclear device was a historic event. Three nations announced 38 nuclear explosions between 1945 and 1952:

On 16 July 1945 the United States detonated *Trinity* on a tower at Alamogordo, New Mexico. This was the first nuclear detonation.

On 6 August 1945 the United States dropped *Little Boy* on Hiroshima, Japan; this was the first combat use of a nuclear weapon.

On 9 August 1945 the United States dropped *Fat Man* on Nagasaki, Japan; this was the second combat use.

Between 30 June 1946 and 31 October 1952 the United States detonated 31 more nuclear devices, the last of which was a hydrogen bomb, the world's first hydrogen bomb.

On 29 August 1949 the Soviet Union detonated Nuclear Test No. 1. On 3 and 22 October that year the Soviet Union detonated two more nuclear devices.

On 3 October 1952 the United Kingdom exploded *Hurricane* on a ship at the Monte Bello Islands, Australia.

This phase of the nuclear arms race ended with the United States still ahead by virtue of being the only nation with the new hydrogen bomb, but the Soviet Union exploded its own hydrogen bomb in 1953. That created a new balance of power.

Berlin Airlift

Unable to agree upon the postwar government of a defeated Germany, the four leading Allies occupied the country and its capital city of Berlin. This compromise arose at the meeting of Allied leaders at Yalta in the Crimea in February 1945. France, Great Britain, and the United States occupied West Germany and West Berlin, and the Soviet Union occupied East Germany and East Berlin. Berlin was in East Germany, within the Soviet controlled zone, yet divided by the four occupation powers.

The Western Allies sought to develop Germany economically whereas the Soviet Union wanted Germany destroyed as a country. This difference came to the forefront in Berlin. In 1948, in an effort to consolidate the western sectors of Germany and of Berlin into a new German nation, the United States, Great Britain, and France introduced a single currency into the sectors they occupied. Stalin opposed any moves that would strengthen Germany, especially any that would increase Western influence in Berlin. He wanted the western powers out of Berlin because he wanted a solid defensive buffer between the communist Soviet Union and the democratic West.

Stalin decided the West would not risk war over Berlin. He tested this idea by temporarily blocking rail access through East Germany to West Berlin. Finally, on 24 June 1948, he imposed a total blockade of West Berlin by closing rail, road, and water access between the western sector of the city and West Germany. These were the supply routes on which the city's population depended for fuel, food, and supplies in general.

Historic Event

The Berlin Airlift began on 26 June 1948 and ended on 30 September 1949. The airlift was the western allies response to the Soviet blockade of Berlin. During the airlift, American and British pilots flew a total of 279,114 missions and carried a total of 2.3 million tons of cargo into West Berlin.

Knowing that the Soviet Union alone had not demobilized after World War II, and with both sides still recovering from the last war, the West did not want a new war. Yet the western powers determined that the Soviets should be prevented from taking control of West Berlin. The question was how to stop the Soviets without provoking the Soviets to combat. The West answered the Soviet blockade with an airlift that used the three air corridors between West Germany and West Berlin. In addition to supporting the airlift, Truman threatened to use nuclear weapons in support of a free West Berlin. He reinforced the threat of atomic retaliation by dispatching B-29 bombers (like those previously used in the atomic attacks on Japan) to Britain and within range of Moscow.

Vittles

The United States called its airlift Operation Vittles, and Great Britain called its effort Operation Knicker and then Operation PlainFare. The United States Air Force initially flew Douglas C-47s into West Berlin and quickly added larger Douglas C-54 Skymasters. The United States Navy assigned R5-Ds to the rescue mission. Later the Douglas C-74 Globemaster and the Fairchild C-82 Flying Boxcar joined the airlift fleet. Alaska Airlines, American Overseas, Pan Am, Seaboard & Western, Slick, Trans-Ocean, and TWA contracted to support the airlift by transporting military personnel and cargo within the United States and across the Atlantic Ocean. The Royal Air Force used C-47 Dakotas, converted Lancaster bombers, and Short Sunderland flying boats, and Great Britain contracted

with private companies to transport cargo to West Berlin. The contract companies were little independents like Freddie Laker's Aviation Traders which had 12 old Handley Page Haltons that went to work carrying supplies to the besieged city. Pratt & Whitney and Rolls-Royce piston engines powered most of the flights. (Figure 8-15)

The airplanes almost always flew at full capacity. At the height of the airlift, planes delivered over 500 tons a day to West Berlin, and on one day in April over 12,000 tons of cargo reached Berlin by air. Coal needed for heat and for electricity was the top priority; 70% of the tonnage delivered was coal. Food too was crucial to the people in Berlin. Medical supplies and other supplies also were flown into blockaded Berlin.

Historical Note

Lieutenant Gail Halvorsen, a pilot from Utah, created tiny parachutes from handkerchiefs, and attached candy. He, his copilot, and flight engineer made many of these units and then dropped the treats out of the aircraft for the children of West Berlin. This proved so popular that other crews too dropped candy on their approach to land. These Candy Bombers proved effective goodwill ambassadors to a people only recently defeated in war by the Allied powers.

Lt. Gail Halvorsen

During the course of the airlift, the United States used about 300 airplanes and Great Britain about 100 to transport cargo into West Berlin. The combined efforts provided up to 700 flights a day into West Berlin. The United States Air Force Base at Rhein-Main Field, near Frankfurt and near the historic Zeppelin base, became a major transfer point where tons of cargo bound for West Berlin were loaded for the flights into the besieged city. Airlift planes also flew from Wiesbaden just west of Rhein Main and from the British Royal Air Force Base at Fassberg in

Figure 8-15. Berlin Airlift aircraft being loaded with supplies.

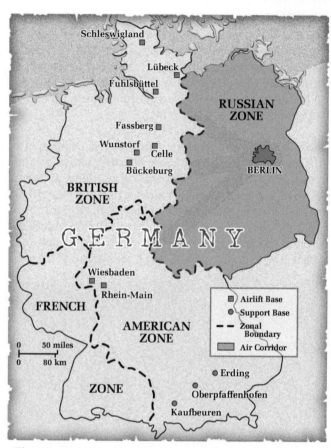

Figure 8-16. The Berlin Airlift used three corridors into and out of Berlin. The pilots flew between Rhein-Main, Wiesbaden, or Fassberg Field in West Germany and Tempelhof Field, Gatow Field, Havel Lake, or the new Tegel Field in West Berlin.

northern Germany. Rhein-Main and Wiesbaden were in the United States zone and Fassberg was in the British zone of West Germany. (Figure 8-16)

West Berlin

The planes flew cargo to Tempelhof Field in the American sector, to Gatow Field in the British sector, and to Havel Lake. The French decided to build Tegel Field in the French sector of West Berlin for use by the airlift, to relieve the congestion at the other fields and, thereby, to improve safety. German workers constructed the field, and Tegel opened in December. Tempelhof added a runway with high-intensity approach lights. German workers provided continual maintenance to the runways at all the fields, which received heavy use by heavy aircraft.

Experienced pilots and pilots who received special training at the Great Falls (Montana) Air Force Base flew the American planes; the Great Falls base duplicated the three West Berlin airways, approach paths, and ground control approach (GCA) systems.

All aircraft participating in the airlift flew at assigned altitudes, headings, and speeds. Radio beacons marked the airways between bases in West Germany and in West Berlin. Flight instruments and navigation equipment proved crucial to the airlift during the winter when the ceiling and the visibility were low.

Flight Lines

"The book said you couldn't land on those steel mats or asphalt with an overweight airplane and stop in time. So we made a habit of touching down right at the end, hitting the brakes as soon as the main wheels touched, and then rotating the nose up until the tailskid hit the runway and slowed you down. It was tough on the airplane, but not as tough as running into something. I saw one C-54 land too fast and too far down. When the guy tried to make the turnoff the nose wheel collapsed. Nobody chewed you out for aborting a landing and going back to base, but tearing up an airplane brought you a lot of unwanted attention."

First Lieutenant William Lafferty, a C-54 pilot, describing landing in West Berlin during the Berlin Airlift, 1948, as quoted in Robert J. Sterling, *When the Airlines Went to War* (New York: Kensington Books, 1997).

GCA guided many flights into Berlin. Incoming aircraft were called Big Easy, and outgoing craft were called Big Willy. Military pilots, like those in the Air Force's new Military Air Transport Service, trusted the ground control approach. Not all runways in West Berlin had precision GCA, but those most heavily used did.

Soviet Response

Soviet planes occasionally harassed the airlift transports, which flew without arms and without fighter escort. Though largely defensive, the Soviet Air Force shot down two British planes. Sometimes a Soviet Yak flew directly at an airlift plane in a game of chicken. As a rule, the transport plane diverted from the fighter's path. Accidents due to fatigue, weather, inexperience, and strict limits on aircraft operation that sometimes stretched beyond safety, proved more fatal than Soviet harassment. In all, 75 airmen — 47 Britons and 28 Americans — died during the airlift.

The Soviet Union lifted the blockade of Berlin on 12 May 1949. The 247-day ordeal was over. The western allies continued the airlift into September in order to provide a stockpile of supplies for the West Berliners. On 30 September 1949 the airlift ceased operations. British and American pilots had flown 279,114 missions and delivered 2.3 million tons of cargo. The Berlin Airlift provided a diplomatic solution short of combat, and the Berlin Crisis demonstrated the value of the nuclear threat as the Soviets responded short of war. Yet Berlin remained a focus of the Cold War conflict as illustrated by the East German uprising of June 1953, the "Berlin Tunnel" — a wiretap — in the Soviet Army's headquarters in Berlin from 1954 to 1956, and the flood of people fleeing communist East Europe by crossing the Berlin border in the late 1950s.

Korean War

Korea had been ruled by Japan since before World War I, and it became spoils of World War II. The Allies discussed Korea at wartime conferences in Cairo, Yalta, and Potsdam. The United States wanted

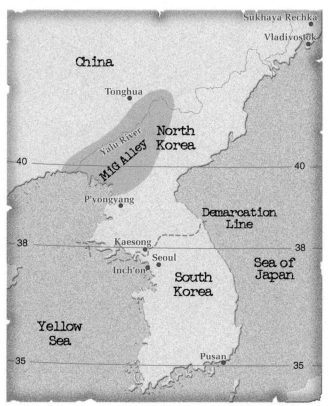

the Soviet Union to join the Pacific war against Japan to relieve the pressure on U.S. troops island hopping toward Japan. In return, the Soviet Union would occupy the northern portion of Korea and acquire the northern Japanese islands (Kiriles and Sakhalins). Korean communists had led nationalist independence movements in Korea during Japanese rule, and communists throughout the land prepared for Korean independence as the world war drew to a close. After the United States dropped an atomic bomb on Hiroshima, and the day before an atomic bomb fell on Nagasaki, the Soviet Union declared war on Japan. Japan surrendered. In Korea the Japanese surrendered to the forces of the Soviet Union north of the 38th Parallel and to forces of the United States south of the 38th.

This partition of Korea was pending an Allied withdrawal and the establishment of a Korean nation with a nationally elected government; but, instead of one Korea, two emerged. The Soviet Union installed a left-wing communist government in the northern sector, and the United States established a hard-line and right-wing anti-communist government in the South. Aided by communists in the North, communists in the south fought for a communist government for all of Korea. The new United Nations encouraged a national election, but only the South held an election. Syngman Rhee, the nationalist ruler in the South, declared the Republic of Korea, which the United Nations promptly recognized. Kim Il-Sung, the nationalist ruler in the North, declared the People's Democratic Republic of Korea, which the Soviet Union promptly recognized. Both the Soviet Union and the United States withdrew forces from Korea. Both superpowers provided funds and arms to support the unification of Korea, and both Kim and Rhee wanted to unify their country. The terms of unification and the nature of the unified government became a continuing source of conflict.

On 25 June 1950 North Korean troops invaded South Korea. The Northern troops rapidly pushed south in order to liberate South Korea from western and capitalist influences. The United States turned to the United Nations (U.N.) for help in containing the communists. The U.N. Security Council, with the Soviet representative absent, voted for a cease fire and for the withdrawal of Northern troops from the South. The Northern troops used Soviet-made tanks, and Soviet aircraft supported the ground troops. Within a week they captured Seoul, the capital of the South, and moved toward the strategic port of Pusan. The United States provided naval and air support for the South. The United Nations created a U.N. command to defend the South, and General Douglas MacArthur became its commander. United States troops constituted most of the U.N. force during the Korean War, although Australia, Belgium, Britain, Canada, Colombia, Ethiopia, France, Greece, New Zealand, Norway, the Netherlands, the Philippines, Thailand, and Turkey also sent ground units. The air war was mainly the United States versus the Soviet Union. (Figure 8-17)

Figure 8-17. The United States used the T-33 "T-Bird" trainer (top). The Soviet Union used the MiG 15 fighter (bottom).

In September the United Nations forces landed behind enemy lines at Inchon; this was a naval and marine landing supported by aircraft. The U.N. forces also counterattacked from Pusan, and they liberated Seoul. The next month South Korean troops moved into North Korea; this expanded the war north of the 38th Parallel. The United Nations forces followed. The North's capital, Pyongyang, fell. South Korean troops pushed to the border with China and forced the North's troops to flee into China. In China the new Communist government felt threatened with the buffer of communist North Korea gone and with the United States supporting nationalist Chinese on Taiwan rather than recognizing the legitimacy of the communist government on the mainland.

Beginning in 1949, communist Chinese airmen received Soviet training and flew Soviet-made aircraft. The communist Chinese government signed a Sino-Soviet Treaty in 1950. This placed China in a position to help Soviet-supported North Korea. In October 1950, two P-80 Shooting Star jet fighters of the United States Air Force strafed the Soviet base at Sukhaya Rechka, just 25 miles northeast of Vladivostok. The Soviets became increasingly concerned about the threat of foreign attack. They increased aid, aircraft, supplies, and training to China, so that China could help defend Asia from western imperialism.

Bombing

On 16 October 1950 the war escalated as 300,000 Chinese troops crossed the Yalu River into North Korea to fight the United Nations and South Korean forces there. B-29 bombers from the United States responded by bombing bridges across the Yalu, but this quickly ceased as the United States wanted to confine the war to Korea and those bridges extended into China. B-29s thereafter routinely flew bombing raids against North Korea, burned cities, and killed perhaps two million civilians before the war ended. The North Korean bombers, in contrast, were old Soviet Polikarpov PO-2 single-engine biplanes left over from World War II. The Chinese used Soviet-supplied Tupolev Tu-2 bombers, which also were war surplus material. (Figure 8-18)

Figure 8-18. The bombers used in the Korean War included the B-29 (top) from the U.S. and the Tu-2 (bottom) from the Soviet Union.

Historical Note

The Korean War revealed differences among countries within the United Nations and within nations participating in the United Nations forces. These differences often focused on the nature of a limited war. This war had limited civil objectives rather than a total military offensive. It was a war limited to the Korean Peninsula and limited to conventional rather than nuclear weapons. Limited war was fighting to negotiate a peace rather than fighting to win a war.

President Harry S. Truman (1884-1972) of the United States wanted to apply sanctions against China, but Britain and other nations favored a negotiated settlement. These other countries identified communist China as distinct from the Soviet Union, but the United States suspected that Soviet influence controlled China. When Truman threatened to use the atomic bomb in Korea, Great Britain objected so strongly that he had to explain that nuclear warfare was a threat but not an option.

General Douglas MacArthur (1880-1964) wanted Nationalist Chinese forces in Taiwan to cross the Formosa Straits and attack mainland China. This would open a second front and enable the armed forces to achieve total victory. MacArthur also wanted to bomb Chinese cities. Other nations participating in the United Nations command in Korea opposed expanding the war to China. Truman tried to reassure these other nations that the United States would not expand the war beyond Korea.

When MacArthur challenged Truman's policies in public, Truman relieved him of command. Truman appointed General Matthew Ridgway (1895-1993) as the new commander of the United Nations forces in Korea.

B-29s in Korea

When Chinese troops broke through United Nations' lines in November 1950, Truman threatened to use the atomic bomb. The Chinese soon pushed troops of the United Nations and South Korea south of the 38th parallel, and the Chinese marched into South Korea, where they soon captured Seoul and Inchon. Truman again considered using nuclear weapons in Korea; in April 1951 he authorized the transfer of atomic-capable B-29s and nine atomic bombs to Guam. The presence of Soviet aircraft in Manchuria discouraged the United States from using the bombs. Using conventional weapons, the United Nations forces finally stopped the advance and slowly recaptured territory.

Jet Fighters

President Truman relieved General MacArthur and replaced him with General Matthew Ridgway. Ridgway

Flight Lines

"The fighter scrambles at Uiju [North Korea] were inconclusive. During the next six weeks we lost three of 30 MiGs and shot down one South Korean propeller P-51 and an American F-80 jet.

"The American bombing of Uiju took a greater toll. I slept with my clothes on every night; at least half a dozen times after dark B-29s droned overhead and plastered our field. . . .

"After six weeks we had reached the limit of our endurance. Our runway, gutted with twenty-foot bomb craters, kept our MiGs virtually grounded. On December 15, 1951, the decision was made to abandon Uiju . . . I and the other MiG pilots happily took off across the Yalu for the sanctuary of Antung, Manchuria . . ."

North Korean pilot Kum Sok No describing a 1951 effort to use Korean jet pilots based in Korea to defend Korea, as quoted in "The Other Side of the Parallel: Red Flier," in *Fighter Pilot, Aerial Combat Aces from 1914 to the Present Day*, edited by Stanley M. Ulanoff (1962; revised edition, New York: Prentice Hall Press, 1986).

MiG 15s

commanded the offensive into North Korea in June 1951, including the relentless B-29 bombing of cities in the North. Soviet pilots and Soviet-trained Chinese and Korean pilots flew Soviet-made MiG fighters; only Soviet pilots flew MiGs equipped with radar for night fighting. In Asia, like Europe, the Soviet motivation was partly defensive: distribute aircraft to allies who help prevent the U.S. B-29 bombers from attacking Manchuria or the Soviet eastern region.

The Soviets tried to keep their pilots away from a direct war with the United States; this is why "MiG Alley," where Soviet and American airmen often engaged in aerial combat, was in the northwest corner of Korea rather than near the front. The communists in Korea also used the Ilyushin Il-10 ground attack airplane, of which the Soviets had built over 40,000 during World War II.

United Nations pilots — mostly from the United States — flew the Lockheed F-80 Shooting Star, Republic F-84 Thunderjet, and North American F-86 Sabre. The Mikoyan-Gurevich MiG-15 and the F-86 Sabre were swept-wing jets, both first flown in 1947 and both introduced to combat during the Korean

Historic Event

On 30 December 1947 the Soviet design bureau of Artyem Ivanovich Mikoyan and Mikhail Iosifovich Gurevich flew a prototype jet plane then designated I-310. A Rolls Royce-built Nene 2 engine powered the fighter design. In 1948 that design went into production as the MiG-15. The MiG-15 was powered by an RD-45 jet engine, the Soviet-built Nene. The MiG entered service in 1948. In 1950 the new version designated MiG-15 *bis* appeared with the VK-1 engine, a Soviet development of the Nene. Other versions followed. The MiG-15 entered combat in Korea in 1950. Soviet factories and Polish and Czechoslovakian licensees produced 12,000 MiG-15s in 17 versions; about half of the production aircraft were trainers. The MiG-17 became the -15's successor and, in 1955, the prototype for what became the MiG-21 first flew.

MiG 15

Flight Lines

"This mission is the type most enjoyed by the fighter pilot. It is a regular fighter sweep, with no worries about escort or providing cover for fighter-bombers. The mission had been well planned and well executed. Best of all, the MiGs had come forth for battle. Our separate flights had probably again confused the enemy radarscope readers, and, to an extent, nullified that tremendous advantage which radar plotting and vectoring gives a fighter on first sighting the enemy. We had put the maximum number of aircraft into the target area at the most opportune time, and we had sufficient fuel to fool the enemy. Our patrolling flights at strategic locations had intercepted split-off MiGs returning toward their sanctuary in at least two instances."

Sabre pilot Colonel Harrison R. Thyng describing a mission over North Korea, in "Sabrejet Leader," by Thyng, in *Fighter Pilot, Aerial Combat Aces from 1914 to the Present Day*, edited by Stanley M. Ulanoff (1962; revised edition, New York: Prentice Hall Press, 1986).

F-86 Sabre

War. The American fighters were based mostly at Kimpo Airfield, whereas the communist jet fighters generally flew from Manchuria.

The United Nations drive during the summer of 1951 and the ensuing stalemate led both sides to the negotiating table, first in Kaesong and later in Panmunjom. Neither side committed significant air resources to combat after this. Both sides compromised. They conceded that a divided Korea was acceptable and that a cease fire would be appropriate. The negotiations faltered at times, but continued.

Other Aircraft

The air war in Korea was dominated by B-29 bombers, Soviet MiGs, and American Sabre jets. Among the other aircraft used in Korea was the little two-seat Cessna L-19 Bird Dog. The U.S. Army used it for liaison, observation, wire laying, communications, and instrument training. The Army also flew the de Havilland Canada L-20 Beaver, Stinson L-5 Sentinel, and North American L-17 Navica fixed-wing aircraft. The Army, Navy, and Marine Corps routinely used Bell and Hiller light helicopters to evacuate wounded personnel. Whereas the top American ace of the war (Air Force Captain Joe McConnell, Jr.) had only 16 kills, the top helicopter pilots tallied hundreds of saves. Army Lieutenant William P. Blake evacuated 900 wounded in 545 missions, and Lieutenant Joseph Bowler carried 824 wounded in 482 missions. Medical evacuation was the primary mission of helicopters in Korea, though the Navy also used the rotorcraft to spot and direct naval gunfire, to spot and destroy enemy mines, to locate and destroy submarines, to transport mail and material, and to perform daylight guard duties. (Figure 8-19)

Figure 8-19. Other aircraft used in Korea were the L-19 Bird Dog (top) and the H-19 Chickasaw (bottom).

Armistice

Ending the Korean War fell to Khrushchev and Eisenhower, two new leaders. Dwight David "Ike" Eisenhower had commanded American forces in Europe during World War II and he led the Allied

invasion of Europe. He became president of the United States in January 1953 and remained in office for two terms (into 1961). Nikita Khrushchev, a long-time supporter of Joseph Stalin, gradually emerged as the new leader of Soviet Union after Stalin's death in March 1953. These two men led the transition to peace. Eisenhower's New Look — policy of nuclear deterrence and the threat of nuclear retaliation — worked in Korea, aided by Soviet reluctance to commit additional resources to the war. On 27 July 1953 the two sides signed an armistice. The war ended in a truce, a draw, with a divided Korea. Neither side extended its influence over both North and South Korea, but the United Nations forces "contained" communism. But the years of Soviet aid and the experience in Korea made China a world power, and the Chinese and Korean experience prompted the Soviet Union to supply arms to other nations in revolt, like Egypt and Algeria.

French Colonial Wars

When France fell in 1941, it lost colonies. Among the Allied wartime considerations were what to do with lands conquered by the Axis Powers and eventually liberated by the Allies. During World War II, for example, President Franklin D. Roosevelt proposed that Vietnam become an Indochina trusteeship under the United Nations. Vietnamese nationalist leader Ho Chi Minh suggested that the United States be the trustee; at the time, Ho was an ally who rescued downed American airmen during the war. Ho was also a leader of the Viet Nam Doc Lap Dong Minh (League for the Independence of Vietnam), better known as the Viet Minh; this group of nationalists, including some communists, fought to oust the Japanese invaders from their homeland. In contrast, Free French leader Charles de Gaulle proposed l'Union Francaise, a French commonwealth that would include the five nations of Indochina (Annam, Cambodia, Cochin China, Laos, and Tonkin). After the war France sought to regain its empire, including these Indochinese lands. This imperialism drew France into wars for independence in Indochina and later in Africa.

Vietnam

At the end of World War II, Japanese troops in Vietnam surrendered — to Chinese forces in northern Vietnam and to British forces in southern Vietnam. The Chinese transferred local rule to the Democratic

Republic of Vietnam, proclaimed by nationalist Ho Chi Minh on VJ Day (2 September 1945). In the southern area, the British ceded power to the French who wished to reclaim its colonies and glory. France wanted all of Vietnam again. The United States acquiesced because of a wartime exchange of French help in North Africa. Vietnam, in the postwar policy of the United States, was a French problem. French imperialism meant war, in this case, the French-Indochina War that began in 1945.

France sent troops and aircraft to protect French settlers and officials throughout the region. The initial aircraft were borrowed British Supermarine Mk VIII Spitfires and abandoned Japanese Nakajima Ki-43 Oscars, also one naval Consolidated PBY-5A Catalina and a few naval Aichi E12A1s. The United States blocked the French use of Republic P-47 Thunderbolts by refusing to supply parts if the aircraft were used in Indochina. The French instead bought British Supermarine Mk IX Spitfires and sent those to Vietnam in early 1946. The Viet Minh tried to win Hanoi and other cities from French troops in December 1946. Fighting continued into 1947, but the French remained in control of the cities and lowlands. The twin-engine de Havilland Mosquitos joined the French fleet in early 1947, but departed months later as the wooden construction was inappropriate for the tropical climate. The Douglas SBD Dauntless dive bomber proved more effective. (Figure 8-20)

Figure 8-20. The French used British Supermarine MK VIII aircraft like the one shown here during the war in Vietnam.

American Aircraft

In 1949 the United States finally permitted aircraft sales to France for use in Vietnam. The U.S. rationale was to wage war against communism because the Viet Minh had become increasingly communistic while fighting the French. The Bell P-63 Kingcobra

fighter and the Douglas SBD-5 Dauntless dive-bomber thus went to Vietnam. Like President Roosevelt before him, President Truman favored strong ties with France more than he opposed colonial rule of Indochina. He wanted France to cooperate in the fight against communism, and for that cooperation, he shipped napalm and sent a Military Assistance Advisory Group to Vietnam in 1950, the same year that the new communist government in China provided assistance to the Viet Minh. A French offensive succeeded only in pushing the Viet Minh into the rural highlands of central and northern Vietnam. The nationalists, led by General Vo Nguyen Giap, fought a guerrilla war against the French. France established two air units to target northern Annam and southern Annam. The Viet Minh won at Cao Bang and Lang Son, but General Jean de Lattre de Tassigny led the French to victory at Vinh Yen and Mao Khe.

The French Armée de l'Air (army air arm) added a third air unit to target central Annam, the Tonkin, and Cochin China more precisely. As of 1951, each air group included fighter, bomber, reconnaissance, and transport aircraft. The fighters were Grumman's F6F Hellcat and soon Grumman's F8F Bearcat. The bombers were heavily armed Douglas B-26s. In the early 1950s the French also used the little Morane-Saulnier M.S. 500 Criquet, the Curtiss SB2C Helldiver, Sikorsky S-55 helicopter, the Douglas C-47 transport, the AAC.1 Toucan (French-built Junkers Ju 52) trimotor, Bristol Type 170 Freighter, and Fairchild C-119 Packet (Flying Boxcar). The French Aéronavale (naval air arm) used the Consolidated PB4F Privateer, the Grumman JRF-5 Goose, and Vought AU-1 (F4U-6) Corsair. (Figure 8-21)

Figure 8-21. The U.S. built Douglas B-26 was used by the French during the war in Vietnam.

By the time the internationally experienced Dwight D. Eisenhower took office as president of the United

States in 1953, the question of Vietnam was: Should the West or the Communists get Asian territory and resources? Regarding the containment of communism, Eisenhower accepted what became known as the Domino Theory. In fact, during the 1954 siege of Dien Bien Phu, Eisenhower publicly introduced the term domino in connection with the spread of communism and the idea of Indochina as the first domino in a row. China's involvement in the Korean War convinced Eisenhower that Chinese support, whether of the North Koreans or the Viet Minh, meant that China was spreading communism in southeast Asia. Britain remained out of the Vietnam conflict, in part, because it did not want to anger China and thereby risk losing Hong Kong.

Dien Bien Phu

France devised a "honeypot" plan. It selected the village of Dien Bien Phu on the Vietnam-Laos border to become the honeypot, a French garrison in Viet Minh territory to be supplied by air and to be the honey that draws the bees — Viet Minh — into the open. Taking off from Bach-Mai and Gia-Lam airports, the French flew 65 C-47 aircraft on the airborne landing at Dien Bien Phu on 20 November 1953. The planes dropped supplies plus five parachute battalions into the valley. The battle began as the paratroopers drifted down. The Viet Minh besieged Dien Bien Phu in March. The United States wanted France to ratify the European Defense Community and to participate in the defense of Western Europe; therefore, the U.S. greatly increased financial support of France in Vietnam during the Dien Bien Phu siege, but the U.S. refused to become a combatant in the Indochinese war.

Historic Event

From 20 November 1953 to 8 May 1954 the French defended Dien Bien Phu. The Viet Minh besieged the French garrison there in March. The long and bloody siege continued until Dien Bien Phu fell to the communist Vietnamese in May. Communist forces and the French signed a ceasefire on 20 July 1954, and the last French forces withdrew from Vietnam in 1956. The United States sent troops to replace the French forces.

The defeat at Bien Dien Phu removed France's already declining will to wage war. Whereas the French fought for imperial territory, the United States fought against the spread of communism. The French wanted to rule Vietnam, and the United States wanted to establish a free democratic government in Vietnam. The battle of Dien Bien Phu and the different objectives of the two Western countries led to the United States replacing France in Vietnam.

Flight Lines

"During the last two days we should have received sixty C-119 aircraft. In reality only twenty-three came and three threw their stuff on the Communist side. The situation with regard to food becomes critical. Units only have one more day of food left. . . ."

Message sent from Dien Bien Phu on 20 April 1954, as quoted in Bernard B. Fall, *Hell in a Very Small Place, the Siege of Dien Bien Phu* (1967; New York: Da Capo Paperback, 1985).

The battle for Dien Bien Phu was long and bloody. Enemy fire forced supply drops to be made at night and damaged the airfield needed to evacuate the wounded. Parachute failures caused damage to French positions on the ground, and some deliveries fell on mine fields. Anti-aircraft fire downed many transport planes until the pilots flew higher. From higher altitudes, supplies often dropped into enemy hands. France lost over 13,000 men who were killed, wounded, or missing. Among the approximately 2,200 dead were French forces, Foreign Legion members, North Africans fighting for France, and Vietnamese, also killed were two Americans employed by the CIA's Civil Air Transport to fly in reinforcements and supplies. About 6,500 soldiers became prisoners as Dien Bien Phu fell on 7-8 May. Soon thereafter a formal ceasefire ended the fighting, a Geneva conference temporarily partitioned Vietnam pending free elections throughout the land, and the French forces withdrew from Vietnam.

The United States replaced the French south of the 17th parallel. Eisenhower applied his "great equation" to Vietnam. He weighed the limitless threat of international communism against the limited resources of the United States. He chose his New Look of nuclear deterrence as the means to affordably contain the Communists. This policy did not help the French at Dien Bien Phu, but it remained U.S. policy in Vietnam through the 1950s, during which time the United States trained southern troops only in conventional warfare. To share the work of policing southeast Asia, the United States organized South East Asia Treaty Organization (SEATO) in 1954. For several years, the United States "fought" by training and financing anti-communist Vietnamese forces. Wanting to avoid being drawn into a succession of Asian wars, the United States limited its involvement in Vietnam from 1955 through 1960 mostly to military training.

Algeria

Having just lost French Indochina, France wanted to hold its Algerian possession. When the nationalist Front de Libération Nationale (National Liberation Front) attacked police and troops across the North African colony in November 1954, a long Algerian War for independence began. From an aviation point of view, the war was significant for its use of helicopters in combat, starting in 1956. French forces used helicopters mostly made in the United States. The

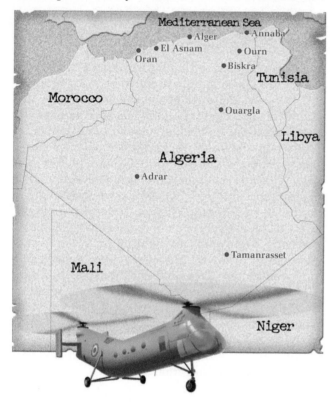

environment were also identified. The French learned that effective inter-service arrangements were necessary for ground forces to control their aviation support, and that decisions regarding aviation support should be made at the front.

As the Algerian War continued year after year, French popular support for the foreign war and for a foreign empire declined. France therefore negotiated an end to war, and Algeria obtained its independence on 5 July 1962.

Limited Wars

Korea, Vietnam, and Algeria were limited wars fought by nationalistic peoples. The Cold War period had additional hot spots. Late in 1949 Chiang Kai-shek's nationalists fled to Taiwan and Mao Tse-tung's communists formed the People's Republic of China. This ended the decades of Chinese civil war, but this also established a communist country in Asia. The nationalist Pathet Lao organized in Laos to oppose France regaining control of Laos and to fight France in the on-going French-Indochina War. Indonesia declared its independence from the Netherlands in 1945 and achieved it in 1949. In contrast, British Malaya became the Federation of Malaya in 1948, but a 12-year Malayan Emergency bought internal conflict, including guerrilla warfare, to the new country.

Army used over 100 Vertol H-21s in Algeria; the Piasecki Helicopter Corporation changed its name to Vertol in 1956, the same year the company sold 50 H-21s to France. The French Air Force used over 100 Sikorsky H-34s. The French also used light utility helicopters produced in both France and the United States.

The experience in Algeria contributed to the development of helicopter technology and tactics, especially as related to transport and gunship helicopters. The French forces demonstrated the effectiveness of suppressive firepower and, thereby, the need to arm helicopters. Helicopter assault missions required specially trained personnel. Combat revealed the need for loading doors on both sides of the fuselage, and the desirability of a rear loading ramp too. The need for reserve engine power and the importance of maintenance appropriate to use in the hot desert

Through much of the 1950s the nationalist Mau Mau rebelled in Kenya. The British finally decided to give Kenya its independence. India too achieved independence during the postwar period. In preparing to grant independence, the British partitioned the land

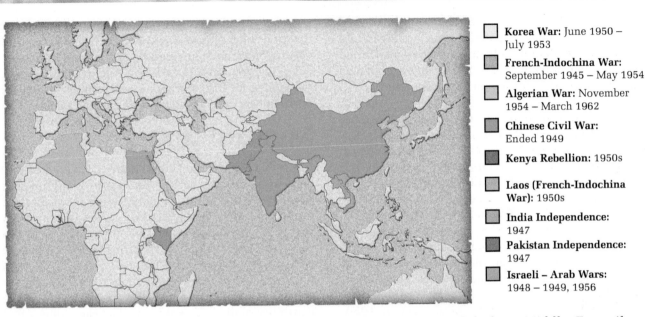

Korea War: June 1950 – July 1953

French-Indochina War: September 1945 – May 1954

Algerian War: November 1954 – March 1962

Chinese Civil War: Ended 1949

Kenya Rebellion: 1950s

Laos (French-Indochina War): 1950s

India Independence: 1947

Pakistan Independence: 1947

Israeli – Arab Wars: 1948 – 1949, 1956

into two parts, the larger section became the Hindu-majority country of India and the smaller section became the Muslim nation of Pakistan. About eight million people relocated to be in the new nation of their choice.

Palestine became Israel and the center of controversy in the Middle East. In 1948 the United Nations decided to partition Palestine, a British mandate since the end of World War I. Jewish residents formed the nation of Israel, and Transjordan (Jordan since 1950) acquired the Arab West Bank of Palestine. When Israel achieved self-determination and statehood in 1948, the Palestinians in the contested land lost their right to self-determination and statehood. A half million Arabs became displaced persons. The new Jewish country of Israel and the neighboring Arab countries fought a war in 1948-1949 that the Israelis called a war for independence and the Arabs called the "Palestine disaster." As a result of this war, Egypt got the Gaza Strip region that had been part of Palestine, but Israel won the war and maintained its independence. This was mainly a land war that ended in a peace brokered by the United Nations.

The Arab-Israeli conflict flared again in 1956. The year before, the Soviet Union began supplying arms, including MiG fighters, to Egypt. Egyptian leader Gamal Abdel Nasser resisted capitalist imperialism and promoted Arab nationalism; for example, he nationalized the Suez Canal. Britain and France urged Israel to invade Egypt, which Israel did by dropping paratroopers into the canal zone. Khrushchev threatened a missile attack if the Western allies did not stop the Suez War, because the war was a Western attempt to force Egypt to not nationalize the Suez

Canal, an essential link to Middle East oil and Britain's interests in the Far East. A settlement led to the withdrawal of British and French troops from Egypt and the return of the Sinai and Gaza Strip to Egypt. The Suez Crisis diverted Western support from the Hungarian uprising of 1956, which the Soviet Union suppressed.

Aircraft played a limited role in these limited wars, but the number and dispersal of conflicts around the globe illustrate that the Cold War was not that cold. President Eisenhower tried to negotiate a stronger peace for those countries caught up in the Cold War nuclear rivalry.

Atoms for Peace

Eisenhower believed that the stockpiling of nuclear weapons by both superpowers to deter the potential aggression should not exceed the amount needed to deter the other. He even advocated a test ban, but not a unilateral one. Eisenhower thought there was an alternative to "atoms for war." He delivered this alternative — his Atoms for Peace speech — before the United Nations on 8 December 1953, during his first year in office. This speech took the nuclear debate beyond the closed doors of governments to the public. Atoms for War was already a reality, as was evident in the destruction of Hiroshima and Nagasaki and in the rhetoric of the Cold War. Eisenhower realized that the atomic bomb was the first weapon that could cripple American industry, the winning factor in all major conflicts of the century thus far. His expressed motive for going public was moral. How could he slow the arms race? He could and did warn the American people of the destructiveness of nuclear weapons, and he offered hope. The hope was based on diverting fissionable material from American and Soviet military stockpiles to civilian use via a United Nations "nuclear bank." He gained French and British support by giving them advance information.

When Eisenhower had entered office, the Atomic Energy Commission (AEC) was a secret, independent, defense-related agency (created in 1946) with a monopoly on nuclear technology, reactors, and fissionable materials. Eisenhower moved the AEC into politics and private enterprise. As a defense-oriented agency, the AEC directed all activities of the vast atomic community that included mines, ore-processing mills, material plants, metal fabrication plants, weapons components plants, weapons assembly plants, government research laboratories, government contractors, plutonium production plants, and nuclear test sites. With the Atomic Energy Act of 1954, Eisenhower broke the government's monopoly, allowed industry to cooperate with the AEC, and opened the way for nuclear power plants. This reflected, in part, Eisenhower's determination to lessen government control of the economy.

Atoms for Peace stimulated international discussions and specific programs, like the international peaceful-uses conferences in Geneva in 1955 and 1958. The International Atomic Energy Agency formed in 1957. EURATOM was a multilateral organization for European atomic energy development. The United States entered into bilateral agreements with numerous nations, like the 1955 agreements with Argentina, Belgium, Brazil, Canada, Republic of China, Denmark, Greece, and other countries. The nuclear-powered merchant ship NS *Savannah* and the civilian power station that opened at Shippingport, Pennsylvania, demonstrated peaceful uses of atomic energy. Atoms for Peace also permitted radioisotope research for medical and other applications.

Atoms for Peace failed to achieve disarmament. Related to his efforts to stop the nuclear weapons race, Eisenhower proposed "open skies" at a Geneva summit of heads of state in 1955; he called upon the United States and the Soviet Union to allow mutual air reconnaissance over their respective military installations. The Soviet Union rejected the proposal. The United States responded by

sending spy planes over Soviet territory, including the new and secret Lockheed U-2. Militaries of various nations continued to participate in atomic weapon programs. By sharing nuclear technology, the Atoms for Peace program contributed to nuclear proliferation and the increase of nuclear waste.

Nuclear Plane

Almost as soon as the United States delivered atomic bombs to Japan by plane, the idea of using nuclear energy to power an airplane with almost unlimited range was entertained by Air Force officers. An early idea was to use a nuclear-powered bomber to carry nuclear weapons; in this scenario, nuclear energy provided both the fuel and warhead. In 1946 the Army Air Forces established a Nuclear Energy Propulsion for Aircraft (NEPA) project to study the feasibility of the different ideas. The Navy developed a nuclear-powered submarine, the *Nautilus*, launched in January 1954, but the Air Force never achieved an operational nuclear-powered airplane. (Figure 8-22)

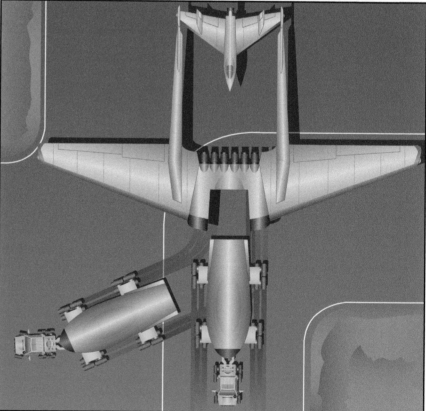

Figure 8-22. This is an artist's rendition of the nuclear-powered bomber. The airplane was never built due to weight and other limitations.

The Atomic Energy Commission spent millions of dollars a year in a frustrating effort to develop a nuclear plane. An airborne reactor needed to be lightweight, powerful and reliable enough for flight, and well-shielded to contain radiation. Private companies contracted to develop the airframe and the jet engine. The Oak Ridge National Laboratory in Tennessee explored several approaches to nuclear-powered aircraft, including a propulsion system fueled with a liquid mixture of fused salts that contained uranium. General Electric experimented with the idea of heating turbines directly in the reactor core. Pratt & Whitney explored nuclear engine technology too. The aircraft nuclear propulsion program promised long range and supersonic speed. the project modified a Convair B-36 bomber to carry a General Electric nuclear reactor, but the flight tests did not involve the reactor powering any of the airplane's systems. The government canceled the program in 1961.

Eisenhower's initial response to the nuclear plane was that it was not a good use of public funds! Yet the Atomic Energy Commission and the Air Force pursued the idea by copying the Navy's nuclear submarine program, but the plane program failed to develop a solid technical base for a nuclear-powered aircraft. In the 1950s the Office of Naval Research also sponsored work on an airborne nuclear power-plant, this one explicitly for Navy use. Publicity releases about the nuclear airplanes tended to lack detail as there was very little news of the secret Soviet efforts to build a nuclear plane. The nuclear arms race was a major feature of the Cold War, and the Atoms for Peace program defined Eisenhower's efforts to stop the arms race. In this context, the nuclear plane was a minor project.

ROCKETS, MISSILES, AND SATELLITES

Rockets, missiles, and satellites were as much part of the "electronics revolution" as they were competitive devices in the space race and the arms race of the Cold War. The electronics revolution began with radio and telephone technology. Turn-of-the-century radio receivers used crystals in which the motion of electricity could be controlled. The crystals — galena, lead sulfide — were what would now be called semiconductors; thus the crystal radio was a solid-state device. A diode, which is a bulb with two electrodes, could receive electromagnetic signals, as could the galena crystal. With the 1906 invention of the triode, receivers with vacuum tubes quickly replaced the crystal-based radios. A triode, which had a third electrode called a grid, could also amplify the radio signal. Vacuum tube electronics dominated radio technology for fifty years. The development of radar relied upon vacuum tubes, called "valves" in British usage and "radio tubes" in lay vocabulary.

Rockets, missiles, and satellites used electronics too. In the 1940s and 1950s these were first-generation electronic devices, characterized by their use of vacuum tubes. The electronics revolution also affected traditional piston planes and jet aircraft, from the new avionics in civil, commercial, and military aircraft to the evolving air defense systems of the Cold War warriors.

Air Defense

President Harry S. Truman had authorized using the long-range B-29 aircraft to drop atomic bombs on Japan in 1945. After the war, he initiated efforts to protect the United States from being attacked by long-range aircraft of an enemy nation. The Soviet Union's Tupolev Tu-4 long-range bomber was based on the Boeing B-29 Superfortress, so the possibility of such an attack existed. With the postwar development of jet bombers and the proposals for nuclear-powered airplanes, the threat to security increased. Distance from foreign enemies no longer protected the United States or any other country from attack. Transpolar and transoceanic flights could bring enemy bombers over distant targets. During Truman's term in office, the Defense Department began generously funding research and development of air defense systems.

The design, development, production, and even management of many electronic technologies involved large numbers of scientists and engineers in the postwar military-industrial-university complex. During the Cold War, with the perceived threat of an enemy attack so great, the military often supported more than one line of research and development. The Air Force, for example, funded different air defense systems under development at both the University of Michigan and the Massachusetts Institute of Technology (MIT) in the late 1940s and early 1950s.

Aeronautical engineer Theodor von Kármán and physicist George E. Valley, Jr., led an Air Defense Systems Engineering Committee that studied the history of air defense, surveyed the ground-based air defense facilities of the United States, and recommended the automation of a nationwide air defense system. In response to the committee's recommendations and to internally perceived needs, the Air Force requested that MIT design and develop a modern air defense system.

In 1951 MIT established a mission-oriented laboratory to pursue the research and development of broadly defined defense electronics, including an automated air defense system. The basis of this new Lincoln Laboratory was MIT's wartime Radiation Laboratory. Under contract to the Air Force, the new laboratory promptly began work on a radar-based and computer-based system initially called the Lincoln Transition System and soon renamed the Semi-Automatic Ground Environment (SAGE). MIT began work without a real-time digital computer. The laboratory collaborated with International Business Machines (IBM) for computers and Bendix Radio for radar.

Michigan was working on a guided-missile program called Air Defense Integrated System for Surveillance and Weapon Control (ADIS) . It began work without an interceptor missile and collaborated with Boeing. Also during this period, Western Electric Company was installing a Distant Early Warning (DEW) System to alert the air defense establishment to incoming communist aircraft.

SAGE

The Semi-Automatic Ground Environment (SAGE) was an air defense project. Its purpose was to defend the United States against enemy bombers. The cathode-ray tube display, automatic communication by telephone lines and by microwave radio, and computer software were among the many features developed for SAGE. The most striking feature was the combat center where digital computers processed data.

MIT's Servomechanisms Laboratory began designing the Whirlwind computer as a Navy project for an airplane simulator before the SAGE project started. Lincoln Laboratory expanded Project Whirlwind to meet the needs of SAGE. Like other early digital computers — Electronic Discrete Variable Calculator (EDVAC), the Manchester University Mark I, and others — Whirlwind used vacuum tube technology, but Whirlwind was also unique and new. It was the first digital computer capable of processing information and automatically controlling processes in real time rather than merely computing arithmetic figures in batches; that is, Whirlwind could process information from radar sensors in real time rather than store the data

Historical Evidence

Original documents record not only what happened, but how the participants perceived the situation. In 1950, for example, the Air Defense Systems Engineering Committee defined an air defense system as an organism. Like any organism, the air defense system needed "sensory components, communication facilities, data analyzing devices, centers of judgement, directors of action, and effectors, or executing agencies." The committee explained, "The stress is not only on pattern and arrangement, but on these also as determined by function, an attribute desired in the Air Defense System. . . . It is the function of an organism . . . to achieve some defined purpose." This organism was automated in the sense defined by Norbert Wiener in his 1948 book *Cybernetics; or, Control and Communication in the Animal and the Machine.* The quotations from the committee's report. A discussion of the committee, and information on the resulting SAGE air defense system are in Thomas P. Hughes, *Rescuing Prometheus* (New York: Pantheon Books, 1998). Hughes' book is a secondary source of information. A primary source is the original document — the committee's report. It is preserved in an archives: Air Defense Systems Engineering Committee, "Air Defense System: ADSEC Final Report," 24 October 1950, MITRE Corporation Archives, Bedford, Massachusetts.

for later batch processing. Field tests demonstrated that Whirlwind connected to 15 radar sites could track "enemy" aircraft and direct interceptor aircraft. This was in the spring of 1953, shortly after Dwight Eisenhower succeeded Truman as president. The air defense system was still in development at the time. (Figure 8-23)

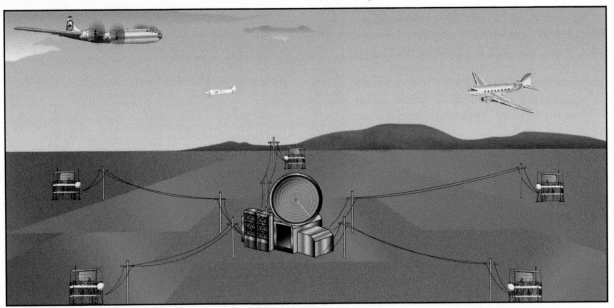

Figure 8-23. The Whirlwind computer was capable of processing and displaying real time data from multiple radar sites. It was a defensive weapon to track enemy aircraft and to direct interceptors against those aircraft.

Whirlwind was the prototype computer, a proof of concepts developed while the machine was being developed. Production versions became the information processing and control centers of SAGE. These were the AN/FSQ-7 and the later AN/FSQ-8 computers; the letters in the designations stood for Army-Navy fixed special equipment. Under MIT contract, IBM manufactured the machines. These computers featured the brand new magnetic flux core memory that allowed random access, which was invented as part of the Whirlwind project. Pulses of electricity could magnetize or demagnetize the memory material, the state of magnetization indicated on or off, and on and off represented data in the digital notation of 0's and 1's. The computers were general-purpose machines with multiple features, including the random-access memory and real-time control needed to track large numbers of attacking and intercepting aircraft.

Systems integration and systems management presented special challenges to the SAGE air defense system. The eventual solution was the creation in 1958 of a non-profit federal contract research center in charge of systems engineering: the MITRE Corporation, (MITRE was not an acronym, but a new word written in capital letters.) Other federal contract research centers also contributed to SAGE; RAND (Research and Development) Corporation and System Development Corporation developed software for the digital computers. More than a hundred contractors supported the program too.

SAGE became operational in one sector in 1958, and soon 22 of the planned 32 computerized direction or combat centers were in operation. By then, SAGE was already obsolete because missiles were replacing bombers as the threatening weapon and because transistors were replacing vacuum tubes in electronic equipment. SAGE AN/FSQ–7 computers each had about 25,000 vacuum tubes. Tubes consumed a lot of power and needed a fairly high voltage to operate. Also, they had a short life and limited reliability. These limitations encouraged work toward a solid-state amplifier — an achievement reached back in 1947 with the invention of the transistor.

Electronics

Military funding fueled the development of electronics in the late 1940s and the 1950s. Vacuum tubes — the first generation of computer technology — persisted despite the

technological and commercial challenge of transistors. Transistors — the second generation of computer technology — evolved from a long line of scientific work in physics, but the technology remained in the laboratory for a few years. The transistor is a device that uses semiconductor material to amplify or switch an electrical signal, and wires that carry the signal to and from the material. The transistor had major advantages over the vacuum tube: small size, reduced voltage, and reduced power requirements. Transistors entered production in 1951 for research and military applications; the first commercial transistor radio appeared in 1954. Transistors reduced computer size, removed the need for cooling hot vacuum tubes, and greatly reduced power consumption. As transistors replaced vacuum tubes, computers got faster, smaller, and cheaper. SAGE AN/FSQ-7 computers were thus replaced before long. (With continual development and updating, SAGE remained in operation into the 1980s.) The third generation of electronics technology already under development in the late 1950s was the integrated circuit — a chip of solid-state semiconductor material on which several circuits could perform functions. These electronic developments affected aerospace equipment of the time. (Figure 8-24)

Electronically guided rockets and missiles were launched in the postwar period and, in an important development of the period, electronics and computers

Figure 8-24. Postwar trends in electronics were toward miniaturization, increased reliability, and lower costs. The technology transitioned from vacuum tubes (left), to transistors (center), to the integrated circuit (right).

became part of the design and development processes as well as the product. Systems engineering firms replaced airframe makers as the prime contractors for defense systems. Science and technology achieved new status in American society, military as well as civil. President Eisenhower appointed the first presidential science adviser, James Killian of MIT, in 1957. Electronics also equipped the strategic bombers that constituted the main defense force in most postwar air forces.

Bombers

The Strategic Air Command, not rockets or missiles, defended the United States during the immediate postwar period. When the Army Air Forces created the Strategic Air Command in 1946, the Soviets promptly reorganized their strategic bombers into the Dalniya Aviatsiya (long-range aviation) group. The Soviets copied the B-29 bomber and introduced it at the Tushino Air Show in 1947. That year in the United States, the North American B-45, Convair B-46, Boeing B-47, and Martin B-48 programs competed to build a medium-range but high-speed jet-powered bomber. Boeing won the competition in 1948 and produced over 1,900 B-47s in the 1950s. The electronic subsystems, like the bombing and navigation systems, remained in development as the

aircraft entered both production and operation. Retrofitting was a part of the B-47 program, because the development of subsystems lagged behind airframe development and, in part, because electronic technology was changing so rapidly during this period. The airplane, for example, had a new defensive armament system. Instead of a manned tail turret, the B-47 had an electronically operated radar remote fire control system.

Long-range bombers were also in development. The B-35, B-36, B-49, B-52, and B-60 programs of the 1940s and 1950s were intercontinental bombers. Propellers drove the Northrop B-35 and Convair B-36. The postwar Northrop B-49 was a turbojet version of the B-35, and the Convair B-60 was a jet version of the B-36. Neither could compete with Boeing's swept-wing B-52 equipped with turbojet engines. In the 1950s the United States also developed the supersonic Convair B-58 bomber (first delivered in 1960), and it funded research into a nuclear-powered bomber and development of a supersonic North American B-70 that was powered by advanced jet engines. Neither of these aircraft ever entered production. The United States produced nearly 2,000 B-47s and about 700 B-52s during the 1950s. Production peaked during the Korean War and again in the mid-1950s when the United States thought the

Historic Event

During 1947 four competing jet bomber programs began flight test programs. The North American B-45 first flew on 17 March, the Convair B-46 on 2 April, the Martin B-48 on 22 June, and the Boeing B-47 on 17 December. The new United States Air Force evaluated the results of the fly-off, actually the results of months of flying by the various prototypes, and selected the Boeing B-47 for production.

North American B-45

Boeing B-47

Consolidated B-46

Martin B-48

Figure 8-25. The swept-wing Boeing B-52 was an eight-engine turbojet that entered service in the 1950s. This aircraft became the main nuclear and conventional weapons delivery system for the United States from its introduction through the end of the century.

Soviet Union was producing more strategic bombers than the U.S. (Figure 8-25)

The main Soviet bomber in the early 1950s was the piston-powered Tupolev Tu-4 Bull, the Soviet version of the B-29. At the May Day celebration in Moscow in 1954 the Soviet Union displayed a new bomber: the turbojet Myasishchev Mya-4 Bison heavy bomber, the prototype of which had first flown in January 1952. To the United States, this bomber appeared capable of delivering a hydrogen bomb, which the Soviets were known to have tested in August 1953. At the Soviet May Day celebration in 1955 the Soviets introduced another new bomber: the turboprop Tupolev Tu-95 Bear, which had first flown in November 1952. Both the Bison and Bear were long-range bombers. At the Aviation Day air show in Tushino in July 1955 Soviet pilots flew 28 Mya-4 Bisons past the reviewing stand. That was four times the number of B-52s then in the Strategic Air Command of the United States Air Force. Unknown to the United States at the time, the same Bison squadron flew past the stand three times; one Bison airplane dropped out after the first pass. (Figure 8-26)

 ## Historic Event

Soviet air shows in 1954 and 1955 led the United States to perceive a "bomber gap," but U-2 spy plane flights over the Soviet Union in 1956 revealed that Soviet bomber production did not exceed that of the United States.

Figure 8-26. The Soviet bombers of the 1950s included the piston engine Tupolev Tu-4 Bull (top), the turbojet Myasishchev Mya-4 Bison (middle), and the turboprop Tupolev Tu-95 Bear (bottom). The Bison and Bear were long-range bombers capable of delivering hydrogen bombs to the United States.

Military leaders, politicians, and the public in the United States perceived a gap between the strategic air forces of the two superpowers, and the U.S. increased bomber production to restore the balance of power. Starting in June 1956, the United States sent Lockheed U-2 spy planes on reconnaissance missions over the Soviet Union. These flights revealed that Soviet production lagged behind American production, and there was no bomber gap for the United States to fill. For example, the Soviets built only about 55 Bears in the 1950s. Soon, however, the United States feared a "missile gap" as it became evident the Soviet Union supported missile development more than bomber production.

Historic Event

On 4 August 1955 test pilot Tony LeVier flew the first Lockheed U-2, *Angel*. He reached a speed of 160 knots (295 km/h) and an altitude of 7,300 feet (2,225 m) on the 36-minute flight.

The public was told, "The Lockheed U-2 is a simple research aircraft" used by the National Advisory Committee on Aeronautics for high-altitude research. This information is from *Jane's All the World's Aircraft 1956-1957*, compiled and edited by Leonard Bridgman (New York: McGraw-Hill Book Company, 1956-1957).

But Lockheed developed the aircraft for the Central Intelligence Agency. It was a spy plane. Mylar-based film developed by Eastman Kodak and high-resolution cameras developed by Edwin Land enabled the Central Intelligence Agency and the Air Force to fly high-altitude photographic reconnaissance missions. Radar and other equipment allowed the U-2 to make electronic reconnaissance flights as well.

Captured V-2 rocket

Rockets and Missiles

Late in World War II the German V-2 rockets carried warheads against enemy targets. The V-2 alerted nations to the range and potential danger of attack by missiles. Both the Soviet Union and the United States sponsored rocket and missile research during the war, but they concentrated their resources on the production and operation of conventional aircraft. The Allies shared the spoils of war from the German rocket group at Peenemünde, but not to the same level. The German rocket team surrendered *en masse* to the Americans; they, their documents, and a number of V-2 rockets soon went to the United States. The rocket center itself was largely destroyed by the Germans before it fell into Soviet hands. The Soviets captured V-2 production plants, but acquired only a few of the German scientific personnel.

The German legacy included much more than the V-2 as the Germans had worked on about 140 different missile programs during the war, including the pilotless jet V-1 (a cruise missile), the Schmetterling (Butterfly) surface-to-air rocket-launched missile, the Fritz X air-to-surface radio-controlled missile (used against Allied ships at Salerno), and the Henschel 298 rocket air-to-air missile. Once Germany had lost supremacy in the European skies, it gave guided missiles high priority. That legacy went to the four occupying powers (France, Great Britain, the Soviet Union, and the United States).

As the Cold War began, it seemed clear to the various nations that the wartime development of the V-2 by the Germans, radar by the British, and atom bomb by the Americans would one day be combined into a single weapon. The race was to be first, but the finish line was off in the future. More immediately, the United States wanted to convert to a peacetime economy, to start the United Nations, and to help reconstruct war-ravaged Europe. Britain, for a European example, helped establish the Australian Weapons Research Establishment (later known as the Woomera Rocket Range) in order to fire British-developed guided missiles in that sparsely populated area. Britain's war-damaged economy could not support major research and development at that time, and most Europeans nations were in similar situations. Britain, to continue the example, maintained a modest missile development program, and in 1957 the Defense

Historical Note

A rocket is a reactive device that dates back as least as far as the early days of gunpowder; that is, about 1,000 years ago. Gunpowder rockets in the form of fireworks have entertained audiences for centuries. Early military rockets were artillery weapons. They provided "the rocket's red glare" during the War of 1812 between Great Britain and the young United States, as commemorated in the song the *Star Spangled Banner*. Nineteenth-century whalers used rocket-powered harpoons. Rocket refers to the reactive nature of the projectile rather than the power source that launches it or the purpose of the projectile. A rocket may be the gunpowder type, or nuclear-powered. The fuel may be in solid, liquid, or gas form.

Congreve solid-fuel rocket.

Dr. Goddard (left) working on liquid-fuel rocket.

Historical Note

A missile is anything capable of being thrown or propelled, hurled or projected. It is a projectile, regardless of how it is projected. It may be launched by rocket or other means. As a weapon, the missile is a warhead meant to strike a distant target, or the missile may carry the warhead. A ballistic missile is like a bullet. Each follows a gravity-defined trajectory after the initial launch or firing. In contrast, a cruise missile can cruise through the air like an unmanned airplane. It may be jet-propelled. Missiles may deliver conventional weapons or nuclear weapons. Missiles are also classed by their launch-to-target mission: air-to-air, air-to-surface, surface-to-surface, surface-to-air, ship-launched or submarine-launched, or even space-to-earth. Missiles may be short range (about 150 miles or 200 kilometers), medium range (about 1,000 miles or 1,500 kilometers), intermediate range (1500 miles, 2500 km), long-range (2,000 miles, 3,000 km or more), or intercontinental range (more than 5,000 miles, 8,000 km).

Short Range 150 miles (200 km)

Medium Range 1,000 miles (1,500 km)

Intermediate Range 1,500 miles (2,500 km)

Long Range 2,000 miles (3,000 km)

Intercontinental Range more than 5,000 miles (8,000 km)

Ministry announced that missiles would gradually replace combat aircraft in the Royal Air Force. In the 1950s, China was emerging from decades of civil war too, so its limited resources went into internal development. Despite nationally important programs in various nations, the main Cold War contenders in the rocket and missile races were the Soviet Union and the United States.

Soviet Rocket Program

The Soviet government had organized its scientific rocket research program as early as 1933, and during World War II they used rocket-artillery units on the Eastern Front. Developing modern new weapons became part of the Soviet effort to modernize its postwar military forces. After the war Sergei Korolov led the Soviet team working with captured German V-2 rockets, which were adapted and improved for use in Soviet experiments. The Soviets reopened Peenemnde as a rocket test center, and they reopened the underground Mittelwerk V-2 factory at Nordhausen. They assigned East German scientists and engineers and factory workers to work on rockets and missiles. In 1947 at an Aviation Day show the Soviet Union flew a MiG-9, an early jet fighter, with a liquid-fuel rocket attached to the tail, and also a Lavochkin La-9 with pulse jet engines. The Soviets improved the German wartime Rheintochter (Daughter of the Rhine surface-to-air missile) and Wasserfall (Waterfall surface-to-air missile). These missiles were installed around Moscow to defend the city. Within five years of the end of the war, the Soviet Union had both nuclear bombs and ballistic missiles, and large long-range missiles and powerful rockets were under development. (Figure 8-27)

Figure 8-27. V-2 rocket engines at the underground Mittelwerk factory at Nordhausen.

Historical Evidence

Science fiction stories in print and on film provide a perspective on historical events. Robert A. Heinlein's *Rocket Ship Galileo* (New York: Scribner, 1947) is the story of three teenage boys who ride an atomic rocket to the moon. Atoms and rockets were popular topics at the time. A movie loosely based on Heinlein's book is *Destination Moon* (Universal/George Pal, 1950). In the movie, American industry is the hero as a team of companies build a rocket-launched, atomic-powered spaceship and beat the Russians to the moon. The fictional General Thayer explained the importance of the mission: "there is absolutely no way to stop an attack from outer space [. . . so] the first country that can use the Moon for the launching of missiles will control the Earth."

U.S. Rocket Program

In general, the immediate postwar rocket and missile programs in the United States remained small because the military relied upon bombers rather than missiles to deliver conventional and nuclear weapons. The military did sponsor several rocket and missile programs. The Army established a missile range at White Sands, New Mexico, in 1945; the Navy established one at Point Mugu, California, in 1946; and the Air Force established the nation's third missile range at Cape Canaveral, Florida, in 1949. The Army contracted with Bell Telephone Laboratories and Western Electric Company for studies, the Air Force worked with Consolidated Vultee (Convair) on a long-range concept, and the Navy converted the USS *Norton Sound* into a guided-missile ship for testing missiles. The Air Force established a guided-missile squadron, then called the First Pilotless Bomber Squadron (Light); it deployed the turbojet-powered Matador surface-to-surface missile. The main program was **Project Paperclip**, a program whereby German scientists and engineers could come to the United States to live and work. This program provided the transition for the V-2 rocket team; 82 team members, including the director Wernher von Braun, came during the summer of 1945, while the war in the Pacific continued.

The V-2 team from Germany experimented with surplus V-2s in upper-atmosphere research. After one V-2 launched from the White Sands firing range in New Mexico wrongly flew into Mexico, the team made improvements on the wartime products. They launched a V-2 from the carrier *Midway*, and they launched a V-2 with a monkey on board. In 1949 they launched a V-2 with a smaller rocket on its nose. The second stage of that rocket, the little rocket called *Wac Corporal*, came out of the Jet Propulsion Laboratory at the California Institute of Technology. It reached outer space. The 78 V-2 launches in the United States were military events, parts of research programs of the Army, Navy, and Air Force. When the Army established a missile development center at the Redstone Arsenal in Alabama in 1949, the V-2 team moved there.

U.S. Missile Programs

The Korean War turned attention to war and sparked interest in missiles, but the presumed minimum weight of a nuclear warhead — 5,000 pounds — raised questions regarding the feasibility of nuclear missiles. The development of thermonuclear devices, hydrogen bombs, in 1952 (United States) and 1953 (Soviet Union) suggested lighter weight warheads were possible. The United States established the Lawrence Livermore Laboratory in Livermore, California, to develop thermonuclear weapons, and the nuclear testing in Operation Castle confirmed the possibility of lighter weights. In 1954 the United States initiated and expanded various missile programs. Corporate competition and interservice rivalry had sponsored numerous small programs before 1954 and supported several large programs thereafter. The largest was Atlas, a military project that produced the first successful American intercontinental missile.

More than 18,000 scientists, engineers, and technicians in the military, industry, and universities worked on the development of the Atlas weapon system, and another 70,000 people in management and production jobs in industry worked to make the missiles. The government employed 17 major contractors, 200 subcontractors, and 200,000 suppliers on this one project. General Bernard Schriever of the Air Force's Western Development Division oversaw the intercontinental missile program. The new electronically oriented Ramo-Wooldridge firm was the prime contractor and systems engineer. Convair made the airframe, North American the propulsion system, General Electric the radio-inertial guidance system and the nose cone, A.C. Spark Plug the all-inertial guidance system, and Burroughs the computer. Testing during development included wind tunnel tests, missile flight tests, and test flights of the Lockheed X-17 with that vehicle representing the missile cone during reentry into the atmosphere. Atlas Series A entered flight testing in 1957. Series B was also a test bed. Some missiles in Series C and D were used in flight tests and others were deployed. Series E missiles went into military service. Titan was a parallel Air Force development, also an intercontinental ballistic missile. Martin, Aerojet General, Bell Telephone, American Bosch, AVCO, and Remington Rand were major contractors, and Ramo-Wooldridge was the systems engineering firm overseeing the concurrent and parallel development of intercontinental missiles. Both Atlas and Titan passed flight tests in 1958. (Figure 8-28)

Historical Evidence

Secondary literature can provide information of a nature not found in primary sources. A historian might use data not available to participants of a program to compare several programs. From such a comparison, the historian can make conclusions and interpret the relative historical significance of events. Historian of technology Thomas P. Hughes, for example, studied many large federally funded technology programs. He concluded that the intercontinental ballistic missile program was "the largest and most costly military-funded research and development program in history — the Manhattan Project [that developed the atom bomb] not withstanding." This conclusion and his account of Project Atlas are in his book *Rescuing Prometheus* (New York: Pantheon Books, 1998).

Figure 8-28. Atlas launch, January 1969.

Personal Profile

Bernard Adolph "Benny" Schriever (1910—2005) was born in Bremen, Germany. With his parents, he came to the United States during World War I. He studied engineering at Texas A&M. Upon graduation he became an Army reserve officer. He learned to fly at Randolph Field, Texas, and worked as a commercial pilot for several years. In 1938 he received a regular Army commission. As an Army engineering officer, he earned a master's degree in mechanical engineering from Stanford University. During World War II he was chief of maintenance for the 19th Bomber Group in Australia, and he flew 38 combat missions with that group. He then became chief of maintenance for the entire Fifth Air Force in the Pacific.

Bernard Schriever

After the war Schriever represented the new breed of Army and later Air Force officers who knew science and engineering and advocated research and development. He served as an Air Force headquarters' liaison with universities and industries. He directed the Air Force's intercontinental ballistic missile program. In succession, he headed the Air Force's Western Development Division, Ballistic Missiles Division, Systems Command, and Air Research and Development Command. He introduced a systems engineering approach to the planning and management of large military programs that involved science and technology as well as university experts and industry contractors. He directed the concurrent development of subsystems and the parallel development of multiple systems, notably the Atlas and Titan missiles. General Schriever retired in 1966.

The Air Force also sponsored the development of the air-to-air missile Falcon to be fired from interceptor aircraft. The intermediate-range surface-to-surface missiles Thor and Jupiter were divided between the Douglas and Chrysler corporations. Thor was an Air Force project, and Jupiter was initially an Army project. The Army worked on the large rocket-launched Redstone missile, first launched in 1953. The Navy developed Polaris, a solid-fuel, intermediate-range, submarine-launched missile. The guidance of these missiles relied upon sturdy electronic components that were strong enough to withstand the launch or firing as well as the flight.

Soviet Missile Programs

In the mid 1950s Nikita Khrushchev won the power struggle that had followed the death of Joseph Stalin. One of Khrushchev's plans was to reduce the military budget by relying more on nuclear deterrents than on conventional forces. He thus strongly supported the Soviet missile program. In the 1950s, mostly behind a screen of secrecy, the Soviet Union developed a variety of missiles, including surface-to-surface missiles like the rocket-launched Comet 1 and 2, the T-1 through 7 series, and the pulse-jet-propelled J-1, 2, and 3; also surface-to-air missiles like the solid-fuel T-8, and

Historical Evidence

Graphic illustrations are an important form of historical evidence. This drawing shows the Rockoon, a Navy research tool. The "rock" was indeed a rocket, a 12-foot Deacon research rocket made by the Allegheny Ballistic Laboratory at Cumberland, Maryland. The "oon" was the Skyhook balloon built by the Winzen Research Corporation of Minneapolis. The balloon lifted the rocket up to about 80,000 feet. There the rocket fired, which sent it higher into the upper atmosphere. The rocket carried both scientific instruments to collect atmospheric data and a radio to transmit that data back to the ground base monitoring the experiments. Much of this work was preparatory to the International Geophysical Year and the scheduled launching of satellites as part of that year's research program. The scientists were collecting information about the upper atmosphere through which the satellites would pass on the way to orbiting the earth.

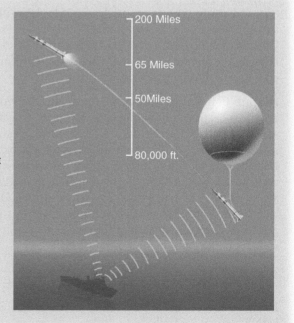

air-to-air missiles like the M-100A. The Soviets experimented with rocket-powered airplanes and developed the unmanned T-4A, a three-stage skip bomber for launching guided missiles and guided bombs. When the Soviets announced their launch of the world's first intercontinental ballistic missile in August 1957, the Tass news agency reported that "no part of the earth is too far away; strategic air forces are obsolete." Sergei Korolov, who had led the Soviet V-2 program, led the design team behind the successful R-7 intercontinental missile. Later in August, a test flight of an R-7 started from Tyuratam and ended, as aimed, 8,000 kilometers away in the Pacific Ocean. The Soviet Union, like the United States, developed rockets and missiles for upper-atmosphere research as well as for military use.

Satellites

Satellites are objects that orbit another body. The moon is a natural satellite of the earth, and the earth and other planets are satellites of the sun. Scientists had long proposed sending man-made satellites into orbit around the earth, and Cold Warriors proposed placing weapon-carrying satellites into orbit for possible use against enemies. Military satellites might also be used for reconnaissance, surveillance, communications, and weather monitoring. In the 1950s the combined effort of research scientists and military interests finally launched artificial satellites into orbit. Both the United States and the Soviet Union announced plans to orbit satellites during the International Geophysical Year of 1957-1958. This 18-month "year" was an international cooperative effort to study the planet earth and its relation to the sky and space. The International Council of Scientific Unions established a Special Committee, headed by British geophysicist Sydney Chapman, to plan and coordinate the Geophysical Year.

Despite being announced, planned, and scheduled, artificial earth satellites became the most sensational aspect of the International Geophysical Year. The satellites achieved their scientific purpose of carrying instruments aloft and broadcasting back information collected about the Earth. Both nations freely exchanged all scientific data gathered by the satellites. During the Cold War the rocket science that launched satellites attracted more attention than the geophysical science conducted using the satellites.

Sputnik

Despite Soviet secrecy in many matters, the Soviet satellite program included public announcements. As early as November 1953 the president of the Soviet Academy of Sciences declared artificial earth satellites feasible given existing technology. In April 1955 the Soviets announced that an earth satellite team had formed. In August 1955 they announced an approximate orbit and launch date of a satellite. On 1 October 1957 they announced the bandwidths for the satellite's transmissions. On 4 October 1957 the Soviet Union launched the first artificial satellite into orbit around the Earth. They called the 184-pound satellite *Sputnik* — "sputnik" being a Russian word that means both "moon" and "companion" (sometimes translated as "fellow traveler"). The Soviets used the military R-7 to launch Sputnik. While the Soviets shared scientific information about Sputnik and their later satellites, as well as the scientific data collected using the satellites, they remained secretive about their launch vehicles. *Sputnik* transmitted radio signals for 21 days; its orbit decayed in early January. (Figure 8-29)

Figure 8-29. The Soviet Union launched the world's first orbiting satellite, *Sputnik*, on 4 October 1957. This was the first man-made object to circle the globe.

Historic Event

On 4 October 1957 the Soviet Union launched the satellite *Sputnik* into orbit. The Soviets thus became the first to place a man-made object in orbit. To the world at that time, this proved that Soviets had powerful rockets assumed capable of delivering nuclear weapons. The Soviets launched *Sputnik II* a month later, on 3 November, with the dog Laika on board, and *Sputnik III* on 15 May 1958. These launches were all part of the Soviet research program for the International Geophysical Year of 1957-1958.

Flight Lines

The Soviet newspaper *Pravda* reported on the flight of *Sputnik*:

"As a result of very intensive work by scientific research institutes and design bureaus the first artificial satellite in the world has been created. On October 4, 1957, this first satellite was successfully launched in the USSR. According to preliminary data, the carrier rocket has imparted to the satellite the required orbital velocity of about 8000 meters per second. At the present time the satellite is describing elliptical trajectories around the earth, and its flight can be observed in the rays of the rising and setting sun with the aid of very simple optical instruments (binoculars, telescopes, etc.).

...

"Scientific stations located at various points in the Soviet Union are tracking the satellite and determining the elements of its trajectory. Since the density of the rarefied upper layers of the atmosphere is not accurately known, there are no data at present for the precise determination of the satellite's lifetime and the point of its entry into the dense layers of the atmosphere. . . ."

Pravda, 5 October 1957, as translated and quoted in *Exploring the Unknown, Selected Documents in the History of the U.S. Civil Space Program, Volume I: Organizing for Exploration* (NASA History Series, Washington: National Aeronautics and Space Administration, 1995).

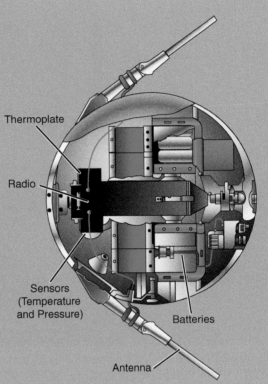

Thermoplate

Radio

Sensors (Temperature and Pressure)

Batteries

Antenna

Sputnik quickly became a symbol of technological achievement and also part of the Cold War rivalry between the world's two superpowers. It demonstrated that Soviet rockets had powerful thrust, clearly enough to deliver nuclear weapons to the United States. It thus raised issues of prestige and military security for the United States, and it contributed to international competition in space flight and arms production. Only twenty-nine days after the launch of *Sputnik*, the Soviets launched *Sputnik II* carrying a laboratory dog. These were blows to American national pride and raised questions about its presumed preeminence in science. From the military point of view, the Soviet achievements were frightful. The reality and images became elements in national strategies for defense and for the arms race.

Vanguard

Unlike the Soviet Union, the United States government became seriously interested in satellites only at the prompting of scientists and not until planning for the International Geophysical Year brought prestige to the topic. The Geophysical Year scientific programs were distinct and separate from the nation's military programs, including development of military satellites, although launching any satellites would entail modifying existing military rockets. In 1955 President Eisenhower approved the proposal to include satellites in the United States' research programs for the Geophysical Year. The question immediately became: what satellite? The Army and Navy offered competing options, the Army's Orbiter with a Redstone missile or the Navy Research Laboratory's satellite scheme on a Viking rocket. The Air Force suggested an Atlas rocket might be used. The Navy's proposal won.

The Navy Research Laboratory then developed and built the Vanguard launch vehicle and the unnamed Vanguard satellite. Glenn L. Martin became the prime Vanguard contractor. The Minneapolis-Honeywell Company developed the rocket's guidance and control system, and Aerojet made the engine. Several subcontractors developed the telemetry system and the scientific instruments installed on board. Vanguard became a three-stage rocket, with flight testing preceding the actual launch. In October 1957, as the United States continued to work on its equipment, *Sputnik* went up. The United States was shocked by the Soviet achievement, which was a psychological blow to a people engaged in a Cold War against communism. Finally on 6 December, the United States was ready to launch Vanguard. The vehicle and satellite burned on the pad. The technical description of the launch was simply that the vehicle

Figure 8-30. The Navy developed the Vanguard rocket based on its Viking rocket which was derived from the German V-2 rocket. The first attempt to launch the Vanguard with a satellite on board failed when the vehicle lost thrust after two seconds, fell back onto the launch pad, and burned.

lost thrust after 2 seconds. The press called Vanguard *Flopnik*. (Figure 8-30)

Von Braun's Army team, and its academic partner — the Jet Propulsion Laboratory — came to the rescue. They used a modified Jupiter-C rocket and placed the 31-pound Explorer I satellite into orbit on 31 January 1958. Explorer I transmitted until May 1958. Instruments on that satellite detected a major discovery of the International Geophysical Year — the Van Allen radiation belts (then believed to be a single belt). Launched in March 1958, the Vanguard I satellite (first satellite successfully placed in orbit by a Vanguard vehicle) transmitted information revealing the "pear shape" of the earth. It continued to transmit data into 1964. The United States finally reached space, but catching up to the Soviet Union remained a goal. (Figure 8-31)

Geophysical Year

By the end of 1958, the Soviet Union had tallied three successful launches, whereas the United States had recorded four successful launches plus ten failed launches and three failed attempts to send a probe in orbit of the moon.

During the International Geophysical Year the Soviets achieved the first successful launch of a satellite, and they launched more powerful vehicles and larger satellites. In contrast, the Americans launched more satellites and equipped them with better scientific instruments. The satellite program dramatically demonstrated the emergence of the Soviet Union as a scientific and technological leader, in a way more dramatic and conclusive than the earlier nuclear weapon tests, bomber gap, or missile gap. (see Appendix C)

Research Planes

Research planes had helped the United States and Soviet Union develop the speeds and altitudes necessary to reach space in 1957. The research programs began as the wartime allies prepared to convert their economies and militaries to peacetime conditions. The initial challenge was supersonic flight, which was an international goal. the **sonic barrier**, or **sound barrier**, is near the speed of sound, which is about 750 mph at sea level and approximately 660 mph above 40,000 feet. The speed of sound is commonly referred to as Mach 1, **Mach** being the ratio of the speed of an object to the speed of

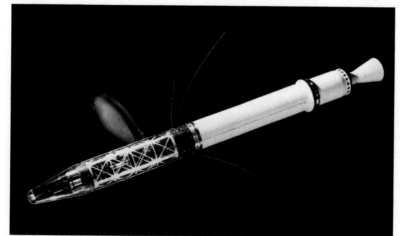

Figure 8-31. The first U.S. satellite was *Explorer I*, launched on 30 January 1958. It was 30.8 pounds, was 80 inches long, and it helped in the discovery of the Van Allen radiation belt (later discovered to be multiple belts).

sound (named after Austrian physicist Ernst Mach). At the sound barrier, the fluid air compresses or piles up. Aircraft designers needed to understand this phenomena in order to design high-speed aircraft.

In Britain, during the summer of 1946, the government cited both cost and safety behind its decision to abandon manned tests at high speeds and to switch to radio-controlled models for research use. A few months later, in a company-developed experimental plane, Geoffrey de Havilland, Jr., died while approaching Mach speed. The jet-powered, swept-wing, tailless de Havilland 108 experimental plane Swallow disintegrated in flight. It and the son of the company's founder went down into Egypt Bay near Hatfield. British authorities salvaged and studied the wreckage and concluded that longitudinal pitching had destroyed the plane. De Havilland was simply the latest to die when flying into the "wall of air" or "sound barrier" at Mach, the speed of sound.

Swallow that killed Geoffrey de Havilland, Jr.

Lacking wind tunnels suitable for transonic research, researchers in the United States conducted dive-flight research, dropped airplane models out of airplanes, fired small solid-propellant rockets, and experimented with rocket-propelled aircraft in order to study high-speed flight. The National Advisory Committee on Aeronautics (NACA) and the Air Force sponsored the development of specialized aerodynamic research airplanes.

The first of these research planes was the Bell X-1, originally designated the X-S-1; X for experimental, S for supersonic, and 1 for the first Air Force contract for a research airplane. Robert J. Woods' team at Bell Aircraft designed the X-1 for supersonic flight and transonic research at high altitude. Bell had eagerly sought the development contract, awarded in 1944, because the end of the war was obviously near and

the company manufactured only military aircraft, like the P-39 fighter. Bell needed a postwar product and designing research aircraft became one of its postwar products; manufacturing helicopters became another product line. The propulsion system of the X-1 was a 6,000-pound-thrust rocket that burned a mixture of liquid oxygen and alcohol-distilled water. The rocket propulsion system provided power for high-speed flight, but burned fuel too quickly to waste on takeoff and climb from the ground, so the aircraft was air-launched from a modified Boeing B-29 Superfortress. (Figure 8-32)

Figure 8-32. The rocket-powered X-1 series of research aircraft had a straight wing. The plane was air-launched from a modified Boeing B-29 bomber.

Having learned from the de Havilland disaster, the Bell-NACA-Air Force team prepared the X-1 aircraft for flight, in part, by installing lots of instruments. As one of the engineers stated, "If we lost the airplane, we could at least find out a little about what happened." The flight test program began in 1946 with glide flights over Muroc Dry Lake in the Mohave Desert of southern California. The presence of the wartime flight test center at Muroc Army Air Field and the features of the flat, hard, dry lakebed drew the NACA and the postwar Air Force to the site. During the course of the X-1 flight test program, NACA established the Muroc Flight Test Unit; this soon became NACA's High-Speed Flight Research Station (and evolved into NASA's Hugh L. Dryden Flight Research Center). The Army air field became an Air Force base in 1947; it acquired the name Edwards two years later. After glide tests of the X-1, engineers added the four-chambered rocket engine. Once the aircraft was released from the mother plane, the pilot fired the rocket engine for powered flight.

Air Force Captain Chuck Yeager flew the Bell X-1 faster than the speed of sound on 14 October 1947. He set the first official Mach record. To be official, the

Historic Event

On 14 October 1947 Captain Charles "Chuck" Elwood Yeager, a test pilot, flew the Bell X-1 rocket plane through the sound barrier, that is, at supersonic speed. He achieved a speed of over Mach 1 — nearly 700 miles per hour at the altitude of 42,000 feet (12,800 m).

Flight Lines

"Suddenly the Mach needle began to fluctuate. It went up to .965 Mach — then tipped right off the scale. I thought I was seeing things! We were flying supersonic! And it was as smooth as a baby's bottom: Grandma could be sitting up there sipping lemonade. I kept the speed off the scale for about twenty seconds, then raised the nose to slow down.

"I was thunderstruck. After all the anxiety, breaking the sound barrier turned out to be a perfectly paved speedway."

. . .

"The guys in the NACA tracking van interrupted to report that they heard what sounded like a distant rumble of thunder: my sonic boom! The first one by an airplane ever heard on earth."

Chuck Yeager describing his ninth flight in the X-1 and the first official supersonic flight of any aircraft, 14 October 1947, in *Yeager, an Autobiography*, by Yeager and Leo Janos.

flight had to break the sound barrier in sustained level flight or a climb. It broke the sound barrier in sustained level flight — the high speed sustained for 20 seconds. To be official, the flight was properly recorded on meters and observed by appropriate personnel. NACA supplied a radar theodolite that monitored Yeager's flights. Pilots Bob Hoover and Dick Frost flew the two chase planes, which were Lockheed single-seat P-80 Shooting Star fighters. Careful research, monitoring, and calculations confirmed Yeager's achievement.

Historical Note

Also testing high-speed aircraft at Muroc in the autumn of 1947 was a North American team working with the new XP-86 Sabre jet fighter; X for experimental, P for pursuit (that P was about to become an F for fighter). The Sabre was designed for high speed and high maneuverability in combat. Its pilot was George "Wheaties" Welch, who, like Chuck Yeager, was a wartime ace. Welch questioned whether he reached Mach on the first flight of the XP-86 on 1 October 1947, but his team lacked the precision Mach meters necessary to confirm the high speed then or on later flights that fall and winter, and Welch put the Sabre into a dive to achieve high speeds. He "officially" dived the Sabre beyond the speed of sound on 26 April 1948. Together Welch and Yeager proved new technology — jet and rocket — and demonstrated there was neither wall nor barrier at the speed of sound.

After the X-1, the next research aircraft came from Douglas Aircraft and Ed Heinemann's design team. This was the Navy-sponsored Douglas D-558. The D-558 came in two basic versions: the D-558-1 Skystreak turbojet version and the D-558-2 Skyrocket rocket-propelled and rocket- and jet-powered versions. The turbojet could takeoff from the ground, while the versions using rocket power were air-launched. The first civilian to break the sound barrier officially was NACA pilot Herb Hoover in a different X-1 than flown by Yeager. That was in March 1948. John Derry became the first British pilot to exceed the speed of sound. He flew the third de Havilland 108 Swallow past Mach in September 1948. In 1953 Jackie Cochran became the first female pilot to fly at supersonic speed; she flew a Canadair Sabre (made in Canada under a North American Aviation license). That same year NACA pilot A. Scott Crossfield exceeded Mach 2 in a dive of the all-rocket Douglas D-558-2, and Yeager in an advanced Bell X-1A achieved 2.5 Mach.

The research plane series tested rocket-propelled advanced, modified, and rebuilt X-1s until NACA retired the aircraft in 1958, by which time new wind tunnels could provide data about supersonic flight and new digital computers could simulate high-speed flight based on flight test results obtained in the research plane program. The rocket-powered, swept-wing Bell X-2 finally flew under power for the first time in 1955. Piloted by Iven "Kinch" Kincheloe, it reached a record altitude the following year. Also in 1956, the X-2 became the first aircraft to reach Mach 3, but that flight went out of control. The pilot and plane smashed into the desert, killing the pilot and destroying the plane.

In addition to the rocket-powered research planes (the X-1 straight-wing, the D-558-2 swept wing, and the X-2 swept wing), the postwar line of research planes included turbojets: the straight-wing, twin-engine Douglas X-3; the swept-wing, semi-tailless, twin-engine Northrop X-4; the variable-wing-sweeping, single-engine Bell X-5; the delta-wing, single-engine Convair XF-92A; and the straight-wing, single-engine Douglas D-558-1. While the rocket-propelled research planes achieved supersonic speeds and jet aircraft achieved lesser high speeds in the 1940s, jet-powered supersonic fighters entered production and service in the United States and the Soviet Union in the 1950s.

Some X-planes were missiles, including the Lockheed X-7, the Aerojet X-8 Aerobee, Bell X-9 Shrike, North American X-10 Navaho, and the Convair X-11 and X-12. The research planes were experimental aircraft

Historic Event

On 7 September 1956 Air Force test pilot Iven "Kinch" Kincheloe flew the rocket-powered Bell X-2 to an altitude of 126,200 feet (38,466 meters). He thus became the first human to fly above 100,000 feet (30,480 meters). The popular news media labeled him "First of the Spacemen." A B-50 launched the X-2 on that flight and on the record speed flight later that month. On 27 September 1956 Air Force test pilot Milburn "Mel" Apt flew the X-2 faster than Mach 3, lost control, and crashed into the desert. The crash killed Apt and destroyed the aircraft.

The history of these flights and the entire research plane series tested at Muroc Dry Lake appears in two books by historian Richard P. Hallion: *Test Pilots, the Frontiersmen of Flight* (1981; revised edition, Washington: Smithsonian Institution Press, 1988) and *On the Frontier, Flight Research at Dryden, 1946-1981* (Washington: National Aeronautics and Space Administration, 1984).

used to explore high altitudes and high speeds in anticipation of future aircraft and spacecraft.

Conclusion

The International Geophysical Year culminated the immediate postwar period, a period that began with the idealism of the new United Nations and ended with the idealism of peaceful international cooperation in scientific research. The postwar transition was complete. World War II technology had yielded to an electronic age of jet planes, rockets, missiles, and spacecraft. The American space program developed rapidly after *Sputnik*. In 1958 the United States created the military Advanced Research Projects Agency and transformed the National Advisory Committee on Aeronautics into the civil National Aeronautics and Space Administration. the Soviet Union also pressed forward its various air and space programs. Aviation was now aerospace, and the competition between the two superpowers spread to outer space.

Study Questions

1. What, where, when, who, and why was the Cold War?

2. Identify the Five Freedoms of the Air that became parts of bilateral agreements regarding civil aviation.

3. Discuss at least three technologies developed during World War II that became part of the postwar civil aviation infrastructure.

4. Explain what the de Havilland Comet, the Tupolev Tu-104, and the Boeing 707 have in common.

5. Describe the airways crisis of the 1950s.

6. Compare and contrast the prewar civil aviation situation in Latin American with the postwar situation.

7. Why and how did Western nations supply West Berlin in 1948-1949?

8. How did the various military forces use aircraft in the Korean War?

9. Identify and discuss at least one specific example of a rocket, a missile, and a satellite of the 1950s.

10. Why were satellites a part of the International Geophysical Year programs?

Bibliography

Brown, Michael E. *Flying Blind, the Politics of the U.S. Strategic Bomber Program*. Ithaca: Cornell University Press, 1992.

Francillon, René J. *Lockheed Aircraft since 1913*. 1982: Annapolis: Naval Institute Press, 1987.

Gunston, Bill. *The Osprey Encyclopedia of Russian Aircraft*, 1875-1995. London: Osprey, 1995.

Mathis, Robert C. *Korea, A Lieutenant's Story*. Philadelphia: Xlibris Corporantion, 2006.

McDougall, Walter A. *The Heavens and the Earth, a Political History of the Space Age*. New York: Basic Books, 1985.

Rochester, Stuart I. *Takeoff at Mid-Century, Federal Civil Aviation Policy in the Eisenhower Years, 1953-1961*. Washington: Federal Aviation Administration, 1976.

Stine, G. Harry. *ICBM, the Making of the Weapon That Changed the World*. New York: Orion Books, 1991.

Sullivan, Walter. *Assault on the Unknown, the International Geophysical Year*. New York: McGraw-Hill Book Company, 1961.

Wilson, John R.M. *Turbulence Aloft, the Civil Aeronautics Administration amid Wars and Rumors of War, 1938-1953*. Washington: Federal Aviation Administration, 1979.

Yeager, Chuck and Leo Janos. *Yeager, an Autobiography*. New York: Bantam Books, 1985.

Timeline

Light blue type represent events that are not directed related to aviation.

1945	May 7. The unconditional surrender of Nazi Germany on this day started the "population transfer" of 12 million ethnic Germans who were expelled from lands occupied by Allied and Associated Nations.
1945	December 3. British Lieutenant Commander E.M. "Winkle" Brown flew a nose-wheel equipped Vampire onto HMS *Ocean* in the first-ever carrier jet trials.
1946	Geoffrey de Havilland, Jr., flew the tailless de Havilland 108 research plane almost to the speed of sound, but the aircraft broke apart at about 0.9 Mach; de Havilland died.

1946   July 4. The Philippines became an independent country, though with a war-ruined economy. In exchange for aid, the Philippines granted the United States 99-year leases for military and naval bases, including Clark Air Force Base and Subic Bay Naval Base.

1947   March 17, April 2, June 22, and December 17. Four companies completed first flights of prototype jet bombers in a competition for United States military contracts. The North American B-45 flew first, then the Convair B-46, the Martin B-48, and finally the Boeing B-47. The new United States Air Force selected the B-47 for production.

1947   Juan Perón won the presidential election in Argentina and promptly established a dictatorship; he was overthrown and forced into exile in 1955.

1947   October 14. Captain Charles Elwood Yeager, a test pilot, flew the Bell X-1 rocket plane through the sound barrier at supersonic speed.

1947   December 30. The Soviet design bureau of Artyem Ivanovich Mikoyan (1905-1970) and Mikhail Iosifovich Gurevich (1893-1976) flew a prototype jet plane designated I-310; this design became the MiG-15 jet fighter plane.

1948   May 14. David Ben-Gurion declared the foundation of the State of Israel. As the Jewish people thus obtained the right of self determination, the Arab people in what had been Palestine lost their right of self determination. The resulting Israeli War for Independence was the first of many Arab-Israeli wars in the unstable region of conflicting nationalist movements.

1948   June 26. In response to the Berlin Blockade, Great Britain and the United States initiated the Berlin Airlift; this was a diplomatic use of aircraft in an effort to avoid war.

1948   South Africa adopted as government policy the apartheid system of racial segregation.

1949   January 27. Pilot John Cunningham and crew of three took the prototype G-5-1/G-ALVG on the first flight of the newly designed Comet jetliner. At a time when jet aircraft meant military aircraft, this commercial program placed Great Britain ahead of other nations in developing civil jet-powered aircraft.

1949   February 24. The United States and its team of German rocket scientists launched a V-2 rocket with a smaller rocket called *Wac Corporal* attached to the V-2 nose and thereby sent a two-stage rocket upward. *Wac Corporal* reached beyond the upper atmosphere into outer space.

1949   April 4. Belgium, Britain, Canada, Denmark, France, Iceland, Italy, Luxembourg, Netherlands, Norway, Portugal, and the United States signed the North Atlantic Treaty that created the North Atlantic Treaty Organization (NATO). This was a response to the Soviet blockade of Berlin in 1948-1949, and it was evidence of a European commitment to defend Europe.

1949   August 29. The Soviet Union detonated its first atomic bomb and achieved a sort of nuclear "parity" with the United States, the only other country with nuclear weapons.

1949   October 1. Mao Tse-tung declared the establishment of a communist Chinese government, and the Chinese Civil War finally ended when Chiang Kai-shek and his nationalist troops fled to the island of Taiwan on 8 December.

1950   June 25. North Korean troops invaded South Korea and thereby started the Korean War. An armistice was signed at Panmunjom on 27 July 1953.

1950   September 17. Both houses of the United States Congress passed the anti-communist Internal Security Act, which President Harry Truman vetoed as "unnecessary, ineffective and dangerous." Congress overrode the veto.

1951   The European Recovery Plan, also known as the Marshall Plan, concluded after delivering $17 billion since 1948 in an effort to stabilize the political situation on the war-ravaged European continent.

1952   January 20. F.F. Opadchi led the Soviet flight crew that flew the first flight of the prototype Myasishchev Mya-4 aircraft, a jet-propelled heavy bomber designed by Vladimir Mikhailovich Myasishchev (1902-1978).

1952   May 2. The de Havilland Comet 1, powered by de Havilland Ghost engines, entered commercial service at London bound for Johannesburg with scheduled stops in Rome, Beirut, Khartoum, Entebbe, and Livingstone. This was the world's first regular passenger jet service.

1952   July 23. The anti-British and anti-monarchist organization called Free Officers, led by Gamal Abdel Nassar, overthrew King Farouk of Egypt.

1952   November 12. Pilot A.D. Perelyot and a flight test crew flew the large turboprop Tupolev Tu-95 bomber on its first flight.

1954   May 1. May Day celebration in Moscow in 1954 the Soviet Union displayed a new bomber: the turbojet Myasishchev Mya-4 Bison heavy bomber. At the next May Day celebration the Soviets demonstrated the new Tupolev Tu-95 Bear bomber.

1954   September 8. Britain, France, the United States, Australia, New Zealand, Pakistan, and Thailand signed the treaty establishing the Southeast Asia Treaty Organization (SEATO), a military alliance.

1954   July. The French agreed to the Geneva Accords on Indochina and Korea, withdrew from Vietnam, and ended the French Indochina War — its effort since 1945 to reestablish colonial rule over Vietnam. The United States rejected the Geneva Accords and moved into Vietnam.

1955   April 5. Britain, Iraq, and Turkey signed the Baghdad Pact (later known as the Central or Middle East Treaty Organization) that strengthened Britain's presence in the Middle East and that represented an effort to contain Soviet influence.

1955   May 14. The Soviet Union, Albania, Bulgaria, Czechoslovakia, East Germany, Hungary, Poland, and Romania signed the Warsaw Treaty of Friendship, Cooperation and Mutual Assistance, commonly known as the Warsaw Pact. This was a communist response to the formation of the North Atlantic Treaty Organization, efforts toward the creation of the European Defense Community, and the rearming of West Germany.

1955   July. At the Aviation Day air show in Tushino, Soviet pilots flew the same squadron of Mya-4 Bison bombers past the reviewing stand three times and thereby fooled the United States into thinking the Soviet Union was producing many strategic aircraft; the United States briefly believed that there was a "bomber gap" and that the United States needed to increase production to close the gap and balance strategic air power with the Soviet Union.

1955   August 4. Test pilot Tony LeVier made the first flight of the U-2 prototype. He took off from Groom Lake, Nevada, and flew the single-engine jet at a speed of 160 knots (295 km/h) on the initial flight test, which lasted 36 minutes.

1956   June 28. Polish workers led an uprising in Poznan. This became known as the Poznan Crisis, and it demonstrated the independent nature of the Polish Communist Party. This sparked the failed Hungarian Revolution in October-November of the same year.

1956   July 26. In response to the United States and Great Britain withdrawing support for the Aswan Dam project, Gamal Abdel Nasser nationalized the Anglo-French Suez Canal Company and, thereby, threatened Western Europe's link with the oil fields of the Persian Gulf and with the Far East. The crisis included an invasion of Egypt by Israel, then an invasion by British and French troops, then occupation of the Canal zone by a United Nations force.

1956   September 15. The Tupolev Tu-104, powered by Mikulin AM-3M jet engines, entered airline service on Aeroflot's Moscow-Omsk-Irkutsk route.

1956   November 5. British and French paratroopers dropped into the Suez Canal zone; this was after the British bombed Egyptian oil fields and the Egyptian bomber command.

1957   July 1. The 18-month International Geophysical Year began. This international effort to study the Earth, air, and space in geophysical terms included the launching of satellites into orbit as part of the formal research programs of the Soviet Union and United States.

1957   August 21. The Soviet Union Launched the R-7 Semyorka (Little Seven); this was the world's first intercontinental ballistic missile.

1957   October 5. The Soviet Union launched the satellite *Sputnik* into orbit and proved that the Soviets had powerful rockets assumed capable of delivering nuclear weapons. The Soviets launched *Sputnik II* a month later, on 3 November, with the dog Laika on board, and *Sputnik III* on 15 May 1958.

1957   December 6. In the United States' first attempt to launch a satellite, a Vanguard — nicknamed *Flopnik* by the press — burned on the launch pad.

1958   January 31. The United States finally achieved its first successful launch of a satellite, Explorer I.

1958   October 1. The National Aeronautics and Space Administration (NASA) came into existence with the possession of the facilities and personnel of the National Advisory Committee for Aeronautics (NACA) that ceased operations the night before.

1958   October 26. Pan American placed the Boeing 707-120 into commercial service. This was the aircraft's first commercial flight and the beginning of commercial jet service using aircraft made in the United States. Great Britain had built and placed the first commercial jet in service, the Soviet Union second, and the United States third.

1958   November 28. The United States successfully launched an Atlas missile, the country's first intercontinental ballistic missile.

1958   December 31. The rebel leader Fidel Castro marched into Havana, Cuba, while the dictator Fulgencio Batista fled the country. Castro quickly established himself as a communist dictator.

CHAPTER 9

SPACE AGE AVIATION (1959-1989)

AVIATION HISTORY

Summary of Events

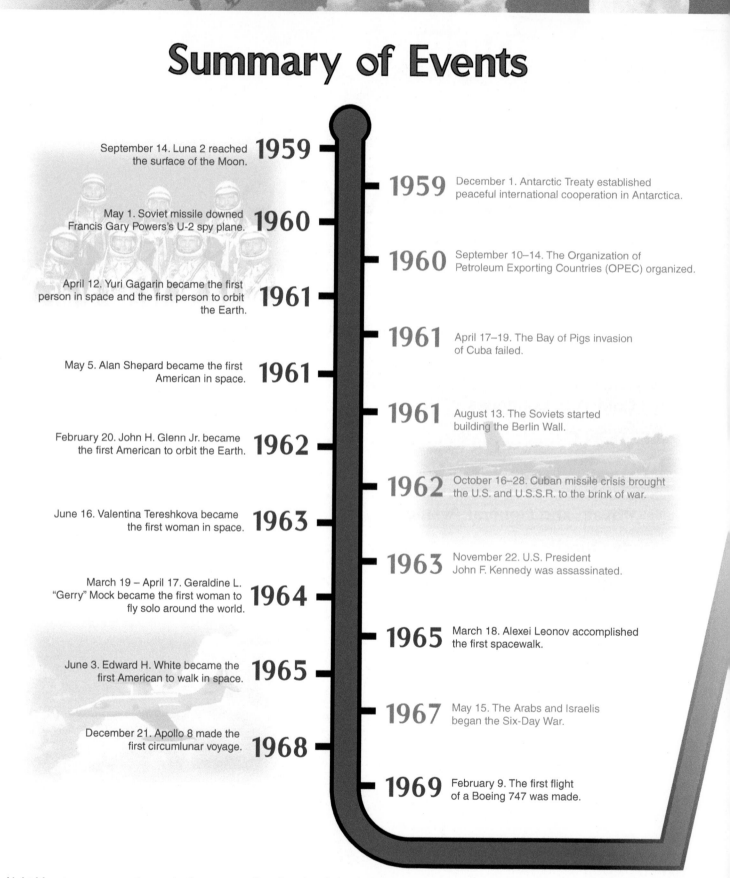

September 14. Luna 2 reached the surface of the Moon. **1959**

1959 December 1. Antarctic Treaty established peaceful international cooperation in Antarctica.

May 1. Soviet missile downed Francis Gary Powers's U-2 spy plane. **1960**

1960 September 10–14. The Organization of Petroleum Exporting Countries (OPEC) organized.

April 12. Yuri Gagarin became the first person in space and the first person to orbit the Earth. **1961**

1961 April 17–19. The Bay of Pigs invasion of Cuba failed.

May 5. Alan Shepard became the first American in space. **1961**

1961 August 13. The Soviets started building the Berlin Wall.

February 20. John H. Glenn Jr. became the first American to orbit the Earth. **1962**

1962 October 16–28. Cuban missile crisis brought the U.S. and U.S.S.R. to the brink of war.

June 16. Valentina Tereshkova became the first woman in space. **1963**

1963 November 22. U.S. President John F. Kennedy was assassinated.

March 19 – April 17. Geraldine L. "Gerry" Mock became the first woman to fly solo around the world. **1964**

1965 March 18. Alexei Leonov accomplished the first spacewalk.

June 3. Edward H. White became the first American to walk in space. **1965**

1967 May 15. The Arabs and Israelis began the Six-Day War.

December 21. Apollo 8 made the first circumlunar voyage. **1968**

1969 February 9. The first flight of a Boeing 747 was made.

Light blue type represents events that are not directly related to aviation.

July 20. *Apollo 11* landed on the Moon, and Neil Armstrong became the first person to walk on the Moon. **1969**

1970 December 18. Airbus Industrie formed.

April 19. The Soviets launched the *Salyut 1* space station. **1971**

1972 September 5. Terrorists killed 11 Israeli athletes and coaches at the Munich Summer Olympic games.

October 6. Arab-Israeli Yom Kippur War began. **1973**

1975 December 26. Supersonic Tupolev TU-144 entered service.

January 21. The supersonic transport Concorde entered service. **1976**

1976 March 24. A military coup overthrew Argentina's Peronist government.

May 25. *Star Wars*, the motion picture, opened. **1977**

1978 October 24. U.S. Congress passed the Airline Deregulation Act.

November 4. Iranian militants took hostages at the American Embassy in Tehran. **1979**

1981 April 12. *Columbia* made the maiden voyage of the space shuttle.

November 12. *Columbia* became the first spacecraft to be reused. **1981**

1982 The personal computer was Time magazine's 1982 Machine of the Year.

September 1. Soviets shot down Korean Air's flight KAL 007. **1983**

1986 January 28. The space shuttle *Challenger* exploded.

February 22. Airbus flew the A320 airliner for the first time. **1987**

1989 June 4. Chinese government massacred protesters at Tiananmen Square.

November 9. The Berlin Wall opened. **1989**

Introduction

The Cold War became a total war with civilian as well as military targets. As an economic competition, the Cold War was first and foremost between communism's public ownership and centrally planned economy and capitalism's private ownership and free trade. That was an ideological and political issue, but the Cold War also tested each side's ability to fund the space race, the science and technology race, and the arms race that were major campaigns of the conflict. Engaged in a "cold" war, the East and West fought with words, but not ordinary words—these were words of terror: atomic bomb, nuclear war, mutually assured destruction. Commercial, general, and private aviation operated within the chilling context of the Cold War.

During the Cold War each superpower tried to demonstrate the superiority of its political and economic systems by showing off science and technology and achieving firsts, mosts, farthests, and bests in aviation and space. The Space Race is the subject of Section A, which covers satellites, probes, space vehicles, astronauts, and the infrastructures of the space programs. Failure is part of the story, as illustrated by the space shuttle *Challenger* disaster in 1986. The military competition of the superpowers is the topic of Section B. Missiles and bombers dominated defense programs of the superpowers, but radar, communications systems, and fighter aircraft were also used to guard the borders between East and West. Aircraft went into combat in limited wars in the Middle East, Africa, South America, and Asia. Section C examines the Jet Age, that period in commercial aviation's history when major airlines adopted and operated jet fleets. As turbine and aerodynamic technologies matured, supersonic flight became a commercial product. Accidents, like the Douglas DC-10 crashes in Paris in 1974 and in Chicago in 1979, and the terrorist threat, which became a reality at Tenerife in 1977, influenced commercial aviation during this period. Section D discusses general aviation during the decades of the Cold War. Given the nature of the Cold War conflict and of the communist centralized control, private and general aviation were confined mainly to the West.

After studying this chapter, you should be able to discuss the Space Race. What was it? When was it? Why was there a race to space? What were some notable events and spacecraft and who were some of the important people associated with the Space Race? Using specific equipment as examples, you should be able to discuss the different roles of missiles, fighters, bombers, helicopters, and reconnaissance aircraft during the Cold War. You should be able to describe the use of aviation in limited wars of the period. You should be able to identify the leading aircraft of the Jet Age, as well as describe the Soviet and British-French achievements in supersonic transports, and explain why the United States did not produce a supersonic transport. Finally, you should be able to outline the development of private and general aviation in the West and explain why private and general aviation failed to develop in the East.

First Lunar Landing

Historical Note

In as much as the Cold War was a diplomatic competition between East and West, between communism and capitalism, between Marxism and democracy, between the United States and the Union of Soviet Socialist Republics, the leaders of the United States and Soviet Union shaped the policies of the opposing sides.

Harry S. Truman and Dwight D. Eisenhower had led the U.S. through the postwar 1940s and the 1950s. With presidential elections every four years, the U.S. had regular opportunities to adjust Cold War policies, and American policies did shift with changes in the presidency: John F. Kennedy, 1961-1963; Lyndon B. Johnson, 1963-1969; Richard M. Nixon, 1969-1974; Gerald Ford, 1974-1977; James E. Jimmy " Carter, 1977-1981; Ronald W. Reagan, 1981-1989; George H. W. Bush, 1989-1993.

After the death of Stalin in 1953, the Soviets also changed leaders periodically, and the various general secretaries of the Communist Party affected Soviet Cold War policies: Nikita Khrushchev, 1953-1964; Leonid Brezhnev, 1964-1982; Yuri Andropov, 1983-1984; Konstantin Chernenko, 1984-1985; and Mikhail Gorbachev, 1985-1991.

SECTION A

SPACE RACE

Q & A

What? The Space Race was an exploration and an adventure. It was also a political event and a scientific and technological challenge. It was an international competition for prestige and power. The race launched satellites, probes, and crewed spacecraft.

When? 1957–1989

Where? Outer space, and the Earth-based facilities of the United States and Soviet Union. A few other nations also established space programs.

Who? The United States and Soviet Union raced toward achievements in space. France and other nations joined the race, not necessarily to win, but to place. Throughout the Cold War, the United States and the Soviet Union set the pace.

Why? Cold War competitors raced to space in an effort to acquire international prestige, to win the loyalty of the people of the world, to gain military control of outer space, to demonstrate the superiority of the political-economic system of the sponsoring nation, and to explore.

Satellites could be used to launch an invasion from outer space. Satellites could be used to spy upon activities anywhere on Earth. Satellites could be tools of the enemy, and the enemy might gain control of outer space. For the United States and the Soviet Union, such ideas formed the plots of their defense policies, as well as of science fiction novels and movies. As U.S. Senator Lyndon B. Johnson said in 1958, "Control of space means control of the world."

Sputnik inspired both the United States and the Soviet Union to accelerate development and production of missiles and nuclear weapons. Sputnik also prodded both superpowers to expand their respective space programs. Control of outer space by one nation could prevent the other nation from achieving control of outer space and, thus, control of the Earth. More immediately, space achievements brought prestige to the sponsoring nation as well as demonstrated what the nation's political-economic system could produce. Defense concerns motivated the superpowers in the Space Race, but both sides maintained official positions supporting only peaceful uses of space. (Figure 9-1)

The United States quickly responded to Sputnik. The country launched its own satellites and did it publicly. Congress in 1958 created House and Senate committees for space policy and established the National Aeronautics and Space Council to advise the President on space matters. Also that year,

Figure 9-1. From 1957 to 1961 ten Sputniks were launched.

Congress passed the organic legislation for two new government agencies dedicated to space. The military Advanced Research Projects Agency (ARPA) worked with existing military services, other federal agencies,

Historical Note

The National Aeronautics and Space Administration (NASA) inherited a vast organization from the National Advisory Committee for Aeronautics (NACA), a body established in 1915. NASA was able to start with 8,000 employees and research facilities that included what is now the Langley Research Center in Virginia, and the Ames Research Center and Dryden Flight Research Center in California. In the years that followed, NASA evolved and expanded by acquiring key personnel from the Navy, Army, and Air Force, as well as key facilities, including the Marshall Space Flight Center in Alabama. By 1989, NASA had facilities around the United States.

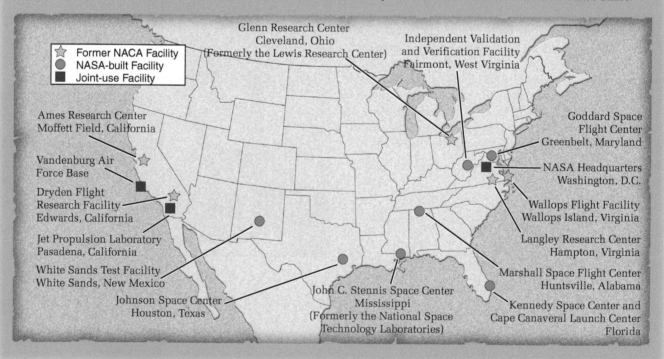

- ☆ Former NACA Facility
- ● NASA-built Facility
- ■ Joint-use Facility

Glenn Research Center
Cleveland, Ohio
(Formerly the Lewis Research Center)

Independent Validation
and Verification Facility
Fairmont, West Virginia

Ames Research Center
Moffett Field, California

Goddard Space
Flight Center
Greenbelt, Maryland

Vandenburg Air
Force Base

NASA Headquarters
Washington, D.C.

Dryden Flight
Research Facility
Edwards, California

Wallops Flight Facility
Wallops Island, Virginia

Jet Propulsion Laboratory
Pasadena, California

Langley Research Center
Hampton, Virginia

White Sands Test Facility
White Sands, New Mexico

Marshall Space Flight Center
Huntsville, Alabama

Johnson Space Center
Houston, Texas

John C. Stennis Space Center
Mississippi
(Formerly the National Space
Technology Laboratories)

Kennedy Space Center and
Cape Canaveral Launch Center
Florida

Historical Note

One of the Soviet Union's first steps into space exploration was the establishment of the Gas-Dynamics Laboratory (GDL), originally located in Moscow in 1921 and later moved to Leningrad in 1925. The name was changed to GDL in 1928. This laboratory implemented N.I. Tikhomirov's work on rocketry. Another group of organizations, called the Groups on Studying Jet Propulsion (GIRD), was formed in 1932. S.P. Korolev was appointed the chief of GIRD on 1 May of that year. The Rocket Research Institution (RNII) was established on the basis of GDL and GIRD on 21 September 1933. Throughout the Soviet Union, research and development of rocket technology continued, both before and during World War II. On 13 May 1946 the USSR Council of Ministers called for a new rocket industry infrastructure. In response to that decision, government organizations, along with the design, research, and industrial organizations, focused on developing, manufacturing, and testing rocket technology. This led to the creation of the powerful R-7 rocket and the launch of the first Earth-orbiting satellite, Sputnik, on 4 October 1957. The various Soviet space programs have evolved through the years and are now controlled by the Russian Space Agency (RKA), which was formed by decree in 1992.

universities, and industry. The civilian National Aeronautics and Space Administration (NASA) replaced the National Advisory Committee on Aeronautics (NACA) and acquired its facilities, equipment, and staff.

Both civil and military agencies became part of the military-industrial complex. As later explained by Roger D. Lanius, then NASA's chief historian, "NASA's projects were clearly cold war propaganda weapons that national leaders wanted to use to sway world opinion about the relative merits of democracy versus communism of the Soviet Union." These projects took probes to planets and astronauts into orbit and to the Moon.

The Soviet Union also responded with a crash program. Nikita Khrushchev used Sputnik to elevate technicians, engineers, and scientists to positions of influence previously held by military officers. He forced a rapid technological transition from conventional military forces and equipment to what he called a "rocket army," consisting of missiles and nuclear missiles. He shifted Soviet defense strategy from combined forces to nuclear deterrence. But winning a nuclear war would require control of outer space, Khrushchev reasoned, and he supported the space program. Sputnik had given the public the perception of a solid space program, but the Soviets needed more than one simple satellite to maintain a strong position in the new Space Race.

SATELLITES

The Soviets had successfully launched into orbit *Sputnik 1* and *Sputnik 2* in 1957, and *Sputnik 2* carried the dog Laika as a passenger. The United States had achieved no launches, as the first Vanguard had exploded during launch. In 1958 both nations successfully launched satellites, the Soviets *Sputnik 3* and the United States several Explorers, but the United States suffered embarrassing failures too. Five Vanguards failed and two of the five Explorers failed to reach orbit. These Soviet and American satellite programs were part of the International Geophysical Year of 1957-1958, a scientific collaboration so successful that it was extended for an additional year. Despite several more failures, the United States launched Discoverer, Pioneer, and Vanguard satellites during 1959, and the Soviet Union placed another Sputnik in space. Nominally, all the Geophysical Year activities were purely scientific, but the Space Race between Cold War competitors had already begun. (Figure 9-2)

Figure 9-2. *Sputnik 2* carried a small dog named Laika.

Communication Satellites

Communication satellites descended from a scientific proof provided in 1946. That January, John D. DeWitt, Jr., of the U.S. Army's Project Diana team demonstrated that radio energy could penetrate the Earth's atmosphere by reflecting radar waves off the Moon. In February the Hungarian physicist Zoltán Bay, of the Budapest Technical University and Tungsram Works, also bounced radar waves off the Moon. Radio waves could penetrate the Earth's atmosphere and could be bounced off objects in space. In 1954 the U.S. Naval Research Laboratory achieved the first voice transmission via the Moon, and in 1958 the U.S. Department of Defense placed into operation the Communication Moon Relay system between Washington, D.C., and Hawaii.

Sputnik opened the way for man-made objects in space to perform the communication relay. A balloon became the first satellite to relay voice communication. NASA launched the giant balloon called *Echo 1* on 12 August 1960. The balloon was folded onboard a Thor-Delta rocket that carried it into orbit, where gases inflated the balloon. The Jet Propulsion Laboratory's Goldstone Dry Lake station sent a voice message that bounced off the balloon to the Bell Telephone Laboratories site in Holmdel, New Jersey. Success! Three days later, in another experiment, a telephone conversation was transmitted via the aluminized polyester satellite. Bouncing microwave signals from satellites worked. (Figure 9-3)

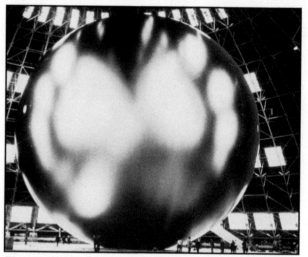

Figure 9-3. The *Echo 1* satellite has been compared to a gigantic aluminum foil beach ball. Communication signals were bounced off its exterior from one ground station to another across great distances.

Later that year, the satellite *Courier 1B* relayed a teletype communication. Launched on 4 October 1960 from Cape Canaveral on a Thor Ablestar vehicle, *Courier 1B* was capable of recording messages from Earth and rebroadcasting them. (Figure 9-4)

The young National Aeronautics and Space Administration decided to pursue research in satellite communications. NASA and AT&T worked together to bring *Telstar 1* into operation; it provided the first transatlantic television broadcast in 1962. Later that year, *Relay 1* broadcast television worldwide. *Syncom 2*, on 26 July 1963, became the first geosynchronous communication satellite in orbit. The U.S. Communication Satellite Act of 1962 provided for an organization to operate the newly evolving communication satellite system: Comsat incorporated that year.

International telecommunications networks formed. In 1962 the European Space Research Organization formed to develop a European satellite, and the

Figure 9-4. The Courier satellites were experimental communication relay satellites.

Figure 9-5. The Soviet Union's *Molniya-1* communications satellite proved the technology of automatic satellite control and 3-axis stabilization.

European Launcher Development Corporation formed two years later to produce a launch vehicle for a European satellite. France and West Germany jointly produced and launched an experimental telecommunications satellite called *Symphonie* in 1974, but it was not until 1983 that Europe placed an operational communication satellite into orbit. The European Space Agency produced the first operational European-made communications satellite, the *European Communication Satellite (ECS)*.

Meanwhile, in 1964, the United States and eleven other nations founded Intelsat, and in 1971 the Soviet Union created Intersputnik in order to break Intelsat's monopoly. In the beginning, Intersputnik used Molniya communication satellites. The Korolev design bureau developed Molniya, the Soviet Union's first communication satellite and network. The first successful launch of a Molniya occurred in secret on 22 August 1964. The Soviet Union announced the successful launch of the next Molniya, *Molniya 1-01*, on 26 April 1965. The Soviet Union continued to launch communications satellites in the Molniya series throughout the Cold War and into the post-Cold War period. (Figure 9-5)

China successfully launched its first satellite in 1970. It placed a geosynchronous experimental communication satellite into orbit in 1984. Soon that satellite became operational and provided communication services, including telephone, telegraph, facsimile, picture, and data transmission.

Observation Satellites

Satellites could observe the weather, the planet's surface, and subjects of defense interest. Weather satellites could transmit images of cloud cover, movement of air masses, and measurements of atmospheric conditions. The first was *TIROS*, *Television and Infra-Red Observation Satellite*, launched on 1 April 1960. (Figure 9-6)

Figure 9-6. The TIROS observation satellites launched between 1960 and 1965 provided important weather data. Over 500,000 photographs were returned to Earth before the final satellite was abandoned on 3 July 1967. These satellites paved the way for more effective long-range weather forecasting.

Earth observation satellites could provide images of the planet's surface in support of geological research, mineral exploration, cartographers' mapping, botanical studies, and environmental monitoring. NASA launched the first, called *Landsat 1* or *ERTS-1 (Earth Resources Technology Satellite-1)*, in July 1972. Everything that these weather and earth observation satellites could do, so could spy satellites, politely called "reconnaissance" satellites. These also could target specific locations for close inspection. (Figure 9-7)

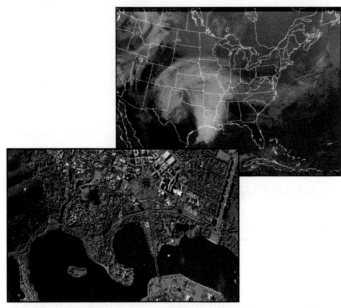

Figure 9-7. Landsat was one of the first satellites to provide detailed infrared and visible image photographs of Earth.

The early Corona satellites took photographs of targets and jettisoned the film in capsules attached to parachutes, which were captured in the air by specially equipped airplanes. Later satellites carried transmitters to send images and data immediately and directly to ground stations. Between 1959 and 1972, there were 144 Corona missions. Initially launched under the cover name Discoverer, the Corona took photographs of targets mostly in the Soviet Union. After Discoverer 38, Corona and other photo-reconnaissance satellite missions were designated KH- for Key Hole. All

Historic Event

President William J. Clinton in 1995 ordered the declassification of the pictures taken by Corona (144 missions), Argon (11 missions), and Lanyard (3 missions) satellites on intelligence missions between 1959 and 1972. The vast majority of the images feature the Soviet Union, the Cold War enemy whose bomber and missile capabilities were of great interest to the United States. The files are now open to the public.

Coronas were launched on Thor-Agena rockets. Corona was clearly a defense program. The line between civil and military projects, even in space, was often obscured by Cold War maneuvers by both East and West.

Probing Space

Early competition in the Space Race involved missions to the Moon, our near-space neighbor and natural satellite, and to the planets Mars and Venus, which have the solar orbits neighboring the Earth's.

Moon Probes

As the space body closest to Earth, the Moon became the first target of space exploration and of competing space programs. The United States and the Soviet Union launched a total of seven lunar probes in 1958. All failed.

The Soviets called their probes Lunas and added numbers only to spacecraft that reached Earth's orbit, so *Luna 1* followed three Lunas that failed to reach orbit. *Luna 1* was the first successful lunar probe. Launched on 2 January 1959, *Luna 1* actually failed to reach its planned destination, the Moon, but it went into orbit around the Sun, which was a notable achievement in itself. *Luna 2*, launched 12 September 1959, hit the Moon. The Soviets thereby achieved a striking first—the first spacecraft to reach another celestial body. The West was watching; Hugh Dryden of NASA observed, "It is further evidence of the excellence of the Soviet capability in the propulsion field." (Figure 9-8)

Figure 9-8. Although *Luna 1* missed its intended target, it sent back valuable data about the Earth's radiation belt, solar wind, and the moon's lack of a magnetic field.

Luna 3 achieved another first for the Soviets. A camera on board took the first photographs of the far side of the Moon. Because the Moon rotates on its axis in the time it takes the Moon to orbit the Earth, the Moon always shows the same side to the Earth. The *Luna 3* photographs enabled cartographers to begin mapping the far side of the Moon.

The United States called its first lunar program Pioneer. The first Pioneer spacecraft exploded seconds after launch. Next, *Pioneer 1* did not escape the Earth's gravitational field, but it returned data about the Earth's radiation belts. *Pioneer 2* failed to reach escape velocity. *Pioneer 3* reached an altitude of 102,320 kilometers (63,580 miles), far short of the intended destination, the Moon. Finally, launched 3 March 1959, *Pioneer 4*, the fourth lunar probe in the country's International Geophysical Year program, passed within 60,200 kilometers (37,300 miles) of the Moon. It was deemed a success, despite not reaching its lunar destination. It followed *Luna 1* into orbit around the Sun. (Figure 9-9)

Figure 9-9. The Pioneer series of spacecraft started as moon probes and evolved to more complex planetary probes.

The Soviet Union and the United States continued to launch lunar missions through the 1960s and into the early 1970s. After a few more Pioneer lunar failures,

and the *Pioneer 5* solar probe success, in 1960, the United States launched a series of Ranger spacecraft designed to fly into the Moon and to take photographs up until the time of impact. The Ranger 1 through 6 missions failed for various reasons, though *Ranger 2* and *Ranger 6* did impact the Moon. *Ranger 7*, launched 28 July 1964, hit the Sea of Clouds, and *Ranger 8*, launched 17 February 1965, hit the Sea of Tranquility. Both returned photographs and data. (Figure 9-10)

Between 1966 and 1968 the United States sent lunar landers and lunar orbiters to the Moon to gather information in preparation for a human mission to the Moon. Six of seven Surveyor probes landed on the Moon. As planned, the Surveyors took close-up pictures of the lunar surface. *Surveyors 3* and *7* scooped soil samples and completed soil mechanic tests of the samples, and *Surveyors 5, 6,* and *7* chemically analyzed lunar soil. *Orbiters 1, 2,* and *3* surveyed Apollo landing sites, and *Orbiters 4* and *5* completed lunar mapping missions.

Meanwhile, the Soviet Union continued the Luna program through *Luna 24* and completed five Zond lunar missions between 1965 and 1970. Like the United States, the Soviet Union studied the Moon in search of feasible landing sites for a manned mission. Launched in April 1963, *Luna 4* flew by the Moon. *Lunas 5, 7,* and *8* achieved lunar impact in 1965. *Luna 6* failed an attempted lunar landing; it missed the Moon. The Soviets opened and closed 1966 with lunar landings by *Luna 9* and *Luna 13*. *Lunas 10, 11,*

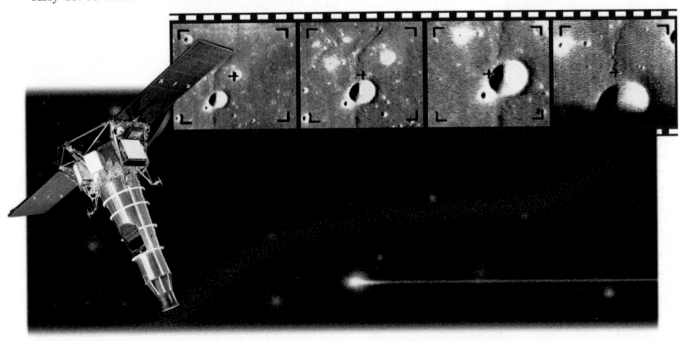

Figure 9-10. The Ranger missions provided valuable information about the Moon's surface.

12, 14, 15, 19, and 22 were lunar orbiters. *Lunas 16* and *17* landed on the Moon in 1970, *Luna 20* in 1972, *Luna 21* in 1973, and *Luna 24*, the final Luna, in 1976. *Luna 17* delivered the lunar rover *Lunokhod 1*, and *Luna 21* delivered the rover *Lunokhod 2*. Ground crews on Earth remotely controlled the rovers. *Lunas 16, 20,* and *24* returned samples of lunar material to Earth for analysis. (Figure 9-11)

Figure 9-12. A few of the Zond probes were modified Soyuz capsules.

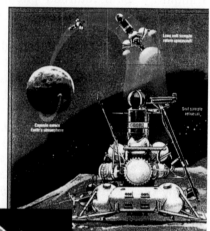

Figure 9-11. Two Luna probes placed robotic rovers on the Moon, and three probes returned lunar material to Earth.

Although several Zond spacecraft went toward planets, *Zond 3* completed a lunar flyby, and four Zonds —numbers 5, 6, 7, and 8—circled the Moon and returned to Earth. *Zond 6* and *Zond 7* landed in Siberia, and *Zond 5* and *Zond 8* in the Indian Ocean. The Soviets recovered these spacecraft. (Figure 9-12)

Historical Note

The Soviet Union won many firsts in the lunar phase of the Space Race: the first probe to impact the Moon, the first flyby, the first image of the far side of the Moon, the first soft landing, and the first circumlunar probe to return to the Earth.

After the United States won the race to put a man on the Moon and sent several more manned missions to the Moon, and after the Soviet Union later abandoned its manned lunar program, interest in the Moon waned. From 1977 through 1989, there were no lunar missions.

Historical Note

The People's Republic of China, Communist China, considered lunar probes in the 1960s, but China's Cultural Revolution hindered the space program in general at that time. In the 1970s Communist Party Secretary Deng Xiao-Ping stated, "China does not need to go to the Moon in order to modernize." In 1986 China began Project 863, which included lunar exploration.

Mars

Astronomers had long studied Mars. Copernicus discovered that the planet moves around the Sun outside the orbit of the Earth. Using telescopes, Galileo Galilei, Christiaan Huygens, Giovanni Cassini, and Robert Hooke observed the planet. William Herschel noted, "The analogy between Mars and the Earth is, perhaps, by far the greatest in the whole solar system." He concluded that Mars is in "a situation similar to ours." In 1877 Giovanni Schiaparelli mapped *canali* (natural channels) on Mars. Percival Lowell transformed Schiaparelli's *canali* into Martian-made canals and hinted that the planet may be inhabited now (in the 1890s). (Figure 9-13.)

Figure 9-13. Mars has always fascinated Earthbound observers.

The unknown inspires awe and fear. Martians in particular have attracted interest. H.G. Wells' novel *War of the Worlds* (1898), Orson Welles' radio broadcast *War of the Worlds* (1938), and George Pal's movie *War of the Worlds* (1953) capitalized on the fear of the unknown Martians. No one had ever seen a Martian, but ancient Greek and Roman mythology had primed the West to associate Mars with war. More conservatively, scientists associated Mars with the possibility of life on another planet similar to and nearby Earth.

Spacecraft offered an opportunity to study Mars up close. The Soviet Union was the first nation to launch missions to Mars. The Soviets launched two interplanetary probes bound for Mars in 1960; both failed to attain Earth orbit, a preliminary position — sometimes called "parking orbit" — from which rockets would send probes on a trajectory toward Mars. A Soviet probe in 1962 traveled over 100 million kilometers (66 million miles) towards Mars

when the communication signal was lost. S.P. Korolev's R-7 rocket, which had launched the Sputnik spacecraft, served as the launch vehicle for the probes. Initially called *Sputnik 30*, *Mars 1* lost communication in 1963.

The United States entered the Mars race in late 1964 with two Mariner launches. One of those, *Mariner 4*, became the first spacecraft to fly by Mars. In 1965 it took close-up pictures of the planet. The images showed an old and lifeless surface. "Close-up" at that time was a mere 9,844 kilometers (6,117 miles) from the planet. *Mariners 6* and *7*, in 1969, passed closer — only 3,430 kilometers (2,131 miles) from Mars. *Mariner 9* became the first U.S. spacecraft to orbit a planet other than Earth. It returned data from Mars for almost a year, from November 1971 until October 1972, and took more than 7,000 photographs. (Figure 9-14)

The Soviet *Mars 2* and *Mars 3* reached the red planet in 1971. Although the *Mars 2* lander crashed, the orbiter circled the planet 362 times while instruments recorded data. *Mars 3* delivered a probe to the surface of Mars, but the probe failed after 20 seconds. The Soviets launched *Mars 4, 5, 6,* and *7* in 1973. All successfully traveled to the Red Planet. *Mars 5* successfully transmitted images from Mars orbit, but the

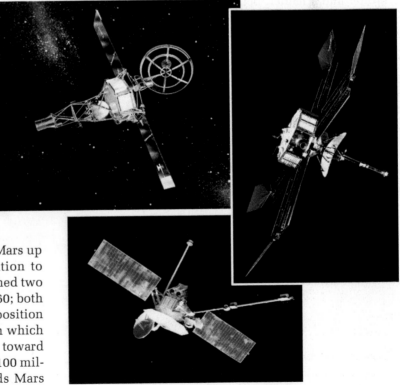

Figure 9-14. Mariner missions explored Mars and Venus between 1962 and 1975.

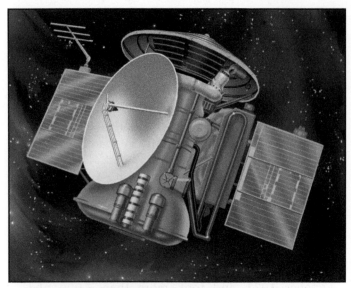

Figure 9-15. The Mars missions achieved the objective of landing a probe on the surface. Of the two probes that reached the surface of Mars, one crashed and the other ceased transmitting 20 seconds after landing.

Launch of Viking 1

Mars 4 and *Mars 7* orbiters missed Mars, and the *Mars 6* lander lost communication just before landing. (Figure 9-15)

The U.S. sent *Viking 1* and *Viking 2* toward Mars in 1975. Each spacecraft consisted of two units, an orbiter and a lander. Both reached Mars in the summer of 1976. The *Viking 1* orbiter returned data until 1980, and its lander continued to operate until late 1982. The *Viking 2* orbiter functioned for over two years, and the lander continued to work until April

1980. The landers searched for life and photographed the landscape. The Viking mission discovered frozen water beneath the soil. The question of life on Mars remained open. (Figure 9-16)

Viking images of the Martian surface

Figure 9-16. The two identical Viking probes landed on Mars in 1976. The orbiting portion of the probe photographed the surface and stayed in orbit. Both landers took pictures of the surface and took meteorological surveys.

Venus

Mars orbits the Sun outside the orbit of the Earth. To the inside of Earth's orbit is Venus.

Venus

Figure 9-17. The Venera probes provided a wealth of information about Venus.

The Soviet Union succeeded in launching 18 probes toward Venus. *Venera 1*, launched in 1961, did not reach the planet for the intended flyby. In 1966 *Venera 2* did fly by Venus. The first lander arrived at the planet in 1966, on 1 March. It was *Venera 3*. Venera probes 4 through 14 were also landers that reached Venus. *Venera 15* and *16* were orbiters that reached the planet in 1983, and in 1984 the Soviet Union launched *Vega 1* and *Vega 2*, two lander/probe spacecraft. The Soviet missions achieved increasingly lengthy experience in the hostile Venusian environment, which the Soviets were the first to explore, document, and map. The Soviets discovered that the atmosphere on Venus is mostly carbon dioxide. (Figure 9-17)

The United States also sent probes to Venus. The Pioneer program that had begun with lunar probes ended with a series of spacecraft exploring Venus. All launched in 1978, these were the *Pioneer Venus Orbiter*, *Pioneer Venus 2* multi-probes, and *Pioneer Venus Probes 1, 2, 3,* and *4*. The *Pioneer Venus Orbiter* achieved an elliptical orbit around Venus, mapped the planet's clouds, measured the atmosphere-solar wind interaction over the planet, and produced radar maps of over 90 percent of the surface. Although designed for an eight-month mission, the *Pioneer Venus Orbiter* remained in operation until 1992, when it burned up in Venus' atmosphere. *Pioneer Venus 2* released one large probe and three small probes into the planet's atmosphere.

Deep Space

Beyond the Moon and Mars beckoned the other planets in the solar system, the Sun, asteroids, comets, and interstellar space. Deep space once referred to anything beyond the Earth's gravitational influence, beyond the Moon. Early probes bound for Mars traveled in deep space. As space exploration reached farther and farther into outer space (all space beyond the Earth's atmosphere), deep space shifted location and meaning: Deep space is beyond the solar system. The Space Race changed the scale of the term and of our perception.

Sun

The United States used Pioneer spacecraft and Helios probes to study the Sun in the 1960s and 1970s. Pioneer spacecraft on solar missions measured solar winds, solar flares, the Sun's magnetic field, cosmic rays, and solar radiation. In cooperation with West Germany, which made the probes, the United States launched *Helios 1* and *Helios 2* in 1974 and 1976 respectively. These probes approached close to the Sun, within 0.3 astronomical unit. An astronomical unit (AU) is a unit of measurement used within the solar system; it is equivalent to the distance between the Earth and the Sun, approximately 150 million kilometers (93 million miles).

Planetary Probes

The United States took the lead in sending spacecraft to the far planets.

Jupiter and Saturn were visited by several spacecraft from the United States. *Pioneer 10* and *Pioneer 11* flew by Jupiter in 1973 and 1974 respectively; these probes were the first and second spacecraft to study Jupiter. Later *Pioneer 10* became the first man-made object to leave the solar system — another first for the United States in the Space Race. The last signals from *Pioneer 10* were received in January 2003, almost 31 years after its launch. *Pioneer 11* also made a flyby of Saturn, another first. Continuing on its solar system escape trajectory, *Pioneer 11* ceased scientific operations and telemetry in 1995 due to a power problem. (Figure 9-18)

Voyagers 1 and *2*, both launched in 1977, went into deep space. Following different trajectories, both made investigatory flybys of Jupiter and Saturn. *Voyager 1* reached Jupiter in 1979 and Saturn in 1980. It also flew close to Saturn's moon, Titan. *Voyager 1* then took a path toward the interstellar space beyond the solar system. Taking the grand tour of planets, *Voyager 2* reached Jupiter in 1979, Saturn in 1981, Uranus in 1986, and Neptune in 1989. Then it too took a new path leading into interstellar space. (Figure 9-19)

Figure 9-18. Pioneer 11 studied the solar system and returned valuable data until it ceased operations in 1995.

The United States closed the 1980s with the launch on 18 October 1989 of the *Galileo* spacecraft. *Galileo* used a complex trajectory through the solar system, gaining energy from close flybys of Venus and Earth, to propel it toward Jupiter. By 1994, *Galileo* was near enough to Jupiter to observe the crash of the comet Shoemaker-Levy 9 into the giant planet. In 1995 *Galileo* released a probe that parachuted into the upper layers of Jupiter's atmosphere, providing detailed information about the structure and composition of the gas giant. In September 2003 the spacecraft was deliberately crashed into Jupiter to avoid contaminating any of Jupiter's moons with Earthly microbes.

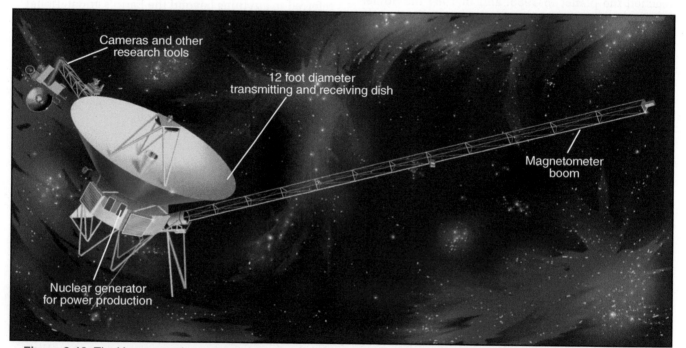

Cameras and other research tools

12 foot diameter transmitting and receiving dish

Magnetometer boom

Nuclear generator for power production

Figure 9-19. The Voyager probes carried recorded greetings in 60 languages as well as sounds of nature and civilization. Instructions for playing the disk were etched on a cover plate.

The closest planet to the Sun was visited by only one probe from Earth in this period. The United States probe *Mariner 10* approached Mercury three times in 1974-1975 and took over 4,000 images of the planet.

Comets

Built in the United States, operated by NASA, and launched in 1978, the *International Sun/Earth Explorer 3 (ISEE-3)* was part of the International Magnetosphere Study. It completed that mission in 1982. It then became the *International Cometary Explorer (ICE)* assigned to intercept a comet. *ICE* achieved the first encounter of a spacecraft with a comet in September 1985 when it flew through the tail of Comet Giacobini-Zinner. It joined the Halley "fleet" the next year. (Figure 9-20)

When Comet Halley returned in March 1986 after a 76-year absence, six spacecraft made observations. Japan's probes *Sakigake* and *Suisei* and the European Space Agency's (ESA) *Giotto* approached the comet. The Soviet Union's two Vega probes and the United States' *ICE* also made observations, *ICE* from a position between the Sun and the comet. These probes had the first close encounter with the comet, which orbits the Sun. The Vega probes carried a television system that produced about 1,500 images of the comet. Czechoslovakian, French, Hungarian, and Soviet scientific and industrial organizations contributed to the onboard television system. Observations showed the comet to be an active place, where frozen gas and dust around the core became a jet stream when exposed to the Sun.

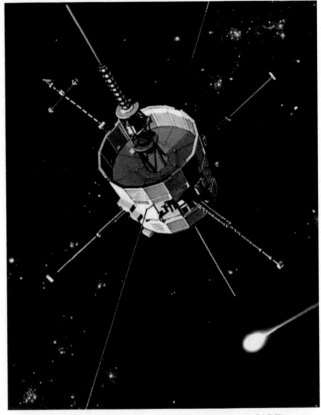

Figure 9-20. The primary scientific objective of ICE was to study the interaction between the solar wind and a cometary atmosphere.

Human Space Flight

After probes, satellites, and even animals had tested space, human beings went into space. The Soviet Union won the race to put the first man in space, the

Historical Note

The tenth and eleventh Pioneer space probes, no matter how far they ultimately travel, will provide evidence of the human race to whoever finds them. They each carry a graphic message in the form of a rectangular plaque bolted to the spacecraft's frame. On the plaque a man and a woman stand before the outline of the spacecraft. The key to translating the plaque is understanding the breakdown of the most common element in the universe, hydrogen. Anyone who can interpret the meaning of the neutral atomic hydrogen will be able to translate the remaining portion of the message. Across the bottom of the gold-plated plaque, a map of the probe's origin and path are inscribed. The plaque was designed by Dr. Carl Sagan and drawn by his wife, Ann Druyan.

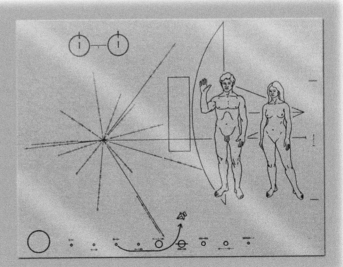

first woman in space, the first multiple-member crew in space, and the first person to perform an extra-vehicular activity or spacewalk, but the United States won the race to the Moon. The conditions of space and space travel, as well as the competition, challenged the capabilities of each country. (Figure 9-21)

Figure 9-21. Every one of the hundreds of human space flights was an awe-inspiring example of human technology.

The two superpowers approached the Space Race with some basic differences. Rocketry in the Soviet Union fell under the Ministry of Armament, and aviation under the Ministry of Aviation Industries. That bureaucracy separated rockets, missiles, and the space program from the aviation community, whereas in the United States, NASA combined expertise from both aviation and space specialties. Unlike the highly visible Wernher von Braun in the United States, his counterpart in the Soviet Union—Sergei Pavlovich "SP" Korolev—remained, in the words of his biographer, "the anonymous chief designer." Soviet leader Nikita Khrushchev explained the secrecy around scientific and technical experts by saying, "We highly value these people, we prize them and protect their safety from hostile agents who might be sent in to destroy these outstanding people, our valuable cadres."

The two superpowers shared some common features in going to space. Each placed central government control over a vast national effort involving dispersed research, development, production, and operations facilities, large numbers of technical workers, and even raw resources. Human space flight was Big Science, costing big money, and involving a big commitment of national resources.

Soviet Space Program

The Soviet Union began the manned space race with a clear advantage in rocketry. The first Soviet ballistic missile was the rocket R-1, a Soviet copy of the German V-2. The R-2 entered service in 1953. The R-2 improved upon the R-1 by doubling the range. The R-3 was an indigenous Soviet design that was never produced. The

Historical Note

The Soviet Union sent several dogs into space: Laika (Barker) on *Sputnik 2* in November 1957, Belka (Squirrel) and Strelka (Little Arrow) on *Sputnik 5* in August 1960, Pchelka (Little Bee) and Mushka (Little Fly) on *Sputnik 6* in December 1960, Chernaushka (Blackie) on *Sputnik 9* and Zvezdochka (Little Star) on *Sputnik 10* in March 1961, and Verterok (Little Wind) and Ugolvok (Little Piece of Coal) on *Voskhod 3* in February 1966.

The United States preferred monkeys and chimpanzees. The monkeys were Gordo on a Jupiter missile in December 1958, Able and Baker on another Jupiter in May 1959, Sam on *Mercury Little Joe 2* in December 1959, and Miss Sam on *Mercury Little Joe 4* in January 1960. The chimps were Ham on *Mercury Redstone 2* in January 1960 and Enos on *Mercury Atlas 5* in November 1961. Able and Baker were the first living beings recovered after a space flight.

SOVIET HUMAN SPACE FLIGHT PROGRAMS

Calendar Year	57	58	59	60	61	62	63	64	65	66	67	68	69	70	71	72	73	74	75	76	77	78	79	80	81	82	83	84	85	86	87	89

Vostok

Voskhod

Soyuz

Salyut

Operational Life

Program

Mir

Note: Apollo-Soyuz 1975

Figure 9-22. It is not clear when some of the Russian space projects actually started. However, they usually built on the accomplishments of prior missions.

R-4 was an intermediate-range (1,200 kilometers) missile, and R-5 was also an intermediate but longer range missile (2,300 kilometers). The R-7 took the Soviets into the Space Age. It achieved two significant firsts—the world's first intercontinental missile and the world's first orbital launch vehicle. It launched *Sputnik 1*, other early satellites, space probes, and the first manned spaceflight, as well as spacecraft throughout the Cold War and thereafter. (Figure 9-22)

Having gone to Germany in 1945 to study the V-2, aeronautical engineer Sergei Pavlovich "SP" Korolev designed the R-3, and later the R-7. The R-7 was a liquid-propelled rocket with Glushko engines. The Ryazanskiy - Pilyugin research institute produced the guidance system, the Sokolov bureau developed the launch pad, and Kuznetsov created the gyro platform. The engines burned Lox/kerosene propellants, rather than the Lox/alcohol mixture used in German-derived rockets. At least 36 factories produced components of the missile, and final assembly took place at Kaliningrad under Korolev's supervision. During test firings, the R-7 program used a unique design concept that suspended the rocket over the flame pit. That concept proved so successful that it became the standard way to launch R-7s thereafter. (Figure 9-23)

Figure 9-23. The R-7 rocket was the workhorse of the Soviet launch vehicles. It was a modified intercontinental ballistic missile.

Personal Profile

Sergei Korolev

Sergei Pavlovich "SP" Korolev (1907-1966) led the Soviet effort to send a human to the Moon. Soviet secrecy kept Korolev obscure during his life. Few people in his own country, let alone in the United States, even knew his name.

Born in Zhutomir, near Kiev, Korolev grew up in the Ukraine. He studied aviation at the Kiev Polytechnic Institute and the Moscow Higher Technical School, where Nikolai Zhukovsky had built a wind tunnel in 1902. Andrei Tupolev was one of Korolev's professors. Korolev earned his pilot's license in 1930.

As a young aviation engineer, Korolev designed the first Russian glider to do loops; the SK-3 Red Star achieved three loops at a 1930 competition. In 1938 he became a victim of the Terror of Stalin and, like millions of innocent Soviet citizens, entered the gulag prison system during the Terror.

In 1940 Korolev joined Tupolev, who had also been arrested, at a prison design bureau in Moscow. That bureau produced the Tupolev Tu-2 light bomber and the Ilyushin-2 attack plane. As the Germans neared Moscow in 1941, Korolev went to the Kazan prison and joined a special design bureau for rocketry. He continued his rocketry work at the bureau after his release from prison in 1944.

As the Russian forces moved into Germany in 1945, Korolev received an Army commission. He joined the team of Russians who went to Germany to transfer German rocket technology, equipment, and personnel to the Soviet Union.

Back in the Soviet Union in 1946, Korolev became chief designer in a special design bureau for long-range ballistic missiles. In a few years he became director of his own design bureau at Podlipki, near Moscow. Korolev contributed to a Soviet achievement notable in the Cold War: the world's first intercontinental ballistic missile (ICBM), the Soviet R-7 Semyorka (Little Seven), launched in 1957 (and designated the SS-6 Sapwood by NATO).

In the early 1960s, Korolev left missile design for the Soviet space program. Under his supervision, Mikhail Khomyakov led the design of the Sputnik satellites. Korolev's R-7 served as the launch vehicle for the early Soviet satellites, lunar and planetary probes, and the first manned spacecraft. Korolev's R-7 helped Yuri Gagarin on 12 April 1961 become the first person in space and the first person to orbit the Earth.

Working in Kaliningrad, Korolev led the Soviet human spaceflight program. He was working on the lunar Soyuz program when he died on 14 January 1966. The city where he worked, once called Podlipki, later called Kaliningrad, has been renamed Korolev. His career is the subject of *Korolev, How One Man Masterminded the Soviet Drive to Beat America to the Moon*, by James Harford (New York: John Wiley & Sons, 1997).

The first launch of the R-7, then with the original 8K62 designation, occurred 15 May 1957. It was not successful. The test program launched twelve prototype missiles between then and the end of January 1958. Among these test launches was a launch demonstrating the first ICBM, without the nuclear warhead it was capable of carrying, on 21 August 1957. Test launches also sent two Sputnik satellites into orbit, on 4 October and 3 November 1957. All these launches used the Baikonur launch site in Kazakhstan. Baikonur, usually called Tyuratam in the Soviet Union, was developed for the R-7 ballistic missile.

During the Cold War, the Soviet Union pursued five human space programs—Vostok, Voskhod, Soyuz, Salyut, and Mir. All the manned spacecraft were launched from Baikonur. Soviet officials justified the huge costs of human spaceflight in military terms and thus secrecy obscured many details of the various programs at the time. Each program received approval and funding as part of five-year plans for the state economy, but the internal competition for favor and funding in the Soviet system hampered the country's space programs. Under the Five Year Plan for 1956-1960, Soviet designers investigated more than 30 space systems.

Historical Note

The Soviet Union successfully used the R-7 as a space launch vehicle over 1,600 times by the end of the 20th century, and the R-7 remained in use into the 21st century.

Vostok

The Soviet Union successfully launched six Vostok (East) spacecraft in the early 1960s. Designed by Korolev, the Vostok craft was a one-person sphere filled with normal atmospheric air under pressure. *Vostok 1* became the first manned spacecraft to orbit the Earth. Launched on 12 April 1961, *Vostok 1* carried 27-year-old Soviet Lieutenant Yuri Gagarin into orbit. Gagarin became the first man in space. After one orbit, he reentered the Earth's atmosphere. There, he ejected from the spacecraft and parachuted safely to the ground. Gagarin superbly demonstrated that human beings could survive spaceflight and reentry. The total time of his historic flight was 108 minutes. (Figure 9-24)

Figure 9-24. The simple yet impressive Vostok series of flights achieved many firsts in space, the most publicly acclaimed being the first man and first woman in space. Korolev's R-7 launched all six Vostoks.

Vostok 2 carried Gherman Titov aloft in August 1961. A year later, in August 1962, *Vostok 3* lifted Andrian Nikolayev into space, and *Vostok 4*, Pavel Popovich. In June 1963 Valeri Bykovski traveled in *Vostok 5* and Valentina Tereshkova in *Vostok 6*. Tereshkova achieved the honor of being the first woman in space. These early Soviet cosmonauts, like early American astronauts, were celebrities. The public knew their names, their faces, their achievements. The Soviet cosmonauts traveled in spacecraft that were controlled from the ground; in other words, they were not in control of the craft. The Soviet Union thereby could select cosmonauts based on their youth and health.

Historic Event

On 12 April 1961 a Soviet R-7 rocket placed Yuri Gagarin and his Vostok spacecraft in Earth orbit. Gagarin's 108 minute, one-orbit flight was a major achievement.

Personal Profile

Yuri Alexeyevich Gagarin (1934-1968) was born into a collective farmer's family. The ambitious former foundry worker graduated from Voroshilov Aviation Technical Academy in 1957. In 1960 he was selected to be a part of the first group of USSR cosmonauts. At 27 years old, he became the first human to orbit the Earth. After his historic 108-minute flight he spent several years performing ceremonial duties before returning to train for a Soyuz mission. He and an instructor pilot died in 1968 when their jet crashed while flying at high speed near the ground.

Yuri Gagarin

Flight Lines

"I can see the clouds! I can see everything! It's beautiful!"

The first description of Earth from outer space was uttered by Russian cosmonaut Yuri Gagarin upon reaching orbit on 12 April 1961.

Voshkod

After the Vostok series, and before the next step in the Soviet manned space program, was a gap in time. Khrushchev wanted to maintain a momentum of flights and therefore demanded a project for the interim period. Korolev modified the Vostok spacecraft into a multiperson Voshkod (Rise) capsule,

Personal Profile

Valentina Vladimirovna Tereshkova (1937-) was born into a collective farmer's family. Her mother moved to the city after her father was killed in the Great Patriotic War. Valentina worked in a tire factory for some time until she joined her mother and sister working at a textile mill. During this time she joined a club for parachutists and took a correspondence course from an industrial school. In 1961 she wrote a letter to the Russian space center asking to join the training program for cosmonauts. At the same time, the program managers had started to search for talented women parachutists who might fit into the program. Ultimately she was chosen based on her experience as a parachutist and became the first women in space at the age of 26. After her flight on the *Vostok 6* mission on 16 June 1963 she never flew another space mission. She went on to serve as a member of the Supreme Soviet in 1966 and later the Central Committee in 1971.

Valentina Tereshkova

which he launched twice using the proven R-7 rocket, with more power than the version used on the Vostok launches. The Voshkod program also introduced a landing system and eliminated the ejection system.

Both Voshkod flights achieved notable firsts. *Voshkod 1*, launched in October 1964, became the first spacecraft carrying multiple people into space. The three-man crew—Vladimir Komarov, Konstantin Feoktistov, and Boris Yegorov—did not wear spacesuits in order to keep the gross weight within safe limits. Launched in May 1965, *Voshkod 2* carried two cosmonauts. One of them, Alexei Leonov, became the first person to perform an extra-vehicular activity in space. He took the first spacewalk! The automatic reentry system failed so commander Pavel Belyayev also faced an extraordinary challenge. He manually achieved retro burn for the reentry. (Figure 9-25)

Soyuz

Working in Kaliningrad, Korolev led the Soviet human spaceflight program. For the lunar flight, he selected the L1 Soyuz spacecraft and the large N-1 launch vehicle. Both were concepts that required development after the Soviet Communist Party Central Committee in 1964 formally established the human lunar program. Space decisions required both party and government approval in the Soviet Union; this bureaucratic maze sometimes slowed the Soviet program.

The Soyuz spacecraft was designed for maneuvering in space so that it could perform orbital rendezvous and docking. It had three modules: the orbiter, the lander, and the Zond (probe). The original plan was to launch three parts of the spacecraft into low-Earth orbit and assemble the craft there. The plan was modified to two launches, then to a single launch. The dual mission was to fly around the Moon and to land on the Moon. Korolev decided upon a two-person lunar orbiter and a detachable one-person lunar lander. The lander would have the capability to launch off the Moon and dock with the orbiter in lunar orbit. (Figure 9-26)

Figure 9-25. Although there were only two missions in the Voshkod program, they accomplished several firsts, including the first multi-person crew and first spacewalk.

Historic Event

On 18 March 1965 Alexei Leonov became the first person to walk in space. To perform the feat, Alexei had to first attach a backpack oxygen system and activate an air lock. The air lock was an inflatable tube that attached to a door in the cabin. When it was ready, he crawled into the tube and began to depressurize the air lock. At 6 psi, the same pressure as his suit, he checked for leaks. When he was sure that none existed, he opened the outer hatch and floated into space. Up to this point things had gone very well. When Leonov decided to return to the craft things began to go awry. He first found that it took more effort to maneuver than was anticipated. In addition, the visor in his spacesuit began to fog, making it more difficult to see. Finally, he was unable to reenter the air lock because the differential pressure between his suit and the void of space had made it very difficult to fit, feet-first, into the air lock. Ultimately he lowered the pressure in his spacesuit and risked getting the bends so that he could fit into the air lock.

Figure 9-26. The Soyuz flew the most missions in the Soviet space program. These included both robotic and human space flight missions.

Korolev's N-1 launch vehicle design underwent years of development, first by Valentin Glushko and later by Nikolai Kuznetsov. During that time, Vladimir Chelomei's design bureau, which employed Khrushchev's son Sergei, developed a competing UR-500 rocket. UR designated Chelomei's Universal Rockets (Universaliskaya Raketa), and N represented Korolev's Carrier (Nositel) series. Kuznetsov's bureau produced the NK-33 super-heavy booster used for the Soyuz launches. The NK-33 used oxygen-kerosene as the fuel for its 30 engines; in contrast, the U.S.-built Saturn had five, large F-1 engines.

In January 1966 Korolev died. His assistant Vassily Mishin succeeded him as head of the Soviet space program. Aware of the progress of the American Apollo lunar program, Mishin rushed the Soyuz program into flight. *Soyuz-1* carried Vladimir Komarov aloft on 23 April 1967. Problems arose in flight and with landing the next day. The parachute deployment system failed, and the *Soyuz-1* capsule crashed to the ground. The crash killed Komarov, the only person on board for the test flight. (Figure 9-27)

During a post-crash suspension of flights, under Mishin's leadership, the Soviets docked two unmanned spacecraft, *Kosmos 186* and *Kosmos 188*, in space; Kosmos spacecraft were unmanned test versions of

Figure 9-27. Cosmonauts Yuri Gagarin (left) and Vladimir Komarov before Komarov's flight on *Soyuz 1*. Komarov died during the landing.

Soyuz. The unmanned *Soyuz 2* and the manned *Soyuz 3* were launched in October 1968. The mission was a space rendezvous, but the docking attempt failed. The following January *Soyuz 4* and *Soyuz 5* achieved a significant first: the two spacecraft, and three cosmonauts, docked in space. *Soyuz 11* docked with the *Salyut 1* space station in 1971, though the *Soyuz 11* crew died upon reentry during a pressurization crisis in which a valve popped open. *Soyuz 12* and later Soyuz were specially designed for ferry operations. *Soyuz 14* docked with the *Salyut 3* space station in 1974 for two weeks of military reconnaissance and science experiments.

Chronically short of funds and lacking modern computers, the Soviet space program lagged behind that of the United States. The Soviet Union had lost the race to the Moon when *Apollo 8* orbited the Moon in 1968 and again when *Apollo 11* landed on the Moon in 1969. While the lunar destination had lost its significance, Soyuz spacecraft proved to be an effective ferry. Finally, in 1974, Leonid Brezhnev fired Mishin and canceled the human lunar project.

Brezhnev helped ease tensions between East and West, and both sides adopted detente policies. In that atmosphere the superpowers undertook a cooperative Apollo-Soyuz Test Project in the mid-1970s. Technical information was exchanged and spacecraft were modified. *Soyuz 19* and an Apollo spacecraft docked in space. Both spacecraft had been launched on 15 July 1975. They gradually aligned their orbits about 130 miles above the Earth. On July 18th, they docked. The three-man U.S. crew—Tom Stafford, Vance Brand, and Donald Slayton—and the two-man U.S.S.R. crew—Alexei Leonov and Valery Kubasov—visited in space. (Figure 9-28)

Although the Soyuz never went to the Moon, it became a space ferry that carried Soviet crews to the Salyut orbiting stations. After 1977, all Soyuz missions supported space stations. Docking had become the Soyuz specialty. Improved versions came into operation, notably the Soyuz-T in 1976 and the Soyuz-TM in 1986. When Brezhnev had fired Mishin in 1974, Valentin Glushko became head of the space design bureau. Under Glushko, and later, Yuri Semenov, the S.P. Korolev Rocket Space Corporation Energia (RSC Energia) designed the *Mir* space station. The Salyut space station system was already in operation.

Historic Event

On 24 April 1967, Soviet cosmonaut Vladimir Komarov died in the crash of *Soyuz 1*. He was the first person to die in the course of a spaceflight.

Salyut

Using a Proton booster rocket for the launch vehicle, the Soviet Union placed the world's first space station into orbit on 19 April 1971. This was *Salyut 1*, also called DOS for long duration orbital station. *Salyut 1* remained in orbit for 176 days. This was two years before the United States launched its *Skylab* space station, and the Salyut program would outlive *Skylab*. (Figure 9-29)

Soviet aerospace engineers in 1970 converted the Soyuz and Almaz designs into the Salyut design.

Figure 9-28. The Apollo-Soyuz mission in 1975 eased tensions between the two superpowers in space. In many respects, the success of the mission helped reinforce the idea that space had no borders or political affiliations.

Historical Evidence

The CIA's National Intelligence Estimate 11-1-1967 entitled "The Soviet Space Program," went to President Lyndon B. Johnson in March 1967. It was the best information the United States had at the time, and it was good information — not complete and not completely accurate, but good information. The Central Intelligence Agency, the Department of Defense, the Department of State, the Atomic Energy Commission, and the National Security Agency participated in preparing the top-secret 36-page document. The "estimate" reported on the recent history of Soviet launches and projected the near-term (five- to ten-year) outlook.

The CIA concluded:

• "The space program has retained a high priority among Soviet national objectives."

• "A continuing high level of development activity and construction of major new launch facilities suggest that a new series of advanced space missions is likely in the next few years."

• "The Soviets have probably planned some form of space spectacular during 1967 in connection with the 50th anniversary of the October Revolution or the 10th anniversary of Sputnik 1."

• "Costs of the Soviets space program have risen sharply over the past few years, but now appear to be leveling off."

• "In view of competing claims on their resources, we believe that the Soviets will not be able to undertake simultaneously all the projects within their technical capabilities."

• "Two years ago, we estimated that the Soviet manned lunar landing program was probably not intended to be competitive with the Apollo program as then projected, i.e. aimed at the 1968-1969 period. We believe this is still the case."

• "The Soviets will probably attempt a manned circumlunar flight during the next few years."

• "We believe that the establishment of a manned space station is also a Soviet objective."

• "The expansion of the Soviet satellite reconnaissance project over the last two years shows that projects of demonstrable strategic value can and will be funded."

• "During the past year, the Soviets have conducted flight tests which could lead to a strategic space weapon system. We estimate that a fractional orbit bombardment system could be deployed in small numbers by late 1967 or early 1968."

Korolev's rival Chelomei had developed the Almaz space station, but it never became a military space station as intended. Salyut was a crash development, because the Soviet officials wanted to beat the American *Skylab* into space.

The Salyut and Soyuz docking system allowed cosmonauts to move between spacecraft without exiting the protective interior environment of spacecraft. But the first attempt to move crew between the *Soyuz 10* with *Salyut 1* failed; the spacecraft docked, but the crew transfer failed. *Soyuz 11* achieved both docking and crew transfer with *Salyut 1* in June 1971, but its three-man crew died when the *Soyuz 11* depressurized upon reentry. The loss of *Salyut 2*

Figure 9-29. The Salyut series of spacecraft were designed for long-duration flights.

(also designated *DOS-2*) was due to a launch vehicle explosion after launch. *Salyut 3* reached orbit, but control of the spacecraft was lost before a crew arrived to man it. *Salyut 4*, the last of the original set, flew successfully in 1974.

Salyut 5 went up in June 1976 and returned a little more than a year later. *Salyut 6* was particularly successful. It remained aloft for five years and ten months, from September 1977 to July 1982. It had two docking ports. Sixteen expeditions, including nine international crews, visited the space station. Soyuz and Progress spacecraft docked. Cosmonauts completed scientific research and experiments. Built as a backup for *Salyut 6*, *Salyut 7* continued providing a research base in space. It was aloft for eight years and ten months. When *Mir* became operational, *Salyut 7* moved out of the limelight. In 1986, two crewmembers from *Mir* visited *Salyut 7* for a few days, then returned to *Mir*. *Salyut 7* fell to Earth on February 7, 1991, showering a small town in Argentina with debris. (Figure 9-30)

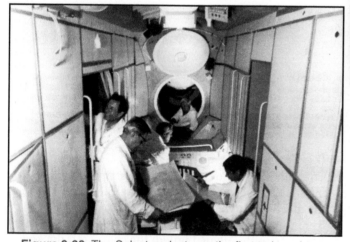

Figure 9-30. The Salyut project was the first to launch several semi-permanent space stations.

Mir

Mir (Peace) was the next generation of Soviet space stations. A decade in development, *Mir* incorporated features and lessons from the Salyut and Almaz programs; for example, *Mir* adopted the digital flight control computer tested on a Salyut and the gyrodyne flywheels from Almaz. *Mir* also incorporated new technology, such as the Kurs automatic rendezvous system and the Altair satellite communication system. The *Mir* base block had compartments for working and living, transferring crews and supplies via the docking ports, for connecting the working compartment to the aft docking port, and for the main engine, fuel tanks, and communication equipment. Getting

the spacecraft down to launch weight proved difficult, so the decision was made to launch some of the equipment later and install it in space. The core module was launched into orbit on 20 February 1986. Additional modules and equipment and instruments went up with various spacecraft visiting *Mir*. The space station remained in operation until it was abandoned in May 2000; it broke apart upon reentry in March 2001. (Figure 9-31)

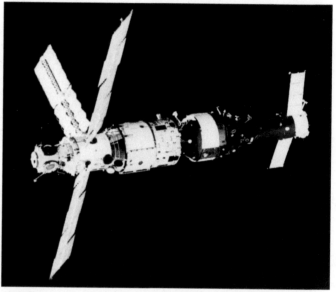

Figure 9-31. MIR as it looked in 1989. It was operational and ready to receive other modules to expand its operation.

Buran

Many proposals, plans, even products stop short of an operational spacecraft. One program that spent years in development, and even diverted substantial resources from the *Mir* development program at one time, was Buran (blizzard or snowstorm). Buran grew out of a 1974 Soviet decision to develop a reusable space system, designated MKS. The Space Transportation System, STS or space shuttle, was already under development in the United States. The Soviet program explored various designs and in 1976 selected Buran.

The development work included converting a Myasishchyev 3M bomber to a 3M-T Energia/Buran transport aircraft. The Buran orbiter flew on the transport during a test flight early in 1983. A Tupolev 154 transport was used in flight trials of the Buran automatic landing system late that year. Another aircraft used in the program was an Antonov An-225 heavy transport, selected to replace the 3M-T.

Originally scheduled for launch in 1983, Buran fell far behind schedule. Trouble with the booster rockets and the resulting delays caused a management shakeup at the Yuzhnoye design bureau. The cryogenic fueling process used super-chilled hydrogen, and the cold flow tests of 1985 were successful. At the Zhukovsky test center near Moscow, cosmonaut Igor Volk flew the Buran on its first test flight in November 1985. Equipment delivery delays and manpower shortage at Baikonur contributed to a reorganization of the Buran program in early 1986.

The first launch of Buran took place on 15 November 1988. This test of the unoccupied spacecraft successfully demonstrated a completely automatic launch, orbital maneuver, deorbit, precision landing, and landing rollout. Proud of the success, the Soviet Union displayed Buran at the Paris Air Show in early June 1989. Four years later Boris Yeltsin canceled the program for lack of a known mission. (Figure 9-32)

Figure 9-32. The Buran (left) was the Soviet attempt to develop a reusable space vehicle. The Energia heavy left booster (right) was the launch vehicle used to place Buran into orbit.

United States

The United States had looked at four different approaches to human space travel. These were the research plane (like the X-15), the ballistic vehicle (like Mercury), the boost-glider (Dyna-Soar spaceplane proposal), and the lifting body (like the proposed Lunex). Whether to develop the space program with civil or military resources was also a question. There were, in fact, many proposals for a human spaceflight program, mostly from the military and military contractors. The U.S. Air Force had Project

7969, the Navy had Project Mer, and the Army had Adam. Project 7969 was also called "Man in Space Soonest." The United States ultimately decided to let the new civilian space agency, NASA, manage the human spaceflight program.

X-15

President Dwight Eisenhower's fiscal conservativeness extended to the space program. He favored a stable economy, even budget surpluses, over an expensive space program, but he did support creating NASA in 1958. The first director of that agency, Keith Glennan, soon announced Project Mercury to put a man in space.

President John F. Kennedy took office in January 1961. Like Eisenhower, Kennedy was a "cold warrior" fighting communism and communists. The Soviets placed the first man in space in April. That bothered Kennedy. He asked Vice President Lyndon Johnson, "Do we have a chance of beating the Soviets by putting a laboratory in space, or by a trip to the moon, or by a rocket to land on the moon, or by a rocket to go to the moon and back with a man. Is there any other space program which promises dramatic results in which we could win?"

Kennedy announced his answer to a joint session of Congress in May. "Finally, if we are to win the battle that is now going on around the world between freedom and tyranny," he began in the rhetoric of the Cold War, and continued, "Now it is time to take longer strides— time for a great new American enterprise—time for this nation to take a clearly leading role in space achievement, which in many ways may hold the key to our future on earth."

"Recognizing the head start obtained by the Soviets with their large rocket engines," Kennedy explained, "We go into space because whatever mankind must undertake, free men must fully share." He concluded, "I believe that this nation should commit itself to achieving the goal, before this decade is out, of landing a man on the moon and returning him safely to the Earth."

The U.S. space program that evolved from Kennedy's decision included the existing Mercury project, also Gemini and Apollo. The *Skylab* and space shuttles also became part of the U.S. manned space program. (Figure 9-33)

Historical Note

The military had been looking at the Moon before Kennedy directed NASA's attention in that direction. In June 1959 the U.S. Army produced the "Project Horizon Report" about establishing a lunar outpost. "The establishment of a manned outpost in the lunar environment will demonstrate United States leadership in space," said one Army report. A lunar base would extend "space reconnaissance and surveillance capabilities and control of space," serve as a communication relay station, support scientific exploration and research, and provide an emergency staging area if needed due to other space activity.

Mercury

Project Mercury began in 1957. NASA decided to use the Atlas intercontinental ballistic missile, existing technology, to launch Mercury. That choice meant that the spacecraft to be carried aloft needed to be small and light. Defense contractor McDonnell won the contract to produce 12 one-person capsules; a capsule is the pressure vessel surrounding the astronaut and containing the controls and communication capabilities. Despite the race against the Soviet Union, NASA proceeded with diligence and care. The failures that had marred the nation's early satellite and probe launches could not be tolerated in a human flight program. (Figure 9-34)

Like the Soviets, NASA turned to the military for astronauts. Project Mercury selected seven. John H. Glenn Jr. came from the Marines. M. Scott Carpenter, Walter M. Schirra, and Alan B. Shepard Jr. were Navy pilots. L. Gordon Cooper Jr., Virgil I. Grissom, and Donald K. Slayton were Air Force pilots. Training was intense and concurrent with technology development and testing of components and systems. The Navy's Mark IV high-altitude pressure suit, made by Goodyear, was modified into a custom-fitted spacesuit.

Figure 9-33. Five major U.S. human space flight projects took place between 1957 and 1989.

Historical Note

In May 1961 the U.S. Air Force presented "Plan Lunex," a proposal for a human lunar expedition to go to the Moon, land, and return to Earth in 1967. The plan specified a Lunex lunar lander as one stage of the spacecraft, a Lunex launching stage, and a Lunex lifting-body reentry vehicle. The Lunex spacecraft would have a three-person crew. The Air Force recognized Cold War priorities. "This one achievement, if accomplished before the USSR, will serve to demonstrate conclusively that this nation possesses the capability to win future competition in technology," according to the proposal.

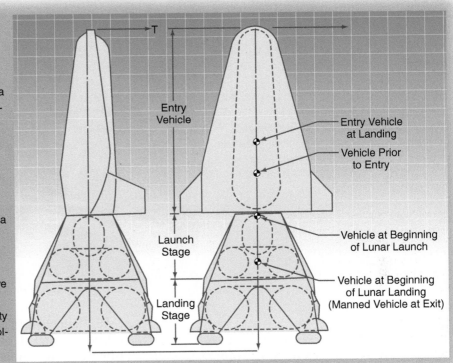

Shepard, in *Freedom 7*, initiated the Mercury system in manned flight when he flew a suborbital mission in May 1961. Grissom in *Liberty Bell 7* flew the next flight, also suborbital, in July. The most famous flight was that of Glenn in *Friendship 7* on 20 February 1962, when he became the first American to orbit the Earth—and third person to orbit, after two Soviet cosmonauts (Gagarin and Titov). Glenn circled the Earth three times and returned safely. The spaceflight lasted four hours and 55 minutes.

The final Mercury flight was unusual. Cooper in *Faith 7* flew 22 orbits over two days, 15-16 May 1963. An electrical malfunction left the automatic stabilization and control system without power. Cooper manually fired the retrorockets for reentry and landed safely in the Pacific Ocean.

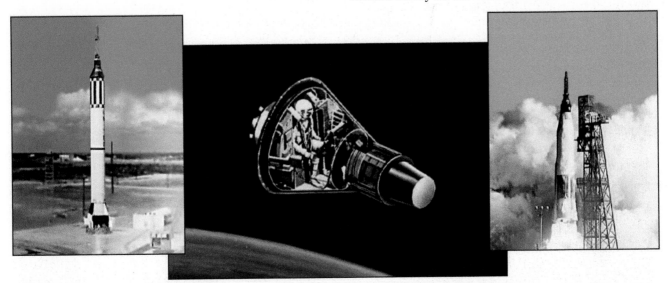

Figure 9-34. The Mercury Project included six flights that took American astronauts from suborbital to orbital flights. The Redstone rocket, on the left, was used for the first two flights of the Mercury project. In the center is the Mercury capsule. The Atlas rocket, on the right, was used for orbital flights.

Historical Note

The original seven astronauts enabled the United States to lay a foundation for space technology, prove the reliability of spacecraft control, and test the advanced tracking and communications network. To honor and commemorate the original seven astronauts, each capsule had "Seven" in its name. At the end of the Mercury program, the United States had a group of highly trained astronauts for further explorations.

Shown here from left to right are Virgil Grissom, Alan Shepard, Jr., Scott Carpenter, Walter Schirra, Donald Slayton, John Glenn, Jr., and Gordon Cooper, Jr.

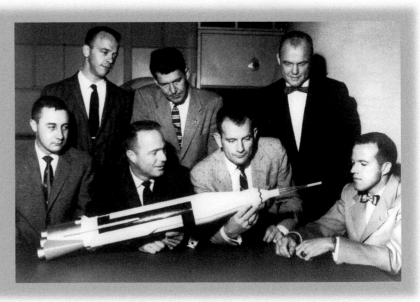

Gemini

Like Voshkod, Gemini was an interim project. Gemini was to continue human space activity between the close of Mercury and the first Apollo flight. For Gemini, NASA enlarged the space capsule to accommodate two crew members and added maneuvering capabilities. Using a modular system, NASA could easily change mounted equipment. The Titan II launch vehicle replaced the Atlas. The goal was simply to gain as much experience with spaceflight, space conditions, and space technology as possible in order to support the upcoming Apollo missions.

NASA launched 12 Gemini flights; 10 of them carried astronauts, and all of them landed in water. *Gemini 1* lifted off unoccupied on 8 April 1964. Ground personnel collected data through the spacecraft's first three orbits. Its mission successfully completed, *Gemini 1* was left in orbit. On its 64th orbit, it reentered the atmosphere and disintegrated. *Gemini 2*, the following January, was also unoccupied. On *Gemini 3* in March 1965, Virgil I. Grissom and John W. Young used rockets to change the orbit of the spacecraft; this was a first. They also performed the first controlled reentry on their way to landing in the Atlantic Ocean. (Figure 9-35)

Personal Profile

John Herschel Glenn Jr. (1921-) was born in Cambridge, Ohio, where he attended primary and secondary school. He studied engineering at Muskingum College in New Concord. He entered the Naval Aviation Cadet Program in March 1942, graduated from this program, and was commissioned in the Marine Corps in 1943. After advanced training, he joined Marine Fighter Squadron 155 and spent a year flying F4U fighters in the Marshall Islands. During his World War II service, he flew 59 combat missions. After the war, from June 1948 to December 1950, Glenn was an advanced flight training instructor at Corpus Christi, Texas. In Korea he flew 63 missions with Marine Fighter Squadron 311. In the last nine days of fighting in Korea, Glenn downed three MIG's in combat along the Yalu River. After Korea, Glenn attended Test Pilot School at the Naval Air Test Center, Patuxent River, Maryland. He was chosen to be one of the original seven astronauts in 1959. In 1962 he became the first American to orbit Earth. Glenn retired from the Marine Corps in 1965 and entered the business world. In 1974 he was elected to the United States Senate. In 1998, at the age of 77, Glenn returned to space.

John Glenn

Like Mercury capsules, Gemini spacecraft were too small for astronauts to move around much inside the vehicles. However, Gemini provided astronauts experience with extra-vehicular activity, including six hours of standing in the

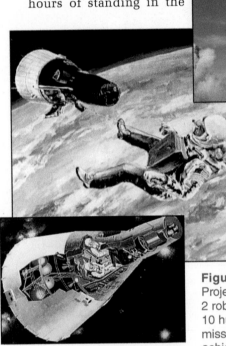

Figure 9-35. The Gemini Project included 12 flights, 2 robotic test flights and 10 human space flight missions. In addition to achieving the major goals of spacewalking, rendezvousing, and docking, the Gemini Project also determined that humans could function in space for up to two weeks with no significant problems.

open hatch and six hours of tethered time. Edward H. White II in *Gemini 4* used a hand-held maneuvering device and a line tethering him to the spacecraft during his historic—first American—extra-vehicular

Figure 9-36. Ed White floats in space on the end of a life line/tether. The line provided oxygen to his spacesuit. White used a gas gun (in his right hand) to help him maneuver.

activity. This was on 3 June 1965, a few months after a Russian cosmonaut had completed the first space-walk. (Figure 9-36)

Historical Note

A reminder to all at the Manned Spacecraft Center in Houston was a poster stating, "WE ARE 301 MAN-ORBITS AND 443 MAN-HOURS BEHIND THE RUSSIANS IN SPACE FLIGHT TIME."

This air of urgency set the stage at the beginning of the manned Gemini flights. At the start of the Gemini missions it had seemed as if the Soviets were always two steps ahead. The engineers, scientists, and astronauts did their best as not only the nation, but also the world, kept a watchful and sometimes critical eye on their efforts.

Flight Lines

"I'm doing great. This is fun."

Outside the Gemini 4 spacecraft, astronaut Edward H. White II said this to the spaceship commander, James A. McDivitt, on 3 June 1965. The next day the New York Times carried this quotation and the story of White's space-walk, the first by an American, on the front page.

Apollo

The Apollo Project had a clear goal—to go to the Moon "before this decade is out." Apollo spacecraft did that repeatedly. Six landed on the Moon! There had been debate about how to reach the moon. NASA finally settled on a method first proposed in about 1916 by the Russian rocket theorist Yuri Vasilievich Kondratyuk and developed in 1962 with the help of NASA engineer John C. Houbolt. The Apollo hardware was impressive to say the least. At the end of a mission, only a small fraction of the initial pre-launch vehicle was left. (Figure 9-37)

Before the first flight, tragedy struck. *Apollo 1* never got off the ground. On 27 January 1967, during a launch pad test in preparation for manned flight, a flash fire broke out. The three astronauts in Spacecraft 012 died. They were veteran astronauts Virgil "Gus" Grissom and Ed White, and rookie astronaut Roger Bruce Chaffee, who was preparing for his first spaceflight. NASA established a review board. That board determined, for one example, that the

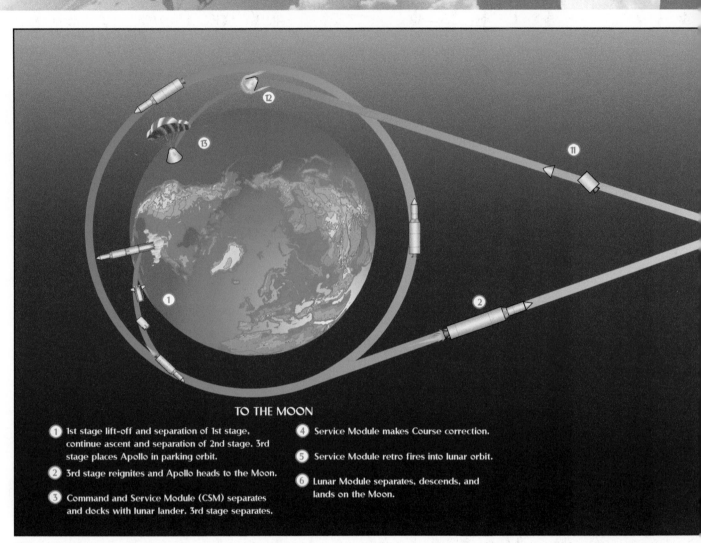

TO THE MOON

① 1st stage lift-off and separation of 1st stage, continue ascent and separation of 2nd stage. 3rd stage places Apollo in parking orbit.

② 3rd stage reignites and Apollo heads to the Moon.

③ Command and Service Module (CSM) separates and docks with lunar lander. 3rd stage separates.

④ Service Module makes Course correction.

⑤ Service Module retro fires into lunar orbit.

⑥ Lunar Module separates, descends, and lands on the Moon.

Figure 9-37. Missions to the moon were complex and required the individual successes of many pieces of equipment and separate tasks. This illustration shows the sequence of events from launch to splashdown.

astronauts did not have time to escape from the capsule. Regarding the inability to make timely and simple egress, the Apollo 204 Review Board found, "Those organizations responsible for the planning, conduct, and safety of this test failed to identify it as being hazardous."

Flights were suspended while NASA addressed the many recommendations of the 204 Board. NASA redesigned the capsule. The first manned Apollo spaceflight finally lifted off in October 1968. That spacecraft, *Apollo 7*, made 163 orbits of the Earth. *Apollo 9* similarly orbited Earth. These missions tested the command and lunar modules. *Apollo 8* circled the Moon on Christmas Eve. *Apollo 10* also orbited the Moon. These flights tested equipment and systems in anticipation of the lunar landing.

Launched by the Saturn V rocket, *Apollo 11* departed Earth on 16 July 1969. Four days later, the command

module *Columbia* released the landing module *Eagle*, which touched down at the Sea of Tranquility on the Moon. This was the first lunar landing! The date was 20 July 1969. Neil A. Armstrong climbed down the lander's ladder and stepped on the Moon, thereby becoming the first person on the Moon. Both feet on the lunar surface, he spoke, "That's one small step for man. One giant leap for mankind." Edwin E. "Buzz" Aldrin joined Armstrong on the ground. Michael Collins remained in the command module, the lunar orbiter, high above the lunar surface. When *Apollo 11* and crew returned to Earth four days later, the mission completed Kennedy's pledge to go to the Moon and to return by the end of the decade. (Figure 9-38)

Apollo 12, 14, 15, 16, and *17* also landed on the Moon. An explosion in an oxygen tank imperiled the *Apollo 13* mission. The crew canceled a scheduled lunar landing and made a lunar flyby instead. Ground personnel directed the astronauts in repairing and

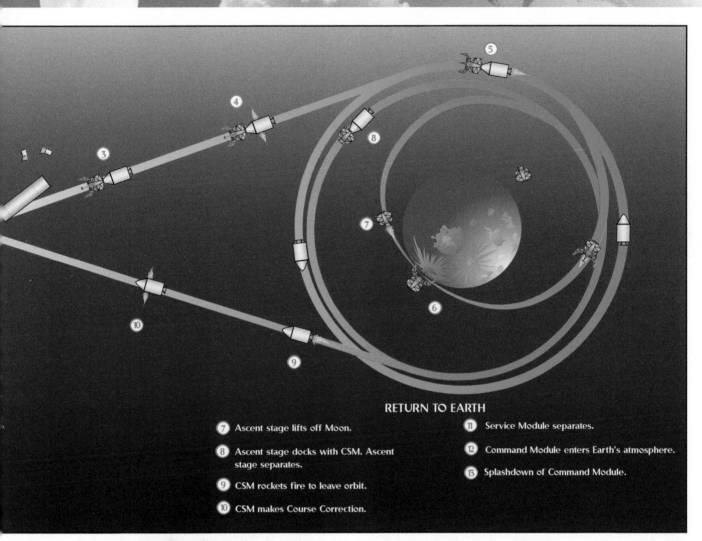

RETURN TO EARTH

7 Ascent stage lifts off Moon.

8 Ascent stage docks with CSM. Ascent stage separates.

9 CSM rockets fire to leave orbit.

10 CSM makes Course Correction.

11 Service Module separates.

12 Command Module enters Earth's atmosphere.

13 Splashdown of Command Module.

Figure 9-38. People around the world had followed the spaceflight and watched the lunar landing on television, the images and voices being broadcast from the Moon. They saw the United States claim undisputed leadership in the Space Race.

bypassing faulty equipment, and the mission came home. Including the crew of *Apollo 11*, twelve astronauts walked on the Moon between July 1969 and April 1972. These people explored the geography and investigated the geology of the Moon. They collected lunar samples and scientific data. They conducted experiments. And then they left. No one has been to the Moon since. (Figure 9-39)

Apollo spacecraft ferried three crews to the Skylab space station, and flew once more, in 1975, to dock with the Soviet *Soyuz 19*.

Historic Event

On 20 July 1969 Neil Armstrong became the first human to set foot on another celestial body. Apollo 11 fulfilled President Kennedy's challenge of landing a man on the moon and returning him safely to Earth.

Figure 9-39. The Apollo project had been the longest running program at NASA when it ended in 1973.

Skylab

Skylab was an experimental program to operate a science and engineering laboratory in space. NASA used a Saturn V rocket to place the unoccupied station, designated *Skylab 1*, in orbit. The launch occurred on 14 May 1973. Using Apollo-style command modules, three missions went to the space station. (Figure 9-40)

Figure 9-40. The *Skylab* project was relatively short lived, but it provided a stable work environment in space.

The first crew arrived in *Skylab 2*, launched 25 May 1973, which docked with the station, made repairs, and deployed parasol sunshades to cool the interior because the meteoroid shield had been torn off during the launch of *Skylab 1*. The crew of three consisted of Charles Conrad, Jr., Paul J. Weitz, and Joseph P. Kerwin. They also conducted a variety of solar, Earth, and medical studies. During their 28-day mission, they performed three extravehicular activities totaling more than six hours.

Skylab 3 spent 59 days in space, from late July to late September 1973. Its crew of three performed maintenance on the space station and spent over 13 hours outside on extravehicular activities. They also conducted experiments and gathered data.

Skylab 4 was the last Skylab mission. The crew spent 84 days aloft. They observed the comet Kohoutek. Crewmembers took four spacewalks and spent a total of 22 hours outside the spacecraft.

As an experimental space station, *Skylab* demonstrated that people could live and work in space for extended periods of time. Unused, the space station descended into the atmosphere. It broke apart over the Southern Hemisphere in July 1979.

Historical Note

EAGLE: "Forward. Drifting right . . . contact light. Okay, engine stop. ACA out of detent. Modes control both auto, descent engine command override off. Engine arm off. 413 is in."

CAPCOM: "We copy you down, Eagle"

ARMSTRONG: "Houston, Tranquility base here. The Eagle has landed."

CAPCOM: "Roger, Tranquility, we copy you on the ground. You've got a bunch of guys about to turn blue. We're breathing again. Thanks a lot."

EAGLE: "Thank you."

Thus went the conversation between the first Apollo moon lander called the *Eagle* and NASA controllers during the landing sequence on the moon. During this sequence, Neil Armstrong had to manually "fly" the lander 300 meters down range of the target landing area to avoid large boulders and moon rocks. The controllers were concerned because the lander was quickly running out of fuel, but it finally touched down with about 20 seconds of propellant remaining. As quoted in David Baker, *The History of Manned Space Flight* (New York: New Cavendish Books, 1981).

Space Shuttle

The space shuttle program produced and operated a small fleet of reusable spacecraft: *Columbia* (OV-102), *Challenger* (OV-099), *Enterprise* (OV-101), *Discovery* (OV-103), and *Atlantis* (OV-104). The concept offered cost savings, as major components could be reused for multiple launches into space. It was to be a space truck, a workhorse, a "space transportation system." (Figure 9-41)

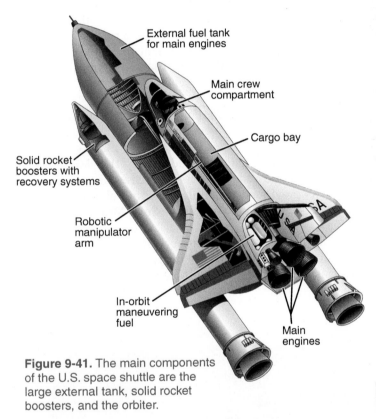

Figure 9-41. The main components of the U.S. space shuttle are the large external tank, solid rocket boosters, and the orbiter.

External fuel tank for main engines

Main crew compartment

Cargo bay

Solid rocket boosters with recovery systems

Robotic manipulator arm

In-orbit maneuvering fuel

Main engines

The concept of reusable spacecraft goes back at least to Eugen Sanger's *Silverbird* of the 1930s, a proposed spaceplane that could fly in near-Earth orbit and, like an airplane, land on Earth. The U.S. Air Force investigated a Dyna-Soar spaceplane concept in the late 1950s and early 1960s. NASA conducted flight tests of manned lifting bodies throughout the 1960s. In 1968 companies like Grumman and North American submitted diverse proposals regarding what a space shuttle might be.

The first flight of the space shuttle required no launch because the spacecraft flew on the back of a Boeing 747. At 23,000 feet, the shuttle released from the plane. The shuttle glided back to the ground. That was in August 1977. The first orbital flight of a space shuttle came four years later.

On 12 April 1981 the space shuttle *Columbia* was launched into orbit. Two days later the space shuttle became the first lifting-reentry vehicle as Robert L. Crippen and John W. Young guided the spacecraft back to Earth. Their landing is the first case of a spacecraft landing like an airplane. The STS-1, as the mission was designated, completed the first orbital flight by a winged spacecraft. The space shuttle also became the first U.S. spacecraft to use solid rocket boosters and the first U.S. spacecraft to be designed with no escape system.

When the *Columbia* lifted off again on 12 November 1981, it became the first spacecraft to be reused.

Using the space shuttle, NASA could deploy, retrieve, and repair satellites. NASA could move people, equipment, laboratories, and spacecraft. The space shuttle opened space wider. In 1983 STS-7 and STS-8 carried Sally Ride, the first United States woman in space, and Guion Bluford, the first black astronaut, to orbit the Earth.

On the 25th shuttle flight, the space shuttle system experienced its first major, catastrophic accident. After nine previous space missions, the *Challenger* had a short and final flight on 28 January 1986. The launch appeared normal, but soon the *Challenger* exploded into a fireball, and debris rained down. (Figure 9-42)

Figure 9-42. The aftermath of the *Challenger* explosion.

The *Challenger* crew of seven died. One crewmember, Christa McAuliffe, was part of the citizen-in-space program. She was there to demonstrate how ordinary spaceflight had become with the space shuttle. The pilot was Francis Scobee. Judith Resnik, Ronald McNair, and Ellison Onizuka were shuttle veterans. Greg Jarvis and Mike Smith were on their first space flight. (Figure 9-43)

Figure 9-43. The crew of mission 51-L, *Challenger's* 10th mission, included (back row, left to right):Ellison Onizuka, Christa McAuliffe, Greg Jarvis, Judy Resnik; (front row, left to right) Mike Smith, Francis Scobee, and Ron McNair.

Flights were suspended. A Presidential Commission investigated. It concluded, "The specific failure was the destruction of the seals that are intended to prevent hot gases from leaking through the joint during the propellant burn of the rocket motor." Plans to commercialize shuttle missions were halted. Modifications were made. An escape system was designed and installed. Finally, on 29 September 1988, the *Discovery* led the space shuttle fleet back into service and space.

The return-to-flight *Discovery* mission was the 26th flight of a space shuttle. There was one more flight in 1988, with a classified Department of Defense payload, and five shuttle flights in 1989. The shuttle was indeed in service again.

The main goal of the *Challenger* mission in February 1984 was to release two commercial communications satellites into space, but both failed to reach geostationary orbit. That justified using the Manned Maneuvering Unit later in the year to rescue the satellites. As previously scheduled, the unit also was utilized on a mission to recover the Solar Max satellite.

During 1984, Manned Maneuvering Units were successfully used on three shuttle missions by six astronauts on nine sorties. As a post-mission report

 ## Historic Event

On 7 February 1984 Navy Captain Bruce McCandless II became the first astronaut to float free in space, not tethered to a spacecraft, yet able to maneuver. When he floated from the payload bay of the *Challenger*, 150 nautical miles above Earth, he noticed "a heck of a big leap." He checked equipment outside the shuttle, floated away from the craft and maneuvered back, and generally tested the Manned Maneuvering Unit on his back. Ten years in development, this unit promised freedom of movement as well as safety for astronauts servicing satellites and performing other duties in space.

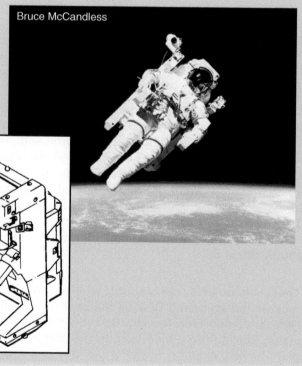

Bruce McCandless

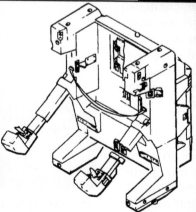

said, the "hardware performed as expected with no anomalies." And yet the units were never used again.

Why? Primarily designed for recovering satellites, the Manned Maneuvering Units were not needed. As shuttle flights of 1984 demonstrated, pilots could maneuver the space shuttle itself with such accuracy that the shuttle's robotic manipulator arm could grab satellites. In fact, most extravehicular activities could be performed effectively without using the unit. Foot restraints, hand grips, tether lines, and self-propelled maneuvering units were adequate. The Manned Maneuvering Units were simply not necessary. Also, new safety concerns raised by the *Challenger* accident in January 1986 made expensive modifications necessary if the units were to be used again. They were not.

CHINA, EUROPE, AND BEYOND

The two superpowers dominated the Cold War and the Space Race, but other nations participated in the world events, and other nations developed scientific and technological capabilities and space programs. China proved to be something of a rogue. Initially in alliance with the Soviet Union, China increasingly became the lone leader of revolutionary communism, something that frightened the West as well as the Soviet East.

China

To start a rocket and space program, the People's Republic of China sought foreign expertise and technology. The first step, in 1955, was to welcome back to China a United States-trained Chinese scientist, and world leader in propulsion theory and applications. Tsien Hsue-Shen had gone to the United States to study in the 1930s and had earned a master's degree at Massachusetts Institute of Technology and a doctorate at the California Institute of Technology. Tsien worked at the Jet Propulsion Laboratory and for the United States Air Force missile program. He returned to China in 1955 and thereafter led the Chinese rocket and space program.

Having recently fought a war with the United States in Korea, and with a leading rocket and missile scientist to lead the program, China included ballistic missile development in the nation's Twelve Year Plan for 1956-1967. China looked to long-range ballistic missiles and nuclear weapons to neutralize the threat of

the United States and the advantage of its communist neighbor, the Soviet Union.

The Soviet Union provided technology to help China, a young communist nation. In the 1950s Chinese engineers studied German and Soviet rocket technology in the Soviet Union, mostly at the Moscow Aviation Institute. China also imported Soviet ballistic missile technology. The Soviet Union sent two R-1 missiles to China in 1956; these were Soviet copies of the German liquid-propellant V-2 missiles of World War II. More advanced R-2 rockets went to China in 1957. The Soviets helped China produce and deploy R-2s by the end of the decade.

The Sino-Soviet cooperation ceased in 1960. For years China's revolutionary leader Mao Tse-Tung had objected to the path the Soviet Union took after the death of Joseph Stalin, to Khrushchev's peaceful coexistence policy, and to the Soviet Union treating China like a satellite country. As Stalin had, Mao wanted the communist revolution to spread worldwide. When the Soviet Union refused to release nuclear technology to China, Sino-Soviet relations collapsed. China decided to develop its own nuclear program, and it tested its first nuclear bomb in 1964 and its first hydrogen bomb in 1967. (Figure 9-44)

Figure 9-44. Manufactured in the early 1960s, the DF-3 was one of China's first ballistic missiles.

With the increase in Western commercial arrangements, western technology went to China in the late 1980s. Companies in the United States, West Germany, and France provided technology, such as the German communication package for the Chinese DFH-3 communication satellites and the American radiation-hardened electronic chips for Chinese meteorological satellites. The United States accused China of stealing technology as far back as 1950 and throughout the Cold War, but whatever evidence of espionage existed usually remained defense classified, closed to the public.

China began development of a human spacecraft in 1966. Using the plans for a recoverable photo-reconnaissance satellite, the Fanhui Shei Weixing FSW-0, as the basis for the design, and planning to use the CZ-2 booster to launch the vehicle, Project 714 developed the *Shuguang 1* spacecraft. China selected astronauts for training in 1971. The first flight was

scheduled for 1973, but in 1972 Mao ruled that terrestrial matters needed funding more than the space program. He closed Project 714 and thereby ended China's development of a human spacecraft.

Tsien's team produced *Dong Fang Hong-1* (*DFH-1* or East is Red-1), China's first satellite, which was successfully launched on 24 April 1970. Tsien's CZ-1 rocket launched the satellite. Four years later, China began launching Fanhui Shei Weixing (FSW) photo-reconnaissance satellites, recoverable satellites used

Personal Profile

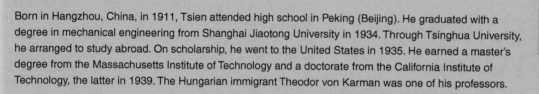

Tsien Hsue-Shen (also known as Qian Xuesen, 1911–) led the Chinese space program from its inception through 1991.

Tsien Hsue-Shen

Born in Hangzhou, China, in 1911, Tsien attended high school in Peking (Beijing). He graduated with a degree in mechanical engineering from Shanghai Jiaotong University in 1934. Through Tsinghua University, he arranged to study abroad. On scholarship, he went to the United States in 1935. He earned a master's degree from the Massachusetts Institute of Technology and a doctorate from the California Institute of Technology, the latter in 1939. The Hungarian immigrant Theodor von Karman was one of his professors.

Tsien joined the rocket research group at the Guggenheim Aeronautical Laboratory, where he conducted theoretical work on supersonic and transonic aerodynamics. He moved to the Jet Propulsion Laboratory, where his expertise on jet propulsion contributed to the Private A missile, the first solid-propellant missile to work in the United States.

At the end of World War II, Tsien went with the United States team of scientists to Germany to obtain German rocket technology and personnel. At this time he met Wernher von Braun. In order to work on the military long-range missiles, Tsien accepted a commission as colonel in the U.S. Army Air Force. He worked on the Titan intercontinental ballistic missile program.

Accused of spying for China during the era of McCarthyism, Tsien lost his security clearance in 1950. The United States kept him under near house arrest for five years, but failed to prosecute him or produce evidence to support the espionage charge. Finally, the United States deported Tsien to China in exchange for American pilots shot down during the Korean War.

Communist Premier Zhou Enlai welcomed him back to China in 1955. Quickly, Tsian prepared a "Proposal for Setting up China's Aerospace Industry for National Defense." In response, the State Council created a Committee of Aerospace Industry and added missiles and missile development to its Twelve Year Plan. In 1956 Tsien founded the Fifth Institute, a rocket and missile research institute (now renamed the China Aerospace Corporation). There he led the development of jet and rocket technology, production of short-range missiles, and the development and production of China's first satellite.

After the Soviet Sputnik success, Tsien proposed a Chinese satellite program. In 1962 he initiated the satellite program by beginning to train Chinese scientists for the tasks of designing, developing, and launching satellites. Tsien's team produced Dong Fang Hong-1, China's first satellite, which was successfully launched on 24 April 1970. Delighted, Mao personally congratulated Tsien.

By then, Tsien was working toward a Chinese manned space program. He designed a winged spaceplane as a manned spacecraft option. Jen Hsin-Min, head of the Chinese Space Agency, publicly announced the manned space program in 1978. The program had launched suborbital tests before the government canceled the program in December 1980, due to costs at a time when basic economic development was a national priority.

In addition to managing all of the ballistic missile programs, Tsien was the chief designer of the DF-5 intercontinental ballistic missile, a nuclear-armed ICBM that was deployed during the 1990s and aimed at targets in the United States.

Tsien won many awards including the honorary rank of Lieutenant General in the People's Liberation Army and the State Scientist of Outstanding Contribution award. He retired in 1991. His story is told in *Thread of the Silkworm,* by Iris Chang (New York: Basic Books, 1995).

by the military. In the 1980s, China used Dong Fang Hong (DFH) and foreign-made communication satellites, and domestic weather satellites. Starting in 1985, China began selling its launch capabilities on the international market and launching foreign satellites into orbit.

Europe

Just as German wartime technology contributed to the space programs of the Soviet Union and the United States, the technology influenced postwar developments in Europe. In 1946 about 80 German rocket experts went to France to help design the Viking rocket that later became part of the Ariane launch vehicle. In 1947 some German rocket experts went to Great Britain, where they assisted in the design of the Black Knight missile; this defense program was later cut from British budgets. The postwar experience contributed to later programs.

The nations of Europe were caught in the middle of the Cold War, but several attempted to maintain a national or European program distinct from the interests of the United States and the Soviet Union. Several invested in rocket, missile, and space technology. In addition to national programs, generally small, there were cooperative efforts involving the European nations.

European states have cooperated through various organizations. The first was called COPERS, which was short for *Commission Préparatoire Européenne pour la Recherche Spatiale*. The main priorities were a European satellite program and a European launch vehicle.

An intergovernmental conference in Paris in 1962 adopted the convention for the European Space Research Organization (ESRO). ESRO established a satellite program. The initial satellite research program continued until 1966. Using the Vandenberg launch site, ESRO launched a series of ESRO satellites on American Scout B launch vehicles during the 1967-1972 period. Vandenberg Air Force Base in California specialized in the launching of polar-orbiting satellites and missile tests across the Pacific Ocean to the Kwajalein Atoll. *ESRO 1A* (also called *Aurorae*), *1B* (*Boreas*), *2B* (*Iris*) and *4* satellites in near-Earth space investigated the polar ionosphere and aurora, the near magnetosphere. ESRO also developed an interest in application satellites, such as communication satellites.

The European Launcher Development Corporation (ELDO) formed in 1964 to develop a satellite launch vehicle for Europe. Great Britain provided the first stage for the launch vehicle, the Blue Streak, from its canceled ICBM program. France provided the second stage and Germany the third. Italy worked on the satellite, and the Netherlands and Belgium worked on tracking and telemetry for the ELDO launch program. Australia became a member of ELDO, because the European organization selected Woomera, Australia, as the site for testing launch vehicles. (Figure 9-45)

Figure 9-45. Woomera's main launch site in the 1960s showing a fully assembled Europa launch vehicle.

In the first phase of the ELDO program, European scientists and engineers achieved three successful launches of the first stage, Blue Streak, in 1964–1965. Phase two involved more test launches in 1966–1967. The first tests involved stage 1 with dummy stages 2 and 3, then tests with stages 1 and 2 with a dummy stage 3. Phase three tested vehicles with all three stages active in 1968–1971. These launches were directed toward orbit. ELDO conducted eleven launches in all, several with equipment failures and problems. Although the first stage performed flawlessly on every launch, not one of the four test satellites reached orbit.

ELDO moved its European launch plans for *Europa II* to Kourou, French Guiana, but the Woomera range remained active. On 29 November 1967, Australia's first satellite, on a U.S. Redstone rocket, lifted off from Woomera into space. This was the Weapons Research Establishment Satellite or *WRESAT*. The satellite completed 642 orbits before reentering the Earth's atmosphere over the Atlantic Ocean.

France had used a launch site in its African colony of Algeria, but with Algerian independence France needed a new location. It selected its South American colony of French Guiana. The Kourou site would allow over-water launches, and from there the Earth's rotation would assist launches into equatorial

Historical Note

In cooperation with Australia, Britain had opened the Woomera, Australia, long-range weapons establishment, a rocket range, in 1947 and began testing there in 1949. Britain tested Black Knight rockets for anticipated use carrying the Blue Streak ICBM warheads. From 1957 to 1987 Britain fired Skylark rockets at the range. The early launches were tests; the latter ones carried scientific payloads.

Among the many missiles launched from Woomera were Europa 1, Sparta, Black Arrow, Aero Mach, Jabiru, Black Knight, Skylark, Long Tom, Aero High, Aeolus, and Koorigal. These were tests by countries in the Western Bloc.

The United States had opened a tracking station on the Island Lagoon dry lake bed at Woomera in 1949. The United States, through NASA, tracked spacecraft from this station until it closed in 1972. By then, the United States was operating its Nurrungar defense satellite monitoring station near Woomera. Built in 1969, the Nurrungar closed in 1999.

At Woomera, Britain launched its *Prospero* satellite on a Black Arrow launch vehicle on 28 October 1971.

orbits. France made the decision in 1964 and completed four rocket launch pads in 1968. These were used for launching sounding rockets.

A Diamant pad completed at Kourou in 1969 was used into 1975. Diamant was a French program, begun in 1961, to develop a French capability for launching satellites. The first launch in 1965, from the Hammaguira, Algeria, site was a success. Hammaguira closed in early 1967. Diamant B and BP vehicles were launched from Kourou.

The *Europa II* launch facilities at Kourou became ready in 1971, the same year that the international First Package Deal in Europe approved the Ariane program. On 5 November of that year, ELDO launched *Europa II*. The third stage failed. ELDO abandoned the Europa program. Over the next three years, the Europa facilities were converted to support the Ariane orbital launch vehicle. The first Ariane 1 was successfully launched at Kourou on 24 December 1979. Ariane was a liquid-propulsion launch system designed for unmanned spacecraft. During the 1980s, the Kourou site, including a new launch pad completed in 1986, launched numerous Ariane 1, 2, 3, and 4 vehicles. Ariane became the first successful

commercial launch vehicle developed in Europe. The French company Aerospatiale manufactured the launch vehicle.

The Second Package Deal of 1973 provided for Europe's participation in Spacelab. Designed and manufactured in Europe, Spacelab was a pressurized module fitted into space shuttle payload bays for missions requiring laboratory capabilities. At the start of the space shuttle program, NASA had tried to lure international partners. That effort produced the Canadian remote manipulator arm, routinely used to grab satellites for retrieval or repair. It also produced the European Spacelab, which enabled astronauts to tend to experiments after Skylab closed in 1973. The first flight of a Spacelab was that of *Spacelab-1* on the space shuttle *Columbia*, mission STS-9, from 28 November to 8 December 1983. (Figure 9-46)

In 1973 ELDO and ESRO had agreed to merge into a new organization, as confirmed in the Second Package Deal. The European Space Agency (ESA) formally came into existence in 1975. Its purposes were European cooperation, space research and technology, space operations, and scientific research—all peaceful aims, no military goals. ESA inherited pro-

Figure 9-46. The European Space Agency designed and produced Spacelab modules so that scientific experiments could be conducted in outer space. *Spacelab-1* went on space shuttle *Columbia* in late 1983, as shown in this picture from that flight.

grams of ELDO and ESRO, including Europa, Ariane, and Spacelab, as well as a variety of satellite programs. It continued to use Kuorou as Europe's spaceport. It adopted new programs too. Headquartered in Paris, France, ESA acquired facilities elsewhere, notably a technology center in Noordwijk, Netherlands; a space operations center in Darmstadt, Germany; and a data processing center in Fracasti, Italy. Representing 15 participating nations, ESA led Europe into near space and deep space.

Southern Space

Nations in the Southern Hemisphere also funded research, development, and even launches during the Space Race. The Republic of South Africa, for example, developed an intermediate-range ballistic missile in the 1980s because of its isolation and the Soviet threat. Israel provided technical assistance. Out of that defense program came the RSA-3 launcher for

surveillance satellites. The first two RSA-3s were launched in 1989, the third in 1990, all as the need for such defense capability declined. During the 1980s, as part of the ballistic missile effort, South Africa's Houwteq company developed the Overberg Test Range on Western Cape, beside the Indian Ocean. The RSA-3s were launched from this site.

Argentina also attempted to develop a ballistic missile in the 1980s, but had not produced an operational device by the end of the decade. Researchers at the Instituto Aerotécnico began development of a liquid-propellant rocket in 1947. Argentina started a solid-propellant program in 1954. The nation began a cooperative sounding-rocket program with NASA in 1961. The launch site at El Chamical, La Rioja, began operations in 1962, and many sounding rockets, such as the *Condor I*, lifted off there. During the 1960s, Argentina launched 16 French Centaure rockets as part of a study of atmospheric dynamics such as wind direction and intensity. The military government of General Juan Carlos Onganía purged the universities in the "night of the long clubs" in 1966, and that hampered space science and technology development. Military repression in 1976 and thereafter again hampered research and development programs.

The space enthusiasm of the late 1950s, resulting largely from Sputnik, also reached Brazil. That nation created the Organizing Group for the National Commission on Space Activities (COGNAE) in 1961. COGNAE became CNAE, which developed laboratories and equipment at Sao José dos Campos. Founded in 1971, the Institute for Space Research (INPE) became the civilian agency in charge of space research and development. The agency used foreign satellites—meteorological, communication, and earth observation satellites. The Complete Brazilian Space Mission (MECB) opened in the late 1970s for the express purpose of developing indigenous space technology. INPE and MECB worked together throughout the 1980s, but had not yet launched a Brazilian-made satellite by the end of the decade.

India

The Indian Committee for Space Research decided to use sounding rockets to enter the Space Age. In 1962 that committee, under the leadership of Vikram A. Sarabhai, developed the Thumba Equatorial Rocket Launching Station at the southern tip of the Indian subcontinent. The first launch occurred 21 November 1963. India used an American Nike-Apache rocket for that launch, but embarked on a program to develop an Indian rocket. The first launch of the resulting single-stage Rohini RH-75 rocket was in 1967. Through various international arrangements, French, German, Japanese, and other nations launched sounding rockets at Thumba.

In 1969 India decided to expand its space program. The Indian Committee for Space Research reorganized into the Indian Space Research Organization (ISRO). To include satellite launch vehicles and large rockets in its space program, ISRO that year began developing a launch station at Sriharikota on the east coast of the country. Sarabhai led the team working toward an Indian satellite launch vehicle; they reached the first launch of the resulting SLV-3 rocket in August 1979. India achieved its first satellite launch, the *Rohini-1B*, on 18 July 1980. At Sriharikota, India launched *Rohini-2* and *Rohini-3* successfully in 1981 and 1983 respectively, but lost the *SROSS-1* and *SROSS-2* satellites launched in 1987 and 1988. India also used foreign launch sites for its satellites.

Sarabhai explained why India, a developing nation, would have a space program. The statement is one of national purpose and pride, applicable to other nations. Sarabhai said, "There are some who question the relevance of space activities in a developing nation. To us, there is no ambiguity of purpose. We do not have the fantasy of competing with the economically advanced nations in the exploration of the Moon or the planets or manned space-flight. But we are convinced that if we are to play a meaningful role nationally, and in the community of nations, we must be second to none in the application of advanced technologies to the real problems of man and society." (Figure 9-47)

Figure 9-47. The first Indian in space was a test pilot named Rakesh Sharma who flew aboard the Soviet Soyuz T-11 spacecraft, launched on 2 April 1984.

SECTION B

Cold War Continues

Sputnik inspired a belief that the Soviet Union had a rocket and missile force. The rockets that launched satellites might power nuclear missiles to any target on Earth. The rockets might also be able to transport other spacecraft into outer space, from where the enemy might control the Earth. Khrushchev maintained this misconception, a bluff, of Soviet superiority in missiles while trying to develop such a force.

Since the end of World War II, Soviet policy relied upon combined forces, including the large Army kept mobilized after the World War. They used conventional deterrence in the form of a threat that the large Soviet military machine could overrun Western Europe. "One cannot win a war with atomic bombs alone," Soviet Defense Minister Georgi Zhukov told Khrushchev. He thereby expressed clearly the Soviet distrust of single-weapon strategies. Soviet strategy through the 1950s combined conventional and nuclear weapons.

Khrushchev, however, changed the strategy. In 1960 he decided nuclear deterrence was to become Soviet policy. It was already the policy of the United States. Upon accepting deterrence, Khrushchev cut funds for the military services and reduced conventional weapons. He claimed to have "powerful missiles" in the Soviet "rocket forces," which continued the bluff begun with Sputnik. The bluff apparently worked, because in 1960, United States presidential candidate John F. Kennedy's campaign featured the "missile gap." Only later did the United States realize that it had held a big lead over the Soviet Union in missiles.

DETERRENCE

Nuclear deterrence was the Cold War strategy of both the West and the East. Both sides sought to avoid attack by maintaining sufficient nuclear weapons and the means of delivering them to destroy any attacker. Dwight D. Eisenhower campaigned for the presidency

Historical Evidence

Historians not only gather evidence about the past, but they analyze the evidence and the source. They place the information in the context of time and place. Also, they ask if the information is factual and accurate or whether it is meant to persuade or otherwise influence opinions. Politicians, for example, often have political purposes behind their statements.

In 1960 Nikita Khrushchev told the Supreme Soviet:

"Our state now has at its disposal powerful missiles. The Air Force and the Navy have lost their former importance in view of the contemporary development of military technology. This type of armament is not being reduced but replaced. Almost the entire Air Force is being replaced with rockets. We have now cut sharply, and will continue to cut sharply, even perhaps discontinue, production of bombers and other obsolete equipment. In the Navy, the submarine fleet assumes great importance, while surface ships can no longer play the part they once did. In our country, the armed forces have to a considerable extent been transformed into rocket forces."

The statement appeared in the Soviet newspaper *Pravda* on 15 January 1960. By greatly overstating Soviet missile capabilities, the statement was false. That made it a bluff, with the United States and its Western Allies as the objects of the bluff. Domestically, the statement affirmed the Communist Party's priority—that is, civilian control over the military. It justified a one-third cut in the size of the Soviet Army. It also shifted prestige from war veterans to technicians, engineers, and scientists. Also, with this statement, Khrushchev signaled a policy shift from combined forces to nuclear deterrence.

Nikita Khrushchev

May Day in Russia

Figure 9-48. NORAD is the nerve center for detecting ballistic missile launches around the world. It is located deep under ground in Cheyenne Mountain, Colorado.

of the United States in 1952 on a platform that included nuclear deterrence. Soviet leader Nikita Khrushchev adopted nuclear deterrence as Soviet policy in 1960. The United States and Union of Soviet Socialist Republics maintained nuclear deterrence policies to the end of the Cold War.

Nuclear deterrence promised massive retaliation in response to any aggressive act. The threat of nuclear destruction extended anywhere within the range of bombers, missiles, and possibly satellites or spacecraft, or within the range of nuclear fallout, which could spread around the globe. Most of the weapons targeted the homelands, both civilian and military locations, of the two superpowers. (Figure 9-48)

Nuclear deterrence allowed reductions in conventional forces and weapons, and it promised defense without combat. Nuclear deterrence is historically significant because it affected military research, development, procurement, and practice. Also, the military spin-offs to civil aviation and the Cold War context affected regulation of airspace and fliers, civil as well as military. Furthermore, nuclear deterrence, particularly mutually assured destruction (MAD), meant that war was not inevitable.

Conventional Weapons

After World War II bombers remained important parts of the air forces of the Soviet Union and the United States, but more so for the United States. Boeing built 744 B-52 bombers, a plane that entered service in 1954 and remained in service throughout the Cold War. Designed to carry nuclear bombs long distances, and modified and upgraded many times, the B-52s went into the air whenever the United States went on alert. (Figure 9-49)

The United States also produced new, supersonic models for the Cold War. The Republic F-105 Thunderchief entered production in 1958. It was a large fighter-bomber designed to carry nuclear weapons, but was later adapted for close-air support and radar suppression. The Convair B-58 Hustler was also supersonic. It was used throughout the 1960s. The General Dynamics FB-111 that appeared in 1968 had variable-geometry wings, which meant that the pilot could change the sweep angle of the wings in flight. (Figure 9-50)

Whereas the United States used bombers as a transitional fleet for delivery of nuclear warheads, the Soviets did not. In sheer numbers, as well as by other criteria, there was a bomber gap. The Soviets had fewer bombers, mostly built by Tupolev. In the mid 1950s, Tupolev introduced the Tu-16 swept-wing, twin-engine jet bomber and the mid-wing, four-engine, propeller-driven Tu-95 bomber. The Tu-95, a mainstay in the Soviet strategic forces, was known in the West by its NATO codename, the Bear. The Tu-142, a long-range naval bomber, entered service in 1968. Both the Tu-22 that appeared in 1961 and the Tu-160 that entered production in the early 1980s were supersonic bombers. (Figure 9-51)

Figure 9-49. One of the mainstays of U.S. Cold War deterrence was the huge B-52 bomber.

Fighters also were conventional weapons, though by the mid-1970s, advanced electronics and precision weapons brought in a new generation of fighters to the United States air forces, notably the Navy's Grumman F-14 Tomcat and the Air Force's McDonnell Douglas F-15 Eagle. The F-14 had a variable-geometry wing, **head-up** display, and radar-guided missiles. The General Dynamics F-16 Falcon, which became operational in 1979, became the first production military aircraft with digital fly-by-wire controls. The stealth Lockheed F-117 Nighthawk first flew in 1981. (Figure 9-52)

Figure 9-50. The Convair B-58 Hustler (top) and the General Dynamics FB-111 (bottom) were designed to deliver nuclear weapons at supersonic speeds.

Figure 9-51. The Tu-22M Backfire (bottom) was intended to replace the Tu-16, but it was not as efficient. The newer Tu-160 Blackjack (top) was comparable to the U.S. B-1.

Figure 9-52. The F-16 Falcon (top) was a supersonic fighter capable of speeds close to Mach 2. The F-117 Nighthawk (bottom) was a subsonic bomber that relied on stealth technology to minimize detection.

The Eastern Bloc primarily used the Soviet MiG-21, a light-weight, single-engine interceptor, which first flew in 1955. More than 11,000 MiG-21s were produced. Mikoyan also produced a large number of MiG-23 fighters between 1969 and 1984. The MiG-29, which entered service in 1983, represented a new generation of fighters. Among its innovations were pulse Doppler radar and a helmet-mounted aiming system for the airplane's missiles. (Figure 9-53)

Both East and West built and flew airborne early warning and command-and-control system aircraft (AWACS) during the Cold War. These were large aircraft equipped with radar and electronic detection equipment. The Boeing E-3 Sentry, Ilyushin Il-76, and Saab 340AEW&C monitored enemy activity, while the E-4B, EC-135, and E-6 probed the skies. (Figure 9-54)

Figure 9-53. The MiG-29 was the top Soviet air-superiority fighter for the majority of the 1980s.

 ## Historic Event

On 22 May 1972 the Flight Research Center at Edwards, California (now NASA Dryden Flight Research Center), made the first test flight of the digital fly-by-wire flight control system. The test bed was a modified Vought F-8 Crusader. The digital fly-by-wire system used electronic flight controls in lieu of conventional mechanical flight controls. The fly-by-wire system came with redundancies for safety. Safety also improved by using wires rather than hydraulic lines, which were more vulnerable to combat damage. Computers could handle more commands and precision than manual input, which resulted in increased aircraft maneuverability. The fly-by-wire system weighed less than hydraulic gear and thereby improved the efficiency of an aircraft. After development, fly-by-wire technology went into military and civil aircraft.

Figure 9-54. The Boeing E-3 Sentry flanked by a McDonnell Douglas F-15 Eagle.

Cargo planes, aerial refueling aircraft, reconnaissance planes, transports, and helicopters were also parts of the conventional fleets of the Cold War.

Missiles

The Soviet Union and the United States both placed intercontinental ballistic missiles into military service in 1959. Both nations had benefited from German V-2 technology captured at the end of World War II.

The Soviet R-7 Semyorka (Little Seven), a liquid-propelled missile first successfully launched in 1957, could carry over five tons of payload, whereas the American Atlas, first launched in 1958, could carry less than two tons. The design difference accommodated the payloads. The Soviet hydrogen bomb

Historic Event

On 24 October 1960 a Soviet R-16 missile, designed by Mikhail Yangel, exploded at the Baikonur launch site. The blast and fire killed 165 people, including the head of the Soviet strategic rocket forces, Mitrofan Nedelin.

weighed much more than the American bomb. The Soviet Union designed the R-7 to carry its heavy bomb, whereas the United States designed a smaller and more technologically sophisticated missile. This difference in sophistication is evident in the fact that the R-7 required 20 hours of preparation before launch and the fuel could not be loaded in advance. The Atlas, however, required only about 15 minutes of preparation before launch. The Soviets recognized, however, that the lift capability of the R-7 could be applied to satellites.

Another first-generation Soviet missile was the fuel-storable R-12 missile, designed by Mikhail Yangel's design bureau in Dnepropetrovsk. Soon Yangel's R-16 displaced Korolev's R-9 design for the second-generation Soviet intercontinental ballistic missile (ICBM), a more practical ICBM than the R-9, few of which were deployed. Yangel became the leader in Soviet ICBM design, and Korolev concentrated his attention on the Soviet space program. (Figure 9-55)

In the United States tests of the Atlas and Thor series of missiles began in 1957. Atlas was an ICBM used to launch Mercury capsules and other space vehicles, and Thor was an intermediate-range ballistic missile (IRBM), used as a space booster or as a stage

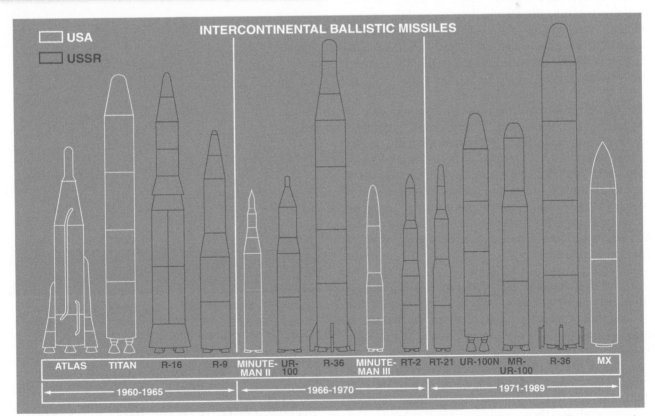

Figure 9-55. The United States and the Soviet Union developed several intercontinental land-based missile systems during this time period. After the basic model was produced several variations were made.

in a multistage space booster. Titan II was a two-stage liquid-propellant ICBM with a man-rating, meaning it could be used as the launch vehicle for the Gemini program. The United States installed Titan I bases in Colorado, South Dakota, California, Washington, and Idaho. Titan IIs went to Kansas, Arizona, California, and Arkansas. Minuteman was a solid-propellant ICBM, rushed into operational status during the Cuban Missile Crisis. Minuteman fields were in North and South Dakota, Montana, Wyoming, Nebraska, Colorado, and Missouri. Titan III was not an armed missile, but a space launch system, based on components of the earlier Titan ICBMs. (Figure 9-56)

The Army's Redstone missile was a surface-to-surface device, which launched two Mercury spacecraft in 1961. The Pershing was a selective-range ballistic missile first deployed to Europe in 1964. The Navy's Polaris was an underwater-to-surface or surface-to-surface missile assigned to nuclear submarines. (Figure 9-57)

Nuclear Weapon Tests

The missile programs of the East and West needed nuclear warheads. Both the United States and the Soviet Union had design, development, testing, and production programs that were top secret. Nuclear tests, however, could usually be detected because atmospheric tests released radiation into the atmosphere and underground explosions generated seismic waves.

The Soviet Union had become a nuclear power in 1949, when it successfully detonated a nuclear bomb at Semipalatinsk, Kazakhstan. The Soviet Union performed 715 nuclear weapon tests between 1949 and 1990. The two major Soviet test sites were at Semipalatinsk and at the Novaya Zemlya archipelago in the Arctic Ocean, where testing began in 1955. Less important test sites were at Azgir and Astrakhan in Kazakhstan and at Orenburg, west of the Ural Mountains.

The first 215 devices were detonated in the atmosphere between 1949 and 1962, the largest being the 58 megaton hydrogen bomb, known as the super bomb, which exploded in October 1961. The Soviets had suspended atmospheric testing of nuclear weapons in late 1958, but resumed atmospheric tests during the tense 1961-1962 period. From 1962 to 1990, the Soviets exploded 500 nuclear devices underground, and three underwater in the Arctic. Not all were weapon tests, however. About one-fifth of the underground tests explored peaceful uses of

Figure 9-56. A Titan missile launch silo under construction in the Western United States.

Figure 9-57. Submarine launched missile systems used by the U.S. during the height of the Cold War included the Polaris, Poseidon, and Trident series of missiles.

nuclear weapons, notably applications in the oil and gas industry.

The United States, the first nuclear power, tested over a thousand devices between 1945 and 1992. The United States used Pacific atolls and islands (Bikini,

Enewetak, Johnston, and Christmas) and the Nevada Test Site for most tests. The United States also conducted tests in Alaska, Colorado, Mississippi, and New Mexico. Following the Soviet example, the United States suspended testing in 1958 but resumed just as the Soviets did in 1961. Both countries ceased atmospheric tests with the Moscow Treaty of 1963 and thereafter relied upon underground testing.

The number of nations with nuclear capability grew slowly: the United Kingdom in 1952, France in 1960, China in 1964, and India in 1974. The Moscow Treaty, signed in August 1963, banned nuclear explosions in the atmosphere, in outer space, and underwater. The Soviet Union, United States, and Great Britain signed the treaty. France continued atmospheric nuclear tests, conducted in the Pacific, until 1980. China also continued testing at Lop Nor until 1984. In 1967, all the nations of Latin America, except Cuba, signed the Treaty of Tlatelolco, Mexico, that prohibited the introduction or manufacture of nuclear weapons.

HOT SPOTS

A "cold" war is a war without combat. In the case of the Cold War, United States and Soviet Union were not in combat, but the two superpowers came close to fighting a number of times, and many limited wars resulted in bloodshed during the Cold War period.

U-2 Incident

The Lockheed U-2 was a spy plane equipped with photographic capabilities made possible by Eastman Kodak's polyester-based film, Edwin Land's high-resolution cameras, and the Hycon Corporation's lenses.

Lockheed U-2

The U-2 could penetrate far across the border of the Soviet Union and high above the altitudes used by Soviet interceptors. Contracts to study the initial concept for a spy plane, designated MK-2147 or Project Bald Eagle, had been awarded in 1953 to Bell, Fairchild, and Martin. These studies led to the Martin RB-57D, which went into limited production, and the Bell X-16, which was never built. At its own expense, Lockheed developed a competitive design and submitted an unsolicited proposal for a high-altitude plane, the CL-282. A presidential committee, the Central Intelligence Agency (CIA), and President Eisenhower selected Lockheed to develop a plane capable of gathering the intelligence on Soviet missile, strategic bomber, and other programs.

Personal Profile

Clarence (Kelly) Johnson (1910-1990) was an innovative and creative engineer born in the town of Ishpeming in the upper part of Michigan. At an early age he had an interest in designing and working with his hands and built many model airplanes. By the age of 12, Johnson had decided that airplane design was his future. He earned a B.S. (1932) and M.S. (1933) from the University of Michigan, and then went to work at the Lockheed Corporation. Eventually, Johnson was chosen to head the "Skunk Works," Lockheed's secret aviation development unit. He was a dedicated man with a strong personality. He is credited with bringing many projects to completion ahead of schedule and under budget. During his 42-year career with Lockheed, he helped design more than 40 airplanes, including the U-2 spy plane, the first plane to fly above 60,000 feet; and the YF-12, the forerunner to the SR-71 Blackbird. Johnson developed the use of the brittle titanium alloy instead of aluminum on the SR-71, which allowed high-speed flying despite intense temperatures. Johnson also worked on a number of commercial airplanes. Among Johnson's many honors and awards was the Medal of Freedom, awarded to him in 1964 by President Lyndon Johnson to recognize his "significant contributions to the quality of American life."

Clarence "Kelly" Johnson

Historic Event

On 1 May 1960 the Soviet Union shot down a U-2 spy plane and
pilot Francis Gary Powers, who was on a CIA spying mission.
Immediately following the loss of the plane, NASA issued a press release stating that a U-2 conducting weather research may have strayed off course after
the pilot "reported difficulties with his oxygen equipment."

To bolster the cover-up, a U-2 was quickly painted in NASA markings, with a ficti-
tious NASA serial number, and put on display for the news media at the NASA
Flight Research Center at Edwards Air Force Base. On 7 May 1960 Soviet Premier
Nikita Kruschev exposed the cover-up by revealing that the pilot had been captured
and espionage equipment had been recovered from the wreckage.

It was the first time that the high flying spy plane had been shot down while conducting a photographic mission over the Soviet
Union. Even with the failure of this mission, the program had served the United States well. It had accurately determined the
Soviet's bomber strength and monitored Soviet rocket development. The exposure of the U-2 put an end to the spy missions over
the Soviet Union as well as to Eisenhower's hopes for a test ban treaty at the upcoming Paris summit. The tensions between the
Soviet Union and the United States grew as a result of the U-2 incident. Powers served 17 months of a 10-year sentence before he
was exchanged for a Soviet spy.

Code-named Aquatone, the plane that became the
U-2 went into development and construction at
Lockheed's Skunk Works in California, under the
direction of engineer Kelly Johnson. The utility, "U,"
designation concealed the plane's real purpose —
reconnaissance overflights of the Soviet Union and
Eastern Bloc countries. Johnson's team adhered to a
tight schedule and began flight testing in the summer
of 1955. Lockheed produced the U-2 for both the CIA
and the Air Force. The U-2A was the initial production version; other versions followed. The CIA began
training pilots in 1956. It organized three Weather

Reconnaissance Squadrons and based them in
Lakenheath, England; Adana, Turkey; and Naha,
Okinawa. The CIA also posted U-2 detachments at
Wiesbaden, Germany, and Peshawar, Pakistan.
Overflights of the Soviet Union began in 1956.

Throughout its design, development, production, and
even its first few years of operation over the Soviet
Union, the U-2 remained obscure. That changed on 1
May 1960, when a Soviet V-750 surface-to-air missile
downed the U-2 flown by an Air Force pilot on
assignment to the CIA, Francis Gary Powers. Powers
was en route from Peshawar to Bodø, Norway. He
went down near Sverdlovsk. Soviet outrage, the fact
that the Soviets had captured Powers, and the fact
that the Soviets had a surface-to-air missile (SAM)
capable of reaching the high-altitude plane, forced
Eisenhower to stop overflights of the Soviet Union.

During the early 1960s the CIA continued overflights
of communist China and even based U-2s in Taiwan.
Overflights of China in 1964 gathered evidence that
China was preparing to explode a nuclear device.

Historical Note

Francis Gary Powers (1929-1977) was an Air
Force lieutenant when he transferred to the
Central Intelligence Agency in 1956. The CIA gave him U-2
training and sent him to Incirlik Air Force Base in Turkey. He
flew reconnaissance over the Soviet Union. The Soviets knew
about the flights but were unable to do anything about aircraft
80,000 feet up, out of range of Soviet aircraft and missiles. The
Soviets secretly developed a surface-to-air missile (SAM), the
V-750, that could reach that altitude. On 1 May 1960 the
Soviets shot down Powers' plane. He parachuted to the
ground, where the Soviets captured him. At a public trial on 17
August 1960 he pleaded guilty to espionage. Sentenced to ten
years in prison, Powers came home in 1962 as part of a prisoner exchange. The United States released Rudolf Abel, convicted of espionage in 1957, in exchange for Powers.

The Air Force also had procured U-2s. These went to
the Strategic Air Command, which used the aircraft
to gather intelligence in Europe and Asia, including
Vietnam, to detect nuclear radiation high over the
Americas, from Argentina to Alaska, and to overfly
revolutionary Cuba, which was under the leadership
of Fidel Castro.

Bay of Pigs

The U-2 incident in 1960 stressed relations between East and West and between Khrushchev and Eisenhower. When a young John Kennedy became president in January 1961, he inherited from the Eisenhower administration a proposal to support an invasion of Cuba by refugees who had fled the island. Trained as a lawyer, Fidel Castro had led the revolution that ousted Cuban dictator Fulgencio Batista in late December 1958. Castro nationalized the sugar cane industry and later oil refineries, both previously owned by companies in the United States. Eisenhower severed ties with Cuba and began training Cuban refugees.

Kennedy began his presidency indecisive about Cuba. In April he allowed the refugees to invade the island — at the Bay of Pigs, but without the promised air and naval support of the United States. By curtailing U.S. air strikes, the United States hoped to preserve deniability of U.S. involvement. The lack of U.S. air support enabled the Cuban Air Force to destroy the ships carrying ammunition and supplies for the invaders. Cuban forces quickly killed or captured the invaders. The Bay of Pigs was a great victory for Castro and a fiasco for Kennedy. It proved to Castro that the United States was a military threat to his regime, and it showed Khrushchev that Kennedy was weak.

After the Bay of Pigs, Khrushchev decided, "In connection with the changes in international relations and the fact the combined amount of test explosions of the Soviet Union is considerably inferior to that of the US, we will resume the test explosions during the autumn of 1961 and achieve a de facto increase of our nuclear power and demonstrate to the imperialists what we are capable of." Nuclear testing was part of the arms race.

Historical Evidence

Key information about the Bay of Pigs invasion remained classified for 36 years. Lyman Kirkpatrick of the CIA wrote a 150-page report entitled "The Inspector General's Survey of the Cuban Operation" in November 1961. The CIA declassified the document in 1998.

Khrushchev did not wait till autumn to test the young American president who had appeared so weak in the failed invasion of Cuba.

Berlin Wall

East Germany, devastated by World War II, was draining the Soviet economy as the Soviet Union tried to rebuild the sector as a communist state. Each month, thousands of East Germans, mostly young and educated people, were fleeing to freedom and prosperity in the West simply by walking from the eastern sector of Berlin to West Berlin. To stop the defections, which was reducing an already too small workforce in the East, the communists erected a wall in Berlin. They began stringing barbed wire on 13 August 1961. Already concerned about Cuba, Kennedy watched the situation in Berlin, but he did not bow to Soviet pressure to withdraw and give West Berlin to the East. The Berlin Wall became concrete.

Despite the geographical distance, the wall became linked with Cuba during the missile crisis of 1962. If the United States got tough in Cuba, would the Soviet Union invade West Berlin? If NATO forces, led by the United States, took action in Berlin, would the Soviets withdraw from Cuba? Should the United States place nuclear missiles in Berlin? What would each side do? Berlin posed questions, but an immediate crisis brought East and West to the brink of war in Cuba.

Cuban Missile Crisis

On 14 October 1962 a U-2 based at Laughlin Air Force Base in Texas flew over Cuba. The Organization of American States had passed a resolution that, in the opinion of the United States, allowed overflights of Cuba, but Cuba and the Soviet Union did not recognize any right of overflight. Nonetheless, the United States had been sending spy planes to monitor the island only ninety miles from the American shore, especially since Cuban refugees had reported Soviet missiles and because unusual ship traffic had been observed. The October 14th flight returned with film, which the CIA developed and analyzed the next day. One photograph showed Soviet medium-range ballistic missiles in Cuba. (Figure 9-58)

The missiles were Yangel's R-12s. Unlike Korolov's earlier design, the R-7, these R-12s could store fuel onboard and would require little preparation before

Figure 9-58. The Soviets had provided not only missiles and aircraft to the Cubans but also trained the crews to use them. The photograph at the right is a reconnaisance photo of Cuba taken in 1962. The map below shows locations of missle sites, military air fields, and support facilities in Cuba.

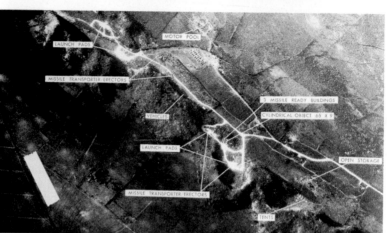

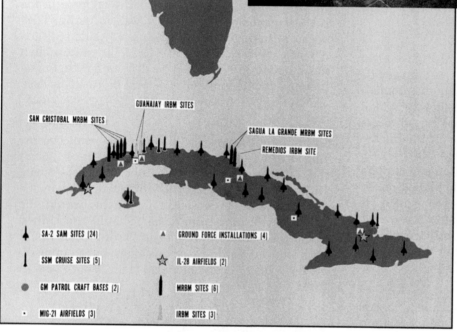

launch. NATO designated the R-12 the SS-4 Sandal. These missiles became the subject of a 13-day international crisis — the Cuban Missile Crisis.

The United States imposed a naval blockade in an effort to prevent Soviet ships en route from delivering more missiles to Cuba. The Soviets tested nine nuclear devices during the Cuban crisis in October. The United States not only continued its nuclear weapons testing, but it rushed a missile silo into operation and placed its ICBM forces on alert to be ready in case deterrence failed. The Strategic Air Command had bombers carrying nuclear weapons in the air. During the tense negotiations, a V-750 missile hit a U-2 that was flying over Cuba; the pilot, Rudolph Anderson, Jr., died.

For the Soviet Union, the missiles served three purposes. One, placing Soviet missiles in Cuba, near the United States, would counter the American-made Jupiter missiles that NATO had installed in Turkey, near the Soviet Union. Two, the Soviets had fewer long-range bombers and intercontinental missiles than the United States, so these missiles could fill the gap in striking capabilities. And three, the missiles would discourage a U.S. invasion, or U.S.-backed invasion, of Cuba. Castro welcomed the missiles and Soviet defense aid.

More secretly than the missiles being delivered to Cuba, the two superpowers reached an agreement for a trade. The United States would remove the missiles from Turkey, and the Soviet Union would remove missiles from Cuba. The United States also promised not to invade Cuba. Castro learned about the agreement from the radio, but only about the Soviets agreeing to remove the missiles from Cuba. He was furious! (Figure 9-59)

The secrecy of the agreement allowed the United States to make subsequent decisions upon the false assumption that the Soviets, when showed force, backed down. Then Secretary of State, Dean Rusk, explained to the press, "We went eyeball to eyeball with the Russkies, and they blinked." The myth of successful brinkmanship remained the popular understanding of the Cuban Missile Crisis for decades. A show of force did not work for the United States or the Soviet Union. Deterrence did not work, though the United States clearly had more weapon power at the time. Diplomacy, and an aversion to all-out war with its nuclear risks, resolved the crisis.

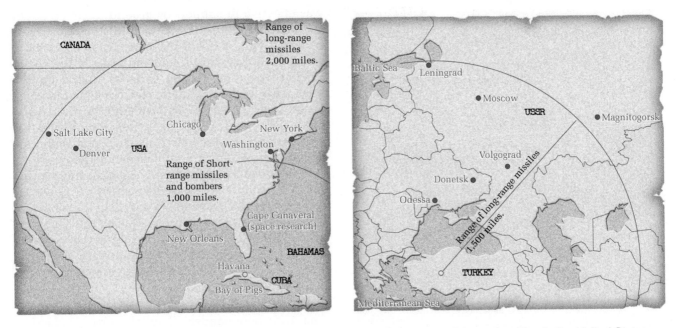

Figure 9-59. The Soviet missiles in Cuba would have been able to strike at most of the major cities in the United States. The Soviet Union wanted the removal of American missiles in Turkey in exchange for the withdrawal of missiles in Cuba. The United States agreed. This deal remained secret until the 1990s

Historical Evidence

After the dissolution of the Union of Soviet Socialist Republics, Russia opened Soviet archives to scholars. Among the files was a cable, dated 27 October 1962, from the Soviet Ambassador to the United States, Anatoly Dobrynin, about a conversation he had that day with the U.S. Attorney General Robert F. Kennedy, brother of the president. Dobrynin's cable contains a transcript of the conversation, a record of the secret deal, and evidence that both sides feared accident, miscalculation, or inadvertence that might start a nuclear war.

The cable and an English translation are in the *Cold War Briefing Book*, prepared by the National Security Archive for the CNN documentary series *Cold War* (Warner Home Video, 1998).

Vietnam War

The withdrawal of French forces and the signing of the Geneva Peace Accords in 1954 left South Vietnam vulnerable to communism. President Eisenhower used the South East Asia Treaty Organization (SEATO) as a way to support and rebuild the Republic of Vietnam south of the 17th parallel. The support involved U.S. advisors and military aid to help train the fledgling South Vietnam Army. The advisors were instructed to defend themselves if need be, but the line between defense and offense often was unclear. In 1959 the Communist Party of Vietnam (Viet Cong) began a campaign of revolutionary violence to overthrow President Ngo Dinh Diem and his anti-Communist government of South Vietnam.

Between 1959 and 1963 military confrontations with the South escalated. North Vietnamese guerrillas infiltrated the South via the Ho Chi Minh Trail and provided arms and ammunition to sympathizers. The trail, named for the leader of North Vietnam, was one of the major supply routes from the North into South Vietnam. The route extended into Laos and Cambodia along the western borders of Vietnam. Diem asked the United States to conduct herbicide spraying to defoliate the route to allow aircraft to more easily spot and attack arms shipments. The defoliant spray was also used in an effort to destroy enemy crops. President Kennedy approved Operation Ranch Hand in November 1962. The Air Force used C-47s, T-28s, B-26s, C-123s, and C-130s to apply the herbicide. A total of 11 million gallons of Agent Orange was used with another 7 million gallons of Agent White, Agent Blue, and other chemical herbicides. The operation finally ended 9 years later after 18 million gallons of chemicals had been sprayed and an estimated 20 percent of South Vietnam's jungles and 36 percent of its mangrove forests had been affected.

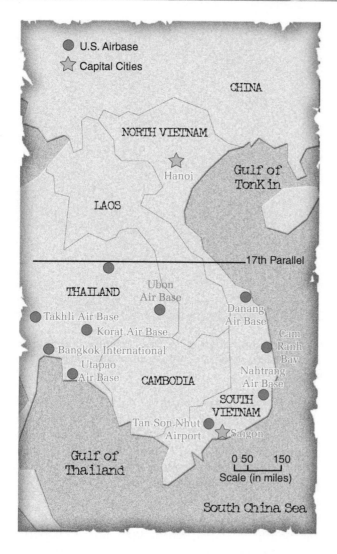

U.S. Airbase
Capital Cities

CHINA

NORTH VIETNAM

Hanoi

Gulf of
TonKin

LAOS

17th Parallel

THAILAND

Ubon
Air Base

Takhli Air Base

Danang
Air Base

Korat Air Base

Cam
Ranh
Bay

Bangkok International

Utapao
Air Base

CAMBODIA

Nahtrang
Air Base

SOUTH
VIETNAM

Tan Son Nhut
Airport

Saigon

Gulf of
Thailand

0 50   150
Scale (in miles)

South China Sea

was effective in supporting ground forces in South Vietnam. Early in 1965 Communist sympathizers attacked two U.S. Army installations in South Vietnam. In retaliation, Johnson ordered the beginning of Operation Rolling Thunder on 24 February 1965. This frequently interrupted bombing campaign lasted until the end of October 1968. Air Force and Navy aircraft engaged in the bombing campaign that was designed to force Ho Chi Minh to abandon his ambition to take over South Vietnam. The operation was intended as a diplomatic signal to impress the North's Communist government with the U.S.'s determination. It also was intended to help the morale of the South Vietnamese forces. During the campaign strict limits were placed on the targets that could be attacked because of the fear that China and the Soviet Union would intervene if the North Vietnamese faced a quick defeat.

The U.S. commander, General Curtis E. LeMay, argued that military targets, rather than the enemy's resolve, should be attacked and that the blows should be rapid and sharp, with the impact felt immediately on the battlefield as well as by the political leadership in Hanoi. The missions struck into North Vietnam with regularity and the aircraft losses due to the Soviet radar-guided anti-aircraft missiles were significant. To counter the air defenses, the Republic F-105 Thunderchief and North American F-100 Super Sabre supersonic fighters became the first aircraft to be used by the United States to destroy the radar systems that were used to guide the missiles. These aircraft were called "Wild Weasels." Several aircraft filled this role over the years, including the

In 1961, 100 military advisors and a special unit of 400 soldiers were in Vietnam. A year later this number had increased to 11,000 advisors. On 1 November 1963, the Communists succeeded in overthrowing the government by capturing and later killing Diem. Three weeks later President Kennedy was assassinated on the streets of Dallas. At the time of the Kennedy and Diem assassinations, 16,000 U.S. advisors were in Vietnam. Kennedy's successor, President Lyndon Johnson, accelerated the undeclared war when two American destroyers were allegedly fired upon by North Vietnamese patrol boats in the Gulf of Tonkin on 4 August 1964. As a result, both the House of Representatives and the Senate passed the Gulf of Tonkin Resolution that gave Johnson broad war powers. The result was a limited reprisal air attack against the North Vietnamese.

By 1964 U.S. forces were actively engaged in the conflict. Many of the confrontations were the first true tests of American air power since the Korean War. Even though it was a limited guerilla war, air power

Operation Ranch Hand

McDonnell F-4 Phantom. In addition to this role, the F-100 was regularly used as a ground support aircraft. (Figure 9-60)

Figure 9-60. This F-100D is firing a rocket salvo at enemy positions on the ground. The unguided rockets were often packed with heavy explosives.

The fighting will of the Communist soldiers proved hard to break, and Rolling Thunder did not accomplish its purpose of causing a significant withdrawal. Late in 1965 the Johnson administration still used air power in an attempt to put political pressure on the North Vietnamese. However, the attacks tended to be directed against the flow of men and supplies from the North. President Johnson restricted the bombing of North Vietnam on 31 March 1968, which effectively brought Operation Rolling Thunder to an end.

The Boeing B-52 was first used in Vietnam during Operation Arc Light. On 18 June 1965, 27 B-52F bombers of the 7th and 320th Bombardment Wings based in Guam were used to attack a Viet Cong jungle stronghold with conventional 750-pound and 1,000-pound bombs. From June through December, the 7th, 320th, and 454th Bombardment Wings completed over 100 missions to South Vietnam. By late June 1966, after one year of participation in the war, the B-52s were dropping approximately 8,000 tons of bombs each month. Missions were flown night and day in all types of weather. In 1966 over 5,000 B-52 sorties were flown, and in 1967 the number increased to approximately 9,700 sorties.

The defense of Khe Sanh in 1968 developed into one of the largest air campaigns in Southeast Asia. Around-the-clock air strikes were made against enemy forces besieging the base. The Strategic Air Command (SAC) bombers dropped approximately 60,000 tons of bombs. With fighter-bomber support limited by the monsoon season, the B-52s were a formidable counter to enemy aggression. Radar directed the B-52s to their targets, where they destroyed supplies and forced the North Vietnamese to withdraw, breaking the siege on Khe Sanh.

Another important development during the Vietnam conflict was the expanded role of helicopters. In addition to their traditional missions of support, supply, and rescue, helicopters were used as offensive weapons for the first time. Again, engine technology proved important in providing long-range, reliable, turbine-power for helicopters like the UH-1 Huey and AH-1 Cobra, as well as the larger CH-47 Chinook and the CH-54 Skycrane. Not only were the turbine engines reliable, but the helicopters were rugged and easy to maintain. (Figure 9-61)

Figure 9-61. The Huey (above) and the Chinook (below) provided transportation and support over hundreds of miles of hostile territory.

The helicopter was easily the most vulnerable aircraft used in Vietnam. Although rugged and versatile, they flew slower and lower to the ground than airplanes, making them easy targets for anti-aircraft gunners. By the end of 1971, 4,200 helicopters had been lost to enemy fire and the rigors of high demand and abusive flying conditions. Even with the high losses, the benefits far outweighed the weaknesses. For example, helicopters allowed for quick reinforcement and rapid evacuations when needed.

The refinement of a close air support system that involved helicopters was also an advancement made during Vietnam. U.S. commanders were committed to using air power to support ground forces to a greater extent than in other conflicts. The military accomplished this by using a number of different aircraft. By 1966, the U.S. Air Force, Navy, and Marines all had fighter/bomber aircraft in place in South Vietnam or on aircraft carriers in the South China Sea and the Gulf of Tonkin. A communication network was set up so ground force units could contact a Tactical Air Control Center (TACC) and request air support any place within the 43 provinces of South Vietnam. The TACCs then directed fighter aircraft to the target area. In an emergency, aircraft already airborne were diverted. Usually, fighters could get to any area within 15 minutes. When a fighter or bomber arrived in an area, it was handed off to a forward air controller (FAC). The FAC would mark the target area

and direct the attack pilot where to drop the bombs. (Figure 9-62)

Figure 9-62. Directed to the target by an FAC, the F-100 Super Sabre would then hit the targets on the ground. It carried different types of bombs and rockets.

In May 1968 preliminary discussions in pursuit of a lasting peace began in Paris but did not succeed. In November, Johnson made another concession, ending

Flight Lines

Captain Don Carson of the U.S. Air Force described flying an F-105 under attack by surface-to-air missiles (SAMs) during a Wild Weasel mission to suppress SAMs in Vietnam. In his account, he quotes his "Bear" — the man in back who was an electronic warfare officer. According to Carson:

"SAMs at two and five ... guns at three," my Bear, Don Brian, coolly calls over the intercom, telling me where the treat is located.

I light up the afterburner, and our speed approaches 600 knots. I turn toward the SAM site which is looking at my flight of four Weasels with his radar. We have the green light in the outboard weapons-pylon buttons, indicating that we are armed and ready to fire our AGM-45 Shrike antiradiation missiles.

"SAMs at twelve o'clock ... a three-ringer." My Bear now has the SAM battery off our nose and is getting very strong signals on his indicating equipment. We press in, pull up our F-105 at the proper range, and hose off a pair of Shrikes just as the SAM site fires at our flight. My skin crawls as the rattlesnake sound in my headset and the flash of the warning-gear light tell me it is for real this time.

"Valid launch ... twelve o'clock," yells my Bear.

"Vampires ... take it down," I call to my flight as I nose over and unload. "Taking it down" is the standard Wild Weasel maneuver of rapidly diving in full afterburner and picking up speed to avoid the SAMs being guided to your aircraft. Sometimes by descending you can even lose the SAM radar tracking you, or force the SAM to overshoot and pass harmlessly by. If this does not work, at least you have one heck of a lot of airspeed you can use to make a break at the last moment and maybe make the SAM miss your aircraft. ...

But now I see the clouds of dust and the "telephone poles" trailing fire as they climb. Our Shrikes are still guiding directly toward the radar van which controls those SAM missiles. It is located in the center of the SAM ring, surrounded by the missile launchers.

The above excerpt is from Captain Don Carson, "Vampires, Take It Down!: 'Wild Weasel' in Action," pages 234-238 in *Fighter Pilot, Aerial Combat Aces from 1914 to the Present Day*, edited by Stanley M. Ulanoff (1962; revised edition, New York: Prentice Hall Press, 1986).

Flight Lines

"Everywhere I looked there were MiGs, and I didn't see any other F-4s around. So I headed east." Randy Cunningham was heading back toward his carrier, the Constellation. As he reached the coast he spotted a lone MiG 17 approaching head on. As the planes converged the MiG opened fire. "His whole nose lit up like a Christmas tree!" recalled the pilot. The F-4 rolled to escape the onslaught and the dogfight began. Usually, the MiGs would make one pass and then turn north, toward home. However, in this case, both aircraft turned back to reengage. Both of the jets fought for the advantage and finally the MiG, probably low on fuel, nosed over and fled nearly straight down. The pilot of the F-4, now with the advantage, pursued and launched a Sidewinder heat-seeking missile. A few seconds latter a quick flash and small puff signified a hit and the MiG flew into the ground. It was later reported that the MiG pilot was a Communist ace called Colonel Toon. At the time it was said that Colonel Toon had shot down 13 American aircraft, more than any pilot during the conflict, but other sources report that Toon was a fictional pilot invented by the North Vietnamese.

The experience of Randy Cunningham and William Driscoll paraphrased from *Fighting Jets* by Bryce Walker (Alexandria, VA: Time-Life Books, 1983).

the bombing throughout the North, and serious peace negotiations began in January 1969.

On 6 April 1972, an aerial interdiction campaign called Linebacker began. It was initially called Freedom Trail, but was quickly designated Linebacker, and then later Linebacker I. The operation was designed to halt a North Vietnamese offensive. On 16 April, B-52s bombed the fuel storage tanks at Haiphong. They were escorted by F-105s, F-4s, F-111s, and Wild Weasel aircraft. Shortly afterward, Navy aircraft joined the fighter-bombers in battering a tank farm and a warehouse complex on the outskirts of Hanoi. When these attacks failed to slow the offensive, naval aircraft began mining the harbors on 8 May; two days later, the Nixon administration extended the aerial interdiction campaign throughout all of North Vietnam.

In terms of tactics employed and results obtained, Linebacker I was a vast improvement over Rolling Thunder. During Linebacker, U.S. aircraft attacked targets like airfields, powerplants, and radio stations, which disrupted the flow of supplies and reinforcements to the units fighting in the South. Laser-guided bombs proved effective, especially against bridges, severing the bridge at Thanh Hoa, which had survived Rolling Thunder, and the highway and railroad bridges over the Red River at Hanoi. North Vietnamese MiGs gave battle throughout Linebacker I, but they failed to gain control of the sky, in part because U.S. radar detected enemy interceptors rising from runways, which enabled controllers to direct Air Force and Navy fighters against them.

Operation Linebacker II began on 18 December 1972. During the eleven-day operation, 3,000 sorties and 40,000 tons of bombs penetrated the most concentrated air defenses of North Vietnam. The decision to proceed with the bombing of the North came from President Richard Nixon, who had by that time turned complete control of the Vietnam War over to the Chairman of the Joint Chiefs of Staff, Admiral Thomas Moorer. Eleven days after the B-52s began Linebacker II, the United States' involvement in Vietnam was essentially over. The peace talks that had come to a stalemate in October 1972 resumed on 8 January 1973. Within 30 days after the final bomb was dropped, Le Duc Tho and Henry Kissinger reached an agreement. They signed the Paris Peace Accords on 27 January 1973.

Linebacker II was very costly to the United States. Over 26 aircraft were shot down by V-750 surface-to-air missiles (SAMs). A total of over 1,200 SAMs had been fired. Fifteen of the aircraft shot down by the

Historical Note

In support of containment, the CIA conducted covert and paramilitary operations in Southeast Asia. It used "front" organizations, proprietary companies wholly owned by the Agency but operating under commercial guise. Organized in the 1960s, the CIA had several airlines: Air America, Air Asia, Civil Air Transport, Intermountain Aviation, and Southern Air Transport. Employed by Bird and Son, Ernest C. Brace was flying people and supplies for a CIA operation in Laos when he was captured at Boum Lao in 1965. Taken to North Vietnam, he remained a civilian prisoner of war for years. His story is told in the book, *A Code to Keep, the True Story of America's Longest-Held Civilian Prisoner of War in Vietnam*, by Ernest C. Brace (New York: St. Martin's Press, 1988).

missiles were Boeing B-52s. Of the 92 B-52 crewmembers shot down, over half were either recovered or captured alive, the remainder were killed or missing. The 129 B-52s that participated in the attacks were sent in three waves of bombers. These missions made up the largest armada of bombers assembled since World War II. The success of Linebacker II forced the North Vietnamese back to the peace negotiations in Paris. Once the North Vietnamese agreed to come back to the negotiation table, Linebacker II bombing raids stopped and peace terms were negotiated.

For the United States, the cost of involvement was high: More than 6.3 million tons of bombs fell during the undeclared war. This was more than three times the amount dropped on Germany and Japan during World War II. More than 2,500 aircraft were lost along with over 2,000 pilots and crewmen. It was estimated that over 150,000 Americans and Vietnamese died during the undeclared war.

Although the U.S. involvement in Vietnam ended in 1973, the war was not over for South Vietnam. The conflict, which had started with the French more than a decade and a half earlier, had been going poorly for the South Vietnamese. In March of 1975 the North mounted its final offensive and in less than four weeks captured the capital of the South, Saigon.

Middle East

The Arab-Israeli conflict of 1956 had left an uneasy peace in the Middle East. Tension between the Arab and Israeli nations increased in the mid-1960s as Egypt, Syria, and Jordan sought and received military aid from the Soviet Union. Israel, one of the smallest countries in the Middle East, received much of its aid from the United States.

The United States and the Soviet Union competed for influence in the Middle East because the region had both strategic location and petroleum reserves. The Suez Canal was a major shipping lane between Europe and the Orient. Flights between Europe and the Orient and between Europe and Africa crossed the Middle East, and the oil there had obvious value. Yet the area was politically unstable with revolutions and coups, which made it susceptible to influence whether by foreign aid or military assistance. In addition to the Arab-Israeli conflict, there were issues of nationalism and anti-imperialism.

THE SIX DAY WAR

Syria and other Arab countries refused to accept the Israeli nation. Israel had a skirmish with Syria on 7

April 1967, when a squadron of Israeli Mirage fighter jets was sent to attack a number of artillery pieces in the Golan Heights. The artillery had been periodically shelling Israel for some time. In defense of the Israeli air strike, the Syrians quickly scrambled a number of MiG-21s. The ensuing air battle resulted in a quick victory for the Israeli fighters. Syria pleaded its case to its Arab neighbors and Egypt responded by moving additional troops into the Sinai Peninsula. By this time Israel had started to feel the pressure as hundreds of thousands of Syrian, Egyptian, Jordanian, and Iraqi troops mobilized. In efforts to avert the mounting tension, diplomatic means of resolving the crisis were explored until 5 June.

On the morning of 5 June, Israel struck its first and most decisive blow. Well after dawn, and after the Egyptian fighter patrols had returned to their bases, the Israeli Air Force took off fully loaded for war. Only a handful of aircraft remained at the Israeli air bases in defense. French-built fighters and bombers like the Super-Mystere, Mirage III, Vautour, Ouragon, and Magister aircraft sped over the Sinai desert and the Mediterranean toward Egypt and its large Air Force. The goal was to destroy the powerful Egyptian Air Force so Israeli ground forces could proceed uninhibited by Egyptian air attacks. When the Israeli attackers arrived they found the Arab aircraft easy targets as they sat on the ground. Anti-aircraft defenses brought down several attackers but, at regular intervals, new Israeli aircraft returned and destroyed the runways, surface-to-air missiles, radar sites, and other air defense weapons. (Figure 9-63)

Figure 9-63. The Mirage III

After the defeat of the Egyptian Air Force, Israel had overwhelming air power that could support the advancing ground infantry and armor. The combined forces quickly defeated the Egyptian Army in the Sinai. The air attacks by Israel destroyed all but one Arab airfield within 375 miles of Jerusalem. By the end of the war, 416 Arab aircraft had been destroyed or disabled compared to 26 for Israel. In addition, Israel had doubled the size of its territory. (Figure 9-64)

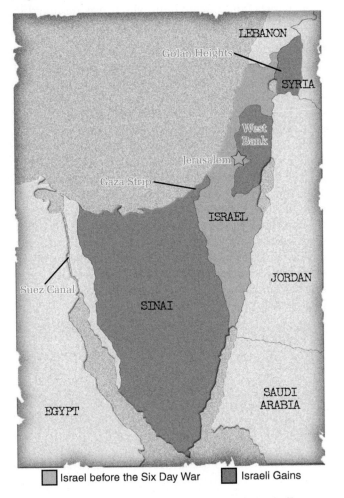

Figure 9-64. After six days of fighting, Israel had effectively doubled its occupied territory.

The Six Day War, named for the number of days it took for Israel to attain victory, changed the political climate as well as the territorial lines in the volatile Middle East. Israel, using overwhelming air power, achieved almost immediate victory. It did so by using surprise air attacks against the large numbers of Arab aircraft, airfields, and air defenses. Israel essentially destroyed the Soviet-built air power in Egypt, Jordan, and Syria before they left the ground in defense.

By the end of the war, Israeli gains included the Golan Heights from Syria, the West Bank and Jerusalem from Jordan; and the entire Sinai Peninsula up to the Suez Canal including the Gaza Strip from Egypt. One of the outcomes of the war was closure of the valuable Suez Canal for eight years due to ongoing skirmishes and fighting. It was reopened again in 1975. The war with Egypt did not

formally end until 1979, when leaders from Israel and Egypt signed a peace treaty.

The Six Day War between Israel and its Arab neighbors dramatically enhanced Dassault Aviation's stature as a manufacturer of military aircraft. Israel used the French-built fighters and bombers and proved their effectiveness. Dassault went on to produce the Mirage IV, which added to the strategic nuclear strike capability of France. It also gave Dassault the opportunity to study and research new technology, notably in the area of high skin temperatures due to high speeds, and to diversify its research into vertical take-off (Mirage III V) and variable swept-wings.

YOM KIPPUR

At the end of the Six Day War, the peace between Israel and the other Arab nations was uneasy. Egyptians regularly employed artillery in an effort to weaken and demoralize the Israelis who had dug in and created a defensive line on the east side of the Suez Canal. The same situation existed in the Golan Heights, where Palestinian guerrillas launched attacks into Israel. All around the new borders of Israel, Arab countries were rearming. The Soviet Union provided top-of-the-line air defense systems designed to counter the U.S.-supplied Israeli aircraft. Soviet fighter-bombers made their way into the Egyptian and Syrian Air Forces. It wasn't long before the Egyptians had rebuilt their Air Force to over 600 aircraft including MiG-21s and MiG-17s. Syria also purchased 360 Soviet fighters and bombers. At the same time, Israel purchased and placed into service A-4 Skyhawks and F-4 Phantoms from the United States. (Figure 9-65)

Figure 9-65. The Douglas A-4 Skyhawk was used extensively as a ground support aircraft by the U.S. Navy and by the Israeli Air Force. The Skyhawk was initially designed to operate from U.S. Navy aircraft carriers. Edward Heinemann of the Douglas Company led the design of the small Skyhawk, which was built as a simple low-cost fighter and ground-attack plane. The A-4 Skyhawk was an amazingly versatile aircraft.

After the Arab alliance determined it had sufficient strength, its members proceeded with an attack. The timing was important. The attack was planned to coincide with both the Arab and Israeli holidays. Because Yom Kippur was a Jewish holiday, it was thought that the Israelis would be off guard. Also, the Arabs thought that the Israelis would not expect an attack during the Muslim holy month of Ramadan. To a great extent they were correct. This time the surprise belonged to the Arab forces as the coordinated attack came from both Syria and Egypt on 6 October 1973.

Like the Six Day War, the surprise started with a preemptive air strike, but this time it was against Israeli air bases. The initial ground attacks came as Arabs mounted an assault to retake the territory that was previously lost in the Six Day War. The Syrians roared into the Golan Heights with heavy tanks and troops. The Syrian anti-aircraft defenses were effective against the Israeli fighters and bombers and the advance into Israel was significant. Egypt used radar-directed 23-millimeter cannons to destroy low flying Israeli aircraft. Effective Soviet-built V-750, S-125, and 3M9 surface-to-air missiles were used against medium-to-high flying fighters.

Israel's first priority was to halt the advance of Syrian tanks in the Golan Heights. The mountains in the northeast of Israel were strategic because of the high terrain and proximity to important Israeli cities and towns. The Syrians also knew the importance of the mission and used hundreds of tanks to spearhead the attack.

While the Syrians moved into the Golan Heights, the Egyptians made an effort to cross the Suez Canal and breach the Israeli defensive Bar Lev Line. Thousands of artillery rounds were sent to soften the Israeli defense line before the attacking troops crossed the canal. The Egyptians quickly breached the defenses and started overtaking strong points. Israel mobilized its air force in an effort to slow the advance on its southern front with Egypt while trying to neutralize the Syrian tanks advancing on the North.

Initially, the Soviet-supplied air defense systems of Syria and Egypt proved deadly against the U.S.-supplied aircraft. Within the first few hours of the war at least 40 Israeli jets were downed; more than had been destroyed in the entire Six Day War. The evasive maneuvers and tactics used by the jets were not effective against the overwhelming number of newer Soviet missiles. In addition, the number of Egyptian heat-seeking missiles and other anti-aircraft weapons produced a virtually impenetrable wall in the air. Israeli Electronic Counter Measures (ECM) could not jam the varying radar frequencies of all the anti-aircraft sys-

tems. Other defense systems like decoy flares, which were used to lure heat-seeking missiles away from their targets, and metal chaff, which was designed to confuse radar, were only moderately successful.

In an effort to neutralize the air defense systems, attacking Israeli aircraft launched radar-homing Shrike missiles. Some missiles found the defensive radar sites and rode the radar's emitting beams down to their origins. The number of air defense sites was reduced and air support started to slow the advance in both the north and south. For the first time, vulnerability on the Israeli side was evident, and both Syria and Egypt proved their new military and organizational strength. The war lasted less than one month and almost brought the United States and the Soviet Union into the conflict. By the end of the war, Israel had advanced even farther into Egyptian and Syrian territory. Some of this land was used as leverage to help attain a peace agreement brokered by the United Nations (U.N.) and the United States and to create U.N. control zones. (Figure 9-66)

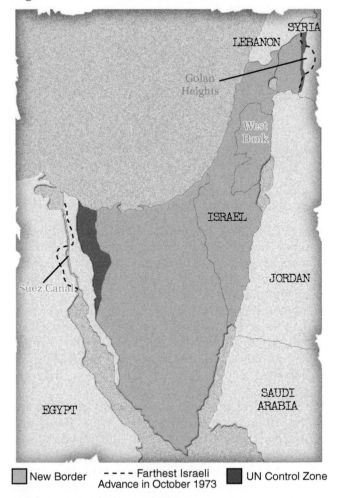

Figure 9-66. Israel occupied territory in Egypt and Syria before the end of the Yom Kippur War. After the war ended Israeli troops withdrew to new borders.

In October of 1973, as a result of the Western support of Israel and to influence the price of oil for economic gain, the Arab countries banded together and enforced an oil embargo. This embargo placed a heavy burden on the American auto and aviation industries and encouraged manufacturers to produce more fuel-efficient automobiles and airplanes. In 1974 and 1975 disengagement agreements were reached between Syria and Israel. The agreements left Syria with a small part of the Golan Heights, and a U.N. force was stationed there to monitor the agreements.

LIMITED WARS

Although a cold war is one without overt military conflict, the Cold War had many armed battles limited in geography to specific locales and limited to conventional, nonnuclear weapons. In addition to Vietnam and the Middle East wars, there were wars in other parts of Asia, in Africa, and Latin America.

Africa

In Cape Town, South Africa, in 1960, British Prime Minister Harold Macmillan observed, "The wind of change is blowing through this continent, and, whether we like it or not, this growth of national consciousness is a political fact." Great Britain, France, and Belgium granted independence to their respective colonies in Africa in the 1960s. Other imperial rulers tried to maintain colonies and control while nationalists demanded both independence and black rule.

Portugal held Angola, Mozambique, and Guinea-Bissau. South Africa held South West Africa (Namibia). White Rhodesians declared independence but formed a white-led republic. The rulers of the southern lands of Africa had routinely used aircraft to control the large holdings with few personnel. Now they used air power for mobility and firepower in wars against insurgencies. They also used aircraft to spray herbicides to reduce cover for rebels, especially along the sides of roads, and to prevent crops from feeding rebels.

The international arms embargoes against Portugal and Rhodesia forced clandestine purchases of aircraft and the modification of civil aircraft. Wealthier South Africa used its professional air force against Cuban and Angolan forces in order to protect the Namibian border. The imperial forces developed strategies and tactics to maximize the use of limited air power.

Encouraged when neighboring Congo gained its independence from Belgium in 1960, nationalists in Angola got guns from the Congo and revolted against Portugal in 1961. Nationalists in the other colonies also caused unrest. Once a great imperial power, but now one of the poorest countries in Europe, Portugal lacked the capability to wage a major war. It immediately expanded its armed forces and recruited natives to fight the rebels.

By 1974 over half the Portuguese military personnel, about 150,000 men, were stationed in Africa. This was a lot for Portugal, but not enough to suppress unrest in three geographically large colonies. The Portuguese studied the experiences of Britain in Malaya, France in Algeria, and the United States in Vietnam, and decided to follow the French model. They organized army and air units as counter-insurgency forces, used both airplanes and helicopters, and built airports.

Portugal used existing North American T-6s and bought more from the French who had a surplus after quitting Algeria. Portugal also bought 100 Dornier Do 27s, high-wing, light utility planes capable of using rough dirt airstrips. Initially, the Portuguese also used the Lockheed PV-2 bomber in the colonies. In the mid-sixties they bought used Fiat G.91R trainers from Germany; these planes could carry machine guns, bombs, and enough fuel for counter-insurgency missions. For logistics, the Portuguese obtained Noratlas transports from France and DC-6 transports from the United States. They even got seven Martin B-26 bombers before the international arms embargo interfered with acquisition of aircraft.

As the French had learned in Angola, the Portuguese discovered that helicopters were particularly well suited for counterinsurgency missions. While fighting in Africa, Portugal bought 143 Alouette III helicopters, made by Sud Aviation in France. It also purchased 12 of Sud Aviation's larger Puma helicopters. (Figure 9-67)

Figure 9-67. Portuguese Alouette III helicopter

In the early 1970s, when the rebel groups acquired shoulder-fired surface-to-air missiles, the nature of the wars changed. By then, Portugal's support for the war and the morale of Portuguese military personnel had declined. A coup in Portugal in 1974 installed a new government, which in 1975 granted independence to the African colonies.

Rhodesia became independent in 1965, but under white rule. Discontent became unrest, which in 1972 became a military matter. The government used cross-border raids to attack rebels taking sanctuary in neighboring countries, but negotiations rather than combat ended the war in 1975. South Africa used covert and overt tactics in an effort to hold South West Africa, which it had controlled since World War I. It made cross-border raids—part of a policy called "forward defense"— into civil war-torn independent Angola, where rebels got military aid from the Communist bloc. Again, negotiations, not combat, brought independence to the black nationalists of Namibia in 1990.

These African conflicts were long-term wars of attrition. Aircraft provided transport, reconnaissance, and firepower—mostly to back up small infantry units. Aircraft helped the ruling governments inflict heavy losses on the rebels. But the wind of change blew the colonial powers away.

Afghanistan

The Soviet Union invaded Afghanistan in 1979 when a coup overthrew the pro-Soviet government of Nur Mohammed Taraki. As Soviet troops moved across the border, airborne divisions landed in the capital, Kabul, and took the city. Within days airborne units had captured most of the cities of Afghanistan. The Soviets installed a pro-Soviet government, but Mujahideen insurgents resisted both the Soviets and the Soviet-installed Afghan government.

The Soviets found themselves in a war of attrition. They had the largest air force in the world, and they used their air resources in Afghanistan. They sent fighter and bomber units to Afghanistan, and they made long-range aircraft in the Soviet Union available. The Sukhoi Su-25 fighter-bomber and ground attack airplane proved effective at supporting combat operations. They used Mil Mi-17 and Mi-8 helicopter transports. They also used Mil Mi-24 gunship helicopters. High temperatures and dust storms affected flying and maintenance of aircraft, particularly the helicopters. (Figure 9-68)

These Soviet air resources went against Mujahideen rebels armed with small arms and rockets—the Strela

Figure 9-68. The Soviet Mi-24 helicopter saw action in Afghanistan as a troop transport and ground attack gunship.

2 shoulder-launched anti-aircraft missile and later the American-made Stinger anti-aircraft missiles. Aircraft swept pockets of resistance, seized high ground, and bombed the rebels. In the end, in 1989, the Soviets evacuated from Afghanistan.

Latin America

Among the many limited wars in Latin America were a series of overlapping rebel movements in Guatemala from the early 1960s onward and a civil war in El Salvador from 1980 to 1992. El Salvador accepted military aid from the United States; Guatemala did not. In the case of Nicaragua, the United States supported the Contras fighting the leftist Sandinista government, which in 1979 had overthrown the Somoza dictatorship; Anatasio Samoza Debayle was the third Samoza to rule. Argentina attacked the British-claimed Falkland Islands in 1982, and the United States invaded Grenada in 1983. Democratic Colombia also had insurgent groups fighting the government. Marxist rebels fought in Argentina and Uruguay, and rural peasants rose in revolt in Peru.

Light planes, like the Cessna A-37 Dragonfly fighter-bomber (a light attack airplane), and helicopters, both transports and gunships, played significant roles in some of the rebel conflicts. Fighters, bombers, and cargo planes participated in various actions. Few rebels had anti-aircraft weapons. They used guerilla warfare tactics. The governments adopted counterinsurgency measures. Guatemala even impressed civil pilots into a military-commanded Comando Especial Reserva Aerea unit. The United States used the Lockheed C-130 Hercules to carry parachute troops to Grenada. The Argentinians used the Dassault Super Entendard jet to launch French-made

Exocet missiles against British ships defending the Falklands, and the British Navy used Sea Harrier jump-jets and Westland Sea King helicopters. The number and variety of wars in Latin America makes generalizing difficult. (Figure 9-69)

Figure 9-69. The British Navy flew Harrier jump jets from carriers during the Falkland conflict.

In a revealing Cold War contrast, Soviet leader Khrushchev considered wars for independence or national liberation as "inevitable and desirable," whereas American president Kennedy suspected Soviet-sponsored subversion and aggression behind such conflicts. Their successors took similar stances.

DEFENSE SYSTEMS

Deterrence was a defense policy, but not the only one. Both the United States and the Soviet Union sought more tangible solutions to the threat of nuclear war—solutions based on military technology.

Flight Lines

"You want to hear early warning radars at least once a month," explained John Bergen, an intelligence officer in the 1950s and 1960s. "And border ones are so critical, so threatening, you might want to hear them—look for that particular radar—every time you flew a mission."

John Bergen as quoted in *By Any Means Necessary, America's Heroes Flying Secret Missions in a Hostile World,* by William E. Burrows (New York: Penguin, 2001).

Flight Lines

"One of the things that I've seen in the recon business is that we push each other. The Russians would never have had to have the Token radar if we hadn't succeeded in adopting tactics and airplanes that could overwhelm what they had prior to that. So they came up with Token radar, which was a very beautiful radar."

Jack Parrish, ferret or intelligence pilot in Siberia during the 1950s, as quoted in *By Any Means Necessary, America's Heroes Flying Secret Missions in a Hostile World,* by William E. Burrows (New York: Penguin, 2001).

Early Warning

Given the fear of nuclear attack, both sides developed systems to warn of inbound missiles or bombers. Radar was a key element. The initial systems were constructed in the early 1950s, and most were replaced with new, more enduring systems by the end of the decade. The United States and Canada, working jointly as the North American Air Defense Command (NORAD), constructed a Distant Early Warning (DEW) line of radar stations from the Aleutian Islands across the top of North America to Greenland. (Figure 9-70)

If radar should detect inbound missiles or bombers, how would anyone at other points along the early warning line know? The communication links we take for granted today did not exist in the 1950s. The United States built the White Alice Communication System, a line of tropospheric scattering communication stations that stretched from the Aleutian Islands across Alaska. This system linked with Canada's section, which extended across northern Canada to Greenland. The North Atlantic Radio System took the line to Iceland and to Great Britain. NATO managed lines between Iceland and both Great Britain and Norway as well as the line south through Europe to Italy to Greece and to Turkey. This communication line basically sat on the West side of the border between East and West. On the East side, the communists also had a long line of troposcattering stations. The United States also maintained troposcattering communication stations at Guantanamo Bay, Cuba, and Florida City, Florida; these stations opened in 1959 and remained operational through the Bay of Pigs invasion and the Cuban missile crisis.

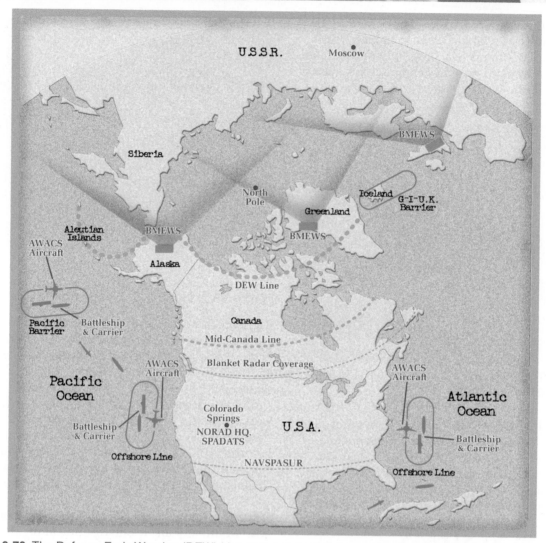

Figure 9-70. The Defense Early Warning (DEW) Line was a radar defense system later sypplemented by the Ballistic Missile Early Warning System (BMEWS) and the Navy Space Survillance (NAVSPASUR) system.

In the late 1970s satellite communications made the troposcattering stations obsolete, and most closed by the end of the decade.

Anti-Ballistic Missile

The superpowers did not fully rely upon deterrence. Each developed an anti-ballistic missile (ABM) defense system to protect their homeland. "It was an umbrella to protect our population against a possible missile strike," Nikolai Detinov of the Soviet Defense Ministry later explained. Each ABM was an interceptor missile. In theory, ABMs could destroy missiles in flight.

The deployment of an effective ABM system by either side could destabilize the nuclear balance of power. ABMs upset mutually assured destruction, the balance of terror, because if one side could neutralize the weapons of the other, that side would have an advantage. ABMs upset the balance of deterrence.

Historical Note

Troposcattering bounced ultra high frequency radio signals off large billboard antennas. The signals bounced toward the troposphere about five miles above ground. The troposphere bounced the signals, at an angle, back to Earth—to a receiving billboard antenna as much as 200 miles from the sending station. The receiving station would then bounce the signals to the next station down the line. Redundancy in the form of dual antennas allowed better capture of the signal, so stations had four antennas—two facing upline and two downline. The troposcattering network in Alaska became operational in 1958. It was called White Alice, and it provided the first wireless telephone and telegraph service to civilian as well as military users in Alaska. In Canada the radar and communication stations used the name DEW Line. Over the North Atlantic, the system was called the North Atlantic Radio System. NATO operated the Ace High system in Europe and the Middle East.

Although both countries had deployed limited ABM systems, they did not rush into production because of the costs of the system and the possibilities of the other side beating the defense system. But balance needed to be maintained, and the United States tried to convince the Soviets to abandon ABMs.

The United States and the Soviet Union reached an agreement to limit ABMs in 1972. The Limitation of Anti-Ballistic Missile Systems Treaty prohibited the superpowers from deploying ABM systems whether "sea-based, air-based, space-based, or mobile land-based." In the preface to the agreement the two nations declared "their intention to achieve at the earliest possible date the cessation of the nuclear arms race and to take effective measures toward reductions in strategic arms, nuclear disarmament, and general and complete disarmament." Each nation was allowed two ABM sites, one defending the nation's capitol and the other defending an intercontinental ballistic missile field.

In 1974 the nations agreed to maintain only one ABM site per nation. The Soviet Union kept its ABM defense of Moscow. The United States chose to defend the ICBMs near Grand Forks, North Dakota. This ABM system was deactivated in 1976.

MRV and MIRV

Rather than maintain a costly ABM system, the United States sought to foil the Soviet ABM. Any ABM system could be overwhelmed by presenting more incoming targets than the system could shoot down. Both sides developed reentry decoys by building multiple reentry vehicles (MRVs) and penetration aids to help their warheads reach their targets in spite of defending ABMs. As smaller nuclear weapons were developed, it became possible to place more than one warhead on each missile. At the height of its trajectory, a missile could jettison multiple warheads to fall separately to their target. Later, more complex multiple independent reentry vehicles (MIRVs) were introduced. Each MIRV had several warheads equipped with guidance systems, so that the falling warheads could be directed to separate targets. Thus, more warheads could be allocated to each target, and even if a few missiles failed or were shot down, enough would get through to ensure destruction of all targets. Defense against a MRV or MIRV would require one missile for each warhead and therefore a huge investment in an ABM system. The Soviets could not afford to make several anti-ballistic missiles to counter each MIRV warhead. Because ABM missiles and radar systems were more expensive than nuclear reentry vehicles, the expense and technical

challenge of creating a workable ABM system became hopelessly prohibitive.

Strategic Defense Initiative

President Ronald Reagan rejected mutually assured destruction. The United States had no anti-ballistic missile system. Reagan wanted a shield. In 1983 he announced what that shield could be. He called it the strategic defense initiative (SDI), but the press and critics labeled it "Star Wars." It would shield the United States from inbound missiles. The proposal was a bargaining chip that put pressure on the Soviet Union. Reagan wanted more. He wanted protection against any kind of missile attack. (Figure 9-71)

Historical Note

In 1981, in the midst of the Cold War and a renewed arms race, President Ronald W. Reagan told a Notre Dame commencement audience, "The years ahead are great ones for this country, for the cause of freedom and the spread of civilization. The West won't contain communism, it will transcend communism. It ... will dismiss it as some bizarre chapter in human history whose last pages are even now being written."

From the transcript of Ronald Reagans' commencement address at Notre Dame on 17 may 1981 as posted on the official website of the Ronald Reagan Presidential Library and Foundation, at http://www.reagan.utexas.edu/archives/speeches/1981/51781a.htm/.

SDI would violate the 1972 Anti-Ballistic Missile Treaty, and upset the balance of deterrence and the status quo of the Cold War. Critics also argued that whatever the defense, an offense could be designed to get around it, and the defense-offensive developments would escalate the arms race. Technologically,

Figure 9-71. Although the Strategic Defense Initiative did not actually produce the "Star Wars" type technology for shooting down ballistic missiles, it did have military spin-offs. These spin-offs included new space technologies and missile tracking technologies.

critics said the system is unfeasible. Supporters noted that if the system worked, an aggressor could not win a war and, therefore, would not attack. But, critics countered, the owner of the system, secure from retaliation, might strike first.

Reagan argued in 1983 that the system would make nuclear weapons obsolete. The Soviet Union tried to tie any Strategic Arms Limitation Talks agreement to halting Star Wars. That did not happen. Throughout Reagan's administration SDI received research and development funds.

THE END

The cliché is that the Cold War began with a bang—the atomic bomb explosions at the end of World War II. In keeping with the cliché, the Cold War ended with a whimper. One side simply quit the fight. In 1989 the Soviet Union watched the opening of the Berlin Wall and the collapse of communist regimes in Eastern Europe. The costs of the Space Race, the arms race, and the Cold War were too much, financially as well as otherwise. Germany unified in 1990. The Warsaw Pact officially disbanded in 1991, and later in the year the Union of Soviet Socialist Republics dissolved. There was no more Soviet Union, no more Cold War.

Did the Cold War accomplish anything? If the goal of the Cold War was to prevent a World War III, and that was certainly the goal behind establishing the United Nations, then yes, it accomplished plenty. The East and West fought a "cold" hard war around the world, but the two sides limited armed conflict to specific geographical areas and to conventional, non-nuclear weapons. There was neither World War III nor nuclear devastation.

Since the United States emerged from the Cold War as the only superpower in the world, it won the direct conflict with the Soviet Union. Japan and West Germany won too. Defeated in World War II and thereafter protected by alliances with the United States and the West, these countries developed domestic, regional, and global economies, and Germany eventually achieved unification.

Because each side tried to force its will and way upon the other, the Cold War was a long, protracted conflict. What has been lost to decades of fear and mistrust, to ubiquitous defense spending, and to the international power struggle? That is a hard question to answer. Gorbachev said, "We all lost the Cold War." Did he mean it, or was he just toying out loud with a thought?

JET AGE

By definition, the term "Jet Age" simply describes the introduction and adoption of jet-powered aircraft in commercial and military aviation. In popular culture, the term meant more. The Jet Age was a new age separating the present from the drab World War II years. The Jet Age featured brand-new, modern, state-of-the-art technology in an age overshadowed by the technological cloud of nuclear weapons tested, stockpiled, and deployed by the two superpowers. Although the Jet Age included the military conversion to jet power (which actually led to the civilian applications), in popular culture the term often applied to what was called a transportation revolution. This term was coined because of how the Jet Age affected the traveling public, even to the point of redefining who the traveling public was. People who had never flown before became regular airline passengers. Airports that once catered to the business traveler now built family-friendly terminals. The Jet Age suggested speed, wealth, mobility, and success. The Jet Age was seen as evidence of the superior Western way of life, because the jetliners, jet passengers, and jet destinations were mostly in the West.

Boeing 727

The De Havilland Comet and the Vickers Viscount, both built in Great Britain, the Boeing 707 and Douglas DC-8, manufactured in the United States, and the Tupolev Tu-104 and Ilyushin Il-62, made in the Soviet Union, ushered in the Jet Age. These jetliners, turbojets developed after World War II and entering production in the 1950s and early 1960s, offered incredible speed and power in comparison to their piston-engined counterparts. The Boeing 707 and 727 were popular new jetliners of the Jet Age.

Both remained in production for more than twenty years. Pan American used the 707 when opening the first around-the-world passenger jet service in 1959. The 727 filled the demand for jet service on shorter routes. The widespread acceptance of the 707 and 727 helped make air travel accessible financially and geographically to the masses. (Figure 9-72)

The East lacked the financial resources and industrial development of the West; nonetheless, the Tupolev factory in the Soviet Union built over 200 Tu-104 jetliners in the 1950s and 1960s. These were primarily to upgrade the service on the national airline, Aeroflot, and secondarily to serve Communist bloc allies.

ENGINE DEVELOPMENT

The engine, of course, was key to the Jet Age. Prior to the development of jet engine technology, large radial reciprocating engines powered most transport aircraft. At the end of World War II, several types of reciprocating or piston engines could produce a couple thousand horsepower. Three examples are the 2,200 horsepower Wright R3350 engine with 18

Figure 9-72. The Pan American 707 *Clipper America* prepares for the inaugural flight from Idlewild Airport in New York to LeBourget Field in Paris, 26 October 1958. The U.S. Army Division band played the Star Spangled Banner as 111 passengers and a crew of 11 boarded.

Flight Lines

"We burst out of the highest cloud layer into the upper air," pilot Sam Saint later recalled, "then it hit me. This was right—the way flying ought to be: smooth, solid, quiet and with obvious power to throw away. Everything about this machine built confidence." Although this reflects the feelings of an airline pilot who was more accustomed to the noise and vibration from the piston-engine transports, the same feelings would be echoed by new travelers. The ability to carry more passengers in newer aircraft such as the 707 opened up the possibility of travel to many people.

American Airlines Captain Sam Saint in regard to flying the Boeing 707 and as quoted in *The Jet Age* by Robert J. Serling (Alexandria, VA: Time-Life Books, 1982).

cylinders in two rows; the 2,700 horsepower Bristol Centaurus with 18 cylinders in two rows; and the Pratt & Whitney R-4360 Wasp Major with 28 cylinders in four rows that yielded 3,000-4,000 horsepower. These radial engines were big, needy machines. They required a lot of maintenance, and they had a relatively short service time between overhauls.

Whereas the big radials were mechanical monsters, the new jets were aerodynamic puzzles. The aerodynamics of the turbojet has antecedents in the theoretical work of Daniel Bernoulli of Switzerland in the 18th century. This work also included early 20th-century theorists like Ludwig Prandtl of Germany, Theodore von Karman of the United States, and A.A. Griffith of England. The pre-war and wartime work of Frank Whittle in Britain and Hans von Ohain in Germany produced the first jet aircraft engines and sparked the aviation industry to developments that, by the 1960s, were creating the new Jet Age.

Turbojet

The early jet engines were not a great improvement over the radial engines in terms of maintenance or

fuel efficiency, but the jet was clearly faster and simpler in some ways. Basically, the early jet consisted of a single shaft, a compressor at one end, a turbine at the other, and some flame cans in the middle combustion area to help stabilize combustion. The jet engine, also called the turbojet, uses a "jet" of air for thrust. The engine draws in air, compresses the air, mixes it with fuel, and ignites the mixture. The resulting combustion increases the volume of the gases and thereby the jet or thrust and also exhaust. As a heat engine, the jet's efficiency depends in part on the temperature of the exhaust; in general, the higher the temperature the more energy released from the fuel. (Figure 9-73)

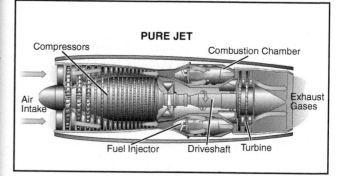

Figure 9-73. The turbojet engine.

Uneven combustion in early engines often caused turbine blade failure. Bleeding some air from the compressor through hollow turbine blades relieved that problem, but also made blades expensive. Water injection cooled the exhaust, and caused the tell-tale smoke when the engine was started and the plane took off, till high-temperature alloys and better throttle control removed the need for carrying cooling water and the injection system. Early Boeing 707s, for example, carried 600 gallons of water for the injection system, but later models could carry more payload in lieu of water. Two-stage or two-spool engines had more than one turbine, each one driving a separate compressor at a different speed, specifically a speed efficient for that particular turbine. More efficient at high altitudes and high speeds, the jets required long runways for takeoff; 5,000 feet was common. Short strips and small fields could not accommodate the aircraft. Takeoff noise was also a factor in the vicinity of an airport.

Technologically, the problems were more difficult to solve than this brief introduction suggests, but engine manufacturers competed to overcome the problems and to produce the most marketable products. New among the postwar engine manufacturers were companies with experience with water pumps, turbine pumps, steam turbines, and turbo air compressors; companies like General Electric in the United States. Some traditional piston-engine makers, like Pratt & Whitney in the United States and Bristol Siddeley and Rolls Royce in Great Britain, made the technological leap to jet engines. (Bristol and Rolls merged in 1966.)

By the early 1960s the jet engine run-time between overhauls was around 1,000 hours, which was comparable to the large radial engines of the time. As jet technology improved, the interval between jet engine overhauls grew. By the mid-1970s, jets had increased the time between overhauls by a factor of five over that of the earliest jet engines. Increased strength of materials and other technological advancements, often developed under military contract, accounted for the rapid improvement of jet engines.

Turbofan

The next major development was the turbofan, sometimes referred to as a fanjet or bypass jet, which came out of research and development at Rolls Royce. The British had initially made turbofan engines or bypass engines like the Conway and Spey, which allowed some air to bypass the combustion section of the engine. The small amount of air going around the combustion section of these early engines did little more than assist in keeping the engine cool. A huge gain in efficiency and noise reduction was made when, in the early 1960s, the high-bypass jet was developed. Instead of running all of the intake air through the engine and exhausting it as high-speed hot gases, a large amount of air was passed through fans and around the combustion portion of the engine. The high-bypass type of engine produced more power while increasing efficiency. An additional benefit was that the relatively cool bypass air

shrouded the hot exhaust gases and the engine produced significantly less noise. (Figure 9-74)

Rolls-Royce created the first production "fanjet" or turbofan jet engine, called the Conway. The engine was tried on several different aircraft, including the Boeing 707 and Douglas DC-8. The increased efficiency produced by the turbofan over the early turbojet engines helped increase the economical operation of the airline fleet and increased the range of airliners. This technology was expanded upon by the high-bypass turbofan that, for the first time, forced the majority of the air around instead of through the engine. Rolls-Royce launched the RB.211 turbofan for the Lockheed L-1011 TriStar in the early 1970s and provided later RB.211s for Boeing B747s in the late 1970s.

Turboprop

Coupling a conventional propeller to a jet engine had been used before 1959; in fact, it was applied on the British Vickers Viscount even before the development of the Comet jet airliner. Basically, the turboprop engine uses the turbine for rotary force rather than jet thrust; that is, to turn the propeller. This combined the smooth operation of the jet engine with the familiar and well-accepted propeller. Also, with the improved power-to-weight ratio, the jet-props were able to carry more payload, use shorter runways, and fly economically at lower altitudes. Other advantages included the propeller's higher efficiency at low altitudes and low speeds. At high speeds, wave drag reduces the efficiency of propellers, but a swept-wing style propeller, like the swept wing on a high-speed airplane, reduces the wave drag. A turboprop using the swept-back propeller is sometimes called a prop-fan. Turbine engines also powered helicopters. (Figure 9-75)

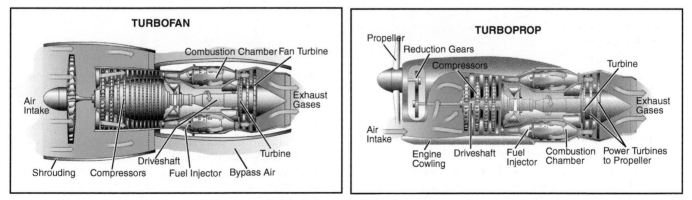

Figure 9-74. The turbofan engine.

Figure 9-75. The turboprop engine.

Historical Note

Maynard Pennell, a Boeing engineer, had this to say about the first "fan" engine produced by General Electric and the competition it produced with Pratt & Whitney.

"In January 1958 we (Boeing) told Pratt & Whitney in New York that if they didn't offer us the turbo-fan we would have no choice but to shift to the GE aft-fan. They acted. On a Saturday morning 4 or 5 days later they invited us to Hartford for a look. Wright Parkins was the guy, outspoken, competent, who turned around at our demand.

We saw an engine that they had put together on paper in a few days. The first two stages of the compressor—the fan stages—were literally taken from a nuclear-powered engine they had given up on after 8 to 10 years. These stages used titanium blades and had considerable running experience and good performance data. They put this in front of a J57 engine. Then they added the new turbine stages to provide the extra power for these large fans, and that was their answer."

As quoted in Carl Solberg's *Conquest of the Skies*, (Boston: Little, Brown and Company, 1979).

Pratt & Whitney J57/JT3C-8

G.E. Aft-fan

Historical Note

In 1962 the development of the C-5 cargo aircraft required the use of a very large and fuel-efficient jet engine. The specifications required a new engine with incredible power that had not yet been developed. The problem required a new approach which was not answered by modifying current production bypass engines, primarily the Conway and the Spey engines, which used some bypass air to keep the engine cool and increase power. The answer was a new engine developed by GE called the TF39. It had a pressure ratio of 23 to 1 and a bypass ratio of 8 to 1. This meant that the engine would produce very high pressure and that

nearly 8 times the amount of air would bypass the engine's combustion process to provide the majority of the thrust. Previous engines had roughly half the pressure ratio and virtually no bypass air. The TF39 was the first high bypass jet engine with a forward fan, and it changed forever the way turbine type engines were designed.

U.S. COMMERCIAL AVIATION

The jet engine needed a jet airframe, the combination of engine and civil airframe was a jetliner. The Jet Age increased the production demands of established aircraft manufacturers as more airlines phased out propeller-driven aircraft and switched to jet aircraft and as the number of airlines around the world increased. The United States maintained a substantial lead in jet aircraft production through the 1970s. Global competition in aircraft manufacturing in the 1980s led to a number of mergers and consolidations. Some manufacturers expanded their military developments into commercial aircraft lines while others concentrated exclusively on military developments and shut down their commercial divisions.

Boeing

The Boeing Company produced several large jet aircraft for the military, including the B-47 and the B-52 bombers, prior to the introduction of the civilian 707. The success and experience gained from the military market helped the company attract and retain customers in the civilian market. Boeing's first commercial jetliner was the 707, which began a highly successful line of 7XX jetliners, each model featuring variations identified by dash numbers.

The 707s were four-engine airliners, most of which were powered by the Pratt & Whitney JT3D engine. Boeing flew the 707 for the first time on 20 December 1957, and soon thereafter, in 1958, Pan American World Airlines placed the first commercial 707 into service. To facilitate international sales, Boeing and other manufacturers provided offsets. In one offset case, for example, British Overseas Airways installed Rolls Royce Conway 50B turbofan engines on 707-400 airliners that the British firm bought. Boeing reduced the price of the airliners to offset the cost of those engines, a cost borne by the buyer. The offset allowed manufacturers in both countries to benefit from making a sale, and the offset allowed the purchaser to use domestic products as well as foreign. Boeing delivered the last commercial 707 in 1979—to Morocco.

The demand for short-to-medium range aircraft intensified after the introduction of the highly successful 707. Boeing responded by producing the 727, a smaller three-engine plane. Pratt & Whitney JT8D engines powered these planes. The first flight of a Boeing 727 occurred on 9 February 1963. The 727 entered airline service the next year. Like the 707, the 727 remained in production for over twenty years. The versatility and reliability of the Boeing 727 made the plane even more popular than the 707. The 727 became the best-selling airliner in history, to that date, when orders passed the 1,000 mark in September 1972. Total sales reached 1,831. (Figure 9-76)

Figure 9-76. The Boeing 727 was the first trijet introduced into commercial service.

Boeing developed a full line of airliners because the airlines operated routes of different distances, with dif-

ferent traffic and different requirements. Training, flight operations, and maintenance would be easier for the airline if it purchased similar equipment that came from the same manufacturer. In response to demand for an aircraft that would efficiently carry fewer than 100 passengers, Boeing started production of the twin-engine 737 in 1965. Like the 727, the 737 used JT8D powerplants. Boeing eventually sold over 4,000 of these airliners. (Figure 9-77)

Figure 9-77. The Boeing 737 production began in February 1965. The first test flight occurred on 9 April 1967, and the first 737 was delivered to Lufthansa airlines on 28 December 1967.

Boeing then looked to the market for larger airplanes. To carry 300 or more passengers, Boeing's next jetliner would be a jumbo jet, a widebody. When the first Boeing 747 rolled out of the factory in September, 1968, it was the largest commercial airliner ever made. The 747 entered commercial service in 1970. (Figure 9-78)

Figure 9-78. Since the introduction of the basic 747 in 1968, Boeing has delivered more than 1,000 747s. The longevity and popularity of the airplane is based on its low seat-mile cost, flexibility, and range.

The 757 and 767 represent a new line of Boeing planes. Both were developed in response to the oil crisis of 1973, when fuel efficiency became critical. The extended-range, two-aisle 767 made its first flight in September 1981, and entered service in September 1982. The narrow-body (single-aisle) 757 first flew in February 1982 and entered service the following year. Both have twin-engines, the 757 powered by either Rolls-Royce RB.211s or Pratt & Whitney PW2000-series engines, and the 767 powered by either Pratt & Whitney 4062 or General Electric CF6 engines. Offering options, like choice of engines, was a marketing tool developed in competitive times. When British Airways ordered the 757, it again received an offset in price by using Rolls-Royce engines. (Figure 9-79)

Douglas and McDonnell

Douglas had dominated the commercial market since the introduction of the popular piston-powered DC-3, DC-6, and DC-7—until the Boeing 707. Douglas answered Boeing's jetliner with a plane very similar in appearance to the 707. The first DC-8 to enter commercial service was flown by Delta Airlines on 18 September 1959. A modified DC-8-40 became the first jet airliner to break the sound barrier on 24 March 1960. Douglas produced 556 DC-8 aircraft, a respectable number, but Boeing produced almost twice as many 707s. Douglas had a good design, fair performance, and a price a few hundred thousand dollars lower than Boeing's 707, but Boeing became more, not less, dominant in the commercial airline industry. (Figure 9-80)

Douglas decided to produce a smaller twin jet to replace the aging piston-powered aircraft used on short routes. The idea was that perhaps a smaller jet could bring the enthusiasm for air travel to smaller and rural communities and thereby capture a new market. Douglas designed its short-haul plane with criteria of simplicity, reliability, maintainability, and economy of operation. The result was the DC-9, which demonstrated that the design criteria had been met

Figure 9-80. The DC-8-61 was 37 feet longer than the original model. It could carry 260 passengers in an all economy configuration.

when it flew for the first time on 25 February 1965. Douglas had a winner. It produced nearly a thousand DC-9s, including several stretched versions, in 17 years of production. (Figure 9-81)

Figure 9-81. The DC-9 was produced in eight different variations. This is a picture of the DC-9-51. It featured a longer fuselage and a new interior.

Just as the DC-9 was going on the market, Douglas was suffering from a cash flow crisis. The leap to jetliners, to the DC-8 and the DC-9, had been costly in terms of expansion, retooling, and training. To avoid a financial

Figure 9-79. The 757 (left) and 767 (right) were similar in design, which saved on crew training.

Historical Note

Franklin Roosevelt was the first President to use air transportation for presidential service. Presidents Truman and Eisenhower used large piston-engined transports. Starting with President Eisenhower, the United States Commander-in-Chief joined the jet age as modified Boeing 707s were purchased by the Air Force to be used specifically for presidential transportation. One of these aircraft, with the tail number 26000, carried President Kennedy to Dallas in 1963, and returned his body to Washington, D.C., following his assassination. Lyndon B. Johnson was sworn into office as the 36th President on board the aircraft at Love Field in Dallas. In 1972 President Richard M. Nixon traveled to China in the same plane. A total of eight presidents were served by the 707s with the military designation of VC-137. In the early 1990s the 707s were phased out of presidential service and replaced with the Boeing 747-200B.

widebody—in 1972. The A300 entered service in 1974. (Figure 9-82)

Figure 9-82. The DC-10 was a trijet widebody. The spacious first class section could seat as many as six across.

crisis, Douglas sought a partner to share the financial burden. Several interested parties met with company officials, who selected the McDonnell Company. The two companies merged in 1967 and became the McDonnell Douglas Corporation. McDonnell retained its military specialty and Douglas continued producing the DC-8 and DC-9.

McDonnell Douglas introduced the DC-10 widebody in 1970; the plane first flew in August of that year. In 1971 the DC-10 entered service. The competition included not only the Boeing 747, but also the new Lockheed L-1011 widebody. Additional competition came from the upstart European consortium called Airbus, which flew its first product—the A300

The competition was hard enough on the DC-10, but then a cargo door came off. An American Airlines flight on the Detroit-to-Buffalo leg of a Los Angeles to New York City flight had only 56 passengers and 11 crew on board one day in June 1972. Without warning, a loud thud came from the rear of the plane and air rushed through the plane. Warning bells and horns sounded in the cockpit. With considerable difficulty, the captain managed to get the plane under some control and to land it. There were no serious injuries, but what had happened? The cargo door had come off in flight. If a locked door could come off in flight once, could the door come off another plane? Was the DC-10 safe? McDonnell Douglas rushed to modify the cargo doors on all planes.

On 3 March 1974 a Turkish Airlines DC-10 crashed just after taking off from Orly Airport in Paris. The crash killed the 346 passengers and crew. It was the deadliest air accident in history, to date. What had happened? The cargo door had opened in flight. Then in May 1979 the left engine of an American Airlines DC-10 came off as the airplane was taking off from Chicago. The engine damaged the wing, causing the airplane to crash. All 271 people on board died, plus two more on the ground. The Federal Aviation Administration grounded all 270 DC-10s being operated by 41 different airlines around the world. Weeks later the planes went back into service.

McDonnell Douglas continued production of the DC-10 for another decade. When McDonnell Douglas finally closed DC-10 production in 1989, only 446 DC-10s had been made. The company had not broken even on the plane.

McDonnell Douglas still had its MD-80 twinjet, successor to the DC-9, which had entered service in 1980, and the derivative MD-90. These two planes sold well through the end of the decade and into the '90s, but

McDonnell Douglas was no longer a major manufacturer of commercial aircraft.

Historical Note

The first airline to use an Inertial Navigation System (INS) as the primary reference for long-distance navigation was Finnair. The aircraft contained two primary systems and a third continuously operating backup. The system was installed on a DC-8-62 used for flights over the Atlantic between northern Europe and New York. The INS was very accurate and allowed extended travel over areas with few geographic features and in areas with few electronic navigational aids.

Figure 9-83. The Convair 880 never achieved the success of other jetliners.

Convair and Lockheed

Lockheed and Convair also produced jetliners for the new Jet Age, but neither manufacturer's commercial branch survived the costly transition from piston engines to jets.

In 1956 Convair, a division of General Dynamics, announced its Convair 880 development program. Convair completed the first flight in January 1959. The 880 was a medium-range transport with General Electric turbojet engines. It was designed to fly fast, about 600 miles per hour. In fact, the 880 designation relates to the speed—600 miles per hour is 880 feet per second. Even before that plane appeared, Convair announced in 1958 the development of a derivative of the 880, a longer plane called the Convair 990 Coronado. The first flight of this new aircraft occurred in January 1961. Costly development and sluggish sales of these airliners almost ruined Convair, which abandoned both programs in 1963. Both models went out of airline service generally in the 1970s, though a few of the planes flew longer. (Figure 9-83)

Lockheed gambled its commercial aircraft division and lost. That is the story of the L-1011 TriStar, a widebody in competition with the Boeing 747, Douglas DC-10, and Airbus A-300. When American Airlines expressed interest in a widebody for use on domestic routes, Lockheed in 1966 began development of a jetliner that catered to American's criteria. Yet in 1968, American selected the DC-10 rather than Lockheed's plane. Lockheed launched the L-1011 with orders from Eastern, TWA, and Air Holdings, the last an offset deal that Lockheed hoped would favorably sway American public opinion about the selection of Rolls-Royce engines over American-made engines. With over 200 planes on order, Lockheed started pro-

duction of the three-engine jetliner. The first flight took place on 16 November 1970. A decade later the company had sold only 195 L-1011s. Having lost billions of dollars on the L-1011, Lockheed stopped production in 1983. (Figure 9-84)

Airline Deregulation

For years the Civil Aeronautics Agency (CAA) had regulated and controlled most aspects of the United States airline industry as well as the development of airports and airways, while the Civil Aeronautics Board (CAB) held regulatory power over airlines. The Federal Aviation Act in 1958 created a new safety and regulatory agency, the Federal Aviation Agency (FAA). The name changed to Federal Aviation Administration (FAA), when Congress created the Department of Transportation in 1967. The FAA had jurisdiction over many of the civil and commercial aviation activities at the time but the Civil Aeronautics Board retained its important role with the airlines. Both the FAA and the CAB attracted critics. The Airline Deregulation Act of 1978 and the air traffic controllers' strike of 1981 exposed some of the problems within the system.

The Airline Deregulation Act of 1978 phased out the authority, responsibility, and duties of the CAB in relation to the airline industry. Proponents of deregulation spoke of an "open skies" policy that allowed the market forces, not the government, to dictate the airline transportation structure. Both the Vietnam War and President Nixon's Watergate scandal had eroded public confidence in government. The Arab oil embargo of 1973 and the economic recession of the 1970s, the increasing passenger capacity of aircraft as reflected in the new widebodies, and the competition from the European Airbus influenced the vote for the Airline Deregulation Act.

Figure 9-84. The L-1011 offered increased comfort and load-carrying capacity, but was not successful competing with the 747 and DC-10.

The results of the new legislation were gradual; for example, the CAB did not dissolve until 1 January 1985. Deregulation gave express carriers the operating freedom to cross state borders and provide new high quality services. As a result, the express delivery business boomed. (Figure 9-85)

Figure 9-85. The express carriers were the first group to be deregulated in 1978.

Regulations can protect as well as hinder, and because some airlines lacked the financial resources to adjust to regulatory changes, deregulation led some airlines to bankruptcy. Others airlines merged as the airline industry consolidated. Yet new carriers formed to provide local and regional service. In 1978, 36 carriers were certified using planes seating 61 or more passengers. By 1984, after deregulation had taken full effect, the number had increased to 123 such carriers; the number declined in the late 1980s as weaker airlines went out of business or were taken over by stronger

carriers. Within 20 years, over 150 airlines would disappear, including nine major carriers.

Free to compete, the airlines created frequent-flier programs, computer reservation systems, and code sharing. Code sharing agreements enabled small regional carriers to share the computer identifier of their large-carrier partners in the reservation system. Because deregulation would leave many small communities without air service, the Department of Transportation administered a new Essential Air Service to subsidize "essential" air service to communities for whom deregulated airlines would not choose to serve because the service would be unprofitable. (Figure 9-86)

Figure 9-86. Regional carriers who flew smaller airplanes, such as this deHavilland DHC-8311A, initially expanded under degregulation.

Airlines developed the hub-and-spoke system. Hubs were strategically located airports used as transfer points for passengers traveling from one community to another in the region surrounding the hub. They also were collection points for passengers traveling to and from the immediate region, other parts of the country, or points overseas. Airlines scheduled "banks" of flights into and out of their hubs several times a day. Dozens of airplanes arrived within minutes of each other. The passengers from those flights would transfer to the planes that would take them to their final destinations.

Controllers Strike

After years of complaints about working conditions, the Professional Air Traffic Controllers Association (PATCO) went on strike 3 August 1981. Over 12,000 controllers walked off the job. PATCO, which had organized in 1968, had long argued that working conditions affect the safety of air travel. The union demanded a $10,000 raise for each controller, a 32-hour work week (rather than 40), and a better retirement package. Controllers thought of the raise as recognition for the pressures they faced at work and the reduction of hours a matter of safety given the increasing volume of air traffic control. The new computer technologies, as well as obsolete and faulty equipment, contributed to stress on the job. (Figure 9-87)

Figure 9-87. Striking air traffic controllers demonstrate in Chicago in 1981.

The FAA monopoly on civil air traffic control, on training as well as hiring, gave the FAA a strong position from which to manage air traffic control. President Ronald Reagan ordered the strikers back to work. Few went. Within 48 hours of the walkout, he fired 11,350 controllers, about 70 percent of the workforce. Furthermore, he placed a lifetime ban on the FAA rehiring any of the strikers. For the Republican president, the issue was not working conditions but control of the workplace. The issue was not air traffic controllers, per se, but organized labor. The massive

firing of controllers destroyed PATCO and signaled a decline in organized labor in the United States.

The FAA used flow control and overtime hours to help the remaining controllers maintain control of scheduled air traffic, but the FAA failed to address the controllers' grievances expressed in 1981 or thereafter. Newly hired controllers soon voiced similar complaints about the FAA's management of labor. Controllers in 1987 organized the National Air Traffic Controllers Association (NATCA) to represent them in talks with their monopolistic FAA employer. Safety remained a concern.

EUROPEAN AIRCRAFT

The first jet engines and the first jet transport aircraft came out of Europe, years ahead of anything from competition across the Atlantic. In the 1960s individual European firms, however, had a difficult time competing in the international market place for modern jetliners. Direct and indirect financial support from the government helped some firms cover the costs of research and development that sales could not recover. Despite the dominance that Boeing acquired in the commercial industry, European companies also produced jetliners. In fact, cooperaion in Europe produced a company that eventually became Boeing's only substantial competition.

France

Sud-Est Aviation in France produced the 210 Caravelle, a short-haul jet that entered service in 1959. The company mounted the twin engines on the rear portion of the fuselage and thereby kept the wings clear and obtained good wing performance. The engine placement also kept noise from the cabin. The Caravelle proved that jets could be operated profitably on short-to-medium length routes, within a 300-mile range. Air France, Scandinavian Airlines, and United Airlines operated the Caravelle with a 60-to-80 seat configuration. This successful early jetliner influenced the subsequent design of aircraft in both Europe and the United States. (Figure 9-88)

Soviet Union

The Iron Curtain and Cold War politics divided the aviation market into East and West. Manufacturers produced and sold their products on their side of the international divide. Soviet transports, for example, were never sold to airlines in the West, and Aeroflot, the Soviet national airline, did not buy planes from western manufacturers. In spite of this, the world's second jetliner was a Soviet product.

Figure 9-88. The French Caravelle influenced the design of modern jet aircraft by placing the engines on the tail.

The Tupolev design bureau produced the Tu-104, a 50- to 100-passenger twin turbojet. Aeroflot introduced it into service in 1956. Within two years the Tu-104 flew scheduled routes east to Petropavlovsk, Vladivostok, and Pyongyang; south to Tashkent and Tiflis in the southern Soviet Union, further south to Cairo and New Delhi, and west to Paris and Copenhagen. Derived from the Tu-16 bomber, the Tu-104 provided the world's first sustained jet service—remaining in continuous service much longer than the De Havilland Comet's two years of service. The Tu-104 remained in service through the 1970s. (Figure 9-89)

Figure 9-89. The Tupolev TU-104 provided regular passenger service with Aeroflot for many years.

Tupolev also produced the Tu-114 turboprop, a large, four-engine, long-range airliner that first flew in 1957. For the next decade, the Tu-114 was the largest airliner in the world. Tupolev made the Tu-124 jetliner, a small short-haul jet that entered service in 1962, and the Tu-134, a bigger short-haul jet that entered service in 1967. The Tupolev Tu-154 trijet entered service in 1972. Tupolev continued production of this economical airliner into the 1990s.

In the mid-1960s Aeroflot was the world's largest airline. It flew more passengers more miles than any other airline in the world. Tupolev provided many of the airliners, but Aeroflot's early workhorse was a turboprop—the Ilyushin Il-18. Sergei Ilyushin's design bureau produced this four-engine turboprop, which went into service with Aeroflot in 1959. The Ilyushin Il-62 became the first Soviet long-haul jet. Heavily influenced by the British Vickers VC10, the Il-62 first flew in 1963, but problems with the Kuznetsov turbofan engines delayed its entrance into service until 1967. The Il-62 became Aeroflot's airliner of choice for long international flights, and the plane remained in service throughout the Cold War period and beyond. Ilyushin also produced the large Il-76 freighter, a four-engine jet that entered service in 1976. (Figure 9-90)

Figure 9-90. The IL-62 had four engines located on the rear of the fuselage much like the British VC10. The Cuban Airlines used the IL-62 on routes between Havana and Mexico City.

Aeroflot, as the only airline in the Soviet Union, also used helicopters in its airline operations. The huge Mil Mi-6 that appeared in 1957 had two turbine engines above the 65-passenger fuselage. Aeroflot used the turbine Mil Mi-8, which first flew in 1961, to service construction projects such as the Baikal-Amur Magistral railroad, and to support polar stations.

Great Britain

The British aviation industry during World War II had concentrated on fighters which, unlike bombers, cannot be altered into transport planes. When the war ended in 1945, Britain had 27 aircraft manufacturers and eight aero-engine makers. Those numbers declined! Some companies failed to make the transition to peace. Others failed to make the transition to the Jet Age, but British companies produced some notable jet airliners.

De Havilland reintroduced the Comet in the late 1950s, and the jet went back into airline service, but the airframe failures of the early 1950s had permanently damaged the reputation of the aircraft. The Comet 4, 4B, and 4C also faced competition from the longer haul capability of the Boeing 707 and Douglas DC-8. Nonetheless, the redesigned aircraft remained in production until 1964. To fill the void of a British long-haul aircraft, Vickers designed the VC10. Flown for the first time on 29 June 1962, this plane became popular.

A few British manufacturers did survive the transition to the Jet Age. But De Havilland needed help. Surrendering its independence and its brand name, De Havilland merged with Hawker Siddeley in 1959. Hawker Siddeley was also making the transition to the Jet Age. It developed a short-haul jet called the Trident, which first flew in January 1962. The Trident entered service in March of 1964. The British Aircraft Company's BAC 1-11, using the Spey engine, attracted customers from around the world, even airlines in the United States such as Braniff and American Airlines. Beginning in 1979, British Aerospace (formerly the British Aircraft Company) transferred the production of the BAC 1-11s to Romania. (Figure 9-91)

Hawker Siddeley began development of what became, with Britain's nationalization of its aircraft industry, the British Aerospace BAe 146 short-haul, small-load airliner. Able to take off and land on short fields, the BAe 146 became popular with small commuter lines.

Supersonic Transports

Throughout the 1960s three major programs developed to produce supersonic transports: the Anglo-French Concorde, Soviet Union's Tupolev Tu-144, and the United States Supersonic Transport or SST program. The goal in all three cases was a supersonic civil transport. All of the design teams selected a similar configuration—four jet engines attached to a delta wing. The Anglo-French team produced the Concorde, and the Soviet Union the Tu-144, but the United States withdrew from what was clearly a race, an economic race for the Anglo-French team and a Cold War competition between the United States and Soviet Union.

SST

In 1960 NASA established a Supersonic Transport (SST) research program. The program quietly investigated theoretical and applied aspects of supersonic flight and supersonic equipment. Boeing, McDonnell Douglas, and Lockheed competed in a government-sponsored contest to design a supersonic transport, and in 1966 Boeing's design won. There was also the international competition. In 1967, for example, *Look* magazine asked, "Will Russia win the SST race?" By 1971, the United States did not care. Having won the lunar race and clearly dominating the aviation industry worldwide, the United States had little support for the expensive SST research and development program.

Figure 9-91. The BAC 1-11 was a successful British design used by airlines on every continent. It entered commercial service in 1965.

Boeing SST mockup

Furthermore, the emerging environmental movement had raised concerns that would plague supersonic transports throughout development and operations. The four main concerns were: (1) emissions, especially the effects of engine emissions on the ozone layer; (2) noise in the vicinity of airports, notably takeoff and landing noise; (3) sonic boom, the noise of cruising flight; and (4) exposure to high-altitude atmospheric radiation, including radiation of galactic and solar origin.

The United States canceled its SST program in 1971 because of environmental and economic concerns and because the SST had lost its support base.

Concorde

At the historic meeting in 1962 when the British and French agreed to collaborate on the design and production of a supersonic transport, the officials present discussed their goal. They wanted Europe to regain world leadership in aviation, something they had lost to the United States in the early 1930s. They wanted to make a leap that would again move them to the forefront of aviation technology.

The British Aircraft Corporation and the French Sud Aviation companies joined to design the airframe, which was eventually assembled in Toulouse, France, by Sud Aviation. British Siddeley and the French SNECMA cooperated to develop the engine, which Bristol Siddeley built at its engineering center in Filton. The aircraft remained in design into 1965, and revisions continued to be made after that while the consortium sought orders for the aircraft. The first Concorde prototype rolled out at Toulouse in December 1967, and the second at Bristol in September of the next year. The Toulouse prototype made its first flight in March 1969, and the Bristol prototype in April. The consortium exhibited both aircraft at the Paris Air Show in June 1969. (Figure 9-92)

The aircraft in supersonic cruise flew 1,350 miles per hour at an altitude up to 60,000 feet (11 miles). Powered by four Rolls-Royce/Snecma Olympus 593 engines, it consumed over 5,500 imperial gallons of fuel per hour. Design changes were made as the aircraft entered production. The British-French consortium of British Aerospace (formerly British Aircraft Corporation) and Aerospatiale (formerly Sud Aviation and other French companies) built 16 production Concorde supersonic jets, for a total of twenty planes. The aircraft completed over 5,000 hours of flight testing before entering service. Both British Airways and Air France introduced Concorde service in January 1976.

Figure 9-92. The Anglo-French Concorde was built of special metal in order to withstand the kinetic heat produced while flying at 1,350 miles per hour. The nose could be dipped during landing so that the pilot had a better view of the runway.

Starting with Malaysia in 1977, nation after nation banned supersonic flight over land because of the noisy sonic boom. The Concorde operated mostly on state-run airlines, notably British Airways and Air France—subsidized by public funds and mostly on transoceanic routes, over water. In 1982 those two airlines discontinued regularly scheduled service to Bahrain and Singapore, Rio de Janeiro and Caracas, Washington and Mexico City. Air France maintained one Concorde route from the mid-80s onward: Paris to New York City. Banned from many airports because of its loud noise and dirty emissions, the aging Concorde could not meet contemporary standards for certification. British Airways also flew transatlantic service into and out of New York, but it also chartered its Concordes as recreational vehicles for the wealthy. Regular passenger service finally ended in October 2003.

Tu-144

Soviet engineers had explored supersonic designs since World War II, initially for military applications, and Soviet predecessors to the Soviet civil supersonic transport included military planes such as the Myasishchev M-50/M-52 Bounder bomber. Civilian predecessors were high-speed aircraft such as the Tupolev Tu-104 and the Tu-114, both of which Tupolev derived from military aircraft.

Tupolev—first the father, then the son, and always the design bureau—led the supersonic aircraft development and production, but the Soviet aerospace industry participated too. Work began in 1961. Ilyushin contributed to the airframe, and Antonov assembled the prototype's wing. Koliesov and Kuznetsov worked on different engines competing for installation. Tupolev displayed a model of its supersonic plane at the Paris Air Show in 1965. The prototype first flew on 31 December 1968, though its first supersonic flight came six months later, on 3 June 1969. Khrushchev declared that the plane represented "a major contribution to the prestige" of the Soviet Union. (Figure 9-93)

Figure 9-93. The Soviet Tu-144 was the first supersonic transport but its service life was short.

The Tu-144 was a 140-passenger supersonic airliner, powered by four Kuznetsov NK-144 turbofan engines. In 1973 a Tu-144 crashed at the Paris Air Show. The plane was not to blame, however, and the Soviet supersonic program continued. The Tu-144 entered mail and freight service with Aeroflot on 26 December 1975. Aeroflot expanded the Tu-144 service to passengers on 1 November 1977, but high maintenance curtailed passenger use of the plane. Tupolev built 16 flying Tu-144 planes, the last in 1981. Cargo flights dominated the Tu-144's service history. Aeroflot withdrew the Tu-144 from service in 1984 because it consumed more fuel and maintenance hours than the airline could afford.

Airbus Industrie

Inspired by the supersonic Concorde alliance between Britain and France, the European aircraft industry decided in 1967 to pool its resources to build a new aircraft, a European airliner. The first project was to build the world's first twin-engine, widebody transport. The new transport was initially designed to carry 300 passengers, hence the name A300. The alliance to produce this aircraft was greatly strengthened in 1970 when the new multinational Airbus Industrie consortium formed. Airbus Industrie initially had two full partners— Aerospatiale of France and Deutsche Aerospace of Germany. Hawker Siddeley of Great Britain and

Fokker of Holland participated, and CASA of Spain became a full member in 1971. British Aerospace became a full member in 1979. (Figure 9-94)

Figure 9-94. The A300 was Airbus Industrie's first aircraft.

Airbus Industrie overcame differences in language, methodologies, and measurement systems, and completed the A300 project ahead of schedule and on budget. After rolling out of Aerospatiale's assembly plant in Toulouse, the first plane made its first flight on 28 October 1972. Air France placed the A300, by then designated the A300B, in service in May 1974. The A300 introduced the supercritical wing to airline service. The supercritical wing offered efficiencies not found in other wings. After a slow start, including an entire year without a single sale, Airbus Industrie sold the A300 to one airline after another. It developed unique marketing, for example, providing not only the planes but also the funding for a sale. Airbus Industrie began to erode Boeing's dominance of the airliner market.

At the end of 1979 Airbus Industrie had 81 aircraft in service with 14 airlines, and it had orders for 256 planes from 32 customers. That year British Aerospace became a full partner in the consortium. Also in 1979 Airbus Industrie added the A320 narrow-body project; the previous year it had launched the A310, a shorter version of the A300. Like Boeing, Airbus Industrie wanted a family of planes so as to be able to stock an airline's entire fleet. The A320 came out in 1984. A new design, it was the first commercial aircraft with fly-by-wire controls. (Figure 9-95)

In 1987 Airbus Industrie decided to launch two larger aircraft products, the twin-engine, medium-range A330 and the four-engine, long-range A340. These were to compete with Boeing's big planes for the transoceanic market. The A330 and A340 had the same basic airframe and wing design, and they

Figure 9-95. The innovative cockpit on the A320 included fewer analog instruments and a sidestick controller instead of the traditional center configuration.

retained the popular twin-aisle cross section of the A300 and A310. In addition, the A320's proven fly-by-wire flight controls went into the A330 and A340. Development of these planes continued into the 1990s.

By 1989 Airbus Industrie had achieved a renaissance in European aviation, it had successfully challenged Boeing's dominance of the industry, and it had acquired a significant share of the world market.

TERRORISM

The Cold War provided a context of threatening violence as a means of deterrence. Terrorism brought the threat of random violence to aviation—to air travelers and to airlines, and it exposed the vulnerability of commercial aviation to acts of violence.

In March 1977, when a terrorist bomb exploded at the passenger terminal at Las Palmas, Grand Canary Island, a Spanish possession, air traffic was diverted to the nearby island of Tenerife. The separatist

Movement for the Independence and Autonomy of the Canaries Archipelago was suspect. Planes went to Tenerife. When Las Palmas reopened, a Pan American flight from Los Angeles via New York City and a KLM flight out of Amsterdam prepared to depart for Las Palmas. There were 396 people on board the Pan American plane, a Boeing 747, and 248 people on board the KLM flight, also a 747. With tired crews and worsening weather, the planes rolled out. They collided, and 583 people died.

Terrorists later attacked planes directly. There were hijackings, such as the TWA flight hijacked to Beriut in June 1984. There were suspected attacks, such as when an Air India Boeing 747 crashed off the coast of Ireland in June 1985. All 329 people on board died. A terrorist bomb was the suspected cause. In December 1988, it was definitely a terrorist bomb that brought down a Pan American flight over Lockerbie, Scotland. Again, all 259 people on the Boeing 747 died, as did eleven people on the ground. Terrorism gave the Jet Age a horrible down-side.

PRIVATE AND GENERAL AVIATION

Airliners, military aircraft, and spacecraft made the news regularly during the Cold War era, but the little planes of general aviation became an increasingly ubiquitous part of aviation. Little planes and little airfields became common throughout the United States, where small planes also lined city airports. The proliferation of general aviation encompassed private planes, air taxis, corporate planes, sporting aircraft, emergency medical transports, fire-fighting tankers, flight school fleets (sometimes just one plane), floatplanes, agricultural spray planes, news helicopters, law enforcement aircraft, homebuilts, experimental planes, restored classics, sailplanes, gliders, and balloons. (Figure 9-96)

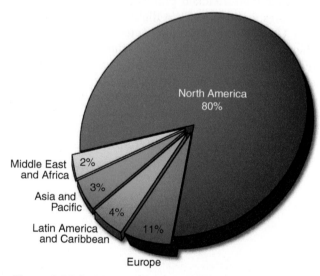

Figure 9-96. In 1989 eighty percent of the world's general aviation aircraft were located in the United States. The percentage had stayed relatively unchanged since the mid-1980s. Source: General Aviation Manufacturers Association and ICAO, International issue of General Aviation Aircraft, 1989.

Light aircraft demonstrated the extent to which aviation had become a part of the daily life of ordinary people. This was more so in the United States than elsewhere, but general aviation spread around the world. Even poor, undeveloped regions attracted general aviation in the form of mail planes, supply planes, missionary planes, and survey aircraft. The "bush pilot" became legend not only in Alaska, but also in Canada, Australia, South America, and Africa. (Figure 9-97)

Figure 9-97. General aviation bush pilots fly to remote areas all around the world. This picture is of a single-engine Cessna 180 with floats in Alaska.

Private Aircraft

In the last half of the 20th century private aviation made flying accessible to millions of people who used aircraft for business as well as pleasure. From the beginning, new ideas had often been developed with the help of small airplanes. During the 60s, 70s, and 80s, creative and skilled amateur builders incorporated new composite and alloy materials, new techniques of construction, and new concepts for design into homemade experimental airplanes. Many of these innovations were soon incorporated into factory production aircraft. Private aviation also continued to be the realm of sports fliers seeking records or adventure. The use of floats attached to aircraft has a long history of use dating back to the Fabre Hydravion of 1910. Although floats fell out of favor for commercial transport service, they experienced a resurgence in general aviation in the 1950s. The utility and opportunity to travel to remote lakes and rivers was intriguing to many general aviation pilots — and practical to people living in rural areas near water but without airfields. Some smaller airplanes were modified to attach floats, and others offered amphibious qualities allowing them to operate on either land or water. Floatplanes allowed access to areas remote from road systems, such as rural Alaska and South America.

Homebuilts and Experimentals

The Wrights and other aviation pioneers began by building their own airplanes. Homebuilding remained a means of affordable access to aviation, and it became quite popular in the second half of the 20th century. New designs were introduced continuously, and new materials became available in the 1970s and thereafter. Homebuilders were also called amateur or experimental builders. The "Experimental" designation provided a means to avoid the expensive certification process required for factory production. Although initially regarded as interesting curiosities, by the 1980s, amateur-built airplanes could be found at most small fields around the United States and in other countries.

The Pitts, the Rutans, the Christen Eagles, the Bedes, and Van's RVs were among the most popular designs among amateur builders around the world. When drawings of the aerobatic Pitts S-1C airplane went on the market in the early 1960s, homebuilders worked in basements, workshops, and garages around the world to build their own. The single-seat biplane never lost its popularity with homebuilders, and the plans remained available for purchase continuously thereafter.

In 1978 Frank Christensen of California introduced his Christen Eagle II kit and with it the concept of fully developed kit planes. Prior to this, the amateur airplane builder usually purchased a set of plans and then set about procuring all the building materials and making most of the component parts. Christensen's kit was both complete and of high quality. An engineer who had specialized in specialty machine tools for the electronics industry, Christensen applied computer-aided design techniques to produce the design and manuals for the Christen Eagle; specifically, he used the IBM Fast Draft system. The Christen Eagle II was a two-seat aerobatic biplane. The Christen Eagle was

Christensen's one business foray into aviation. The kit included the engine for the plane, many finished parts, and lots of manuals. Construction of the Eagle required no welding.

In 1969 aeronautical engineer Jim Bede of the United States introduced the BD-4 kit plane, which sold in the thousands and demonstrated the potential of a larger homebuilt market than previously assumed. The BD-4 was a high-wing monoplane. Unlike Christensen, Bede stayed in the homebuilt business. His BD-5, with retractable tricycle gear, appeared in 1971. Bede ran into difficulties when, after accepting thousands of deposits on the kit, the manufacturer of the engine he intended to include in the kit went bankrupt—without providing the engines. Switching to another engine, Bede had more troubles when the Japanese government would not allow the engines to leave Japan. With customers becoming unhappy after years of delays, Bede dropped the BD-5 project in 1978. Despite the challenges, many BD-5s have been built and flown. One of the models, the Bede micro-jet, actually used a small jet engine and could fly at over 300 miles per hour. One of the 12 BD-5J jet planes built—"the world's smallest jet"—appeared in the James Bond movie *Octopussy* (1983).

Founded in 1973, Van's Aircraft introduced the single-seat sport RV-3 that year, the tandem two-seat RV-4 in 1981, and the side-by-side two-seat RV-6 in the mid 1980s. Van's, Bede, Christen, and Pitts are successful examples of the hundreds of companies that sold designs, kits, parts, accessories, manuals, and instruction to homebuilders. Homebuilders and designers included among their lot sporting folks who made planes for amazing flights. Among those were Burt Rutan and Paul MacCready.

Sports Planes Extraordinaire

In 1975 Burt Rutan's plan for the VariEze amazed the aviation world with its composite construction and forward canard design. It was soon followed by the larger Long-EZ, which set many world records, including a 1979 record for distance over a closed circuit without landing—a distance of 4,800 miles (7,725 kilometers)! Rutan later designed the *Voyager*, a trimaran with wings and two engines. Constructed of lightweight composite materials, the plane flew around the world in 1986, circling the Earth without stopping and without refueling! Burt's brother Dick Rutan and Jeana Yeager were at the controls for the nine-day trip, from the long Edwards Air Force Base runway in the Mojave Desert, west, to the same airfield. With 7,011 pounds

Personal Profile

Elbert L "Burt" Rutan (1943-) was born in Dinuba, California. Before he was even ten years old, Burt Rutan was building model airplanes and dreaming about flying them. His aspirations lead him to an aeronautical engineering degree in 1965 and a job as a civilian flight test engineer for the U.S. Air Force. Rutan launched his own business in 1974 to sell designs for several of his light aircraft to homebuilders. Scaled Composites, Inc., later developed prototypes of seven aircraft that utilized lightweight composite material. The famed aerospace engineer designed and built many innovative and cutting edge composite aircraft, including the VariEze, Quickie, and the Long-EZ. Probably his most famous airplane was the Voyager, which in 1986 made a record-breaking around the world trip without refueling. Many of Burt Rutan's designs incorporated a forward canard that made the airplane look as if the tail was in front of the airplane.

Burt Rutan

of fuel on board at takeoff, the plane required 14,000 feet of runway. (Figure 9-98)

Human-powered flight, a concept going back to the Daedalus myth, proved difficult to attain despite numerous attempts over the centuries. Aircraft designer Paul MacCready met the challenge. His *Gossamer Condor*, a human-powered plane, flew into

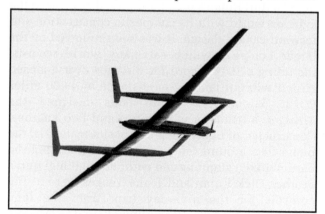

Figure 9-98. In 1986 Burt Rutan's *Voyager* flew around the world without stopping or refueling.

the record books on 23 August 1977. The pilot was Bryan Allen; the place, Shafter Airport in California. MacCready's *Gossamer Albatross*, also human powered, flew across the English Channel on 12 June 1979. He then turned to solar power, the bane of Daedalus. MacCready's *Solar Challenger*, a solar-powered single-seater, flew for the first time on 20 November 1980. Piloted by Stephen Ptacek, the *Solar Challenger* flew across the English Channel on 7 July 1981. In celebration of the Greek myth of Daedalus, Greek bicycling champion Kanellos Kanellopoulos flew the MIT-designed, human-powered *Daedalus* across the Aegean Sea, from Crete to Santorin, 72.4 miles, on 23 April 1988. Kanellopoulos thereby set a world record for human-powered flight, officially recorded as 115.11 km by the Fédération Aéronautique Internationale, the official keeper of aerospace records.

Gliding and Soaring

Gliding refers to descending flight in an unpowered heavier-than-air craft. The weight of the airplane—a glider or paraglider—provides the motive force. Gliders may be airplanes with enclosed cabins, or the person may literally hang below a fabric wing — hang glide. Gliding gave us a new definition of "outstanding." The noun "outstanding" is a landing away from the home field, a common type of landing in cross-country gliding. Paragliding combines elements of hang gliding and parachuting. It is a form of free flying in descent. Soaring, in contrast to gliding, is achieved by flying the aircraft into air that is ascending faster than the sailplane is descending. The most common ascending air masses are thermals, or bubbles of rising warm air. Ridge lift is created when wind hitting the side of a hill is forced to rise. A larger scale version of ridge lift can set up a series of standing waves downwind from a mountain range. Mountain waves can lift sailplanes into the stratosphere, and can exist hundreds of miles downwind from the mountains.

As part of the space program, NASA investigated the Rogallo wing, patented by Francis Rogallo in 1948. The space agency wondered if the Rogallo wing, which had no rigid elements, could assist a spacecraft upon reentry into the Earth's atmosphere. News of NASA's interest sparked public interest in hang gliding. Hang gliding and paragliding gained popularity in the 1970s because the "aircraft" were inexpensive to purchase and operate, because gliders required little maintenance and little training, and because gliding remained relatively unregulated throughout the world. (Figure 9-99)

In the early 1970s many hang gliders were homemade, but companies soon began producing and selling high-performance hang gliders and equipment. The new hang gliders were made from lightweight rigid or semi-rigid frame material with polyester cloth stretched between the members. The paragliders were made from the same polyester type material but did not have any rigid materials. Companies also produced the airplane-like gliders and sailplanes that required a substantial financial investment on the part of the purchaser. Some of the most popular glider manufacturers included Schweizer, Grob, Schleicher, Schempp-Hirth, and Scheibe. The vast majority of manufacturers were in Europe because the sport

military interest had helped support the airship division of Goodyear, historically **the** airship maker in the United States. After World War II, Goodyear used airships for

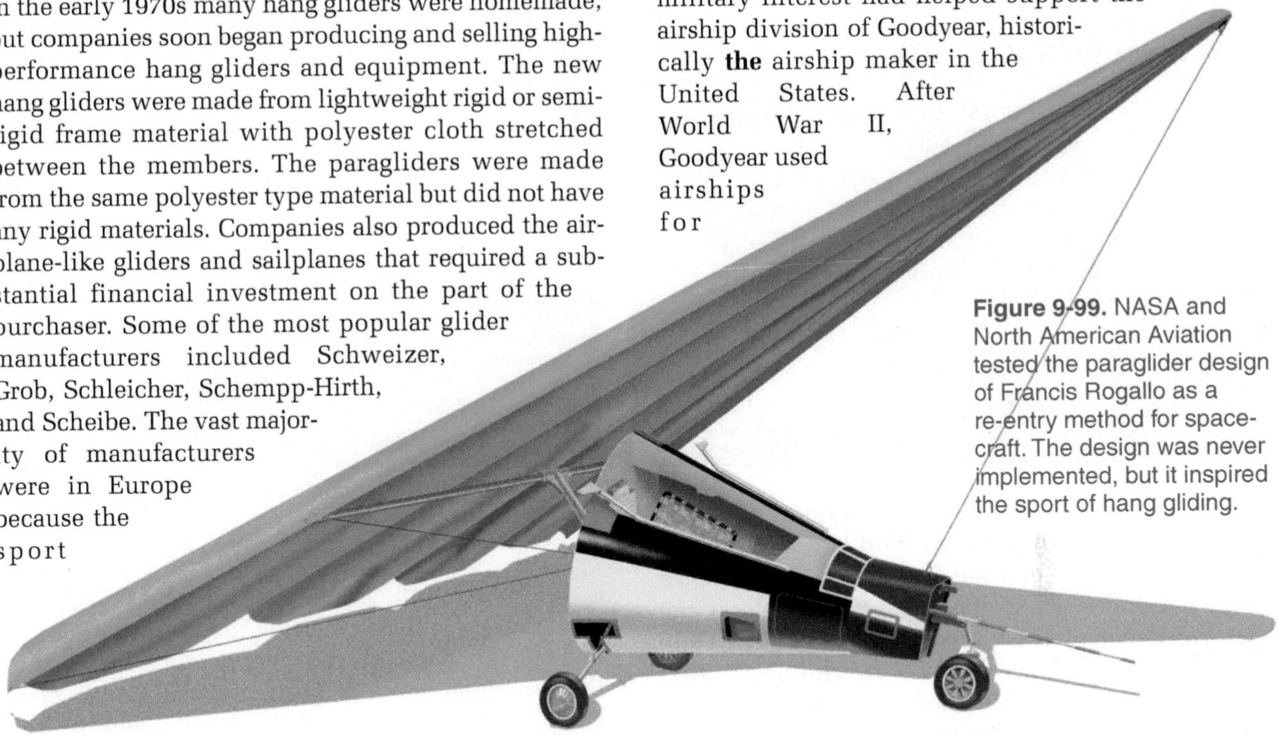

Figure 9-99. NASA and North American Aviation tested the paraglider design of Francis Rogallo as a re-entry method for spacecraft. The design was never implemented, but it inspired the sport of hang gliding.

had a rich European history and because private planes were not as easily available there as in the United States. (Figure 9-100)

Figure 9-100. Control of the hang gliders was done by shifting the weight of the pilot, and control for paragliders was done by pulling on control cables.

Airships and Balloons

Rigid airships had lost much of their usefulness prior to World War II; however, the U.S. Navy continued to use nonrigid airships until 1962. The Navy attempted to create a new airship program in the 1980s, but Congress terminated funds for the project in 1989. The

aerial advertising, and in 1963 began to cover major sporting events with airborne television cameras. It had several airships in operation, each based in a different location around the country. The Gefa-Flug company in Germany developed airships for the European market. The airship might, according to various proposals, be used to lift logs in logging operations, for transporting passengers, or for carrying cargo, but in practice the airship remained a novelty.

Balloons retained their importance in atmospheric research and weather monitoring. Large plastic balloons carried instruments into the atmosphere to measure pressure, temperature, wind, radiation, dust particles, and magnetic phenomena. The space program used ballooning to explore the upper reaches of the atmosphere and to prove the concept of high altitude escape. The Man-High I Program tested high-altitude escape equipment and procedures that would later be used for high-altitude airplanes. Man-High II performed experiments in the near-space environment to learn how that region would affect humans. On the *Excelsior III* balloon mission on 16 August 1960, U.S. Air Force Captain Joseph Kittinger jumped out of a balloon at 102,800 feet. He fell for nearly five minutes at speeds above 600 miles per hour before the atmosphere slowed him down. He opened his parachute at 18,000 feet.

Balloons became became a popular sport vehicle. Raven Industries revived hot air ballooning, which

Goodyear Blimp

Figure 9-101. Maxie Anderson and Ben Abruzzo floating over the Pacific Ocean.

had been neglected for more than a hundred years. The forerunner of the modern sport balloon was first flown on 10 October 1960 at Bruning, Nebraska. It had a revolutionary 30,000 cubic-foot envelope that was constructed of a polyurethane coated nylon. Propane powered its burner. In the mid-1960s Cameron, Thunder & Colt, and Raven dominated balloon manufacturing. The sport of ballooning grew slowly until the 1970s when Sid Cutter started the Albuquerque International Balloon Fiesta. That annual festival became the largest gathering of balloons and balloon pilots in the world.

Balloon pilots and their support teams attempted many flights that had challenged balloonists since the 19th century. The American team of Ben Abruzzo, Maxie Anderson, and Larry Newman, all of Albuquerque, New Mexico, achieved the first Atlantic crossing in August 1978. They flew the *Double Eagle II* from Presque Isle, Maine, on the 11th, and landed at Miserey, France, on the 17th. Their flight was the 18th documented attempt to cross the Atlantic Ocean and the first successful crossing. In November 1981 another Ben Abruzzo team, which also included Larry Newman formerly of the *Double Eagle II*, flew the *Double Eagle V* in the first Pacific crossing. They left Nagashima, Japan, flew 5,768 miles, and landed at Coorla, California. Earlier that year, in January, Maxie Anderson and Don Ida had attempted the first round-the-world balloon flight. They started in Luxor, Egypt, but their flight landed in India, a good distance from Egypt but far short of the goal. (Figure 9-101)

Helicopters

Helicopters have become popular in the civilian sector for executive transportation, search and rescue, logging, police surveillance, medical transportation, and agricultural application. Bell, Sikorsky, Hughes, McDonnell Douglas, Agusta, and Aerospatiale produced helicopters. Aerospatiale produced some of the more popular models, including the Super Puma, Dauphin, Panther, the A-Star, Gazelle, and the ever-popular Alouette III. In the United States the Bell 206 JetRanger became popular for air taxi and charter operations. It entered service in 1967. Six years later, Bell delivered the 1,000th commercial JetRanger. Bell delivered the 2,000th in 1976, and the 4,000th in 1988. Bell transferred production of the JetRanger from the United States to Canada in 1986. The little Robinson R22 became popular for training and for personal use, as well as for herding reindeer in Alaska. First flown in 1975 and introduced into service in 1979, the R22 was a piston-engine powered helicopter. (Figure 9-102)

Figure 9-102. The two-seat Robinson R22 helicopter weighs less than two thousand pounds when fully loaded at takeoff. It has served as a police helicopter as well as in agricultural, military, and training roles.

Historical Note

One of the most prevalent applications for helicopters has been in the offshore oil industry. Oil rigs in the North Sea and the Gulf of Mexico relied on helicopters to transport supplies and workers to and from the rigs that are miles offshore. The use of helicopters could cut a 14-hour boat ride down to a 1-hour helicopter flight.

U.S. Airplane Makers

General aviation encompassed both personal aircraft and business machines, the latter including air taxi, charter, and corporate aircraft. In the late 1950s many light planes were still manufactured with fabric that covered metal airframes. Among these were some Piper, Champion, and Bellanca planes. Piper replaced its fabric-covered Tri-Pacer series with the new all-metal Cherokee series in the 1960s, but kept the fabric-covered Super Cub in production through the 1980s. Composite materials, fiberglass, and high-strength plastics started making their way into production aircraft in the late 1970s. An increasing number of airplane makers began using new construction materials and techniques.

Aircraft manufacturers in the United States introduced many new models, and their combined efforts produced an average of 9,000 airplanes a year in the 1960s. The national airspace system was handling more traffic than ever before, with increasing numbers of general aviation aircraft, commercial airliners, and military aircraft. This stressed the communication, navigation, and airspace infrastructures around the world. Founded in 1939, the Aircraft Owners and Pilots Association (AOPA) represented the interests of general aviation in negotiations with industry and government as all sought solutions to the problems.

Historical Note

What happened to the radial airplane engine?

In the light plane market, the flat horizontally opposed engine replaced the radial and in the large plane market, the radial was replaced by the gas turbine engine. During the 1960s flat engines got larger and turbines got smaller, and they squeezed radials out of business.

The flat horizontally opposed engine provided:

• Better visibility over the nose than a radial engine.

• Improved streamlining.

• No weight penalty, as a radial requires more cylinders for the same power.

• Less vibration, because pistons come together and move apart in pairs, so fewer and larger cylinders are possible.

• Higher revolutions per minute, which require smaller propeller diameters.

The jet engine provided:

• Higher, faster, farther flight than the radial.

• Greater reliability, with less maintenance time and lower maintenance costs than the radial.

• Smooth, vibration-free flight.

• Lighter weight.

• Higher efficiency.

In addition to companies whose business was to make general aviation aircraft, manufacturers of airliners and military aircraft also produced some business planes for general aviation use. Designed as a military light utility jet, the Lockheed L-1329 JetStar is an example. It went into corporate service in 1961. North American followed with the Sabreliner business jet in April 1963. In 1975 an estimated 40 percent of general aviation aircraft were used for business purposes. Although Lockheed and North American experienced slow initial sales, the corporate aircraft market appeared ready for an expansion. Soon other manufacturers in the United States and Europe took steps to expand their general aviation market presence.

Figure 9-103. The Gulfstream III increased the comfort of business jets. It had a large cabin and could carry over ten passengers.

Lockheed JetStar

Grumman and Gulfstream

From the late 1950s into the 1970s, the Grumman American Aviation Corporation produced for private use large turboprops that rivaled the size of small regional or commuter-sized aircraft. The Gulfstream I was a twin-engine turboprop capable of carrying up to 19 passengers. Before production ended in 1969, 200 aircraft had been built. The Gulfstream II (G-II) became the first corporate jet capable of carrying 14–16 passengers and a crew of two for long distances and at jet airliner speeds. As the production of the G-II came to a close in 1978, the company American Jet Industries purchased an 80 percent share in Grumman American, a subsidiary of Grumman Corporation. What had been Grumman American became Gulfstream American. By then, 258 of the popular G-II had been delivered. NASA extensively modified one to train astronauts to fly the Space Shuttle. After the G-II, Gulfstream American brought out the G-III in 1979 and the G-IV in 1985 to serve the corporate customer. (Figure 9-103)

Personal Profile

William Powell Lear (1902-1977) was born in Hannibal, Missouri. The creative genius and entrepreneur never received a formal education past the eighth grade. At the age of 20 Bill established his first company and developed the first practical automobile radio. He sold his invention in 1924 to what would become the giant Motorola Corporation. From 1930 to 1950 he was granted more than 100 patents. He was a very successful owner of an electronics business. His autopilot innovations became world famous and included the development of the autopilot for the French Caravelle jetliner which made the first automatic landings while carrying passengers. He sold his electronics business in 1962 and used over $10 million of the proceeds to produce the first Learjet. The overwhelming success of the sleek business jet propelled the development of several models before the company was sold in 1969.

William Lear

Learjet

William P. Lear developed the Learjet just as demand for private and business jets exploded in the mid-1960s. Although heavily influenced by the Swiss P-16 fighter-bomber, the Lear 23 was a completely new aircraft, and it became one of the most successful corporate jets in history. Its efficiency, speed, and relatively low cost made it an instant hit in the market; however, noise from the engines bothered people in the cabin. The Lear 23 went into production at a new manufacturing plant in Wichita, Kansas, entering service in 1963. Learjet merged with Gates Rubber in 1969 and became Gates Learjet. During the boom years in general aviation in the 1970s, Gates Learjet produced their 500th jet and set numerous engineering and aeronautical milestones. The company produced several series of Learjets, including the 23, 24, 25, 28, 29, 35, 36, 54, 55, and 56. They all had similar characteristics, including two engines mounted on the tail and a sleek pointed nose. Some Learjet models feature winglets, the upturned end of the wing tip, which garnered them the nickname Longhorns.

Learjet

Cessna

Cessna Aircraft made private planes and business planes. Its line included the highly popular 172, 182, and 150. Cessna started producing the 172 in 1956 and by 1978, had produced over 30,000. The 182 also entered production in 1956. Cessna had made over 18,000 182s by 1978, and both the 172 and 182 remained in production. The 172 and 182 were four-seat, high-wing monoplanes with tricycle gear. A smaller two-place trainer, the 150, entered production in 1958. By 1978, Cessna had made over 23,000 150s, and this plane also remained in production. Included in the production figures for the 172, 182,

and 150 are airplanes made under license by Reims Aviation in France. As the numbers suggest, Cessna was the world's leading airplane maker in terms of number of planes produced. (Figure 9-104)

Figure 9-104. The Cessna 172 was the most popular light single-engine airplane in the world.

Cessna also built larger and more complex single and twin-engine aircraft. They also added performance features like turbocharging and introduced the P-210, a pressurized single-engine airplane. The Cessna 300 and 400 twin-engine series gained a large share of the business transport market. Cessna added the small Cessna Citation jet, and then the Citation II and Citation III. The market for the business jets remained relatively steady even after the peak in total general aviation production in 1978. Market saturation, especially in the private plane arena, and high fuel prices pushed production down. The product liability crisis, a general business problem in the United States in the 1980s, hurt Cessna and other small plane makers. Frivolous lawsuits, abandonment of fault-based standards, and the expense of insuring against lawsuits forced the companies to curtail production of small private aircraft. In 1985 Cessna became a subsidiary of General Dynamics, and the next year Cessna stopped production of all single-engine aircraft. It continued production of business jets, twins, and turboprops. (Figure 9-105)

Piper

Descended from the Taylor Aircraft Company of the 1930s, Piper Aircraft Corporation made the light single-engine Cub and Super Cub from 1938 until 1982. The low-wing Comanche series entered production in 1958 and the Cherokee series of trainers and light aircraft became available in 1961. Beginning in 1952, Piper offered a modified Super

Figure 9-105. The Cessna Citation evolved into several very popular models.

Figure 9-107. Piper was the first company to design an aircraft for agricultural use; that plane, the PA-25 Pawnee, and its successor, the PA-36 Pawnee Brave, remained in production from 1957 into the early 1980s. Cessna introduced the AgWagon (pictured above) in 1965.

Cub for agricultural spraying, the PA-18A. In 1957 Piper introduced the first airplane designed specifically for agricultural use, the PA-25 Pawnee. In the 1970s Piper added turbocharged engines to some of its popular aircraft, including the Piper Arrow. In the 1980s the product liability crisis particularly hurt Piper Aircraft. Piper reintroduced the Warrior and Archer aircraft as new variations of the Cherokee design and added the new high performance single-engine Malibu, but sales were sparse. The twin-engine Seneca, Navajo, and Cheyenne aircraft sold just enough to keep the company afloat during the hard times of the '80s, but Piper finished the decade financially weak. (Figures 9-106 and 9-107)

Beech

Beech produced the all-metal, low cantilever wing Model 18 Twin Beech from 1937 to 1969, with wartime production going to the military. The truss-type construction of the center section and the welded chrome steel tubing helped make the plane durable in use as well as successful in sales. The four-seat Model 35 Bonanza, with its distinctive V-tail, entered production in 1947 and remained in production until 1981. Beech produced over 10,000 Bonanzas, and the successful design became the basis of subsequent designs, like the single-fin Model 33 Debonair, first flown in 1959, and the six-seat Model 36 Bonanza, introduced in 1968. The Model 65 Queen Air, first flown in 1958, was the successor to the Twin Beech. The Queen Air was a business airplane that could be operated as a cargo

Figure 9-106. The Piper Cheyenne grew out of the Navajo family of twin-engine aircraft.

carrier. Fewer than 350 had been produced before production ceased in 1971. Introduced in 1964, the King Air 90 was the next Beech business plane. It had a pressurized fuselage and turboprop engines, and it sold well. The Travel Air and Baron series, both entering service in the early 1960s, also sold well to business customers. Beech also produced a line of less expensive airplanes for the flight training and personal flying market from 1963 through 1983. Diversification, such as making fuselages for the Bell JetRanger, proved profitable. In 1981 Beech became a subsidiary of the Raytheon Company. The merger enabled Beech to pursue development of the modern all-composite Model 2000 Starship, a business plane, which used Burt Rutan's canard layout and had twin turboprop pusher engines. A total of 53 Starships were produced, with the first entering service in 1988. (Figure 9-108)

Beechcraft Starship

Figure 9-108. The V-tail Bonanza was one of the most popular high performance aircraft through the 1970s. It was later refitted with a more conventional tail and continued its production run.

COMPETING MANUFACTURERS

The products of various international manufacturers sold overseas, so most domestic manufacturers were in competition with someone else making a product for their targeted customers. Among the products were Aérospatiale's line of helicopters; the CASA C-212 Aviocar, a light utility transport introduced by Construcciones Aeronáuticas SA of Spain; the Do.228 commuter airliner designed by Dornier of Germany but also produced in India during the 1980s; the Embraer EMB-110 Bandeirante low-wing turboprop produced in Brazil in the 1970s and 1980s; the Fuji FA-200 Aero Subaru light plane built in Japan between 1967 and 1986; the Mitsubishi MU-300 Diamond, a twin turbofan business plane

first flown in 1978; the Partenavia P-68 piston twin produced in Italy; and the DR.400 light plane made by Avions Pierre Robin. Dassault in France, De Havilland Canada, Morane-Saulnier and Socata of France, and Israel Aircraft Industries are examples of firms outside the United States that succeeded in producing business and personal aircraft during the Jet Age.

Dassault

Avions Marcel Dassault's first business jet flew for the first time in 1963 and remained in production into the 1990s. Derived from Dassault's Mystère fighter, the plane was initially called the Mystere 20. A marketing campaign by Dassault's U.S. partner

Historical Note

In addition to the decline in demand for light aircraft in the United States, Congress inflicted another wound on the general aviation industry called the Tax Equity and Fiscal Responsibility Act (TEFRA) in 1982. The tax increased the federal tax on aviation fuel for general aviation from 4 cents per gallon to 12 cents per gallon. The authors of the bill insisted that those who used the air traffic control system should pay a tax directly related to its use. Although this seemed logical, it was argued that the majority of the system was in place for the commercial operators, which was true to a certain extent. In fact, even the amount of fuel used for each segment was significantly different. Even though general aviation had 98 percent of all aircraft, it used only 8.6 percent of civil aviation fuels while 91.4 percent was used by commercial operators. In addition, many of the smaller and lighter aircraft could get by with a less complicated air traffic control system. In the end operators of general aviation aircraft had to pay the tax.

dubbed it the Fanjet Falcon, and it became called the Falcon 20/200. It was the product of a joint effort with Sud Aviation in France. A scaled-down version, the Falcon 10, flew in 1971. The Falcon 20 also served as the basis for the three-engine, intercontinental-range Falcon 50, first flown in 1976. An improved version of the Falcon 10, the Falcon 100 was available with an early Electronic Flight Instrumentation System (EFIS) starting in 1986. Dassault quickly became Europe's preeminent business aircraft manufacturer. It produced over 500 Falcon 20/200s. (Figure 9-109)

Figure 9-109. The Dassault Falcon.

De Havilland Canada

Once a subsidiary of the British De Havilland company, De Havilland Aircraft of Canada became a part of Boeing in 1986, then was purchased by Bombardier in 1992. The six-seat DHC-2 Beaver, first flown in 1947, went into production that reached 1,692 planes total. The Turbo Beaver, first flown in 1963, went out of production in 1968. The DHC-3 Otter, first flown in 1951, remained in production until 1966, and had a capacity of 9–14 passengers. The Beaver and Otter became renowned as bush transports. The DHC-4 Caribou was a twin-engine military transport with a rear loading ramp. Its first test flight was in 1958. While the DHC-4 Caribou and DHC-5 Buffalo were basically military planes, the DHC-6 Twin Otter was a commuter transport. It entered production in 1965 and remained in production through 1988. The DHC-7 Dash Seven was also a commuter transport, but with four turboprop engines and room for 44–50 passengers. It first flew in 1975 and remained in production till 1988. The more successful planes were the bush planes. Over time, turboprops began replacing the large radial engines found in earlier models. (Figure 9-110)

Figure 9-110. The de Havilland Beaver.

Morane-Saulnier and Socata

The Morane-Saulnier and Socata companies made general aviation aircraft. In 1958 the flight training and air sports department of the French Government conferred with aircraft manufacturers about the possibility of building a general aviation airplane. Morane-Saulnier responded by proposing the MS 880 Rallye, a 90-horsepower aircraft that seated up to three people. The Rallye made its first flight in June 1959. Over the next two decades, more than 3,500 of these airplanes were produced and purchased in some 65 countries worldwide. In spite of the eventual success of the Rallye series, Morane-Saulnier fell into a period of hard economic times. By the end of 1962, Morane-Saulnier closed its doors and filed for bankruptcy protection. The firm passed through a receivership phase, first with Potez and then with the Groupe Sud-Aviation. Socata (Société de Construction d'Avions de Tourisme et d'Affaires), created on 25 July 1966 as a subsidiary of the Groupe Sud-Aviation, developed a complete line of training and corporate aircraft. Aircraft were sold around the world in the Tarbes (TB) line. They included the TB9 Tampico Club, TB10 Tabago, TB200 Tabago XL, TB20 and TB21 Trinidads, and the twin-engine TB360 Tangara. (Figure 9-111)

Israel Aircraft Industries

In 1967 North American and Rockwell Standard, both of the United States, merged. Both companies had business jet programs. North American produced the Sabreliner, and Rockwell the Jet Commander. Because of the overlap and conflict in

Figure 9-111. The TB-10 Tabago is a popular single engine 4-5 person aircraft. It is often used for training.

the new North American Rockwell Company, Jet Commander went on the market. Founded in 1954, Israel Aircraft Industries (IAI) bought the Jet Commander production line in 1968. The Jet Commander was a new plane, having first flown in 1963. IAI developed, updated, and manufactured the Jet Commander, and it derived the larger, more powerful Westwind from the Jet Commander. IAI delivered the first Westwind in 1972. The Astra was a further development and also a light utility transport. The prototype flew in 1986. IAI sold these jets on the international market. (Figure 9-112)

Figure 9-112. Israel Aircraft Westwind.

Pilot Training

After World War II there was a lull in pilot training, as veterans trained by the various military-preparedness and military programs and experienced with wartime air duty returned to civilian life. They were the postwar private pilots, as were the females who had served in support of the military and who had filled aviation jobs vacated by men going to war. But some of the flight schools that had opened before and during the war continued instruction after the war, and some veterans opened their own flight training operations. In the United States, the number of "student starts" (people enrolling for flight training) gradually climbed out of the postwar slump. Student starts peaked at 160,000 in 1966. After a decline, student starts increased again—to about 200,000 in 1977, and in that year alone more than 14,000 single-engine planes were sold in the United States. (Figure 9-113)

The United States had the economy, aviation infrastructure undamaged by combat, and population to lead the way, but people in other nations also learned to fly. However, just as the overwhelming majority of private aircraft were in the United States, the vast majority of private pilots flew in the United

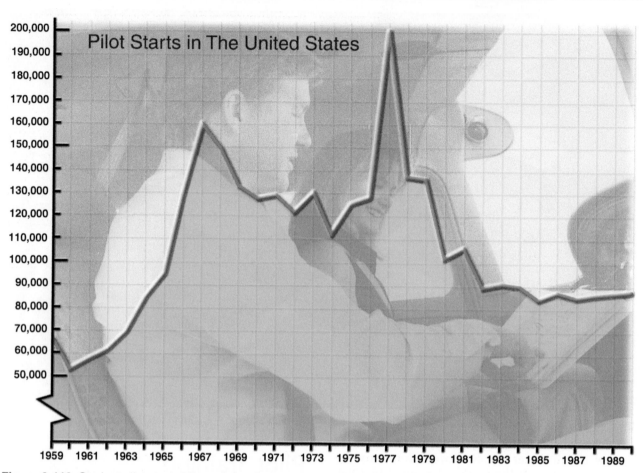

Figure 9-113. Student pilot starts hit an all time high in the late 1970s. The decline thereafter corresponded with the decrease in activity by aircraft manufacturers.

States. Manufacturers like Cessna and Piper developed flight instruction packages tailored to their aircraft to support pilot training at their respective dealerships around the world. Fixed-base operators (FBOs) also adopted the courses. (Figure 9-114)

Figure 9-114. Ground school involved new learning aids and techniques as the world of aviation grew more complex.

Since the implementation of licensing requirements in the various nations, training has consisted of ground school and flight instruction. Ground schools have taught the theory and regulations of flight as well as weather, controls, instruments, and human factors. The instructor talking, showing slides, and using a blackboard, gave way to film strips, and then videos, supplementing the classroom teacher. Flight instruction consisted of both dual and solo flying. During the aircraft sales slump of the 1950s, manufacturers offered flight training, both ground school and flight instruction, as a marketing tool. For example, a customer could buy a plane and learn to fly it from the manufacturer or from the manufacturer's dealer. The military services maintained their own flight training, though many would-be military pilots began with civilian instruction. (Figure 9-115)

Founded in 1947, the University Aviation Association (UAA) promoted aviation education at universities. The UAA has supported teaching pilots and other aviation professionals, supported the National Intercollegiate Flying Association, and in the 1980s established an accreditation program for

Figure 9-115. Manufacturers like Cessna (below) and Piper (right) set up training centers around the world to train new pilots and distribute aircraft.

Personal Profile

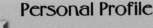

Paul E. Sanderson (1922–) improved flight education by introducing the latest multimedia instructional techniques and materials for general aviation use.

Born and raised in Ohio, Sanderson went into the Navy after high school. During World War II, he went from the Patuxent River Naval Air Test Center in Maryland to the Pacific. He served at Pearl Harbor, at the Enewetak and Kwajalein atolls in the Marshall Islands, and on the carrier USS *Boxer*. Still in the Navy after the war, he became an instructor at the Aircraft Instrument and Link Trainer School in Jacksonville, Florida.

After the Navy, Sanderson taught at the Pittsburgh Institute of Aeronautics and Airline Training and the Embry Riddle School of Aviation, both in Miami, Florida. He founded his own ground school in 1956. Sanderson introduced multimedia techniques

Paul Sanderson

into the ground school program, including slides illustrating course content and reel-to-reel tapes of his lectures. He also preprinted his notes for students. In sum, he produced the first Audio Visual Pilot Training Course for general aviation. The Strategic Air Command acquired Sanderson's course for Air Force flying clubs.

The Sanderson family moved to Wichita, Kansas, where, in 1958, Paul became head of the Yingling Aircraft ground and flight school. Yingling was a Cessna dealer. There Sanderson developed what he called Preflight Fact packages featuring the Cessna 150. In 1961 Cessna ordered 100 complete Private Pilot courses that featured Cessna aircraft. Piper, Beechcraft, and other aviation companies thereafter ordered customized flight courses. The packages were available during the aircraft sales boom of the early- to mid-1960s, and Sanderson sold 3,000 courses by 1968.

Sanderson Films became part of the Times Mirror Company in 1968. Times Mirror merged Sanderson with Jeppesen & Company in 1974. Jeppesen Sanderson has continued to produce training materials ever since, including newer computer-based learning systems and on-line courses. Paul Sanderson served as vice chairman of the board for Jeppesen Sanderson for more than 20 years before he retired in 1997. (Boing acquired Jeppesen Sanderson in 2000.)

university aviation programs. Student pilots from around the world began coming to the United States for their private and commercial licenses, as well as for various ratings. As airline pilots who had been trained during World War II and Korea began retiring in the 1960s, the airlines gradually started recruiting civilian-trained pilots. This opened the door for women to become airline pilots.

AIR SHOWS

Air shows ranged from local fly-ins to international events. They helped publicize and popularize aviation. Flight demonstrations and static displays showed the general public what was happening in aviation, and Cold Warriors showed their military and economic might by bringing their newest and fanciest products. The Paris Air Show, for example, showed the latest weapons and commercial products, whereas the EAA Fly-In at Oshkosh, Wisconsin, showcased sport and amateur-built aircraft. Since 1968, the International Council of Air Shows has promoted air shows in North America.

At the big two international air shows — Paris and Farnborough — commercial, military aircraft, and space hardware grabbed the headlines, but general aviation participated too. Begun in 1908, the Paris Air Show moved to Le Bourget field in 1951. At the 1969 Paris Air Show the Concorde prototype and the Boeing 747 made the headlines. In 1973 the new European Airbus and Aerospatiale helicopters were top draws. In 1977 the Dassault Mirage F1 full-size plexiglass model got a lot of attention. In 1983 it was the space shuttle *Enterprise* on a Boeing 747, and in 1989 the Soviet Buran space shuttle on an Antonov.

Begun as a British air show in 1932, the big air show in Great Britain has been at Farnborough since 1948. It was a British show through 1970, a European show in 1972, and an international air show since 1974. At the 1982 show, for one example, there were 480 exhibitors. Airship Industries of Britain showed its Skyship 500 nonrigid airship, which represented a limited revival of airships. Boeing introduced its

Historical Note

Some of the "firsts" related to the Paris Air Show include:

1957: The Soviet Union made its first appearance at the show.

1967: Two Sikorsky HH-3E Jolly Green Giant helicopters made the first nonstop transatlantic helicopter flight being refueled in midair a total of nine times each. The helicopters made a dramatic appearance, circling the field in refuel formation.

1969: Fourteen different countries came together to witness prototypes of both the Concorde and the Boeing 747.

1973: The European Airbus made its first appearance and Aerospatiale's helicopters impressed the crowd with record-breaking performances.

1979: The Mirage 2000 and 4000 were first presented along with the Ariane rocket.

1983: The attendees witnessed the arrival of the American Space Shuttle Enterprise, carried atop a Boeing 747.

1987: The Airbus A320 was introduced, along with the Rafale fighter, and China made its first appearance as an exhibitor.

1989: The USSR put on extensive displays, showcasing SU 25, SU 27, MIG 29, and the Antonov 225 carrying the space shuttle Buran.

757 and 767, while Airbus introduced its A310, and British Aerospace its Jetstream 31. Incorporated in 1916, the Society of British Aircraft Constructors (SBAC) changed its name to the Society of British Aerospace Companies (SBAC) in 1964. It has always sponsored the British air show.

The Experimental Aircraft Association held its first fly-in as part of the Milwaukee, Wisconsin, Air Pageant in 1953. The show became an annual event, relocating to Rockford, Illinois, in 1959, then to Oshkosh, Wisconsin, in 1970. Often simply called

Oshkosh, this show has always been a fly-in as well as an air show. The open-invitation nature of the fly-in allowed tremendous growth in the number of aircraft attending over the years — from less than 50 in 1953 to over 10,000 a year in the 1980s. This became the air show par excellence for private pilots, and by far the largest aviation event in the United States. (Figure 9-116)

Air races also displayed aircraft in public performance, but air racing declined in popularity. Accidents, new safety regulations, and insurance costs led to fewer airfields willing to host racing. The Reno National Air Races gained in popularity as the number of races elsewhere declined.

Aerobatics, classic aircraft, powerful military planes, new commercial airliners, specialty planes like agricultural applicators, homebuilts, balloons, and private planes have entertained audiences around the world. From big international events to local fly-ins, air shows represented aviation—the manufacturers, the aircraft owners, the pilots—and involved the public in celebrating aircraft and aviation.

Figure 9-116. The Oshkosh Airshow is one of the worlds largest.

Study Questions

1. Why did the Cold War lead the United States and the Soviet Union into a Space Race?

2. Compare and contrast American and Russian human space flight programs.

3. What caused the space shuttle Challenger accident in 1986?

4. Compare and contrast the use of aircraft in the Vietnam and Middle East wars?

5. Describe the role of missiles in the Gary Powers incident, the Cuban Missile Crisis, and the Strategic Defense Initiative.

6. Why did European nations cooperate in the production of the Concorde and Airbus airliners?

7. What is the historical significance of the Airline Deregulation Act passed by the U.S. Congress in 1978?

8. Given the technological and commercial rivalry, as well as the ideological conflict, between the Soviet Union and the United States, explain why the Soviet Union built a supersonic transport and the United States did not.

9. What European and American manufacturers produced business aircraft during the 1960s–1980s?

10. Describe three adventure or expedition flights that helped popularize private flying?

Bibliography

Barbree, Jay and Martin Caidin with Susan Wright. *Destination Mars, in Art, Myth, and Science.* New York: Penguin Studio, 1997.

Davies, R.E.G. Airlines of Asia since 1920. London: Putnam Aeronautical Books and McLean, VA:Paladwr Press, 1997.McLean, VA: Paladwr Press, 1997.

Harford, James. *Korolev, How One Man Masterminded the Soviet Drive to Beat America to the Moon.* New York: John Wiley & Sons, 1997.

Higham, Robin, John T. Greenwood, and Von Hardesty, editors. *Russian Aviation and Air Power in the Twentieth Century.* London: Frank Cass Publishers, 1998.

Jenkins, Dennis R. *Space Shuttle, the History of Developing the National Space Transportation System.* Marceline, MO: Walsworth Publishing Company, 1992.

Kent, Richard J. Jr. *Safe, Separated, and Soaring, a History of Federal Civil Aviation Policy, 1961-1972.* Washington: Federal Aviation Administration, 1980.

Lynn, Mathew. *Birds of Prey: Boeing vs. Airbus: A Battle for the Skies.* 1995; revised, New York: Four Walls Eight Windows, 1998.

McDougall, Walter A. *... the Heavens and the Earth, a Political History of the Space Age.* New York: Basic Books, 1985.

Stewart, Stanley. *Air Disasters.* London: Arrow Books, 1988.

Von Braun, Wernher and Frederick I. Ordway III. *History of Rocketry and Space Travel.* 1966; 3rd edition, New York: Crowell, 1976.

Timeline

Light blue type represents events that are not directly related to aviation.

Year	Event
1959	January 2. The Soviet Union launched the lunar probe Luna 1, which failed to impact the Moon, but became the first spacecraft to orbit the Sun.
1959	January 3. Alaska became the 49th state of the United States.
1959	August 21. Hawaii became the 50th state of the United States.
1959	September 14. The Soviet probe Luna 2 became the first spacecraft to reach the Moon.
1959	December 1. Signed on this day, the Antarctic Treaty established peaceful international cooperation in Antarctica, a continent open for scientific research.
1960	May 1. Francis Gary Powers, flying an American U-2 spy plane over the Soviet Union, is shot down and captured.
1960	September 10-14. The Organization of Petroleum Exporting Countries (OPEC) was organized at a conference in Baghdad.
1960	October 24. A Soviet R-16 missile, designed by Mikhail Yangel's bureau, exploded at the Baikonur launch site. The blast and fire killed 165 people, including the head of the Soviet strategic rocket forces, Mitrofan Nedelin.

1961   April 12. Soviet cosmonaut Yuri Gagarin became the first person in space and the first person to orbit the Earth.

1961   April 17-19. Fidel Castro's communist forces crushed an invasion of Cuba by a guerrilla force of Cuban refugees, who had trained in the United States and who landed at the Bay of Pigs.

1961   May 5. Astronaut Alan Shepard in a Mercury capsule called Freedom 7 reached suborbital space and thereby became the first American in space.

1961   May 25. President John F. Kennedy announced the American goal, "before this decade is out, of landing a man on the moon and returning him safely to the earth."

1961   August 13. The Soviets sealed West Berlin with barriers that became the Berlin Wall.

1961   October 30. The Soviet Union exploded a 58 megaton hydrogen bomb, the most powerful hydrogen bomb detonated during the Cold War.

1962   February 20. Astronaut John H. Glenn Jr. in a Mercury capsule called Friendship 7 completed three orbits of the Earth; he was the first American to orbit the Earth.

1962   April 26. The Soviets launched the spy satellite Kosmos 4, later renamed Zenit; this was the first Soviet spy satellite.

1962   September 27. Nature writer Rachel Carson published Silent Spring about the dangers of pesticides and herbicides.

1962   October 16-28. The United States and the Soviet Union came to the brink of war over the placement of Soviet missiles in Cuba.

1963   June 16. Selected because of her parachute skills, Valentina Vladimirovna Tereshkova in Vostok 6 became the first woman in space.

1963   June 26. Visiting West Berlin, a city bound by the communist-built Berlin Wall, U.S. President John F. Kennedy proclaimed, "Ich bin ein Berliner" ("I am a Berliner").

1963   August 5. The Soviet Union, United States, and Great Britain signed the Moscow Treaty banning nuclear explosions in the atmosphere, in outer space, and under water.

1963   November 22. The President of the United States, John F. Kennedy, was assassinated, and Lyndon B. Johnson became president.

1964   April 17. Geraldine L. "Jerrie" Mock became the first woman to fly solo around the world.

1964   July 2. The Civil Rights Act of 1964 became effective; it was the first major piece of civil rights legislation to pass the United States Congress since the 19th century.

1964   October 12-13. The Soviet Union achieved the world's first three-man spaceflight; Konstantin Feoktistov, Vladimir Komarov, and Boris Yegorov made 16 orbits in Voskhod 1.

1965   February 27. The large four-engined turboprop Antonov An-22 Antheus flew for the first time.

1965   March 18. A Soviet cosmonaut, Alexei Leonov, accomplished the first spacewalk when he left Voskhod 2 for twenty minutes.

1965	June 3. Edward H. White became the first American to walk in space, to complete an extravehicular activity (EVA) when he exited Gemini 4.
1966	February 3. The Soviet probe Luna 9 made the first soft landing on the Moon.
1966	March 16. The United States achieved the first space docking when the manned Gemini 8 and an unmanned Agena target vehicle docked in outer space.
1967	January 27. Three astronauts—Virgil Grissom, Roger Chaffee, and Edward White—died in a fire in an Apollo capsule during a simulated countdown.
1967	April 9. Boeing used a production airplane for the first flight of the twin-engine, short-range Boeing 737.
1967	May 15. The Arabs and Israelis began the Six Day War.
1967	October 30. The Soviet Union achieved the first automatic docking in space when the unmanned Kosmos 186 and Kosmos 188 docked.
1967	December 3. South African surgeon Christian N. Barnard performed the world's first successful heart transplant operation; the recipient lived for 18 days.
1968	January 30. Viet Cong and North Vietnamese forces began the surprise Tet offensive, which continued through March.
1968	December 21. Apollo 8 lifted off on the first circumlunar voyage; it orbited the Moon ten times.
1968	December 31. The supersonic Tupolev Tu-144 flew for the first time.
1969	January 14-15. Soyuz 4 and Soyuz 5 docked; this was the first time that two separately manned spacecraft docked in space.
1969	February 9. Using a production Boeing 747-100, Boeing flew the 747 "jumbo jet" for the first time.
1969	July 20. Apollo 11 landed on the Moon, and Neil Armstrong became the first person to walk on the Moon.
1969	November 14-24. Apollo 12 completed the second lunar landing.
1970	December 18. Aerospatiale of France and MBB and VFW-Fokker of Germany established the consortium GIE (Groupement d'Intéret Economique) Airbus Industrie—Airbus; CASA of Spain became a full partner in 1971, and British Aerospace of the United Kingdom became a partner in 1979.
1971	March 26. East Pakistan seceded from Pakistan and proclaimed itself the independent nation of Bangladesh; by defeating West Pakistan in December, the Bengalis secured their independence.
1971	April 19. The Soviets launched Salyut 1, a space station.
1972	February 21. United States President Richard M. Nixon arrived in People's Republic of China for a historic meeting with Chairman Mao Tse-Tung and Premier Zhou En-Lai.

1972   May 25. Test pilot Gary Krier made the first flight in an aircraft equipped with a digital fly-by-wire control system; the aircraft was a modified F-8 Crusader.

1972   May 26. The United States and the Soviet Union signed a treaty limiting anti-ballistic missile systems.

1972   September 5. Terrorists killed 11 Israeli athletes and coaches at the Munich Summer Olympic games.

1973   October 6. On this Jewish Day of Atonement, Egyptian and Syrian forces made a surprise attack on Israel and thereby started the brief Yom Kipper War.

1974   May 20. The Airbus A300 twin-engine, wide-body transport entered service with Air France.

1975   July 18. The American Apollo 18 and the Soviet Soyuz 19 docked in space 222 kilometers over the Atlantic Ocean; this was the first cooperative space program involving the two Cold War rivals.

1975   November 20. Spanish dictator Francisco Franco died; he had already named Juan Carlos, grandson of the former king, to succeed him and restore the Spanish monarchy.

1975   December 26. The supersonic Tupolev TU-144 entered mail service; it entered passenger service in February 1977, but the plane went out of service in June 1978.

1976   March 24. A military coup in Argentina overthrew the Peronist government and established a military regime that ruled until 1982.

1976   January 21. Built by France's Aerospatiale and the British Aircraft Corporation, the supersonic transport Concorde entered service by flying for Air France and British Airways.

1977   May 25. Star Wars, the movie, opened; it won eight Academy Awards, and the sequels The Empire Strikes Back and Return of the Jedi appeared in 1980 and 1983 respectively.

1977   August 23. Pilot Bryan Allen demonstrated sustained, controlled, maneuverable man-powered flight by flying Paul B. MacCready's Gossamer Condor.

1978   August 22. Mzee Jomo Kenyatta, president of Kenya since 1964, the first president of independent Kenya, died.

1978   October 24. The United States Congress passed the Airline Deregulation Act, which phased out government control of airfares, services, and routes.

1979   November 4. Iranian militants, encouraged by the new government of the Ayatollah Ruhollah Khomeini, took nearly a hundred hostages at the United States Embassy in Tehran; they held 54 captive for 444 days.

1979   December 12. The Soviet Politburo decided to invade Afghanistan.

1980   July 19. The Olympic Games opened in Moscow, but 45 nations boycotted the Moscow games to protest the Soviet invasion of Afghanistan.

1980   August 31. Lech Walesa, leader of the strikers in Gdansk, Poland, signed an agreement with the government whereby the government allowed independent trade unions.

1981	April 12. The maiden launch of the Space Transportation System—also called the space shuttle—sent the orbiter Columbia into space.
1981	August 3. Over ten thousand air traffic controllers went on strike in the United States.
1981	November 12. The space shuttle Columbia became the first spacecraft to be reused when it was launched on its second mission.
1982	April 3. The Airbus first flew the A310 derivative of the larger A300 airliner.
1982.	The personal computer was the Machine of the Year for 1982, as declared by Time magazine (3 January 1983).
1983	September 1. A Soviet SU-14 pursuit plane shot down a civil airliner, Korean Air Lines flight KAL 007, over Sakhalin Island; 269 people on the Boeing 747 died.
1984	January 1. After 95 years under British protectorate, Brunei became an independent country.
1984	February 7 Wearing a manned maneuvering unit on his back, Bruce McCandless II became the first person to float free in space, not tethered to a spacecraft.
1985	November 13. The eruption of the volcano Nevado del Ruiz killed an estimated 25,000 people in Columbia.
1986	January 28. The space shuttle Challenger exploded just after liftoff; the crew of seven, including a school teacher flying as payload specialist, died.
1986	April 26. An accident at the nuclear power station at Chernobyl in the Ukraine, within the Soviet Union, released a radiation cloud, and radiation burns killed more than 50 people, but the Soviet authorities tried to suppress information about the accident and the radiation released.
1986	December 23. Dick Rutan and Jeana Yeager finished flying Burt Rutan's Voyager around the world in the first nonstop circumnavigation without refueling.
1987	February 22. Airbus flew the A320 airliner for the first time; this plane was the first airliner with the fly-by-wire flight control system.
1988	January 2. Canada and the United States signed a free trade agreement.
1989	April 23. Kanellos Kanellopoulos flew the MIT-designed, human-powered Daedalus across the Aegean Sea, from Crete to Santorini, 72 miles (115.11 kilometers).
1989	June 4. The communist Chinese government sent tanks to squelch a pro-democracy demonstration in Tiananmen Square, Beijing; thousands of protestors died.
1989	September 10. Hungary opened its border for refugees fleeing East Germany.
1989	November 9. The Berlin Wall opened.

CHAPTER 10

MODERN AEROSPACE (1990-Present)

AVIATION HISTORY

Summary of Events

April 24. *Hubble Space Telescope* launched **1990**

October 3. Germany reunited. **1990**

January 18. Eastern Airlines went out of business. **1991**

August 19-21. A coup failed in Russia. **1991**

December 8. Commonwealth of Independent States formed. **1991**

December 2-13 Space shuttle mission STS-61 repaired the *Hubble Space Telescope*. **1993**

February 10. Jeannie Flynn became first U.S. mission-qualified fighter pilot. **1994**

May 10. Nelson Mandela became the first black president of South Africa. **1994**

August 17. General Aviation Revitalization Act was signed into U.S. law. **1994**

June 2. Scott O'Grady's F-16 Fighting Falcon shot down over Bosnia. **1995**

September 24. Comprehensive Test Ban Treaty signed. **1996**

July 4. Mars *Pathfinder* landed on the red planet. **1997**

1990 August 2. Iraq invaded Kuwait.

1991 January 16 - March 3. Gulf War fought.

1991 July 1. Piper Aircraft filed for bankruptcy protection.

1991 November 19. DGV Dauphin helicopter flew 372 kilometers per hour.

1992 August 4. Airbus 310 became the first foreign jetliner in Russian service.

1994 January 1. The North American Free Trade Agreement became effective.

1994 April-July. Genocidal tribal warfare in Rwanda killed approximately 800,000 Tutsis and Hutus.

1994 June 12. Boeing 777 made its maiden flight.

1995 Martha McSally became the first U.S. Air Force female pilot to fly a combat mission.

1995 June 29. Space shuttle *Atlantis* docked at the space station *Mir*.

1997 July 1. Hong Kong reverted to Chinese control.

Light blue type represents events that are not directly related to aviation.

Historical Evidence

A famous, perhaps infamous, case of product liability is that of Cleveland v. Piper Aircraft. The case concerns a pilot who crashed while attempting to take off from the Mid-Valley Airport in Los Lunas, New Mexico, in July 1983.

The pilot, Edward Charles Cleveland, had removed the front pilot's seat and installed a motion picture camera in his Piper Super Cub, a 1970 taildragger. To film a commercial, a cinematographer stood with his back against the instrument panel during the attempted takeoff. He and the camera were facing the rear, where a glider was being towed by a rope attached to the aircraft's tail. The pilot sat in the rear pilot's seat for the takeoff.

Concerned about the safety of the proposed flight, the owner of the airport closed the airfield and parked a van on the runway to prevent takeoffs and landings. When Cleveland attempted to take off, his aircraft struck the van and his head struck the camera. He suffered serious brain injury, and, on his behalf, his wife sued.

Piper's defense included evidence that the basic Cub design dates from 1937, that the particular aircraft, when sold, met all Federal Aviation Administration requirements of the time, that a rear seat harness was offered as an option but was not required for the plane, and that tens of thousands of Cubs and Super Cubs had flown safely for decades.

Nonetheless, in May 1986, the jury decided that Piper had been negligent in designing an aircraft without adequate forward visibility from the rear pilot's seat and without a rear shoulder harness. The jury awarded Cleveland $2.5 million. The trial judge reduced the award to $1,042,500.

The historical evidence of this case includes the court records and the records of the subsequent appeal that Piper made to the 10th Circuit Court; for example, a document cited as Cleveland v. Piper Aircraft, 985 F.2d 1438, 10th Circuit, U.S. Court of Appeals, February 16, 1993.

Other evidence appeared in news reports and commentaries, such as Mike Overly's article "A Mirror for the Emperor" that appeared in the Aviation Safety Institute's Aviation Safety Monitor, June 1992. Using the decision in Cleveland v. Piper as an example of why the light plane business was "dying," Overly urged revising regulatory priorities and liability limitations.

Revitalization

The main attempts to revitalize the general aviation industry in the United States involved foreign certification standards for aircraft, limiting the liability of aircraft manufacturers, and recreational and sport pilot certificates. These measures helped general aviation in different ways and to different degrees. Research and development efforts were also undertaken to help revitalize the industry.

The Experimental Aircraft Association supported the adoption of certain European certification standards for certain small aircraft. The Federal Aviation Administration (FAA) accepted the European standards in 1992; also, the FAA's Small Airplane Directorate promoted general aviation.

The General Aviation Revitalization Act (GARA) of 1994 addressed the product liability problem that plagued general aviation in the United States in the 1980s and early 1990s. The act established an 18-year limit for manufacturer's liability. The time limit applied to aircraft with 19 or fewer seats not engaged in scheduled passenger service — to general aviation's light and business aircraft. In legal terms, the 1994 law is a statute of repose rather than a statute of limitation because it ends the opportunity for a

SECTION A

GENERAL AVIATION

 Q & A

What? Internationalism

When? Since the end of the Cold War, marked by the fall of the Berlin Wall in 1989 and the collapse of the Soviet Union in 1991, civil aviation organizations, commercial manufacturers and airlines, military air forces and defense suppliers, and space programs have cooperated in a variety of ways.

Where? Worldwide

Who? The aerospace community, including private pilots flying across borders, domestic airlines delivering passengers to international hubs, international airlines, military air forces, government agencies, and international organizations.

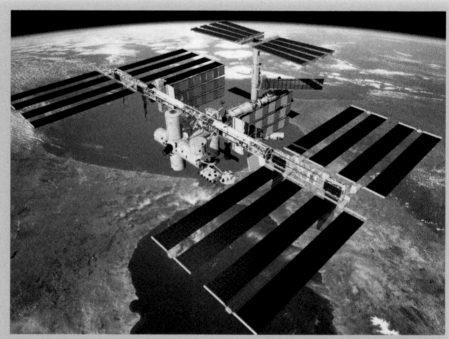

Why? The end of the Cold War reduced tensions and barriers between nations. Cooperation spread the cost and risk as well as the employment and income. The European Community attempted to elevate Europe's role in world affairs, including the global economy. United States companies sought to escape antitrust regulations that applied to domestic deals. International terrorism required international counterterrorism measures. Also, international cooperation provided access to markets, products, and services.

GENERAL AVIATION

General aviation in the United States declined after the peak production years of the 1970s. From the 1978 peak of 17,877 planes shipped to a low of 928 units shipped in 1994, production of general aviation aircraft declined 95 percent. Factories closed and an estimated 100,000 jobs were lost. Cessna ceased making single-engine airplanes. Piper went into bankruptcy in 1991. The number of flight students declined. The United States lost market share to manufacturers in other countries.

Manufacturers blamed product liability, and even the public thought some of the publicized cases were frivolous considering the old age of the particular aircraft and other factors contributing to an accident. Under law, there was no time limit regarding liability. Also, the legal doctrine of "joint and several liability" allowed a manufacturer to be sued even when poor maintenance, bad weather, unauthorized modifications, or pilot error were clearly major factors in an accident. The more aircraft a manufacturer sold and the longer the aircraft remained in service, the more liable the manufacturer became.

Introduction

General aviation, commercial aviation, military aerospace, and space flight have shared a trend toward internationalism since the end of the Cold War hostilities. Some general aviation manufacturers shared development of new aircraft. Sales via imports and exports crossed borders routinely. Private pilots and their aircraft literally circled the globe. Business and charter planes carried passengers and cargo between nations. Manufacturers of large airliners also obscured borders as they shared the costs and risks of developing new aircraft, a practice that had begun with the widebodies in the 1960s. Military contractors shared the production of aircraft, and air forces worked in joint multinational operations. Space programs shared astronauts, equipment, and launches internationally. (Figure 10-1)

The initial goodwill after the end of the Cold War yielded to the harsh realities of the bloody peace that followed, with ethnic cleansing on the Balkan Peninsula, ethnic genocide attempted in Rwanda, two wars in Iraq, a generally unstable situation in the Middle East, civil wars and coups in Africa, troubles in Afghanistan, tension between Pakistan and India, unrest in Northern Ireland, nuclear ambitions in North Korea, and the rise and spread of fanatical, fundamentalist terrorism. These events coupled with the changing world economy and the growth of the European Community, affected aviation activities and space programs.

Section A of this chapter discusses general aviation, including the revitalization of the industry, new aircraft production, and research and development. Section B covers commercial aviation, including the manufacturers, the airlines, and the terrorist attacks carried out on commercial aviation. Section C discusses various military aerospace developments and deployments, including the increasing use of remotely piloted or crewless aerial vehicles. Section D describes space programs, including the tragic loss of the space shuttle *Columbia*. The chapter and the book close with a question: what will the future of aerospace be?

After studying this chapter, you should be able to discuss various efforts to revitalize the general aviation industry and give several specific examples of research and development of the recent past. You should also be able to explain the consolidation and cooperation in the commercial aviation industry and use case studies to illustrate points in the explanation. In addition, you should be able to discuss the changing nature of warfare, compare and contrast the use of military force as retaliatory and preemptive to terrorist acts, and describe the military aircraft in use since 1990. Finally, you should be able to summarize space activities by nation and by type of activity, illustrating the summary with historical cases.

Figure 10-1. The Bombardier Global Express is a high-end corporate jet. Canada's Bombardier helped consolidate the general aviation industry by acquiring four companies: Learjet, founded in the United States in the early 1960s; Canadair, established in Canada in the 1920s and operating under the Canadair name since the 1940s; DeHavilland Canada, another company dating back to the 1920s; and Short Brothers, founded by the Short brothers in Britain in 1908.

August 6. AeroVironment's *Pathfinder* reached 80,400 feet. **1998**

1998 August 7. Bombs exploded at U.S. embassies in Kenya and Tanzania.

October 21. First successful launch achieved for European Ariane 5 launch vehicle. **1998**

1999 March 1-21. *Breitling Orbiter 3* made the first balloon round-the-world flight.

March 24. NATO began an 11-week bombing campaign in Yugoslavia. **1999**

2000 July 25. An Air France Concorde crashed, killing 109 people, in Paris.

October 31. A Soyuz spacecraft launched with the first crew of the *International Space Station.* **2000**

2001 March 23. Russian space station *Mir*, as intended, dropped into Pacific Ocean.

August 13. Solar-powered *Helios* reached 96,863 feet. **2001**

2001 September 11. Terrorists crashed four hijacked airliners in the United States.

December 13. United States withdrew from the 1972 Anti-Ballistic Missile Treaty. **2001**

2002 January 1. The euro became the common currency in 12 European countries.

July 20. African Union formed. **2002**

2002 November 19. Oil tanker *Prestige* caused an environmental disaster off Spain.

December 9. United Airlines filed for bankruptcy protection **2002**

2003 February 1. The space shuttle *Columbia* broke up during reentry.

September 27. ESA launched *SMART-1* toward the Moon. **2003**

2003 October 15-16. Yang Liwei in *Shenzhou 5* orbited Earth.

November 16. NASA's scramjet-powered *X-43A* aircraft established a speed record of Mach 9.6. **2004**

2004 December 26. A deadly tsunami struck southern Asia and eastern Africa.

October 12. China launched the *Shenzhou 6*, with two astronauts on board, for a five-day flight. **2005**

2006 January 19. NASA launched the *New Horizons* spacecraft on a journey to Pluto.

plaintiff to sue. If an accident occurs more than 18 years after delivery of the aircraft, the manufacturer is immune.

Citing the new law as incentive, Cessna built a new factory at Independence, Kansas, and resumed production of single-engine aircraft in 1996. Organized in 1995, the New Piper Aircraft carried the Piper name out of bankruptcy protection. Manufacturers of equipment also responded to the more favorable liability environment. Unison finally introduced a new electronic ignition that was under development in the 1980s but not brought to market earlier due to the product liability climate that existed then.

Historic Event

Passage of the General Aviation Revitalization Act of 1994 established an 18-year statute of repose for product liability. The act thereby protected manufacturers of light planes and parts for light planes from lawsuits resulting from crashes of aircraft over 18 years old. The act stimulated a recovery in the general aviation industry. On 17 August 1994 President Bill Clinton signed GARA into law.

Planes

The number of general aviation planes shipped rose gradually from the low of 928 aircraft in 1994 to 2,816 in 2000. The recovery during the mid- to late-1990s favored single-engine piston-powered airplanes, the shipments of which went from 444 in 1994 to 1,810 in 2000. Shipments of multiengine piston-powered airplanes almost doubled during the same period, from 55 in 1994 to 103 in 2000. Shipments, including exports, of turboprops and jets doubled, from a turbine total of 429 in 1994 to 903 in 2000. U.S. manufacturers exported a larger percentage of production before revitalization than after, but the percentage was already in decline. In 1990, for example, the industry exported 458 airplanes, or 40 percent of the total production. By 1994, the percentage of production export was down to 30 percent (277 airplanes). The export of 569 airplanes in 2000 accounted for 20 percent of the annual production.

Fifteen U.S. manufacturers shipped 2,816 general aviation planes in 2000. By number of units shipped, Cessna led with 1,256 planes. These were Skyhawks, Skylanes, Stationairs, Caravans, and various Citation models. Raytheon Aircraft produced 476 airplanes — Beechcraft Bonanzas, Barons, King Airs, and 1900D Airliners, plus Beechjets and Hawkers. The New Piper Aircraft made 395 units, including Warriors, Archers, Arrows, Saratogas, Senecas, Seminoles, and Malibu Mirages and Meridians. Learjet shipped 133 Learjets of three models, and Mooney shipped 100 Bravos, Ovations, and Eagles. The other ten manufacturers produced less than a hundred planes each. American Champion, Aviat Aircraft, and Cirrus Design achieved shipments in the 90s; Gulfstream in the 70s, and Maule in the 50s. Bellanca, Boeing Business Jets, Commander Aircraft, Lancair, and Micco Aircraft each produced fewer than 25 planes that year.

When Cessna and Piper resumed production of single-engine airplanes, they relied upon proven designs, which were somewhat improved versions of planes that were already popular. Aviat, founded by Frank Christensen, maker of the Christen Eagle kit plane, developed its Husky bush plane in the 1980s — after deciding that the high price and the assumption of product liability for previously manufactured planes made it impractical to purchase the rights for the Piper Super Cub, the Champion line, or the Interstate Arctic Tern. Aviat advertised the Husky as a new airplane of conventional design. Development and certification of aircraft, as well as establishing a manufacturing facility and a marketing program, were costly and beyond the industry's willingness to leap to an entirely new design. (Figure 10-2)

Figure 10-2. New Piper Malibu Meridian.

While legal, regulatory, and economic factors hampered manufacturers of light planes, the designers and builders of homebuilt aircraft adopted new materials, new construction techniques, and aeronautical advances from the military and commercial sectors. Homebuilders also used personal computers, computer-aided design, and aerodynamic modeling. Some, such as Richard VanGrusvenen, creator of the popular Van RV series, used the same riveted sheet aluminum technology as Cessna, Piper, and Mooney. Some kits, like the Pulsar, provided a plane at a price less than a small economy car. The high-performance Glasair III Turbo, Lancair IV, and Questair Venture could cruise at nearly 300 knots, and some homebuilt planes incorporated pressurized cabins, retractable landing gear, constant-speed propellers, autopilots, and moving-map navigation displays. According to government regulation, a homebuilder had to perform at least 51 percent of the work constructing the aircraft. Most builders performed more to save money, to ensure quality, and to enjoy the building process. Manufacturers provided parts that would have been difficult to fabricate or assemble at home.

In the 1990s, general aviation manufacturing became a stronger industry than it had been when the decade began, but also an industry much smaller than during the heyday of the 1960s and 1970s. Most of the general aviation manufacturers that survived lost their independence. Beech became a subsidiary of Raytheon in 1979. Cessna became part of General Dynamics in 1985; then was purchased by Textron in 1992. Learjet became a division of Gates Rubber Company in 1967. It became Learjet again in 1988, and then, in 1990, the Canadian Bombardier company purchased Learjet. In a final example, New Piper Aircraft gradually became the property of American Capital Strategies, which began investing in the company in 1998 and completed the acquisition in 2003. The large parent corporations provided financial, managerial, technological, and marketing resources for the makers of general aviation planes. (Figure 10-3)

Recovery was the news and the reality for general aviation until the September 11, 2001, terrorist attacks on the United States caused a downturn in the indus-

 ## Historical Note

Without question, the Cessna 172 is one of the most successful airplane designs ever; more than 37,000 of them have been built. Production totals of other aircraft don't even come close: perhaps 30,000 Messerschmitt Me-109s were built, if all the different Me-109 versions are counted. Worldwide production of the Douglas DC-3 was close to 13,000, followed by the MiG 21 at around 12,000. Even though the 172 was out of production from 1986 to 1996, there are still more of them flying than any other airplane. It is estimated that one out of every ten airplanes in the world is a C-172. Cessna has built over 180,000 airplanes, which means that fully half of all the airplanes flying in the world are Cessnas.

The 1973-75 C-172M is the most produced variant at 4,926 units.

The appearance of the C-172 has changed over the years. The top photograph is the 1956 model, with straight tail and no rear windows. The swept tail appeared in 1960, and "Omni-Vision" windows were introduced in 1963. The new 172 is shown in the lower photograph.

try. General aviation, like all of civil aviation, suffered from the public's loss of confidence and from the new security regulations that resulted from the attacks. General aviation's low accident rate and low fatality rate remained admirable, but the industry slumped. In 2001 U.S. manufacturers shipped 2,632 airplanes, and the next year only 2,214 planes. New student pilot starts and the total number of active pilots also declined in 2001, but those numbers had been declining for a decade. The use of commercial airlines in the September attacks raised the question of terrorists using or targeting private or business aircraft, and new security measures helped to cause fear among the public, made private air travel less convenient, and reduced recreational flying.

Pilots

The recreational pilot certificate, introduced in 1990, was intended to stimulate general aviation by luring more people into flying, but the number of recreational pilots remained quite small: 87 in 1990, 161 in 1991, 187 in 1992, and up to 343 in 1999; in 2001 the number dropped to 318.

The sport pilot certificate, introduced in July 2004, has proven more popular. Under the new rules, a sport pilot could usually substitute a current driver's license for the aviation medical certificate required for private, commercial, and airline transport pilots. The amount of training required was less than for the recreational pilot certificate, with emphasis on the skills needed by a sport pilot. The Aircraft Owners and Pilots Association (AOPA), Experimental Aircraft Association (EAA), and other organizations had fought hard for these new regulations, which enable people to fly at less expense.

Between 1990 and 2001, the numbers of student pilots, women pilots, private pilots, and total pilots

Personal Profile

Richard VanGrunsven learned to fly in 1955 at the age of 16. Throughout high school and college he flew from a short grass strip on his parents' farm in Oregon. After obtaining an engineering degree, he served in the Air Force for three years. While in the Air Force, he began using his engineering knowledge to modify the airframe of a Stits Playboy homebuilt for better performance. By August of 1971, he had designed and built an essentially new airplane, based loosely on the Playboy, but with all-aluminum construction, cantilever wings, and the looks, performance, and handling characteristics that distinguished all of his subsequent designs.

Vangrunsven emphasized versatility in his designs. He wanted his airplanes to perform well by many different standards, without sacrificing one measure of performance for another. Thus, his designs had high cruise speeds without high landing speeds, were moderately aerobatic without being unstable or difficult to control, efficient without being uncomfortable, and good looking without being too difficult or expensive to build. Although the first RVs were created for his own personal use and enjoyment, he was quick to make his airplane designs accessible to other builders, developing highly-regarded kits and providing excellent support for builders. He has apparently made service to the customer the main focus of his company, Van's Aircraft, Inc. Although much of the popularity of his airplanes was due to their looks and performance, many builders credited the support they received from Van's Aircraft, the quality of the kits, or the integrity of Vangrunsven himself.

Historical Note

General aviation in the United States in 2000 covered 217,533 active aircraft engaged in corporate, business, personal, instructional, agricultural, aerial observation, sight-seeing, air tours, air taxis, medical, and other uses.

Aircraft Type	Active General Aviation Aircraft	Aircraft Type	Active General Aviation Aircraft
ALL AIRCRAFT — Total	217,533	ROTORCRAFT — Total	7,150
PISTON — Total	170,513	Piston	2,680
One-Engine	149,422	Turbine	4,470
Two-Engine	20,951		
Other Piston	140	GLIDERS — Total	2,041
TURBOPROP — Total	5,762		
One-Engine	678	LIGHTER-THAN-AIR — Total	4,660
Two-Engine	5,040		
Other Turboprop	45	EXPERIMENTAL — Total	20,407
TURBOJET — Total	7,001	Amateur	16,739
Two-Engine	6,215	Exhibition	1,973
Other Turbojet	786	Other	1,694

Private pilots used most of the piston planes (148,192), gliders (1,732) lighter-than-air craft (3,770), and experimental aircraft (18,910) for personal use. Corporate and business operators used most of the turboprop aircraft (3,976), and corporate fliers used most of the turbojets (5,078). These numbers from the FAA appear in the General Aviation Statistical Databook 2002, published by the General Aviation Manufacturers Association.

Historical Note

Air ambulances have a history of military service dating back to airplane rescues during World War I. The Australian Royal Flying Doctor Service, established in 1928, brought the concept to civil customers. The first government-certified air ambulance company in the United States was Schaefer Air Service, established in Los Angeles in 1947. While helicopters and piston planes still provide local services, jet air ambulances have made medical transport available to travelers worldwide. Among the jet aircraft used by various air ambulances companies are the Learjet, Cessna Citation, Dassault Falcon, King Air, and Hawker.

declined, while the average age of pilots increased. The number of student certificates held dropped from 120,000 in 1990 to fewer than 95,000 in 2001. Women pilots numbered about 40,000 in 1990 and less than 36,000 in 2001. There were 299,000 private pilots in 1990 and only 251,500 in 2000, and fewer than 244,000 in 2001. The total number of pilots declined from over 702,000 in 1990 to 631,000 in 2000, and down to 620,000 in 2001. During this period the average age of pilots rose from 40 to 44 years.

The AOPA, however, reported a record membership of more than 404,000 members at the end of 2004. The organization promotes general aviation by protecting existing airports, opposing user fees, questioning security rules, limiting temporary flight restrictions, and trying to reduce the cost of flying.

Figure 10-3. This Raytheon business jet has a carbon fiber composite fuselage.

Research and Development

Established in 1994 as part of the national effort to revitalize general aviation, NASA's Advanced General Aviation Transport Experiments (AGATE) project brought together 70 companies and universities to research and develop new general aviation technologies. The main focus was single-engine, single-pilot airplanes. The FAA became a partner in the AGATE program. Under AGATE, the National Aeronautics and Space Agency (NASA) helped develop the "Highway in the Sky" or HITS display technology. NASA exhibited AGATE's advanced integrated cockpit system that included HITS, simplified flight controls, and electronic systems, at the AirVenture air show in Oshkosh, Wisconsin, in 2001. Avidyne Corporation is an example of a corporate participant. In an academic example, the University of Kansas and Kansas State University have cooperated under AGATE to develop reliable instrumentation for advanced control, guidance, and display systems. NASA's Langley Research Center in Virginia did much of the crash survivability testing for the AGATE Project. (Figure 10-4)

A significant part of AGATE is the General Aviation Propulsion (GAP) program, begun in 1996. NASA undertook work with Teledyne Continental Motors to develop a two-cycle 200-horsepower diesel engine for general aviation use. NASA also contracted with Williams International to develop a small lightweight turbine engine for general aviation aircraft. The turbine specifications refer to single-engine and twin-engine aircraft with a capacity for up to six seats. The goals included affordable, reliable powerplants that are quieter and more fuel efficient, and require less maintenance than the existing engines.

To further stimulate general aviation, in 2001, NASA began a Small Aircraft Transportation System (SATS) program to integrate general aviation into the national airways system and to increase air access to small communities. Both AGATE and SATS were created to further what NASA official Robert Whitehead in 1997 called, "NASA's vision for a small aircraft transportation system that brings safe, affordable and convenient air transportation to far more of America's population."

The FAA established Capstone to improve general aviation safety by bringing near-real-time weather information to the cockpit using a very high frequency data link. Capstone also includes a cockpit display of terrain, with the color of the representations varying according to the plane's

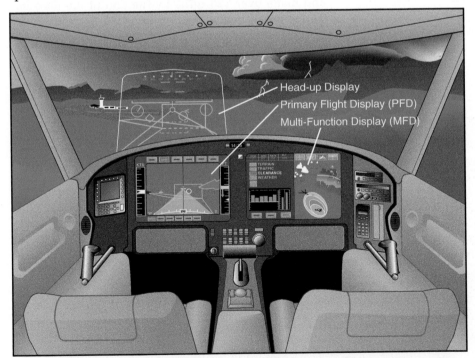

Head-up Display
Primary Flight Display (PFD)
Multi-Function Display (MFD)

Figure 10-4. This is an artist conception of the AGATE aircraft cabin. It incorporates side-stick flight controls, a multi-function display (MFD), a head-up display, and a primary flight display (PFD).

Flight Lines

height above the ground. By providing the cockpit equipment free of charge to several bush airlines, the FAA initially tested the Capstone system in Alaska in 2000. The Flight Information Service - Broadcast (FIS-B) became available continuously and automatically to equipped cockpits. The FIS data link was designed to provide service through the United States to aircraft flying 5,000 feet above ground level and higher, up to 17,500 feet above mean sea level.

These are public examples of research and development in general aviation. Proprietary research and development programs lack the open access that government agencies provide.

International Production

While the United States continued to dominate general aviation in terms of airplane shipments, number of aircraft in operation, and number of pilots, manufacturers outside the United States shipped aircraft too. Airbus, Bombardier, Dassault, Piaggio, Pilatus, and Socata all produced general aviation airplanes. Airbus introduced the ACJ, a spacious corporate jet (CJ) with seating for up to 50 passengers and crew members and with a range of 4500 miles, first flown and first delivered in 1998. Bombardier made Learjets, Challengers, and Global Express planes. Dassault continued its popular Falcon line. Piaggio made the Avanti, Pilatus the PC-12, and Socata the TB series. One of the destinations for these aircraft was the United States, which imported 282 civil aircraft in 1998, 432 in 1999, 460 in 2000, 519 in 2001, and 597 in 2003. (Figures 10-5, 10-6, and 10-7)

Piaggio's Avanti had begun in the 1980s as a joint venture with Gates Learjet. First flown in 1986, the Avanti was a nine-passenger twin-engine turboprop, powered by Pratt & Whitney PT6 engines in a pusher configuration. In the 1990s, such twins faced competition from new single-engine turboprops. Socata of France and Mooney of the United States jointly designed the TBM 700, a six-seat pressurized plane. Socata produced the TBM starting in 1990 and made over 125 units by the end of the decade. The versatile Swiss-made Pilatus PC-12 could be a nine-passenger airliner, a six-passenger executive plane, or a cargo carrier. The prototype first flew in 1991. Capable of taking off and landing at unimproved airstrips, the PC-12 became popular, and

Figure 10-5. Regional jets, such as this Canadair regional jet, are becoming a familiar sight on shorter routes.

Pilatus built more than 200 of them over the next decade.

Dassault unveiled the Falcon 7X at the Paris Air Show in 2005. The three-engine 7X is a digitally designed business jet that includes 40,000 parts and 200,000 fasteners. The first flight of the 7X had occurred a month before the air show, but because of the digital design, that aircraft was a production model rather than a prototype. Dassault told prospective customers that digital design would facilitate customizing the aircraft too. Dassault also sold the design technology to Boeing, which planned to use it in developing the 787 passenger jetliner.

Figure 10-7. The Socata TBM 700 turboprop.

races were canceled due to the grounding of aircraft following the terrorist attacks of September 11.

Incentives to race included winning prize money, meeting technical challenges, testing flying skills, demonstrating aircraft, setting records, and simply having fun. Although rules changed each year, and weather occasionally canceled a race, races were held in six basic classes. The biplane class allowed small, single-seat aerobatic planes, such as the Pitts Special and Smith Miniplane, to compete. The Formula One class, as in auto racing, provided technical specifications to which the competing airplanes must have been built. The T-6 or Harvard class raced stock North American T-6 Texan, Harvard, or SNJ aircraft. Unlimited meant any piston plane.

The sports class covered high-performance, commercially available, kit-built airplanes. It joined the Reno schedule in 1998. Dave Morss, in a Lancair IV, won the Gold Race in the sports class in 1998, 1999, and 2000; his speeds were respectively 308 mph, 319 mph, and 328 mph. Darryl Greenamyer, in a Lancair Legacy, won both in 2002 with a speed of over 328 mph, and in 2003 with a speed of 324 mph.

Figure 10-6. Pilatus PC-12.

Flight Records

Pilots still reached for records — the first, the fastest, or the farthest, now often qualified as the first, fastest, or farthest in a particular type or model of aircraft over a particular route. The Reno National Championship Air Races, for example, provided the venue for pilots seeking to establish the fastest times. In other examples, there was an international race to make the first balloon flight around the world, and AeroVironment made a series of solar powered aircraft that flew farther above the earth than any piston-, jet-, or other solar-powered airplane.

Reno Races

The Reno Air Racing Association continued sponsoring annual Reno National Championship Air Races that had begun in 1964. The only interruption in the annual races occurred in 2001, when the September

Historic Event

At the Reno National Championship Air Races on 12 September 2003, *Dago Red*, a modified North American P-51D Mustang piloted by Skip Holm, flew an average speed of 507.105 miles per hour and thereby shattered the world unlimited-class speed record. The six laps of the race covered 50.33 miles. Two days later *Dago Red* won the eight-lap, 67.29-mile Gold race with a speed of 497.938 mph. At the 2003 Air Races, *Dago Red* won its fifth Reno national championship in the unlimited class.

The Racing Association added the sixth class, jet class, as a special attraction to draw people to the 2002 races, the year after the 2001 Reno races had been canceled. The jet class was limited to L-39 Albatross jets. Curt Brown won the 2002 Gold Race with a speed of just over 456 mph, and Mary Dilda won the 2003 Gold Race with a speed of 434 mph.

The biplane class had several repeat winners. *Rags*, a Rose Peregrine flown by Dave Rose, won the Biplane Gold races in 1999, 2000, and 2002. *Glass Slipper*, a Mong Sport piloted by Jim Smith, won in 1992 and 1998, and *Class Action*, a Pitts Special, with Earl Allen in the pilot's seat, in 1994 and 1997. Patti Johnson-Nelson in *Full Tilt Boogie*, a Boland Mong, finished first in 1993, 1995, and 1996. Takehisa "Ken" Ueno, in the *Samurai*, won in 1991, and Danny Mortensen flew the *Amsoil Pacific Flyer*, a Mong, to first in the 1990 race. Winning speeds varied between 192 mph in 1990 and 224 mph in 2002.

A few pilots and planes dominated the unlimited class. Lyle Shelton won four consecutive years (1988-1991) with speeds between 450 and 482 mph. He flew *Rare Bear*, a Grumman F8F-2 Bearcat. Bill "Tiger" Destefani won 1992–1993 and 1995–1997. His North American P-51 Mustang *Strega* achieved a top racing speed of 468 mph. John Penney in *Rare Bear* won in 1994 with a speed of 424 mph. Bruce Lockwood won in 1998 with a speed of 451 mph, and in 1999 at 472 mph. He flew *Dago Red*, a P-51D Mustang. Skip Holm flew *Dago Red* to win the 2000, 2002, and 2003 Gold races in the unlimited class. This airplane became the first unlimited-class plane to break the 500 miles-per-hour mark. Holm flew the plane at the record-setting pace of 507 mph in 2003.

Balloon Race

The team of Maxie Anderson, Ben Abruzzo, and Larry Newman, in the balloon *Double Eagle II*, crossed the Atlantic Ocean in 1978, and Abruzzo, Newman, Ron Clark, and Rocky Aoki, in the *Double Eagle 5*, crossed the Pacific Ocean in 1981. They reflected the boom in recreational ballooning that came with the availability of lightweight materials, such as nylon for the envelope, and the adaptation of propane and later kerosene burners to balloons. Only one great balloon challenge remained — a flight around the world. Billed as the "last great race," this challenge attracted long-distance balloonists.

Several round-the-world attempts failed in the early 1990s, yet the competition intensified. Steve Fossett of the United States made his first attempt at a round-the-world flight in January 1996. He piloted the balloon *Solo Challenger*, built by Cameron Balloons of England, from South Dakota to a landing three days later in eastern Canada. The next year, in a rebuilt and renamed balloon, now called the *Solo Spirit*, he tried again. He left from St. Louis in January, and flew eastward, but landed in India. In December he tried again. The *Solo Spirit* landed this time in Krasnodar, Russia, still short of his round-the-world goal.

An international team also tried in 1997. Bertrand Piccard of Switzerland, Wim Verstraeton of Belgium, and Andy Elson of the United States departed from Switzerland in the *Breitling Orbiter*, made by Cameron, but ditched in the Mediterranean Sea. Piccard's team returned to the air in early 1998, in the

Dago Red and *Rare Bear* in 2003

balloon now called *Breitling Orbiter 2*. The name Breitling came from the sponsoring Swiss watchmaker. This time they traveled as far as Myanmar (Burma), when China's refusal to grant permission for the balloon to enter Chinese airspace forced a landing.

Among the competition were Kevin Uliassi and Dick Rutan. Uliassi lifted off from a field in Illinois in December 1997, but he landed only a few hours later in Indiana. His balloon was the *J. Renee*, made by Cameron. Uliassi tried again in March 1998, and this time he made it as far as Myanmar. Dick Rutan and Dave Melton had to parachute from their *Global Hilton* only 70 minutes after launch in January 1998. The helium bag exploded on both the *J. Renee* and *Global Hilton*.

At least seven teams were preparing balloons for a round-the-world attempt in late 1998. Virgin Group executive Richard Branson and his *ICO Global Challenger*, made by Lindstrand Balloons of England and referred to by the name of the sponsoring company, ICO. The *Dymocks Flyer* and *Team RE/MAX* balloons incorporated features borrowed from NASA's high-altitude research balloons. John Wallington and Bob Martin were the crew. The *Spirit of Peace, Global Conqueror,* and *Cable & Wire* were Cameron products. Fossett attempted round-the-world flights twice in 1998. He, Richard Branson, and Per Lindstrand took off from Argentina and ditched near Australia in one attempt, and took off from Marrakech, Morocco, and landed near Hawaii in their next attempt. Meanwhile, Rutan and Melton prepared the *World Quest*, designed by Burt Rutan, for a 1999 attempt to circumnavigate the globe in the Southern Hemisphere.

Piccard's turn came again on 1 March 1999, when he and Brian Jones on the *Breitling Orbiter 3* launched from Switzerland, meridian 9.27 degrees East. On 20

Historic Event

On 20 March 1999 Bertrand Piccard and Brian Jones pass 9.27° west, the meridian that marks the completion of the first circumnavigation of the Earth in a balloon. They landed the following morning at 1:02 am near Mut in Egypt, after having spent 19 days, 21 hours, and 55 minutes aloft, which also set a new balloon flight duration record.

March, over the Islamic Republic of Mauritania, they achieved the round-the-world goal by crossing 9.27 degrees East. They landed the next day near Mut, Egypt. The flight logged 19 days, 21 hours, and 55 minutes of flight time. They won! And they established duration and distance records in the process.

Record-setting continues to be a sport of the wealthy, as Fossett illustrates. He flew around the world in the *Bud Light Spirit of Freedom* in June-July 2002. His flight began at Northam, Western Australia, on 19 June, and concluded at Lake Yamma Yamma, a dry lake, in the east Australian outback on 4 July. With this flight, Fossett achieved the first solo round-the-world balloon flight, the longest-distance solo flight, and the longest-duration solo flight. Another example is Vijaypat Singhania of India. Singhania broke the altitude record for hot air balloons in 2005, when he in the *Envelope* reached 69,852 feet in November 2005.

High Flight

Founded by Paul MacCready, the AeroVironment company continued developing high-altitude aircraft throughout the 1990s. The goal became a high-altitude aircraft that could replace communication, reconnaissance, and research satellites. Having worked on the *Solar Challenger* high-altitude piloted aircraft,

Historical Note

Flying a balloon around the world was not enough for Steve Fossett, who continued to chase world records. In the Virgin Atlantic *Global Flyer* airplane, in March 2005, he set a new speed record of 67 hours and 01 minute for flying a plane without refueling around the world. Also in the *Global Flyer*, in February 2006, he established a new long-distance record of 26,389 miles; this broke Dick Rutan and Jeanna Yeager's 1986 *Voyager* airplane record of 24,987 miles and also exceeded the Bertrand Piccard and Brian Jones's 1999 *Breitling Orbiter 3* balloon distance record of 25,361 miles.

Personal Profile

Bertrand Piccard is a Swiss medical doctor and psychiatrist, but his place in the history books was assured when he, along with British pilot Brian Jones, became the first to fly nonstop around the world in a balloon. Piccard is only the latest in a line of pioneers and high acheivers. He is the son of Jacques Piccard, who descended nearly seven miles below the surface of the ocean in the bathyscaphe *Trieste* in 1960. That dive, made with U.S. Navy Lt. Don Walsh, went to the deepest known point on Earth, the bottom of the Mariana Trench in the Pacific Ocean. Jacques had previously set a world record for the deepest ocean descent in 1953, along with Bertrand's grandfather, Auguste, who actually designed the bathyscaphe. A world-renowned Swiss engineer and scientist, Auguste had also set a world altitude record in 1931, ascending to an altitude of 51,961 feet in a stratospheric balloon. Bertrand's great-uncle Jean was the twin brother of Auguste, and also a distinguished physicist. Jean flew balloons into the stratosphere too, ascending to 57,549 feet in 1934.

Bertrand Piccard

AeroVironment turned to unmanned aerial vehicles (UAVs) to reach higher altitudes. Each of the AeroVironment planes converted solar energy into electrical energy to drive multiple propellers on a large wing. The company adapted engines and propellers for high altitudes. NASA's Environmental Research Aircraft and Sensor Technology (ERAST) project became a sponsor of the company's high-alti-tude solar-electric airplane program in 1997. ERAST sought aircraft for monitoring floods, fires, and crops.

AeroVironment's six-engine *Pathfinder* broke the *Solar Challenger's* altitude record for solar-powered aircraft. The *Pathfinder* reached 50,500 feet in 1995 and 71,500 in 1997. The modified and larger *Pathfinder Plus* achieved 80,400 feet in 1998. After low-altitude tests in 1998, the *Centurion* was modified, its wing expanded from 206 feet to 247 feet, and its name changed to *Helios*. This *Helios* prototype shattered the piston, jet, and solar altitude records in 2001, when it reached 96,863 feet. The Lockheed SR-71 spy plane had held the altitude record of 85,068 feet since 1976. (Figure 10-8)

In 2001, AeroVironment's Sky Tower subsidiary, the Japanese Ministry of Post and Telecommunications, and NASA conducted telecommunication tests with commercial signals transmitted from over 60,000 feet in the stratosphere. Sky Tower is developing a High Altitude Platform Station for use by wireless service providers of a wide range of communication applications. AeroVironment is also developing a commercial version of *Helios*, which is to be equipped with fuel cells for storing energy to support night flight; that would enable the aircraft to achieve be long-duration flights, rather than land daily as the source of solar energy sets.

The crash of the *Helios* prototype in September 2003 was an unfortunate event, but not something that would deter ongoing or future work. NASA had opened a UAV Technology Center at the Ames Research Center the month before, and development continued at AeroVironment and other companies. The Association for Unmanned Vehicle Systems International already included Boeing, General Dynamics, and Northrop Grumman among its many corporate members, and BAE of Great Britain, Schiebel of Germany, Mitsui of Japan, Israeli Aircraft Industries, and Korea Aerospace — as well as AeroVironment. Some of the members had military UAV programs, but some, such as AeroVironment, were developing civil UAVs.

General aviation since 1990 has been changing — getting simpler in the example of ultralight flight and getting more technologically sophisticated in other cases, and an industry that once was centered in the United States has become more international.

Figure 10-8. On August 6, 1998, the solar-powered *Pathfinder* aircraft climbed to 80,400 feet over Hawaii. Beginning at 8:00 a.m., it climbed throughout the morning and reached its peak altitude around 3:15 p.m. Larger versions of the aircraft are expected to reach 100,000 feet.

Historic Event

On 13 August 2001, above the U.S. Navy Pacific Missile Range on Kauai Island, Hawaii, the unmanned solar-powered *Helios* flew to 96,863 feet, an altitude higher than any piston, jet, or solar aircraft in history.

Flight Lines

"If you play with toy airplanes, you get expertise in things that are really important."

Paul Macready, founder of AeroVironment, used these words to explain his career in aviation, as quoted in *Popular Science*, June 2003.

SECTION B

Commercial Aviation

Worldwide, the air transport industry suffered several years of losses until the upturn of 1993. The airline industry as a whole had posted operating losses in 1990, 1991, and 1992. The world's airlines posted an operating profit of about $2.3 billion in 1993, $8.4 billion in 1994, and $14 billion in 1995. Both passenger and freight traffic increased significantly from the lows of 1991. Total passenger kilometers increased from 1,844,000 million in 1991 to 2,230,000 million in 1995, which represented in 1992 a 4.6 percent increase over the previous year, in 1993 a 1.1 percent increase, in 1994 a 7.6 percent increase, and in 1995 a 6.3 percent increase. Freight ton kilometers went from 58,530 million in 1991 to 83,940 million in 1995, which represented in 1992 a 6.9 percent increase over the previous year, in 1993 a 7.9 percent increase, in 1994 a whopping 14.3 percent increase, and in 1995 an 8.7 percent increase. The International Civil Aviation Organization (ICAO) compiled these figures and predicted that the industry results through 1995 were sufficient to produce a net profit for the entire period 1990-1995. During the period of upturn, airlines reduced operating costs, fuel prices remained stable, and airlines began ordering new aircraft.

In 1995 international traffic accounted for 56 percent of the total passenger-kilometers flown and 84 percent of the freight ton-kilometers performed, according to ICAO. The routes were international, and industry also represented many nations. Of the worldwide revenues from scheduled operations in 1995, airlines of the United States accounted for about 35 percent. Airlines of other nations, especially in Europe and Asia, drew 65 percent of the revenues. By total passenger-kilometers and by ton-kilometers, by international operations and by total operations, the countries performing the most commercial airline service were the United States, United Kingdom, and Japan, in that order.

The upturn continued until the end of the century when the Asian currency crisis cut Japanese financing for equipment (which had been substantial in the mid 1990s), reduced the number of routes and the number of passengers, and generally soured the economy and by extension commercial aviation. The downturn deepened with the terrorist events of September 11, 2001, and the subsequent decline in travel. Contagious diseases such as the West Nile virus and severe acute respiratory syndrome (SARS) also discouraged air travel for a while.

A common thread in the story of commercial aviation since the end of the Cold War is internationalism. Through the ICAO and other forums, many nations moved toward the worldwide implementation of the new aeronautical meteorological codes, such as the METAR, SPECI, and TAF codes. Many problems were also international in scope, like the fuel crisis of 2005.

Historical Note

The top 25 airports in the world handled about 877 million passengers, including 423 million international passengers, in 1995. Ranked by volume of international passengers, the top 25 were: London Heathrow, Frankfurt, Hong Kong, Paris Charles de Gaulle, Amsterdam Schipol, Singapore, Toyko Narita, London Gatwick, New York Kennedy, Bangkok, Miami, Zurich, Los Angeles, Seoul, Brussels, Manchester, Rome Fiumicino, Copenhagen, Paris Orly, Palma de Mallorca, Dusseldorf, Toronto, Madrid, Munich, and Vienna.

Bangkok

Airliners

The worldwide commercial fleet reflected the increasing internationalism. In the mid 1990s the fleet included aircraft built by North American, European, and Brazilian manufacturers. The jetliners were Airbus A300, A310, A319, A320, A321, A330, and A340; Boeing 737, 747, 757, 767, and 777; British Aerospace 146-100/200/300 and RJ70/85/100; Canadair Regional Jet; Embraer EMB-145, Fokker 70 and 100; and McDonnell-Douglas MD-80/90 and MD-11. The fleet also included turboprops made by Aérospatiale-Aeritalia, British Aerospace, DeHavilland Canada, Dornier, Embraer, Fokker, and Saab. The Russian Federation and its customers had fleets that included the jetliners Ilyushin Il-76, Yakovlev Yak-42, Ilyushin Il-86, Antonov An-124, and — in the case of Russia — the Airbus A310, which in 1992 became the first foreign airliner in Aeroflot's fleet.

Competition between European and American manufacturers intensified, particularly the competition between Airbus and Boeing. Carefully avoiding intra-European rivalries, the international Airbus consortium continued to reinvigorate the European aviation industry and to capture market share. Airbus announced its first operating profits in early 1991, the same year it obtained its first orders from United Airlines. Selling to United represented a major achievement because United and Boeing had strong ties going back to the early 1930s when both United and Boeing were part of United Aircraft and Transport Corporation. Airbus had already sold aircraft to American Airlines in the mid 1980s by accepting American's innovative proposal for a "walkaway lease." The lease permitted the airline to walk away, that is — return a leased plane, with only 30 days advance notice. The lease resembled a rental arrangement, and it had the advantage that an airline could equip its fleet without showing any liability (long-term financial commitment) on the balance sheet.

Airbus sales captured half of the widebody sector in 1990, and Boeing responded by launching the 777 twinjet project that year. This twin-engine, twin-aisle plane was about the same size as the Boeing 747, but large for a twin. Initially proposed as an extended Boeing 767, the 777 became a new design and the world's longest aircraft. The design process was new in the sense that all design work was done on computers; engineers used software rather than hardware to resolve aerodynamic and engineering issues. The computer-aided design process answered questions previously addressed by wind tunnel and flight tests.

The 777 came with fly-by-wire controls, a technology that Airbus had pioneered. Boeing developed and brought into production the 777-200 and -300 during the 1990s. (Figure 10-9)

Subsidies have long been an issue. Boeing accused Airbus of unfair trade practice due to the government subsidies that helped the European consortium, and Airbus responded that Boeing received indirect government subsidies in the form of research, development, and military contracts. Nonetheless, the European Commission and the United States agreed in 1992 to establish clear rules applicable to both manufacturers. By terms of the agreement, direct subsidies were limited to 30 percent or less of the total development costs and indirect subsidies were limited to 5 percent of the manufacturer's civil turnover. Also, the various governments were not to pressure any other government to buy aircraft of its make. That agreement held for seven years, until aircraft came under the General Agreement on Tariffs and Trade, which, as Airbus had insisted, included the provision that royalties not count as subsidies. These agreements recognized and legitimized different ways of doing business. Airbus, nonetheless, considered becoming more corporate in its structure. Airbus planned to restructure into a Single Corporate Entity (SCE) in 1999, but postponed doing so indefinitely. Both sides eventually agreed to use the World Trade

Figure 10-9. Boeing 777-300

10-20

Historical Note

Because the partner companies of the Airbus consortium are scattered throughout several European countries, many large components (such as wings and fuselage sections) must be transported between plants in different parts of Europe. The A300-600ST shown below is one of the aircraft to handle that task. Development work on the "Beluga" began in 1991, and it first flew in September of 1994.

Organization's definition of subsidy, yet subsidies remain an issue in 2006. Does this tax or that tax constitute a subsidy? Do cost-plus defense contracts subsidize Boeing?

At the Farnborough Air Show in 1992, Airbus displayed its new A340. Post-Soviet Russia also brought a new transport, the Tupolev Tu-204 with Rolls-Royce engines, because the Russians hoped to sell planes on the world market. For a few years, Airbus and Boeing reluctantly explored a joint superjumbo jet project, but those discussions ended in 1995. About that time, the 1994 sales figures were released: Airbus had sold more airplanes than Boeing for the first time.

The United States responded to the Airbus challenge by giving NASA more funds for civil aerospace research so that the United States might reclaim the technological leadership. NASA investigated topics applicable to commercial aircraft. In the late 1980s and early 1990s laminar flow control was developed to reduce drag over a wing and thereby improve fuel efficiency. In a concurrent program, NASA and the FAA jointly studied the causes of wind shear and explored possible corrective actions. In the mid-1990s, NASA engineers and scientists developed flight control from engine thrust. The agency also worked to improve the configuration of aircraft to

reduce sonic boom, which had implications for the second-generation supersonic transport under development at NASA and Boeing (since cancelled) as well as military aircraft. More recently, NASA teams have been developing a windowless cockpit, new airport designs, and improved flight control centers.

In 1997 Boeing acquired McDonnell Douglas, a financially troubled competitor that had only 5 percent of the commercial market at the time. The deal helped Boeing more on the military side. Worried more about foreign competition than antitrust enforcement, the United States government supported the merger. Boeing was important to the country, and Boeing's success on the world market was important, because Boeing was the country's single largest exporter. When the European Commission approved the merger, the commission required that Boeing share certain patent information with Airbus.

The industry experienced other mergers as well. Mergers allowed companies to reduce costs by eliminating redundancies in administrative functions, facilities, and personnel, but mergers also contributed to unemployment in the industry.

Meanwhile, Airbus decided to extend its product line into business aircraft, and it did so in a big way. The spacious Airbus Corporate Jet (ACJ), with a capacity to seat up to 50 passengers and crew, was essentially an A319 with a luxurious interior. Airbus made the first delivery of an ACJ in 1998. At that time Embraer of Brazil was developing a new line of aircraft to compete in the business plane sector, with the twin-turboprop 50-seat ER-145, and in the regional airline sector, with the 70- to 110-seat Embraer 170/175/190/195 family. Embraer advertised nearly 90 percent commonality among the models, and all models used the same cabin crew trainer. Founded in 1969 as a government venture, Embraer had become a private company in 1994. First in the

Historic Event

On 25 July 2000, an Air France Concorde crashed in Paris, killing the 109 people on board the plane and four people on the ground. Despite a good safety record since entering service in 1976, the Concorde had serious design flaws, as revealed by the investigation into the Paris crash. The cause of that crash was a design flaw: the aircraft lacked protection from debris, such as that from a bursting tire.

Historical Note

Only Air France and British Airways flew the supersonic Concorde, and both took the plane out of service after the fatal crash in Paris on 25 July 2000. The crash did not affect the airline industry as a whole. Air France and British Airways resumed Concorde service in November 2001 with modified planes, sturdier tires, and lined fuel tanks. But the crash investigation had revealed design flaws, and maintenance costs were high. Both airlines retired the Concorde in 2003.

The Concorde had been the only supersonic airliner in service. Aeroflot had taken the Tupulev Tu-144 out of service in 1984, and the U.S. closed the NASA high speed research program in 1999, before any American supersonic design entered production. The future of civil supersonic flight is uncertain.

Boeing had been a contractor on the NASA high speed research program. At the 2001 Paris Air Show, Boeing unveiled a model of the Sonic Cruiser, a commercial plane designed to fly at speeds up to Mach .98 — just short of supersonic. But Boeing canceled the Sonic Cruiser program in December 2002.

NASA, the U.S. Defense Advanced Research Projects Agency, the Japanese Aerospace Exploration Agency, and QunetiQ of the United Kingdom are experimenting with scramjet aircraft designed to fly at hypersonic speeds. Flight testing of scramjets — supersonic combustion ramjets — has been underway at the Woomera test range in Australia since 2002; on March 27, 2006, the Hyshot III was tested there. NASA's scramjet-powered X-43A aircraft established a speed record of Mach 9.6 on 16 November 2004. But any commercial application of the scramjet appears to be a long way off.

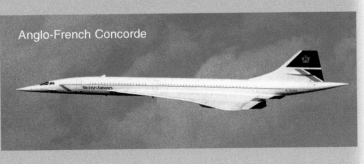

Anglo-French Concorde

More practical is a supersonic passenger plane under study by the Society of Japanese Aerospace Companies and the French Aerospace Industries Association. At the Paris Air Show in 2005 these groups signed an agreement to cooperate on a successor to the Concorde.

Historical Note

Airbus and Boeing were big companies that made big planes with big price tags. They were big in another way too. In 1990, when Airbus opened its new factory in Toulouse, France, the factory was the largest building in Europe. Boeing's 747 plant on the outskirts of Seattle was the largest in the world.

new family to fly was a 170 in February 2002, while development continued on the other airliners in the family. The maiden flight of a stretched version, the 175, occurred in June 2003. Embraer scheduled delivery of the Embraer 170 to its launch customer, Swiss International, and to US Airways Express Fleet late in 2003. US Airways, by the way, was under bankruptcy protection from August 2002 to March 2003.

Airbus committed to designing and producing a superjumbo jet in 2000, when it launched the new A380. Airbus specifications required the latest composite materials, state-of-the-art industrial processes, fuel efficiency, and environmentally friendly operations. Although the airliner was still a few years from anticipated production, Federal Express placed an order in 2003 for aircraft to be used on its cargo route between North America and Southeast Asia. The A380 completed its first test flight in April 2005.

Boeing meanwhile took under development what it called the Dreamliner, initially designated 7E7, which would have only half the passenger capacity of the Airbus superjumbo. The 7E7 was being designed for high-speed, long-distance routes. The 7E7 became the 787.

Developing new airplanes involved a gamble, and the companies placed their bets. Boeing bet on the 777 and 787, and Airbus bet on the A380. Whether a winner or a loser emerges is yet to be determined. Boeing's record-setting 777 flight nonstop from Hong Kong to London in November 2005, over a distance of 13,422 miles, was part of the stakes. It was Boeing's way of saying, "my plane can go farther than yours," yours being the Airbus A340 with a range of less than 11,000 miles.

Some companies also hedged their bets; Pratt & Whitney, for example, announced in early 2006 its decision to produce parts for rival General Electric's commercial CFM56 engines, which is built by General Electric and the French company Snecma Moteurs, a subsidiary of Safran S.A. The lucrative spare-parts business that had long supported third-party suppliers would now, Pratt & Whitney hoped, help the competition.

Airlines

In addition to aircraft, bilateral and multilateral agreements, as well as infrastructure technology, helped open international air routes to commercial traffic. In July 1996, for example, the Caribbean Community agreed to more liberal and transparent exchange of commercial trade routes, and in December the six South American countries in the Mercosur trade area decided to encourage subregional air services to cities not served by bilateral agreements. The North Pole, or Arctic, air routes provided great-circle savings in distance, but involved many nations. In 2001 Canada, China, Finland, Germany, Iceland, Japan, Mongolia, Norway, the Russian Federation, and the United States agreed upon the new structure for air routes crossing the Arctic Ocean. All contracting states got the right to use the routes. The increasing development and implementation of global satellite-based communication, navigation, and surveillance systems for air traffic management replaced line-of-sight systems and enabled the development of new routes, such as those across the South Pacific Ocean.

Air Afrique

Some airlines were international in more ways than routes traveled. Air Afrique represented 11 partners states: Benin, Burkina Faso, Central African Republic,

Chad, Congo, Cote d'Ivoire, Mali, Mauritania, Niger, Senegal, and Togo. Similarly, Denmark, Norway, and Sweden were members of a consortium called the Scandinavian Airlines System. Bahrain, Oman, Qatar, and United Arab Emirates were partners in Gulf Air.

By the international Treaty of Yaounde, Cameroon, in 1961, Air Afrique organized to serve 11 former French colonies. As a proud symbol of African independence, Air Afrique developed routes to other African nations, as well as Asia, the Middle East, Europe, and North and South America. By the 1990s, the airline had grown to over 5,000 employees, and its fleet included Airbuses and DC-10s.

Air Afrique, however, operated with chronic financial problems, and it accumulated a heavy debt load. In 2001 the member states decided to liquidate the airline. In its place, they planned a new airline. The 11 partner states would own 20 percent of the successor airline, employees would receive 5 percent, and Air France, minority shareholder in Air Afrique, would acquire 35 percent of the new company. The remaining stock would go to institutional investors. That was the plan for a new company with the familiar name Air Afrique. Despite assistance from the World Bank, the restructuring plan collapsed. The September 11 terrorist attacks on targets in the United States depressed commercial aviation and hampered the restructuring effort. Political instability in various African countries and the sheer amount of debt were other factors. In January 2002 Air Afrique returned the last of the aircraft it had leased, and in February the defunct airline formally went into bankruptcy.

Air Afrique was but one African airline. Many others continued to fly, and some had problems. When a Sosoliso Airlines plane crashed in December 2005, over a hundred people died; 71 were students of one boarding school. Another Nigerian airline, Bellview Airlines, had crashed a plane in October 2005, also killing over a hundred people. Nigeria's President Olusegun Obasanjo temporarily grounded the fleets of Sosoliso and Chanchangi and complained of corruption in the aviation sector that resulted in multiple crashes and needless deaths. Crashes make news. The safely operated airlines rarely crash, whether in Africa or elsewhere. So when the European Union in March 2006 banned dozens of African airlines from flying in European airspace, the African Airlines Association promptly objected. According to the association, none of the banned airlines did fly in European airspace, so the ban tainted African airlines that did fly in European airspace, airlines with good safety standards.

United Airlines

United Airlines, long a major national airline in the United States, expanded into a global airline, restructured its employee relations, struggled, and eventually fell into bankruptcy. The expansion began in 1990. That year United acquired routes between the United States and Paris, Tokyo, London, and Madrid. The next year it expanded to Amsterdam, Berlin, Madrid, and Munich, and the following year to Caracas, Buenos Aires, Rio de Janeiro, Sao Paolo, and other South American cities. United was expanding as fuel prices rose due to the Gulf War, and while no-frill airlines were initiating service as low-price alternatives to the business-class service that was United's specialty. Moreover, new routes required planes, and United placed large orders. The airline lost hundreds of million dollars a year in 1991, 1992, and 1993. United kept its global goal, however, and in 1995, with the addition of service to New Delhi, India, it succeeded in covering the globe.

To cut costs, United froze hiring, grounded its inefficient older aircraft, and sold flight kitchens. Labor remained a high cost, and difficult negotiations finally produced contracts with the Air Line Pilots Association and the International Association of Machinists. Yet in December 1993 United approved an employee ownership plan in order to further reduce its outflow of money. Accordingly, the airline's 54,000 employees in the United States exchanged part of their salaries and benefits for shares in the company. When the employee stock ownership plan became effective in July 1994, United became the largest employee-owned company in the world. In another innovation adopted in 1994, representatives of the International Association of Machinists and the Air Line Pilots Association joined the airline's board of directors. Initially, the employee stock ownership plan covered only employees in the United States, but the airline gradually expanded the coverage.

To be more competitive, United in 1994 established the Shuttle regional airline to serve the western region of the United States with prices and routes designed to compete with other regional airlines. Regional airlines in general provided two valuable services: they carried passengers to airline hubs, at which passenger could catch flights on major airlines

to more distant destinations, and they delivered passengers to destinations within their service areas.

United joined Air Canada, Lufthansa, Scandinavian Airlines, and Thai Airways to found the Star Alliance in 1997. They ambitiously called this alliance "the airline network for Earth." This was code sharing on a grand scale. Code sharing, by which partner airlines (regionals and majors cooperating at a hub, airlines operating overlapping but different routes, and even international airlines connecting at airports to transfer passengers) could share in the computer database a code to enable passengers to book passage with the same "airline" despite different legs of the flight being flown by different sharers of the code. Frequent flier mileage that accumulated over an entire trip went to the passenger's frequent flier account. Star Alliance attracted new members: Air New Zealand, All Nippon Airways, Asian Airlines, BMI (formerly British Midland), Lauda, Mexicana, Singapore Airlines, Tyrolean Airways, and VARIG Brazilian Airlines. Star Alliance indeed became a global network.

But United Airlines still had problems, especially money problems. The global economic recession, troubled labor negotiations following the end of the investment period in the employee stock ownership plan, a proposed merger with US Airways; the loss of planes, personnel, and passengers on September 11, 2001; and the decline in passenger travel after September 11 compounded the company's financial problems, and the company continued to invest in technology to improve service. Efforts to refinance failed, and in December 2002 United Airlines filed for Chapter 11 bankruptcy protection. That allowed the airline to continue operating while seeking a solution to its financial problems. The company sought wage reductions, but rising fuel costs overshadowed cost savings elsewhere. The company based its plan to emerge from bankruptcy on crude oil prices of $50 barrel, but prices reached over $70 in 2005 and stayed in the high $60s into the next year. United Airlines remained under Chapter 11 protection in early 2006, as it celebrated the 25th anniversary of its frequent-flier mileage program.

One problem for United and other legacy airlines in the United States has been low-fare competitors. Southwest Airlines, for example, hedged aggressively on fuel and therefore managed to keep fares too low for legacy airlines to recover their costs when fuel prices rose. But even low-fare operators have had problems; for example, Independence Air quit flying in January 2006. Incidents of bad management and the effects from terrorism, including the cost of increased aviation security following the September 11 attacks, have contributed to the industry's problems. Some problems apparently date farther back in time — to deregulation and the absence of a coherent national aviation policy.

China

In the mid-1980s communist China decided to decentralize the Civil Aviation Administration of China (CAAC), the national airline. A variety of airlines formed, including local-service, regional, and domestic lines between major cities. The three regional divisions of the CAAC became international and mainline airlines: Air China, China Eastern, and China Southern. By 1995, over 25 airlines had begun operations in China. The new government policy allowed the formation of independent airlines, and among the airlines that formed were Shanghai Airlines, Xiamen, Shenzhen, Hainon (Haikou), Wuhan, China Great Wall (Chongqing), and China Xinhau (Beijing).

These airlines needed airliners, and they turned to the west for the planes. Some purchased used, others new. Among the western models in Chinese fleets in 1995 were Boeing 707, 737, 747, 757, 777; Airbus A300, A310, A330, A340; MD-11, MD-82; BAe 146 ; Short 360; Fokker 100, and DeHavilland Canada DHC-8 — more Boeing planes than all others combined. The

Historical Evidence

"Is flying safe? It is not safe enough." In these few words consumer activist Ralph Nader and author Wesley J. Smith summarize their 1994 book called *Collision Course, the Truth about Airline Safety*. They found evidence of safety lapses throughout the aviation industry, including bureaucratic complacency, cost-benefit analyses in lieu of safety-based decisions, economic deregulation weakening safety regulation, the FAA having the conflicting jobs of promoting both aviation and safety, the FAA rule-shopping to accommodate airlines, mismanaged inspectors, unhappy air traffic controllers, troubled technologies, inadequate crash survivability, ineffective passenger screening, airport runway incursions, crowded airways, controlled flight into terrain, and stormy weather. The problems were generally known in the aviation community. In closing, Nader and Smith advised air passengers to "protect yourself."

Historical Evidence

The Federal Aviation Administration (FAA) and the National Transportation Safety Board (NTSB) keep track of aviation accidents and safety statistics. Airline industry organizations such as the Air Transport Association (ATA), Regional Airline Association (RAA), and International Air Transport Association (IATA) usually keep statistics relating to their business. Organizations like the General Aviation Manufacturers Association (GAMA) keep records of general information on production, revenue, and industry trends. Organizations like the Experimental Aircraft Association (EAA) and the Aircraft Owners and Pilots Association (AOPA) assemble statistical information that may be helpful or interesting to their members. Often you can access this information through their websites.

ATA - www.airlines.org	GAMA - www.gama.aero
AOPA - www.aopa.org	IATA - www.iata.org
EAA - www.eaa.org	ICAO - www.icao.org
FAA - www.faa.gov	NTSB - www.ntsb.gov
FAI - www.fai.org	RAA - www.raa.org

Chinese airlines also operated Russian-made airliners, mostly Tupolev Tu-154s, but also Antonov AN-24s and AN-30s, Ilyushin Il-14s, Il-76s and Il-86s, and Yakovlev Yak-42s. Based on the AN-24 design and built by Xi'an Aircraft, the Yun-7 appeared in many of the airline fleets. Xi'an Aircraft delivered 131 of the Yun-7 between 1986 and 2000. When a Yun-7 crashed in June 2000 with a loss of 42 lives, China grounded the Yun for several weeks. Aviation authorities determined that the aircraft was not at fault, and the planes returned to service.

Western manufacturers courted China because of the liberal policy that allowed airlines to proliferate, because of the country's large size in terms of geography (fourth largest in the world) and in terms of population (largest in the world), and because of the great opportunity for sales in China. Yet China's government policy also encouraged development of a domestic industry; for example, Aviation Industries of China started the new century designing a 60-90 seat plane for China's regional market and looking toward developing a 150-200 seat aircraft.

TERRORISM

The end of the Cold War eased tensions between the United States and the former republics of the Soviet Union, notably Russia, but the United States and the western world got new enemies in the form of terrorists who opposed Western and American influence. Terrorism was not new, but the magnitude grew and the nature changed. Fanaticism and fundamentalism became factors. Terrorists sought not only publicity, but destruction, and no longer considered civilians innocent. Aircraft became both target and weapon.

The U.S. Navy mistakenly shot down Iran Air Flight 655 over the Persian Gulf in July 1988 and caused 290 fatalities, all passengers and crew on the civilian airliner. This greatly soured relations between the United States and Iran. When Pan American Flight 103 was destroyed by terrorists in December 1988, suspicion fell on the possibility that Iran was retaliating. The Pan American case continued in the courts through the 1990s and beyond. Finally in 2001, a Scottish court found one Libyan, Abdel Basset al-Megrahi, guilty of murdering 259 passengers and crew and 11 people on the ground at Lockerbie, Scotland.

In 1994 people wanting to crash airplanes into buildings tried to hijack two airliners. In the first instance, in April, an upset Federal Express flight engineer tried to hijack a Douglas DC-10 for the purpose of crashing it into the Federal Express building in Memphis, but the cockpit crew, all three injured, subdued the man. In the second incident, in December, four agents of the Armed Islamic Group, which used the French initials GIA, hijacked an Air France Airbus A300 in Algiers, Algeria. The GIA stated that it was trying to rid Islamic Algeria of western, particularly French, influence. The plane flew to Marseille. There the terrorists released some of the hostages and requested 27 tons of fuel for a flight to Paris, and stated they had 20 sticks of dynamite with them. Released hostages were unsure whether the terrorists planned to explode the plane over Paris or to crash it into the Eiffel Tower. French troops stormed the plane in Marseille and killed the hijackers.

When TWA Flight 800 crashed off of Long Island in July 1996, the cause was not obvious. Terrorism was one of the possibilities considered, but a lengthy government investigation concluded a fuel tank exploded, the explosion probably caused by an electrical problem.

By the late 1990s, terrorist Osama bin Laden, a Saudi in exile in Afghanistan, was leading his al-Qaeda organization and other followers in a jihad or holy war against the United States. Bin Laden and his followers objected to westernizing and modernizing influences of the United States in Arabic and Islamic nations. Bin Laden organized the 1998 terrorist attacks on U.S. embassies in Nairobi, Kenya, and Dar es Salaam, Tanzania. President Bill Clinton responded to those attacks with retaliatory missile strikes against terrorist-associated sites in Afghanistan and Sudan. This military force was a new level of response to terrorism. The United States eventually filed criminal charges against more than 20 men in connection with the embassy attacks. Bin Laden became a suspect again when terrorists blew a hole in the USS Cole at Aden, Yemen, in October 2000; 17 sailors died.

September 11, 2001

On 11 September 2001 terrorists hijacked four airliners: American Airlines Flight 11 and United Airlines Flight 175, both out of Boston bound for Los Angeles, American Airlines Flight 77 out of Washington Dulles Airport bound for Los Angeles, and United Airlines Flight 93 out of Newark bound for San Francisco. The 19 hijackers then used the aircraft as weapons. Flight 11 crashed into the North Tower of the World Trade Center in New York City at 8:46 a.m. local time. At 9:03 Flight 175 crashed into the South Tower. After the second crash, the Federal Aviation Administrated grounded all flights in the United States; this was the first nationwide closure of the national airspace. At 9:38 Flight 77 hit the Pentagon in Arlington, Virginia, near Washington, DC. At 10:10 Flight 93 crashed in rural Pennsylvania after the people on board interfered with the hijackers. The damage and death toll of the September 11 attacks were shocking. Both towers of the World Trade Center collapsed — live on television and with hundreds of rescue workers trapped inside. The 266 people on the planes, over 2,600 people at the World Trade Center, and 125 people at the Pentagon died. Hundreds more suffered injuries.

The use of aircraft as weapons by terrorists was new, and the magnitude of destruction was new. Aircraft remained grounded for days. National Guard troops moved into airports to provide security, and they stayed for months. Meanwhile, Congress nationalized airport security by transferring the responsibility from local security firms to a newly created

Transportation Safety Administration. Given the fear of biological or chemical weapons, the government grounded crop-dusting planes even after other aircraft were allowed to resume operation. Security expanded not only over passengers and luggage, but also cargo and mail. Airports, towers, and navigation and communication sites received security.

Missiles

A big fear arose that man-portable, shoulder-launched surface-to-air missiles, such as the Strela and the Stinger, could bring down commercial airliners. The Russian-made Kolomna Strela-2 (designated

Historical Evidence

"Whereas the future development of international civil aviation can greatly help to create and preserve friendship and understanding among the nations and peoples of the world, yet its abuse can become a threat to general security," so begins the Convention on International Civil Aviation signed at Chicago on 7 December 1944. That convention came into force in 1947 when the 26th country ratified it. At that time the International Civil Aviation Organization (ICAO) became the official agency for international civil aviation.

At ICAO's 33rd Assembly session in Montreal in late September 2001, within weeks of the September 11 terrorist attacks in the United States, ICAO passed a declaration on "the misuse of civil aircraft as weapons of destruction and other terrorist acts involving civil aviation." In that resolution, ICAO acknowledged that "the threat of terrorist acts, unlawful seizure of aircraft and other acts of unlawful interference against civil aviation, including acts aimed at destruction of aircraft, as well as acts aimed at using the aircraft as a weapon of destruction, have serious adverse effect on the safety, efficiency and regularity of international civil aviation, endanger the lives of persons on board and on the ground and undermine the confidence of the peoples of the world in the safety of international civil aviation."

September 11, as the 2001 events came to be called, affected more than the targeted nation. As ICAO noted, it undermined "the confidence of the peoples of the world in the safety of international civil aviation." ICAO collected the data that document the resulting worldwide decline in the civil aviation industry, as the organization had grown to represent 188 member states. The data appears in ICAO's reports, including the annual reports on civil aviation, published in the ICAO Journal.

Historical Note

A British citizen who converted to a fundamentalist version of Islam, Richard C. Reid (also known as Abdel Raheem) boarded American Airlines Flight 63 in Paris in December 2001. During the flight to Miami, Florida, he tried to ignite the plastic explosive in his shoes by lighting matches. The matches attracted attention, and flight attendants and passengers subdued Reid. The flight was diverted to Boston, where Reid was arrested.

Reid claimed his act was part of the jihad, in his words, "part of the ongoing war between Islam and disbelief … between us and the U.S." Convicted in January 2003, Reid was sentenced to life in prison. During the sentencing, U.S. District Judge William Young told Reid: "You are not an enemy combatant. You are a terrorist. You are not a soldier in any war. You are a terrorist. … And we do not negotiate with terrorists. … We hunt them down one by one and bring them to justice. … You are a terrorist."

the SA-7 or Grail by NATO) is a man-portable surface-to-air missile that debuted in the 1960s. The improved Strela-2M entered Soviet service in the 1970s. The 2M went into production in Egypt, China, the former Yugoslavia, and in the former communist republics of East Europe. It is widely available. The United States provided a more sophisticated shoulder-launched missile, the Raytheon FIM-92A Stinger, to Mujahedeen rebels fighting the Soviet occupation of Afghanistan in the 1980s.

In Sri Lanka, the Liberation Tigers of Tamil Eelam used the Strela repeatedly against government aircraft, killing about 180 people in the attacks. Terrorists also fired two SA-7s at an Israeli Arkia Airlines Boeing 757 departing Mombasa, Kenya, in 2002, but the attack failed. The American-made Stingers became a threat to commercial aircraft overflying Afghanistan, and might be used anywhere by terrorists who obtain weapons through the black market or terrorist networks.

Technologically, two Israeli companies combined efforts to develop Flight Guard. The Flight Guard joined Elta radar to detect shoulder-launched missiles, and Israeli Military Industries developed a counter-measures dispensing system to lead missiles away from the airliner. The United States Congress discussed possibly requiring on-board missile-defense systems on commercial airlines. The cost would be high for installation, maintenance, and upgrades, as well as the cost of weight and drag on the aircraft. To reduce the threat to U.S. commercial flights from attack by shoulder-fired, heat-seeking missiles, in 2003 the United States sent aviation safety investigators to airports in Asia and Europe to

Historical Note

The United States started screening passengers at airports in 1973, in response to then-recent aircraft hijackings. After September 11, 2001, the National Guard moved into airports to provide security while Congress established a Transportation Security Administration to assume responsibility for screening passengers and baggage. Thereafter, federal employees performed the screening.

investigate how commercial airports could defend against terrorists with such weapons.

Historical Note

Terrorists and rebels have launched shoulder-fired surface-to-air missiles against civil aviation:

April 1994. President Juvenal Habyarimana of Rwanda and President Cyprien Ntaryamira of Burundi died when Habyarimana's presidential jet, a Dassault Falcon 50, was shot down by two missiles; the responsible group was never identified. Their deaths precipitated ethnic genocide.

December 1997. A Yugoslav Air Transport plane with five aboard went down near Pristina, Kosovo, when struck by a missile launched by Kosovar rebels, the UCK (Ushtria Clirimtare E Kosoves, also known as the Kosovo Liberation Army or KLA).

September 1998. A Lionair Antonov AN-24 was shot down by rebels near Mannar, Sri Lanka; 55 people died.

October 1998. A Congo Airlines Boeing 727 with 40 people aboard went down when a missile hit the aircraft shortly after takeoff from Kindu, Congo.

November 1999. An old Douglas DC-3 fell to a missile when attacked by FARC (Fuerzas Armadas Revolucionarias de Colombia) rebels in Colombia.

December 1999. A United Nations Lockheed C-130 Hercules crashed and killed 14 in Angola when struck by a missile launched by UNITA (National Union for the Total Independence of Angola) rebels.

June 2001. A United Nations Boeing 727 over Angola was damaged by a UNITA-launched missile.

November 2002. Two SA-7 missiles missed an Israeli Arkia Airlines Boeing 757 departing Mombasa, Kenya.

August 2003. A man was arrested for trying to bring an Igla portable, surface-to-air missile into the United States for the purpose, he said, of attacking Air Force One, the presidential airplane.

Recovery

Airlines worldwide experienced a sharp downturn 2001, and only some improvement in 2002, according to the ICAO annual report for 2002. The problems began with the terrorist attacks of September 11, 2001, that shattered public confidence in air travel. The threat of a war between the United States and the Saddam Hussein-led Ba'ath-government of Iraq, and the subsequent war, hampered recovery of the air transport industry. So did the new and highly contagious disease called severe acute respiratory syndrome (SARS), which apparently flew out of China with air passengers. Both freight ton-kilometers and passenger-kilometers declined in 2001, marking the first decrease in passenger volume since 1993. Mail traffic fell too, partly due to the restrictions imposed by the United States on carrying mail on passenger flights.

Security became key. The United States established a Homeland Security Department and therein a Transportation Security Administration, and the nation increased security measures at the borders, including international airports. Airports installed security check points and adopted crowd control lines to funnel people through security. Frank C. Lanza's L-3 Communications company, founded in 1997, boomed with government orders for electronic detection systems for use at airports to scan luggage, at land ports of entry to scan trucks, and at seaports to scan shipping containers. Aviation schools, once popular with foreign students, attracted new scrutiny, as the September 11 terrorists had trained at several flight schools in the United States. In fact, all foreign students became subject to new screening procedures. The government conducted criminal background checks of airport workers, and banned flights near large public gatherings. The FAA designed a new airman certificate with a hologram for added security. The FAA also tried to protect the infrastructure of aviation, but a power blackout in the northeast and north central United States and southern Canada in August 2003 caused the cancellation of 700 flights and demonstrated the vulnerability of the infrastructure to nonterrorist factors, such as age and overuse.

International airports and airlines around the world increased security in response to September 11 and subsequent threats of terrorist activity. The United Nations, ICAO, NATO, and other international bodies increased efforts to stop terrorist acts. Is it enough?

Military Aerospace

The end of the Cold War did not end limited warfare around the world. In 1991, the year the Soviet Union dissolved, there was the Gulf War, or first Iraq War, in which Iraq fought a United States-led coalition of 30 countries (17 of which provided combat troops); also, the Iraqi government fought off a coup attempt by the Shi'a group. That same year in Africa, Algeria fought the Armed Islamic Group (GIA), and rival clans fought a civil war in Somalia and drew United Nations intervention. A Balkan war started in 1992 when Bosnia and Herzegovina declared independence from Yugoslavia. It was a bloody ethnic conflict between Muslim, Croat, and Serb, and it continued until the United Nations dropped bombs in 1995. In 1994 Chechen independence advocates fought Russian troops, who stayed to contain the sustained movement for independence. That conflict has continued into 2006.

The Congo fought rebels in 1997. Long-term rebel conflicts continued in Angola, Indonesia, and Sri Lanka. The Israel-Lebanon War that had begun in 1982 continued until 2003. Also, Chad fought Muslim separatists, Sierra Leone fought rebels, Tajikistan fought the United Tajik Opposition, and Ethiopia battled Eritrea. In 1999 Kosovo became a bloody ethnic battleground. In 2001 a coalition of the United States, the Afghan Northern Alliance, and NATO countries fought the Taliban government and al-Qaeda militants in Afghanistan. In 2003 the United States and United Kingdom fought Iraq in Operation Iraqi Freedom. This was the Second Iraq War.

The aerospace industry, as represented by its products, participated in the battles, wars, and conflicts to different degrees and in different ways. Satellites provided reconnaissance, as did aircraft, including drones in some cases. Fighters, bombers, helicopters, and transports contributed to the conflicts defensively and offensively. Missiles and missile countermeasures also influenced the course of the conflicts.

Although dominated by conventional weapons (albeit at times state-of-the-art), some of these conflicts raised the fear of nuclear war and nuclear holocaust. At least seven nations had nuclear weapons: Britain, China, France, India, Pakistan, Russia, and the United States. Israel is widely believed to have nuclear weapons. South Africa had abandoned its nuclear capability by disarming its bombs. The newly independent republics of Belarus, Kazakhstan, and Ukraine gave remaining Soviet nuclear technology back to Russia. The status remained unclear about Iran, Iraq, and North Korea, and the fear remained that some of the former Soviet nuclear technology had reached terrorists.

Manufacturers

Both in Europe and in the United States, the military aerospace industry consolidated after the end of the Cold War. In the early 1990s Ford, General Dynamics, and IBM sold off their aerospace businesses. General Dynamics, for example, sold its general aviation airplane maker, Cessna, to Textron, its missile program to Hughes, its fighter business to Lockheed, and its space subsidiary to Martin Marietta. In the mid 1990s Lockheed and Martin merged, as did Northrop and Grumman, and Boeing acquired McDonnell Douglas. Rockwell's aerospace divisions went to Boeing too. Boeing, Lockheed, and Raytheon emerged as the big three defense contractors. Boeing and Lockheed competed for military airplane contracts, whereas Lockheed and Raytheon competed for air-traffic control contracts. Suppliers also consolidated; for example, United Technologies purchased Sundstrand and merged it with Hamilton Standard, and Honeywell merged with AlliedSignal.

The European aerospace community experienced some consolidation too. Aerospatiale and Matra merged in 1999. Daimler/Chrysler Aerospace (DASA) and Aerospatiale-Matra joined to form European Aeronautic, Defense and Space (EADS). The Franco-German EADS became the largest aerospace company in Europe. British Aerospace and Marconi Electronics merged, as did DASA and Construcciones Aeronáuticas S.A. (CASA). Stork Aerospace, the successor of Werkspoor, acquired Fokker Aviation in 1996, which was the year after the diversified Fokker aerospace corporation had collapsed in bankruptcy. Several years later Stork, of the Netherlands, and Saab Ericsson, of Sweden, acquired Fokker Space, which changed its name to Dutch Space Industry.

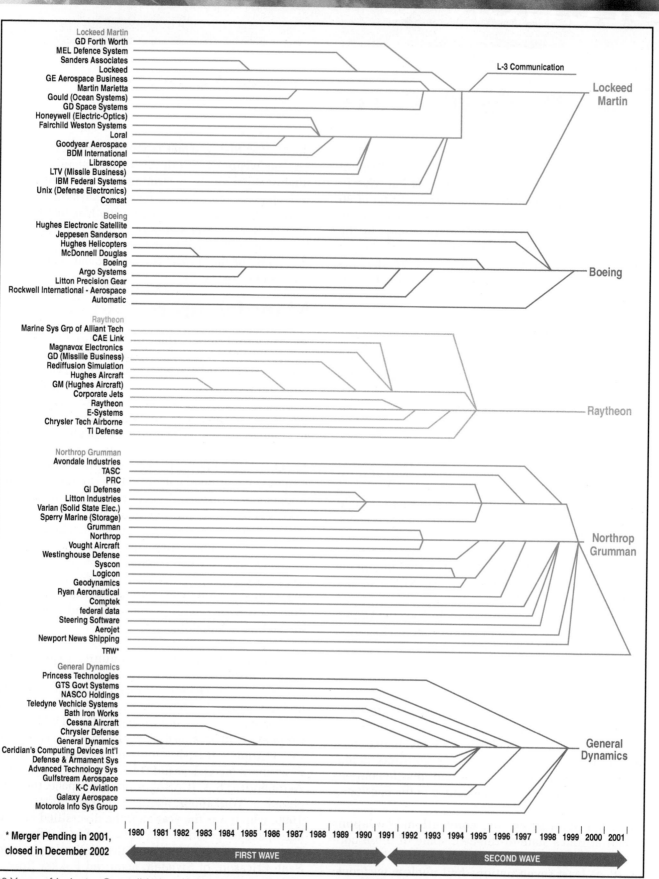

Lockeed Martin
- GD Forth Worth
- MEL Defence System
- Sanders Associates
- Lockeed
- GE Aerospace Business
- Martin Marietta
- Gould (Ocean Systems)
- GD Space Systems
- Honeywell (Electric-Optics)
- Fairchild Weston Systems
- Loral
- Goodyear Aerospace
- BDM International
- Librascope
- LTV (Missile Business)
- IBM Federal Systems
- Unix (Defense Electronics)
- Comsat

L-3 Communication

Lockeed Martin

Boeing
- Hughes Electronic Satellite
- Jeppesen Sanderson
- Hughes Helicopters
- McDonnell Douglas
- Boeing
- Argo Systems
- Litton Precision Gear
- Rockwell International - Aerospace
- Automatic

Boeing

Raytheon
- Marine Sys Grp of Alliant Tech
- CAE Link
- Magnavox Electronics
- GD (Missille Business)
- Rediffusion Simulation
- Hughes Aircraft
- GM (Hughes Aircraft)
- Corporate Jets
- Raytheon
- E-Systems
- Chrysler Tech Airborne
- TI Defense

Raytheon

Northrop Grumman
- Avondale Industries
- TASC
- PRC
- GI Defense
- Litton Industries
- Varian (Solid State Elec.)
- Sperry Marine (Storage)
- Grumman
- Northrop
- Vought Aircraft
- Westinghouse Defense
- Syscon
- Logicon
- Geodynamics
- Ryan Aeronautical
- Comptek
- federal data
- Steering Software
- Aerojet
- Newport News Shipping
- TRW*

Northrop Grumman

General Dynamics
- Princess Technologies
- GTS Govt Systems
- NASCO Holdings
- Teledyne Vechicle Systems
- Bath Iron Works
- Cessna Aircraft
- Chrysler Defense
- General Dynamics
- Ceridian's Computing Devices Int'l
- Defense & Armament Sys
- Advanced Technology Sys
- Gulfstream Aerospace
- K-C Aviation
- Galaxy Aerospace
- Motorola Info Sys Group

General Dynamics

1980 1981 1982 1983 1984 1985 1986 1987 1988 1989 1990 1991 1992 1993 1994 1995 1996 1997 1998 1999 2000 2001

* Merger Pending in 2001, closed in December 2002

FIRST WAVE

SECOND WAVE

20 Years of Industry Consolidation. (Adapted from Chart 7-4, *The Final Report of the Commission on the Future of the United States Aerospace Industry*, U.S. Government, November 2002.)

Historical Evidence

In late 2002 the Commission on the Future of the United States Aerospace Industry warned, "The contributions of aerospace to our global leadership have been so successful that it is assumed U.S. preeminence in aerospace remains assured. Yet the evidence would indicate this to be far from the case. The U.S. aerospace industry has consolidated to a handful of players — from what was once more than 70 suppliers in 1980 to 5 prime contractors today. Only one U.S. commercial prime aircraft manufacturer remains. Not all of these surviving companies are in strong business health. ... We noted with interest how other countries that aspire for a great global role are directing intense attention and resources to foster an indigenous aerospace industry. This is in contrast to the attitude present here in the United States. We stand dangerously close to squandering the advantage bequeathed to us by prior generations of aerospace leaders."

The Final Report of the Commission on the Future of the United States Aerospace Industry (November 2002) studied civil air transportation, space, and military aerospace. Regarding defense, the Commission recommended that the nation develop a national military industrial base policy, sustain the currently robust defense industrial base, and maintain and enhance the critical national infrastructure.

Austrian Aerospace was already a subsidiary of Saab Ericsson. Meanwhile, Stork purchased a major share in Société Anonyme Belge de Constructions Aéronautiques (SABCA), the Belgian aerospace company. Also, international cooperative programs enabled companies in different countries to participate as partners or contractors in the production of European aircraft and spacecraft, such as Airbus, Eurofighter, Eurocopter, and Ariane.

Fighters

The military services cooperated and consolidated programs. The Joint Strike Fighter (JSF) program involved the U.S. Air Force, Marines, and Navy, and the British Navy and Royal Air Force. These services sought an affordable, lethal, survivable, supportable, and multipurpose combat aircraft. Boeing and Lockheed Martin competed for the contract that might lead to production of 3,000 of the next-generation fighters. Lockheed won the concept demonstration contract in 1996. It completed the initial design review the next year, the same year it took Northrop Grumman and BAE Systems (a British Aerospace division) as partners. The design included stealthy, rather than fully stealth, characteristics, stealthy in this case meaning radar-evading.

Lockheed built two demonstrator aircraft in Palmdale, California. These F-35 prototypes, designated X-35s, passed flight tests in 2000 and 2001. The first flight was on 24 October 2001, when the X-35A moved to nearby Edwards Air Force Base. The X-35A with conventional takeoff and landing (CTOL) established numerous flight-test records during its flight test program in the autumn of 2000, including supersonic flight. After completing the X-35A flight test program, Lockheed converted the aircraft into the X-35B. Meanwhile, in early 2001, the X-35C demonstrated carrier-suitable qualities in tests at the Naval Air Station Patuxent River, Maryland. The transcontinental flight from California to Maryland was in itself an achievement for a new prototype. The 35C had larger wing and control surfaces than the other variants. During the test program, naval test pilots performed field carrier landing practices (FCLPs) as well as carrier approaches. The X-35B had a short takeoff / vertical landing (STOVL) system, with a shaft-driven light fan engine. It completed flight and carrier tests successfully in March 2001. Lockheed continued flight-testing the aircraft. (Figure 10-10)

Later in 2001, the team of Lockheed Martin, Northrop Grumman, and BAE won the government's System Development and Demonstration Contract. This was

Figure 10-10. The Lockheed X-35A was one of three versions of the Joint Strike Fighter, all highly compatible.

a production contract that called for an initial output of 22 fighters. In 2003 the X-35C flew into history and took its place at the Naval Air Museum in Pensacola, Florida. The Joint Strike Fighter passed Preliminary Design Review in 2003 and prepared for the Critical Design Review scheduled for 2004. Three production variants remain in the plan: F-35A for conventional takeoff and landing, the F-35B for short takeoff and vertical landing on small carriers and at forward-deployed areas on land, and the F-35C for catapult launches and arrested landings on large carriers. (Figures 10-11 and 10-12)

The Joint Strike Fighter program became international with the addition of eight international partners: Australia, Canada, Denmark, Italy, the Netherlands, Norway, Turkey, and the United Kingdom. Fighters offered potential of production for export, especially to nations participating in the production. Lockheed selected foreign and domestic contractors to help with best-value components and to establish economies of scale. Stork Fokker, for example, delivered hardware to Pratt & Whitney for testing the production propulsion system for the fighter, and the Dutch company worked with the engine maker to develop production processes. Rolls-Royce provided the lift-fan engine for the STOVL system, and Hamilton-Sundstrand made the control system. Such international partnerships were part of what had become known as global risk-sharing.

The plan was for the F-35 to replace the General Dynamics F-16, the way Lockheed's F-22 Raptor was to replace the McDonnell Douglas F-15. More generally, the new fighters were to replace aging aircraft in military fleets. Although eager for F-35 contracts, European aerospace companies remained interested

Figure 10-11. A flight test of the X-35B engaged the short-takeoff and vertical landing (STOVL) system.

Historical Note

In 1982 the Republic of China on the island of Taiwan established an Indigenous Defense Fighter (IDF) program. Called An-Hsiang (Safe Fight), the program had four sections. Ying-Yang (Soaring Eagle) developed the airframe. Yun-Hun (Cloud Men) worked on the jet engine for a fighter. Tien-Lei (Sky Thunder) focused on radar and avionics. Tien-Chien (Sky Sword) worked with missiles, the weapon technology for the fighter. First flown in 1989, the aircraft neared production in the early 1990s, when the United States and France agreed to sell General Dynamics F-16s and Dassault Mirages respectively to Taiwan. The Ching Kuo indigenous fighter entered production with Han Hsiang Aerospace Industry (HHAI). It entered service with the RoC Air Force of Taiwan in January 2000. The RoC Air Force acquired 130 Ching Kuo fighters that year.

in European military independence and self-sufficiency. While the F-22 remained in the late stages of test and evaluation, the Navy decided in 2003 to base F/A-18E/F Super Hornet strike fighter squadrons on the east coast of the United States, at Naval Air Station Oceana, Virginia, and at the Marine Corps Air Station Cherry Point, North Carolina.

Historic Event

First flown on 24 October 2000, the Lockheed Joint Strike Fighter X-35A broke the sound barrier and achieved the supersonic speed of Mach 1.05 on 21 November 2000.

These three aircraft — the F/A-18E/F newly entered into service, the F-22 entering production, and the F-35 still under development — formed the aerial fleet projected to defend the United States in the 21st century.

Europe wanted to sell European fighters, such as the Eurofighter Typhoon, Dassault's Rafale and Mirage, Saab's Gripen, and Russia's Mikoyan MiG and Sukhoi planes. The Gripen became operational in 1995 and began the gradual replacement of older Saab Viggen fighters. The French Navy inaugurated the Rafale into operational service in 1997. Britain, Germany, Italy, and Spain cooperated on the Eurofighter Typhoon. Two Eurojet turbofan engines provided the power. In February 2003 the first production Eurofighters all flew within a few days of each other, each in its own country. Eurofighter GmbH, the organization manag-

Figure 10-12. The supersonic X-35C carrier variant (CV) completed a naval test program in March 2001.

Figure 10-13. Swedish JAS 39 Gripen fighter.

ing the program for the four participating countries, delivered the first production Eurofighters to the Royal Air Force in June 2003, the German Air Force in August 2003 and to the Spanish Air Force in September 2003. Europe thus offered competition to the U.S. military aerospace industry. (Figures 10-13, 10-14, and 10-15)

Historic Event

In 1993 Lieutenant Jeannie Flynn became the first American woman to be accepted for combat pilot training. She became an F-15E Eagle fighter pilot.

Figure 10-14. French Dassault Rafale.

Figure 10-15. The Eurofighter 2000.

F/A-18 Hornet

European Self-Sufficiency

Charles de Gaulle, President of France from 1958 to 1969, had argued for French and European independence from the influence of the Cold War superpowers and from dependence upon a superpower for French national defense, so he had initiated a French nuclear program. Willy Brandt, Chancellor of Germany from 1969 to 1974, also did not want to be caught in the middle of any Cold War conflict between the superpowers, so he urged detente to lessen Cold War tensions. Margaret Thatcher, Prime Minister of Great Britain from 1979 to 1990, similarly wanted to protect the sovereignty of her country and the safety of Europe. All three supported cooperation among European states, and during their terms in office they furthered cooperation among European nations. By 1990, the European Community members had experience in commercial, economic, and political cooperation, but the United States military forces in Europe still overshadowed the forces of the individual European nations.

Throughout the 1990s, a European military transport was under development, but bringing a new product to market, even the military market, often was a long process filled with failures, shifting priorities, resource deficiencies, and design changes. Buying military aircraft from the United States would not financially benefit the people in Europe, but purchasing European-made aircraft would, and thus obtaining funds to purchase aircraft might garner political approval more easily if the product were European. Among the needs for military readiness were transports that could move people and materiel to out-of-area destinations. They chose to build a four-engine turboprop competitive with the Boeing C-17 and the latest Lockheed C-130 variants.

The European airlifter went through several organizations and configurations since it began back in 1982. Originally, it was the Future International Military Airlifter (FIMA), a concept pursued jointly by British Aerospace, Aerospatiale, MBB, and Lockheed. The goal was to produce about 300 airplanes for sales to Germany, France, the United Kingdom, Italy, Spain, Turkey, Belgium, and Portugal. The program moved in 1991 to a newly formed multinational company called Euroflag. Euroflag's purpose was to design and build a medium-lift military transport aircraft. It called the program the Future Large Aircraft (FLA). But in 1994 Euroflag transferred the FLA program to Airbus Industrie and dissolved.

Airbus worked on the project for several years, and in 1999 established Airbus Military Company to handle what it was calling the A400M. In 2003 Airbus selected the Europrop International (EPI) engine for the transport. The company was actively trying to sell enough A400Ms to place the plane into production. And Europrop, itself an international consortium, needed to develop the proposed large engine. Britain's Rolls-Royce, France's Snecma, Germany's MTU, and Spain's Industria de Turbo-Propulsors (ITP) were partners in Europrop. The companies were jointly designing the big TP400-D6 engines and planned to share production and marketing. Europe was moving toward self-sufficiency in military transport — and in helicopters.

Helicopters

European companies cooperatively produced European helicopters, a goal once referred to as Eurocopter. The program that eventually produced the NH90 began as a simple memorandum of understanding in 1990. The party nations were France, Germany, Italy, and the Netherlands. Each country submitted its own military specifications for the aircraft under consideration. Two years later, Agusta of Italy, Eurocopter of France, Eurocopter Deutschland of Germany, and Fokker of the Netherlands signed an intercompany agreement and created the NATO Helicopter Management Agency (NAHEMA) to manage the venture and NHIndustries to design and develop the helicopter. Three years later the first prototype flew, and NHIndustries, based in Aix-en-Provence, France, assumed program management, marketing, and sales responsibilities. NHIndustries became a subsidiary of Eurocopter, which was a subsidiary of Aerospatiale and Daimler/Chrysler Aerospace, then of EADS.

The four partner companies shared design and production responsibilities. In 2000 they signed a production contract, and Portugal joined the cooperative effort the next year. In 2001 the Nordic Standard Helicopter Program selected the NH-90 as the common helicopter for the Finnish, Norwegian, and Swedish navies, for antisubmarine and antisurface-vessels missions. The aircraft produced was a twin-engine, medium-size military helicopter. The two versions were designated TTH for Tactical Transport Helicopter and NFH for NATO Frigate Helicopter. The all-composite fuselage was crashworthy and the self-sealing fuel tanks crash-resistant. The design also incorporated fly-by-wire controls, multifunction cockpit displays, titanium main rotor hub, and other modern technologies. Equipment, instruments, and systems were flight-tested on five prototypes. NHIndustries assembled the first production NH90s in 2003. (Figures 10-16 and 10-17)

The NH-90 was but one of the Eurocopters built. The Eurocopter brand covered cooperative efforts that also produced the Eurocopter AS532 Cougar, Eurocopter BO105, Eurocopter AS-565 Panther, Eurocopter Tiger, and civil helicopters such as the Eurocopter EC635. The Tiger appeared in three versions: the Tiger UHT—a multi-role fire support helicopter, the Tiger HAC—an anti-tank helicopter, and the Tiger HAP—an air-to-air combat and fire-support machine. The Tiger entered service in 2003. The Panther came in shipboard and transport versions. European companies also produced their own products, such as Aerospatiale's Fennec AS550 anti-tank helicopter, which entered production in France in the 1980s, and the newer Agusta A129 Mangusta antitank and area-suppression helicopter made in Italy.

Europe kept an eye toward future helicopters too. In 2001 the French ONERA company, German DLR research organization, and the multinational Eurocopter signed an agreement to join a research and technology partnership.

While European production provided the chief competition to U.S. manufacturers, Denal Aviation in South Africa also introduced a military helicopter. Denal produced the Rooivalk AH-2 attack helicopter that entered service in 1999. Requiring a two-person crew (pilot and weapons officer), the Rooivalk went first to the South African Air Force. Denal advertised its missions as anti-armor, ground suppression, anti-helicopter, ferry, reconnaissance, and counter-insurgency. Original armament included anti-tank missiles, air-to-air missiles, unguided rockets, and cannons.

Figure 10-16. The NH90 helicopter flies over Europe.

United States manufacturers also brought new products to market. The Bell AH-1Z, a 1997 design, had 84 percent commonality with the UH-1Y, both derivatives of the 40-year-old UH-1. Over 16,000 UH-1 helicopters have been produced, each generation gradually improving upon the basic design. The AH-1Z, designed for the U.S. Marine Corps, brought new features for combat survivability and crashworthiness, including instruments that warn of missiles. The four-bladed rotor was constructed of new composite materials, the targeting system used state-of-the-art technology, and the helmet-mounted sight and display system reduced cockpit workload and modernized the cockpit. The weaponry included the supersonic AIM-9 Sidewinder air-to-air missile. Bell also continued development of the V-22 Osprey, a tiltrotor with vertical and short takeoff and landing (V/STOL) capability.

Sikorsky Aircraft also developed new helicopter technology. It generated derivatives of proven designs, such as the UH-60M derivative of the Black Hawk. The UH-60M first flew on 17 September 2003. Sikorsky also developed new aircraft, such as the

Historic Event

On 19 November 1991 the European-made DGV Dauphin helicopter flew 372 kilometers per hour over a three-kilometer course and thereby broke a couple of world records previously held by Sikorsky helicopters. As a reward, the American Helicopter Society awarded the French crew the Igor Sikorsky Trophy. The flight crew consisted of pilot Guy Dabadie, flight engineer Michel Sudre, and flight observer Bernard Fouques. The French-made experimental DGV was a testbed for new technology.

Figure 10-17. A naval NH90 lands on a ship's deck.

H-92 (the military version of the S-92), which made a demonstration tour of Europe in 2003. The H-92 Superhawk joined the Black Hawk and Seahawk in Sikorsky's military line, which also included the CH/MH-53E. Designed as an all-weather, board-range of missions aircraft, the H-92 was being marketed for military utility use, transport, anti-submarine warfare, and combat search and rescue. Sikorsky partnered with Boeing on the RAH-66 Comanche; the Comanche program was canceled in 2004.

Missiles

The Soviet Union and China, the largest communist nations during the Cold War, provided nuclear expertise and technology to North Korea, Pakistan, and Iran. In search of employment, nuclear scientists and engineers from post-Soviet Union republics went as civilians to provide additional help. North Korea, Pakistan, and Iran violated international non-proliferation agreements that apply to nuclear weapons technology and missiles as well as chemical and biological weapons.

China was a major proliferator of ballistic missile technology. It transferred complete ballistic missile systems to Pakistan in 1992. That gave Pakistan the capability to launch conventionally-armed ballistic missiles. Pakistan exploded a nuclear device it 1998, and, even while still developing its own nuclear capability, Pakistan transferred nuclear technology to Iran.

Iran first fired its medium-range Shahab-3 missile in 1998. In September 2003 it displayed the missiles on mobile launchers while celebrating the 23rd anniversary of the war with Iraq. At that time President Muhammad Khatami spoke of "self-sufficiency" and "becoming stronger — militarily." The country claims its nuclear program is strictly for energy production, not for weapons. The UN's International Atomic Energy Agency continued investigating Iran's nuclear program despite such disclaimers.

The Korean peninsula and people have remained divided since the end of World War II. North Korea's effort to develop nuclear weapon capabilities included friendly transfers of technology as well as black-market purchases and smuggled cargo. China transferred missile technology to North Korea in the 1990s.

Historical Note

The top ten prime contractors in the defense industry in the United States at the end of the last century, in order from largest down, were Lockheed Martin, Boeing, General Dynamics, Northrop Grumman, United Technologies, Textron, Litton Industries, Newport News Shipbuilding, and TRW.

Despite international protest that such a shield would damage the international system of arms control, United States President George W. Bush in December of 2001 announced the withdrawal of the United States from the 1972 Anti-Ballistic Missile (ABM) Treaty. The nation embarked on a program to build a missile defense shield.

The U.S. Secretary of Defense reported to Congress in 2005 that China had nuclear missiles capable of reaching most of the world, including liquid-fueled and silo-based CSS-4 intercontinental ballistic missiles; solid-fueled and road-mobile DF-31 ICBMs, and sea-based JL-2 ballistic missiles. Moreover, China had developed an anti-air raid doctrine that includes offensive and defensive counter-air measures involving aircraft, missiles, artillery, special forces, and naval forces, and China is developing space-based capabilities for reconnaissance, communication, and navigation. A key U.S. concern is Taiwan, and the Taiwan Strait, as China seeks to deter any independence movement and to unify Taiwan with the Chinese mainland.

Historical Note

The Inuit, an indigenous people of Greenland, Canada, Alaska (USA), and Chukotka (Russia), have objected to the militarization of the North as a violation of their human rights, such as the right to participate in decisions affecting them as a people. They also argued that militarization infringes their land rights and pollutes their lands.

Thule provided a historical example. Built in 1951-53, Thule is a U.S. Air Force Base in western Greenland. To build it, the U.S. forced the move of Inuits from the area. Recently leaked documents reveal the U.S. military later dumped toxic wastes at more than 50 sites in Greenland.

In December 2001, when President George W. Bush announced the withdrawal the United States from the 1972 Anti-Ballistic Missile (ABM) Treaty, the Inuit Circumpolar Conference (ICC) protested. "For Inuit, the unilateral action by Mr. Bush is especially troublesome, as the next American step will be to upgrade military infrastructure across the Arctic and in our back yard," said ICC President Aqqaluk Lynge of Greenland. By 2003, the U.S. was upgrading Thule for the national missile defense program.

War Experience

War tested equipment, personnel, and policies.

Israel-Lebanon War

To protect Israel's northern border from attacks by the Palestine Liberation Organization (PLO), Israel fought the Israel-Lebanon War of 1982. Israel used conventional weapons against conventional weapons to weaken the PLO, but the unconventional Hezbollah entered into protracted guerrilla warfare against Israelis occupying southern Lebanon. The Hezbollah (the Party of God) were willing to suffer heavy losses, and they continued their insurgency against the Israeli presence. Israel refrained from using extensive bombing, strafing, and missiles against an enemy hiding among innocent civilians, so the war became one of attrition and one in which the Palestinians accepted casualties. The United States had Vietnam, the Soviets had Afghanistan, and Israel had Lebanon.

U.S.-made General Dynamics F-16 Fighting Falcons and McDonnell Douglas F-15 Eagles flew support for Israel's McDonnell Douglas F-4 Phantom fighter-bombers, but the Hezbollah were a few people hiding among many, and Israel did not accept heavy civilian losses. Israel turned to helicopters to attack Hezbollah, often relying on the Bell AH-1 Cobra and the Boeing AH-64 Apache attack helicopters. In 1992, a remotely piloted vehicle (RPV) relayed data to guide an Apache with Hellfire missiles on an effective raid that killed a Hezbollah leader and his family.

Under development by Israel since 1970, unmanned aerial vehicles (UAVs) had been used in the Yom Kippur War of 1973. UAVs are also called remotely controlled aerial vehicles, drones, remotely operated aircraft, or robots. Israel Aircraft Industries introduced its indigenous UAV, the Mastiff, in 1978, and followed with the larger Scout, and then the Searcher. Israel sent the Scout into war in southern Lebanon during the invasion of 1982; the target was Syrian missile batteries. The Scouts relayed information to Grumman E-2C Hawkeyes. The Syrians could neither shoot down the little Scouts nor jam their microwave communication. During the seven-week Operation Peace for Galilee campaign, Israel destroyed 19 SA-6 missile launch sites and 85 Syrian fighters, while losing only three Israeli fighters and several UAVs.

Israel continued to deploy UAVs in the continuing conflict in southern Lebanon. In Operation Grapes of Wrath in April 1996, Israel used UAVs for 24-hour watch during the 16 days of air, naval, and artillery bombardment of the Hezbollah. The Arava early-warning aircraft, an Israeli Aircraft Industries plane, controlled some of the UAVs. The Israelis flew over 1200 hours and lost no aircraft during that sustained battle. One of the legacies of this televised conflict was the development by other nations of twin-boomed UAVs similar to the Israeli model.

Yet the Hezbollah killed over 100 Israelis in 1993–1997, and Israel lost 77 soldiers when two helicopters accidentally collided in the buffer zone in 1997. Finally, in the year 2000, Israel withdrew from Lebanon.

Gulf War

Iraq, under the dictatorial rule of Saddam Hussein, invaded Kuwait in August 1990. Iraq resisted international pressure to withdraw. The United States sent troops to the Middle East in September and attacked Iraqi forces in January 1991. During the Gulf War, the allies employed the principle of overwhelming force. Their forces totaled 975,500 troops, 56 percent of whom were U.S. personnel, but also Turkish,

British, French, Egyptians, Saudis, Syrians, and troops from ten other nations.

The United States had Pioneer UAVs, made by Israeli Aircraft Industries, and deployed them in Operation Desert Storm. The U.S. Navy and Marine Corps operated the UAVs from ships, and the U.S. Army operated them from the desert. The Pioneer used rocket-assisted take-off (RATO). The U.S. launched more than 300 UAV missions during the war.

Stealth had been important since Egyptian radar-guided surface-to-air missiles had inflicted heavy damage on the Israeli Air Force's McDonnell Douglas F-4 Phantom fighters in the Yom Kippur War of 1973, and since late in the Vietnam War when radar suppression became as important as bombing for aircraft assignments. The research and development of stealth aircraft and remotely controlled airborne "smart weapons" had proceeded. Lockheed designed surfaces to reflect radar away from receptors, covered surfaces with radar-absorbent material, and cooled, diffused, and shielded engine exhaust to thwart heat-seeking weapons. Carrying fuel and weapons inside the aircraft and retracting antennas under the skin further hid the stealth aircraft from detection. Lockheed first flew this concept, called the F-117, in 1981. The United States flew six F-117A missions as part of the invasion of Panama in 1989, and radar detected none. (Figure 10-18)

In the successful 1991 campaign to force Saddam Hussein's Iraqi forces out of Kuwait, the United States sent 42 F-117As against Baghdad, knocking out radar sites, surface-to-air missile sites, and other targets. Both the offense and defense were aerial. Baghdad had 75 surface-to-air missile launchers and

Figure 10-18. F117

Historic Event

In 1995 Martha McSally became the first U.S. Air Force female pilot to fly a combat mission when she flew over the no-fly zone in Iraq. In 1995 and 1996 she flew 100 hours over southern Iraq to enforce the no-fly zone. She called her plane "an ugly down-and-dirty tank killer." It was the Fairchild Republic A-10 Thunderbolt II (also called the Warthog), equipped with a Gatling gun.

Some female pilots wrote books about their military experience, like Rhonda Cornum's *She Went to War* (Novato, CA: Presidio Press, 1992) and Loree Draude Hirschman's *Just Another Navy Pilot, an Aviator's Sea Journal* (Annapolis, MD: Naval Institute Press, 2000). Cornum flew a helicopter during the Gulf War, and she became a prisoner of war. Hirschman flew the jet S-3B Viking from the USS *Abraham Lincoln* in the Persian Gulf in 1995.

nearly 3,000 antiaircraft artillery guns. Stealth technology freed the pilots from the need to dodge antiaircraft fire. No Iraqi aircraft engaged the stealth F-117As in combat.

Iraq agreed to a ceasefire in March 1991. The Gulf War pushed Iraq out of Kuwait, but left Saddam Hussein in power. The allies had lost about 300 people in the war, Iraq lost thousands, perhaps tens of thousands. As part of the peace settlement, Iraq agreed to disarm nuclear, biological, and chemical weapons and all missiles with ranges exceeding 90 miles (150 kilometers). That set the stage for the United Nations to inspect Iraqi sites to ensure that the illicit weapons were indeed destroyed. Meanwhile, British and American forces enforced two no-fly zones, and periodically drew Iraqi fire.

Bosnian War

Devoid of authoritarian control after the collapse of the Soviet Union, the Balkan Peninsula reverted to ethnic conflicts reminiscent of the three Balkan Wars in the early 1900s, the third of which evolved into the Great War, World War I. This time the United Nations sent forces to quell the violence. The United States launched Pioneer UAVs to confirm the location of mobile targets identified by Boeing E-8s. The Bosnian War of 1992–1995 closed on a horrible note in July 1995, when Christian Serbs invaded a United Nations safe zone at Srebrenica and massacred about 8,000 Muslims. The massacre provided the emergency and justification for NATO to bomb Bosnia-Herzegovina to achieve peace. This was an ethnic war that killed over 250,000 people and forced nearly two million to flee their homes. Experience in the Balkans suggested that allies needed compatible equipment for, at least, communication, identification, and operations.

Kosovo Conflict

The conflict in Kosovo began in 1989 as a peaceful protest by Kosovo's ethnic Albanians against the loss of autonomy for the province due to Serbian actions. In 1996 the Kosovo Liberation Army began occasional attacks against Serbian police units. That escalated in 1998 into an armed uprising. When the Serbian government tried to exert control in 1999, ethnic warfare resulted. Claiming that unrest in the Balkans threatened the stability of Europe, NATO ordered air strikes against Serbian military targets. The air raids began on 24 March 1999, and the campaign lasted 78 days. During that time, Operation Allied Force launched 34,300 sorties, dropped over 11,000 bombs, launched over 11,000 missiles, and lost no airmen or women in combat-related action.

The United States conducted many of the air strikes over Serbia, but not as effectively as planned. The Northrop Grumman B-2 bombers flying from Whiteman Air Force Base in Missouri all returned safely, but a Lockheed F-117A Nighthawk and UAVs were shot down. Collateral damage in the form of civilians killed was also high. The Human Rights Watch organization reported that at least 500 civilians were killed during air raids. Twenty-four F-117As participated in the NATO campaign, and the pilot of the one shot down in March was rescued only a few hours after the plane was hit. B-1s and B-52s flew from European bases. The U.S. also deployed radar-jamming equipment on the Grumman EA-6B Prowlers, Boeing's Joint Direct Attack Munition (JDAM) on the B-2s, the Joint Surveillance and Target Attack Radar System (JSTARS) on the E-8s, and conventional air-launch cruise missiles. (Figure 10-19)

The war demonstrated a need for commonality among allies in air equipment, procedures, and practices. Over 100 aircraft were destroyed, as well as over 300 artillery pieces, ten military airfields, and all of Yugoslavia's oil refineries. Serbians suffered about 10,000 casualties. The United States lost two soldiers in a helicopter accident. Rather than submit to international pressure, the Serbs forced Kosovo's ethnic Albanians to flee into neighboring lands, Albania, Macedonia, and Montenegro. A negotiated peace in June allowed displaced Albanians to return, and the United Nations peace-keeping forces moved into position.

Historic Event

On 2 June 1995 a Serbian-launched SAM-6 surface-to-air missile downed a U.S. Air Force General Dynamics F-16 Fighting Falcon over Serbian territory in Bosnia. Under the cover of NATA air forces suppressing anti-aircraft fire, the 24th Marine Expeditionary Unit rescued the pilot, Captain Scott O'Grady, six days later. With the help of co-author Jeff Coplon, O'Grady later told his story in *Return with Honor* (New York: Doubleday, 1995).

Afghanistan War

Whereas Kosovo was an ethnic war, Afghanistan was a war against the Taliban regime that had come to power in 1996 and that supported terrorism, at least to the extent of harboring Osama bin Laden and his al-Qaeda terrorist organization; it was perhaps also a war for the oil resources in Central Asia.

As did Kosovo, Afghanistan proved the importance of aircraft for force projection and expeditionary operations. Satellite-gathered intelligence and satellite-based communication informed the aerial side of

Figure 10-19. The Northrop Grumman B-2 Spirit bomber was used in combat for the first time during the 1999 Kosovo conflict.

Historical Evidence

NATO conducted an 11-week bombing campaign in 1999 to stop the genocidal war between ethnic Serbs and ethnic Albanians in the Kosovo region of Yugoslavia. The B-2 bomber went into combat for the first time during this war. After the war, the Military Procurement Subcommittee of the U.S. House of Representatives held a hearing on "The Performance of the B-2 Bomber in the Kosovo Air Campaign," 106th Congress, 1st session, 30 June 1999. At the hearing, Norm Dicks, of the Defense Appropriation Subcommittee, observed, "But the story of the B-2 success in Yugoslavia was not just an issue of technological superiority that helped end the conflict early; it was a story of using military force without putting enormous numbers of U.S. service men and women at risk. Flying from the U.S. with global reach and with the advantage of low observability — stealth — that the B-2 gives us, this aircraft was able to operate during the worst weather conditions in a manner that put fewer lives at risk. Stealth truly saves lives, and the initial operational campaign was certainly proof of that. The B-2 pilots all returned home safely." The procurement subcommittee noted that the Air Force had only 21 B-2s.

both wars. The United States policy was to use overwhelming force. Airstrikes opened the way, and thereafter, aircraft supported the ground war.

The bombing started on 7 October 2001. The air campaign followed an out-of-harm's-way strategy that relied upon high technology, but the attacks from safe distance caused unintended casualties among civilians, including at least 54 fatalities among civilians in Oruzgan Province. The civilian casualties strained relations with Afghan allies, some of whom demanded participation in planning future air raids. Most of the civilian casualties were later attributed to poor information received from Afghans on the ground. Given that fewer than 50 U.S. military men and women died in Afghanistan, the air war had indeed proved out of harm's way. But the war proved all too personal for the Afghan people.

The experimental Predator UAV proved effective in Afghanistan. Being crewless, the Predator could enter military service early in development, and it did. The U.S. Air Force used it as part of the new Force Protection Surveillance System, first deployed in Afghanistan. The U.S. launched the planes from neighboring countries. Pilots at television screens monitored the flights, identified targets spotted by the Predators, and even launched missiles carried by the planes. General Atomics Aeronautical Systems produced the Predator, a medium-altitude UAV. A top Predator pilot tracked Taliban and al-Qaeda leadership movements and launched Hellfire anti-tank missiles. The Air Force withheld her name for security reasons. As aerial drones surveyed outdoor movements, unmanned ground vehicles called PackBots, each carrying a television camera, traveled into caves and tunnels.

After the war had "ended," Afghanistan remained an armed nation involved in armed conflict. Rival war-

lords fought for influence and territory. When 300 rockets hit Gardez in April of 2002, over 100 civilians were killed. That was an internal matter, particularly since the warlords tended to fight within clans rather than between ethnic groups, but the weapons came from outside. The continued conflict also endangered British and American troops stationed in Afghanistan.

Second Iraq War

Starting in 1998, Iraq refused United Nations inspectors access to the country. The United States adopted preemptive strike as military policy with Operation Iraqi Freedom in early 2003. The United States military attacked the government of Iraq to prevent the Iraqi government from using weapons of mass destruction and from supporting terrorism. This was justified as homeland defense, and hotly debated.

The operation involved prepositioning of aircraft carriers, missile-launching ships, and naval support in general. Airlift also contributed to the operation. Technology and speed enabled the United States to employ fewer forces than a traditional invasion would have required, and the Air Force, naval air support, and mobile artillery supported the ground troops. Special forces moved to destroy weapons and prevent escalation of conflict.

Preemptive strike as applied to Iraq involved heavy use of aircraft, including missiles, drones, and "smart" munitions, and included surveillance and communication technologies. Suppression of enemy air defense capabilities was key, and both Air Force and Navy aircraft tackled that chore.

UAVs posed a problem for the military: how to recruit pilots from cockpits to fly aircraft by remote control from the ground. Recruiting Predator pilots was a problem in late 2002 as the United States prepared for war against Iraq. The Air Force had fewer than 100 Predator pilots. The Air Force addressed the problem by awarding flight time and therefore flight pay to pilots guiding the unmanned Predator. The U.S. sent Predators in search of chemical and biological weapons, for mobile laboratories, and for launch systems.

The United States used a variety of UAVs in the Iraqi war in addition to the Predator, including the Global Hawk, Pointer, Silver Fox, Phoenix, Pioneer, and Remus. Northrop Grumman's Global Hawk was a high-altitude, long-endurance (HALE) UAV. The Army used the AeroVironment Pointer, the AAI Shadow 200, and the TRW/AIA Hunter. The Marine Corps flew the TRW/IAI Pioneer and AeroVironment Dragon Eye. The Air Force deployed the Lockheed Martin Desert Hawk for airbase security. The Naval Research Laboratory had flight tested the Flight Inserted Detector Expendable for Reconnaissance (FINDER), but the Navy did not say whether it was used over Iraq. The FINDER is air-launched from under the wings of a Predator UAV and carries a chemical and biological weapons sensor. The Navy did deploy the Silver Fox, a drone developed at the Office of Naval Research and built by Advanced Ceramics Research. The six-foot long, 20-pound Silver Fox was launched from a compressed-air catapult, and could reach altitudes up to 12,000 feet. The Marines used a laptop computer to operate the Dragon Eye. (Figure 10-20)

To a limited extent, the Iraqi war was a joint operation, as Great Britain sent army and marine forces into combat, but international opinion saw the war as a unilateral action by the United States, because the

war began without the support of the United Nations. Technology and speed enabled the United States to employ fewer forces than a traditional invasion would have required, but the Iraqi use of "anti-access" and "area-denial" defense tactics inflicted losses.

The Second Iraq War toppled the regime of Saddam Hussein, but, like Afghanistan, Iraq failed to ease peacefully into post-war reconstruction. The policy of preemptive strike and the Second Iraq War broadened the rift between the United States and Europe and provided additional incentive for Europe to develop military self-sufficiency.

Historical Note

Piloting aircraft is one of the direct combat roles open to women in the U.S. military services. Captain Sarah Piro of the Army flew a Bell Kiowa scout helicopter repeatedly on raids in Iraq. Ladda "Tammy" Duckworth, a pilot with the Illinois Army National Guard, lost her legs when a rocket-propelled grenade hit the Sikorsky Black Hawk helicopter she was flying in Iraq. By early 2006, about 50 women in the military services have been killed in Iraq, and another 350 or so injured.

Space Defense

Key to all major defense programs, and some offensive programs, are satellites. Reconnaissance (or spying) satellites are prevalent in the international space community. But the threat of terrorism extends beyond general, commercial, and military aviation into outer space. Iran, for example, joined the "space club" in October 2005, when a Russian company under Iranian contract launched an Iranian satellite made by another Russian company. The Iran Space

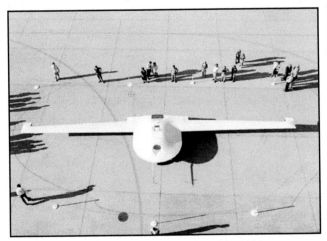

10-20. The DarkStar UAV was canceled in 1999.

Agency, established in 2003, is developing boosters, rockets, and other space technologies. The current state of Iranian space technology is not a security concern for either the delivery capabilities or the reconnaissance aspects, but the direction in which Iran is going in space and with atomic weapons has raised security issues, particularly given the techni-cal assistance Iran has also received from China, India, and North Korea. Iran has ballistic missiles capable of reaching Israel. The United Nation's Security Council is watching this rogue nation. But too many nations have aeronautical and astronautical programs for the international community to monitor all potential threats.

Space Exploration

The United Nations Office for Outer Space Affairs maintains a registry of objects launched into outer space. Since 1990, launch reports have been submitted from Algeria, Argentina, Australia, Brazil, Canada, China, Chile, Czech Republic, the European Space Agency, the European Organization for the Exploitation of Meteorological Satellites, France, Germany, India, Israel, Italy, Japan, Luxembourg, Malaysia, the Republic of Korea, the Russian Federation, Philippines, Spain, Sweden, Ukraine, the United Arab Emirates, the United Kingdom, and the United States. In 1990, for example, the Soviet Union reported launching 11 objects, the United Kingdom three, France two, the United States two, China one, Czechoslovakia one, Germany one, India one, and Japan one. Ten years later, in 2000, Argentina, Brazil, China, France, Japan, Russia, South Korea, Spain, Sweden, the United Kingdom, and the United States reported launches. While many countries have purchased commercial spacecraft, and several are capable of building their own satellites, relatively few have launch vehicles or the ability to actually place anything in orbit. The countries with indigenous space programs that have successfully launched at least one satellite into orbit include the United States, Russia, Canada, France, Japan, China, the United Kingdom, India, and Israel. Almost all spacecraft are launched by the United States, Russia, China, and the European Union (through its European Space Agency). Space has become an international destination. Space has also become commercialized, with revenue-generating launches and payloads, even paying passengers. Communication satellites, meteorological satellites, and space probes have extended far beyond the former Cold War programs of the East and West.

Exploration

Planetary probes, lunar probes, and space observatories explored the mysteries of space. Nearby Mars is a popular subject of study, as is the solar system in general.

Mars

Mars attracted a lot of interest in the 1990s and especially during its close encounter with Earth in 2003. The 1988-1989 failures of *Phobos 1* and *Phobos 2* had ended Soviet planetary exploration, and post-Soviet Russia unsuccessfully tried to send *Mars 96* to the Red Planet in 1996. Meanwhile, the U.S. sent *Mars Observer*, which failed in 1993; *Mars Global Surveyor,* which reached the planet in 1997; *Pathfinder,* which landed and deployed a rover on the surface in 1997; and *Mars Climate Orbiter,* which was lost in 1999. In 1999 the U.S. launched the *Mars Polar Lander* carrying microprobes called *Amundsen* and *Scott*; the lander lost communication when it reached the Mars atmosphere. (Figure 10-21)

Figure 10-21. *Sojourner* rover (left), and the rocky Martian landscape (right).

On 27 August 2003 the planet Mars came closer to Earth than it had been in the past 50,000 years. Mars was only 55,760,000 kilometers (a little more than 300 million miles) from Earth. The last people to see Mars up close like this were Neanderthals! The scientific term for this event is perihelial opposition. Mars was closest to both the Sun and the Earth. Perihelial describes its position closest to the Sun. Opposition describes the straight line from the Sun, though the Earth, to Mars; the Sun and Mars were on opposite sides of the Earth.

The Planetary Society designated Mars Day to recognize the event, which prompted multiple probes to be launched toward the Red Planet. The European Space Agency's *Beagle 2* lander and both of NASA's *Mars Exploration* Rovers, *Spirit* and *Opportunity*, landed in January 2004 on the Red Planet, where they searched for evidence of present or past life. Japan's *Nozomi (Hope)* probe was damaged en route to the planet and abandoned.

A key question concerning Mars remains the possibility of life. "This is a desolate, dry, barren world today, yet when we look at Mars from orbit we see tantalizing clues it was once wetter and warmer," said Steve Squyres of Cornell University, principle investigator for the *Opportunity* mission. Water suggests life, so the search for the origin of life extends to Mars.

The *Mars Global Explorer*, which reached the planet in 1997, remains in orbit. It has remained functional for far longer than its intended lifetime, and continued to transmit information into 2006.

Galileo

As initially approved in 1977, the Jet Propulsion Laboratory in Pasadena designed, built, and operated NASA's *Galileo* mission. Despite delays caused by redesigns and by the space shuttle *Challenger* disaster, the space probe *Galileo* rode the space shuttle *Atlantis* into space in 1989. *Galileo* had a troubled early life with the main antenna unable to deploy and with the electronic shutdowns. Despite many technical difficulties, *Galileo* provided valuable scientific data from flybys of Earth and Venus, encounters with asteroids (the first ever by spacecraft), observation of Comet Shoemaker-Levy 9's dive into the atmosphere of Jupiter, and orbits of Jupiter with flybys of five of the planet's moons.

In 1991 *Galileo* became the first spacecraft to encounter an asteroid, the asteroid Gaspra. In passing within 1000 miles (1,600 kilometers) of the asteroid's

center, the probe captured photos and data. Two years later, *Galileo* became the second spacecraft to encounter an asteroid when it made observations of Ida. The data that *Galileo* gathered on Ida enabled scientists to discover that the asteroid has a moon, little Dactyl, with a diameter of less than one mile (about 1.5 kilometers). In 1994 *Galileo* observed Comet Shoemaker-Levy 9 as it collided with Jupiter. The comet had broken into pieces two years before, and 21 separate impacts were observed over a period of six days.

In 1995 *Galileo* achieved Jovian orbit. *Galileo* surveyed the planet and five of its moons — Europa, Ganymede, Callisto, Io, and Amalthea — and it sent a 750-pound probe with two radio transmitters and six scientific instruments into Jupiter's atmosphere. Through numerous flybys, *Galileo* collected data about the icy moon Europa and the volcanic moon Io. Data revealed that Ganymede has a magnetic field, the first identified for a satellite, and that liquid salt water may exist below the surfaces of Europa, Ganymede, and Callisto. The mission also revealed that Jupiter's rings are formed by dust from meteoroids striking the four inner moons. (Figure 10-22)

Figure 10-22. This composite picture shows the planet Jupiter and its stormy Red Spot, and the four moons (from top to bottom) Io, Europa, Ganymede, and Callisto. The Red Spot is more than 300 years old. The storm's diameter is about twice the size of Earth, and its winds blow about 250 miles per hour (400 kilometers per hour). Europa is about the size of the Earth's Moon. Ganymede is the largest moon in the solar system. The photographs came from *Galileo*, except for the Callisto image, which was taken on the earlier *Voyager* mission, because *Galileo's* cameras focused only on regional details rather than global coverage of that moon.

Historical Note

This is Europa, one of four moons of Jupiter discovered by Galileo in 1610. Europa's surface features suggest that a vast liquid ocean exists just beneath the fractured icy surface. The ocean is warmed by continuous tidal stretching and squeezing as Europa orbits Jupiter. Liquid water is considered one of the most important ingredients for life.

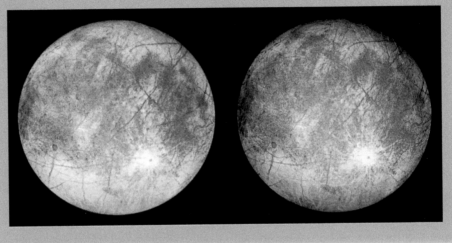

By 2003, *Galileo* was running low on fuel, and electronic problems were increasing. Among the Galilean discoveries were the possibility of subsurface briny oceans on three of Jupiter's moons. Because the presence of water means the possibility of life, rather than risk the spacecraft crashing into one of these moons and thereby introducing contaminating germs from Earth, NASA decided to destroy *Galileo*. After its 35th and final orbit of Jupiter, on 21 September 2003 the probe descended into the Jovian atmosphere. Freefalling faster than 100,000 miles per hour, *Galileo* disintegrated. NASA estimated that *Galileo* traveled 2.8 billion miles (4.6 billion kilometers) between its launch in 1989 and its disintegration in 2003. (Figure 10-23)

Space Probes

In addition to the Mars probes and *Galileo*, other spacecraft enabled scientists to study space.

Launched in May 1989 and named after the Portuguese explorer who sailed around the Earth, the NASA spacecraft *Magellan* arrived at Venus in August of 1990 and orbited around this second planet from the Sun. For the first two years, *Magellan* gathered radar images and altimetry data that yielded a map of 98 percent of the planet at a resolution of approximately 100 meters. The data revealed a geologically active planet covered mostly by volcanic materials, and the relatively few impact craters suggested a young age for the surface of the planet. Although the planet itself is 4.5 billion years old, the

volcanic surface was only 500 million years old. The planet's tectonics appeared to be the result of upwelling and subsidence, rather than the continental drift and ocean-floor spreading that characterizes the Earth's tectonics.

Figure 10-23. *Galileo* probe nears Jupiter.

Magellan ready for release

Magellan completed three cycles of mapping, which enabled scientists to see changes, if any, over time. During the subsequent two years, *Magellan* measured the gravitational field of Venus, also via three orbital cycles. As a part of that effort, the NASA controllers at Earth experimented successfully with aerobraking by using the technique to maneuver the spacecraft from elliptical orbit to circular orbit. Aerobraking tilted the spacecraft into the atmosphere, and the atmospheric drag slowed the spacecraft, which then moved into a lower orbit. The mission ended with a planned crash into Venus on 11 October 1994.

The International Solar-Polar Mission with two spacecraft had developed by 1990 into the *Ulysses* program. The United States had canceled its spacecraft in 1981, but the European partners built their spacecraft *Ulysses*. It was a solar probe, launched by NASA from the space shuttle *Discovery* in 1990. Equipped to study solar winds, the magnetic field of the Sun, solar bursts, and waves and rays of various sorts, *Ulysses* made a swingby of Jupiter in 1992 to gain speed and place it into an orbit that would pass high over the Sun's north and south poles. In 1994 it passed over the star's south pole at a distance of two astronomical units (186,000,000 miles), and it passed over the solar north pole in 1995. That concluded the primary mission. The international partners decided to continue operations for another solar orbit, 6.2 years, and in 2000 they again extended operations.

One of the spacecraft's achievements was the discovery that some of the stardust traveling outward from the Sun passes through the Sun's magnetic field and reaches Earth and other planets. When the sun is highly active, at what is called solar maximum, the magnetic field is disturbed and an increased amount of dust escapes. In 2003, after the solar activity from the last solar maximum had calmed down, the amount of escaping dust increased. This was a surprising discovery from *Ulysses*, which had been the first spacecraft to study the solar environment above the solar poles. While *Ulysses* orbited the Sun, NASA sent the probe *Genesis* to gather sample particles from the solar wind. After three years in space, it crashed in the Utah desert when its recovery parachute failed to deploy.

Japan succeeded in two lunar missions launched in 1990. The Institute of Space and Astronautical Science launched a swingby satellite called *Hiten* and a lunar orbiter called *Hagoromo*. These missions provided Japan with experience, data, proven technology and techniques. *Hayabusa* is a more recent example of a Japanese spaceprobe. Launched in May 2003, *Hayabusa* made a successful soft-landing on asteroid 25143 Itokawa in September 2005, and is expected to return to Earth with samples collected from the asteroid in June 2010.

While space probes in general were civil, scientific spacecraft, in 1994 NASA cooperated with the U.S. Department of Defense in launching *Clementine*, a lunar and deep space probe. The mission was to test equipment in the space environment, map the lunar surface, and fly to an asteroid. What made the mission military was the Ballistic Missile Defense Organization (BMDO), the missile defense program. The BMDO within the Defense Department wanted specific information that *Clementine* was designed to

Huygens

gather. Launched in January 1994, the spacecraft made two Earth flybys, completed two cycles of mapping the Moon, and exited lunar orbit. A computer malfunction in May ended the mission prematurely; however, the spacecraft provided tantalizing evidence of water ice at the Moon's south pole.

The *Lunar Prospector*, a NASA spacecraft launched by an Athena II rocket, traveled from Earth to lunar orbit in January 1998. Its mission was to find ice, if any, on the Moon. It went into low polar orbit, mapped the surface below, and measured the magnetic and gravitational fields. Its instruments indicated perhaps 3 billion metric tons of water ice in permanently shadowed craters. In July 1999 the *Prospector* made a controlled crash into the Moon near the South Pole. Instruments on Earth watched for water vapor during impact, but no vapor was observed.

Launched by a Titan IV rocket, *Cassini* departed Earth in 1997 on its way to Saturn, with flybys of Earth, Jupiter, and Venus during the travels preceding its arrival at Saturn in June of 2004. At Saturn, the mission sought information about the structure and dynamics of Saturn's rings, the composition and geological history of many of the moons, the nature of the dark matter on the moon Iapetus, the dynamics of Saturn's atmosphere, and the variability of clouds on the moon Titan. The flybys of three planets en route were gravity-assist maneuvers. *Cassini*, an orbiter, carried the *Huygens* probe, which in January of 2005 descended through Titan's atmosphere and landed on that moon, Saturn's largest moon. Fourteen European nations, as well as the United States, participated in planning, building, equipping, and launching *Cassini*. Those partners tracked the progress of the space probe while it traveled toward Saturn and delighted in the photographs of Titan's surface.

In March 2004 the European Space Agency launched *Rosetta* toward a rendezvous with the Comet 67P/Churyumov-Gerasimenko in 2014. It carries a landing probe designed to explore the comet's surface. According to the plan, *Rosetta* will fly to Mars and get a gravity assist from that planet, return for an Earth flyby, then fly by the asteroid 2867 Steins, and again fly by the Earth, this time for a gravity assist as it heads for a flyby of asteroid 21 Lutetia and on to the Comet 67P/Churyumov-Gerasimenko.

The first European spacecraft designed to orbit the Moon, the *SMART-1*, came from the European Space Agency. ESA launched the lunar mission on 27 September 2003 from the European spaceport in Kourou, French Guiana. An Ariane 5 rocket carried

Cassini

the *SMART-1* spacecraft into Earth orbit, from whence it transferred to Moon orbit. The twofold mission was to test the spacecraft's ion drive system and use miniaturized instruments to explore the Moon's geochemistry and South Pole region. ESA installed an infrared spectrometer and an experimental X-ray spectrometer for analyzing the composition of the Moon. *SMART-1* arrived at the Moon on schedule in January 2005 and sent back close-up photographs. (Figure 10-24)

Figure 10-24. Rollout and lift-off of the European Space Agency's lunar probe *SMART-1* occurred at the Kourou spaceport in French Guiana.

Mission planners intend to crash it into the Moon in September 2006 to gather more data.

In January 2006 NASA launched a mission to Pluto and beyond to objects in the Kuiper Belt. Despite a speed of 36,000 miles per hour, the *New Horizons* spacecraft is expected to spend nine years en route to Pluto. The results are future events. *New Horizons* will not only probe the farthest "major" body in our solar system, but also complete the interplanetary exploration begun with the launch of *Mariner 2* toward Venus in 1962.

Observatories

Numerous observatories placed into orbit during the 1990s provided views into space and insights into the origin of the universe and the nature of its features.

NASA used the space shuttle *Discovery* to carry the *Hubble Space Telescope* to orbit in April 1990. *Hubble* was an international observatory, a product and tool of the European Space Agency and NASA. Designed for long-term use, *Hubble* was constructed and equipped for routine on-orbit servicing, so astronauts from visiting spacecraft could perform maintenance. Initially, a mirror problem hindered the effectiveness of the optical system, but a repair mission, carried on the space shuttle *Endeavour*, enabled the telescope to operate with full functionality. The precision pointing and powerful optics thereafter provided vast quantities of high quality data. Using *Hubble* data, scientists concluded that black holes exist at the centers of galaxies, confirmed that quasars are active galactic nuclei, and found evidence that the expansion of the universe is accelerating. Service missions refurbished instruments, replaced parts, installed new instruments, and generally upgraded the observatory in 1993, 1997, 1999, and 2002. In 2003 scientists using *Hubble* imagery discovered two small moons orbiting Uranus and brought the total number of that distant planet's moons to 24.

Hubble was the first of several space telescopes launched in the 1990s. They shared one purpose: astronomy. *Hubble* observed primarily ultraviolet, visible, and infrared light, and the *Compton Gamma-Ray Observatory* studied gamma rays. Launched aboard the space shuttle *Atlantis* in April 1991, *Compton* had four instruments that covered six decades of the electromagnetic spectrum. It observed spectral energy until a gyro failure prompted controllers to lower the spacecraft from orbit. It reentered the Earth's atmosphere in June of 2000.

The European Space Agency and NASA cooperated on the *Solar and Heliospheric Observatory (SOHO)* that was launched aboard an Atlas 2-AS rocket from Cape Canaveral, Florida, in December 1995. Built in Europe by Matra, *SOHO* carried instruments from a variety of European and American scientists. *SOHO* collected data about the Sun's corona, solar winds, and the interior structure of the star. Initially designed for a two-year mission, *SOHO* remained in operation in halo orbit in 2006.

The *Chandra X-ray Observatory* and *XMM–Newton Observatory* observed X-rays. NASA launched *Chandra* into orbit in July 1999, and the European Space Agency launched *Newton* in December 1999. A spacecraft is necessary to study x-rays in space because the Earth's atmosphere absorbs x-rays. *Chandra* and *Newton* have observed dark matter, black holes, white dwarfs, supernovas, stars, and background x-rays in space.

Satellites

Many countries focused their space programs on satellites. India, for example, had sent satellites into space in the 1970s, launched its own satellite in 1980, and continued developing satellites. India built

Hubble Space Telescope

the INSAT-2 geostationary communication and meteorological satellite, finished in 1992. The Indian-built Polar Satellite Launch Vehicle failed to reach orbit in 1993, but it did prove component technology. India successfully launched the Geosynchronous Satellite Launch Vehicle in 2001; this gave India the capacity to launch large communication and weather satellites and to launch space probes.

Brazil sent data collection satellites (Satelites de Coleta de Dados), the SCD-1 and SCD-2, aloft in 1993 and 1998 respectively, but used commercial launch services due to the lack of an indigenous launch vehicle and delays in the national program to develop a launch vehicle. Orbital Sciences Corporation used the Pegasus air-launched space booster system to launch the SCD-1 and SCD-2 from Cape Canaveral, Florida. The rocket dropped from a Lockheed L-1011. The SCD satellites gathered meteorological and environmental information.

On 14 October 1999, after 11 years of planning, China launched the China-Brazil Earth Resources Satellite, CBERS-1. CBERS was a remote sensing probe designed to monitor the environment of Brazil. China launched it from Taiyuan, China, on board a Chinese Long March 4B rocket. The second CBERS satellite was launched from Taiyuan on 21 October 2003. Brazil's goal was development of an indigenous space program, but in 1997 a strap-on booster failed to ignite on its launch vehicle, the VLS-1, and in 1999 the second stage failed. After a second domestic launch failure in 1999, a Brazilian satellite engineer at the National Space Research Institute noted, "Other countries have seen many more rockets burst before something started working."

But the Brazilian space program suffered a major loss in August 2003 when a VLS-1 rocket exploded on the launch pad during pre-launch tests at the Alcantara Launch Center near Sao Luis. The accident killed 21 people, mostly civilian technicians. It destroyed two research satellites and hurt the country's effort to be the first South American nation to use an indigenous launch vehicle to place an indigenous satellite into orbit.

NASA launched South Africa's first satellite in 1999, and South Africa operated the Satellite Applications Center at Hartebeesthoek, near Johannesburg, which had evolved from a NASA-operated satellite tracking program. The South African center supported satellites of France and the United States.

Algeria's first satellite, the British-built ALSAT 1, went into space on board a Russian rocket in November of 2002. It was the first in an international network of five satellites in the Disaster-Monitoring Constellation. Nigeria became the third African nation to have a satellite in space. Almost a year later, on 27 September 2003, a Russian Kosmos 3M rocket carried three more of the spacecraft into orbit, including: Nigeria's NigeriaSat-1 (the first satellite for this West African country), Turkey's BILSAT-1, and Britain's *UK-DMC*. The satellites were designed to monitor water resources, soil erosion, deforestation, and oil pipelines. The satellites were also meant to serve military and communication needs. The Rosoboronexport company launched the Omsk Polyot-made rocket from Plesetsk, which had also served as launch site for the Algerian satellite.

The development of constellations of telephone and data transfer satellites in the late 1990s was a major technological achievement, though financially an initial flop represented by Iridium, Globalstar, and Orbcomm Global. These companies offered mobile, personal satellite phones with nearly global coverage provided by networks or constellations of satellites in orbit around the globe. Iridium began in 1998 with Motorola's backing and equipment. It filed for bankruptcy protection in August 1999. Finding a buyer for its network of 66 small satellites in low orbit proved difficult. (Figure 10-25)

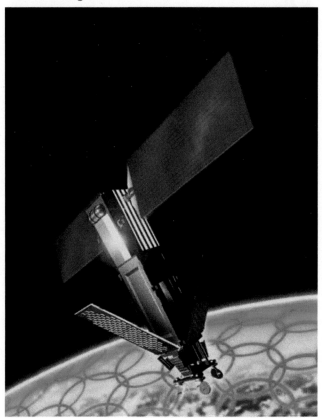

Figure 10-25. Iridium is a global satellite communication system.

The economic failure of the satellite communication companies affected commercial small-launch companies such as Orbital Sciences, founded in 1982, and large corporations, such as Lockheed, that considered commercial launches. The subsequent Iridium Satellite LLC company purchased the assets of the original Iridium, but not the liabilities or operating costs. The successor provided satellite phones used by the military during the Iraq War of 2003 and was subsequently approved for commercial communication in post-war Iraq.

Space Programs

Once the domain of the Soviet Union and the United States, space opened to many nations, as the satellite programs of many countries illustrated. The Russians operated the space station *Mir* as long as possible, but turned to commercial and cooperative ventures to nurture its space program during a time of limited funds. The United States continued launching its aging space shuttle fleet to the point of disaster. The European Space Agency and China pursued respective efforts to establish a strong presence in space. (Figure 10-26)

Mir

Post-Soviet Russia had to find new ways to do many things, including funding its space program. The space program featured the *Mir* space station, Soyuz transports, and the *International Space Station*. Starsem, the company that markets commercial use of the Soyuz spacecraft, relied upon the Baikonur Cosmodrome for launches. The Samara Space Center built the Soyuz spacecraft and the unmanned Progress.

On 20 February 1986 a Proton booster launched the core 17KS module of *Mir* (*Peace*); the core had six docking ports. The Cosmos-1700 satellite *Luch* (*Beam*) had been launched before the core module to be in place for communication between *Mir* and ground stations.

At *Mir*, Russian cosmonauts installed the Kvant-1 module in 1987, Kvant-2 in 1989, Kristall in 1990, Spektr and Space Shuttle Docking Compartment in 1995, and Priroda in 1996. Soyuz transports and unmanned Progress vehicles resupplied the space station, which remained operational for 15 years, long beyond its planned life. (Figure 10-27)

During that time, Russians cosmonauts became hosts to an international array of astronauts, some paying

Historic Event

On 28 August 2000, two Russian cosmonauts and one French astronaut closed the space station Mir. Launched in 1986, the Russian space station far exceeded its planned operational life.

guests as post-Soviet Russia sold time on the *Mir* space station to various countries undertaking space research and that wanted space time for their astronauts. The Soviets had brought Afghani, Syrian, and French astronauts to the space station in 1988, and in 1990 the Japanese television reporter Toyohiro Akiyama broadcast live reports to Tokyo viewers from *Mir*. Austrian, British, and Kazakhstani astronauts visited in 1991, as did German and French astronauts in 1992. Norman Thagard became the first U.S. astronaut at *Mir* in 1995.

Historic Event

On 23 March 2001 the Russian space station Mir returned to Earth. The spacecraft fell into the Pacific Ocean.

Figure 10-26. Lockheed Martin sells launch services on the Proton launch vehicles through International Launch Services.

Figure 10-27. *Mir* orbits serenely 215 miles above the Earth.

Historic Event

On 29 June 1995 a United States space shuttle, the Atlantis, docked at the Russian space station Mir for the first time. The Atlantis performed a crew exchange for the Mir.

In June 1995 the *Atlantis* docked with *Mir*. It had been two decades since the Apollo-Soyuz dockings. There were three astronauts in the *Mir* and seven astronauts in the shuttle. The *Atlantis* performed a crew exchange. Russia continued international cooperation; for example, Thomas Reiter represented the European Space Agency at *Mir* in 1996. U.S. astronaut Shannon Lucid spent 170 days on *Mir* that year; she set a U.S. endurance record. Other American astronauts visited *Mir* for stays of more than 100 days. In 1999 Slovakian and French astronauts visited.

Finally two Russian cosmonauts and a French astronaut closed *Mir* in 2000. *Mir* reentered the Earth's atmosphere and broke up over the Pacific Ocean in March 2001. *Mir* had maintained a Russian presence in space, proven space station technology and techniques, and opened diplomatic channels.

Historical Note

On 22 March 1995 Valeri Vladimirovich Polyakov (1942–) completed a spaceflight of record duration: 437 days, 17 hours, and 58 minutes. The Soyuz TM-18 had carried him into space on 9 January 1994, and he had spent the interim on board the space station *Mir*. A graduate of the Moscow Medical Institute, Polyakov specialized in astronautics medicine. He had been in space once before, for 240 days, 22 hours, and 34 minutes. On that trip, he departed on the Soyuz TM-6 on 29 August 1988, visited the *Mir*, and returned to Earth on 27 April 1989. On his two spaceflights, Polyakov logged a total of 678 days in space. He was studying the effects of long-term stays in space on the human body.

Personal Profile

Nikolai Mikhailovich Budarin (1953–), Russian cosmonaut, flew two missions on board U.S. space shuttles.

Budarin was born in Kirya, Chuvashia, in the Russian Republic of the Soviet Union. He studied mechanical engineering at the Moscow Aviation Institute. He rose through the engineering ranks at RSC Energia (the S.P. Korolev Rocket Space Corporation Energia), which designed the *Mir* space station. In 1989 Budarin became a candidate cosmonaut. He completed training at the Gagarin Cosmonaut Training Center and passed a government examination to qualify as a cosmonaut. He then trained for the Soyuz-TM transport vehicle and the *Mir* space station. In 1995 he went aboard the space shuttle *Atlantis* to perform a *Mir* crew upload. On that mission, the *Atlantis* achieved the 100th manned U.S. space launch and the first docking of a space shuttle with the Russian space station. After duty on board *Mir*, Budarin landed in the Soyuz TM-21. In 2002 Budarin flew his second shuttle flight, this time on board the *Endeavour*, on a mission for routine assembly work on the *International Space Station*. That was the last shuttle flight of 2002.

Space Shuttle

By the end of the 1980s, the Space Shuttle program had launched 32 spaceflights, including the disastrous 1986 launch of the *Challenger* and seven successful launches thereafter. The first flight of a space shuttle in the 1990s launched a satellite, retrieved a satellite from orbit, set a record for the longest space shuttle flight to date (261 hours), and made a night landing.

Atlantis and *Discovery* enjoyed successful missions, but then hydrogen leaks on the orbiter *Columbia* delayed a launch later in 1990. The *Atlantis* moved to the pad, but an umbilical disconnect fitting on its external tank also leaked hydrogen. While it was being repaired, the *Columbia* moved back to the launch pad, but a tropical storm delayed its launch, so *Discovery* moved to the pad and was launched on October 6. Leaks remained, but NASA raised the level of allowed leakage and thereby determined the leakage to be within acceptable levels. The agency also worked to develop a new disconnect unit. In November 1990 *Atlantis* became the fifth launch of the year. It carried a classified defense payload. In December, *Columbia* became the sixth.

Throughout the 1990s NASA sent space shuttles into outer space. The Space Shuttle program included the *Enterprise*, *Columbia*, *Discovery*, *Atlantis*, and, as of 1992, the *Endeavour*. It made the "golden" fiftieth space shuttle flight in May of 1992, and that launch was the first "on time" launch since 1985. Beginning in 1998, the shuttles visited the *International Space Station* and provided crew rotation flights.

During the 1990s and thereafter, space shuttles carried foreign astronauts from Canada, France, Germany, Japan, Russia, and Switzerland. The astronauts served as mission and payload specialists, as illustrated in the following examples. Chris A. Hadfield of the Canadian Space Agency flew as a mission specialist on two missions and accomplished 14 hours of extravehicular activity. As mission specialists, Julie Payette, Steve Maclean, Robert B. Thirsk, and Dafydd (Dave) Rhys Williams of the Canadian Space Agency each flew on one flight. Mission specialist Claude Nicollier of Switzerland and the European Space Agency flew four shuttle missions and accumulated over 1,000 hours of spaceflight time. Hans Schlegel of Germany and Michel Tognini of France also represented the European Space Agency when they went as mission specialists on shuttle missions. Japanese astronauts flew the 50th and 100th shuttle missions, Mamoru Mohri on the

Historical Note

The 50th flight of the Space Shuttle program began with the launch of the *Endeavour* on 12 September 1992. The historic flight carried the first black woman into space, mission specialist Mae R. Jemison, and a Japanese astronaut, payload specialist Mamoru Mohri. Mohri was the second Japanese man in space; a Japanese reporter had flown on a Soviet spacecraft earlier. In Japan, September 12 became Space Day because this was the anniversary of the first Japanese astronaut going into space. The *Endeavour* also carried on that flight the first married couple to travel in space together, payload specialist Mark C. Lee and mission specialist N. Jan Davis. It was a Spacelab mission with experiments in the life sciences, so on board were hornets, frogs, and carp. The flight completed 126 orbits of the Earth. It landed at the Kennedy Space Center on 19 September. This was the fourth spaceflight for commander Robert H. "Hoot" Gibson, formerly a naval pilot.

Endeavour in 1992 and Koichi Wakata on the *Discovery* in 2000.

Russian cosmonauts also participated in the U.S. space program. Nikolai Budarin, for example, represented the new, post-Soviet Russian Space Agency. A mechanical engineer by training, he rose through the engineering ranks in the Soviet space program. In 1989 he became a cosmonaut candidate. He completed training at the Gagarin Cosmonaut Training Center and passed a government examination to qualify as a cosmonaut. He then trained for Soyuz-TM transport vehicle and the *Mir* space station. He performed a *Mir* crew upload in 1995. On that mission the *Atlantis* achieved the 100th manned U.S. space launch and the first docking of a space shuttle with the Russian space station. Launched by the *Atlantis*, Budarin landed by Soyuz TM-21. In 2002 Budarin flew his second shuttle flight, this time on board the *Endeavour* on a mission for routine assembly work on the *International Space Station*. That was the last shuttle flight of 2002.

NASA had launched 32 space shuttle missions in the 1980s and 96 missions by the end of the 20th century. The agency launched four shuttle missions in 2000, seven in 2001, five in 2002, and one in 2003. The first flight of 2003 broke up upon reentry and thereby prompted NASA to ground the Space Shuttle program for investigation of the accident and in the interests of safety of the astronauts who fly aboard the spacecraft.

Columbia Accident

The space shuttle *Columbia* had become operational in 1981. It flew the first space shuttle mission; in fact, it flew the first five shuttle spaceflights between 1981 and 1982. More than twenty years later the same *Columbia* flew the 113th shuttle mission. The mission began on 16 January 2003, when *Columbia* lifted off from Cape Canaveral. The shuttle accomplished its science experiments. On 1 February it returned to

Historic Event

John Glenn was the first US astronaut to orbit the Earth. On 29 October 1998 he demonstrated that age need not be a barrier to space travel.

The world was fascinated with the idea of John Glenn, the first American to orbit the Earth, flying again at the age of 77. His first spaceflight in 1962 gave the United States a measure of pride in the face of many humiliating firsts by the Soviets in space. His 1998 flight rekindled memories of the excitement and anticipation felt at the dawn of the space age. The flight facilitated a great deal of intergenerational communication, and those too young to remember his first flight may have gotten a sense of the enthusiasm and optimism of the 1960s.

Flight Lines

"In space one has the inescapable impression that here is a virgin area of the universe in which civilized man, for the first time, has the opportunity to learn and grow without the influence of ancient pressures. Like the mind of a child, it is as yet untainted with acquired fears, hate, greed, or prejudice."

John Glenn, Jr., U.S. astronaut and senator, as quoted in *The Home Planet*, edited by Kevin W. Kelley. (Reading MA: Addison-Wesley Publishing, 1988).

Historic Event

The 100th mission of the space shuttle passed routinely. Designated STS-92, this flight of the *Discovery* took the zenith-port truss, control moment gyros, and two heat pipes to the *International Space Station*. The *Discovery* spent seven days docked at the space station. The crew included commander Brian Duffy, pilot Pamela A. Melroy, and five mission specialists, one of whom was Japanese astronaut Koichi Wakata. The other mission specialists were Leroy Chiao, Michael E. Lopez-Alegria, William S. McArthur, and Peter J.K. Wisoff, all of whom completed spacewalks. Launched on 11 October 2000, STS-92 landed at Edwards Air Force Base, California, on 24 October.

the earth's atmosphere to land. On the reentry path something went terribly, fatally wrong. The spacecraft disintegrated, and the seven astronauts on board died.

A piece of insulating foam was quickly identified as the suspected cause of the disaster. After launch, while the shuttle traveled upward at more than 1,600 miles per hour, the foam tore loose from the external propellant tank (a 15-story high fuel can). The supersonic air stream carried the foam about 60 feet to the leading edge of the left wing. Traveling about 530 mph, the spinning foam struck the wing with about a ton of force. The blow knocked off reinforced carbon panels installed to insulate the wing against the extremely high temperatures of reentry. The blow made a hole in the wing. Upon reentry, the hole allowed super-hot gasses into the wing. The gasses burned the wing until it fell off. The shuttle suffered catastrophic failure.

The loose piece of foam from the external fuel tank breached the thermal protection system on the wing. That was the physical cause of the tragedy, concluded the *Columbia* Accident Investigation Board, but the board also determined that NASA's culture and history contributed to the accident. Compromises had been made in the beginning to gain approval for the program. After the successful Apollo lunar program, NASA often faced resource constraints; it did not have enough money. According to the accident board, NASA was "an agency trying to do too much with too little." Priorities fluctuated, yet schedules applied pressure. According to the board, NASA wrongly considered the shuttle operational rather than developmental technology. NASA's space program developed a culture "detrimental to safety." It relied on past success as a substitute for sound engineering practices, such as testing to understand why systems were not

Personal Profile

The astronaut with the most space shuttle missions (as of 2006) came from Costa Rica. He logged seven spaceflights and over 1,600 hours in space between 1986 and 2002. When he first went into space in 1986, he became the first Latin American in space.

Franklin R. Chang-Díaz (1950–) was born in San José, Costa Rica. He graduated from the Colegio de la Salle there and then from Hartford, Connecticut, High School. He studied mechanical engineering at the University of Connecticut and studied applied plasma physics at the Massachusetts Institute of Technology, from which he received a doctorate degree in 1977. Shortly after becoming a naturalized citizen of the United States, Chang-Díaz joined NASA. He began astronaut training in 1981.

Chang-Díaz reached space for the first time in 1986 on board the *Columbia*. That mission deployed a communication satellite and performed scientific experiments. Chang-Díaz returned to space in 1989 on the *Atlantis*. This mission deployed *Galileo* on its mission to Jupiter. On his third spaceflight, on the *Atlantis* in 1992, he helped deploy the European Space Agency's *European Retrievable Carrier (EURECA)*. That *Atlantis* mission also attempted to deploy the joint NASA-Italian Space Agency Tethered Satellite System (TSS), but the tether got tangled. Chang-Díaz also flew on a *Discovery* mission in 1994 that carried the Wake Shield Facility for a free-flight attempt to grow film materials for use in electronics. It also carried the first Russian astronaut on a shuttle, Sergei K. Krikalev. (An experienced cosmonaut, Krikalev had already completed two long-duration stays on board the *Mir*.) On the *Columbia* in 1996, Chang-Díaz returned to space in a second attempt to deploy the TSS. At almost full deployment, the tether broke. On the *Discovery* in 1998, Chang-Díaz participated in the final Shuttle-*Mir* docking mission, a series of dockings in preparation for the *International Space Station*. His seventh spaceflight was in 2002 on board the *Endeavour*. This was the second utilization flight to the *International Space Station*. The flight carried three astronauts to the *International Space Station*, made a crew exchange, and brought three astronauts down.

In addition to flying in space, Chang-Díaz conducted scientific research, published technical papers, gave lectures, and taught. In the 1980s and 1990s, as a visiting scientist with MIT, he led a plasma propulsion program that was developing rocket technology with a view toward manned flight to Mars. When NASA established the Advanced Space Propulsion Laboratory at the Johnson Space Center in 1993, Chang-Díaz became director of the laboratory. He led the laboratory and its development of plasma rocket technology for a Mars mission. He retired from NASA in 2005.

performing in accordance with requirements. Organizational barriers also prevented effective communication of critical safety information. Professional differences of opinion were stifled. And the informal chain of command and the decision-making processes operated outside NASA rules. In summary, the history and culture of NASA let the agency fly the shuttle for years with known foam debris problems. The history and culture also allowed the agency to disregard the safety concerns of its engineers.

The *Columbia* Accident Investigation Board recommended that the space shuttle return to flight "at the earliest date consistent with an overriding consideration: safety." "The recognition of human spaceflight as a developmental activity," the board cautioned, "requires a shift in focus from operations and meeting schedules to a concern with the risks involved."

Why do we need a space program? This question arose repeatedly in the days after the *Columbia* acci-

dent. The scientific and technological challenges and the romance of space exploration remained, but what was the purpose, the objective? Only months before the *Columbia* accident, the Commission on the Future of the U.S. Aerospace Industry had concluded that the United States must continue to be "a space-faring nation in order to be the global leader in the 21st century — our freedom, mobility, and quality of life will depend on it." How NASA, Congress, the President, and the nation will answer the question after the *Columbia* accident is a matter of speculation, not history.

The Space Shuttle program returned to flight with the launch of *Discovery* on 26 July 2005. This was a test flight for the spacecraft and the program. *Discovery* landed safely at Edwards Air Force Base in California on 9 August, but the foam insulating the external tank remained a concern, as does the age of the space shuttle fleet. *Discovery* was first launched in 1984. It is an old spacecraft. Safety remains a major issue. What is in the future?

Historic Event

On 1 February 2003, after re-entering the earth's atmosphere for landing, the space shuttle *Columbia* broke apart. The seven-member crew died. Commander Rick D. Husband was an Air Force colonel and test pilot who had logged 627 hours in space. Pilot William C. McCool was a Navy pilot. This was his only space flight. Payload Commander Michael P. Anderson was an Air Force officer and experienced space traveler. The four mission spe-

cialists were: David M. Brown, a naval aviator and flight surgeon on his first spaceflight; Kalpana Chawla, an aerospace engineer with 759 hours of spacetime; Laurel Blair Salton Clark, a naval flight surgeon; and Ilan Ramon, a payload specialist and colonel in the Israeli Air Force, also on his first spaceflight.

European Space Agency

Founded on the international cooperation of the 1960s, and established in the mid-1970s, the European Space Agency had developed a strong satellite program by the 1980s. In the 1990s ESA emerged as a major space program that continued the now expanded effort to develop a European space capability for the benefit of Europe. Over the years, ESA identified many goals for the European space program: to keep Europe in the scientific discovery of space, to conduct medical research in space, to generate new technologies, to contribute to the strength of European industry, to protect the Earth's environment via satellite monitoring, to improve weather forecasting for agriculture and transportation, to create maps, to increase science and technology employment, to reduce Europe's brain drain, and to explore space.

The 15 member states — Austria, Belgium, Denmark, Finland, France, Germany, Ireland, Italy, the Netherlands, Norway, Portugal, Spain, Sweden, Switzerland, and the United Kingdom — have established ESA as the organization to coordinate financial, scientific, and technical resources to undertake activities beyond the means of any individual country.

ESA and other customers hired launched services from the France-based Arianespace company with corporate shareholders representing 12 European nations. Founded in 1980, Arianespace had sold hun-

dreds of launch contracts since its founding. The launch family has included the Ariane 1, first launched in 1979, Ariane 3, first launched in 1984, Ariane 2, first launched in 1987, Ariane 4, first launched in 1988, the generic Ariane 5, first successfully launched in 1997, and the Ariane 5 heavy-lift launcher, which entered service in 2005. Arianespace also used Soyuz launchers, operated by Starsem, a French-Russian joint venture in which Arianespace held shares. Under development for a projected 2007 first launch is the Vega, a solid-propellant, single-body launcher for small payloads. Arianespace had more than 50 percent of the world market for geostationary satellites by the turn of the century. In March 2006 Arianespace launched the 170th rocket in the Ariane line. (Figure 10-28)

Arianespace launched the Egyptian Nilesat, the Brazilian Brazilsat B4, the Italian defense Circal, the British defense Skynet 4F, the ESA's Envisat, EUTELSAT's Atlantic Bird, the European Meteorological Satellite (EUMETSAT) organization's MSG-1, and many Intelsat communication satellites. The Ariane's 100th launch carried an Intelsat telecommunication satellite into space in 1997. On the final launch of an Ariane 4 in 2003, the 116th launch of an Ariane vehicle, the rocket carried an Intelsat satellite into space. An Ariane 5 launch in September of 2003 carried two satellites into space — the INSAT-3E for the Indian Space Research Organization and the e-BIRD, built by Boeing, for the European operator Eutelsat. It also launched an ESA spacecraft, the lunar probe *SMART-1*.

Figure 10-28. Ariane 5

Historical Note

By the end of 2005, Arianespace's Ariane 5 launch vehicle had completed more than 20 successful launches. The Ariane 5ECA version has a liftoff mass of 780 metric tons, including payload of 9.6 metric tons. The 5ECA can carry multiple satellites and place them in orbit. When the generic Ariane 5 carried the *SMART-1* lunar orbiter aloft, it also took up the INSAT-3C and e-BIRD satellites. The first Ariane launch of 2006, in March, was of an Ariane 5ECA that placed Hot Bird 7A and Spainsat satellites into orbit.

ESA entered the 21st century with a clear strategy defined by the councils of ESA and the European Union. The three actions required by the strategy were: strengthen the foundations for space activities, enhance scientific knowledge, and reap the benefits for society and markets. Foundations for space meant launch vehicles to ESA, because access to space required launch capability. The second action meant scientific research, space research and also Earth research from space. The *International Space Station* fell under this rubric, as did the proposed Aurora program for robotic and manned exploration of the solar system. The third action required close cooperation between the space agency and the European Union. This encompassed satellite communication, satellite navigation, and industrial development.

Regarding manned spaceflight, ESA had selected its first astronauts in 1977. Two went to Spacelab. The first ESA astronaut to reach outer space was Ulf Merbold, in 1983; the second went in 1985, and Merbold went again in 1992. By the end of 2000, ESA

Historical Evidence

Questioning *why* is a difficult proposition in history. Statements of why may mislead by omission or commission, or the statements may inform. Why must Europe invest in space? The European Space Agency answered:

"Today's space systems are the key to the understanding and management of the World, to the provision of goods and services in the global marketplace, and to regional and global security and peacekeeping."

This statement is from ESA's website at http://www.esa.int/.

astronauts had flown on 14 space shuttle flights and completed three long-duration stays on the Russian space station *Mir*. In 1998 Europe and ESA established a Single European Astronaut Corps, which had grown by the year 2000 to 16 astronauts. The first ESA astronaut to reach the *International Space Station* was Umberto Guidoni in 2001.

China

Like the European Space Agency, the People's Republic of China also planned to go to the Moon, but China prepared for a manned mission. The government approved the manned space program in 1992. Called Project 921, this national program had several stages. One was to be a manned space capsule and manned flight. Stage two was to be a Chinese space station, and stage three a space transportation system using a delta-wing orbiter. There was a lot of work to be done.

Familiar with Soviet technology, early Chinese capsule designs resembled the Soyuz. When Russian leader Boris Yeltsin visited Beijing in 1996, China purchased Soyuz capsules, though the Chinese were also building their own manned spacecraft, with some systems such as the escape tower, spacesuits, and docking mechanisms purchased from Russia. The Chinese also purchased astronaut training and other services from the Russian program, which was short of funds after the collapse of the Soviet Union just a few years earlier. The Chinese indigenous spacecraft program designed the Shenzhou, which incorporated the Soyuz influence.

China operated three satellite launch centers — Xichang for launch to geosynchronous orbits, Jiuquan for mid-inclination orbits, and Taiyuan for polar orbits. It developed the Long March line of modular rockets, and it developed cryogenic engines used in the launches. By 2000, China had launched 47 satellites of various types, including the indigenous FSW (Fanhui Shei Weixing, recoverable test satellite) series begun in the 1980s, the DFH (Hongfanghong) telecommunication satellites also begun in the 1980s, the FY (Fengyun) meteorological satellites, and the SJ (Shijian) scientific satellites. (Figure 10-29)

China sold commercial launch services on the international market. In 1990, for example, China used a Long March 3 rocket to carry the U.S.-made and Hong Kong-owned Asiasat 1 satellite into orbit. China launched 27 foreign-made satellites between 1985 and 2000.

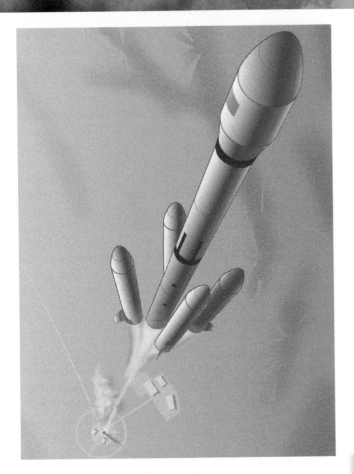

Figure 10-29. A Chinese Long March 3.

landed on 16 January in Inner Mongolia. *Shenzhou 3* lifted off on 25 March 2002, made 107 orbits around Earth, and landed on 1 April in Inner Mongolia. Launched on 29 December 2002, *Shenzhou 4* completed 108 revolutions around Earth and landed on 5 January 2003 in Inner Mongolia. It was equipped to accommodate three people in manned flight.

On 15 October 2003, at the Juiquan spaceport in the Gobi Desert in Gansu Province, China used a Long March 2F rocket to launch the *Shenzhou 5* spacecraft into orbit around the Earth. Yang Liwei rode the spacecraft into space, orbited Earth 14 times, and parachuted safely to ground on October 16th. With this flight, China became the third nation, behind Russia and the United States, to have achieved manned spaceflight, and Yang became the first Chinese astronaut. He was chosen from a team of astronauts, all military pilots, who had been training for years for spaceflight. These astronauts the Chinese called "yuhang yuans" but they are often called "taikonauts" in Western media. China's manned space program, under the leadership of Li Junai, had already announced plans for shuttles, space stations, lunar bases, and Mars missions. The *Shenzhou 5* was the proving flight.

Still under communist control, China kept secrets about its space program, but it openly pursued a manned spaceflight program. It launched four unmanned Shenzhou spacecraft between November 1999 and January 2003, preparatory to manned spaceflight. *Shenzhou 1*, launched on 19 November 1999, made 14 orbits around Earth and landed on 20 November in Inner Mongolia. *Shenzhou 2,* launched on 9 January 2001, completed 107 orbits around Earth. It carried a monkey, a dog, a rabbit, some snails, and other scientific payloads. *Shenzhou 2*

Flight Lines

"It looks extremely splendid around here," China's first astronaut Yang Liwei said from his seat on board China's first manned spacecraft, the *Shenzhou 5*, as it orbited Earth, as reported by the Associated Press.

Two years later, on 5 October 2005, China launched the *Senzhou 6*, with two astronauts on board for a five-day flight. They were Commander Fèi Jùnlóng and Flight Engineer Niè Haishèng. As the China Daily boasted, "Two years, two big steps, and the Chinese are getting closer and closer to the Moon."

Commercial Space Flight

Just as the Archdeacon Prize encouraged Alberto Santos-Dumont to develop and fly an airplane in France in 1906, and just as the Orteig Prize prompted Charles Lindbergh's flight from New York to Paris in 1927, the X Prize has been funded to stimulate manned spaceflight in spacecraft privately developed and privately operated. By 2003, 25 groups from seven nations had registered as competitors for the X Prize.

Historic Event

On 15-16 October 2003 China achieved manned spaceflight and thereby became the third country in the world with a successful manned space program. Launched by a Long March 2F rocket, the spacecraft *Shenzhou 5* lifted off from the Jiuquan spaceport in the Gobi Desert. China's first astronaut, Yang Liwei, rode the spacecraft into orbit. After orbiting the Earth repeatedly, Yang landed by parachute.

Historical Note

When placed in orbit in 1990, the AsiaSat 1 was already a spacecraft with a history. Built in the early 1980s by Hughes Aircraft, it was first launched from the Space Shuttle *Challenger* in February 1984 as Westar 6. The failure of an attached rocket motor that should have kicked it into a higher orbit left it in a useless orbit — essentially space junk. In November of 1984, it was retrieved from orbit by astronauts from the space shuttle *Discovery* and returned to Earth (photo). After a thorough refurbishment it was ready for launch again, this time on an expendable Chinese launch vehicle. The AsiaSat 1 spacecraft provides telecommunications and broadcast services over much of South Asia and Australia.

Most of the competitors were based in the United States, but registrations also came from Argentina, Canada, Israel, Romania, Russia, and the United Kingdom. Burt Rutan's Scaled Composites and John Carmack's Armadillo Aerospace, of Texas, received regulatory approval for their respective rocket ships. Privately funded, Bristol Spaceplanes Limited of the United Kingdom began developing a suborbital spaceplane it called the *Ascender*. Bristol designed the *Ascender* as a passenger plane and as one that might win the X Prize.

According to the rules of the competition, the manned spacecraft must reach 62 miles above Earth and return safely twice within a 14-day period. The craft must have a capacity of three people, though only one pilot plus the weight equivalent to two passengers needed to be on board during the competition. The spacecraft would only graze space briefly during the competition, but the X Prize Foundation foresaw such an achievement as opening "the flood gates" for commercial human spaceflight.

Paul Allen's Mojave Aerospace Ventures team, led by designer Burt Rutan of Scaled Composites, won the Ansari X Prize on 4 October 2004. Their pilot, Brian Binnie, flew *SpaceShipOne* to the record altitude of 367,442 feet (69.6 miles or 112 kilometers) on that day, while making the second flight to space within the stipulated 14-day period. (Figure 10-30)

Commercial spaceflights, long a subject of science fiction, have become a limited reality with Russia taking paying passengers on board a few of their space flights. The commercial seats on Soyuz transports were expensive, about $20 million USD, and customers had to meet flight qualifications. In April 2001 Dennis Tito of California rode a Soyuz to the International Space Station. He was the first space tourist. The second was Mark Shuttleworth of South Africa, who went aloft in April 2002. He rode Soyuz TM-34 from Kazakhstan's Baikonur launchpad.

Now a variety of commercial ventures promise competition for the Russian passengers. Richard Branson of Great Britain bought the X Prize-winning technology and announced plans to take passengers into suborbital space. Rocketplane Limited Inc. also announced plans to launch commercial flights from a former air base converted into a spaceport, near Burns Flat, Oklahoma, albeit initially for only a few minutes of space time per flight and only at the relatively low space altitude of 330,000 feet.

International Space Station

The United States, the European Space Agency (in 1995), Japan, Russia, and Canada became partners in a venture called the *International Space Station*. Soyuz and space shuttle spacecraft carried the

Figure 10-30. Burt Rutan was the first to register for the X Prize competition. *SpaceShipOne*, shown above with its carrier aircraft *White Knight*, that won the $10 million prize in 2005.

modules of the space station, the construction crews, and station crews into space. The first two modules of the station went into orbit in 1988, one on a Russian Proton rocket and the other on the space shuttle *Endeavour*. In space, astronauts joined the two modules. Other modules followed. The space station was still under construction when in 2000 a Soyuz spacecraft carried a crew to the station, and continuous occupation began. The fifth shuttle mission to the space station carried the Z-1 truss for installation as part of the station's ongoing assembly. That was in 2000, and the *Discovery* made the delivery. The central truss was built by stages toward the 90-meter length in the design.

While the station design followed the modular example of *Mir*, it did not follow the developmental example. The space station was designed to be a permanent base for scientific research in space — comparable to the research stations on the continent of Antarctica. The different nations designed their own respective modules for the space station. For emergency descent, a Soyuz transport was attached to the space station.

ESA began building 15 major components or assemblies of the Crew Return Vehicle (CRV), based on the U.S. X-38 spacecraft, and intended as a successor to the Soyuz emergency vehicle. ESA also designed and began building Europe's Columbus general-purpose-laboratory module. ESA planned to use the Ariane 5 launcher and an Automated Transfer Vehicle (ATV) for supplying the station, as redundant to, not as a replacement of, the Soviet Progress ferry. ESA's ATV is larger than the Russian Progress transport. ESA also began work on a European robotic arm (ERA) to be mounted on the Russian module, again to be redundant rather than as a replacement of the Canadian arm.

The international partners bartered goods and services to build the Space Station. NASA, for example, agreed to carry Europe's *Columbus* laboratory to the station in exchange for ESA building two connecting nodes. ESA let that job go to the Italian Space Agency. ESA, in fact, approached the space station as a barter arrangement, not a cash investment.

The United States launched its second utilization mission (in contrast to an assembly mission) to the *International Space Station* in 2002. The *Endeavour* transported the three members of the expedition crew up to the station. The mission also installed Canada's 17-meter-long robotic arm developed for use in assembly and maintenance. The arm could "inchworm" along the truss to work sites.

By October 2002 a total of 15 people had visited the *International Space Station*. Soyuz spacecraft and space shuttles carried the people back and forth until the *Columbia* disaster. Then, Soyuz spacecraft provided all of the transport to and from the *International Space Station*. Expedition crews have occupied the station continuously since October 2000. Most of the crew members are from the United States or Russia, but the Italian Roberto Vittori, the Spaniard Pedro Duque, the Brazilian Marcos Pontes, and astronauts of other nationalities have also visited the station.

Spaceplanes

Both the Soyuz and the space shuttle represented old worn technology by the 21st century. Since the Soyuz 1 launch of 1967, the Soyuz had been launched 1,682 times by the end of August 2003. Since their first launch in 1981, space shuttles had been launched 113 times, and two shuttles had been destroyed in fatal accidents. Future access to the International Space Station and to space in general motivated several efforts to develop new launchers, perhaps modern spaceplanes.

Attempts at newer designs had been made. Tsien Hsue-Shen of China had drafted a spaceplane proposal in the 1970s. He incorporated a booster-launcher and two strap-on boosters. Since the 1980s, Japan had been investigating high-speed technology with a spaceplane in mind. At the start of the 21st century, Japan was exploring the possibility of building a civilian spaceliner with scramjet propulsion. Japan recognized that a civil spaceplane required international effort, and it sought international partners and funds for the spaceplane it had under development.

Russia decided to adapt the Soyuz, one of Sergei Korolev's legacies. For the *International Space Station* missions, the Soyuz TMA replaced the Soyuz TM, which had been used from May 1986 to November 2002 to ferry crews for *Mir* and the *International Space Station*. The TMA version was smaller, the computers more efficient, the cabin space able to accommodate larger crew members, the instrumentation presented in the new "glass cockpit" displays, and the landing speed reduced. In 2004 Russia announced the ongoing development of the Kliper (Clipper) spacecraft, a partial lifting body design or a winged spacecraft, the configuration not yet determined, but to be launched by rocket.

NASA developed the concept and technology for an X-30 National AeroSpace Plane (NASP) program in the late 1980s and early 1990s, but no plane was constructed. In 1996 the agency turned development to the X-33 spaceplane and the X-34 reusable launch vehicle. The X-33 was a single-stage-to-space project involving NASA and Lockheed Martin. The smaller X-34 was a test-bed vehicle designed to be air-launched from Orbital Science's Lockheed L-1011 aircraft; Orbital Sciences had the design and construction contract. Both were hypersonic, the X-33 with Mach 15 capability and the X-34 with Mach 8. The X-33 engineering was troubled, including the wedge-shape body, the aerospike engine development, and the liquid-hydrogen fuel tank. Industry was cost-sharing on the X-33, which fell behind schedule and over budget. NASA canceled both the X-33 and X34 in early 2001. In the summer of 2002 NASA also canceled its X-38 Crew Return Vehicle project. Rising costs were a factor. The X-37 was a flight demonstrator for the Orbital Space Plane.

In the 1990s and early 21st century, NASA developed the Orbital Space Plane concept to assure access to and from the *International Space Station* and low-Earth orbit. NASA studied fiscal risks and accountability as well as technology for the Orbital Space Plane so that any forthcoming NASA decision could be based on a sound business plan as well as solid engineering. NASA selected this Orbital Space Plane to replace the space shuttle. For the *International Space Station*, this aircraft was intended to transport astronauts to and from the station and to serve as a "life boat" for astronauts. A Crew Escape System provided an added element of safety. NASA's budget remained a challenge.

The Future?

History happened in the past. Historians analyze the past by asking questions: What changed? What continued? Why? And why at that time and place? The questions of change and continuity may also be applied to the future, but we lack the evidence for definitive answers about the future. History can inform strategic, long-term planning, but it cannot predict or forecast the future because the unique element of time introduces variables not present in past cases.

Will the Chinese, Russian, and East European markets open to general aviation? Will the economies and regulatory environments of Africa, Latin America, and Southeast Asia allow expansion of private flying? Will the United States continue to dominate the general aviation industry, or will the fear of terrorists place a permanent damper on private flying? Will vertical takeoff, hover, or other technology make the automobile-plane a means of personal transportation? Will the European Union continue to grow in aerospace influence? Will the addition of more European and East European nations change the aerospace direction of the European Union? Will the economic and regulatory cooperation in Europe challenge the dominance of the United States in general aviation or in military aerospace? Will the United States maintain a world position in air transportation with only one manufacturer of commercial airliners? Will the U.S. space program find focus and support for major space activities? Will any nation build a base on the Moon or Mars? Will Communist China initiate a space race with the United States? Or will Europe, Russia, Japan, or India achieve leadership in outer space?

Forecasters, policy analysts, strategic planners, corporate executives, and government officials may attempt to answer these questions about the future. Historians will wait and see.

Study Questions

1. Discuss efforts to revitalize the general aviation industry and give at least three specific examples.

2. What feats did sports aviators accomplish during the period since 1990?

3. How did the commercial aviation industry consolidate?

4. How did Airbus successfully challenge Boeing in the commercial air transport market?

5. When and how did terrorists attack commercial aviation, including the attacks of September 11, 2001, and how did the attacks affect commercial aviation?

6. Why did the military aerospace industry internationalize and in what ways did it internationalize? Use specific examples in your answer.

7. What is the difference between retaliatory and preemptive strikes? Illustrate your answer with examples from conflicts of the period.

8. Why are an increasing number of countries going into space, and how are they getting there? Use specific examples in your answer.

9. Why did the space shuttle *Columbia* break apart upon reentry in 2003?

10. Based on the history of aviation and space to 2006, what variables do you think remain influential in aerospace?

Bibliography

Bonnet, Roger M. and Vittorio Manno. *International Cooperation in Space, the Example of the European Space Agency*. Cambridge, MA: Harvard University Press, 1994.

Gordon, Yefim and Alan Dawes. *Russian Air Power*. London: Airlife, 2002.

Guttery, Ben R. *Encyclopedia of African Airlines*. Jefferson, NC: McFarland & Company, 1998.

Jane's Information Group. *China's Aerospace and Defence Industry*. Coulsdon, Surrey, UK: Jane's Information Group, 2000.

Jackson, Paul, editor. *Jane's All the World's Aircraft 2000-2001*. London: Jane's Information Group, 2000.

McDaid, Hugh and David Oliver. *Smart Weapons, Top Secret History of Remote Controlled Airborne Weapons*. New York: Orion Books, 1997.

Nader, Ralph and Wesley J. Smith. *Collision Course, the Truth about Airline Safety*. Blue Ridge Summit, PA: TAB Books, 1994.

Kelly, Mary Pat. *"Good to Go," the Rescue of Scott O'Grady from Bosnia*. Annapolis, MD: Naval Institute Press, 1996.

U.S. Central Intelligence Agency, Center for the Study of Intelligence. *At the Cold War's End: US Intelligence on the Soviet Union and Eastern Europe, 1989-1999*. CIA, 1999.

U.S. Commission on the Future of the United States Aerospace Industry. *Final Report of the Commission on the Future of the United States Aerospace Industry*. Commission on the Future of the United States Aerospace Industry, November 2002.

Timeline

1990 February 11. Afrikaner President F.W. de Klerk in South Africa released Nelson Mandela from prison after the anti-apartheid activist had served decades of a life sentence.

1990 April 24. The joint NASA-ESA Hubble program used the space shuttle *Discovery* to launch the *Hubble Space Telescope* for a long-term mission to observe from orbit above the Earth's atmosphere.

1990 August 2. Claiming Kuwait was stealing oil from a field near the border, Iraq invaded Kuwait.

1990 September 29. Test pilot Dave Ferguson made the first flight in the Lockheed-Boeing-General Dynamics prototype YF-22A fighter.

1990 October 3. Eastern and Western Germany reunited under the economic and political system of the Federal Republic of Germany.

1990 October 6. The European Space Agency launched *Ulysses* to probe stardust.

1990 October 24. At the Novaya Zemlya test site in the Arctic, the Soviet Union conducted its last nuclear test; ventilation allowed radiation to escape into the atmosphere in violation of the 1963 Moscow Treaty.

1991 January 16. An international coalition led by the United States attacked Iraq, which had invaded Kuwait the preceding summer and had ignored pressure to withdraw; aircraft led the attack.

1991 January 18. Dating back to 1926, and operating as Eastern Air Lines since 1938, Eastern Airlines ceased trading and went out of business.

1991 June 15. Mount Pinatubo volcano erupted and caused the United States to close Clark Air Force Base in the Philippines.

1991 July 1. Piper Aircraft filed for bankruptcy protection.

1991 August 19–21. A coup failed in Russia; rebels placed Soviet leader Mikhail Gorbachev under house arrest at his Black Sea summer home, but President Boris Yeltsin led the government's successful effort to survive the challenge from communist hardliners opposed to capitalist reforms.

1991 November 19. The DGV Dauphin AS 365X helicopter flew 372 kilometers per hour and broke two speed records previously held by Sikorsky helicopters.

1991 December 8. Twelve of the former 15 Soviet republics formed the Commonwealth of Independent States.

1991 December 25. The eighth and final Soviet leader, Mikhail Gorbachev, resigned, and the United States recognized six independent republics, former Soviet socialist republics: Armenia, Belarus, Kazakhstan, Kyrgyzstan, Russia, and the Ukraine.

1992 August 4. An Airbus 310 entered service with Aeroflot, the national airline of the Russian Federation, and became the first foreign jetliner in Russian service.

1992 September 23. The United States detonated its last nuclear test; the U.S. had conducted more than a thousand nuclear tests since 1945.

1993 September 21–October 4. Pro-Western President Boris Yeltsin dissolved the Russian parliament, an action that prompted a coup attempt and bloody fighting in Moscow in early October; the coup failed.

1993 December 2. The space shuttle *Endeavour* was launched on a service mission to the *Hubble Space Telescope,* where an optical problem was resolved.

1994 January 1. The North American Free Trade Agreement (NAFTA) became effective and bound Canada, Mexico, and the United States to free trade according to the terms of the agreement.

1994 February 10. Jeannie Flynn, the first woman accepted for combat training by the U.S. Air Force, completed her F-15 training and became a mission-qualified fighter pilot; by the end of 2002, she had logged over 2,000 hours in the McDonnell Douglas F-15E Eagle fighter, including 200 hours of combat time.

1994 April-July. Genocidal tribal warfare in Rwanda killed approximately 800,000 Tutsis and Hutus.

1994 May 10. Nelson Mandela became the first black president of South Africa; he held the position until his retirement in June 1999.

1994 June 12. The Boeing 777, a twin-engine, twin-aisle jetliner, made its maiden flight.

1994 August 17. President Bill Clinton signed into law the General Aviation Revitalization Act that established an 18-year statute of repose for product liability on general aviation airplanes and airplane parts.

1994 October 11. NASA crashed the spacecraft *Magellan* into the planet Venus so that instruments could collect and relay data during the descent.

1994 October 26. The kingdom of Jordan and the state of Israel signed a peace treaty that ended the 46-year period in which the two nations were in an official state of war.

1995. Martha McSally became the first U.S. Air Force female pilot to fly a combat mission when she flew a Fairchild Republic A-10 Thunderbolt II (also called the Warthog) over the no-fly zone in Iraq.

1995 April 19. A truck bomb destroyed the Murrah Federal Building in Oklahoma City and killed 168 people; Timothy McVeigh, an anti-government terrorist, was later executed for the crime.

1995 June 2. A surface-to-air missile downed a U.S. F-16 Fighting Falcon over Bosnia, over Serbian territory; pilot Scott O'Grady was rescued six days later.

1995 June 7. The world's biggest twin-engine jet, the Boeing 777, made its first commercial flight, a United Airlines flight from London to Washington.

1995 June 29. A United States space shuttle, the *Atlantis*, docked at the Soviet space station *Mir* for the first time and performed a crew exchange for the *Mir*.

1997 February 28. The European Space Agency accomplished the first successful launch of an Ariane 5 rocket; it carried the first in a new series of INTELSAT satellites, developed by the International Telecommunications Satellite Organization.

1997 July 1. Under British rule since 1941, Hong Kong reverted to Chinese control; China agreed to "one country, two systems," that is, not to impose communism and socialism on the former British colony.

1997 July 4. The *Pathfinder* landed on Mars, the "Red Planet."; the spacecraft and the rover *Sojourner* operated on the surface of the planet for months.

1998 August 6. AeroVironment's solar-powered *Pathfinder* reached the record altitude of 80,400 feet.

1784	Balloonists made **the first manned flights in Ireland, Scotland, England, and the United States, as well as Italy**; this illustrates how quickly the French invention of the balloon inspired international interest and activity in aviation.
1784 June	Madame Thible became **the first female on board a balloon in free** flight; other women had gone aloft in tethered flight before this date.
1785 January 7	French balloonist Jean-Pierre Blanchard and American doctor John Jeffries flew in a hydrogen balloon across the English Channel; this was **the first flight across the English Channel.**
1785 June 15	Jean-François Pilâtre de Rozier and Pierre Romain became **the first aviation fatalities** when they crashed a balloon that had caught fire in flight; the balloon used both hot air and hydrogen for lift.
1786	An American expatriate living in England, John Jeffries, wrote A Narrative of the Two Aerial Voyages of Doctor Jeffries with Mons. Blanchard, **the first aviation book written by an American.**
1793 January 9	French balloonist Jean-Pierre Blanchard made **the first free flight of a manned balloon in all of the Americas** when he flew from Philadelphia, Pennsylvania, into nearby New Jersey on this date.
1793	Napoleon Bonaparte's revolutionary government confiscated a balloon and gave it to the French Republican army; thus making that balloon **the world's first military aircraft.**
1794	The French army established **the world's first military air force**, a balloon unit called Compagnie d'Aerosteirs.
1794 June	The French balloon Entreprenant became **the first military aircraft used in combat**; the hydrogen balloon flew observation missions against the Austrian army.
1796 September	The Austrian army at Würzburg captured French balloonists and a French balloon — **the first airmen to be prisoners of war and the first aircraft to be captured in war.**
1797 October 22	French balloonist André Jacques Garnerin made **the first parachute jump from substantial height** when he dropped from a balloon about 3,000 feet above the ground.
1808 July 24	Balloonist R. Jordarki Kuparanto abandoned his burning hot air balloon over Warsaw and parachuted to a safe landing in **the first known case of an aviator parachuting to safety**.
1819 July 7	Balloonist Madeleine Sophie Blanchard, widow of Jean-Pierre Blanchard, became **the first woman to die in a flying accident** when fireworks over Paris ignited her balloon, which crashed.
1836 November 7-8	In **the first major demonstration of night flight**, English aerial pilot Charles Green and two passengers flew a balloon from England to Germany, a distance of 480 miles (772 kilometers) in 18 hours; this flight also demonstrated the utility of the dragline and the feasibility of long-distance flying.
1848 June	John Stringfellow in Great Britain launched a steam-powered model of a monoplane from an overhead wire; this was **one of the first powered flights of a heavier-than-air machine**, albeit an unmanned ten-foot model.

1849 Spring	George Cayley tested a full-size airplane with a boy on board during some test flights; this triplane with powered-flappers flew like a powered glider.
1852	**The first major society devoted to flying** was the Sociéte Aérostatique et Météorologique de France, founded in this year.
1852 September 24	Henri Giffard used a three-horsepower steam engine to power **the first known flight of a dirigible balloon.**
1853 Summer	George Cayley's full-size glider and his coachman made **the first manned free flight of a heavier-than-air machine.**
1861	The Union Army of the United States converted the coal barge G.W. Parke Custis into **the first aircraft carrier**, the aircraft being an observation balloon.
1870-1871	**The first sustained airmail service** was the Balloon Post that carried mail out of Paris when the Prussian army besieged the city in 1870-1871.
1871 August 18	Alphonse Pénaud made **the first public flight of his planophore**, a model aircraft driven by twisted rubber.
1874	Félix du Temple achieved what may have been **the first powered takeoff of an airplane** when a sailor rode his steam-powered tractor plane on a hop into the air; the plane failed to fly.
1890 October 9	Clement Ader became airborne in **the first takeoff of his Ecole**, but he was unable to achieve sustained flight.
1897 July 11	Swedish explorer Salmon Auguste Andrée, physicist Nils Strindberg, and engineer Knut Fraenkel ascended in the balloon Eagle for **the first major attempt to fly over the North Pole**; they disappeared.
1899 August	Wilbur and Orville Wright flew **the first Wright aircraft** — a biplane kite equipped with aeronautical controls by which the operator on the ground could twist or "warp" the wings.
1900 July 2	Count Ferdinand von Zeppelin witnessed **the first flight of the first Zeppelin**, the Luftschiff-Zeppelin 1 or LZ 1 airship.
1900	Wilbur and Orville Wright built and flew **the first Wright glider**, a biplane equipped with wing-warping so the pilot could control lateral stability.
1901	The Wright Brothers constructed **their first wind tunnel** in order to obtain information about wing performance; wind tunnels were research tools used in various laboratories of the time.
1903 March 23	The Wright Brothers filed **their first application for a flying-machine patent**, which the United States rejected.
1903 December 17	Wilbur and Orville Wright piloted the Wright Flyer in **the first manned, powered, controlled, and sustained flights of a heavier-than-air aircraft**; Orville Wright was **the first airplane pilot**, but each brother made two flights on this date.

1904 May 26	**The first flight of the Wright Flyer No. 2** took place at Huffman Prairie, near Dayton, Ohio; the Wright Brothers had converted the Huffman Prairie pasture into the first airport for airplanes.
1904 September 20	Wilbur Wright flew **the first known circuit flight of an airplane**; that is, he flew in a circle.
1904 October	Robert Esnault-Pelterie flew a glider of his design in **the first known flight of a full-size airplane with ailerons installed on the wings**.
1905	Balloonists organized **the first major international aviation organization**, the Féderation Aéronauticque Internationale.
1905	In France, Gabriel Voisin and Ernest Archdeacon organized Syndicat d'Aviation, possibly **the first airplane manufacturing company** in the world.
1906 May 22	Orville and Wilbur Wright received **their first United States patent for a flying-machine**; Belgium, France, and Great Britain had already granted the Wrights patents.
1906	Harry Harper of the Daily Mail of London became **the first full-time aviation reporter**.
1906 September 30	Balloonists from several nations ascended from Paris in **the first Gordon Bennett balloon race**, which Frank P. Lahm of the United States Army won.
1906 November 12	Brazilian pilot Alberto Santos-Dumont made **the first officially recognized airplane flight in Europe** when he flew his 14-bis box-kite-style airplane a distance of over 100 meters.
1907 September 2	Walter Wellman, Melvin Vanigman, and Felix Reisenberg made **the first motorized flight in the Arctic**, but their airship America failed to reach the North Pole.
1907 Autumn	Inventor Alexander Graham Bell organized the Aerial Experiment Association, **the first organization formed to build and fly research planes**, with the goal of developing a practical airplane.
1907 November 13	Paul Cornu flew a helicopter to a height of about one foot (30 centimeters) above the ground for about 20 seconds; this was **the first well-documented flight of a helicopter**.
1908 January 13	Henry Farman in a Voisin biplane flew **the first circular flight of an airplane in Europe**.
1908 February	The United States Army entered into a contract with the Wright Brothers for the purchase of one airplane, designated Model A, which upon delivery became **the first military plane in the United States**.
1908 May 15	Wilbur Wright took mechanic Charlie Furnas for a ride in the refurbished and now two-seat Wright Flyer No. 3; thereby, Furnas became **the world's first airplane passenger** and the Flyer No. 3 became **the world's first passenger airplane**.
1908 September 17	When pilot Orville Wright crashed the Wright Model A airplane during a military demonstration flight, his passenger Lieutenant Thomas Etholen Selfridge became **the first airplane fatality**.
1908	Horace, Albert, and Hugh Short organized **the first airplane manufacturing company in Great Britain**.

1909	Motorcycle maker Glenn H. Curtiss organized **the first airplane manufacturing company in the United States**.
1909 April 24	Over Italy, in a plane piloted by Wilbur Wright, a photographer took **the first aerial motion pictures shot from an airplane**.
1909 July 25	Louis Blériot flew the Blériot XI monoplane in **the first airplane flight across the English Channel**.
1909 August	Wilbur and Orville Wright began **aviation's first patent war** by obtaining a restraining order prohibiting the exhibition of a competitor's airplane.1909 August Rheims (now Reims), France, hosted the first international air show and the first Gordon Bennett or Blue Ribbon airplane race.
1909 September 7	Eugene Lefebvre died when he crashed a Wright Model A plane in France; he was **the first pilot killed in an airplane accident**.
1909	Fred T. Jane published **the first edition of *Jane's All the World's Aircraft***.
1910 March 28	French pilot Henry Fabre flew his Hydroavion floatplane off water and landed on water in **the first known flight that took off from and landed on water**.
1910 Spring	Aero clubs in various nations began issuing **the first airplane pilot licenses**, and soon the Baroness Raymonde de la Roche became **the first female pilot or aviatrix in the world to obtain a pilot license.**
1910 June 19	Zeppelin airships went into service with the new Deutsche Luftschiffahrts Aktiengesellschaft (DELAG) company, **the first commercial airline**.
1910 October 15	Walter Wellman and his crew sent **the first radio distress signal from an aircraft** when they needed assistance because the airship America lost an engine over the Atlantic Ocean.
1911 January 18	Pilot Eugene Ely in a Curtiss pusher biplane landed on and took off from the USS Pennsylvania in **the first convincing demonstration of the practicality of using ship-based airplanes.**
1911 February 18	The Universal Postal Exhibition in Allahabad, India, prompted **the first official airmail service**, which started between Allahabad and Naini Junction on this date.
1911 Summer	Paris was the site of **the First International Congress of Aerial Law**; this congress granted each country the right to regulate flight in the airspace over the respective nation.
1911 August 2	Harriet Quimby became **the first woman in the United States to earn an airplane pilot license.**
1913	Igor I. Sikorsky built the *Grand*, a four-engine airplane with an enclosed cabin and an observation deck; the *Grand* was **Russia's first large airplane** and one of the first large airplanes in the world.
1913 June 21	Georgia Broadwick parachuted from an airplane over Los Angeles in **the first known parachute jump from an airplane by a female**.
1913 September 21	Adolphe Pégoud flew his Blériot monoplane in sustained inverted flight, **the first known upside-down flying under the control of the pilot.**

1914 January 1	Pilot Anthony Jannus of the Benoist Company flew one passenger from St. Petersburg, Florida, to Tampa, Florida; this opened **the first scheduled service of an airline using airplanes in scheduled service.**
1914 August 3	A German Taube airplane dropped three bombs on Lunéville, France, in **the first known bombing of the war** that had begun only two days earlier; the pilot threw the hand bombs from the open-cockpit as no air force at the time had airplanes specially designed as bombers.
1914 August 6	The German airship Zeppelin Z 6 bombed Liège, Belgium, in **the first documented use of an airship as a bomber during the war**, for aircraft started the war flying reconnaissance missions.
1914 October 5	The crew of a French two-seat Voisin shot down a German two-seat Aviatik in air-to-air combat, perhaps **the first successful victory of one airplane over another in battle.**
1915 January 19	**German airships raided England for the first time**; the naval airships dropped bombs on Yarmouth.
1915 February 15	**The Russian bomber Il'ya Mourometz flew its first bombing mission**; the Sikorsky bomber was one of the first airplanes to be designed for special military missions.
1915 August 1	German pilot Max Immelmann in the new Fokker E.1 monoplane with a synchronized, forward-firing machine gun scored **the first confirmed victory by an Eindecker, one of the first airplanes specially designed as a fighter.**
1916 September 2	British pilot William Leefe Robinson in a B.E.2 scored a victory over a German Schütte-Lanz airship, **the first airship to be shot down during the war.**
1917 February	**The first flight of the Junkers J4** demonstrated an all-metal airplane with corrugated duralumin skin.
1917 April 5-6	The British Royal Flying Corps sent its new **special night-bombing squadron on its first raid**; this Squadron No. 100 bombed Douai airfield that night.
1918 May 15	The United States Army began **the first regularly scheduled airmail service in the United States**; the Army proved the initial route and concept, then the Post Office Department's new Air Mail Service assumed responsibility for flying the mail.
1918 April 1	Great Britain established **the first air force organization independent of army and navy organizations**, and this Independent Air Force soon became the Royal Air Force.
1918 December	The French airline Latécoère opened **the first Latécoère international airmail service** with flights between Toulouse, France, and Barcelona, Spain, as a step toward linking France by air with the French colonies in Africa.
1919 May 8-31	A.C. Read and his naval crew flew the Navy-Curtiss flying boat NC-4 from stop to stop across the Atlantic Ocean and thereby completed **the first transatlantic flight.**
1919 June 14-15	Pilot John Alcock and navigator Arthur Whitten Brown flew a modified Vickers Vimy biplane from Newfoundland to Ireland in **the first nonstop transatlantic flight.**

1919 July 2-13	The British-made airship R.34 flew a round-trip across the Atlantic Ocean and in the process became the first lighter-than-air aircraft to cross the Atlantic Ocean, **the first aircraft to cross the Atlantic from the east to the west, the first aircraft to make a round-trip flight across the Atlantic, and the first airship to attempt to use a direction-finding radio on a transoceanic flight.**
1919 December 10	The brothers Ross and Keith Smith in a Vickers Vimy completed a flight from England to Australia; they were **the first to fly between England and Australia in less than a month's time**, and they were part of the postwar enthusiasm for flying first to this or that destination or flying there first in a certain amount of time.
1921 July 21	The United States Army Air Service used Martin MB-2 bombers to bomb the captured German battleship *Ostfriesland* in **the first effective postwar demonstration of the air power's effectiveness against naval ships.**
1922 June 16	Two Portuguese pilots, Gago Coutinho and Sacadura Cabral, finished **the first flight across the South Atlantic Ocean**, a flight they had begun in March.
1923 January 9	Spanish designer Juan de la Cierva made **the first official flight of the first successful de la Cierva autogiro**, the C.4.
1923 September 4	**The first helium airship** was also **the first rigid airship made in the United States**: the ZR-1 *Shenandoah*, which made **the first flight of a helium airship** on this date.
1923 June 17	The United States Army conducted **the first aerial refueling** using a De Havilland D.H. 4B light bomber modified into **the first aerial tanker.**
1924 September 28	The United States Army team won the international competition to be **the first to fly around the world**: four airmen and two Douglas World Cruisers completed the flight that departed from Seattle in April, flew westward around the world, and returned to Seattle in September.
1926 May 9	Explorer Richard E. Byrd and pilot Floyd Bennett flew a Fokker Trimotor over the North Pole; this was **the first flight over the North Pole.**
1926 May 12	Norwegian explorer Roald Amundsen and American adventurer Lincoln Ellsworth, and their crew that included Italian airshipman Umberto Nobile, flew in the airship *Norge* over the North Pole; this was **the first airship flight over the North Pole.**
1927 May 20-21	Charles Lindbergh made **the first nonstop flight between New York and Paris and the first solo transatlantic air crossing** when he flew from New York to Paris in the Orteig Prize competition.
1927 August 26	Two planes completed **the first major Pacific air race** — the Pacific Air Race's nonstop flight from Oakland, California, to Honolulu, Hawaii; the race demonstrated the possibility of transpacific flight and the high cost in terms of aircraft and lives, but a military plane in June and a civilian plane in August had already flown from California to Hawaii.
1927 October 14-15	Dieudonné Costes and Joseph le Brix completed **the first nonstop airplane flight across the South Atlantic Ocean**; they flew a Breguet 19 from Saint-Louis, Senegal, to Port Natal, Brazil.
1928 April 12-13	Hermann Köhl and Baron von Hünefeld of Germany and James Fitzmaurice of Ireland flew the Junkers W 33 *Bremen* in **the first transatlantic nonstop airplane flight from east to west**, against the prevailing winds.

1928 Nov. 28-29	Richard Byrd, Bernt Balchen, Harold June, and Ashley McKinley in a Fokker Trimotor made **the first flight over the South Pole**, and Byrd became **the first person to fly over both the North and South poles.**
1929 August 8-29	The German airship *Graf Zeppelin* made **the first airship flight around the world.**
1932 May 20-21	Amelia Earhart — the Lady Lindy — became **the first female pilot to make a solo and nonstop transatlantic flight**; she flew a Wright-powered Lockheed Vega 5B.
1933 April 3	Lord Clydesdale and Stewart Blacker in a Westland PV.3 torpedo bomber and David McIntyre and cameraman Sidney Bonnet in a Westland Wallace military plane made **the first flights over Mount Everest.**
1935 November 22	Pan American started the **first transpacific airmail service** with a flight from San Francisco via Honolulu, Wake, and Guam, to Manila in the Philippines; Edwin C. Musick was the captain of the Martin M.130 flying boat named *China Clipper* that made the flight.
1936 June 26	Ewald Rohlfs flew **the first flight of the Focke-Achgelis Fa 61 dual-rotor helicopter**, which stayed aloft for 28 seconds.
1937 June 20	The three-man crew — pilot Valeri Chkaloff, co-pilot Georgi Baidukoff, and navigator Alexander Beliakoff — of a Russian ANT-25 completed **the first non-stop, great-circle flight from the Soviet Union to the United States**; their flight began in Moscow and ended in Vancouver, Washington.
1939 August 3	Britain's new chain of radar stations detected and tracked the German airship *Graf Zeppelin II* that was on a spy mission over eastern England and Scotland; this was **the first radar detection of secret foreign activity against any nation.**
1939 August 27	Hans von Ohain's jet engine powered **the first flight of a jet-propelled airplane; the first jet plane** was the Heinkel He178, and the first jet pilot was Erich Warsitz.
1939 September 14	**Igor I. Sikorsky made his "first hop" (his words) in a helicopter**, the VS-300A, which was not the first helicopter but was the prototype of the first helicopter to enter volume production.
1941 May 15	Frank **Whittle's jet engine first powered an aircraft**, the Gloster E28/39.
1942 March 7	**The first African-American airmen in United States military service received their wings** as they graduated from the Army's experimental Tuskegee, Alabama, training program: Lemuel Custis, Benjamin O. Davis, Jr., Charles DeBow, George Roberts, and Mac Ross.
1942 May	At a training facility in Engels, beside the Volga River, in the Soviet Union, **the first class of female combat pilots** graduated and went to their combat assignments in bomber, fighter, and night bomber units of the Red Air Force; they became **the first female pilots to fly into combat in the world.**
1942 May 18	The United States Army accepted the XR-4 helicopter on this date and soon thereafter the YR-4A for service evaluation; Army orders that year enabled the Sikorsky R-4 to become **the first helicopter in volume production.**
1942 July 18	German pilot Fritz Wendel flew **the first jet-powered flight of the Messerschmitt Me 262**, which was equipped with two Junkers turbojets.

1942 October 1	**The first flight of the Bell XP-59 on this date demonstrated the first turbojet aircraft designed and built in the United States**, known in production and service as the P-59 Airacomet fighter; the General Electric engines were developed from Frank Whittle's jet engine.
1943 May 31	Tuskegee Airmen in the segregated United States Army completed **the first combat mission flown by African-American airmen in U.S. military service**; they flew fighter cover for a bombing raid against the Italian island of Pantelleria.
1944 May	A German fighter wing received **the first manned operational rocket-powered planes to enter military service**, the Messerschmitt Me 163 Komet, a single-seat interceptor.
1944 June 5	The long-range and high-altitude **Boeing B-29 Superfortress entered combat action for the first time** in a bombing raid against Japanese forces in Bangkok, Thailand.
1944 June 13	Germany launched **the first V-1 jet-powered flying bombs to hit London**.
1944 July 10	The Messerschmitt Me 262 became **the world's first jet-powered airplane to enter operational service**; it went into action over Juvincourt, France, on this date.
1944 August 4	The newly operational British jet-powered **Gloster Meteor interceptors scored their first combat victories** by shooting down two unmanned German V-1 flying bombs over southern England.
1944 September 8	**Germany launched rocket-propelled V-2 missiles against London and Paris for the first time**.
1945 August 6	The United States dropped **the first atomic bomb** from a Boeing B-29 Superfortress onto the Japanese city of Hiroshima.
1945 August 25	Lockheed completed **the first flight of a commercial version of the Constellation**, an aircraft initially designed for the commercial market, but which entered production during the war as a military transport, and which Lockheed was now rushing to convert for the postwar commercial market.
1946 March 8	The United States issued **the world's first commercial certification, an approved type certificate, for a helicopter**, the Bell Model 41 helicopter.
1947 October 14	Charles "Chuck" Elwood Yeager of the United States Air Force flew a Bell X-1 research plane in **the first official supersonic flight** of a manned aircraft in sustained level flight faster than the speed of sound.
1947 December 17	The **prototype Boeing B-47 first flew** and entered the fly-off competition between the North American B-45, Convair B-46, and Martin B-48 prototypes for the prize of an Air Force contract for production bombers.
1947 December 30	A British Rolls Royce Nene jet engine powered **the first flight of prototype Soviet jet fighter designated I-310**; designed by the Mikoyan-Gurevich design bureau, the fighter went into production and service the next year as the MiG-15.
1948 March 10	In **the first official supersonic flight by a civilian pilot**, Herbert H. Hoover of the National Advisory Committee on Aeronautics flew a Bell X-1 faster than sound.

1948 June 26	The postwar East and West met in **the first major confrontation of the Cold War**, a confrontation that remained short of armed combat, as the democratic West began an airlift over the blockade that the communist East placed around Berlin.
1948 September 6	John Derry in an experimental de Havilland Swallow became **the first British pilot to achieve officially recognized supersonic flight**.
1949 January 27	The de Havilland company in Great Britain completed **the first flight of a jetliner designed for commercial service**, the G-5-1/G-ALVG prototype for what became the Comet.
1950 June 25	The North Korean invasion of South Korea on this date started **the first major though limited war of the Cold War era**, a war in which East and West fought opposing ideologies as well as troops and a war in which helicopters and jet fighters assumed new military roles.
1952 April 15	Boeing completed **the first flight of the jet-powered YB-52 prototype** of the B-52 bomber; the engines were Pratt & Whitney J57s.
1952 May 2	**The first commercial jetliner service in the world began** when British Overseas Airways Corporation placed a de Havilland Comet in service, departing London, bound for Johannesburg, and powered by de Havilland Ghost engines.
1952	The United States Civil Aeronautics Administration made operational **the first Victor (V) airways** featuring very-high-frequency omnidirectional ranges (VORs) on the ground to help pilots navigate in the air.
1953 May 20	Pilot Jackie Cochran flew a Canadair Sabre, made in Canada under a North American Aviation license, faster than the speed of sound and thereby became **the first women to break the sound barrier**.
1953 November 20	Civilian test pilot Scotty Crossfield flew an all-rocket powered Douglas D-558-2 Skyrocket in **the first piloted flight to achieve Mach 2**.
1954 May 1	The **Soviet Union displayed for the first time its new turbojet Myasishchev Mya-4 Bison heavy bomber** at an air show in Moscow, and this sparked concern in the United States that the Soviets might be capable of delivering nuclear bombs to the United States.
1954 July 15	Boeing made **the first flight of the Model 367-80, prototype of the 707 jetliner**.
1955 August 4	**The first flight of a Lockheed U-2 high-altitude reconnaissance plane** lasted 36 minutes.
1956 September 7	Air Force test pilot Iven C. Kincheloe became **the first person to fly above 100,000 feet** when he flew the rocket-powered Bell X-2 to 126,200 feet; the press called him **"First of the Spacemen."**
1956 September 15	**The first Soviet-made jetliner entered service** when Aeroflot began using the Tupolev Tu-104, powered by Mikulin engines, on the Moscow-Omsk-Irbutsk route on this day.
1956 September 27	The rocket-powered Bell X-2 research plane became **the first manned aircraft to exceed Mach 3**, although the flight ended with a crash that killed pilot Milburn "Mel" Apt and destroyed the airplane.

1956 November 17	The Dassault firm in France made **the first flight of the prototype Mirage III**, powered by one French-made Atar turbojet engine and designed as a high-altitude and high-speed interceptor; the Mirage-line of fighters became a major French export in the 1960s and 1970s.
1957 February 13	**The first launch at the Woomera, Australia, launch site** sent a British Skylark aloft; Great Britain had developed Woomera as a long-range weapons test site, a missile range.
1957 May 15	The **Soviet Union's first launch of an R-7, the world's first intercontinental ballistic missile,** failed 98 seconds after liftoff; the fourth launch on 21 August 1957 was **the first successful launch of the R-7**, which became a highly reliable and often used launch vehicle.
1957 October 4	The Soviet Union launched **the first artificial earth-orbiting satellite**, *Sputnik* (later designated *Sputnik 1*).
1958 March 25	Test pilot Jan Zurakowski flew the prototype Avro Canada FC-105 Arrow, **the first fighter plane with fly-by-wire controls**, but due to high costs Canada cancelled the program short of production in February 1959.
1958 October 4	The British Overseas Aircraft Corporation (BOAC) used the de Havilland Comet 4 to inaugurate **the first transatlantic passenger jet service**.
1958 October 26	**The first regularly scheduled service of a jetliner made in the United States** began when Pan American placed the Boeing 707-120 into service; this was also **the first commercial service of a Pratt & Whitney jet engine**, the JT-3.
1959 January 2	The Soviet Union began launching **the first successful moon probes**: *Luna 1* on this date, *Luna 2* on 12 September, and *Luna 3* on 4 October.
1959 January–April	Aerolíneas Argentinas started **the first commercial jet service in South America** in January; the airline flew a de Havilland Comet 4 on a proving flight from Buenos Aires, Argentina, to Rio de Janeiro, Brazil, on 7 April, and flew the Comet via Trinidad to New York on the 8th, thereby opening **the first jet service between South America and North America.**
1959 May 28	After a suborbital flight 300 miles above Earth, in a nose cone launched by a Jupiter AM-18 missile, Able, a female rhesus monkey, and Baker, a female squirrel monkey, became **the first living beings recovered after spaceflight**.
1959 September 14	The Soviet probe *Luna 2* reached the surface of the Moon and thereby became **the first spacecraft to land on the Moon**.
1960 April 1	**The first weather satellite**, TIROS — Television and Infra-Red Observation Satellite — was launched.
1960 May 1	In **the first major demonstration of the Soviet air defense system and its surface-to-air missiles,** the Soviet Union shot down the Lockheed U-2 high-altitude reconnaissance plane that Gary Powers of the United States was flying on a spy mission over Soviet territory.
1961 April 12	Soviet cosmonaut Major Yuri Alekseyevich Gagarin on board the *Vostok I* became **the first person to orbit the Earth.**
1961 May 5	Astronaut Alan Shepard in a Mercury capsule called *Freedom 7* reached suborbital space and thereby became **the first American in space.**

1962 February 20	John Herschel Glenn in the Mercury spacecraft *Friendship 7* achieved **the first United States manned orbital flight**; he completed three orbits.
1962 April 26	The Soviets launched the spy satellite *Kosmos 4*, later renamed *Zenit 2*; this was **the first Soviet spy satellite**.
1962 June 29	The Rolls-Royce Conway engine, **the first fan jet, bypass gas turbine to enter service**, made its maiden flight on a Vickers prototype VC10 jetliner.
1962 July 10	Designed and built by Bell Telephone Laboratories and launched on this date, the satellite *Telstar 1* relayed **the first transatlantic television broadcast**; later in the year Relay 1 provided **the first worldwide television broadcast**.
1962 November 1	The Soviet Union launched the *Mars I* planetary probe into space; *Mars I* was **the first Soviet planetary probe to fly by another planet**, but communications with the craft were lost while it was en route to Mars.
1962 December 14	Launched in August, **the first successful United States planetary probe**, *Mariner 2*, made the first "near approach" to another planet, Venus.
1963 February 9	Boeing made **the first flight of the Boeing 727**, which entered airline service the next year, remained in production for 20 years, and became the best selling jetliner of the time; Boeing sold 1,831 727s.
1963 June 16	The Soviet Union launched **the first woman in space**; selected for her parachute skills, Lieutenant Valentina Vladimirovna Tereshkova on board *Vostok 6* orbited the Earth.
1963 July 26	*Syncom 2* became **the first communication satellite in geosynchronous orbit**.
1963 October 7	Bill Lear's **first successful light Lear jet**, the Lear 23, made its first flight.
1963 November 21	The successful launch of a sounding rocket became **the first launch at Thumba Equatorial Rocket Launching Station** (also known as TERLS) on the Indian subcontinent.
1964 April 17	Geraldine L. "Jerrie" Mock became **the first woman to fly solo around the world**; she flew a Cessna 180 called the *Spirit of Columbus*.
1964 October 12	*Voshkod 1* became **the first spacecraft carrying multiple people**, and its three-man crew of Vladimir Komarov, Konstantin Feoktistov, and Boris Yegorov made the first live television transmission from space.
1965 February 27	The large four-engined turboprop **Antonov An-22 Antheus flew for the first time**.
1965 March 18	A Soviet cosmonaut, Alexei Leonov, accomplished **the first spacewalk** when he left *Voshkod 2* for twenty minutes.
1965 June 3	Edward H. White became **the first American to walk in space** during the *Gemini 4* space flight.
1966 February 3	The Soviet probe *Luna 9* made **the first soft landing on the Moon**.
1966 March 1	The Soviet *Venera 3* probe became **the first spacecraft to impact Venus**; several other *Venera* spacecraft also landed on Venus.

1966 March 16	Neil Armstrong and David Scott in *Gemini 8* docked with an Agena target vehicle and thereby accomplished **the first docking of two vehicles in space**.
1967 March 1	The Ilyushin Il-62, **the first Soviet long-range jetliner**, entered service with Aeroflot; Ilyushin built 230 of this popular four-engine airliner.
1967 April 9	Boeing conducted **the first flight test of the Boeing 737**, a short-range jetliner.
1967 April 24	When the parachute deployment failed while *Soyuz 1* returned to Earth, Soviet cosmonaut Vladimir Komarov died and thereby became **the first person to die in the course of a spaceflight**.
1967 October 30	The Soviet Union achieved **the first automatic docking in space** when two unmanned spacecraft, *Kosmos 186* and *Kosmos 188*, docked.
1968 December 21	*Apollo 8* orbited the Moon ten times; this was **the first human circumlunar voyage**.
1968 December 31	The prototype Tupolev Tu-144, **the world's first supersonic airliner**, made its first flight on this date — months before the 2 March 1969 first flight of the supersonic Concorde airliner; the Tu-144 achieved supersonic speed for the first time on 3 June 1969.
1969 January 14-15	*Soyuz 4* and *Soyuz 5* docked; this was **the first time two manned spacecraft docked in space**.
1969 February 9	Using a production Boeing 747-100, Boeing **flew the 747 "jumbo jet" for the first time**.
1969 July 20	*Apollo 11* landed on the Moon, and Neil Armstrong became **the first person to walk on the Moon**.
1970 April 24	The People's Republic of China launched **the first Chinese satellite**, the *Dong Fang Hong-1* (East is Red-1), into orbit; as it floated around Earth, the satellite broadcast the patriotic song "The East Is Red."
1970 December 15	Launched by the Soviet Union on 17 August, *Venera 7* made **the first successful soft landing on another planet** when the spacecraft landed on Venus; *Venera 7* transmitted data for 23 minutes after landing.
1971 April 19	The Soviets launched *Salyut 1*, **the first space station**.
1972 May 25	Test pilot Gary Krier made **the first flight in an aircraft equipped with a digital fly-by-wire control system**; the aircraft was a modified Vought F-8 Crusader.
1972 July 23	The National Aeronautics and Space Administration launched *Landsat*, **the first of the series of Landsat satellites** that photographed the Earth's resources.
1972 October 28	The European consortium **Airbus flew the twin-engine A300 widebody for the first time**.
1973 December 3	Launched on 2 March 1972, *Pioneer 10* performed **the first flyby of Jupiter** and continued on a flight through the Solar System; *Pioneer 10* remained in service providing telemetry data until 27 April 2002.
1974 February 22	Lieutenant Barbara Ann Allen became **the first woman designated a naval pilot** when she received her Gold Wings at Naval Air Station Corpus Christi; the Army began training the Army's first woman helicopter pilots in 1974, and the Air Force admitted the first women to pilot training in 1976.

1974 May 20	Air France initiated **the first commercial service of the Airbus A300.**
1975 July 18	The American *Apollo 18* and the Soviet *Soyuz 19* docked in space 222 kilometers over the Atlantic Ocean; this was **the first cooperative space program involving the two Cold War rivals.**
1975 December 26	**The first supersonic transport in service,** the Tupolev TU-144, entered mail service, and it entered passenger service in February 1977, but the plane went out of service in June 1978.
1976 January 21	Built by France's Aerospatiale and the British Aircraft Corporation, **the first supersonic Concordes in service** began flying for Air France and British Airways.
1977 August 23	Powered by pilot Bryan Allen, the *Gossamer Condor* demonstrated sustained, maneuverable, human-powered flight and thereby won the Kremer Prize for **first human-powered flight.**
1978 August 10	Ben L. Abruzzo, Maxie L. Anderson, and Larry M. Newman began **the first successful balloon transatlantic crossing;** the *Double Eagle II* made the flight in five days.
1979 June 12	Paul MacCready's human-powered *Gossamer Albatross* became **the first airplane pedaled across the English Channel.**
1979 December 24	The European Space Agency launches **the first Ariane commercial launch vehicle** from Kourou, French Guiana, breaking the monopoly of the United States on commercial launch services.
1980 July 18	India achieved **the first Indian satellite launched on an Indian launch vehicle** by sending *Rohini-1B* aloft on an SLV-3 rocket.
1981 April 12-14	**The first launch and flight of the Space Transportation System** — also called the space shuttle — sent the orbiter *Columbia* into space; John W. Young and Robert L. Crippen flew what was also **the first orbital flight of a winged spacecraft.**
1981 June 18	The Lockheed F-117 completed its first flight, **the first flight of a low-observable stealth-technology aircraft;** the company delivered 59 F-117s to the U.S. Air Force between the first delivery in 1982 and the last delivery in 1990.
1981 November 9-12	Ben Abruzzo, Larry Newman, Ron Clark, and Rocky Aoki flew the *Double Eagle V* in **the first Pacific balloon crossing;** they left Nagashima, Japan, flew a record distance of 5,768 miles, and landed at Covelo, California.
1981 November 12	The space shuttle *Columbia* became **the first spacecraft to be reused** as it was launched on its second mission.
1983 June 18-24	On the seventh space shuttle mission, flying aboard the *Challenger*, physicist Sally Ride became **the first American woman in space;** she returned to space on the *Challenger* in 1984.
1983 August 30	Aerospace engineer and astronaut, former Air Force pilot, Guion S. Bluford Jr. became **the first African-American in space** when he went aloft on the *Challenger* on the first of four space flights he would make; the 1983 mission included **the first night launch of a shuttle** on 30 August and **the first night landing of a shuttle** on 5 September.

1984 February 7	Astronaut Bruce McCandless performed **the first untethered spacewalk and first free flight in space** when he left the shuttle *Challenger* and used the backpack-style Manned Maneuvering Unit to fly 300 feet from the orbiter.
1986 January 28	In **the first catastrophic accident of a space shuttle**, the *Challenger* exploded after liftoff; the seven-person crew of teacher-in-space Christa McAuliffe, pilot Francis Scobee, Judith Resnik, Ronald McNair, Ellison Onizuka, Greg Jarvis, and Mike Smith died.
1986 December 14-23	Dick Rutan and Jeana Yeager flew the *Voyager* to a world absolute distance record of 40,212 kilometers (26,366 statute miles) on what was **the world's longest flight; this was the first unrefueled nonstop airplane flight around the world.**
1987 February 22	**Airbus flew the A320 airliner for the first time;** this plane was **the first airliner with a fly-by-wire flight control system.**
1988 April 23	In **the first human-powered flight across the Aegean Sea** since the mythical Icarus, father of Daedalus, Greek bicycling champion Kanellos Kanellopoulos flew the MIT-designed *Daedalus* from Crete to Santorin.
1988 November 15	The Soviet Union successfully launched the *Buran* transport without anyone aboard in **the first successful demonstration of a Soviet reusable spacecraft**, but it never flew again; Russian leader Boris Yeltsin canceled the program four years later.
1990 February 21	Brazil launched a *Sonda 2* sounding rocket in **the first launch at the Alcantara launch site.**
1990 September 29	Test pilot Dave Ferguson made **the first flight in the Lockheed-Boeing-General Dynamics prototype YF-22A fighter.**
1991 November 19	The DGV Dauphin AS 365X became **the first helicopter to fly 372 kilometers per hour.**
1992 September 12	Mission specialist Mae Carol Jemison became **the first African-American woman in space** and payload specialist Mamoru Mohri **the first Japanese astronaut in space** when they launched on board the space shuttle *Endeavour*.
1994 February 10	Jeannie Flynn, **the first woman accepted for combat training by the U.S. Air Force**, completed her F-15 training and became a mission-qualified fighter pilot; by the end of 2002, she had logged over 2,000 hours in the McDonnell Douglas F-15E Eagle fighter, including 200 hours of combat time.
1994 June 12	Boeing made **the first flight of the 777**, a twin-engine, twin-aisle jetliner; United Airlines flew the first commercial flight of the 777 in June 1995.
1995 June 29	A United States space shuttle, the *Atlantis*, docked at the Soviet space station *Mir* for the first time; the *Atlantis* performed a crew exchange for the *Mir*.
1997 February 28	The European Space Agency accomplished **the first successful launch of an Ariane 5 rocket**; it carried **the first in a new series of INTELSAT satellites**, developed by the International Telecommunications Satellite Organization.
1997 June	Airbus launched the Airbus Corporate Jut (ACJ), a derivative of the A319, in competition with the Boeing Businsess Jet (BBJ), derivative of the Boeing 737.
1999 March 1-21	Bertrand Piccard of Switzerland and Brian Jones of Britain in the balloon *Breitling Orbiter 3* completed **the first balloon round-the-world flight.**

1999 July 23	The commander of the space shuttle Columbia, on mission STS-93 was Colonel Eileen M. Collins, **the first woman to command a Space Shuttle mission.**
2000 January–July	The Republic of China (RoC) Air Force of Taiwan accepted delivery of the complete production run of 1130 indigenous Ching-Kuo fighter planes; the Ching-Kuo was **the first fighter developed and manufactured in Taiwan.**
2000 October 31	A Russian Soyuz spacecraft launched with **the first crew to live on board the International Space Station**; U.S. astronaut Bill Shepherd and Russian cosmonauts Sergei Krikalev and Yuri Gidzenko.
2001 April 30	Dennis Tito became **the first space tourist** when he as a paying passenger on Soyuz TM32/31 lifted off on a ten-day mission to the International Space Station.
2001 August 13	The solar-powered and unmanned Helios reached the altitude of 96,863 feet and thereby broke previous altitude records; it was **the first aircraft powered by piston-, jet-, or solar-power to reach that altitude.**
2001 September 11	In **the first use of airliners as weapons of terror**, terrorists hijacked four airliners and crashed them into targets in the eastern United States; more than 2,700 people died.
2002 June 19 - July 4	Steve Fossett of the United States in the balloon *Bud Light Spirit of Freedom* completed **the first solo balloon flight around the world.**
2002 November 28	A Russian rocket launched **the first Algerian satellite**, *ALSAT-1*, into orbit.
2003 September 27	The European Space Agency launched **the first European lunar probe** *SMART-1* on a mission to orbit the Moon, which reached a successful conclusion in 2006.
2003 October 15-16	**China achieved its first manned spaceflight** when Yang Liwei flew the *Shenzhou 5* repeatedly around the Earth.
2004 October 4	Paul Allen's Mojave Aerospace Ventures team, led by designer Burt Rutan, became **the first commercial venture to place a passenger spacecraft in space** twice within a 14-day period and thereby won the X Prize that was established to encourage commercial space travel.
2005 October 12	China launched the *Shenzhou 6*, **the first Chinese spacecraft with multiple crew members**, two astronauts, for a five-day flight.
2006 January 19	NASA launched *New Horizons* on a journey to Pluto; this is **the first space mission to Pluto.**

UNITED STATES PATENT OFFICE.

ORVILLE WRIGHT AND WILBUR WRIGHT, OF DAYTON, OHIO.

FLYING-MACHINE.

No. 821,393.   Specification of Letters Patent.   Patented May 22, 1906.

Application filed March 23, 1903   Serial No. 149,220

To all whom it may concern:

Be it known that we, ORVILLE WRIGHT and WILBUR WRIGHT, citizens of the United States, residing in the city of Dayton, county
5 of Montgomery, and State of Ohio, have invented certain new and useful Improvements in Flying-Machines, of which the following is a specification.

Our invention relates to that class of fly-
10 ing-machines in which the weight is sustained by the reactions resulting when one or more aeroplanes are moved through the air edgewise at a small angle of incidence, either by the application of mechanical power or by
15 the utilization of the force of gravity.

The objects of our invention are to provide means for maintaining or restoring the equilibrium or lateral balance of the apparatus, to provide means for guiding the machine
20 both vertically and horizontally, and to provide a structure combining lightness, strength, convenience of construction, and certain other advantages which will hereinafter appear.
25 To these ends our invention consists in certain novel features, which we will now proceed to describe and will then particularly point out in the claims.

In the accompanying drawings, Figure 1 is
30 a perspective view of an apparatus embodying our invention in one form. Fig. 2 is a plan view of the same, partly in horizontal section and partly broken away. Fig. 3 is a side elevation, and Figs. 4 and 5 are detail
35 views, of one form of flexible joint for connecting the upright standards with the aeroplanes.

In flying-machines of the character to which this invention relates the apparatus is supported in the air by reason of the contact
40 between the air and the under surface of one or more aeroplanes, the contact-surface being presented at a small angle of incidence to the air. The relative movements of the air and aeroplane may be derived from the mo-
45 tion of the air in the form of wind blowing in the direction opposite to that in which the apparatus is traveling or by a combined downward and forward movement of the machine, as in starting from an elevated posi-
50 tion or by combination of these two things, and in either case the operation is that of a soaring-machine, while power applied to the machine to propel it positively forward will cause the air to support the machine in a simi-
55 lar manner. In either case owing to the varying conditions to be met there are numer-ous disturbing forces which tend to shift the machine from the position which it should occupy to obtain the desired results. It is the chief object of our invention to provide
60 means for remedying this difficulty, and we will now proceed to describe the construction by means of which these results are accomplished.

In the accompanying drawings we have
65 shown an apparatus embodying our invention in one form. In this illustrative embodiment the machine is shown as comprising two parallel superposed aeroplanes 1 and 2, and this construction we prefer, although our
70 invention may be embodied in a structure having a single aeroplane. Each aeroplane is of considerably greater width from side to side than from front to rear. The four corners of the upper aeroplane are indicated by
75 the reference-letters *a*, *b*, *c*, and *d*, while the corresponding corners of the lower aeroplane 2 are indicated by the reference-letters *e*, *f*, *g*, and *h*. The marginal lines *a b* and *e f* indicate the front edges of the aeroplanes, the
80 lateral margins of the upper aeroplane are indicated, respectively, by the lines *a d* and *b c*, the lateral margins of the lower aeroplane are indicated, respectively, by the lines *e h* and *f g*, while the rear margins of the upper
85 and lower aeroplanes are indicated, respectively, by the lines *c d* and *g h*.

Before proceeding to a description of the fundamental theory of operation of the structure we will first describe the preferred mode
90 of constructing the aeroplanes and those portions of the structure which serve to connect the two aeroplanes.

Each aeroplane is formed by stretching cloth or other suitable fabric over a frame
95 composed of two parallel transverse spars 3, extending from side to side of the machine, their ends being connected by bows 4, extending from front to rear of the machine. The front and rear spars 3 of each aeroplane
100 are connected by a series of parallel ribs 5, which preferably extend somewhat beyond the rear spar, as shown. These spars, bows, and ribs are preferably constructed of wood having the necessary strength, combined
105 with lightness and flexibility. Upon this framework the cloth which forms the supporting-surface of the aeroplane is secured, the frame being inclosed in the cloth. The cloth for each aeroplane previously to its at-
110 tachment to its frame is cut on the bias and made up into a single piece approximately

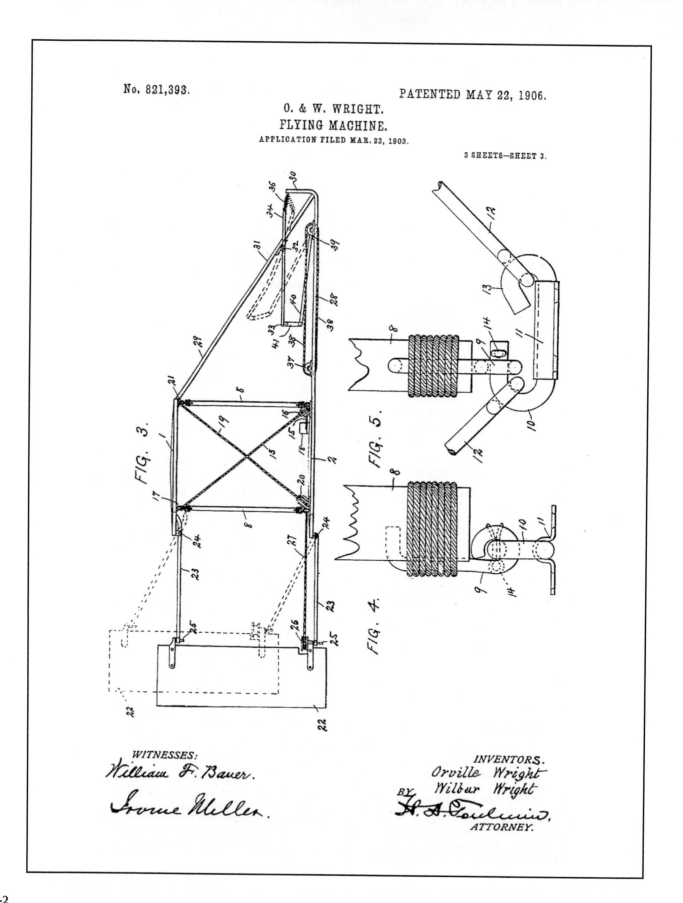

No. 821,393.

PATENTED MAY 22, 1906.

O. & W. WRIGHT.
FLYING MACHINE.
APPLICATION FILED MAR. 23, 1903.

3 SHEETS—SHEET 3.

FIG. 3.

FIG. 4.

FIG. 5.

WITNESSES:
William F. Bauer.
Ivone Miller.

INVENTORS.
Orville Wright
Wilbur Wright
BY H. A. Toulmin.
ATTORNEY.

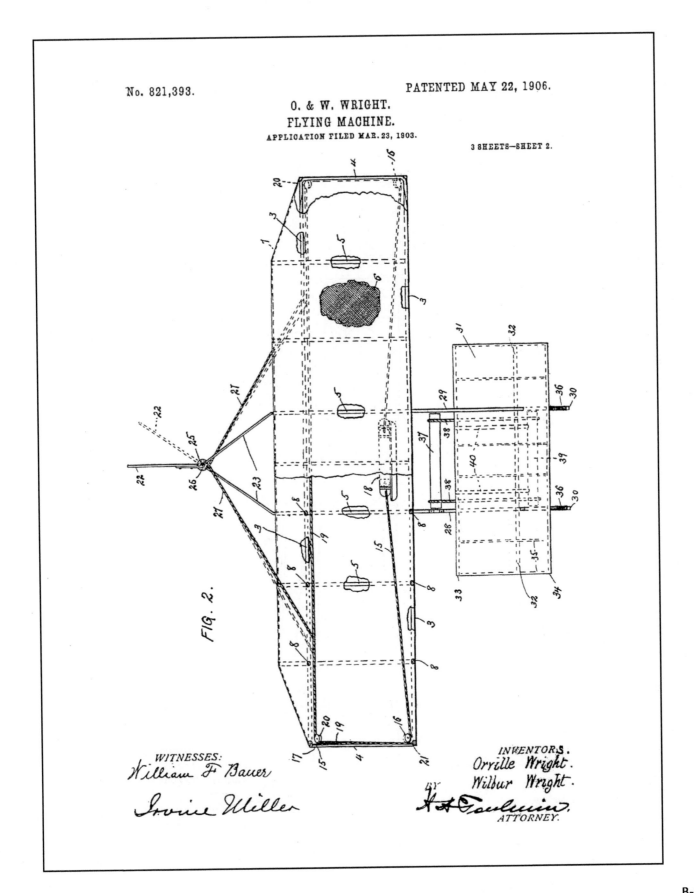

No. 821,393.

PATENTED MAY 22, 1906.

O. & W. WRIGHT.
FLYING MACHINE.
APPLICATION FILED MAR. 23, 1903.

3 SHEETS—SHEET 2.

FIG. 2.

WITNESSES:
William F Bauer

Irvine Miller

INVENTORS.
Orville Wright.
Wilbur Wright.
BY
H. A. Toulmin
ATTORNEY.

No. 821,393.

PATENTED MAY 22, 1906.

O. & W. WRIGHT.
FLYING MACHINE.
APPLICATION FILED MAR. 23, 1903.

3 SHEETS—SHEET 1.

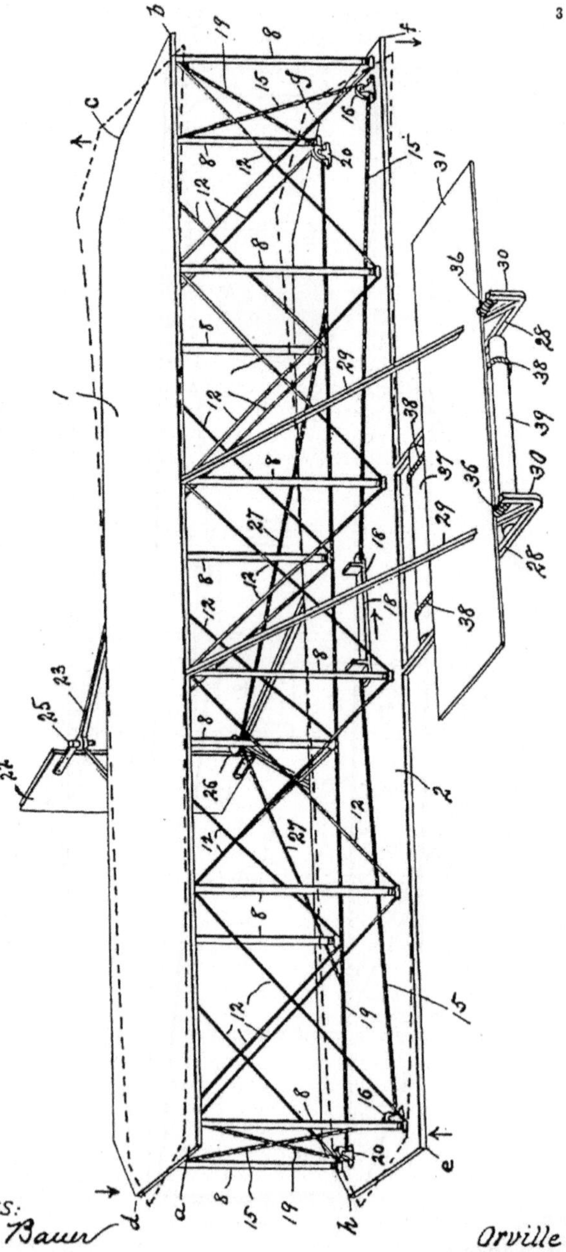

FIG. 1.

WITNESSES:
William F. Bauer

Irvine Miller

INVENTORS.
Orville Wright
Wilbur Wright
BY
H. A. Toulmin
ATTORNEY.

2   §21,393

the size and shape of the aeroplane, having the threads of the fabric arranged diagonally to the transverse spars and longitudinal ribs, as indicated at 6 in Fig. 2. Thus the diag-
5 onal threads of the cloth form truss systems with the spars and ribs, the threads consti-tuting the diagonal members. A hem is formed at the rear edge of the cloth to receive a wire 7, which is connected to the ends of
10 the rear spar and supported by the rear-wardly-extending ends of the longitudinal ribs 5, thus forming a rearwardly-extending flap or portion of the aeroplane. This con-struction of the aeroplanes gives a surface
15 which has very great strength to withstand lateral and longitudinal strains, at the same time being capable of being bent or twisted in the manner hereinafter described.

When two aeroplanes are employed, as in
20 the construction illustrated, they are con-nected together by upright standards 8. These standards are substantially rigid, be-ing preferably constructed of wood and of equal length, equally spaced along the front
25 and rear edges of the aeroplane, to which they are connected at their top and bottom ends by hinged joints or universal joints of any suitable description. We have shown one form of connection which may be used
30 for this purpose in Figs. 4 and 5 of the draw-ings. In this construction each end of the standard 8 has secured to it an eye 9, which engages with a hook 10, secured to a bracket-plate 11, which latter plate is in turn fas-
35 tened to the spar 3. Diagonal braces or stay wires 12 extend from each end of each stand-ard to the opposite ends of the adjacent standards, and as a convenient mode of at-taching these parts I have shown a hook 13
40 made integral with the hook 10 to receive the end of one of the stay-wires, the other stay-wire being mounted on the hook 10. The hook 13 is shown as bent down to retain the stay-wire in connection to it, while the
45 hook 10 is shown as provided with a pin 14 to hold the stay-wire 12 and eye 9 in position thereon. It will be seen that this construc-tion forms a truss system which gives the whole machine great transverse rigidity and
50 strength, while at the same time the jointed connections of the parts permit the aero-planes to be bent or twisted in the manner which we will now proceed to describe.

15 indicates a rope or other flexible con-
55 nection extending lengthwise of the front of the machine above the lower aeroplane, pass-ing under pulleys or other suitable guides 16 at the front corners e and f of the lower aero-plane, and extending thence upward and
60 rearward to the upper rear corners c and d of the upper aeroplane, where they are at-tached, as indicated at 17. To the central portion of this rope there is connected a lat-erally-movable cradle 18, which forms a
65 means for moving the rope lengthwise in one

direction or the other, the cradle being mov-able toward either side of the machine. We have devised this cradle as a convenient means for operating the rope 15, and the machine is intended to be generally used with 70 the operator lying face downward on the lower aeroplane, with his head to the front, so that the operator's body rests on the cra-dle, and the cradle can be moved laterally by the movements of the operator's body. It 75 will be understood, however, that the rope 15 may be manipulated in any suitable manner.

19 indicates a second rope extending trans-versely of the machine along the rear edge of the body portion of the lower aeroplane, pass- 80 ing under suitable pulleys or guides 20 at the rear corners g and h of the lower aeroplane, and extending thence diagonally upward to the front corners a and b of the upper aero-plane, where its ends are secured in any suit- 85 able manner, as indicated at 21.

Considering the structure so far as we have now described it and assuming that the cradle 18 be moved to the right in Figs. 1 and 2, as indicated by the arrows applied to the 90 cradle in Fig. 1 and by the dotted lines in Fig. 2, it will be seen that that portion of the rope 15 passing under the guide-pulley at the corner e and secured to the corner d will be under tension, while slack is paid out 95 throughout the other side or half of the rope 15. The part of the rope 15 under tension exercises a downward pull upon the rear up-per corner d of the structure and an upward pull upon the front lower corner e, as indi- 100 cated by the arrows. This causes the corner d to move downward and the corner e to move upward. As the corner e moves upward it carries the corner a upward with it, since the intermediate standard 8 is substantially rigid 105 and maintains an equal distance between the corners a and e at all times. Similarly, the standard 8, connecting the corners d and h, causes the corner h to move downward in uni-son with the corner d. Since the corner a 110 thus moves upward and the corner h moves downward, that portion of the rope 19 con-nected to the corner a will be pulled upward through the pulley 20 at the corner h, and the pull thus exerted on the rope 19 will pull the 115 corner b on the other side of the machine downward and at the same time pull the cor-ner g at said other side of the machine up-ward. This results in a downward movement of the corner b and an upward movement of 120 the corner c. Thus it results from a lateral movement of the cradle 18 to the right in Fig. 1 that the lateral margins a d and e h at one side of the machine are moved from their normal positions, in which they lie in the nor- 125 mal planes of their respective aeroplanes, into angular relations with said normal planes, each lateral margin on this side of the ma-chine being raised above said normal plane at its forward end and depressed below said nor- 130

821,393　　　　　　　　**8**

mal plane at its rear end, said lateral margins being thus inclined upward and forward. At the same time a reverse inclination is imparted to the lateral margins *b c* and *f g* at the
5　other side of the machine, their inclination being downward and forward. These positions are indicated in dotted lines in Fig. 1 of the drawings. A movement of the cradle 18 in the opposite direction from its normal po-
10　sition will reverse the angular inclination of the lateral margins of the aeroplanes in an obvious manner. By reason of this construction it will be seen that with the particular mode of construction now under consider-
15　ation it is possible to move the forward corner of the lateral edges of the aeroplane on one side of the machine either above or below the normal planes of the aeroplanes, a reverse movement of the forward corners of the lat-
20　eral margins on the other side of the machine occurring simultaneously. During this operation each aeroplane is twisted or distorted around a line extending centrally across the same from the middle of one lateral margin to
25　the middle of the other lateral margin, the twist due to the moving of the lateral margins to different angles extending across each aeroplane from side to side, so that each aeroplane-surface is given a helicoidal warp or
30　twist. We prefer this construction and mode of operation for the reason that it gives a gradually-increasing angle to the body of each aeroplane from the central longitudinal line thereof outward to the margin, thus giv-
35　ing a continuous surface on each side of the machine, which has a gradually increasing or decreasing angle of incidence from the center of the machine to either side. We wish it to be understood, however, that our invention is
40　not limited to this particular construction, since any construction whereby the angular relations of the lateral margins of the aeroplanes may be varied in opposite directions with respect to the normal planes of said
45　aeroplanes comes within the scope of our invention. Furthermore, it should be understood that while the lateral margins of the aeroplanes move to different angular positions with respect to or above and below the
50　normal planes of said aeroplanes it does not necessarily follow that these movements bring the opposite lateral edges to different angles respectively above and below a horizontal plane, since the normal planes of the
55　bodies of the aeroplanes are inclined to the horizontal when the machine is in flight, said inclination being downward from front to rear, and while the forward corners on one side of the machine may be depressed below the nor-
60　mal planes of the bodies of the aeroplanes said depression is not necessarily sufficient to carry them below the horizontal planes passing through the rear corners on that side. Moreover, although we prefer to so construct
65　the apparatus that the movements of the lat-

eral margins on the opposite sides of the machine are equal in extent and opposite in direction, yet our invention is not limited to a construction producing this result; since it may be desirable under certain circumstances　70 to move the lateral margins on one side of the machine in the manner just described without moving the lateral margins on the other side of the machine to an equal extent in the opposite direction. Turning now to the pur-　75 pose of this provision for moving the lateral margins of the aeroplanes in the manner described, it should be premised that owing to various conditions of wind-pressure and other causes the body of the machine is apt to be-　80 come unbalanced laterally, one side tending to sink and the other side tending to rise, the machine turning around its central longitudinal axis. The provision which we have just described enables the operator to meet　85 this difficulty and preserve the lateral balance of the machine. Assuming that for some cause that side of the machine which lies to the left of the observer in Figs. 1 and 2 has shown a tendency to drop downward, a　90 movement of the cradle 18 to the right of said figures, as hereinbefore assumed, will move the lateral margins of the aeroplanes in the manner already described, so that the margins *a d* and *e h* will be inclined downward　95 and rearward and the lateral margins *b c* and *f g* will be inclined upward and rearward with respect to the normal planes of the bodies of the aeroplanes. With the parts of the machine in this position it will be seen that the lateral　100 margins *a d* and *e h* present a larger angle of incidence to the resisting air, while the lateral margins on the other side of the machine present a smaller angle of incidence. Owing to this fact, the side of the machine present-　105 ing the larger angle of incidence will tend to lift or move upward, and this upward movement will restore the lateral balance of the machine. When the other side of the machine tends to drop, a movement of the cradle　110 18 in the reverse direction will restore the machine to its normal lateral equilibrium. Of course the same effect will be produced in the same way in the case of a machine employing only a single aeroplane.　115

In connection with the body of the machine as thus operated we employ a vertical rudder or tail 22, so supported as to turn around a vertical axis. This rudder is supported at the rear ends of supports or arms　120 23, pivoted at their forward ends to the rear margins of the upper and lower aeroplanes, respectively. These supports are preferably V-shaped, as shown, so that their forward ends are comparatively widely separated.　125 their pivots being indicated at 24. Said supports are free to swing upward at their free rear ends, as indicated in dotted lines in Fig. 3, their downward movement being limited in any suitable manner. The vertical pivots　130

4   821,393

of the rudder 22 are indicated at 25, and one of these pivots has mounted thereon a sheave or pulley 26, around which passes a tiller-rope 27, the ends of which are extended out laterally and secured to the rope 19 on opposite sides of the central point of said rope. By reason of this construction the lateral shifting of the cradle 18 serves to turn the rudder to one side or the other of the line of flight. It will be observed in this connection that the construction is such that the rudder will always be so turned as to present its resisting-surface on that side of the machine on which the lateral margins of the aeroplanes present the least angle of resistance. The reason of this construction is that when the lateral margins of the aeroplanes are so turned in the manner hereinbefore described as to present different angles of incidence to the atmosphere that side presenting the largest angle of incidence, although being lifted or moved upward in the manner already described, at the same time meets with an increased resistance to its forward motion, and is therefore retarded in its forward motion, while at the same time the other side of the machine, presenting a smaller angle of incidence, meets with less resistance to its forward motion and tends to move forward more rapidly than the retarded side. This gives the machine a tendency to turn around its vertical axis, and this tendency if not properly met will not only change the direction of the front of the machine, but will ultimately permit one side thereof to drop into a position vertically below the other side with the aeroplanes in vertical position, thus causing the machine to fall. The movement of the rudder hereinbefore described prevents this action, since it exerts a retarding influence on that side of the machine which tends to move forward too rapidly and keeps the machine with its front properly presented to the direction of flight and with its body properly balanced around its central longitudinal axis. The pivoting of the supports 23 so as to permit them to swing upward prevents injury to the rudder and its supports in case the machine alights at such an angle as to cause the rudder to strike the ground first, the parts yielding upward, as indicated in dotted lines in Fig. 3, and thus preventing injury or breakage. We wish it to be understood, however, that we do not limit ourselves to the particular description of rudder set forth, the essential being that the rudder shall be vertical and shall be so moved as to present its resisting-surface on that side of the machine which offers the least resistance to the atmosphere, so as to counteract the tendency of the machine to turn around a vertical axis when the two sides thereof offer different resistances to the air.

From the central portion of the front of the machine struts 28 extend horizontally forward from the lower aeroplane, and struts 29 extend downward and forward from the central portion of the upper aeroplane, their front ends being united to the struts 28, the forward extremities of which are turned up, as indicated at 30. These struts 28 and 29 form truss-skids projecting in front of the whole frame of the machine and serving to prevent the machine from rolling over forward when it alights. The struts 29 serve to brace the upper portion of the main frame and resist its tendency to move forward after the lower aeroplane has been stopped by its contact with the earth, thereby relieving the rope 19 from undue strain, for it will be understood that when the machine comes into contact with the earth further forward movement of the lower portion thereof being suddenly arrested the inertia of the upper portion would tend to cause it to continue to move forward if not prevented by the struts 29, and this forward movement of the upper portion would bring a very violent strain upon the rope 19, since it is fastened to the upper portion at both of its ends, while its lower portion is connected by the guides 20 to the lower portion. The struts 28 and 29 also serve to support the front or horizontal rudder, the construction of which we will now proceed to describe.

The front rudder 31 is a horizontal rudder having a flexible body, the same consisting of three stiff cross-pieces or sticks 32, 33, and 34, and the flexible ribs 35, connecting said cross-pieces and extending from front to rear. The frame thus provided is covered by a suitable fabric stretched over the same to form the body of the rudder. The rudder is supported from the struts 29 by means of the intermediate cross-piece 32, which is located near the center of pressure slightly in front of a line equidistant between the front and rear edges of the rudder, the cross-piece 32 forming the pivotal axis of the rudder, so as to constitute a balanced rudder. To the front edge of the rudder there are connected springs 36, which springs are connected to the upturned ends 30 of the struts 28, the construction being such that said springs tend to resist any movement either upward or downward of the front edge of the horizontal rudder. The rear edge of the rudder lies immediately in front of the operator and may be operated by him in any suitable manner. We have shown a mechanism for this purpose comprising a roller or shaft 37, which may be grasped by the operator so as to turn the same in either direction. Bands 38 extend from the roller 37 forward to and around a similar roller or shaft 39, both rollers or shafts being supported in suitable bearings on the struts 28. The forward roller or shaft has rearwardly-extending arms 40, which are connected by links 41 with the rear edge of the rudder 31. The normal position of the

821,393   5

rudder 31 is neutral or substantially parallel with the aeroplanes 1 and 2; but its rear edge may be moved upward or downward, so as to be above or below the normal plane of said rudder through the mechanism provided for that purpose. It will be seen that the springs 36 will resist any tendency of the forward edge of the rudder to move in either direction, so that when force is applied to the rear edge of said rudder the longitudinal ribs 35 bend, and the rudder thus presents a concave surface to the action of the wind either above or below its normal plane, said surface presenting a small angle of incidence at its forward portion and said angle of incidence rapidly increasing toward the rear. This greatly increases the efficiency of the rudder as compared with a plane surface of equal area. By regulating the pressure on the upper and lower sides of the rudder through changes of angle and curvature in the manner described a turning movement of the main structure around its transverse axis may be effected, and the course of the machine may thus be directed upward or downward at the will of the operator and the longitudinal balance thereof maintained.

Contrary to the usual custom, we place the horizontal rudder in front of the aeroplanes at a negative angle and employ no horizontal tail at all. By this arrangement we obtain a forward surface which is almost entirely free from pressure under ordinary conditions of flight, but which even if not moved at all from its original position becomes an efficient lifting-surface whenever the speed of the machine is accidentally reduced very much below the normal, and thus largely counteracts that backward travel of the center of pressure on the aeroplanes which has frequently been productive of serious injuries by causing the machine to turn downward and forward and strike the ground head-on. We are aware that a forward horizontal rudder of different construction has been used in combination with a supporting-surface and a rear horizontal rudder; but this combination was not intended to effect and does not effect the object which we obtain by the arrangement hereinbefore described.

We have used the term "aeroplane" in this specification and the appended claims to indicate the supporting-surface or supporting-surfaces by means of which the machine is sustained in the air, and by this term we wish to be understood as including any suitable supporting-surface which normally is substantially flat, although of course when constructed of cloth or other flexible fabric, as we prefer to construct them, these surfaces may receive more or less curvature from the resistance of the air, as indicated in Fig. 3.

We do not wish to be understood as limiting ourselves strictly to the precise details of construction hereinbefore described and shown in the accompanying drawings, as it is obvious that these details may be modified without departing from the principles of our invention. For instance, while we prefer the construction illustrated in which each aeroplane is given a twist along its entire length in order to set its opposite lateral margins at different angles we have already pointed out that our invention is not limited to this form of construction, since it is only necessary to move the lateral marginal portions, and where these portions alone are moved only those upright standards which support the movable portion require flexible connections at their ends.

Having thus fully described our invention, what we claim as new, and desire to secure by Letters Patent, is—

1. In a flying-machine, a normally flat aeroplane having lateral marginal portions capable of movement to different positions above or below the normal plane of the body of the aeroplane, such movement being about an axis transverse to the line of flight, whereby said lateral marginal portions may be moved to different angles relatively to the normal plane of the body of the aeroplane, so as to present to the atmosphere different angles of incidence, and means for so moving said lateral marginal portions, substantially as described.

2. In a flying-machine, the combination with two normally parallel aeroplanes, superposed the one above the other, of upright standards connecting said planes at their margins, the connections between the standards and aeroplanes at the lateral portions of the aeroplanes being by means of flexible joints, each of said aeroplanes having lateral marginal portions capable of movement to different positions above or below the normal plane of the body of the aeroplane, such movement being about an axis transverse to the line of flight, whereby said lateral marginal portions may be moved to different angles relatively to the normal plane of the body of the aeroplane, so as to present to the atmosphere different angles of incidence, the standards maintaining a fixed distance between the portions of the aeroplanes which they connect, and means for imparting such movement to the lateral marginal portions of the aeroplanes, substantially as described.

3. In a flying-machine, a normally flat aeroplane having lateral marginal portions capable of movement to different positions above or below the normal plane of the body of the aeroplane, such movement being about an axis transverse to the line of flight, whereby said lateral marginal portions may be moved to different angles relatively to the normal plane of the body of the aeroplane, and also to different angles relatively to each other so as to present to the atmosphere different angles of incidence, and means for si-

6   821,393

multaneously imparting such movement to said lateral marginal portions, substantially as described.

4. In a flying-machine, the combination, with parallel superposed aeroplanes, each having lateral marginal portions capable of movement to different positions above or below the normal plane of the body of the aeroplane, such movement being about an axis transverse to the line of flight, whereby said lateral marginal portions may be moved to different angles relatively to the normal plane of the body of the aeroplane, and to different angles relatively to each other, so as to present to the atmosphere different angles of incidence, of uprights connecting said aeroplanes at their edges, the uprights connecting the lateral portions of the aeroplanes being connected with said aeroplanes by flexible joints, and means for simultaneously imparting such movement to said lateral marginal portions, the standards maintaining a fixed distance between the parts which they connect, whereby the lateral portions on the same side of the machine are moved to the same angle, substantially as described.

5. In a flying-machine, an aeroplane having substantially the form of a normally flat rectangle elongated transversely to the line of flight, in combination with means for imparting to the lateral margins of said aeroplane a movement about an axis lying in the body of the aeroplane perpendicular to said lateral margins, and thereby moving said lateral margins into different angular relations to the normal plane of the body of the aeroplane, substantially as described.

6. In a flying-machine, the combination, with two superposed and normally parallel aeroplanes, each having substantially the form of a normally flat rectangle elongated transversely to the line of flight, of upright standards connecting the edges of said aeroplanes to maintain their equidistance, those standards at the lateral portions of said aeroplanes being connected therewith by flexible joints, and means for simultaneously imparting to both lateral margins or both aeroplanes a movement about axes which are perpendicular to said margins and in the planes of the bodies of the respective aeroplanes, and thereby moving the lateral margins on the opposite sides of the machine into different angular relations to the normal planes of the respective aeroplanes, the margins on the same side of the machine moving to the same angle, and the margins on one side of the machine moving to an angle different from the angle to which the margins on the other side of the machine move, substantially as described.

7. In a flying-machine, the combination, with an aeroplane, and means for simultaneously moving the lateral portions thereof into different angular relations to the normal plane of the body of the aeroplane and to each other, so as to present to the atmosphere different angles of incidence, of a vertical rudder, and means whereby said rudder is caused to present to the wind that side thereof nearest the side of the aeroplane having the smaller angle of incidence and offering the least resistance to the atmosphere, substantially as described.

8. In a flying-machine, the combination, with two superposed and normally parallel aeroplanes, upright standards connecting the edges of said aeroplanes to maintain their equidistance, those standards at the lateral portions of said aeroplanes being connected therewith by flexible joints, and means for simultaneously moving both lateral portions of both aeroplanes into different angular relations to the normal planes of the bodies of the respective aeroplanes, the lateral portions on one side of the machine being moved to an angle different from that to which the lateral portions on the other side of the machine are moved, so as to present different angles of incidence at the two sides of the machine, of a vertical rudder, and means whereby said rudder is caused to present to the wind that side thereof nearest the side of the aeroplanes having the smaller angle of incidence and offering the least resistance to the atmosphere, substantially as described.

9. In a flying-machine, an aeroplane normally flat and elongated transversely to the line of flight, in combination with means for imparting to said aeroplane a helicoidal warp around an axis transverse to the line of flight and extending centrally along the body of the aeroplane in the direction of the elongation of the aeroplane, substantially as described.

10. In a flying-machine, two aeroplanes, each normally flat and elongated transversely to the line of flight, and upright standards connecting the edges of said aeroplanes to maintain their equidistance, the connections between said standards and aeroplanes being by means of flexible joints, in combination with means for simultaneously imparting to each of said aeroplanes a helicoidal warp around an axis transverse to the line of flight and extending centrally along the body of the aeroplane in the direction of the elongation of the aeroplane, substantially as described.

11. In a flying-machine, two aeroplanes, each normally flat and elongated transversely to the line of flight, and upright standards connecting the edges of said aeroplanes to maintain their equidistance, the connections between such standards and aeroplanes being by means of flexible joints, in combination with means for simultaneously imparting to each of said aeroplanes a helicoidal warp around an axis transverse to

821,393   7

the line of flight and extending centrally along the body of the aeroplane in the direction of the elongation of the aeroplane, a vertical rudder, and means whereby said rudder
5 is caused to present to the wind that side thereof nearest the side of the aeroplanes having the smaller angle of incidence and offering the least resistance to the atmosphere, substantially as described.

10 12. In a flying-machine, the combination, with an aeroplane, of a normally flat and substantially horizontal flexible rudder, and means for curving said rudder rearwardly and upwardly or rearwardly and down-
15 wardly with respect to its normal plane, substantially as described.

13. In a flying-machine, the combination, with an aeroplane, of a normally flat and substantially horizontal flexible rudder pivotally
20 mounted on an axis transverse to the line of flight near its center, springs resisting vertical movement of the front edge of said rudder, and means for moving the rear edge of said rudder above or below the normal plane
25 thereof, substantially as described.

14. A flying-machine comprising superposed connected aeroplanes, means for moving the opposite lateral portions of said aeroplanes to different angles to the normal
30 planes thereof, a vertical rudder, means for moving said vertical rudder toward that side of the machine presenting the smaller angle of incidence and the least resistance to the atmosphere, and a horizontal rudder pro-
35 vided with means for presenting its upper or under surface to the resistance of the atmosphere, substantially as described.

15. A flying-machine comprising superposed connected aeroplanes, means for mov-
40 ing the opposite lateral portions of said aeroplanes to different angles to the normal planes thereof, a vertical rudder, means for moving said vertical rudder toward that side of the machine presenting the smaller angle
45 of incidence and the least resistance to the atmosphere, and a horizontal rudder provided with means for presenting its upper or under surface to the resistance of the atmosphere, said vertical rudder being located at the rear
50 of the machine and said horizontal rudder at the front of the machine, substantially as described.

16. In a flying-machine, the combination, with two superposed and connected aeroplanes, of an arm extending rearward from 55 each aeroplane, said arms being parallel and free to swing upward at their rear ends, and a vertical rudder pivotally mounted in the rear ends of said arms, substantially as described.

17. A flying-machine comprising two su- 60 perposed aeroplanes, normally flat but flexible, upright standards connecting the margins of said aeroplanes, said standards being connected to said aeroplanes by universal joints, diagonal stay-wires connecting the 65 opposite ends of the adjacent standards, a rope extending along the front edge of the lower aeroplane, passing through guides at the front corners thereof, and having its ends secured to the rear corners of the upper aero- 70 plane, and a rope extending along the rear edge of the lower aeroplane, passing through guides at the rear corners thereof, and having its ends secured to the front corners of the upper aeroplane, substantially as described. 75

18. A flying-machine comprising two superposed aeroplanes, normally flat but flexible, upright standards connecting the margins of said aeroplanes, said standards being connected to said aeroplanes by universal 80 joints, diagonal stay-wires connecting the opposite ends of the adjacent standards, a rope extending along the front edge of the lower aeroplane, passing through guides at the front corners thereof, and having its ends 85 secured to the rear corners of the upper aeroplane, and a rope extending along the rear edge of the lower aeroplane, passing through guides at the rear corners thereof, and having its ends secured to the front corners of the 90 upper aeroplane, in combination with a vertical rudder, and a tiller-rope connecting said rudder with the rope extending along the rear edge of the lower aeroplane, substantially as described.

ORVILLE WRIGHT.
WILBUR WRIGHT.

Witnesses:
CHAS. E. TAYLOR,
E. EARLE FORRER.

SPACE FLIGHTS

The space flights listed in this appendix represent the significant satellites, probes, and human space flights from 1957 to 1999. Some of the programs are summarized because there were a number of flights that achieved essentially the same objective, such as the later Soyuz flights that resupplied Mir and the numerous Space Shuttle flights. Some of the early programs such as the Vanguard and Explorer series are not covered in depth.

Satellites and Probes

International Geophysical Year Satellite Launches _____

The International Geophysical Year (IGY) of 1957-1958 was an 18-month period of international cooperative effort to study the planet Earth and its relation to the sky and space. This list represents a chronology of the launches during the IGY and either the success or failure of the launch. Some launches are described in more detail in other lists of this appendix.

Mission	Date	Country, Description
Sputnik 1	4 October 1957	USSR, successful launch.
Sputnik 2	3 November 1957	USSR, successful launch.
Vanguard	6 December 1957	U.S., failed launch.
Explorer 1	31 January 1958	U.S., successful launch.
Vanguard	5 February 1958	U.S., failed launch.
Explorer 2	5 March 1958	U.S., failed launch.
Vanguard 1	17 March 1958	U.S., successful launch.
Explorer 3	26 March 1958	U.S., successful launch.
Vanguard 5	28 April 1958	U.S., failed launch.
Sputnik 3	15 May 1958	USSR, successful launch.
Vanguard SLV-1	27 May 1958	U.S., failed launch.
Vanguard SLV-2	26 June 1958	U.S., failed launch.
Explorer 4	26 July 1958	U.S., successful launch.
(Pioneer)	17 August 1958	U.S., failed launch.
Explorer 5	24 August 1958	U.S., failed launch.
Vanguard SLV-3	26 September 1958	U.S., failed launch.
Pioneer 1	11 October 1958	U.S., failed to orbit the moon.
Beacon	23 October 1958	U.S., failed launch.
Pioneer 2	8 November 1958	U.S., failed to orbit the moon.
Pioneer 3	6 December 1958	U.S., failed to pass the moon.

TIROS Satellites _____

Mission	Date	Description
TIROS 1	1 April 1960	First weather satellite. 22,952 photographs until 17 June 1960.
TIROS 2	23 November 1960	36,156 photographs until 4 December 1961.
TIROS 3	12 July 1961	35,033 photographs until 27 February 1962.
TIROS 4	8 February 1962	32,593 photographs until 10 June 1962.
TIROS 5	19 June 1962	58,226 photographs until May 1963.
TIROS 6	18 September 1962	66,674 photographs until 11 October 1966
TIROS 7	19 June 1963	Over 125,000 photographs until 3 February 1966.
TIROS 8	21 December 1963	Over 100,000 photographs until 1 July 1967.

TIROS 9	22 January 1965	In near-polar orbit gave first photographs of earth's entire cloud cover until 15 February 1967.
TIROS 10	2 July 1965	Final Tiros; polar orbit; abandoned 3 July 1967.

Landsat Satellites

Mission	Date	Description
Landsat 1	23 July 1972	First U.S. earth resource satellite.
Landsat 2	22 January 1975	Carried the same payload as Landsat 1.
Landsat 3	5 March 1978	Same as Landsat 1 with a thermal band scanner.
Landsat 4	16 July 1982	Remained in service until 1987.
Landsat 5	1 March 1984	Included a thematic mapper.
Landsat 6	5 October 1993	Contact lost during launch.
Landsat 7	15 April 1999	Had a 15 meter resolution and 185 kilometer swath.

Ranger Project

Mission	Date	Description
Ranger 1	23 August 1961	Test launch into earth orbit.
Ranger 2	18 November 1961	Test launch into earth orbit.
Ranger 3	26 January 1962	Missed moon by 22,862 miles. (36,793 km)
Ranger 4	23 April 1962	Onboard command system failed, impacted moon's far side.
Ranger 5	18 October 1962	Missed moon by 450 miles. (724 km)
Ranger 6	30 January 1964	Television system failed and impacted moon.
Ranger 7	28 July 1964	Returned 4,308 photographs and impacted moon.
Ranger 8	17 February 1965	Television system failed and impacted moon.
Ranger 9	21 March 1965	Returned 5,814 photographs and impacted moon.

Surveyor Probes

Mission	Date	Description
Surveyor 1	30 May 1966	Landed in Oceanus Procellanum and returned 11,150 photographs until 13 July.
Surveyor 2	20 September 1966	Impacted moon after the control system failed.
Surveyor 3	17 April 1967	A surface sampler dug into the lunar soil. Returned 6,315 photographs until 3 May.
Surveyor 4	14 July 1967	Landed in Sinus Medii; but radio contact was lost prior to touchdown.
Surveyor 5	8 September 1967	Landed by remote control from earth. It carried a box to analyze soil by bombardment with alpha particles.
Surveyor 6	7 November 1967	Landed in Sinus Medii; analyzed soil and refired landing rockets causing Surveyor to lift off and resettle 8 feet (2.5m) away.
Surveyor 7	7 January 1968	First highland landing; carried sampling scoop and chemical analysis device.

Pioneer Probes

Mission	Date	Description
Pioneer	17 August 1958	Launch failure.
Pioneer 1	11 October 1958	Intended lunar orbiter to send back television pictures reached 0.717 miles (113,800 km) from earth, mapping extent of Van Allen radiation belts.
Pioneer 2	8 November 1958	Launch failure.

Pioneer 3	6 December 1958	Intended lunar flyby; however, it had insufficient thrust, and only reached 63,580 miles (102,300 km) from earth.
Pioneer 4	3 March 1959	Passed 37,300 miles (60,000 km) from moon.
Pioneer	26 November 1959	Intended lunar orbiter, launch failure.
Pioneer 5	11 March 1960	Interplanetary probe orbiting Sun between Earth and Venus, sent data on solar flares and particles until 26 June 1960.
Pioneer	25 September 1960	Intended lunar orbiter, launch failure.
Pioneer	15 December 1960	Intended lunar orbiter, launch failure.
Pioneer 6	16 December 1965	Interplanetary probe orbiting Sun between Earth and Venus.
Pioneer 7	17 August 1966	Interplanetary probe orbiting Sun between Earth and Mars.
Pioneer 8	13 December 1967	Interplanetary probe orbiting Sun slightly farther than Earth.
Pioneer 9	8 November 1968	Interplanetary probe orbiting Sun between Earth and Venus.
Pioneer E	27 August 1969	Intended interplanetary monitor; launch failure.
Pioneer 10	3 March 1972	Bypassed Jupiter at 81,000 miles (130,000 km) on 3 December 1973.
Pioneer 11	5 April 1973	Bypassed Jupiter at 26,725 miles (43,000 km) on 3 December 1974. Passed Saturn in mid-1979.
Pioneer 12	20 May 1978	Long-term mission to Venus carrying 17 different experiments.
Pioneer 13	8 August 1978	Dropped four probes into the Venus atmosphere. The four probes provided atmospheric information while descending to surface.

Mariner Probes

Mission	Date	Description
Mariner 1	22 July 1962	Launch failure; intended Venus probe.
Mariner 2	26 August 1962	Flew past Venus 14 December at a distance of 21,594 miles (34,752 km)
Mariner 3	5 November 1964	Intended Mars probe; contact lost when the spacecraft shroud failed to jettison.
Mariner 4	28 November 1964	Flew past Mars 14 July 1965, a distance of 5,118 miles (9,846 km)
Mariner 5	14 June 1967	Flew past Venus 19 October 1967, at a distance of 2,480 miles (3,990 km)
Mariner 6	25 February 1969	Flew past Mars 31 July at a distance of 2,120 miles (3,412 km)
Mariner 7	27 March 1969	Flew past Mars 5 August at a distance of 2,190 miles (3,534 km)
Mariner 8	8 May 1971	Launch failure
Mariner 9	30 May 1971	Went into Mars orbit. First man made device to orbit another planet.
Mariner 10	3 November 1973	Flew past Venus 5 February 1974, at a distance of 3,585 miles (5,769 km). Passed Mercury on 29 March at a distance of 431 miles (694 km).

Sputnik Probes

Mission	Date	Description
Sputnik 1	4 October 1957	First satellite to orbit earth; two radio transmitters aboard.
Sputnik 2	3 March 1957	First biomedic experiments; dog Laika aboard.
Sputnik 3	15 May 1958	Discovered earth's outer radiation belt.
Sputnik 4	15 May 1960	Carried "dummy" cosmonaut to test environmental control. Broke into 8 pieces after 64 orbits.
Sputnik 5	19 August 1960	First space vehicle to be retrieved. Had "dummy" cosmonaut, two dogs, and TV monitor.
Sputnik 6	11 December 1960	Medical and biological experiments; recovery attempt failed.
Sputnik 7	4 February 1961	Believed to be Venus probe abort.
Sputnik 8	12 February 1961d	Launched Venus 1 from parking orbit.
Sputnik 9	9 March 1961	Sputnik and dog aboard recovered after one orbit.
Sputnik 10	25 March 1961	Recovered after one orbit with dog Zvezdochka.

Venera Probes

Mission	Date	Description
Venera 1	12 February 1961	Contact lost at 4.7 million miles. Bypassed Venus at 60,000 miles.
Venera 2	12 November 1965	Passed Venus at 15,000 miles, but failed to return data.
Venera 3	16 November 1965	Impacted Venus 1 March 1966, but failed to return data.
Venera 4	12 June 1967	Ejected capsule into Venus atmosphere and provided the first direct measurements of the planet's makeup.
Venera 5	5 January 1969	Ejected capsule into Venus atmosphere on 16 May, and transmitted data for 53 minutes during descent.
Venera 6	10 January 1969	Ejected capsule into Venus atmosphere, data returned for 51 minutes during descent.
Venera 7	17 August 1970	Ejected capsule into Venus atmosphere on December 15, which transmitted data from surface for 23 minutes.
Venera 8	27 March 1972	Ejected capsule into atmosphere, which soft-landed and returned data, including the presence of uranium.
Venera 9	8 June 1975	Lander capsule descended and returned panoramic photographs and other date from surface for 53 minutes. Orbiter section continued in orbit around Venus.
Venera 10	14 June 1975	Lander capsule descended and returned panoramic photographs and other data from surface for 65 minutes. Orbiter section continued in orbit around Venus.
Venera 11,12	9 August 1978	Measured chemical components of the planet's lower atmosphere.
Venera 13,14	30 October 1981	Two probes were launched within 5 days of each other. It had a similar design to the 9th - 12th probes and included a soil sampler.
Venera 15,16	2 June 1981	Identical probes with radar designed for mapping.

Luna Missions

Mission	Date	Description
Luna 1	2 January 1959	Missed moon and became first satellite.
Luna 2	12 September 1959	First man-made object to impact moon.
Luna 3	4 October 1959	Sent back first photographs of lunar far side.
Luna 4	2 April 1963	Missed moon, mission failure.
Luna 5	9 May 1965	Failed soft-lander.
Luna 6	8 June 1965	Missed moon, failed soft-lander.
Luna 7	4 October 1965	Impacted moon, failed soft-lander.
Luna 8	3 December 1965	Impacted moon, failed soft-lander.
Luna 9	31 January 1966	Soft-landed on moon. Returned photos for 3 days.
Luna 10	31 March 1966	Entered lunar orbit and measured magnetic field, meteoroids.
Luna 11	24 August 1966	Successor to Luna 10, entered lunar orbit.
Luna 12	22 October 1966	Entered lunar orbit, took photographs and made measurements.
Luna 13	21 December 1966	Soft-landed on moon, returned photos, tested soil.
Luna 14	7 April 1968	Entered lunar orbit, measured near-moon conditions such as magnetic and gravitational field, solar wind particles.
Luna 15	13 July 1969	Impacted moon, failed sample-return attempt.
Luna 16	12 September 1970	Landed and returned to earth with 0.2 lb. of moon soil.
Luna 17	10 November 1970	Landed on moon carrying Lunokhod 1 automatic moon rover.
Luna 18	2 September 1971	Impacted moon, failed landing attempt.
Luna 19	28 September 1971	Entered lunar orbit. Studied lunar surface and near-lunar space.
Luna 20	14 February 1972	Landed and returned a small soil sample to earth.
Luna 21	8 January 1973	Landed carrying the Lunokhod 2 lunar rover.
Luna 22	29 May 1974	Entered lunar orbit. Studied moon and near-lunar space.
Luna 23	28 October 1974	Landed on moon, but a damaged drill prevented sample return.
Luna 24	14 August 1976	Returned soil samples in 1976.

Zond Probes

Mission	Date	Description
Zond 1	2 April 1964	Launched toward Venus; communications failed.
Zond 2	30 November 1964	Launched toward Mars; communications failed.
Zond 3	18 July 1965	Photographed the far side of the moon and headed toward mars. It then retransmitted lunar photographs back to Earth.
Zond 4	2 March 1968	Unsuccessful test of circumlunar spacecraft.
Zond 5	15 September 1968	First flight to moon and back. Carried biological experiments to assess radiation hazard and tape recording to test voice transmission between capsule and earth.
Zond 6	10 November 1968	Photographed lunar far side. Used a skip-glide re-entry using aerodynamic lift.
Zond 7	8 August 1969	First Soviet color pictures of moon.
Zond 8	20 October 1970	Similar to previous Zonds, with modified re-entry trajectory. It splashed down in the Indian Ocean 27 October.

Human Space Flight

Mercury Project

Mission	Date	Crew	Description
Freedom 7	5 May 1961	Alan Shepard	Suborbital flight; First American in space.
Liberty Bell 7	21 July 1961	Virgil Grissom	Second successful suborbital flight.
Friendship 7	20 February 1962	John Glenn	Three orbit flight, first American to orbit.
Aurora 7	24 May 1962	Scott Carpenter	Second American orbital flight.
Sigma 7	3 October 1962	Walter Schirra	Engineering test flight with six orbits.
Faith 7	15 May 1963	Gordon Cooper	Last Mercury mission achieved one day in space.

Gemini Project

Mission	Date	Crew	Description
Gemini 1	8 April 1964	No crew	Test of Titan-II rocket and Gemini capsule
Gemini 2	19 January 1965	No crew	Suborbital launch and test.
Gemini 3	23 March 1965	Virgil Grissom John Young	First manned Gemini flight.
Gemini 4	3 June 1965	Jim McDivitt Ed White	Over 4-day flight. First EVA by an American.
Gemini 5	21 August 1965	Gordon Cooper Charles Conrad	Test of fuel cells, guidance, and navigation systems for rendezvous.
Gemini 6	15 December 1965	Wally Schirra Tom Stafford	Rendezvous with Gemini 7
Gemini 7	4 December 1965	Frank Borman Jim Lovell	14-day mission to test endurance and prepare for docking.
Gemini 8	16 March 1966	Neil Armstrong David Scott	First docking with another space vehicle.
Gemini 9	3 June 1966	Tom Stafford Eugene Cernan	Space walks and docking practice.
Gemini 10	18 July 1966	John Young Michael Collins	1 hr, 28 minute space walk and docking procedures with Gemini 8.
Gemini 11	12 September 1966	Charles Conrad Richard Gordon	Record Gemini orbit of 739.2 miles (1,189.3 km).
Gemini 12	11 November 1966	Jim Lovell Edwin Aldrin	Final Gemini flight rendezvous and docking with Agena target.

Apollo Project

Mission	Date	Crew	Description
Apollo 1	26 February 1966	No crew	Suborbital test launch with Saturn 1B.
Apollo 2	5 July 1966	No crew	Orbital test of Saturn 1B, no CSM.
Apollo 3	25 August 1966	No crew	Suborbital test with Saturn 1B and CSM.
Apollo 4	9 November 1967	No crew	First launch of a Saturn 5 rocket, and Apollo CSM in orbit. Successful test of the CSM.
Apollo 5	22 January 1968	No crew	Test flight of the lunar module; launched into earth orbit by Saturn 1B.
Apollo 6	4 April 1968	No crew	Second test flight of Saturn 5 and CSM in Earth orbit.
Apollo 7	11 October 1968	Walter Schirra Donn Eisele Walter Cunningham	Earth-orbital test flight of 3-man CSM; launch by Saturn 1B.
Apollo 8	21 December 1968	Frank Borman James Lovell William Anders	First manned Saturn 5 launch; 10 orbits of moon in Apollo CSM.
Apollo 9	3 March 1969	James McDivitt David Scott Russell Schweickart	Earth orbital test of CSM and lunar module; launched by Saturn 5.
Apollo 10	18 May 1969	Thomas Stafford John Young Eugene Cernan	Full dress rehearsal of moon landing, in lunar orbit; 2.5 days were spent orbiting the moon.
Apollo 11	16 July 1969	Neil Armstrong Edwin Aldrin Michael Collins	Armstrong and Aldrin make the first manned lunar landing in the Sea of Tranquility.
Apollo 12	14 November 1969	Charles Conrad Richard Gordon Alan Bean	Conrad and Bean land in the Ocean of Storms.
Apollo 13	11 April 1970	James Lovell John Swigert Fred Haise	Landing attempt was canceled after an explosion in an oxygen tank damaged the spacecraft.
Apollo 14	31 January 1971	Alan Shepard Stuart Roosa Edgar Mitchell	Shepard and Mitchell landed in Frau Mauro region of the moon.
Apollo 15	26 July 1971	David Scott Alfred Worden James Irwin	Scott and Irwin land at Hadley Hill; first use of the lunar roving vehicle.
Apollo 16	27 April 1972	John Young Thomas Mattingly Charles Duke	Young and Duke land in the Descartes high lands to collect varying rock samples.
Apollo 17	7 December 1972	Eugene Cernan Ronald Evans Harrison Schmitt	Cernan and Schmitt make the longest moon walk and collect the largest amount of moon samples.

Skylab Project

Mission	Date	Crew	Description
Skylab 1	14 May 1973	Station launch	Worlds largest payload launched by a two-stage Saturn V.
Skylab 2	25 May 1973	Charles Conrad Joseph Kerwin Joseph Kerwin	Deployed a parasol sunshade to cool the space station, freed a solar wing during a space walk.

| Skylab 3 | 28 July 1973 | Alan Bean
Owen Garriott
Jack Lousma | Installed a new sun shield during a space walk, made earth surveys and solar observations. |
| Skylab 4 | 16 November 1973 | Gerald Carr
Edward Gibson
William Pogue | Performed a seven hour space walk to change film in a telescope mount and observe comet Kohoutek. |

Space Shuttle Project

Significant Space Shuttle missions are included in the following list. For a complete list and description see the NASA web site (www.nasa.gov).

Mission	Launch Date	Crew	Description
STS-1 Columbia	12 April 1981	John Young Robert Crippen	First Space Shuttle mission.
STS-5 Columbia	11 November 1982	Vance Brand Robert Overmyer Joseph Allen William Lenoir	First operational mission
STS-7 Challenger	19 June 1983	Robert L. Crippen Frederick H. Hauck John M. Fabian Sally K. Ride Norman E. Thagard	The first U.S. woman, Sally Ride, to travel in space.
STS-8 Challenger	30 August 1983	Richard H. Truly Daniel C. Brandenstein Dale A. Gardner Guion S. Bluford, Jr. William E. Thornton	First African-American to fly in space, Guion Bluford.
STS-9 Columbia	28 November 1983	John W. Young Brewster H. Shaw, Jr. Owen K. Garriott Robert A. R. Parker Byron K. Lichtenberg Ulf Merbold	First Spacelab mission and ESA astronaut, Ulf Merbold.
STS-41B Challenger	3 February 1984	Vance D. Brand Robert L. Gibson Bruce McCandless II Ronald E. McNair Robert L. Stewart	First untethered flight by McCandless using MMU.
STS 51-L Challenger	28 January 1986	Francis R. Scobee Michael J. Smith Judith A. Resnik Ellison S. Onizuka Ronald E. McNair Sharon Christa McAuliffe Gregory B. Jarvis	Explosion 73 seconds after liftoff claimed crew and vehicle.
STS-49 Endeavour	7 May 1992	Daniel C. Brandenstein Kevin P. Chilton Bruce E. Melnick Thomas D. Akers Richard J. Hieb Kathryn C. Thornton Pierre J. Thuot	Successfully captured and redeployed INTELSAT VI (F-3) satellite.

STS-71 Atlantis	27 June 1995	Robert L. "Hoot" Gibson Charles J. Precourt Ellen S. Baker Gregory J. Harbaugh Bonnie J. Dunbar Embarking to Mir Anatoly Y. Solovyev Nikolai M. Budarin Returning from Mir Vladimir N. Dezhurov Gennady M. Strekalov Norman E. Thagard	First Shuttle- Mir docking.
STS-95 Discovery	20 November 1998	Curtis L. Brown, Jr. Steven W. Lindsey Scott E. Parazynski Stephen K. Robinson Pedro Duque Chiaki Mukai John H. Glenn, Jr.	Return of John Glenn to space, geriatric tests.
STS- 96 Discovery	27 May 1999	Kent V. Rominger Rick D. Husband Ellen Ochoa Tamara E. Jernigan Daniel T. Barry Julie Payette Valery Ivanovich Tokarev	First shuttle mission to the International Space Station; the International Space Station became the destination and mission of all but two shuttle flights in 2000-2002
STS-93 Columbia	22 July 1999	Eileen M. Collins Jeffrey S. Ashby Michel Tognini Steven A. Hawley Catherine G. Coleman	Deployed X-ray Observatory, first female Commander.
STS-92	11 October 2000	Brian Duffy Pamela A. Melroy Koichi Wakata Leroy Chiao Peter J.K. Wisoff Michael Lopez-Alegria William S. McArthur	Marks the 100th shuttle flight.
STS-109 Columbia	1 March 2002	Scott D. Altman Duane G. Carey John M. Grunsfeld Nancy J. Currie James H. Newman Richard M. Linnehan Michael J. Massimino	Hubble Space Telescope service mission.
STS-107 Columbia	1 February 2003	Rick Husband Willie McCool Michael Anderson Kalpana Chawla David Brown Laurel Clark Ilan Ramon	Spacecraft broke up after reentry on on 1 February 2003, crew lost.

STS-114 Discovery	26 July 2005	Eileen Collins	NASA's return to flight and return to the International Space Station
		James Kelly	
		Charles Camarda	
		Wendy Lawrence	
		Soichi Noguchi	
		Stephen Robinson	
		Andrew Thomas	

Vostok Project

Mission	Date	Crew	Description
Vostok 1	12 April 1961	Yuri Gagarin	First manned space flight; made one orbit of earth.
Vostok 2	6 August 1961	Gherman Titov	First day-long flight.
Vostok 3	11 August 1962	Andrian Nikolayev	Orbited the earth 64 times before returning to earth.
Vostok 4	12 August 1962	Pavel Popovich	Completed 48 orbits simultaneously with Vostok 3
Vostok 5	14 June 1963	Valery Bykovsky	Longest to date individual flight, 81 oribts.
Vostok 6	16 June 1963	Valentina Tereshkova	First women in space makes 48 orbits.

Voskhod Project

Mission	Date	Crew	Description
Voskhod 1	12 October 1964	Vladimir Komarov	First multiple person space capsule made a day long 16-orbit flight.
		Konstantin Feoktistov	
		Boris Yegorov	
Voskhod 2	18 March 1965	Alexei Leonov	Alexei Leonov made the first space walk, returned to earth after 18 orbits.
		Pavel Belyaev	

Soyuz Project

Mission	Date	Crew	Description
Soyuz 1	23 April 1967	Vladimir M. Komarov	Cosmonaut killed during re-entry.
Soyuz 2	25 October 1968	No crew	Target for Soyuz 3 docking test.
Soyuz 3	26 October 1968	Georgii T. Beregovoi	Maneuvered close to Soyuz 2 but did not dock.
Soyuz 4	14 January 1969	Vladimir A. Shatalov	Docked with Soyuz 5.
Soyuz 5	15 January 1969	Boris V. Volynov	Alexei Yeliseyev and Yevgeni Khrunov transferred to Soyuz 4 on a space walk.
		Aleksei S. Yeliseyev	
		Yevgeni V. Khrunov	
Soyuz 6	11 October 1969	Georgi S. Shonin	In space welding experiments.
		Valerii N. Kubasov	
Soyuz 7	12 October 1969	Anatoli V. Filipchenko	Maneuvered with Soyuz 6 and 8.
		Vladislav N. Volkov	
		Viktor V. Gorbatko	
Soyuz 8	12 October 1969	Vladimir A. Shatalov	Maneuvered with Soyuz 6 and 7.
		Aleksei S. Yeliseyev	
Soyuz 9	2 June 1970	Andrian G. Nikolayev	Record breaking 17.5-day flight.
		Vitali I. Sevastyanov	
Soyuz 10	23 April 1971	Vladimir Shatalov	Docked with Salyut 1 but did not enter.
		Alexei Yeliseyev	
		Nikolai Rukavishnikov	

Soyuz 11	6 June 1971	Georgi Dobrovolsky Viktor Patsayev Vladislav Volkov	Docked and entered Salyut 1 for 23 days. Soyuz capsule failed upon re-entry and all aboard died.
Soyuz 12	27 September 1973	Vasily G. Lazarev Oleg G. Makarov	Two-day test flight of a simplified Soyuz spacecraft for space station ferry missions.
Soyuz 13	18 December 1973	Pyotr I. Klimuk Valentin V. Lebedev	Scientific flight.
Soyuz 14	3 July 1974	Pavel Popovich Yuri Artyukhin	Docked with Salyut 3 for a 16 day mission.
Soyuz 15	26 August 1974	Gennady Sarafanov Lev Demin	Attempted to automatically dock with Salyut 3.
Soyuz 16	2 December 1974	Anatoli V. Filipchenko Nikolai N. Rukavishnikov	Rehearsal for Apollo-Soyuz flight.
Soyuz 17	11 January 1975	Alexei Gubarev Georgi Grechko	Docked with Salyut 4 in a 29 day mission.
Soyuz 18	24 May 1975	Pyotr Klimuk Vitaly Sevasyanov	64-day mission aboard Salyut 4.

Soyuz 19 was the Apollo-Soyuz Test Project (see below). Ongoing missions performed by Soyuz, Soyuz-T, Soyuz-TM, and Progress resupply ships were flown in support of the Salyut series of space stations and the Mir space station. The Soyuz spacecraft became the sole transport for the International Space Station (ISS) from February 2003 to July 2005 due to grounding of the space shuttle fleet, and remained the prime transport for the ISS after NASA's return to flight.

Apollo-Soyuz Test Project

Mission	Date	Crew	Description
Soyuz 19	15 July 1975	Alexei Leonov Valeri Kubasov	Joint effort to dock U.S. and Soviet spacecraft in earth orbit.
Apollo 18/ASTM		Thomas Stafford Donald Slayton Vance Brand	The Apollo module remained in orbit 6 days after the docking was done.

Salyut Project

Mission	Date	Description
Salyut 1	19 April 1971	Soyuz 10 failed to enter the space station but Soyuz 11 spent 23 days aboard the station.
Salyut 2	3 April 1973	Disintegrated in orbit and re-entered the atmosphere.
Salyut 3	24 June 1974	Soyuz 14 crew docked and transferred, Soyuz 15 rendezvous failed.
Salyut 4	26 December 1974	Soyuz 17 docked for a 29 day mission and the Soyuz 18 crew had a 63 day mission. And robotic Soyuz 20 docked automatically.
Salyut 5	22 June 1976	Three Soyuz missions were flown to the station, two were successful.
Salyut 6	29 September 1977	The most successful space station to date. The first automatic Progress resupply ships were used to set new space endurance records.
Salyut 7	19 April 1982	Second Soviet female cosmonaut, Svetlana Savitskaya served aboard the last Salyut spacecraft.

Mir Project

Dates represent major additions to Mir

Mission	Date
Mir Primary Module	20 February 1986
Kvant Module	31 March 1987
Kvant 2 Module	26 November 1989
Kristall Module	31 May 1990
Spektr Module	20 March 1995
Docking Module	12 November 1995
Piroda Module	23 April 1996
Deorbit	22 March 2001

International Space Station

Expedition	Date	Launch Vehicle	Crew
Expedition 1	31 October 2000 21 March 2001	Soyuz	William M. (Bill) Shepherd of USA Yuri Pavolich Gidzenko of Russia Sergei K. Krikalev of Russia
Expedition 2	8 March 22 August 2001	Space shuttle *Discovery*	Yury Usachev of Russia James Voss of USA Susan Helms of USA
Expedition 3	10 August 17 December 2001	Space shuttle *Discovery*	Frank Culbertson Vladimir Dezhurov Mikhail Tyurin
Expedition 4	5 December 2001 19 June 2002	Space shuttle *Endeavour*	Yury I. Onufrienko of Russia Daniel W. Bursch of USA Carl E. Walz of USA
Expedition 5	5 June 7 December 2002	Space shuttle *Endeavour*	Valery Korzun of Russia Peggy Whitson of USA Sergei Treschev of Russia
Expedition 6	23 November 2002 3 May 2003	Space shuttle *Endeavour*	Kenneth Bowersox of USA Donald Pettit of USA Nikolai Budarin of Russia
Expedition 7	25 April 27 27 October 2003	Soyuz TMA-2	Yuri Malenchenko of Russia Ed Lu of USA
Expedition 8	18 October 2003 29 April 2004	Soyuz TMA-3	Michael Foale of USA Alexander Kaleri of Russia Pedro Duque of Spain, European Space Agency
Expedition 9	18 April 23 October 2004	Soyuz TMA-4	Gennady Pedalka of Russia Mike Fincke of USA *Andr Kulpers of The Netherlands, European Space Agency * Returned with Expedition 8 on Soyuz TMA-3

Expedition 10	13 October 2004 24 April 2005	Soyuz TMA-5	Leroy Chiao of USA Salizhan Sharipov of Russia *Yuri Shargin of Russia *Returned with Expedition 9 on Soyuz TMA-4
Expedition 11	14 April 2005 10 October 2005	Soyuz TMA-6	Sergei Krikalev of Russia John Phillips of USA *Roberto Vittori of Italy, European Space Agency *Returned with Expedition 10 on Soyuz TMA-5
Expedition 12	30 September 2005 8 April 2006	Soyuz TMA-7	Bill McArthur of USA Valery Tokarev of Russia *Gregory Olsen under commercial contract with Russian Federal Space Agency *Returned with Expedition 11 on Soyuz TMA-6
Expedition 13	29 March 2006	Soyuz TMA-8	Pavel Vinogradov of Russia Jeffrey Williams of USA Thomas Reiter, European Space Agency, joined the ISS crew from space shuttle Discovery STS-121 on July 6, 2006. *Marcos Pontes of Brazil, Brazilian Space Agency *Returned with Expedition 12 on Soyuz TMA-7

Chinese Space Flights

Spacecraft	Date	Crew
Shenzhou 5	15-16 October 2003	Yang Liwei
Shenzhou 6	12-17 October 2005	Fei Junlong Nie Haisheng

APPENDIX D

PICTURE CREDITS

Each list is in a specific sequence. The owner of the photograph is in bold followed by the page number in the book and a brief description of the photograph.

Aerial Age 1911, by Walter Wellman. 1-31: Portrait of Walter Wellman

Airbus Industrie. 9-81: A-320 cockpit

Archiv der Luftschiffbau Zeppelin GmbH, Friedrichshafen. 3-36: German Ships and Airship; 4-12: Daimler L-Motor; 4-12: Zeppelin L 30 in 1916; 4-12: Zeppelin works in Germany; 4-13: Zeppelin L 48; 5-21: Hugo Eckener; 5-43: Bodensee LZ 120

ArianeSpace ESA. 10-3: Ariane 5 liftoff

Bell Helicopter. 7-26: Bell Model 30 Helicopter

Boeing. 10-2: McDonnell Douglas C-17; 10-21: 747 under construction

Bombardier Aerospace. 10-4: Global Express 10-12: Canadair Regional Jet

Breitling. 10-15: Breitling Orbiter; 10-16: Bertrand Piccard

Brown Brothers, Sterling, PA. 1-24: 1906 Gordon Bennett Balloon

Canada Aviation Museum. 3-16: A.E.A. Silver Dart

Capelotti, P.J. 1-32: "Capelotti surveying Wellman's base camp on Danskoya, August 1993"

Carneiro, Daniel R. 8-28: Brazilian Airliner

Cessna Aircraft Corp. 9-90: Cessna Citation; 10-8: 1956 C-172; 10-8: 1965 C-172; 10-8: New C-172

Cirrus Designs. 10-3: Cirrus SR-20

City of Santos-Dumont. 3-2 and 3-6: Alberto Santos-Dumont's 14-bis

Colonel Richard Gimbel Aeronautical History Collection, United States Air force Academy Library. 1-5: Lana's ship; 1-6: Montgolfier Balloon; 1-7: Joseph Montgolfier Portrait; 1-7: Jacques Montgolfier Portrait; 1-8: Montgolfier Balloon - redrawn; 1-9: First balloon ascent at Annonay; 1-9: J.A.C. Charles Portrait; 1-10: People attacking Charles Balloon; 1-11: 1st manned balloon; 1-11: Montgolfier unmanned ascent; 1-12: Making hydrogen; 1-13: Map of Charles flight path over Paris; 1-14: Flesselles Balloon Ascent; 1-15: Battle at Fleurus; 1-15: Garnerin parachute jump; 1-16: Ballooning circa 1800; 1-16: Blanchard and Jeffries; 1-18: Charles Green

dragline - redrawn; 1-18: Blanchard Portrait; 1-19: Charles Green Portrait; 1-21: Eagle Hydrogen Balloon; 1-26: Blanchard Balloon; 1-27: Henri Giffard's steam-powered dirigible; 2-29: Wright Flyer over Paris

Corbis Bettman Archives. 1-20: Eugene Godard portrait; 3-3: Eugene Ely takeoff from ship; 3-6: Voisin Airplane; 3-8: Henry Farman and Voisin airplane; 3-8: Henry Farman; 3-10: Bleriot flying over the English Channel on 25 July 1909; 3-10: Louis Charles-Joseph Bleriot; 3-17: 1913 Curtiss Seaplane; 3-17: Julia Clark in Curtiss Pusher; 3-18: Exhibition flying: Curtiss Rheims Racer; 3-18: Curtiss Pusher landing on the USS Pennsylvania 18 Jan 1911; 3-18: Curtiss Pusher taking off from the USS Birmingham 10 Nov 1910; 3-20: Cal Rodgers crash; 3-20: Charles Rolls crash; 3-26: Curtiss Biplane at Atlantic City; 3-32: ENV and Anzani aircraft engines; 4-16: German Caquot balloons; 4-39: Geoffrey de Havilland; 4-40: Curtiss H-16 Flying Boat; 4-41: Jennies being assembled; 4-44: Paris Peace Conference; 5-2: R.34; 5-2: Vickers Vimy; 5-6: NC-4; 5-7: NC-4; 5-8: Alcock and Brown; 5-9: Vickers Vimy; 5-10: Alcock and Brown Memorial; 5-11: John Alcock; 5-12: R.34 on the ground; 5-19: Shenandoah; 5-22: Barnstormers; 5-24: Barnstorming; 5-25: Major General Mason Patrick; 5-31: The Boston crash; 5-35: Richard Byrd; 5-36: Amundsen's Dornier-Wals aircraft; 5-36: Josephine Ford Fokker; 5-38: Pescara and Berliner helicopters; 5-42: Paris Peace Conference; 5-45: U.S. Army airmail plane; 6-6: Spirit of St. Louis; 6-7: Davis-Wooster crash; 6-7: Spirit of St. Louis; 6-8: Lindbergh in Paris; 6-13: James Mollison; 6-20: Saint Exupery; 6-29: Aeropostale airplane; 6-32: Airmail airplane catapulted from Bremen; 6-33: Depot ship Schwabenland; 6-35: Knute Rockne; 6-36: Mapmakers; 6-36: Weather Bureau; 6-38: Ellen Church; 6-40: Pan American Fokker Trimotor; 6-40: Ford Trimotor; 6-43: Hindenburg explosion; 6-44: Hindenburg crash; 6-51: Amelia Earhart; 6-53: Francisco Franco; 6-55: K1-15-I Karigane; 7-9: Maginot Line fortification; 7-11: Paratroopers leaving airplane; 7-11: Heinkels over Paris; 7-13: Winston Churchill; 7-17: I-16 fighter plane; 7-18: Ship convoy in North Atlantic; 7-19: Craig Field Cadet; 7-20: Tuskegee airmen in training; 7-21: First Tuskegee class; 7-22: Female bomber pilots; 7-24: German helicopter; 7-28: Frank Whittle; 7-28: Gloster E28/39; 7-30: Bell P-59A; 7-31: Hanna Reitsch; 7-33: British Navy radar station; 7-34: B-24D; 7-34: PBY in the Aleutians; 7-38: North American B-25 and P51 Mustang; 7-39: P-40s in the Mediterranean; 7-40: Tuskegee airmen in Africa; 7-41: Benjamin O. Davis, Jr.; 7-42: B-17s near Munich; 7-43: Consolidated PBY-5 Catalina; 7-43: PBY-5 in storm; 7-45: Unexploded German V1 Missile; 7-48: Erich Hartmann; 7-52: Explosion at Pearl Harbor; 7-55: Japanese bombing of

Prince of Wales; 7-57: Battle of the Coral Sea; 7-57: Battle of Midway; 7-57: Torpedoed Aircraft Carrier; 7-58: Guadalcanal; 7-58: Saburo Sakai; 7-59: Admiral Isoroku Yamamoto; 7-60: Richard Ira Bong; 7-61: Air base in China; 7-61: Kamikaze attack on US ship; 7-61: Kamikaze pilots; 8-6: Chicago; 8-7: Juan Trippe; 8-18: Douglas DC-3; 8-18: New York Airport; 8-3 and 8-24: Tupolev Tu-104; 8-24: Vickers Viscount; 8-29: DC-3 "Lansa" at La Ceiba; 8-31: Harry Truman; 8-33: Pilot Halvorsen; 8-34: Berliners Watching Airlift Plane; 8-36: MiG-15; 8-40: Supermarine Spitfire; 8-49: Consolidated B-46; 8-50: Tu-95 Bear and F-4s; 8-53: Mittelwerk underground plant; 8-60: Lt. Col. Chuck Yeager; 9-6: Sputnik; 9-8: Laika; 9-44: May Day parade; 9-48: Trident missile launch; 9-49: Kelly Johnson; 9-52: Map and aerial photo of Cuba; 9-54: Defoliant spraying in Vietnam; 9-68: Interior of 707; 9-73: Air Force One; 9-75: Cargo operation; 9-76: Striking air traffic controllers; 9-77: Tu-104; 9-80: Tu-144 at the Paris Air Show; 9-84: Burt Rutan; 9-86: Maxie Anderson's balloon; 9-87: Helicopter on oil rig

Corel Corporation. 5-4: Vickers Vimy; 5-5: Curtiss Jenny; 5-15: Vickers Vimy; 5-23: Curtiss Jenny JN-4; 5-35: Polar ice; 6-8: Ocean; 6-18: de Havilland 88 Comet; 6-20: Tiger Moth; 6-21: Piper J-3 Cub; 6-21: Stinson Straight Wing; 6-21: Taylor E-2 Cub; 6-21: Waco Straight Wing; 6-24: Flying Flea; 7-4: North American P-51 Mustang; 7-10: Hawker Hurricane; 7-10: German Bf109 and Spitfire; 7-13: Spitfire; 7-45: North American P-51 Mustang; 7-45: Republic P-47; 7-52: Zeros; 7-59: Chance Vought F4U Corsair; 8-2: Comet; 8-5: TU-95 Bear; 8-14: 1946 Taylorcraft; 8-40: Douglas A-26; 8-51: Lockheed U-2; 9-2: B-52; 9-2: Learjet; 9-3: Concorde; 9-45: B-52; 9-45: FB-111; 9-45: Tu-22M; 9-46: F-16 and F-117; 9-46: MiG-29; 9-55: Hueys and Chinook; 9-57: F-4 Phantom II; 9-58: Mirage; 9-59: A-4 Skyhawks; 9-62: Mi-24 Hind; 9-63: Harrier; 9-67: Boeing 727; 9-70: GE TF39 engine; 9-70: C-5B; 9-71: Boeing 737; 9-71: Boeing 747; 9-72: Douglas DC-8 and DC-9. 9-72: Boeing 757 and 767; 9-75: Lockheed L-1011; 9-75: DeHavilland DHC-8311A; 9-77: Il-62; 9-80: Airbus A300; 9-81: Airbus A320; 9-85: Hang glider; 9-86: Goodyear blimp; 9-92: Dassault Falcon; 9-92: de Havilland Beaver; 9-93: IAI Westwind; 10-2: F-117A; 10-6: Piper Super Cub; 10-13: Air racer; 10-21 Concorde; 10-33: JAS 39 Gripen; 10-33: Dassault Rafale; 10-33: Eurofighter 2000; 10-38: F-117A

Denver Public Library. 5-18: Crash of R.38

Deutsche Lufthansa AG. 1-33: Von Zeppelin Portrait; 1-34: Zeppelin LZ 10; 4-8: Von Zeppelin; 4-8: Zeppelin Airship L 26; 5-17: Airship Bodensee; 5-21: LZ 127 Graf Zeppelin; 5-40: Loading Junkers; 5-44: Luft Hansa aircraft; 6-2: Graf Zeppelin; 6-3: Hindenberg; 6-31: Duetsche Luft Hansa airliner; 6-32: Rohrbach Roland; 6-33: Depot ship Schwabenland; 6-40: Dornier Do X; 6-42: Inflight over New Jersey; 6-42: Graf Zeppelin moored; 6-43: Hindenburg and Graf Zeppelin in flight; 8-25: Lufthansa Aircraft

Deutches Museum. 2-5: Laurence de Gusmao — Passarola

Diercks, LeAnna Jo. 6-2: Lindbergh

Dornier Historical Archive. 6-15: Dornier Wal

Dover AFB Museum. 8-33: Berlin Airlift Aircraft

Eastman, Jug. 8-39: L-19 Birddog

European Space Agency. 10-55: Ariane 5; 10-47: SMART-1 rollout and launch

Farrell, Jerry. 9-74: F-100 in Vietnam; 9-76: F-100 dropping bomb

Fenemore, Sidney. 3-3: Louis Paulhan; 3-25: Louis Paulhan; 5-38: de Havilland Moth

Franklin Institute. 2-6: 1903 Wright Flyer 3-view

Gable, Michelle. 5-21: LZ 127 Graf Zeppelin

Goehler, Dave. 6-11: Spirit of St. Louis

Helix Interactive. www.warbird.com. 10-14: Reno Air Race, copyright 2003

Hemry, David. 9-82: Cessna 180 floatplane in Alaska

Husar, Mike/EAA. 9-97: Oshkosh air show

International Launch Services. 10-50: Proton launch, courtesy of International Launch Services and Lockheed Martin Corporation. All rights reserved.

Iridium Satellite. 10-49: Iridium satellite

Jacobacci, Capt. Juan. 8-27: Argentina Airline

Jane's All The Worlds Aircraft. 3-34: Cover of Jane's All the World's Aircraft 1909

Jeppesen Aviation Foundation. 4-48: Photo from the movie "Wings"; 5-4 and 5-19: Shenandoah in flight; 5-20: Shenandoah; 6-18: SM.55X flying boat

Kennedy, Gary. 2-7: Windmill; 3-16: Alexander Graham Bell Museum

Kidby, Lang. 5-4: Ross/Smith Vimy; 5-13: Smith Brothers; 5-14: Ross Smith

LaFayette Foundation, 6298 South Killarney Court, Aurora, CO 80016. 4-2: Spad XI of Escadrille 36 on the Italian Front late 1918; 4-3: Lothar von Richthofen; 4-3: Major Raoul Lufbery; 4-20: Lafayette Escadrille pilots and/or aircraft; 4-21: French airfield circa 1914; 4-23: Richtofen Airfield; 4-24: Gun mounted on aircraft; 4-25: Artillery battery; 4-27: Morane Type N; 4-27: Anthony Fokker; 4-29: Manfred von Richtofen; 4-29: Max Immelmann; 4-30: Ernst Udet; 4-30: Richtofen; 4-33: Italian bomber; 4-34: Handley Page Bomber; 4-34: various German Bombers; 4-35: Short 184 Seaplane, Felixtowe F.5 flying boat, Zeppelin-Staaken Type L Seaplane, and Brandenburg W.33 seaplane; 4-39: Sopwith 1 1/2 Strutter and Sopwith Pup; 4-40: de Havilland D. H. 4; 5-23: JN-4 (Canuck) on ground

Latecoere. 5-40: Pierre-Georges Latecoere; 6-31: pilot Henry Guillamet; 6-28: Late 28

LearJet Corporation. 9-88: Bill Lear; 9-89: Learjet

Library of Congress. 3-25: Cal Rodgers

Lockheed-Martin. 10-2: YF-22A; 10-31: X-35A; 10-32: X-35B; 10-33; X-35C

McCray, Velma. 3-4 and 3-24: 1911 Chicago International Meet

Mentzer, Ray. 3-36: Lloyd George; 4-2: Anthony Fokker testing machine gun; 4-2: Framework of Zeppelin shot down; 4-3: Breguet bomber in flight; 4-23: Cameraman in position; 4-27: Roland Garros

Montana Historical Society, Helena, MT. 3-4 and 3-34: Katherine Stinson

Montana State University, Burlingame Special Collection. 3-4 and 3-19: Cromwell Dixon

NASA. 8-2 and 8-59: X-1 and B-29; 8-60: SP-86 Sabre; 9-2: Mercury astronauts; 9-3: Challenger explosion; 9-4: First lunar landing; 9-5: Earth; 9-5: U.S. launch; 9-9: Courier satellite; 9-9: TIROS satellite; 9-10: Landsat images; 9-10: Luna 1; 9-11: Pioneer; 9-11: Ranger; 9-12: Luna probes; 9-13: Mars; 9-13: Mariners; 9-14: Viking launch; 9-16: Viking montage; 9-15: Venera; 9-16: Pioneer; 9-16: Voyager; 9-17: ICE; 9-18: Saturn launch; 9-18: Monkey; 9-19: Soviet space systems; 9-23: Gagarin with Komarov; 9-24: Apollo-Soyuz; 9-26: Mir in 1989; 9-28: U.S. space programs; 9-29: Mercury montage; 9-30: Mercury astronauts; 9-30: John Glenn; 9-31: Gemini summary; 9-31: Ed White spacewalk; 9-33: Apollo 11 montage; 9-34: Lunar rovers; 9-34: Skylab; 9-35: Challenger explosion; 9-36: Challenger crew; 9-36: MMU; 9-41: ESA Spacelab in Columbia; 9-74: Convair 880; 9-88: Lockheed JetStar; 10-3: Cassini; 10-5: International Space Station; 10-43: Sojourner and Martian landscape; 10-44: Jupiter and moons; 10-45: Europa; 10-45: Galileo nearing Jupiter; 10-46: Magellan; 10-46: Huygens; 10-47: Cassini; 10-48: Hubble; 10-51: Mir; 10-51: Nikolai Budarin; 10-53: John Glenn; 10-54: Franklin Chang-Diaz; 10-55: Columbia STS 107 crew; 10-58: Satellite retrieval

NASA Dryden Flight Research Center. 9-49: U-2; 10-17: Pathfinder; 10-41: DarkStar

National Archives. 1-29: Dumont dirigible No. 6; 2-16: Wright tethered kit; 2-19: Wright's wind tunnel; 2-27: Wright Flyer No. 2 at Huffman Prairie; 2-29: Selfridge crash; 3-20: Wright crash on 17 Sept 1908 that killed Thomas Selfridge; 4-9: Downed Zeppelin in France; 4-33: Sikorsky Il'ya Mourametz bomber; 5-3: Macchi M.39 racer; 5-8: Commander A.C. Read; 5-20: Los Angeles (LZ 126); 5-34: Macchi M.39 racer; 6-12: Dole's 1927 Pacific Air Race; 6-14: Doug "Wrong Way" Corrigan; 6-18: Soviet ANT-25; 6-53:

Benito Mussolini; 6-54: Adolph Hitler; 7-2: Doolittle B-25; 7-3: Atomic bomb; 7-4: Flying Tigers P-40s; 7-12: Aircraft Spotter in Britain; 7-18: Attack on Pearl Harbor; 7-6: Dynamic Static from F6F; 7-12: St. Paul's Cathedral; 7-35: War production line; 7-36: Women working in a war plant; 7-39: Rommel in North Africa; 7-44: Bombing of ball-bearing plant; 7-46: Eisenhower gives the order for D-Day; 7-48: B-17 bombers; 7-51: USS Arizona burning in Pearl Harbor; 7-52: Zero taking off 7 Dec 1941; 7-55: Doolittle Raid; 7-62: Navy pilots 7-62: TBMs & SB2Cs dropping bombs on Hokadate, Japan; 7-64: Nagasaki Blast; 7-65: F4Us and F6Fs flying in formation; 7-65: MacArthur signing Japanese surrender; 8-31: Joseph Stalin

National Postcards. 3-24: Claude Grahame-White of Great Britain

NH Industries. 10-35: NH-90 helicopter; 10-36: NH-90 landing on ship

Norwegian Polar Institute Archives. 1-32: Wellman's airship "America" being towed; 1-32: Wellman's hangar on Danes Island

Pan American Historical Foundation. 8-20: Boeing 707 rollout at Boeing Plant; 9-38: Pan Am 707

Penguin Putnam, Inc. 1-22: Andree's arctic flight path map; 1-22: S.A. Andree portrait. From *Andree's Story* by S.A. Andree, Nils Strindberg & K. Fraenkel, translated by Edward Adams-Ray, Translation copyright 1930 by Albert Bonniers Forlag & Hearst Enterprises Inc. ©1930 Viking Press, Inc., translation. Used by permission of Viking Penguin, a division of Penguin Putnam, Inc.

Pietenpol, Don. 6-23: Air Camper; 6-23: Bernie Pietenpol

Polish Museum, Krakow. 7-7: P.11c

Raytheon Aircraft Company. 8-13: General Aviation Aircraft; 9-91: Beech Starship; 9-91: V-tail Beechcraft Bonanza; 10-3: Raytheon Business Jet

Rogers, Tony , U.K. 9-77: Sud Aviation caravelle; 9-78: BAC 1-11

Schoeman, Captain Scott D. "Shoe", USMC. 10-34: F/A-18C Hornet

Short Brothers. 3-9: Short Brothers; 5-3 and 5-45: NC-3 Cromarty 1921; 6-34: Empire Flying Boat

Socata Aircraft. 9-93: Socata aircaft; 10-13: Socata TBM 700

Sohmura, Takuji. 10-19: Boeing 777-300

Stache, Sammlung. 8-56: Sputnik launch; 9-5: Soviet launch; 9-19: R-7 rocket; 9-21: Vostok diagram; 9-21: Yuri Gagarin; 9-22: Valentina Tereshkova; 9-22: Voskhod diagram and launch; 9-23: Soyuz montage; 9-23: Soviet spacewalk; 9-25: Salyut spacecraft; 9-26: Salyut interior; 9-27: Buran and Energia

Swanson, Bob. 4-42: Spruce logging

U.S. Air Force. 9-45: Tu-160; 9-46: E-3 Sentry AWAC; 10-20: Beluga; 10-39: B-2; 10-33: Jeannie Flynn

U.S. Air Force Academy Special Collections. 2-15: Wilbur and Orville on front porch; 2-18: Wright glider; 2-29: Flyer No. 3 with two people on board; 2-29: Wright military flight; 2-31: Portrait of Orville; 2-31: Portrait of Wilbur; 3-9: Passenger carrying flight of the Wrights; 3-31: 1911 Wright Glider; 3-33: Flight instruction in 1910; 4-23: Aerial photography; 4-24: Bombing mission; 4-30: Frank Luke; 4-44: Armistice Day; 5-2: Douglas World Cruiser Aircraft; 5-4: Army World Flight Crew; 5-26: Airmen of Army World Flight; 5-26: Douglas World Cruiser aircraft; 5-27: Seattle and Boston at Santa Monica; 5-28: DWC aircraft before departure; 5-30: "World Flight Team in Bagdad, Iraq"; 5-30: World Flight Team in Shanghai and Calcutta; 5-31: The DWC Boston; 6-39: DC-3; 7-2: VS-300; 7-2: Supermarine MK VIII; 7-25: VS-300; 7-32: V-1; 7-32: V-2; 7-49: Me262 jet; 7-60: P-80A jet; 7-63: B-29; 7-63: B-29s bombing; 8-32: Berlin Airlift; 8-37: B-29 on an air raid; 8-38: MiG-15; 8-49: B-45 and B-47; 8-50: Mya- 4 Bison; 8-54: Atlas launch; 8-55: General Bernard Adolph Schriever; 9-27: X-15 on the ground

Unisys Corporation. 3-31: Sperry Gyros; 6-47: 1930s airplane radios

United Technologies. 3-3: 1911 Glenn Curtiss takeoff from water; 3-11: Sikorsky's first helicopter; 3-11: Sikorsky's pilot's license; 3-12: Sikorsky at the wheel of the S-21 "Grand" in 1913; 4-41: DeHavilland; 5-4: Boeing 40A mail plane; 5-5: NC-4 Flying Boat; 5-47: Airmail Service; 5-48: Airmail aircraft; 6-2: Amelia Earhart; 6-3: Pan American China Clipper; 6-3: Howard Hughes; 6-4: Charles Lindbergh; 6-6: Lindbergh and Robertson mailplane; 6-6: Charles Lindbergh; 6-6: St. Louis Backer of Lindbergh; 6-7: Sikorsky & Fonck Waving; 6-7: Spirit of St. Louis; 6-9: Lindbergh Whirlwind engine; 6-15: Wiley Post and the Winnie Mae; 6-16: Winnie Mae; 6-19: Gee-Bee 7-11 Super Sportster; 6-19: Wiley Post's pressure suit; 6-30: Collier Trophy winners, Hamilton Standard and Chief Engineer Frank Caldwell; 6-35: Boeing 247 Airliner; 6-39: Frederick B. Rentscler; 6-48: Martin and Osa Johnson; 6-49: Martin and Osa Johnson in Borneo; 6-50: Martin M-130 flying boat; 7-8: Vickers Wellington in 1939; 7-23: Jacqueline Cochran; 7-25: Igor Sikorsky; 7-27: Sikorsky R-4; 8-15: Post war flying boat; 8-21: L.S.Hobbs

Van Dyk, Herman. 4-15: Drachenballoon; 5-37: Norge airship

Van's Aircraft. 10-9: Richard Vangrunsven; 10-9: RV-4 airplane

Virgin Galactic. 10-58: White Knight and SpaceShip One

Wade, Mark, Astronautix.com. 9-9: Molniya satellite, copyright Mark Wade

White House. 10-7: GARA Signing

Whitman, Paul F. 7-54: Computer drawn map of Corregidor

Wilke, Lanny. 4-8: Von Zeppelin; 4-37: Albatros production

Wings Over the Rockies Air and Space Museum. 7-53: B-17 in Philippines; 8-32: Nuclear Explosion; 8-36: T-33; 8-36: US & Soviet bombers in Korea; 8-37: MiG-15; 8-38: Sabre F-86 in Korea; 8-46: Military aircraft firing missile; 8-49: Martin XB-48; 8-50: B-52; 8-52: Air-to-surface missile; 8-52: Surface-to-surface missile; 9-44: Entrance to NORAD and inside; 9-45: B-58 hustler; 9-48: Missile silo under construction